bedfordstmartins.com/bedguide

Integrated with the text and now even easier to use. Look for notes in the margins of *The Bedford Guide* that direct you to specific resources on the book's Web site. Most of the notes include keywords, which you can type into the Web search box to find immediately relevant writing help. You can also find information on the Web site by browsing a menu of common writing concerns—your own or those raised by an instructor or peer editor.

---

276   Chapter 16 • Strategies for Planning   A Writer's Guide

TOO VAGUE	Native American blankets are very beautiful.
TOO BROAD	Native Americans have adapted to modern civilization.
POSSIBLE TO SHOW	Members of the Apache tribe are skilled workers in high-rise construction.

■ Exercise
Examining Thesis Statements

Discuss each of the following thesis sentences with your classmates. Answer these questions for each:

> Is the thesis stated exactly?
> Does the thesis state just one idea?
> Is the thesis stated positively?
> Is the thesis sufficiently limited for a short essay?
> How might the thesis be improved?

■ For exercises on choosing effective thesis statements, visit <bedfordstmartins.com/bedguide> and do a keyword search: 🔍 thesis

1. Teenagers should not get married.
2. Cutting classes is like a disease.
3. Students have developed a variety of techniques to conceal inadequate study from their instructors.
4. Older people often imitate teenagers.
5. Violence on television can be harmful to children.
6. I don't know how to change the oil in my car.

HOW TO USE A THESIS TO ORGANIZE

Often a good, clear thesis will suggest an organization for your ideas.

WORKING THESIS	Despite the disadvantages of living in a downtown business district, I wouldn't live anywhere else.
FIRST ¶S	Disadvantages of living in the business district
NEXT ¶S	Advantages of living there
LAST ¶	Affirmation of your fondness for downtown city life

A clear thesis will also help to organize you, keeping you on track as you write. Just putting your working thesis into words can stake out your territory. Your thesis can then guide you as you select details and connect sections of the essay. Its purpose is to guide you on a quest, not to limit your ideas.

As you write, however, you don't have to cling to a thesis for dear life. If further investigation changes your thinking, you can change your thesis.

| WORKING THESIS | Because wolves are a menace to people and farm animals, they ought to be exterminated. |

---

the BEDFORD GUIDE for COLLEGE WRITERS   SEVENTH EDITION

X. J. KENNEDY
DOROTHY M. KENNEDY
MARCIA F. MUTH
SYLVIA A. HOLLADAY

A Writer's Guide | A Writer's Reader | A Writer's Research Manual | A Writer's Handbook

WELCOME

This site gives you more examples, activities, and resources related to every part of **The Bedford Guide.** You can find resources by browsing through the menu bar above, searching by keyword (right), or following links matched to your instructor's concerns, to comments from a peer editor, or to your own concerns (below).

>> site requirements

🔍 KEYWORD SEARCH

Notes in the margins of **The Bedford Guide** include keywords to help you find resources on this Web site. To get to a particular resource, type the relevant keyword into this box:

[thesis]   [SEARCH]

SEARCH by WRITING CONCERN

| Your instructor wants you to ... ▶ |
| A peer editor says ... ▶ |
| You are concerned about ... ▶ |

You may be seeking help with your writing based on something an instructor or peer said, or based on your own concerns. Roll your cursor over one of the prompts to the left to find resources on this site that can help.

LOG-ON

E-mail address: [   ]

Password: [   ]

[LogOn]

I am not registered.
Sign me up as a(n):
+ Student
+ Instructor

Forget your password?

COMMENT

If you're using Comment with **The Bedford Guide,** click here to get to it.

INSTRUCTOR RESOURCES

Materials and resources to support your work with **The Bedford Guide** include conversation starters, classroom ideas, and sample syllabi.

>> Go to Instructor Resources

Bedford/St. Martin's | Composition | About This Book | Order a Book | Contact Us | Tech Support

---

Practical support for each part of the book. Want to read more writing samples to spark your imagination? Need help revising your paper? Interested in creating a schedule for your research project? From the home page of *The Bedford Guide,* you can access resources to supplement whatever part of the book you're using. You can also get to TopLinks — a database of links to the best sites on the Web for writing papers on popular culture, education, and other topics.

More practice to make you a better writer. Exercise Central, a huge bank of online exercises, gives you immediate feedback to help make you a better editor of your own writing. Now it includes a new set of writing and research exercises to give you practice with choosing and supporting main ideas, organizing your writing, citing sources, and more.

X.J. KENNEDY ◆ DOROTHY M. KENNEDY
MARCIA F. MUTH ◆ SYLVIA A. HOLLADAY

The BEDFORD GUIDE *for* COLLEGE WRITERS

SEVENTH EDITION

with Reader, Research Manual, and Handbook

BEDFORD / ST. MARTIN'S ◆ Boston ◆ New York

FOR BEDFORD/ST. MARTIN'S

Developmental Editors: Beth Castrodale, Karin Halbert
Production Editor: Deborah Baker
Senior Production Supervisor: Joe Ford
Senior Marketing Manager: Richard Cadman
Editorial Assistants: Stefanie Wortman, Caryn O'Connell
Copyeditor: Jane Zanichkowsky
Text Design: Claire Seng-Niemoeller
Cover Design and Art: Hannus Design Associates
Composition: Monotype Composition Company, Inc.
Printing and Binding: R.R. Donnelley & Sons Company

President: Joan E. Feinberg
Editorial Director: Denise B. Wydra
Editor in Chief: Karen S. Henry
Director of Marketing: Karen Melton Soeltz
Director of Editing, Design, and Production: Marcia Cohen
Managing Editor: Elizabeth M. Schaaf

Library of Congress Control Number: 2004102166

Manufactured in the United States of America.

9 8 7 6 5
f   e   d   c

For information, write: Bedford/St. Martin's, 75 Arlington Street, Boston, MA 02116 (617-399-4000)

ISBN: 0–312–41808–6   EAN: 978–0–312–41808–3 (Instructor's Annotated Edition)
ISBN: 0–312–41251–7   EAN: 978–0–312–41251–7 (hardcover Student Edition)
ISBN: 0–312–41252–5   EAN: 978–0–312–41252–4 (paperback Student Edition)

ACKNOWLEDGMENTS

Michael Abernethy, "Male Bashing on TV" from PopMatters.com (January 9, 2003). Copyright © 2003 by PopMatters.com. Reprinted with permission.

Russell Baker, "The Art of Eating Spaghetti" from *Growing Up.* Copyright © 1982 by Russell Baker. Reprinted with the permission of the McGraw-Hill Companies, Inc.

Dave Barry, "From Now On, Let Women Kill Their Own Spiders" from *The Miami Herald* (February 12, 1999). Copyright © 1999 by Dave Barry. Reprinted with the permission of the author.

A. Scott Berg, "Travels with 'My Aunt,'" (excerpt) from *Kate Remembered.* Copyright © 2003 by A. Scott Berg. Reprinted with the permission of G. P. Putnam's Sons, a division of Penguin Group (USA) Inc.

Judy Brady, "I Want a Wife" from *Ms.* (December 1971). Copyright © 1970 by Judy Brady. Reprinted with the permission of the author.

Suzanne Britt, "Neat People vs. Sloppy People" from *Show and Tell* (Raleigh, North Carolina: Morning Owl Press, 1982). Copyright © 1982 by Suzanne Britt. Reprinted with the permission of the author.

Elinor Burkett, "Unequal Work for Unequal Pay" from *The Baby Boon: How Family-Friendly America Cheats the Childless.* Copyright © 2000 by Elinor Burkett. Reprinted with the permission of the Free Press, a division of Simon & Schuster Adult Publishing Group. All rights reserved.

Acknowledgments and copyrights are continued at the back of the book on pages A-65–67, which constitute an extension of the copyright page. It is a violation of the law to reproduce these selections by any means whatsoever without the written permission of the copyright holder.

Preface: To the Instructor

The *Bedford Guide for College Writers* has always emphasized learning by doing, helping students improve their writing through practice and feedback. That emphasis carries into this seventh edition, which continues to offer four coordinated composition books integrated into one convenient text. This single volume offers a process-oriented rhetoric, a thematically arranged reader, a full research manual, and a comprehensive handbook — all of the textbooks you and your students will need for a solid writing course. (*The Bedford Guide* is available in two other versions as well: as three books in one, without a handbook, and as two books in one, comprising a rhetoric and a reader.)

The seventh edition does even more to build essential writing and research skills — from devising a sound thesis to finding the best evidence to support it. In addition, the book provides new diagrams, flowcharts, and other visuals to reinforce key writing concepts and expanded coverage of using and analyzing visuals (such as photographs, tables, and other graphics).

Overview of **The Bedford Guide**

BOOK ONE: *A Writer's Guide*

The first book is a process-oriented rhetoric with readings; it addresses all of the assignments and topics typically covered in the first-year writing course. For convenience, the rhetoric is divided into four parts.

Part One, "A College Writer's Processes," introduces students to processes for writing (Chapter 1), reading (Chapter 2), and critical thinking (Chapter 3) — essential skills for meeting college expectations. Each chapter ends with a new two-page chart that shows where students can find helpful resources for writing, active reading, or critical thinking in the text, in its accompanying Writing Guide Software, and on the companion Web site. (See p. x for an example.)

In Part Two, "A Writer's Situations," eight core chapters — each including two sample readings (one by a student) — guide students step-by-step through a full range of common first-year writing assignments. If followed sequentially, these chapters lead students gradually into the rigorous analytical writing that will comprise most of their college writing. The rhetorical situations in Part Two include recalling an experience (Chapter 4), observing a scene (Chapter 5), interviewing a subject (Chapter 6), comparing and contrasting (Chapter 7), explaining causes and effects (Chapter 8), taking a stand (Chapter 9), proposing a solution (Chapter 10), and evaluating (Chapter 11).

Part Three, "Special Writing Situations," offers helpful strategies and plenty of examples to support students' efforts in three additional situations: responding to literature (Chapter 12), writing in the workplace (Chapter 13), and writing for assessment (Chapter 14).

Part Four, "A Writer's Strategies," is a convenient resource for approaching all aspects of writing. The first five chapters explain and exemplify the stages of the writing process: generating ideas (Chapter 15), planning (Chapter 16), drafting (Chapter 17), developing (Chapter 18), and revising and editing (Chapter 19). Marginal annotations in the earlier parts guide students to these chapters, which collectively serve as a writer's toolbox. Part Four also includes two chapters on using and analyzing visuals: "Strategies for Designing Your Document" (Chapter 20) and "Strategies for Understanding Visual Representations" (Chapter 21). Both chapters, included in the popular Bedford/St. Martin's supplement *Getting the Picture*, have been thoroughly updated and include new visual examples, such as Web sites, *PowerPoint* slides, and brochures.

BOOK TWO: *A Writer's Reader*

A Writer's Reader offers provocative content and clear models, accompanied by apparatus that moves students smoothly from reading and thinking to writing. Thirty-two brief selections — 14 new — are arranged according to five themes: families (Chapter 22), men and women (Chapter 23), popular culture (Chapter 24), the workplace (Chapter 25), and education (Chapter 26), a new theme added in response to reviewer requests. These diverse readings are coordinated with *A Writer's Guide* and serve as models of the writing situations assigned there; a rhetorical table of contents helps students see these connections (see p. xxxix).

Each reading is introduced by a biographical headnote and a brief reading tip. Each is followed by questions on meaning, writing strategies, critical reading, vocabulary, and connections to other selections; journal prompts; and suggested writing assignments, one personal and the other analytical. These questions move students from reading carefully for both thematic and rhetorical elements to applying new strategies and insights in their own writing.

BOOK THREE: *A Writer's Research Manual*

A Writer's Research Manual covers all the essential steps for print, electronic, and field research: planning and managing a research project (Chapter 27), finding sources (Chapter 28), evaluating sources (Chapter 29), integrating sources (Chapter 30), writing the research paper (Chapter 31), and documenting sources (Chapter 32). Integrating sources is now a separate and fully developed chapter, emphasizing the importance of this crucial skill. In addition, the comprehensive *Research Manual* concludes with an extensive collection of documentation models — 74 in MLA style and 44 in APA style.

BOOK FOUR: *A Writer's Handbook*

With thorough coverage of all the standard topics, reference tabs, highlighted rules, boxed charts, and ESL guidelines, *A Writer's Handbook* looks and works like a conventional handbook. It also includes forty-eight exercise sets for practice in and out of class. Answers to half of the questions in each set are provided in the back of the book so that students can check their understanding.

QUICK RESEARCH GUIDE

This new resource (included in all versions of *The Bedford Guide*) targets challenging research tasks, making it an ideal reference for all research projects and an especially helpful guide for papers drawing on just a few sources. It's full of handy checklists, charts, and other visuals designed to make information quickly accessible to students. For more details, see page x.

QUICK EDITING GUIDE

This resource (also included in all versions of *The Bedford Guide*) gives special attention to the most troublesome grammar and editing problems. It also includes basic guidelines for manuscript format.

Cross-references in the book to both the Quick Research Guide and Quick Editing Guide help students make optimal use of these helpful resources.

New to the Seventh Edition

The revisions in this new edition reflect trends in composition and incorporate the suggestions of a host of reviewers. The changes have resulted in an even more practical book that helps students with their most challenging writing tasks.

MORE ATTENTION TO ESSENTIAL WRITING AND READING SKILLS IN THE BOOK—AND ONLINE

Users and other reviewers have told us that students need more help — in every type of writing situation — with formulating and supporting a thesis. Students also need guidance in the critical reading that supports thoughtful and engaged writing. We've responded with the following features.

More Emphasis Throughout on Thesis and Support.   New aids include examples of working and revised thesis statements keyed to various writing situations and unique highlighting of thesis, support, and other features in the professional essays in *A Writer's Guide*. These elements help students analyze effective thesis statements and support in context.

REVISING AND EDITING

Because explaining causes and effects takes hard thought, you'll want to set aside plenty of time for rewriting. As Yun Yung Choi approached her paper's final version, she wanted to rework her thesis, developing it with greater precision and more detail.

WORKING THESIS   The turnabout for women resulted from the influence of Confucianism in all aspects of society.

REVISED THESIS   This turnabout in women's place in Korean society was brought about by one of the greatest influences that shaped the government, literature, and thoughts of the Korean people — Confucianism.

From his sister at Swarthmore, I'd heard about a kid in Florida whose mother picked him up after school every day, drove him straight to the mall, and left him there until it closed — all at his insistence. I'd heard about a boy in Washington who, when his family moved from one suburb to another, pedaled his bicycle five miles every day to get back to his old mall, where he once belonged.   **1**

Their stories aren't unusual. The mall is a common experience for the majority of American youth; they have probably been going there all their lives. Some ran within their first large open space, saw their first fountain, bought their first toy, and read their first book in a mall. They may have smoked their first cigarette or first joint or turned them down, had their first kiss or lost their virginity in the mall parking lot. Teenagers in America now spend more time in the mall than anywhere else but home and school. Mostly it is their choice, but some of that mall time is put in as the result of two-paycheck and single-parent households, and the lack of other viable° alternatives. But are these kids being harmed by the mall?   **2**

I wondered first of all what difference it makes for adolescents to experience so many important moments in the mall. They are, after all, at play in the fields of its little world and they learn its ways; they adapt to it and make it adapt to them. It's here that these kids get their street sense, only it's mall sense. They are learning the ways of a large-scale artificial environment: its subtleties and flexibilities, its particular pleasures and resonances,° and the attitudes it fosters.   **3**

Introduction

Situation described in transitional paragraph

Question raised about effects

THESIS specifying effects

More Help with Reading. The seventh edition features stronger coverage of critical reading (in Chapter 2) and improved apparatus for the model readings in the core writing chapters. This apparatus includes helpful annotations of professional essays (see above) and provocative questions in the margins of student essays to encourage close reading.

> For me, growing up in a small suburb on the outskirts of Seoul, the adults' preference for boys seemed quite natural. All the important people that I knew--doctors, lawyers, policemen, and soldiers--were men. On the other hand, most of the women that I knew were either housekeepers or housewives whose duty seemed to be to obey and please the men of the family. When my teachers at school asked me what I wanted to be when I grew up, I would answer, "I want to be the wife of the president." Because all women must become wives and mothers, I thought, becoming the wife of the president would be the highest achievement for a woman. I knew that the birth of a boy was a greatly desired and celebrated event, whereas the birth of a girl was a disappointing one, accompanied by the frequent words of consolation for the sad parents: "A daughter is her mother's chief help in keeping house."

How would you have answered this question?

New Exercises in Exercise Central, an Online Bank of Practice Items. The new exercises, developed especially for *The Bedford Guide* and available at <bedfordstmartins.com/bedguide>, cover such writing basics as identifying thesis and support, organizing support, identifying effective introductions and conclusions, integrating source material and avoiding plagiarism, and documenting sources.

STRENGTHENED RESEARCH COVERAGE

Every version of *The Bedford Guide* offers improved research coverage, helping students use sources more effectively throughout the writing process.

A More Comprehensive *Research Manual*. Every chapter in the *Research Manual* has been strengthened and updated, sharpening coverage of purpose and thesis, project organization, effective searches, recommended electronic sources, source integration, and other research skills. New charts help students recognize different types of sources and identify the best print and electronic sources to meet the needs of their research project and the expectations of their readers.

Finding Evidence and Opinions in Electronic Sources	Source for Facts and Statistics	Source for Expert Testimony	Source for Opinions
Online Reference Site	List of topics or links may lead to specialized facts or statistics	Expert academic sources available	Academic topic links to a variety of approaches and views on research topics
Gateway Site for a Topic or Field	Site pages with facts or links, such as *Polling Report* at <www.pollingreport.com>	Expert academic and field sources available	Academic topic links; opinion sites, such as *Opinion-Pages* at <www.opinion-pages.org> or *Public Agenda* at <www.publicagenda.com>

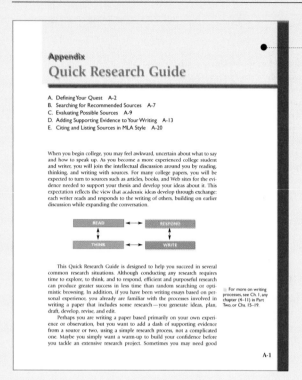

A New Quick Research Guide. This new guide, offered with every version of the book, helps students with key research processes: defining a research quest, seeking sources that meet their needs, evaluating and integrating sources, and citing and listing sources in MLA style. Cross-references throughout the book to this resource help students find a few useful sources no matter what assignment they're tackling.

New Research Exercises in Exercise Central. These new items cover evaluating, integrating, and citing sources, and more.

A MORE VISUALLY ACCESSIBLE AND APPEALING BOOK

New visuals serve two important purposes: to make the book and the writing concepts it covers even more accessible and to illustrate the types of visuals that students can use in their own writing.

Colorful New Flowcharts. Concluding each of the three chapters in Part One and the very end of the book itself, these flowcharts show students where they can get help on writing, reading, and critical thinking in the book, on its companion Web site, and in the Writing Guide Software.

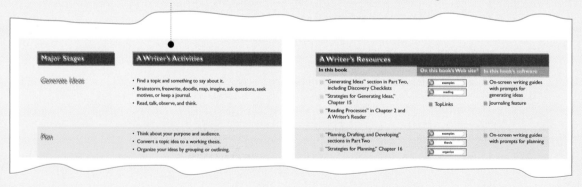

More Visuals to Help Students Structure Ideas and Think Through Writing Tasks. Convenient and easy-to-understand diagrams, tables, and flowcharts show students how to organize their writing processes and their writing itself.

SPATIAL MOVEMENT	top → bottom	left → right	near → far	center → edge

PROMINENT FEATURES	*least:* Sunday suit, light blue blouse, dramatic flowered hat ↓ *most:* grandma's sharp eyes, finding the best in others

SPECIFIC DETAILS TO GENERAL IMPRESSION	souvenir sellers calling, tour boats slapped by small waves, and pungent fish frying on Fisherman's Wharf ↓ In all this commotion, a visitor sees the wharf's vitality.

COMMON AND ORDINARY TO UNUSUAL FEATURES	mounds of bright leaves, crisp fall air, children bouncing ↓ the sheer joy of every moment at the playground across from the pediatric cancer center

More Coverage of Using Visuals Throughout the Writing Process. The assignment chapters in "A Writer's Situations" now advise students about using visuals to generate ideas, illustrate documents, and make writing more convincing and visually accessible. Additionally, Chapters 20 and 21, on designing documents and analyzing visuals, expand advice on adding visuals to support content and supply many more sample documents.

Consider Sources of Support. Because your memory drops as well as retains, you may want to check your recollections against those of a friend or family member who was there. Did you keep a journal at the time? Was the experience a turning point (big game, graduation) that your family would have documented with photos? Was it sufficiently public (such as a demonstration) or universal (such as a campus orientation) to have been recorded in a newspaper? If so, perhaps you can refresh your memory and rediscover details or angles that you had forgotten.

Family photograph

AN IMPROVED AND INTEGRATED SUITE OF ELECTRONIC RESOURCES

These resources help students with every step of writing, from drafting to peer review to revising. Marginal references in the book direct students to this additional help wherever it might be useful.

Comment. This Web-based writing-response tool, now tailored for *The Bedford Guide*, allows students and teachers to comment on others' writing quickly and easily while drawing on helpful material from the book, such as peer-response advice and handbook content. (To order Comment packaged with your students' books, see the box on p. xvi.)

Writing Guide Software. This software transforms the essential advice in *The Bedford Guide* into an on-screen tutorial, making the book accessible where and when students actually do their writing. (To order the Writing Guide software packaged with your students' books, see the box on p. xvi.)

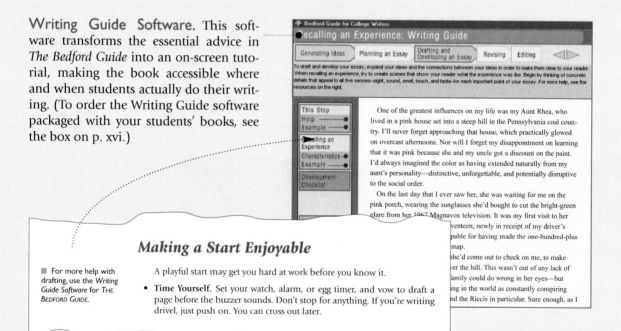

For more help with drafting, use the *Writing Guide Software* for THE BEDFORD GUIDE.

Making a Start Enjoyable

A playful start may get you hard at work before you know it.

- **Time Yourself.** Set your watch, alarm, or egg timer, and vow to draft a page before the buzzer sounds. Don't stop for anything. If you're writing drivel, just push on. You can cross out later.

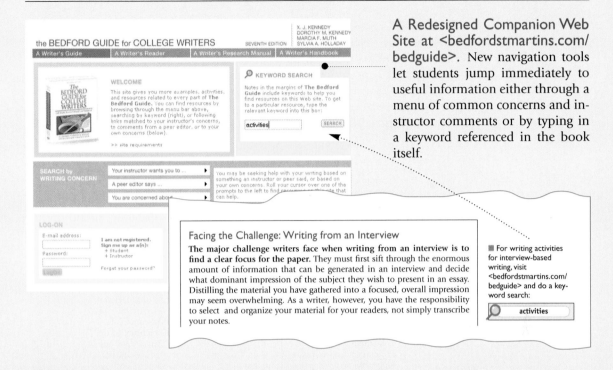

A Redesigned Companion Web Site at <bedfordstmartins.com/bedguide>. New navigation tools let students jump immediately to useful information either through a menu of common concerns and instructor comments or by typing in a keyword referenced in the book itself.

Facing the Challenge: Writing from an Interview

The major challenge writers face when writing from an interview is to find a clear focus for the paper. They must first sift through the enormous amount of information that can be generated in an interview and decide what dominant impression of the subject they wish to present in an essay. Distilling the material you have gathered into a focused, overall impression may seem overwhelming. As a writer, however, you have the responsibility to select and organize your material for your readers, not simply transcribe your notes.

■ For writing activities for interview-based writing, visit <bedfordstmartins.com/bedguide> and do a keyword search:

activities

Print Ancillaries

The Bedford Guide for College Writers, seventh edition, is accompanied by a full ancillary package that offers instructors and students a wide array of useful resources. Providing flexibility and support for experienced and beginning instructors alike, this package includes a variety of supplements, all newly revised and updated, to help you tailor your course to your students' needs.

Instructor's Annotated Edition of *The Bedford Guide for College Writers* puts information right where busy instructors need it: on the pages of the book itself. The marginal annotations offer teaching tips, new analysis tips with readings, last-minute in-class activities, vocabulary glosses, additional assignments, and cross-references to other ancillaries.

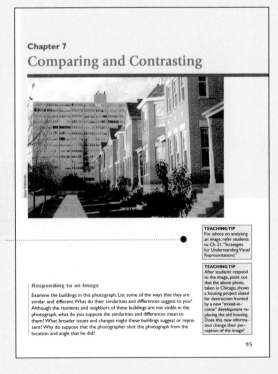

Chapter 7
Comparing and Contrasting

TEACHING TIP
For advice on analyzing an image, refer students to Ch. 21, "Strategies for Understanding Visual Representations."

TEACHING TIP
After students respond to the image, point out that the above photo, taken in Chicago, shows a housing project slated for destruction fronted by a new "mixed-income" development replacing the old housing. Does this new information change their perception of the image?

Responding to an Image

Examine the buildings in this photograph. List some of the ways that they are similar and different. What do their similarities and differences suggest to you? Although the residents and neighbors of these buildings are not visible in the photograph, what do you suppose the similarities and differences mean to them? What broader issues and changes might these buildings suggest or represent? Why do suppose that the photographer shot the photograph from the location and angle that he did?

95

Practical Suggestions for Teaching with *The Bedford Guide for College Writers,* by Sylvia A. Holladay, Shirley Morahan, and Dana Waters, helps instructors plan and teach their composition course. This text includes practical advice on designing an effective course, sample syllabi, chapter-by-chapter support (including answers to all exercises), and suggestions for using the electronic media package. It also includes new advice about helping students avoid plagiarism.

..., such as .... on the ....ents shoul...
....ine what gives a person authority or expertise. To help students ask questions that will prompt recall about the problem, have them role-play an interview during class. Then have them write a report on their understanding of the people they interviewed.

3. Organize an oral-history project in which each student interviews an older person who has been successful in the career or profession the student wants to enter. Assign an essay in which students define the critical issues in their profession by incorporating what they learned from the people they interviewed.

Here's an Idea . . .

Ask students to write a letter to Robert G. Schreiner about his essay, What Is a Hunter? Then have them discuss in groups how they would feel and react if they received those comments about their own work. Are the suggestions specific enough to be helpful? Would any of the comments make them angry or defensive? How might the comments be phrased to make them more helpful or more palatable to the writer? These discussions will make students aware of how their comments need to be specific but supportive in order to be helpful. For more about collaborative learning, see Chapter 2 of this manual.

BEDFORD/ST. MARTIN'S PROFESSIONAL RESOURCES

Second Edition

TEACHING COMPOSITION

Background Readings

T. R. Johnson

Teaching Composition: Background Readings, edited by T. R. Johnson of Tulane University, has been revised to accompany the seventh edition of *The Bedford Guide.* Its thirty readings covering theory, research, and pedagogy have been selected to help novice and experienced instructors get the most out of this composition textbook as they develop or refine their teaching techniques. Introductions and suggested activities connect the readings to the writing course.

Transparency Masters to Accompany *The Bedford Guide* *for College Writers* provides supplemental examples of writing strategies, visual representations of rhetorical and grammatical concepts, and other materials useful for classroom discussion.

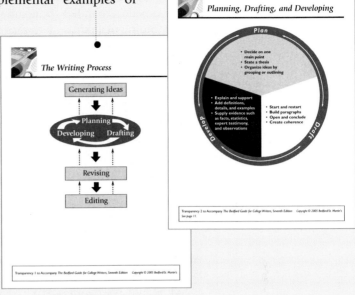

Study Skills for College Writers, by Laurie Walker of Eastern Michigan University, offers many practical tips and strategies for managing time, taking notes, taking tests, and accessing college resources. This supplement is full of activities designed to help underprepared students improve their study skills. (To order this ancillary packaged with your students' books, see the box on p. xvi.)

PREPARATION

The best way to prepare for a test is little by little, day by day. It is easier, less stressful, and more productive to study for tests in this incremental, methodical fashion than to cram.

Cramming may be better than not studying at all, but not much better. It increases anxiety and decreases stamina, the energy your brain needs to function at its best. If you have been studying little by little, day by day, the time you might otherwise spend cramming would be better spent getting an extra hour of sleep. Attend class faithfully, take notes, review your notes, and read all assigned material. Reread, whenever possible.

Try It!

Working backward from your exam date, construct a three- or four-day study schedule. Write down specific hours and specific tasks. Consider inviting a classmate or two to join you for one or two of these times. Be sure to set — and meet — a reasonable goal for each session.

Electronic Ancillaries

The Bedford Guide for College Writers is available with Comment, Writing Guide Software, and a companion Web site, all described on pp. xi–xiii. The following electronic resources are also offered.

Exercise Central, accessible through *The Bedford Guide*'s Web site at <bedfordstmartins.com/bedguide>, includes thousands of editing exercises

—conveniently arranged by topic—that provide immediate feedback on students' progress. For the seventh edition of *The Bedford Guide*, Exercise Central has been expanded to include new exercises on writing, integrating sources, avoiding plagiarism, and more.

The Bedford/St. Martin's Writing and Grammar Test Bank CD-ROM allows instructors to create secure, customized tests and quizzes to assess students' writing and grammar competency and gauge their progress as the course progresses. Nearly 2,000 test items are included.

Blackboard and WebCT content is also available with this book.

Ordering Information

To order any of the ancillaries for *The Bedford Guide*, please contact your Bedford / St. Martin's sales representative, e-mail sales support at sales _support@bfwpub.com, or visit our Web site at <bedfordstmartins.com>.

When ordering Comment with your students' books, use the package ISBN for the version of *The Bedford Guide* that you are using :

- with Reader, Research Manual, and Handbook (hardcover): 0–312–43579–7

- with Reader, Research Manual, and Handbook (paperback): 0–312–43550–9

- with Reader and Research Manual (paperback only): 0–312–43593–2

- with Reader (paperback only): 0–312–43580–0

When ordering the Writing Guide Software with your students' books, use the package ISBN for the version of *The Bedford Guide* that you are using:

- with Reader, Research Manual, and Handbook (hardcover): 0–312–43302–6

- with Reader, Research Manual, and Handbook (paperback): 0–312–43314–X

- with Reader and Research Manual (paperback only): 0–312–43246–1

- with Reader (paperback only): 0–312–43241–0

When ordering *Study Skills for College Writers* with your students' books, use the ISBN for the version of *The Bedford Guide* that you are using:

- with Reader, Research Manual, and Handbook (hardcover): 0–312–43799–4

- with Reader, Research Manual, and Handbook (paperback): 0–312–43800–1

- with Reader and Research Manual (paperback only): 0–312–43801–X

- with Reader (paperback only): 0–312–43802–8

Thanks and Appreciation

Many individuals have contributed significantly to the seventh edition of *The Bedford Guide for College Writers,* and we extend our sincerest thanks to all of them.

EDITORIAL ADVISORY BOARD

As we began to prepare the seventh edition, we assembled an Editorial Advisory Board to respond to the many significant changes we planned and to share ideas about how to make the book more useful to both students and teachers. These dedicated instructors responded thoroughly and insightfully to just about every new feature of the text, and we are extremely grateful to each and every one of them:

- Jan Bone, Roosevelt University and Harper College
- Kaye Kolkmann, Modesto Junior College
- Leigh A. Martin, Community College of Rhode Island
- Miles S. McCrimmon, J. Sargeant Reynolds Community College
- Elizabeth Metzger, University of South Florida
- Mark Reynolds, Jefferson Davis Community College
- Carol Westcamp, University of Arkansas, Ft. Smith
- Mary Zacharias, San Jacinto Community College Central

OTHER COLLEAGUES

We also extend our gratitude to instructors across the country who took time and care to review the sixth edition and previous editions, to participate in a focus group, and to send us their suggestions gleaned from experience with students. For this we thank Alice B. Adams, Prestonsburg Community College; Rosemary R. Adams, Eastern Connecticut State University; Ted Allder, University of Arkansas Community College at Batesville; Patricia Allen, Cape Cod Community College; Steve Amidon, University of Rhode Island; David Auchter, San Jacinto Junior College; Renee Bangerter, Fullerton College; Stuart Barbier, Delta College; Marci Bartolotta, Nova Southeastern University; Randolph A. Beckham, Germanna Community College; Pamela J. Behrens, Alabama A&M University; Carmine J. Bell, Pasco Hernando Community College; Kay Berg, Sinclair Community College; Jan Bone, Roosevelt University; Jeannie Boniecki, Naugatuck Valley Community College; Ty Buckman, Wittenberg University; Joan Campbell, Wellesley College; Tom Casey, El Paso Community College; Steve Cirrone, Tidewater Community College; Susan Romayne Clark, Central Michigan University; Ted Contreras, Long Beach City College; Nancy Cook, Sierra College; Jane Corbly, George Peabody College for Teachers; Monica Cox, Community

College of Rhode Island; Carolyn Craft, Longwood College; Sheilah Craft, Marian College; Mary Cullen, Middlesex Community College; P. R. Dansby, San Jacinto Community College; Fred D'Astoli, Ventura College; Ed Davis, Sinclair Community College; Patricia Ann Delamar, University of Dayton; Irene Duprey-Gutierrez, University of Massachusetts, Dartmouth; Corinna Evett, Fullerton and Santa Ana Colleges; Carol Luers Eyman, St. Joseph School of Practical Nursing; Leora Freedman, Modesto Junior College; Sandy Fuhr, Gustavus Adolphus College; Jan Fulwiler, Lethbridge Community College; Pamela Garvey, St. Louis Community College–Meramec; Mary Ann Gauthier, St. Joseph College; Michael Gavin, Prince George's Community College; Olga Geissler, San Joaquin Delta College; Robert Gmerlin, Sierra College; Aaron Goldweber, Heald College; Daniel Gonzales, Louisiana State University; Sherry F. Gott, Danville Community College; Robert Grindy, Richland Community College; Joyce Hall, Border Institute of Technology; Jefferson Hancock, San Jose State University; Alyssa Harad, University of Texas at Austin; Johnnie Hargrove, Alabama A&M University; Judy Hatcher, San Jacinto College Central; Elaine Hays, University of Rhode Island; Diana Hicks, American River College; Marita Hinton, Alabama A&M University; Tom Hodges, Amarillo College; Patricia Hunt, Catonsville Community College; Elizabeth Jarok, Middlesex Community College; Barbara Jensen, Modesto Junior College; Greg Jewell, Madisonville Community College; Jean L. Johnson, University of North Alabama; Ted Johnston, El Paso Community College; Andrew Jones, University of California at Davis; Anne D. Jordan, Eastern Connecticut State University; M. L. Kayser, Heald College; Cynthia Kellogg, Yuba College; Dimitri Keriotis, Modesto Junior College; Kate Kiefer, Colorado State University; Yoon Sik Kim, Langston University; Fred A. Koslowski III, Delaware Valley College; Sandra Lakey, Pennsylvania College of Technology; Norman Lanquist, Eastern Arizona College; Colleen Lloyd, Cuyahoga Community College; Stephen Ma, University of Alberta; Susan Peck MacDonald, California State University at Long Beach; Jennifer Madej, Milwaukee Area Technical College; Janice Mandile, Front Range Community College; Gerald McCarthy, San Antonio College; Jenna Merritt, Eastern Michigan University; Eric Meyer, St. Louis Community College–Meramec; Libby Miles, University of Rhode Island; Sandra Moore, Mississippi Delta Community College; Cleatta Morris, Louisiana State University at Shreveport; Sheryl A. Mylan, Stephen F. Austin State University; Clement Ndulute, Mississippi Valley State University; Peggy J. Oliver, San Jacinto College South; Mike Palmquist, Colorado State University; Geraldine C. Pelegano, Naugatuck Valley Community College; Laurel S. Peterson, Norwalk Community Technical College; Mary F. Pflugshaupt, Indiana State University; John F. Pleimann, Jefferson College; Kenneth E. Poitras, Antelope Valley College; Michael Punches, Oklahoma City Community College; Patrice Quarg, Cantonsville Community College; Jeanie Page Randall, Austin Peay State University; Betty Ray, Jones College; Joan Reteshka, Sewickley Academy; Kira Roark, University of Denver; Dawn Rodrigues, University of Texas at Brownsville; Ann Westmoreland Runsick, Gateway Technical College; Nancy J. Schneider, University of Maine at Augusta; Janis Schulte, Colby Community College; Susan Schurman, Ventura College; Patricia C. Schwindt, Mesa Community College; Herbert Shapiro, SUNY Empire State College; Elizabeth Smart, Utah State University; Ognjen Smiljanic, Eastern Michigan University; David Sorrells, Lamar State College–Port Arthur; Ann Spencer-Livingstone, SUNY Morrisville Norwich Campus; Scott R. Stankey, Anoka-Ramsey Community College; Leroy Sterling, Alabama A&M University; Dean Stover, Gateway Community College; Monnette Sturgill, Prestonsburg Community College; Ronald Sudol, Oakland University; Darlene Summers, Montgomery College; David Tammer, Eastern Arizona College; William G. Thomas, Saddleback College; Dave Waddell, California State University at Chico; Christopher Walker, Prince George's Community College; Laurie Walker, Eastern Michigan University; Dana Waters, Dodge City Community College; Patricia South White, Norwich University; Susan Whitlow, University of Arkansa–Fort Smith; Jim Wilcox, Southern Nazarene University; Carmiele Wilkerson, Wittenberg University; and Valerie P. Zimbaro, Valencia Community College.

CONTRIBUTORS

The seventh edition could not have been completed without the help of numerous individuals. For the sixth edition, Karla Saari Kitalong (University of Central Florida) contributed two outstanding chapters to the rhetoric — one on document design and one on understanding visual texts — and, with Marcia F. Muth, helped to refine and expand these chapters for the seventh edition. Art researcher Jason Reblando helped us take the book in an even more visually rich direction, finding many new photographs and other images that truly enhance and extend the book's pedagogy. He also cleared permission for much of the art. Kathleen Beauchene (Community College of Rhode Island) wrote excellent apparatus for the new reading selections and also new "Analysis Tips" for the *Instructor's Annotated Edition.* Tammy S. Sugarman (Georgia State University) thoroughly reviewed the *Research Manual* and Quick Research Guide and provided many specific suggestions for improving the content of both. Carolyn Lengel, who has contributed handbook content for the text, wrote engaging new writing and research exercises for Exercise Central, an online bank of practice items that accompanies *The Bedford Guide.* A special thanks to Dana Waters (Dodge City Community College) for contributing new annotations to the *Instructor's Annotated Edition,* for revising the *Practical Suggestions,* and for suggesting many excellent student essays, some of which we have included in the book. Once again, T. R. Johnson (Tulane University) edited *Teaching Composition: Background Readings* with energy and insight, and Linda Bonney helped with manuscript preparation. Fred Courtright cleared text permissions skillfully and efficiently. Finally, warm thanks go to Jennifer Smith, who skillfully redesigned *The Bedford Guide*'s companion Web site to make it more focused on the needs and goals of students.

STUDENT WRITERS

We offer sincere thanks to all the students who have challenged us over the years to find better ways to help them learn. In particular we would like to thank those who granted us permission to use their essays in the seventh edition. Focused as this textbook is on student writing, student essays are the linchpin of *A Writer's Guide*. The writings of Robert G. Schreiner, Dawn Kortz, Tim Chabot, Yun Yung Choi, Heather Colbenson, Jonathan Burns, and Sarah E. Goers were included in earlier editions as well as this one. New to the seventh edition are the writings of Michael Coil, LaBree Shide, Theresa H. Nguyen, Lindsey Schendel, and Carrie Williamson.

EDITORIAL

At Bedford/St. Martin's three individuals merit special recognition. President Joan E. Feinberg and Editorial Director Denise B. Wydra (also a former editor of *The Bedford Guide*) have been a never-ending source of ideas for making the book even more practical for both students and instructors. We also deeply appreciate the creative guidance and perceptive advice of Editor in Chief Karen Henry, who has helped sustain the direction of the book throughout many editions.

The editorial effort behind this edition was truly a team endeavor. First off, we wish to thank the editors of the sixth edition, who laid invaluable groundwork for this new edition, streamlining the book and moving it in a more visually engaging direction that we have continued. These editors were Michelle Clark, Maura Shea, Amanda Bristow, and Genevieve Hamilton. Marcia F. Muth, instrumental in streamlining and harmonizing the sixth edition, assumed a major authorial role in the seventh edition, answering needs expressed by users with many exciting new features described earlier in this Preface. She is as tireless as she is innovative, and every part of this book has benefited from her perceptiveness and careful attention to detail. Beth Castrodale skillfully managed all aspects of the seventh edition, thoughtfully encouraging textual and visual innovation and cheerfully filling numerous gaps, all the while keeping us on track and, most importantly, on schedule. Karin Halbert, a resourceful and extremely talented editor, developed *A Writer's Reader*, finding many excellent selections and helping to craft the apparatus. Karin also developed the *Practical Suggestions* and *Teaching Composition: Background Readings* with skill and insight. Caryn O'Connell also helped find selections for *A Writer's Reader* among many other tasks. Stefanie Wortman assisted with details too numerous to mention, helping to locate art, preparing the rhetorical table of contents, and overseeing production of the Web site and Exercise Central. Other members of the Bedford/St. Martin's staff contributed greatly to the seventh edition. Many thanks and heartfelt appreciation go to Deborah Baker, whose exacting eye, careful hand, and great patience shepherded the book through production.

We especially appreciate her care in overseeing the production of the book's growing art program. Marcia Cohen, Elizabeth Schaaf, and John Amburg were immensely helpful in overseeing production. Donna Dennison oversaw the impressive redesign of the book's cover, giving us a fresh look that still preserves the integrity of *The Bedford Guide*. Billy Boardman also provided invaluable design assistance, and Angela Dambrowski coordinated the routing of cover copy. We are fortunate to have an excellent New Media team, which helped with every aspect of producing the book's electronic ancillaries, from the companion Web site to Comment to the Writing Guide Software; warm thanks to Nick Carbone, Katie Schooling, Chad Crume, Coleen O'Hanley, David Mogolov, Tari Fanderclai, Steve Abrams, and Gemma Barnes. Karen Melton Soeltz and Richard Cadman skillfully coordinated the marketing of the book, while its promotion was ably handled by Tom Macy and Pelle Cass. Sandy Schechter oversaw the process of clearing text permissions. We are grateful for Jane Zanichkowsky's copyediting and, last but not least, for Claire Seng-Niemoeller's attractive and accessible designs of the many new visual elements included in this edition.

Marcia Muth is especially grateful to the School of Education at the University of Colorado at Denver for sponsoring her writing workshops. Finally, we thank our friends and families for their unwavering patience, understanding, and encouragement.

How to Use The Bedford Guide for College Writers

Just as you may be unsure of what to expect from your writing course, you may also be unsure of what to expect from your writing textbook. You may even be wondering how any textbook can improve your writing. In fact, a book can't make you a better writer, but practice can, and *The Bedford Guide for College Writers* guides your practice. This text offers help — easy to find and easy to use — for writing the essays most commonly assigned in the first-year composition course.

Underlying *The Bedford Guide* is the idea that writing is a necessary and useful skill in and beyond the writing course. What this book also provides is help with writing for other college courses, writing on the job, and writing as a member of a community. In other words, the skills you will learn throughout this book are transferable to other areas of your life, making *The Bedford Guide* both a time-saver and a money-saver.

The following sections describe how you can get the most out of this text. *The Bedford Guide* is designed so that you can move quickly and easily to the section you need. And once you are there, several key features can help you improve your writing by guiding your practice. Let us show you what we mean.

Finding Information in The Bedford Guide

It's easy to find what you need when you need it in *The Bedford Guide*. Each of the tools described here will direct you to useful information — fast.

Brief List of Contents.   Open the book to the inside front cover. At a glance you can see a list of the topics within *The Bedford Guide*. If you are looking for a specific chapter, this brief list of contents is the quickest way to find it.

Detailed List of Contents.   Beginning on p. xxxi, the longer, more detailed list of contents breaks down the topics covered within each chapter of the book. Use this list to find a specific part of a chapter. For example, if you have been assigned to read Russell Baker's "The Art of Eating Spaghetti," a quick scan of the detailed contents will show you that it begins on page 48.

Rhetorical List of Contents.   This list, which begins on page xxxix, includes all of the readings in *The Bedford Guide*, organized by writing strategy. You can use this list to help you locate additional examples of a particular kind of writing such as comparing and contrasting or explaining causes and effects.

Resource Charts.   If you open the book to the inside back cover and its facing page, you'll find a chart showing where you can get help in the text and its software, or on its Web site, no matter where you are in the writing process. If you find yourself stuck at a particular stage, consider turning here

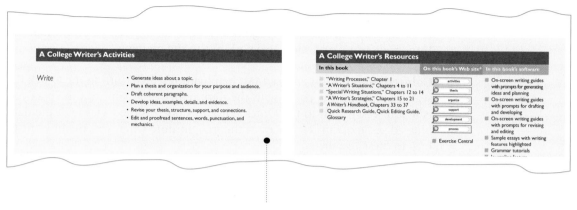

for help. This chart is much like the three charts in Part One, which show you how to find resources specifically for writing (pp. 16–17), reading (pp. 30–31), and critical thinking (pp. 40–41).

Index.   An index is a complete list of a book's contents in alphabetical order. Turn to page I-1 when you want to find all of the information available in the book for a particular topic. This example shows you all the places to look for help with your thesis.

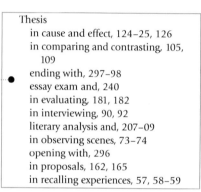

List of Visuals.   At the back of the book, you'll find a list of different types of visuals in the book (organized by genre). Refer to this for ideas about how to use images effectively.

Guide to the Handbook.   Just before the resource chart in the back of the book, you'll find a guide that shows you at a glance the entire contents of *A Writer's Handbook*. Turn to this guide when you need help editing your essays. It gives exact page numbers for each handbook topic, such as "sentence fragments."

Marginal Cross-References.   You can find additional information quickly by using the references in the margins — notes on the sides of each page that tell you exactly where to turn in the book or on the Web site for more help or for other activities related to what you are reading. Many of the Web

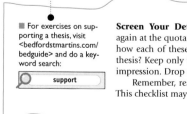

■ For exercises on supporting a thesis, visit <bedfordstmartins.com/bedguide> and do a keyword search:

    support

Screen Your Details.   Using your revised thesis as a touchstone, look again at the quotations and other details you have included. Will readers see how each of these strengthens the dominant impression expressed in your thesis? Keep only those that support your thesis and enhance the dominant impression. Drop all the others, even if they are vivid or catchy.

Remember, readers will be interested in your observations and insights. This checklist may help you revise your work to strengthen them.

references now include keywords. Simply type these words into a search box at <bedfordstmartins.com/bedguide> to get to the relevant information. Handbook pages also include definitions in the margins.

Colored Edges.   If you need fast help with research, turn to the Quick Research Guide on the pages with the dark red edge. If you need help as you edit your essay, turn to the Quick Editing Guide on the pages with the dark blue edge. Frequent references in the margin note when you might want to turn to these resources.

If you are writing a research paper and are looking for guidelines for MLA documentation, check the pages with the brown edge. If you need to find APA guidelines, check the pages with the green edge.

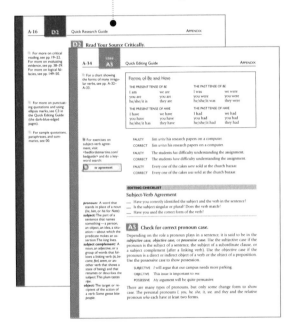

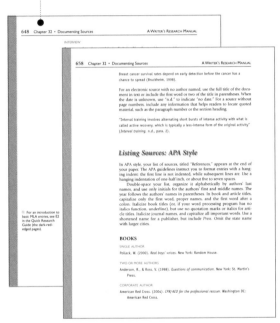

Colored Tabs.   Your instructor may use correction symbols, such as "agr" for subject-verb agreement, to indicate areas in your draft that need editing. Blue tabs at the top of each page in *A Writer's Handbook* link these common correction symbols with explanations, examples, and exercises related to the particular editing problem. The example below shows a page from handbook Chapter 33, section 4, on subject-verb agreement.

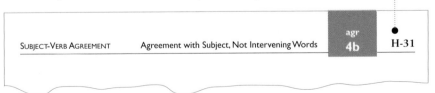

Answers to Exercises. As you complete the exercises in the handbook, you will want to know if you're on track. Turn to pages A-59–A-64 in the back of the book to find the correct answers to the lettered exercises.

Becoming a Better Writer by Using The Bedford Guide

The Bedford Guide includes readings, checklists, computer tips, and other help you can use to complete each writing assignment.

Model Readings. *The Bedford Guide* is filled with examples of both professional and student essays to help you as you write your own. These essays are located on the blue-shaded pages in *A Writer's Guide* and in *A Writer's Reader*. All the essays in the book include informative notes about the author, helpful prereading questions, definitions of difficult words, questions for thinking more deeply about the reading, and suggestions for writing.

Reading Annotations. The professional essays in *A Writer's Guide* begin with some annotations to point out notable features, such as the thesis and the first of the points supporting it. The student essays include a few intriguing questions in the margins to spark your imagination as you read.

2 The notion of becoming a writer had flickered off and on in my head since the Belleville days, but it wasn't until my third year in high school that the possibility took hold. Until then I'd been bored by everything associated with English courses. I found English grammar dull and baffling. I hated the assignments to turn out "compositions," and went at them like heavy labor, turning out leaden, lackluster paragraphs that were agonies for teachers to read and for me to write. The classics thrust on me to read seemed as deadening as chloroform.

THESIS stating main idea

Major event I

3 When our class was assigned to Mr. Fleagle for third-year English I antici-

🔵 *Why do you think that the writer reacts as he does?*

The whole episode sickened me to some degree, and at the time I did not know why. We continued to hunt throughout the afternoon, and feigning boredom, I allowed my cousin and grandfather to shoot all of the rabbits. Often, the shots didn't kill the rabbits outright so they had to be killed against the pickup. The thump, thump, thump of the rabbits' skulls against the metal began to irritate me, and I was

102   Chapter 7 • Comparing and Contrasting   A WRITER'S GUIDE

Learning by Writing

THE ASSIGNMENT: COMPARING AND CONTRASTING

■ You can complete each of the steps in this assignment by using the *Writing Guide Software for THE BEDFORD GUIDE.*

Write a paper in which you compare and contrast two items to enlighten readers about both subjects. The specific points of similarity and difference will be important, but you will go beyond them to draw a conclusion from your analysis. This conclusion, your thesis, needs to be more than "point A is different from point B" or "I prefer subject B to subject A." You will need to explain why you have drawn your conclusion. You'll also need to provide specific supporting evidence to explain your position and to convince your readers of its soundness. You may choose two people, two kinds of people, two places, two objects, two activities, or two ideas, but be sure to choose two you care about. You might write an impartial paper that distinctly portrays both subjects, or you might show why you favor one over the other.

Among the engaging student papers we've seen in response to similar assignments are these:

An American student compared and contrasted her home life with that of her roommate, a student from Nigeria. Her goal was to deepen her understanding of Nigerian society and her own.

A student who was interested in history compared and contrasted millennial fears for the years 1000 and 2000, considering whether popular responses had changed.

Another writer compared and contrasted conditions at two city facilities, making a case for a revised funding formula.

GENERATING IDEAS

■ For strategies for generating ideas, see Ch. 15.

Find Two Subjects. Pick subjects you can compare and contrast purposefully. An examination question may give them to you, ready-made: "Compare and contrast ancient Roman sculpture with that of the ancient Greeks." But suppose you have to find your subjects for yourself. You'll need to choose things that have a sensible basis for comparison, a common element.

moon rocks + stars = no common element

Dallas + Atlanta = cities to consider settling in

Montel Williams + Oprah Winfrey = television talk show hosts

Besides having a common element, the subjects should have enough in common to compare but differ enough to throw each other into sharp relief.

sports cars + racing cars = common element + telling differences

sports cars + oil tankers = limited common element + unpromising differences

---

PART TWO • A WRITER'S SITUATIONS   Learning by Writing   103

Try generating a list or brainstorming. Recall what you've recently read, discussed, or spotted on the Web. Let your mind skitter around in search of pairs that go together. You can also play the game of *free association,* jotting down a word and whatever it brings to mind: *Democrats? Republicans. New York? Los Angeles. King Kong? Godzilla.* Or whatever. You might find the following questions useful as you look for a topic:

■ For more on brainstorming, see pp. 254–56.

DISCOVERY CHECKLIST

____ Do you know two people who are strikingly different in attitude or behavior (perhaps your parents or two brothers, two friends, two teachers)?

____ Can you think of two groups of people who are both alike and different (perhaps two teams or two clubs)?

____ Have you taken two courses that were quite different but both valuable?

____ Do you prefer one of two places where you have lived or visited?

____ Can you recall two events in your life that shared similar aspects but turned out to be quite different (perhaps two sporting events or two romances or the births of two children)?

____ Can you compare and contrast two holidays or two family customs?

____ Are you familiar with two writers, two artists, or two musicians who seem to have similar goals but quite different accomplishments?

Once you have a list of pairs, put a star by those that seem promising. Ask yourself what similarities immediately come to mind. What differences? Can you jot down several of each? Are these striking, significant similarities and differences? If not, move on until you discover a workable pair.

> **Facing the Challenge: Comparing and Contrasting**
>
> **The major challenge that writers face when comparing and contrasting two subjects is to determine their purpose.** Writers who skip this step run the risk of having readers ask, "So, what's the point?" Suppose you develop brilliant points of similarity and difference between the films of Oliver Stone and those of Stanley Kubrick. Do you want to argue that one director is more skilled than the other? Or perhaps you want to show how they treat love or war differently in their films? Consider the following questions as you determine your primary purpose for comparing and contrasting:
>
> • Do you want to inform your readers about these two subjects in order to provide a better understanding of each?
>
> • Do you want to persuade your readers that one of the two subjects is preferable to the other?
>
> Asking what you want to demonstrate, discover, or prove *before* you begin to draft will help you to write a more effective comparison and contrast essay.

■ For writing activities for comparing and contrasting, visit <bedfordstmartins.com/bedguide> and do a keyword search:

| activities |

Clear Assignments.   The "Learning by Writing" section in Chapters 4 to 11 presents the assignment for the chapter and guides you through the process of writing that type of essay. The "Facing the Challenge" box in each of these sections helps you through the most complicated step in the assignment.

Computer Advice.   Each "Writing with a Computer" box offers handy tips for using technology wisely as you write your paper.

You can use the Table menu in your word processor to help you assess the importance of causes and effects. Open a file, go to the Table menu, insert a table, and enter "4" for the number of columns. Label the columns "Major Cause," "Minor Cause," "Major Effect," and "Minor Effect." Divide up your causes and effects accordingly, making entries under each heading. You can create more rows automatically by placing your cursor outside the last cell of the table and hitting the Return key. Each box should expand automatically to fit whatever you type into it. Refine your table as you relate, order, or limit your points.

WRITING WITH A COMPUTER

Applying What You Learn: Some Uses of Taking a Stand

In College Courses. When assignments and examination questions ask you to take a stand on a controversy, your responses indicate clearly to your instructor how firmly you grasp the material.

- In a health-care course, you might be asked to criticize this statement: "There's too much science and not enough caring in modern medicine."
- In a criminal justice course, you might be asked to state and defend your opinion on juvenile sentencing.
- In your research paper for an economics course, you might be asked to take a stand on the state budget allocations in terms of their effects on college tuition.

In the Workplace. In nearly every professional position — lawyer, teacher, nurse, business manager, journalist — you will be invited to state and support your views for the benefit of others in your profession or the general public.

- Scientists who do original research must persuade the scientific community that their findings are valid, writing and publishing accounts of their work in journals for evaluation by their peers.
- Social workers write documents to persuade courts and other agencies that certain actions or services are best for the welfare of their clients.
- Facing fierce competition, executives must convince their CEO that their ideas will result in impressive benefits for the company.

In Your Community. As an active citizen, you may feel compelled to inform and influence the public on matters of concern to all.

- You may want to write a letter to the editor of your newspaper or to your political representative debating a controversial issue faced by your community — controlling violence in your schools, funding a new drainage system, enforcing the leash law.
- You may represent the tenants in your apartment building by writing a letter of protest to a landlord who wants to raise rents.
- You may write a letter and design a poster to protest a company's operating and marketing policies.

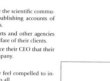

Useful Visuals. Watch for images, figures, charts, tables, visual examples, and other graphics throughout the text. Although we hope that these visuals contribute to an attractive book, they have been selected or designed to help you learn more effectively. Some may suggest ideas for writing or expand your thinking about a topic; others present information so that it's easy to absorb.

Helpful Checklists. Easy-to-use checklists help you to discover something to write about, get feedback from a peer, revise your draft, and edit using references to the Quick Editing Guide.

...ls to review your proposal and solution, an-

...n to this proposal? Does it make you want to ...out the problem?

- Are you convinced that the problem is of concern to you? If not, why not?
- Are you persuaded that the writer's solution is workable?
- Has the writer paid enough attention to readers and their concerns?
- Restate what you understand to be the proposal's major points:
  Problem
  Explanation of problem
  Proposal
  Explanation of proposal
  Procedure to implement proposal
  Advantages and disadvantages
  Response to other solutions
  Final recommendation
- If this were your paper, what is the one thing you would be sure to work on before handing it in?

FOR PEER RESPONSE

For general questions for a peer editor, see pp. 328–29.

Here are some questions to get you started editing and proofreading:

EDITING CHECKLIST

___ Is it clear what each pronoun refers to? Is any *this* or *that* ambiguous? Does each pronoun agree with (match) its antecedent?	A6
___ Is your sentence structure correct? Have you avoided writing fragments, comma splices, or fused sentences?	A1, A2
___ Do your transitions and other introductory elements have commas after them, if these are needed?	C1
___ Have you spelled and capitalized everything correctly, especially names of people and organizations?	D1, D2

■ For more help, turn to the dark-blue-edged pages, and find the sections of the Quick Editing Guide noted here.

Editing Advice.   Editing advice in the Quick Editing Guide, Handbook, and Glossary helps you write correctly and concisely. The Handbook also includes ESL guidance.

Applying What You Learn.   You can apply the writing skills that you learn using *The Bedford Guide* to writing in other college courses, at your job, in your community, and in your everyday life. The "Applying What You Learn" section that ends Chapters 4 through 11 shows how you might use different kinds of writing — for example, using observation to write a case study on the job or using evaluation to assess a public service in your community.

Contents

A WRITER'S READER

Introduction: Reading to Write   389

A WRITER'S RESEARCH MANUAL

A WRITER'S HANDBOOK

Introduction: Grammar, or The Way Words Work   H-3

Rhetorical Contents

(essays listed in order of appearance)

TELLING A STORY

A
Writer's
Guide

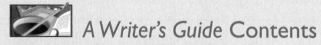 *A Writer's Guide* Contents

Introduction: Writing in College

As a college writer you probably wrestle with the question *What should I write?* You may feel you have nothing to say or nothing worth saying. Sometimes your difficulty lies in understanding the requirements of your writing situation, sometimes in finding a topic, and sometimes in uncovering pertinent information about it. Perhaps you, like many other college writers, have convinced yourself that professional writers are different in some way, that they have some special way of discovering ideas for writing. But they have no magic. In reality, what they have is experience and confidence, the products of lots of practice writing.

In *The Bedford Guide for College Writers,* we want you to become a better writer by actually writing. To help you do so, we'll give you a lot of practice as well as useful advice about writing to help you build your skills and confidence. Because writing and learning to write are many-faceted tasks, each part of *A Writer's Guide* is devoted to a different aspect of writing.

Part One, "A College Writer's Processes."   This part introduces writing, reading, and thinking critically — essential processes for meeting college expectations.

Part Two, "A Writer's Situations."   The eight chapters in Part Two form the core of *The Bedford Guide.* Each presents a writing situation and then guides you as you write a paper in response. You'll develop skills in recalling, observing, interviewing, comparing and contrasting, explaining causes and effects, taking a stand, proposing a solution, and evaluating.

Part Three, "Special Writing Situations."   This part leads you through three special situations that most students encounter at some point — writing about literature, writing in the workplace, and writing for assessment.

Part Four, "A Writer's Strategies."   Part Four is packed with tips and activities that you can use to generate ideas, plan, draft, develop, revise, and edit. You'll also find strategies for designing documents and analyzing images.

Together, these four parts contribute to a seamless whole, much like the writing process itself. Read them at a leisurely pace, study them when you need help, browse through them for ideas, or turn to them in a pinch. They will guide you as you write — and as you become a more skillful and confident writer.

PART ONE

A
College Writer's
Processes

Introduction

Your composition course may be one of your first college classes. For this reason, the course will both introduce you to college expectations and equip you with the skills that you need to meet these expectations. You may already feel confident that your past education and experiences have prepared you well for higher education. On the other hand, like many students, you may feel worried about your skills or uncertain about what will be expected and how you will fare in the academic world. In either case, *The Bedford Guide for College Writers* will give you concrete advice to help you succeed.

You already know a good deal about what college instructors expect. Like other teachers you've had, they'll require you to come to class, contribute to discussions, and hand in assignments. But they hope and expect that you'll do far more than this — that you'll engage fully in what's sometimes called "the college experience." The richness of this experience depends on your active response to the intellectual exchanges, resources, and opportunities that surround you in college. Sometimes this environment seems intimidating, and you may feel that you are simply drifting with the current, passively absorbing ideas as they flow through your classrooms. But you can learn how to ask questions about your writing, reading, and thinking — and how to navigate your own voyage of discovery.

As you undertake the process of becoming a well-educated person, your college instructors will expect you to show how you have grown as a writer, a reader, and a thinker. More specifically, they will want you to write thoughtful, purposeful papers, appropriately directed to your audience. They will want you not only to rely on your own ideas but also to read the writings of others, to ask questions about what you read, and to conduct research in complex disciplines, sometimes using and documenting many sources. And they will expect you to think critically and to state your points clearly as you write, integrating and supporting your own ideas with those drawn from your reading. The first three chapters in this book briefly introduce the processes — writing, reading, and thinking critically — that will help you meet these essential academic expectations.

Chapter 1
Writing Processes

You are already a writer with long experience. In school you have taken notes, written book reports and term papers, answered exam questions, perhaps kept a journal. In community meetings you have recorded minutes, and on the job you've composed memos. You've e-mailed friends, made shopping lists, maybe even tried your hand at writing poetry. All this experience is about to pay off for you.

Unlike parachute jumping, writing in college is something you go ahead and try without first learning all there is to know. In truth, nothing anyone can tell you will help as much as learning by doing. In this book our purpose is to help you to write better, deeper, clearer, and more satisfying papers than you have ever written before and to learn to do so by actually writing. Throughout the book we'll give you a lot of practice — in writing processes, patterns, and strategies — to build confidence. And we'll pose various writing situations and say, "Go to it!"

Writing, Reading, and Critical Thinking

In college you will add new techniques and perform challenging tasks that expand what you already know about writing. You may be asked not only to recall an experience but also to reflect upon its significance. Or you may be asked to go beyond summarizing varied positions about an issue by presenting your own position or proposing a solution. Above all, you will be reading and thinking critically — not just stacking up facts but analyzing what you discover, deciding what it means, and weighing its value.

In your composition course, you can view each writing task as a problem to solve, often through careful reading and objective thinking. You will

■ For more on reading critically, see Ch. 2. For more on thinking critically, see Ch. 3.

need to read — and write — actively, engaging with the ideas of others. At the same time, you will need to think critically, analyzing and judging those ideas. To help you assess your own achievement, you will use criteria — models, conventions, principles, standards. As you write and rewrite, you can evaluate what you are doing by considering specific questions:

- Have you achieved your purpose?
- Have you considered your audience?
- Have you made your point clear by stating it in a thesis or unmistakably implying it?
- Have you supported your point with enough reliable evidence to persuade readers?
- Have you arranged your ideas logically so that each follows from, supports, or adds to the one before it?
- Have you made the connections among ideas clear to a reader?
- Have you established an appropriate tone?

In large measure, learning to write well is learning what questions to ask as you write. Throughout *A Writer's Guide*, we include questions and suggestions designed to help you accomplish your writing tasks and reflect on your own processes as you write, read, and think critically.

A Process of Writing

Writing can seem at times an overwhelming drudgery, worse than scrubbing floors; at other moments, it's a sport full of thrills — like whizzing downhill on skis, not knowing what you'll meet around a bend. Surprising and unpredictable as the process may seem, nearly all writers do similar things:

- They generate ideas.
- They plan, draft, and develop their papers.
- They revise and edit.

▇ You can complete each of these steps for any essay you write using the *Writing Guide Software* for *THE BEDFORD GUIDE*.

These three activities form the basis of most effective writing processes, and they lie at the heart of each chapter in Part Two, "A Writer's Situations." These activities aren't lockstep stages: you don't always proceed in a straight line. You can skip around, taking up parts of the process in whatever order you like, work on several parts at a time, or circle back over what's already done. For example, while gathering material, you may feel an urge to play with a sentence until it clicks. Or while writing a draft, you may decide to look for more material. You may leap ahead, cross out, backtrack, adjust, question, test a fresh approach, tinker, polish — and then in the end look up unfamiliar punctuation and spell-check the tricky words.

GENERATING IDEAS

For strategies for generating ideas, see Ch. 15.

The first activity in writing—finding a topic and something to say about it—is often the most challenging and least predictable. Each chapter in Part Two includes a section called "Generating Ideas," which is filled with examples, questions, checklists, and visuals designed to trigger ideas and associations that will help you begin the chapter's writing assignment.

Discovering What to Write About.   Finding a topic is not always easy, but you may discover an idea while talking with friends, riding your bike, or staring out the window. Sometimes a topic lies near home, in a conversation or an everyday event you recall. Often, your reading will raise questions that call for investigation. Even if a particular writing assignment holds little personal appeal for you, your challenge is to find a slant that does interest you. Find it, and words will flow—words that can engage readers as you accomplish your purpose.

Discovering Material.   You'll need information to shape and support your ideas—facts and figures, reports and opinions, examples and illustrations. How do you find supporting material that makes your slant on a topic clear and convincing to your readers? Luckily you have numerous sources at your fingertips. You can recall your own experience and knowledge, you can observe things around you, you can converse with others who are knowledgeable, you can read enlightening materials that draw you to new approaches and views, and you can think critically about all these sources around you.

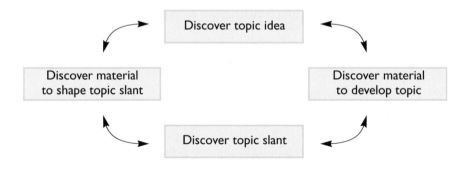

PLANNING, DRAFTING, AND DEVELOPING

After discovering a topic and beginning to gather material about it, you will plan your paper, write a draft, and then develop your ideas further. Each chapter in Part Two has a section titled "Planning, Drafting, and Developing," designed to help you through these stages of the writing process for the assignment in that chapter.

Planning. Having discovered a burning idea to write about (or at least a smoldering one) and some supporting material (but maybe not enough yet), you will sort out what matters most. If right away you see one main point, or thesis, for your paper, test various ways of stating it, given your purpose and audience:

For planning strategies, see Ch. 16.

> MAYBE   Parking in the morning before class is annoying.
>
> OR   Campus parking is a big problem.

Next arrange your ideas and material in a sensible order that will clarify your point. For example, you might group and label the ideas you have generated, make an outline, or analyze the main point, breaking it down into its parts:

For practice choosing a main point, visit <bedfordstmartins.com/bedguide> and do a keyword search:

thesis

> Campus parking is a problem for students because of the long lines, inefficient entrances, and poorly marked spaces.

But if no clear thesis emerges quickly, don't worry. You may find one while you draft — that is, while you write an early version of your paper.

Drafting. When your ideas first start to flow, you want to welcome them — lure them forth, not tear them apart — or they might go back into hiding.

For drafting strategies, see Ch. 17.

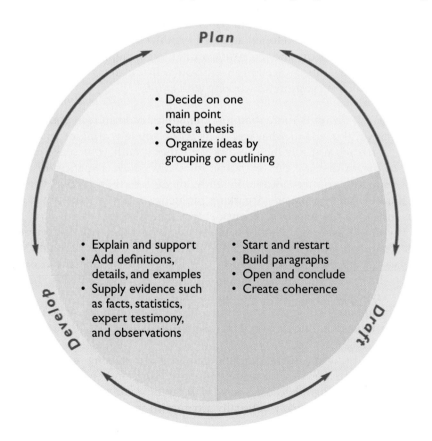

Plan
- Decide on one main point
- State a thesis
- Organize ideas by grouping or outlining

Develop
- Explain and support
- Add definitions, details, and examples
- Supply evidence such as facts, statistics, expert testimony, and observations

Draft
- Start and restart
- Build paragraphs
- Open and conclude
- Create coherence

Processes for Planning, Drafting, and Developing

Don't be afraid to take risks at this stage: you'll probably be surprised and pleased at what happens, even though your first version will be rough. Writing takes time; a paper usually needs several drafts and may need a clearer introduction, stronger conclusion, more convincing evidence, or a revised plan. Especially for an unfamiliar or complicated subject, you may throw out your first attempt and start all over if a stronger idea hits you.

For strategies for developing ideas, see Ch. 18. For strategies for generating ideas, see Ch. 15. For advice on using a few sources, see the Quick Research Guide (the dark-red-edged pages).

Developing.   As you draft, you'll weave in explanations, definitions, and evidence to make your ideas clear. For example, you may need to define an at-risk student, illustrate the problems faced by a single parent, or supply statistics about hit-and-run accidents. If you lack specific support for your main point, you can use strategies for developing ideas — or return to strategies for generating ideas. You'll keep gaining insights and drawing conclusions while you draft. By all means, welcome these ideas, and work them in if they fit. For a summary of this process, see the graphic on page 11.

REVISING AND EDITING

For revising and editing strategies, see Ch 19.

You might want to relax once you have a draft, but for most writers, revising begins the work in earnest. Revising means both reseeing and rewriting, making major changes so that your paper accomplishes what you want it to. After you have a well-developed and well-organized revision, you are ready to edit: to correct errors and improve wording. Each chapter in Part Two has a "Revising and Editing" section where you will find revision and editing checklists with a suggestion for working with a peer.

Revising.   Revision is more than just changing words: in fact, you may revise what you know and what you think while you're writing or when you pause to reread. You can then rework your thesis, shift your plans, decide what to put in or leave out, rearrange for clarity, move sentences or paragraphs around, connect ideas differently, or express them better. Perhaps you'll add costs to a paper on parking problems or switch attention to fathers instead of mothers as you consider teen parenthood.

If you put aside your draft for a few hours or a day, you can reread it with fresh eyes and a clear mind. As humorist Leo Rosten has said, "You have to put yourself in the position of the negative reader, the resistant reader, the reader who doesn't surrender easily, the reader who is alien to you as a type, even the reader who doesn't like what you are writing." Other students can also help you — sometimes more than a textbook or an instructor can — by responding to your drafts as engaged readers.

For editing advice, see the Quick Editing Guide (the dark-blue-edged pages).

Editing.   Editing means refining the details and correcting any flaws that may stand in the way of your readers' understanding and enjoyment. Don't edit too early, though, because you may waste time on some part that you later revise out. In editing, you usually accomplish these repairs:

- Get rid of unnecessary words.
- Choose livelier and more precise words.
- Rearrange words in a clearer, more emphatic order.
- Combine short, choppy sentences, or break up long, confusing sentences.
- Refine transitions for continuity of thought.
- Check grammar, usage, punctuation, and mechanics.

Proofreading.   Finally you'll proofread your paper, taking a last look, checking correctness, and catching doubtful spellings or word-processing errors.

For more on proofreading, see pp. 338–39.

REVISE	← PEER RESPONSE →	EDIT	→	PROOFREAD
• Purpose		• Grammar		• Spelling
• Thesis		• Sentences		• Incorrect words
• Audience		• Word choice		• Missing words
• Structure		• Punctuation		• Minor errors
• Support		• Mechanics		• Minor details
• Emphasis		• Format for paper		

ACTIVITY: DESCRIBING YOUR WRITING PROCESS

Describe your writing process. How do you get started? How do you keep writing? What process do you go through to reach a final draft? Do your steps ever vary depending upon the type of writing you're doing? What step or strategy in your writing process would you most like to change?

Audience and Purpose

At any moment in the writing process, two questions are worth asking:

Who is my audience?   **Why am I writing?**

WRITING FOR READERS

Your audience, or your readers, may or may not be defined in your assignment. Consider the following examples:

ASSIGNMENT 1   Discuss the advantages and disadvantages of home schooling.

ASSIGNMENT 2   In a letter to parents of school-aged children, discuss the advantages and disadvantages of home schooling.

■ For more on planning for your readers, see pp. 269–70.

Notice how the first assignment differs from the second. Because the first leaves the audience undefined, you can assume that your primary readers would be your instructor and your classmates. Writing for these readers will give you practice in writing for more general academic audiences. If your assignment defines an audience, as in the second example, you will need to think about how to approach those readers and what to assume about their relationship to your topic. For example, what points would you include in a discussion aimed at parents? How would you organize your ideas? Would you discuss advantages first? Or disadvantages? Consider how your approach might differ if the assignment read this way:

ASSIGNMENT 3   In a letter to public school teachers, discuss the advantages and disadvantages of home schooling.

When you analyze what readers know, believe, and value, you can aim your writing toward them with a better chance of hitting your mark.

Use these questions to help you write and revise for your audience:

■ For more on revising for audience, see p. 326.

- Who are your readers? What is their relationship to you?
- What do your readers already know about this topic? What do you want them to learn?
- How much detail will they want to read about this topic?
- What objections are they likely to raise as they read? How can you anticipate and overcome their objections?
- What's likely to convince them?
- What's likely to offend them?

ACTIVITY: CONSIDERING AUDIENCE

Write a short paragraph describing in detail a "worst" event — your worst date, worst dinner, worst car repair, or some similar catastrophe. Then revise that paragraph so that your audience is a person involved in the event — the person who went on that date with you, cooked or served the dinner, worked on your car. Now revise the paragraph once again — this time writing to a person you plan to date soon, a cook at a restaurant you want to try, or a repair person working at another garage. Compare the three paragraphs. How are they similar? How do they differ?

WRITING FOR A REASON

■ For more on planning with your purpose in mind, see pp. 269–70. For more on revising for purpose, see pp. 324–25.

Like most college writing assignments, every assignment in this book asks you to write for a definite reason. For example, in Chapter 4 you'll be asked to recall a memorable experience in order to explain its importance for you;

in Chapter 9, you'll take a stand on a controversy in order to convey your position and persuade readers to respect it. Be careful not to confuse the sources and strategies you are asked to apply in these assignments with your ultimate purpose for writing. "To compare and contrast two things" is not a very interesting purpose; "to compare and contrast two Web sites *in order to explain their differences*" implies a real reason for writing. In most college writing, your ultimate purpose will be to explain something to your readers or to convince them of something.

To sharpen your concentration on your purpose, ask yourself from the start: What do I want to do? And, in revising, Did I do what I meant to do? You'll find that these practical questions will help you slice out irrelevant information and remove other barriers to getting your paper where you want it to go.

ACTIVITY: CONSIDERING PURPOSE

Return to the three paragraphs you wrote for the previous activity (p. 14). Write a sentence or two summing up your purpose in writing each paragraph. Given these three purposes, how might you revise your paragraphs?

What Matters Most

Like a hard game of basketball, writing a college paper is strenuous. As the following chart shows, you can find help throughout the writing process in this book and its electronic supplements. Without getting in your way, we want to lend you all possible support and guidance. So, no doubt, does your instructor, someone closer to you than any textbook writers. Still, like even the best coaches, instructors and textbook writers can improve your game only so far. Advice on how to write won't make you a better writer. You'll learn more and have more fun when you take a few sentences to the hoop and make points yourself. After you sink a few baskets, you'll gain confidence in your ability and find the process of writing easier.

Major Stages	A Writer's Activities
Generate Ideas	• Find a topic and something to say about it. • Brainstorm, freewrite, doodle, map, imagine, ask questions, seek motives, or keep a journal. • Read, talk, observe, and think.
Plan	• Think about your purpose and audience. • Convert a topic idea to a working thesis. • Organize your ideas by grouping or outlining.
Draft	• Start and restart. • Write paragraphs and topic sentences. • Write openings and conclusions. • Create coherence with transitions, repetitions, and pronouns.
Develop	• Weave in supporting examples, details, and definitions. • Analyze subject, divide and classify, analyze process, compare and contrast, or identify cause and effect. • Supply evidence—facts, statistics, expert testimony, and firsthand observation.
Revise	• Reconsider purpose, thesis, and audience. • Rework structure, support, and connections. • Stress what counts; cut or whittle what doesn't. • Work with a peer editor.
Edit	• Refine grammar, sentences, and word choice. • Correct punctuation and mechanics. • Check the paper's format and document design.
Proofread	• Check for misspellings. • Check for incorrect or missing words. • Check for minor errors and details.

A Writer's Resources

In this book	On this book's Web site*	In this book's software
■ "Generating Ideas" section in Part Two, including Discovery Checklists ■ "Strategies for Generating Ideas," Chapter 15 ■ "Reading Processes" in Chapter 2 and *A Writer's Reader*	🔍 activities 🔍 reading ■ TopLinks	■ On-screen writing guides with prompts for generating ideas ■ Journaling feature
■ "Planning, Drafting, and Developing" sections in Part Two ■ "Strategies for Planning," Chapter 16	🔍 thesis 🔍 organize	■ On-screen writing guides with prompts for planning
■ "Planning, Drafting, and Developing" sections in Part Two ■ "Strategies for Drafting," Chapter 17 ■ Advice on using graphics in Chapter 20	🔍 activities 🔍 open_end 🔍 coherence	■ On-screen writing guides with prompts for drafting and developing ■ Sample essays with writing features highlighted
■ "Planning, Drafting, and Developing" sections in Part Two ■ "Strategies for Developing," Chapter 18 ■ Advice on sources in Quick Research Guide	🔍 examples 🔍 development 🔍 support	■ On-screen writing guides with prompts for drafting and developing ■ Sample essays with writing features highlighted
■ "Revising and Editing" sections in Part Two ■ "Strategies for Revising and Editing," Chapter 19	🔍 process	■ On-screen writing guides with prompts for revising
■ "Revising and Editing" sections in Part Two ■ "Strategies for Revising and Editing," Chapter 19 ■ Format for academic papers in Chapter 20 ■ Quick Editing Guide or MLA style in Quick Research Guide	🔍 process ■ Exercise Central	■ On-screen writing guides with prompts for editing ■ Grammar tutorials ■ Grammar assessment
■ "Revising and Editing" sections in Part Two ■ "Strategies for Revising and Editing," Chapter 19	🔍 process ■ Exercise Central	■ On-screen writing guides with prompts for revising and editing ■ Grammar tutorials ■ Grammar assessment

*At <bedfordstmartins.com/bedguide>, use the search box shown to find writing resources or exercises by keyword.

Chapter 2
Reading Processes

What's so special about college reading? Don't you just pick up the book, start on the first page, and keep going? Certainly this approach works for much reading, and you probably have been reading this way ever since you met *The Cat in the Hat*. Reading from beginning to end works especially well when you are eager to find out what happens next, as in a thriller or a romance, or what to do next, as in a cookbook.

On the other hand, much of what you read in college — whether textbooks, scholarly articles, books, research reports, or the papers of your peers — is complicated and challenging. Dense material like this may require special reading strategies such as rereading, identifying main points, or annotating key passages. Most important, college reading often requires closer reading and deeper thinking — in short, a process for reading critically.

Reading critically is a useful skill. For assignments in this course alone, you will need to evaluate the strengths and weaknesses of essays by professionals and students. If you research any topic, you will need to figure out what your sources say, how you might use their information, and whether they are reliable. Critical reading is important in other courses, too. For example, you might analyze a sociology report on violent children for its assumptions and implications as well as the soundness of its argument. On the job, you may be required to verify that your product meets technical specifications, while in the community, you may want to respond to a proposal for a tax hike. Whenever your writing relies on critical reading, you need to explain what is going on in the text and then go further, making your own point based on its ideas.

A Process of Critical Reading

Reading critically means approaching whatever you read in an active, questioning manner. This essential college-level skill changes reading from a spectator sport to a contact sport. You no longer sit in the stands, watching graceful skaters glide by. Instead, you charge right into a rough-and-tumble hockey game, gripping your stick and watching out for your teeth.

Critical reading, like critical thinking, is not a specialized, isolated activity. It is a continuum of strategies that thoughtful people use every day to grapple with new information, to integrate it with existing knowledge, and to apply it to problems in daily life and in academic courses. Many readers do similar things:

For more on critical thinking, see Ch. 3.

- They get ready to do their reading.
- They read on a literal level.
- They read on an analytical level.

Educational expert Benjamin S. Bloom[1] identified six levels of cognitive activity: knowledge, comprehension, application, analysis, synthesis, and evaluation. Each level becomes more complex and demands higher thinking skills than the previous one. The first three levels are literal skills. When you show that you know a fact, comprehend its meaning, and can apply it to a new situation, you demonstrate your mastery over building blocks of thought. The other three levels — analysis, synthesis, and evaluation — are critical skills. These skills take you beyond the literal level: you break apart the building blocks to see what makes them work, recombine them in new and useful ways, and judge their worth or significance.

See the reading skills figure on p. 23.

ACTIVITY: DESCRIBING YOUR OWN READING PROCESS

How do you read a magazine, newspaper, or popular novel? What are your goals when you do this kind of reading? What's different about reading the material assigned in college? What techniques do you use for reading assignments? How might you read more effectively? Do you use strategies that might help your classmates, especially in classes with a lot of reading?

Getting Started

College reading is active reading. Before you read, think ahead about how to approach the reading process — how to make the most of the time you spend reading.

[1] Benjamin S. Bloom et al., *Taxonomy of Educational Objectives, Handbook 1: Cognitive Domain* (New York: McKay, 1956).

PREPARING TO READ

Thinking about Your Purpose.   Naturally enough, your overall goal for doing most college reading is to be successful in your courses. When you begin to read, ask questions like these about your immediate purpose:

- What are you reading?
- Why are you reading?
- What do you want to do with the reading?
- What does your instructor expect you to learn from the reading?
- Do you need to memorize the details, find the main points, or connect the ideas?
- How does this reading build on, add to, contrast with, or otherwise relate to other reading assignments in the course?

Planning Your Follow-Up.   When you are assigned a specific essay, chapter, or article or are required to choose a reading about a certain topic, your instructor probably expects something to follow the reading.

- Do you need to be ready to discuss the reading during class?
- Will you need to mention it or analyze it during an examination?
- Will you need to write an essay or paper about it or its topic?
- Do you need to find its main points? Sum it up? Compare it? Question it? Spot its strengths and weaknesses? Draw useful details from it?

Skimming the Text.   Before you actively read a text, begin by skimming it — quickly reading only enough to introduce yourself to its content and organization. If the reading has a table of contents or subheadings, read those first to figure out what the material covers and how it is organized. Read the first paragraph and then the first (or first and last) sentence of each paragraph that follows. If the material has any illustrations or diagrams, read the captions.

RESPONDING TO READING

Keeping a Reading Journal.   A reading journal is an excellent place to record not just what you read but how you respond to it. It helps you read actively and build a reservoir of ideas for follow-up writing. You can use a special notebook or computer file to address questions like these:

- What is the subject of the reading? What is the writer's stand?
- What does the writer take for granted? What assumptions does he or she begin with? Where are these stated or suggested?
- What evidence supports the writer's main points?

- Do you agree with what the writer has said? Do his or her ideas clash with your ideas or question something you take for granted?

- What conclusions can you draw from the reading? Has the writer failed to tell you something you wish you knew?

For advice on keeping a writer's journal, see Ch. 15.

- Has the reading opened your eyes to new ways of viewing the subject?

Annotating the Text.   Writing notes on the page (or on a photocopy if the material is not your own) is a useful way to trace the author's points, question them, and add your own comments as they pop up. You can underline key points, mark checks and stars by ideas when you agree or disagree, and jot questions in the margins. One student decided to analyze an article called "Why Men Fear Women's Teams" by Kate Rounds from the January–February 1991 issue of *Ms.* She annotated a key passage in the article like this:

For more on evaluating what you read, see C1–C3 in the Quick Research Guide (the dark-red-edged pages).

For a Critical Reading Checklist, see p. 25.

different case from individual sports

By contrast, women's professional (team) sports have failed   *key point*
spectacularly. Since the mid-seventies, every professional league —
✓ softball, basketball, and volleyball — has gone belly-up. In 1981, after a
example four-year struggle, the Women's Basketball League (WBL), backed by   *bitter tone*
backs up sports promoter Bill Byrne, folded. The league was drawing fans in a
point number of cities, but the sponsors weren't there, TV wasn't there, and
✓ nobody seemed to miss the spectacle of a few good women fighting for
a basketball.   *our team never got these either*

Something I know about!   Or a (volleyball,) for that matter. Despite the success of (bikini) — *Why does she call it this?*
volleyball, an organization called MLV (Major League Volleyball) bit the   *2nd example*
dust in March of 1989 after nearly three years of struggling for
sponsorship, fan support, and television exposure. [As with pro
basketball, there was a man behind women's professional volleyball,] real   *She's suspicious of men*
estate investor Robert (Bat) Batinovich. Batinovich admits that, unlike
oh, great court volleyball, beach volleyball has a lot of "visual T&A mixed into it." ←

What court volleyball does have, according to former MLV executive   *seems like these are only two options*
credential director Lindy Vivas, is strong women athletes. Vivas is assistant
volleyball coach at San Jose State University. "The United States in
Why do guys always think we're weak and prissy?   general," she says, "has problems dealing with women athletes and   *good quote*
strong, aggressive females. The perception is you have to be more
aggressive in team sports than in golf and tennis, which aren't contact
sports. Women athletes are looked at as masculine and get the stigma of ←
being gay."

This student's annotations helped her to deepen her reading of the article and generate ideas for her writing.

ACTIVITY: ANNOTATING A PASSAGE

For a sample annotated passage, see p. 21.

Annotate the following passage from the middle of Ellen Goodman's essay "Kids, Divorce, and the Myth."

> Not that long ago, when the divorce statistics first began to rise, many Americans comforted themselves with the belief that parents and children shared the same perspective. A child in an unhappy home would surely know it, surely suffer from it. What was right for parents — including divorce — was right for children.
>
> But today that seems like a soothing or perhaps self-serving myth.
>
> One of the myth-busters is Judith Wallerstein, who has been studying the children of divorce for over twenty-five years. Her latest book about *The Unexpected Legacy of Divorce* is written about and for the offspring of splintered families, children who carry the family rupture into their adulthood.
>
> This psychologist has followed 131 children of 80 California families, a small and not-so-random sample of the one million children whose parents divorce each year. Today a quarter of all adults under forty-four come from divorced homes, and Wallerstein takes a handful of these children to show in rich detail the way divorce was and remains a life-transforming event.
>
> Her book echoes with the laments of their tribe. These are adults who spent childhood negotiating between two parents and two homes. Some were emotionally abandoned, others were subject to the crazy postdivorce years. Some still wait for disaster, and others are stronger for the struggle.
>
> But as the elder to their tribe, Wallerstein makes one central and challenging point: "The myth that if the parents have a poor marriage the children are going to be unhappy is not true."

Reading on a Literal Level

To read critically, you must engage with a piece on both a literal level and an analytical level. As the diagram on page 23 shows, each skill acts as a foundation for the next. When you read literally, you decode the words in the passage, figure out the meaning, and connect the information to what you already know. For example, suppose you read in your history book a passage about Franklin Delano Roosevelt (FDR), the only American president elected to four consecutive terms of office.

KNOWING, COMPREHENDING, AND APPLYING

Becoming Aware of the Information.   Once you read the passage, even if you have little background in American history, you know and can recall the information it presents about FDR and his four terms in office.

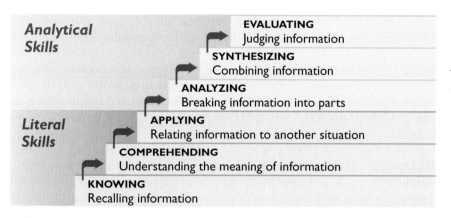

Literal and Analytical Reading Skills
The information in this figure is adapted from Benjamin S. Bloom et al., Taxonomy of Educational Objectives, Handbook 1: Cognitive Domain *(New York: McKay, 1956).*

Comprehending the Information.   To comprehend the information, you need to know that a term for a U.S. president is four years and that *consecutive* means "continuous." Thus, FDR was elected to serve for sixteen years.

Applying the Information.   To apply this knowledge, you think of other presidents — George Washington, who served two terms; Grover Cleveland, who served two terms but not consecutively; Jimmy Carter, who served one term; and Bill Clinton, who served two terms. Then you realize that being elected to four terms is quite unusual.

Reading on an Analytical Level

After mastering a passage on the literal level, you need to read on the analytical level, probing deeply into the meaning beneath the surface. First you analyze the information, considering its parts and implications from various angles. Then you gather related material and synthesize all of it, recombining it to achieve new insights. Finally, you evaluate the significance of the information.

ANALYZING, SYNTHESIZING, AND EVALUATING

Analyzing.   To return to FDR's four terms as president, you can ask questions to scrutinize this information from various angles, selecting a principle for analysis that suits your purpose. Then you can use this principle to break the information into its components or parts. For example, you might analyze FDR's tenure in office in relation to the political longevity of other presidents. Why has FDR been the only president elected to serve four terms? What circumstances during his terms contributed to three reelections? How is FDR different from other presidents?

Synthesizing.   To answer your questions, you may have to read more or review material you have read in the past. Then you begin synthesizing —

recombining information, pulling together all the facts and opinions, identifying the evidence accepted by all or most sources, examining any controversial evidence, and drawing whatever conclusions reliable evidence seems to support. For example, it would be logical to conclude that the special circumstances of the Great Depression and World War II contributed to FDR's four terms. On the other hand, it would not be logical to conclude that Americans reelected him out of pity because he was a victim of polio.

Evaluating.   Finally, you evaluate your new knowledge to determine its significance, both to your understanding of depression-era politics and to your assessment of your history book's approach. For instance, you might ask yourself, Why has the book's author chosen to make this point? How does it affect the rest of the discussion? Does this author seem reliable? And you may also have formed your own opinion about FDR's reelections. Based on your critical reading and the evidence you have gathered, you might conclude that FDR's four-term presidency is understandable in light of the events of the 1930s and 1940s, that the author has mentioned this fact to highlight the unique political atmosphere of that era, and that, in your opinion, it is evidence neither for nor against FDR's excellence as a president.

ACTIVITY: READING ANALYTICALLY

■ For additional critical reading activities, visit <bedfordstmartins.com/bedguide> and do a keyword search:

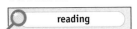

Think back to something you have read recently that helped you make a decision, perhaps a newspaper article, a magazine article, an electronic posting, or a college brochure. How did you analyze what you read, breaking the information into parts? How did you synthesize it, combining it with what you already knew? How did you evaluate it, judging its significance for your decision?

GENERATING IDEAS FROM READING

Like flints that strike against one another and cause sparks, readers and writers provoke one another. For example, when your class discusses an essay, you may be surprised by the range of insights reported by other readers. If you missed some of their insights during your reading, remember that they may be equally surprised by what you see.

■ For more on generating ideas, see Ch. 15.

Often you look to other writers — in books or magazines — to stimulate your ideas by suggesting a topic, providing information about it, or helping you explain it or back it up with evidence. You may read because you want to understand ideas, test them, or debate with the writer, but reading is a dynamic process; your reading may change your ideas instead of supporting them. Here are suggestions for unlocking the potential hidden in a good text.

Log Your Reading.   For several days keep a log of the articles that you find. Record the author, title, and source for each promising piece so that you can easily find it again. Briefly note the subject and point of view as well, so you identify a range of possibilities.

Look for Meaty Pieces.   Spur your thinking by browsing through essay collections or current magazines in the library or online. Try *Atlantic Monthly, Harper's, New Republic, Commentary,* or special-interest magazines — such as *Architectural Digest* or *Black History Magazine* — on subjects that intrigue you. Check the editorials and op-ed columns in your local newspaper, the *New York Times,* or the *Wall Street Journal.* Also search the Internet for articles on an interesting subject that challenges you to think seriously (such as film classics or the effects of poverty on children). Look for articles that are meaty, not superficial, and that are written to inform and convince, not to entertain or amuse.

Recall Something You Have Already Read.   What have you read lately that started you thinking? Return to a recent reading — a chapter in a humanities textbook, an article assigned in a sociology course, a research study for a biology course.

Read Critically.   Once you select a thought-provoking piece, read it slowly and carefully. Read first on the literal level, so that you are aware of the information and can comprehend and apply it. Then read on the analytical level, analyzing, synthesizing, and evaluating. Instead of just soaking up what the reading says, engage in a dialogue or conversation with the writer. Criticize. Wonder. Argue back. Demand convincing evidence. Use the following checklist to get you started as a critical reader.

CRITICAL READING CHECKLIST

____ What problems and issues does the author raise?

____ What is the author's purpose? Is it to explain or inform? To persuade? To amuse? In addition to this overall purpose, is the author trying to accomplish some other agenda?

____ Where do you agree, and where do you disagree? Where do you want to say "Yeah, right!" or "I don't think so!"?

____ How does this piece relate to your own experiences or thoughts? Have you encountered anything similar? Is the topic or approach personally intriguing to you?

____ Are there any important words or ideas that you don't understand? If so, do you need to reread or turn to a dictionary or reference book?

____ What is the author's point of view? What does the author assume or take for granted? Where does the author reveal these assumptions? Do they make the selection seem weak or biased?

■ For more on facts and opinions, see p. 36.

■ For more on evaluating evidence, see pp. 38–39 and C1–C3 in the Quick Research Guide (the dark-red-edged pages).

____ Which statements are facts that can be verified by observation, firsthand testimony, or research? Which are opinions? Does one or the other dominate the piece?

____ Is the writer's evidence accurate, relevant, and sufficient? Do you find it persuasive?

Analyze the Writing Strategies.   For some readings in this book, notes in the margin illustrate how to identify key features such as the introduction, thesis statement or main idea, major points, and supporting evidence. Ask questions such as these to help you identify writing strategies:

WRITING STRATEGIES CHECKLIST

____ How does the author introduce the reading?

____ Where does the author state or imply the main idea or thesis?

____ How is the text organized? What are the main points used to develop the thesis?

____ How does the author supply support — facts, data, statistics, expert opinions, personal experiences, observations, explanations, examples, or other information?

____ How does the author connect or emphasize ideas?

____ How does the author conclude the reading?

____ What is the author's tone? How do the words and examples reveal the author's attitude, biases, or assumptions?

■ For a sample annotated passage, see p. 21.

■ For more practice reading critically, read and annotate "Women and Men Talking on the Job" (pp. 441–46) or "Male Bashing on TV" (pp. 463–67) from A Writer's Reader.

ACTIVITY: READING CRITICALLY

Using the advice in this chapter, critically read the following essay from the *Washington Post* Web site. First, add your own notes and comments in the margin, responding on both literal and analytical levels. Second, add notes about the writer's writing strategies. (Sample annotations are supplied to help you get started.) Next, write out your own well-reasoned conclusions about the reading.

Jay Mathews

Class Struggle: Is Homework Really So Terrible?

Writer uses family example as introduction

Sounds good to me!!
Writer uses humor to bond with readers

My daughter recently announced, with dramatic emphasis, that she is now a second semester high school senior. This is an important milestone. The college applications have all been written. The last grades that count for much have been recorded. Time to party.   1

Except that it is not her style. She said she was going to start taking it easy, but she is still doing a lot of homework. Last week her friends told her   2 they were going to organize an intervention because they caught her spending several hours preparing for an exam.

What should I do about her? Like most American parents, I am proud of my children when they meet their academic responsibilities. But I also worry when it seems too much. We want our children to have balanced lives. We often see our children's teachers as insensitive taskmasters who steal time from family life. *3 Writer sets up conflict*

I was fascinated by a recent report about all this on CBS *Sunday Morning.* I decided to check on some of the facts and experts the program cited in hopes that would help me make up my own mind. *4 Writer notes TV source but digs deeper*

The CBS report said a University of Michigan study showed more than a 50 percent increase in the amount of homework done by American school children twelve and under. But the actual study had some surprises. *5*

The university's Panel Study of Income Dynamics, directed by economist Frank Stafford of the Institute for Social Research, has been gathering data for decades on how people use their time. They surveyed a representative sample of 3,586 children aged twelve and under in 1997, and compared the results to a similar 1981 study. As CBS reported, homework time increased 59.5 percent. *6*

Poor kids!

But it is like raising my bowling score. A nearly 60 percent improvement sounds big until you learn that my previous average was a 53. The average child in 1981 spent just one hour and twenty-four minutes a week on homework. By 1997 that had increased to two hours and fourteen minutes. That means that this allegedly overburdened American child, innocent victim of callous teachers, is averaging less than a half hour of homework each school night. *7 Oops—not really*

Hmm. I found books written by two experts on the CBS show. One was Etta Kralovec, coauthor with John Buell of the 2000 book *The End of Homework: How Homework Disrupts Families, Overburdens Children, and Limits Learning,* and Janine Bempechat, author of the 2000 book *Getting Our Kids Back on Track: Educating Children for the Future.* *8*

I was disappointed by the Kralovec-Buell book, although that may be my fault. The authors and I seem to be on different planes of existence. Their proof that homework is an important cause of suicide among school children is a news clipping from the Harare [Zimbabwe] *Herald* referring to the case of an eleven-year-old in Hong Kong who left a note saying he jumped out of a thirty-four-story building because he didn't finish his lessons. They argue that homework is bad, in part, because it gives middle class children an unfair advantage over less financially fortunate classmates. They suggest that the problem can only be solved by a social and cultural revolution in the United States as well as the rest of the world and, I imagine, the eternal cosmos. *9*

In other words, if you are worried because it is 1 A.M. and your daughter hasn't finished her environmental studies report, Kralovec and Buell aren't much help. *10*

Bempechat has a more practical approach. She gets quickly to what research says about homework: It has no effect on achievement in early *11* elementary grades and not much effect in the higher elementary grades, but does raise achievement in middle school and high school. Middle schoolers do better if they study at home five to ten hours a week, but more than that doesn't add anything. The greatest benefits from homework occur for high schoolers who study five to ten hours a week, and students who do more than that experience additional gains.

So should we forget about homework in the first and second grades? 12 Bempechat says no, for an intriguing reason. Children need to develop habits of work, she says, and it is likely to be easier if they start early with appropriately small obligations.

"The fifteen-minute assignment of first grade gradually stretches into the 13 three-week assignment of fifth grade," she says. "The years in between will be the training ground for our children's development into (relatively) organized and mature learners. Early experiences with homework may not contribute to children's academic development, but they certainly promote their motivational development. . . . As school gets increasingly difficult and courses become more complex, your children need to be persistent when the going gets tough. Homework, as much as you and they may hate it, will foster these strengths of character."

Kralovec and Buell will argue, perhaps, that Bempechat has given in to 14 the capitalist worship of productivity and ignores the importance of spiritual growth. That may make sense on their planet, but the need to develop habits of consistency and persistence appeals to me. The research I have done about college admissions over the past three years convinces me that success in life, as opposed to success in the application game, is the direct result of those character traits Bempechat is talking about, and they develop long before anyone ever takes an SAT.

Once we establish that homework is necessary, we can discuss possible 15 changes in the nature of the beast. My colleague Karin Chenoweth, who does the Homeroom column on this Web site and in the *Washington Post*, suggests that elementary and middle school homework be no more than an hour a day of reading and fifteen minutes of writing about that reading, with maybe twenty extra minutes of math and vocabulary work. That would certainly reduce parental struggles with dioramas, collages, and my wife's most horrific memory, the log cabin that our daughter had to construct out of Tootsie Rolls in the first grade.

There is also a very firm approach to homework, used by the KIPP 16 schools to keep low-income children on track, that might work in more affluent schools for different reasons. San Francisco–based KIPP (Knowledge Is Power Program) has fifteen schools around the country that have significantly raised the academic achievement of fifth through eighth graders in communities where such high test scores are rare. The KIPP schools enshrine homework by giving each of their teachers a cell phone and insisting that students call their teachers at any time if they have any problem completing the assignment that night. If a child appears the next day with an assignment incomplete, the parents are called to the school to talk about it.

This builds Bempechat's motivational habits, which regular public 17
schools in KIPP neighborhoods often neglect. But consider the impact such
a policy might have in affluent communities where the anti-homework
movement has taken root. An open invitation — indeed, a requirement —
that the teacher be called about any inexplicable instructions or incomprehensible problems is likely to be accepted by middle class parents with a
vengeance. After a few evenings handling such calls, the teachers are likely to
think more carefully about their assignments before they hand them out,
and that will be good for everybody.

Of course, even good habits can be overdone. But when I think about 18
cautioning my daughter about working too hard, I remind myself that that
was the way I behaved in high school. Like most people reflecting on
courses and teachers that challenged them when they were teenagers, I have
no regrets about those late nights.

Unless there are clear signs of emotional illness, or a daily schedule that 19
is nothing but books and papers, students like Katie are better off making
their own decisions. They have acquired the character traits that Bempechat
extols. They are determined to handle the responsibilities they have been
given.

They may find their homework boring or frustrating, but when they 20
start earning a living they are going to have jobs with some of that, and it is
best to develop coping skills early. Schools that demand a half hour a day of
academic work at home, less than a fifth of the time these same children
spend watching television, do not seem to me to be overdoing it.

Major Stages	A Reader's Activities
Get Started	• Prepare to read by thinking about your purpose. • Plan your follow-up in class discussions, exams, or essays. • Skim the text.
Respond to Reading	• Keep a reading journal. • Annotate the text.
Read on a Literal Level	• Know and recall what you read. • Comprehend the information. • Apply the information to other situations.
Read on an Analytical Level	• Analyze by breaking into parts or components. • Synthesize by combining with other materials. • Evaluate and assess.
Generate Ideas from Reading	• Log your reading. • Look for meaty pieces. • Recall previous reading. • Read critically. • Analyze the writing strategies in what you read.

A Reader's Resources

In this book	On this book's Web site*	In this book's software

- Information about a writer's purposes in Chapter 1
- Common academic and other writing situations in Parts Two and Three
- "Getting Started" as a reader (pp. 19–22) and "Getting Ready" as a writer (pp. 266–68)

🔍 reading
🔍 examples

- TopLinks

- Critical Reading Guides
- Sample essays with writing features highlighted

- Advice on journals and generating ideas in Chapter 15
- Annotated readings in Part Two and *A Writer's Reader*
- Reading questions in Part Two and *A Writer's Reader*

🔍 reading

- TopLinks

- Journaling feature
- Critical Reading Guides (see annotating exercise)

- "Questions to Start You Thinking" about meaning after each reading
- "As You Read" questions before the readings in Part Two and *A Writer's Reader*
- "Responding to an Image" prompts in *A Writer's Reader* and "Observing the Characteristics of an Image" in Chapter 21 for advice about "reading" images

🔍 reading
🔍 visual

- TopLinks

- Critical Reading Guides
- Sample essays with writing features highlighted

- "Questions to Start You Thinking" about reading critically and making connections after each reading in *A Writer's Reader*
- Advice in Chapters 12 and 18 and the Quick Research Guide on summarizing, analyzing, and evaluating
- Advice on interpreting the meaning of an image in Chapter 21

🔍 reading
🔍 evaluate
🔍 visual

- TopLinks

- Critical Reading Guides
- Sample essays with writing features highlighted

- Advice on finding and evaluating sources in the Quick Research Guide
- Specialized advice about reading literature in Chapter 12
- Paired and related readings in *A Writer's Reader*
- Sample annotations and reading questions in Part Two and *A Writer's Reader*
- "Questions to Start You Thinking" about writing strategies after each reading

🔍 reading
🔍 evaluate

- TopLinks

- Journaling feature
- Sample essays with writing features highlighted
- Critical Reading Guides

---

*At <bedfordstmartins.com/bedguide>, use the search box shown to find writing resources or exercises by keyword.

31

Chapter 3

Critical Thinking Processes

*C**ritic,* from the Greek word *kritikos,* means "one who can judge and discern" — in short, someone who thinks critically. College will have given you your money's worth if it leaves you better able to judge and discern — to determine what is more and less important, to make distinctions and recognize differences, to generalize from specifics, to draw conclusions from evidence, to grasp complex concepts, to choose wisely. The effective thinking that you will need in college, on the job, and in your daily life is active and purposeful, not passive and ambling. It is critical thinking.

A Process of Critical Thinking

You use critical thinking every day to solve problems and make decisions. Suppose you don't have enough money both to pay your tuition and to buy the car you need. First, you might pin down the causes of your financial problem. Next, you might examine your options to find the best solution, as shown in the graphic on page 33.

ACTIVITY: THINKING CRITICALLY TO SOLVE A CAMPUS PROBLEM

With classmates, identify a common problem for students at your college — juggling a busy schedule, parking on campus, making a class change, joining a social group, or some other issue. Working together, use critical thinking to explore the problem and identify possible solutions.

*Critical Thinking
Processes in Action*

? **Problem**
You can't afford both your college tuition and the car you need.

Solution

1 **IDENTIFY CAUSES**

Causes in your control:
Expensive vacation?

Causes out of your control:
Medical emergency?
Job loss?
Tuition increase?
Financial aid policy change?

2 **ANALYZE, SYNTHESIZE, AND EVALUATE OPTIONS**

Do without a car	*(how?)*	• Get rides with family or friends? • Take public transportation?
Decrease your tuition	*(how?)*	• Take fewer courses?
Get more money	*(how?)*	• Get a loan from the bank? • Get a loan from the college? • Get a loan from a family member? • Get another job?

3 **REACH A LOGICAL CONCLUSION**

Apply for a short-term loan through the college for tuition.

Getting Started

Using critical thinking, you've explored your problem step by step and reached a reasonable solution. Critical thinking, like critical reading, draws on a cluster of intellectual strategies and skills.

■ For more on critical reading, see Ch. 2.

CRITICAL THINKING SKILL	DEFINITION	APPLICATIONS FOR READERS	APPLICATIONS FOR WRITERS
Analysis	Breaking down information into its parts and elements	Analyzing the information in articles, reports, and books to grasp the facts and concepts they contain	Analyzing events, ideas, processes, and structures to understand them and explain them to readers

(continued on next page)

CRITICAL THINKING SKILL	DEFINITION	APPLICATIONS FOR READERS	APPLICATIONS FOR WRITERS
Synthesis	Putting together elements and parts to form new wholes	Synthesizing information from several sources, examining implications, and drawing conclusions supported by reliable evidence	Synthesizing source materials with your own thoughts in order to convey the unique combination to others
Evaluation	Judging according to standards or criteria	Evaluating a reading by determining standards for judging, applying them to the reading, and arriving at a conclusion about its significance or value	Evaluating something in writing by convincing readers that your standards are reasonable and that the subject either does or does not meet those standards

These three activities — analysis, synthesis, and evaluation — are the core of critical thinking. They are not new to you, but applying them rigorously in college-level reading and writing may be. When you approach college reading and writing tasks, instructors will expect you (and you should expect yourself) to think, read, write, and think some more.

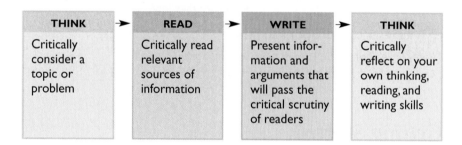

Sometimes your assignments, such as those in Part Two of this book, will give you explicit opportunities to use your reading and thinking skills. Other times, you'll simply dive into an assignment without considering whether you're analyzing at one moment or synthesizing at the next. Instead, you'll concentrate on your destination, where you want to go in your paper and what your assignment requires. Later you can look back on your route as a critical thinker, reconsidering the curves in the road and the scenery along the way — thinking critically about your own skills.

ACTIVITY: THINKING CRITICALLY TO EXPLORE AN ISSUE

You have worked hard on a group presentation that will be a major part of your grade — and each member of the group will get the same grade. Two days before the project is due, you discover that one group member has plagiarized heavily from various sources. Although everyone in your group likes the presentation, you believe that your instructor knows the plagiarized sources well. Working together with classmates, use critical thinking to explore your problem and determine what you might do.

Supporting Critical Thinking with Evidence

As you write a college paper, you try to figure out your purpose, the position you want to take, and ways to get readers to follow your logic and accept your points. Your challenge, of course, is not just to think clearly but to demonstrate your thinking to others, to persuade them to pay attention to what you say. And sound evidence is what critical readers want to see.

Sound evidence supports your main idea or thesis, substantiating your points for readers. It also bolsters your stance as a credible writer, demonstrating the merit of your position. When you write, you need to marshal enough appropriate evidence to clarify, explain, and support your ideas. You need to weave claims, evidence, and your own interpretations together into a clearly reasoned explanation or argument. And as you do so, you need to select and test your evidence so that it will convince your readers.

For advice on using a few sources, see the Quick Research Guide (the dark-red-edged pages).

TYPES OF EVIDENCE

What is evidence? It is anything that demonstrates the soundness of a claim. Facts, statistics, firsthand observations, and expert testimony are four reliable forms of evidence. Other evidence might include examples, illustrations, details, and opinions. Depending on the purpose of your assignment, some kinds of evidence weigh more heavily than others. For example, readers might appreciate your memories of livestock care on the farm in an essay recalling your childhood summers. However, they would probably discount your memories in an explanatory or argumentative paper about agricultural methods unless you could show that your memories are representative or that you are an expert on the subject. Personal experience may strengthen an argument but generally is not sufficient as the sole support. If you are in doubt about the type of evidence an assignment requires, ask your instructor whether you should use sources or rely on personal experience and examples.

For more on using evidence in a paper that takes a stand, see pp. 143–44.

Facts.   Facts are statements that can be verified objectively, by observation or by reading a reliable account. They are usually stated dispassionately: "If you pump the air out of a five-gallon varnish can, it will collapse." Of course, we accept many of our facts based on the testimony of others. For example, we believe that the Great Wall of China exists although we may never have seen it with our own eyes.

Sometimes people say facts are true statements, but truth and sound evidence may be confused. Consider the truth of these statements:

The tree in my yard is ten feet tall.	*True* because it can be verified
A kilometer is 1,000 meters.	*True* using the metric system
The speed limit on the highway is sixty-five miles per hour.	*True* according to law
Fewer fatal highway accidents have occurred since the new exit ramp was built.	*True* according to research studies
My favorite food is pizza.	*True* as an opinion
More violent criminals should receive the death penalty.	*True* as a belief
Murder is wrong.	*True* according to value judgment

Some would claim that each statement is true, but when you think critically, you should avoid treating opinions, beliefs, judgments, or personal experience as true in the same sense that verifiable facts and events are true.

Statistics.   Statistics are facts expressed in numbers. What portion of American children are poor? According to statistics from the U.S. Census Bureau, 12.1 million children (or 16.7 percent of all children) lived in poverty in 2002 compared with 11.7 million (or 16.3 percent) in 2001. Clear as such figures seem, they may raise complex questions. For example, how significant is the increase in the poverty rate over one year? What percentage of children were poor over longer terms such as ten years or twenty?

Most writers, without trying to be dishonest, interpret statistics to help their causes. The statement "Fifty percent of the populace have incomes above the poverty level" might substantiate the fine job done by the government of a developing nation. Putting the statement another way — "Fifty percent of the populace have incomes below the poverty level" — might use the same statistic to show the inadequacy of the government's efforts.

Even though a writer is free to interpret a statistic, statistics should not be used to mislead. On the wrapper of a peanut candy bar, we read that a one-ounce serving contains only 150 calories. The claim is true, but the bar weighs 1.6 ounces. Gobble it all — more likely than eating 62 percent of it — and you'll ingest 240 calories, a heftier snack than the innocent statistic on the wrapper suggests. Because abuses make some readers automatically distrustful, use figures fairly when you write, and make sure they are accurate. If you doubt a statistic, compare it with figures reported by several other sources. Distrust a statistical report that differs from every other report unless it is backed by further evidence.

▧ Should you want to contact a campus expert, turn to Ch. 6 for advice about interviews.

Expert Testimony.   By "experts," we mean people with knowledge gained from study and experience of a particular field. The test of an expert is whether his or her expertise stands up to the scrutiny of others who are knowledgeable in that field. Basketball player Michael Jordan on how to play offense or economist John Kenneth Galbraith on what causes inflation carries authority, but an exchange of topics would not be credible. Also consider whether the expert has any bias or special interest that would affect reliability. Statistics on cases of lung cancer attributed to smoking might be better taken from government sources than from the tobacco industry.

Firsthand Observation.   Firsthand observation is persuasive. It can add concrete reality to abstract or complex points. You might support the claim "The Meadowfield waste recycling plant fails to meet state guidelines" by recalling your own observations: "When I visited the plant last January, I was struck by the number of open waste canisters and by the lack of protective gear for the workers who handle these toxic materials daily."

For more on observation, see Ch. 5.

As readers, most of us tend to trust the writer who declares, "I was there. This is what I saw." Sometimes that trust is misplaced, however, so always be wary of a writer's claim to have seen something that no other evidence supports. Ask yourself, Is this writer biased? Might the writer have (intentionally or unintentionally) misinterpreted what he or she saw? Of course, your readers will scrutinize your firsthand observations, too; take care to reassure them that your observations are unbiased and accurate.

ACTIVITY: LOOKING FOR EVIDENCE

Using the issue you explored with classmates for the activity on page 33, what would you need to support your identification, explanation, or solution of the problem? Working with classmates, identify the kinds of evidence that would be most useful. Where or how might you find such evidence?

Testing Evidence

As both a reader and a writer, you should always critically test and question evidence to see whether it is strong enough to carry the weight of the writer's claims. Use these questions to determine whether evidence is useful and trustworthy.

For more on selecting evidence to persuade readers, see p. 144.

EVIDENCE CHECKLIST

___ Is it accurate?
  • Do the facts and figures seem accurate based on what you have found in published sources, reports by others, or reference works?
  • Are figures or quoted facts copied correctly?
___ Is it reliable?
  • Is the source trustworthy and well regarded?

- Does the source acknowledge any commercial, political, advocacy, or other bias that might affect the quality of its information?
- Does the writer supplying the evidence have appropriate credentials or experience? Is the writer respected as an expert in the field?
- Do other sources agree with the information?

___ Is it up-to-date?

- Are facts and statistics — such as population figures — current?
- Is the information from the latest sources?

___ Is it to the point?

- Does the evidence back the exact claim made?
- Is the evidence all pertinent without resorting to interesting — but unrelated — fact or opinion that obscures the absence of relevant evidence?

___ Is it representative?

- Are examples typical of all the things included in the writer's position?
- Are examples balanced to avoid stacking the evidence?
- Are contrary examples acknowledged?

For information on mistakes in thinking called logical fallacies, see pp. 149–51.

___ Is it appropriately complex?

- Is it sufficient to account for the claim made?
- Does it avoid treating complex things superficially?
- Does it avoid needlessly complicating simple things?

___ Is it sufficient and strong enough to back the claim and persuade readers?

- Is the amount and quality of the evidence appropriate for the claim and for the readers?
- Is the evidence aligned with the existing knowledge of readers?
- Does the evidence answer the questions a reader is likely to ask?
- Is the evidence vivid and significant?

Using Evidence to Support an Appeal

For more on appeals, see pp. 146–47.

One way to select evidence and to judge whether it is appropriate and sufficient is to consider the types of appeal — logical, emotional, and ethical. Most effective arguments work on all three levels, using all three types of appeals with evidence that supports all three.

LOGICAL APPEAL (LOGOS)

When writers use a logical appeal (*logos* or "word" in Greek), they appeal to the reader's mind or intellect. This appeal relies on evidence that is factual, objective, clear, and relevant. Critical readers expect logical evidence to support major claims and statements. For example, if a writer were arguing for term limits for legislators, she wouldn't want to base her argument on the evidence that some long-term legislators weren't reelected last term (irrelevant) or that the current system is unfair to young people who want to get into politics (not logical). Instead, she might argue that the absence of term limits encourages corruption, using evidence of legislators who repaid lobbyists for campaign contributions by siding with them in key votes.

EMOTIONAL APPEAL (PATHOS)

When writers use an emotional appeal (*pathos* or "suffering" in Greek), they appeal to the reader's heart. They choose language, facts, quotations, examples, and images that evoke emotional responses. Of course, convincing writing does touch readers' hearts as well as their minds. Without this heartfelt tug, a strict logical appeal may seem cold and dehumanized. If a writer opposed hunting seals for their fur, he might combine statistics about the number of seals killed each year and the overall population decrease with a vivid description of baby seals being slaughtered. Some writers use emotional words and sentimental examples to manipulate readers — to arouse their sympathy, pity, or anger in order to convert them without any logical evidence — but dishonest emotional appeals may alienate readers. Instead of basing an argument against a political candidate on pitiful images of scrawny children living in roach-infested squalor, a good writer would report the candidate's voting record on issues that affect children.

ETHICAL APPEAL (ETHOS)

When writers use an ethical appeal (*ethos* or "character" in Greek), they call on the reader's sense of fairness and trust. They select and present evidence in a way that will make the audience trust them, respect their judgment, and believe what they have to say. The best logical argument in the world falls flat when readers don't take the writer seriously. How can you use an ethical appeal to establish your credibility as a writer? First you need to establish your credentials in the field through experience, relevant reading, or interviews that helped you learn about the subject. If you are writing about environmental pollution, tell your readers that your allergies have been irritated by chemicals in the air. Identify medical or environmental experts you have contacted or whose publications you have read. Demonstrate your knowledge through the information you present, the experts and sources you cite, and the depth of understanding you convey. Establish a rapport with readers by indicating values and attitudes that you share with them and by responding seriously to opposing arguments. Finally, use language that is precise, clear, and appropriate in tone.

ACTIVITY: IDENTIFYING TYPES OF APPEALS

Bring to class the editorial or opinion page from a newspaper or newsmagazine. Read some of the letters or articles. Identify the types of appeals used by each author to support his or her point.

Major Stages	A Critical Thinker's Activities
Get Started	• Analyze by breaking into parts or components. • Synthesize by combining with other materials. • Evaluate and assess.
Apply Critical Thinking Skills	• Think through topics and problems. • Think critically as a reader. • Think critically as a writer.
Supply Evidence to Support Thinking	• Find facts. • Add statistics. • Look for expert testimony. • Observe.
Test Evidence	• Read to confirm accuracy, reliability, and currency. • Select what is pertinent and representative. • Monitor complexity. • Supply enough strong evidence to persuade readers.
Use Evidence to Support Appeals	• Appeal to logic. • Appeal to emotions. • Appeal to ethical issues of fairness and trust.

A Critical Thinker's Resources

In this book	On this book's Web site*	In this book's software

- Summarizing, analyzing, synthesizing, and evaluating advice in Chapters 11 and 18 and the Quick Research Guide
- Criteria for evaluating print and electronic sources in the Quick Research Guide
- Advice on interpreting the meaning of an image in Chapter 21

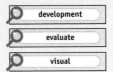

- Critical Reading Guides
- Sample essays with features highlighted

- Logical thinking advice in Chapter 9, "Taking a Stand"
- *A Writer's Reader* and Part Two (for applying your critical thinking skills as a reader)
- Writing situations in Parts Two and Three (for applying your critical thinking skills as a writer)

reading

examples

- Critical Reading Guides
- Sample essays with features highlighted
- On-screen writing guides

- Search strategies and tips for finding sources in the Quick Research Guide
- "Using Visuals to Reinforce Your Content" section in Chapter 20
- Advice about evaluating sources in the Quick Research Guide
- Observing and interviewing advice in Chapters 5 and 6

support

visual

evaluate

- On-screen writing guides with prompts for developing
- Sample essays with writing features highlighted
- Critical Reading Guides and writing prompts for observing and interviewing

---

- Advice on critical reading in Chapter 2 as well as questions and annotations with readings throughout
- "Strategies for Developing," in Chapter 18
- Critical thinking skills for researchers in the Quick Research Guide
- Part Two, especially Chapters 7 to 11 (for applying these skills)

reading

development

support

- Critical Reading Guides
- Sample essays with writing features highlighted
- On-screen writing guides with prompts for developing

- Advice on making compelling appeals to readers in Chapters 9, 10, and 11
- Advice on purpose and audience in Chapters 1 (pp. 13–15) and 16 (pp. 269–271)
- Advice on avoiding logical fallacies (pp. 147–48)

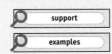

- On-screen writing guides with prompts for developing

---

*At <bedfordstmartins.com/bedguide>, use the search box shown to find writing resources or exercises by keyword.

PART TWO

A Writer's Situations

Introduction

In Part Two, we present a sequence of writing situations that require you to use processes for writing, reading, and thinking critically. The eight writing assignments—recalling an experience, observing a scene, interviewing a subject, comparing and contrasting, explaining causes and effects, taking a stand, proposing a solution, and evaluating—are arranged roughly in order of increasing complexity—that is, according to the level of critical reading and thinking required. Some require analysis—breaking something down into its components to understand it better. Others require synthesis—combining information from various sources with your own ideas and conclusions in order to achieve a new perspective. The most complex task, evaluating, can incorporate several of the other critical strategies. Let's look at these writing situations in more detail.

Recalling an Experience.   Recalling an event depends on your richest resource as a writer—your memory. Chapter 4 guides you in focusing and shaping your writing from memory so that you can present recollections effectively and convey their importance to your readers.

Observing a Scene.   Observation relies on using your senses to see, hear, smell, touch, and taste what's around you. Chapter 5 helps you select and arrange compelling details in order to convey your insights about what you have observed.

Interviewing a Subject.   Interviewing adds the freshness of conversation, the liveliness of exchange with someone else, and the informed viewpoint of an expert to your writing. Chapter 6 encourages you to bring the subject of an interview to life as you distill the impression and information gained during your interview.

Comparing and Contrasting.   Comparing and contrasting focuses on the similarities and differences of two (or more) items or groups. Chapter 7 guides you first in analyzing each item and then in lining up the characteristics of each, side by side, to determine how they are alike and how they are different. Most important, because effective comparison and contrast points out likenesses and differences for some significant purpose, you will convey your conclusion about how each alternative operates or which alternative is preferable.

Explaining Causes and Effects.   As you focus on an action, event, or situation, identifying causes means ferreting out roots and origins. Determining effects means figuring out results. Sometimes as you analyze, you will find a chain of causes and effects: a situation causes specific effects, which in turn cause other effects. Chapter 8 helps you to analyze and explain causes, effects, or both in order to support an overall point that helps you and your readers understand the issue better.

Taking a Stand.   When you take a stand, you argue for one side or another of an issue. Chapter 9 helps you develop your position in a controversy and present your opinion so that readers will respect it even if they do not agree with you. You may come to a debate with strong views, or you may develop a position while looking into the matter. In either case, once you reach a clear position, you will present your case persuasively to your readers using solid, pertinent evidence — facts, statistics, expert opinion, and direct observation.

Proposing a Solution.   Proposing a solution requires not only taking a stand but also presenting a feasible solution to the problem at hand. Chapter 10 helps you identify a problem and then propose a convincing, workable solution. You will use two main methods of persuading readers that the problem should be solved as you recommend: showing readers why the problem matters to them and supplying evidence to support your solution.

Evaluating.   Evaluating means judging: deciding whether an idea, a presentation, a product, a work of art, or some other thing is good or bad, effective or ineffective. As Chapter 11 explains, you will identify, implicitly or explicitly, specific criteria for judging your subject. Once your standards are clear, based on your personal preferences or the views of experts in the field, you can analyze your subject to see how well it meets the criteria you propose. As you explain your judgment, you will also try to persuade your readers that your view is reasonable.

Taken together, these eight chapters present many of the writing situations you will encounter in other college courses and in your career. Use the processes outlined in these chapters as resources when you meet unfamiliar writing situations or need to marshal appropriate evidence for essays.

Chapter 4
Recalling an Experience

© Larry Williams/CORBIS

Responding to an Image

In your view, when was this photograph taken? Who might the people be?
Where are they, and why are they there? What are they doing? What relationships among these people does the picture suggest with its focal point and
arrangement? What emotions can you detect in individual facial expressions and
body language? Write about an experience the image helps you recall or about
a possible explanation of events in this picture. Use vivid detail to convey what
happened to you or what might have happened to the people in the picture.

Writing from recall is writing from memory, a writer's richest — and handiest — resource. Recall is clearly necessary when you are asked to write of a personal experience, a favorite place, a memorable person. But even when an instructor hands you a subject that seems to have nothing to do with you, your memory is the first place to look. Suppose you have to write a psychology paper about how advertisers play on consumers' fears. Begin with what you remember. What ads have sent chills down your back? What ads have suggested that their products could save you from a painful social blunder, a lonely night, or a deadly accident? All by itself, memory may not give you enough to write about, but you will rarely go wrong if you start by jotting down something remembered.

Learning from Other Writers

■ For more on thesis and support, see Chs. 16 and 18.

Here are two samples of good writing from recall — one by a professional writer, one by a college student. To help you begin to analyze the first reading in this chapter, look for the notes in the margin. They identify features such as the main idea, or thesis, and the first of the main events that support it in a paper written from recall.

As You Read These Recollections

As you read these essays, ask yourself the following questions:

■ For more examples of writing from recall, visit <bedfordstmartins.com/bedguide> and do a key-word search:

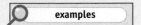

1. Is the perspective of the essay primarily that of a child or an adult? Why do you think so?
2. What does the author realize after reflecting on the events recalled? Does the realization come soon after the experience or later, when the writer examines the events from a more mature perspective?
3. How does the realization change the individual?

In this essay from his autobiography Growing Up *(1982), columnist Russell Baker recalls being sixteen in urban Baltimore and wondering what to do with his life.*

Introduction

Russell Baker
The Art of Eating Spaghetti

The only thing that truly interested me was writing, and I knew that sixteen-year-olds did not come out of high school and become writers. I thought of writing as something to be done only by the rich. It was so obviously not real work, not a job at which you could earn a living. Still, I had begun to think of myself as a writer. It was the only thing for which I seemed to have the smallest talent, and, silly though it sounded when I told people I'd like to be a writer, it gave me a way of thinking about myself which satisfied my need to have an identity.

48

The notion of becoming a writer had flickered off and on in my head [2]
since the Belleville days, but it wasn't until my third year in high school that
the possibility took hold. Until then I'd been bored by everything associated
with English courses. I found English grammar dull and baffling. I hated the
assignments to turn out "compositions," and went at them like heavy labor,
turning out leaden, lackluster paragraphs that were agonies for teachers to
read and for me to write. The classics thrust on me to read seemed as deadening as chloroform.

*[margin: **THESIS** stating main idea]*

When our class was assigned to Mr. Fleagle for third-year English I antici- [3]
pated another grim year in that dreariest of subjects. Mr. Fleagle was notori-
ous among City students for dullness and inability to inspire. He was said to
be stuffy, dull, and hopelessly out of date. To me he looked to be sixty or seventy and prim to a fault. He wore primly severe eyeglasses, his wavy hair was
primly cut and primly combed. He wore prim vested suits with neckties
blocked primly against the collar buttons of his primly starched white shirts.
He had a primly pointed jaw, a primly straight nose, and a prim manner of
speaking that was so correct, so gentlemanly, that he seemed a comic antique.

[margin: Major event 1]

I anticipated a listless,° unfruitful year with Mr. Fleagle and for a long [4]
time was not disappointed. We read *Macbeth*. Mr. Fleagle loved *Macbeth* and
wanted us to love it too, but he lacked the gift of infecting others with his
own passion. He tried to convey the murderous ferocity of Lady Macbeth
one day by reading aloud the passage that concludes

[margin: Support for major event 1]

> . . . I have given suck, and know
> How tender 'tis to love the babe that milks me.
> I would, while it was smiling in my face,
> Have plucked my nipple from his boneless gums. . . .

The idea of prim Mr. Fleagle plucking his nipple from boneless gums was
too much for the class. We burst into gasps of irrepressible snickering. Mr.
Fleagle stopped.

"There is nothing funny, boys, about giving suck to a babe. It is the — [5]
the very essence of motherhood, don't you see."

He constantly sprinkled his sentences with "don't you see." It wasn't a [6]
question but an exclamation of mild surprise at our ignorance. "Your pronoun needs an antecedent, don't you see," he would say, very primly. "The
purpose of the Porter's scene, boys, is to provide comic relief from the horror, don't you see."

Late in the year we tackled the informal essay. "The essay, don't you see, [7]
is the . . ." My mind went numb. Of all forms of writing, none seemed so
boring as the essay. Naturally we would have to write informal essays. Mr.
Fleagle distributed a homework sheet offering us a choice of topics. None
was quite so simpleminded as "What I Did on My Summer Vacation," but
most seemed to be almost as dull. I took the list home and dawdled until
the night before the essay was due. Sprawled on the sofa, I finally faced up

listless: Lacking energy or enthusiasm.

to the grim task, took the list out of my notebook, and scanned it. The topic on which my eye stopped was "The Art of Eating Spaghetti."

This title produced an extraordinary sequence of mental images. Surging up out of the depths of memory came a vivid recollection of a night in Belleville when all of us were seated around the supper table — Uncle Allen, my mother, Uncle Charlie, Doris, Uncle Hal — and Aunt Pat served spaghetti for supper. Spaghetti was an exotic treat in those days. Neither Doris nor I had ever eaten spaghetti, and none of the adults had enough experience to be good at it. All the good humor of Uncle Allen's house reawoke in my mind as I recalled the laughing arguments we had that night about the socially respectable method for moving spaghetti from plate to mouth. 8

Suddenly I wanted to write about that, about the warmth and good feeling of it, but I wanted to put it down simply for my own joy, not for Mr. Fleagle. It was a moment I wanted to recapture and hold for myself. I wanted to relive the pleasure of an evening at New Street. To write it as I wanted, however, would violate all the rules of formal composition I'd learned in school, and Mr. Fleagle would surely give it a failing grade. Never mind. I would write something else for Mr. Fleagle after I had written this thing for myself. 9

When I finished it the night was half gone and there was no time left to compose a proper, respectable essay for Mr. Fleagle. There was no choice next morning but to turn in my private reminiscence° of Belleville. Two days passed before Mr. Fleagle returned the graded papers, and he returned everyone's but mine. I was bracing myself for a command to report to Mr. Fleagle immediately after school for discipline when I saw him lift my paper from his desk and rap for the class's attention. 10

"Now, boys," he said, "I want to read you an essay. This is titled 'The Art of Eating Spaghetti.'" 11

And he started to read. My words! He was reading *my words* out loud to the entire class. What's more, the entire class was listening. Listening attentively. Then somebody laughed, then the entire class was laughing, and not in contempt and ridicule, but with openhearted enjoyment. Even Mr. Fleagle stopped two or three times to repress a small prim smile. 12

I did my best to avoid showing pleasure, but what I was feeling was pure ecstasy at this startling demonstration that my words had the power to make people laugh. In the eleventh grade, at the eleventh hour as it were, I had discovered a calling. It was the happiest moment of my entire school career. When Mr. Fleagle finished he put the final seal on my happiness by saying, "Now that, boys, is an essay, don't you see. It's — don't you see — it's of the very essence of the essay, don't you see. Congratulations, Mr. Baker." 13

Conclusion restating thesis — For the first time, light shone on a possibility. It wasn't a very heartening possibility, to be sure. Writing couldn't lead to a job after high school, and it was hardly honest work, but Mr. Fleagle had opened a door for me. After that I ranked Mr. Fleagle among the finest teachers in the school. 14

reminiscence: Memory.

Questions to Start You Thinking

Meaning

1. In your own words, state what Baker believes he learned in the eleventh grade about the art of writing. What incidents or statements help identify this lesson for readers? What lesson, if any, did you learn from the essay?

2. Why do you think Baker included this event in his autobiography?

3. Have you ever changed your mind about something you had to do, as Baker did about writing? Or about a person, as he did about Mr. Fleagle?

Writing Strategies

4. What is the effect, in paragraph 3, of Baker's repetitions of the words *prim* and *primly*? What other devices does he use to characterize Mr. Fleagle vividly? Why do you think Baker uses so much space to portray his teacher?

5. What does the quotation from *Macbeth* add to Baker's account? Had the quotation been omitted, what would have been lost?

6. How does Baker organize the essay? Why does he use this order?

STUDENT ESSAY

Robert G. Schreiner

What Is a Hunter?

What is a hunter? This is a simple question with a relatively straightforward answer. A hunter is, according to <u>Webster's New Collegiate Dictionary</u>, a person who hunts game (game being various types of animals hunted or pursued for various reasons). However, a second question is just as simple but without such a straightforward answer: What characteristics make up a hunter? As a child, I had always considered the most important aspect of the hunter's person to be his ability to use a rifle, bow, or whatever weapon was appropriate to the type of hunting being done. Having many relatives in rural areas of Virginia and Kansas, I had been exposed to rifles a great deal. I had done extensive target shooting and considered myself to be quite proficient in the use of firearms. I had never been hunting, but I had always thought that since I could fire a rifle accurately I would make a good hunter.

One Christmas holiday, while we were visiting our grandparents in Kansas, my grandfather asked me if I wanted to go jackrabbit hunting with him. I eagerly accepted, anxious to show off my prowess° with a rifle. A younger cousin of mine also wanted to come, so we all went out into the garage, loaded two .22 caliber rifles and a 20-gauge shotgun, hopped into the pickup truck, and drove out of town. It

In this college essay, Robert G. Schreiner uses vivid details to bring to life a significant childhood event.

1

2

prowess: Superior skill.

had snowed the night before, and to either side of the narrow road swept six-foot-deep powdery drifts. The wind twirled the fine crystalline snow into whirling vortexes° that bounced along the icy road and sprayed snow into the open windows of the pickup. As we drove, my grandfather gave us some pointers about both spotting and shooting jackrabbits. He told us that when it snows, jackrabbits like to dig out a hollow in the top of a snowdrift, usually near a fencepost, and lie there soaking up the sunshine. He told us that even though jackrabbits are a grayish brown, this coloration is excellent camouflage in the snow, for the curled-up rabbits resemble rocks. He then pointed out a few rabbits in such positions as we drove along, showing us how to distinguish them from exposed rocks and dirt. He then explained that the only way to be sure that we killed the rabbit was to shoot for the head and, in particular, the eye, for this was on a direct line with the rabbit's brain. Since we were using solid point bullets, which deform into a ball upon impact, a hit anywhere but the head would most likely only wound the rabbit.

❓ How does the writer convey his grandfather's definition of hunting?

My grandfather then slowed down the pickup and told us to look out for the rabbits hidden in the snowdrifts. We eventually spotted one about thirty feet from the road in a snow-filled gully. My cousin wished to shoot the first one, so he hopped out of the truck, balanced the .22 on the hood, and fired. A spray of snow erupted about a foot to the left of the rabbit's hollow. My cousin fired again, and again, and again, the shots pockmarking the slope of the drift. He fired once more and the rabbit bounced out of its hollow, its head rocking from side to side. He was hit. My cousin eagerly gamboled into the snow to claim his quarry.° He brought it back holding it by the hind legs, proudly displaying it as would a warrior the severed head of his enemy. The bullet had entered the rabbit's right shoulder and exited through the neck. In both places a thin trickle of crimson marred the gray sheen of the rabbit's pelt. It quivered slightly and its rib cage pulsed with its labored breathing. My cousin was about to toss it into the back of the pickup when my grandfather pointed out that it would be cruel to allow the rabbit to bleed slowly to death and instructed my cousin to bang its head against the side of the pickup to kill it. My cousin then proceeded to bang the rabbit's head against the yellow metal. Thump, thump, thump, thump; after a minute or so my cousin loudly proclaimed that it was dead and hopped back into the truck.

3

❓ Why do you think that the writer reacts as he does?

The whole episode sickened me to some degree, and at the time I did not know why. We continued to hunt throughout the afternoon, and feigning boredom, I allowed my cousin and grandfather to shoot all of the rabbits. Often, the shots didn't kill the rabbits outright so they had to be killed against the pickup. The thump, thump, thump of the rabbits' skulls against the metal began to irritate me, and I was

4

vortex: Rotation around an axis, as in a whirlwind.   **quarry:** Prey.

strangely glad when we turned around and headed back toward home. We were a few miles from the city limits when my grandfather slowed the truck to a stop, then backed up a few yards. My grandfather said he spotted two huge "jacks" sitting in the sun in a field just off the road. He pointed them out and handed me the .22, saying that if I didn't shoot something the whole afternoon would have been a wasted trip for me. I hesitated and then reluctantly accepted the rifle. I stepped out onto the road, my feet crunching on the ice. The two rabbits were about seventy feet away, both sitting upright in the sun. I cocked and leveled the rifle, my elbow held almost horizontal in the military fashion I had learned to employ. I brought the sights to bear on the right eye of the first rabbit, compensated° for distance, and fired. There was a harsh snap like the crack of a whip and a small jolt to my shoulder. The first rabbit was gone, presumably knocked over the side of the snowdrift. The second rabbit hadn't moved a muscle; it just sat there staring with that black eye. I cocked the rifle once more and sighted a second time, the bead of the rifle just barely above the glassy black orb that regarded me so passively. I squeezed the trigger. Again the crack, again the jolt, and again the rabbit disappeared over the top of the drift. I handed the rifle to my cousin and began making my way toward the rabbits. I sank into powdery snow up to my waist as I clambered to the top of the drift and looked over.

On the other side of the drift was a sight that I doubt I will ever forget. There 5 was a shallow, snow-covered ditch on the leeward side of the drift and it was into this ditch that the rabbits had fallen, at least what was left of the rabbits. The entire ditch, in an area about ten feet wide, was spattered with splashes of crimson blood, pink gobbets of brain, and splintered fragments of bone. The twisted corpses of the rabbits lay in the bottom of the ditch in small pools of streaming blood. Of both the rabbits, only the bodies remained, the heads being completely gone. Stumps of vertebrae protruded obscenely from the mangled bodies, and one rabbit's hind legs twitched spasmodically. I realized that my cousin must have made a mistake and loaded the rifle with hollowpoint explosive bullets instead of solid ones.

I shouted back to the pickup, explaining the situation, and asked if I should 6 bring them back anyway. My grandfather shouted back, "No, don't worry about it, just leave them there. I'm gonna toss these jacks by the side of the road anyway; jackrabbits aren't any good for eatin'."

Looking at the dead, twitching bodies I thought only of the incredible waste of 7 life that the afternoon had been, and I realized that there was much more to being a hunter than knowing how to use a rifle. I turned and walked back to the pickup, riding the rest of the way home in silence.

Why do you think the writer returns in silence?

compensate: Counterbalance.

Questions to Start You Thinking

Meaning

1. Where in the essay do you first begin to suspect the writer's feelings about hunting? What in the essay or in your experience led you to this perception?

2. How would you characterize the writer's grandfather? How would you characterize his cousin?

3. How did the writer's understanding of himself change as a result of this hunting experience?

Writing Strategies

4. How might the essay be strengthened or weakened if the opening paragraph were cut out? Without this paragraph, how would your understanding of the author and his change be different?

5. Would Schreiner's essay be more or less effective if he explained in the last paragraph what he means by "much more to being a hunter"?

6. What are some of Schreiner's memorable images?

7. Using highlighters or marginal notes, identify the essay's introduction, thesis, major events, support for each event, and conclusion. How effective is the organization of this essay?

Learning by Writing

THE ASSIGNMENT: RECALLING A PERSONAL EXPERIENCE

■ You can complete each of the steps in this assignment by using the *Writing Guide Software* for *THE BEDFORD GUIDE*.

Write about one specific experience that changed how you acted, thought, or felt. Use your experience as a springboard for reflection. Your purpose is not merely to tell an interesting story but to show your readers — your instructor and your classmates — the importance of that experience for you.

We suggest you pick an event that is not too personal or too subjective. Something that happened to you or that you observed, an encounter with a person who greatly influenced you, a decision that you made, or a challenge or an obstacle that you faced will be easier to recall (and to make vivid for your readers) than an interior experience like a religious conversion or falling in love.

Memorable student papers have recalled experiences heavy and light:

One writer recalled guitar lessons with a teacher who at first seemed harsh but who turned out to be a true friend.

Another student recalled a childhood trip when everything went wrong and she discovered the complexities of change.

Another recalled competing with a classmate who taught him a deeper understanding of success.

Facing the Challenge: Writing from Recall

The major challenge writers confront when writing from recall is to focus their essays on a main idea. When writing about a familiar — and often powerful — experience, it is tempting to include every detail that comes to mind and equally easy to overlook familiar details that would make the story's relevance clearer to the reader.

Once you are certain of your *purpose* in writing about a particular event — what you want to show readers about your experience — you can transform a laundry list of details into a narrative that connects events clearly around a main idea. You can select details that work together to convey the significance of your experience. To help you decide what to show your readers, respond to each of the following questions in a few sentences:

- What was important to you about the experience?
- What did you learn from it?
- How did it change you?
- How would you reply to a reader who asked "So what?" about it?

Once you have decided on your main point about the experience, you should select the details that best illustrate that point and show readers why the experience was important to you.

■ For writing activities for recalling an experience, visit <bedfordstmartins.com/bedguide> and do a keyword search:

activities

GENERATING IDEAS

You may find that the minute you are asked to write about a significant experience, the very incident will flash to mind. Most writers, though, will need a little time for their memories to surface. Often, when you are busy doing something else — observing the scene around you, talking with someone, reading about someone else's experience — the activity can trigger a recollection. When a promising one emerges, write it down. Perhaps, like Russell Baker, you found success when you ignored what you thought you were supposed to do in favor of what you really wanted to do. Perhaps, like Robert Schreiner, you learned from a painful experience.

■ For more strategies for generating ideas, see Ch. 15.

Try Brainstorming.   When you brainstorm, you just jot down as many ideas as you can. You can start with a suggestive idea — *disobedience, painful lesson, childhood, peer pressure* — and list under it whatever occurs through free association. You can also use the questions in the following checklist:

■ For more on brainstorming, see pp. 254–56.

DISCOVERY CHECKLIST

___ Did you ever break an important rule or rebel against authority? Did you learn anything from your actions?

___ Did you ever succumb to peer pressure? What were the results of going along with the crowd? What did you learn?

___ Did you ever regard a person in a certain way and then have to change your opinion of him or her?

___ Did you ever have to choose between two equally attractive alternatives? How might your life have been different if you had chosen differently?

___ Have you ever been appalled by witnessing an act of prejudice or insensitivity? What did you do? Do you wish you had done something different?

For more on freewriting, see pp. 256–57.

Try Freewriting.   You might also spend ten or fifteen minutes freewriting—simply writing without stopping. If you get stuck, write "I have nothing to say" over and over, until ideas come. They will come. After you are finished, you can circle or draw lines between related items, considering what main idea connects events.

For more on doodling or sketching, see pp. 258–59.

Try Doodling or Sketching.   As you remember an experience such as breaking your arm during a soccer tournament, try sketching or doodling whatever helps you recollect the event and its significance. Begin turning your doodles into words by adding comments on main events, notable details, and their impact on you.

For more on mapping, see pp. 259–60.

Try Mapping Your Recollections.   Identify a specific time period such as your birthday last year, the week when you decided to enroll in college, or a time when you changed in some way. On a blank page, on movable sticky notes, or in a computer file, record all the details you can recall about that time—people, statements, events, locations, and related physical descriptions.

For more on using a reporter's questions, see pp. 262–63.

Try a Reporter's Questions.   Once you recall an experience you want to write about, ask "the five *W*'s and an *H*" that journalists find useful.

- Who was involved?
- What happened?
- Where did it take place?
- When did it happen?
- Why did it happen?
- How did the events unfold?

WRITING WITH A COMPUTER

As you keyboard words onto a screen and use the Edit menu to copy, cut, or paste, you can see how easily you can manipulate your writing to answer the writing task. You may start generating ideas by brainstorming, freewriting, answering reporter's questions, outlining a chronology, or writing directly about the experience you recall. Some students find it helpful to write out notes or guidelines in bold type to remind themselves about their tasks and their assignment's challenges. Just as your teacher will encourage you to find and develop your own writing processes, you should actively create your own electronic writing space to support these processes.

Any question might lead to further questions — and to further discovery.

- **Who** was involved? ———→ What did the others look like?

  What did they say or do?

  Would their words supply any lively quotations?

- **What** happened? ———→ What did you think as the event unfolded?

  When did you see the importance of the experience?

Consider Sources of Support.   Because your memory drops as well as retains, you may want to check your recollections against those of a friend or family member who was there. Did you keep a journal at the time? Was the experience a turning point (big game, graduation) that your family would have documented with photos? Was it sufficiently public (such as a demonstration) or universal (such as a campus orientation) to have been recorded in a newspaper? If so, perhaps you can refresh your memory and rediscover details or angles that you had forgotten.

Family photograph

PLANNING, DRAFTING, AND DEVELOPING

Now, how will you tell your story? If the experience is still fresh in your mind, you may be able simply to write a draft, following the order of events and shaping your story as you go along. If you want to plan before you write, here are some suggestions.

For more strategies for planning, drafting, and developing papers, see Chs. 16, 17, and 18.

Start with a Main Idea, or Thesis.   As you think about the experience, jot down a few words that identify it and express its importance to you. Next, begin to shape these words into a sentence that states the significance of the experience — the main idea that you want to convey to a reader. If you aren't certain yet about what that idea is or how to put it into words, just begin writing. You can work again on your thesis as you revise.

For more on stating a thesis, see pp. 271–77.

For exercises on choosing effective thesis statements, visit <bedfordstmartins.com/bedguide> and do a keyword search:

[🔍   thesis   ]

TOPIC IDEA + SLANT   reunion in Georgia + really liked meeting family

WORKING THESIS   When I went to Georgia for a family reunion, I enjoyed meeting many relatives.

Establish a Chronology.   Retelling an experience is called *narration*, and the simplest way to organize is chronologically — relating the essential

For examples of time markers and other transitions, see pp. 300–01.

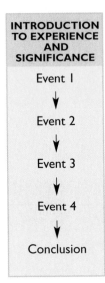

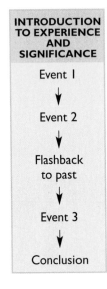

events in the order in which they occurred. On the other hand, sometimes you can start an account of an experience in the middle and then, through *flashback*, fill in whatever background a reader needs to know.

Richard Rodriguez, for instance, begins *Hunger of Memory* (Boston: David R. Godine, 1982), a memoir of his bilingual childhood, with an arresting sentence:

> I remember, to start with, that day in Sacramento, in a California now nearly thirty years past — when I first entered a classroom, able to understand about fifty stray English words.

The opening hooks our attention. In the rest of his essay, Rodriguez fills us in on his family history, on the gulf he came to perceive between the public language (English) and the language of his home (Spanish).

For more on providing details, see pp. 307–09.

For exercises on supporting a thesis, visit <bedfordstmartins.com/bedguide> and do a keyword search:

For more on the placement of visuals, see p. 368.

Show Readers What Happened.   How can you make your recollections come alive for your readers? Look again at Russell Baker's account of Mr. Fleagle teaching *Macbeth* and at the way Robert G. Schreiner depicts his cousin putting the wounded rabbits out of their misery. These two writers have not merely told us what happened; they have *shown* us, by creating scenes that we can see in our mind's eye.

As you tell your story, zoom in on at least two or three such specific scenes. Show your readers exactly what happened, where it occurred, what was said, who said it. Use details and words that appeal to all five senses — sight, sound, touch, taste, and smell. Because photographs and illustrations can clarify visual details for readers, carefully select the best placement for any images you decide to include. (Be sure that your instructor approves such additions.)

REVISING AND EDITING

For more revising and editing strategies, see Ch. 19.

After you have written an early draft, put it aside for a day or two — or a few hours if your deadline is looming. Then read it over carefully. Try to see everything through the eyes of one of your readers, noting both the pleasing parts and the confusing spots. Revise to ensure that you've expressed your thoughts and feelings clearly and strongly in a way that will reach your readers; edit to repair any distracting weaknesses in grammar or expression.

Focus on a Main Idea, or Thesis.   As you read over the essay, ask yourself: What was so important about this experience? Why is it so memorable? Will readers be able to see why this experience was a crucial one in your life? Will they understand how your life has been different ever since? Be sure that you convey a genuine and specific difference, reflecting the incident's

Learning to Be a Peer Editor

To practice peer response before trying your skills on a classmate's paper, select any student-written paper from this book's table of contents, and write a short but detailed letter to the writer. Tell the writer what is effective and ineffective about the essay, and explain why. Get together with others in your class who chose the same paper, and compare comments. What did you notice in the essay? Is its main idea or thesis clear to you? What did you miss that others noticed? As you will see, several people can notice far more than one individual can.

FOR GROUP LEARNING

real impact on you. In other words, revise to keep your essay focused on a single main idea or thesis.

> WORKING THESIS   When I went to Georgia for a family reunion, I enjoyed meeting many relatives.
>
> REVISED THESIS   Meeting my Georgia relatives showed me how powerfully two values — generosity and resilience — unite my family.

For more on stating a thesis, see pp. 271–77.

Add Concrete Detail.   Ask whether you have made events come alive for your readers by recalling them in sufficient concrete detail. Be specific enough that your readers can see, smell, taste, hear, and feel what you experienced. Make sure that all your details support your main idea or thesis. Notice again Robert Schreiner's focus in his second paragraph on the world outside his own skin: his close recall of the snow, of his grandfather's pointers about the habits of jackrabbits and the way to shoot them. As you revise, you may well recall more vivid details to include.

For more about providing details, see pp. 307–09.

Follow a Clear Sequence.   Reconsider the order of events in terms of your readers, looking for changes that might make your essay easier for them to follow. For example, if a classmate reads your draft and seems puzzled about the sequence, you might want to make a rough outline or list of the main events to check the clarity of your arrangement. Or you might add more transitions to connect events so that readers can tell exactly where your account is going.

For more on transitions, see pp. 300–03.

Revise and rewrite until you've related your experience and its impact as well as you can. Here are some useful questions about revising your paper:

REVISION CHECKLIST

___ Where have you shown why this experience was important and how it changed your life?

___ How have you engaged readers so that they will want to keep reading? Will they find your paper dramatic, instructive, or revealing? Will they see and feel what you experienced?

_____ Why do you begin your narration as you do? Is there another place in the draft that would make a better beginning?

_____ If the events are not in chronological order, how have you made the organization easy for readers to follow?

_____ In what ways does the ending provide a sense of finality?

_____ Do you stick to a point? Is everything relevant to your main idea or thesis?

_____ If you portray any people, how have you made their importance clear? Which details make them seem real, not just shadowy figures?

_____ Does any dialogue have the ring of real speech? Read it aloud. Try it on a friend.

■ For more editing and proofreading strategies, see pp. 336–39.

After you have revised your recall essay, edit and proofread it. Carefully check the grammar, word choice, punctuation, and mechanics — and then correct any problems you find. Here are some questions to get you started:

■ For more help, turn to the dark-blue-edged pages, and find the sections of the Quick Editing Guide noted here.

EDITING CHECKLIST	
_____ Is your sentence structure correct? Have you avoided writing fragments, comma splices, or fused sentences?	A1, A2
_____ Have you used correct verb tenses and forms throughout? When you present a sequence of past events, is it clear what happened first and what happened next?	A3
_____ When you use transitions and other introductory elements to connect events, have you placed any needed commas after them?	C1
_____ In your dialogue, have you made sure that commas and periods are inside the closing quotation mark?	C3
_____ Have you spelled everything correctly, especially the names of people and places? Have you capitalized names correctly?	D1, D2

When you have made all the changes you need to make, print out a clean copy of your paper — and hand it in.

OTHER ASSIGNMENTS

1. Choose a person outside your immediate family who had a marked effect on your life, either good or bad. Jot down ten details that might help a reader understand what that person was like. Consider the person's physical appearance, way of talking, and habits as well as any memorable incidents. When your list is finished, look back at "The Art of Eating Spaghetti" to identify the kinds of detail Baker uses in his portrait of Mr. Fleagle, noting any you might add to your list. Then write a paper in which you portray that person, including the details that help explain his or her impact on you.

2. Recall a place you were once fond of — your grandmother's kitchen, a tree house, a library, a locker room, a vacation retreat. If you have a pho-

Have a classmate or friend read your draft and suggest how you might present the main idea about your experience more clearly and vividly. Ask your peer editor questions such as these about writing from recall:

FOR PEER RESPONSE

- What do you think the writer's main idea, or thesis is? Where is it stated or clearly implied? Why was this experience significant?

- What emotions do the people in the essay feel? How did *you* feel while reading the essay?

- Where does the essay come alive? Underline images, descriptions, and dialogue that seem especially vivid.

- If this were your paper, what is the one thing you would be sure to work on before handing it in?

For general questions for a peer editor, see pp. 328–29.

tograph of the place, looking at it may help to jog your memory. Write a paper that emphasizes why this place was memorable. What made it different from every other place? Why was it important to you? What do you feel when you remember it?

3. Write a paper in which you recall some traditional ceremony, ritual, or observation familiar to you. Such a tradition can pertain to a holiday, a rite of passage (confirmation, bar or bat mitzvah, college orientation, graduation), a sporting event, a family custom. Explain the importance of the tradition to you, using whatever information you recall. How did the tradition originate? Who takes part? How has it changed through the years? What does it add to the lives of those who observe it?

Applying What You Learn: Some Uses of Recalling Experience

In College Courses.   Virtually every paper, no matter what it sets out to accomplish, can benefit from vivid examples that you recall.

- Recalling a relevant personal experience can engage your readers' interest and provide a springboard for your investigation, analysis, explanation, or argument. For example, your recollections of visiting or living in another country might introduce a sociology paper on cultural differences or a psychology paper on adaptation to change.

- Your recollection of events may provide the foundation for the reflective journal you keep during an internship or clinical experience.

- Your personal experience can add authority to the judgments and conclusions you offer in your academic writing assignments. In a paper for an anthropology course, you might recall your impressions of visiting the Anasazi ruins at Mesa Verde. In a paper for a human development course, you might include memories of caring for your grandmother.

Career day, Iowa State University

In the Workplace. You will also use recall as you write on the job.

- Recalling your past jobs and your workplace skills might help you identify new opportunities at the next campus career day.

- Detailed data that help you recall past successes, failures, or customer comments can provide compelling reasons for adopting proposals that you offer or changing a product or service.

- Recalling past contacts with customers or clients can remind them of your company's valuable product or service and help to personalize your letters, e-mail messages, or other contacts with them.

Reunion Memories

Brown Family
Gathering
September 6-7, 2003
Marion, Virginia

In Your Community. In your private life, your memory is the source not only for personal journals, diaries, or correspondence, but also for much of your writing as an involved member of your community.

- Your personal experiences can lend enormous impact to an appeal for changes in city plans, school policies, or government funding. If your child has been upset by her school's use of standardized tests, recalling her frustration could alert school board members to the problems inherent in the testing policies.

- Recalling and recording how you have organized or implemented plans can save time and improve an event the next time around.

- Recalling events from your childhood or from your happiest or most difficult days with your family can make your next reunion or holiday gathering even more meaningful for you.

Chapter 5
Observing a Scene

Responding to an Image

A scene like this one might look and feel very different to different observers, depending on their vantage points, emotions, background, and experience. In this image, what prominent element attracts your attention? Who is the observer? What details might be important for this observer? Although visual details are obviously central, feel free to describe sound, smell, and touch, as well as any emotions that might come into play. Next, identify a second person who might be observing this scene. Which details might matter most to this other observer? In what ways are your two lists of details similar or different?

Most writers begin to write by recalling what they know. Then they look around and add what they observe. Some writing consists almost entirely of observation — a reporter's eyewitness account of a fire, an anthropologist's field notes, a clinical report by a doctor or nurse detailing a patient's condition, a scientist's account of a laboratory experiment. So does any writing that describes a person, place, or thing. In other instances, observation provides supporting details to make the primary ideas clear or convincing.

Not enough to write about? Open your eyes — and your other senses. Take in not only what you can see but also what you can hear, smell, touch, and taste. Then when you write, report your observations in concrete detail. Of course, you can't record everything your senses bring you. You must be selective. Keep in mind your purpose in writing and your audience to help you choose the important and relevant details. To make a football game come alive for readers of your college newspaper, you might briefly mention the overcast cold weather and the buttery smell of popcorn. But if your purpose is primarily to explain which team won and why, you might stress the muddy playing field, the most spectacular plays, and the players who scored.

Learning from Other Writers

Here are two essays by writers who observe their surroundings and reflect on their observations. To help you begin to analyze the first reading in this chapter, look for the notes in the margin. They identify features such as the main impression created in the observation and stated in the thesis, the first of the locations observed, and the supporting details that describe the location.

■ For more on thesis and support, see Chs. 16 and 18.

■ For more examples of writing from observation, visit <bedfordstmartins.com/bedguide> and do a keyword search:

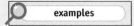
examples

As You Read These Observations

As you read these essays, ask yourself the following questions:

1. Specifically, what does the writer observe? Places? People? Behavior? Nature? Things?

2. What senses does the writer rely on? What sensory images does each writer develop? Find some striking passages in which the writer reports his or her observations. What makes these passages memorable to you?

3. Why does the writer use observation? What conclusion does the writer draw from reflecting on the observations?

Eric Liu

The Chinatown Idea

In this selection from The Accidental Asian *(1998), Eric Liu describes a childhood visit to Chinatown in New York City.*

Another family outing, one of our occasional excursions to the city. It was a Saturday. I was twelve. I remember only vaguely what we did during the day — Fifth Avenue, perhaps, the museums, Central Park, Carnegie Hall. But I recall with precision going to Chinatown as night fell. `1`

Introduction

We parked on a side street, a dim, winding way cluttered with Chinese placards° and congested with slumbering Buicks and Chevys. The license `2`

Vantage point 1

plates — NEW YORK, EMPIRE STATE — seemed incongruous here, foreign. We walked a few blocks to East Broadway. Soon we were wading through thick crowds on the sidewalk, passing through belts of aroma: sweat and breath, old perfume, spareribs. It was late autumn and chilly enough to numb my cheeks, but the bustle all around gave the place an electric warmth. Though it was evening, the scene was lit like a stage, thanks to the aluminum lamps hanging from every produce stand. Peddlers lined the street, selling steamed buns and chicken feet and imitation Gucci bags. Some shoppers moved along slowly. Others stopped at each stall, inspecting the greens, negotiating the price of fish, talking loudly. I strained to make sense of the chopped-off twangs of Cantonese coming from every direction, but there were more tones than I knew: my ear was inadequate; nothing was intelligible.

Supporting detail

This was the first time I had been in Chinatown after dark. Mom held `3` Andrea's hand as we walked and asked me to stay close. People bumped us, brushed past, as if we were invisible. I felt on guard, alert. I craned my neck as we walked past a kiosk° carrying a Chinese edition of *Playboy*. I glanced sidelong at the teenage ruffians on the corner. They affected an air of menace with their smokes and leather jackets, but their feathery almost-mustaches and overpermed hair made them look a bit ridiculous. Nevertheless, I kept my distance. I kept an eye on the sidewalk, too, so that I wouldn't soil my shoes in the streams of putrid° water that trickled down from the alleyways and into the parapet° of trash bags piled up on the curb.

I remember going into two stores that night. One was the Far Eastern `4` Bookstore. It was on the second floor of an old building. As we entered, the sounds of the street fell away. The room was spare and fluorescent. It looked like an earnest community library, crowded with rows of chest-high shelves. In the narrow aisles between shelves, patrons sat cross-legged on the floor, reading intently. If they spoke at all it was in a murmur. Mom and Dad each found an absorbing book. They read standing up. My sister and I, meanwhile, wandered restlessly through the stacks, scanning the spines for stray English words or Chinese phrases we might recognize. I ended up in children's books and leafed through an illustrated story about the three tigers. I couldn't read it. Before long, I was tugging on Dad's coat to take us somewhere else.

---

placards: Posters, signs.   **kiosk:** Booth.   **putrid:** Rotten; decaying.   **parapet:** Wall; suggesting a castle.

The other shop, a market called Golden Gate, I liked much more. It was 5
noisy. The shoppers swarmed about in a frenzy. On the ground level was an
emporium° of Chinese nonperishables: dried mushrooms, spiced beef, sea-
weed, shredded pork. Open crates of hoisin sauce° and sesame chili paste.
Sweets, like milky White Rabbit chews, coconut candies, rolls of sour "haw
flakes." Bags of Chinese peanuts, watermelon seeds. Down a narrow flight of
stairs was a storehouse of rice cookers, ivory chopsticks, crockery, woks that
hung from the wall. My mother carefully picked out a set of rice bowls and
serving platters. I followed her to the long checkout line, carrying a basket
full of groceries we wouldn't find in Poughkeepsie. I watched with wonder
as the cashier tallied up totals with an abacus.

THESIS
stating main impression

We had come to this store, and to Chinatown itself, to replenish our 6
supply of things Chinese: food and wares, and something else as well. We
had ventured here from the colorless outer suburbs to touch the source, to
dip into a pool of undiluted Chineseness. It was easier for my parents, of
course, since they could decode the signs and communicate. But even I,
whose bond to his ancestral culture had frayed down to the inner cord of
appetite — even I could feel somehow fortified by a trip to Chinatown.

Conclusion drawn
from observation

Yet we knew that we couldn't stay long — and that we didn't really want 7
to. We were Chinese, but we were still outsiders. When any peddler addressed us in Cantonese, that became obvious enough. They seemed so familiar and so different, these Chinatown Chinese. Like a reflection distorted
just so. Their faces were another brand of Chinese, rougher-hewn. I was fascinated by them. I liked being connected to them. But was it because of
what we shared — or what we did not? I began that night to distinguish between my world and theirs.

It was that night, too, as we were making our way down East Broadway, 8
that out of the blur of Chinese faces emerged one that we knew. It was Po-
Po's° face. We saw her just an instant before she saw us. There was surprise
in her eyes, then hurt, when she peered up from her parka. Everyone hugged
and smiled, but this was embarrassing. Mom began to explain: we'd been
uptown, had come to Chinatown on a whim, hadn't wanted to barge in on
her unannounced. Po-Po nodded. We made some small talk. But the realization that her daily routine was our tourist's jaunt,° that there was more
than just a hundred miles between us, consumed the backs of our minds
like a flame to paper. We lingered for a minute, standing still as the human
current flowed past, and then we went our separate ways.

Afterward, during the endless drive home, we didn't talk about bump- 9
ing into Po-Po. We didn't talk about much of anything. I looked intently
through the window as we drove out of Chinatown and sped up the FDR
Drive, then over the bridge. Manhattan turned into the Bronx, the Bronx
into Yonkers, and the seams of the parkway clicked along in soothing intervals as we cruised northward to Dutchess County. I slipped into a deep,

emporium: Marketplace.   **hoisin sauce:** A sweet brown sauce that is a popular Chinese condiment.   **Po-Po:** The narrator's grandmother.   **jaunt:** trip, outing.

open-mouthed slumber, not awakening until we were back in Merrywood, our development, our own safe enclave. I remember the comforting sensation of being home: the sky was clear and starry, the lawn a moon-bathed carpet. We pulled into our smooth blacktop driveway. Silence. It was late, perhaps later than I'd ever stayed up. Still, before I went to bed, I made myself take a shower.

Questions to Start You Thinking

Meaning

1. Why do Liu and his family go to Chinatown?

2. How do Liu and his family feel when they encounter Po-Po? What observations and descriptions lead you to that conclusion?

3. What is the significance of the last sentence? How does it capture the essence of Liu's Chinatown experience?

Writing Strategies

4. In which paragraphs or sections does the writer's use of sensory details capture the look, feel, or smell of Chinatown? In general, how successfully has Liu included various types of observations and details?

5. How does Liu organize his observations? Is this organization effective? Why or why not?

6. Which of the observations and events in this essay most clearly reveal that Liu considers himself to be a "tourist"?

STUDENT ESSAY

Michael Coil
Communications

Walking into the county government building, a visitor would not imagine what goes on in the basement twenty-four hours a day, seven days a week. The building is so quiet, and nobody is in sight. I make my way down the stairs and into the basement. A long hallway and an inconspicuous,° unmarked brown wooden door lead me to the communications center, where the radio traffic for all of Dodge City and Ford County is handled. Nothing along the way even hints at the amount of emotion that is felt in this small space.

For his first-year composition class, Michael Coil took a fresh look at a familiar location.

? *What kinds of places does this building bring to mind?*

Inside the center a kitchen is connected to a workspace with a large glass window that looks in on the main room. An office for the supervisor sits closed and locked, and a bathroom hides around the corner. The smell of constantly brewing coffee is thick, as though permanently tattooed on the air. I step through the

inconspicuous: Not noticeable.

❓ *When have you had a similar change in perception?*

kitchen and past the long window into the Dispatch Room. As a police officer for the city, I have been in the Dispatch Room many times, but I have never sat and thought of everything that goes on there. I begin to see things through new eyes.

The first thing to attract my attention is the number of computers at the work-stations. I see three individual stations, each with a tall leather chair and a computer keyboard. At each station is a line of computer screens of various shapes and sizes, all brightly lit and streaming with information. A large green digital clock on the wall keeps the time, and a stack of printers taller than I am decorates the wall beside me. I notice a quiet hum from the many hard drives and printer fans. It is cold outside, but still the heat of the machines makes it necessary to run the air conditioner.

A television hangs from the ceiling in the corner. I can tell it's muted because it makes no sound though lines streaming with information slide off the screen. The reporters on the screen appear to be talking about Iraq. The anchorman looks angry, but nobody in the room pays him any attention. The only real noise is from the three 911 dispatchers talking happily. The mood is light, and conversation seems to come very easily.

A phone rings, and one of the dispatchers answers. She enters something on her screen and then hangs up. She tells me that the hospital was calling to ask them to page one of the on-call doctors. The dispatchers resume their conversation. They are casual and friendly, and their conversation ranges from what they ate today to the personalities of their dogs at home. I find it easy to talk with them, and I can tell that spending so much time side by side in this room brings the three dispatchers together like close friends.

❓ *How can a ring be "obnoxious"?*

After a few minutes the phone rings again. The situation is different this time. The first phone that rang was a normal ring without unusual volume or tone, but this one makes my blood churn. It is loud, obnoxious,° and ugly. It's like combining the screech of a vulture and the wail of a dying animal. The air becomes thick and tense. The conversation stops in mid-sentence, and I can feel all of the dispatchers tense up in anticipation of what they are about to hear. The three of them pick up the phone, and one begins to talk. Another begins to type on the computer screen, and the third gets on the radio and dispatches the call to the police. From where I am sitting at the rear of the workspace, I can hear the woman on the phone screaming. I can't quite decipher° what she is saying, but by the dispatcher's rising tone, I can tell it is not good. Repeatedly the caller is told to calm down and tell what's going on. With each command the dispatcher's voice gets more edgy. Hearts are racing now, and the room fills with dread. "Somebody is breaking into my house," the voice on the line finally pushes out. I read the screen and see that she lives not far from

obnoxious: Offensive, intolerable.   **decipher:** Interpret.

3

4

5

6

where we are sitting. It only takes a minute or two for the first unit to arrive, but sitting and listening to that poor woman's plea for help makes that short time feel like an eternity. The officers inform the dispatcher that they are in front of the house, and they don't see anybody. The person must have left just moments before they got there. The dispatcher speaking with the woman leans back slowly in her chair, causing it to groan softly. She rubs her hands on her face as though she were sweating and suddenly goes back into her casual mode. She politely tells the woman to answer the door because the police are standing out front, then pauses a moment and says goodbye.

How have you responded to the sounds that the writer has described?

Several minutes pass before I can collect myself and begin to process everything I just saw and heard. I feel as though I had been sitting in the house with that distraught woman watching helplessly. I feel suddenly tired, stressed, and still my nerves are shaking from the adrenaline. The dispatchers, however, return to their conversation without missing a beat. The tension filters silently away, and the mood becomes friendly again. Only a unique and brave person could willingly face challenges like that one on a day-to-day basis.

7

As I walk out of the communications room, I see multiple cartoons cut out of the newspaper and taped to the doorway. I think to myself, What a difficult task it must be to come back down after eight hours on the emotional rollercoaster. It would be so easy for the dispatchers to become bitter, angry people, but they are quite the opposite. They are inviting and friendly, and though they will always deny it, they are modern-day heroes waiting to come to our rescue. Day and night they sit, behind the brown unmarked wooden door, at the end of the long marble hallway, always ready to help.

8

Questions to Start You Thinking

Meaning

1. Is the Dispatch Room as "quiet" as Coil originally suspects as he enters the building? Which paragraph best supports your answer?

2. In paragraph 8, Coil uses the term "modern-day heroes" to describe the dispatchers. What details in his account support that description?

3. What does Coil learn about himself from his visit to the Dispatch Room?

Writing Strategies

4. How does comparing and contrasting the dispatchers' behavior before a call and during a call help Coil create a vivid impression of the room?

5. Which sense does Coil use most effectively? Point to a few examples that support your choice.

6. Paragraph 6 includes the only dialogue in the essay. What effect does it have?

7. Using highlighters or marginal notes, identify the essay's introduction, thesis, major vantage points for observation, details supporting each part of the observation, and conclusion. How effective is the organization of this essay?

Learning by Writing

THE ASSIGNMENT: OBSERVING A SCENE

■ You can complete each of the steps in this assignment by using the *Writing Guide Software* for THE BEDFORD GUIDE.

Observe a place near your campus, home, or job and the people who frequent this place. Then write a paper in which you describe the place, the people, and their actions so as to convey the spirit of the place and offer some insight into the impact of the place on the people.

This assignment is meant to start you observing closely. Go somewhere nearby, and station yourself where you can mingle with the people there. Open your senses — all of them, so that you see, smell, taste, hear, and feel. Jot down what you immediately notice, especially the atmosphere and how it affects the people there. Take notes describing the location, the people, and the actions and events you see. Then use your observations to convey the spirit of the scene. What is your main impression of the place? Of the people there? Of the relationship between the people and the place?

■ For writing activities for observing a scene, visit <bedfordstmartins.com/ bedguide> and do a key-word search:

activities

Facing the Challenge: Observing a Scene

The major challenge writers face when writing from observation is to include compelling details that fully convey the main impression of a scene. As we experience the world, we are bombarded by sensory details, but our task as writers is to choose the details that make a subject come alive for readers. For example, describing an oak as "a big tree with green leaves" is too vague to help readers envision the tree or grasp what is unique about it.

Use these questions to help you notice sensory details:

- What colors, shapes, and sizes do you see?
- What tones, pitches, and rhythms do you hear?
- What textures, grains, and physical features do you feel?
- What fragrances and odors do you smell?
- What sweet, spicy, or other flavors do you taste?

After recording the details that define the scene, ask two more questions:

- What overall main impression do these details establish?
- Which specific details will best show the spirit of this scene to a reader?

Your answers will help you decide which details to include in your paper and which to leave out.

Remember, your purpose is not only to describe the scene but also to express thoughts and feelings connected with what you observe.

Three student writers wrote about these observations:

One student, who works nights in the emergency room, observed the scene and the community that abruptly forms when an accident victim arrives: doctors, nurses, orderlies, the patient, and friends or relatives.

Another observed a bar mitzvah celebration that reunited a family for the first time in many years.

Another observed the activity in the bleachers in a baseball stadium before, during, and after a game.

GENERATING IDEAS

Although setting down observations might seem a cut-and-dried task, to many writers it is true discovery. Here are some ways to generate such observations.

Brainstorm.   First, you need to find a scene to observe. What places interest you? Which are memorable? Start brainstorming — listing rapidly any ideas that come to mind. Here are a few questions to help you start your list:

For more strategies for generating ideas, see Ch. 15.

For more on brainstorming, see pp. 254–56.

DISCOVERY CHECKLIST

___ Where do people gather for some event or performance (a stadium, a theater, an auditorium)?

___ Where do people get together for some activity (a church, a classroom)?

___ Where do crowds form while people are getting things or services (a shopping mall, a dining hall or student union, a dentist's waiting room)?

___ Where do people go for recreation or relaxation (an arcade, a ballpark)?

___ Where do people gather (a fire, a party, a wedding, a graduation)?

Get Out and Look.   If nothing on your list strikes you as compelling, plunge into the world to see what you see. Visit a city street or a country hillside, a campus building or a practice field, a lively scene — a mall, an airport, a fast-food restaurant, a student hangout — or one with only a few people sunbathing, walking dogs, or tossing Frisbees. Stand off in a corner for a while, and then mix with the group to gain different views of the scene.

Record Your Observations. Michael Coil's essay "Communications" began as

Band practice at University of California, Berkeley

For more on journal keeping, see pp. 265–66.

some notes Coil made about his county communications center and the phone traffic it receives. He was able to mine those notes for details to bring his subject to life.

Your notes on a subject — or tentative subject — can be taken in any old order or methodically. To draw up an "observation sheet," fold a sheet of paper in half lengthwise. Label the left column "Objective," and impartially list exactly what you see, like a zoologist looking at a new species of moth. Then label the right column "Subjective," and list your thoughts and feelings about what you observe. If possible, keep looking at your subject while you write.

Objective	Subjective
The ticket holders form a line outside the old brick hall, standing two or three deep all the way down the block.	This place has seen concerts of all kinds — you can feel the history as you wait, as if the hall protects the crowds and the music.
Groups of friends talk, a few couples hug, and some guys laugh as they tell jokes.	The crowd seems relaxed and friendly, all waiting to hear their favorite group.
Everyone shuffles forward when the doors finally open, looking around at the crowd and edging toward the entrance.	The excitement and energy grow with the wait, but it's just the concert ritual — the prelude to a perfect night.

The quality of your paper will depend in large part on the truthfulness and accuracy of your observations. Your objective notes on an observation sheet will trigger more subjective notes. As your list grows, write on one side of your paper only: later you can spread out your notes and look at them all in one glance. Even in the sample observation sheet made at the concert venue, a main impression is starting to take shape. The old hall shelters concertgoers and musicians alike, channeling their energy and enthusiasm into the music.

Include a Range of Images.   Have you captured not just sights but sounds, touches, odors? Have you observed from several vantage points or on several occasions to deepen your impressions? Have you added sketches or doodles to your notes, perhaps drawing the features or mapping the shape of the place? Can you begin writing as you continue to observe your subject? Have you noticed how other writers use *images*, evoking sensory experience, to record what they sense, as in naturalist Henry Beston's memoir *Northern Farm* (New York: Rinehart, 1948)? Here he describes a remarkable sound: "the voice of ice," the midwinter sound of a whole frozen pond settling and expanding in its bed.

Sometimes there was a sort of hollow oboe sound, and sometimes a groan with a delicate undertone of thunder. [. . .] Just as I turned to go, there came from below one curious and sinister crack which ran off into a sound like the whine of a giant whip of steel lashed through the moonlit air.

PLANNING, DRAFTING, AND DEVELOPING

After recording your observations, look over your notes or your observation sheet, circling whatever looks useful. Maybe you can rewrite your notes into a draft, throwing out details that don't matter, leaving those that do. Maybe you'll need a plan to help you organize all the observations, laying them out graphically or in a simple scratch outline.

For more strategies for planning, drafting, and developing, see Chs. 16, 17 and 18.

Start with a Main Impression or Thesis.   What main insight or impression do you want to get across? Answering this question will help you decide which details to include and which to omit. It will also help you avoid a dry recitation of observed facts.

For more on stating a thesis, see pp. 271–77.

PLACE OBSERVED   Smalley Green after lunch

MAIN IMPRESSION   relaxing activity is good after a morning of classes

WORKING THESIS   After their morning classes, students have fun relaxing on Smalley Green with their dogs and Frisbees.

For exercises on choosing effective thesis statements, visit <bedfordstmartins.com/ bedguide> and do a keyword search:

```
🔍          thesis
```

Organize to Show Readers Your Point.   How do you map out a series of observations? Your choice will depend on your purpose in writing and the main impression that you want to create. Whatever your choice, be sure to add transitions — words or phrases that guide the reader from one vantage point, location, or idea to the next. Experiment with options such as the ones at the top of the next page.

For more organization strategies, see pp. 277–87.

As you create your "picture," you bring a place to life using the details that capture its spirit. If your instructor approves, consider whether adding a photograph, sketch, diagram, or other illustration would enhance your written observation.

For transitions that mark place or direction, see p. 300.

REVISING AND EDITING

Your revising, editing, and proofreading will all be easier if you have taken accurate notes on your observations. But what if, when you look over your draft, you find that you don't have enough detail? If you have any doubts, go back to the scene, and take more notes to flesh out your draft.

For more revising and editing strategies, see Ch. 19.

Focus on a Main Impression or Thesis.   As you begin to revise, ask a friend to read your observation, or read it yourself as if you had never visited the place you observed. While reading, you might notice gaps that would

Sequential Organization

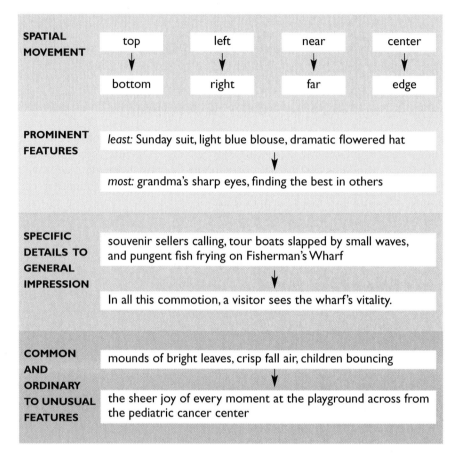

| SPATIAL MOVEMENT | top → bottom | left → right | near → far | center → edge |

PROMINENT FEATURES

least: Sunday suit, light blue blouse, dramatic flowered hat

↓

most: grandma's sharp eyes, finding the best in others

SPECIFIC DETAILS TO GENERAL IMPRESSION

souvenir sellers calling, tour boats slapped by small waves, and pungent fish frying on Fisherman's Wharf

↓

In all this commotion, a visitor sees the wharf's vitality.

COMMON AND ORDINARY TO UNUSUAL FEATURES

mounds of bright leaves, crisp fall air, children bouncing

↓

the sheer joy of every moment at the playground across from the pediatric cancer center

puzzle a reader or decide that the spirit of the place seems understated. Consider whether the main impression you want to convey would be clearer if you sharpened its description in your thesis.

■ For more on stating a thesis, see pp. 271–77.

WORKING THESIS   After their morning classes, students have fun relaxing on Smalley Green with their dogs and Frisbees.

REVISED THESIS   When students, dogs, and Frisbees accumulate on Smalley Green after lunch, they show how much campus learning takes place outside of class.

■ For exercises on supporting a thesis, visit <bedfordstmartins.com/bedguide> and do a keyword search:

🔍 **support**

Add Relevant and Powerful Details.   Next, check your selection of details. Does each detail contribute to your main impression? Should any details be dropped or added? Should any be rearranged so that your organization, moving from point to point, is clearer? Could any observations be described more vividly or powerfully? Could more precise or more concrete wording strengthen the way you present the details?

Let a classmate or friend respond to your draft, suggesting how to use detail to convey your main impression more powerfully. Ask your peer editor to answer questions such as these about writing from observation:

- What is the main insight or impression you carry away from this writing?

- Which sense does the writer use particularly well? Are any senses neglected that could be used?

- Can you see and feel what the writer experienced? Would more details make this writing more compelling? Put check marks wherever you want more detail.

- How well has the writer used evidence from the senses to build a main impression? Which sensory impressions contribute most strongly to the overall picture? Which seem superfluous?

- If this were your paper, what is the one thing you would be sure to work on before handing it in?

FOR PEER RESPONSE

For general questions for a peer editor, see pp. 328–29.

To see where your draft could need work, you might consider these questions:

REVISION CHECKLIST

___ Have you accomplished your purpose—to convey to readers your overall impression of your subject and to share some telling insight about it?

___ What can you assume your readers know? What do they need to be told?

___ Have you gathered enough observations to describe your subject? Have you observed with *all* your senses? (Smell isn't always useful, but it might be.)

___ Have you been selective, including details that effectively support your overall impression?

___ Which observations might need to be checked for accuracy? Which might need to be checked for richness or fullness?

___ Is your organizational pattern the most effective for your subject? Is it easy for readers to follow? Would another pattern work better?

After you have revised your observation essay, edit and proofread it. Carefully check the grammar, word choice, punctuation, and mechanics—and then correct any problems you find. If you have added more details while revising, consider whether they have been sufficiently blended with the ideas already there.

Here are some questions to get you started when editing and proofreading your observation paper:

For more editing and proofreading strategies, see pp. 336–39.

For more help, turn to the dark-blue-edged pages, and find the sections of the Quick Editing Guide noted here.

EDITING CHECKLIST

— Is your sentence structure correct? Have you avoided writing fragments, comma splices, and fused sentences?   A1, A2

— Have you used an adjective whenever describing a noun or pronoun? Have you used an adverb whenever describing a verb, adjective, or adverb? Have you used the correct form when comparing two or more things?   A7

— Is it clear what each modifier in a sentence modifies? Have you created any dangling or misplaced modifiers?   B1

— Have you used parallel structure wherever needed, especially in lists or comparisons?   B2

FOR GROUP LEARNING

Reading Your Writing Aloud

Try reading your draft aloud to your group. Rehearse your reading beforehand, and deliver it with feeling. Ask your audience to stop you when something isn't clear. Have a pencil in hand to mark such problems, or ask someone else to note them for you. After you've finished reading aloud, ask for reactions. (Or ask your listeners any of the questions in the peer response checklist on page 75.) Have someone record the most vital suggestions and reactions that your draft provokes. If possible, audiotape your reading and the reactions. Review both the notes and the tape when you revise.

WRITING WITH A COMPUTER

When you write an observation, you will want to use modifiers (adjectives or adverbs) to qualify other words so that your observations are clear. However, adverbs like *very* and *really* or adjectives like *beautiful* and *great* are vague rather than concrete and precise. Read your draft aloud, and note any vague or imprecise modifiers you have used. Then, use the Find function in your word processor's Edit menu to help you locate all of the places in your paper where you have used *really*, for example, or another potentially vague modifier. As you find each modifier, ask, "Is it specific enough?" "Will it guide my reader through my way of seeing?" Delete any weak modifiers, or replace them with more specific words.

OTHER ASSIGNMENTS

1. To develop your powers of observation, go for a walk, recording your observations in two or three detailed paragraphs. Let your walk take you through either an unfamiliar scene or a familiar scene worth a closer look than you normally give it (such as a supermarket, a city street, an open field). Avoid a subject so familiar that you would struggle to see it

from a fresh perspective (such as a dormitory corridor or a parking lot). Sum up your impression of the place, including any opinion you form through your close observations.

2. Try this short, spontaneous writing exercise. Begin the assignment immediately after class, and turn it in the same afternoon.

> Go to a nearby public place—burger joint, library, copy center, art gallery—and select a person who catches your eye, who somehow intrigues you. Try to choose someone who looks as if she or he will stay put for a while. Settle yourself where you can observe your subject unobtrusively. Take notes, if you can do so without being observed.
>
> Now, carefully and tactfully (we don't want any fistfights or lawsuits) notice everything you can about this person. Start with physical characteristics, but focus on other things too. How does the person talk? Move? What does the person's body language tell you?
>
> Write a paragraph describing the person. Pretend that the person is going to hold up a bank ten minutes from now, and the police will expect you to supply a full and accurate description.

3. The perspective of a tourist, an outsider alert to details, often reveals the distinctive character of places and people. Think of some place you have visited as an outsider in the past year, and jot down any notable details you recall. Or spend a few minutes as a tourist right now. Go to a busy spot on or off campus, and record your observations of anything you find amusing, surprising, puzzling, or intriguing. Then write an essay on the unique character of the place.

Applying What You Learn: Some Uses of Observing a Scene

In College Courses.   Observing and accurately recording your observations is critical to your success in many courses besides English, especially those that involve labs, field trips, or practica that prepare you for your career.

- Students in the social sciences—sociology, criminal justice, psychology, anthropology—often take field trips requiring them to observe behavior closely and report their observations. Similarly, students in the humanities or fine arts may be expected to observe and record their impressions of a play, concert, exhibit, or historical site.

- Classes in health, education, or other professional fields may include clinical or field observations.

- Science classes—biology, anatomy, physics, or chemistry—may call for lab reports, recording observations of experiments, or field reports on animal life within a habitat.

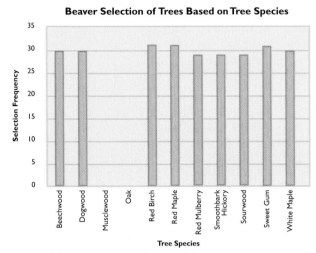

Beaver Selection of Trees Based on Tree Species

From a lab report on beaver foraging behavior

In the Workplace.   In many careers and professions, observation and analysis provide valuable information and lend credibility to your writing.

- If you choose a career in nursing, teaching, or social work, you will probably write case studies based on observation, sometimes for publication, sometimes for reference.

- Journalists must draw on what they observe to report news events or write feature articles. During interviews, body language, tone of voice, and surroundings may be as revealing as words spoken by the subject.

- Many careers will require you to make field observations and report your findings to your superiors. Architects and engineers observe at a building site; biologists and conservationists observe animals in the wild; astronomers observe movement in the night sky.

In Your Community.   Observation is a primary resource for your writing as an active member of your community.

- Vivid observations in an editorial or proposal calling for resolution of a neighborhood problem—a dangerous intersection, a poorly lighted park, a run-down building—will make the hazards real for readers.

A fraternity house destroyed during a three-day party

- Joining the planning group for a community project, such as a sports arena or a performing arts center, may require you to observe facilities in other communities and report your findings. Observing another community's festival also can provide ideas and identify logistical details for planning an event in your own community.

- You may need to report to authorities and to insurance agents what you've observed at the site of an accident, a natural disaster, or a crime. Photos of the scene can be useful support.

Chapter 6
Interviewing a Subject

Scott Olson/Getty Images

Responding to an Image

You may or may not have heard of Ira Glass, but suppose you have been assigned to interview him. What does the photograph suggest you might learn about his personality and interests? How do his pose, clothing, and expression contribute to your impression of him? Look also at the equipment shown in the photograph. What do you suppose he does for a living? What do you think the photographer finds interesting about Ira Glass?

Don't know what to write about? Go talk with someone. Meet for half an hour with an anthropology professor, and you probably will have plenty of material for a paper. Just as likely, you can get a paper's worth of information from a ten-minute exchange with a mechanic who relines brakes. Both the mechanic and the professor are experts. But even people who aren't usually considered experts may tell you things you didn't know and provide you with material.

As this chapter suggests, you can direct a conversation by asking questions to elicit what you want to find out. You do so in an *interview* — a special kind of conversation with a purpose — usually to help you understand the other person or to find out what that person knows.

Learning from Other Writers

■ For more on thesis and support, see Chs. 16 and 18.

Here are two essays whose writers talked to someone and reported the conversations, using direct quotations and telling details to reveal engaging personalities. To help you begin to analyze the first reading in this chapter, look for the notes in the margin. They identify features such as the thesis, and the quotations providing support.

■ For more examples of writing based on interviews, visit <bedfordstmartins.com/ bedguide> and do a keyword search:

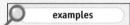
examples

As You Read These Interview Essays

As you read these essays, ask yourself the following questions:

1. Was the conversation reported from an informal discussion or planned as an interview? Does the writer report the conversation directly or indirectly?
2. What does the interview show about the character and personality of the individual speaking? What does it show about the author who is listening?
3. Why do you think the writer draws on conversation?

A. Scott Berg published the memoir Travels with "My Aunt," *from which this excerpt was taken, shortly after the 2003 death of his famous subject, actress Katharine Hepburn.*

Extended introduction — giving context for subject

A. Scott Berg
Travels with "My Aunt"

The lives of the biggest movie stars — the "superstars" — are generally as "unreal" offstage as the characters they portray. There is a near-constant frenzy around them — the whirl of managers and agents and publicists and assistants tending to the constant demands for the star's time: interviews; photograph sessions; public appearances. The ringing telephone becomes an addiction, often sending a star into withdrawal when it stops.

For those who became famous under the old studio system, the lack of reality to their lives was even greater. Because the contract stars of the thirties, forties, and fifties had worked constantly, everything off the set was less important than what they did before the cameras. The studio heads paying the bills protected their own interests and took care of everything in their stars' lives. On the set, doubles were always available for the dangerous or unpleasant duties, whether it was performing a stunt or standing under the hot lights. Off-camera, everything was tended to. Not just clothing and grooming and personal chores but even indecent, occasionally illegal, activities were cleaned up, swept under the carpet, fixed.

> 2 Extended introduction (continued)

Many stars begin to believe their own encomiastic° press releases. After a year or a decade, and, in a few cases, a lifetime of fabulous salaries and fringe benefits, there naturally comes a sense of great expectations. With most movie stars, there also comes a sense of entitlement.

> 3

Perhaps the most attractive aspect of Katharine Hepburn's personality was that she held no such feelings. She made plenty of demands; indeed, she knew how to get what she wanted long before she was a star. In part, that's how she got to be a star. But she always remained grounded. In twenty years I never found a trail of bodies she trampled over in order to reach her goal. For all her impatience, there was always a sense of humility and humanity, even a sense of gratitude for her good fortune. She was never above making a bed, cooking a meal, chopping wood, or working her garden. Indeed, she found pleasure in those activities. Almost every time I saw her in the kitchen in Fenwick,° she was wiping a sponge across the countertop, cleaning up after somebody.

> 4 THESIS stating dominant impression
>
> Elaboration of dominant impression

In short, she never lost her work ethic. She believed the point of making money was to allow you to live comfortably enough to work some more, until you simply could work no longer.

> 5

"Retire?" she had exclaimed one night at dinner, when Irene Selznick° had found a gentle way of broaching° the topic. "What's the point? Actors shouldn't walk away from the audience as long as the audiences aren't walking away from them. As long as people are buying what I'm selling," she added, "I'm still selling." Kate never understood how people got stuck in jobs they didn't enjoy.

> 6 Quotations showing subject's personality

Stars who bemoaned° the hardships of their profession — the impositions, the loss of privacy — rankled° her, as though she were embarrassed to be one of them. "These actors who complain in interviews about twelve-hour days!" she said with incomprehension. "You sit there for eleven of them. It's not as if we're carrying sacks of feed all day!"

> 7

"What does he expect?" she said upon reading about Sean Penn punching out a photographer. "You can't go around saying, 'I'm special. I make my

> 8

---

encomiastic: Full of praise.   **Fenwick:** The Hepburn family's Connecticut home. **Irene Selznick:** Theater producer and former wife of David O. Selznick.   **broaching:** Bringing up.   **bemoaned:** Complained about.   **rankled:** Angered.

living asking you to look at me, to pay to see me,' and then get upset at somebody for taking a picture. If you don't want to be a public figure, don't pick a public profession and don't appear in public. Because in public you're fair game." She also didn't understand stars who sued newspapers over printing lies about them. "I never cared what anybody wrote about me," Hepburn said, "as long as it wasn't the truth."

While she sought the limelight all her life, Hepburn believed actors re-   9 ceived too much attention and respect. "Let's face it," she said once, "we're prostitutes. I've spent my life selling myself — my face, my body, the way I walk and talk. Actors say, 'You can look at me, but you must pay me for it.'" I said that may be true, but actors also offer a unique service — the best of them please by inspiring, by becoming the agents for our emotional catharses.° "It's no small thing to move people," I said, "and perhaps to get people to think differently, maybe even behave differently." I pointed out to Hepburn that she had used her celebrity over the years for numerous causes — whether it was marching in parades for women's equality or campaigning for Roosevelt, speaking out against McCarthyism, or supporting Planned Parenthood. "Not much, really," Kate said. "I could've done more. A lot more. . . . It really doesn't take all that much to show up for a dinner with the President or to accept an award from an organization so it can receive some publicity. Oh, the hardship! Oh, the inconvenience! Oh, honestly!"

Provocative ending quotation — [the bracketed final two sentences: "receive some publicity. Oh, the hardship! Oh, the inconvenience! Oh, honestly!"]

Questions to Start You Thinking

Meaning

1. What, according to Berg, is the difference between Hepburn and "superstars"? What evidence does he use to support this view?

2. What is Hepburn's criticism of stars who complain about the "hardships" of their profession?

3. In paragraph 9, Hepburn compares actors to prostitutes. What evidence does she give for that comparison?

Writing Strategies

4. In paragraphs 1 through 3, Berg defines "superstars" and their expectations. Why do you suppose he starts this way? Do you find this opening effective? Why or why not?

5. What is Berg's general impression of Hepburn? What observations and details does he include to affect your impression of her?

6. Throughout this essay, Berg uses quotations from Hepburn to reveal her personality and philosophy. Are the quotations sufficient? Do they "sound" real? Would this essay be just as effective, or more so, if the writer chose to paraphrase rather than quote? Why or why not?

catharses: Releases of emotions or tensions, often through art.

STUDENT ESSAY

Dawn Kortz

Listen

Mic-Leo's Café--named after the two sisters that own it, Mickey and Lee--is tucked into a corner of the Eckles Building, a former department store located in downtown Dodge City, Kansas. The first time I saw the café, I fell in love. It is decorated in warm tones of green and burgundy, with plants in almost every corner. The tables are of every shape, size, and color imaginable, giving the room a cozy, comfortable feeling. Warm sunlight wafts through the café during business hours through the large plate windows that make up the front of the café. The people that come to Mic-Leo's Café are, for the most part, regulars--folks we all know by name. In the mornings the local businessmen and farmers can be seen gathering around the tables, drinking coffee, and sharing stories of grandchildren, politics, and golf. Among these regulars is Emmett Sherwood, who taught me how to appreciate the past.

I first met Emmett when I began working at Mic-Leo's Café as a part-time waitress trying to earn some extra money for college. Emmett, a grandfatherly man, has a gift for making everyone around him laugh with his colorful personality and stories. Interested in Emmett and how much of Dodge City's history he has lived through, I arrange to meet with him at the café early one afternoon. As we settle ourselves into a quiet corner I take notice of the deliberate, professional way that Emmett is dressed. It is obvious from his clothing that he is from another generation. Unlike my generation, which believes comfort is the most important quality in clothing, Emmett dresses for style. Today, like every other day, he is wearing dress slacks and a starched white shirt and tie. When I ask him about his clothing and why he wears a tie every day, he replies, "Going to town requires dignity." The only casual thing Emmett is wearing is his signature bright red beret. The red color matches Emmett's bright personality. Everyone who knows Emmett recognizes him by his hat.

I can tell that Emmett is excited to have a captive audience listen to his stories by the eagerness with which he accepts my invitation for this interview. As we begin to talk, I notice the far-off look in his eyes, as if he is trying to remember the old days, his youth, and how the city he loves looked when he first arrived. After each of us is served a cup of steaming coffee, Emmett begins by telling me he was born in Oklahoma but grew up in St. Johns, Kansas. As a young man of fourteen, he became attracted to the big city and in 1920 moved to Dodge City, Kansas, where he was married, raised a family, and continues to live.

Emmett points out the window and shows me where, on Saturdays, the farmers would come to town and set up open-air markets for the town folks to trade for

1   *Dawn Kortz, who wrote this as a student at Dodge City Community College, creates a lively portrait of an elderly man.*

2   ❓ *Can you identify with Kortz's relationship with Emmett? In what way?*

3

4

baked goods, produce, and eggs. "For me," he says, "going shopping at Wal-Mart can't compare to the feeling I got when I dressed up to go to town, see friendly folks, and help my neighbor." Emmett fondly remembers the 1920s as a time of growth for the nation and for Dodge City and as a happy, carefree time. With a smile and a mischievous twinkle, Emmett remembers the saloons and harlot houses--and especially the popular Harvey House restaurant where the waitresses wore black and white outfits which "sported the shortest skirts anyone in Dodge had seen until then." He blushes and his voice drops to a hush as he recalls this detail. He recovers and goes on to describe Front Street, the only street at the time to be paved with the distinctive red brick that now covers most of downtown. Front Street was the center of business for Dodge City; the Eckles Building, too, is located here. Emmett explains that all of the most prominent establishments were located in the downtown square, including the famous O'Neal Hotel. Emmett glows as he remembers the dances and shows he saw there, but his eyes glaze over as he recounts the fire that destroyed the beautiful, majestic building.

I ask Emmett what Dodge City was like during the Great Depression. Emmett re-   5
calls with sadness families and children that he knew then. Many went hungry while the men went to look for jobs, sometimes even leaving the state in search of an opportunity. Other men, who before the depression worked in stores, were forced to work fields for local farmers for enough food to feed their families. "I am lucky to have always had a decent job and a place to sleep," Emmett says reflectively. "People these days think they need so much; they're wrong." Emmett's words are especially meaningful in today's material world.

How are Emmett's words "especially meaningful" today?

The time after World War II was important for Dodge City. Emmett remembers it   6
as a period of economic boom when everyone had a renewed sense of pride in the United States. After the war ended, the communities came together to celebrate the return of their fathers, sons, and husbands. For the first time in history, it was common for women to work outside of the home, and Emmett remarks, "We never could get them back home!" I know he is teasing by his smile.

As we wind down our interview, coffee cups sitting cold and empty, I thank   7
Emmett for taking the time to talk. The café has emptied, and the sun has started going down--leaving a chill in the air. As Emmett slowly rises to leave, stretching his weak back from the long period of inactivity, I appreciate his age for the first time. As he walks down the sidewalk toward his car, he turns and with a tip of his head waves good-bye.

Do you agree with Kortz's conclusion about the importance of history?

Today, when I look around the city in which I live, I realize that what I see is   8
not what Dodge City has always been. Emmett has given me a new appreciation of the past. He has instilled in me the importance of history--my family history, my town's history, my country's history, and my world's history. Every day when he

comes into Mic-Leo's and I serve him coffee, I remember our talk, and I can only hope that there are others like Emmett sharing their life stories with people of another generation. I also hope that there are more people of my generation willing to take the time to listen.

Questions to Start You Thinking

Meaning

1. What is the main point of Kortz's essay?

2. What kind of man is Emmett Sherwood? How does Kortz feel about him?

3. How is Emmett's history the history of Dodge City? Is an interview an effective method of relating the history of a place? Why, or why not?

Writing Strategies

4. Why does Kortz begin her essay with a description of Mic-Leo's Café? What sensory details does she use to create the scene for a reader? How does Kortz's description serve as a frame for her conversation with Emmett?

5. What details does Kortz use to describe Emmett? What senses does she draw on? Does she provide enough detail for you to form a clear image in your head?

6. How much of what Emmett says does Kortz quote directly? Why does she choose to quote directly rather than paraphrase in these places? Would her essay be stronger if she used more of Emmett's own words?

7. Using highlighters or marginal notes, identify the essay's introduction, thesis, major emphases, supporting quotation and description for each emphasis, and conclusion. How effective is the organization of this essay?

Learning by Writing

THE ASSIGNMENT: INTERVIEWING

Write a paper about someone who interests you and base the paper primarily on a conversation with that person. Write about any acquaintance, friend, relative, or person you have heard about whose traits, interests, activities, background, or outlook on life might interest your readers. Your purpose is to show this person's character and personality — to bring your subject to life for your readers — through his or her conversation.

Notable student papers from a similar assignment included these:

One student wrote about a high school science teacher who had quit teaching for a higher-paying job in the computer industry, only to return three years later to the classroom.

One writer recorded the thoughts and feelings of a discouraged farmer she had known since childhood.

▓ You can complete each of the steps in this assignment by using the *Writing Guide Software* for THE BEDFORD GUIDE.

▓ To interview someone for information about something, see Other Assignments on p. 93.

Another learned about adjustment to life in a new country by talking to his neighbor from Vietnam.

GENERATING IDEAS

For strategies for generating ideas, see Ch. 15.

If an image of the perfect subject has flashed into your mind, consider yourself lucky, and set up an appointment with that person at once. If you have drawn a blank, you'll need to cast about for a likely interview subject.

For more on brainstorming, see pp. 254–56.

Brainstorm for Possible Subjects.   Try brainstorming for a few minutes, seeing what pops into mind. Your subject need not be spectacular or unusual; ordinary lives can make fascinating reading. As you begin examining the possibilities, you may find the following questions helpful:

DISCOVERY CHECKLIST

___ Are you acquainted with anyone whose life has been unusually eventful, stressful, or successful?

___ Are you curious about why someone you know made a certain decision or how that person got to his or her current point in life?

___ Is there an expert or leader whom you admire or are puzzled by?

___ Do you know someone whose job or hobby interests you?

___ What older person could tell you about life thirty or even fifty years ago?

___ Among the people you know, who is actively engaged in a cause? Who has passionate convictions about society, politics, sex, or childrearing?

___ Whose background and life history would you like to know more about?

___ Whose lifestyle, values, or attitudes are utterly different from your own and from those of most people you know?

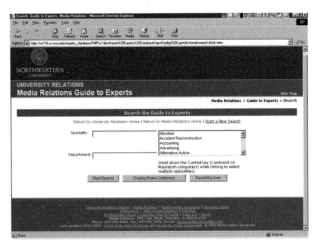

Experts' database on a university Web site

Tap Local Interview Resources.   Investigate campus resources such as the directory, student guide, Web page, departmental faculty lists, student activity officers and sponsors, recent yearbook photographs, stories from the newspaper archives, or facilities such as the theater, media, or sports centers. Look for students, staff, or faculty with intriguing backgrounds or experiences. Campuses and libraries often maintain lists or databases of local authorities, researchers, and authors available for press contacts or expert advice. Identify several prospects in case your first choice isn't available.

Set Up an Interview.   First find out whether your prospective source will grant you an interview. Make sure that the person can talk with you at some length — an hour, say — and has no objection to appearing in your paper. If you sense any reluctance, your wisest course is to find another subject.

Don't be timid about asking for an interview. After all, your request is flattering, acknowledging that person as someone with valuable things to say. Try to schedule the interview on your subject's own ground — his or her home or workplace. You can learn a great deal from those physical surroundings, making the interview more realistic and the essay more vivid because of the details you can observe.

Prepare Questions.   The interview will go better if you have prepared questions in advance. Questions about the person's background, everyday tasks, favorite activities, hopes, and aspirations are likely to encourage your subject to open up. Asking your subject to do a little imagining may elicit a revealing response. (If your house were on fire, what are the first objects you'd try to save? If you had your life to live over, what would you do differently?)

For more on asking a reporter's questions, see pp. 262–63.

Facing the Challenge: Writing from an Interview

The major challenge writers face when writing from an interview is to find a clear focus for the paper. They must first sift through the enormous amount of information that can be generated in an interview and decide what dominant impression of the subject they wish to present in an essay. Distilling the material you have gathered into a focused, overall impression may seem overwhelming. As a writer, however, you have the responsibility to select and organize your material for your readers, not simply transcribe your notes.

To identify possible angles suggested by your notes, jot down answers to these questions:

- What did you find most interesting about the interview?
- What topics did your subject talk about the most?
- What did he or she become most excited or animated about?
- What topics generated the most interesting quotations?

Your answers should help you to determine a dominant impression — the aspect of your interviewee's character or personality that you want to emphasize for your readers. Once you have this focus, you need to pick the details and direct quotations from the interview that best illustrate the points you want to make. Use direct quotations strategically and sparingly to reveal the character traits that you wish to emphasize. Select colorful quotations that allow readers to "hear" your subject's distinctive voice. Make sure that the quotations — long or short — are accurate. To capture the dynamic of conversation, include your own observations as well as actual quotations.

For writing activities for interview-based writing, visit <bedfordstmartins.com/bedguide> and do a keyword search:

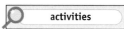
activities

FOR PEER RESPONSE

Ask a classmate to read the questions you plan to use in your interview and then to respond to the following:

- Are the questions appropriate for the person who will be interviewed?
- Will the questions help gather the information you are seeking?
- Are any of the questions unclear? How could you rephrase them?
- Do any of the questions seem redundant? Irrelevant?
- What additional questions might you ask?

You can't find out everything about the person you're interviewing, but you should focus on whatever aspects best reveal his or her personality. Good questions will help you lead the conversation where you want it to go, get it back on track when it strays, and avoid awkward silences. For example, if you were to interview someone with an unusual occupation or hobby, you might ask questions like these:

- How long have you been a park ranger?
- How did you get involved in this work?
- How have you learned about the physical features and ecological balance in your park?
- What happens in a typical day on the job?
- Has this job changed your life or your concerns in any way?
- What are your plans and hopes for the future?

One good question can get some people talking for hours, and four or five may be enough for any interview, but it's better to prepare too many than too few. You can easily skip any that seem irrelevant during the interview.

■ For more on using observation, see Ch. 5.

Be Flexible and Observant.   Sometimes a question won't interest your subject as much as you'd hoped it would. Or the person may seem reluctant to answer, especially if you're unwittingly trespassing into private territory, such as someone's love life. Don't badger. If you wait silently for a bit, you might be rewarded. But if the silence persists, just go on to the next question. Anytime the conversation heads toward a dead end, you can always steer it back: "But to get back to what you were saying about . . ."

If the discussion moves in a worthwhile direction, don't be a slave to your questions. Sometimes the most rewarding question simply grows out of what the subject says or an item you note in the environment. Observing your subject's clothing, expressions, mannerisms, and equipment may also suggest unexpected facets of personality. For example, Kortz describes both the café and Emmett's clothing as she introduces his character.

Decide How to Record the Interview.   Many interviewers use only paper and pen or pencil to take notes unobtrusively. Even though they can't write

After you have conducted your interview, follow the lead of reporters who routinely transcribe conversations and interviews into computer files. Try to type in the exact conversation from your tape or as much of the interview as possible from your notes. If you have used both tape and notes, combine them in a single computer file, but use bold to distinguish your notes. Save the complete, unedited conversation transcript and original notes with a descriptive name.

Open a new file when you begin your first draft. As you quote and summarize your subject's words and ideas in your draft, you can return to your transcript and notes to copy or check his or her own wording. In this way you can refine your interview while maintaining your original research in the first file. Use the menu in your word processor to go back and forth between two open files as you copy and paste quotations into your draft. Be sure to add quotation marks to indicate exact words from the interview.

WRITING WITH A COMPUTER

down everything the person says, they want to look the subject in the eye and keep the conversation lively. As you take notes, be sure to record or sketch details on the scene — names and dates, numbers, addresses, surroundings, physical appearance. Also jot down memorable words just as the speaker says them. Put quotation marks around them so that when you transcribe your notes later, you will know that they are quoted directly.

A telephone interview sounds easy, but lacks the lively interplay you can achieve face-to-face. You'll miss observing the subject's possessions and environment, which so often reveal personality, or seeing your subject's smiles, frowns, or other body language. Meet with your subject if possible.

Many professionals advise against using a tape recorder because it may inhibit the subject and make the interviewer lazy about concentrating on the subject's responses. Too often, the objections go, it tempts the interviewer simply to quote the rambling conversation from the tape without shaping it into good writing. If you do bring a tape recorder to your interview, be sure that the person you're talking with has no objections. Arm yourself with a pad of paper and a pen or pencil just in case the recorder malfunctions or the tape runs out. And don't let your mind wander. Perhaps the best practice is to tape-record the interview but at the same time take notes. Write down the main points of the conversation, and use your tape as a backup to check the accuracy of your notes or to expand an idea or quotation.

As soon as the interview ends, rush to the nearest desk, and write down everything you remember but couldn't record. The questions you prepared for the interview will guide your memory, as will any notes you took while talking.

PLANNING, DRAFTING, AND DEVELOPING

After your interview, you may have a good notion of what to include in your first draft, what to emphasize, what to quote directly, what to summarize. But if your notes seem a confused jumble, what should you do?

For more strategies for planning, drafting, and developing, see Chs. 16, 17, and 18.

For strategies for using examples and details, see Ch. 18.

Evaluate Your Material.   Remember that your purpose in this assignment is to reveal your subject's character and personality through his or her conversation. Start by listing the details you're already likely to include. As you sift your material, you may find these questions useful:

What part of the conversation gave you the most insight into your subject's character and circumstances?

Which direct quotations reveal the most about your subject? Which are the most amusing, pithy, witty, surprising, or outrageous?

Which objects in the subject's environment provide you with valuable clues about his or her interests?

What, if anything, did your subject's body language reveal? Did it suggest discomfort, pride, self-confidence, shyness, pomposity?

What did tone or gestures tell you about the person's state of mind?

How can you summarize your subject's character or personality?

Does one theme run through your material? If so, what is it?

In addition to your notes, you may want to turn to photographs, sketches, or your own doodles to help you clarify the dominant impression and main emphases you want to develop in your paper.

For more on stating a thesis, see pp. 271–77.

For exercises on choosing effective thesis statements, visit <bedfordstmartins.com/bedguide> and do a keyword search:

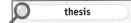
thesis

Focus Your Thesis on a Dominant Impression.   Most successful portraits focus on a single dominant impression of the interview subject. If you had to characterize your subject in a single sentence, how would you describe him or her? See if you can state a single main impression that you want to convey about your subject. Then eliminate anything that doesn't contribute to this view.

DOMINANT IMPRESSION   Del talked a lot about the freedom of the press.

WORKING THESIS   Del Sampat is a true believer in the freedom of the press.

If you have lots of material and if, as often happens, your conversation rambled, you may want to develop the dominant impression by emphasizing just a few things about your subject — personality traits, views on particular topics, or the influences that shaped those views. If such a focus is not immediately evident, try grouping your details to help you discover one. Try filling in three layers of notes, following the pattern in the graphic below, to help you figure out what to emphasize and how to relate your materials.

For more on grouping ideas, see Ch. 16.

1. Dominant Impression
2. Main Emphases
     points about traits, views, influences
3. Supporting Details
     quotations, reported words, description

Have a classmate or a friend read your draft and suggest how to make the portrait more vivid, complete, and clear. Ask your peer editor to answer questions such as these about writing from an interview:

FOR PEER RESPONSE

- Does the essay opening make you want to know the person portrayed? If so, how has the writer interested you? If not, what gets in your way?

- What seems to make the person interviewed interesting to the writer?

- What is the writer's dominant impression of the person interviewed?

- Does the writer include any details that contradict or are unrelated to the dominant impression or insight?

- Do the quoted words or reported speech "sound" real to you? Do any quotations seem at odds with the dominant impression of the person?

For general questions for a peer editor, see pp. 328–29.

- Would you leave out any of the conversation the writer used? Mark anything you would omit.

- Do you have questions about the subject that aren't answered?

- If this were your paper, what is the one thing you would be sure to work on before handing it in?

Bring Your Subject to Life for Readers.   At the beginning of your paper, can you immediately frame the person you interviewed? A quotation, a bit of physical description, a portrait of your subject at home or at work can bring the person instantly to life in your reader's mind. If your instructor approves adding an image, consider where to place it so that it supplements your text but does not overshadow your essay.

For more on the placement of visuals, see p. 368.

From time to time you'll want to quote your subject directly. Be as accurate as possible, and don't put into quotation marks anything your subject didn't say. Sometimes you may want to quote a whole sentence or more, sometimes just a phrase. Keep evaluating and selecting your quotations until they all convey the essence of your subject.

For more on selecting and presenting quotations, see D3 and D6 in the Quick Research Guide (the dark-red-edged pages). For more on punctuating quotations, see C3 in Quick Editing Guide (the dark-blue-edged pages).

Double-Check Important Information.   You may find that you can't read your hasty handwriting or that some crucial bit of information somehow escaped when you were taking notes. In such a case, telephone the person you interviewed to ask specific questions so that you will not take much time. You may also want to read back to your subject any direct quotations you intend to use, so that he or she can confirm their accuracy.

REVISING AND EDITING

As you read over your first draft, keep in mind that your purpose was to make the person you interviewed come alive for your reader.

For more revising and editing strategies, see Ch. 19.

FOR GROUP LEARNING

Conducting a Collective Interview

With your whole class or your writing group, interview someone with special knowledge or expertise. Public figures often visit schools and are used to facing class questions. Or someone on campus might visit to discuss a problem that interests your group. Plan the interview in advance:

- What do you want to find out?
- What lines of questioning will you pursue?
- What topic will each student ask about?
- How much time will each group member have to ask a series of questions?
- Who will take notes?

Preview each other's questions to avoid duplication. Ask open-ended, rather than yes/no, questions to encourage discussion. Your group's product can be many individual papers or one collaborative paper based on a fair division of responsibilities.

Focus on Your Main Idea or Thesis.   Once you have finished a draft, you may realize that you still feel swamped by too much information. Will your readers feel that your essay is overloaded? Will they understand the dominant impression you want to convey about the person you have interviewed? To be certain that they will, first polish and refine your thesis.

■ For more on stating a thesis, see pp. 271–77.

WORKING THESIS   Del Sampat is a true believer in the freedom of the press.

REVISED THESIS   Del Sampat, news editor for the *Campus Times,* sees every story he writes as an opportunity to exercise and defend the freedom of the press.

■ For exercises on supporting a thesis, visit <bedfordstmartins.com/ bedguide> and do a keyword search:

Screen Your Details.   Using your revised thesis as a touchstone, look again at the quotations and other details you have included. Will readers see how each of these strengthens the dominant impression expressed in your thesis? Keep only those that support your thesis and enhance the dominant impression. Drop all the others, even if they are vivid or catchy.

Remember, readers will be interested in your observations and insights. This checklist may help you revise your work to strengthen them.

REVISION CHECKLIST

___ Are the details focused on a dominant impression you want to emphasize? Are all the details in your paper relevant to this impression? How do you convey the impression to readers?

___ How do the parts of the conversation you've reported reveal the subject's unique personality, character, mood, or concerns?

___ Should your paper have a stronger beginning? Is your ending satisfactory?

___ Should some quotations be summarized or indirectly quoted? Should some explanation be enlivened by adding specific quotations?

—— When the direct quotations are read out loud, do they sound as if they're from the mouth of the person you're portraying?

—— Where might you need to add revealing details about the person's surroundings, personal appearance, or mannerisms?

—— Have you included your own pertinent observations and insights?

—— Does any of your material strike you now as irrelevant or dull?

If your portrayal still lacks life and focus, you may want to skim your notes or listen again to parts of your tape recording. Do additional details seem necessary after all? Is there anything you now wish you had asked your interview subject? It may not be too late to add new material.

After you have revised your essay, edit and proofread it. Carefully check the grammar, word choice, punctuation, and mechanics — and then correct any problems you find. Here are some questions to get you started when editing and proofreading your paper:

For more editing and proofreading strategies, see pp. 336–39.

EDITING CHECKLIST

—— Is it clear what each pronoun refers to so that the *he*'s and *she*'s are not confusing? Does each pronoun agree with (match) its antecedent?   **A6**

—— Have you used the correct case (*he* or *him*) for all your pronouns?   **A5**

—— Is your sentence structure correct? Have you avoided writing fragments, comma splices, or fused sentences?   **A1, A2**

—— Have you used quotation marks, ellipses (to show the omission of words), and other punctuation correctly in all your quotations?   **C3**

For more help, turn to the dark-blue-edged pages, and find the sections of the Quick Editing Guide noted here.

OTHER ASSIGNMENTS

1. Interview someone from whom you can learn, possibly someone whose profession interests you or whose advice can help you solve a problem or make a decision. Your purpose will be to communicate what you have learned, not to characterize the person you interview.

2. Write a paper based on an interview with at least two members of your extended family about some incident that is part of your family lore. Direct your paper to younger relatives. If accounts of the event don't always agree, combine them into one vivid account, noting that some details may be more trustworthy than others. Give credit to your sources.

3. After briefly talking with fifteen or twenty students on your campus to find out what careers they are preparing for, write a short essay summing up what you find out. What are their reasons for their choices? Are most students intent on earning money or on other pursuits? How many want lucrative careers because they have to pay back college loans? Provide some quotations to flesh out your survey. From the information you have gathered, characterize your classmates. Are they materialists? Idealists? Practical people?

Applying What You Learn:
Some Uses of Writing from an Interview

In College Courses. Often you will find yourself interviewing people who can contribute valuable insights into what you are studying.

- In a human development course, you might interview people at various stages of the life cycle—asking about the transition from student life to the working world, about parenthood, or about widowhood or retirement.

- History students may interview people who have firsthand knowledge of an event or era they are studying—a veteran of the Vietnam War, a farmer who remembers a major drought, a woman who participated in the famous Selma to Montgomery civil rights march.

- Education students may interview classroom teachers to gain an understanding of the demands and rewards of teaching.

In the Workplace.   Interviewing is a useful tool, too, for writing on the job.

- Journalists interview "informed sources" to give readers the complete story; conversely, political figures, authors, or actors often use interviews to air their opinions.

- Businesses interview customers to gain feedback on a product or service so they can meet consumer demands. Interviewers compile and report results from general surveys or from more extensive interviews.

- Professional investigators conduct interviews to gather evidence—insurance adjusters settling a claim, lawyers preparing a case, medical researchers tracking a disease.

In Your Community.   As a citizen of the larger community, you will find conversation can provide the support you need in many writing tasks.

- Interviewing experts can help you make informed evaluations of community proposals. If county commissioners propose raising taxes to build a new sewage treatment center, you might talk to a waste water management expert about the merits of the plan.

- Information from experts or citizens can support your position on civic issues, such as the need for a traffic light, a highway bypass, or more transit police.

- Interviewing the missionary group speaking at your church is a good way to create a flyer or pamphlet seeking support for the group's work.

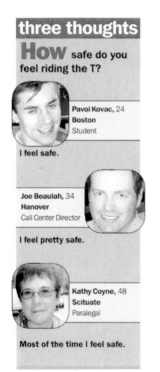

three thoughts

How safe do you feel riding the T?

Pavol Kovac, 24
Boston
Student

I feel safe.

Joe Beaulah, 34
Hanover
Call Center Director

I feel pretty safe.

Kathy Coyne, 48
Scituate
Paralegal

Most of the time I feel safe.

Newspaper interviews

Chapter 7
Comparing and Contrasting

Jason Reblando

Responding to an Image

Examine the buildings in this photograph. List some of the ways that they are similar and different. What do their similarities and differences suggest to you? Although the residents and neighbors of these buildings are not visible in the photograph, what do you suppose the similarities and differences mean to them? What broader issues and changes might these buildings suggest or represent? Why do suppose that the photographer shot the photograph from the location and angle that he did?

95

Which city — Dallas or Atlanta — has more advantages and more drawbacks for a young single person thinking of settling down to a career? As songwriters, how are Sarah McLachlan and Sheryl Crow similar and dissimilar? Such questions invite answers that set two subjects side by side.

When you compare, you point out similarities; when you contrast, you discuss differences. When you write about two complicated subjects, usually you will need to do both. Considering Mozart and Bach, you might find that each has traits the other has — or lacks. Instead of concluding that one is great and the other inferior, you might conclude that they're two distinct composers, each with an individual style. On the other hand, if your main purpose is to judge between two subjects (as when you'd recommend moving either to Dallas or to Atlanta), you would look especially for positive and negative features, weigh the attractions of each city and its faults, and then stick your neck out and make your choice.

Learning from Other Writers

In this chapter you will be asked to write a paper setting two subjects side by side, comparing and contrasting them. Let's see how other writers have used these familiar habits of thought in writing. To help you begin to analyze the first reading in this chapter, look for the notes in the margin. They identify features such as the main idea or thesis, the sequence of the broad subjects considered, and the specific points of comparison and contrast.

■ For more on thesis and support, see Chs. 16 and 18.

■ For more examples of writing based on comparing and contrasting, visit <bedfordstmartins.com/bedguide> and do a keyword search:

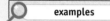 examples

As You Read These Comparisons and Contrasts

As you read these essays, ask yourself the following questions:

1. What two (or more) items are compared and contrasted? Does the writer use comparison only? Contrast only? A combination of the two? Why?

2. What is the purpose of the comparison and contrast? What idea does the information support or refute?

3. How does the writer organize the essay? Why?

Suzanne Britt takes a lighthearted look at neat and sloppy people in this selection from her essay collection Show and Tell *(1983).*

Suzanne Britt
Neat People vs. Sloppy People

Introduction
THESIS
Setting up subjects
Subject A

I've finally figured out the difference between neat people and sloppy   1
people. The distinction is, as always, moral. Neat people are lazier and meaner than sloppy people.

Sloppy people, you see, are not really sloppy. Their sloppiness is merely   2
the unfortunate consequence of their extreme moral rectitude.° Sloppy people

rectitude: Correctness, decency.

96

carry in their mind's eye a heavenly vision, a precise plan, that is so stupen- — Point 1
dous, so perfect, it can't be achieved in this world or the next.

Point 2

Sloppy people live in Never-Never Land. Someday is their métier.° 3
Someday they are planning to alphabetize all their books and set up home
catalogs. Someday they will go through their wardrobes and mark certain
items for tentative mending and certain items for passing on to relatives of
similar shape and size. Someday sloppy people will make family scrapbooks
into which they will put newspaper clippings, postcards, locks of hair, and
the dried corsage from their senior prom. Someday they will file everything
on the surface of their desks, including the cash receipts from coffee purchases at the snack shop. Someday they will sit down and read all the back
issues of *The New Yorker.*

For all these noble reasons and more, sloppy people never get neat. 4
They aim too high and wide. They save everything, planning someday to
file, order, and straighten out the world. But while these ambitious plans
take clearer and clearer shape in their heads, the books spill from the
shelves onto the floor, the clothes pile up in the hamper and closet, the
family mementos accumulate in every drawer, the surface of the desk is
buried under mounds of paper, and the unread magazines threaten to reach
the ceiling.

Sloppy people can't bear to part with anything. They give loving atten- 5
tion to every detail. When sloppy people say they're going to tackle the
surface of a desk, they really mean it. Not a paper will go unturned; not a
rubber band will go unboxed. Four hours or two weeks into the excavation,
the desk looks exactly the same, primarily because the sloppy person is — Exaggeration to make a
meticulously creating new piles of papers with new headings and scrupu-   point and add humor
lously stopping to read all the old book catalogs before he throws them
away. A neat person would just bulldoze the desk.

Neat people are bums and clods at heart. They have cavalier° attitudes 6
toward possessions, including family heirlooms. Everything is just another
dust-catcher to them. If anything collects dust, it's got to go and that's that.
Neat people will toy with the idea of throwing the children out of the house
just to cut down on the clutter.

Neat people don't care about process. They like results. What they want 7
to do is get the whole thing over with so they can sit down and watch the
rasslin' on TV. Neat people operate on two unvarying principles: Never handle
any item twice, and throw everything away.

The only thing messy in a neat person's house is the trash can. The 8
minute something comes to a neat person's hand, he will look at it, try to
decide if it has immediate use and, finding none, throw it in the trash.

Neat people are especially vicious with mail. They never go through 9
their mail unless they are standing directly over a trash can. If the trash can
is beside the mailbox, even better. All ads, catalogs, pleas for charitable contributions, church bulletins, and money-saving coupons go straight into
the trash can without being opened. All letters from home, postcards from

métier: Trade, specialty.   **cavalier:** Dismissive.

Europe, bills, and paychecks are opened, immediately responded to, then dropped in the trash can. Neat people keep their receipts only for tax purposes. That's it. No sentimental salvaging of birthday cards or the last letter a dying relative ever wrote. Into the trash it goes.

Neat people place neatness above everything, even economics. They are 10 incredibly wasteful. Neat people throw away several toys every time they walk through the den. I knew a neat person once who threw away a perfectly good dish drainer because it had mold on it. The drainer was too much trouble to wash. And neat people sell their furniture when they move.

Another exaggeration for effect —— They will sell a La-Z-Boy recliner while you are reclining in it.

Neat people are no good to borrow from. Neat people buy everything in 11 expensive little single portions. They get their flour and sugar in two-pound bags. They wouldn't consider clipping a coupon, saving a leftover, reusing plastic nondairy whipped cream containers, or rinsing off tin foil and draping it over the unmoldy dish drainer. You can never borrow a neat person's newspaper to see what's playing at the movies. Neat people have the paper all wadded up and in the trash by 7:05 A.M.

Neat people cut a clean swath° through the organic as well as the inor- 12 ganic world. People, animals, and things are all one to them. They are so insensitive. After they've finished with the pantry, the medicine cabinet, and

Concluding exaggeration for effect the attic, they will throw out the red geranium (too many leaves), sell the dog (too many fleas), and send the children off to boarding school (too many scuff marks on the hardwood floors).

Questions to Start You Thinking

Meaning

1. Does Britt favor one group over the other? Which details or statements support your response?

2. Based on the details presented here, to which group do you belong? What specific details describe you most accurately?

3. What is Britt's purpose in contrasting neat people and sloppy people? Is her goal to explain or to convince? Or is it something else?

Writing Strategies

4. In the introductory paragraph, Britt jumps right into the essay. Is that technique effective? How else might she have begun her essay?

5. Which method of organization does Britt use to arrange her essay? How effectively does she switch between her two subjects of "sloppy" and "neat?"

6. From reading this essay, are readers to assume that "sloppy" and "neat" people have nothing in common? Why?

swath: Path.

STUDENT ESSAY

Tim Chabot
Take Me Out to the Ball Game, but Which One?

For much of the twentieth century, baseball has been considered the national
pastime of the United States. Hank Aaron, home runs, and hot dogs seem as American as Thanksgiving. Many American presidents, from Eisenhower to Clinton, have
participated in the tradition of a celebrity throwing out the first ball on opening day
of a new baseball season. But in the 1990s, baseball stars are being eclipsed by the
stars of another game invented in America--basketball. Michael Jordan and Shaquille
O'Neal, basketball greats and household names, have become more famous than any
current pitcher or home run king. In addition, the 1994 to 1995 baseball strike has
pushed the sport further out of the limelight as the public has become disillusioned
with the greed of both players and managers. The strike has raised a question in the
minds of many: Should baseball continue to be considered our national pastime, or
should basketball take its place?

Both sports are very popular with American sports fans. In addition, both games 2
attract fans of all races--white, African American, Asian American, Hispanic--and all
classes, rich and poor, educated and uneducated. Baseball has become a national
treasure through its appeal to a wide, wide audience. At a Saturday afternoon game,
men, women, grandparents, and kids of all ages wait to catch a fly ball. The appeal
of basketball is growing, the sport having become popular in urban and rural areas,
on high school and college campuses. Both sports are played in quite a variety of locations. Baseball games occur on neighborhood sandlots as well as official diamonds.
Basketball requires little space and equipment, so pickup basketball games occur in
almost every neighborhood park and virtually anywhere that a hoop can be rigged up.

Although both sports are popular with American fans, attending a baseball game 3
is quite different from attending a basketball game. Baseball is a family-oriented
spectator sport. Because of the widely diverse baseball fans with varied attention
spans, attending a baseball game is like going to an open-air carnival, and the game
itself is only one of the many spectacles. If fans are bored with the game, they can
listen to the vendors hawking ice cream, watch a fight brewing in the bleacher
seats, stand in line to buy peanuts or hot dogs, participate in "the wave," or just
bask in the sun. Only diehard fans keep a constant eye on the game itself because
there are frequent breaks in the play.

In contrast, the central spectacle of any basketball arena is definitely the game 4
itself. Few distractions to entertain a casual fan occur, except for cheerleaders for
college teams. Basketball arenas are always indoors, and the games are usually at
night, creating an atmosphere that is urban and adult. The constant motion of the

*Student Tim Chabot
compares and contrasts
baseball and basketball,
asking which deserves
the title of America's
national pastime.*

*Why do you think
the writer raises this
question here?*

*Do you agree with
the analogy between
baseball and an "open-
air carnival"?*

What other differences in attending the games come to mind?

sport rivets° attention to the game itself. Attending a basketball game can be compared to an exciting night on the town, while watching a baseball game is like relaxing with the family in the backyard.

The pace of the two games is also quite different. The leisurely pace of a base-   5
ball game contributes to its popularity because it offers relaxation to harried Americans. Each batter may spend several minutes at the plate, hit a few foul balls, and reach a full count of three balls and two strikes before getting on base, hitting a routine pop fly, or striking out. While batters slow things down by stepping out of the box to practice their swing, pitchers stall the play by "holding the runners on" to prevent stolen bases. The substitution of relief pitchers suspends the game and gives spectators an opportunity to purchase junk food or memorabilia. In games in which star pitchers duel, the audience may see only a few men on base in nine innings and a very low score. Also, the tradition of the seventh-inning stretch underscores baseball's appeal to a person who wants to take it easy and relax.

On the other hand, the quick pace of basketball has contributed to its popular-   6
ity in our fast-paced society. Players run down the court at sometimes exhausting speed for a "fast break," successful baskets can occur merely seconds apart, each team may score as many as one hundred points a game, and the ball changes sides hundreds of times, as opposed to every half-inning in baseball. Games can be won or lost in the few seconds before the final buzzer. Basketball players are always in motion, much like American society. The pounding excitement of basketball appeals to people who play hard as well as work hard.

These two sports require different athletic abilities from the players. Although   7
baseball games are slow-paced, the sport places a premium on athletic precision and therefore showcases strategy and skill rather than brute physical strength. The choice of a pitch, the decision to bunt or to steal a base, and the order of batters are all careful strategic moves that could affect the outcome of the whole game. Baseball has been called the "thinking person's game" because of its emphasis on statistics and probabilities. Although mental strategy and dexterity° are emphasized, physical strength is important, too. A strong arm obviously increases the power of a player's throw or of his swing, and speed is essential in running bases. But intimidating physical ability is not necessarily a required element to become a major league player, and even out-of-shape players can become stars if their bats are hot. The importance of skill over brawn has contributed to baseball's popularity not merely as a spectator sport but also as a sport in which millions of Americans participate, from Little League to neighborhood leagues for adults.

Do you agree that baseball requires "skill" and basketball "brawn"?

Unlike baseball, basketball emphasizes physical power, stamina, and size since   8
jumping high, running fast, and just being tall with long legs and big hands usually

rivets: Commands or fixes attention to.   **dexterity:** Skill in using the hands or body.

contribute to a player's success. Skill and dexterity are certainly necessary in executing a slam dunk or dribbling past a double team, but these skills are usually combined with physical strength. In order to be a successful rebounder, a player needs to be extremely aggressive and occasionally commit fouls. Many more injuries occur on basketball courts than on baseball fields. Perhaps the physical power and intimidation required in basketball have led to the media's focus on individual players' star qualities. Magic, Bird, Jordan, and Shaq are icons° who have taken the place of baseball stars of previous generations like Joe DiMaggio, Ted Williams, and Babe Ruth. Furthermore, in the international arena of the Olympics, basketball came to be seen as a symbol of American strength and power, as the 1992 Dream Team demolished all of its opponents.

If the rest of the world now equates basketball with America, should we consider it to be our true national pastime? The increasing popularity of basketball seems to reflect the change in American society in the past few decades, a change to a more fast-paced and aggressive culture. But basketball doesn't yet appeal to as diverse an audience as does baseball, and thus it doesn't seem to deserve to be called a national phenomenon--yet. Until kids, women, and grandparents are as prevalent at a Lakers game as are young males, baseball will retain its title as the national pastime. But when the leisurely pace of the baseball game grinds to a halt because of players' strikes, impatient fans may turn to the exciting speed of basketball to rejuvenate their faith in American sports.

9

Why do you agree or disagree with this conclusion?

Questions to Start You Thinking

Meaning

1. In what specific ways does Chabot claim that baseball and basketball are similar? In what ways are these two sports different? Do the similarities outweigh the differences, or vice versa?

2. Can you think of other ways these two sports are similar and different?

3. Would you nominate another sport, say soccer or ice hockey, for the national pastime? If so, why?

Writing Strategies

4. Is Chabot's support for his comparison and contrast sufficient and balanced? Explain.

5. What transitional devices does Chabot use to indicate when he is comparing and when he is contrasting?

6. What is Chabot's thesis? Why does Chabot state it where he does?

7. Using highlighters or marginal notes, identify the essay's introduction, thesis, contrasting subjects, points of comparison and contrast, and conclusion. How effective is the organization of this essay?

icons: Images or symbols.

Learning by Writing

THE ASSIGNMENT: COMPARING AND CONTRASTING

■ You can complete each of the steps in this assignment by using the *Writing Guide Software* for THE BEDFORD GUIDE.

Write a paper in which you compare and contrast two items to enlighten readers about both subjects. The specific points of similarity and difference will be important, but you will go beyond them to draw a conclusion from your analysis. This conclusion, your thesis, needs to be more than "point A is different from point B" or "I prefer subject B to subject A." You will need to explain why you have drawn your conclusion. You'll also need to provide specific supporting evidence to explain your position and to convince your readers of its soundness. You may choose two people, two kinds of people, two places, two objects, two activities, or two ideas, but be sure to choose two you care about. You might write an impartial paper that distinctly portrays both subjects, or you might show why you favor one over the other.

Among the engaging student papers we've seen in response to similar assignments are these:

An American student compared and contrasted her home life with that of her roommate, a student from Nigeria. Her goal was to deepen her understanding of Nigerian society and her own.

A student who was interested in history compared and contrasted millennial fears for the years 1000 and 2000, considering whether popular responses had changed.

Another writer compared and contrasted conditions at two city facilities, making a case for a revised funding formula.

GENERATING IDEAS

■ For strategies for generating ideas, see Ch. 15.

Find Two Subjects.   Pick subjects you can compare and contrast purposefully. An examination question may give them to you, ready-made: "Compare and contrast ancient Roman sculpture with that of the ancient Greeks." But suppose you have to find your subjects for yourself. You'll need to choose things that have a sensible basis for comparison, a common element.

moon rocks + stars = no common element

Dallas + Atlanta = cities to consider settling in

Montel Williams + Oprah Winfrey = television talk show hosts

Besides having a common element, the subjects should have enough in common to compare but differ enough to throw each other into sharp relief.

sports cars + racing cars = common element + telling differences

sports cars + oil tankers = limited common element + unpromising differences

Try generating a list or brainstorming. Recall what you've recently read, discussed, or spotted on the Web. Let your mind skitter around in search of pairs that go together. You can also play the game of *free association*, jotting down a word and whatever it brings to mind: *Democrats? Republicans. New York? Los Angeles. King Kong? Godzilla.* Or whatever. You might find the following questions useful as you look for a topic:

For more on brainstorming, see pp. 254–56.

DISCOVERY CHECKLIST

___ Do you know two people who are strikingly different in attitude or behavior (perhaps your parents or two brothers, two friends, two teachers)?

___ Can you think of two groups of people who are both alike and different (perhaps two teams or two clubs)?

___ Have you taken two courses that were quite different but both valuable?

___ Do you prefer one of two places where you have lived or visited?

___ Can you recall two events in your life that shared similar aspects but turned out to be quite different (perhaps two sporting events or two romances or the births of two children)?

___ Can you compare and contrast two holidays or two family customs?

___ Are you familiar with two writers, two artists, or two musicians who seem to have similar goals but quite different accomplishments?

Once you have a list of pairs, put a star by those that seem promising. Ask yourself what similarities immediately come to mind. What differences? Can you jot down several of each? Are these striking, significant similarities and differences? If not, move on until you discover a workable pair.

Facing the Challenge: Comparing and Contrasting

The major challenge that writers face when comparing and contrasting two subjects is to determine their purpose. Writers who skip this step run the risk of having readers ask, "So, what's the point?" Suppose you develop brilliant points of similarity and difference between the films of Oliver Stone and those of Stanley Kubrick. Do you want to argue that one director is more skilled than the other? Or perhaps you want to show how they treat love or war differently in their films? Consider the following questions as you determine your primary purpose for comparing and contrasting:

• Do you want to inform your readers about these two subjects in order to provide a better understanding of the two?

• Do you want to persuade your readers that one of the two subjects is preferable to the other?

Asking what you want to demonstrate, discover, or prove *before* you begin to draft will help you to write a more effective comparison and contrast essay.

For writing activities for comparing and contrasting, visit <bedfordstmartins.com/bedguide> and do a keyword search:

activities

**WRITING WITH
A COMPUTER**

After deciding on the items you will compare, open a file and record what you know about Subject A and then about Subject B. (Separate them with a page break if you wish.) Next, click on "table" in your word processor menu to create a table with three columns (up and down) and at least half a dozen rows (across). Use the first row to label the columns: Categories on the left, then Subject A in the middle, and Subject B on the right.

Now read over your notes on Subject A. When you spot related details, identify a logical category that encompasses them. Enter the category name in the left column of the second row of your table, and copy the related details for Subject A into the middle column. Repeat this process, labeling more rows as categories and moving corresponding details into the Subject A column for each row. (Insert new rows at the end of your table as needed.)

Next review your notes on Subject B. If some details fall into categories already listed in your table, copy those details into the Subject B column for each category. If new categories emerge, add them in new rows along with the Subject B details. After you finish categorizing your notes, round out the table — adding details to fill in empty cells, combining similar categories, or adding entirely new categories. Select the most promising categories from your table as common features for logical comparison and contrast in your essay.

▪ For more on tables, see pp. 366–67.

Limit the Scope of Your Paper.   If you propose to compare and contrast Japanese literature and American literature in 750 words, your task is probably impossible. But to cut down the size of this subject, you might compare and contrast, say, a haiku of Bashō about a snake with a short poem about a snake by Emily Dickinson. This topic you could cover adequately in 750 words.

Explore Each Member of Your Pair to Build Support.   As you examine in depth each of your two subjects, your goal is twofold. You want to analyze each using a similar approach so that you have a reasonable basis for comparison and contrast. You also want to find the details and examples that you'll need to support your points. Consider the following sources of support:

▪ For more on using a reporter's questions, see pp. 262–63.

▪ For more on interviewing, see Ch. 6.

• Two events, processes, procedures	Ask a reporter's questions — 5 W's (who, what, where, when, why) and an H (how).
• Two events from the past	Using the same questions, interview or converse with someone at each event, or read newspaper or other accounts.
• Two perceptions (public and private)	Interview someone behind the scenes; read or listen to contrasting views.

- Two approaches or viewpoints

- Two subject ideas

- Two policies or options

Browse online for Web sites or pages that supply different examples.

Read a few articles to test the possibilities.

Look for studies or government statistics like those below.

For advice on finding a few useful sources, turn to B1–B2 in the Quick Research Guide (the dark-red-edged pages).

State	2002 Personal Income (in thousands)	2002 Population (in thousands)	2002 Per Capita Personal Income
Illinois	$419,857,924	12,601	$33,320
Indiana	$173,889,313	6,159	$28,233
Michigan	$303,745,428	10,050	$30,223
Ohio	$334,832,201	11,421	$29,317
Wisconsin	$163,216,142	5,441	$29,997

Per Capita Personal Income in Great Lakes States, 2002
Sources: Personal income data from U.S. Bureau of Economic Analysis <www.bea.gov> and population data from U.S. Census Bureau <www.census.gov>.

PLANNING, DRAFTING, AND DEVELOPING

As you start planning your paper, be certain that you are prepared to cover both subjects in a similar fashion. If you use two columns (one for each subject), a table, or a scratch outline to record your ideas, you can easily identify promising major points of comparison or contrast, consolidate supporting details, and spot gaps in your information. Remind yourself once more of your goal in comparing and contrasting the two subjects. What is it you want to demonstrate, argue, or find out?

For more on planning, drafting, and developing, see Chs. 16, 17, and 18. For more on outlines, see pp. 280–87.

State Your Purpose in a Thesis.   You need a reason to place two subjects side by side — a reason that you and most of your readers will find compelling and worthwhile. Ask yourself if you prefer one subject in the pair over the other. What reasons can you give for your preference? It's also all right not to have a preference; you can try instead to understand both subjects more clearly, making a point about each or both of them. Comparing and contrasting need not be a meaningless exercise. Try instead to think clearly and pointedly in order to explain an idea about which you care.

For more on stating a thesis, see pp. 271–77.

For exercises on choosing effective thesis statements, visit <bedfordstmartins.com/bedguide> and do a keyword search:

TWO SUBJECTS	two teaching styles in required biology courses
REASON	to show why one is better
WORKING THESIS	Although students learn a lot in both of the required introductory biology courses, one class teaches information and the other teaches how to be a good learner.

thesis

■ For exercises on sup-
porting a thesis, visit
<bedfordstmartins.com/
bedguide> and do a key-
word search:

Select a Pattern to Help Readers Follow Your Organization. Besides understanding your purpose and thesis, readers also need to follow your supporting evidence — the clusters of details that reveal the nature of each subject you consider. They're likely to expect you to follow one of two ways to organize a comparison-and-contrast essay.

OPPOSING PATTERN, SUBJECT BY SUBJECT	ALTERNATING PATTERN, POINT BY POINT
Subject A	Point 1
Point 1	Subject A
Point 2	Subject B
Point 3	Point 2
Subject B	Subject A
Point 1	Subject B
Point 2	Point 3
Point 3	Subject A
	Subject B

Although both patterns present the same information, each has its own advantages and disadvantages.

■ For another example using the opposing pattern, see pp. 319–20.

Use the Opposing Pattern of Organization. When you use the *opposing pattern* of *subject by subject,* you state all your observations about subject A and then do the same for subject B. As an example, in Chapter 15 of *Educational Policies in Crisis: Japanese and American Perspectives* (New York: Praeger, 1986), the book's editors, William K. Cummings and others, use the opposing pattern to compare and contrast how the two countries think about education. For each country, they cover similar points, first the attitude toward career opportunities and then the attitude toward educational institutions.

Subject A:
American attitude

Point 1: Careers

Point 2:
Educational institutions

Shift to Subject B:
Japanese attitude

Point 1: Careers

More salient, however, than these structural characteristics is the way that the two nations think about education. The United States fosters a myth of limitless opportunity. Football players can earn more than corporation presidents, and the local shoe store of today has the possibility of becoming one of *Fortune*'s Top 100 in 20 years. School is but one of several routes to success. For the individual who seeks the educational route, being a late bloomer is not necessarily an obstacle to upward mobility. Thus even when they enter college, many Americans have poorly developed intellectual skills. Most Americans are also relaxed about choosing their educational institutions, believing that what happens outside school and later in life may have more influence on their chances for success than what takes place in school. In contrast with the American belief in limitless opportunity, the Japanese assign great importance to a small number of career choices in the central government bureaucracy and the top corporations. They rank other careers in descending order and assume that an individual's educational performance will determine where he or she ends up in this hierarchy. Most Japanese parents seek to manage the lives of their children, from a surprisingly young age, so that the children will have the best chances of entering the top careers. Because admission to a prestigious university is known to be essential for gaining access to these attractive careers, parents are deeply concerned with the educational performance of their children. They exert every effort to ensure that their children earn good grades and enter the best schools. The large number of parents sharing this common belief results in severe academic competition. In contrast to Americans, Japanese children develop from an early age a realistic sense of the opportunities they can expect as they grow up.

Point 2:
Educational institutions

This opposing pattern of organization is workable for a single paragraph or a short essay where it can effectively unify all the details about each individual subject, like neat versus sloppy people in Suzanne Britt's essay. For a long essay or a more complicated subject, it has a drawback: readers might find it difficult to remember all the separate information about subject A while reading about subject B.

For another example using the alternating pattern, see p. 320.

Use the Alternating Pattern of Organization.   There's a better way to organize most longer papers: the *alternating pattern* of *point by point.* Using this method, you take up one point at a time, applying it first to one subject and then to the other. If your paper will have headings, you can use them to identify these points as well, thus helping readers preview the overall structure at a glance and anticipate the information covered in each section. Tim Chabot uses this pattern of organization to lead the reader along clearly and carefully, looking at each subject before moving on to the next point. His outline might have looked like the following:

For more on headings, see pp. 357–61.

Thesis: Despite the popularity of basketball in the 1990s, baseball should continue to be considered our national pastime.

You may want a classmate or friend to respond to your draft, suggesting how to present your two subjects more clearly. Ask your peer editor to answer questions like these about comparison and contrast:

- How does the introduction motivate you to read the entire essay?

- What is the point of the comparison and contrast of the two subjects? Is the thesis stated in the essay, or is it implied?

- Is the essay organized by the opposing pattern or by the alternating pattern? Is the pattern appropriate, or would the other one work better?

- Are the same categories discussed for each item? If not, should they be?

- Are there enough details for you to understand the comparison and contrast? Put a check where more details or examples would be useful.

- If this were your paper, what is the one thing you would be sure to work on before handing it in?

FOR PEER RESPONSE

For general questions for a peer editor, see pp. 328–29.

For more on outlines, see pp. 280–87. For Tim Chabot's full paper, see pp. 99–101.

I. Similarities of fans
  A. Appeal to diverse groups
      1. Baseball
      2. Basketball
  B. Varied locations
      1. Baseball
      2. Basketball

II. Difference in atmosphere at game
  A. Baseball as a diverse family-oriented spectator sport
      1. Many distractions
      2. Frequent breaks in play
  B. Basketball as game-focused sport
      1. Few distractions
      2. Constant game activity

III. Difference in pace of game
  A. Leisurely pace of baseball
      1. Slow batters
      2. Stalling pitchers
      3. Substitution of relief pitchers
      4. Low score
      5. Seventh-inning stretch
  B. Quick pace of basketball
      1. Fast players
      2. High scores
      3. Frequent changes of sides
      4. Constant motion

IV. Different athletic abilities of players
  A. Baseball as a mental game
      1. Emphasis on athletic precision
          a. Strategy
          b. Skill
          c. Decision-making
      2. Physical strength less important
  B. Basketball as a physical game
      1. Emphasis on physical power
          a. Jumping high
          b. Running fast
          c. Being tall and big
          d. Being aggressive
      2. Importance of skill and dexterity

For more on transitions, see pp. 300–03.

Add Transitions.   Once your essay is organized, you can bring cohesion to it through effective transitional words and phrases — *on the other hand, in*

Comparing and Contrasting Yourself with a Partner

Work with a partner to develop a single comparison-and-contrast essay for assignment 3 on page 113. Decide together what the focus of your essay will be: Your family backgrounds? Your hobbies? Your career goals? Your study habits? Your taste in music or clothes? Your political beliefs? Then each partner should work alone to generate a detailed analysis of himself or herself, given this focus. Come together again to compare your analyses, to decide how to shape the essay, and to draft, revise, and edit the paper.

FOR GROUP LEARNING

contrast, also, both, yet, although, finally, unlike. Your choice of wording will depend on the content of your paragraphs, but make sure that your transitions are varied and smooth. Jarring, choppy transitions will distract attention from your main point instead of contributing to a unified essay, each part working to support a meaningful thesis.

REVISING AND EDITING

Focus on Your Thesis.   Reconsider your purpose when you begin to review your draft. If your purpose is to illuminate two subjects impartially, ask yourself whether you have given your reader a balanced view. Obviously it would be unfair to set forth all the advantages of Oklahoma City and all the disadvantages of Honolulu and then conclude that Oklahoma City is superior to Honolulu on every count.

For more on revising and editing strategies, see Ch. 19.

Of course, if you love Oklahoma City and can't stand Honolulu, or vice versa, go ahead: don't be balanced; take a stand. Even so, you will want to include the same points about each city and to admit, in all honesty, that Oklahoma City has its faults. One useful way to check your comparison and contrast for either balance or thoroughness is to make an outline of your first draft and then give the outline a critical squint.

For more on outlines, see pp. 280–87.

If your classmates have made suggestions, perhaps about clarifying wording to sharpen distinctions, use their ideas to help you rework your thesis.

For more on stating a thesis, see pp. 271–77.

WORKING THESIS   Although students learn a lot in both of the required introductory biology courses, one class teaches information and the other teaches how to be a good learner.

REVISED THESIS   Although students learn the basics of biology in both of the required introductory courses, one class teaches how to memorize information and the other teaches an invaluable lesson: how to be an active learner.

Vary Your Wording.   Make sure, as you go over your draft, that you have escaped a monotonous drone: A does this, B does that; A has these advantages, B has those. Comparison and contrast needn't result in a paper as

■ For strategies for increasing coherence, see pp. 300–03.

symmetrical as a pair of sneakers. Revising and editing give you a chance to add lively details, transitions, dashes of color, and especially variety, as the following example illustrates:

The menu is another major difference between the Cozy Cafe and the Wilton

Inn. For lunch, the Cozy Cafe offers sandwiches, hamburgers, and chili. ~~For~~ ^L^unch, ^at^

the Wilton Inn ~~offers~~ *features* dishes such as fajitas, shrimp salads, and onion soup topped

with Swiss cheese. ~~For dinner, the Cozy Cafe continues to serve the lunch menu and~~

~~adds~~ *adding* home-style comfort foods such as meatloaf, stew, macaroni and cheese, and

barbecued ribs. ~~By dinner,~~ *after five o'clock* the Wilton's specialties for the day are posted--perhaps

marinated buffalo steak or orange-pecan salmon.

In critiquing your draft as you rewrite, this checklist may prove handy:

REVISION CHECKLIST

___ Does your introduction present your topic and main point clearly? Is it interesting enough to make a reader want to read the whole essay?

___ Is your reason for doing all the comparing and contrasting unmistakably clear? What do you want to demonstrate, argue for, or find out? Do you need to reexamine your goal?

___ Have you used the same categories for each item so that you treat them fairly? In discussing each feature, do you always look at the same thing?

___ What have you concluded about the two? Do you prefer one to the other? If so, is this preference (and your rationale for it) clear?

___ Does your draft look thin at any point for lack of evidence? If so, how might you develop your ideas?

___ Are there any spots where you need to revise a boringly mechanical, monotonous style ("On one hand, . . . now on the other hand")?

■ For more editing and proofreading strategies, see pp. 336–39.

After you have revised your comparison-and-contrast essay, edit and proofread it. Carefully check the grammar, word choice, punctuation, and mechanics — and then correct any problems you may find. Here are some questions to get you started editing and proofreading your paper:

EDITING CHECKLIST

■ For more help, turn to the dark-blue-edged pages and find the sections of the Quick Editing Guide noted here.

___ Have you used comparative forms (for two things) and superlative forms (for three or more) correctly for adjectives and adverbs?   A7

___ Is your sentence structure correct? Have you avoided writing fragments, comma splices, or fused sentences?   A1, A2

—— Have you used parallel structure in your comparisons and   B2
    contrasts? Are your sentences as balanced as your ideas?
—— Have you used commas correctly after introductory phrases and   C1
    other transitions?

OTHER ASSIGNMENTS

1. Listen to two different recordings of the same piece of music as per-
    formed by two different groups, orchestras, or singers. What elements of
    the music does each stress? What contrasting attitudes toward the music
    do you detect? In an essay, compare and contrast these versions.

2. Write an essay in which you compare and contrast the subjects in any of
    the following pairs for the purpose of throwing light on both. In a short
    paper, you can trace only a few similarities and differences, but don't
    hesitate to use your own observations, go to the library, or interview a
    friendly expert if you need material.

    Women and men as single parents
    Living at home and living away from home
    The coverage of a world event on television and in a newspaper
    The state of AIDS research at two moments—ten years ago and today
    The styles of two athletes playing in the same position (two pitchers,
        two quarterbacks, two goalies)
    English and another language
    Your college and a rival college
    Two differing views of a current controversy
    Northern and southern California (or two other regions)
    The experience of watching a film on a DVD and in a theater
    Two similar works of architecture (two churches, two skyscrapers, two
        city halls, two museums)

3. In an essay either serious or nonserious, for the purpose of introducing
    yourself to other members of your class, compare and contrast yourself
    with someone else. You might choose either a real person or a character
    in a film, a TV series, a novel, or a comic strip, but you and this other
    person should have much in common. Choose a few points of compari-
    son (an attitude, a habit, or a way of life), and deal with each.

Applying What You Learn: Some Uses of Comparing and Contrasting

In College Courses.   College instructors know that distinguishing subtle
similarities and differences between two subjects requires close attention, so
they frequently ask students to demonstrate that understanding by comparing and contrasting.

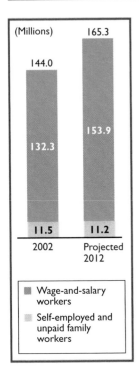

Employment by class of worker, 2000 and projected 2010
Source: Occupational Outlook Quarterly

- You would compare and contrast to "evaluate" the relative merits of Norman Rockwell and N. C. Wyeth in an art history course.

- An assignment to "consider" the consequences of doing business as a small corporation and as a partnership calls for comparison and contrast.

- When you are asked to "describe" a subject, comparing or contrasting it with a similar, more familiar subject might be the best way to accomplish the task. If your instructor asks you to write a paper describing the funeral customs in medieval England, comparing and contrasting them with modern traditions could give your readers a frame of reference.

In the Workplace.   At work, you will constantly compare and contrast products or services of one company with those of another, merits of one proposal with those of another, or benefits of option A with those of option B.

- Labor-market analysts compare employment data and projections to inform employers and workers about labor trends and help them plan for the future.

- When you recommend a new procedure for your department, you will want to emphasize its strong points by comparing and contrasting it with the existing procedure.

- When hiring personnel, organizations compare and contrast applicants' management style, work experience, educational levels, and personal attributes.

In Your Community.   Comparing and contrasting is an effective method of analyzing alternatives in your community life as well.

- The advantages of one option over another quickly become apparent when you compare or contrast them, whether you want to choose a childcare provider, a fitness center, or backup aid cameras for your car or truck.

- You can create an effective pamphlet urging voters to support building a new elementary school by contrasting the costs and benefits of a new building with those of a renovated one.

- If you were appointed to recommend a resort for your organization's annual conference, you would want to compare and contrast accommodations, meeting facilities, food services, and dates of availability in your report for the executive board.

| | | Excellent | Very good | Good | Fair | Poor |

CAMERAS
In order of display clarity.

Brand	Price	Clarity of display	Screen size (in.)
HitchCAM HC-001	$900	○	2.75x2
Magna Donnelly Video Mirror Reverse Aid 22336	400	◒	2x1.5

Consumer Reports, *October 2003*

Chapter 8
Explaining Causes and Effects

Fred Voetsch

Responding to an Image

This image shows both causes and effects—environmental, social, economic, psychological, and more. What causes can you identify? What effects? Also consider artistic choice—the selection of the scene and the vantage point from which it was photographed. What mood does the photograph create? What attitudes does it suggest? How does it affect you personally?

When a house burns down, an insurance company assigns a claims adjuster to look into the disaster and answer the question Why? He or she investigates to find the answer — the *cause* of the fire, whether lightning, a cooking mishap, or a match that someone deliberately struck — and presents it in a written report. The adjuster also details the *effects* of the fire — what was destroyed or damaged, what repairs will be needed, how much they will cost.

Often in college you are asked to investigate and think like the insurance adjuster, tracing causes or identifying effects. To do so, you have to gather information to marshal evidence. Effects, by the way, are usually easier to identify than causes. Results of a fire are apparent to an onlooker the next day, although its cause may be obscure. For this reason, seeking causes and effects may be an uncertain pursuit, and you are unlikely to set forth definitive explanations with absolute certainty.

Learning from Other Writers

■ For more on thesis and support, see Chs. 16 and 18.

The following essays explore causes and effects, each examining a different environment. To help you begin to analyze the first reading in this chapter, look for the notes in the margin. They identify features such as the thesis and the first of the causes or effects that develop it in a paper analyzing cause and effect.

■ For more examples of writing that explains causes and effects, visit <bedfordstmartins.com/bedguide> and do a keyword search:

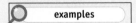

examples

As You Read These Cause-and-Effect Essays

As you read these essays, ask yourself the following questions:

1. Does the writer explain causes? Or effects? Or both? Why?
2. Does the writer perceive and explain a chain or series of causal relationships? If so, how are the various causes and effects connected?
3. What evidence does the writer supply? Is the evidence sufficient to clarify the causal relationships and to provide credibility to the essay?

William Severini Kowinski examines some of the underlying reasons for "mall culture" in this excerpt from his book The Malling of America *(1985).*

Quotation used to preview writer's focus

William Severini Kowinski
Kids in the Mall: Growing Up Controlled

Butch heaved himself up and loomed over the group. "Like it was different for me," he piped. "My folks used to drop me off at the shopping mall every morning and leave me all day. It was like a big free baby-sitter, you know? One night they never came back for me. Maybe they moved away. Maybe there's some kind of a Bureau of Missing Parents I could check with."

–Richard Peck, *Secrets of the Shopping Mall,* a novel for teenagers

114

From his sister at Swarthmore, I'd heard about a kid in Florida whose mother picked him up after school every day, drove him straight to the mall, and left him there until it closed—all at his insistence. I'd heard about a boy in Washington who, when his family moved from one suburb to another, pedaled his bicycle five miles every day to get back to his old mall, where he once belonged.

— Introduction

Their stories aren't unusual. The mall is a common experience for the majority of American youth; they have probably been going there all their lives. Some ran within their first large open space, saw their first fountain, bought their first toy, and read their first book in a mall. They may have smoked their first cigarette or first joint or turned them down, had their first kiss or lost their virginity in the mall parking lot. Teenagers in America now spend more time in the mall than anywhere else but home and school. Mostly it is their choice, but some of that mall time is put in as the result of two-paycheck and single-parent households, and the lack of other viable° alternatives. But are these kids being harmed by the mall?

— Situation described in transitional paragraph

— Question raised about effects

I wondered first of all what difference it makes for adolescents to experience so many important moments in the mall. They are, after all, at play in the fields of its little world and they learn its ways; they adapt to it and make it adapt to them. It's here that these kids get their street sense, only it's mall sense. They are learning the ways of a large-scale artificial environment: its subtleties and flexibilities, its particular pleasures and resonances,° and the attitudes it fosters.

— **THESIS** specifying effects

The presence of so many teenagers for so much time was not something mall developers planned on. In fact, it came as a big surprise. But kids became a fact of mall life very early, and the International Council of Shopping Centers found it necessary to commission a study, which they published along with a guide to mall managers on how to handle the teenage incursion.°

The study found that "teenagers in suburban centers are bored and come to the shopping centers mainly as a place to go. Teenagers in suburban centers spent more time fighting, drinking, littering, and walking than did their urban counterparts, but presented fewer overall problems." The report observed that "adolescents congregated in groups of two to four and predominantly at locations selected by them rather than management." This probably had something to do with the decision to install game arcades, which allow management to channel these restless adolescents into naturally contained areas away from major traffic points of adult shoppers.

The guide concluded that mall management should tolerate and even encourage the teenage presence because, in the words of the report, "The vast majority support the same set of values as does shopping center management." *The same set of values* means simply that mall kids are already preprogrammed to be consumers and that the mall can put the finishing

viable: Effective or practical.   **resonances:** Profound and lasting impacts.
incursion: Invasion.

touches to them as hard-core, lifelong shoppers just like everybody else. That, after all, is what the mall is about. So it shouldn't be surprising that in spending a lot of time there, adolescents find little that challenges the assumption that the goal of life is to make money and buy products, or that just about everything else in life is to be used to serve those ends.

Growing up in a high-consumption society already adds inestimable 7 pressure to kids' lives. Clothes consciousness has invaded the grade schools, and popularity is linked with having the best, newest clothes in the currently acceptable styles. Even what they read has been affected. "Miss [Nancy] Drew wasn't obsessed with her wardrobe," noted the *Wall Street Journal.* "But today the mystery in teen fiction for girls is what outfit the heroine will wear next." Shopping has become a survival skill and there is certainly no better place to learn it than the mall, where its importance is powerfully reinforced and certainly never questioned.

Use of contrast —

The mall as a university of suburban materialism, where Valley Girls 8 and Boys from coast to coast are educated in consumption, has its other lessons in this era of change in family life and sexual mores° and their economic and social ramifications.° The plethora° of products in the mall, plus the pressure on teens to buy them, may contribute to the phenomenon that psychologist David Elkind calls "the hurried child": kids who are exposed to too much of the adult world too quickly, and must respond with a sophistication that belies their still-tender emotional development. Certainly the adult products marketed for children — form-fitting designer jeans, sexy tops for preteen girls — add to the social pressure to look like an adult, along with the home-grown need to understand adult finances (why mothers must work) and adult emotions (when parents divorce).

Education comparison: negative —

Kids spend so much time at the mall partly because their parents allow 9 it and even encourage it. The mall is safe, it doesn't seem to harbor any unsavory activities, and there is adult supervision; it is, after all, a controlled environment. So the temptation, especially for working parents, is to let the mall be their babysitter. At least the kids aren't watching TV. But the mall's role as a surrogate mother may be more extensive and more profound.

Karen Lansky, a writer living in Los Angeles, has looked into the subject 10 and she told me some of her conclusions about the effects on its teenaged denizens of the mall's controlled and controlling environment. "Structure is the dominant idea, since true 'mall rats' lack just that in their homelives," she said, "and adolescents about to make the big leap into growing up crave more structure than our modern society cares to acknowledge." Karen pointed out some of the elements malls supply that kids used to get from their families, like warmth (Strawberry Shortcake dolls and similar cute and cuddly merchandise), old-fashioned mothering ("We do it all for you," the fast-food slogan), and even home cooking (the "homemade" treats at the food court).

mores: Moral principles or codes of conduct.   **ramifications:** Consequences stemming from an initial plan, act, or process.   **plethora:** Abundance.

The problem in all this, as Karen Lansky sees it, is that while families 11
nurture children by encouraging growth through the assumption of responsibility and then by letting them rest in the bosom of the family from the
rigors° of growing up, the mall as a structural mother encourages passivity
and consumption, as long as the kid doesn't make trouble. Therefore all
they learn about becoming adults is how to act and how to consume.

Kids are in the mall not only in the passive role of shoppers — they also 12
work there, especially as fast-food outlets infiltrate the mall's enclosure. There
they learn how to hold a job and take responsibility, but still within the same
value context. When *CBS Reports* went to Oak Park Mall in suburban Kansas
City, Kansas, to tape part of their hour-long consideration of malls, "After the
Dream Comes True," they interviewed a teenaged girl who worked in a fast-
food outlet there. In a sequence that didn't make the final program, she described the major goal of her present life, which was to perfect the curl on
top of the ice-cream cones that were her store's specialty. If she could do that,
she would be moved from the lowly soft-drink dispenser to the more prestigious ice-cream division, the curl on top of the status ladder at her restaurant.
These are the achievements that are important at the mall.

Other benefits of such jobs may also be overrated, according to Lau- 13
rence D. Steinberg of the University of California at Irvine's social ecology
department, who did a study on teenage employment. Their jobs, he found,
are generally simple, mindlessly repetitive, and boring. They don't really
learn anything, and the jobs don't lead anywhere. Teenagers also work primarily with other teenagers; even their supervisors are often just a little
older than they are. "Kids need to spend time with adults," Steinberg told
me. "Although they get benefits from peer relationships, without parents
and other adults it's one-sided socialization. They hang out with each other,
have age-segregated jobs, and watch TV."

Perhaps much of this is not so terrible or even so terribly different. Now 14
that they have so much more to contend with in their lives, adolescents
probably need more time to spend with other adolescents without adult impositions, just to sort things out. Though it is more concentrated in the mall
(and therefore perhaps a clearer target), the value system there is really the
dominant one of the whole society. Attitudes about curiosity, initiative, self-
expression, empathy, and disinterested learning aren't necessarily made in
the mall; they are mirrored there, perhaps a bit more intensely — as through
a glass brightly.

Besides, the mall is not without its educational opportunities. There are 15
bookstores, where there is at least a short shelf of classics at great prices, and
other books from which it is possible to learn more than how to do sit-ups.
There are tools, from hammers to VCRs, and products, from clothes to
records, that can help the young find and express themselves. There are
older people with stories, and places to be alone or to talk one-on-one with
a kindred spirit. And there is always the passing show.

Education comparison: positive

---

rigors: Harsh difficulties.

The mall itself may very well be an education about the future. I was   16
struck with the realization, as early as my first forays into Greengate,[1] that
the mall is only one of a number of enclosed and controlled environments
that are part of the lives of today's young. The mall is just an extension, say,
of those large suburban schools — only there's Karmelkorn instead of chem
lab, the ice rink instead of the gym: It's high school without the imperti-
nence of classes.

Growing up, moving from home to school to the mall — from enclosure   17
to enclosure, transported in cars — is a curiously continuous process, without
much in the way of contrast or contact with unenclosed reality. Places must
tend to blur into one another. But whatever differences and dangers there are
in this, the skills these adolescents are learning may turn out to be useful in
their later lives. For we seem to be moving inexorably° into an age of pre-
planned and regulated environments, and this is the world they will inherit.

Conclusion; writer ends with another quotation

Still, it might be better if they had more of a choice. One teenaged girl   18
confessed to *CBS Reports* that she sometimes felt she was missing something
by hanging out at the mall so much. "But I'm here," she said, "and this is
what I have."

Questions to Start You Thinking

Meaning

1. According to Kowinski, what do teenagers seek at the mall?

2. In paragraph 6, Kowinski quotes a study concluding that mall management
   and teens share "the same set of values." What are the values they share?
   What is the effect of these values on teenagers?

3. How do mall experiences shape the kinds of adults these teens become?

4. Kowinski compares the mall experience to high school. In what ways is it
   similar to high school? How is it different?

Writing Strategies

5. Kowinski examines both negative and positive effects of mall life on teens.
   In which paragraphs do you find negative effects? Where does he include
   positive effects? How well does this organization work?

6. Does Kowinski's essay deal predominantly with causes or effects? Where
   and to what degree does he examine each of these? How would his essay
   change if he limited his focus to only causes or only effects?

7. Kowinski begins his essay with a quotation from Richard Peck's *Secrets of the
   Shopping Mall*. Is this an effective beginning? Why or why not? In what
   other ways might he have begun his essay?

inexorably: Incapable of being stopped or deterred.

[1] Greengate Mall in Greensburg, Pennsylvania, where Kowinski began his research
on malls. [Eds.]

STUDENT ESSAY

Yun Yung Choi
Invisible Women

Yun Yung Choi examines the adoption of a new state religion in her native Korea and the effects of that adoption on Korean women.

For me, growing up in a small suburb on the outskirts of Seoul, the adults' pref- 1
erence for boys seemed quite natural. All the important people that I knew--doctors,
lawyers, policemen, and soldiers--were men. On the other hand, most of the women
that I knew were either housekeepers or housewives whose duty seemed to be to
obey and please the men of the family. When my teachers at school asked me what I
wanted to be when I grew up, I would answer, "I want to be the wife of the president." Because all women must become wives and mothers, I thought, becoming the
wife of the president would be the highest achievement for a woman. I knew that
the birth of a boy was a greatly desired and celebrated event, whereas the birth of a
girl was a disappointing one, accompanied by the frequent words of consolation for
the sad parents: "A daughter is her mother's chief help in keeping house."

How would you have answered this question?

These attitudes toward women, widely considered the continuation of an unbro- 2
ken chain of tradition, are, in fact, only a few hundred years old, a relatively short
period considering Korea's long history. During the first half of the Yi dynasty, which
lasted from 1392 to 1910, and during the Koryo period, which preceded the Yi dynasty, women were treated almost as equals with many privileges that were denied
them during the latter half of the Yi dynasty. This turnabout in women's place in
Korean society was brought about by one of the greatest influences that shaped the
government, literature, and thoughts of the Korean people--Confucianism.°

Throughout the Koryo period, which lasted from 918 to 1392, and throughout 3
the first half of the Yi dynasty, according to Laurel Kendall in her book View from
the Inner Room, women were important and contributing members of the society and
not marginal and dependent as they later became. Women were, to a large extent, in
command of their own lives. They were permitted to own property and receive inher-
itances from their fathers. Wedding ceremonies were held in the bride's house, where
the couple lived, and the wife retained her surname. Women were also allowed freedom of movement--that is, they were able to go outside the house without any feelings of shame or embarrassment.

With the introduction of Confucianism, however, the rights and privileges that 4
women enjoyed were confiscated. The government of the Yi dynasty made great efforts to incorporate into society the Confucian ideologies, including the principle of
agnation. This principle, according to Kendall, made men the important members of

Confucianism: Ethical system based on the teachings of Chinese philosopher Confucius
(551–479 B.C.)

How do you re-spond to this historical background?

society and relegated° women to a dependent position. The government succeeded in Confucianizing the country and encouraging the acceptance of Confucian proverbs such as the following: "Men are honored, but women are abased." "A daughter is a 'robber woman' who carries household wealth away when she marries."

The unfortunate effects of this Confucianization in the lives of women were numerous. The most noticeable was the virtual confinement of women. They were forced to remain unseen in the anbang, the inner room of the house. This room was the women's domain, or, rather, the women's prison. Outside, a woman was carried through the streets in a closed sedan chair. Walking outside, she had to wear a veil that covered her face and could travel abroad only after nightfall. Thus, it is no wonder that Westerners traveling through Korea in the late nineteenth century ex-pressed surprise at the apparent absence of women in the country.   5

Women received no formal education. Their only schooling came from govern-ment textbooks. By giving instruction on the virtuous° conduct of women, these books attempted to fit women into the Confucian stereotype--meek, quiet, and obe-dient. Thus, this Confucian society acclaimed particular women not for their talent or achievement but for the degree of perfection with which they were able to mimic the stereotype.   6

A woman even lost her identity in such a society. Once married, she became a stranger to her natal° family, becoming a member of her husband's family. Her name was omitted from the family chokpo, or genealogy book, and was entered in the chokpo of her in-laws as a mere "wife" next to her husband's name.   7

Even a desirable marriage, the ultimate hope for a woman, failed to provide financial and emotional security for her. Failure to produce a son was legal grounds for sending the wife back to her natal home, thereby subjecting the woman to the greatest humiliation and to a life of continued shame. And because the Confucian ideology stressed a wife's devotion to her husband as the greatest of womanly virtues, widows were forced to avoid social disgrace by remaining faithfully unmar-ried, no matter how young they were. As women lost their rights to own or inherit property, these widows, with no means to support themselves, suffered great hard-ships. Thus, as Sandra Martielle says in Virtues in Conflict, what the government considered "the ugly custom of remarriage" was slowly eliminated at the expense of women's happiness.   8

This male-dominated system of Confucianism is one of the surviving traditions from the Yi dynasty. Although the Constitution of the Republic of Korea proclaimed on July 17, 1948, guarantees individual freedom and sexual equality, these ideals failed to have any immediate effect on the Korean mentality that stubbornly adheres   9

---

relegated: Reduced to a less important position.   **virtuous:** Moral, honorable.
natal: Relating to one's birth.

to its belief in the superiority of men. Women still regard marriage as their prime objective in life, and little girls still wish to become the doctor's wife, the lawyer's wife, and even the president's wife. But as the system of Confucianism is slowly being forced out of existence by new legal and social standards, perhaps a day will come, after all, when a little girl will stand up in class and answer, "I want to be the president."

Why do you think the writer ends with this quotation?

Questions to Start You Thinking

Meaning

1. What effect does Choi observe? What cause does she attribute it to?

2. What specific changes in Korean culture does Choi attribute to the introduction of Confucianism?

3. What evidence do you find of the writer's critically rethinking an earlier belief and then revising it? What do you think may have influenced her to change her belief?

Writing Strategies

4. What does Choi gain by beginning and ending with her personal experience?

5. Where does Choi use the strategy of comparing and contrasting? Do you think this is effective?

6. How does Choi consider readers for whom her culture might be foreign?

7. Using highlighters or marginal notes, identify the essay's introduction, thesis, major causes or effects, supporting explanations and details for each of these, and conclusion. How effective is the organization of this essay?

Learning by Writing

THE ASSIGNMENT: EXPLAINING CAUSES AND EFFECTS

Pick a disturbing fact or situation that you have observed, and seek out the causes and effects to help you and your readers understand the issue better. In your essay, you may limit your ideas to the causes *or* the effects, or you may include both but emphasize one more than the other. Yun Yung Choi uses the last approach when she briefly identifies the cause of the status of Korean women (Confucianism) but spends most of her essay detailing the effects of this cause.

The situation you choose may have affected you and people you know well, such as student loan policies, the difficulty of working while going to school, or divorce in the family. It might have affected people in your city or region—a small voter turnout in an election, decaying bridge supports, or

■ You can complete each of the steps in this assignment by using the *Writing Guide Software* for THE BEDFORD GUIDE.

pet owners not using pooper-scoopers. It may affect society at large — identity theft, immigration laws, or the high cost of health care. It might be gender or racial stereotypes on television, binge drinking at parties, spouse abuse, teenage suicide, pollution, the shortage of male elementary school teachers, or the use of dragnets for ocean fishing. Don't think you must choose an earthshaking topic to write a good paper. On the contrary, you will do a better job if you are personally familiar with the situation you choose.

Papers written in response to this assignment have included the following:

One student cited her observations of the hardships faced by Indians in rural Mexico as one cause of the recent rebellions there.

Another analyzed the negative attitudes of men toward women in the company where she worked and the resulting tension among workers, inefficiency, and low production.

A third contended that buildings constructed in Miami are not built to withstand hurricane-force winds due, for one reason, to the inadequate inspection system.

GENERATING IDEAS

■ For more strategies for generating ideas, see Ch. 15.

Find a Topic.   What familiar situation would be informative or instructive to explore? This assignment leaves you the option of writing from personal experience, from what you know, what you can find out, or a combination of the two. Begin by letting your thoughts wander over the results of an undesirable situation. Has the situation always been this way? Or has it changed in the last few years? Have things gotten better or worse?

The ideas in the following list may help you search your memory:

DISCOVERY CHECKLIST

___ Has a difficult situation resulted from a change in your life (a new job; a fluctuation in income; personal or family upheaval following death, divorce, accident, illness, or good fortune; a new school)?

___ Has the environment changed (due to air pollution, a flood or a storm, a new industry, the failure of an old industry)?

___ Has a disturbing situation been caused by an invention (the computer, the VCR, the television, the ATM, the cell phone)?

___ Do certain employment trends cause you concern (for women in management, for blacks in the military, for white males in nursing)?

___ Is a situation on campus or in your neighborhood, city, or state causing problems for you (traffic, pollution, population, health care)?

■ For more on brainstorming, see pp. 254–56.

When your thoughts begin to percolate, jot down a list of likely topics. Then choose the idea that you care most about and that promises to be neither too large nor too small. A paper confined to the causes of a family's move from New Jersey to Montana might be only one sentence long: "My father's company transferred him." But the subsequent effects of the move on the family might form the basis of an interesting essay. On the other hand, you might need hundreds of pages to study all the effects of gangs in urban high schools. Instead, you might consider just one unusual effect, such as gang members staking out territory in the parking lot of a local school.

List Causes and Effects.   Your choice tentatively made, write for ten or fifteen minutes, identifying likely causes and effects. After noting those you see, consider which are immediate (evident and close at hand), which are remote (underlying, more basic, or earlier), and how you might arrange them in a logical sequence or causal chain.

FOCUS ON CAUSAL CHAIN					
Remote Causes	→ Immediate Causes →	**SITUATION**	→ Immediate Effects	→	Remote Effects
Foreign competition →	Sales, profits drop →	Clothing factory closing →	Jobs vanish	→	Town flounders

Once you have figured out the basic causal relationships, focus on the complexity or the implications of the causes, effects, or both. Probe more deeply for contributing, related, or even hidden factors.

FOCUS ON IMMEDIATE EFFECTS			FOCUS ON REMOTE EFFECTS
Factory workers lose jobs	→	Households curtail spending	Town economy undermined
Grocery and other stores suffer	→	Businesses fold	Food pantry, social services overwhelmed
Workers lose health coverage	→	Health needs ignored	Hospital limits services and doctors leave
Retirees fear benefits lost	→	Confidence erodes	Unemployed and young people leave

When you begin to draft your paper, these ideas will be a rich resource, allowing you to concentrate on the causes or effects you find most important and skip any that are minor.

Try Mapping the Situation.   If a visual technique might help you analyze the situation, try mapping. Using a blank page, movable sticky notes, or a computer file, identify and position causes and effects in order to show their relationships or relative importance.

■ For more on mapping, see pp. 259–60.

Consider Sources of Support.   After identifying causes and effects, note your evidence next to each item. You can then see at a glance exactly where you need to generate more material. Star or underline any causes and effects

■ For advice on finding a few pertinent sources, turn to the Quick Research Guide (the dark-red-edged pages).

■ For writing activities for cause and effect, visit <bedfordstmartins.com/bedguide> and do a key-word search:

🔍 **activities**

Facing the Challenge: Causes and Effects

The major challenge writers face when exploring causal relationships is how to limit the subject. When you explore a given phenomenon — from teenage drug use to the success of your favorite band — devoting equal space to all possible causes and effects will either overwhelm your readers or put them to sleep. Instead, you need to decide what you want to show your readers — and then emphasize the causal relationships that help achieve this purpose.

Rely on your purpose to help you decide which part of the relationship — cause or effect — to stress and how to limit your ideas to strengthen your overall point. If you are writing about your parents' divorce, for example, you may be tempted to discuss all the possible *causes* for their separation and then analyze all the *effects* it has had on you. Your readers, however, won't want to know about every single argument your parents had. Both you and your readers will have a much easier time if you make some decisions about your focus:

- Do you want to concentrate on *causes* or *effects*?
- Which of your explanations are most and least effective?
- How can you emphasize the points that are most important to you?
- Which relatively insignificant or irrelevant ideas can you omit?

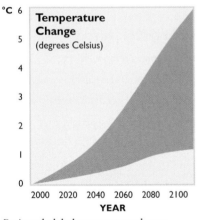

Projected global temperature change

that stand out as major ones. A way to rate the items on your list is to ask, How significant is this cause? Would the situation not exist without it? (This major cause deserves a big star.) Or would the situation have arisen without it, for some other reason? (This minor cause might still matter but be less important.) Has this effect had a resounding impact? Is it necessary to explain the results adequately?

As you set priorities — identifying major causes or effects and noting missing information — you may wish to talk with others, use a search engine, or browse the library Web site for sources of supporting ideas, concrete details, and reliable statistics. For example, you might look for illustrations of the problem, accounts of comparable situations, or charts showing current data and projections.

PLANNING, DRAFTING, AND DEVELOPING

■ For Choi's complete essay, see pp. 119–21.

Start with a Scratch Outline and Thesis. Yun Yung Choi's "Invisible Women" follows a clear plan. The essay was written from a brief scratch outline that simply lists the effects of the change:

Intro — Personal anecdote

—Tie with Korean history

> *—Then add working thesis: The turnabout for women resulted from the influence of Confucianism in all aspects of society.*
>
> *Comparison and contrast of status of women before and after Confucianism*
>
> *Effects of Confucianism on women*
>
>   *1. Confinement*
>   *2. Little education*
>   *3. Loss of identity in marriage*
>   *4. No property rights*
>
> *Conclusion: Impact still evident in Korea today but some hints of change*

For more about informal outlines, see pp. 281–84.

For exercises on choosing effective thesis statements, visit <bedfordstmartins.com/bedguide> and do a keyword search:

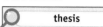

thesis

The paper makes its point: it identifies Confucianism as the reason for the status of Korean women and details four specific effects of Confucianism on women in Korean society. And it shows that cause and effect are closely related: Confucianism is the cause of the change in the status of Korean women, and Confucianism has had specific effects on Korean women.

For more about stating your main point in a thesis, see pp. 271–77.

Organize to Show Causes and Effects to Readers. The main part of your paper — showing how the situation came about (the causes) or what followed as a result (the effects) or both — more than likely will follow one of these patterns:

I. The situation	I. The situation	I. The situation
II. Its causes	II. Its effects	II. Its causes
		III. Its effects

You can begin planning your paper by grouping the causes and effects and then classifying them as major or minor. If, for example, you are writing about the reasons more college students accumulate credit card debt now than they did a generation ago, you might list the following:

For more planning strategies, see Ch. 16.

1. easy credit
2. high credit limits
3. compulsive buying

On reflection you might decide that compulsive buying — especially of CDs, DVDs, software, games, and electronic equipment — is a major cause and that the availability of credit actually is a minor one.

You could then organize the causes from least important to most important, emphasizing the major one by giving it more space and the final place in your essay. After you have organized in a way that seems logical to you, discuss your plans or share your draft with a classmate, a friend, or your instructor. Ask whether your organization will make sense to someone else.

Introduce the Situation. When you draft the first part of your paper, describe the situation you want to explain in no more than two or three paragraphs. Make clear to your readers which task — explaining the causes, explaining the effects, or explaining both — you intend to accomplish. Instead of doing this in a flat, mechanical fashion ("Now I am going to explain the causes of this situation"), you can announce your task casually, naturally, as if you were talking to someone: "At first, I didn't realize that keeping six pet cheetahs in our backyard would bother the neighbors." Or, you might tantalize your readers as one writer did in a paper about her father's sudden move to a Trappist monastery: "The real reason for Father's decision didn't become clear to me for a long while."

■ For exercises on supporting a thesis, visit <bedfordstmartins.com/bedguide> and do a keyword search:

■ For more on the placement of visuals, see p. 368.

Work in Your Evidence.   Some writers want to rough out a cause-and-effect draft, positioning all the major points first and then circling back to pull in supporting explanations and details. Others want to plunge deeply into each section — stating the main point, elaborating, and working in the evidence all at once. Because tables, charts, and graphs can often consolidate information that substantiates or illustrates causes or effects, consider whether such additions would strengthen your essay. If so, place your graphics near the related text discussion, supporting but not duplicating it.

REVISING AND EDITING

■ For more revising and editing strategies, see Ch. 19.

Because explaining causes and effects takes hard thought, you'll want to set aside plenty of time for rewriting. As Yun Yung Choi approached her paper's final version, she wanted to rework her thesis, developing it with greater precision and more detail.

■ For more on stating a thesis, see pp. 271–77.

WORKING THESIS   The turnabout for women resulted from the influence of Confucianism in all aspects of society.

REVISED THESIS   This turnabout in women's place in Korean society was brought about by one of the greatest influences that shaped the government, literature, and thoughts of the Korean people — Confucianism.

She also faced a problem pointed out by classmates who had read her draft: how to make a smooth transition from recalling her own experience to probing causes.

, a relatively short time, considering Korea's long history

(emphasize that everyone thinks that) ——→ *widely*

These attitudes toward women, ~~which I once~~ believed to be the continuation of an unbroken chain of tradition, are, in fact, only a few hundred years old. During the *[tell when]* first half of the Yi dynasty, which lasted from 1392 to 1910, and during [the Koryo period,] women were treated almost as equals, with many privileges that were denied them during the latter half of the Yi dynasty. This upheaval in women's place in Korean society was brought about by one of the greatest influences that shaped the government, literature, and thoughts of the Korean people: Confucianism. Because of Confucianism, my birth was not greeted with joy and celebration but rather with these words of consolation: "A daughter is her mother's chief help in keeping house."

(Belongs in opening paragraph)

In revising a paper that traces causes, effects, or both, you might consider questions like these:

REVISION CHECKLIST

___ Have you shown your readers your purpose in presenting causes or effects?

___ Is your explanation thoughtful, searching, and reasonable?

___ Where might you need to reorganize or add transitions so your paper is easy for readers to follow?

If you are tracing causes,

___ Have you made it clear that you are explaining causes?

___ Do you need to add any significant causes?

___ At what points might you need to add more evidence to convince readers that the causal relationships are valid, not just guesses?

___ Do you need to drop any remote causes you can't begin to prove? Or any assertions made without proof?

___ Have you oversimplified by assuming only one small cause accounts for a large phenomenon or that one thing caused another just because the one preceded the other?

If you are determining effects,

___ Have you made it clear that you are explaining effects?

___ What possible effects have you left out? Are any of them worth adding?

___ At what points might you need to supply more evidence that these effects have occurred?

___ Could any effect have resulted not from the cause you describe but from some other cause?

For more on evidence, see pp. 35–40. For mistakes in thinking called logical fallacies, see pp. 149–50.

You can use the Table menu in your word processor to help you assess the importance of causes and effects. Open a file, go to the Table menu, insert a table, and enter "4" for the number of columns. Label the columns "Major Cause," "Minor Cause," "Major Effect," and "Minor Effect." Divide up your causes and effects accordingly, making entries under each heading. You can create more rows automatically by placing your cursor outside the last cell of the table and hitting the Return key. Each box should expand automatically to fit whatever you type into it. Refine your table as you relate, order, or limit your points.

WRITING WITH A COMPUTER

For more editing and proofreading strategies, see pp. 336–39.

After you have revised your cause-and-effect essay, edit and proofread it. Carefully check the grammar, word choice, punctuation, and mechanics — and then correct any problems you find. Here are some questions to get you started when editing and proofreading your paper:

For more help, turn to the dark-blue-edged pages, and find the sections of the Quick Editing Guide noted here.

EDITING CHECKLIST

____ Have you used correct verb tenses and forms throughout? When you describe events in the past, is it clear what happened first and what happened next?   **A3**

____ Have you avoided creating fragments when filling in additional causes or effects? (Check revisions carefully, especially those beginning "*Because . . .*" or "*Causing . . . .*") Have you avoided writing comma splices or fused sentences when trying to integrate ideas smoothly?   **A1, A2**

____ Do your transitions and other introductory elements have commas after them, if these are needed?   **C1**

FOR PEER RESPONSE

For general questions for a peer editor, see pp. 328–29.

Let a classmate or friend read your draft, considering how you've analyzed causes or effects. Ask your peer editor to answer questions such as the following: If the writer explains causes,

- Does the writer explain, rather than merely list, causes?
- Do the causes seem logical and possible?
- Are there other causes that the writer might consider? If so, list them.

If the writer explains effects,

- Do all the effects seem to be results of the situation the writer describes?
- Are there other effects that the writer might consider? If so, list them.

For all cause-and-effect papers,

- What is the writer's thesis? Does the explanation of causes or effects help the writer accomplish the purpose of the essay?
- Is the order of supporting ideas clear and useful? Can you suggest a better organization?
- Are you convinced by the writer's logic? Do you see any logical fallacies?
- Point out any causes or effects you find hard to accept.

For more on evidence, see pp. 35–40. For mistakes in thinking called logical fallacies, see pp. 149–50.

- Do the writer's evidence and detail convince you? Put stars where more or better evidence is needed.
- If this were your paper, what is the one thing you would be sure to work on before handing it in?

Explaining the News

In class or in your writing group, tell aloud a two-minute story that you invent to explain the causes behind any surprising event reported in the morning's news. Either realistic explanations or tall tales are acceptable, but be sure to prepare some brief notes about your story in advance. Invite the others to comment on it, and, with their reactions in mind, set it down on paper to turn in at the next class, embellished and improved as much as you wish. If your group wants to videotape its version of the news, select an anchor, decide on the order of your stories, and rehearse first. Invite your whole class to watch and evaluate your video.

FOR GROUP LEARNING

OTHER ASSIGNMENTS

1. Pick a change that has taken place during your lifetime — a noticeable, lasting transformation produced by an event or series of events. Seek out its causes and effects to help you and your readers understand that change better. The change might be one that has affected only you, such as a move to another location, a decision you made, or an alteration in a strong personal opinion or belief. It might be a change that has also affected other people in your neighborhood or city (a new zoning law), in a region (the growth of a new industry such as high technology), or in society at large (general access to the Internet). Or it might be a new invention, a medical breakthrough, or a deep-down shift in the structure or attitudes of society.

2. Explore your own motives and explain your reasons for taking some step or for doing something in a routine way.

3. Read one newspaper or magazine article that probes the causes of some contemporary problem: the shortage of reasonable day-care options, for instance, or tuition increases in your state. Can you suggest causes that the article writer seems to have ignored? Write an essay in which you argue that the author has or has not done a good job of explaining the causes of this problem.

Applying What You Learn:
Some Uses of Explaining Causes and Effects

In College Courses.   Both writing assignments and examination questions often pose problems in causality.

- One or two paragraphs that explore the causes of a phenomenon or its effects might add depth to a paper assigned on almost any subject — a sociology paper about teenage parenthood or a literature paper on characteristics of romanticism in American fiction.

- Exam questions may call for you to identify causes ("Trace the causes of the decline of foreign automobile sales in America") or survey effects ("What economic effects were immediately evident when Prohibition was repealed in 1933?").

- Instructors in many courses will ask you to write about causal relationships. In a speech pathology course, you might investigate effects of head trauma, fetal alcohol syndrome, or learning disabilities.

In the Workplace. Understanding causal relationships, often driving issues of the workplace, can make the difference between success or failure.

- Advertising agencies and marketing departments examine causes and effects to determine what strategies will convince consumers to buy.

- State department officials and military officers analyze international relations and issue causality reports — the possible consequences of an impending war between Pakistan and India, the effects of a military coup in South America, or the causes of genocide in Rwanda.

- Economic analysts look at circumstances that will produce changes in the workforce.

In Your Community. Understanding why a problem exists in your community or what might result from a proposed action allows you to add your voice to those who wish to maintain the status quo or to initiate changes.

- Your professional or civic organization may respond to a controversy by outlining likely consequences of a current or proposed practice and making clear the group's stance.

- Images of the long-term effects of dumping in your city's landfill can help build a persuasive poster campaign for recycling.

- A letter to your school board sharing evidence of the effects of a dress code on student behavior in other school districts can assist board members in making the decision most beneficial to your child.

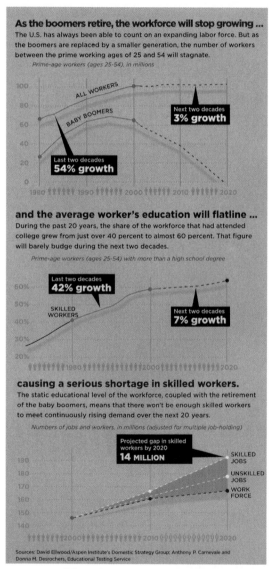

As the boomers retire, the workforce will stop growing ...
The U.S. has always been able to count on an expanding labor force. But as the boomers are replaced by a smaller generation, the number of workers between the prime working ages of 25 and 54 will stagnate.

Prime-age workers (ages 25-54), in millions

ALL WORKERS
BABY BOOMERS

Next two decades
3% growth

Last two decades
54% growth

1980   1990   2000   2010   2020

and the average worker's education will flatline ...
During the past 20 years, the share of the workforce that had attended college grew from just over 40 percent to almost 60 percent. That figure will barely budge during the next two decades.

Prime-age workers (ages 25-54) with more than a high school degree

Last two decades
42% growth

SKILLED WORKERS

Next two decades
7% growth

1980   2000   2020

causing a serious shortage in skilled workers.
The static educational level of the workforce, coupled with the retirement of the baby boomers, means that there won't be enough skilled workers to meet continuously rising demand over the next 20 years.

Numbers of jobs and workers, in millions (adjusted for multiple job-holding)

Projected gap in skilled workers by 2020
14 MILLION

SKILLED JOBS
UNSKILLED JOBS
WORK FORCE

2000   2010   2020

Sources: David Ellwood/Aspen Institute's Domestic Strategy Group; Anthony P. Carnevale and Donna M. Desrochers, Educational Testing Service

Data on workforce changes. Source: Business 2.0

Chapter 9
Taking a Stand

Responding to an Image

This image appeared on the cover of *Play Fair at the Olympics,* a report published in advance of the 2004 games. What is the stance being taken? What issues and concerns might have led to this position? Is the image effective and convincing? Based on the image, what do you think are the missions and goals of those who produced the report (Oxfam, the Clean Clothes Campaign, and Global Unions)?

Both in class and outside of class, you'll hear controversial issues discussed — prayer in the schools, Internet copyright issues, health care. Even in academic fields, experts don't always agree, and issues may remain controversies for years. Taking a stand in response to such issues will help you understand the controversy and clarify what you believe.

Writing of this kind has a twofold purpose — to state an opinion and to win your readers' respect for it. What you say might or might not change a reader's opinion. But if you fulfill your purpose, a reader at least will see good reasons for your views. In taking a stand, you do these things:

- You state your opinion or stand.
- You give reasons with evidence to support your position.
- You enlist your readers' trust.
- You consider and respect what your readers probably think and feel.

Learning from Other Writers

■ For more such writings, visit <bedfordstmartins.com/bedguide> and do a key-word search:

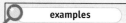

examples

■ For more on thesis and support, see Chs. 16 and 18.

As a result of persuasive efforts such as Suzan Shown Harjo's essay, the Native American Graves Protection and Repatriation Act was passed in 1990.

Let's look at two essays in which the writers take a stand effectively on issues of importance to them. To help you begin to analyze the first reading in this chapter, look for the notes in the margin. They identify features such as the thesis and the first of the main points that support it in a paper that takes a stand.

As You Read These Essays That Take a Stand

As you read these essays, ask yourself the following questions:

1. What stand does the writer take? Is it a popular opinion, or does it break from commonly accepted beliefs?

2. How does the writer appeal to readers?

3. How does the writer support his or her position? Is the evidence sufficient to gain your respect? Why, or why not?

Suzan Shown Harjo

Last Rites for Indian Dead

Introduction appeals to readers

What if museums, universities, and government agencies could put your dead relatives on display or keep them in boxes to be cut up and otherwise studied? What if you believed that the spirits of the dead could not rest until their human remains were placed in a sacred area?

The ordinary American would say there ought to be a law — and there is, for ordinary Americans. The problem for American Indians is that there

132

are too many laws of the kind that make us the archeological property of the
United States and too few of the kind that protect us from such insults.

     THESIS
     taking a stand
     Point 1

Some of my own Cheyenne relatives' skulls are in the Smithsonian Institution today, along with those of at least 4,500 other Indian people who
were violated in the 1800s by the U.S. Army for an "Indian Crania Study." It
wasn't enough that these unarmed Cheyenne people were mowed down by
the cavalry at the infamous Sand Creek massacre; many were decapitated
and their heads shipped to Washington as freight. (The Army Medical Museum's collection is now in the Smithsonian.) Some had been exhumed°
only hours after being buried. Imagine their grieving families' reaction on
finding their loved ones disinterred° and headless.

Some targets of the Army's study were killed in noncombat situations
and beheaded immediately. The officer's account of the decapitation of the
Apache chief Mangas Coloradas in 1863 shows the pseudoscientific nature
of the exercise. "I weighed the brain and measured the skull," the good doctor wrote, "and found that while the skull was smaller, the brain was larger
than that of Daniel Webster."

     — Supporting evidence

These journal accounts exist in excruciating detail, yet missing are any
records of overall comparisons, conclusions, or final reports of the Army
study. Since it is unlike the Army not to leave a paper trail, one must wonder
about the motive for its collection.

The total Indian body count in the Smithsonian collection is more than
19,000, and it is not the largest in the country. It is not inconceivable that the
1.5 million of us living today are outnumbered by our dead stored in museums, educational institutions, federal agencies, state historical societies, and
private collections. The Indian people are further dehumanized by being exhibited alongside the mastodons and dinosaurs and other extinct creatures.

Where we have buried our dead in peace, more often than not the sites
have been desecrated. For more than two hundred years, relic-hunting has
been a popular pursuit. Lately, the market in Indian artifacts has brought
this abhorrent activity to a fever pitch in some areas. And when scavengers
come upon Indian burial sites, everything found becomes fair game, including sacred burial offerings, teeth, and skeletal remains.

One unusually well-publicized example of Indian grave desecration occurred two years ago in a western Kentucky field known as Slack Farm, the site
of an Indian village five centuries ago. Ten men — one with a business card
stating "Have Shovel, Will Travel" — paid the landowner $10,000 to lease dig-
ging rights between planting seasons. They dug extensively on the forty-acre
farm, rummaging through an estimated 650 graves, collecting burial goods,
tools, and ceremonial items. Skeletons were strewn about like litter.

What motivates people to do something like this? Financial gain is
the first answer. Indian relic-collecting has become a multimillion-dollar
industry. The price tag on a bead necklace can easily top $1,000; rare pieces
fetch tens of thousands.

     Question used as
     transition

---

exhumed: Dug up out of the earth.   **disinterred:** Taken out of a place of burial.

And it is not just collectors of the macabre° who pay for skeletal re- 10
mains. Scientists say that these deceased Indians are needed for research that
someday could benefit the health and welfare of living Indians. But just how
many dead Indians must they examine? Nineteen thousand?

There is doubt as to whether permanent curation of our dead really 11
benefits Indians. Dr. Emery A. Johnson, former assistant Surgeon General,
recently observed, "I am not aware of any current medical diagnostic or
treatment procedure that has been derived from research on such skeletal remains. Nor am I aware of any during the thirty-four years that I have been
involved in American Indian . . . health care."

Indian remains are still being collected for racial biological studies. 12
While the intentions may be honorable, the ethics of using human remains
this way without the full consent of relatives must be questioned.

Some relief for Indian people has come on the state level. Almost half 13
of the states, including California, have passed laws protecting Indian burial
sites and restricting the sale of Indian bones, burial offerings, and other sacred items. Rep. Charles E. Bennett (D-Fla.) and Sen. John McCain (R-Ariz.)
have introduced bills that are a good start in invoking the federal government's protection. However, no legislation has attacked the problem head-
on by imposing stiff penalties at the marketplace, or by changing laws that
make dead Indians the nation's property.

Some universities — notably Stanford, Nebraska, Minnesota, and Seattle — 14
have returned, or agreed to return, Indian human remains; it is fitting that
institutions of higher education should lead the way.

Congress is now deciding what to do with the government's extensive 15
collection of Indian human remains and associated funerary objects. The secretary of the Smithsonian, Robert McC. Adams, has been valiantly° attempting to apply modern ethics to yesterday's excesses. This week, he announced
that the Smithsonian would conduct an inventory and return all Indian
skeletal remains that could be identified with specific tribes or living kin.

Transition to concluding proposal

But there remains a reluctance generally among collectors of Indian re- 16
mains to take action of a scope that would have a quantitative impact and a
healing quality. If they will not act on their own — and it is highly unlikely
that they will — then Congress must act.

Conclusion proposes action

The country must recognize that the bodies of dead American Indian 17
people are not artifacts to be bought and sold as collector's items. It is not
appropriate to store tens of thousands of our ancestors for possible future
research. They are our family. They deserve to be returned to their sacred
burial grounds and given a chance to rest.

The plunder of our people's graves has gone on too long. Let us rebury 18
our dead and remove this shameful past from America's future.

---

macabre: Gruesome, ghastly.   **valiantly:** Bravely.

Questions to Start You Thinking

Meaning

1. What is the issue Harjo identifies? How extensive does she show it to be?

2. What is Harjo's position on this issue? Where does she first state it?

3. What evidence does Harjo present to refute the claim that housing skeletal remains of Native Americans in museums is necessary for medical research and may benefit living Indians?

Writing Strategies

4. What assumptions do you think Harjo makes about her audience?

5. What types of evidence does Harjo use to support her argument? How convincing is the evidence to you?

6. How does Harjo use her status as a Native American to enhance her position? Would her argument be as credible if it were written by someone of another background?

7. How does she appeal to the emotions of the readers in the essay? In what ways do these strategies strengthen or detract from her logical reasons?

8. Why does Harjo discuss what legislatures and universities are doing in response to the situation?

STUDENT ESSAY

LaBree Shide

ANWR: Not a Place for Profit

America is a fast-changing country. Everywhere Americans look, new buildings are popping up. Civilization seems to be reaching every corner of the United States. There are a few places that remain untouched by commercialism and capitalism, as well as places that are meant to be protected from any future attempts to industrialize the land. One such place is the Arctic National Wildlife Refuge (ANWR). ANWR is one of the largest refuges in America and can be found in northeastern Alaska. According to the Yale Political Union, "the Refuge contains some of the most diverse wildlife in the arctic, including 36 fish species, 36 land mammals, nine marine mammals, and over 160 migratory and resident bird species." ANWR's future, however, is being threatened, as businesses and government want to open up the refuge to oil drilling. Yet drilling goes against everything that brought about ANWR's existence: ANWR was established "for the purpose of preserving the area's unique wildlife, wilderness, and recreational values" (Yale Political Union). Oil drilling should not be allowed in ANWR because the wild land would become industrialized, undermining the purpose of setting aside a wildlife refuge.

LaBree Shide's opinion piece appeared in Harvest, a collection of essays by students at the University of Oregon.

Do you feel affected by the drilling issue? Why or why not?

In your view, what needs do "sanctuaries" and "refuges" serve?

If drilling is allowed in ANWR, something very special would be lost, something   2
that cannot be restored, and that is nature. In a letter on behalf of the National
Resources Defense Council, Robert Redford, an environmental activist, wrote, "the
preservation of irreplaceable wild lands like the Arctic Refuge and Greater Yellowstone is a core American value" (2). Redford touches on the fact that when nature is
destroyed, drilling threatens our society. Just because most people live in the cities
or suburbs doesn't mean they would not be affected by drilling in ANWR. ANWR is a
place that people can visit, but more importantly it is a place that creates pride.
With pollution and overcrowded conditions, Americans can look at ANWR and be
proud of the fact that they were able to preserve this land in its natural state. ANWR
is something more than just a place to visit; it is a place where "in the sanctuary of
a forest or the vastness of the desert or the silence of grassland, we can touch a
timeless force larger than ourselves and our all-too-human problems" (Redford 3).
Any unnatural activity on ANWR land would defeat the purpose of preserving a
refuge in its natural state; moreover, ANWR's animals would be unprotected and
would eventually go extinct.

If worse comes to worst, and bills are passed allowing drilling in ANWR, the end   3
will in no way justify the means. First of all, there is no way to predict how much oil
will actually be found. After all of the destruction of the land, the drillers may find
themselves with less oil than predicted. Even if they reach their goal, the oil still
wouldn't be enough to change America's dependence on other countries for oil. As
Robert Redford states, "we could drill the Arctic Refuge, Greater Yellowstone, and
every other wild land in America and we'd still be importing oil" (2). The way to reduce dependence is to change what we are already doing. Americans need to cut
down on what they are using: "The Sierra Club, for example, points out that we could
save far more oil by taking reasonable steps to increase the efficiency of automobiles" (Yale Political Union). Americans need to reduce car emissions, use less oil,
preserve, and save, rather than ask for more. The way for Americans to "declare energy independence [. . . is] to reduce our appetite for oil" (Redford 2). If we lose
sight of our values and drilling is allowed in ANWR, it will all be for nothing, as we
would find ourselves with the same oil deficiency, except, unfortunately, without a
wildlife refuge.

Aside from changing because of drilling, ANWR would eventually become an in-   4
dustrialized area. The U.S. Geological Survey determined that "the oil is expected to
occur in a number of accumulations rather than a single large accumulation." Supporters of drilling say that even the little sites added together don't equal very much
land. This may be true, but the fact is that "oil development would spread over a
large region connected by roads, pipelines, power plants, processing plants, airports,
gravel mines, power lines, and other infrastructure"° (Yale Political Union). So more

infrastructure: Construction that supports human and industrial activity.

land would be affected than the original estimate. Furthermore, a precedent° would be set for all of ANWR: if it is okay to drill there, why not here? Oil companies will be asking this very question. As the Yale Political Union notes, "ANWR drilling will inevitably industrialize the Coastal Plain. The entire 1.5 million acre Coastal Plain area would be opened to oil leasing under pending Congressional legislation." Drilling in one place would only give permission to future drillers to continue until all of the land is industrialized.

Supporters of drilling in ANWR argue that drilling companies will touch very lit-   5
tle land. Arctic Power, a supporter of drilling, reported, "only 1.5 million acres or 8 percent of the northern coast of ANWR is being considered for development" (ANWR). This may be true, but the question must be asked: Where do we draw the line? Such drilling would set a precedent, and drillers will continue arguing that it is just a little bit of land, until little by little, there is no more land left. The land will be affected in several indirect ways as well. The U.S. Department of the Interior estimated that 12,500 acres would be "directly impacted in a web of roads, drill pads, processing facilities, and airports extending over hundreds of square miles, not in a compact area" (Yale Political Union). The claim that only a small area will be affected does not accurately reflect the amount of land that will be impacted.

Arctic Power has argued that ANWR is hardly visited by people, implying that   6
gives the "okay" to drill there. Arctic Power reported, "only a few hundred people visit ANWR each year" (ANWR). This may be true, but the sole purpose of ANWR is not to be a recreational place. ANWR was established "for the purpose of preserving the area's unique wildlife, wilderness, and recreational values" (Yale Political Union). The very people trying to turn ANWR into a consumer-driven, developed area are reducing it to a place for humans to have fun, when in truth it is primarily a place for animals to live undisturbed.

Another disturbing fact is one that drilling proponents have failed to mention: 7
the exploration company seeking to drill in Alaska has gotten in trouble for illegally dumping hazardous wastes. According to the Yale Political Union:

> In February 2000, BP Exploration was sentenced to pay $15.5 million in criminal fines and to implement a new environmental management program, and to serve five years of probation for failure to report illegal dumping of hazardous wastes down Endicott oil wells.

ANWR is threatened not only by drilling but also by hazardous wastes that could damage the land and kill the animals. Even if this particular company is not allowed to explore, similar companies might pose a threat. Too many risks would be taken if drilling were allowed in ANWR.

precedent: A case or decision that could be used to justify similar cases or decisions in the future.

ANWR is a place where animals of the Arctic can live naturally, without human   8
disturbance. Those who want to drill are more concerned with money and short-term
oil supplies and are not considering the welfare of the animals. Fortunately, many
Americans do not hold the same values as the drilling proponents. According to a
poll by the Associated Press, "Most [Americans] oppose exploring for more oil in
Alaska's Arctic National Wildlife Refuge" (Lester). Supporters of drilling in ANWR
should consider the opinion of most Americans, as well as the need for the animals
and landscape of ANWR to remain undisturbed, and change their minds.

(?) Do you side with
"most Americans" on
this issue?

Works Cited

For details on citing
and listing sources see D6
and E1–E2 in the Quick
Research Guide (the
dark-red-edged pages).

Arctic National Wildlife Refuge (ANWR). Arctic National Wildlife Refuge. 6 Dec. 2001
<http://www.anwr.org>.

Lester, Will. "Poll Shows Concern about Energy." 1 Feb. 2001. Associated Press report
on International Communications Research. 5 Dec. 2001 <http://www
.icrsurvey.com/ICRInTheNews/AP_Energy.html>.

Redford, Robert. Letter on behalf of the Natural Resources Defense Council.
21 Nov. 2001.

U.S. Geological Survey. 17 Nov. 2001. U.S. Geological Survey. 6 Dec. 2001
<http://www.usgs.gov>.

Yale Political Union. 5 Nov. 2001. Yale Political Union. 5 Dec. 2001
<http://yale.edu/ypunion>.

Questions to Start You Thinking

Meaning

1. What points does Shide make to support her position that drilling should
not be allowed in the Arctic National Wildlife Refuge?

2. Shide suggests that all Americans share some responsibility for the pressures
to drill in the refuge. What actions does she suggest that Americans take?

3. What negative effects of oil exploration, aside from the drilling itself, does
Shide identify?

Writing Strategies

4. What kind of support does Shide use to back up her claims about the dangers of drilling in the wildlife refuge? Do you find her argument effective?
Why, or why not?

5. What source or sources does Shide draw on the most? Does her use of
sources seem balanced overall? Why, or why not?

6. At what point in the essay does Shide consider opposing points of view?
Does she adequately address these views? Explain.

7. Using highlighters or marginal notes, identify the essay's introduction, thesis, major points or reasons, supporting evidence for each point, and conclusion. How effective is the organization of this essay?

Learning by Writing

THE ASSIGNMENT: TAKING A STAND

Find a controversy that rouses your interest. It might be a current issue, a long-standing one, or a matter of personal concern: military benefits for national guard troops sent to war zones, the contribution of sports to a school's educational mission, or the need for menu changes at the cafeteria to accommodate ethnic, religious, and personal preferences. Your purpose in this paper isn't to try to solve a large social or moral problem but to make clear exactly where you stand on an issue and to persuade your readers to respect your position, perhaps even to accept it. As you reflect on your topic, you may change your position, but don't shift positions in the middle of your essay.

■ You can complete each of the steps in this assignment by using the *Writing Guide Software* for *THE BEDFORD GUIDE*.

Assume that your readers are people who may or may not be familiar with the controversy, so provide some background or an overview to help them understand the situation. Furthermore, your readers may not have taken sides yet or may hold a position different from yours. You'll need to consider their views and choose strategies that will enlist their support.

Here are brief summaries of a few good papers that take a stand:

A writer who pays her own college costs disputed the opinion that working during the school year provides a student with valuable knowl-

---

Facing the Challenge: Taking a Stand

The major challenge writers face when taking a stand is to gather enough relevant evidence to support their position. Without such evidence, you'll convince only those who agreed with you in the first place. You also won't persuade readers by raving emotionally about an issue or insulting them as ignorant if they hold different opinions. Moreover, few readers respect a wishy-washy writer who avoids taking a stand.

What does work is respect — yours for the views of readers who will, in turn, respect your opinion, even if they don't agree with it. You convey — and gain — respect when you anticipate readers' possible objections or counterarguments, demonstrate knowledge of these alternate views, and present evidence that addresses others' concerns as it strengthens your argument.

To anticipate and find evidence that acknowledges other views, list groups that might have strong opinions on your topic. Then try putting yourself in the shoes of a member of each group by writing a paragraph on the issue from *her* point of view.

- What would her opinion be?
- On what grounds might she object to your argument?
- How can you best address her concerns and overcome her objections?

Your paragraph will suggest additional evidence to support your claims.

■ For writing activities for taking a stand, visit <bedfordstmartins.com/bedguide> and do a keyword search:

 activities

edge. Citing her painful experience, she maintained that devoting full time to studies is far better than juggling school and work.

Another writer challenged his history textbook's portrayal of Joan of Arc as "an ignorant farm girl subject to religious hysteria."

A member of the wrestling team argued that the number of weight categories in wrestling should be increased because athletes who overtrain to qualify for the existing categories often damage their health.

GENERATING IDEAS

For more strategies for generating ideas, see Ch. 15.

For this assignment, you will need to select an issue, take a stand, develop a clear position, and assemble evidence that supports your view.

For more on brainstorming, see pp. 254–56. For more on keeping a journal, see pp. 265–66.

Find an Issue.   The topic for this paper should be an issue or controversy that interests both you and your readers. Try brainstorming a list of possible topics. To get started, look at the headlines of a newspaper or newsmagazine, review the letters to the editor, check the political cartoons on the opinion page, or watch for stories or photos on civic demonstrations or protests. You might also consult the indexes to *CQ Researcher* or *Opposing Viewpoints* in the library, watch a news broadcast, use a search engine to browse on the Web, talk with your friends, or consider topics raised in class. If you keep a journal, look over your entries to see what has perplexed or angered you. If you need to understand the issue better or you aren't sure you want to take a stand on it, investigate by freewriting, reading, or turning to other sources.

Student war protest

Once you have a list of possible topics, drop those that seem too broad or complex or those that you don't know much about. Weed out anything that looks as if it might not hold your interest or that of your readers. From your new, shorter list, pick the issue or controversy for which you think you can make the strongest argument.

For advice on finding a few sources, see B1–B2 in the Quick Research Guide (the dark-red-edged pages).

Start with a Question and a Thesis.   At this stage, many writers find it useful to pose the issue as a question—a question that will be answered through the position they take. Remember that you need to skip vague questions that most readers wouldn't debate or convert them to questions that allow different stands.

VAGUE QUESTION   Is sexism bad?

CLEARLY DEBATABLE   Should we fight sexist stereotypes in advertising?

You can help focus your position by stating it in a sentence — a thesis, or statement of your stand. Your statement can answer your question:

WORKING THESIS   We should expect advertisers to fight rather than reinforce sexist stereotypes.

OR   Most people who object to sexist stereotypes in advertising need to get a sense of humor.

For more on stating a thesis, see pp. 271-77.

Your thesis should invite continued debate, not state a fact, by taking a strong position that could be argued.

FACT   Hispanics constitute 16 percent of the community but only 3 percent of our school population.

WORKING THESIS   Our school should increase its outreach to the Hispanic community, which is currently underrepresented on campus.

Select Evidence to Support Your Position.   As you begin to look for evidence to support your position or claim, consider the issue in terms of the three general types of claims — claims that require substantiation, claims that provide evaluation, and claims that endorse policy.

1. Claims of substantiation require examining and interpreting information in order to resolve disputes about facts, circumstances, causes or effects, definitions, or the extent of a problem, as in these examples:

- Certain types of cigarette ads, such as the once-popular Joe Camel ads, significantly encourage smoking among teenagers.

- Police brutality in this country is not a major problem but a distorted perception based on a few well-publicized exceptions to the rule.

- On the whole, bilingual education programs actually help students learn English faster than total immersion.

2. Claims of evaluation consider right or wrong, appropriateness or inappropriateness, worth or lack of worth involved in issues, as in these instances:

Making a Claim

Have each member of your writing group write out, in one complete sentence, the core claim or position he or she will support. Drop all these "position statements" into a hat, with no names attached. Then, draw and read each aloud in turn. For each position, invite the group to suggest useful supporting evidence, counterevidence, and possible sources for both. Ask the group's recorder to list suggestions on a separate page for each claim. Finally, match up writers with claims, and share reactions. If this activity causes you to alter your stand, be thankful: it will be easier to revise now than later.

FOR GROUP LEARNING

- Research using fetal tissue is unethical in a civilized society.
- English-only legislation promotes cultural intolerance in our society.
- Keeping children in foster care for years, instead of releasing them for adoption, is wrong.

3. Claims of policy challenge or defend approaches for achieving generally agreed-upon goals, as in the following:

- The federal government should support the distribution of clean needles to reduce the rate of HIV infection among intravenous drug users.
- Denying illegal immigrant children enrollment in American public schools will reduce the problem of illegal immigration.
- Underage teenagers accused of murder should be tried as adults.

Consider Your Audience as You Develop Your Claim.   The nature of your audience might influence the type of claim you choose to make. For example, suppose you wish to promote the distribution of free condoms in high school. The following table illustrates how the responses of your audience might vary with your claim.

These three types of claims may also be used as support for a position. Stating supporting claims as supporting points can provide topic sentences to help your reader follow your line of reasoning. Each topic sentence can help readers see one of your subpoints as it introduces supporting examples, statistics, or other evidence.

AUDIENCE	TYPE OF CLAIM	POSSIBLE EFFECT ON AUDIENCE
Conservative parents who believe that free condoms would promote immoral sexual behavior	*Evaluation:* In order to save lives and prevent unwanted pregnancies, distributing free condoms in high school is our moral duty.	Counterproductive if the parents feel that you are accusing them of immorality for not agreeing with you
Conservative parents who believe that free condoms would promote immoral sexual behavior	*Substantiation:* Distributing free condoms in high school can effectively reduce pregnancy rates and the spread of STDs, especially AIDS, without substantially increasing the rate of sexual activity among teenagers.	Possibly persuasive, based on effectiveness, if parents feel that you recognize their desire to protect their children from harm, no matter what, and your evidence deflates their main fear (promoting sexual activity)
School administrators who want to do what's right but don't want hordes of angry parents pounding down the school doors	*Policy:* Distributing free condoms in high school to prevent unwanted pregnancies and the spread of STDs, including AIDS, is best accomplished as part of a voluntary sex education program that strongly emphasizes abstinence as the primary preventative.	Possibly persuasive if administrators see that you address health and pregnancy issues without setting off parental outrage (by proposing a voluntary program that would promote abstinence, thus addressing a primary concern of parents)

Assemble Supporting Evidence.   Your claim stated, you'll need evidence to support it. What is evidence? It is anything that demonstrates the soundness of your position and the points you make in your argument—facts, statistics, observations, expert testimony, illustrations, examples, and case studies.

For more about forms of evidence, see pp. 35–40.

The three most important sources of evidence are these:

1. *Facts, including statistics.*   Facts are statements that can be verified by objective means; statistics are facts expressed in numbers. Facts usually form the basis of a successful argument.
2. *Expert testimony.*   Experts are people with knowledge of a particular field gained from study and experience.
3. *Firsthand observation.*   Your own observations can be persuasive if you can assure your readers that your account is accurate.

For more about using sources, see the Quick Research Guide (the dark-red-edged pages).

Of course, evidence must be used carefully to avoid defending logical fallacies—common mistakes in thinking—and making statements that lead to wrong conclusions.

For more on logical fallacies, see pp. 149–50.

One logical fallacy that often crops up in position papers is the misuse of examples (claiming proof by example or using too few examples). Because two professors you know are dissatisfied with state-mandated testing programs, you can't claim that all or even most professors are. Even if you surveyed more professors at your school, you could speak only generally of "many professors." To claim more, you might need to conduct scientific surveys, access reliable statistics in the library or on the Internet, or solicit the views of a respected expert in the area.

If you are having trouble thinking of types of evidence, consider the following questions:

DISCOVERY CHECKLIST

___ What experiences in your own life have shaped your opinions?

___ What have you observed, or what might you observe, that would support your stand?

___ What expert might you interview?

___ What reading might you do?

___ What precise information do you want to find?

Record Evidence.   For this assignment, you will need to record your evidence in written form. Take notes in a notebook, on index cards, or in a computer file. Be sure to note exactly where each piece of information comes from. Keep the form of your notes flexible so that you can easily rearrange them as you plan your draft.

Test and Select Evidence to Persuade Readers.   Now that you've collected some evidence, you need to sift through it to decide which pieces of

For more on testing evidence, see pp. 37–38.

information to use. Evidence is useful and trustworthy when it is accurate, reliable, up-to-date, to the point, representative, appropriately complex, and sufficient and strong enough to back the claim and persuade your readers. You may find that your evidence supports a stand different from the one you intended to take. Might you find some facts, testimony, and observations that would support your original position after all? Or should you rethink your position? If so, rework your working thesis. Does your evidence cluster around several points or reasons? If so, use your evidence to help plan the sequence of your essay.

■ For more on the use of visuals and their placement, see pp. 363–69.

In addition, consider whether information presented visually would strengthen your case or make your evidence easier for readers to grasp. For example, graphs can effectively show facts or figures, tables can convey terms or comparisons, and photographs or other illustrations can substantiate situations. Test each visual as you would test other evidence to ensure accuracy, reliability, and relevance. Mention each visual in your text, and place the visual close to that text reference. Be sure to cite the source of any visual you use and of any data you consolidate in your own graph or table.

Most effective arguments take opposing viewpoints into consideration whenever possible. Use these questions to help you assess your evidence from this standpoint.

ANALYZE YOUR READERS' POINTS OF VIEW

- What are their attitudes? Interests? Priorities?
- What do they already know about the issue?
- What do they expect you to say?
- Do you have enough appropriate evidence that they will find convincing?

FOCUS ON THOSE WITH DIFFERENT OR OPPOSING OPINIONS

- What are their opinions or claims?
- What is their evidence?
- Who supports their positions?
- Do you have enough appropriate evidence to show why their claims are weak, only partially true, misguided, or just plain wrong?

ACKNOWLEDGE AND REBUT THE COUNTERARGUMENTS

- What are the strengths of other positions? What might you want to concede or grant to be accurate or relevant?
- What are the limitations of other positions? What might you want to question or challenge?
- What facts, statistics, testimony, observations, or other evidence would support questioning, qualifying, challenging, or countering other views?

PLANNING, DRAFTING, AND DEVELOPING

Reassess Your Position and Your Thesis.   Now that you have looked into the issue, what is your current position? If necessary, revise the thesis that you formulated earlier. Then summarize your reasons for holding this view, and list your supporting evidence.

For more on stating a thesis, see pp. 271–77.

WORKING THESIS   We should expect advertisers to fight rather than reinforce sexist stereotypes.

REFINED THESIS   Consumers should spend their shopping dollars thoughtfully in order to hold advertisers accountable for reinforcing rather than resisting sexist stereotypes.

For exercises on choosing effective thesis statements, visit <bedfordstmartins.com/bedguide> and do a keyword search:

thesis

Organize Your Material to Persuade Readers.   Arrange your notes into the order you think you'll follow, perhaps making an outline. One useful pattern is the classical form of argument:

1. Introduce the subject to gain the readers' interest.
2. State your main point or thesis.
3. If useful, supply the historical background or an overview of the situation.
4. Provide evidence to support your points or reasons.
5. Refute the opposition.
6. Reaffirm your main point.

For more on outlines, see pp. 280–87.

Especially when you expect readers to be hostile to your position, you may want to take the opposite approach: refute the opposition first, then replace those views by building a logical chain of evidence that leads to your main point, and finally state your position. If you state your position too early, you might alienate resistant readers or make them defensive. Of course, you can always try both approaches to see which one works better. Note also that some papers will be mostly based on refutation (countering

For exercises on supporting a thesis, visit <bedfordstmartins.com/bedguide> and do a keyword search:

support

As you plan a paper taking a stand, try making three columns to write about your logical, emotional, and ethical appeals. Using the Format menu, select "Columns," and click on the number "3." Begin the first column with the heading "Logical Appeals." Here write the claims and support that rely on reasoning and sound evidence. When you have completed as much as you can in this column, create the next column, generally by going to the Insert menu, clicking on "Break," selecting "Column break," and clicking "OK." Begin your second column with the heading "Emotional Appeals," and note the claims and support that may affect readers' emotions. Now create a third column, headed "Ethical Appeals." Record here the claims and support showing that your beliefs are based on values and that you understand the values of opposing points of view. To move back and forth between columns, simply move your cursor. As you reread each column, consider how to relate your claims and support across columns, how to organize your ideas persuasively, and how best to merge or separate your logical, emotional, and ethical appeals. Try color coding if you want to identify related ideas.

WRITING WITH A COMPUTER

opposing views) and some mostly on confirmation (directly supporting your position). Others might even alternate refutation and confirmation rather than separating them.

Define Your Terms.   To prevent misunderstanding, make clear any unfamiliar or questionable terms used in your thesis. If your position is "Humanists are dangerous," give a short definition of what you mean by *humanists* and by *dangerous* early in the paper.

■ For more on appeals, see pp. 39–40.   **Attend to Logical, Emotional, and Ethical Appeals.**   The logical appeal engages readers' intellect; the emotional appeal touches their hearts; the ethical appeal draws on their sense of fairness and reasonableness. A persuasive argument usually operates on all three levels. For example, you might develop a thesis about the need to curb accidental gunshot deaths, as the following table illustrates.

TYPE OF APPEAL	WAYS OF MAKING THE APPEAL	POSSIBLE SUPPORTING EVIDENCE
Logical (logos)	• Rely on clear reasoning and sound evidence to influence a reader's thinking. • Demonstrate what you claim, and don't claim what you can't demonstrate. • Test and select your evidence.	• Supply current and reliable statistics about gun ownership and accidental shootings. • Prepare a bar graph that shows the number of incidents each year in Lion Valley during the past ten years, using data from the county records. • Describe the immediate and long-term consequences of a typical shooting accident.
Emotional (pathos)	• Choose examples and language that will influence a reader's feelings. • Include effective images, but don't overdo them. • Complement logical appeals, but don't replace them.	• Describe the wrenching scenario of a father whose college-age son unexpectedly returns home at 3 A.M. The father mistakes his son for an intruder and shoots him, throwing the family into turmoil. • Use quotations and descriptions from newspaper accounts to show reactions of family members and neighbors.
Ethical (ethos)	• Use a tone and approach that appeal to your reader's sense of fairness and reasonableness. • Spell out your values and beliefs, and acknowledge values and beliefs of others with different opinions.	• Establish your reasonable approach by acknowledging the views of hunters and others who store guns at home and follow recommended safety procedures. • Supply the credentials or affiliation of experts ("Raymond Fontaine, public safety director for the town of Lion Valley").

(continued on next page)

TYPE OF APPEAL	WAYS OF MAKING THE APPEAL	POSSIBLE SUPPORTING EVIDENCE
Ethical (ethos) *(continued)*	• Establish your credentials, if any, and the credentials of experts you cite. • Instill confidence in your readers so that they see you as a caring, trustworthy person with reliable views.	• Note ways in which experts have established their authority ("During my interview with Ms. Dutton, she related several recent incidents involving gun accidents in the home, testifying to her extensive knowledge of this issue in our community.")

Credit Your Sources.   As you write, make your sources of evidence clear. One simple way to do so is to incorporate your source into the text: "According to an article in the December 10, 2000, issue of *Time*" or "According to my history professor, Dr. Harry Cleghorn..."

▓ For pointers on documenting sources, see D6 and E1–E2 in the Quick Research Guide (the dark-red-edged pages).

REVISING AND EDITING

When you're writing a paper taking a stand, you may be tempted to fall in love with the evidence you've gone to such trouble to collect. Taking out information is hard to do, but if it is irrelevant, redundant, or weak, the evidence won't help your case. Play the crusty critic as you reread your paper. Consider outlining what it actually includes so that you can check for missing or unnecessary points or evidence. Pay special attention to the suggestions of friends or classmates who read your draft for you. Apply their advice by ruthlessly cutting unneeded material, as in the following passage:

▓ For more revising and editing strategies, see Ch. 19.

Enlist several other students to read your draft critically and tell you whether they accept your arguments. For a paper in which you take a stand, ask your peer editors to answer questions such as these:

• Can you state the writer's claim?

• Do you have any problems following or accepting the reasons for the writer's position? Would you make any changes in the reasoning?

• How persuasive is the writer's evidence? What questions do you have about that evidence? Can you suggest some good evidence the writer has overlooked?

• Has the writer provided enough transitions to guide you through the argument?

• Has the writer made a strong case? Are you persuaded to his or her point of view? If not, is there any point or objection that the writer could address to make the argument more compelling?

• If this were your paper, what is the one thing you would be sure to work on before handing it in?

FOR PEER RESPONSE

For general questions for a peer editor, see pp. 328–29.

The school boundary system requires children who are homeless or whose families move frequently to change schools repeatedly. ~~They often lack clean clothes, winter coats, and required school supplies.~~ As a result, these children struggle to establish strong relationships with teachers, to find caring advocates at school, and even to make friends to join for recess or lunch.

As you revise, here are some questions to consider:

REVISION CHECKLIST

___ Is your main point, or thesis, clear? Do you stick to it rather than drifting into contradictions?

___ Does your view convince you? Where might you need better evidence?

___ Have you tried to keep in mind your readers and what would appeal to them? Where have you answered their likely objections?

___ Have you defined all necessary terms and explained your points clearly?

___ Is your tone suitable for your readers? Are you likely at any places to alienate them, or, at the other extreme, to sound weak or apologetic?

___ Might your points seem stronger if arranged in a different sequence?

___ Have you unfairly omitted any evidence that would hurt your case?

___ In rereading your paper, do you have any excellent, fresh thoughts? If so, where might you make room for them?

For more editing and proofreading strategies, see pp. 336–39.

After you have revised your argument, edit and proofread it. Carefully check the grammar, word choice, punctuation, and mechanics — and then correct any problems you find. Wherever you have given facts and figures as evidence, check for errors in names and numbers. This advice may seem trivial, but there's a considerable difference between "10,000 people" and "100,000 people." Here are some questions to get you started editing and proofreading:

EDITING CHECKLIST

For more help, turn to the dark-blue-edged pages, and find the sections of the Quick Editing Guide noted here.

___ Is it clear what each pronoun refers to? Does each pronoun agree with (match) its antecedent? Do pronouns used as subjects agree with their verbs? Carefully check sentences making broad claims about *everyone, no one, some, a few,* or some other group identified by an indefinite pronoun. **A6**

___ Have you used an adjective whenever describing a noun or pronoun? Have you used an adverb whenever describing a verb, adjective, or adverb? Have you used the correct form when comparing two or more things? **A7**

___ Have you set off your transitions, other introductory elements, and interrupters with commas, if these are needed? **C1**

| ____ | Have you spelled and capitalized everything correctly, especially names of people and organizations? | D1, D2 |
| ____ | Have you correctly punctuated quotations from sources and experts? | C3 |

RECOGNIZING LOGICAL FALLACIES

Logical fallacies are common mistakes in thinking that may lead to wrong conclusions or distort evidence. Here are a few of the most familiar logical fallacies.

TERM	EXPLANATION	EXAMPLE
Non Sequitur	Stating a claim that doesn't follow from your first premise or statement; Latin for "It does not follow"	Jenn should marry Mateo. In college he got all As.
Oversimplification	Offering easy solutions for complicated problems	If we want to end substance abuse, let's send every drug user to prison for life. (Even aspirin users?)
Post Hoc Ergo Propter Hoc	Assuming a cause-and-effect relationship where none exists even though one event preceded another; Latin for "after this, therefore because of this"	After Jenny's black cat crossed my path, everything went wrong, and I failed my midterm.
Allness	Stating or implying that something is true of an entire class of things, often using *all, everyone, no one, always,* or *never*	Students enjoy studying. (All students? All subjects? All the time?)
Proof by Example or Too Few Examples	Presenting an example as proof rather than as illustration or clarification; overgeneralizing (the basis of much prejudice)	Armenians are great chefs. My neighbor is Armenian, and can he cook!
Begging the Question	Proving a statement already taken for granted, often by repeating it in different words or by defining a word in terms of itself	Rapists are dangerous because they are menaces. Happiness is the state of being happy.
Circular Reasoning	Supporting a statement with itself; a form of begging the question	He is a liar because he simply isn't telling the truth.
Either/Or Reasoning	Oversimplifying by assuming that an issue has only two sides, a statement must be true or false, a question demands a yes or no answer, or a problem has only two possible solutions (and one that's acceptable)	What are we going to do about acid rain? Either we shut down all the factories that cause it, or we just learn to live with it.

(continued on next page)

TERM	EXPLANATION	EXAMPLE
Argument from Dubious Authority	Using an unidentified authority to shore up a weak argument or an authority whose expertise lies outside the issue, such as a television personality selling insurance	According to some of the most knowing scientists in America, smoking two packs a day is as harmless as eating oatmeal cookies.
Argument *ad Hominem*	Attacking an individual's opinion by attacking his or her character, thus deflecting attention from the merit of a proposal; Latin for "against the man"	Carruthers may argue that we need to save the whales, but he's the type who gets emotional over nothing.
Argument from Ignorance	Maintaining that a claim has to be accepted because it hasn't been disproved or that it has to be rejected because it has not been proved	Despite years of effort, no one has proved that ghosts don't exist; therefore, we should expect to see them at any time. No one has ever shown that life exists on any other planet; clearly the notion of other living things in the universe is absurd.
Argument by Analogy	Treating an extended comparison between familiar and unfamiliar items, based on similarities and ignoring differences, as evidence rather than as a useful way of explaining	People were born free as the birds; it's cruel to expect them to work.
Bandwagon Argument	Suggesting that everyone is joining the group and readers who don't may miss out on happiness, success, or a reward	Purchasing the new Swallowtail admits you to the nation's most elite group of drivers.

OTHER ASSIGNMENTS

1. Write a letter to the editor of your newspaper or a newsmagazine in which you agree or disagree with the publication's editorial stand on a current question or with the recent words or actions of some public figure. Make clear your reasons for holding your view.

2. Write a short paper expressing your view on one of these topics or another that comes to mind. Make clear your reasons for believing as you do.

Bilingual education	Raising the minimum wage
Nonsmokers' rights	Protecting the rainforests
Dealing with date rape	Controlling terrorism
Salaries of professional athletes	Prayer in public schools

3. Write one claim each of substantiation, of evaluation, and of policy for or against censoring pornographic Web sites. Indicate an audience each claim might address effectively. Then list reasons and types of evidence you might need to support one of these claims. Finally, for the same claim, indicate what opposing viewpoints you would need to consider and how you could best do so.

Applying What You Learn: Some Uses of Taking a Stand

In College Courses.   When assignments and examination questions ask you to take a stand on a controversy, your responses indicate clearly to your instructor how firmly you grasp the material.

- In a health-care course, you might be asked to criticize this statement: "There's too much science and not enough caring in modern medicine."

- In a criminal justice course, you might be asked to state and defend your opinion on juvenile sentencing.

- In your research paper for an economics course, you might be asked to take a stand on the state budget allocations in terms of their effects on college tuition.

In the Workplace.   In nearly every professional position — lawyer, teacher, nurse, business manager, journalist — you will be invited to state and support your views for the benefit of others in your profession or the general public.

- Scientists who do original research must persuade the scientific community that their findings are valid, writing and publishing accounts of their work in journals for evaluation by their peers.

- Social workers write documents to persuade courts and other agencies that certain actions or services are best for the welfare of their clients.

- Facing fierce competition, executives must convince their CEO that their ideas will result in impressive benefits for the company.

In Your Community.   As an active citizen, you may feel compelled to inform and influence the public on matters of concern to all.

- You may want to write a letter to the editor of your newspaper or to your political representative debating a controversial issue faced by your community — controlling violence in your schools, funding a new drainage system, enforcing the leash law.

- You may represent the tenants in your apartment building by writing a letter of protest to a landlord who wants to raise rents.

- You may write a letter and design a poster to protest a company's operating and marketing policies.

Chapter 10
Proposing a Solution

If you polluted the air in the 80's,
here's your chance to redeem yourself

Riders wanted.

Responding to an Image

This advertisement appeared as a "spoof ad" on Adbusters, a Web site that advocates a critical eye toward advertisements of all kinds (<www.adbusters.org>). What is the problem posed by the ad? What techniques are used to help viewers understand the problem? What solution does the ad propose? Is this solution realistic and workable? What is the significance of the "Riders wanted" logo, and how does it affect the credibility of the ad's message? Compare this ad to the Volkswagen ad that appears on page 377, noting the similarities and differences between the two images. How does awareness of Volkswagen's advertising help to make this a more effective spoof?

Sometimes when you learn of a problem such as the destruction of the rain forest, homelessness, or famine, you say to yourself, "Something should be done about that." You can do something constructive yourself — through the powerful and persuasive activity of writing.

Your purpose in such writing, as political leaders and advertisers well know, is to rouse your audience to action. Even in your daily life at college, you can write a letter to your college newspaper or to someone in authority and try to stir your readers to action. Does some college policy irk you? Would you urge students to attend a rally for a cause or a charity?

The uses of such writing go far beyond these immediate applications. In Chapter 9, you took a stand and backed it up with evidence. Now go a step further, writing a *proposal* — a recommendation for taking action. If, for instance, you have made the claim "Our national parks are in sorry condition," you might urge readers to act — to write to their representatives in Congress or to visit a national park and pick up trash. On the other hand, you might suggest that the Department of the Interior be given a budget increase to hire more park rangers, purchase additional park land to accommodate more visitors, and buy more cleanup equipment. You might also suggest that the department could raise funds through sales of park videos as well as increased revenues from visitors attracted by the videos. The first paper would be a call to immediate action on the part of your readers; the second, an attempt to forge a consensus about what needs to be done.

Learning from Other Writers

The writers of the following two essays propose sensible solutions for pressing problems. To help you begin to analyze the first reading in this chapter, look for the notes in the margin. They identify features such as the introduction of the problem, the thesis, and the introduction of the proposed solution.

■ For more on thesis and support, see Chs. 16 and 18.

As You Read These Proposals

As you read these essays, ask yourself the following questions:

1. What problem does the writer identify? Does the writer rouse you to want to do something about the problem?
2. What solution does the writer propose? What evidence supports the solution? Does the writer convince you to agree with this solution?
3. How is the writer qualified to write on this subject?

■ For more examples of writing that proposes a solution, visit <bedfordstmartins.com/bedguide> and do a keyword search:

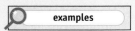

examples

Wilbert Rideau, editor of the Angolite, *the Louisiana State Penitentiary newsmagazine, offers a voice seldom heard in the debate over crime control — that of the criminal.*

Introduction of
the problem

THESIS
stating the problem

Wilbert Rideau
Why Prisons Don't Work

I was among thirty-one murderers sent to the Louisiana State Penitentiary in 1962 to be executed or imprisoned for life. We weren't much different from those we found here, or those who had preceded us. We were unskilled, impulsive, and uneducated misfits, mostly black, who had done dumb, impulsive things — failures, rejects from the larger society. Now a generation has come of age and gone since I've been here, and everything is much the same as I found it. The faces of the prisoners are different, but behind them are the same impulsive, uneducated, unskilled minds that made dumb, impulsive choices that got them into more trouble than they ever thought existed. The vast majority of us are consigned to suffer and die here so politicians can sell the illusion that permanently exiling people to prison will make society safe.

Getting tough has always been a "silver bullet," a quick fix for the crime and violence that society fears. Each year in Louisiana — where excess is a way of life — lawmakers have tried to outdo each other in legislating harsher mandatory penalties and in reducing avenues of release. The only thing to do with criminals, they say, is get tougher. They have. In the process, the purpose of prison began to change. The state boasts one of the highest lockup rates in the country, imposes the most severe penalties in the nation, and vies to execute more criminals per capita than anywhere else. This state is so tough that last year, when prison authorities here wanted to punish an inmate in solitary confinement for an infraction,° the most they could inflict on him was to deprive him of his underwear. It was all he had left.

If getting tough resulted in public safety, Louisiana citizens would be the safest in the nation. They're not. Louisiana has the highest murder rate among states. Prison, like the police and the courts, has a minimal impact on crime because it is a response after the fact, a mop-up operation. It doesn't work. The idea of punishing the few to deter the many is counterfeit because potential criminals either think they're not going to get caught or they're so emotionally desperate or psychologically distressed that they don't care about the consequences of their actions. The threatened punishment, regardless of its severity, is never a factor in the equation. But society, like the incorrigible° criminal it abhors, is unable to learn from its mistakes.

Introduction of the
proposed solution

Prison has a role in public safety, but it is not a cure-all. Its value is limited, and its use should also be limited to what it does best: isolating young criminals long enough to give them a chance to grow up and get a grip on their impulses. It is a traumatic experience, certainly, but it should be only a temporary one, not a way of life. Prisoners kept too long tend to embrace the criminal culture, its distorted values and beliefs; they have little choice — prison is their life. There are some prisoners who cannot be returned to society — serial killers, serial rapists, professional hit men, and the like — but

---

infraction: Violation.   **incorrigible:** Incapable of reform.

the monsters who need to die in prison are rare exceptions in the criminal landscape.

Crime is a young man's game. Most of the nation's random violence is committed by young urban terrorists. But because of long, mandatory sentences, most prisoners here are much older, having spent fifteen, twenty, thirty, or more years behind bars, long past necessity. Rather than pay for new prisons, society would be well served by releasing some of its older prisoners who pose no threat and using the money to catch young street thugs. Warden John Whitley agrees that many older prisoners here could be freed tomorrow with little or no danger to society. Release, however, is governed by law or by politicians, not by penal professionals. Even murderers, those most feared by society, pose little risk. Historically, for example, the domestic staff at Louisiana's Governor's mansion has been made up of murderers, hand-picked to work among the chief-of-state and his family. Penologists° have long known that murder is almost always a once-in-a-lifetime act. The most dangerous criminal is the one who has not yet killed but has a history of escalating offenses. He's the one to watch.

Rehabilitation can work. Everyone changes in time. The trick is to influence the direction that change takes. The problem with prisons is that they don't do more to rehabilitate those confined in them. The convict who enters prison illiterate will probably leave the same way. Most convicts want to be better than they are, but education is not a priority. This prison houses 4,600 men and offers academic training to 240, vocational training to a like number. Perhaps it doesn't matter. About 90 percent of the men here may never leave this prison alive.

The only effective way to curb crime is for society to work to prevent the criminal act in the first place, to come between the perpetrator° and crime. Our youngsters must be taught to respect the humanity of others and to handle disputes without violence. It is essential to educate and equip them with the skills to pursue their life ambitions in a meaningful way. As a community, we must address the adverse life circumstances that spawn criminality. These things are not quick, and they're not easy, but they're effective. Politicians think that's too hard a sell. They want to be on record for doing something now, something they can point to at reelection time. So the drumbeat goes on for more police, more prisons, more of the same failed policies.

Ever see a dog chase its tail?

Transitions (underlined) for coherence

Conclusion summing up solution

Questions to Start You Thinking

Meaning

1. Does Rideau convince you that the belief that "permanently exiling people to prison will make society safe" is an "illusion" (paragraph 1)?

2. According to Rideau, why don't prisons work?

3. What does he propose as solutions to the problem of escalating crime? What other solutions can you think of?

penologist: One who studies prison management and criminal justice.   **perpetrator:** One who is responsible for an action or crime.

Writing Strategies

4. What justifications, if any, for the prison system has Rideau left out of his essay? Do these omissions help or hurt his essay? Why, or why not?

5. What evidence does the author provide to support his assertion that Louisiana's "getting tough" policy has not worked? Does he provide sufficient evidence to convince you? Does he persuade you that action is necessary?

6. What would make Rideau's argument in favor of his proposals more persuasive?

7. Other than himself, what authorities does Rideau cite? Why do you think he does this?

8. Does the fact that the author is a convicted criminal strengthen or weaken his argument? Why do you think he mentions this fact in his very first sentence?

9. How do you interpret the last line, "Ever see a dog chase its tail?" Is this line an effective way for Rideau to end his essay? Explain.

STUDENT ESSAY

Heather Colbenson
Missed Opportunities

Heather Colbenson's proposal, written for a course in agricultural business, addresses a problem she had encountered personally—the lack of funds to support agricultural programs in rural high schools.

❓ *What comparable local problems have you experienced or observed?*

A terrible problem is occurring within some small high schools in Minnesota: the agriculture classes are being reduced or even cut from the curriculum. When agriculture classes are cut, the FFA program is also cut because a student must take an ag class to be in the FFA. At one time the FFA stood for the Future Farmers of America; however, the organization has grown to encompass things other than farming, so it is now called the National FFA Organization, and it has become the largest youth organization in the United States. This is an important organization because it helps students develop leadership skills that they will use to be successful in business and in life. Therefore, the FFA programs in small schools should be saved.

Why would high schools in farming communities drop agriculture classes and the FFA program? One reason is that many colleges require that high school students take specific courses for entry into college. When funding decreases, these courses for college-bound students are seldom cut. Also, students must choose between general education college-prep courses and elective courses such as agriculture. For example, Minnesota colleges now require two years of foreign language. In small schools, like my own, the students could take either foreign language or ag classes. Most students choose the language classes to fulfill the college requirement. When the students leave the ag classes to take foreign language, the ag enrollment declines, making it easy for school administrators to cut ag classes.

The main reason that small schools are cutting ag programs is that the state   3
has not provided significant funding for the schools to operate. When schools have
to make cuts, some decide that the agriculture classes are not as important as other
courses--basic education courses such as English, math, and science and college-
prep courses such as foreign language, calculus, and physics. When there is not
enough money, something has to go, and ag often gets cut.

What are your views about the problem of pitting classes against each other?

If cuts have to be made, why should schools keep their ag courses and the FFA   4
programs? If schools do cut these programs, students lose many opportunities. The
FFA and ag classes are not just about cows and corn; they teach leadership, teamwork, and self-motivation. The FFA provides many different ways for a student to
develop skills in these areas through holding offices, competing in contests, and
making friends.

The main goal of the FFA is leadership development, and one significant benefit   5
of the FFA is the opportunity for high school students to develop leadership skills.
This opportunity is lost if ag classes and FFA organizations are cut in the schools.
Through FFA projects students learn to identify problems, to research solutions,
to formulate plans to solve problems, and to direct and guide other people in
implementing° the plans. Through these activities, they develop self-confidence and
self-motivation. This organization definitely helped me develop leadership and confidence. When an FFA program is cut from a school, a major resource of leadership
development is gone because students may never find out that they can develop
the ability to lead. George Bush, former president of the United States and a former
member of the FFA, praises this organization for its leadership opportunities. If FFA
programs are cut, students may not have other avenues to help them develop these
skills.

Learning teamwork is another benefit of the FFA, and the chance to work as a   6
team is also lost when an ag program is cut. Of course, students learn teamwork
from sports, but what sport has a team that consists of seventy people, as my FFA
did? When FFA programs are cut, students have fewer opportunities to learn to work
cooperatively with other people.

What is "team-work"? Can you provide an example from your own experience?

A third advantage of FFA programs is that students discover that they can com-   7
pete successfully against other students outside of the sports arena. The FFA has
competitions at the local, district, and state levels. If the FFA is cut, a student may
never know the pride of representing his or her school at all these levels and might
never experience the thrill of competing with people from all over the nation at a
national contest.

A fourth advantage is that FFA offers opportunities for students to explore vari-   8
ous careers. FFA activities and competitions deal with livestock, business, sales,

implementing: Putting into effect.

horticulture,° floriculture,° and public speaking. Cutting the program would result in the lost opportunity of trying different possible career areas. I might never have found my desire to be a business major had I not been in the FFA.

A fifth benefit from the FFA is meeting other people. If I had not been in the FFA, one of the greatest losses for me would have been missing the opportunity to meet other people. I gained friends from many different schools and states. Now many of those same friends attend the University of Minnesota with me. The loss of ag classes and an FFA program would result in a lot of missed opportunities for the students. I believe that there is no other student organization that can provide the opportunities the FFA does.

Can you think of another student organization that provides such opportunities?

With all of these benefits from FFA programs for students in small high schools, these programs definitely should be saved. But what can be done to save them? Consolidation° of programs, fundraising, education, and support are all things that can very easily keep a program going strong. First, schools that are having financial trouble can consolidate FFA programs. Small schools that have consolidated have been able to save their ag program, making the chapter stronger and dividing the cost. A second activity that can help the financial situation is local fundraising. This is a great way to keep an FFA program. My chapter sells fruit and raffle tickets every year to raise money. The school doesn't pay for any of the activities. Third, the FFA members themselves must educate the administration, teachers, younger students, and businesspeople of the town as to how the FFA supports and helps students beyond their increased knowledge of agriculture. If these people realize the range of benefits that students receive from the FFA, then they will ensure that the program remains in the local school. Fourth, FFA members must support their own program from within. If even one FFA member says negative things about the FFA, it will hurt the program; people always remember negative things. Instead, members should share their concerns with other members and work within the group to change the situation.

I believe that ag classes and the FFA should remain available for the benefit of students. Small schools do have financial trouble and do have to make cuts, yet the FFA is the wrong place to cut because many students would miss out on opportunities that could very easily change their lives. I want other students to be members of this great organization from which I have benefited so much.

9

10

11

horticulture: The science or art of cultivating plants.   floriculture: The science or art of cultivating flowering plants.   consolidation: The process of merging or uniting separate systems into a whole.

Questions to Start You Thinking

Meaning

1. What problem does Colbenson identify? Does she convince you that this is an important problem? Why, or why not?

2. What solutions does she propose? Which is her strongest suggestion? Her least convincing? Can you think of any other suggestions she might have included?

3. Does Colbenson convince you of the benefits of the FFA program? Does she convince you that these benefits can be gained more readily from involvement in the FFA than in other activities? Why, or why not?

Writing Strategies

4. Is Colbenson's argument easy to follow? Why or why not? What kinds of transitions does she use to lead readers through her points? How effective do you find them?

5. Is her evidence specific and sufficient? Explain.

6. What qualifies Colbenson to write about this topic? How do these qualifications contribute to her ability to persuade?

7. Using highlighters or marginal notes, identify the essay's introduction, thesis, explanation of the problem, proposal to solve the problem, and conclusion. How effective is the organization of this essay?

Learning by Writing

THE ASSIGNMENT: PROPOSING A SOLUTION

In this essay you'll first carefully analyze and explain a specific social, economic, political, civic, or environmental problem—a problem you care about and strongly wish to see resolved. The problem may be large or small, but it shouldn't be trivial. It may affect the whole country or mainly people in your city, campus, or classroom. Show your readers that this problem really exists and that it matters to you and to them. Write for an audience who, once aware of the problem, may be expected to help do something about it. After setting forth the problem, you may want to explain why it exists, as Colbenson does in her essay "Missed Opportunities."

The second thing you are to accomplish in the essay is to propose one or more ways to solve the problem or at least alleviate it. In making a proposal, you urge action by using words like *should, ought,* and *must*: "This city ought to have a Bureau of Missing Persons"; "Small private aircraft should be banned from flying close to a major commercial airport." Lay out all the reasons why your proposal deserves to be implemented, and supply evidence that your solution is reasonable and that it can work. Remember that your purpose is to convince your readers that something should be done about the problem.

■ You can complete each of the steps in this assignment by using the *Writing Guide Software* for THE BEDFORD GUIDE.

Students cogently argued for action in the following papers:

Using research studies and statistics, one student argued that using the scores from standardized tests such as the SAT and the ACT as criteria for college admissions is a problem because it favors aggressive students from affluent families. His proposal was to abolish using the scores in this way.

Another argued that one solution to vacation frustration is to turn everything — planning, choosing a location, arranging transportation, reserving lodging — over to a travel agent.

A third argued that the best solution to the problem of her children's poor education is homeschooling.

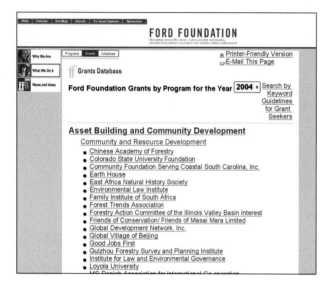

GENERATING IDEAS

Identify a Problem.   Brainstorm by writing down all the possible topics that come to mind. Observe events around you to identify irritating campus or community problems you would like to solve. Watch for ideas as you read the newspaper or listen to the news. Browse through issue-oriented Web sites. Look for sites sponsored by large nonprofit foundations that accept grant proposals and fund innovative solutions to societal issues. Then star the ideas that seem to have the most potential. Here are a few questions to help ideas start flowing:

DISCOVERY CHECKLIST

___ Can you recall any problem that needs a solution? What problems do you meet every day or occasionally? What problems concern people near you?

___ What conditions in need of improvement have you observed on television or in your daily activities? What action is called for?

___ What problems have been discussed recently on campus or in class?

___ What problems are discussed in the newspaper or a newsmagazine such as *Time, Newsweek,* or *U.S. News & World Report?*

For more on brainstorming, see pp. 254–56. For more on imagining, see p. 261.

Think about Solutions.   Once you've chosen a problem, brainstorm — alone or with classmates — for possible solutions, or use your imagination. Some problems, such as reducing international tensions, present no easy

Facing the Challenge: Proposing a Solution

The major challenge writers face when writing a proposal is to develop a detailed and convincing solution. Finding solutions is much harder than finding problems. Convincing readers that you have found a reasonable, workable solution is harder still. For example, suppose you propose the combination of a rigorous exercise program and a low-fat diet as a solution for obesity. While these solutions seem reasonable and workable to you, readers who have lost weight and then gained it back might point out that their main problem is not losing weight but maintaining weight loss over time. To account for their concerns and enhance your credibility, you might revise your solution to focus on realistic long-term goals and strategies for sticking to an exercise program. For instance, you might recommend that friends join a health club together to encourage each other to participate or that they walk together two or three times a week.

To develop a realistic solution that fully addresses a problem and satisfies the concerns of readers, consider questions such as these:

- How might the problem affect different groups of people?
- What range of concerns are your readers likely to have?
- What realistic solution addresses the concerns of readers about *all* aspects of the problem?

■ For writing activities for proposing a solution, visit <bedfordstmartins.com/bedguide> and do a keyword search:

activities

solutions. Still, give some thought to any problem that seriously concerns you, even if it has thwarted teams of experts. Sometimes a solution will reveal itself to a novice thinker, and even a small contribution to a partial solution is worth offering. You can use several strategies to think about problems and solutions:

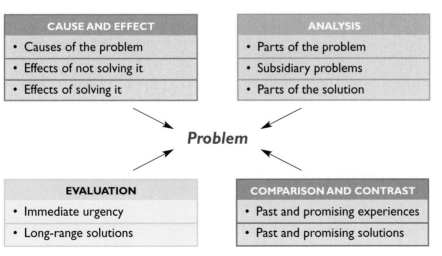

CAUSE AND EFFECT
- Causes of the problem
- Effects of not solving it
- Effects of solving it

ANALYSIS
- Parts of the problem
- Subsidiary problems
- Parts of the solution

Problem

EVALUATION
- Immediate urgency
- Long-range solutions

COMPARISON AND CONTRAST
- Past and promising experiences
- Past and promising solutions

▨ For more on causes and effects, see Ch. 8 and pp. 320–27. For more on analysis, see pp. 311–13.

▨ For more on comparison and contrast, see Ch. 7 and pp. 318–20. For more on evaluation, see Ch. 11.

Consider Your Readers.   Readers need to believe that your problem is real and your solution is feasible. If you are addressing your classmates, maybe they haven't thought about the problem before. Try to discover ways to make it personal for them, to show that it affects them and deserves their attention. Here are some questions to ask yourself about your readers:

- Who are your readers? How would you describe them?

- Why should your readers care about this problem? Does it affect their health, welfare, conscience, or pocketbook?

- Have they ever expressed any interest in the problem? If so, what has triggered their interest?

- Do they belong to any organization or segment of society that makes them especially susceptible to — or uninterested in — this problem?

- What attitudes about the problem do you share with your readers? Which of their assumptions or values that differ from yours will affect how they view your proposal?

■ For more on evidence, see Ch. 3. For more on using evidence to support an argument, see pp. 141–44.

Consider Sources of Support.   To show that the problem really exists, you'll need evidence and examples. If you feel that further research in the library will help you know more about the problem, now is the time to do it. In addition, previous efforts to solve the problem may help you develop your solution. Consider whether local history archives, past newspaper stories or photographs, accounts of public meetings, interviews with others, or Web sites sponsored by interested organizations might raise concerns of readers or practical limitations of solutions.

■ For advice on finding a few sources, see A and B in the Quick Research Guide (the dark-red-edged pages).

PLANNING, DRAFTING, AND DEVELOPING

■ For more on stating a thesis, see pp. 271–77. For strategies for planning, drafting, and developing, see Chs. 16, 17, and 18.

Start with Your Proposal and Your Thesis.   A basic approach is to state your proposal in a sentence that can act as your thesis.

PROPOSAL	Let people get divorced without going to court.
WORKING THESIS	The legislature should pass a law allowing couples to divorce without having to go to court.

From such a statement, the rest of the argument may start to unfold, often falling naturally into a simple two-part shape:

1. *A claim that a problem exists.* This part explains the problem and supplies evidence of its significance — for example, the costs, adversarial process, and stress of divorce court for a couple and their family.
2. *A claim that something ought to be done about it.* This part proposes a solution to the problem — for example, legislative action to authorize other options such as mediation.

You can make your proposal more persuasive by including some or all of the following elements:

■ For exercises on choosing effective thesis statements, visit <bedfordstmartins.com/bedguide> and do a keyword search:

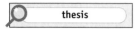
thesis

Knowledge or experience that qualifies you to propose a solution (your experience as a player or a coach, for example, that establishes your credibility as an authority on Little League)

Values, beliefs, or assumptions that have caused you to feel strongly about the need for action

An estimate of the resources — money, people, skills, material — required to implement the solution (perhaps including what is readily available now and what needs to be obtained)

Step-by-step actions that need to be taken to achieve your solution

An estimate of the time needed to implement the solution

Possible obstacles or difficulties that may need to be overcome

Reasons your solution is better than others proposed or tried already

Controls or quality checks to monitor implementing your solution

Any other evidence that shows that your suggestion is practical, reasonable in cost, and likely to be effective

For exercises on supporting a thesis, visit <bedfordstmartins.com/bedguide> and do a keyword search:

Organize with an Outline.   Following is the informal outline that Heather Colbenson used as she wrote her essay "Missed Opportunities." Note the kinds of evidence she chose to include and the order she chose for organizing that evidence.

For more on outlines, see pp. 280–87.

THESIS: FFA PROGRAMS IN SMALL SCHOOLS SHOULD BE SAVED.
1. Reasons FFA programs are being cut
   –College requirements
   –Decreased funds
2. Reasons FFA programs should not be cut: benefits of FFA
   –Leadership training
   –Teamwork
   –Competition
   –Career exploration
   –Meeting people
3. Suggestions for saving FFA programs
   –Consolidation
   –Fundraising
   –Education
   –Support from within

You can increase the likelihood that readers will accept your proposal in two ways. First, state your proposal by claiming that a problem exists. Then, when you turn to your claim that something should be done, begin with a simple and inviting suggestion. For example, a claim that national parks need better care might begin by suggesting that readers head for such a park and personally size up the situation.

WRITING WITH A COMPUTER

To propose a solution persuasively, you must show that you understand a problem well enough to suggest solutions while addressing specific audience needs. Considering these ideas in columns can help you see them differently than you do as you write. After drafting your ideas in one file, open a new file, go to the Format menu and choose "Columns," and then click on "3." Label the first column "Problems," the second column "Solutions," and the third "Readers' Objections." Now return to your draft file, using it to copy and paste your ideas into the appropriate column in your new file. Add points as needed so that you move logically from problem to solution and answer readers' objections point by point. Now return again to your draft to reorder and develop your points more effectively.

Imagine Your Readers' Objections.   Perhaps you can think of objections your readers might raise — reservations about the high cost, the complexity, or the workability of your plan, for instance. You can persuade your readers by anticipating an objection that might occur to them and laying it to rest.

For pointers on integrating and documenting sources, see D6 and E1–E2 in the Quick Research Guide (the dark-red-edged pages).

Cite Sources Carefully.   When you collect ideas and evidence from outside sources, you need to document your evidence — that is, tell where you found everything. Check with your instructor on the documentation method he or she wants you to use. You may also want to identify sources as you introduce them to assure a reader that they are authoritative.

According to Newsweek correspondent Josie Fair, . . .

In his biography FDR: The New Deal Years, Davis reports . . .

While working as a Senate page in the summer of 1999, I observed . . .

For more advice about integrating visuals, see pp. 363–69.

You can introduce a table, graph, drawing, map, photograph, or other visual evidence in much the same way.

As the 2000 census figures in Table 1 indicate, . . .

The photograph illustrating the run-down condition of the dog park (see Fig. 2) . . .

REVISING AND EDITING

For more revising and editing strategies, see Ch. 19.

As you revise, concentrate on a clear explanation of the problem and solid supporting evidence for the solution. Keep your purpose of convincing your readers uppermost in your thoughts. Be sure to make your essay coherent and its parts clear for your readers.

Clarify Your Thesis.   Your readers are likely to rely on your thesis to identify the problem and possibly to preview your solution. Look again at your
thesis from a reader's point of view.

For more on stating a thesis, see pp. 271–77.

WORKING THESIS   The legislature should pass a law allowing couples to
divorce without having to go to court.

REVISED THESIS   Because divorce court can be expensive, adversarial, and
stressful, passing a law that allows couples to divorce
without a trip to court would encourage simpler and
more harmonious ways of ending a marriage.

Reorganize for Unity and Coherence.   In drafting her essay, Heather
Colbenson had problems with organization and coherence. As she revised
paragraphs 2 and 3 from her first draft, she tackled these problems by setting
three priorities: (1) identify the two primary reasons for cutting FFA programs more clearly for readers, (2) place the main reason (decreased funds)
last for emphasis, and (3) rework her discussion of course options to focus
on courses pitted against each other, college requirements. She also discovered that part of her solution—school consolidations—had crept into her
problem section, so she decided to move that point to later in her essay.

For Heather Colben-son's revised version, see pp. 156–58.

Why would high schools in farming communities drop agriculture classes and the

The main reason that   is that

FFA program? ʌSmall schools are cutting ag programs ~~because~~ the state has not pro-

vided significant funding for the schools to operate. The small schools have to make

cuts, and some small schools are deciding that the agriculture classes are not as im-

portant as other courses. Some small schools are consolidating to receive more aid.

Many of these schools have been able to save their ag program.

— *Move last for emphasis*

Why did I put a solution here? Move to end!

One reason is that m

ʌMany colleges are demanding that students have two years of foreign language.

In small schools, like my own, the students could take either foreign language or ag

classes. Therefore, students choose language classes to fill the college requirement.

When the students leave the ag classes to take foreign language, the number of stu-

dents declines, which makes it easier for school administrators to cut ag classes.

Rewrite this! Not really college require-ments but college-prep courses vs. others when budget is tight

Her revised paper was more forcefully organized and more coherent,
making it easier for readers to follow. The bridges between ideas were now
on paper, not just in her mind. Colbenson also eliminated unnecessary
words and generally improved the paper's style and precision of expression.

For strategies for achieving coherence see pp. 300–03.

Exchanging Written Reactions

Exchange proposals with another student, and read each other's draft. Then take turns sharing first reactions — positive as well as negative. After this exchange, take your partner's draft home for a day or two. Before your next meeting, write a review letter to your partner in which you thoughtfully critique the draft and suggest revisions. (To help the writer, mark the draft as you comment, pointing out any problems with the organization, thesis, support, and so forth.) Exchange letters during your next meeting, and discuss your experiences. What did you learn about proposing solutions? About writing? About peer editing?

Be Reasonable.   Exaggerated claims for your solution will not persuade your readers. Neither will oversimplifying the problem so that the solution seems more likely to apply. Don't be afraid to express your own reasonable doubts about the completeness of your solution. If necessary, rethink both the problem and the solution.

For more on errors in reasoning, see pp. 149–50.

In looking back over your draft once more, consider these questions:

REVISION CHECKLIST

___ Does your introduction invite the reader into the discussion?

___ Is your problem clear? How have you made it relevant to readers?

___ Have you clearly outlined the steps necessary to solve the problem?

___ Where have you demonstrated the benefits of your solution?

___ Have you considered other solutions before rejecting them for your own?

___ Have you anticipated the doubts readers may have about your solution?

___ Do you come across as a well-meaning, reasonable writer willing to admit that you don't know everything? If you sound preachy, have you overused *should* and *must*?

___ Have you avoided promising that your solution will do more than it can possibly do? Have you made believable predictions for its success?

For more editing and proofreading strategies, see pp. 336–39. For more on documenting sources, see E1–E2 in the Quick Research Guide (the dark-red-edged pages).

After you have revised your proposal, edit and proofread it. Carefully check the grammar, word choice, punctuation, and mechanics — and then correct any problems you find. If you have used sources, be sure that you have cited them correctly in your text and added a list of works cited.

Make sure your sentence structure helps you make your points clearly and directly. Don't let yourself slip into the passive voice, a grammatical construction that represents things as happening without any obvious agent: "The problem should be remedied by spending more money on prevention." Instead, every sentence should specify who should take action: "The dean of students should remedy the problem by spending more money on prevention."

Ask several classmates or friends to review your proposal and solution, answering questions such as these:

- What is your overall reaction to this proposal? Does it make you want to go out and do something about the problem?

- Are you convinced that the problem is of concern to you? If not, why not?

- Are you persuaded that the writer's solution is workable?

- Has the writer paid enough attention to readers and their concerns?

- Restate what you understand to be the proposal's major points:

  Problem
  Explanation of problem
  Proposal
  Explanation of proposal
  Procedure to implement proposal
  Advantages and disadvantages
  Response to other solutions
  Final recommendation

- If this were your paper, what is the one thing you would be sure to work on before handing it in?

FOR PEER RESPONSE

For general questions for a peer editor, see pp. 328–29.

Here are some questions to get you started editing and proofreading:

EDITING CHECKLIST

___ Is it clear what each pronoun refers to? Is any *this* or *that* ambiguous? Does each pronoun agree with (match) its antecedent?	A6
___ Is your sentence structure correct? Have you avoided writing fragments, comma splices, or fused sentences?	A1, A2
___ Do your transitions and other introductory elements have commas after them, if these are needed?	C1
___ Have you spelled and capitalized everything correctly, especially names of people and organizations?	D1, D2

For more help, turn to the dark-blue-edged pages, and find the sections of the Quick Editing Guide noted here.

OTHER ASSIGNMENTS

1. If you followed the assignment in Chapter 9 and took a stand, now write a few paragraphs extending that paper, going on to propose a solution that argues for action. You may find it helpful to brainstorm with classmates first.

2. Write a memo to your supervisor at work in which you propose an innovation (related to procedures, schedules, policies, or similar matters) that could benefit your department or company.

3. Choose from the following list a practice that seems to you to be an in-efficient, unethical, unfair, or morally wrong solution to a problem. In a few paragraphs, give reasons for your objections. Then propose a better solution:

Censorship	Genetic engineering
Corporal punishment for children	Outsourcing jobs
Laboratory experiments on animals	Dumping wastes in the ocean

Applying What You Learn: Some Uses of Proposals

In College Courses.   In many courses, writing a proposal will be re-quired, often a plan to be approved before implementation.

- Students embarking on a research project may be required to submit to an adviser or a committee a proposal that sets forth what they intend to investigate and how they will conduct their study.

- In social science courses, you may examine a current issue and propose a solution to the disclosure of adoption records, the rising costs of pre-scription drugs, prison overcrowding, or racial profiling.

- Students who object to a grade can file a grievance proposing a grade change. Like writers of persuasive essays, they state a claim and supply evidence in support of it.

In the Workplace.   Proposals often suggest new projects, recommend purchases or changes in procedure, and solve personnel problems.

- After gathering comments from workers and financial analyses, the human resources office prepares proposals outlining benefits such as medical and dental insurance.

- When a company decides to build or renovate a building, the ar-chitect submits a proposal outlining the plans, and then contrac-tors submit bids, proposing to complete the work for a certain cost.

- Every job application is a proposal. Applicants propose that an employer hire them and support that proposal by selecting the best possible evidence for their résumés and letters or applica-tions.

In the Spotlight
Companies are recognizing that providing benefits to low-wage employees—stretched thin by the demands of work and life—can yield big returns. [more]

From Ford Foundation Web site

In Your Community.   Every day we encounter proposals for solu-tions—in editorials, in books, in public service announcements, in political debate.

- You might write to the board proposing that your congregation begin a building fund to expand your overcrowded fellowship hall. Your proposal would include evidence of the need for more space, the cost of the addition, ways of raising the money, and a time frame for completion.

- In a speech to your local service club, you might inform them about the drop-out rate at your local high school and propose that members donate their time to work with at-risk teens.

- Alarmed by the low literacy rate of many adults in your community, you propose a tutoring program to the library and design posters to promote the effort.

Chapter 11
Evaluating

Lou Beach

Responding to an Image

This image originally appeared on the cover of an issue of *Utne,* next to these lines promoting a featured article: "Clear your head. Too many choices? How to make up your mind without losing it." What does this image suggest about decision making, a critical step in evaluation? How does the image guide a viewer's eye to its focal point? What details contribute to the overall impression it conveys? In what ways does it reflect the feelings of writers and others who must repeatedly make and present thoughtful choices? In your journal, notebook, or laptop, record your responses—as a writer—to this image.

Evaluating means judging. You do it when you decide what candidate to vote for, pick which camera to buy, or recommend a new restaurant to your friends. All of us pass judgments — often snap judgments — as we move through a day's routine. A friend asks, "How was that movie you saw last night?" and you reply, "Terrific — don't miss it" or maybe "Pretty good, but it had too much blood and gore for me."

But to *write* an evaluation calls for you to think more critically. As a writer you first decide on *criteria*, or standards for judging, and then come up with evidence to back up your judgment. Your evaluation zeroes in on a definite subject that you inspect carefully in order to reach a considered opinion. The subject might be a film, a book, a sports team, a group of performers, a product, a body of research: the possibilities are endless.

Learning from Other Writers

Here are evaluations by a professional writer and by a student. To help you begin to analyze the first reading in this chapter, look for the notes in the margin. They identify features such as the thesis, the criteria for evaluation, and the evidence supporting the writer's judgment, all typical of essays that evaluate.

For more on thesis and support, see Chs. 16 and 18.

For more examples of evaluative writing, visit <bedfordstmartins.com/ bedguide> and do a keyword search:

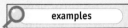

examples

As You Read These Evaluations

As you read these essays, ask yourself the following questions:

1. Do you consider the writer qualified to evaluate the subject he or she chose? What biases and prejudices might the writer bring to the evaluation?

2. What criteria for evaluation does the writer establish? Are these reasonable standards for evaluating the subject?

3. What is the writer's assessment of the subject? Does the writer provide sufficient evidence to convince you of his or her evaluation?

Robert Hartwell Fiske
Don't Look It Up! The Decline of the Dictionary

Merriam-Webster's Collegiate Dictionary *Eleventh Edition,* **edited by** *Frederick C. Mish, et al.*

Robert Hartwell Fiske regularly comments on contemporary language usage at his Web site, www .vocabula.com, home of the online Vocabula Review. *Here he reviews the newest edition of a popular dictionary.*

This new slang-filled edition of the *Merriam-Webster's Collegiate Dictionary* does as much as, if not more than, the famously derided° *Webster's Third International Dictionary* to discourage people from taking lexicographers° seriously. "Laxicographers" all, the Merriam-Webster staff remind us that

Introduction presenting overall judgment

derided: Ridiculed.   **lexicographers:** Dictionary authors.

dictionaries merely record how people use the language, not necessarily how it ought to be used. Some dictionaries, and certainly this new *Merriam-Webster*, actually promote illiteracy.

Several years ago, the editors of *The American Heritage Dictionary* caused 2 a stir by deciding to include four-letter words in their product. Since the marketing strategy of including swear words has not been adopted by all dictionary makers, Merriam-Webster, apparently not knowing how else to distinguish its dictionary from competing ones, has decided to include slang words in its eleventh edition. There's nothing wrong with trying to distinguish their product, of course, but when it means tampering with the English language — by including idiotic slang and omitting infinitely more useful words — it's reprehensible.

THESIS
presenting judgment

Merriam-Webster proclaims it has added some ten thousand words to 3 its *Collegiate Dictionary*. To do so, as a company spokesman admitted, "some words had to be kicked out" of the earlier edition. More interesting than this new edition would be a book of the words abandoned. Were they ses-quipedalian° words that few people use or know the meaning of, or even disyllabic° words that few people use or know the meaning of? For it's quite true that Americans are increasingly monosyllabic;° many people cannot even manage to say "disparage" or "disrespect" or "insult," so enamored° are they of the repugnant° "dis" (included in the *Collegiate* tenth and eleventh).

Introduction to criteria

What word did Merriam-Webster decide to omit to make room for "fun-4 plex" (an entertainment complex that includes facilities for various sports and games and often restaurants)? What word did they omit in order to add "McJob" (a low-paying job that requires little skill and provides little oppor-tunity for advancement)? What words did they omit in order to add "head-banger" (a musician who performs hard rock), "dead presidents" (United States currency in the form of paper bills), and "Frankenfood" (genetically engineered food)? Frankly, I rather like the coinage "Frankenfood." But if people do not enjoy or feel comfortable eating genetically altered foods, which I suspect is likely, the word will be fleeting.

Supporting evidence

Almost all slang, the people at Merriam-Webster should know, is 5 ephemeral.° Most of the slang added to the eleventh edition will never see the twelfth — or at least ought not to. The editors at Merriam-Webster, though, seem altogether perverse in their insistence on welcoming and then holding on to silly slang. Several editions ago, they added the term "far-out," and they have yet to remove it — even though almost no one (certainly no one I know) uses the word today.

As most people know by now, dictionary makers today merely record 6 how the language is used, not how the language ought to be used. That is, lexicographers are descriptivists, language liberals. People using "disinter-ested" when they mean "uninterested" does not displease a descriptivist.

Introduction to contrast

A prescriptivist, <u>by contrast</u>, is a language conservative, a person inter-7 ested in maintaining standards and correctness in language use. To prescrip-

Transitions (underlined)
for coherence

sesquipedalian: Long; having many syllables.   disyllabic: Having two syllables.
monosyllabic: Having one syllable.   enamored: In love with.   repugnant: Disgust-ing.   Ephemeral: Short-lived, temporary.

tivists, "disinterested" in the sense of "uninterested" is the result of uneducated people not knowing the distinction between the two words. <u>And</u> if
there are enough uneducated people saying "disinterested" (and I'm afraid
there are) when they mean "uninterested" or "indifferent," lexicographers
enter the definition into their dictionaries. <u>Indeed</u>, the distinction between
these words has all but vanished owing largely to irresponsible writers and
boneless lexicographers.

Transitions (underlined) for coherence

Words, we are told, with the most citations are included in Merriam- 8
Webster dictionaries. Are then words with the fewest omitted, or in danger
of being omitted? The *Merriam-Webster's Collegiate Dictionary* includes "alright," but what word was "kicked out" so that an inanity,° an illiteracy like
"alright" could be kept in? All it seems to take for a solecism° to become
standard English is people misusing or misspelling the word. And if enough
people do so, lexicographers will enter the originally misused or misspelled
word into their dictionaries, and descriptive linguists° will embrace it as a
further example of the evolution of English.

Repetition of word for effect

Merriam-Webster's laxicographers, further disaffecting careful writers and 9
speakers, assign the meaning "reluctant" to the definition of "reticent." "Reticent" means disinclined to speak; taciturn; quiet. "Reluctant" means disinclined to do something; unwilling; loath. Because some people mistakenly
use "reticent" to mean "reluctant," dictionaries now maintain "reticent" does
mean "reluctant." There are other examples of Merriam-Webster's inexcusably
shoddy° dictionary-making. According to the dictionary's editors, the spelling
"accidently" is as valid as "accidentally"; the verb "predominate" is also an adjective meaning "predominant"; "enormity" means the same as "enormous-
ness"; "infer" means the same as "imply"; and "peruse" means not only to
examine carefully but to read over in a casual manner. The *Merriam-Webster's
Collegiate Dictionary* actually promotes the misuse of the English language.

Of course, it's in the financial interest of dictionary makers to record the 10
least defensible of usages in the English language, for without ever-changing
definitions — or as they would say, an evolving language — there would be
less need for people to buy later editions of their product.

A few months ago (before the new edition of the *Merriam-Webster Colle-* 11
giate was published), I took a poll of *Vocabula Review* readers and discovered
that 68 percent of the respondents rejected the strong descriptivist° idea of
dictionary-making, and only 4 percent would necessarily bow to the definitions and spellings found in the dictionary. More than that, though, the new
Merriam-Webster is a sign that dictionaries, at least, as they are now being
compiled, have outlived their usefulness. Dictionaries are no longer sacrosanct,° no longer sources of unimpeachable° information. Dictionaries are,
indeed, no longer to be trusted.

Conclusion

---

inanity: Something that is shallow or silly.   **solecism:** An error or mistake.   **lin-
guists:** Those who study language.   **shoddy:** Careless, substandard.   **descriptivist:**
Describing what something *is,* as opposed to prescribing what it *should be.*   **sacrosanct:**
Sacred.   **unimpeachable:** Flawless, above criticism.

Questions to Start You Thinking

Meaning

1. In Fiske's view, how does the new *Merriam-Webster's Collegiate Dictionary* promote illiteracy?

2. In paragraph 7, why does Fiske use the term "boneless lexicographers"?

3. In paragraph 10, what reason does Fiske provide for the "ever-changing" definitions in dictionaries? Does his reason seem logical to you? Why, or why not?

Writing Strategies

4. What is Fiske's overall judgment of the dictionary, and what criteria does he use to make this judgment?

5. In your view, how well does he support his judgment? Point to some specific examples in making your case.

6. Where does Fiske use comparison and contrast to make his point? How effective is this strategy?

7. Who is the intended audience for this essay? How can you tell?

8. How would you describe Fiske's tone, the quality of his writing that reveals his attitude toward his topic and his readers? What specific words, phrases, or sentences contribute to his tone? Does this tone seem appropriate for his purpose and audience?

STUDENT ESSAY

Theresa H. Nguyen
Antiterrorist Law Violates Civil Rights

Writing this opinion piece in November 2002 for the Yale Herald, *Theresa H. Nguyen evaluates the USA PATRIOT Act passed shortly after the September 11 terrorist attacks.*

What other reactions to this act do you recall?

On Wednesday, November 13, a special federal appeals court gave the Justice Department broad new power to use wiretaps for intelligence investigations. The court's ruling came under the deceptively titled Uniting and Strengthening America by Providing Appropriate Tools Required to Intercept and Obstruct Terrorism Act (USA PATRIOT Act), passed just over a year ago. This piece of legislation dramatically changed the legal structure within which law enforcement and foreign intelligence agencies operate, allowing significant expansion of surveillance° and information-gathering power in response to the September 11 terrorist attacks. However, considerable bipartisan° concern regarding the act's ineffectiveness in combating terrorism, its reliance on executive command rather than congressional and judicial oversight, and, most important, its infringements° on individual civil liberties, have

surveillance: Watching, monitoring.   **bipartisan:** Pertaining to both major political parties (Republicans and Democrats).   **infringements:** Trespasses on a right or privilege.

proved this act unworthy for a nation that claims personal liberty as a founding principle.

National policy has hitherto° separated domestic criminal investigations from the collection of foreign intelligence, as the requirements for obtaining a wiretap for intelligence-gathering are more lax than the strict standards required to wiretap in a criminal investigation. In their decision, the judges affirmed Attorney General John Ashcroft's assertion that the USA PATRIOT Act eliminates any distinction between the foreign and domestic sides of national security operations, going further to declare that this separation was never required or intended by Congress. "Effective counter-intelligence,"° the panel wrote, "requires the wholehearted cooperation of all the government's personnel who can be brought to the task." The USA PATRIOT Act facilitates this cooperation by removing barriers that also serve as significant safeguards to American liberty.

Section 203 of the USA PATRIOT Act allows information obtained through confidential grand jury proceedings and criminal investigations to be disclosed to "any federal law enforcement, intelligence, protective, immigration, national defense, or national security official" when it involves "foreign intelligence or counterintelligence . . . or foreign intelligence information." These terms are not only vague but also expose law-abiding citizens to government intrusion and exploitation.°

Section 206 of the act allows for a roaming wiretap that permits "roving authority" to intercept communications without distinction of the specific computer or cellular device. This authority allows the government to tap all devices within a given area if the target of investigation is suspected to be within that area, violating the fourth amendment guarantee that search warrants "particularly describe the place to be searched." Where the private communications of law-abiding individuals are incidental° interception becomes a matter of distress.

Section 218 of the act requires that foreign intelligence gathering be only a "significant purpose" of an investigation, rather than the former requirement that it be "the purpose." With the addition of ambiguous° terminology like this, the opportunity for privacy intrusions, surveillance, and monitoring becomes increasingly ominous.

The legislative proposals that provided the basis for the USA PATRIOT Act were introduced in Congress within a week of the terrorist attacks, passing through both houses with minimal discussion, criticism, and debate. Acting under extreme pressure from Attorney General John Ashcroft and the Bush administration and in a national climate of fear, uncertainty, emotion, and mounting patriotism, Congress members voted on the act even before the finalized text of the bill was available for assessment.

hitherto: Until now.   **counterintelligence:** Means taken to gather information about those with opposing views or interests.   **exploitation:** The unjust use of something. **incidental:** Accidental.   **ambiguous:** Vague, poorly defined.

Nor have the media provided the necessary scrutiny.° An informed citizenry is   7
essential to democracy, and the media are the primary means by which American citizens obtain information about new laws. Through thorough political discourse,° the
public holds its government accountable. Yet in the months immediately following
the September 11 attacks, news coverage, while heavy in terms of quantity, lacked
journalistic quality in regard to breadth and completeness. Media inquiry has been
overwhelmingly deficient, promoting a jingoistic° national atmosphere that discourages dissent.° In order to remain consistent with the popular public sentiment of
patriotism, little was said in opposition to the USA PATRIOT Act. Indeed, even a
year after its passage, most Americans are not even aware of its existence or know of
the act simply as "anti-terrorism" legislation. The implication, for both legislators
and citizens, is that dissent is unpatriotic. Thus, the act persists in a country in
which national security is the premium, and to these ends, some sacrifice of liberty
is acceptable.

*How do you view
dissent and patriotism?*

However, war does not legitimize disregarding the Bill of Rights and other con   8
stitutional provisions that limit the powers of the government. Our history reveals a
fallible° nation prone to imprudent° legislation in times of war: the Alien and Sedition Acts, the suspension of habeas corpus° during the Civil War, the internment° of
Japanese Americans during World War II, the McCarthy-era witch-hunt of supposed
Communist sympathizers, and the Church Committee's surveillance and harassment of
Dr. Martin Luther King Jr. In his majority opinion for *Kennedy v. Mendoza Martinez,* a
Supreme Court case involving draft evasion, Justice Arthur Goldberg wrote, "It is
fundamental that the great powers of Congress to conduct war and to regulate the
nation's foreign relations are subject to the constitutional requirements of due
process.° The imperative necessity for safeguarding these rights to procedural due
process under the gravest of emergencies has existed throughout our constitutional
history, for it is then, under the pressing exigencies° of crisis, that there is the
greatest temptation to dispense with fundamental constitutional guarantees, which,
it is feared, will inhibit governmental action."

The Supreme Court has asserted the fundamental right to privacy, although this   9
right is not explicit in the Constitution. Despite such judicial precedent, the USA PA
TROIT Act flaunts° this right. Expansion of governmental surveillance and information-

scrutiny: Close study or evaluation.   **discourse:** Discussion.   **jingoistic:** Devoted to
a national stance or cause to such an extent that other views are not tolerated. **dissent:**
Disagreement.   **fallible:** Given   to   making   mistakes.   **imprudent:** Incautious.
habeas corpus: A legislative order aimed at preventing unlawful imprisonment.   **internment:** Imprisonment.   **due process:** Legal processes and safeguards to which all
are entitled under the law.   **exigencies:** Needs or demands.   **flaunts:** Disregards,
disrespects.

gathering powers affects all United States residents, not just the terrorists for whom it is intended.

Congressional oversight of the USA PATRIOT Act is limited to a sunset provision   10 mandating the expiration of many sections of the act. However, while it applies to the expanded powers of the surveillance authorities, it does not apply to many other controversial provisions, including the aforementioned section allowing the sharing of grand jury information with intelligence agencies. Such legislative oversight is integral° to monitoring the implementation of new legislation, and to prevent abuses by the executive. In a case concerning jurisdiction of military courts over civilians, the court ruled, "If society is disturbed by civil commotion--if the passions of men are aroused and the restraints of law weakened, if not disregarded--these safeguards need, and should receive, the watchful care of those entrusted with the guardianship of the Constitution and laws. In no other way can we transmit to posterity° unimpaired the blessings of liberty, consecrated° by the sacrifices of the Revolution."

Without a doubt, such passions have been stirred in the war on terrorism, and   11 likewise, Congress and the judiciary must be called upon to exert governmental checks and balances, prevent abuses, and provide the necessary guardianship of privacy rights to ensure the protection of our liberties.

Do you agree with the writer's judgment? Why, or why not?

Questions to Start You Thinking

Meaning

1. Why, in Nguyen's view, is the USA PATRIOT Act "unworthy for a nation that claims personal liberty as a founding principle" (paragraph 1)? What evidence does she use to back this view?

2. Why, according to Nguyen, has there been minimal debate about or criticism of the act?

3. Based on her evaluation, what does Nguyen recommend?

Writing Strategies

4. What criteria does Nguyen use to judge the PATRIOT Act? What criteria might she be overlooking?

5. Based on her criteria, do you find her evaluation of the act persuasive? Why, or why not?

6. Would the addition of other types of sources or viewpoints enrich her analysis? If so, what additions would you suggest?

7. Using highlighters or marginal notes, identify the essay's introduction, thesis, criteria for evaluation, supporting evidence, and conclusion. How effective is the organization of this essay?

integral: Essential.   **posterity:** Future generations.   **consecrated:** Made sacred.

Learning by Writing

THE ASSIGNMENT: WRITING AN EVALUATION

■ You can complete each of the steps in this assignment by using the *Writing Guide Software* for THE BEDFORD GUIDE.

Pick a subject to evaluate — one you have personal experience with and feel competent to evaluate. This might be a movie, a TV program, a piece of music, an artwork, a new product, a government agency, a campus facility or policy, or anything else you can think of. Then in a thoughtful essay, analyze your subject and evaluate it. You will need to determine specific criteria for evaluation and make them clear to your readers. In writing your evaluation, you will have a twofold purpose: (1) to set forth your assessment of the quality of your subject and (2) to convince your readers that your judgment is reasonable.

Among the lively student-written evaluations we've seen are these:

A music major evaluated several works by American composer Aaron Copland and found Copland a trivial and imitative composer "without a tenth of the talent or inventiveness that George Gershwin or Duke Ellington had in his little finger."

A student planning a career in business management evaluated a computer firm in which he had worked one summer. His criteria were efficiency, productivity, appeal to new customers, and employee satisfaction.

A student from Brazil, who had seen firsthand the effects of industrial development in the Amazon rainforest, evaluated the efforts of the U.S. government to protect the ozone layer, comparing them with the efforts of environmentalists in her own country.

GENERATING IDEAS

Find Something to Evaluate.   Try using *brainstorming* or *mapping* to identify as many possible topics as you can think of. Select the ones with most potential — the ones that are most familiar or easiest to find out about. Spend enough time investigating these possibilities that you can comfortably choose one subject for your essay.

Consider Sources of Support.   You'll want to spend time finding material to help you develop a judgment. You may recall a program on television or hunt for an article to read. You might observe a performance or a sports team. An interview or conversation could reveal what others think. Perhaps you'll want to review several examples of your subject: watching several films, listening to several

College production of Romeo and Juliet

Developing a Consensus

Meet with your writing group to discuss the subject you plan to evaluate, and see whether the group can help you arrive at a sound judgment of it. The other group members will need to see or hear your detailed report about what you're evaluating. If possible, pass around a product, show a photograph of artwork, play a song on a CD, or read aloud a short literary work or an idea expressed in a reading. Ask your listeners to explain the reasons for their own evaluations. Maybe they'll suggest criteria or evidence that hadn't occurred to you.

FOR GROUP LEARNING

CDs, examining several works of art, or testing several products. You might also browse for information about your subject at several Web sites or attend a campus concert or play.

Establish Your Criteria.   Jot down criteria, standards to apply to your subject based on the features of the subject worth considering. How well, for example, does a popular entertainer score on musicianship, onstage manner, rapport with the audience, selection of material, originality? In evaluating the desirability of Portland as a home for a young careerist, you might ask: Does it provide an ample choice of decent-paying entry-level positions in growth firms? Any criterion you use to evaluate has to fit your subject, your audience, and your purpose. After all, ample entry-level jobs might not matter to an audience of retirees.

For more strategies for generating ideas, see Ch. 15.

Try Comparing and Contrasting.   Often you can readily size up the worth of a thing by setting it next to another of its kind. (When you *compare*, you point to similarities; when you *contrast*, you note differences.) To be comparable, of course, your two subjects need to have plenty in common. The quality of a Harley Davidson motorcycle might be judged by contrasting it with a Honda but not with a Sherman tank.

For more on comparing and contrasting, see Ch. 7.

For example, if you are writing a paper for a film history course, you might compare and contrast the classic German horror movie *The Cabinet of Dr. Caligari* with the classic Hollywood movie *Frankenstein*, concluding that *Caligari* is the more artistic film. In planning the paper, you might make two columns in which you list the characteristics of each film:

	CALIGARI	FRANKENSTEIN
SETS	Dreamlike and impressionistic	Realistic, but with heavy Gothic atmosphere
	Sets deliberately angular and distorted	Gothic sets
LIGHTING	Deep shadows that throw figures into relief	Torches highlighting monster's face in night scene

And so on, point by point. By jotting down each point and each bit of evidence side by side, you can outline your comparison and contrast with great efficiency. Once you have listed them, decide on a possible order for the points.

For more on defining, see pp. 310–11.

Try Defining Your Subject.   Another technique for evaluating is to define your subject, indicating its nature so clearly that your readers can easily distinguish it from others of its kind. In defining, you help your readers understand your subject — its structure, its habitat, its functions. In evaluating a classic television show such as *Roseanne* or *The Mary Tyler Moore Show,* you might want to do some *extended* defining, discussing the nature of sitcoms over the years, their techniques, their views of women, their effects on the audience. Unlike a *short definition,* such as you'd find in a dictionary, an extended definition is intended not simply to explain but to judge: What is the nature of my subject? What qualities make my subject unique, unlike others of its sort?

Develop a Judgment That You Can Explain to Readers.   In the end, you will have to come to a decision: Is your subject good, worthwhile, significant, exemplary, preferable — or not? Most writers find themselves coming to a judgment gradually as they explore their subjects and develop criteria.

For writing activities for evaluating, visit <bedfordstmartins.com/ bedguide> and do a keyword search:

activities

Facing the Challenge: Evaluating

The major challenge writers face when writing evaluations is to make clear to their readers the criteria they have used to arrive at their opinion. While you may not be an expert in any field, you should never underestimate your powers of discrimination. When reviewing a movie, for example, you may begin by simply summarizing the story of the film and saying whether you like it or not. However, for readers who are wondering whether to see the movie, you need to go beyond these comments. For example, you might find a movie's special effects, exotic sets, and rollicking plot effective but wish that the characters had seemed more believable. Based on these criteria, you might come up with the thesis that the movie may not be realistic but is extremely entertaining and well worth seeing.

Once you've chosen a topic, use the following questions to help you clarify and apply standards for evaluating it:

- What features or standards do you plan to use as criteria for evaluating your topic?

- How could you briefly explain each of the criteria for a reader?

- What judgment or evaluation about your topic do these criteria support?

After identifying your criteria, you can examine each in turn. Explaining your criteria will ensure that you move beyond a summary to an opinion or judgment that you can justify to your readers.

To close in on a promising subject, you might ask yourself a few questions:

DISCOVERY CHECKLIST

___ What criteria do you plan to use in making your evaluation? Are they clear and reasonably easy to apply?

___ What evidence can back up your judgments?

___ Would comparing or contrasting help in evaluating your subject? If so, with what might you compare or contrast your subject?

___ What specific qualities define your subject, setting it apart from all the rest of its class?

PLANNING, DRAFTING, AND DEVELOPING

Start with a Thesis.   Reflect a moment: What is your purpose in this evaluation? What main point do you wish to make? Try writing a paragraph that sums up the purpose of your evaluation, or work on stating a thesis that summarizes your main point.

For more on stating a thesis, see pp. 271–77.

TOPIC + JUDGMENT	campus performance of *Lobby Hero* — liked the seniors featured in it plus the problems the play raised
WORKING THESIS	Chosen to showcase the achievements of graduating seniors, the play *Lobby Hero* also brings up ethical problems.

For exercises on choosing effective thesis statements, visit <bedfordstmartins.com/bedguide> and do a keyword search:

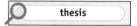
thesis

Consider Your Criteria.   Many writers find that a list of specific criteria gives them confidence and provokes ideas. Consider making a chart with three columns — criteria, evidence, and judgment — and filling it in to help focus your thinking.

Develop an Organization.   You may want to begin with a direct statement of your judgment: Based on durability, cost, and comfort, the Classic 7 is an ideal campus backpack. On the other hand, you may want to reserve judgment by opening with a question about your subject: How good a film is *Master and Commander*? Each approach suggests a different organization for your essay:

For more on outlining, see pp. 280–87.

Thesis or main point	→	Supporting evidence	→	Return to thesis
Opening question	→	Supporting evidence	→	Overall judgment

In either case, you'll supply plenty of evidence — details, examples, possibly comparisons or contrasts — so that readers find your case compelling. You'll also cluster your evidence around your points or criteria for judgment so that readers know how and why you have reached your judgment. If appropriate

For exercises on supporting a thesis, visit <bedfordstmartins.com/bedguide> and do a keyword search:

support

FOR PEER RESPONSE

For general questions for a peer editor, see pp. 328–29.

Enlist the advice of a classmate or friend as you determine your criteria for evaluation and your judgment. Ask your peer editor to answer questions like these about your evaluation:

- What is your overall reaction to this essay? Does the writer persuade you to agree with his or her evaluation?

- When you finish the essay, can you tell exactly what the writer thinks of the subject? Where does the writer express this opinion?

- How do you know what criteria the writer is using for evaluation?

- Does the writer give you sufficient evidence for his or her judgment? Put stars wherever more or better evidence is needed.

- What audience does the writer seem to have in mind?

- Would you recommend any changes in the essay's organization?

- If this were your paper, what is the one thing you would be sure to work on before handing it in?

and approved by your instructor, you might include a sketch, photograph, or other illustration of your subject or develop a comparative table summarizing the features of similar items you have compared.

You might try both patterns of organization (or a different one altogether) and see which works better for your subject and purpose. Most writers find that an outline—even a rough list—helps them keep track of points to make.

■ For more on comparison and contrast, see Ch. 7 and pp. 318–20.

If you intend to compare and contrast your subject with something else, one way to arrange the points is *subject by subject:* discuss subject A, and then discuss subject B. For a longer comparison, a better way to organize is *point by point,* applying each point first to one subject and then to the other.

REVISING AND EDITING

■ For more on stating a thesis, see pp. 271–77. For more revising and editing strategies, see Ch. 19.

Focus on Your Thesis.   As you begin to revise, make your thesis as precise and clear as possible.

| WORKING THESIS | Chosen to showcase the achievements of graduating seniors, the play *Lobby Hero* also brings up ethical problems. |
| REVISED THESIS | This year's senior showcase play, *Lobby Hero* by Kenneth Lonergan, spotlights outstanding performers and raises timely ethical issues. |

Be Fair.   Make your judgments reasonable, not extreme. A reviewer can find fault with a film and still conclude that it is worth seeing. There's noth-

After you have written a draft of your evaluative essay, you will need to consider how well you have linked specific support to your judgments. Scroll through the draft, and highlight each judgment or opinion with color. (Look under "format" to find "font" choices, including color.) Then go back to the beginning, and this time highlight all facts and evidence with a different color. Are your judgments followed by or related to the evidence to support your claims? Do you need to modify your judgments or revise your support? Do you need to add more support at any points or move sentences around so that your support is more closely linked to your judgments? Writing an evaluation is not simply about being right: connecting your claims with your evidence makes your evaluation persuasive and interesting.

WRITING WITH A COMPUTER

ing wrong, of course, with a fervent judgment ("This is the trashiest excuse for a play I have ever suffered through"), but consider your readers and their likely reactions. Read some reviews in your local newspaper or watch some movie critics on television to see how they balance their judgments. Because readers will have more confidence in your opinions if you seem fair and reasonable, revise your tone and your wording where needed. For example, one writer revised his opening after he realized that he was evaluating the audience rather than the performance.

> The most recent performance by a favorite campus group--Rock Mountain--
> *disappointing concert   Although t*
> was an ~~incredibly revolting~~ experience. ~~T~~he ~~outlandish~~ crowd ignored the DJ who
> *people*
> introduced the group/ and a few ~~nameless members of one social group spent~~
> *ed*
> ~~their time~~ tossing around trash cans in front of the stage/, *the opening number*
> *still announced the group's powerful musical presence.*

Use this handy checklist as you think critically about your draft:

REVISION CHECKLIST

___ Is the judgment you pass on your subject unmistakably clear?

___ Have you given your readers evidence to support each point you make?

___ Have you been fair? If you are championing something, have you deliberately skipped over any of its disadvantages or faults? If you are condemning your subject, have you omitted any of its admirable traits?

___ Have you anticipated and answered readers' possible objections?

___ If you compare one thing with another, do you look consistently at the same points in both?

For more on comparison and contrast, see Ch. 7 and pp. 318–20.

For more editing and proofreading strategies, see pp. 336–39.

After you have revised your evaluation, edit and proofread it. Carefully check grammar, word choice, punctuation, and mechanics — and then correct any problems you find. Pay attention to sentences in which you describe the subject of your evaluation, making them as precise and useful as possible. If you have used comparisons or contrasts, make sure these are clear: don't lose your readers in a thicket of vague pronouns or confusing references.

Here are some questions to help you start editing and proofreading:

For more help turn to the dark-blue-edged pages, and find the sections in the Quick Editing Guide noted here.

EDITING CHECKLIST

___ Is the reference of each pronoun clear? Does each pronoun agree with (match) its antecedent?   **A6**

___ Is it clear what each modifier in a sentence modifies? Have you created any dangling or misplaced modifiers, especially in descriptions of your subject?   **B1**

___ Have you used parallel structure wherever needed, especially in lists or comparisons?   **B2**

OTHER ASSIGNMENTS

1. Write an evaluation of a college course you have taken or are now taking. Analyze its strengths and weaknesses. Does the instructor present the material clearly, understandably, and interestingly? Can you confer with the instructor if you need to? Are the assignments pointed and purposeful? Is the textbook helpful, readable, and easy to use? Does this course give you your money's worth?

For more on responding to literature, see Ch. 12.

2. Read these two poems on a similar theme critically, and decide which seems to you the better poem. Then, in a brief essay, set forth your evaluation. Some criteria to apply might be the poet's choice of concrete, specific words that appeal to the senses and his awareness of his audience.

> **Putting in the Seed**
> ROBERT FROST (1874–1963)
>
> You come to fetch me from my work tonight
> When supper's on the table, and we'll see
>
> If I can leave off burying the white
> Soft petals fallen from the apple tree
> (Soft petals, yes, but not so barren quite,
> Mingled with these, smooth bean and wrinkled pea),
> And go along with you ere you lose sight
> Of what you came for and become like me,
> Slave to a springtime passion for the earth.
> How Love burns through the Putting in the Seed
> On through the watching for that early birth

When, just as the soil tarnishes with weed,
The sturdy seedling with arched body comes
Shouldering its way and shedding the earth crumbs.

Between Our Folding Lips
T. E. BROWN (1830–1897)

Between our folding lips
God slips
An embryon life, and goes;
And this becomes your rose.
We love, God makes: in our sweet mirth
God spies occasion for a birth.
Then is it His, or is it ours?
I know not — He is fond of flowers.

3. Visit a restaurant, a museum, or a tourist attraction, and write an evaluation of it for others who might consider a visit. Or evaluate a magazine
   you do not often read, one of the essays in this textbook, or a proposal
   under consideration at work or in your local community. Be sure to
   specify your criteria for evaluation.

Applying What You Learn: Some Uses of Evaluating

In College Courses.   In writing assignments and on exams, you'll be
asked over and over to evaluate. Evaluation demonstrates to your instructor
your sound understanding and considered opinion of a topic.

- Speech pathology students might be asked to consider the long-standing controversy that rages in education for the deaf by describing and
  then evaluating three currently disputed teaching methods — oral/aural,
  signing, and a combination of the two.

- Students of language and linguistics might be asked to evaluate Skin-
  ner's behaviorist theory of articulation therapy.

- Students often are asked to evaluate their instructors and courses; outside class, students on some campuses are invited to evaluate their campus facilities or student services.

In the Workplace.   Every executive or professional needs to evaluate people,
projects, goals, and results.

- Political commentators and newspaper editors evaluate the state of the
  economy, the actions of the administration or Congress, the decisions
  of the Supreme Court, and the merits of proposed legislation.

Evaluating Job Offers

- To evaluate all the factors associated with the position offered and the organization, ask for sufficient time to consider the offer. Sufficient time will depend on your needs and the needs of the organization. The amount of time you need may be different from what the company needs. You may be asked to give your decision sooner than you wish. If, at the end of that time, you have not been able to make a decision, ask for an extension, which may or may not be granted.

- Consider the position, the goals established for the position, the company's track record, what is projected for the company's future, opportunity for promotion, personalities of supervisor and coworkers, management style, and corporate culture.

- Follow up with other organizations that are considering you for employment in which you still have interest. Explain that you have received another offer, but because of your interest in their organization/position, you are following up with them to learn the status of your candidacy.

Web page from George Mason University Career Services

- Agencies such as police departments, civil defense units, rescue squads, or the Red Cross evaluate their performance in crisis situations in an attempt to refine and perfect responses.

- Every job applicant is evaluated by the employer—and every job applicant also evaluates the employer, the workplace, and the job offer.

In Your Community.   Familiar kinds of written evaluation abound in our daily lives.

- In a posting to an electronic discussion group, you might explain your evaluation of the topic or of comments of others in the group.

- Friends, peers, or co-workers may ask you to write a letter of recommendation for a job or a commendation for an award. In either case, you'll evaluate relevant characteristics of performance or merit.

- When friends plan to get together, they may turn to the local newspaper to check the restaurant reviews or film ratings—and then share their own ratings.

flicks in a flash

Compiled by Amelia Lennon

legend

★ rave review, a gem;

▨ mixed response, crap shoot;

🦃 turkey

Variety's Top 10 for the weekend ending 11/23/03	BOSTON PHOENIX	BOSTON GLOBE	BOSTON HERALD	NY TIMES	PEOPLE	TIME	NEWSWK	NEW YORKER	VILLAGE VOICE	WASHINGTON POST	NEW YORK
1 Dr. Seuss' The Cat in the Hat	🦃	🦃	🦃	🦃					🦃		
2 Gothika	🦃	🦃	▨	🦃						🦃	🦃
3 Elf	★	★	★	★	▨		★		▨	▨	▨
4 Master and Commander	★	★	★	★					▨	▨	▨
5 Love Actually	▨	▨	▨	🦃		▨	▨		▨	▨	▨
6 The Matrix Revolution	▨	★	▨	🦃	🦃	▨	▨	▨	▨	🦃	🦃
7 Brother Bear	★	▨	▨	▨	▨					▨	▨
8 Looney Tunes: Back in Action	▨	★	▨	▨				★	★	▨	
9 Scary Movie 3	▨	▨	▨	▨	🦃			🦃	▨	▨	
10 Radio	▨	🦃	★	🦃	▨					🦃	🦃

Summary movie ratings chart from a newspaper

PART THREE

Special Writing
Situations

Introduction

Much of your writing during college will fall into one of the categories covered in Part Two. However, three common situations that you're likely to encounter will call for specialized forms of writing—writing about literature, writing for the workplace, and writing for assessment.

In college English and humanities classes, you'll write papers about literature. You may need to write a personal response, a synopsis, a paraphrase, a review, a comparison and contrast, or—most common in college—a literary analysis. Chapter 12 provides brief advice on writing a synopsis or a paraphrase of a literary work. It concentrates on the literary analysis, explaining how to analyze a piece of literature, how to develop a coherent interpretation, and how to present it persuasively.

Whether you are working while you attend college or looking forward to a career once you finish, you'll need to use your writing skills in the workplace. As a consumer, a client, or an employee, you may need to write a business letter to straighten out a bill or lodge a complaint. You may need to write memos and e-mail messages as part of your current job. In addition, when you apply for a new position, you may need to write a résumé and letter of application. To simplify such tasks, Chapter 13 offers recommendations and samples for workplace writing.

Finally, as a student you'll face testing situations in which you must demonstrate your knowledge of a subject as well as your proficiency in writing, often constrained by a time limit. Writing essay examinations, short-answer quizzes, impromptu essays, and portfolio entries requires you to use special skills—reading carefully, planning globally, composing quickly, and proofreading independently. Chapter 14 gives valuable tips on how not only to survive but also to thrive in such situations.

Chapter 12

Responding to Literature

As countless readers know, reading fiction gives pleasure and delight. Whether you are reading Stephen King or Stephen Crane, you can be swept up into an imaginative world where you journey to distant lands and meet exotic people. You may also meet characters like yourself and encounter familiar as well as new ways of viewing life. By sharing the experiences of literary characters, you gain insight into your own problems and tolerance of others.

More often than not, a writing assignment in a literature or humanities course will require you first to read closely a literary work (short story, novel, play, or poem), and then to divide it into its elements, explain its meaning, and support your interpretation with evidence from the work. Such analysis is not an end in itself; its purpose is to illuminate the meaning of the work, to help you and others understand it better.

There are certain basic ways of writing about literature, each with its own purpose. We emphasize the *literary analysis*, which requires you to analyze, interpret, and evaluate what you read (pp. 190–210). We also introduce the synopsis, a summary of the events in a narrative, and the paraphrase, an expression of the content of a work in your own words (pp. 000–00). Because literary analysis has its own vocabulary—as do fields as diverse as scuba diving, gourmet cooking, and engineering—we also supply a handy glossary of terms used to discuss the elements of fiction, poetry, and drama (see pp. 202–03).

Literary Analysis

LEARNING FROM OTHER WRITERS

In a composition course, Jonathan Burns was given an assignment to write a literary analysis of "The Lottery," a provocative short story by Shirley Jackson. Read this story yourself to understand its meaning. Then read on to see what Jonathan Burns made of it.

Shirley Jackson

The Lottery

The morning of June 27th was clear and sunny, with the fresh warmth of 1
a full-summer day; the flowers were blossoming profusely and the grass
was richly green. The people of the village began to gather in the square, between the post office and the bank, around ten o'clock; in some towns there
were so many people that the lottery took two days and had to be started on
June 26th, but in this village, where there were only about three hundred
people, the whole lottery took less than two hours, so it could begin at ten
o'clock in the morning and still be through in time to allow the villagers to
get home for noon dinner.

The children assembled first, of course. School was recently over for the 2
summer, and the feeling of liberty sat uneasily on most of them; they
tended to gather together quietly for a while before they broke into boister-
ous play, and their talk was still of the classroom and the teacher, of books
and reprimands. Bobby Martin had already stuffed his pockets full of stones,
and the other boys soon followed his example, selecting the smoothest and
roundest stones; Bobby and Harry Jones and Dickie Delacroix — the villagers pronounced his name "Dellacroy" — eventually made a great pile of
stones in one corner of the square and guarded it against the raids of the
other boys. The girls stood aside, talking among themselves, looking over
their shoulders at the boys, and the very small children rolled in the dust or
clung to the hands of their older brothers or sisters.

Soon the men began to gather, surveying their own children, speaking 3
of planting and rain, tractors and taxes. They stood together, away from the
pile of stones in the corner, and their jokes were quiet and they smiled
rather than laughed. The women, wearing faded house dresses and sweaters,
came shortly after their menfolk. They greeted one another and exchanged
bits of gossip as they went to join their husbands. Soon the women, standing by their husbands, began to call to their children, and the children came
reluctantly, having to be called four or five times. Bobby Martin ducked
under his mother's grasping hand and ran, laughing, back to the pile of
stones. His father spoke up sharply, and Bobby came quickly and took his
place between his father and his oldest brother.

The lottery was conducted — as were the square dances, the teenage 4
club, the Halloween program — by Mr. Summers, who had time and energy
to devote to civic activities. He was a round-faced, jovial man and he ran the
coal business, and people were sorry for him, because he had no children
and his wife was a scold. When he arrived in the square, carrying the black
wooden box, there was a murmur of conversation among the villagers, and
he waved and called, "Little late today, folks." The postmaster, Mr. Graves,
followed him, carrying a three-legged stool, and the stool was put in the
center of the square and Mr. Summers set the black box down on it. The villagers kept their distance, leaving a space between themselves and the stool,

and when Mr. Summers said, "Some of you fellows want to give me a hand?" there was a hesitation before two men, Mr. Martin and his oldest son, Baxter, came forward to hold the box steady on the stool while Mr. Summers stirred up the papers inside it.

The original paraphernalia for the lottery had been lost long ago, and 5 the black box now resting on the stool had been put into use even before Old Man Warner, the oldest man in town, was born. Mr. Summers spoke frequently to the villagers about making a new box, but no one liked to upset even as much tradition as was represented by the black box. There was a story that the present box had been made with some pieces of the box that had preceded it, the one that had been constructed when the first people settled down to make a village here. Every year, after the lottery, Mr. Summers began talking again about a new box, but every year the subject was allowed to fade off without anything's being done. The black box grew shabbier each year; by now it was no longer completely black but splintered badly along one side to show the original wood color, and in some places faded or stained.

Mr. Martin and his oldest son, Baxter, held the black box securely on the 6 stool until Mr. Summers had stirred the papers thoroughly with his hand. Because so much of the ritual had been forgotten or discarded, Mr. Summers had been successful in having slips of paper substituted for the chips of wood that had been used for generations. Chips of wood, Mr. Summers had argued, had been all very well when the village was tiny, but now that the population was more than three hundred and likely to keep on growing, it was necessary to use something that would fit more easily into the black box. The night before the lottery, Mr. Summers and Mr. Graves made up the slips of paper and put them in the box, and it was then taken to the safe of Mr. Summers's coal company and locked up until Mr. Summers was ready to take it to the square next morning. The rest of the year, the box was put away, sometimes one place, sometimes another; it had spent one year in Mr. Graves's barn and another year underfoot in the post office, and sometimes it was set on a shelf in the Martin grocery and left there.

There was a great deal of fussing to be done before Mr. Summers declared the lottery open. There were the lists to make up — of heads of families, heads of households in each family, members of each household in each family. There was the proper swearing-in of Mr. Summers by the postmaster, as the official of the lottery; at one time, some people remembered, there had been a recital of some sort, performed by the official of the lottery, a perfunctory, tuneless chant that had been rattled off duly each year; some people believed that the official of the lottery used to stand just so when he said or sang it, others believed that he was supposed to walk among the people, but years and years ago this part of the ritual had been allowed to lapse. There had been, also, a ritual salute, which the official of the lottery had had to use in addressing each person who came up to draw from the box, but this also had changed with time, until now it was felt necessary only for the official to speak to each person approaching. Mr. Summers was very good at all this; in his clean white shirt and blue jeans, with one hand resting carelessly on the black box, he seemed very proper and important as he talked interminably to Mr. Graves and the Martins.

Just as Mr. Summers finally left off talking and turned to the assembled villagers, Mrs. Hutchinson came hurriedly along the path to the square, her sweater thrown over her shoulders, and slid into place in the back of the crowd. "Clean forgot what day it was," she said to Mrs. Delacroix, who stood next to her, and they both laughed softly. "Thought my old man was out back stacking wood," Mrs. Hutchinson went on, "and then I looked out the window and the kids was gone, and then I remembered it was the twenty-seventh and came a-running." She dried her hands on her apron, and Mrs. Delacroix said, "You're in time, though. They're still talking away up there." 8

Mrs. Hutchinson craned her neck to see through the crowd and found her husband and children standing near the front. She tapped Mrs. Delacroix on the arm as a farewell and began to make her way through the crowd. The people separated good-humoredly to let her through; two or three people said, in voices just loud enough to be heard across the crowd, "Here comes your Missus, Hutchinson," and "Bill, she made it after all." Mrs. Hutchinson reached her husband, and Mr. Summers, who had been waiting, said cheerfully, "Thought we were going to have to get on without you, Tessie." Mrs. Hutchinson said, grinning, "Wouldn't have me leave m'dishes in the sink, now, would you, Joe?" and soft laughter ran through the crowd as the people stirred back into position after Mrs. Hutchinson's arrival. 9

"Well, now," Mr. Summers said soberly, "guess we better get started, get this over with, so's we can go back to work. Anybody ain't here?" 10

"Dunbar," several people said. "Dunbar, Dunbar." 11

Mr. Summers consulted his list. "Clyde Dunbar," he said. "That's right. He's broke his leg, hasn't he? Who's drawing for him?" 12

"Me, I guess," a woman said, and Mr. Summers turned to look at her. "Wife draws for her husband," Mr. Summers said. "Don't you have a grown boy to do it for you, Janey?" Although Mr. Summers and everyone else in the village knew the answer perfectly well, it was the business of the official of the lottery to ask such questions formally. Mr. Summers waited with an expression of polite interest while Mrs. Dunbar answered. 13

"Horace's not but sixteen yet," Mrs. Dunbar said regretfully. "Guess I gotta fill in for the old man this year." 14

"Right," Mr. Summers said. He made a note on the list he was holding. Then he asked, "Watson boy drawing this year?" 15

A tall boy in the crowd raised his hand. "Here," he said. "I'm drawing for m'mother and me." He blinked his eyes nervously and ducked his head as several voices in the crowd said things like "Good fellow, Jack," and "Glad to see your mother's got a man to do it." 16

"Well," Mr. Summers said, "guess that's everyone. Old Man Warner make it?" 17

"Here," a voice said, and Mr. Summers nodded.   18

A sudden hush fell on the crowd as Mr. Summers cleared his throat and   19
looked at the list. "All ready?" he called. "Now, I'll read the names — heads
of families first — and the men come up and take a paper out of the box.
Keep the paper folded in your hand without looking at it until everyone has
had a turn. Everything clear?"

The people had done it so many times that they only half listened to the   20
directions; most of them were quiet, wetting their lips, not looking around.
Then Mr. Summers raised one hand high and said, "Adams." A man disengaged himself from the crowd and came forward. "Hi, Steve," Mr. Summers
said, and Mr. Adams said, "Hi, Joe." They grinned at one another humor-
lessly and nervously. Then Mr. Adams reached into the black box and took
out a folded paper. He held it firmly by one corner as he turned and went
hastily back to his place in the crowd, where he stood a little apart from his
family, not looking down at his hand.

"Allen," Mr. Summers said. "Anderson. . . . Bentham."   21

"Seems like there's no time at all between lotteries anymore," Mrs.   22
Delacroix said to Mrs. Graves in the back row. "Seems like we got through
with the last one only last week."

"Time sure goes fast," Mrs. Graves said.   23

"Clark. . . . Delacroix."   24

"There goes my old man," Mrs. Delacroix said. She held her breath   25
while her husband went forward.

"Dunbar," Mr. Summers said, and Mrs. Dunbar went steadily to the box   26
while one of the women said, "Go on, Janey," and another said, "There she
goes."

"We're next," Mrs. Graves said. She watched while Mr. Graves came   27
around from the side of the box, greeted Mr. Summers gravely, and selected
a slip of paper from the box. By now, all through the crowd there were men
holding the small folded papers in their large hands, turning them over and
over nervously. Mrs. Dunbar and her two sons stood together, Mrs. Dunbar
holding the slip of paper.

"Harburt. . . . Hutchinson."   28

"Get up there, Bill," Mrs. Hutchinson said, and the people near her   29
laughed.

"Jones."   30

"They do say," Mr. Adams said to Old Man Warner, who stood next to   31
him, "that over in the north village they're talking of giving up the lottery."

Old Man Warner snorted. "Pack of crazy fools," he said. "Listening to   32
the young folks, nothing's good enough for *them*. Next thing you know,
they'll be wanting to go back to living in caves, nobody work anymore, live
that way for a while. Used to be a saying about 'Lottery in June, corn be
heavy soon.' First thing you know, we'd all be eating stewed chickweed and
acorns. There's *always* been a lottery," he added petulantly. "Bad enough to
see young Joe Summers up there joking with everybody."

"Some places have already quit lotteries," Mrs. Adams said.   33

"Nothing but trouble in *that*," Old Man Warner said stoutly. "Pack of   34
young fools."

"Martin." And Bobby Martin watched his father go forward. "Over-   35
dyke. . . . Percy."

"I wish they'd hurry," Mrs. Dunbar said to her older son. "I wish they'd   36
hurry."

"They're almost through," her son said.   37

"You get ready to run tell Dad," Mrs. Dunbar said.   38

Mr. Summers called his own name and then stepped forward precisely   39
and selected a slip from the box. Then he called, "Warner."

"Seventy-seventh year I been in the lottery," Old Man Warner said as he   40
went through the crowd. "Seventy-seventh time."

"Watson." The tall boy came awkwardly through the crowd. Someone   41
said, "Don't be nervous, Jack," and Mr. Summers said, "Take your time, son."

"Zanini."   42

After that, there was a long pause, a breathless pause, until Mr. Sum-   43
mers, holding his slip of paper in the air, said, "All right, fellows." For a
minute, no one moved, and then all the slips of paper were opened. Suddenly, all the women began to speak at once, saying, "Who is it?" "Who's
got it?" "Is it the Dunbars?" "Is it the Watsons?" Then the voices began to
say, "It's Hutchinson. It's Bill." "Bill Hutchinson's got it."

"Go tell your father," Mrs. Dunbar said to her older son.   44

People began to look around to see the Hutchinsons. Bill Hutchinson   45
was standing quiet, staring down at the paper in his hand. Suddenly, Tessie
Hutchinson shouted to Mr. Summers, "You didn't give him time enough to
take any paper he wanted. I saw you. It wasn't fair!"

"Be a good sport, Tessie," Mrs. Delacroix called, and Mrs. Graves said,   46
"All of us took the same chance."

"Shut up, Tessie," Bill Hutchinson said.   47

"Well, everyone," Mr. Summers said, "that was done pretty fast, and   48
now we've got to be hurrying a little more to get done in time." He consulted his next list. "Bill," he said, "you draw for the Hutchinson family. You
got any other households in the Hutchinsons?"

"There's Don and Eva," Mrs. Hutchinson yelled. "Make *them* take their   49
chance!"

"Daughters draw with their husbands' families, Tessie," Mr. Summers   50
said gently. "You know that as well as anyone else."

"It wasn't *fair*," Tessie said.   51

"I guess not, Joe," Bill Hutchinson said regretfully. "My daughter draws   52
with her husband's family, that's only fair. And I've got no other family except the kids."

"Then, as far as drawing for families is concerned, it's you," Mr. Sum-   53
mers said in explanation, "and as far as drawing for households is concerned, that's you, too. Right?"

"Right," Bill Hutchinson said.   54

"How many kids, Bill?" Mr. Summers asked formally.   55

"Three," Bill Hutchinson said. "There's Bill, Jr., and Nancy, and little   56
Dave. And Tessie and me."

"All right, then," Mr. Summers said. "Harry, you got their tickets back?"   57

Mr. Graves nodded and held up the slips of paper. "Put them in the box,   58
then," Mr. Summers directed. "Take Bill's and put it in."

"I think we ought to start over," Mrs. Hutchinson said, as quietly as she   59
could. "I tell you it wasn't *fair*. You didn't give him time enough to choose.
*Every*body saw that."

Mr. Graves had selected the five slips and put them in the box, and he   60
dropped all the papers but those onto the ground, where the breeze caught
them and lifted them off.

"Listen, everybody," Mrs. Hutchinson was saying to the people around   61
her.

"Ready, Bill?" Mr. Summers asked, and Bill Hutchinson, with one quick   62
glance around at his wife and children, nodded.

"Remember," Mr. Summers said, "take the slips and keep them folded   63
until each person has taken one. Harry, you help little Dave." Mr. Graves
took the hand of the little boy, who came willingly with him up to the box.
"Take a paper out of the box, Davy," Mr. Summers said. Davy put his hand
into the box and laughed. "Take just *one* paper," Mr. Summers said. "Harry,
you hold it for him." Mr. Graves took the child's hand and removed the
folded paper from the tight fist and held it while little Dave stood next to
him and looked up at him wonderingly.

"Nancy next," Mr. Summers said. Nancy was twelve, and her school   64
friends breathed heavily as she went forward, switching her skirt, and took a
slip daintily from the box. "Bill, Jr.," Mr. Summers said, and Billy, his face
red and his feet overlarge, nearly knocked the box over as he got a paper out.
"Tessie," Mr. Summers said. She hesitated for a minute, looking around defi-
antly, and then set her lips and went up to the box. She snatched a paper
out and held it behind her.

"Bill," Mr. Summers said, and Bill Hutchinson reached into the box and   65
felt around, bringing his hand out at last with the slip of paper in it.

The crowd was quiet. A girl whispered, "I hope it's not Nancy," and the   66
sound of the whisper reached the edges of the crowd.

"It's not the way it used to be," Old Man Warner said clearly. "People   67
ain't the way they used to be."

"All right," Mr. Summers said. "Open the papers. Harry, you open little   68
Dave's."

Mr. Graves opened the slip of paper and there was a general sigh   69
through the crowd as he held it up and everyone could see that it was blank.
Nancy and Bill, Jr., opened theirs at the same time, and both beamed and
laughed, turning around to the crowd and holding their slips of paper above
their heads.

"Tessie," Mr. Summers said. There was a pause, and then Mr. Summers 70 looked at Bill Hutchinson, and Bill unfolded his paper and showed it. It was blank.

"It's Tessie," Mr. Summers said, and his voice was hushed. "Show us her 71 paper, Bill."

Bill Hutchinson went over to his wife and forced the slip of paper out of 72 her hand. It had a black spot on it, the black spot Mr. Summers had made the night before with the heavy pencil in the coal-company office. Bill Hutchinson held it up, and there was a stir in the crowd.

"All right, folks," Mr. Summers said. "Let's finish quickly." 73

Although the villagers had forgotten the ritual and lost the original 74 black box, they still remembered to use stones. The pile of stones the boys had made earlier was ready; there were stones on the ground with the blowing scraps of paper that had come out of the box. Mrs. Delacroix selected a stone so large she had to pick it up with both hands and turned to Mrs. Dunbar. "Come on," she said. "Hurry up."

Mrs. Dunbar had small stones in both hands, and she said, gasping for 75 breath, "I can't run at all. You'll have to go ahead and I'll catch up with you."

The children had stones already, and someone gave little Davy Hutchin- 76 son a few pebbles.

Tessie Hutchinson was in the center of a cleared space by now, and she 77 held her hands out desperately as the villagers moved in on her. "It isn't fair," she said. A stone hit her on the side of the head.

Old Man Warner was saying, "Come on, come on, everyone." Steve 78 Adams was in the front of the crowd of villagers, with Mrs. Graves beside him.

"It isn't fair, it isn't right," Mrs. Hutchinson screamed, and then they 79 were upon her.

Questions to Start You Thinking

Meaning

1. Where does this story take place? When?

2. How does this lottery differ from what we usually think of as a lottery? Why would people conduct a lottery such as this?

3. What does this story mean to you?

Writing Strategies

4. Can you see and hear the people in the story? Do they seem to be real or based on fantasy? Who is the most memorable character to you?

5. Are the events believable? Does the ending shock you? Is it believable?

6. Is this story realistic, or is Jackson using these events to represent something else?

■ For Burns's synopsis of "The Lottery," see p. 211. For more on writing a summary, see D5 and D6 in the Quick Research Guide (the dark-red-edged pages).

■ For examples of annotated passages, see p. 21 and pp. 26–27.

Read Closely.   As Jonathan Burns read "The Lottery," he was carried along quickly to the startling ending. After the immediate impact of the story wore off, Burns reread it, savoring some of the details he had missed during his first reading. Then he wrote a summary or *synopsis* of "The Lottery" to get a clear fix on the literal events in the story.

But Burns knew that he could not write a good essay without reading the story closely, marking key points in the text. By rereading *at least* three times, he could check his interpretations and be sure that evidence from the story supported his claims. When you analyze a complex work of literature, allow time for several close readings, each for a different reason.

READING CHECKLIST

■ For more on literal and critical reading, see Ch. 2.

Reading to Comprehend

___ What is the literal meaning? Write a few sentences briefly explaining the overall situation — what happens to whom, where, when, why, and how.

___ What are the facts of the situation — the events of the plot, the aspects of the setting, the major attributes of the characters, the words and actions of the characters?

___ What does all the vocabulary mean, especially in titles and in poems? Look up any unfamiliar words or words whose familiar meanings don't seem to fit the context.

Reading to Analyze

___ What are the main components, parts, or elements of the work? Read, read aloud, mark, or make notes on what you seek — theme, character, language, style, symbol, form.

___ What does the literary work mean? What does it imply?

___ What does it suggest about the human condition? How does it expand your understanding? What insights can you apply to your own life?

Reading to Evaluate

___ How do you assess the soundness and plausibility of what the author says?

___ Are the words and tone appropriate for the purpose and audience?

___ Does the author achieve his or her purpose? Is it a worthwhile purpose?

Plan and Organize an Analysis.   Jonathan Burns knew he had to analyze the important elements — such as setting, character, and tone — in "The Lottery" to understand the story well enough to write about it. He immediately thought of the story's undertone of violence but decided that it was so subtle that writing about it would be difficult. Then he considered the especially memorable characters, Mr. Summers and Old Man Warner. And of course there was Tessie Hutchinson; he could hear her screams as the stones hit her. But he could not think of much to say except the vague statement that they were memorable. All of a sudden, he hit on the surprise ending. How did Jackson manipulate all the details to generate such a shock?

To begin to focus his thinking, he brainstormed for possible essay titles having to do with the ending, some serious, others flippant: Death Comes as a Surprise, The Unsuspected Finish, Patience of the Devil. He chose the straightforward title "The Hidden Truth." After reviewing his notes, Burns realized that Jackson uses characterization, symbolism, and ambiguous description to build up to the ending. He listed details from the story under those three headings to make an informal plan for his paper:

For more on brainstorming, see pp. 254–56. For more on seeking motives of characters, see pp. 263–65.

> Title: The Hidden Truth
> Working Thesis: In "The Lottery" Jackson effectively crafts a shock ending.
> 1. Characterization that contributes to the shock ending
>   –The children of the village
>   –The adults of the village
>   –Conversations among the villagers
> 2. Symbols that contribute to the shock ending
>   –The stones
>   –The black box
> 3. Ambiguous description that contributes to the shock ending
>   –The word "lottery"
>   –Comments
>   –"clean forgot"
>   –"wish they'd hurry"
>   –"It isn't fair."
>   –Actions
>   –Relief
>   –Suspense

For more on stating a thesis, see pp. 271–77. For more on organizing ideas and outlining, see pp. 280–87.

Then he drafted the following introduction:

For more on introductions, see pp. 294–96.

Unsuspecting, the reader follows Shirley Jackson's softly flowing tale of a rural community's timeless ritual, the lottery. Awareness of what is at stake--the savage murder of one random member--comes slowly. No sooner does the realization set in than the story is over. It is a shock ending.

What creates the shock that the reader experiences reading "The Lottery"? Shirley Jackson takes great care in producing this effect, using elements such as language, symbolism, and characterization to lure the reader into not anticipating what is to come.

With his synopsis, his plan, his copy of the story, and this beginning of a draft, Burns revised the introduction and wrote the following essay.

STUDENT ESSAY

Jonathan Burns

The Hidden Truth: An Analysis of Shirley Jackson's "The Lottery"

It is as if the first stone thrown strikes the reader as well as Mrs. Hutchinson.   1
And even though there were signs of the stoning to come, somehow the reader is
taken by surprise at Tessie's violent death. What factors contribute to the shock
ending to "The Lottery"? On closer examination of the story, the reader finds that
through all the events leading up to the ending, Shirley Jackson has used unsus-
picious characterizations, unobtrusive symbolism, and ambiguous descriptions to
achieve so sudden an impact.

By all appearances, the village is a normal place with normal people. Children   2
arrive at the scene first, with school just over for the summer, talking of teachers
and books, not of the fact that someone will die today (191). And as the adults
show up, their actions are just as stereotypical: the men talk of farming and taxes,
while the women gossip (191). No trace of hostility, no sense of dread in anyone:
death seems very far away here.

The conversations between the villagers are no more ominous. As the husbands   3
draw slips of paper for their families, the villagers make apparently everyday comments about the seemingly ordinary event of the lottery. Mr. Summers is regarded as
a competent and respected figure, despite the fact that his wife is "a scold" (191).
Old Man Warner brags about how many lotteries he's seen and rambles on criticizing
other towns that have given up the tradition (194–95). The characters' comments
show the crowd to be more a closely knit community than a murderous mob.

The symbols of "The Lottery" seem equally ordinary. The stones collected by the   4
boys (191) are unnoticed by the adults and thus seem a trivial detail. The reader
thinks of the "great pile" (191) as children's entertainment, like a stack of imaginary
coins rather than an arsenal. Ironically, no stones are ever thrown during the children's play, and no violence is seen in the pile of stones.

Similarly, Jackson describes the box and its history in great detail, but nothing   5
seems unusual about it. It is just another everyday object, stored away in the post
office or on a shelf in the grocery (192). Every other day of the year, the box is in
plain view but goes virtually unnoticed. The only indication that the box has lethal
consequences is that it is painted black (192), yet this is an ambiguous detail, as
a black box can also signify mystery or magic, mystical forces that are sometimes
thought to exist in any lottery.

In her ambiguous descriptions, Jackson refers regularly to the village's lottery   6
and emphasizes it as a central ritual for the people. The word <u>lottery</u> itself is ironic,
as it typically implies a winning of some kind, like a raffle or sweepstakes. It is par-

The numbers in paren-
theses are page-number
citations following MLA
style. For more advice on
citing and listing sources,
see D6 and E in the
Quick Research Guide
(the dark-red-edged
pages).

alleled to square dances and to the teenage club, all under the direction of Mr. Summers (191), activities people look forward to. There is no implied difference between
the occurrences of this day and the festivities of Halloween: according to Jackson,
they are all merely "civic activities" (191). Equally ambiguous are the people's emotions: some of the villagers are casual, such as Mrs. Hutchinson, who arrives late because she "'clean forgot'" what day it is (193), and some are anxious, such as Mrs.
Dunbar, who repeats to her son, "'I wish they'd hurry,'" without any sign of the cause
of her anxiety (195). With these descriptive details, the reader finds no threat or
malice in the villagers, only vague expectation and congeniality.

Even when it becomes clear that the lottery is something no one wants to win,   7
Jackson presents only a vague sense of sadness and mild protest. The crowd is relieved
that the youngest of the Hutchinsons, Davy, doesn't draw the fatal slip of paper (196).
One girl whispers that she hopes it isn't Nancy (196), and when the Hutchinson children discover they aren't the winners, they beam with joy and proudly display their
blank slips (196). Suspense and excitement grow only when the victim is close to
being identified. And when Tessie is revealed as the winner of the lottery (197), she
merely holds her hands out "desperately" and repeats, "'It isn't fair'" (197).

With a blend of character, symbolism, and description, Jackson paints an overall   8
portrait of a gentle-seeming rural community, apparently no different from any other.
The tragic end is sudden only because there is no recognition of violence beforehand,
despite the fact that Jackson has provided the reader with plenty of clues in the ample
details about the lottery and the people. It is a haunting discovery that the story
ends in death, even though such is the truth in the everyday life of <u>all</u> people.

Questions to Start You Thinking

Meaning

1. What is Burns's thesis?
2. What major points does he use to support the interpretation stated in his
   thesis? What specific elements of the story does he include as evidence?

Writing Strategies

3. How does this essay differ from a synopsis, a summary of the events of the
   plot? (For a synopsis of "The Lottery," see pp. 211–12.)
4. Does Burns focus on the technique of the short story or on its theme?
5. Is his introduction effective? Compare and contrast it with his first draft
   (p. 201). What did he change? Which version do you prefer?
6. Why does he explain characterization first, symbolism second, and description last? How effective is this organization? Would discussing these elements in a different order have made much difference?
7. Is his conclusion effective?
8. How does he tie his ideas together as he moves from paragraph to paragraph? How does he keep the focus on ideas and technique instead of plot?

A Glossary of Terms for Literary Analysis

Characters. Characters are imagined people. The author shows you what they are like through their actions, speech, thoughts, attitudes, and background. Sometimes a writer also includes physical characteristics or names or relationships with other people. For example, in "The Lottery," the description of Mr. Summers introduces the lottery official as someone with civic interests who wants to avoid slip-ups (paragraphs 4, 9, and 10).

Figures of Speech. Figures of speech are lively or fresh expressions that vary the expected sequence or sense of words. Some common types of figurative language are the *simile,* a comparison using *like* or *as;* the *metaphor,* an implied comparison; and *personification,* the attribution of human qualities to inanimate or nonhuman creatures or things. In "The Lottery," three boys *guard* their pile of stones "against the *raids*" of others (paragraph 2).

Imagery. Images are words or groups of words that refer to any sense experience: seeing, hearing, smelling, testing, touching, or feeling. The images in "The Lottery" help readers envision the "richly green" grass (paragraph 1), the smooth and round stones the children gather (paragraph 2), the "hush" that comes over the crowd (paragraph 19), and Mrs. Dunbar "gasping for breath" (paragraph 75).

Irony. Irony results from readers' sense of discrepancy. A simple kind of irony, *sarcasm,* occurs when you say one thing but mean the opposite: "I just love scrubbing the floor." In literature, an *ironic situation* sets up a wry contrast or incongruity. In "The Lottery," cruel and horrifying actions take place on a sunny June day in an ordinary village. *Ironic dialogue* occurs when a character says one thing, but the audience or reader is aware of another meaning. When Old Man Warner reacts to giving up the lottery as "wanting to go back to living in caves" (paragraph 32), he implies that such a change would return the villages to a more primitive life. His comment is ironic because the reader is aware that this lottery is a primitive ritual. A story has an *ironic point of view* when readers sense a difference between the author and the narrator or the character who perceives the story; Jackson, for instance, clearly does not condone the actions of the villagers.

Plot. Plot is the arrangement of the events of the story — what happens to whom, where, when, and why. If the events follow each other logically and are in keeping with the characters, the plot is *plausible,* or believable. Although the ending of "The Lottery" at first may shock readers, the author uses *foreshadowing,* hints or clues such as the villagers' nervousness about the lottery, to help readers understand future events or twists in the plot.

Most plots place the *protagonist,* or main character, in a *conflict* with the *antagonist,* some other person or group. In "The Lottery," a reader might see Tessie as the protagonist and the villagers as the antagonist. *Conflict* consists of two forces trying to conquer each other or resist being conquered —

not merely vaguely defined turmoil. *External conflicts* occur outside an individual—between two people, a person and a group (Tessie versus the villagers), two groups (lottery supporters and opponents), or even a character and the environment. *Internal conflicts* between two opposing forces or desires occur within an individual (such as fear versus hope as the lottery slips are drawn). The *central conflict* is the primary conflict for the protagonist that propels the action of the story. Events of the plot *complicate* the conflict (Tessie arrives late, Bill draws the slip) and lead to the climax, the moment when the outcome is inevitable (Tessie draws the black dot). This outcome is the *resolution,* or conclusion (the villagers stone Tessie). Some stories let events unfold without any apparent plot—action and change occur inside the characters.

Point of View. The point of view, the angle from which a story is told, might be the author's or a character's. The *narrator* is the one who tells the story and perceives the events, perhaps with limited knowledge or a part to play. Three common points of view are those of a *first-person narrator (I),* the *speaker* who tells the story; a *third-person narrator* (*he* or *she*) who participates in the action (often as the protagonist); and a *third-person narrator* who simply observes. The point of view may be *omniscient* (told through several characters' eyes); *limited omniscient* (told through one character's eyes); or *objective* (not told through any character's eyes). In "The Lottery," a third-person objective narrator seemingly looks on and reports what occurs without knowing what the characters think.

Setting. Setting refers to the time and place of events and may include the season, the weather, and the people in the background. The setting often helps establish a literary work's *mood* or *atmosphere,* the emotional climate that a reader senses. For example, the first sentence of "The Lottery" establishes its setting (paragraph 1).

Symbols. Symbols are tangible objects, visible actions, or characters that hint at meanings beyond themselves. In "The Lottery," the black box suggests outdated tradition, resistance to change, evil, cruelty, and more.

Theme. A theme is a work's main idea or insight—the author's observation about life, society, or human nature. Sometimes you can sum up a theme in a sentence ("Human beings cannot live without illusion"); other times, a theme may be implied, hard to discern, or one of several in a work.

To state a theme, go beyond a work's topic or subject by asking yourself, What does the author say about this subject? Details from the story should support your statement of theme, and your theme should account for the details. "The Lottery" treats subjects such as the unexpected, scapegoating, outmoded rituals, and violence; one of its themes might be stated as "People are selfish, always looking out for number one."

LEARNING BY WRITING

The Assignment: Analyzing a Literary Work. For this assignment, you are to be a literary critic—analyzing, interpreting, and evaluating a literary selection for your classmates. Your purpose is to deepen their understanding because you will have devoted time and effort to digging out the meaning and testing it with evidence from the work itself. Even if they too have studied the work carefully, you will try to convince them that your interpretation is valid.

Write an essay interpreting a literary work that intrigues you or expresses a worthwhile meaning. Your instructor may want to approve your selection. After careful analysis of the work, you will become the expert critic, explaining the meaning you discern, supporting your interpretation with evidence from the work, and evaluating the effectiveness of literary elements used by the author and the significance of the theme.

You cannot include everything about the work in your paper, so you should focus on one element (such as character, setting, or theme) or the interrelationship of two or three elements (as Jonathan Burns did when he analyzed characterization, symbolism, and description in his interpretation of "The Lottery"). Although a summary, or *synopsis,* of the plot is a good beginning point, retelling the story is not a satisfactory literary analysis.

These college writers successfully responded to such an assignment:

One showed how the rhythm, rhymes, and images of Adrienne Rich's poem "Aunt Jennifer's Tigers" mesh to convey the poem's theme of tension between a woman's artistic urge and societal constraints.

Another writer who was a musician analyzed the credibility of Sonny as a musician in James Baldwin's "Sonny's Blues"—his attitudes, actions, struggles, relationship with his instrument and with other musicians—and concluded that Sonny is a believable character.

A psychology major concluded that the relationship between Hamlet and Claudius in Shakespeare's *Hamlet* represents in many ways the tension, jealousy, and misunderstanding between stepsons and stepfathers.

Find a Subject. Read several literary works to find two or three you like. You might start with a favorite author or a favorite short story among those read for this course. Next, reread the works that interest you and select one to concentrate on. Choose the one that strikes you as especially significant—realistic or universal, moving or disturbing, believable or shocking—with a meaning that you wish to share with your classmates.

▓ For more on analysis, see pp. 311–13.

Generate Ideas. Analyzing a literary work is the first step in interpreting meaning and evaluating literary quality. As you read the work, identify its elements and analyze them as Jonathan Burns did for "The Lottery." Then focus on *one* significant element or a cluster of related elements. When you write your interpretation, restrict your discussion to that focus.

We provide three checklists to guide you in analyzing different types of literature. Each of these is an aid to understanding, *not* an organizational outline for writing about literature. The first checklist focuses on short stories and novels, but some of its questions can help you analyze setting, character, theme, or your reactions as a reader for almost any kind of literary work.

DISCOVERY CHECKLIST

Analyzing a Short Story or a Novel

For a glossary of literary terms, see pp. 202–03.

____ What is your reaction to the story? Jot it down.

____ Who is the *narrator* — not the author, but the one who tells the story?

____ What is the *point of view?*

____ What is the *setting* (time and place)? What is the *atmosphere* or *mood?*

____ How does the *plot* unfold? Write a synopsis, or summary, of the events in time order, including relationships among those events.

____ What are the *characters* like? Describe their personalities, traits and motivations based on their actions, speech, habits, and so on. What strategies does the author use to develop the characters? Who is the *protagonist?* The *antagonist?* Do any characters change? Are the changes believable?

____ How would you describe the story's *style,* or use of language? Is it informal, conversational or formal? Does the story use dialect or foreign words?

____ What are the *external conflicts* and the *internal conflicts?* What is the *central conflict?* Express the conflicts using the word *versus,* such as "dreams versus reality" or "the individual versus society."

____ What is the *climax* of the story? Is there any *resolution?*

____ Are there important *symbols?* What might they mean?

____ What does the *title* of the story mean?

____ What are the *themes* of the story? Are they universal (applicable to all people everywhere at all times)? State your interpretation of the main theme. How is this theme related to your own life?

____ What other literary works or experiences from life does the story make you think of? Jot them down.

When looking at a poem, consider the elements specific to poetry and those shared with other genres, as the following checklist suggests.

DISCOVERY CHECKLIST

Analyzing a Poem

____ What is your reaction to the poem? Jot it down.

____ Who is the *speaker* — not the author, but the one who narrates?

____ Is there a *setting?* How does it relate to the meaning of the poem? What *mood* or emotional *atmosphere* does it suggest?

—— Can you put the poem into your own words — paraphrase it?

—— What is striking about the poem's language or *repetition* of words? Identify any unusual words, words used in an unusual sense, or *archaic* words (no longer commonly used). Consider *connotations,* the suggestions conjured by the words: *house* has a different connotation from *home,* although both may refer to the same place. Is the level of language colloquial or formal? Does the poem use irony or figurative language: *imagery, metaphor, personification?*

—— Is the poem *lyric* (expressing emotion) or *narrative* (telling a story)?

—— What is the structure of the poem? How is it divided? Does it consist of *couplets* (two consecutive rhyming lines) or *quatrains* (units of four lines) or some other units? How do the beginning and the end relate to each other and to the poem as a whole?

—— Does the poem use *rhyme* (words that sound alike)? If so, how does the rhyme contribute to the meaning?

—— Does the poem have *rhythm* (regular meter or beat, patterns of accented and unaccented syllables)? How does the rhythm contribute to the meaning?

—— What does the *title* of the poem mean?

—— What is the major *theme* of the poem? How does this underlying idea unify the poem? How is it related to your own life?

—— What other literary works or experiences from life does the poem make you think of? Jot them down.

A play is written to be seen and heard, not read. When you analyze a play, you may ask what kind of play it is and how it would appear onstage, as the following checklist suggests.

DISCOVERY CHECKLIST

Analyzing a Play

—— What is your reaction to the play? Jot it down.

—— Is the play a *tragedy* (a serious drama that arouses pity and fear in the audience and usually ends unhappily with the death or downfall of the *tragic hero*)? Or is it a *comedy* (drama that primarily aims to amuse and usually ends happily)?

—— What is the *setting* of the play? What is its *mood?*

—— In brief, what happens? Summarize each act of the play.

—— What are the characters like? Who is the *protagonist?* Who is the *antagonist?* Are there *foil characters* who contrast with the main character and reveal his or her traits? Which characters are in conflict? Which change?

—— Which speeches seem especially significant?

—— What is the plot? Identify the *exposition* or background information needed to understand the story. Determine the main *external* and *internal* conflicts. What is the *central conflict?* What events *complicate* the central conflict? How are these elements of the plot spread throughout the play?

—— What is the *climax* of the play? Is there a *resolution* to the action?

—— What does the *title* mean?

—— Can you identify any *dramatic irony*, words or actions of a character that carry meaning unperceived by the character but evident to the audience?

—— What is the major *theme* of the play? Is it a universal idea? How is it related to your own life?

—— What other literary works or experiences from life does the play make you think of? Jot them down.

Consider Your Readers. When you write your analysis, don't try to impress readers with your brilliance. Stick to terms that you understand. Regard your readers as friends in whose company you are discussing something familiar to all of you, though they may not have studied the work as carefully as you have. Your purpose is to explain the work's deeper meaning, which your readers may not see after a cursory reading. This assumption will help you determine how much evidence from the work to include and will save you a lot of wordy summarizing.

Identify Your Support. After you have determined the major element or cluster of elements that you intend to focus on, go through the work again to find all the passages that relate to your main point. Mark them as you find them, or put these relevant passages on note cards or in a computer file, along with the page references. If you use any quotations, quote exactly.

For more on planning, drafting, and developing, see Chs. 16, 17, and 18.

Develop Your Main Idea or Thesis. Begin writing by trying to express your main point in a thesis statement that identifies the literary work and the author. Suppose you start with a working thesis on the theme of "The Lottery":

For more on stating a thesis, see pp. 271–77.

WORKING THESIS   In "The Lottery," Shirley Jackson reveals the theme.

But this statement is too vague, so you rewrite it to be more precise:

IMPROVED   In "The Lottery" by Shirley Jackson, the theme is tradition.

This thesis is better but still doesn't state the theme clearly or precisely. You try several other ways of expressing what Jackson implies about tradition:

IMPROVED   In "The Lottery" by Shirley Jackson, one of the major themes is that outmoded traditions can be harmful.

Adding the qualifier *one of* indicates that this theme is not the only one in the story, but the rest of the thesis is vague. What does "outmoded" mean? How are the traditions harmful?

MORE PRECISE   In "The Lottery" by Shirley Jackson, one of the major themes is that traditions that have lost their meaning can still move people to act abnormally without thinking.

This is a better thesis, but it may change as you start writing the analysis. For instance, you might decide to go beyond interpretation of Jackson's ideas by adding the word *tragic* to convey your evaluation of her observation of the human condition:

EVALUATION   In "The Lottery," Shirley Jackson reveals the tragic theme that
ADDED   traditions that have lost their meaning can still move people to abnormal and thoughtless action.

Or you might say this, alerting readers to your main points:

PREVIEW   In "The Lottery," Shirley Jackson effectively uses symbolism
ADDED   and irony to reveal the theme that traditions that have lost their meaning can still move people to abnormal and thoughtless action.

When planning your essay, focus on analyzing ideas, not retelling events. One way to maintain that focus is to analyze your thesis, dividing it into parts and then developing each part in turn in your essay. The thesis

FOR PEER RESPONSE

For general questions for a peer editor, see pp. 328–29.

Ask one of your classmates to read your draft, considering how effectively you have analyzed the literary work and presented your analysis. Ask your peer editor to answer specific questions such as these:

- What is your first reaction to the literary analysis?

- In what ways does the analysis add to your understanding of the literary work? In what ways does it add to your insights into life?

- Does the introduction make you want to read the rest of the analysis? What changes would you suggest to strengthen the opening?

- Is the main idea clear? Is there sufficient relevant evidence from the work to support that point? Put stars wherever additional evidence is needed. Put a check mark by any irrelevant information.

- Does the writer go beyond plot summary to analyze elements, interpret meaning, and evaluate literary merit? If not, how might the writer revise?

- Is the analysis organized by ideas instead of events? What changes in organization would you suggest?

- Do the transitions guide you smoothly from one point to the next? Do the transitions focus on ideas, not on time or position in the story? Note any places where the writer might add transitions.

- If this were your paper, what is the one thing you would be sure to work on before handing it in?

just presented could be divided into (1) use of symbolism to reveal theme and (2) use of irony to reveal theme. Similarly, you might divide a thesis about character change into the character's original traits or attitudes, the events that cause change, and the character's new traits or attitudes.

For a story that shows character change, see "The Story of an Hour," pp. 213–15.

Introduce Your Essay.   Tie your beginning to your main idea, or thesis. If you are uncertain how to begin, try one of these openings:

For more on introductions, see pp. 294–96.

- Focus on the universality of the character (pointing out that most people might feel as Tessie in "The Lottery" did and shout "'It isn't fair, it isn't right'" if their name were drawn).
- Focus on the universality of the theme (discussing briefly how traditions seem to be losing their meaning in modern society).
- Quote a striking line from the work ("and then they were upon her" or "'Lottery in June, corn be heavy soon'").
- Start with a statement of what the work is about, with your reaction to the work when you read it, with a parallel personal experience, or with a comment about a technique that the writer uses.
- Ask a "Have you ever?" question to draw readers into your interpretation.

Support Your Interpretation.   In the paragraphs that develop your analysis, include evidence that supports your interpretation — descriptions of setting and character, summaries of events, quotations of dialogue, and other specifics from the story. Cite the page numbers (for prose) or line numbers (for poetry) where these details can be found in the work. Integrate evidence from the story with your own comments and ideas.

For more on citing and listing literary works, see E1 and E2 in the Quick Research Guide (the dark-red-edged pages).

Keep the focus on ideas, not events, by using transition markers that refer to character traits and personality change, not to time. Say "Although Mr. Summers was . . ." instead of "At the beginning of the story Mr. Summers was . . . ." Write "Tessie became . . ." instead of "After that Tessie was . . ." State "The villagers in 'The Lottery' changed . . . ," not "On the next page . . ."

For a list of transitions showing logical connections, see pp. 300–01.

Conclude Your Essay.   When you reach the end, don't just stop writing. Use the same techniques you use for introductions — anecdote, personal experience, comment on technique, quotation — to provide a sense of finality and closing for your readers. Refer to or reaffirm your thesis. Often an effective conclusion ties in directly with the introduction.

For more on conclusions, see pp. 296–98.

Revise and Edit.   Consider these questions as you shape your draft:

For more revising and editing strategies, see Ch. 19.

REVISION CHECKLIST

___ Have you clearly identified the literary work and the author near the beginning of the analysis?

___ Is your main idea or thesis clear? Does everything else relate to it?

—— Have you focused on one element or a cluster of related elements in your analysis? Have you organized around these ideas rather than events?

—— Do your transitions focus on ideas, not on plot or time sequence? Do they guide readers easily from one section or sentence to the next?

—— Are your interpretations supported by evidence from the literary work? Do you need to add specific examples of dialogue, action, or description to support your interpretation? Are the details that you select relevant to the points of analysis, or are they just interesting sidelights?

—— Have you woven the details from the work smoothly into your text? Have you cited their correct page or line numbers? Have you quoted and cited carefully instead of lifting language and sentence structure from the work without proper attribution?

—— Do you understand all the words and literary terms you use?

—— Have you tried to share your insights into the meaning of the work with your readers, or have you slipped into trying to impress them?

■ For more editing and proofreading strategies, see pp. 336–39.

After you have revised your literary analysis, edit and proofread it. Carefully check the grammar, word choice, punctuation, and mechanics — and then correct any problems you find. Make sure that you smoothly introduce all of your quotations and references to the work and weave them into your own discussion. Here are some questions to get you started editing and proofreading your paper:

■ For more help, turn to the dark-blue-edged pages, and find the Quick Editing Guide section noted here.

EDITING CHECKLIST

—— Have you used the present tense for events in the literary work and   **A 3**
for comments about the author's presentation?

—— Have you used quotation marks correctly whenever you give the   **C 3**
exact words of the literary work?

—— Have you used correct manuscript format for your paper?   **D 3**

Strategies for Writing about Literature: Synopsis and Paraphrase

LEARNING FROM OTHER WRITERS: SYNOPSIS

■ For more on summarizing and paraphrasing, see section D in the Quick Research Guide on the dark-red-edged pages.

In your literature courses you will often be asked to write synopses of short stories and novels and to paraphrase poems. Both skills are valuable because they require you to get the chronology straight and to pick out the significant events and details. Synopsis and paraphrase also help you relate the parts of a work to each other and to the themes of the work.

A *synopsis* is a summary of the plot of a narrative — a short story, a novel, a play, or a narrative poem. It describes the first level of meaning, the literal layer. It condenses the story to only the major events and the most significant details. You do not include your own interpretation, but you summarize the work in your own words, taking care not to lift language or sentence structure from the work itself. Like a synopsis, a *paraphrase* conveys the meaning of the original piece of literature and the relationships of its parts in your own words. A paraphrase, however, converts the original poetry to your own prose or the original prose to your own words in a passage about as long as the original.

In preparation for writing his literary analysis of "The Lottery" — to make sure he had the sequence of events clear — Jonathan Burns wrote the following synopsis of the story.

■ For "The Lottery," see pp. 191–97.

STUDENT EXAMPLE

Jonathan Burns
A Synopsis of "The Lottery"

Around ten o'clock on a sunny June 27, the villagers gathered in the square for a lottery, expecting to be home in time for lunch. The children came first, glad that school was out for the summer. The boys romped and gathered stones, the girls talked quietly in small groups, and the little ones hovered near their brothers and sisters. Then the men came, followed by the women. When parents called, the children came reluctantly.   1

Mr. Summers, who always conducted the town lottery, arrived with the black wooden box and set it on the three-legged stool that Mr. Graves had brought out. The villagers remained at a distance from these men and didn't respond when Mr. Summers asked for help. Finally, Mr. Martin and his son held the shabby black box as Mr. Summers mixed the papers in it. Although the townspeople had talked about replacing the box, they never had, but they had substituted paper slips for the original wooden chips. To prepare for the drawing, they listed the members of every household and swore in Mr. Summers. Although they had dropped many aspects of the original ritual, the official still greeted each person individually.   2

Tessie Hutchinson rushed into the square, telling her friend Mrs. Delacroix she had almost forgotten what day it was. Then she joined her husband and children.   3

When Mr. Summers asked if everyone was present, he was told that Clyde Dunbar was absent because of a broken leg but that his wife would draw for the family. Summers noted that the Watson boy was drawing for his mother and checked to see if Old Man Warner was present.   4

The crowd got quiet. Mr. Summers reminded everybody of what they were to do and began to call the names in alphabetical order. People in the group joked   5 nervously as the names were called. Mrs. Delacroix and Mrs. Graves commented on how fast time had passed since the last lottery, and Old Man Warner talked about how important the lottery was to the villagers. When Mr. Summers finished calling the roll, there was a pause before the heads of households opened their slips. Everybody wondered who had the special slip of paper, who had won the lottery. They discovered it was Bill Hutchinson. When Tessie complained that the drawing hadn't been done fairly, the others told her to be a "good sport."

Mr. Graves put five slips into the box, one for each member of Bill Hutchinson's   6
family. Tessie kept charging unfairness. The children drew first, then Tessie, then Bill. The children opened their slips, smiled broadly, and held blank pieces of paper over their heads. Bill opened his and it was blank too. Tessie wouldn't open hers; Bill had to do it for her. Hers had a black spot on it.

Mr. Summers urged the villagers to complete the process quickly. They picked up   7
stones, even little Davy Hutchinson, and started throwing them at Tessie, as she kept screaming, "It isn't fair, it isn't right." Then they stoned her.

Questions to Start You Thinking

Meaning

1. In what ways does this synopsis help you understand the story better?

2. Why isn't a synopsis as interesting as a short story?

3. Can you tell from this synopsis whether Burns understands Jackson's story beyond the literal level?

Writing Strategies

4. Does Burns retell the story accurately and clearly? Does he get the events in correct time order? How does he show the relationships of the events to each other and to the whole?

5. Does Burns select the details necessary to indicate what happened in "The Lottery"? Why do you think he omits certain details?

6. Are there any details, comments, or events that you would add to his synopsis? Why, or why not?

7. How does this synopsis differ from Burns's literary analysis (pp. 200–01)?

LEARNING BY WRITING: SYNOPSIS

The Assignment: Writing a Synopsis of a Story by Kate Chopin. Whenever you have trouble understanding a story or have a lot of stories to read, you may benefit from writing a synopsis so that you can easily review a story's specifics. Keep your synopsis of the plot true to the original, noting accurate details in time order. Condensing five pages to a few hundred words forces you to focus on the most important details in the story and the sequence of events. This focus often leads you to a statement of theme.

Kate Chopin was a nineteenth-century American writer whose female characters search for their own identity and for freedom from domination and oppression. For practice, write a synopsis of two hundred to three hundred words of Chopin's short story "The Story of an Hour." Consider the following questions to help you get started:

DISCOVERY CHECKLIST

___ What are the major events and details of the story?

___ In what time order do events take place?

___ How are the parts of the story related (without adding your own opinions or interpretations)?

___ Which of the author's words might you want to quote?

Kate Chopin
The Story of an Hour

Knowing that Mrs. Mallard was afflicted with a heart trouble, great care was taken to break to her as gently as possible the news of her husband's death. 1

It was her sister Josephine who told her, in broken sentences, veiled 2
hints that revealed in half concealing. Her husband's friend Richards was there, too, near her. It was he who had been in the newspaper office when intelligence of the railroad disaster was received, with Brently Mallard's name leading the list of "killed." He had only taken the time to assure himself of its truth by a second telegram, and had hastened to forestall any less careful, less tender friend in bearing the sad message.

She did not hear the story as many women have heard the same, with a 3
paralyzed inability to accept its significance. She wept at once, with sudden, wild abandonment, in her sister's arms. When the storm of grief had spent itself she went away to her room alone. She would have no one follow her.

There stood, facing the open window, a comfortable, roomy armchair. 4
Into this she sank, pressed down by a physical exhaustion that haunted her body and seemed to reach into her soul.

She could see in the open square before her house the tops of trees that 5
were all aquiver with the new spring life. The delicious breath of rain was in the air. In the street below a peddler was crying his wares. The notes of a distant song which someone was singing reached her faintly, and countless sparrows were twittering in the eaves.

There were patches of blue sky showing here and there through the 6
clouds that had met and piled one above the other in the west facing her window.

She sat with her head thrown back upon the cushion of the chair, quite 7
motionless, except when a sob came up into her throat and shook her, as a child who has cried itself to sleep continues to sob in its dreams.

She was young, with a fair, calm face, whose lines bespoke repression   8
and even a certain strength. But now there was a dull stare in her eyes,
whose gaze was fixed away off yonder on one of those patches of blue sky. It
was not a glance of reflection, but rather indicated a suspension of intelligent thought.

There was something coming to her and she was waiting for it, fearfully.   9
What was it? She did not know; it was too subtle and elusive to name. But
she felt it, creeping out of the sky, reaching toward her through the sounds,
the scents, the color that filled the air.

Now her bosom rose and fell tumultuously. She was beginning to recog-   10
nize this thing that was approaching to possess her, and she was striving to
beat it back with her will — as powerless as her two white slender hands
would have been.

When she abandoned herself a little whispered word escaped her   11
slightly parted lips. She said it over and over under her breath: "Free, free,
free!" The vacant stare and the look of terror that had followed it went from
her eyes. They stayed keen and bright. Her pulses beat fast, and the coursing
blood warmed and relaxed every inch of her body.

She did not stop to ask if it were not a monstrous joy that held her. A   12
clear and exalted perception enabled her to dismiss the suggestion as trivial.

She knew that she would weep again when she saw the kind, tender   13
hands folded in death; the face that had never looked save with love upon
her, fixed and gray and dead. But she saw beyond that bitter moment a long
procession of years to come that would belong to her absolutely. And she
opened and spread her arms out to them in welcome.

There would be no one to live for during those coming years; she would   14
live for herself. There would be no powerful will bending her in that blind
persistence with which men and women believe they have a right to impose
a private will upon a fellow creature. A kind intention or a cruel intention
made the act seem no less a crime as she looked upon it in that brief moment of illumination.

And yet she had loved him — sometimes. Often she had not. What did   15
it matter! What could love, the unsolved mystery, count for in face of this
possession of self-assertion which she suddenly recognized as the strongest
impulse of her being.

"Free! Body and soul free!" she kept whispering.   16

Josephine was kneeling before the closed door with her lips to the   17
keyhole, imploring for admission. "Louise, open the door! I beg; open the
door — you will make yourself ill. What are you doing, Louise? For heaven's
sake open the door."

"Go away. I am not making myself ill." No; she was drinking in a very   18
elixir of life through that open window.

Her fancy was running riot along those days ahead of her. Spring days,   19
and summer days, and all sorts of days that would be her own. She breathed
a quick prayer that life might be long. It was only yesterday she had thought
with a shudder that life might be long.

She arose at length and opened the door to her sister's importunities. 20
There was a feverish triumph in her eyes, and she carried herself unwittingly
like a goddess of Victory. She clasped her sister's waist, and together they descended the stairs. Richards stood waiting for them at the bottom.

Someone was opening the front door with a latchkey. It was Brently 21
Mallard who entered, a little travel-stained, composedly carrying his grip-
sack and umbrella. He had been far from the scene of the accident, and did
not even know there had been one. He stood amazed at Josephine's piercing
cry; at Richards's quick motion to screen him from the view of his wife.

But Richards was too late. 22

When the doctors came they said she had died of heart disease — of joy 23
that kills.

LEARNING BY WRITING: PARAPHRASE

The Assignment: Writing a Paraphrase of a Poem.   When you study poetry, you can benefit from paraphrasing — expressing the content of a poem
in your own words without adding your opinions or interpretations. You
may write your paraphrase in the margin next to the poem or in a notebook,
journal, or file. Writing a paraphrase forces you to divide the poem into logical sections, to figure out what the poet says in each section, and to discern
the relationships of the parts. After paraphrasing a poem, you should find it
easier to state its theme — its main idea or insight — in a sentence or two.

Consider the following questions to help you get started:

> For more on para-
> phrasing, see D4 and D6
> in the Quick Research
> Guide (the dark-red-
> edged pages).

DISCOVERY CHECKLIST

___ What are the major sections of the poem? What does the poet say in each
section?

___ How are the sections of the poem related?

___ Are there any words whose meanings you don't know? Are there any words
used in a special sense, different from the usual meanings? What do those
words mean in the context of the poem?

___ Does the poet use images to create sensory pictures or figurative language,
such as similes or metaphors, to create comparisons? How do these contribute to the meaning?

Other Assignments for Writing about Literature

1. Use a poem, a play, or a novel instead of a short story to write the literary analysis assigned in this chapter (p. 204).

> For more on writing a
> comparison and contrast
> essay, see Ch. 7.

2. Write an essay comparing and contrasting a literary element in two or three short stories or poems.

3. Paraphrase "The Road Not Taken" or "Richard Cory," poems included with the next two assignments. Express the content of the poem in your own words, paying attention to the sections of the poem and their relationships. Make sure you figure out what all the words mean and how any images or figures of speech contribute to the meaning.

4. Read the following poem by Robert Frost (1874–1963). Then write an essay in which you use a paraphrase of this poem as a springboard for your thoughts on a fork in the road of your life — a decision that made a big difference for you.

The Road Not Taken

Two roads diverged in a yellow wood,
And sorry I could not travel both
And be one traveler, long I stood
And looked down one as far as I could
To where it bent in the undergrowth;

Then took the other, as just as fair,
And having perhaps the better claim,
Because it was grassy and wanted wear;
Though as for that the passing there
Had worn them really about the same,

And both that morning equally lay
In leaves no step had trodden black.
Oh, I kept the first for another day!
Yet knowing how way leads on to way,
I doubted if I should ever come back.

I shall be telling this with a sigh
Somewhere ages and ages hence:
Two roads diverged in a wood, and I —
I took the one less traveled by,
And that has made all the difference.

For more on writing a comparison and contrast essay, see Ch. 7.

5. Read the following poem by Edwin Arlington Robinson (1869–1935). Have you known and envied someone similar to Richard Cory, someone who everyone else thought had it all? What happened to him or her? What did you discover about your impression of this individual? Write a personal response essay in which you compare and contrast the person you knew with Richard Cory. This assignment requires that you analyze the poem as well as draw on your own experience.

Richard Cory

Whenever Richard Cory went down town,
We people on the pavement looked at him:

He was a gentleman from sole to crown,
Clean favored, and imperially slim.

And he was always quietly arrayed,
And he was always human when he talked;
But still he fluttered pulses when he said,
"Good-morning," and he glittered when he walked.

And he was rich — yes, richer than a king —
And admirably schooled in every grace:
In fine, we thought that he was everything
To make us wish that we were in his place.

So on we worked, and waited for the light,
And went without the meat, and cursed the bread;
And Richard Cory, one calm summer night,
Went home and put a bullet through his head.

6. Write a critical analysis of a song, a movie, or a television program. Because you won't have a written text in front of you, you probably will need to hear the work or view it several times to pull out the specific evidence necessary to support your interpretation.

For more about analyzing visuals, see Ch. 21. For more on analysis in general, see pp. 311–13.

Chapter 13
Writing in the Workplace

M ost of the world's workplace communication takes place in writing. Although a conversation or voice mail message may be forgotten or ignored, a letter or memorandum (memo) is a physical thing that sits on a desk, calling for action and providing a permanent record of business exchanges.

Personnel managers, the people who do the hiring in large corporations, tend to be keenly interested in applicants who can write clearly, accurately, and effectively. A survey conducted at Cornell University asked executives to rate in importance the qualities they would like employees to possess. Skill in writing was ranked in fourth place, ahead of managerial skill and skill in analysis, suggesting the practical value of a writing course.

In this chapter, we first outline some general guidelines for workplace writing and then show you four kinds likely to prove useful — letters, memoranda, e-mail, and résumés.

EFFECTIVE WORKPLACE WRITING

Respectful tone

Clear purpose

Concise, clear, well-organized presentation

Reader's point of view

Guidelines for Writing in the Workplace

Good workplace writing succeeds in achieving a clear purpose. When you write to a business, your writing represents you; when you write as part of your job, your writing represents your company as well.

KNOW YOUR PURPOSE

Your purpose, or reason for writing, helps you select and arrange information; it gives you a standard against which to measure your final draft. Most likely, you will want to create a certain response in your readers, informing them about something or motivating them to take a specific action.

DISCOVERY CHECKLIST

___ Do you want to inform? (For example, do you want to make an announcement, update your readers on a developing situation, explain a specialized piece of knowledge, or reply to a request?)

___ Do you want to motivate some action? (For example, do you want a question answered, a wrong corrected, a certain decision made, or a personnel director to hire you?)

___ When your readers are finished reading what you've written, what do you want them to think? What do you want them to do?

KEEP YOUR AUDIENCE IN MIND

Consider everything in your workplace writing from your readers' point of view. After all, your purpose is not to express your ideas but to have your readers act on them, even if the action is simply to notice your grasp of the situation. If you don't know the person to whom you are writing, make educated guesses based on what you know about her or his position or company.

DISCOVERY CHECKLIST

___ What do your readers already know about the subject? Are they experts in the field? Have they been kept up to date on the situation?

___ What do your readers need to know? What information do they expect you to provide? What information do they need before they can take action?

___ What can you assume about your readers' priorities and expectations? Are they busy executives, deluged with mail and messages? Are they conscientious administrators who will appreciate your attention to detail?

___ What is most likely to motivate your readers to take the action you want?

Especially in letters and memoranda where the purpose is to motivate, it's useful to focus on how "you, the reader" will benefit instead of focusing on what "I, the writer" would like.

"I" ATTITUDE   Please send me the form so that I can process your order.

"YOU" ATTITUDE   So that you can receive your shipment promptly, please send me the form.

USE AN APPROPRIATE TONE

Tone is the quality of writing that reveals your attitude toward your topic and your readers. If you show readers that you respect them, their intelligence, and their feelings, they are far more likely to view you and your message favorably. Most workplace writing today ranges from the informal to the slightly formal. Gone are the extremely formal phrases that once dotted business correspondence: *enclosed herewith, be advised that, pursuant to the stated request.* At the other extreme, however, slang, overfriendliness, and a too casual style might cast doubts on your seriousness or credibility. Strive for a relaxed and conversational style, using simple sentences, familiar words, and the active voice.

TOO CASUAL   I hear that thing with the new lackey is a definite go.

TOO FORMAL   This office stands informed that the administration's request for supplementary personnel has been honored.

APPROPRIATE   I understand that a new office assistant has been hired.

In all your business writing, be courteous and considerate. If you are writing to complain, remember that your reader may not be the one who caused the problem — and you are more likely to win your case with courtesy than with sarcasm or insults. When delivering bad news, remember that your reader may interpret a bureaucratic response as cold and unsympathetic. And if you have made a mistake, acknowledge it.

REVISION CHECKLIST

___ Have you avoided slang terms and extremely casual language?

___ Have you avoided unnecessarily formal or sophisticated words?

___ Are your sentences of a manageable length?

___ Have you used the active voice ("I am sending it") rather than the passive voice ("It is being sent")?

___ Does anything you've written sound blaming or accusatory?

___ Do you hear a friendly, considerate, competent person behind your words?

___ Have you asked someone else to read your writing to check for tone?

PRESENT INFORMATION CAREFULLY

In business, time is money: time wasted reading irrelevant, poorly written material is money wasted. To be effective, your business writing should be concise, clear, and well organized.

For advice on document design, see Ch. 20.

Concise writing shows that you respect your readers' time. In most cases, if a letter, memo, or résumé is longer than a page or two, it's too long. You might need to find a better way to present the material, or you might need to cut unneeded information or details.

Clear writing ensures that the information you convey is accurate, complete, and unambiguous. Put the most important information in a prominent spot (usually at the beginning). Let your readers know exactly what you want them to do — politely, of course. If you have a question, ask it. If you want something, request it.

Well-organized writing helps readers move through it quickly and easily. Every piece of business correspondence should be written so that it can be skimmed. Make sure the topic of the document is absolutely clear from the very beginning, usually the first paragraph of a letter or the subject line of a memo or e-mail message. Use a conventional format that your readers will expect (see Figures 13.2 and 13.4 later in this chapter). Break information into easily processed chunks; order these chunks logically and consistently. Finally, use topic sentences and headings (when appropriate) to label each chunk of information and to give your readers an overview of your document.

> Clear presentation and organization are also important for PowerPoint slides and Web presentations. For examples, see p. 356, p. 359, and p. 363.

REVISION CHECKLIST

____ Have you kept your letter, memo, or résumé to a page or two?

____ Have you cut all unnecessary or wordy explanation?

____ Have you scrutinized every word to ensure that it can't be misinterpreted? Have you supplied all the background information readers need?

____ Have you emphasized the most important part of your message? Will readers know what you want them to do?

____ Have you followed a consistent, logical order and a conventional format?

____ If appropriate, have you included labels and headings?

> For more revising and editing strategies, see Ch. 19.

The sample message in Figure 13.1 illustrates how successful workplace writing combines attention to purpose, audience, tone, and presentation.

Business Letters

To correspond with outside parties, either individual people or other groups, organizations use business letters to request and provide information, motivate action, respond to requests, and sell goods and services. Because letters become part of the permanent record, they can be checked later to determine exactly who said what and when. You should keep a copy of every letter you write, a printout as well as a backup on disk or network.

A good business letter is brief — limited to one page if possible. It supplies whatever information the reader needs, no more. For example, a letter of inquiry might simply request a booklet, a sample, or some other promotional material. When you make a special request, however, you might add why you are writing, what you need, and when you need it. On

> For advice on job application letters, see pp. 231–32.

Figure 13.1
Sample Workplace
Communication

INTERLINK SYSTEMS, INC.

Uses standard format to
identify readers, writer, topic,
and date

TO: All Employees
FROM: Erica Xiang   *EX*
SUBJECT: Changes in employee benefits
DATE: October 21, 2003

Each fall the Human Resources group looks closely at the company's health insurance benefits to make certain that we are providing an excellent level of coverage
in a way that makes economic sense. To that end, we have made some changes to
our plan, effective January 1, 2004. Let me outline the three major changes.

Explains purpose, noting
reader's priorities

Previews clear organization
in blocks

Uses friendly tone to note
new benefit for employees

Offers assistance

1. We are pleased to be able to offer employees the opportunity, through a
   Flexible Spending Account, to pay for dependent care and unreimbursed
   health expenses on a pre-tax basis, a feature that can result in considerable
   savings. I will distribute additional information on this benefit at our staff
   meeting tomorrow, October 22, at 10:30 A.M. I will be available immediately
   after the meeting to answer any specific questions.

Introduces benefit change
with positive background

2. Those of you who have taken advantage of our **vision care benefit** in the past
   know that it offers significant help in paying for eye exams, eyeglasses, and
   contact lenses. The current plan will change slightly on January 1. Employees
   and covered dependents will be eligible to receive up to $50 each year toward
   the cost of a routine eye exam and up to $100 every two years toward the cost
   of eyeglasses or contact lenses. If you see a provider within our health insurance network, you will pay only $10 per office visit.

Presents increased cost
carefully, noting coverage
quality and high employer
contribution

3. We at Interlink Systems feel strongly that our health insurance benefits are
   excellent, but as you know, the cost of such plans continues to rise every year.
   In the interest of maintaining excellent coverage for our employees, we will
   raise our **employee contribution**. Starting January 1, we are asking employees
   with single coverage to contribute $12.50 per pay period toward the cost of
   medical insurance, and employees who cover dependents to contribute $40
   per pay period. Even with this increase, the amount the company asks its
   employees to contribute towards the premiums (about 8%) is significantly
   less than the nationwide average of 30%.

Offers more help and
supplies contact information

Please contact me if you have questions or concerns about the changes that I have
outlined in this memo. You can reach me at x462 or at exiang@interlink.net.

the other hand, a letter of complaint needs to focus on your problem — what product is involved, when and where you purchased it, exactly why you are unhappy, and how you'd like the problem solved. Include specifics such as product numbers and dates, and maintain a courteous tone. Because they are so brief, business letters are often judged on the basis of small details — grammar, punctuation, format, appearance, and openings and closings.

FORMAT FOR BUSINESS LETTERS

The format of business letters (see Figure 13.2) is well established by convention. Remember that the physical appearance of a letter is very important.

See the sample letters on pp. 224 and 232.

- Use 8½-by-11-inch bond paper, with matching envelopes. Write on only one side of the page.

- Single-space and use an extra line of space to separate paragraphs and the different elements of the letter. In very short letters, it's acceptable to leave additional space before the inside address.

- Leave margins of at least one inch on both sides; try to make the top and bottom margins fairly even, although you may have a larger bottom margin if your letter is very short.

- Pay attention to grammar, punctuation, and mechanics. Your readers will.

Return Address.   This is your address or the address of the company for which you are writing. Use no abbreviations except the two-letter postal abbreviation for the state. A return address is not needed on preprinted letterhead stationery that already provides this information.

Date.   Supply this on the line after the return address, without any extra space above. Spell out the month, and follow it by the day, a comma, and the year.

Inside Address.   This is the address of the person to whom you are writing. Begin with the person's full name and title (*Mr., Ms., Dr., Professor*); when addressing a woman who does not have a professional title, use *Ms.* unless you know that she prefers *Miss* or *Mrs.* The second line should identify the position the person holds (if any), and the third line should name the organization (if you are writing to one). If you don't know who will read your letter, it is acceptable to start with the name of the position, department, or organization. Avoid abbreviations in the address except for the two-letter state abbreviation.

Salutation.   Skip a line, and then type *Dear* followed by the person's title, last name, and a colon. If you don't know the name of the person who will read your letter, you can use the position that person holds (*Dear Editor*) or the name of the organization (*Dear Angell's Bakery*) in place of a name.

Figure 13.2   Letter Using Modified Block Style

Return address

Date

Inside address

Salutation

Introduction to situation

Request for action

Expectation of resolution

Closing

Signature

Name

1453 Illinois Avenue
Miami, FL 33133
January 26, 2004

Customer Service Department
Fidelity Products, Inc.
1192 Plymouth Avenue
Little Rock, AR 72210

Dear Customer Service Representative:

On January 12 I purchased a Fidelity media cabinet (Model XAR) from my local Tech-Mart. I have been unable to assemble the cabinet because the instructions are unclear. These instructions are incomplete (step 6 is missing) and are accompanied by diagrams so small and dark that it is impossible to distinguish the numbers for the different pieces.

Please send me usable instructions. If I do not receive clear instructions within the next three weeks, I will have to return my media cabinet to the Tech-Mart where I purchased it and request a full refund.

— Body

I have used your equipment for more than ten years and have been very satisfied, so I was particularly disappointed to find that the media cabinet did not come with clear directions for assembly. I look forward to a prompt resolution of this problem.

Sincerely,

James Winter

James Winter

Body.   This is your message. Leave one line of space between paragraphs, and begin each paragraph even with the left margin (no indentations). Paragraphs should generally be no longer than seven or eight typed lines.

Closing.   Leave one line of space after the last paragraph, and then use a conventional closing followed by a comma: *Sincerely, Sincerely yours, Respectfully yours, Yours truly.*

Typed Name with Position.   Leave four lines of space after the closing, and type your name in full, even if you will sign only your first name. Do not include a title before your name. If you are writing on behalf of an organization, you can include your position on the next line.

Signature.   After you have printed the letter, sign your name in the space between the closing and the typed name. Unless you have established a personal relationship with the person to whom you are writing, use both your first and last names. Do not include a title before your name.

Abbreviations at End.   Leave at least two lines of extra space between your typed name and any abbreviations used to communicate more information about the letter. Put each abbreviation on a separate line. If you send a copy to someone other than the recipient, use *cc:* followed by the name of the person or organization receiving a copy. If the letter is accompanied by another document in the same envelope, use *Enc.* or *Enclosure.* If the letter has been typed by someone other than the person who wrote and signed it, the writer's initials are given in capital letters, followed by a slash and the initials of the typist in lowercase letters: *VW/dbw.*

Modified and Full Block Style.   Two standard formats specify the placement of the elements on the page. To align a letter using *modified block style* (see Figure 13.2), you need to imagine a line running down the center of the page from top to bottom. The return address, date, closing, signature, and typed name are placed so that the left side of each aligns with this center line. The *full block style* is generally used only on letterhead stationery with the name and address of the organization. Omit typing the return address, and align all the elements at the left margin.

Envelope Formats.   The U.S. Postal Service recommends a format that uses all capital letters, standard abbreviations, and no punctuation; this style makes the information on the envelope easier for the Postal Service to scan and process. However, the conventional envelope format (see Figure 13.3) may be preferred and is always safe to use.

Memoranda

A *memorandum* (*memo* for short) is a form of communication used within a company to request or exchange information, to make announcements, and to confirm conversations. Memos are frequently used to convey information to large groups — an entire team, department, or organization. Generally, the topic of a memo is quite narrow and should be apparent to the reader in a glance. Memos tend to be written in the first person (*I* or *we*) and can range from the very informal (if written to a peer) to the extremely formal (if written to a high-ranking superior on an important matter). Most are short, but the memo format can be used to convey proposals and reports; long memos freely use headings, subheadings, lists, and other features that are easy to scan. (For a sample, see Figure 13.4.)

Figure 13.3
Envelope Formats

U.S. Postal Service format

JAMES WINTER
1453 ILLINOIS AVE
MIAMI FL 33133-3955

CUSTOMER SERVICE DEPT
FIDELITY PRODUCTS INC
1192 PLYMOUTH AVE
LITTLE ROCK AR 72210-4687

Conventional format

Maria Solis
Customer Service Department
Fidelity Products, Inc.
1192 Plymouth Avenue
Little Rock, AR 72210-4687

Mr. James Winter
1453 Illinois Avenue
Miami, FL 33133-3955

FORMAT FOR MEMORANDA

 See also Fig. 13.1 on p. 222.

Although every organization has its own format for memos, the heading generally consists of a series of lines with clear labels (followed by colons).

Date:	(date on which memo is sent)
To:	(person or persons to whom it is primarily addressed)
cc:	(names of anyone else who receives a copy)
From:	(name of the writer)
Subject: *or* Re:	(concise, accurate statement of the memo's topic)

The subject line often determines whether a memo is read. (The old-fashioned abbreviation *Re:* for *regarding* is still used, but we recommend the more common *Subject.*) Accurately summarize the topic in a few words ("Agenda for 12/10 meeting with Ann Kois," "Sales estimates for new product line").

Electronic Mail

Electronic mail (*e-mail* for short) is popular in business settings because it is easy, speedy, and convenient, combining immediacy with the permanence of letters and memos. It is commonly used both within organizations and between organizations and outside parties. However, letters and memos are often still preferred for formal, official correspondence.

Figure 13.4
Memorandum

memorandum

Date: February 9, 2004   Standard heading labels

To: Edward Copply, Director, Product Support

cc: Justin Blake

From: Maria Solis, Customer Service Supervisor   *MS*

Subject: Customer dissatisfaction with instructions for Model XAR

As I mentioned in our conversation of January 30, the Customer Service Department has   Confirmation of
recently received many letters and phone calls regarding the instructions for assembling our   conversation
new media cabinet, Model XAR. Customers find these instructions confusing and often ask
us to arrange a refund. (A copy of the instructions is attached.)

After examining the letters in our files, I've concluded that customers have two specific   Specific issues
concerns. The first concern is that the written instructions skip words and entire steps. If
you look at the attached copy, you will notice that there is no step 6 and that step 3 reads
"Connect the to leg one." The second concern is that the drawings are too dark. Customers
complain that dark shading obscures the numbers and makes it difficult to determine where
one section begins and the other ends.

The number of calls and letters we're getting suggests that these poor instructions are
creating frustration and resentment among both our loyal customers and first-time buyers.
In most cases, the customers who contact us are satisfied when we send them a photocopied
set of the corrected instructions we've created here in Customer Service, but I feel strongly
that the instructions sent out with the product should be improved.

I know that you're planning to review and revise the entire line of product information   Recommendation
sheets and instructions, Ed. I recommend that the instructions for Model XAR be put at
the top of the list.

Please let me know if I can provide further information.   Offer of assistance

Enclosure   Enclosure noted

Because it seems so conversational, e-mail may not be polished like other written messages. People who correspond regularly through e-mail tend to forgive one another's infelicities; however, you should remember that your e-mail messages are a part of the official record and have no guarantee of privacy. You may feel that you are having a confidential chat with a trusted friend or colleague, but the chat can be intercepted, recorded on other computers, and distributed either in print or over a network.

FORMAT FOR E-MAIL

The headings for e-mail are predetermined by the systems that generate and transmit it; these almost universally use a standard memo format. The computer will prompt you to enter information in the header lines: *To:*, *cc:*, and *Subject:*, for example. Then you simply type your message. The person receiving your message sees your headers as well as a *From* line with your name.

E-mail is a flexible form with a wide range of acceptable practices. Many e-mail messages will be read and answered while displayed on the computer screen. If possible, keep messages short. If a message runs long, make it easy to navigate by stating at the beginning what it covers and by using clear headings and noticeable dividers (extra space between sections, for example).

Résumés and Application Letters

The most important business correspondence you write may be the résumé and letter you use to apply for a job. Direct, persuasive, correct prose can help you stand out above the crowd.

RÉSUMÉS

In a résumé, you present yourself as someone who has the qualifications needed to excel at a job, someone who will be an asset to the organization. Job seekers often have multiple copies of a single résumé on hand, but you may want to customize your résumé for each job application if you can easily print out attractive copies.

Although a résumé is a highly formatted document, it also allows a wide variety of decisions about style, organization, and appearance. In this section, we describe a typical résumé, but many formats are acceptable. Unless you have a great deal of relevant work experience, your résumé should be no longer than one page. The standard résumé consists of a heading and labeled sections that detail your experience and qualifications. Within each section, use brief, pointed phrases and clauses rather than complete sentences. Use action verbs (*supervised, ordered, maintained*) and the active voice whenever possible. Highlight labels with underlining, boldface, or a larger type size. Arrange information on the page so that it is pleasing to the eye; use the best paper and clearest printer you can. (For an example of a résumé, see Figure 13.5.)

■ For more on document design, see Ch. 20.

If you submit electronic applications, you may need to prepare your résumé in several different forms: a text file that you can attach to an e-mail message, an electronically readable version that a company can scan into its database, or a Web version that you can post on your site or a job site (see Figure 13.6). For all these versions, format carefully so that recipients can easily read what you supply. Turn to your campus career center for résumé samples and advice about using alternate formats to your advantage.

Figure 13.5
Conventional Résumé

Anne Cahill
402 Pigeon Hill Road
Windsor, CT 06095
(860) 555-5763
acahill@mediaone.com

Heading with
contact information

Section labels

Objective	Position as Registered Nurse in pediatric hospital setting
Education	**University of Connecticut**, Storrs, CT. Bachelor of Science, Major in nursing, May 2004. GPA: 3.5.

Specific background
and experience

Manchester Community Technical College, Manchester, CT. Associate degree in occupational therapy, May 1998. GPA: 3.3.

Work Experience
9/99–present   **Certified Occupational Therapy Assistant**, Johnson Memorial Hospital, Stafford Springs, CT
• Assist children with delayed motor development and cerebral palsy to develop skills for the activities of daily life

9/97–9/99   **Nursing Assistant**, Woodlake Healthcare Center, Tolland, CT
• Helped geriatric residents with activities of daily living
• Assisted nursing staff in treating acute care patients

Current information
placed first

9/95–9/97   **Cashier**, Stop and Shop Supermarket, Vernon, CT
• Trained newly hired cashiers

Clinical Internships   **St. Francis Hospital**, Hartford CT
• Student Nurse, Maternity and Postpartum, spring 2004

Hartford Hospital, Hartford, CT
• Student Nurse, Pediatrics, fall 2003

Visiting Nurse and Community Health, Mansfield, CT
• Student Nurse, Community, spring 2003

Manchester General Hospital, Manchester, CT
• Student Nurse, Medical-Surgical, fall 2002

Computer Skills   • Proficient with Microsoft Office, Database, and Windows 2000 applications
• Experienced with Internet research

Activities   • Student Union Board of Governors, University of Connecticut, class representative
• Intramural soccer

References   Available upon request

Figure 13.6
Résumé for the Web

Heading

Menu for available
information

Web design using bullets and
white space

Anne Cahill

Objective: **Position as a Registered Nurse in pediatric hospital setting**

- Education
- Experience
- Other Activities
- References
- Contact Me

Profile

New nursing graduate combines proficiency in the latest nursing techniques with significant clinical experience

- Experienced in providing professional, compassionate health-care services to children, others

- Able to work proficiently and productively in hospital settings

- Accustomed to working in a team with a broad range of health professionals and administrators

- Proficient with Microsoft Office, Database, and Windows 2000 applications and with Internet research

Heading.   The heading is generally centered (or otherwise pleasingly aligned) on the page with separate lines for your name; street address; city, state, and zip code; phone number; and e-mail address.

Employment Objective.   This optional section allows personnel officers to see at a glance your priorities and goals. Try to sound confident and eager but not pompous or presumptuous.

Education.   This section is almost always included, generally first. For each postsecondary school you've attended, specify the name of the institution, your major, your date of graduation (or expected graduation), and your grade point average (if it reflects well on you). You can also mention any awards, honors, or relevant course work.

Experience.   In this key section of the résumé, list each job separately with the most recent one first. You can include both full-time and part-time jobs.

For each, give the name of the organization, your position, your responsibilities, and the dates you held the job. If you were involved in any unusual projects or were responsible for any important developments, describe them. Highlight details that show relevant work experience and leadership ability. Minimize information about jobs or responsibilities that are unconnected to the job for which you're applying.

Skills. If your special skills (data processing, technical drawing, knowledge of a foreign language) aren't obvious from the descriptions of your education and work experience, you can list them.

Activities. You can specify either professional interests and activities (*Member of Birmingham Bricklayers Association*) or personal pursuits (*skiing, hiking, needlepoint*) showing that you are dedicated and well-rounded.

References. If a job advertisement requests references, provide them. Always contact your references in advance to make sure they are willing to give you a good recommendation. For each person, list the name, his or her organization and position, and the organization's address and phone number. If references have not been requested, you can simply note "Available on request."

APPLICATION LETTERS

When writing a letter applying for a job, you should follow all the guidelines for other business letters. Remember that your immediate objective is to obtain an interview. As you compete against other candidates, your letter and résumé are all the employer has to judge you on.

For general guidelines for business letters, see pp. 221–25.

If you're responding to an advertisement, read it critically. What qualifications are listed? Ideally, you should have all the required qualifications, but if you lack one, try to find something in your background that compensates, some similar experience in a different form. What else can you tell about the organization or position from the ad? How does the organization represent itself? (If you're unfamiliar with the organization and you can't glean much about it from the ad, check the company's Web site.) How does the ad describe the ideal candidate? As a team player? A dynamic individual? If you feel that you are the person this organization is looking for, you'll want to portray yourself this way in your letter.

In your letter, you want to spark your readers' interest, convince them that you're a qualified and attractive candidate, and motivate them to interview you. Whenever possible, address your letter to the person responsible for screening applicants and setting up interviews; you may need to call the organization to find out this person's name. In the first paragraph, identify the job, indicate how you heard about it, and summarize your qualifications. In the second paragraph, expand on your qualifications, highlighting key information on your résumé and supplementing it with additional details, if necessary. At this point, you need to show your readers that you're a better candidate than the other applicants. In the third paragraph, restate your interest in the job, ask for an interview, and let your prospective employer know how to reach you. (For a sample application letter, see Figure 13.7 below.)

Figure 13.7
Application Letter

Follows standard
letter format

Addresses specific person

Identifies job sought and
specifies interest

Explains qualifications

Confirms interest and
supplies contact information

Encloses résumé and proof
of certification

---

402 Pigeon Hill Road
Windsor, CT 06095
July 8, 2004

Sheryl Sullivan
Director of Nursing
Center for Children's Health and Development
St. Francis Hospital and Medical Center
114 Woodland Street
Hartford, CT 06105

Dear Ms. Sullivan:

I am writing to apply for the full-time position as a pediatric nurse at the Center for Children's Health and Development at St. Francis Hospital, which was advertised on the Eastern Connecticut Health Network Web site. I feel that my varied clinical experiences and my desire to work with children ideally suit me for the job. In addition, I am highly motivated to grow and succeed in the field of health care.

I have worked for the past five years as a certified occupational therapy assistant. In this capacity, I help children with delayed motor function acquire the skills necessary to achieve as high a level of independence as possible. While working as a COTA, I attended nursing school with the ultimate goal of becoming a pediatric nurse. My varied clinical experiences as a student nurse and my previous experience as a nurse's aide in a geriatric center have exposed me to many types of care. I feel that these experiences have helped me to become a well-rounded caregiver; they also, however, have reinforced my belief that my skills and talents are best suited to working with children.

I believe that I would be a strong addition to the medical team at the Children's Center. My clinical experiences have prepared me to deal with a wide range of situations. In addition, I am dedicated to maintaining and enhancing the well-being of children. I am enclosing proof of my recent certification as a Registered Nurse in the state of Connecticut. Please write to me at the address above, e-mail me at acahill783@yahoo.com, or call me at (860) 555-5763. Thank you for your consideration. I look forward to hearing from you.

Sincerely,

Anne Cahill

Anne Cahill

Enclosures

Chapter 14
Writing for Assessment

Most college writing is done for assessment—that is, most of the papers you hand in are eventually evaluated and graded. But some college writing tasks exist *only* as methods of assessment: they are designed not to help you expand your writing skills (or content knowledge) but to allow you to demonstrate that you have mastered them. You often need to do such writing on the spot—a quiz to finish in twenty minutes, a final exam to complete in a few hours, an impromptu essay to dash off in one class period. How do you discover and shape your ideas in a limited time?

In this chapter we provide tips for three types of in-class writing that are commonly used for assessment—the essay exam, the short-answer exam, and the timed writing assignment. We also discuss the writing portfolio, a collection of writing samples that demonstrates your strengths as a writer.

Essay Examinations

In many courses an essay exam is the most important kind of in-class writing. Instructors believe that such writing shows that you haven't just memorized a batch of material but that you have examined it critically and can clearly communicate your thoughts about it to someone else.

PREPARING FOR THE EXAM

Some instructors favor open-book exams, in which you bring your books and perhaps your notes to class for reference. In an open-book exam, ability to memorize and recall is less important than ability to reason and to select what matters most. On the other hand—if the exam will be closed book—it's a good idea to fix in your memory any vital names, dates, and definitions.

But when you review, don't clutter your mind with random details. Instead, look for the main ideas in each textbook chapter. Then ask yourself: What do these ideas have to do with each other? How might they be combined? What conclusions can I draw from all the facts?

A good way to prepare for any exam, whether the books are closed or open, is to imagine questions you might be asked and then plan answers. If your instructor has supplied sample questions, pattern new questions after them.

LEARNING FROM ANOTHER WRITER

To start looking at techniques for answering *any* exam question, let's take one concrete example. A final exam in developmental psychology posed this question:

> What evidence indicates innate factors in perceptual organization? You might find it useful to recall any research that shows how infants perceive depth and forms.

In response, David Ian Cohn sat back in his chair for a few minutes and thought over the reading he'd done for the course. What perception research had used babies for subjects? He jotted down ideas, crossed out a couple of weak ones, and drew lines linking ideas that went together. Then he took a deep breath and wrote this straightforward answer:

■ For an illustration of linking, see p. 278.

> Research on infants is probably the best way to demonstrate that some factors in perceptual organization are innate. As the cliff box experiment shows, an infant will avoid what looks like a drop-off, even though its mother calls it and even though it can feel glass covering the drop-off area. The same infant will crawl to the other end of the box, which appears (and is) safe. Apparently, infants do not have to be taught what a cliff looks like.
>
> Psychologists have also observed that infants are aware of size constancy. They recognize a difference in size between a 10 cm box at a distance of one meter and a 20 cm box at a distance of two meters. If this phenomenon is not innate, it is at least learned early, for the subjects of the experiment were infants of sixteen to eighteen months.
>
> When shown various patterns, infants tend to respond more noticeably to patterns that resemble the human face than to those that appear random. This seemingly innate recognition helps the infant identify people (such as its mother) from less important inanimate objects.
>
> Infants also seem to have an innate ability to match sight with sound. When simultaneously shown two television screens, each depicting a different subject, while being played a tape that sometimes matched one screen and sometimes the other, infants looked at whichever screen matched what they heard — not always, but at least twice as often.

Questions to Start You Thinking

Meaning

1. What is the main idea of Cohn's answer?

2. If you were the psychology instructor, how could you immediately see that Cohn had thoroughly dealt with the question and only with the question?

Writing Strategies

3. In what places is Cohn's answer concrete and specific, not vague and general?

4. Suppose Cohn had tacked on a concluding sentence: "Thus I have conclusively proved that there are innate factors in perceptual organization, by citing much evidence showing that infants definitely can perceive depth and forms." Would that sentence have strengthened his answer?

GENERATING IDEAS

Once you are in the classroom, beginning your race with the clock, resist the temptation to start scribbling. First read over all the questions on the exam carefully. If you are offered a choice, just cross out any questions you are *not* going to answer so you don't waste time on them by mistake. If you don't understand what a question calls for, ask your instructor right away.

Plan a Concrete Answer.   Few people can dash off an excellent essay exam answer without first taking time to plan. Instructors prefer answers that are concrete and specific rather than those that wander in the clouds of generality. David Cohn's answer to the psychology question cites evidence all the way through — particular experiments in which infants were subjects. Take a little time — as Cohn did — to generate concrete examples.

Organize around the Question.   Instructors also prefer answers that are organized and coherent rather than rambling. Often a question will contain directive words that help you define your task: *evaluate, compare, discuss, explain, describe, summarize, trace the development of.* You can put yourself on the right track if you incorporate a form of such a word in your first sentence.

QUESTION	Define romanticism, citing its major characteristics and giving examples of each.
ANSWER	Romanticism is defined as . . .
ANSWER	Romanticism is a complex concept, difficult to define. It . . .

PLANNING: RECOGNIZING TYPICAL EXAM QUESTIONS

Most exam questions fall into types. If you can recognize them, you will know how to organize and begin to write. Here are examples.

For more on explaining cause and effect, see Ch. 8 and pp. 320–21.

The Cause and Effect Question.   These questions usually mention *causes* and *effects*.

> What were the immediate causes of the stock market crash of 1929?

> Describe the principal effects on the economy that commonly result from a low prime rate of interest.

For more on comparing and contrasting, see Ch. 7 and pp. 318–20.

The Compare or Contrast Question.   This popular type of question calls on you to point out similarities (comparing), discuss differences (contrasting), or do both, in the process explaining not one subject but two. Be sure to pay attention to both subjects, paralleling the points you make about each, giving both equal space.

> Compare and contrast *iconic memory* and *eidetic imagery.* (1) Define the two terms, indicating the ways in which they differ, and (2) state the way or ways in which they are related or alike.

After supplying a one-sentence definition of each term, a student proceeded first to contrast and then to compare, for full credit.

> *Iconic memory is a picturelike impression that lasts for only a fraction of a second in short-term memory. Eidetic imagery is the ability to take a mental photograph, exact in detail, as though its subject were still present. But iconic memory soon disappears. Unlike an eidetic image, it does not last long enough to enter long-term memory. IM is common; EI is unusual: very few people have it. Both iconic memory and eidetic imagery are similar, however: both record visual images, and every sighted person of normal intelligence has both abilities to some degree.*

A question of this kind doesn't always use the words *compare* and *contrast.*

> Signal at least three differences between Copernicus's and Kepler's models of the solar system. In what respects was Kepler's model an improvement on that of Copernicus? [*contrast and show superiority*]

> Distinguish between agnosia and receptive aphasia. In what ways are the two conditions similar? [*contrast and then compare*]

> Briefly explain the duplex theory of memory. What are the main differences between short-term memory and long-term memory? [*contrast only*]

The Demonstration Question.   This kind of question gives you a statement and asks you to back it up.

> Demonstrate the truth of Freud's contention that laughter may contain elements of aggression.

In other words, you are asked to explain Freud's claim and supply evidence to support it. You might refer to crowd scenes you have experienced, analyze a joke or a scene in a TV show, or use examples from your reading.

The Discussion Question.   A discussion question may tempt the unwary to shoot the breeze.

> Discuss three events that precipitated Lyndon B. Johnson's withdrawal from the 1968 presidential race.

This question looks like an open invitation to ramble about Johnson and Vietnam, but it isn't. Try rewording the question to help you focus your discussion: "Why did President Johnson decide not to seek another term? Analyze the causes and briefly explain each."

Sometimes a discussion question won't announce itself with the word *discuss*, but with *describe* or *explain* or *explore*.

> Describe the national experience following passage of the Eighteenth Amendment. What did most Americans learn from it?

Provided you know that this amendment banned the sale, manufacture, and transportation of alcoholic drinks and that it was finally repealed, you can discuss its effects — or perhaps the reasons for its repeal.

The Divide or Classify Question.   Sometimes you are asked to slice the subject into sections, sort things into kinds, or break the idea, place, person, or process into its parts.

For more on division and classification, see pp. 314–16.

> Identify the ways in which each inhabitant of the United States uses, on the average, 1,595 gallons of water a day. How and to what degree might each person cut down on this amount?

For a start, you would divide up water use into several parts — drinking, cooking, bathing, washing cars, and so on. Then, after that division, you would give tips for water conservation and tell how effective each is.

> What different genres of film did King Vidor direct? Name at least one outstanding example of each kind.

This classification question asks you to sort films into categories — possibly comedy, war, adventure, mystery, musical, western.

The Definition Question.   When you write an extended definition, illustrate it with an example.

For more on definition, see pp. 310–11.

> Explain the three dominant styles of parenting — *permissive, authoritarian-restrictive,* and *authoritative.*

This question calls for a trio of definitions. The next, however, asks you to explain a single method and give examples.

> Define the Stanislavsky method of acting, citing outstanding actors who have followed it.

The Evaluation Question.   This favorite calls on students to think critically and to present an argument.

For more on evaluating, see Chs. 9 and 11.

Present and evaluate the most widely accepted theories to account for the disappearance of the dinosaurs.

Evaluate *one* of the following suggestions, giving reasons for your judgments:

a. Cities should stop building highways to the suburbs and instead build public monorail systems.

b. Houses and public buildings should be constructed to last no longer than twenty years.

Other argument questions might begin "Defend the idea of . . ." or "Show weaknesses in the concept of . . ." or otherwise call on you to take a stand.

The Respond to the Comment or Quotation Question.   A question might supply a statement for close reading, asking you to test the writer's opinion against what you know.

Discuss the following statement: high-minded opposition to slavery was only one cause, and not a very important one, of the animosity between North and South that in 1861 escalated into civil war.

Carefully read the statement a few times, and then jot down contrary or supporting evidence.

Was the following passage written by Gertrude Stein, Kate Chopin, or Tillie Olsen? On what evidence do you base your answer?

She waited for the material pictures which she thought would gather and blaze before her imagination. She waited in vain. She saw no pictures of solitude, of hope, of longing, or of despair. But the very passions themselves were aroused within her soul, swaying it, lashing it, as the waves daily beat upon her splendid body. She trembled, she was choking, and the tears blinded her.

The passage is taken from a story by Kate Chopin. If you were familiar with Chopin, who specializes in physical and emotional descriptions of impassioned women, you would know this answer, and you might point to language (*swaying, lashing*) that marks it as hers.

■ For more on process analysis, see pp. 316–18.   **The Process Analysis Question.**   Often you can spot this kind of question by the word *trace*:

Trace the stages through which a bill becomes a federal law.

Trace the development of the medieval Italian city-state.

Both questions want you to tell how something occurs or occurred. In brief, you divide the process into steps and detail each step. The other type of process analysis, the "how-to" variety, is called for in this question:

An employee has been consistently late for work, varying from fifteen minutes to a half hour daily. This employee has been on the job only five months but shows promise of learning skills that your firm needs badly. How would you deal with this situation?

The Imaginative Question.   Sometimes an instructor will throw in a question that at first glance might seem bizarre. On second glance, you may see that the question reaches deep.

> Imagine yourself to be a trial lawyer in 1921, charged with defending Nicola Sacco and Bartolomeo Vanzetti, two anarchists accused of murder. Argue for their acquittal on whatever grounds you can justify.

This question calls on a prelaw student to show familiarity with a famous case (which ended with the execution of the defendants). In addition, it calls for knowledge of the law and of trial procedure. Such a question might be fun to answer; moreover, in being asked to imagine a time, a place, and dramatic circumstances, you might learn something.

DRAFTING: THE ONLY VERSION

When the clock on the wall is ticking away, generating ideas and shaping an answer often take place at the same time. If you can do your preliminary work right on the exam sheet, you will save time: annotate questions, underline important points, scribble short definitions. Write reminders that you will notice while you work: TWO PARTS TO THIS QUES.! or GET IN EXAMPLE OF ABORIGINES. To make sure that you include all necessary information without repetition, you might jot down a brief, informal outline. This was David Cohn's outline for his answer on his psychology exam:

For David Cohn's complete answer, see p. 234.

> *Thesis: Research on infants is probably the best way to demonstrate that some factors in perceptual organization are innate.*
> *Cliff box — kid fears drop despite glass, mother, knows shallow side safe*
> *Size constancy — learned early if not intrinsic*
> *Shapes — infants respond more/better to face shape than nonformed*
> *Match sound w/ sight — 2 TVs, look twice as much at right one*

Budget Your Time.   When you have two or more essay questions to answer, block out your time roughly based on the points or minutes your instructor allots to each. Give extra minutes to a complicated question (such as one with several parts). Then pace yourself as you write. For example, make a little schedule so you'll wrap up question 2 at 10:30 and move on.

Begin with the Easy Questions.   Many students find that it helps their morale to start with the question they feel best able to answer. Unless your instructor specifies that you have to answer the questions in order, why not skip around? Just make sure you clearly number each answer or label the item as your instructor does. Then begin each answer in such a way that the instructor will immediately recognize which question you're answering. If the task is "Compare and contrast the depression of the 1930s with the recession that began in 2001," an answer might begin in this way:

Compared to the paralyzing depression that began in 1929, the latest recession seems like a bad case of measles.

For more on thesis statements, see pp. 271–77. For David Cohn's complete answer, see p. 234.

Try Stating Your Thesis at the Start.   Some students make their opening sentence a thesis statement—a sentence that immediately makes clear the main point. Then they proceed in the rest of the answer to back up that statement. Stating a clear thesis often makes good sense; you'll be less likely to ramble, and your instructor will know right away what you're talking about. That's how David Cohn opens his answer to the psychology question. An easy way to get started is to turn the question into a statement and use it to begin an answer.

QUESTION
Can adequate reasons for leasing cars and office equipment, instead of purchasing them, be cited for a two-person partnership?

ANSWER
I can cite at least four adequate reasons for a two-person partnership to lease cars and office equipment. For one thing, under present tax laws, the entire cost of a regular payment under a leasing agreement may be deducted....

Stick to the Point of the Question.   You may be tempted to throw into your answer everything you have learned in the course. But to do so defeats the purpose of the examination—to use your knowledge, not to parade it. Answer by selecting and shaping *what matters*.

Answer the Whole Question.   Often a question will have two parts.

Name the most common styles of contemporary architecture and then evaluate one of them.

When the dragon of a question has two heads, make sure you cut off both.

Stay Specific.   Pressed for time, some exam takers think, "I haven't got time to get specific here. I'll just sum this up in general." That's a mistake. Every time you throw in a broad statement ("The Industrial Revolution was beneficial for the peasant"), take time to add specific examples ("In Dusseldorf, as Taine tells us, the mortality rate from starvation among displaced Prussian farmworkers dropped from a peak of almost 10 percent a year").

Leave Room to Revise.   Give yourself room for second thoughts by writing on only one side of the page in your examination booklet and skipping every other line. Then later, should you wish to add words or sentences or even a whole paragraph, you can do so with ease.

REVISING: REREADING AND PROOFING

If you have paced yourself, you'll have at least a few minutes left to look over your work. Check how clear your ideas are and how well they hang together. Add sentences wherever you think new ones are needed. If you recall an important point, you can add a paragraph on a blank left-hand page. Just draw an arrow indicating where it goes.

Naturally, errors occur more often when you write under pressure than when you have time to proofread and edit carefully. On an exam, what you say and how forcefully you say it matter most. Still, no instructor will object to careful corrections. You can easily add words with carets (^):

foreign
Israeli ^ policy

Or you can neatly strike out a word by drawing a line through it.

When your paper or blue book is returned, consider these questions as you look it over:

ESSAY EXAM CHECKLIST

___ Did you answer the whole question, not just part of it?

___ Did you stick to the point, not throw in unrequested information?

___ Did you make your general statements clear by citing evidence or examples?

___ Does your answer sprawl, or is it focused?

___ Did you inflate your answer with hot air, or did you stay close to earth, giving plenty of facts, examples, and illustrations?

___ Did you proofread for omissions and lack of clarity?

___ On what question or questions do you feel you did a good job that satisfies you, no matter what grade you received?

___ If you had to write this exam over again, how would you now go about it?

Short-Answer Examinations

The *short-answer exam* may call on you to identify names or phrases from your reading, in a sentence or a few words.

Identify the following: Clemenceau, Treaty of Versailles, Maginot line.

You might answer the question as follows:

Georges Clemenceau — This French premier, nicknamed The Tiger, headed a popular coalition cabinet during World War I and at the Paris Peace Conference demanded stronger penalties against Germany.

▓ For more about writing definitions, see pp. 310–11.

Writing a short identification is much like writing a short definition. Be sure to mention the general class to which a thing belongs.

> *Treaty of Versailles — pact between Germany and the Allies that . . .*
> *Maginot line — fortifications that . . .*

If you do so, you won't lose points for writing an answer like this, which fails to make clear the nature of the thing being identified:

> *Maginot line — The Germans went around it.*

Timed Writings

Many composition instructors, to give you experience in writing on demand, assign impromptu in-class essays. For such writings, your time is limited (usually forty-five minutes to an hour), the setting is controlled (usually you're at a desk and not allowed to use a dictionary or a spell checker), and you can't choose your own subject. The purpose of timed writings is to test your writing skills, not to see how much information you can recall.

Though this rapid-fire type of writing seems a lot different from the leisurely think-plan-draft-revise method of composing, your usual methods of writing can serve you well, even used in a hurry.

Budget Your Time.   For an in-class essay, if you have forty-five minutes to write, a good rule of thumb is to spend ten minutes preparing, thirty minutes writing, and five minutes rereading and making last-minute changes. Take care not to spend so much time thinking and planning that you must rush through getting your ideas down on paper in an essay — the part you will be graded on.

Choose Your Topic Wisely.   For on-the-spot writing, the trick is to make the topic your own. If you have a choice at all, choose the one you know the most about, not the one you think will impress your readers. They'll be most impressed by logical argument and solid evidence. If you have to write on a broad abstract subject (say, a world problem that affects many people), bring it down to something personal, something you have observed or experienced. Have you witnessed traffic jams, brownouts, or condos ruining beaches? Then write about increased population, using these examples.

Think and Plan before You Write.   Despite your limited time, read the instructions and the topics or questions carefully, choose your topic thoughtfully, restrict it to something you know about, form a main idea for focus, and jot down the major divisions for development. If a good hook for the introduction or conclusion occurs to you, make a note of it. Just don't spend so much time on planning that you can't finish the essay.

Don't Try to Be Perfect.   No one expects extemporaneous essays to read as smoothly as reports written over several weeks. You can't polish every sentence or remember the exact word for every spot. And never waste time recopying. Devote your time to the more important parts of writing.

Save Time to Proofread.   The last few minutes when you read over your work and correct glaring errors may be the best-spent minutes of all. Cross out and make corrections neatly. Use asterisks (*), arrows, and carets (^). Especially check for the following:

> ■ For more on making corrections, see the Quick Editing Guide (the dark-blue-edged pages).

- omitted letters (*-ed* or *-s*)
- added letters (develop*e*)
- inverted letters (rec*ie*ve)
- wrong punctuation (a comma instead of a period)
- omitted apostrophes (*dont* instead of *don't*)
- omitted words ("She going" instead of "She *is* going")
- wrong words (*except* instead of *accept*)
- misspelled words (*mispelled*)

TYPES OF TOPICS

Often you can expect the same types of questions or topics for in-class writings as for essay exams. If you know how to organize those types, you can do well. Remember to look for the key words and do what they say.

> ■ For common types of exam questions, see pp. 235–39.

Thinking Fast

To practice planning quickly for timed writing or tests, brainstorm as a class to explore approaches to writing on the sample topics provided in this chapter. Select one class member (or three, in turn) to record ideas on the board. Devote exactly ten minutes of discussion per topic to these key parts of a successful response:

FOR GROUP LEARNING

- possible thesis sentences
- possible patterns of organization
- possible kinds and sources of evidence

Expect a wide range of ideas. Spend the last part of class evaluating them.

What were the *causes* of World War I?

Compare and contrast the theories of capitalism and socialism.

Define civil rights.

If you are given a general subject on which thousands of diverse students can write, add your personal twist. Again, pay attention to key words.

Analyze a problem in education that is *difficult to solve.*

Discuss ways to cope with stress.

Standardized tests often ask you to respond to a short passage, testing not only your writing ability but also your reading comprehension.

Thomas Jefferson stated, "If a nation expects to be ignorant and free, in a state of civilization, it expects what never was and never will be." *How* is his comment *relevant* to education today?

Writing for Portfolio Assessment

The writing portfolio has become a popular method of assessment for college classes. Portfolio courses typically emphasize revision and reflection — the ability to identify and discuss your choices, strengths, or learning processes. In such a course, you'll need to save all your drafts and notes, keep track of your choices and changes, and near the end of the term select and submit your best writing.

A writing portfolio is a collection of pieces of writing that represent the writer's best work. Collected over time and across projects, a portfolio showcases a writer's talent, hard work, and ability to make thoughtful choices about content and presentation. For a single course, the portfolio is usually due at the end of the term and includes pieces you have written and revised for that course. Most portfolios need some kind of introduction (usually a self-assessment or rationale) addressed to readers, who might be teachers, supervisors, evaluators, parents, or classmates.

UNDERSTANDING PORTFOLIO ASSESSMENT

The portfolio is a method of evaluation and teaching that shapes the whole course from beginning to end. For example, your portfolio course will probably emphasize responses to your writing — from your classmates and your instructor — but not necessarily grades on your separate papers. The portfolio method attempts to shift attention to the writing process itself — to discovery, planning, drafting, peer response, revision, editing — allowing time for your skills to develop before the writing "counts" and the portfolio is graded.

The portfolio method is flexible, but you need to read your instructor's syllabus and assignment sheets carefully and listen well in class to determine what kind of portfolio you'll be expected to keep. Below are a few typical types, and more than one might be used in a course.

A Writing Folder.   Students are asked to submit all drafts, notes, outlines, scribbles, doodles, and messy pages—in short, all writing done for the course, whether finished or unfinished. Students may also be asked to select from the folder two or three of their most promising pieces to revise for a "presentation portfolio." The folder is usually not accompanied by a reflective introduction or cover letter.

A Learning (or Open) Portfolio.   Students are free to submit a variety of materials that have contributed to their learning. They may even be free to determine the contents, organization, and presentation of the portfolio. A learning portfolio for a composition class might include photos or other nonprint objects collected to demonstrate learning.

A Closed Portfolio.   Students must turn in assignments that are specified by the instructor, or their options for what to include may be limited.

A Midterm Portfolio.   The portfolio is given a trial run at midterm, or the midterm grade is determined by one or two papers that are submitted for evaluation, perhaps accompanied by a brief self-assessment.

A Final or Presentation Portfolio.   The portfolio is evaluated at the end of the course after being revised, edited, and polished for presentation.

A Modified or Combination Portfolio.   The student has some, but not unlimited, choice in what to include. For example, the instructor may ask for three entries that show certain features or parts of the course.

Find out when your course begins what kind of portfolio your instructor has in mind. Here's one likely scenario. You are required to submit a modified or combination portfolio—one that contains, for example, three revised papers (out of the five or six drafts required). You decide, late in the term, which three to include or where to concentrate on revision and editing. You also may be asked to reflect on what those choices say about you as a writer, to demonstrate your learning in the course, or to explain the decisions you made in the process of writing a paper. Here are some typical questions your instructor, the syllabus, or assignment sheets may answer:

- How many papers should you include in the portfolio?
- Do all these papers need to be revised? If so, what level of revision is expected?

- How much of the course grade is determined by the portfolio grade? Are the portfolio entries graded separately, or does the entire portfolio receive one grade?

- May you include papers written for other courses?

- May you include entries other than texts or documents — such as photos, videos, maps, disks with downloaded Web pages, or other visuals?

- Should you preface the portfolio with a cover letter?

- Does each entry need a separate cover sheet?

- What is expected in your introduction: Description? Explanation? Reflection? Self-assessment?

TIPS FOR KEEPING A PORTFOLIO

Keep Everything, and Stay Organized.   Don't throw anything away! Keep all your notes, lists, drafts, outlines, clusters, responses from readers, photocopied articles, and references for works cited. If you have your own computer, *back up everything* to a disk. If you use the computer lab, save your work to a disk, and keep an extra blank disk in your backpack. Use a system to organize everything. Invest in a good folder with pockets, and label the contents of each pocket. Include the drafts, notes, outlines, and peer review forms for each assignment.

Manage Your Time.   The portfolio isn't due until the end of the course (or at midterm), but planning ahead will save you time and frustration. For example, as your instructor returns each assignment with comments, make some changes in response to those suggestions while the ideas are fresh. If you don't understand or know how to approach one of your instructor's comments, ask right away — at the end of class or during office hours that same week. Make notes about what you think you want to do. Then, even if you want to let a paper simmer, you will have both a plan and some fresh insight when you work on it again.

Practice Self-Assessment.   For complex activities, it's important to your improvement to step back and evaluate your own performance. Maybe you have great ideas but find it hard to organize them. Maybe you write powerful thesis statements but run out of things to say in support of them. Don't wait until the portfolio cover letter is due to begin tracking your learning or assessing your strengths, weaknesses, or preferences.

You can practice self-assessment from the first day of class. For example, after reviewing the syllabus carefully, write one or two paragraphs about how you think you will do in this course. Which assignments or activities do you expect to do well on, and why? Which may be hard for you, and why? In addition, for each paper you share with peers or hand in, write a journal entry about what you think the paper does well and what it still needs. Keep track, in a log or journal, of your process to plan, research, or draft each paper — where you get stuck and where things click.

For more on keeping a journal, see pp. 265–66.

Choose the Entries Carefully. If you can select what to include, consider your choices in light of the course emphasis. Of course, you want to select pieces your evaluator will think are "the best," but also consider which show the most promise or potential and which you might want to revisit. Which drafts show creativity, insight, or an unusual approach to the assignment? Which show variety — different purposes, audiences, or voices? Which show depth — your ability to do thorough research or stay with a topic for several weeks? Also consider the order of the entries — which piece might work best first or last, and how each placement affects the whole.

Write a Strong Reflective Introduction or Cover Letter. Your introduction — usually a self-assessment in the form of a cover letter, a statement, or a description for each of your entries — could be the most important text you write all semester. Besides introducing readers to your collection and portraying you as a writer, it explains your choices in putting the portfolio together and demonstrates that you can evaluate your work and your writing process. For many portfolio-based courses, the reflective introduction or cover letter is the "final exam," testing what you've learned about good writing, about readers' needs, and about the importance of details — in this case, the details of a careful self-presentation.

If your instructor has not assigned a reflective introduction or cover letter, it could be that you've been asked to assemble course materials for a writing folder and not a portfolio. But it also could be that descriptions of your process or your choices are expected to appear throughout the portfolio — perhaps at the end or in brief introductions to each entry. Here are some questions you can ask about writing a reflective introduction or cover letter:

DISCOVERY CHECKLIST

___ Who will read the cover letter in this portfolio?

___ What qualities of writing will your reader value?

___ Will the reader suggest changes or evaluate your work?

___ What will the outcome of the reading be? How much can you influence it?

___ What do you want to emphasize about your writing? What are you proud of? What have you learned? What did you have trouble with?

___ How can you present your writing ability in the best light?

If your reader or evaluator is also your classroom instructor, look back over his or her responses on your returned papers, and review the course syllabus and assignment sheets. What patterns do you see in your instructor's concerns or directions? What information could you give a friend about your instructor's expectations—or pet peeves? Use what you've learned about your instructor's values as a reader to compose a convincing, well-developed introductory statement or cover letter for your portfolio.

For more on appeals, see pp. 39–40.

If your readers or evaluators are unknown, ask your instructor to give you as much information as possible so that you can decide which logical, ethical, or emotional appeals might be most effective. Although you won't know your readers personally, it's safe to assume that they will be trained in portfolio assessment and will share many of your instructor's ideas about good writing. If your college writing program has guidelines or grading criteria, consult them, too.

How long should your introduction or cover letter be? Check with your instructor, but regardless of length, develop your ideas or support your claims as in any effective writing. If you are asked to write a letter, follow the format for a business letter: include the date, a salutation, and a closing.

In the reflective introduction, you might try some of the following (but don't try to use all of them):

- Discuss your best entry and why it is your best.
- Detail your revisions—the improvements and changes that you want readers to notice.
- Review everything included, touching on the strengths of each.
- Outline the writing and revising process that you used for one or more of your entries.
- State what the portfolio illustrates about you as a writer, student, researcher, or critical thinker.
- Acknowledge your weaknesses, but show how you've worked to overcome them.
- Acknowledge your reader-respondents and their influence on your portfolio pieces.
- Reflect on what you've learned about writing, reading, and other topics of the course.
- Lay the groundwork for a positive evaluation of your work.

Polishing the Final Portfolio.   From the first page to the last, your portfolio should be ready for public presentation, a product you can take pride in or show to others. Besides careful editing and proofreading, think about creative ways to give your portfolio a final distinctive feature. For example, consider having the portfolio bound at your local copy shop, adding a colorful cover or illustrations, or including a table of contents or a running header. Although a cheerful cover will not make up for weak writing or careless editing, readers will value the extra effort you put into the final product.

PART FOUR

A Writer's Strategies

Introduction

The following seven chapters constitute a manual offering in-depth advice on writing strategies. The word *strategy* may remind you of warfare: in the original Greek sense of the word, it is a way to win a battle. Writing a college paper, you'll probably agree, is a battle of a kind. In this manual you'll find an array of small weapons to use — and perhaps some heavy artillery.

Here are techniques you can learn, methods you can follow, good practices you can observe. The first five chapters offer a wealth of suggestions for approaching each of the stages of the writing process: generating ideas, planning, drafting, developing, and revising and editing. In Part Two, each stage was covered for each assignment, and relevant strategies were mentioned briefly. Here, each stage of the writing process gets a full chapter, and the strategies for each are explained and illustrated more fully. The last two chapters here offer advice on strategies of increasing importance — designing your own document and understanding visual representations.

No strategy will appeal to every writer, and no writer uses every one for every writing task. Consider this part of the book a reference guide or instruction manual. Turn to it when you need more help, when you're curious, or when you'd like to enlarge your repertoire of writing skills. We can't tell you which of the ideas and techniques covered in these pages will work for you, but we can promise that if you try some of them, you'll be rewarded.

Chapter 15

Strategies for Generating Ideas

For most writers, the hardest part of writing comes first—confronting a blank sheet of paper. Fortunately, you can prepare for that moment, both for finding ideas and for getting ready to write. All of the tested techniques that follow have worked for some writers—both professionals and students—and some may work for you.

Finding Ideas

For more help with finding ideas, use the *Writing Guide Software* for *THE BEDFORD GUIDE.*

When you begin to write, you need to start the ideas flowing. Sometimes ideas appear effortlessly on the paper or screen, perhaps triggered by the opportunities and resources around you—something you read, see, hear, discuss, or think about. (See the top half of the graphic on p. 253.) But at other times you need an arsenal of idea generators, strategies you can use at any point in the writing process—whenever your ideas dry up or you need more examples or evidence. If one strategy doesn't work for a particular writing task, try another. (See the strategies presented in the lower half of the graphic, all detailed in the following pages.)

BUILDING FROM YOUR ASSIGNMENT

Learning to write is learning what questions to ask yourself. Sometimes your assignment begins this process by raising some questions and answering others. For example, Ben Martinez jotted his notes in his book as his instructor and classmates discussed the first assignment for his composition class—recalling a personal experience.

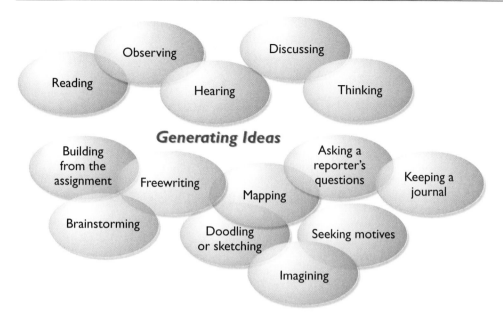

Generating Ideas

Reading • Observing • Discussing • Hearing • Thinking • Building from the assignment • Freewriting • Asking a reporter's questions • Keeping a journal • Mapping • Brainstorming • Doodling or sketching • Seeking motives • Imagining

The assignment answered several questions such as which readers to address and what purpose to try to accomplish in the paper. It clarified three big questions for Ben: Which experience should I pick? How did it change me? Why was it so important for me? His classmates asked their instructor other questions about the length, format, and due date for the essay. As class ended, Ben didn't know what he'd write about, but he had figured out which questions he needed to tackle first, using other strategies for generating ideas.

■ For more detail about this assignment, turn to p. 54 in Ch. 4.

Write about one specific experience that changed how you acted, thought, or felt. Use your experience as a springboard for reflection. Your purpose is not merely to tell an interesting story but to show your readers--your instructor and your classmates--the importance of that experience for you.

What readers? class + prof.

Need to pick one event with consequences

What purpose? 2 parts! Tell the story but do more—reflect & show importance

Try these steps as you examine an assignment:

1. *Read through the assignment once* simply to discover its overall direction.
2. *Read it again,* this time highlighting or marking any information that answers questions about your situation as a writer. Does the assignment identify or suggest the readers you should address, your purpose in writing, the type of paper expected, the parts usually included in that kind of writing, or the format required?
3. *Jot down the questions that the assignment raises for you.* Figure out exactly what you need to decide — the type of topic to pick, the focus to develop, the issues or aspects to consider, or other guidelines to follow.

4. *Finally, list any questions that the assignment doesn't answer or ask you to answer.* Ask your instructor about these questions during or after class.

■ Exercise

Building from Your Assignment

Select an assignment from this book, another textbook, or another class, and jot down some notes about it. What questions does the assignment answer for you? Which questions or decisions does it direct to you? What other questions about the assignment might you want to ask your instructor? When you finish your notes, exchange assignments with a classmate, and make notes about that assignment, too. Working with your partner, compare your responses to both assignments.

BRAINSTORMING

A *brainstorm* is a sudden insight or inspiration. As a writing strategy, brainstorming uses free association to stimulate a chain of ideas, often to personalize a topic and break it down into specifics. When you brainstorm, you start with a word or phrase and spend a set period of time simply scribbling a list of ideas as rapidly as possible, writing down whatever comes to mind with no editing or going back.

Brainstorming can be a group activity. In the business world, it is commonly used to fill a specific need—a name for a product, a corporate emblem, a slogan for an advertising campaign. In college, you can try group brainstorming with a few other students or your entire class. Members of the group sit facing one another. They designate one person to record on paper or a chalkboard whatever the others suggest or the best idea in the air at a busy moment. After several minutes of calling out ideas, the group can look over the recorder's list to identify useful results.

On your own, you might brainstorm to define a topic, generate an example while writing, or come up with a title for a finished paper. Martha Calbick brainstormed after her instructor assigned a paper ("Demonstrate from your own experience how the computer has significantly changed our lives"). First, she wrote the word *computer* at the top of the page and set her alarm for fifteen minutes. Then she began to scribble words and phrases. Her first thought—how her kid brother constantly played computer games—quickly led, by free association, to several more.

> *Computer*
> *My kid bro. thinks computers are for kids—always trading games*
> *In 3rd grade they teach programming*
> *Hackers—software pirates—become a programmer? big future?*
> *Some get rich—Ed's brother wrote a program for accountants*
> *Computers in subway stations—print tickets*

Group Brainstorming

Working with a small group of your classmates — or with the entire class — choose one subject from the list on page 256 that each person knows about. Brainstorm about it individually for ten minutes. Then compare and contrast the brainstorming lists of everyone in the group. Although the group began with the same subject, each writer's treatment will be unique because of differences in experience and perspective. What does this exercise tell you about group brainstorming as a strategy for generating topics for writing?

FOR GROUP LEARNING

Banks — shove in your plastic card

Newspaper story on man who lucked out — deposited $100 but computer credited $10,000

Class schedules and grades — all online

My report card showed a D instead of a B — big fight to correct it

Are we just numbers now?

When her alarm went off, Calbick took a break. After returning to her list, she crossed out ideas that did not interest her, such as her brother's games. She circled the promising question "Are we just numbers now?" and noted how other items, such as the mindless $10,000 credit at the bank, expressed that very idea, too. From her rough list, an idea began to emerge: the dehumanizing effects of computer errors.

In her paper, Calbick recalled the time and effort involved in correcting the simple mistake that had momentarily robbed her of a good grade. She mentioned the consequences of other computer errors, including the man who had struck it rich at the bank. She concluded with a wry complaint about computerized society: "A computer knows your name and number, but it doesn't know who you are."

When you want to brainstorm, try this advice:

1. *Start with a key word or phrase* — one that will launch your thoughts in a productive direction. If you need a topic, begin with a general word or phrase (for example, *computer*); if you need an example for a paragraph in progress, use a specific word or phrase (for example, *financial errors computers make*).
2. *Set a time limit.* Ten to fifteen minutes is long enough for strenuous thinking.
3. *Write rapidly.* List brief items — words, ideas, short sentences — that you can quickly scan later.
4. *Don't stop.* Don't worry about spelling, repetition, absurdity, or relevance. Don't judge, and don't arrange: just produce. Record whatever comes into your head, as fast as your fingers can type or your pen can fly. If your mind goes blank, keep moving, even if you only repeat what you've just written.

When you finish, circle or check anything that suggests a provocative direction. Scratch out whatever looks useless or dull. Then try some conscious organizing: Are any thoughts related? Can you group them? If so, does the group suggest a topic?

■ Exercise

Brainstorming

From the following list, choose a subject that interests you, that you know something about, and that you'd like to learn more about — in other words, that you might like to write on. Then brainstorm for ten minutes.

travel	fear	exercise
dieting	dreams	automobiles
family	technology	sports
advertisements	animals	education

Now look over your brainstorming list, and circle any potential topic for a paper. How well did this brainstorming exercise work for you? Can you think of any variations that would make it more useful?

FREEWRITING

To tap your unconscious by *freewriting*, you simply write a series of sentences without stopping for fifteen or twenty minutes. The sentences don't have to be grammatical or coherent or stylish; just keep them flowing to unlock an idea's potential.

For Calbick's brainstorming, see pp. 254–55.

Generally, freewriting is most productive if it has an aim — for example, finding a topic, a purpose, or a question you want to answer. Martha Calbick wrote her topic at the top of a page — and then explored her rough ideas.

> *Computer errors — so how do they make life impersonal? You push in your plastic card and get some cash. Just a glassy screen. No human teller behind a window. When the computer says you have no money left in your account, that's terrible. Worse than when a person won't cash your check. At least the person looks you in the face, maybe even smiles. Computers make mistakes, too. That man in Utica — from the story in the paper — deposited $100.00 to his account and the computer misplaced a decimal point and said he had put in $10,000.*

The result, as you can see, wasn't polished prose. It was full of false starts and little asides to herself. Still, in twenty minutes she produced a paragraph that served as a springboard for her finished essay.

If you want to try freewriting, here's what you do:

1. *Write a sentence or two at the top of your page or computer screen* — the idea you plan to develop by freewriting.

Invisible writing is a kind of freewriting done on a word processor. After typing your topic at the beginning of a file, darken or turn off your monitor so that you cannot read what's on the screen. Then freewrite. If you feel uneasy, try to relax and concentrate on the ideas. After ten minutes, turn the monitor back on, scroll to the beginning, and read what you have written.

WRITING WITH A COMPUTER

2. *For at least ten minutes, write steadily without stopping.* Express whatever comes to mind, even "My mind is blank," until some new thought floats into view.
3. *Don't censor yourself.* Don't cross out false starts, misspellings, or grammar errors. Don't worry about connecting ideas or finding perfect words.
4. *Feel free to explore.* Your initial sentences can serve as a rough guide, but they shouldn't be a straitjacket. If you find yourself straying from your original idea, a change in direction may be valuable.
5. *Prepare yourself*—if you want to. While you wait for your pencil to start racing, you may want to ask yourself some of these questions:

   What interests you about the topic? What aspects do you care most about?

   What do you recall about this topic from your own experience? What do you know about it that the next person doesn't?

   What have you read about it? Observed about it? Heard about it?

   How might you feel about this topic if you were someone else (a parent, an instructor, a person from another country)?

6. *Repeat the process, looping back to expand a good idea if you wish.* You can poke at the parts that look most interesting to see if they will further unfold:

   What does that mean?

   If that is true, what then? So what?

   What other examples or evidence does this statement call to mind?

   What objections might a reader raise? How might they be answered?

■ Exercise

Freewriting

Select an idea from your current thinking or from a brainstorming list. Write it at the top of a page or screen. Freewrite about it for fifteen minutes. Share your freewriting with your classmates. If you wish, repeat this process, looping back to explore a provocative idea from your freewriting.

DOODLING OR SKETCHING

If you fill the margins of your notebooks with doodles, harness this artistic energy to generate ideas for writing. As Elena Lopez started thinking about an accident during a soccer tournament, she began to sketch her collision with a teammate (Figure 15.1). She added stick figures, notes, symbols, and color as she outlined a series of events and their consequences.

Try this advice as you develop ideas by doodling or sketching:

1. *Give your ideas room to grow.* Open a new file using a drawing program, doodle in pencil on a blank page, or sketch on a series of pages to capture a sequence of events.

■ See Ch. 20 for ways to add effective visuals to your writing.

2. *Concentrate on your topic, but welcome new ideas.* Begin with a key visual in the center or at the top of a page. Add new sketches or doodles as

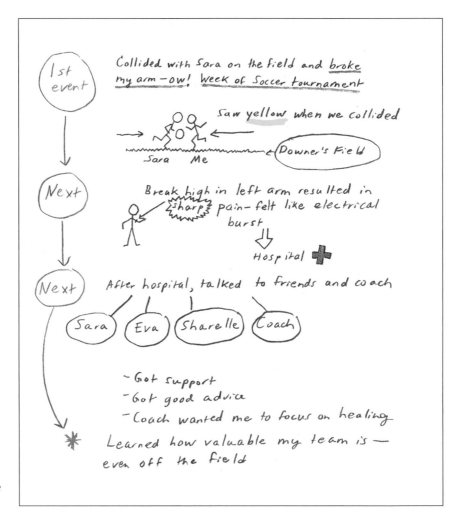

Figure 15.1   Doodling or Sketching to Generate Ideas

they occur to you; you may find that they embellish, expand, define, or redirect your initial topic.

3. *Add icons, symbols, colors, figures, labels, notes, or questions.* Freely mix visual and textual material, recording ideas spontaneously without stopping to refine them.

4. *Follow up on your discoveries.* After a break, return to your pages to see how your ideas have evolved. Jot notes by your doodles, making connections, identifying sequences, noting details, or converting visual concepts into descriptive sentences.

■ Exercise

Doodling or Sketching

Start with a doodle or sketch that illustrates your topic. Add related events, ideas, or details to develop your topic visually. Share your material with classmates, and then use their observations or questions to help you refine your direction as a writer.

MAPPING

Mapping taps your visual and spatial creativity as you generate ideas. When you use mapping, you position ideas on the page or in a file to show their relationships or relative importance — radiating outward from a key term in the center, dropping down from a key word at the top, sprouting upward from a root idea, branching out from a trunk, flowing across the page or screen in a chronological or causal sequence, or following a circular, spiral, sequential, or other familiar form.

Andrew Choi used mapping to gather ideas for his proposal for revitalizing the campus radio station (Figure 15.2). He noted ideas on colored sticky notes — blue for problems, yellow for solutions, and pink for implementation details. Then he moved the sticky notes around on a blank page, arranging them as he connected ideas.

Here are some suggestions for mapping:

1. *Allow space for your map to develop.* Open a new computer file, find some posterboard for arranging sticky notes or cards, or use a large page for jotting notes.

2. *Begin with your topic or a key idea.* Drawing on your imagination, memory, class notes, or reading, place a key word at the center or top of a page or screen.

3. *Add related ideas, examples, issues, or questions.* Place these points above, below, or beside your key word, adding them quickly and spontaneously.

4. *Refine the connections.* As your map evolves, use lines, arrows, or loops to connect ideas; box or circle them to focus attention; add colors to relate comparable points or to distinguish source materials from your own ideas.

Figure 15.2   Mapping to Generate Ideas

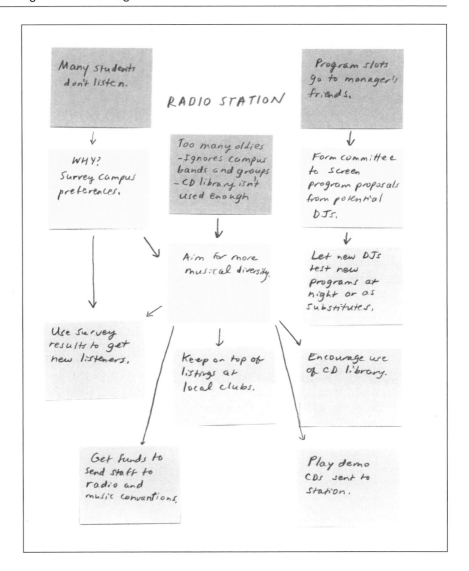

■ See Ch. 20 for ways to add effective visuals to your writing. See also pp. 279–80 on clustering.

After a break, continue mapping to probe one part more deeply, refine the structure, add detail, or build an alternate map from a different viewpoint. Because mapping is so versatile, use it also to develop graphics that present ideas in visual form.

■ Exercise

Mapping

Start with a key word or idea that you know about. Map related ideas, using visual features to show how they connect. Share your map with classmates, and then use their questions or comments to refine your mapping.

For Group Learning

Working with a group of three to five classmates, write on a notecard the word or phrase your instructor assigns to the entire class — for example, *campus dining* or *balancing work and college.* Then spend ten or fifteen minutes writing other ideas on new note cards and arranging them around the central card. Move the cards around, and draw connecting arrows if that helps to relate your ideas. Share each group's ideas with the entire class.

FOR GROUP LEARNING

IMAGINING

Your imagination is a valuable resource for exploring possibilities — analyzing an option, evaluating an alternative, or solving a problem. Through imagination, you can discover surprising ideas, original examples, striking expressions, and unexpected relationships.

Suppose that you asked, "What if the average North American life span were more than a century?" No doubt a longer life span would mean that more of the populace would be old. How would that fact affect doctors and nurses, hospitals, and other medical facilities? How might city planners respond to the needs of so many more old people? What would the change mean for shopping centers? For television programming? For leisure activities? For the social security system? For taxes?

Use some of the following strategies to unleash your imagination:

1. *Speculate about changes, alternatives, and options.* What common assumption — something we all take for granted — might you question or deny? What problem or deplorable condition would you like to remedy? What changes in policy, practice, or attitude might avoid problems you foresee for the future? What different paths in life — each with challenges and successes — might you take?

2. *Shift perspective.* Experiment by taking a point of view other than the usual one. Assume a perspective held by another person or group (someone on the opposite side of an issue) or invented by you (a plant, an animal, or a Martian). Try shifting the debate (to whether people over sixty-five, not teenagers, should be allowed to drink) or the time frame (from present to past or future).

3. *Envision what might be.* Join the many other writers who have imagined a utopia (an ideal state) or an anti-utopia. By envisioning, you can conceive of other possible alternatives — a better way of treating illness, of electing a president, or of finding meaningful order in a chaotic jumble.

4. *Synthesize.* Synthesizing (generating new ideas by combining previously separate ideas) is the opposite of analyzing (breaking down into component parts). Synthesize to make fresh connections, fusing materials — perhaps old or familiar — into something new.

For more about analysis and synthesis, see pp. 34–35.

■ Exercise

Imagining

Begin with a problem that cries out for a solution, a condition that requires a remedy, or a situation that calls for change. Ask "What if?" or use "Suppose that" as a starter to trigger your imagination. Speculate about what might be, record your ideas, and share them with your classmates.

ASKING A REPORTER'S QUESTIONS

Journalists, assembling facts to write a news story, ask themselves six simple questions — the five *W*'s and an *H:*

Who?	Where?	Why?
What?	When?	How?

In the *lead,* or opening paragraph, of a good news story, the writer tries to condense the whole story into a sentence or two, answering all six questions.

> A giant homemade fire balloon [*what*] startled residents of Costa Mesa [*where*] last night [*when*] as Ambrose Barker, 79, [*who*] zigzagged across the sky at nearly 300 miles per hour [*how*] in an attempt to set a new altitude record [*why*].

Later in the news story, the reporter will add details, using the six basic questions to generate more about what happened and why.

For your college writing you can use these six helpful questions to generate specific details for your essays. They can help you explore the significance of a childhood experience, analyze what happened at some moment in history, or investigate a campus problem. Their purpose is to help you gather ideas. Don't worry if some of them go nowhere, seem irrelevant, or lead to repetitious answers. Later, you'll weed out irrelevant points, keeping only those that look promising for your topic.

For a topic that is not based on your personal experience, you may need to do reading or interviewing to answer some of the questions. Take, for example, the topic of the assassination of President John F. Kennedy, and notice how each question can lead to further questions.

- *Who* was John F. Kennedy? What was his background? What kind of person was he? What kind of president? Who was with him when he was killed? Who was nearby? Who do most people believe shot him?

- *What* happened to Kennedy — exactly? What events led up to the assassination? What happened during the assassination itself? What did the people around him do? What did the media representatives do? What did everyone across the country do? Ask someone who remembers this event what he or she did on hearing about it.

- *Where* was Kennedy assassinated? The city? The street? Where was he going? What was he riding in? Where was he sitting? Where did the shots likely come from? Where did the shots hit him? Where did he die?

- *When* was he assassinated—the day, month, year, time? When did Kennedy decide to go to this city? When—precisely—were the shots fired? When did he die? When was a suspect arrested?

- *Why* was Kennedy assassinated? What are some of the theories of the assassination? What solid evidence is available to explain it? Why has this event caused so much controversy?

- *How* was Kennedy assassinated? What kind of weapon was used? How many shots were fired? Specifically what caused his death? How can we get at the truth of this event?

■ Exercise
Asking a Reporter's Questions

Choose one of the following topics, or use one of your own:

A memorable event in history
An unforgettable event in your life
A concert that you have seen
An accomplishment on campus
An occurrence in your city
An important speech
A proposal for change
A questionable stand someone has taken

Answer the six reporter's questions about the topic. Then write a sentence or two synthesizing the answers to the six questions. Incorporate that sentence into an introductory paragraph for an essay that you might write later.

SEEKING MOTIVES

In a surprisingly large part of your college writing, you will try to explain the motives behind human behavior. In a history paper, you might consider how George Washington's conduct shaped the presidency. In a psychology report, you might try to explain the behavior of participants in an experiment. In a literature essay, you might analyze the motives of Hester Prynne in *The Scarlet Letter*. Because people, including characters in fiction, are so complex, this task is challenging.

■ For more on writing about literature, see Ch. 12.

If you want to understand any human act, according to philosopher–critic Kenneth Burke, you can break it down into a set of five basic components, a pentad, and ask questions about each one. While covering much the same ground as the reporter's questions, Burke's pentad differs in that it can show how the components of a human act affect one another. This line of thought can take you deeper into the motives for human behavior than most reporters' investigations ever go.

Suppose that you are preparing to write a political science paper on President Lyndon Baines Johnson, known as LBJ. Right after President Kennedy's assassination in 1963, Vice President Johnson was sworn in as president. A year later, in 1964, he was elected to the post by a landslide. By 1968, however, Johnson had decided not to run for a second term as president. You decide to use Burke's pentad to investigate why he made this decision.

1. *The act:* What was done?
   Announcing the decision to leave office without standing for reelection.
2. *The actor:* Who did it?
   President Johnson.
3. *The agency:* What means did the person use to make it happen?
   A televised address to the nation.
4. *The scene:* Where and when did the act happen and in what circumstances?
   Washington, D.C., March 31, 1968. Protesters against the Vietnam war were gaining numbers and influence. The press was increasingly critical of the escalating war. Senator Eugene McCarthy, an antiwar candidate for president, had made a strong showing against LBJ in the New Hampshire primary election.
5. *The purpose or motive for acting:* What could have made the person do it?
   Possible motives might include avoiding a probable defeat, escaping further personal attacks, sparing his family, making it easier for his successor to pull the country out of the war, and easing bitter dissent among Americans.

To carry Burke's method further, you can pair the five components and begin fruitful lines of inquiry by asking questions, as illustrated below, about the pairs:

actor to act	act to scene	scene to agency
actor to scene	act to agency	scene to purpose
actor to purpose	act to purpose	agency to purpose

PAIR   actor to agency

QUESTION What did LBJ [actor] have to do with his televised address [agency]?

ANSWER   Commanding the attention of a vast audience, LBJ must have felt he was in control—even though his ability to control the situation in Vietnam was slipping.

Not all the questions will prove fruitful, and some may not even apply. But one or two pairs of questions might reveal valuable answers and start you writing.

■ Exercise

Seeking Motives

Choose an action that puzzles you such as something you, a family member, or a friend has done; a decision of a historical or current political figure; or something in a movie, television program, or literary selection. Then apply Burke's pentad to this action to try to determine the individual's motives. If you wish, you can also pair up the components (see p. 263) to perceive deeper relationships. When you believe you understand the individual's motivation, write a paragraph explaining the action, and share it with your classmates.

KEEPING A JOURNAL

Journal writing richly rewards anyone who engages in it every day or several times a week. You can write anywhere or anytime: All you need is a notebook, a writing implement, and a few minutes to record an entry. To keep a valuable journal, you need only the honesty and willingness to set down what you genuinely think and feel. No one will criticize how you spell, punctuate, organize your ideas, or express yourself.

For ideas about keeping a reading journal, see pp. 20–21.

For the faithful journal keeper, a journal is a mine studded with priceless nuggets — thoughts and observations, reactions and revelations that are yours for the taking. When you write, you can rifle your well-stocked journal freely — not only for writing topics, but for insights, examples, and other material.

Reflective Journal Writing.   What do you write in your journal? When you make an entry, put less emphasis on recording what happened, as in a diary, than on *reflecting* about what you do or see, hear or read, learn or believe. Here you can explore dreams, try out ideas, vent fears and frustrations, for an audience of one: yourself. An entry can be a list or an outline, a paragraph or a full-blown essay, a poem or a letter you don't intend to send, even a page of brainstorming or doodling. Describe a person or a place, set down a conversation, or record any insights into your actions or those of others. Consider your pet peeves, your treasures, your convictions or moral dilemmas, or the fate of the world — or the country — if you were in charge. Use your challenges and successes as a writer to nourish and inspire your writing, recording what worked, what didn't, and how you reacted to each.

Responsive Journal Writing.   Sometimes you *respond* to something in particular — to your reading for an assignment, to classroom discussions, to a movie, to a conversation or observation. This type of journal entry is more focused than the reflective entry. Faced with a long paper to write, you might assign *yourself* a response journal. Then when the time comes to draft your paper, you will have plenty of material to quarry.

For more on responding to reading, see Ch. 2.

For responsive journal prompts, see the end of each selection in *A Writer's Reader.*

Warm-Up Journal Writing.   You can also use your journal to prepare for an assignment. You can group ideas, scribble outlines, sketch beginnings, capture stray thoughts, record relevant material. Of course what starts as a quick warm-up comment on an essay you've read (or a responsive journal entry) may turn into the draft of a paper. In other words, don't let the categories we've given straitjacket you. A journal can be just about anything you want it to be, and the best journal is the one that's most useful to *you*.

WRITING WITH A COMPUTER

Keeping an e-journal is as simple as creating a file and making entries by date or subject. Record ideas, feelings, impressions, images, memories, quotations, and any other writing you wish. You also will quickly notice how easy it is to copy and paste inspiring parts of e-mail, interesting quotations from Web pages, or even digitized images and sounds into your e-journal. Just be sure that you identify the source of material that you copy so that you won't later confuse it with your original writing. As your e-journal grows, you will develop a ready supply of "seeds" and support for your writing assignments.

■ Exercise

Keeping a Journal

Keep a journal for at least a week. Each day record your thoughts, feelings, observations, and reactions. Reflect on what happens, and respond to what you read. Try at least one of the responsive prompts following a selection in *A Writer's Reader*. At the end of the week, bring your journal to class, and read aloud to your classmates the entry you like best.

Getting Ready

Once you have generated a suitable topic and some ideas related to that topic, you are ready to get down to the job of actually writing.

SETTING UP CIRCUMSTANCES

Get Comfortable.   If you can write only with your shoes off or with a can of soda nearby, set yourself up that way. Some writers need a radio blaring rap music; others need quiet. Create an environment that puts you in the mood for writing.

Devote One Special Place to Writing.   Your place should have good lighting and space to spread out. It may be a desk in your bedroom, the dining room table, or a quiet cubicle in the library — someplace where no one will bother you and where your mind and body will be ready to settle in for work. Try to make it a place where you can leave your projects and keep handy your pens, paper, computer, dictionary, and other reference materials.

Establish a Ritual.   Some writers find that a ritual relaxes them and helps them get started. You might open a soda, straighten your desk, turn the radio on (or off), and create a new file on the computer.

Relocate.   If you're not getting anywhere with your writing, try moving from the college library to home or from the kitchen to your bedroom. Try an unfamiliar place — a bowling alley, a restaurant, an airport; block out the noises around you, and concentrate hard on your writing.

Reduce Distractions.   Most of us can't prevent interruptions, but we can reduce them. If you are expecting your boyfriend to call, call him before you start writing. If you have small children, write when they are asleep or at school. Use your voice mail to record any calls. Let people around you know you are serious about writing, and allow yourself to give your full attention to it.

Exhaust Your Excuses.   If you, like most writers, are an expert procrastinator, help yourself run out of reasons not to write. Is your room annoyingly jumbled? Straighten it. Sharpen those pencils, throw out that trash, and make that phone call. Then, with your room, your desk, and your mind swept clean, sit down and write.

Yield to Inspiration.   Sometimes ideas, images, or powerful urges to write will arrive like sudden miracles. When they come, even if you are taking a shower or getting ready to go to a movie, yield to impulse and write. Your words probably will flow with little exertion.

Write at the Time Best for You.   Some people think best early in the morning, while others favor the small hours when the world is still and their stern self-critic might be asleep, too. Writing at dawn or in the wee hours also reduces distractions from other people.

Write on a Schedule.   Many writers find that it helps to write at a predictable time of day. This method worked marvels for English novelist Anthony Trollope, who would start at 5:30 A.M., write 2,500 words before 8:30 A.M., and then go to his job at the General Post Office. (He wrote more than sixty books.) Even if you can't set aside the same time every day, it may help to decide, "Today from four to five, I'll sit down and write." Or if you get stuck, vary your schedule.

PREPARING YOUR MIND

Talk about Your Writing.   Discuss your ideas with a classmate, friend, or roommate, encouraging questions, comments, and suggestions. Talk in person, by phone, through e-mail, or on tapes. Or talk to yourself, using a voice-activated tape recorder, while you sit through traffic jams during your commute to campus or while you jog, walk your dog, or ride your bike.

Lay Out Your Plans.   Tell any nearby listener — student down the hall, spouse, parent, friend — why you want to write this particular paper, what material you'll put into it, how you're going to lay it out. If the other person says, "That sounds good," you'll be encouraged. Even if the reaction is a yawn, you'll have set your own thinking in motion.

For advice about journals, see pp. 265–66.

Keep a Notebook or Journal Handy.   Always have some paper in your pocket or backpack or on the night table to write down good ideas that pop into your mind. Imagination may strike in the checkout line of the supermarket, in the doctor's waiting room, or during a lull on the job.

Read.   The step from reading to writing is a short one. Even when you're just reading for fun, you start to involve yourself with words. Who knows? You might also hit on something useful for your paper. Or read purposefully. If you have a topic, set out to read and take notes.

Chapter 16
Strategies for Planning

Starting to write often seems a chaotic activity, but you can use the strategies in this chapter to help create order. For most papers, you will first want to consider your audience and purpose and then focus on a central point or thesis. To help you sensibly arrange your material, the chapter also includes advice on grouping ideas and on outlining.

Shaping Your Topic for Your Audience and Your Purpose

As you work on your college papers, you may feel as if you're performing a juggling act—selecting weighty points and lively details, tossing them into the air, catching each one as it falls, deftly keeping them all moving in sequence. Busy as you are simply juggling, however, your performance almost always draws a crowd—your instructor, your classmates, or other readers. They'll expect you to attend to their concerns as you try to achieve your purpose—probably informing, explaining, or persuading.

For critical questions about audience and more about purpose, see p. 270.

269

Thinking carefully about your audience and purpose can help you plan a paper more effectively. If you want to show your classmates and instructor the importance of an event, you'll need to decide how much detail about the event those readers need. If most of them have gotten speeding tickets, for instance, they'll need less information about that experience than bus riders or other city commuters might. However, to achieve your purpose, you'll need to go beyond what happened to why the event mattered to you. No matter how many tickets your readers have gotten, they won't know exactly how that experience changed you unless you share that information effectively. In fact, they may incorrectly assume that you ended up worrying about being late to class or paying higher insurance rates when, in fact, you had suddenly realized how close you had come to having an accident like your cousin's and how that recognition motivated you to change your driving habits.

Similarly, if you want to persuade county officials to adopt your proposal for changing the way absentee ballots are distributed to college students, you'll need to support your idea with reasons and evidence — drawing on the state election laws and legal precedents familiar to these readers as well as the experiences of student voters. In fact, you may need to show not only how your proposal would solve existing problems but also why it would improve the situation more effectively than other proposals.

Although your assignment may help you begin to define your purpose and audience, you can continue to refine your understanding using questions such as these:

- *Who are your readers?* If they are not clearly identified in your assignment or by your situation, whom do you assume that they are? What do these readers know or want to know? What opinions do they hold? What do they find informative or persuasive? How might you plan your writing to appeal effectively to them?

- *What is your general purpose?* What specifically would you like to accomplish in your paper? How would you like your readers to react to your paper — for example, do you want them to smile, think, or agree? To understand, learn, accept, respect, care, change, or reply? How might you plan your writing to accomplish your aims?

- *What qualities of good writing have been discussed in your class,* explained in your syllabus, or identified in assigned readings? What criteria for college writing have emerged from exchanges of drafts with classmates or comments from your instructor? How might you shape your writing to demonstrate desirable qualities to your readers?

- *How might you narrow and focus your ideas about the topic,* given what you know or assume about your audience and purpose? Which slant would best accomplish your purpose? What points about the topic would appeal most strongly to your readers? What details would engage or persuade them?

■ Exercise

Considering Audience and Purpose

Think back to a recent writing task — a college essay, a job application, a report or memo at work, a message to a relative, a letter to a campus office, or some other piece. Write a brief description of your situation as a writer at that time. Who — exactly — were your readers? What was your purpose? How did you account for both as you planned your writing? How might you have increased the effectiveness of your writing?

Stating and Using a Thesis

Most pieces of effective writing are unified around one main point. That is, all the subpoints and details are relevant to that point. Generally, after you have read an essay, you can sum up the writer's main point in a sentence, even if the author has not stated it explicitly. We call this summary statement a *thesis*.

■ For more help with stating and using a thesis, use the *Writing Guide Software* for THE BEDFORD GUIDE.

Often the thesis — the writer's main point — will be *explicit*, plainly stated, in the piece of writing itself. In "Don't Misread My Signals" (reprinted in *A Writer's Reader*; see p. 438), Judith Ortiz Cofer states her thesis in the last sentence of the first paragraph — "[y]ou can leave the island of Puerto Rico, master the English language, and travel as far as you can, but if you are a Latina, especially one who so clearly belongs to Rita Moreno's gene pool, the island travels with you." This clear statement, strategically placed, helps readers see her main point.

Sometimes a thesis may be *implicit*, implied rather than directly stated. In "The Niceness Solution" (from *Beyond Queer*, 1996) Paul Varnell describes an ordinance "banning rude behavior, including rude speech," passed in Raritan, New Jersey. After discussing a 1580 code of conduct, he identifies four objections to such attempts to limit free speech. He concludes with this sentence: "Sensibly, Raritan Police Chief Joseph Sferro said he would not enforce the new ordinance." Although Varnell does not state his main point in one concise sentence, readers know that he opposes the law passed in New Jersey and any other attempts to legislate "niceness."

The purpose of most academic and workplace writing is to inform, to explain, or to convince, and to achieve any of these purposes you must make your main point crystal clear. A thesis sentence helps you clarify that idea in your own mind and stay on track as you write. It also helps your readers readily see your point and follow your discussion. Sometimes you may want to imply your thesis, but if you state it explicitly, you ensure that readers cannot miss it.

DISCOVERING YOUR WORKING THESIS

■ Look for specific advice under headings that mention a thesis in Chs. 4 to 11.

It's rare for a writer to develop a perfect thesis statement early in the writing process and then write an effective essay that fits it exactly. What you should aim for is a *working thesis* — a statement that can guide you but that you will ultimately refine. Ideas for a working thesis are probably all around you.

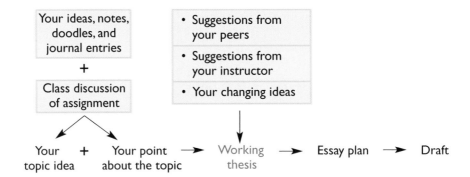

A useful thesis contains not only the key words that identify your *topic* but also the *point* you want to make or the *attitude* you intend to take. Your topic identifies the area you want to explore.

> TOPIC   old-fashioned formal courtesy

To convert a topic to a thesis, you need to add your own slant, attitude, or point.

> Topic   +   Slant or Attitude or Point   =   Working Thesis

Be sure that you make an actual point rather than repeating the topic.

> CIRCULAR REPETITION   Old-fashioned formal courtesy is a thing of the past.
>
> TOPIC IDEA + SLANT   old-fashioned formal courtesy + its decline as roles have changed
>
> WORKING THESIS   As the roles of men and women have changed in our society, old-fashioned formal courtesy has declined.

FOR GROUP LEARNING

Identifying Theses

Working in a small group, select five essays from Part Two of this book to read carefully (or your instructor may choose the essays for your group). Then, individually, write out the thesis for each essay. Some thesis sentences are stated outright (explicit), but others are implied (implicit). Compare and contrast the thesis statements that you identified with those your classmates found, and discuss the similarities and differences. How can you account for the differences? Try to agree on a thesis statement for each essay.

Beginning with this working thesis, you could focus on how changing societal attitudes toward gender roles have caused changes in courtesy. Later, when you revise, you may refine your thesis further—perhaps restricting it to courtesy toward the elderly, toward women, or, despite stereotypes, toward men. The chart suggests ways of developing a thesis.

For advice about revising a thesis, see pp. 324–25.

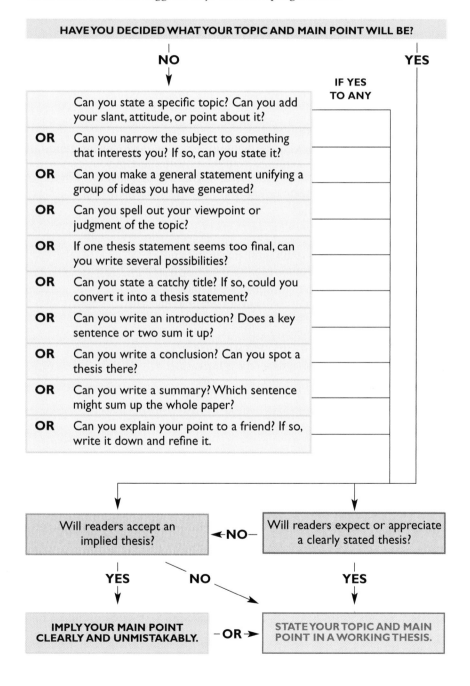

Sometimes the requirements of a college assignment may distract you from its purpose. For example, if you plan to compare and contrast two local newspapers' coverage of a Senate election, ask yourself what the point of that comparison and contrast is. Simply noting a difference won't be enough to satisfy most readers.

NO SPECIFIC POINT   The *Herald*'s coverage of the Senate elections was different from the *Courier*'s.

WORKING THESIS   The *Herald*'s coverage of the Senate elections was more thorough than the *Courier*'s.

■ Exercise

Discovering a Thesis

Write a sentence, a working thesis, that unifies each of the following groups of details. Then compare and contrast your theses with those of your classmates. What other information would you need to write a good paper on each topic? How might the thesis statement change as you write the paper?

1. Cigarettes are expensive.
   Cigarettes can cause fires.
   Cigarettes cause unpleasant odors.
   Cigarettes can cause health problems to the smoker.
   Secondhand smoke from cigarettes can cause health problems.

2. Clinger College has a highly qualified faculty.
   Clinger College has an excellent curriculum in my field.
   Clinger College has a beautiful campus.
   Clinger College is expensive.
   Clinger College has offered me a scholarship.

3. Crisis centers report that date rape is increasing.
   Most date rape is not reported to the police.
   Often the victim of date rape is not believed.
   Sometimes the victim of date rape is blamed or blames herself.
   The effects of date rape stay with a woman for years.

HOW TO STATE A THESIS

Once you have a notion of your topic and main point, these four suggestions may help you state a workable thesis that will guide your planning and drafting.

- *State the thesis sentence exactly.* Replace vague or general wording with concise, detailed, and down-to-earth language.

TOO GENERAL   There are a lot of troubles with chemical wastes.

Are you going to deal with all chemical wastes, throughout all of history, all over the world? Are you going to list all the troubles they can possibly cause?

MORE SPECIFIC   Careless dumping of leftover paint is to blame for a recent outbreak of skin rashes in Atlanta.

- *State just one central idea in the thesis sentence.* If your paper is to focus on one point, your thesis should state only one main idea.

   TOO MANY IDEAS   Careless dumping of leftover paint has caused a serious problem in Atlanta, and a new kind of biodegradable paint offers a promising solution to one chemical waste dilemma.

   ONE CENTRAL IDEA Careless dumping of leftover paint has caused a serious problem in Atlanta.

   OR   A new kind of biodegradable paint offers a promising solution to one chemical waste dilemma.

- *State your thesis positively.* You can usually find evidence to support a positive statement, but you'd have to rule out every possible exception in order to prove a negative one. Negative statements also may sound half-hearted and seem to lead nowhere.

   NEGATIVE   Medical scientists do not know what causes breast cancer.

   POSITIVE   The causes of breast cancer remain a challenge for medical scientists.

Presenting the topic positively as a "challenge" might lead to a paper about an exciting quest. Besides, to show that medical scientists are working on the problem would be relatively easy, given an hour of on-line or library research.

- *Limit your thesis to a statement that is possible to demonstrate.* A workable thesis is limited so that you can support it with sufficient convincing evidence. It should stake out just the territory that you can cover thoroughly within the length assigned and the time available, and no more.

   DIFFICULT TO SHOW   For centuries, popular music has announced vital trends in Western society.

   DIFFICULT TO SHOW   My favorite piece of music is Beethoven's Fifth Symphony.

The first thesis above could inform a whole encyclopedia of music; the second would require that you explain why that symphony is your favorite, contrasting it with all the other musical compositions you know. The following thesis sounds far more workable for a brief essay.

   POSSIBLE TO SHOW   In the past two years, a rise in the number of pre-teenagers has resulted in a comeback for heavy metal on our local concert scene.

Unlike a vague statement or a broad, unrestricted claim, a limited thesis statement narrows and refines your topic, thus restricting your essay to a reasonable scope.

TOO VAGUE	Native American blankets are very beautiful.
TOO BROAD	Native Americans have adapted to modern civilization.
POSSIBLE TO SHOW	Members of the Apache tribe are skilled workers in high-rise construction.

■ Exercise

Examining Thesis Statements

■ For exercises on choosing effective thesis statements, visit <bedfordstmartins.com/bedguide> and do a key-word search:

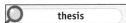
thesis

Discuss each of the following thesis sentences with your classmates. Answer these questions for each:

Is the thesis stated exactly?
Does the thesis state just one idea?
Is the thesis stated positively?
Is the thesis sufficiently limited for a short essay?
How might the thesis be improved?

1. Teenagers should not get married.
2. Cutting classes is like a disease.
3. Students have developed a variety of techniques to conceal inadequate study from their instructors.
4. Older people often imitate teenagers.
5. Violence on television can be harmful to children.
6. I don't know how to change the oil in my car.

HOW TO USE A THESIS TO ORGANIZE

▨ For more on using a thesis to develop an outline, see pp. 280–82.

Often a good, clear thesis will suggest an organization for your ideas.

WORKING THESIS	Despite the disadvantages of living in a downtown business district, I wouldn't live anywhere else.
FIRST ¶S	Disadvantages of living in the business district
NEXT ¶S	Advantages of living there
LAST ¶	Affirmation of your fondness for downtown city life

A clear thesis will also help to organize you, keeping you on track as you write. Just putting your working thesis into words can stake out your territory. Your thesis can then guide you as you select details and connect sections of the essay. Its purpose is to guide you on a quest, not to limit your ideas.

As you write, however, you don't have to cling to a thesis for dear life. If further investigation changes your thinking, you can change your thesis.

WORKING THESIS	Because wolves are a menace to people and farm animals, they ought to be exterminated.

REVISED THESIS   The wolf, a relatively peaceful animal useful in nature's scheme of things, ought to be protected.

You can restate your thesis at any time: as you write, as you revise, as you revise again.

Organizing Your Ideas

When you organize an essay, you select an order for the parts that makes sense and shows your readers how the ideas are connected. Often your organization will not only help a reader follow your points but also reinforce your emphases by moving from beginning to end or from least to most significant, as the table below illustrates.

GROUPING YOUR IDEAS

While exploring a topic, you will usually find a few ideas that seem to belong together — two facts on New York traffic jams, four actions of New York drivers, three problems with New York streets. But similar ideas seldom appear together in your notes because you did not discover them all at the

ORGANIZATION	MOVEMENT	TYPICAL USE	EXAMPLE
Spatial	Left to right, right to left, bottom to top, front to back, outside to inside	• Describing a place or a scene • Describing a person's physical appearance	You might describe an ocean vista, moving from the rocky beach with its tidepools to the plastic buoys floating off shore to the sparkling water meeting the glowing sky at sunset.
Chronological	What happens first, second, and next, continuing until the end	• Narrating an event • Explaining steps in a procedure	You might narrate the events that led up to an accident: leaving home late, stopping to do an errand, rushing along the highway, racing up to the intersection.
Logical	General to specific, specific to general, least important to most important, cause to effect, problem to solution	• Explaining an idea • Persuading readers to accept a stand or a proposal	You might analyze the effects of the 1997 El Niño by selecting four major consequences, placing the most important one last for emphasis.

same time. To identify an effective order for your ideas, you'll need to sort your ideas into groups, arrange them in sequences. Here are five common ways to work:

1. *Rainbow connections.* List all the main points you're going to express. Don't recopy the rest of your material. Use highlighting or colored pencils to mark points that go together with the same color. When you write, follow the color code, and deal with related ideas at the same time.

2. *Linking.* Make a list of major points, and then draw lines (in color if you wish) to link related ideas. Number each linked group to identify a sequence for discussing the ideas. Figure 16.1 illustrates a linked list for an essay to be called "Manhattan Driving." The writer has drawn lines connecting related points and has supplied each linked group with a heading. When he writes his draft, each heading will probably inspire a topic sentence to introduce each major division of his essay. He will leave out one point that failed to relate to any other: "Chauffeured luxury cars."

3. *Solitaire.* Collect notes and ideas on roomy (5-by-8-inch) file cards. To organize, spread out the cards; arrange and rearrange them, as in a game of solitaire. When each idea seems to lead to the next, gather all the cards into a deck in this order. As you write, deal yourself a card at a time and translate its contents into sentences. This technique is particularly helpful when you write about literature or when you write from research.

4. *Slide show.* If you are familiar with presentation software such as Microsoft PowerPoint, write your notes and ideas on "slides" (the software equivalent of blank sheets). When you're done, the program gives you

Figure 16.1
The Linking Method for Grouping Ideas

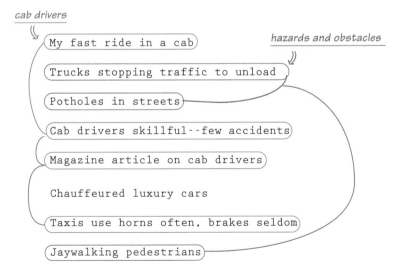

the option of viewing your slides one by one or viewing the entire collection (in Microsoft PowerPoint, choose "View," then "Slide Sorter"). In the slide sorter view, you can shuffle and reshuffle your slides into the most promising order.

5. *Clustering.* Like mapping, clustering is a visual method useful for coming up with ideas as well as grouping those ideas. In the middle of a piece of paper, write your topic in a word or a phrase. Then think of the major divisions into which this topic might be organized. For an essay called "Manhattan Drivers," the major divisions might be the *types* of Manhattan drivers: (1) taxi drivers, (2) bus drivers, (3) truck drivers, (4) drivers of private cars — New Yorkers, and (5) drivers of private cars — out-of-town visitors. Arrange these divisions around your topic, and circle them too. Draw lines out from the major topic to the subdivisions. You now have a rough plan for an essay. (See Figure 16.2.)

For more about mapping, see pp. 259–60.

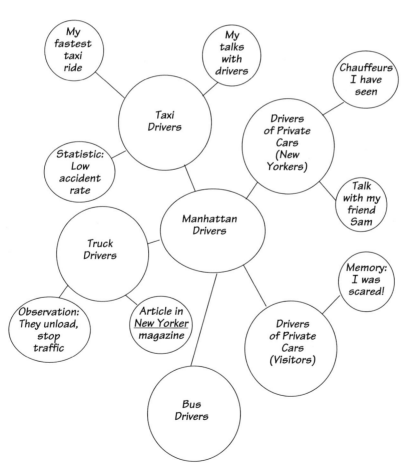

Figure 16.2
The Clustering Method for Grouping Ideas

Around each division, make another cluster of details you might include — examples, illustrations, facts, statistics, bits of evidence, opinions. Circle each specific item, and connect it to the appropriate type of driver. When you write your paper, you can expand the details into one paragraph for each type of driver.

This technique lets you know where you have enough specific information to make your paper clear and interesting — and where you don't. If one subtopic has no small circles around it (such as "bus drivers" in Figure 16.2), you should think of some specifics to expand it or drop it.

■ Exercise

Clustering

Generate clusters for three of the following topics. With your classmates, discuss which one of the three would probably help you write the best paper.

teachers	fast food	civil rights
Internet sites	leisure activities	substance abuse
my favorite restaurants	musicians	technology

OUTLINING

A familiar way to organize is to outline. A written outline, whether brief or detailed, acts as a map that you make before a journey. It shows where to leave from, where to stop along the way, and where to arrive. If you forget where you are going or what you want to say, you can consult it to get back on track. When you turn in your essay, your instructor may request an outline as both a map for readers and a skeletal summary of your material.

**WRITING WITH
A COMPUTER**

Here are some of the easy computer tools you can use to highlight, categorize, and shape your thinking by distinguishing your points on a screen.

Highlighting

Boxing

Showing color

Using **bold**, *italics*, underlining

- Adding bullets

1. Numbering

Changing fonts

Varying print sizes

To use these features, click on their icons on your toolbar or use your menu. You can also see your experiments with organization by using an option like "Track Changes" or by creating a table or column of ideas in a separate window to the left of your text.

How can you arrive at a useful outline? Some writers like to begin with a working thesis. If it's clear, it may suggest how to develop or expand an outline, allowing the plan for the paper to grow naturally from the idea behind it. Others prefer to start with a loose informal outline — perhaps just a list of points to make. If readers find your papers mechanical, such an outline may free up your writing. Still others, especially for research papers or complicated arguments, like to lay out a complex job very carefully in a detailed formal outline. If readers find your writing disorganized and hard to follow, this more detailed plan might be especially useful. In any case, your thesis can be a good guide for planning.

For more on thesis statements, see pp. 271–77.

Thesis-Guided Outlines. Your working thesis statement may identify points that you can use to organize your paper. (Of course, if it doesn't, you may want to revise your thesis and then return to your outline or vice versa.) Try questioning your thesis in order to generate a useful organization, as the table on page 282 illustrates.

Informal Outlines. For in-class writing, brief essays, and familiar topics, a short or informal outline, also called a *scratch outline,* may serve your needs. Jot down a list of points in the order you plan to make them. Use this outline, for your eyes only, to help you get organized, stick to the point, and remember good ideas under pressure. The following example outlines a short paper explaining how outdoor enthusiasts can avoid illnesses carried by unsafe drinking water. It simply lists each of the methods for treating potentially unsafe water that the writer would explain in the paper.

Working Thesis: Campers and hikers need to ensure the safety of the water that they drink from rivers or streams.

Introduction: Treatments for potentially unsafe drinking water

1. *Small commercial filter*
   —Remove bacteria and protozoa including salmonella and E. coli
   —Use brands convenient for campers and hikers

2. *Chemicals*
   —Use bleach, chlorine, or iodine
   —Follow general rule: 12 drops per gallon of water

3. *Boiling*
   —Boil for 5 minutes (Red Cross) to 15 minutes (National Safety Council)
   —Store in a clean, covered container

Conclusion: Using one of three methods of treating water, campers and hikers can ensure the safety of water from natural sources.

KEY ELEMENT OF THESIS	EXAMPLES OF KEY ELEMENT	SAMPLE THESIS STATEMENT	QUESTION YOU MIGHT ASK	POSSIBLE ORGANIZATION OF OUTLINE
Plural word	Words such as *benefits, advantages, teenagers,* or *reasons*	A varied personal exercise program has four main *advantages.*	What are the types, kinds, or examples of this word?	List outline headings based on the categories or cases you identify.
Key word identifying an approach or vantage point about a topic	Words such as *claim, argument, position, interpretation,* or *point of view*	Wylie's *interpretation* of Van Gogh's last paintings unifies aesthetic and psychological considerations.	What are the parts, aspects, or elements of this approach?	List outline headings based on the components that you identify.
Key word identifying an activity	Words such as *preparing, harming,* or *improving*	*Preparing* a pasta dinner for surprise guests can be an easy process.	How is this activity accomplished, or how does it happen?	Supply a heading for each step, stage, or element that the activity involves.
One part of the sentence subordinate to another	Sentence part beginning with *because, since,* or *although*	*Although* the new wetland preserve will protect only some wildlife, it will bring several long-term benefits to the region.	What does the qualification include, and what does the main statement include?	Use a major heading for the qualification and another for the main statement.
General evaluation that assigns a quality or value to someone or something	Evaluative words such as *typical, unusual, valuable, notable,* or other specific qualities	When other parents meet Sandie Burns on the soccer field sidelines, they may be surprised to see her wheelchair, but they soon discover that she is a *typical* soccer Mom.	What examples, illustrations, or clusters of details will show this quality?	Add a heading for each extended example or each group of examples or details you want to use.
Claim or argument advocating a certain decision, action, or solution	Words such as *should, could, might, ought to, need to,* or *must*	Despite these tough economic times, the student Senate *should* strongly recommend extended hours for the library computer lab.	Which reasons and evidence will justify this opinion? Which will counter the opinions of others who disagree with it?	Provide a heading for each major justification or defensive point; add headings for countering reasons.

Outlining

Discuss the formal topic outline on page 284 with some of your classmates or the entire class, considering the following questions:

FOR GROUP LEARNING

- Would this outline be useful in organizing an essay?

- How is the organization logical? Is it easy to follow? What are other possible arrangements for the ideas?

- Is this outline sufficiently detailed for a paper? Can you spot any gaps?

- What possible pitfalls would the writer using this outline need to avoid?

This simple outline could easily fall into a five-paragraph essay or grow to eight paragraphs — introduction, conclusion, and three pairs of paragraphs in between. You probably won't know until you write the paper exactly how many paragraphs you'll need.

An informal outline can be even briefer than the preceding one. To answer an exam question or prepare a very short paper, your outline might be no more than an *outer plan* — three or four phrases jotted in a list:

Isolation of region
Tradition of family businesses
Growth of electronic commuting

On the other hand, suppose that you are assigned an anthropology paper on the people of Melanesia. You decide to focus on the following idea:

Working Thesis: Although the Melanesian pattern of family life may look strange to Westerners, it fosters a degree of independence that rivals our own.

Laying out ideas in the same order that they follow in the two parts of this thesis statement, you might make a short, simple outline like this:

1. *Features that appear strange to Westerners*
   –A woman supported by her brother, not her husband
   –Trial marriages common
   – Divorce from her children possible for any mother

2. *Admirable results of system*
   –Wives not dependent on husbands for support
   –Divorce between mates uncommon
   –Greater freedom for parents and children

This informal outline suggests an essay that naturally falls into two parts — features that seem strange and admirable results of the system.

Say you plan a "how-to" essay analyzing the process of buying a used car, beginning with this thesis:

Working Thesis: Despite traps that lie waiting for the unwary, preparing yourself before you shop can help you find a good used car.

The key word in this thesis is *preparing,* and you ask yourself *how* the buyer should prepare before shopping for a used car.

–Read car magazines and <u>Consumer Reports.</u>
–Check ads in the newspapers.
–Make phone calls to several dealers.
–Talk to friends who have bought used cars.
–Know what to look and listen for when you test drive.
–Have a mechanic check it out.

After starting your paper with some horror stories about people who got taken by car sharks, you can discuss, point by point, your bits of advice. Of course, you can always change the sequence, add or drop an idea, or revise your thesis as you go along.

For sample formal outlines, see pp. 285–87.

Formal Outlines.   A *formal outline* is an elaborate guide, built with time and care, for a long, complex paper. Because major reports, research papers, and senior theses require so much work, some professors and departments ask a writer to submit a formal outline at an early stage and to include one in the final draft. Because a formal outline shows how ideas relate one to another—which ones are equal and important (*coordinate*) and which are less important (*subordinate*), it clearly and logically spells out where you are going. If you outline again after writing a draft, the outline checks your logic then as well, perhaps indicating where to revise.

When you make a full formal outline, follow these steps:

- Place your thesis statement at the beginning.
- List the major points that support and develop your thesis, labeling them with roman numerals (I, II, III).
- Break down the major points into divisions with capital letters (A, B, C), subdivide those using arabic numerals (1, 2, 3), and subdivide those using small letters (a, b, c). Continue until your outline is fully developed. If a very complex project requires further subdivision, use arabic numerals and small letters in parentheses.
- Indent each level of division in turn: the deeper the indentation, the more specific the ideas. Align like-numbered or -lettered headings under one another.

For more on parallelism, see B2 in the Quick Editing Guide (the dark-blue-edged pages).

- Cast all headings in parallel grammatical form: phrases or sentences, but not both in the same outline.

A *formal topic outline* for a long paper about city and small-town drivers might be constructed as follows:

Drivers in Cities and Small Towns

Working Thesis: Different lifestyles cause city drivers to be more aggressive than small-town drivers.

I. Lifestyles of drivers
    A. Fast-paced, stress-filled lifestyle of city drivers
        1. Aggressive
        2. Impatient
        3. Tense
        4. Often frustrated
    B. Slow-paced lifestyle of small-town drivers
        1. Laid-back
        2. Patient
        3. Relaxed
        4. Not easily upset
II. Resulting behavior as drivers
    A. City drivers
        1. Little consideration for other drivers
            a. Blowing horn
            b. Shouting
            c. Not using proper signals
                (1) Turning across lanes
                (2) Stopping without warning
        2. Disregard for pedestrians
        3. Violation of speed limits
            a. Running red lights
            b. Having many accidents
    B. Small-town drivers
        1. Consideration of other drivers
            a. Driving defensively
            b. Yelling less
            c. Signaling
                (1) Turning
                (2) Stopping
        2. Regard for pedestrians
        3. Attention to speed limits
            a. Observing traffic lights
            b. Having fewer accidents

A topic outline may not be thorough enough to pinpoint what you want to say, how to say it, or how ideas relate. If so, consider a *formal sentence outline,* simply writing complete sentences for the headings or turning topic headings into sentences—specifying ideas, changing wording, and even reworking your thesis as needed. A sentence outline can clarify what you intend to say and help you draft topic sentences and paragraphs, but you cannot be sure how everything fits together until you write the draft itself.

Drivers in Cities and Small Towns

Working Thesis: Because of their more stressful lives, city drivers are more aggressive than small-town drivers.

I. The lives of city drivers are more stress-filled than are the lives of small-town drivers.
   A. City drivers are always in a hurry.
      1. They are impatient.
      2. They are often frustrated.
   B. Small-town drivers live slower-paced lives.
      1. They are relaxed.
      2. They are seldom frustrated on the streets.

II. As a result of the tension they live with constantly, city drivers are more aggressive than are small-town drivers.
   A. City drivers are aggressive.
      1. They show little consideration for other drivers.
         a. They blow their horns often.
         b. They shout at other drivers frequently.
      2. They show little respect for pedestrians.
      3. They do not obey traffic laws.
         a. They do not use proper signals.
         b. They turn across lanes.
         c. They stop without warning.
         d. They speed.
      4. They have many accidents.
   B. Small-town drivers are laid-back.
      1. They are considerate of other drivers.
         a. They drive carefully.
         b. They rarely yell or honk at other drivers.
      2. They show concern for pedestrians.
      3. They obey traffic laws.
         a. They use proper signals.
         b. They turn properly.

c. They stop slowly.

d. They speed less.

4. They have fewer accidents.

CAUTION: Because an outline divides or analyzes ideas, some readers and instructors disapprove of categories with only one subpoint, reasoning that you can't divide anything into one part. Let's say that your outline on earthquakes lists a 1 without a 2:

For more on analysis and division, see pp. 311–13.

D. Probable results of an earthquake include structural damage.

1. Houses are stripped of their paint.

Logically, if you are going to discuss the *probable results* of an earthquake, you need to include more than one result:

D. Probable results of an earthquake include structural damage.

1. Houses are stripped of their paint.

2. Foundations crack.

3. Road surfaces are damaged.

4. Water mains break.

Not only have you now come up with more points, but you have also placed the most important last for emphasis.

■ Exercise

Outlining

1. Using one of your groups of ideas from the exercises in Chapter 15, construct a formal topic outline that might serve as a guide for an essay.

2. Now turn that topic outline into a formal sentence outline.

3. Discuss both outlines with your classmates and your instructor, bringing up any difficulties you encountered. If you get any better notions for organizing your ideas, change the outline.

4. Write an essay based on your outline.

■ For exercises on organizing support effectively, visit <bedfordstmartins.com/bedguide> and do a keyword search:

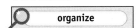

organize

Chapter 17
Strategies for Drafting

Learning to write well involves learning what key questions to ask yourself: How can I begin this draft? What should I do if I get stuck? How can I flesh out the bones of my paper? How can I end effectively? How can I keep my readers with me? In this chapter we offer advice to get you going and keep you going, drafting the first paragraph to the last.

Making a Start Enjoyable

For more help with drafting, use the *Writing Guide Software* for THE BEDFORD GUIDE.

A playful start may get you hard at work before you know it.

- **Time Yourself.** Set your watch, alarm, or egg timer, and vow to draft a page before the buzzer sounds. Don't stop for anything. If you're writing drivel, just push on. You can cross out later.

- **Slow to a Crawl.** If speed quotas don't work, time yourself to write with exaggerated laziness, maybe a sentence every fifteen minutes.

- **Scribble on a Scrap.** If you dread the blank sheet of paper, try starting on scrap paper, the back of a list, or a small tablet.

- **Begin Writing the Part You Find Most Appetizing.** Start in the middle or at the end, wherever the thoughts come easily to mind. As novelist Bill Downey observes, "Writers are allowed to have their dessert first."

For more about purpose and audience, see pp. 13–15 and pp. 269–70.

- **State Your Purpose.** Set forth what you want to achieve: To tell a story? To explain something? To win a reader over to your way of thinking?

- **Slip into a Reader's Shoes.** Put yourself in a reader's place. Start writing what you'd like to find out from the paper.

- **Nutshell It.** Tersely summarize the paper you want to write. Condense your ideas into one small, tight paragraph. Later you can expand each sentence until the meaning is clear and all points are adequately supported.

- **Shrink Your Immediate Job.** Break the writing task into smaller parts, and do only the first one. Vow to turn out, say, just the first two paragraphs.

- **Seek a Provocative Title.** Write down a dozen possible titles for your paper. If one sounds strikingly good, don't let it go to waste!

- **Tape-Record Yourself.** Talk a first draft into a tape recorder. Then play it back. Then write. Even if you find it hard to transcribe your spoken words, this technique may set your mind in motion.

- **Speak Up.** On your feet, before an imaginary cheering crowd, spontaneously utter an opening paragraph. Then — quick! — tape it or write it down.

- **Take Short Breaks.** Even if you don't feel tired, take a regular break every half hour or so. Get up, walk around the room, stretch, or get a drink of water. Two or three minutes should be enough to refresh your mind.

Restarting

When you have to write a long or demanding essay that you can't finish in one sitting, you may return to it only to find yourself stalled. You tromp your starter and nothing happens. Your engine seems reluctant to turn over. Try the following suggestions for getting back on the road.

WRITING WITH A COMPUTER

Use your word processor menu options to set the margin widths, line spacing, print size, and other aspects of your paper's format and page layout. If your instructor has not specified formatting, customize your files to produce pages with one-inch margins and double spacing, using 12-point type.

Whether you store your work on disks or on the hard drive of your own computer, a simple file-naming convention and folder system will make it easy for you to keep track of your work. Some students prefer file names that identify the course, term, assignment, and draft number, while others note the paper topic or activity with the draft number — Eng101F2004-1-1 or Recall-1. When you revise a draft, be sure to duplicate and rename the file — Eng101F2004-1-2 or Recall-2 — instead of simply rewriting the original file. Then all the versions of your paper will be available in case you want to retrieve writing from an early draft or your instructor wants to review the stages of your writing process. Use the menu or the help screen to create a folder for each course; store all your drafts for the class there.

For more advice on document design, see Ch. 20.

- **Leave Hints for How to Continue.** If you're ready to quit, jot down any remaining ideas. Tell yourself what you think might come next, or write the first sentence of the next section. When you come back to work, you will face not a blank wall but rich and suggestive graffiti.

- **Pause in Midstream.** End a writing session by breaking off in midsentence or midparagraph. Just leave a sentence trailing off into space, even if you know what its closing words should be. When you return to your task, you can start writing again immediately.

- **Repeat.** If the next sentence refuses to appear, simply recopy the last one until that shy creature emerges on the page.

- **Reread.** When you return to work, spend a few minutes rereading what you have already written or what you have planned.

- **Switch Instruments.** Do you compose on the computer? Try writing in longhand. Or drop your pen to type. Try writing on note cards or colored paper.

- **Change Activities.** When words won't come, do something quite different from writing. Run, walk your dog, cook your favorite meal, or nap. Or reward yourself — after you arrive at a certain point in your labors — with a trip to the vending machine, a phone call to a friend, or a TV show. All the while, your unconscious mind will be working on your writing task.

Paragraphing

For more on developing ideas within paragraphs, see Ch. 18.

An essay is written not in large, indigestible lumps but in *paragraphs* — small units, each more or less self-contained, each contributing some new idea in support of the thesis or main point of the essay. Writers dwell on one idea at a time, stating it, developing it, illustrating it with examples or a few facts — *showing* readers, with plenty of detailed evidence, exactly what they mean.

Paragraphs can be as short as one sentence or as long as a page. Sometimes the length is governed by the audience, the purpose of the writing, or the medium in which it appears. Journalists expect newspaper readers to gobble up facts like popcorn, quickly skimming articles with short one- or two-sentence paragraphs. College writers, in contrast, should assume their readers' willingness to read through well-developed paragraphs.

When readers see a paragraph indentation, they interpret it as a pause, a chance for a deep breath. After that signpost, they expect you to concentrate on a new aspect of your thesis for the rest of that paragraph. The following sections in this chapter give you advice on guiding readers through your writing — using opening paragraphs to draw them in, topic sentences to focus and control body paragraphs within an essay, and concluding paragraphs to wrap up the discussion.

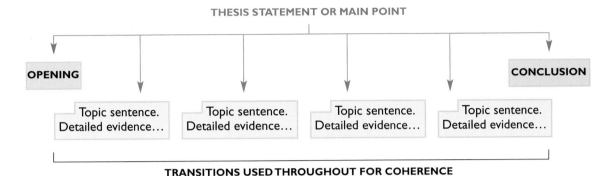

Using Topic Sentences

A *topic sentence* spells out the main idea of a paragraph in the body of an essay. It guides you as you write, and it hooks your readers as they discover what to expect and how to interpret the rest of the paragraph. As the topic sentence establishes the focus of the paragraph, it also relates the paragraph to the thesis of the essay, supporting the topic and main point of the essay as a whole. (For this reason, much of the advice on writing topic sentences for paragraphs also extends to writing thesis statements for essays.) To convert an idea to a topic sentence, you need to add your own slant, attitude, or point.

For more on thesis statements, see pp. 271–77.

> Main Idea   +   Slant or Attitude or Point   =   Topic Sentence

How can you write a good topic sentence? Make it interesting, accurate, and limited. The more pointed and lively your topic sentence, the more it will interest your readers. Even a dull and vague start can be enlivened once you zero in on a specific point.

MAIN IDEA + SLANT	television + everything that's wrong with it
DULL START	There are many things wrong with television.
POINTED TOPIC SENTENCE	Of all the faulty television programming, what I dislike most is the melodramatic news.
¶ PLAN	Illustrate the point with two or three melodramatic news stories.

A topic sentence also should be an accurate guide to the rest of the paragraph so that readers expect just what the paragraph delivers.

INACCURATE GUIDE	An emergency may not be a common event, but emergency preparedness should be. [The paragraph explains several types of household emergencies, not preparedness.]

| ACCURATE TOPIC SENTENCE | Although an emergency may not be a common event, emergency preparedness should be routine at every home. |
| ¶ PLAN | Explain how a household can prepare for an emergency with a medical kit and a well-stocked pantry. |

Finally, a topic sentence should be limited so you don't mislead or frustrate readers about what the paragraph covers.

MISLEADING	Seven factors have contributed to the increasing obesity of the average American. [The paragraph discusses only one.]
LIMITED TOPIC SENTENCE	Portion size is a major factor that contributes to the increasing obesity of average Americans.
¶ PLAN	Define healthy portion sizes, contrasting them with the large portions common in restaurants and packaged foods.

KINDS OF TOPIC SENTENCES

Topic Sentence as First Sentence.   Usually the topic sentence appears first in the paragraph, followed by sentences that clarify, illustrate, and support what it says. It is typically a statement but can sometimes be a question, alerting the reader to the topic without giving away the punchline. In the following example from James David Barber's *The Presidential Character: Predicting Performance in the White House,* 3rd ed. (Englewood Cliffs: Prentice, 1985), as in all the following examples, we have put the topic sentences in *italics.*

> *The first baseline in defining Presidential types is activity-passivity.* How much energy does the man invest in his Presidency? Lyndon Johnson went at his day like a human cyclone, coming to rest long after the sun went down. Calvin Coolidge often slept eleven hours a night and still needed a nap in the middle of the day. In between, the Presidents array themselves on the high or low side of the activity line.

This paragraph moves from general to specific. The topic sentence clearly states at the outset what the paragraph is about. The second sentence defines *activity-passivity.* The third and fourth sentences, by citing extreme ends of the baseline, supply illustrations — active Johnson, passive Coolidge. The final sentence makes a generalization that reinforces the central point.

Topic Sentence near the Beginning of Paragraph.   Sometimes the first sentence of a paragraph acts as a transition, linking what is to come with what has gone before. Then the *second* sentence might be the topic sentence. This pattern is illustrated in this paragraph from "On Societies as Organisms" in *The Lives of a Cell* (New York: Viking, 1974) by physician Lewis

Thomas. It follows one about insects that ends "and we violate science when we try to read human meanings in their arrangements."

> It is hard for a bystander not to do so. *Ants are so much like human beings as to be an embarrassment.* They farm fungi, raise aphids as livestock, launch armies into wars, use chemical sprays to alarm and confuse enemies, capture slaves. The families of weaver ants engage in child labor, holding their larvae like shuttles to spin out the thread that sews the leaves together for their fungus gardens. They exchange information ceaselessly. They do everything but watch television.

Topic Sentence at End of Paragraph.   Occasionally a writer, especially one trying to persuade the reader to agree, piles detail on detail. Then, with a dramatic flourish, the writer *concludes* with the topic sentence, as student Heidi Kessler does.

> A fourteen-year-old writes to an advice columnist in my hometown newspaper that she has "done it" lots of times and sex is "no big deal." At the neighborhood clinic where my aunt works, a hardened sixteen-year-old requests her third abortion. A girl-child I know has two children of her own, but no husband. A college student in my dorm now finds herself sterile from a "social disease" picked up during casual sexual encounters. Multiply these examples by thousands. *It seems clear to me that women, who fought so hard for sexual freedom equal to that of men, have emerged from the battle not as joyous free spirits but as the sexual revolution's walking wounded.*

This paragraph moves from the particular to the general — from four examples about individuals to one large statement about American women at the end. By the time you come to the end of the paragraph, you might be ready to accept the conclusion in the topic sentence.

Topic Sentence Implied.   It is also possible to find a perfectly unified, well-organized paragraph that has no topic sentence at all, like the following from "New York" (*Esquire*, July 1960) by Gay Talese:

> Each afternoon in New York a rather seedy saxophone player, his cheeks blown out like a spinnaker, stands on the sidewalk playing "Danny Boy" in such a sad, sensitive way that he soon has half the neighborhood peeking out of windows tossing nickels, dimes, and quarters at his feet. Some of the coins roll under parked cars, but most of them are caught in his outstretched hand. The saxophone player is a street musician named Joe Gabler; for the past thirty years he has serenaded every block in New York and has sometimes been tossed as much as $100 a day in coins. He is also hit with buckets of water, empty beer cans and eggs, and chased by wild dogs. He is believed to be the last of New York's ancient street musicians.

No one sentence neatly sums up the writer's idea. Like most effective paragraphs that do not state a topic sentence, this one contains something just as good — a *topic idea*. The author doesn't allow his paragraph to wander aimlessly. He knows exactly what he wants to achieve—a description of how Joe Gabler, a famous New York street musician, plies his trade. Because Talese keeps this purpose firmly in mind, the main point—that Gabler meets both reward and abuse—is clear to the reader as well.

■ Exercise

Topic Sentences

Discuss each of the following topic sentences with your peer group, answering these questions:

> Will it catch readers' attention?
> Is it accurate?
> Is it limited?
> How might you develop the idea in the rest of the paragraph?
> Can you improve it?

1. Television commercials stereotype people.
2. Living away from home for the first time is hard.
3. It's good for a child to have a pet.
4. A flea market is a good place to buy jewelry.
5. Pollution should be controlled.
6. Everybody should recycle wastes.

Writing an Opening

Even writers with something to say may find it hard to begin. Often they are so intent on writing a brilliant opening that they freeze, unable to write at all. They forget even the essentials—setting up the topic, sticking to what's relevant, and establishing a thesis. If you feel like a deer paralyzed by headlights when you face your first page, try these ways of tackling the opening:

- Start with your thesis statement, with or without a full opening paragraph. Fill in the rest later.
- Write your thesis statement—the one you planned or one you'd now like to develop—in the middle of a page. Go back to the top of the page, and concisely add the background a reader needs to appreciate where you're going.
- Write a long beginning for your first draft; then cut it down to the most dramatic, exciting, or interesting essentials.
- Simply set words—any words—on paper, without trying for an arresting opening. Rewrite later.

- Write the first paragraph last, after you know exactly where your essay goes.
- Move your conclusion to the beginning, and write a new ending.
- Write a summary for yourself and your readers.

KINDS OF OPENINGS

Your opening paragraph should intrigue readers — engaging their minds and hearts, exciting their curiosity, drawing them away from their preoccupations into the world set forth in your writing. Use this checklist as you hunt for an effective opening that fits your paper. Then read the sample opening paragraphs that follow.

DISCOVERY CHECKLIST

___ What vital background might readers need?

___ What general situation might help you narrow down to your point?

___ What facts or statistics might make your issue compelling?

___ What powerful anecdote or incident might introduce your point?

___ What striking example or comparison would engage a reader?

___ What question will your thesis — and your essay — answer?

___ What lively quotation would set the scene for your essay?

___ What assertion or claim might be the necessary prelude for your essay?

___ What preview of the points to come might usefully prepare a reader?

___ What would compel someone to keep on reading?

Begin with a Story.   Often a simple anecdote can capture your readers' interest and thus serve as a good beginning. Here is how Harry Crews opens his essay "The Car" in *Florida Frenzy* (Gainesville: UP of Florida, 1982):

> The other day, there arrived in the mail a clipping sent by a friend of mine. It had been cut from a Long Beach, California, newspaper and dealt with a young man who had eluded police for fifty-five minutes while he raced over freeways and through city streets at speeds up to 130 miles per hour. During the entire time, he ripped his clothes off and threw them out the window bit by bit. It finally took twenty-five patrol cars and a helicopter to catch him. When they did, he said that God had given him the car and that he had "found God."

Most of us, after such an anecdote, want to read on. What will the writer say next? What has the anecdote to do with the essay as a whole?

Introduce a Topic or Position and Comment on It.   Sometimes a writer expands on a topic, bringing in vital details, as in this opening by David Morris, from his article "Rootlessness" (*The Utne Reader*, May/June 1990):

Americans are a rootless people. Each year one in six of us changes residences; one in four changes jobs. We see nothing troubling in these statistics. For most of us, they merely reflect the restless energy that made America great. A nation of immigrants, unsurprisingly, celebrates those willing to pick up stakes and move on: the frontiersman, the cowboy, the entrepreneur, the corporate raider.

After stating his point baldly, Morris supplies statistics to support his contention and briefly explains the phenomenon. This same strategy can be used to open with a controversial opinion, then back it up with examples.

Ask a Question.   An essay can begin with a question and answer, as James H. Austin begins "Four Kinds of Chance," in *Chase, Chance, and Creativity: The Lucky Art of Novelty* (New York: Columbia UP, 1978):

What is chance? Dictionaries define it as something fortuitous that happens unpredictably without discernible human intention. Chance is unintentional and capricious, but we needn't conclude that chance is immune from human intervention. Indeed, chance plays several distinct roles when humans react creatively with one another and with their environment.

Beginning to answer the question in the first paragraph leads readers to expect the rest of the essay to continue the answer.

For more on thesis statements, see pp. 271–77.

End with the Thesis Statement.   Opening paragraphs can often end by stating the essay's main point. After capturing readers' attention with an anecdote, gripping details, or examples, you lead readers in exactly the direction your essay is to go. Such a thesis statement can be brief, as in this powerful opening of an essay by George B. Leonard called "No School?":

The most obvious barrier between our children and the kind of education that can free their enormous potential seems to be the educational system itself: a vast, suffocating web of people, practices and presumptions, kindly in intent, ponderous in response. Now, when true educational alternatives are at last becoming clear, we may overlook the simplest: no school.

Writing a Conclusion

The final paragraphs of an essay linger longest in readers' minds, as does E. B. White's conclusion to "Once More to the Lake" (p. 000). In the essay, White describes his return with his young son to a vacation spot he had loved as a child. As the essay ends in an unforgettable image, he recalls how old he really is and realizes the inevitable passing of generations.

When the others went swimming my son said he was going in, too. He pulled his dripping trunks from the line where they had hung all through the shower and wrung them out. Languidly, and with no thought of going in, I watched him, his hard little body, skinny and bare, saw him wince slightly as he pulled up around his vitals the small, soggy, icy garment. As he buckled the swollen belt, suddenly my groin felt the chill of death.

White's classic example of an effective ending opens with a sentence that points back to the previous paragraph as it also looks ahead. Then White leads us quickly to his final, chilling insight. And then he stops.

KINDS OF CONCLUSIONS

It's easy to suggest what *not* to do at the end of an essay: don't leave your readers half expecting you to go on. Don't restate everything you've already said. Don't introduce a brand-new topic that leads away from your point. And don't signal that the end is near with an obvious phrase like "As I have said."

"How *do* you write an ending, then?" you might well ask. Use this checklist as you tackle your conclusion. Then read the sample concluding paragraphs that follow.

DISCOVERY CHECKLIST

___ What restatement of your thesis would give readers a satisfying sense of closure?

___ What provocative implications of your thesis might answer "What now?" or "What's the significance of what I've said?"

___ What snappy quotation or statement would wrap up your point?

___ What closing facts or statistics might confirm the merit of your point?

___ What final anecdote, incident, or example might round out your ideas?

___ What question has your essay answered?

___ What assertion or claim might you want to restate?

___ What summary might help a reader pull together what you've said?

___ What would make a reader sorry to finish such a satisfying essay?

End with a Quotation.   An apt quotation can neatly round out an essay, as literary critic Malcolm Cowley shows in *The View from Eighty* (New York: Viking, 1980), his discussion of the pitfalls and compensations of old age.

> "Eighty years old!" the great Catholic poet Paul Claudel wrote in his journal. "No eyes left, no ears, no teeth, no legs, no wind! And when all is said and done, how astonishingly well one does without them!"

State or Restate Your Thesis.   In a sharp criticism of American schools, humorist Russell Baker in "School vs. Education" ends by stating his main point, that schools do not educate.

Afterward, the former student's destiny fulfilled, his life rich with Oriental carpets, rare porcelain, and full bank accounts, he may one day find himself with the leisure and the inclination to open a book with a curious mind, and start to become educated.

End with a Brief Emphatic Sentence.   For an essay that traces causes or effects, evaluates, or argues, a deft concluding thought can reinforce your main idea. In *The Long Count* (New York: Atheneum, 1969), former heavyweight champion Gene Tunney analyzes his two victorious fights with Jack Dempsey, whose boxing style differed markedly from Tunney's own. Notice the definite click with which Tunney closes the door on "The Long Count."

> Jack Dempsey was a great fighter — possibly the greatest that ever entered a ring. Looking back objectively, one has to conclude that he was more valuable to the sport or "The Game" than any prizefighter of his time. Whether you consider it from his worth as a gladiator or from the point of view of the box office, he was tops. His name in his most glorious days was magic among his people, and today, twenty years after, the name Jack Dempsey is still magic. This tells a volume in itself. As one who has always had pride in his profession as well as his professional theories, and possessing a fair share of Celtic romanticism, I wish that we could have met when we were both at our unquestionable best. We could have decided many questions, to me the most important of which is whether "a good boxer can always lick a good fighter."
> I still say yes.

Stop When the Story Is Over.   Even a quiet ending can be effective, as long as it signals clearly that the essay is finished. Journalist Martin Gansberg simply stops when the story is over in his true account of the fatal stabbing of a young woman, Kitty Genovese, in full view of residents of a Queens, New York, apartment house. The residents, unwilling to become involved, did nothing to interfere. Here is the last paragraph of his account, "Thirty-eight Who Saw Murder Didn't Call Police" (*New York Times,* 17 Mar. 1964):

> It was 4:25 A.M. when the ambulance arrived to take the body of Miss Genovese. It drove off. "Then," a solemn police detective said, "the people came out."

◼ Exercise

Openings and Conclusions

Openings and conclusions frame an essay, contributing to the unity of the whole. The opening sets up the topic and main idea; the conclusion reaffirms the thesis and rounds off the ideas. Discuss the following with your classmates.

I.   Here are two possible opening paragraphs from a student essay on the importance of teaching children how to swim.

   A. Humans inhabit a world made up of over 70 percent water. In addition to these great bodies of water, we have built millions of swimming

◼ For more exercises on openings and conclusions, visit <bedfordstmartins.com/bedguide> and do a keyword search:

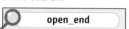

   open_end

pools for sports and leisure activities. At one time or another most people will be faced with either the danger of drowning or the challenge of aquatic recreation. For these reasons, it is essential that we learn to swim. Being a competitive swimmer and a swimming instructor, I fully realize the importance of knowing how to swim.

B. Four-year-old Carl, curious like most children, last spring ventured out onto his pool patio. He fell into the pool and, not knowing how to swim, helplessly sank to the bottom. Minutes later his uncle found the child and brought him to the surface. Since Carl had no pulse, his uncle immediately administered CPR until the paramedics arrived. Eventually he was revived. During his stay in the hospital, his mother signed him up for beginning swimming classes. Carl was a lucky one. Unlike thousands of other children and adults, he got a second chance.

1. Which introduction is more effective? Why?
2. What would the body of this essay consist of? What kinds of evidence would be included?
3. Write a suitable conclusion for this essay.

II. If you were to read each of the following introductions from professional essays, would you want to read the entire essay? Why?

A. During my ninth hour underground, as I scrambled up a slanting tunnel through the powdered gypsum, Rick Bridges turned to me and said, "You know, this whole area was just discovered Tuesday." (David Roberts, "Caving Comes into Its Golden Age: A New Mexico Marvel," *Smithsonian* Nov. 1988: 52)

B. From the batting average on the back of a George Brett baseball card to the interest rate fluctuations that determine whether the economy grows or stagnates, Americans are fascinated by statistics. (Stephen E. Nordlinger, "By the Numbers," *St. Petersburg Times* 6 Nov. 1988: 11)

C. "What does it look like under there?"

It was always this question back then, always the same pattern of hello and what's your name, what happened to your eye and what's under there. (Natalie Kusz, "Waiting for a Glass Eye," *Road Song* [New York: Farrar, 1990], rpt. in *Harper's* Nov. 1990)

III. How effective are these introductions and conclusions from student essays? Could they be improved? If so, how? If they are satisfactory, explain why. What would be a catchy yet informative title for each essay?

A. Recently a friend down from New York astonished me with stories of several people infected — some with AIDS — by stepping on needles washed up on the New Jersey beaches. This is just one incident of pollution, a devastating problem in our society today. Pollution is increasing in our world because of greed, apathy, and Congress's inability to control this problem. . . .

Wouldn't it be nice to have a pollution-free world without medical wastes floating in the water and washing up on our beaches? Without garbage scattered on the streets? With every corporation abiding by the laws set by Congress? In the future we can have a pollution-free world, but it is going to take the cooperation of everyone, including Congress, to ensure our survival on this Planet Earth.

B. The divorce rate has risen 700 percent in this century and continues to rise. More than one out of every two couples who are married end up in divorce. Over one million children a year are affected by divorce in the family. From these statistics it is clear that one of the greatest problems concerning the family today is divorce and the adverse effects it has on our society. . . .

Divorce causes problems that change people for life. The number of divorces will continue to exceed the 700 percent figure unless married couples learn to communicate, to accept their mates unconditionally, and to sacrificially give of themselves.

IV. Choose one of the topics that you generated in Chapter 15, and write at least three different introductions with conclusions. Ask your classmates which is the most effective.

Achieving Coherence

Effective writing proceeds in some sensible order, each sentence following naturally from the one before it. Yet even well-organized prose can be hard to read unless it is *coherent*. To make your writing coherent, you can use various devices that tie together words in a sentence, sentences in a paragraph, paragraphs in an essay.

DEVICES THAT CREATE COHERENCE

Transitional Words and Sentences.   You use transitions every day to help your readers and listeners follow your train of thought. For example, you might say to a friend, "Well, *on the one hand*, a second job would help me save money for tuition. *On the other hand*, I'd have less time to study." But some writers rush through, omitting links between thoughts or mistakenly assuming that connections they see will automatically be clear to readers. Often just a word, phrase, or sentence of transition inserted in the right place will transform a disconnected passage into a coherent one.

Many words and phrases specify connections between or within sentences. In the chart on page 301, *transitional markers* are grouped by purpose or the kind of relation or connection they establish.

Occasionally a whole sentence serves as a transition. As in this excerpt from an essay by Marsha Traugot about adopting older and handicapped children, the opening of a paragraph may hark back to the one before while simultaneously suggesting the new direction. We have italicized the transitional sentences.

■ For another example, see the paragraph by Lewis Thomas on p. 302.

Some exchanges hold monthly meetings where placement workers looking for a match can discuss waiting children or families, and they also sponsor parties where children, workers, and prospective parents meet informally.

COMMON TRANSITIONS	
TO MARK TIME	then, soon, first, second, next, recently, the following day, in a little while, meanwhile, after, later, in the past
TO MARK PLACE OR DIRECTION	in the distance, close by, near, far away, above, below, to the right, on the other side, opposite, to the west, next door
TO SUMMARIZE OR RESTATE	in other words, to put it another way, in brief, in simpler terms, on the whole, in fact, in a word, to sum up, in short, in conclusion, to conclude, finally, therefore
TO RELATE CAUSE AND EFFECT OR RESULT	therefore, accordingly, hence, thus, for, so, consequently, as a result, because of
TO ADD OR AMPLIFY OR LIST	and, also, too, besides, as well, moreover, in addition, furthermore, in effect, second, in the second place, again, next
TO COMPARE	similarly, likewise, in like manner
TO CONCEDE	whereas, on the other hand, with that in mind, still, and yet, even so, in spite of, despite, at least
TO CONTRAST	on the other hand, but, or, however, unlike, nevertheless, on the contrary, conversely, in contrast, instead
TO INDICATE PURPOSE	to this end, for this purpose, with this aim
TO EXPRESS CONDITION	although, though
TO GIVE EXAMPLES OR SPECIFY	for example, for instance, in this case, in particular, to illustrate
TO QUALIFY	for the most part, by and large, with few exceptions, mainly, in most cases, generally, some, sometimes, typically
TO EMPHASIZE	it is true, truly, indeed, of course, to be sure, obviously, without doubt, evidently, clearly, understandably

> *And if a match still cannot be made?* Exchanges and other child welfare organizations now employ media blitzes as aggressive as those of commercial advertising. . . .

By repeating the key word *match* in her transitional sentence and by inserting the word *still*, Traugot makes clear that what follows will build on what has gone before. At the same time, by making the transitional sentence a rhetorical question, Traugot promises that the new paragraph will introduce fresh material, in this case answering the question.

Transition Paragraphs.   Transitions may be even longer than sentences. In a long and complicated essay, moving clearly from one idea to the next will sometimes require a short paragraph of transition.

> So far, we have been dwelling on the physical and psychological effects of driving nonstop for more than two hundred miles. Now let's reflect on causes. Why do people become addicted to their steering wheels?

Use a transition paragraph only when you sense that your readers might get lost if you don't patiently lead them by the hand. If your essay is short, one question or statement at the beginning of a new paragraph will be enough.

A transition paragraph can also aid your return from one branch of argument to your main trunk. In "Things Unflattened by Science" from *Late Night Thoughts on Listening to Mahler's Ninth Symphony* (New York: Viking, 1983), Lewis Thomas has been complaining that biologists keep expecting medical researchers to come up with quick answers to intractable problems—cancer, schizophrenia, stress. Then, to return to the essay's main idea—what biological problems he would like to see solved—Thomas inserts a transition paragraph.

> But I digress. What I wish to get at is an imaginary situation in which I am allowed three or four questions to ask the world of biomedical science to settle for me by research, as soon as possible. Can I make a short list of top-priority puzzles, things I am more puzzled by than anything else? I can.

In a new paragraph, he continues: "First, I want to know what goes on in the mind of a honeybee," whether a bee is programmed like a robot or can think and imagine, even a little bit. Neatly and effectively, the transition paragraph has led to this speculation and to several paragraphs to come.

Repetitions.   Another way to clarify the relationship between two sentences, paragraphs, or ideas is to repeat a key word or phrase. Such purposeful repetition almost guarantees that readers will understand how all the parts of a passage fit together. Note the repetition of the word *anger* in the following paragraph (italics ours) from *Of Woman Born* (New York: Norton, 1976) by poet Adrienne Rich. In this complex paragraph, the writer explores her relationship with her mother. The repetition holds all the parts together and makes clear the unity and coherence of the paragraph's ideas.

> And I know there must be deep reservoirs of *anger* in her; every mother has known overwhelming, unacceptable *anger* at her children. When I think of the conditions under which my mother became a mother, the impossible expectations, my father's distaste for pregnant women, his hatred of all that he could not control, my *anger* at her dissolves into grief and *anger* for her, and then dissolves back again into *anger* at her: the ancient, unpurged *anger* of the child.

Pronouns.   Because they always refer back to nouns or other pronouns, pronouns serve as transitions by making readers refer back as well. Note how certain pronouns (in italics) hold together the following paragraph by columnist Ellen Goodman:

> I have two friends who moved in together many years ago. *He* looked upon this step as a trial marriage. *She* looked upon it as, well, moving in together. *He* was sure that in a matter of time, after *they* had built up trust and confidence, *she* would agree that marriage was the next logical step. *She*, on the other hand, was thrilled that here at last was a man *who* would never push *her* back to the altar.

The paragraph contains other transitions, too: time markers like *many years ago, in a matter of time,* and *after; on the other hand,* which indicates a contrast; and repetition of synonyms like *trial marriage, marriage,* and *the altar.* All serve the main purpose of transitions — keeping readers on track.

■ Exercise

Identifying Transitions

Go over one of the papers you have already written for this course, and circle all the transitional devices you can detect. Then share your paper with a classmate. Can the classmate find additional transitions? Does the classmate think you need transitions where you don't have any?

■ For more exercises on transitions, visit <bedfordstmartins.com/bedguide> and do a keyword search:

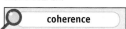
coherence

Chapter 18
Strategies for Developing

■ For more help with developing an essay, use the *Writing Guide Software* for *THE BEDFORD GUIDE*.

■ For examples of development strategies, visit <bedfordstmartins.com/ bedguide> and do a key-word search:

development

How can you spice up your general ideas with the stuff of real life? How can you tug your readers deeper and deeper into your essays until they say, "I see just what you mean"? Well-developed essays have such power because they back up general points with evidence that comes alive for readers. In this chapter we cover eight indispensable methods of development—giving examples, providing details, defining, analyzing a subject, dividing and classifying, analyzing a process, comparing and contrasting, and showing causes and effects. Although you may choose to use only one method within a single paragraph, a strong essay almost always requires a combination of developmental strategies.

Whenever you develop a piece of writing or return to it to revise, you face a challenge: How do you figure out what to do? Sometimes you may suspect that you've wandered into the Writer's Grill, a local hang-out offering a huge buffet lunch. You watch others load their plates, but you still hesitate. Which foods will taste best? Which will be healthy choices? Which will make your meal a relaxing experience? How much will fit on your plate? Whether you're hesitating in the buffet line or struggling to wrap up your essay, the answers to such questions are all individual. For you as a writer, the answers depend on your situation, the clarity of your main idea or thesis, and the state of your draft, as the following checklist suggests.

DISCOVERY CHECKLIST

Purpose

___ Does your assignment recommend or require specific methods of development?

___ Which developmental strategies might be most useful to explain, inform, or persuade?

___ What type of development might best achieve your specific purpose?

Audience

___ Which developmental strategies would best clarify your topic for readers?

___ Which would best demonstrate your thesis to your readers?

___ What kinds of evidence will your specific readers prefer? Which developmental strategies might present this evidence most effectively?

Thesis

___ What kinds of development does your thesis promise or imply that you will supply?

___ What sequence of developmental strategies would best support your thesis?

Essay Development

___ Has a reader or peer editor pointed out any ideas in your draft that need fuller development?

___ Where might your readers have trouble following or understanding without more or better development?

Paragraph Development

___ Should any paragraphs with one or two sentences be developed more fully?

___ Should any long paragraphs with generalizations, repetition, and wordy phrasing be developed differently so that they are richer and deeper?

Giving Examples

An example — the word comes from the Latin *exemplum*, "one thing chosen from among many" — is a typical instance that illustrates a whole type or kind. Giving examples to support a generalization is probably the most often used means of development. This example, from *In Search of Excellence* (New York: Harper and Row, 1982) by Thomas J. Peters and Robert H. Waterman Jr., explains the success of America's top corporations:

> Although he's not a company, our favorite illustration of closeness to the customer is car salesman Joe Girard. He sold more new cars and trucks, each year, for eleven years running, than any other human being. In fact, in a typical year, Joe sold more than twice as many units as whoever was in second place. In explaining his secret of success, Joe said: "I sent out over thirteen thousand cards every month."
>
> Why start with Joe? Because his magic is the magic of IBM and many of the rest of the excellent companies. It is simply service, overpowering service, especially after-sales service. Joe noted, "There's one thing that I do that a lot of salesmen don't, and that's believe the sale really begins *after* the sale — not before. . . . The customer ain't out the door, and my son has made up a thank-you note." Joe would intercede personally, a year later, with the service manager on behalf of his customer. Meanwhile he would keep the communications flowing.

Notice how Peters and Waterman focus on the specific, Joe Girard. They don't write *corporation employees* or even *car salespeople.* Instead, they zero in on one particular man to make the point come alive.

Joe Girard	Level 4: Specific Example
car salespeople	Level 3: Even More Specific Group
corporation employees	Level 2: More Specific Group
America's top corporations	Level 1: General Group or Category

This ladder of abstraction moves from the general — America's top corporations — to a specific person — Joe Girard. The specific example of Joe Girard makes closeness to the customer *concrete* to readers: he is someone readers can relate to. To check the level of specification in one of your paragraphs or outlines, draw a ladder of abstraction for it. Do the same to restrict a broad subject to a topic manageable in a short essay. If you haven't gone up to the fourth or fifth level, you are probably being too general and need to add specifics.

An example doesn't always have to be a specific individual. Sometimes you can create a picture of something readers have never encountered or give an abstraction a recognizable personality and identity. Using this strategy, Jonathan Kozol makes real the plight of illiterate people in our health-care system in this paragraph from *Prisoners of Silence: Breaking the Bonds of Adult Illiteracy in the United States* (New York: Continuum, 1980):

> Illiterates live, in more than literal ways, an uninsured existence. They cannot understand the written details on a health insurance form. They cannot read waivers that they sign preceding surgical procedures. Several women I have known in Boston have entered a slum hospital with the intention of obtaining a tubal ligation and have emerged a few days later after having been subjected to a hysterectomy. Unaware of their rights, incognizant of jargon, intimidated by the unfamiliar air of fear and atmosphere of ether that so many of us find oppressive in the confines even of the most attractive and expensive medical facilities, they have signed their names to documents they could not read and which nobody, in the hectic situation that prevails so often in those overcrowded hospitals that serve the urban poor, had ever bothered to explain.

Examples aren't trivial doodads you add to a paragraph for decoration; they are what holds your readers' attention and shows them that your writing makes sense. By using examples, you make your ideas more concrete and tangible. To give plenty of examples is one of the writer's chief tasks. When you need more, you can generate them at any point in the writing process. Begin with your own experience, even with a topic about which you know little, or try conversing with others, reading, digging in the library, or browsing on the Web.

For ways to generate ideas, see Ch. 15.

Consider these questions when you use examples in your writing:

___ Are your examples relevant to your main idea or thesis?
___ Are your examples the best ones you can think of? Will readers find them strong and appropriate?
___ Are your examples really specific? Or do they just repeat generalities?
___ From each paragraph, can you draw a ladder of abstraction to at least the fourth level?

■ Exercise

Giving Examples

To help you get in the habit of thinking specifically, fill in a ladder of abstraction for five of the following general subjects. Then share your ladders with classmates, and compare and contrast your specifics with theirs. Examples:

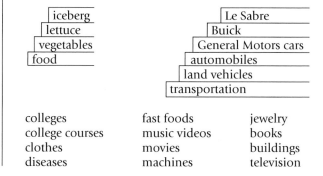

colleges	fast foods	jewelry
college courses	music videos	books
clothes	movies	buildings
diseases	machines	television

Providing Details

A *detail* is any specific, concrete piece of information — a fact, a bit of the historical record, your own observation. Details make scenes and images more realistic and vivid for readers. They also back up generalizations, convincing readers that the writer can make broad assertions with authority.

Mary Harris "Mother" Jones told the story of her life as a labor organizer in *The Autobiography of Mother Jones* (Chicago: Kerr, 1980). She lends conviction to her general statement about a coal miner's lot at the end of the nineteenth century with ample evidence from her own experience and observations.

> Mining at its best is wretched work, and the life and surroundings of the miner are hard and ugly. His work is down in the black depths of the earth. He works alone in a drift. There can be little friendly companionship as there is in the factory; as there is among men who build bridges and houses, working together in groups. The work is dirty. Coal dust grinds itself

into the skin, never to be removed. The miner must stoop as he works in the drift. He becomes bent like a gnome.

His work is utterly fatiguing. Muscles and bones ache. His lungs breathe coal dust and the strange, damp air of places that are never filled with sunlight. His house is a poor makeshift and there is little to encourage him to make it attractive. The company owns the ground it stands on, and the miner feels the precariousness of his hold. Around his house is mud and slush. Great mounds of culm [the refuse left after coal is screened], black and sullen, surround him. His children are perpetually grimy from playing on the culm mounds. The wife struggles with dirt, with inadequate water supply, with small wages, with overcrowded shacks.

Although Mother Jones, not a learned writer, relies on short, simple sentences, her writing is clear and powerful because of the specific details she uses. Her opening makes two general statements: (1) "Mining is wretched work," and (2) the miner's life and surroundings are "hard and ugly." She supports these generalizations with a barrage of factual evidence and detail, including well-chosen verbs: "Coal dust *grinds* itself into the skin." The result is a moving, convincingly detailed portrait of the miner and his family.

N. Scott Momaday ("To the Singing, to the Drums" [*Natural History*, Feb. 1975]) uses many details to describe the scene of the Kiowa celebration of the Gourd Dance on the Fourth of July at Carnegie, Oklahoma.

The celebration is on the north side. We turn down into a dark depression, a large hollow among trees. It is full of camps and cars and people. At first there are children. According to some centrifugal social force, children function on the periphery. They run about, making festival noises. Firecrackers are snapping all around. We park and I make ready; the girls help me with my regalia. I am already wearing white trousers and moccasins. Now I tie the black velvet sash around my waist, placing the beaded tassels at my right leg. The bandoleer of red beans, which was my grandfather's, goes over my left shoulder, the V at my right hip. I decide to carry the blanket over my arm until I join the dancers; no sense in wrapping up in this heat. There is deep, brick-red dust on the ground. The grass is pale and brittle here and there. We make our way through the camps, stepping carefully to avoid the pegs and guy lines that reach about the tents. Old people, imperturbable, are lying down on cots and benches in the shadows. Smoke hangs in the air. We smell hamburgers, popcorn, gunpowder. Later there will be fried bread, boiled meat, Indian corn.

■ For more on transitions, see pp. 300–03.

Momaday arranges his vivid details both spatially and chronologically. Notice his spatial transitions: *on the north side, turn down, on the periphery, all around, on the ground, here and there, through the camps, in the shadows, in the air.* Look also at the time markers: *At first, Now, until, Later.* These transitions guide readers through the experience.

Quite different from Momaday's personal details are Paula Gunn Allen's hard facts and objective statistics, heaped up to convince readers that ever since Native Americans began making pacts with the U.S. government, their survival has been threatened.

Some researchers put our pre-contact population at more than 45 million, while others put it at around 20 million. The U.S. government long put it at 450,000 — a comforting if imaginary figure, though at one point it was put at around 270,000. If our current population is around one million; if, as some researchers estimate, around 25 percent of Indian women and 10 percent of Indian men in the United States have been sterilized without informed consent; if our average life expectancy is, as the best-informed research presently says, 55 years; if our infant mortality rate continues at well above national standards; if our average unemployment for all segments of our population — male, female, young, adult, and middle-aged — is between 60 and 90 percent; if the U.S. government continues its policy of termination, relocation, removal, and assimilation along with the destruction of wilderness, reservation land, and its resources, and severe curtailment of hunting, fishing, timber harvesting, and water-use rights — then existing tribes are facing the threat of extinction which for several hundred tribal groups has already become fact in the past five hundred years.

Providing details is one of the simplest yet most effective ways of developing ideas. All it takes on your part is close attention and precise wording to communicate the details to readers. If readers were on the scene, what would they see? What would they hear, smell, or feel? Which small details from your reading are most meaningful to you? Would a bit of research turn up just the right fact or statistic? Remember that effective details have a specific purpose: they must help make your images more evocative or your point more convincing. Every detail should support — in some way — your main idea.

Here are some questions to consider when you use details:

DISCOVERY CHECKLIST

___ Do all your details support your point of view, main idea, or thesis?

___ Do you have details of sights? Sounds? Tastes? Touch? Smells?

___ Have you included enough details to make your writing clear and interesting?

___ Have you arranged your details in an order that is easy to follow?

■ Exercise

Providing Details

To practice generating and using specific details, brainstorm with classmates or alone on one of the following subjects. Be sure to include details that appeal to all five senses. Group the details in your list (see pp. 277–80), and write a paragraph or two using your specific details. Begin by stating a main idea that conveys an engaging impression of your subject (not "My grandmother's house was in Topeka, Kansas" but "My grandmother's house was my childhood haven").

■ For more on brainstorming, see pp. 254–56.

■ For more exercises on supporting details, visit <bedfordstmartins.com/bedguide> and do a keyword search:

support

the things in my room	a memorable event	my job
my grandmother's home	an unusual person	a classroom
a haunted house	my favorite pet	the cafeteria
my old car	a hospital room	an incident

Defining

Define, from the Latin, means "to set bounds to." You define a thing, a word, or a concept by describing it so that it is distinguished from all similar things. If people don't agree on the meaning of a word or an idea, they can't share knowledge about it. Scientists in particular take special care to define their terms precisely. In his article "A Chemist's Definition of pH," Gessner G. Hawley begins with a brief definition:

> pH is a value taken to represent the acidity or alkalinity of an aqueous solution; it is defined as the logarithm of the reciprocal of the hydrogen-ion concentration of a solution:
>
> $$pH = 1n \frac{1}{[H^+]}$$

If you use a word in a special sense or coin a word, you have to explain it or your readers will be lost. Prolific word coiner and social prophet Alvin Toffler in *The Third Wave* (New York: Morrow, 1980) invents the word *techno-sphere*, which he defines as follows:

> All societies — primitive, agricultural, or industrial — use energy; they make things; they distribute things. In all societies the energy system, the production system, and the distribution system are interrelated parts of something larger. This larger system is the *techno-sphere*.

In his later book *PowerShift* (New York: Bantam, 1990), Toffler picks up the word *screenie* from Jeffrey Moritz, president of National College Television, and adds his own boundaries to this coined term:

> Moritz uses the term *screenie* to describe this video-drenched generation, which has digested thousands of hours of television, imbibing its "video-logic." To that must be added, for many of them, more hours of interactive video games and, even more important, of work on their own personal computers. They not only follow a different logic, but are accustomed to make the screen do things, thus making them good prospects for the interactive services and products soon to hit the market. Above all, they are accustomed to choice.

Sometimes you may define a standard word not often used, to save your readers a trip to the dictionary, or a familiar but often misunderstood concept. What is intelligence, socialism, HMO, or minimum wage? The more complex or ambiguous an idea, a thing, a movement, a phenomenon, or an organization, the longer the definition you will need to clarify the term for your readers.

Here are some questions to consider when you use definitions:

DISCOVERY CHECKLIST

____ Have you used definitions to help your readers understand the subject matter, not to show off your knowledge?

____ Have you tailored your definition to the needs of your audience?

____ Is your definition specific, clear, and accurate?

____ Would your definition benefit from an example or from details?

■ Exercise

Defining

Write an extended definition (a paragraph or so) of one of the following words. Begin with a one-sentence definition of the word. Then, instead of getting most of your definition from a dictionary or textbook, expand and clarify your ideas using some of the strategies in this chapter — examples, details, subject analysis, division and classification, process analysis, comparison and contrast, and causal analysis. You may also use *negation* (explaining what something is by stating what it is not). Share your definition with your classmates.

education	abuse	exercise	literacy
privacy	jazz	dieting	success
taboo	rock music	gossip	fear
prejudice	AIDS	security	gender

Analyzing a Subject

When you *analyze* a subject, you divide it into its parts and then deal with one part at a time. If you have taken any chemistry, you probably analyzed water: you separated it into hydrogen and oxygen, its two elements. You've heard many a television commentator analyze the news, telling us what made up an event — who participated, where it occurred, what happened. Analyzing a news event may produce results less certain and clear-cut than analyzing a chemical compound, but the principle is similar — to take something apart for the purpose of understanding it better.

Analysis helps readers understand something complex: they can more readily take in the subject in a series of bites than in one gulp. For this reason, college textbooks do a lot of analyzing: an economics book divides a labor union into its component parts, an anatomy text divides the hand into its bones, muscles, and ligaments. In your college papers, you might

For more on division and classification, see pp. 314–16. For more on process analysis, see pp. 316–18. For more on cause and effect, see pp. 320–21.

analyze and explain to readers anything from a contemporary subculture (What social groups make up the homeless population of Los Angeles?) to an ecosystem (What animals, plants, and minerals coexist in a rainforest?). Analysis is so useful that you can apply it in many situations: breaking down the components of a subject to classify them, separating the stages in a process to see how it works, or identifying the possible results of an event to project consequences.

In *Cultural Anthropology: A Perspective on the Human Condition* (St. Paul: West, 1987), Emily A. Schultz and Robert H. Lavenda briefly but effectively demonstrate by analysis how a metaphor like "the Lord is my shepherd" makes a difficult concept ("the Lord") easy to understand.

> The first part of a metaphor, the metaphorical subject, indicates the domain of experience that needs to be clarified (e.g., "the Lord"). The second part of a metaphor, the metaphorical predicate, suggests a domain of experience which is familiar (e.g., sheep-herding) and which may help us understand what "the Lord" is all about.

Lillian Tsu, a government major at Cornell University, opens her essay "A Woman in the White House" in a similar manner, using analysis to identify major difficulties faced by female politicians in the United States.

The past twenty years have witnessed the rise of several powerful female leaders in world politics. In 1979, Margaret Thatcher became the first female prime minister of Great Britain; in 1986, Corazón Aquino ended a twenty-year dictatorship in the Philippines; and in 1988, Benazir Bhutto became the first woman to head a modern Muslim state when she became the prime minister of Pakistan. However, the success of these women may not translate into the future success of prospective female presidential candidates in the United States. Though these women rose to the top of their respective political ladders, their successes can be categorized as political anomaly or the result of a highly unusual set of circumstances. Although traditionally paternalistic societies like the Philippines and Pakistan and socially conservative states like Great Britain have elected female leaders, particular characteristics of the United States' own electoral system make it unlikely that this country will follow suit and elect a female president. Despite social modernization and the progress of the women's movement, the voters of the United States still lag far behind those of other nations in their willingness to trust in the leadership of a female executive. While the women's movement has succeeded in changing Americans' attitudes as to what roles are socially acceptable for women, female candidates still face a more difficult task in U.S. elections than their male counterparts face. Three factors are responsible for this situation--political socialization, lack of experience, and open discrimination.

Next, Tsu treats these factors in turn, beginning each of the first three sections with a transition phrase emphasizing the difficulties U.S. female candidates face: "One obstacle," "A second obstacle," "A third obstacle." The opening list and the transitions give readers clear direction in a complicated essay, guiding them through the explanation of the three factors to the final section on the implications of the analysis.

When you plan an analysis, you might label slices in a pielike circle or arrange subdivisions in a list running from smallest to largest or from least to most important. Make sure that your analysis has a purpose — that it will demonstrate something about your subject or tell your readers something they didn't know before. For example, you might want to analyze New York City for the purpose of showing its ethnic composition. If so, you might divide the city geographically into neighborhoods — Harlem, Spanish Harlem, Yorkville, Chinatown, Little Italy. If you want to explain New York's social classes, however, you might start with homeless people and work up to the cream of society. The way you slice your subject into pieces will depend in part on the point you want to make about it — and the point you end up making will depend in part on how you've sliced it up. As you develop your ideas, you may also find that you have a stronger point to make — that New York City's social hierarchy is oppressive and unstable, for example.

How can you ensure that your readers will be able to follow your thinking as you analyze? Some writers like to begin by identifying the subdivisions into which they are going to slice their subject ("The federal government has three branches"). If you invent a name or label for each part you mention, define the terms you use, and clarify with examples, you will also help distinguish each part from all the others. You can make your essay as readable as possible by using transitions, leading readers from one part to the next.

For more on transitions, see pp. 300–03.

Here are some questions to consider when you use analysis:

DISCOVERY CHECKLIST

___ Exactly what will you try to achieve in your analysis?

___ How does your analysis support your main idea or thesis?

___ How will you break your subject into parts?

___ How can you make each part clear to your readers?

___ What definitions, details, and examples can help clarify each part?

■ Exercise

Analyzing a Subject

Analyze one of the following subjects by making a list of its basic parts or elements. Then use your list as the basis for a paragraph or short essay explaining each part. Be sure to identify the purpose or point of your analysis. Compare your analysis with those of others in your class who chose the same subject.

a college	a choir, orchestra, or other musical group
a newspaper	a computer or other technological device
a reality TV show	a basketball, baseball, hockey, or other team
effective teaching	a family
a healthy lifestyle	leadership

Dividing and Classifying

For more on analysis, see pp. 311–13.

To divide is to break something down, identifying or analyzing its components. It's far easier to take in a subject, especially a complex subject, one piece at a time. The thing divided may be as concrete as Chicago (which a writer might divide into neighborhoods) or as abstract as a person's knowledge of art (which the writer might divide into knowledge of sculpture, painting, drawing, and other forms). To classify is to make sense of a complicated and potentially bewildering array of things — works of literature, this year's movies — by sorting them into categories (*types* or *classes*) that you can deal with one at a time. Literature is customarily arranged by genre — novels, stories, poems, plays. Movies might be sorted by audience (movies for children, teenagers, or mature audiences).

These two methods of development are like two sides of the same coin. In theory, any broad subject can be *divided* into components, which can then be *classified* into categories. In practice, it's often difficult to tell where division stops and classification begins.

In the following paragraph from his college textbook *Wildlife Management* (San Francisco: Freeman, 1978), Robert H. Giles Jr. uses division to simplify an especially large, abstract subject: the management of forest wildlife in America. To explain which environmentalists assume which duties and responsibilities, Giles divides forest wildlife management into six levels or areas of concern, arranged roughly from large to small, all neatly explained in fewer than 175 words.

There are six scales of forest wildlife management: (1) national, (2) regional, (3) state or industrial, (4) county or parish, (5) intra-state region, management unit, or watershed, and (6) forest. Each is different. At the national and regional levels, management includes decisions on timber harvest quotas, grazing policy in forested lands, official stance on forest taxation bills, cutting policy relative to threatened and endangered species, management coordination of migratory species, and research fund allocation. At the state or industrial level, decision types include land acquisition, sale, or trade; season setting; and permit systems and fees. At the county level, plans are made, seasons set, and special fees levied. At the intra-state level, decisions include what seasons to recommend, what stances to take on bills not affecting local conditions, the sequence in which to attempt land acquisition, and the placement of facilities. At the forest level, decisions may include some of those of the larger management unit but typically are those of maintenance schedules, planting stock, cutting rotations, personnel employment and supervision, road closures, equipment use, practices to be attempted or used, and boundaries to be marked.

In a textbook lesson on how babies develop, Kurt W. Fischer and Arlyne Lazerson, writing in *Human Development* (New York: Freeman, 1984), describe a research project that classified individual babies into three types according to temperament.

> The researchers also found that certain of these temperamental qualities tended to occur together. These clusters of characteristics generally fell into three types — the easy baby, the difficult baby, and the baby who was slow to warm up. The *easy infant* has regular patterns of eating and sleeping, readily approaches new objects and people, adapts easily to changes in the environment, generally reacts with low or moderate intensity, and typically is in a cheerful mood. The *difficult infant* usually shows irregular patterns of eating and sleeping, withdraws from new objects or people, adapts slowly to changes, reacts with great intensity, and is frequently cranky. The *slow-to-warm-up infant* typically has a low activity level, tends to withdraw when presented with an unfamiliar object, reacts with a low level of intensity, and adapts slowly to changes in the environment. Fortunately for parents, most healthy infants — 40 percent or more — have an easy temperament. Only about 10 percent have a difficult temperament, and about 15 percent are slow to warm up. The remaining 35 percent do not easily fit one of the three types but show some other pattern.

When you divide and classify, your point is to make order out of a complex or overwhelming jumble of stuff. Make sure the components and categories you identify are sensible, given your purpose, and follow the same principle of classification or analysis for all categories. For example, if you're trying to discuss campus relations, it makes sense to divide the school population into *instructors, students,* and *support staff;* it would make less sense to divide it into *people from the South, people from the other states,* and *people from overseas.* Also, try to group apples with apples, not with oranges, so that all the components or categories are roughly equivalent. For example, if you're classifying television shows and you've come up with *sitcoms, dramas, talk shows, children's shows, news,* and *cartoons,* then you've got a problem: the last category is probably part of *children's shows.* Finally, check that your final system is simple and easy for your readers to understand. Most people can handle only about seven things at once. If you've got more than six or seven components or categories, perhaps you need to combine or eliminate some.

Consider these questions when you use division or classification:

DISCOVERY CHECKLIST

___ How does your division or classification support your main idea or thesis?

___ Do you use the most logical principle of division or classification for your purpose?

___ Do you stick to one principle throughout?

___ Have you identified components or categories that are comparable?

___ Have you arranged your components or categories in the best order?

___ Have you given specific examples for each component or category?

___ Have you made a complex subject more accessible to your readers?

■ Exercise

Dividing and Classifying

For more on brain-
storming, see pp. 254–56.

To practice dividing and classifying, choose one or two of the following sub-jects. Brainstorm for five minutes on each, trying to come up with as many components as you can. With your classmates, create one large list by combining items from all students who chose each subject. Working as a group, take the largest list and try to classify the items on it into logical categories. Feel free to add or change components or categories if you've overlooked something.

students	customers	sports	families
teachers	Web sites	vacations	drivers

Analyzing a Process

Analyzing a process means telling step by step how something is or was done or how to do something. You can analyze an action or a phenomenon — how a skyscraper is built, how a revolution begins, how sunspots form, how to make chili. This strategy can also explain large, long-ago happenings that a writer couldn't possibly have witnessed or complex technical processes that a writer couldn't personally duplicate. Here, for instance, is a paragraph from "The Case for Cloning" (*Time*, 9 Feb. 1998) in which Madeleine Nash describes the process of cloning cells.

> Cloning individual human cells [. . .] is another matter. Biologists are already talking about harnessing for medical purposes the technique that produced the sheep called Dolly. They might, for example, obtain healthy cells from a patient with leukemia or a burn victim and then transfer the nucleus of each cell into an unfertilized egg from which the nucleus has been removed. Coddled in culture dishes, these embryonic clones — each genetically identical to the patient from which the nuclei came — would begin to divide. The cells would not have to grow into a fetus, however. The addition of powerful growth factors could ensure that the clones develop only into specialized cells and tissue. For the leukemia patient, for example, the cloned cells could provide an infusion of fresh bone marrow, and for the burn victim, grafts of brand-new skin. Unlike cells from an unrelated donor, these cloned cells would incur no danger of rejection; patients would be spared the need to take powerful drugs to suppress the immune system.

This paragraph illustrates an *informative* process analysis that sets forth how something happens.

The *directive* or "how-to" process analysis instructs readers how to do something (how to box, invest for retirement, clean a painting) or how to make something (how to draw a map, blaze a trail, set up a computer). In the following example from *The Little Windows Book, 3.1 Edition* (Berkeley: Peachpit, 1992), technical writer Kay Yarborough Nelson uses a directive process description to teach her readers how to use a computer mouse.

> You can use the mouse in three basic ways: by clicking, double-clicking, and dragging.
>
> To select an item on the screen, you can move the mouse pointer to it and click once with the left mouse button. (If you're left-handed, you can change it to the right mouse button, as you'll see in the chapter on customizing Windows.) Selecting an item makes it active, so that you can work with it. For example, you might click on a document's icon so that you could copy or move it.
>
> You can also double-click on an item to make it active and actually start it. To double-click, quickly click twice with the left mouse button. For example, double-clicking on a program's icon will open a window and start the program. . . .
>
> A third way of using the mouse is dragging. To drag, put the mouse pointer on what you want to drag, press and hold the left mouse button down, and then move the mouse.

Nelson takes care to make each step seem simple and logical. Her clear divisions (*three basic ways*), unambiguous commands (*move, click, put*), concrete examples (*For example*), and helpful transitions (*a third way, and then*) help guide readers through the process step by step.

Although generally used to supply accurate directions, process analysis can also be turned to humorous ends, as illustrated in this paragraph from "How to Heal a Broken Heart (in One Day)" by student Lindsey Schendel.

> To begin your first day of mourning, you will wake up at 11 a.m., thus banishing any feelings of fatigue. Forget eating a healthy breakfast; toast two waffles, and plaster them with chocolate syrup instead of maple. Then make sure you have a room of serenity so you may cry in peace. It is important that you go through the necessary phases of denial and depression. Call up a friend or family member while you are still in your serious, somber mood. Explain to that person the hardships you are facing and how you don't know if you can go on. Immediately afterwards, turn on any empowering music, get up, and dance.

Like more serious process directions, this paragraph includes steps or stages (sleeping late, eating breakfast, crying and calling through denial and depression, and getting up and dancing). They are arranged in chronological order with transitions marking the movement from one to the other (*To begin, then, while, immediately afterwards*).

Process analyses are wonderful ways to show your readers the inside workings of events or systems, but they can be difficult to follow. Be sure to

For more on transitions, see pp. 300–03.

divide the process into logical steps or stages and to put the steps in a sensible chronological order. Add details or examples wherever your description may become ambiguous or abstract, and use transitions to mark the end of one step and the beginning of the next.

Here are some questions to consider when you use process analysis:

DISCOVERY CHECKLIST

___ Do you thoroughly understand the process you are analyzing?

___ Do you have a good reason to analyze a process at this point in your writing? How does your analysis support your main idea or thesis?

___ Have you broken the process into logical and useful steps?

___ Is the order in which you present these steps the best one possible?

___ Have you used transitions to guide your readers from one step to the next?

■ Exercise

Analyzing a Process

Analyze one of the following processes or procedures as the basis of a paragraph or short essay. Then share your process analysis with classmates. Can they follow your analysis easily? Do they spot anything you left out?

registering for college classes	falling in love
studying for a test	buying a used car
having influenza (or another disease)	moving

Comparing and Contrasting

For advice on writing a comparison and contrast essay, see Ch. 7.

Often you can develop ideas by setting a pair of subjects side by side, comparing and contrasting them. When you compare, you point out similarities; when you contrast, you discuss differences. Working together, these twin strategies use one subject to clarify another. The dual method works well for a pair similar in nature — two cities, two films, the theories of two economists. Because this method shows that you have observed and understood both subjects, college instructors will often ask you to compare and contrast on exams ("Discuss the chief similarities and differences between nineteenth-century French and English colonial policies in West Africa").

In daily life, we compare and contrast to decide which menu item to choose, which car (or other product) to buy, which college course to sign up for. A comparison and contrast can lead to a final evaluation and a decision about which thing is better, but it doesn't have to. In a travel essay, "Venezuela for Visitors" from *Hugging the Shore* (New York: Knopf, 1983), novelist John Updike sees Venezuelan society as polarized. It consists of rich people and Indians, two classes Updike compares and contrasts without choosing between them.

> Missionaries, many of them United States citizens, move among the Indians. They claim that since Western civilization, with all its diseases and detritus, must come, it had best come through them. Nevertheless, Marxist anthropologists inveigh against them. Foreign experts, many of them United States citizens, move among the rich. They claim they are just helping out, and that anyway the oil industry was nationalized five years ago. Nevertheless, Marxist anthropologists are not mollified. The feet of the Indians are very broad in front, their toes spread wide for climbing avocado trees. The feet of the rich are very narrow in front, their toes compressed by pointed Italian shoes. The Indians seek relief from tension in the use of *ebene*, or *yopo*, a mind-altering drug distilled from the bark of the ebene tree and blown into the user's nose through a hollow cane by a colleague. The rich take cocaine through the nose, and frequent mind-altering discotheques, but more customarily imbibe cognac, *vino blanco*, and Scotch, in association with colleagues.

Updike simply sets the two side by side, noting the foreigners among them, the state of their feet, and their drug preferences. By doing so, he throws the two groups into sharp relief.

You can use two basic methods of organization for comparison and contrast — the opposing pattern and the alternating pattern. Using the *opposing pattern,* you discuss all the characteristics or subdivisions of the first subject in the first half of the paragraph or essay and then discuss all the characteristics of the other subject. Using the *alternating pattern,* you move back and forth between the two subjects. This pattern places the specifics close together for immediate comparison and contrast. For example, a writer using the opposing pattern to compare and contrast two brothers would discuss Jim's physical appearance, personality traits, and interests and then Jack's appearance, personality, and interests — discussing in both parts the same characteristics in the same order. A writer using the alternating pattern would discuss Jim's physical appearance, then Jack's physical appearance; Jim's personality, then Jack's; Jim's interests, then Jack's. Whichever pattern you choose, be sure to cover the same subpoints for each subject and to follow the same order in each part.

For more on these organizing patterns, see pp. 106–08

In the paragraph above about Venezuelan society, John Updike uses the alternating pattern to compare and contrast rich people and Indians. In the following paragraph, Jacquelyn Wonder and Priscilla Donovan, management consultants, use the opposing pattern of organization to explain the differences in the brains of females and males.

For a sample paper and outline using the alternating pattern, see pp. 99–101 and pp. 107–08.

> At birth there are basic differences between male and female brains. The female cortex is more fully developed. The sound of the human voice elicits more left-brain activity in infant girls than in infant boys, accounting in part for the earlier development in females of language. Baby girls have larger connectors between the brain's hemispheres and thus integrate information more skillfully. This flexibility bestows greater verbal and intuitive skills.

For another example using the opposing pattern, see pp. 106–07.

Male infants lack this ready communication between the brain's lobes; therefore, messages are routed and rerouted to the right brain, producing larger right hemispheres. The size advantage accounts for males having greater spatial and physical abilities and explains why they may become more highly lateralized and skilled in specific areas.

After the topic sentence that begins the paragraph, the authors first explain the development of the female brain and how it accounts for specific thinking styles in females. Then they explain the development of the male brain and the effects on males' abilities.

Consider these questions when you use comparison and contrast:

DISCOVERY CHECKLIST

___ Is your reason for comparing and contrasting unmistakably clear? Does it support or develop your main idea or thesis?

___ Have you chosen to write about the *major* similarities and differences?

___ Have you compared or contrasted like things? Have you discussed the same categories or features for each item?

___ Have you used the best possible arrangement, given your subject and the point you're trying to make?

___ If you are making a judgment, have you treated both subjects fairly?

___ Have you avoided a boring, monotonous style, moving mechanically from "On the one hand" to "Now on the other hand"?

■ Exercise

Comparing and Contrasting

Write a paragraph or two in which you compare and contrast the subjects in one of the following pairs:

> baseball and football (or two other sports)
> living in an apartment (or dorm) and living in a house
> two cities or towns you are familiar with
> two musicians
> communicating by telephone and e-mail
> watching a sports event on television and in person

Identifying Causes and Effects

For advice on writing a cause and effect essay, see Ch. 8.

From the time we are children, we ask why. Why can't I go out and play? Why is the sky blue? Why did my goldfish die? Seeking causes and effects continues into adulthood, so it's natural that explaining causal relationships is a common method of development. To use this method successfully, you must think about the subject critically, gather evidence, draw judicious conclusions, and show relationships clearly.

In the following paragraph from "What Pop Lyrics Say to Us" (*New York Times*, 24 Feb. 1985), Robert Palmer speculates on the causes that led young people to turn to rock music for inspiration as well as the effects of their expectations on the musicians of the time.

> By the late '60's, the peace and civil rights movement were beginning to splinter. The assassinations of the Kennedys and Martin Luther King had robbed a generation of its heroes, the Vietnam War was escalating despite the protests, and at home, violence was on the rise. Young people turned to rock, expecting it to ask the right questions and come up with answers, hoping that the music's most visionary artists could somehow make sense of things. But rock's most influential artists — Bob Dylan, the Beatles, the Rolling Stones — were finding that serving as the conscience of a generation exacted a heavy toll. Mr. Dylan, for one, felt the pressures becoming unbearable, and wrote about his predicament in songs like "All Along the Watchtower."

Instead of focusing on causes *or* effects, often writers trace a *chain* of cause and effect relationships, as Charles C. Mann and Mark L. Plummer do in "The Butterfly Problem" (*Atlantic Monthly*, Jan. 1992).

> More generally, the web of species around us helps generate soil, regulate freshwater supplies, dispose of waste, and maintain the quality of the atmosphere. Pillaging nature to the point where it cannot perform these functions is dangerously foolish. Simple self-protection is thus a second motive for preserving biodiversity. When DDT was sprayed in Borneo, the biologists Paul and Anne Ehrlich relate in their book *Extinction* (1981), it killed all the houseflies. The gecko lizards that preyed on the flies ate their pesticide-filled corpses and died. House cats consumed the dying lizards; they died too. Rats descended on the villages, bringing bubonic plague. Incredibly, the housefly in this case was part of an intricate system that controlled human disease. To make up for its absence, the government was forced to parachute cats into the area.

Consider these questions when you identify causes and effects:

DISCOVERY CHECKLIST

____ Is your use of cause and effect clearly tied to your main idea or thesis?

____ Have you identified actual causes? Can you find evidence to support them?

____ Have you identified actual effects, or are they conjecture? If conjecture, are they logical possibilities? Can you find evidence to support them?

____ Have you judiciously drawn conclusions concerning causes and effects? Have you avoided fallacies, such as hasty generalization and stereotyping?

____ Have you presented your points clearly and logically, so that your readers can follow them easily?

For more on logical fallacies, see pp. 149–50.

■ Exercise

Identifying Causes and Effects

1. Identify some of the *causes* of *five* of the following. Discuss possible causes with your classmates.

failing an exam	stage fright	losing a job
an automobile accident	losing/winning a game	losing weight
poor health	stress	going to college
good health	getting a job	getting a scholarship

2. Identify some of the *effects* of *five* of the following. Discuss possible effects with your classmates.

an insult	dieting	divorce
a compliment	speeding	traveling to another country
learning to read	winning the lottery	drinking while driving

3. Identify some of the *causes and effects* of *one* of the following. You may need to do a little research to identify the chain of causes and effects for the event. How might you use what you have discovered as part of an essay? Discuss your findings with your classmates.

the online shopping boom	the SARS outbreak
the Vietnam War	recycling
the attack on September 11, 2001	a gay marriage court case
the discovery of atomic energy	the uses of solar energy
a major U.S. Supreme Court decision	the hole in the ozone layer
	racial tension

Chapter 19
Strategies for Revising and Editing

Good writing is rewriting. When Ernest Hemingway was asked what made him rewrite the last page of the novel *A Farewell to Arms* thirty-nine times, he replied, "Getting the words right." His comment reflects the care that serious writers take in revising their work. In this chapter we provide strategies for revising and editing—ways to rethink muddy ideas and emphasize important ones, to rephrase obscure passages and restructure

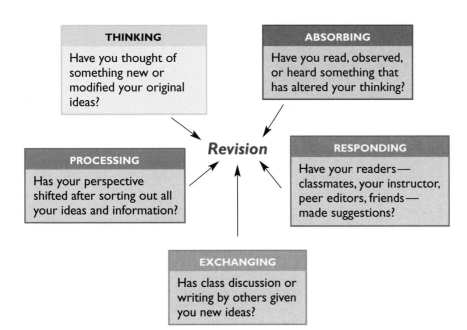

THINKING

Have you thought of something new or modified your original ideas?

ABSORBING

Have you read, observed, or heard something that has altered your thinking?

PROCESSING

Has your perspective shifted after sorting out all your ideas and information?

Revision

RESPONDING

Have your readers—classmates, your instructor, peer editors, friends—made suggestions?

EXCHANGING

Has class discussion or writing by others given you new ideas?

garbled sentences. Our advice applies not only to rewriting whole essays but also to rewriting sentences and paragraphs. In addition, we give you tips for editing and proofreading grammar, spelling, punctuation, and mechanics.

Re-viewing and Revising

Revision means "seeing again" — discovering again, conceiving again, shaping again. As an integral aspect of the total writing process, it may occur at any and all stages of the process, and most writers do a lot of it. *Macro revising* is making large, global, or fundamental changes that affect the overall direction or impact of writing — its purpose, organization, or audience. On the other hand, *micro revising* is paying attention to the details. It involves the language aspects of writing — sentences, words, punctuation, grammar — including ways to create emphasis and eliminate wordiness.

MACRO REVISING	MICRO REVISING
• **PURPOSE:** Have you refined what you want to accomplish?	• **EMPHASIS:** Do you need to position your ideas more effectively?
• **THESIS:** Do you need to state your main point more accurately?	• **CONCISENESS:** Can you spot extra words that you might cut?
• **AUDIENCE:** Should you address your readers differently?	• **CLARITY:** Can you make any sentences and words clearer?
• **STRUCTURE:** Should you reorganize any part of your writing?	
• **SUPPORT:** Do you need to add, drop, or rework your support?	

REVISING FOR PURPOSE AND THESIS

When you revise for purpose, you make sure that your writing really accomplishes whatever you want it to do. If your goal is to create an interesting profile of a person, have you done so? If you want to persuade your readers to take a certain course of action, have you succeeded? Of course, if your complex project has evolved or your assignment is now clearer to you, the purpose of your final essay may be different from your purpose when you began. To revise for purpose, try to step back and see your writing as other readers will. Concentrate on what's actually in your paper, not what you assume is there.

At this point you'll probably want to revise your working thesis statement (if you've developed one) or create a thesis sentence (if you haven't). First scrutinize your working thesis statement. Reconsider how it is worded:

■ For more help with revising, use the *Writing Guide Software* for THE BEDFORD GUIDE.

■ For more on stating a working thesis, see pp. 272–74.

- Is it stated exactly in concise, detailed language?
- Is it focused on only one main idea?
- Is it stated positively rather than negatively?
- Is it limited to a demonstrable statement?

Then consider how accurately your thesis now represents your main idea and your draft as a whole:

- Does each part of your essay directly relate to your thesis?
- Does each part of your essay develop and support your thesis?
- Does your essay carry out everything your thesis promises?

If you find unrelated or contradictory passages, you have two options: revise the thesis, or revise the essay.

You may find that your ideas have deepened, your topic has become more complex, or your essay has developed along new lines during the process of writing. If so, you may want to refine or expand your thesis statement so that it accurately represents this evolution.

WORKING THESIS	The *Herald*'s coverage of the Senate elections was more thorough than the *Courier*'s.
REVISED THESIS	The *Herald*'s coverage of the Senate elections was less timely but more thorough and less biased than the *Courier*'s.
WORKING THESIS	As the roles of men and women have changed in our society, old-fashioned formal courtesy has declined.
REVISED THESIS	As the roles of men and women have changed in our society, old-fashioned formal courtesy has declined not only toward women but also toward men.

Here are helpful questions about revising for purpose and thesis:

REVISION CHECKLIST

___ Do you know exactly what you want your essay to accomplish? Can you put it in one sentence: "In this paper I want to . . ."?

___ Is your thesis stated outright in the essay? If not, have you provided clues so that your readers will know precisely what it is?

___ Does every part of the essay work to achieve the same goal?

___ Have you tried to do too much? Does your coverage of your topic seem too thin? If so, how might you reduce the scope of your essay?

___ Does your essay say all that needs to be said? Is everything — ideas, connections, supporting evidence — on paper, not just in your head?

___ In writing the essay, have you changed your mind, rethought your assumptions, made a discovery? Does anything now need to be recast?

___ Do you have enough evidence? Is every point developed fully enough to be clear? To be convincing?

■ To see one student's
revising and editing
process, visit
<bedfordstmartins.com/
bedguide> and do a key-
word search:

process

REVISING FOR AUDIENCE

An essay is successful only if it succeeds with its particular audience, and what works with one audience can fall flat with another. Visualize one of your readers poring over the essay, sentence by sentence, reacting to what you have written. What expressions do you see on that reader's face? Where does he or she have trouble understanding? Where have you hit the mark? Your organization, your selection of details, your word choice, and your tone all affect your readers, so pay special attention to these aspects.

Here are some helpful questions about revising for your audience:

REVISION CHECKLIST

— Who will read this essay?

— Does the essay tell them what they want to know rather than what they probably know already?

— Are there any places where readers might fall asleep? If so, can such passages be shortened or deleted or livened up?

— Does the opening of the essay mislead your readers by promising something that the essay never delivers?

— Do you unfold each idea in enough detail to make it both clear and interesting? Would readers appreciate more detailed evidence?

— Have you anticipated questions readers might ask?

— Where might readers raise serious objections? How might you anticipate these objections and answer them?

— Have you used any specialized or technical language that your readers might not understand? If so, have you worked in brief definitions?

— What is your attitude toward your readers? Are you chummy, angry, superior, apologetic, condescending, preachy? Should you revise to improve your attitude? Ask your peers for an opinion.

— Will your readers be convinced that you have told them something worth knowing?

REVISING FOR STRUCTURE AND SUPPORT

When revising for structure and support, you make sure that the order of your ideas, your selection of supporting material, and its arrangement are as effective as possible. You may have all the ingredients of a successful essay — but they may be a jumbled, confusing mess.

▨ For more on para-
graphs, topic sentences,
and transitions, see Ch. 17.
In a well-structured essay, each paragraph, sentence, and phrase fulfills a clear function. Are your opening and closing paragraphs relevant, concise, and interesting? Is everything in each paragraph on the same topic? Are all ideas adequately developed? Are the paragraphs arranged in the best possible order? Finally, review each place where you lead readers from one idea to the next to be certain that the transition is clear and painless.

An outline can be useful for diagnosing a draft that you suspect doesn't quite make sense. Instead of using outlining to plan, now you want to show what you've succeeded in getting on paper. Start by finding the topic sentence of each paragraph in your draft (or creating one, if necessary) and listing them in order. Label the sentences *I., II., A., B.,* and so on to indicate the logical relationships of ideas in your essay. Do the same with the supporting details under each topic sentence, labeling them also with letters and numbers and indenting appropriately. Now look at the outline. Does it make sense on its own, without the essay to explain it? Would any different order or arrangement be more effective? Does any section look thin and need more evidence? Are the connections between parts in your head but not on paper? Maybe too many ideas are jammed into too few paragraphs. Maybe you don't include as many specific details and examples as you need — or maybe you need stronger ones. Work on the outline until you get it into strong shape, and then rewrite the essay to follow it.

For more on using outlining for planning, see pp. 280–87.

Try these helpful questions about revising for structure and support:

REVISION CHECKLIST

—— Does your introduction set up the whole essay? Does it both grab readers' attention and hint at what is to follow?

—— Does the essay fulfill all that you promise in your opening?

—— Would any later passage make a better beginning?

—— Is your thesis clear early in the essay? If explicit, is it given a position of emphasis?

—— Do the paragraph breaks seem logical?

—— Is the main idea of each paragraph clear? Have you used a topic sentence in every paragraph?

—— Is the main idea of each paragraph fully developed? Where might you need more details or better evidence to be convincing?

—— Within each paragraph, is each detail or piece of evidence relevant to the topic sentence? If you find a stray bit, should you omit it altogether or move it to another paragraph?

—— Are all the ideas directly relevant to the main point of the essay?

—— Would any paragraphs make more sense in a different order?

—— Does everything follow clearly? Does one point smoothly lead to the next? Would transitions help make the connections clearer?

—— Does the conclusion follow from what has gone before, or does it seem arbitrarily tacked on?

WORKING WITH A PEER EDITOR

Of course, there's no substitute for having someone else go over your writing. Most college assignments ask you to write for an audience of classmates, but even if your essay is written for a different group (the town council or

WRITING WITH A COMPUTER

E-mail can be an efficient way for writers and readers to exchange drafts. You can either copy and paste a document into the e-mail message or attach a document. Sometimes copying the draft into the message will remove some formatting, such as italics or bold, but this process usually works well and avoids spreading computer viruses. If you want to preserve the formatting of a document and believe your reader has compatible software, you may attach the document instead. If you use the Save As option, probably under the File menu, you can create a duplicate version of your file in another format such as Rich Text Format (rtf) which can be opened in any word-processing software.

readers of *Newsweek* magazine, for example), having a classmate read over your essay is a worthwhile revision strategy. To get all you can as a writer from a peer review, you need to play an active part in the discussion of your work:

- Ask your reader questions. (If this prospect seems difficult, write a "Dear Editor" letter or memo ahead of time, and bring it to your meeting.)
- Be open to new ideas — for focus, organization, details, or material.
- Use what's helpful, but trust yourself as the author.

To be a helpful, supportive peer editor, try to offer honest, intelligent feedback, not judgment.

- Look at the big picture: purpose, focus, clarity, coherence, organization, support.
- When you spot strengths or weaknesses, be specific: note examples.
- Answer the writer's questions, and also use the questions supplied throughout this book to concentrate on essentials, not details.

See specific checklists in the "Revising and Editing" sections in Chs. 4 to 11.

As a writer, you can ask your peer editor to begin with your specific questions or use applicable questions from the following general checklist:

Questions for a Peer Editor

FIRST QUESTIONS FOR A PEER EDITOR
What is your first reaction to this paper?
What is this writer trying to tell you?
What are this paper's greatest strengths?
Does it have any major weaknesses?
What one change would most improve the paper?

QUESTIONS ON MEANING
Do you understand everything? Is the draft missing any information that you need to know?

Does this paper tell you anything you didn't know before?

Is the writer trying to cover too much territory? Too little?

Does any point need to be more fully explained or illustrated?

When you come to the end, has the paper delivered what it promised?

Could this paper use a down-to-the-ground revision?

QUESTIONS ON ORGANIZATION

Has the writer begun in a way that grabs your interest and quickly draws you into the paper's main idea? Or can you find a better beginning at some later point?

Does the paper have one main idea, or does it juggle more than one?

Would the main idea stand out better if anything were removed or added?

Might the ideas in the paper be more effectively arranged? Do any ideas belong together that now seem too far apart?

Can you follow the ideas easily? Are transitions needed? If so, where?

Does the writer keep to one point of view — one angle of seeing?

Does the ending seem deliberate, as if the writer meant to conclude rather than running out of gas? How might the writer strengthen the conclusion?

QUESTIONS ON WRITING STRATEGIES

Do you feel that this paper addresses you personally?

Do you dislike or object to any statement the writer makes or any wording the writer uses? Is the problem word choice, tone, or inadequate support to convince you? Should the writer keep or change this part?

Does the draft contain anything that distracts you or seems unnecessary?

Do you get bored at any point? How might the writer keep you reading?

Is the language of this paper too lofty and abstract? If so, where does the writer need to come down to earth and get specific?

Do you understand all the words used? Do any specialized words need clearer meanings?

A simple way to work with another person's help is to start by saving your file with a new title. Add a "+" and your peer editor's initials to the file name to help keep track of different drafts. When you and your peer exchange texts, you may each want to use all capitals for the comments you make in each other's drafts. The capitalized comments will be easy to distinguish from the original.

Some word processors also offer editing systems, such as "Track Changes" in your Tools menu. This resource allows peer editors to highlight possible changes in your draft using underlining, color differences, and strikeouts. You can easily see suggestions, even from several readers.

**WRITING WITH
A COMPUTER**

Stressing What Counts

An ineffective writer treats all ideas as equals. An effective writer decides what matters most and shines a bright light on it. You can't emphasize merely by <u>underlining</u>, putting things in "quotation marks," or throwing them into CAPITAL LETTERS. Such devices soon grow monotonous, stressing nothing at all. This section suggests how to emphasize things that count using the most emphatic positions in an essay, a paragraph, or a sentence — the beginning and the end.

STATING FIRST

In an essay, you might start with what matters most. For an economics paper on import quotas (such as the number of foreign cars allowed into a country), Donna Waite summed up her findings.

Although an import quota has many effects, both for the nation imposing the quota and for the nation whose industries must suffer from it, I believe that the most important effect is generally felt at home. A native industry gains a chance to thrive in a marketplace of lessened competition.

A paper that takes a stand or makes a proposal might open with the writer's position.

Our state's antiquated system of justices of the peace is inefficient.

The United States should orbit a human observer around Mars.

In a single sentence, as in an essay, you can stress things at the start. Consider the following unemphatic sentence:

When Congress debates the Hall-Hayes Act removing existing protections for endangered species, as now seems likely to occur on May 12, it will be a considerable misfortune if this bill should pass, since the extinction of many rare birds and animals would certainly result.

The debate and its probable date consume the start of the sentence. The writer might have made better use of this emphatic position:

The extinction of many rare birds and animals would certainly follow passage of the Hall-Hayes Act.

Now the writer stresses what he most fears — dire consequences. (A later sentence might add the date and his opinion about passage.)

STATING LAST

To place an idea last can throw weight on it. Emphatic order, proceeding from least important to most, is dramatic: it builds up and up. In papers on import quotas and justices of the peace, however, dramatic buildups might look contrived. Still, in an essay on how city parks lure visitors to the city, the thesis sentence — summing up the point of the essay — might stand at the very end: "For the inner city, improved parks will bring about a new era of prosperity." Giving the evidence first and leading up to the thesis at the end is particularly effective in editorials and informal persuasive essays.

A sentence that uses climactic order, suspending its point until the end, is a *periodic* sentence. Notice how novelist Julian Green builds to his point of emphasis.

> Amid chaos of illusions into which we are cast headlong, there is one thing that stands out as true, and that is — love.

Cutting and Whittling

Like pea pickers who throw out dirt and pebbles, good writers remove needless words that clog their prose. One of the chief joys of revising is to watch 200 paunchy words shrink to a svelte 150. To see how saving words helps, let's first look at some wordiness. In what she imagined to be a gracious style, a New York socialite once sent this dinner invitation to Hu Shi, the Chinese ambassador:

> O learned sage and distinguished representative of the numerous Chinese nation, pray deign to honor my humble abode with your noble presence at a pouring of libations, to be followed by a modest evening repast, on the forthcoming Friday, June Eighteenth, in this Year of the Pig, at the approximate hour of eight o'clock, Eastern Standard Time. Kindly be assured furthermore, O most illustrious sire, that a favorable reply at your earliest convenience will be received most humbly and gratefully by the undersigned unworthy suppliant.

In reply, the witty diplomat sent this telegram:

> CAN DO. HU SHI.

Hu Shi's reply disputes a common assumption — that the more words an idea takes, the more impressive it will seem. Most good contemporary writers know that the more succinctly they can state an idea, the clearer and more forceful it will be.

Cut the Fanfare.   Why bother to announce that you're going to say something? Cut the fanfare. We aren't, by the way, attacking the usefulness of transitions that lead readers along.

For more on transitions, see pp. 300–03.

WORDY   As far as getting ready for winter is concerned, I put antifreeze in my car.

REVISED   To get ready for winter, I put antifreeze in my car.

WORDY   The point should be made that . . .
Let me make it perfectly clear that . . .
In this paper I intend to . . .
In conclusion I would like to say that . . .

Be Direct.   The phrases *on the subject of, in regard to, in terms of, as far as . . . is concerned,* and their ilk often lead to wind.

WORDY   He is more or less a pretty outstanding person in regard to good looks.

REVISED   He is strikingly handsome.

Words can also tend to abound after *There is* or *There are.*

WORDY   There are many people who dislike flying.

REVISED   Many people dislike flying.

Use Strong Verbs.   Forms of the verb *be* (*am, is, are, was, were*) followed by a noun or an adjective can make a statement wordy. Such weak verbs can almost always be replaced by active verbs.

WORDY   The Akron game was a disappointment to the fans.

REVISED   The Akron game disappointed the fans.

Use Relative Pronouns with Caution.   When a clause begins with a relative pronoun (*who, which, that*), you often can whittle it to a phrase.

WORDY   Venus, which is the second planet of the solar system, is called the evening star.

REVISED   Venus, the second planet of the solar system, is called the evening star.

Cut Out Deadwood.   The more you revise, the more shortcuts you'll discover. Try reading the sentences below without the words in *italics*.

Howell spoke for the sophomores, and Janet *also spoke* for the seniors.

He is *something of* a clown but *sort of* the lovable *type.*

As a major in *the field of* economics, I plan to concentrate on *the area of* international banking.

The decision as to whether *or not* to go is up to you.

Cut Descriptors.   Adjectives and adverbs are often dispensable. Contrast these two versions:

WORDY   Johnson's extremely significant research led to highly important major discoveries.

REVISED   Johnson's research led to major discoveries.

Be Short, Not Long.   While a long word may convey a shade of meaning that a shorter synonym doesn't, in general shun a long word when you can pick a short one. Instead of *the remainder,* write *the rest*; instead of *activate, start* or *begin*; instead of *adequate* or *sufficient, enough.* Look for the right word — one that wraps an idea in a smaller package.

WORDY   Andy has a left fist that has a lot of power in it.

REVISED   Andy has a potent left.

By the way, it pays to read. From reading, you absorb words like *potent* and set them to work for you.

Keep It Clear.   Finally, recall what you want to achieve — clear communication with your readers using specific, unambiguous words arranged in logical order. Try to read your draft as a brand-new reader would. Be sure to return, after a break, to passages that you have struggled to write; reduce any battle scars by focusing on clarity.

UNCLEAR   Thus, after a lot of thought, it should be approved by the board even though the federal funding for all the cow-tagging may not be approved yet because it has wide support from local cattle ranchers.

CLEAR   In anticipation of federal funding, the Livestock Board should approve the cow-tagging proposal widely supported by local cattle ranchers.

Here is a list of questions to use in slimming your writing:

REVISION CHECKLIST

____ Are you direct, straightforward, and clear?

____ Do you announce an idea before you utter it? If so, consider chopping out the announcement.

____ Can you recast any sentence that begins *There is* or *There are*?

____ Can you substitute an active verb wherever you use a form of the verb *be* (*is, was, were*)?

____ Can you reduce to a phrase any clause beginning with *which, who,* or *that*?

____ Have you used too many adjectives and adverbs?

____ Do you see any long words where short words would do?

John Martin, a business administration major, wrote the following economics paper to fulfill the assignment "Briefly discuss a current problem in international trade. Venture an opinion or propose a solution." You can see the thoughtful cuts and condensations that Martin made with the help of his English instructor and his peer editor. His large changes — macro revisions — are highlighted in the margin. Both these macro revisions and his smaller micro revisions are marked in the text. Following the edited draft you'll find the paper as he resubmitted it — in fewer words.

FIRST DRAFT

Japan's Closed Doors: Should the U.S. Retaliate?

State problems more clearly for readers

~~There is currently a~~ *A* serious problem brewing in ~~the world of~~ *is* international trade ~~which may turn out to be a real tempest in a teapot, so to speak.~~ According-

a cliché to cut

ing to the latest National Trade Estimates report, several ~~of the countries that~~ the U.S. ~~has been doing business with~~ *trading partners* deserve to be condemned for ~~what the report has characterized as~~ "unfair trade practices." The government has said it will use the report to single out ~~specific~~ countries ~~which it is then going to go~~ ahead and *to* punish under the Super 301 provisions of the trade law.

Rework paragraph to move more directly to point about Japan

The Super 301 section ~~of the trade law~~ requires Carla Hills, ~~who is~~ the U.S. trade representative, to ~~try to get rid of~~ *attack* what she ~~has officially designated to be~~ *calls* "priority unfair practices." She will ~~be~~ slashing at the ~~whole~~ web of impedi-

same as impediments

ments ~~and obstacles~~ that have ~~slowed down or~~ denied ~~the various products of~~ *American* the many United States firms ~~much~~ *fast* access to Japanese markets.

Move paragraph to follow background

Some American businesspeople would ~~like to~~ take aim at Japan immediately. However, Clyde Prestowitz, ~~who is~~ a former Commerce Department official, ~~seriously~~ doubts that ~~in the last analysis~~ it would be ~~a good idea to come out~~ *wise to* and name Japan ~~to feel the terrible effects of~~ *for* retaliation under Super 301 ~~in view of the fact that in his opinion,~~ *;* "It's hard to negotiate with guys you are calling cheats." No doubt ~~there are~~ many other observers ~~who~~ share his view.

Strengthen paragraph focus by opening with the point

~~It is important for the reader to note here that for a long time, longer than anyone can remember,~~ Japan has been the ~~leading~~ *long* prime candidate for a dose

of Super 301. Over the past decade, ~~there have been many years of negotiations~~
                                    have battered
~~and battering by different~~ industry groups at the unyielding doors of ~~the~~
                              with
Japanese markets, ~~which have yielded~~ some successes, but have ~~pretty much~~
                    make them swing wide.
failed ~~miserably~~ to ~~dent the invisible trade barriers that stand looming between~~

~~us and the Japanese markets, preventing the free access of U.S. goods to~~
                        The
~~Japanese consumers. As far as the~~ U.S. trade deficit with Japan~~, is concerned,~~

~~it was somewhat~~ more than $50 billion last year~~, and it~~ shows ~~very~~ little sign of
improving
~~getting significantly much better~~ this year.
                          The   *has*   *help*
     ~~Evidently it is the task of the~~ administration to try to ~~pave the way for~~   *State opinion more*
                                                                                                clearly to achieve
U.S. exports ~~to~~ wedge their way into the protected Japanese markets while   *paper's purpose*
                                                  nations
keeping ~~it firmly~~ in mind that the interests of both ~~the United States and Japan~~
        stronger
call for ~~strengthening of the~~ economic and military ties~~.that bind both coun-~~

~~tries into a sphere of friendly relationship. It is my personal conclusion that if~~
If
the administration goes ahead~~, with this,~~ it will ~~certainly~~ need to plan ~~ahead~~

~~for the future~~ carefully.

REVISED VERSION

       Japan's Closed Doors: Should the U.S. Retaliate?
A serious problem is brewing in international trade. According to the latest National Trade Estimates report, several U.S. trading partners deserve to be condemned
for "unfair trade practices." The government has said it will use the report to single
out countries to punish under the Super 301 provisions of the trade law.
    The Super 301 section requires Carla Hills, the U.S. trade representative, to
attack what she calls "priority unfair practices." She will slash at the web of impediments that have denied American firms fast access to Japanese markets.
    Japan has long been the prime candidate for a dose of Super 301. Over the past
decade, industry groups have battered at the unyielding doors of Japanese markets,
with some success, but have failed to make them swing wide. The U.S. trade deficit
with Japan, more than $50 billion last year, shows little sign of improving this year.
    Some American businesspeople would take aim at Japan immediately. However,
Clyde Prestowitz, a former Commerce Department official, doubts that it would be

wise to name Japan for retaliation under Super 301: "It's hard to negotiate with guys you are calling cheats." No doubt many other observers share his view.

The administration has to try to help U.S. exports wedge their way into protected Japanese markets while keeping in mind that the interests of both nations call for stronger economic and military ties. If the administration goes ahead, it will need to plan carefully.

Editing and Proofreading

Editing means correcting and refining grammar, punctuation, and mechanics. Don't edit and proofread too soon. In your early drafting, don't fret over the correct spelling of an unfamiliar word; it may be revised out in a later version. If the word stays in, you'll have time to check it later. After you have revised, however, you are ready to refine and correct. Proofreading means taking a final look at your paper to check correctness and to catch spelling or word-processing errors. In college, good editing and proofreading can make the difference between a C and an A. On the job, it may help you get a promotion. Readers, teachers, and bosses like careful writers who take time to edit and proofread.

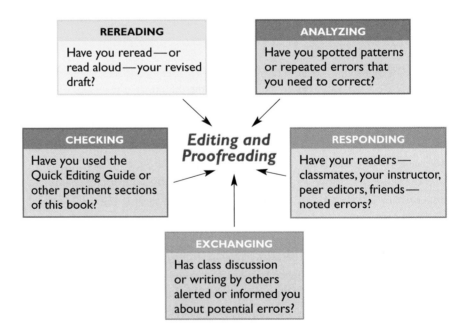

REREADING
Have you reread—or read aloud—your revised draft?

ANALYZING
Have you spotted patterns or repeated errors that you need to correct?

CHECKING
Have you used the Quick Editing Guide or other pertinent sections of this book?

Editing and Proofreading

RESPONDING
Have your readers—classmates, your instructor, peer editors, friends—noted errors?

EXCHANGING
Has class discussion or writing by others alerted or informed you about potential errors?

EDITING

As you edit, whenever you doubt whether a word or construction is correct, consult a good reference handbook. Learn the grammar conventions you don't understand so you can spot and eliminate problems in your own writing. Practice until you easily recognize major errors such as fragments and comma splices. Ask for assistance from a peer editor or a tutor in the writing center if your campus has one.

EDITING	PROOFREADING
• **GRAMMAR:** Are your sentences and their parts correct?	• **SPELLING:** Have you spell-checked and reread attentively?
• **SENTENCES:** Are your sentences clear and effective?	• **INCORRECT WORDS:** Have you used any words by mistake?
• **WORD CHOICE:** Are your words correct and well selected?	• **MISSING WORDS:** Have you left out any words?
• **PUNCTUATION:** Do you need to add, correct, or drop any marks?	• **MINOR ERRORS:** Can you see any incorrect details?
• **MECHANICS:** Do you need to correct capitals, italics, or other matters?	
• **FORMAT:** Do you need to adjust margins, spacing, or headings?	

Use the "Quick Editing Guide" at the end of this book to get you started (look for the pages with dark blue edges). It briefly reviews grammar, style, punctuation, and mechanics problems typically found in college writing. For each problem, it supplies definitions, examples, and a checklist to help you tackle the problem. Here is an editing checklist for the problems explained there, along with the section letter and number:

EDITING CHECKLIST

Common and Serious Problems in College Writing

Grammar Problems

    —— Have you avoided writing sentence fragments?   A1

    —— Have you avoided writing comma splices or fused sentences?   A2

    —— Have you used the correct form for all verbs in the past tense?   A3

    —— Do all verbs agree with their subjects?   A4

    —— Have you used the correct case for all pronouns?   A5

▨ For more help, turn to the dark-blue-edged pages, and find the Quick Editing Guide section noted here.

For help documenting any sources in your paper, turn to the dark-red-edged pages, and find D6 and E1–E2 in the Quick Research Guide there.

___ Do all pronouns agree with their antecedents?   A6
___ Have you used adjectives and adverbs correctly?   A7

Sentence Problems

___ Does each modifier clearly modify the appropriate sentence element?   B1
___ Have you used parallel structure where necessary?   B2

Punctuation Problems

___ Have you used commas correctly?   C1
___ Have you used apostrophes correctly?   C2
___ Have you punctuated quotations correctly?   C3

Mechanics and Format Problems

___ Have you used capital letters correctly?   D1
___ Have you spelled all words correctly?   D2
___ Have you used correct manuscript form?   D3

PROOFREADING

Careful proofreading is especially important because many errors in writing occur unconsciously and easily become habits. If you have never looked closely at the spelling of *environment*, you may never have noticed the second *n*. Split-second inattention or a break in concentration can also cause errors. Because the mind works faster than the pencil (or the word processor), when you are distracted by someone talking or a telephone ringing, you may omit a word or put in the wrong punctuation.

The very way our eyes work also leads to errors. When you read normally, you usually see only the shells of words—the first and last letters. You fix your eyes on the print only about three or four times per line. To proofread effectively, you must look at the letters in each word and the punctuation marks between words without sliding over these symbols. Proofreading requires time and patience but is a skill you can develop.

WRITING WITH A COMPUTER

Spell checkers are handy tools, but they aren't foolproof. They can't tell you that you've used *their* when you meant *there*, *affect* when you meant *effect*, or *won* when you meant *own*. Grammar checkers also can alert you to many types of sentence problems, but you have to reason through the suggestions carefully. A checker may question long sentences and unusual constructions that are perfectly correct. As the writer, you, not the software, should always have the final word. (See also p. A-1.)

Proofreading in Pairs

Select a passage, from this textbook or elsewhere, that is about one hundred words long. Type up the passage, intentionally adding ten errors in grammar, spelling, punctuation, or capitalization. Swap passages with a classmate; proofread, then check each other's work against the originals. Share your proofreading strategies.

FOR GROUP LEARNING

TIPS FOR PROOFREADING

1. *All* writers make mistakes as they put ideas on paper. Making mistakes isn't bad — but then you need to take the time to find and correct them.
2. Let a paper sit several days, overnight, or at least a few hours before proofreading it.
3. Budget enough time to proofread thoroughly.
4. Read what you have written very slowly, looking at every word and letter. See what you have actually written, not what you think is there.
5. Read your paper aloud. Speaking forces you to slow down and see more, and sometimes you will hear a mistake you haven't seen.
6. Read the essay backward. This will force you to look at each word because you won't get caught up in the flow of ideas.
7. Use a dictionary or a spell checker whenever you can.
8. Double-check for your own habitual errors (such as leaving off *-s* or *-ed* or putting in unnecessary commas).
9. Read your essay several times, focusing each time on a specific area of difficulty (once for spelling, once for punctuation, once for a problem that recurs in your writing).
10. Ask someone else to read your paper and tell you if it is free of errors. But take pride in your own work. *Don't* let someone else do it for you.

■ Exercise

Editing and Proofreading

Read the following passage carefully. Assume that the organization of the paragraph is satisfactory, but look for ten errors in the paragraph. Find these mistakes in sentence structure, grammar, spelling, punctuation, and capitalization, and correct them. After you have corrected the passage, discuss with your classmates the changes you have made and your reasons for making those changes.

> Robert Frost, one of the most popular American poets. He was born in San Francisco in 1874, and died in Boston in 1963. His family moved to new England when his father died in 1885. There he completed highschool and attended colledge but never graduate. Poverty and problems filled his life. He worked in a woolen mill, on a newspaper, and on

■ For editing exercises, visit Exercise Central at <bedfordstmartins.com/bedguide>.

varous odd jobs. Because of ill health he settled on a farm and began to teach school to support his wife and children. Throughout his life he dedicated himself to writing poetry, by 1915 he was in demand for public readings and speaking engagements. He was awarded the Pulitzer Prize for poetry four times-in 1924, 1931, 1937, and 1943. The popularity of his poetry rests in his use of common themes and images, expressed in everyday language. Everyone can relate to his universal poems, such as "Birches" and "Stopping by Woods on a Snowy Evening." Students read his poetry in school from seventh grade through graduate school, so almost everyone recognize lines from his best-loved poems. America is proud of it's son, the homespun poet Robert Frost.

Chapter 20

Strategies for Designing Your Document

Whether the document you prepare is an essay, a research paper, or a business letter, creating an effective design for it helps you achieve your purpose and meet the expectations of your audience. Through your own reading, you may have noticed that you respond differently to documents depending upon their appearance. For example, look quickly at Figure 20.1. Which of the two newspapers there seems more appealing to you?

If you prefer *USA Today*, you're like many Americans — you like the look of a colorful, casual newspaper and may even consider it easier to read. But if someone asked which of the two newspapers seems more credible or trustworthy, many would say the *Wall Street Journal*. Its closely typed text, narrow columns, and limited use of color create a look more "respectable" than that of the open, friendly *USA Today* with its abundant pictures, more colorful design, and playful tone. As you can see, the same features that make the *Wall Street Journal* seem more credible than *USA Today* may also make it less inviting to read. Like other newspapers, however, the *Wall Street Journal* freely uses headlines, short paragraphs, column dividers, white space, page numbers, and other visual markers that help the reader grasp the structure of the text at a glance and decide where to plunge in. Without such visual markers, the pages of the *Wall Street Journal* would provide the reader few pathways into its content.

Occasionally, college students are assigned a composition that looks and reads like a newspaper. But most of the papers you will write are not as visually complex as the *Wall Street Journal* or *USA Today*. Instead of calling for multiple columns, headlines, and graphs, your teacher will most likely expect to see double-spacing, one-inch margins, numbered pages, and indented block quotations — visual markers typical of college compositions. Figure 20.2 shows two pages — the first page and the list of sources — of a typical college composition that follows the guidelines of the Modern Language Association (MLA).

For more on manuscript format, turn to D3 in the Quick Editing Guide (the dark-blue-edged pages).

341

Figure 20.1
Front Pages of USA Today
and the Wall Street
Journal *(with common
features labeled)*

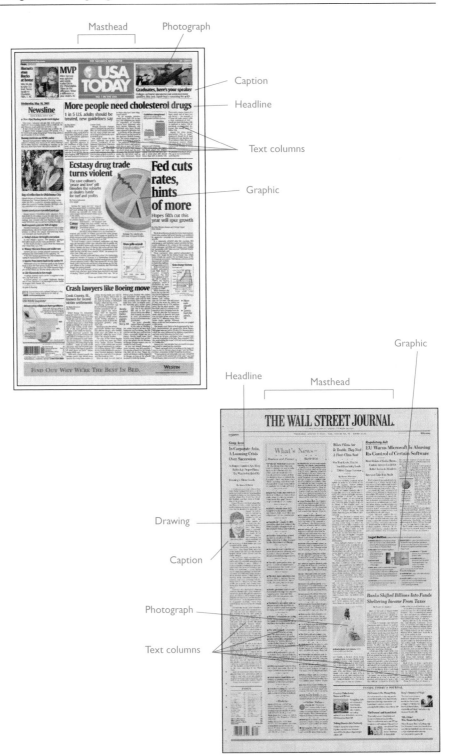

Masthead

Photograph

Caption

Headline

Text columns

Graphic

Graphic

Headline

Masthead

Drawing

Caption

Photograph

Text columns

Figure 20.2
The First Page and Works Cited Page of a Student Research Paper in MLA Format

1"

1/2"
Goers 1

Sarah E. Goers — Writer's name

Professor Day — Instructor's name

English 101 — Course

28 January 2004 — Date

1/2" or 5 spaces

Is Inclusion the Answer? — Title, centered

Writer's last name and page number

⟶Inclusion is one of the most passionately debated issues in public education today. Full inclusion, defined as
placing all students with disabilities in general education
classes, has three main components: the integration of
special education students into the mainstream classroom, educational planning and programming, and the
clarification of responsibility for appropriate instruction
(Heinich 292). Although the intent is to provide the best
care for all children

education students

lieve that the full in

stream classrooms m

ther type of student

from a general educa

prepared to accomm

school where their n

unprepared teachers

they most likely suff

full inclusion over p

are questionable.

Title, centered

Double-spacing throughout

Citation with author's name and page number in parentheses

1"

1"

1"

List of works cited on a separate page

Works Cited

1"

Centered heading

1/2"
Goers 10

Block, Martin E. "Did We Jump on the Wrong Bandwagon?
Problems with Inclusion." Palestra 15.3 (1999) 4-10.
10 Dec. 2003 <http://www.palestra.com/Inclusion.html>.

Gaskins, Jacob. "Teaching Writing to Students with
Learning Disabilities: The Landmark Method."
Teaching English in the Two-Year College 22.2
(1995): 71-76.

Heinich, Robert, ed. Educating All Handicapped Children.
Englewood Cliffs: Educational Technology Publications, 1979.

Hewett, Beth. "Helping Students with Learning
Disabilities: Collaboration between Writing Centers
and Special Services." Writing Lab. 25.3 (2000):
1-4.

Jacobson, Linda. "Disabled Kids Moving into Regular
Classrooms." Atlanta Journal 5 May 1994: C1.

Maushard, Mary. "Special Schools Fall Victim to 'Inclusion.'
Sun [Baltimore] 13 June 1993: B1. NewsBank.
1/2" Boston Public Lib. 21 Dec. 2003 <http://
www.newsbank.com>.

Radebaugh, Barbara. "NEA vs. AFT." Education 201-002
Lecture. William Rainey Harper Coll., Palatine, IL.
21 Jan. 1999.

Rios, Denise A. "Special Students Joining Regular Classrooms." Orange County Register 9 June 1994: A24.
NewsBank. Boston Public Lib. 11 Dec. 2003.
<http://www.newsbank.com>.

List alphabetized by author's last name

First line of entry at left margin

Subsequent lines indented 1/2" or 5 spaces

Understanding Four Basic Principles of Document Design

Four key principles of document design will help you to produce effective documents in and out of the classroom. Use the following questions based on these principles to help you plan an appropriate design for your college papers or other documents:

DISCOVERY CHECKLIST

___ Who are your readers? What are their key concerns? How might your document design acknowledge their concerns?

___ What form or genre do readers expect? What features do readers see as typical characteristics of that form? What visual evidence would they expect or accept as appropriate?

___ What problems or constraints will your readers face? How can your document design help to address these constraints?

___ What is the purpose of your document? How can its design help achieve this purpose? How can it enhance your credibility as a writer?

PRINCIPLE 1: KNOW YOUR READERS

For questions to help identify your readers, see p. 326.

Whether you are writing an essay for class or preparing an entirely different type of document, identifying your audience is a good first step toward creating an effective design. For most papers that you write in a first-year composition course, your primary reader is your teacher and your secondary readers include your peers. For some assignments, you might be asked to include other readers as well.

For more on purpose and audience, see pp. 13–15 and pp. 269–70.

Suppose you've written a paper explaining the benefits of a longer school year to a real-world audience. An audience of parents would have different concerns than an audience of community leaders or of school officials or teachers. Teachers, for example, would need to be assured that their paychecks would keep pace with the longer work year. The school board would need to be convinced that the increased costs for salaries, building operations, and transportation would pay off in higher student achievement. And other civic leaders might want to know the effects on community safety, traffic congestion, and seasonal employment rates.

In deciding how to design your document, you might consider ways to acknowledge, even highlight the key concerns of your particular audience, perhaps using headings, white space, and variations in type style. You might also consider whether your audience is likely to read every word of your argument or to skim it for key points. Perhaps visuals, such as tables, graphs, or diagrams, would make information more accessible. Thinking about such issues as you plan and draft means you'll have a better chance of reaching your audience.

PRINCIPLE 2: SATISFY YOUR READERS' EXPECTATIONS

When you think about a newspaper, a particular type of publication comes to mind because the newspaper is a familiar *genre,* or form. As Figure 20.1 shows, almost all newspapers share a set of defined features, such as a masthead, headlines, pictures with captions, graphics, and articles arranged in columns of text. Even if details of the form vary, newspapers are still recognized as newspapers. Similarly, *Forbes* and *Parenting* both belong to the genre of the magazine: both feature glossy pages, articles arranged in columns, notable quotations set in larger type, and photographs. Despite significantly different content, magazines share a common genre identification, as Figure 20.3 illustrates.

For samples of workplace genres, see Ch. 13.

Like the newspaper and the magazine, the college paper can be thought of as a genre. Readers, including your teacher and your peers, have expectations about what topics are appropriate for such documents, how they should be written, and how they should look. Readers also have expectations about appropriate visual evidence, such as graphs, tables, photographs, or other illustrations, depending on the field and the assignment. Check your course syllabus to see if a specific document design is required.

For advice about a general format for papers, see D3 in the Quick Editing Guide (the dark-blue-edged pages).

Usually your readers expect your paper to be word-processed with numbered pages. Other conventions may also be expected. Some teachers want

Unless your teacher encourages unusual or creative formatting, don't experiment too much with the appearance of a college paper. In fact, you can easily apply expected features to your papers by creating a template to use for all papers with the same specifications. First, format your paper the way you want it to look. Then, create a document template that you can access any time you begin a new paper. Depending on your word processor, you will follow a sequence like the following:

WRITING WITH A COMPUTER

1. Create a duplicate copy of your formatted file.
2. Delete all of the text in the document.
3. Use the "save as" feature to save the file as a document template.
4. Give the template a name, such as "English paper" or "Paper form."
5. When you create a new file, choose this template from the options in your template folder. (Use the Help box for more on templates.)

Figure 20.3
Common Features in Magazine Design: Page Spread from Forbes, *April 2, 2001 (top) and* Parenting, *June/July 2003 (bottom)*

Quotation emphasized   Photograph   Text columns

Text column   Photograph   Quotation emphasized

you to include a cover page with your name, the title of your paper, your course number and section, the date, and perhaps other information. Others may prefer that you follow the MLA paper format, simply supplying a four-line identifier and a centered title on the first page (see Figure 20.2). Some will ask you to include your last name or a shortened title with the page number at the top or bottom of each page.

For sample pages from an MLA paper, see Figure 20.2 on p. 343.

Although you should follow any specific guidelines that your instructor supplies, some genre features are flexible. For example, you might use larger, boldface type for your paper title or use underlining or boldface to set off any headings. Perhaps you might want to separate your page numbers from the rest of the text with a horizontal line or insert a little extra white space between paragraphs. Such features could help to make your standard paper distinctive and easier for your teacher to read.

PRINCIPLE 3: CONSIDER YOUR READERS' CONSTRAINTS

Your teacher probably expects you to print your paper in a crisp, black, 12-point type, double-spaced, on one side of a white sheet of paper with one-inch margins. You also may be asked to reprint a paper if your toner cartridge is nearly empty. Before accusing your teacher of being overly picky, remember that he or she may read and grade compositions in batches of a hundred or more. Papers that are printed clearly in a standard format are easier on the eyes than those with faint print or unusual formats. In addition, your teacher needs sufficient margin space for comments. If you try to save paper by using a smaller point size, narrower margins, or single spacing, the paper may be more difficult to read and harder to grade.

When you address readers besides your teacher, they too will have some constraints. Some may read your document on a computer screen if it arrives as an e-mail attachment. Others may skim a text's main points during the morning commute or sort through a stack of résumés before lunch. Just as you want to write an effective paper that addresses your readers' information needs, you also want to design a usable, readable paper—one that readers can readily absorb regardless of constraints.

PRINCIPLE 4: REMEMBER YOUR PURPOSE

Like most writers, you have in mind a particular reason for writing. As you take into account your readers' concerns, their expectations, and the conditions under which they read, your challenge is to write convincingly for them. When you do so, you also increase your credibility as a writer. Although good document design is no substitute for a clear and orderly essay, it can help you achieve your purpose and enhance the message you are trying to convey, as the rest of this chapter will explain.

For more on purpose, see pp. 13–15 and pp. 269–70.

Creating an Effective Design for Your Document

When you design a document, you direct a reader's attention using tools such as type options, lists, white space, headings, repetition, color, and visuals. Although you may not be accustomed to thinking about design issues, you already make design choices whenever you type something in your word processor. The following guidelines can help you design effective documents that achieve your purpose and appeal to your audience.

USING A PROMINENT ELEMENT

Artists and designers aim to attract readers' attention by giving important elements prominence. Consider Figure 20.4, for example, which shows two of six panels of a student-designed brochure. The image of the mannequin on the brochure's cover immediately draws the eye, but the pattern of light guides readers to the central question: "Is your life out of control?" Other words on the left panel (such as "broken," "stuck," "lost," and "depressed") serve as a suggestive backdrop, but there is no mistaking the main message.

For more on white space, see pp. 354–56; for more on headings, see pp. 357–61; and for more on color, see p. 362.

Providing a prominent element helps your readers focus on what you think is most important. As you begin work on any visual document ask, "What is the main message I want to get across?" Once you have decided on that message, think of ways to give it prominence. For example, if you are designing a brochure, flyer, poster, or postcard, you might want to surround one large headline by a significant amount of space, as the designer of the brochure did in the left panel. Note also in the right panel how the headings — all questions, parallel in form — appear in color, separated by white space so that readers clearly see the breaks between topics. The inside panels of the brochure respond to the questions posed in the headings, pointing readers toward helpful resources.

For more on understanding visuals, see Ch. 21.

You can get ideas about how to present prominent elements by looking at visual documents designed by others. Learning to spot these elements — and figure out how they are given prominence — can also help you analyze and interpret visual documents.

CHOOSING FONTS

Typography refers to the appearance of typeset letters on a page. When you add boldface type, use all capital letters, or change type size, you are making a typographic choice. Such choices can make your document clearer and more attractive, but inappropriate or excessive use of an option can clutter your work.

Current word-processing software allows changing typefaces, commonly called *fonts*, to increase readability, achieve special effects, add emphasis, or set a particular tone. Although most college papers use a conventional font

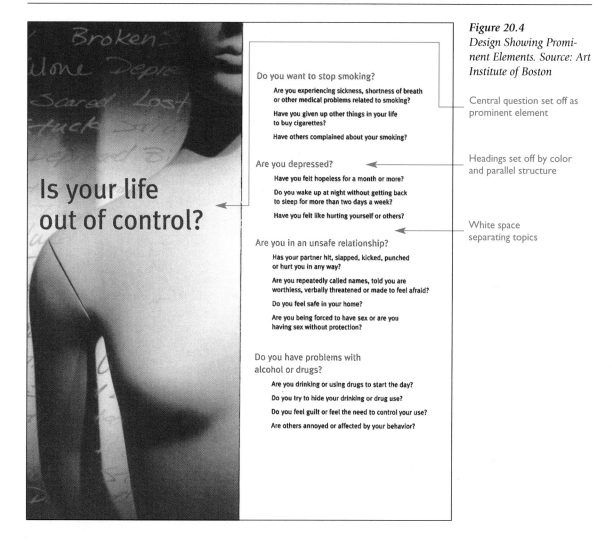

Figure 20.4
Design Showing Promi-
nent Elements. Source: Art
Institute of Boston

Central question set off as
prominent element

Headings set off by color
and parallel structure

White space
separating topics

in a 12-point size, sometimes you may need to use larger size type for signs, posters, and visuals (such as *PowerPoint* slides) for oral presentations. Test such materials for readability by printing samples in various type sizes and standing back from them at the distance of your intended audience.

For examples of *PowerPoint* slides, see p. 356.

Figure 20.5 shows the same sentence written in four different 12-point fonts: Times New Roman, Courier New, Arial, and Comic Sans MS. Although the examples are all written in the standard 12-point size, the typefaces occupy different amounts of horizontal space on the page.

Serif or Sans Serif Fonts.   Times New Roman and Courier New are called *serif* fonts. A serif font has small tails, or serifs, at the ends of the letters. Arial and Comic Sans MS, in contrast, are *sans serif* — without serifs.

Figure 20.5
Space Occupied by
Different Typefaces

Times New Roman	An estimated 40 percent of young children have an imaginary friend.
Courier New	An estimated 40 percent of young children have an imaginary friend.
Arial	An estimated 40 percent of young children have an imaginary friend.
Comic Sans MS	An estimated 40 percent of young children have an imaginary friend.

These fonts have solid, straight lines and no tails at the tips of the letters. You can see the difference between a serif and sans serif font in these examples:

Times New Roman (serif) B b C c   Arial (sans serif) B b C c

Sans serif fonts have a clean look but are less readable than serif fonts, especially in long passages. If you look over your local newspaper, you may notice a combination of serif and sans serif fonts. Typically, sans serif fonts are used for headlines and other display type, such as advertisements and "pull quotes" (interesting quotations "pulled out" of an article and printed in larger type to catch the reader's eye). On the other hand, most newspapers choose serif fonts for their article (or "body") text. In fact, Times New Roman, the default font on many word processors, was developed for *The Times* newspaper in London for its own use. Other common serif fonts include Palatino and New Century Schoolbook. A combination of fonts can provide maximum readability and emphasis, as Figure 20.6 shows.

If you decide to combine two different fonts, keep these points in mind:

- Serif and sans serif fonts can be combined in the same document, though document designers recommend using only one of each.
- For further emphasis, you may vary the type size or type style, such as italics or bold, for each font.

Novelty Fonts.   For most college and professional writing, novelty fonts — those that are unusual or decorative — are inappropriate. **Comic Sans MS** is a novelty font, as are *Brush Script* and **Tempus Sans**. While these casual playful typefaces may suit some writing situations, novelty fonts can set the wrong tone for your paper, especially if your subject is technical or serious.

For example, if you are writing a paper about civil liberties, Comic Sans MS might suggest that readers don't need to take your arguments seriously

> ## Watching TV with a Critical Eye
>
> By second grade, kids have figured out, often from personal experience, that the toys they see in commercials don't always measure up in real life. Children this age are old enough to get into more sophisticated discussions about fact and opinion.

Figure 20.6
Sans Serif Heading Used with Serif Body Font.
Source: Kiplinger's, February 2000

or that you lack respect for a serious subject. Figure 20.7 shows two versions of the same text — one set in Times New Roman, which is appropriate for an academic setting, and the other set in Comic Sans MS, which generally is not. In academic or other serious writing, stick with standard fonts that are familiar to readers and that set a professional tone.

For more on typefaces in visual images, see pp. 378–81.

Italics.   When you *italicize* words, you call the reader's attention to them.

- Use italics for book, film, or software titles.
  My favorite novel is *Wuthering Heights.*
- Use italics for foreign words.
  My Finnish grandmother called me *Kultani* ("my golden one").

Times New Roman	*Comic Sans MS*
Does Heightened Surveillance Make Us More or Less Secure? Since the terrorist attacks of September 11, 2001, a wide-ranging debate has ensued over whether face-recognition systems and other surveillance tools should be used to identify potential terrorists. While proponents see these tools as an essential defense when loosely organized terrorist "cells" might strike at any time, opponents say these systems are flawed at best and jeopardize the civil liberties of all citizens.	**Does Heightened Surveillance Make Us More or Less Secure?** Since the terrorist attacks of September 11, 2001, a wide-ranging debate has ensued over whether face-recognition systems and other surveillance tools should be used to identify potential terrorists. While proponents see these tools as an essential defense when loosely organized terrorist "cells" might strike at any time, opponents say these systems are flawed at best and jeopardize the civil liberties of all citizens.

Figure 20.7   *Identical Text Set in Two Fonts. Sources: See Figure 20.9*

WRITING WITH A COMPUTER

Your word-processing program is likely to supply several ways of changing type style. When you look at the screen, your toolbar probably includes boxes that identify the font you are using (such as Times New Roman) and the point size of the characters (such as 12). Nearby you may spot other small boxes or icons that, with a click, shift what you type to bold, italics, or underlined text — all necessary in academic papers if only for the various styles of documenting sources. You can also use your mouse to highlight sections of text and then click on these icons to change the text style for that passage. Clicking on the Format menu and then on "Font" generally supplies a menu of possible changes, including design elements such as shadows or small capitals.

- Use italics for your first use of a technical or scientific term, and provide a definition for the reader. After that, use regular type without emphasis.

    AIDS patients monitor their levels of *helper T-cells* because these cells detect antigens in the body and activate other cells to fight the antigens. Because HIV destroys helper T-cells, this information indicates the status of a patient's immune system.

Italicized words appear lighter in weight than nonitalicized words. This lightness, coupled with the slant of the letters, makes italics unsuitable for sustained reading. Use italics for emphasis, not for large blocks of text.

■ For examples of bold-face type in résumés, see p. 229.

Boldface.   Boldface type is suitable for emphasis only. Too much produces the "raisin bread" effect, a random scattering of dark spots across a light page, illustrated in Figure 20.8. Because this scattering encourages the reader to "hear" the words as emphasized, it creates a choppy, unnatural rhythm.

Many teachers expect you to choose emphatic words, not to rely on boldface type for emphasis in academic papers. In other documents, be selective about using boldface, highlighting only words that you want the reader to see or "hear" with emphasis added. In general, reserve boldface type primarily for headings, key points in a list of factors, or similar uses.

Longevity.   People are living longer today, so Social Security funds need to stretch to accommodate these longer lives.

Inflation.   Dollars paid into the system in 1980 are worth less today, and interest on the fund has not kept pace with the need for the dollars.

Figure 20.8
The Raisin-bread Effect Produced by Too Much Boldface

Treating Carpal Tunnel Syndrome

Physicians **generally** suggest one of **three** methods of treating patients with carpal tunnel syndrome. **First,** reducing the amount of repeated **wrist** movement **can** allow the median nerve to heal. **This** can be accomplished by changing habits or **positions** or by using a wrist **splint**. . . .

PREPARING LISTS

The organization or placement of material on a page—its layout—can make information more accessible for readers. For example, lists are easier to read when they are displayed rather than integrated.

INTEGRATED LIST   Movies are rated by the film-rating board of the Classification and Rating Administration (CARA) based on several criteria, including these: overall theme, use of language, presence of violence, presence of nudity and sexual content, and combined use of these elements in the context of an individual film.

DISPLAYED LIST   Movies are rated by the film-rating board of the Classification and Rating Administration (CARA) based on several criteria, including these:
- overall theme
- use of language
- presence of violence
- presence of nudity and sexual content
- combined use of these elements in the context of an individual film

Bulleted List.   One type of displayed list uses a mark called a *bullet* to set off a fragment of information. The most common bullet is the small round one often available in a word processor's bulleted list function (•).

Use a bulleted list to enumerate steps, reasons, or items, especially when the order isn't significant, as in this example:

Controversy surrounding the 2000 presidential election climaxed in Florida, where several balloting issues converged.

- A controversial Palm Beach County ballot was blamed for several thousand votes possibly cast in error for a third-party candidate, Pat Buchanan.

- A Florida law triggered a statewide ballot recount when the votes for the two main candidates were separated by less than 1 percent.

Your word-processing program may supply several options for preparing lists automatically. Your toolbar may show small icons or boxes for developing bulleted or numbered lists. If so, one click on an icon adds a number or bullet to your text, while a second click removes it from a passage. When you type a return at the end of one listed item, the next symbol (another bullet or another number) appears. Your Insert menu probably also includes a "Symbol" option. Clicking here reveals alternative symbols—for example, square bullets or different sizes of round bullets. Generally, a click on the selected item adds it to your text. For academic papers, use such devices conservatively, always following any specific directions from your instructor or from the style guide preferred by the field. If these directions differ from the available options in your software, simply type out the expected style, such as a list within a sentence using letters inside pairs of parentheses: (a), (b), and (c).

WRITING WITH A COMPUTER

- Outstanding absentee ballots had to be counted to determine which candidate had received the most votes.

■ For examples of the use of bullets in résumés, see p. 229.

Bullets — perhaps combined with headings, white space, and boldface type — can effectively highlight skills or titles in a résumé, making it easier for readers to spot a job applicant's relevant experience. Web résumés, like other Web pages, divide information to fit the screen. They may use design devices to emphasize links and categories, such as education and experience.

Numbered List.   Another type of displayed list, the numbered list, can emphasize important sequences, especially in activity plans, how-to advice, instructional writing, or other process descriptions. Here is a simplified sequence of activities for making an article of clothing:

1. Select your pattern and fabric.
2. Lay out the pattern and pin it to the fabric, paying careful attention to the arrows and grain lines.
3. Cut out the fabric pieces following the outline of the pattern.
4. Sew the garment together using the pattern's step-by-step instructions.

USING WHITE SPACE STRATEGICALLY

■ For examples of the use of white space in print and Web résumés, see p. 229 and p. 230. For more about white space in visual images, see p. 376.

White space is just that: space within a document that is free of text. Areas of blank space give the eye a rest and can frame important information. As a design device, white space allows you to increase emphasis as you guide the reader through your document.

■ For sample pages from an academic paper, see p. 343. For advice on the format for a college paper, see D3 in the Quick Editing Guide (the dark-blue-edged pages).

College Papers.   If you have already written college papers, you have probably used white space to assist your readers. For example, one-inch margins and double-spacing provide some respite for the reader's eyes. Adding extra white space to indent the first line of your paragraphs helps the reader immediately differentiate one paragraph from the next. In addition, indenting an extended "block" quotation sets it off and marks it as a special kind of text.

As you can see in Figure 20.9, white space is crucial to the appearance of your papers. Were this example single-spaced, its closely spaced lines would be much too cramped, interfering with readers' ability to keep their place in the text and possibly intimidating them. When text elements are close together and look fairly uniform, readers may feel as if they are trying to merge onto a congested freeway. Some may give up if they don't see openings where they can easily jump in and begin to navigate the text.

However, if you simply separate sections of your paper by hitting the enter key an extra time or two — especially if your paper is double-spaced — you will trap too much white space between sections. This extra space may create a gap that prevents the reader's eye from making natural connections within the text, thus interfering with the perception of your paper as a cohesive unit.

Does Heightened Surveillance Make Us More or Less Secure? ←— Centered title with space on both sides

Indented paragraph —→ Since the terrorist attacks of September 11, 2001, a wide-ranging debate has ensued over whether face-recognition systems and other surveillance tools should be used to identify potential terrorists. While proponents see these tools as an essential defense when loosely organized terrorist "cells" might strike at any time, opponents say these systems are flawed at best and jeopardize the civil liberties of all citizens.

Barry Steinhardt, director of the Technology and Liberty Program of the American Civil Liberties Union, sees a clear threat to personal freedom:

> Many people still do not grasp that Big Brother surveillance is no longer the stuff of books and movies.... Given the capabilities of today's technology, the only thing protecting us from a full-fledged surveillance society are the legal and political institutions we have inherited as Americans. Unfortunately, the September 11 attacks have led some to embrace the fallacy that weakening the Constitution will strengthen America. ("'Big Brother'")

Extended quotation indented as a block

However, others argue that technology can make us safer — and, in fact, already has. Video monitoring systems using closed-circuit televisions have been in use for years in such places as the United Kingdom, where officials say that crime has declined significantly as a result ("Law, Order, and Terrorism").

Figure 20.9
Text Using White Space. Sources: "'Big Brother' Is No Longer a Fiction, ACLU Warns in New Report," American Civil Liberties Union, 15 January 2003, 23 June 2003, www.aclu.org/Privacy/ Privacy.cfm?ID=11612. "Law, Order, and Terrorism: Other Nations' Remedies," Dahlia Lithwick, Slate, 5 October 2001, 23 June 2003, <www.slate.msn.com/ id/116673>.

Readable double-spaced lines

Text framed by margins

Visuals. Effective use of space is also important in visuals — such as transparencies or *PowerPoint* slides — for presentations. Providing ample space and limiting the text on each slide helps readers absorb your major points. For example, the slide in Figure 20.10 contains too much text, making it hard to read and potentially distracting for the audience. In contrast, Figure 20.11 contains less text and more open space, making each point easier to read. It also uses bullets effectively to highlight the main points. These points are meant only to summarize major issues and themes, not to detail all of them; you can flesh out your main points during your talk. Though the

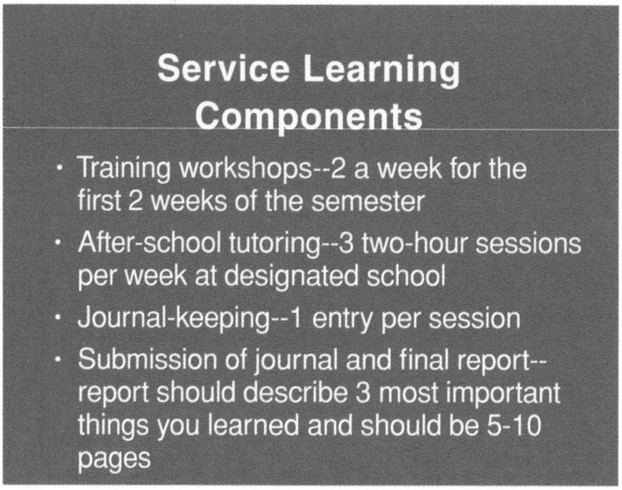

Figure 20.10
PowerPoint *Slide with
Too Much Text and Too
Little Space*

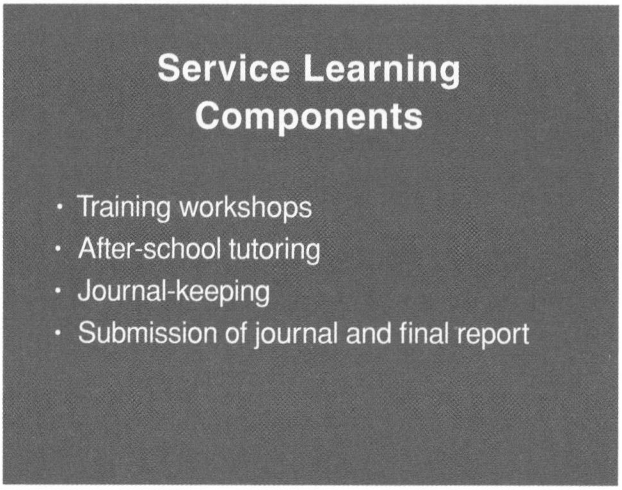

> ## Service Learning Components
>
> - Training workshops--2 a week for the first 2 weeks of the semester
> - After-school tutoring--3 two-hour sessions per week at designated school
> - Journal-keeping--1 entry per session
> - Submission of journal and final report--report should describe 3 most important things you learned and should be 5-10 pages

Figure 20.11
PowerPoint *Slide with
Brief Text and Effective
Use of Space*

> ## Service Learning Components
>
> - Training workshops
> - After-school tutoring
> - Journal-keeping
> - Submission of journal and final report

slides have been reduced to fit in this book, the original type sizes were large enough to be viewed by the presenter's classmates: 44 points for the heading and 32 points for the body.

Finally, as you can see, the "white space" without text in these slides is actually blue. Some public-speaking experts believe that black type on a white background can be too stark for a slide; instead, they recommend a dark blue background with yellow or white type. However, others believe that black on white is fine and may in fact be what the audience is accustomed to. Presentation software like *PowerPoint* makes it easy for you to experiment with these options.

USING HEADINGS AND ALIGNMENT

Readers of both texts and visuals look for cues about what's most important and about how various components are related to one another. Effective document design provides just such cues through features like headings and subheadings. Clear headings help your readers navigate by showing a document's hierarchy of ideas. Appropriately aligned headings guide the reader's eye.

Heading Levels.   The relative size and prominence of the section headings indicate how a document is structured and which sections are most important. Headings also name the sections so that readers know where they are and where they are going. Though headings are often unnecessary in short essays, they can focus the attention of readers while providing a useful pathway through complex documents such as research papers, lab reports, business proposals, and Web-based documents.

Use typographical elements to distinguish clearly between levels of headings and subheadings within your document. Once you decide what a major section (or *level-one*) heading should look like — boldfaced and italicized, for example — be consistent with the comparable headings throughout your document. Treat minor headings consistently as well. In this book, you'll notice that all of the major headings within a chapter are set like this:

Level-One Heading   [17-point, boldfaced, italicized, in color]

Level-two and level-three headings are set like this:

LEVEL-TWO HEADING   [12-point, capitalized, boldfaced]

Level-Three Heading   [10-point, boldfaced]

Each of these styles is used consistently in order to offer readers visual cues to both content and organization. The headings differ from each other and from the main text in size, style, and color. Differentiating headings in such ways makes your text easier to read and easier to use whether your reader is scrutinizing every word or scanning only key points.

If your instructor asks you to follow the guidelines of a particular style, you may have less flexibility in formatting headings. For example, the American Psychological Association (APA) illustrates five levels of headings, all in the same regular font style and size as the body text but varying capitalization, placement (centered or left), and underlining to distinguish the levels. MLA, however, does not recommend headings or discuss their design.

▨ For more on MLA style, see E1–E2 in the Quick Research Guide (the dark-red-edged pages), consult the *MLA Handbook for Writers of Research Papers*, or go to <www.mla.org/style>. For more on APA style, consult the *Publication Manual of the American Psychological Association* or <www.apastyle.org>.

Heading Consistency.   The headings in your document should be brief, clear, and informative. The four most common styles of headings are *-ing* phrases, noun phrases, questions, and imperative sentences. Effective writers maintain consistent parallel phrasing, whatever the style they choose. In other words, if you write a level-one heading as an *-ing* phrase, make certain that all of the level-one headings that follow are also *-ing* phrases.

Here are some examples of each style of heading:

■ For more on parallel structure, see B2 in the Quick Editing Guide (the dark-blue-edged pages).

-ING PHRASES
Using the College Catalog
Choosing Courses
Declaring a Major

NOUN PHRASES
The Benefits of Electronic Commerce
The Challenges of Electronic Commerce
The Characteristics of the Online Shopper

QUESTIONS
What Is Hepatitis C?
Who Is at Risk?
How Is Hepatitis C Treated?

IMPERATIVE SENTENCES
Initiate Your IRA Rollover
Learn Your Distribution Options
Select New Investments

The Web page shown in Figure 20.12 uses nouns and noun phrases as main headings. Under the headings are links to other content at the site, listed in a comparable fashion. In general, Web pages — especially home pages and site guides — tend to have more headings than other types of documents because they are designed to help readers find information quickly, within a small viewing frame. If you are designing a Web page, consider what different users might want to find on your site, and clearly connect your headings and content to users' needs.

■ For more information on Web design, visit the Web Style Guide at <www.webstyleguide.com>.

Heading Alignment.   Besides being consistently styled and phrased, headings should also be consistently placed, or aligned, along the same vertical line. Figure 20.13 illustrates confusing alignment, mixing left-aligned, right-aligned, and fully justified text running out to both the left and right margins. Because your title is generally centered, you might be tempted to center all of your headings, but doing so may introduce nonfunctional white space that detracts from the effectiveness of your paper. Instead, rely on the graphic designer's principle of alignment: each element should be aligned with at least one other item, rather than having an alignment all its own.

But centering *is* an alignment, you might protest. Indeed, centering all of your headings and subheadings should create a uniform alignment

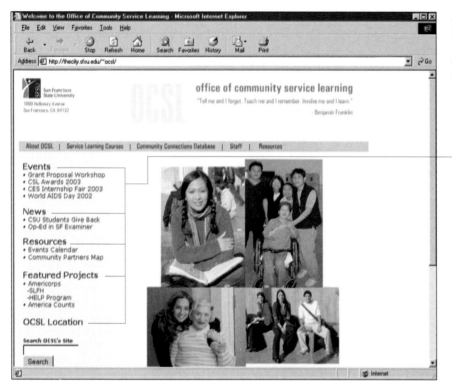

Figure 20.12
Parallel Headings on a
Web Page. Source: Office
of Service Learning, San
Francisco State University

Headings using nouns
and noun phrases

The Progressive Party Platform of 1912

Centered title

The Rule of the People

The National Progressive party, committed to the principles of government by a self-controlled democracy expressing its will through representatives of the people, pledges itself to secure such alterations in the fundamental law of the several States and the United States as shall insure the representative character of the government.

Left-aligned text

In particular, the party declares for direct primaries for the nomination of State and National officers; for nationwide preferential primaries for candidates for presidency; for the direct election of the United States Senators by the people; and we urge on the States the policy of the short ballot, with responsibility to the people secured by the initiative, referendum and recall.

Amendment of Constitution

The Progressive party, believing that a free people should have the power from time to time to amend their fundamental law so as to adapt it progressively to the changing needs of the people, pledges itself to provide a more easy and expeditious method of amending the Federal Constitution. . . .

Figure 20.13
Centered Title over Text
with Varying Alignments.
Source: "The Progressive
Party Platform of 1912."
From National Party
Platforms 1840–1964.
Kirk H. Porter and Don-
ald Bruce Johnson, comps.
U of Illinois P., 1966,
175–78.

Equal Suffrage

The Progressive party, believing that no people can justly claim to be a true democracy which denies political rights on account of sex, pledges itself to the task of securing equal suffrage to men and women alike.

Fully justified text, aligned
at left and right

Right-aligned text

throughout your paper. Except in cases of coincidence, however, each centered heading will be a different length and thus will have a different alignment, as you can see in Figure 20.14.

In contrast, in Figure 20.15 the headings are positioned at the left margin (or "flush left," as designers call it) to create a strong line down the left side of the page. This line helps keep the reader's eye moving downward and forward through the paper. The indented paragraphs also line up with each

Figure 20.14
Centered Headings
(no strong alignment).
Source: See Figure 20.13

The Progressive Party Platform of 1912

The Rule of the People

The National Progressive party, committed to the principles of government by a self-controlled democracy expressing its will through representatives of the people, pledges itself to secure such alterations in the fundamental law of the several States and the United States as shall insure the representative character of the government.

In particular, the party declares for direct primaries for the nomination of State and National officers; for nationwide preferential primaries for candidates for presidency; for the direct election of the United States Senators by the people; and we urge on the States the policy of the short ballot, with responsibility to the people secured by the initiative, referendum and recall.

Amendment of Constitution

The Progressive party, believing that a free people should have the power from time to time to amend their fundamental law so as to adapt it progressively to the changing needs of the people, pledges itself to provide a more easy and expeditious method of amending the Federal Constitution. . . .

Equal Suffrage

The Progressive party, believing that no people can justly claim to be a true democracy which denies political rights on account of sex, pledges itself to the task of securing equal suffrage to men and women alike.

Figure 20.15
Left-aligned Title, Headings, and Text (strong alignment). Source: See Figure 20.13

The Progressive Party Platform of 1912

The Rule of the People

The National Progressive party, committed to the principles of government by a self-controlled democracy expressing its will through representatives of the people, pledges itself to secure such alterations in the fundamental law of the several States and the United States as shall insure the representative character of the government.

In particular, the party declares for direct primaries for the nomination of State and National officers; for nationwide preferential primaries for candidates for presidency; for the direct election of the United States Senators by the people; and we urge on the States the policy of the short ballot, with responsibility to the people secured by the initiative, referendum and recall.

Amendment of Constitution

The Progressive party, believing that a free people should have the power from time to time to amend their fundamental law so as to adapt it progressively to the changing needs of the people, pledges itself to provide a more easy and expeditious method of amending the Federal Constitution. . . .

Equal Suffrage

The Progressive party, believing that no people can justly claim to be a true democracy which denies political rights on account of sex, pledges itself to the task of securing equal suffrage to men and women alike.

other, creating another strong alignment on the page. The text itself lines up along the left margin. The Web page in Figure 20.12 also aligns the headings in its menu.

Much of the time you will use both left-aligned text and left-aligned headings in your document. Right-aligned text is rare in a college paper, except for special elements such as running headers and footers (discussed below). Some people like the tidy look of fully justified text, but you should use it with caution. The computer justifies text by adding extra white space between words and by hyphenating words that don't fit on a line; both of these techniques make text more difficult to read. Many teachers prefer left alignment only and no automatic hyphenation, as the MLA and APA guidelines advise.

USING REPETITION PURPOSEFULLY

Though common in poetry and in technical writing, too much verbal repetition may be frowned upon in academic writing. *Visual* repetition, however, can assist a reader. If you were driving along a freeway and the familiar navigation signs — the green and white rectangles — suddenly changed to purple triangles, you might wonder whether you had strayed into a different country. Similarly, if the font or alignment suddenly changes in a paper, the reader immediately asks: What is this new navigational cue? What am I expected to do now?

To avoid disorienting readers, you can repeat one or two fonts throughout your paper to sustain a clean and uncluttered look. Consistent headings and subheadings also serve as a kind of road map to guide the readers' progress. Another simple design strategy is the use of running, or repeated, headers and footers. A *running header* is a line of information that appears consistently at the top of each page of your document, while a *running footer* appears consistently at the bottom of each page. Check the top of this page and the few after it or before it to figure out the pattern for this book's running headers. As part of either the header or the footer, writers sometimes include information such as the document title, its file name, or a distinctive graphic. Once you create a header or footer, your word processor can automatically insert it on each page with the page number, if you've selected that option, or with the date. Figure 20.16 illustrates the type of header required in MLA style.

Fallon 2

Claremont's third message is that activism is needed to combat this

terrorism and hatred, and he provides clear models for activism. . . .

Figure 20.16
Sample Header (running head) in MLA Style, from Geoffrey Fallon's "Hatred within an Illustrated Medium: Those Uncanny X-Men"

**WRITING WITH
A COMPUTER**

Although word-processing programs differ, you can set most to add running headers to your academic papers, automatically supplying your last name and the page number (or other information) at the top of each page. Check the View or Format menu for a "Header or Footer" option. In the header box, use the tab key or your mouse to move to the header location you desire — generally the far right side for an academic paper. Type the header information — such as your last name (in MLA style), a key word from your title (in APA style), or your own identifier for a draft — and then click on the page number option or icon. Each page will be correctly numbered in sequence even if you delete or add text passages.

USING COLOR EFFECTIVELY

Until recently, college papers typically have not included much color. However, word-processing software and other programs now make it possible to include color graphics, photographs, and other images in papers. Make sure that color serves a purpose — for instance, to highlight key information — instead of being used merely as decoration. For example, a good use of color would be to distinguish the slices in a pie chart (see p. 366).

If you are creating documents beyond college papers, you may have even more opportunities to use color. For example, on a Web page you can use color to highlight headings and other key information, as Figure 20.17 shows. On any given page — in Web sites or paper documents — avoid using too many different colors because they can overload readers and defeat the purpose of helping them find important information. Also, choose your colors carefully. For example, although yellow is an attention-getting color, as school buses and traffic signs illustrate, words written in yellow on a white background are difficult to read.

Using Visuals to Reinforce Your Content

Some of your documents may benefit from the addition of graphs, diagrams, maps, photographs, or other materials that add visual interest, convey information, and reinforce the content in your text. You might prepare these yourself or incorporate such materials from other sources, giving credit and requesting permission, if needed (see p. 367). In either case, visual materials should be appropriate for your purpose and your audience, not used as decoration. Check your software for special tools for creating graphics like pie charts, bar charts, and tables. If you are unfamiliar with these functions, ask for advice at the computer lab.

ADDING VISUALS

When could your document benefit from visuals? To answer this question, think about the ways in which visual material can support your point.

- To discuss a conflict in a certain geographical area, supply a map.
- To illustrate an autobiographical essay, scan an image of yourself as a baby or at some important moment in your life.
- To clarify the stages or steps in a process, a procedure, or a set of directions, include a diagram.

Process Diagrams and Illustrations.   A paper explaining a process such as wastewater treatment in King County, Washington, might include a diagram, as in Figure 20.18. On the other hand, Figure 20.19 shows another way to illustrate a process. Notice how the drawings and descriptions work together to provide an overview of the work that is done at an archaeological site.

Colorful images draw the eye
and point out key events

Figure 20.17
Use of Color on a Web
Page. Source: The Smith-
sonian Institution

Blue headers indicate links to
various museums

Green headers indicate
online sources at the
Smithsonian

Additional color images
illlustrate links

Figure 20.18
A Diagram Showing the Process of Wastewater Treatment in King County, Washington. Source: King County, Washington, Department of Natural Resources Wastewater Treatment Division <dnr.metrokc.gov/wtd/ntf/link.htm>

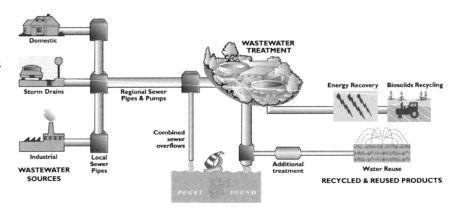

Figure 20.19
Illustration of Work at an Archaeological Dig. Source: Dorling Kindersley Children's Illustrated Encyclopedia

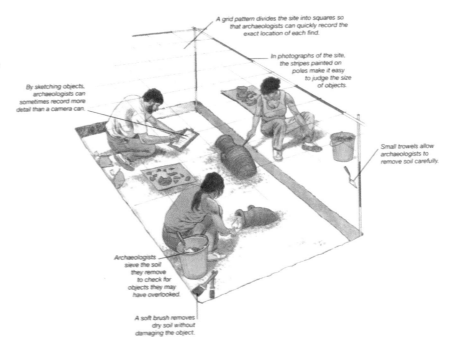

Comparative Graphs and Charts.   Graphics in college papers, magazines, Web sites, and other publications also consolidate information — both numbers and words — in visual form.

- To illustrate a trend, a relationship, or a contrast — the number of school-aged children who use the Internet or the ratio of men to women at your college — create a graph in a spreadsheet. For example, the one in Figure 20.20 shows a trend, the rising oil prices, as it contrasts prices in different regions.

How can you add visuals to your paper? In a few cases—such as using material from a print source with a deadline only hours away—your simplest method may be the old-fashioned one: add an extra page break in your text where you want to place the material, print the final version of your file, and then use the numbered blank page to photocopy or present the material in your paper. Much of the time, however, you can create your own material right in your text file. To prepare a table, use the Insert or the Table menu; the table will appear wherever you add it in the text. Simply add page breaks before and after it if you wish to present it on its own page, as some instructors and academic style manuals prefer.

WRITING WITH A COMPUTER

Other options for adding boxes, graphs, pie charts, bar charts, or art may be available through the Insert menu, a Drawing or Clip Art option, or related spreadsheet or presentation software. Use a scanner to integrate printed material, or try an image editor to scan photographs or add digital photos. Turn to your computer lab for help in learning to use more sophisticated software applications or to gain access to software and equipment more advanced than your own. When you are working on a complex project, get help well ahead of your deadline, and allow plenty of time to learn new techniques for integrating visuals. Be sure to request permission to use images when needed, and acknowledge visual sources as carefully as textual sources.

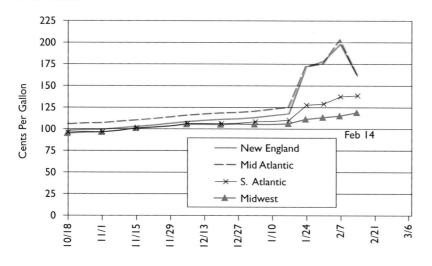

Regional Residential Heating Oil Prices

Figure 20.20
A Graph Showing Prices for Residential Heating Oil in Different Regions from October 1999 to March 2000. Source: Energy Information Administration/State Energy Office Data <www.eia.doe.gov/ pub/oil_gas/petroleum/ presentations/2000/ senate022400/ senate022400.htm>

Figure 20.21
A Pie Chart Showing
Shares of a Whole. Source:
Discover *magazine,*
December 2002, page 13

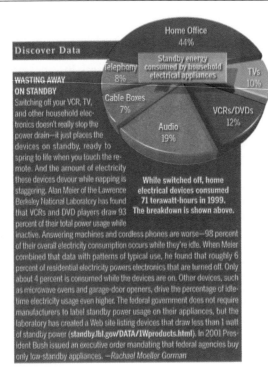

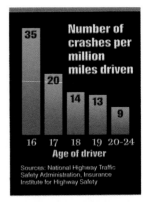

Figure 20.22   *A Bar*
Chart Presenting Numerical
Comparisons. Source: U.S.
News & World Report,
April 8, 2002, page 48

- To illustrate percentages or shares of a whole, add a pie chart, such as the one in Figure 20.21. This chart, shown with the brief article that it illustrates, indicates how much of the total (100%) "standby energy" various types of appliances use. Notice how color is also used to distinguish the "slices" of the pie.

- To compare various values or amounts, provide a bar chart like the one in Figure 20.22. This chart, used to illustrate an article about increased driving restrictions for teens, supplies an at-a-glance comparison of the number of car crashes occurring in various age groups.

Comparative Tables.   Consider using a table to organize textual information for easier reading. Typically, tables have columns (running up and down) and rows (running across). Tables are common in academic and workplace writing, but they are also used in popular magazines, as Figure 20.23 shows. The information in this table could have been explained in a paragraph, but a block of text would have been less accessible for readers — and far less visually interesting. Notice how the little photographs of the various objects described bring the design to life.

Figure 20.23
A Table Organiz-
ing Textual Data.
Source: Health,
May 2002, page
35

CREDITING SOURCES

If you include visual materials from another source, printed or electronic, credit that source in your essay. Be sure to ask permission, if required, to use an image so that you don't risk violating the copyright. If you download an image from the Web, check the site for its guidelines for the use of images. Follow these guidelines, asking permission if necessary and giving credit to the owner of the copyright. If you are uncertain about whether you can use an image from a source, check with your teacher.

For more on the MLA documentation style, see E1–E2 in the Quick Research Guide (the dark-red-edged pages).

ARRANGING VISUALS AND TEXT IN YOUR DOCUMENT

Using visuals can create problems in *layout,* the arrangement of text and graphics on a page. Here are some guidelines for ensuring that your layout is effective and appropriate for your purpose and audience.

Integration of Visuals and Text.   Because you are including the visual to support an idea in your text, your reader will make better sense of the graph, chart, diagram, or photograph if you provide a context for it. In an introductory sentence, you should give your reader this information:

- The number or letter of the visual (for example, Figure 6)
- Its location (on page 9, in section 3)
- Its content
- The point that it helps you to make

Also supply a label with your visual to identify its topic and number.

Placement and Alignment of Visuals.   Placing a visual close to the related discussion will make your document easy for readers to follow. Readers may get distracted if they must flip from the body of the text to an appendix, for example. In addition, when your headings and text are aligned at the left margin to sustain a strong forward flow through the document, you may not want to disrupt the flow by centering your visuals. Let your eye be the judge.

Balance between Visuals and Text.   The visuals should support, not overshadow, the content of your paper. Try to strike a balance between the size of any single graphic or image and the related chunks of text. Though a reader's eye should be drawn to the visual, try to give it an appropriate — rather than excessive — share of the page layout.

Consider the following questions as you design your document:

DOCUMENT DESIGN CHECKLIST

____ Does your document design meet your readers' expectations and acknowledge their constraints?

____ Does your document design help to achieve your purpose, that is, your reason for writing? Does it help emphasize your key points and demonstrate a clear organization?

____ Have you used appropriate fonts, or typefaces, in your document? Do you use boldface and italic type sparingly for emphasis? Have you used displayed lists when appropriate to call out information?

____ Does the white space in your document work strategically, calling attention to or linking certain portions of text rather than creating gaps between textual elements?

____ Do your headings, subheadings, and alignment provide your reader with clear and purposeful navigational cues?

____ Have you used repeated elements, such as running headers or footers, that increase visual coherence?

____ Do your diagrams, photographs, or other illustrations clarify your content? Do your graphs, charts, or tables present numerical or textual information "at a glance"?

____ Have you used color effectively to highlight, distinguish, or organize information?

___ Does your layout integrate the visuals using appropriate placement, sizing, and alignment?

___ Have you secured any permission needed to use copyrighted material? Have you credited the source of each visual?

■ Exercises

1. Experiment with the fonts that are available on your computer. Using a paragraph or two from a recent paper, go through the font list to see how your sentences look in various fonts available to you. Test different sizes as well as the bold and italic versions. How readable is each font?

2. Look at a bulletin board, literature rack, magazine shelf, or other location where many different examples of printed material are displayed. Identify several different uses of fonts to establish a mood or convey a message. Select one example that you find particularly effective, and briefly explain how the font helps to convey the desired mood or message to the audience. If possible, include a copy of the example with your paper.

3. Using your favorite search engine (Google or Yahoo!, for example), locate an online example of a research paper or report. (The keywords "research paper" or "research report" should return several examples.) Or find a technical or government report online or in the library. Read the abstract or introduction to get an idea of the author's topic. Then quickly skim the report in order to answer the following questions:

   a. What is the purpose of the report?

   b. Who is the intended audience or reader? How can you tell?

   c. In what ways does the writer use document design strategies to address readers' needs and constraints?

   d. How does the writer use document design strategies to help make his or her point?

   e. What design revisions would you recommend to the writer? How might these changes improve the reading experience of the intended audience?

   Write a brief essay presenting your findings.

4. FOR GROUP WORK: Assemble several different documents that you are reading or might read — perhaps a textbook, a newspaper, a magazine, a brochure, a catalog, or a campus publication. Examine each document carefully, considering which aspects of the design seem effective or ineffective in achieving the writer's purpose and meeting the reader's needs. Then, bring your documents and notes to class. In groups of three to five students, share your findings.

5. FOR GROUP WORK: In a small group, examine several different documents — one supplied by each group member or one or two of the document sets prepared for exercise 4. For each document, consider what other design choices might have made the visual presentation more effective. When you've finished your analysis, share your findings with the rest of the class.

Chapter 21
Strategies for Understanding Visual Representations

O n a street-corner billboard, a man is biting into a jelly doughnut while driving, a look of horror on his face. He's horrified because a big blob of purple jelly (captured in midair) is about to land in the middle of his white dress shirt. The only other picture on the billboard is a detergent manufacturer's logo.

Other billboards on this corner advertise such diverse commodities as fast food, cell-phone services, and the radiology department at a local hospital. Thousands of drivers pause at this intersection to wait out a red light — a captive audience for aggressive and compelling visual representations. It's a good location for the detergent ad: drivers who pass the billboard, especially those who are eating in their cars, will relate to the problem of food spills on nice clothes. Obviously, the company that sponsored the ad hopes these people will remember its brand — the one that can tackle even the worst stains on the whitest shirts — the next time they buy laundry detergent.

The specific images on these billboards change with time, but images are a constant and persistent presence in our lives. The sign atop a taxi invites us to try the new ride at a local tourist attraction. A celebrity sporting a milk moustache smiles from the side of a city bus, accompanied by the familiar question, "Got milk?" The lettering on a pickup truck urges us to call for a free landscaping estimate. On television, video, and the Web, advertising images surround us, trying to shape our opinions about everything from personal hygiene products to snack foods to political candidates.

Advertisements are not the only visual representations that affect us. Cartoons, photographs, drawings, paintings, logos, graphics, and other two-dimensional media originate from a variety of sources with a variety of purposes — and all work to evoke responses. The critical skills you develop for analyzing these still images also apply to other types of visual representations, including television commercials, films, and stage productions. We can't help but notice visual images, and whether we respond with a smile or a frown, one thing is certain: visuals help to structure our views of reality.

Using Strategies for Visual Analysis

Begin a visual analysis by conducting a *close reading* of the image. Like a literal and critical reading of a written text, a close reading of an image involves careful, in-depth examination of the advertisement, photograph, cartoon, artwork, or other visual representation. Your close reading should focus on the following three levels of questions:

- **What is the big picture?** What is the source of the image? What is its purpose? What audience does it address? What prominent element in the image stands out? What focal point draws the eye?

- **What characteristics of the image can you observe?** What story does the image tell? What people or animals appear in the image? What are the major elements of the image? How are they arranged?

- **How can you interpret what the image suggests?** What feeling or mood does it create? What is its cultural meaning? What are the roles of any signs, symbols, or language that it includes? What is the image about?

The rest of the chapter explains these three levels of visual analysis in more detail. You may discover that your classmates respond differently to some images than you do. Your personal cultural background and your experiences may influence how you interpret the meaning of an image. If you plan

■ For a model visual analysis and visual-analysis activity, visit <bedfordstmartins.com/bedguide> and do a keyword search:

visual

■ For more on literal and critical reading of texts, see Ch. 2. For a checklist for analyzing images, see pp. 384–85.

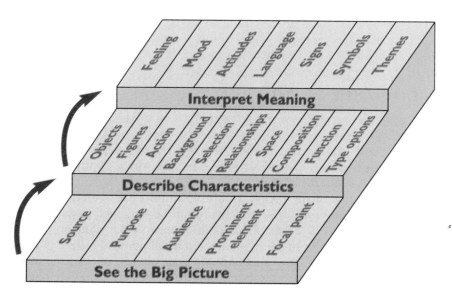

to write about the image you analyze, take notes or use your journal to record your observations and interpretations. Be sure to include a copy of the image, if one is available, when you solicit peer review of your essay or submit it to your teacher.

Level One: Seeing the Big Picture

Begin your close reading of an image by discovering what you can about its source and overall composition. If you include the image in a paper, you will need to cite the source and its "author" or artist, just as you would if you were including text from a reading, an article, or a literary work.

PURPOSE AND AUDIENCE

For more on purpose and audience, see pp. 13–15 and pp. 269–70.

Identifying the purpose and intended audience for an image is sometimes complicated. For example, an image may appear in its original context or in a different situation, used seriously, humorously, or allusively. Use the following checklist to help you find out as much as you can about the purpose and audience for the image:

DISCOVERY CHECKLIST

___ What is the context for the image? For example, if it is an advertisement, when and where did it run? If it is a photograph, painting, or other work of art, who is the artist? Where has it been published or exhibited?

___ What is the purpose of the image?

___ What audience does the image aim to attract?

Next, examine the overall composition of the image. The photograph in Figure 21.1 will serve as a guide to this process.

PROMINENT ELEMENT

Start with the overall view. Look carefully at the whole image and ask yourself, "Is there one prominent element — object, person, background, writing — in the image that immediately attracts my attention?" Examine that element in detail, and ask yourself how and why that prominent element draws you into the image.

In Figure 21.1, many people would first notice the dark-haired Caucasian girl. Her prominence in the picture can be explained in part by her position at the left side of the photograph, framed by the white porch railing. People who read from left to right and top to bottom — including most Americans and Europeans — also typically read photographs in the same way, which means that the viewer's eye is likely to be drawn into the photograph at the upper left corner. For this reason, artists and photographers often position key elements—those they want viewers to see right away—somewhere in the upper left quadrant of the image. (See Figure 21.2, p. 374.)

FOCAL POINT

There is another reason the reader's eye might be drawn first to the girl on the left: notice that all of the other children are turned slightly toward her, straining to see the pages of the magazine she is holding. Not only is she positioned so as to provide a focal point for the viewer, but she is also the focal point of action within the photograph.

Now, take a look at the child on the right side of the picture. You may have noticed her first. Or, once you did notice her, you may have been surprised that she didn't attract your attention right away. After all, she provides some contrast within the photograph because she sits apart from the other girls, seems to be a little younger, and does not appear to be included in their little group. What's more, she's not wearing any clothes. Still, most people won't notice her first because of the path the eye typically travels within a photograph. Because of the left-to-right and top-to-bottom reading pattern that Americans and Europeans take for granted, most of us view photographs in a *Z* pattern, as depicted in Figure 21.3 (p. 374). Even though most viewers would notice the child on the far right last, they would still pause to look at her. Thus, the bottom right corner of an image is a second very important position that a skilled photographer can use to retain the viewers' attention. When you look at the "big picture" in this way, you can see the overall composition of the image, identify its prominent element, and determine its focal point.

Level Two: Observing the Characteristics of an Image

As you concentrate on the literal reading of a written text, you become aware of the information it presents, you comprehend what it means, and you are able to apply it in relation to other situations. Similarly, your close reading of an image includes observing its *denotative* or literal characteristics. At this stage, you focus on exactly what the image depicts—observing it objectively—rather than probing what it means or signifies.

For more about reading on a literal level, see pp. 22–23. For a checklist for analyzing images, see pp. 384–85.

CAST OF CHARACTERS

Objects.   Examine the condition, colors, sizes, functions, and positions of the objects included in the image. In Figure 21.1, for example, only one object is depicted in the image: a large magazine. Everything else in the image is either a figure or part of the background.

Figure 21.1 (top)
Photograph of Four Children,
Kodak Picture of the Day,
October 22, 2000

Figure 21.2 (above left)
Photograph Divided into
Quarters

Figure 21.3 (above right)
Z Pattern Often Used to Read
Images

Figure 21.4 (right)
Close-up Detail of Photograph

Figures.   Look closely at any figures (men, women, children, animals) in the image. Consider their facial expressions, poses, hairstyles and colors, ages, sexes, ethnicity, possible education, suggested occupations, apparent relationships to each other, and so on.

Figure 21.1 shows four girls, three about eight or nine years old and the fourth a few years younger. Three of the girls are Caucasian, and one is African American. The dark-haired Caucasian girl is wearing a colorful bathing suit as is the African American girl. Between them sits a light-haired Caucasian girl, wearing shorts and a short-sleeved blue and white flowered T-shirt. All three appear to be dressed appropriately for the weather. The three girls pore over the magazine held by the dark-haired Caucasian girl. Judging from their facial expressions, they are totally engrossed in the contents of the magazine, as well as a little puzzled. The girls seem to be looking at a picture; the magazine is turned sideways with the spine at the bottom.

The fourth child, the youngest in the photograph, sits slightly apart from the others. Her light hair appears damp — possibly from swimming, we might conclude, because two of the other girls are attired in swimsuits. We can see that her skin is tanned and that she has several small bruises on her legs, probably acquired during normal play. Her right leg is crossed over her left, causing her body to turn slightly away from the other girls. Her face is turned toward them, however, and she seems to be trying to see what they are looking at. Her hands are raised, her eyes are bright, and she's smiling at whatever she is able to see of the magazine.

STORY OF THE IMAGE

Action.   The action shown in an image suggests its "plot" or story, the events surrounding the moment captured in the image. In Figure 21.1, four children are seated on the steps of a house looking at a magazine on a summer day. Because no adults appear in the picture and the children look puzzled, we might assume that they are looking at something they don't understand, possibly something adults might frown on. On the other hand, they are not acting secretive, so this impression may not be accurate.

Background.   The background in an image shows where and when the action takes place. In Figure 21.1, the children are seated on the wooden steps of a blue house. We might conclude that the steps are part of a back porch rather than a front porch because the porch is relatively small and the steps begin immediately: there is no deck and consequently nowhere to sit except on the steps themselves. The top step is painted blue, and the railing is painted white to match the white metal door and window frames. In a few places the paint is chipped or worn away. But these signs of disrepair simply seem to indicate that the house is lived in and comfortable; they are not severe enough to suggest that the occupants are poor. In the windows next to the steps and on the door, we can see the reflections of trees. The children's clothes identify the season as summer.

DESIGN AND ARRANGEMENT

Selection of Elements.   When you look at the design of an image, you might reflect on both the elements within the image and their organization.

- What are the major colors and shapes?

- How are they arranged?

- Does the image appear balanced? Are light and dark areas arranged symmetrically?

- Does the image appear organized or chaotic?

- Is one area of the picture darker (heavier) or brighter (lighter) than other areas?

- What does the design make you think of—does it evoke a particular emotion, historical period, or memory?

In Figure 21.1, the most prominent shape is the white porch railing that frames the children and draws the viewer's eye in toward the action. The image appears balanced, in that the white door provides the backdrop for the youngest child, while the blue siding and white porch railing frames the other girls. Therefore, the image is split down the center, both by the separation of the figures and by the shapes that make up the background. The brightly colored summer clothing worn by the girls on the left side also accentuates the youngest child's monochromatic nakedness.

Relationship of Elements.   Visual elements may be related to one another or to written material that appears with them. As you notice such relationships, consider what they tell you. In Figure 21.1, for instance, the three older girls are grouped together around the magazine, and the youngest child is clearly not part of their group. She is separated physically from the others by a bit of intervening space and by the vertical line formed by the doorframe, which splits the background in two. Moreover, her body is turned slightly away from them, and she is not clothed. However, her gaze, like the other girls', is on the magazine that they are scrutinizing; this element of the picture connects all of the children together.

For more information on white space in document design, see pp. 354–56.

Use of Space.   An image may be surrounded by a lot of "white space" — empty space without text or graphics — or it may be "busy," filled with visual and written elements. White space is effective when it provides relief from an otherwise busy layout or when it directs the reader's eye to key elements of the image. The image in Figure 21.1 does not include any empty space; its shapes and colors guide the viewer's eye.

In contrast, look at the image in Figure 21.5. It specifically uses white space to call attention to the Volkswagen's small size. When this advertisement was produced back in 1959, many American cars were large and heavy. The VW, a German import, provided consumers with an alternative type of vehicle, and the advertising emphasized this contrast.

Figure 21.5
Volkswagen Advertisement, about 1959

ARTISTIC CHOICES

Whether an image is a photograph, a drawing, or another form of representation, the person who composes it considers its artistic effect, its function, and its connection to related text.

Composition Decisions.   Aesthetic or artistic choices may vary with the preferences of the designer and the characteristics of the medium. For example, if an image is a photograph, the photographer might use a close-up, medium, or wide-angle shot to compose it — and also determine the angle of the shot, the lighting, and the use of color.

The picture of the four children in Figure 21.1 is a medium shot and has been taken at the children's eye level. If the photograph were a close-up, only one aspect of the image would be visible. Notice in Figure 21.4 how the meaning of the picture changes when we view the girls' faces as a close-up. We have no way of telling where the picture was taken or what the girls are doing; moreover, by moving in closer, this view completely cuts out the youngest child. The girls' attentiveness is still apparent, but we can't quite tell what its object is.

In contrast, in the Volkswagen ad (Figure 21.5), the white space creates the effect of a long shot taken from below with a telephoto lens. We see the car as it might appear if we were looking down at it through the wrong end of a pair of binoculars. This vantage point shrinks the car so that an already small vehicle looks even smaller.

For more about the ways visuals support content, see pp. 362–69.

Function Decisions.   When using an image to illustrate a point, either alone or in connection with text, a writer must make sure that the illustration serves the overall purpose of the document; in other words, form should follow function. For example, the 1959 Oldsmobile ad, Figure 21.6, shows people who seem to be having a good time; in fact, one scene is set near the shore. These illustrations suggest that those who purchase the cars will enjoy life, a notion that undoubtedly suits the advertiser's goals.

For a sample pie chart, see Figure 20.21, p. 366. For sample photographs, turn to the images opening Chs. 4 to 11 and 22 to 26.

Writers have many choices available to them for illustrations — not only photographs and drawings but also charts, graphs, and tables. Certain types of these visuals are especially suited to certain functions. For example, a pie chart is perhaps the best way to convey parts of a whole visually. A photograph effectively captures the drama and intensity of the moment — a child's rescue, a family's grief, or an earthquake's toll. When you look at newspapers, magazines, and other publications, consider how the visuals function and why the writer might have chosen to include them.

For more on typefaces, see pp. 348–52.

Typeface Options.   Many images, especially advertisements, combine image and text, using the typeface to set a particular mood and convey a particular impression. For example, Times New Roman is a common typeface, easy to read and somewhat conservative, whereas Comic Sans MS is considered informal — almost playful — and looks like handwriting. Any printed element included in an image may be trendy or conservative, large or small, in relation to the image as a whole. Further, it may be meant to inform, evoke an emotion, or decorate the page.

For a definition and example of sans serif type, see pp. 349–50.

Look back at Figure 21.5, the 1959 Volkswagen ad. The words "Think small" are printed in a sans serif typeface — spare and unadorned, just like the VW itself. The ad also includes a significant amount of text across the

DYNAMIC 88 HOLIDAY SPORTSEDAN—
sports car flair, full family size! Features
new, improved Econ-O-Way Carburetion
and exclusive 2-stage, fuel-saving automatic choke!

OLDSMOBILE FOR '59 brings you the "Linear Look" . . . alive with advanced ideas! Everything is new! The view is Vista-Panoramic . . . there's more passenger room and luggage space, too. Rocket Engine power is quieter and smoother . . . the ride is best described as a "Glide". To step out of the ordinary, step into a '59 Olds at your dealer's today!   OLDSMOBILE DIVISION. GENERAL MOTORS CORPORATION

1959

NINETY-EIGHT HOLIDAY SCENICOUPE—
luxury, roominess, visibility as never before!
Huge, tinted rear window—specially processed to block sun's rays—is standard equipment!

Figure 21.6
Oldsmobile Advertisement, 1959

bottom of the page. While this text is difficult to read in the reproduction in this book, it humorously points out the benefits of driving a small imported vehicle instead of one of the many large, roomy cars common at the time.

In contrast to the VW ad campaign, the 1959 Oldsmobile marketing strategy promoted a big vehicle, not a small one, as Figure 21.6 illustrates.

Figure 21.7   Stairway.
Source: Design for Communication:
Conceptual Graphic Design Basics

Figure 21.8   Type as Cultural Cliché.
Source: Publication Design

Here the cars are shown in medium to close-up view to call attention to their length. Happy human figures positioned in and beside the cars emphasize their size, and the cars are painted in bright colors, unlike the VW's serviceable black. The type in the ad, like the other visual elements, reflects and promotes the Oldsmobile's size. The primary text in the center of the page is large enough to be read in the reproduction here. It introduces the brand name by opening the first sentence with the Oldsmobile '59 logo and praises the cars' expansive size, space, power, and other features. Near the bottom of each car image, however, are a few lines of "fine print" that are difficult to read in the reproduction — brief notes about other features of the car.

Other images besides advertisements use type to set a mood or convey feelings and ideas. Figure 21.7 is a design student's response to an assignment that called for using letters to create an image. The student used a simple typeface and a stairlike arrangement to help viewers "experience" the word *stairway.* Figure 21.8 illustrates how certain typefaces have become associated with particular countries — even to the point of becoming clichés. In fact, designers of travel posters, travel brochures, and other such publications often draw on predictable typographical choices like these to suggest a feeling or mood — for example, boldness, tradition, adventure, history.

Just as type can establish a mood or tone, the absence of any written language in an image can also affect how we view that image. Recall Figure 21.1, the photograph of the children sitting on the porch looking at a magazine. Because we can't see the magazine's title, we are left to wonder — perhaps with amusement — about what has so engrossed the children. If the title of the magazine — *Sports Illustrated, Wired, People* — were revealed to us, the photograph might seem less intriguing. By leaving us to speculate about the identity of the magazine, the photographer may keep us looking longer and harder at the image.

Level Three: Interpreting the Meaning of an Image

When you read a written text on an analytical level, you engage actively with the text. You analyze its parts from different angles, synthesize the material by combining it with related information, and finally evaluate or judge its significance. When you interpret an image, you do much the same, actively questioning and examining what the image *connotes* or suggests, speculating about what it signifies.

For more on reading analytically, see pp. 23–24. For a checklist for analyzing images, see pp. 384–85.

Because interpretation is more personal than observation, this process can reveal deep-seated individual and cultural values. In fact, interpreting an image is sometimes emotional or difficult because it may require you to examine beliefs that you are unaware of holding. You may even become impatient with visual analysis, perhaps feeling that too much is being read into the image. Like learning to read critically, however, learning to interpret images is a valuable skill. When you see an image that attracts you, chances are good that you like it because it upholds strong cultural beliefs. Through close reading of images, you can examine how image makers are able to perpetuate such cultural values and speculate about why — perhaps analyzing an artist's political motivations or an advertiser's economic motivations. When you interpret an image, you go beyond literal observation to examine what the image suggests and what it may mean.

GENERAL FEELING OR MOOD

To begin interpreting an image, consider what feeling or mood it creates and how it does so. If you are a woman, you probably recall huddling, around age eight or nine, with a couple of "best friends" as the girls do in Figure 21.1. As a result, the interaction in this photograph may seem very familiar and may evoke fond memories. If you are a man, this photograph may call up somewhat different memories. Although eight-year-old boys also cluster in small groups, their motivations may differ from those behind little girls' huddles. Moreover, anyone who was ignored or excluded at a young age may feel a rush of sympathy for the youngest child; her separation from the older children may dredge up age-old hurt feelings.

For many viewers, the image may also suggest a mood associated with summer: sitting on the back porch after a trip to the swimming pool, spending a carefree day with friends. This "summer" mood is a particular cultural association related to the summers of childhood. By the time we reach college, summer no longer has the same feeling. Work, summer school, separations, and family responsibilities — maybe even for children like those in the picture — obliterate the freedoms of childhood summer vacations.

SOCIOLOGICAL, POLITICAL, ECONOMIC, OR CULTURAL ATTITUDES

On the surface, the Volkswagen ad in Figure 21.5 is simply an attempt to sell a car. But its message might be interpreted to mean "scale down" — lead a less consumer-oriented lifestyle. If Volkswagen had distributed this ad in the 1970s, it would have been unremarkable — faced with the first energy crisis that adversely affected American gasoline prices, many advertisers used ecological consciousness to sell cars. In 1959, however, energy conservation was not really a concern. Contrasted with other automobile ads of its time, the Volkswagen ad seems somewhat eccentric, making the novel suggestion that larger cars are excessively extravagant.

Whereas the Volkswagen ad suggests that "small" refers both to size and affordability, the Oldsmobile ad in Figure 21.6 depicts a large vehicle and implies a large price tag. By emphasizing the Vista-Panoramic view and increased luggage space and by portraying the car near a seashore, the ad leads viewers to think about going on vacation. It thus implies luxury and exclusivity — not everyone can afford this car or the activities it suggests.

Sometimes, what is missing from an image is as important as what is included. Viewers of today might readily notice the absence of people of color in the 1959 Oldsmobile ad. An interesting study might investigate what types of magazines originally carried this ad and whether (and if so, how) Oldsmobiles were also advertised in publications aimed at Asian Americans, African Americans, or Spanish-speaking people.

LANGUAGE

Just as you would examine figures, colors, and shapes when you observe the literal characteristics of an image, so you need to examine its words, phrases, and sentences when you interpret what it suggests. Does its language provide information, generate an emotional response, or do both? Do its words repeat a sound or concept, signal a comparison (such as a "new, improved" product), carry sexual overtones, issue a challenge, or offer a definition or philosophy of life? The words in the center of the Oldsmobile ad in Figure 21.6, for instance, are calculated to associate the car with a leisurely, affluent lifestyle. On the other hand, VW's "Think small" ad in Figure 21.5 turns compactness into a goal, a quality to be desired in a car and, by extension, in life.

Frequently advertisements employ wordplay — lighthearted or serious — to get their messages across. Consider, for example, the public-service advertisement in Figure 21.9, which was created by a graphic-design student. This ad features a play on the word *tolerance,* which is scrambled on the chalkboard so that the letters in the center read *learn.* The chalkboard, a typical feature of the classroom, suggests that tolerance is a basic lesson to be learned. Also, the definition of tolerance at the bottom of the ad is much like other definitions students might look up in a dictionary. (It reads, "The capacity for, or practice of, recognizing or respecting the behavior, beliefs, opinions, practices, or rights of others, whether agreeing with them or not.")

Figure 21.9
Public-service Advertisement Showing Wordplay.
Source: Design for Communication: Conceptual Graphic Design Basics

SIGNS AND SYMBOLS

Signs and symbols, such as product logos, are images or words that communicate key messages. In the Oldsmobile ad in Figure 21.6, the product logo doubles as the phrase that introduces the description of the 1959 model. Sometimes a product logo alone may be enough, as in the Hershey chocolate company's holiday ads that include little more than a single Hershey's Kiss. The shape of the Kiss serves as a logo or symbol for the company.

If you look back at the second magazine spread in Figure 20.3 (see p. 346), you'll see a prominent symbol — the U.S. flag. The flag is held by a little boy who is sitting on a man's shoulders. (Presumably, the man is the boy's father.) In this spread, the flag is associated not only with the Fourth of July, the article's subject, but also with a family's values. Even without the headings and quotations, the symbolism comes across clearly.

THEMES

The theme of an image is not the same as its plot. When you identify the plot, you identify the story that is told by the image. When you identify the theme, on the other hand, you explain what the image is about. An ad for a diamond ring may tell the story of a man surprising his wife with a ring on their twenty-fifth wedding anniversary, but the advertisement's theme could be sex, romance, longevity, or some other concept. Similarly, the theme of a soft-drink ad might be competition, community, compassion, or individualism. A painting of the ocean might be about cheerfulness, fear, or loneliness. Through a close reading, you can unearth clues and details to support your interpretation of the theme and convince others of its merit.

Ask the following questions as you analyze an image or as you prepare to present your analysis in an essay:

VISUAL ANALYSIS CHECKLIST

Seeing the Big Picture

___ What is the source of the image? What is its purpose and audience?

___ What prominent element in the image immediately attracts your attention? How and why does it draw you into the image?

___ What is the focal point of the image? How do the elements of the image direct your attention to this point? What path does your eye follow as you observe the image?

Observing the Characteristics of an Image

___ What objects are included in the image?

___ What figures (people or animals) appear in the image?

___ What action takes place in the image? What is its "plot" or story?

___ What is in the background of the image? Where does the action of the image take place? What kind of place is it?

___ What elements contribute to the design of the image? What colors and shapes does it include? How are they arranged or balanced? What feeling, memory, or association does the design evoke?

___ How are the pictorial elements related to one another? How are they related to any written material? What do these relationships tell you as a viewer?

___ How does the image use space? Does it include a lot of white space, or does it seem cluttered and busy?

___ What composition decisions has the designer or artist made? What type of shot, shot angle, lighting, or color is used?

___ What is the function of the image? How does form support function?

___ What typefaces are used? What impressions do they convey?

Interpreting the Meaning of an Image

___ What general feeling do you get from looking at the image? What mood does the image create? How does it create this mood?

___ What sociological, political, economic, or cultural attitudes are reflected in the image?

___ What language is included in the image? How does the language function?

___ What signs and symbols can you identify? What role do these play?

___ What theme or themes can you identify in the image?

■ Exercises

1. Find a print ad that evokes a strong emotional response. Study the ad closely, observing its characteristics and interpreting its meaning. Write an essay in which you explain the techniques by which the ad evokes your emotional response. Include a copy of the ad with your essay, and consult others to determine whether they have the same response to the ad.

2. Volkswagen continues to produce thought-provoking advertisements like the one shown in Figure 21.5 on page 377. Video clips of some of the company's recent television ads can be found at <www.vw.com/musicpillar/ads.htm>. View one or two of these advertisements, considering such features as their stories or "plots"; the choice of figures, settings, and images; the angles from which subjects are filmed; and any text messages included. Based on your analysis of the ads, decide what message you think that the company wants to communicate about its cars. In an essay, describe this message and the audience that Volkswagen seems to be aiming for, and discuss how the artistic choices in the ads might appeal to this audience.

3. Compile a design notebook. Over the course of several weeks, collect ten or twelve images that appeal to you. You may wish to choose examples of a particular genre, or your teacher may assign a genre or theme. For example, you might select advertisements, portraits, or landscape photographs, or you might choose snack food advertisements from magazines aimed at several different audiences. On the other hand, your collection might revolve around a theme, such as friendship, competition, community, or romance. As you collect these images, "read" each one closely, and write short responses explaining your reactions to the images. At the end of the collection period, choose two or three images. Write an essay in which you compare or contrast them, analyzing how they illustrate the same genre, convey a theme, or appeal to different audiences.

4. Visit a music store, and find a CD cover whose design interests you. Make notes about design choices such as its prominent element and focal point, the use of color and imagery, and the use of typography. Based on the design, try to predict what kind of music is on the CD. If the store has CD-listening stations, try to listen to a track or two. Did the music match your expectations based on the CD design? If you were the CD designer, would you have made any different artistic choices? Write a brief essay discussing your observations, and attach a copy of the CD cover, if possible. (You might be able to print it out from the Web.) As an alternative assignment, listen to some music that's new to you, and design a CD cover for it, applying the elements described in this chapter. Describe in a brief paper the visual elements you would include in your CD cover. If you wish, sketch your design for the cover, using colored pencils or markers or pasting in images or type from print sources, such as magazines or newspapers.

5. FOR GROUP WORK: Select some type of image (for example, an advertisement; a visual from a magazine or image database; a CD, DVD, or videocassette cover) and, on your own, make notes on its "literal" characteristics. (For guidance, see "Observing the Characteristics of an Image," pp. 373–81.) Then, bring your image and notes to class. In small groups of three to five students, share your images and discuss your literal readings.

6. FOR GROUP WORK: In a small group, pick one or two of the images that the group members analyzed for exercise 5. Ask each group member, in turn, to suggest possible interpretations of the images. (For guidance, see "Interpreting the Meaning of an Image," pp. 381–84.) What different interpretations do group members suggest? How do you account for their differences? Share your findings with the rest of the class.

A
Writer's
Reader

 *A Writer's Reader* Contents

Introduction: Reading to Write 389

Introduction:
Reading to Write

A Writer's Reader is a collection of thirty-two carefully selected professional essays. We hope, first of all, that you will read these pieces simply for the sake of reading—enjoying and responding to the ideas presented. Good writers read widely, and in doing so, they increase their knowledge of the craft of writing. Second, we hope that you will actively study these essays as solid examples of the situations and strategies explored in *A Writer's Guide*. The authors represented in this reader, experts from varied fields, have faced the same problems and choices you do when you write. You can learn from studying their decisions, structures, and techniques. Finally, we hope that you will find the content of the essays intriguing—and that the essays, along with the questions posed after each one, will give you ideas to write about.

Each chapter in *A Writer's Reader* concentrates on a familiar broad theme—families, men and women, popular culture, the workplace, and education. In some essays the writers focus on the inner world and write personal experience and opinion papers. In others the authors turn their attention to the outer world and write informational and persuasive essays. Within each chapter, the last two selections are a pair of essays on the same subject. We've provided these pairs so that you can see how different writers use different strategies to address similar issues.

Each chapter in the reader begins with an image, a visual activity, and a Web search activity, all intended to stimulate your thinking and writing. Each reading selection is preceded by biographical information about the author, placing him or her—and the piece itself—into a cultural and informational context. Next a reading note, As You Read, suggests a way to consider the selection. Following each reading are five Questions to Start You Thinking that consistently cover the same ground: meaning, writing strategies, critical thinking, vocabulary, and connections with one or more of the other selections in *A Writer's Reader*. Each paired essay is also followed by a question that asks you about a link between the essays. After these questions come a couple of journal prompts designed to get your writing juices flowing. Finally, two possible assignments make specific suggestions for writing. The first assignment is directed toward your inner world, asking you to draw generally on your personal experience and your understanding of the essay. The second is outer directed, asking you to look outside yourself and write an evaluative or argumentative paper, one that may require further reading or research.

For more on journal writing, see pp. 265–66.

Chapter 22
Families

Zack Townsend and His Family / Bruccoli Clark Layman

Responding to an Image

What does the composition of this family photograph suggest to a viewer? Carefully examine the photograph, making thorough notes about the clothing, positions, facial expressions, posture, race, gender, and other attributes of the people in the photograph. What might these attributes indicate about the occasion? Where do you think this photograph was taken? What kind of family does this photograph portray? Does this family portrait remind you of any others you've seen?

Web Search

Search the Library of Congress online archive called American Memory (<http://memory.loc.gov/ammem/>) by entering a subject related to your family's history, such as a state or city where your ancestors or family have lived, an industry a relative has worked in, or a historical event or natural disaster that affected your family in some way. Locate and study a specific photograph or document on this subject. Imagine that your family has a direct connection to the photo or document you have found. Write an imaginary narrative about one or more members of your family based on your finding.

■ For reading activities linked to this chapter, visit <bedfordstmartins.com/bedguide> and do a keyword search:

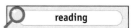

reading

E. B. White
Once More to the Lake

E. B. (Elwyn Brooks) White *(1899–1985) was born in Mount Vernon, New York. After serving in the army, he graduated from Cornell University and moved to Seattle to work as a reporter. His career led him back to the East Coast, where he joined the staff of the recently established* New Yorker *magazine in 1927. For half a century, his satires, poems, and essays helped define that magazine's distinctive style of elegant wit and social comment. He moved to Maine in 1933, and his widely read books for children,* Stuart Little *(1945),* Charlotte's Web *(1952), and* The Trumpet of the Swan *(1970), draw on his familiarity with the country to celebrate life's blend of sadness, happiness, love, and loss. In the following essay, first published in* Harper's *magazine in 1941, White reflects on the experience of returning with his son to a favorite scene from his own childhood.*

AS YOU READ: *Notice what, according to White, changes a person's perspective from childhood to adulthood.*

August 1941

One summer, along about 1904, my father rented a camp on a lake in Maine and took us all there for the month of August. We all got ringworm from some kittens and had to rub Pond's Extract on our arms and legs night and morning, and my father rolled over in a canoe with all his clothes on; but outside of that the vacation was a success and from then on none of us ever thought there was any place in the world like that lake in Maine. We returned summer after summer—always on August 1 for one month. I have since become a salt-water man, but sometimes in summer there are days when the restlessness of the tides and the fearful cold of the sea water and the incessant wind that blows across the afternoon and into the evening make me wish for the placidity of a lake in the woods. A few weeks ago this feeling got so strong I bought myself a couple of bass hooks and a spinner and returned to the lake where we used to go, for a week's fishing and to revisit old haunts.

I took along my son, who had never had any fresh water up his nose and 2
who had seen lily pads only from train windows. On the journey over to the
lake I began to wonder what it would be like. I wondered how time would
have marred this unique, this holy spot—the coves and streams, the hills
that the sun set behind, the camps and the paths behind the camps. I was
sure that the tarred road would have found it out, and I wondered in what
other ways it would be desolated. It is strange how much you can remember
about places like that once you allow your mind to return into the grooves
that lead back. You remember one thing, and that suddenly reminds you of
another thing. I guess I remembered clearest of all the early mornings, when
the lake was cool and motionless, remembered how the bedroom smelled of
the lumber it was made of and of the wet woods whose scent entered
through the screen. The partitions in the camp were thin and did not extend
clear to the top of the rooms, and as I was always the first up I would dress
softly so as not to wake the others, and sneak out into the sweet outdoors
and start out in the canoe, keeping close along the shore in the long shadows
of the pines. I remembered being very careful never to rub my paddle against
the gunwale° for fear of disturbing the stillness of the cathedral.

The lake had never been what you would call a wild lake. There were 3
cottages sprinkled around the shores, and it was in farming country although the shores of the lake were quite heavily wooded. Some of the cottages were owned by nearby farmers, and you would live at the shore and
eat your meals at the farmhouse. That's what our family did. But although it
wasn't wild, it was a fairly large and undisturbed lake and there were places
in it that, to a child at least, seemed infinitely remote and primeval.

I was right about the tar: it led to within half a mile of the shore. But 4
when I got back there, with my boy, and we settled into a camp near a farmhouse and into the kind of summertime I had known, I could tell that it was
going to be pretty much the same as it had been before—I knew it, lying in
bed the first morning smelling the bedroom and hearing the boy sneak quietly out and go off along the shore in a boat. I began to sustain the illusion
that he was I, and therefore, by simple transposition, that I was my father.
This sensation persisted, kept cropping up all the time we were there. It was
not an entirely new feeling, but in this setting it grew much stronger. I seemed
to be living a dual existence. I would be in the middle of some simple act, I
would be picking up a bait box or laying down a table fork, or I would be saying something and suddenly it would be not I but my father who was saying
the words or making the gesture. It gave me a creepy sensation.

We went fishing the first morning. I felt the same damp moss covering 5
the worms in the bait can, and saw the dragonfly alight on the tip of my rod
as it hovered a few inches from the surface of the water. It was the arrival of
this fly that convinced me beyond any doubt that everything was as it always
had been, that the years were a mirage, and that there had been no years.
The small waves were the same, chucking the rowboat under the chin as we

---

gunwale: Upper edge of the side of a boat.

fished at anchor, and the boat was the same boat, the same color green and the ribs broken in the same places, and under the floorboards the same fresh water leavings and debris — the dead hellgrammite, the wisps of moss, the rusty discarded fishhook, the dried blood from yesterday's catch. We stared silently at the tips of our rods, at the dragonflies that came and went. I lowered the tip of mine into the water, tentatively, pensively dislodging the fly, which darted two feet away, poised, darted two feet back, and came to rest again a little farther up the rod. There had been no years between the ducking of this dragonfly and the other one — the one that was part of memory. I looked at the boy, who was silently watching his fly, and it was my hands that held his rod, my eyes watching. I felt dizzy and didn't know which rod I was at the end of.

We caught two bass, hauling them in briskly as though they were mack- 6 erel, pulling them over the side of the boat in a businesslike manner without any landing net, and stunning them with a blow on the back of the head. When we got back for a swim before lunch, the lake was exactly where we had left it, the same number of inches from the dock, and there was only the merest suggestion of a breeze. This seemed an utterly enchanted sea, this lake you could leave to its own devices for a few hours and come back to, and find that it had not stirred, this constant and trustworthy body of water. In the shallows, the dark, water-soaked sticks and twigs, smooth and old, were undulating in clusters on the bottom against the clean ribbed sand, and the track of the mussel was plain. A school of minnows swam by, each minnow with its small individual shadow, doubling the attendance, so clear and sharp in the sunlight. Some of the other campers were in swimming, along the shore, one of them with a cake of soap, and the water felt thin and clear and unsubstantial. Over the years there had been this person with the cake of soap, this cultist, and here he was. There had been no years.

Up to the farmhouse to dinner through the teeming dusty field, the 7 road under our sneakers was only a two-track road. The middle track was missing, the one with the marks of the hooves and the splotches of dried, flaky manure. There had always been three tracks to choose from in choosing which track to walk in; now the choice was narrowed down to two. For a moment I missed terribly the middle alternative. But the way led past the tennis court, and something about the way it lay there in the sun reassured me; the tape had loosened along the backline, the alleys were green with plantains° and other weeds, and the net (installed in June and removed in September) sagged in the dry noon, and the whole place steamed with midday heat and hunger and emptiness. There was a choice of pie for dessert, and one was blueberry and one was apple, and the waitresses were the same country girls, there having been no passage of time, only the illusion of it as in a dropped curtain — the waitresses were still fifteen; their hair had been washed, that was the only difference — they had been to the movies and seen the pretty girls with the clean hair.

plantains: Common wild plants.

Summertime, oh, summertime, pattern of life indelible° with fade-   8
proof lake, the wood unshatterable, the pasture with the sweetfern and the
juniper forever and ever, summer without end; this was the background,
and the life along the shore was the design, the cottages with their innocent
and tranquil design, their tiny docks with the flagpole and the American flag
floating against the white clouds in the blue sky, the little paths over the
roots of the trees leading from camp to camp and the paths leading back to
the outhouses and the can of lime for sprinkling, and at the souvenir counters at the store the miniature birchbark canoes and the postcards that
showed things looking a little better than they looked. This was the American family at play, escaping the city heat, wondering whether the newcom-
ers in the camp at the head of the cove were "common" or "nice," wondering whether it was true that the people who drove up for Sunday dinner at
the farmhouse were turned away because there wasn't enough chicken.

It seemed to me, as I kept remembering all this, that those times and   9
those summers had been infinitely precious and worth saving. There had
been jollity and peace and goodness. The arriving (at the beginning of August) had been so big a business in itself, at the railway station the farm
wagon drawn up, the first smell of the pine-laden air, the first glimpse of the
smiling farmer, and the great importance of the trunks and your father's
enormous authority in such matters, and the feel of the wagon under you
for the long ten-mile haul, and at the top of the last long hill catching the
first view of the lake after eleven months of not seeing this cherished body
of water. The shouts and cries of the other campers when they saw you, and
the trunks to be unpacked, to give up their rich burden. (Arriving was less
exciting nowadays, when you sneaked up in your car and parked it under a
tree near the camp and took out the bags and in five minutes it was all over,
no fuss, no loud wonderful fuss about trunks.)

Peace and goodness and jollity. The only thing that was wrong now,   10
really, was the sound of the place, an unfamiliar nervous sound of the
outboard motors. This was the note that jarred, the one thing that would
sometimes break the illusion and set the years moving. In those other
summertimes all motors were inboard; and when they were at a little distance, the noise they made was a sedative, an ingredient of summer sleep.
They were one-cylinder and two-cylinder engines, and some were make-and-
break and some were jump-spark, but they all made a sleepy sound across
the lake. The one-lungers throbbed and fluttered, and the twin-cylinder ones
purred and purred, and that was a quiet sound, too. But now the campers
all had outboards. In the daytime, in the hot mornings, these motors made
a petulant, irritable sound; at night in the still evening when the afterglow
lit the water, they whined about one's ears like mosquitoes. My boy loved
our rented outboard, and his great desire was to achieve single-handed mastery over it, and authority, and he soon learned the trick of choking it a little
(but not too much), and the adjustment of the needle valve. Watching him I

indelible: Unable to be removed.

would remember the things you could do with the old one-cylinder engine with the heavy flywheel,° how you could have it eating out of your hand if you got really close to it spiritually. Motorboats in those days didn't have clutches, and you would make a landing by shutting off the motor at the proper time and coasting in with a dead rudder. But there was a way of reversing them, if you learned the trick, by cutting the switch and putting it on again exactly on the final dying revolution of the flywheel, so that it would kick back against compression and begin reversing. Approaching a dock in a strong following breeze, it was difficult to slow up sufficiently by the ordinary coasting method, and if a boy felt he had complete mastery over his motor, he was tempted to keep it running beyond its time and then reverse it a few feet from the dock. It took a cool nerve, because if you threw the switch a twentieth of a second too soon you would catch the flywheel when it still had speed enough to go up past center, and the boat would leap ahead, charging bull-fashion at the dock.

We had a good week at the camp. The bass were biting well and the sun   11
shone endlessly, day after day. We would be tired at night and lie down in the accumulated heat of the little bedrooms after the long hot day and the breeze would stir almost imperceptibly outside and the smell of the swamp drift in through the rusty screens. Sleep would come easily and in the morning the red squirrel would be on the roof, tapping out his gay routine. I kept remembering everything, lying in bed in the mornings — the small steamboat that had a long rounded stern like the lip of a Ubangi,° and how quietly she ran on the moonlight sails, when the older boys played their mandolins° and the girls sang and we ate doughnuts dipped in sugar, and how sweet the music was on the water in the shining night, and what it had felt like to think about girls then. After breakfast we would go up to the store and the things were in the same place — the minnows in a bottle, the plugs and spinners disarranged and pawed over by the youngsters from the boys' camp, the Fig Newtons and the Beeman's gum. Outside, the road was tarred and cars stood in front of the store. Inside, all was just as it had always been, except there was more Coca-Cola and not so much Moxie and root beer and birch beer and sarsaparilla. We would walk out with the bottle of pop apiece and sometimes the pop would backfire up our noses and hurt. We explored the streams, quietly, where the turtles slid off the sunny logs and dug their way into the soft bottom; and we lay on the town wharf and fed worms to the tame bass. Everywhere we went I had trouble making out which was I, the one walking at my side, the one walking in my pants.

One afternoon while we were at that lake a thunderstorm came up. It   12
was the revival of an old melodrama that I had seen long ago with childish awe. The second-act climax of the drama of the electrical disturbance over a

---

flywheel: A heavy wheel revolving on a shaft to regulate machinery.   **Ubangi:** People who live near the Ubangi River in the Central African Republic and Zaire. The women traditionally pierce and stretch their lips around flat wooden disks.   **mandolins:** Small stringed instruments often used in ballads and folk music.

lake in America had not changed in any important respect. This was the big scene. The whole thing was so familiar, the first feeling of oppression and heat and a general air around camp of not wanting to go very far away. In midafternoon (it was all the same) a curious darkening of the sky, and a lull in everything that had made life tick; and then the way the boats suddenly swung the other way at their moorings with the coming of a breeze out of the new quarter, and the premonitory° rumble. Then the kettle drum, then the snare, then the bass drum and cymbals, then crackling light against the dark, and the gods grinning and licking their chops in the hills. Afterward the calm, the rain steadily rustling in the calm lake, the return of light and hope and spirits, and the campers running out in joy and relief to go swimming in the rain, their bright cries perpetuating the deathless joke about how they were getting simply drenched, and the children screaming with delight at the new sensation of bathing in the rain, and the joke about getting drenched linking the generations in a strong indestructible chain. And the comedian who waded in carrying an umbrella.

When the others went swimming my son said he was going in, too. He   13
pulled his dripping trunks from the line where they had hung all through the shower and wrung them out. Languidly, and with no thought of going in, I watched him, his hard little body, skinny and bare, saw him wince slightly as he pulled up around his vitals the small, soggy, icy garment. As he buckled the swollen belt, suddenly my groin felt the chill of death.

Questions to Start You Thinking

1. CONSIDERING MEANING: How have the lake and the surrounding community, as White depicts them, changed since he was a boy?

2. IDENTIFYING WRITING STRATEGIES: Notice the details White uses to describe life at the lake. How many different sensory experiences do his images evoke? Identify and then analyze at least four memorable images from the essay, explaining what makes each memorable.

3. READING CRITICALLY: White compares the past with the present to show that "there had been no years" since his childhood at the lake (paragraph 5). How does this comparison shape the tone of White's essay? How does the tone change at the end? What is the effect of this sudden change?

4. EXPANDING VOCABULARY: Define *primeval* (paragraph 3), *transposition* (paragraph 4), *hellgrammite* (paragraph 5), *undulating, cultist* (paragraph 6), and *petulant* (paragraph 10). What is White's purpose in using adult words rather than a child's words to look back on his childhood experience?

5. MAKING CONNECTIONS: Both White and Danzy Senna ("The Color of Love," pp. 411–15) write about a relationship with a close family member. While they both use narration to reveal the intricacies of these relationships, Senna adds dialogue to her narration. As a reader, are you affected more by one approach than the other? Which approach do you find more successful? Or do you find each effective in its own way?

premonitory: Warning.

Journal Prompts

1. Describe a place that has special meaning for you. Why is it special?
2. Use White's description of a thunderstorm (paragraph 12) as a model to describe a natural event that you have witnessed.

Suggestions for Writing

1. Think of a place you knew as a child and then visited again as an adult. Write an essay explaining how the place had changed and not changed. Use observation and recall to make the place as memorable for your readers as it was for you.
2. How do you think nostalgia—the desire to return to an important and pleasant time in the past—influences the way we remember our own experiences? Use examples from White's essay and from your experience to illustrate your explanation.

Amy Tan
Mother Tongue

Amy Tan *was born in 1952 in Oakland, California, a few years after her parents immigrated to the United States from China. After receiving a B.A. in English and linguistics and an M.A. in linguistics from San Jose State University, Tan worked as a specialist in language development for five years before becoming a freelance business writer in 1981. Tan wrote her first short story in 1985; it became the basis for her first novel,* The Joy Luck Club *(1990), which was a phenomenal best-seller and was made into a movie. Tan's second novel,* The Kitchen God's Wife *(1991), was equally popular. She has also written children's books,* The Moon Lady *(1992) and* The Chinese Siamese Cat *(1994), and edited* Best American Short Stories *(1999). With* The One Hundred Secret Senses *(1995), Tan's ambitious third novel, she returned to themes of familial relationships, loyalty, and ways of reconciling the past with the present. Most recently she published* The Bonesetter's Daughter *(2001) and* The Opposite of Fate: A Book of Musings *(2003). "Mother Tongue" first appeared in* Threepenny Review *in 1990; in this essay, Tan explores the effect of her mother's "broken" English—the language Tan grew up with—on her life and writing.*

AS YOU READ: *Identify the difficulties Tan says exist for a child growing up in a family that speaks nonstandard English.*

I am not a scholar of English or literature. I cannot give you much more 1 than personal opinions on the English language and its variations in this country or others.

I am a writer. And by that definition, I am someone who has always 2 loved language. I am fascinated by language in daily life. I spend a great deal of my time thinking about the power of language — the way it can evoke an emotion, a visual image, a complex idea, or a simple truth. Language is the tool of my trade. And I use them all — all the Englishes I grew up with.

Recently, I was made keenly aware of the different Englishes I do use. I was giving a talk to a large group of people, the same talk I had already given to half a dozen other groups. The nature of the talk was about my writing, my life, and my book, *The Joy Luck Club*. The talk was going along well enough, until I remembered one major difference that made the whole talk sound wrong. My mother was in the room. And it was perhaps the first time she had heard me give a lengthy speech, using the kind of English I have never used with her. I was saying things like, "The intersection of memory upon imagination" and "There is an aspect of my fiction that relates to thus-and-thus" — a speech filled with carefully wrought° grammatical phrases, burdened, it suddenly seemed to me, with nominalized° forms, past perfect tenses, conditional phrases, all the forms of Standard English that I had learned in school and through books, the forms of English I did not use at home with my mother.

Just last week, I was walking down the street with my mother, and I again found myself conscious of the English I was using, and the English I do use with her. We were talking about the price of new and used furniture and I heard myself saying this: "Not waste money that way." My husband was with us as well, and he didn't notice any switch in my English. And then I realized why. It's because over the twenty years we've been together I've often used that same kind of English with him, and sometimes he even uses it with me. It has become our language of intimacy, a different sort of English that relates to family talk, the language I grew up with.

So you'll have some idea of what this family talk I heard sounds like, I'll quote what my mother said during a recent conversation which I video-taped and then transcribed.° During this conversation, my mother was talking about a political gangster in Shanghai who had the same last name as her family's, Du, and how the gangster in his early years wanted to be adopted by her family, which was rich by comparison. Later, the gangster became more powerful, far richer than my mother's family, and one day showed up at my mother's wedding to pay his respects. Here's what she said in part:

"Du Yusong having business like fruit stand. Like off the street kind. He is like Du Zong — but not Tsung-ming Island people. The local people call putong, the river east side, he belong to that side local people. That man want to ask Du Zong father take him in like become own family. Du Zong father wasn't look down on him, but didn't take seriously, until that man big like become a mafia. Now important person, very hard to inviting him. Chinese way, came only to show respect, don't stay for dinner. Respect for making big celebration, he shows up. Mean gives lots of respect. Chinese

wrought: Crafted.   **nominalized:** Made into a noun from a verb.   **transcribed:** Made a written copy of what was said.

custom. Chinese social life that way. If too important won't have to stay too long. He come to my wedding. I didn't see, I heard it. I gone to boy's side, they have YMCA dinner. Chinese age I was nineteen."

You should know that my mother's expressive command of English be- 7 lies° how much she actually understands. She reads the *Forbes* report, listens to *Wall Street Week*, converses daily with her stockbroker, reads all of Shirley MacLaine's books with ease—all kinds of things I can't begin to understand. Yet some of my friends tell me they understand fifty percent of what my mother says. Some say they understand eighty to ninety percent. Some say they understand none of it, as if she were speaking pure Chinese. But to me, my mother's English is perfectly clear, perfectly natural. It's my mother tongue. Her language, as I hear it, is vivid, direct, full of observation and imagery. That was the language that helped shape the way I saw things, expressed things, made sense of the world.

Lately, I've been giving more thought to the kind of English my mother 8 speaks. Like others, I have described it to people as "broken" or "fractured" English. But I wince when I say that. It has always bothered me that I can think of no way to describe it other than "broken," as if it were damaged and needed to be fixed, as if it lacked a certain wholeness and soundness. I've heard other terms used, "limited English," for example. But they seem just as bad, as if everything is limited, including people's perceptions of the limited English speaker.

I know this for a fact, because when I was growing up, my mother's 9 "limited" English limited *my* perception of her. I was ashamed of her English. I believed that her English reflected the quality of what she had to say. That is, because she expressed them imperfectly her thoughts were imperfect. And I had plenty of empirical evidence to support me: the fact that people in department stores, at banks, and at restaurants did not take her seriously, did not give her good service, pretended not to understand her, or even acted as if they did not hear her.

My mother has long realized the limitations of her English as well. 10 When I was fifteen, she used to have me call people on the phone to pretend I was she. In this guise, I was forced to ask for information or even to complain and yell at people who had been rude to her. One time it was a call to her stockbroker in New York. She had cashed out her small portfolio and it just so happened we were going to go to New York the next week, our very first trip outside California. I had to get on the phone and say in an adolescent voice that was not very convincing, "This is Mrs. Tan."

And my mother was standing in the back whispering loudly, "Why he 11 don't send me check, already two weeks late. So mad he lie to me, losing me money."

And then I said in perfect English, "Yes, I'm getting rather concerned. 12 You had agreed to send the check two weeks ago, but it hasn't arrived."

belies: Shows to be false.

Then she began to talk more loudly. "What he want, I come to New 13
York tell him front of his boss, you cheating me?" And I was trying to
calm her down, make her be quiet, while telling the stockbroker, "I can't
tolerate any more excuses. If I don't receive the check immediately, I am
going to have to speak to your manager when I'm in New York next week."
And sure enough, the following week there we were in front of this astonished stockbroker, and I was sitting there red-faced and quiet, and my
mother, the real Mrs. Tan, was shouting at his boss in her impeccable broken English.

We used a similar routine just five days ago, for a situation that was far 14
less humorous. My mother had gone to the hospital for an appointment, to
find out about a benign brain tumor a CAT scan had revealed a month ago.
She said she had spoken very good English, her best English, no mistakes.
Still, she said, the hospital did not apologize when they said they had lost
the CAT scan and she had come for nothing. She said they did not seem to
have any sympathy when she told them she was anxious to know the exact
diagnosis, since her husband and son had both died of brain tumors. She
said they would not give her any more information until the next time and
she would have to make another appointment for that. So she said she
would not leave until the doctor called her daughter. She wouldn't budge.
And when the doctor finally called her daughter, me, who spoke in perfect
English—lo and behold—we had assurances the CAT scan would be
found, promises that a conference call on Monday would be held, and
apologies for any suffering my mother had gone through for a most regret-
table mistake.

I think my mother's English almost had an effect on limiting my possi- 15
bilities in life as well. Sociologists and linguists probably will tell you that a
person's developing language skills are more influenced by peers. But I think
that the language spoken in the family, especially in immigrant families
which are more insular, plays a large role in shaping the language of the
child. And I believe that it affected my results on achievement tests, IQ tests,
and the SAT. While my English skills were never judged as poor, compared
to math, English could not be considered my strong suit. In grade school I
did moderately well, getting perhaps B's, sometimes B-pluses, in English and
scoring perhaps in the sixtieth or seventieth percentile on achievement tests.
But those scores were not good enough to override the opinion that my true
abilities lay in math and science, because in those areas I achieved A's and
scored in the ninetieth percentile or higher.

This was understandable. Math is precise; there is only one correct an- 16
swer. Whereas, for me at least, the answers on English tests were always a
judgment call, a matter of opinion and personal experience. Those tests
were constructed around items like fill-in-the-blank sentence completion,
such as, "Even though Tom was _____ , Mary thought he was _____ ." And
the correct answer always seemed to be the most bland combinations of
thoughts, for example, "Even though Tom was shy, Mary thought he was
charming," with the grammatical structure "even though" limiting the cor-

rect answer to some sort of semantic° opposites, so you wouldn't get answers like, "Even though Tom was foolish, Mary thought he was ridiculous."
Well, according to my mother, there were very few limitations as to what
Tom could have been and what Mary might have thought of him. So I never
did well on tests like that.

The same was true with word analogies, pairs of words in which you   17
were supposed to find some sort of logical, semantic relationship — for example, "*Sunset* is to *nightfall* as _____ is to _____ ." And here you would be
presented with a list of four possible pairs, one of which showed the same
kind of relationship: *red* is to *stoplight*, *bus* is to *arrival*, *chills* is to *fever*, *yawn*
is to *boring*. Well, I could never think that way. I knew what the tests were
asking, but I could not block out of my mind the images already created
by the first pair, "*sunset* is to *nightfall*" — and I would see a burst of colors
against a darkening sky, the moon rising, the lowering of a curtain of stars.
And all the other pairs of words — *red, bus, stoplight, boring* — just threw up a
mass of confusing images, making it impossible for me to sort out something as logical as saying: "A sunset precedes nightfall" is the same as "a chill
precedes a fever." The only way I would have gotten that answer right would
have been to imagine an associative situation, for example, my being dis-
obedient and staying out past sunset, catching a chill at night, which turns
into feverish pneumonia as punishment, which indeed did happen to me.

I have been thinking about all this lately, about my mother's English,   18
about achievement tests. Because lately I've been asked, as a writer, why
there are not more Asian Americans enrolled in creative writing programs.
Why do so many Chinese students go into engineering? Well, these are
broad sociological questions I can't begin to answer. But I have noticed in
surveys — in fact, just last week — that Asian students, as a whole, always do
significantly better on math achievement tests than in English. And this
makes me think that there are other Asian American students whose English
spoken in the home might also be described as "broken" or "limited." And
perhaps they also have teachers who are steering them away from writing
and into math and science, which is what happened to me.

Fortunately, I happen to be rebellious in nature and enjoy the challenge   19
of disproving assumptions made about me. I became an English major my
first year in college, after being enrolled as pre-med. I started writing nonfiction as a freelancer the week after I was told by my former boss that
writing was my worst skill and I should hone my talents toward account
management.

But it wasn't until 1985 that I finally began to write fiction. And at first I   20
wrote using what I thought to be wittily crafted sentences, sentences that
would finally prove I had mastery over the English language. Here's an example from the first draft of a story that later made its way into *The Joy Luck*

---

semantic: Relating to the meaning of language.

Club, but without this line: "That was my mental quandary in its nascent° state." A terrible line, which I can barely pronounce.

Fortunately, for reasons I won't get into today, I later decided I should 21 envision a reader for the stories I would write. And the reader I decided upon was my mother, because these were stories about mothers. So with this reader in mind — and in fact she did read my early drafts — I began to write stories using all the Englishes I grew up with: the English I spoke to my mother, which for lack of a better term might be described as "simple"; the English she used with me, which for lack of a better term might be described as "broken"; my translation of her Chinese, which could certainly be described as "watered down"; and what I imagined to be her translation of her Chinese if she could speak in perfect English, her internal language, and for that I sought to preserve the essence, but neither an English nor a Chinese structure. I wanted to capture what language ability tests can never reveal: her intent, her passion, her imagery, the rhythms of her speech, and the nature of her thoughts.

Apart from what any critic had to say about my writing, I knew I had 22 succeeded where it counted when my mother finished reading my book and gave me her verdict: "So easy to read."

Questions to Start You Thinking

1. CONSIDERING MEANING: What are the Englishes that Tan grew up with? What other Englishes has she used in her life? What does each English have that gives it an advantage over the other Englishes in certain situations?

2. IDENTIFYING WRITING STRATEGIES: What examples does Tan use to analyze the various Englishes she uses? How has Tan been able to synthesize her Englishes successfully into her present style of writing fiction?

3. READING CRITICALLY: Although Tan explains that she writes using "all the Englishes" she has known throughout her life (paragraph 21), she doesn't do that in this essay. What are the differences between the English Tan uses in this essay and the kinds she says she uses in her fiction? How does the language she uses here fit the purpose of her essay?

4. EXPANDING VOCABULARY: In paragraph 9, Tan writes that she had "plenty of empirical evidence" that her mother's "limited" English meant that her mother's thoughts were "imperfect" as well. Define *empirical*. What does Tan's use of this word tell us about her present attitude toward the way she judged her mother when she was growing up?

5. MAKING CONNECTIONS: Tan and Richard Rodriguez ("Public and Private Language," pp. 524–29) recount learning English as they grew up in homes where English was a second language. What similarities do you find in their experiences and the obstacles they faced? How did learning English affect their self-images? How did it influence their relationships with their families?

---

nascent: Beginning; only partly formed.

Journal Prompts

1. Describe one of the Englishes you use to communicate. When do you use it, and when do you avoid using it?

2. In what ways are you a "translator," if not of language, then of current events and fashions, for your parents or other members of your family?

Suggestions for Writing

1. In a personal essay explain an important event in your family's history, using your family's various Englishes or other languages.

2. Take note of and, if possible, transcribe one conversation you have had with a parent or other family member, one with a teacher, and one with a close friend. Write an essay comparing and contrasting the "languages" of the three conversations. How do the languages differ? How do you account for these differences? What do you think would happen if someone used "teacher language" to talk to a friend or used "friend language" in a class discussion or paper?

Anna Quindlen
Evan's Two Moms

Anna Quindlen *was born in 1953 in Philadelphia. After graduating from Barnard College in 1974, she worked briefly as a reporter for the* New York Post *before moving to the* New York Times. *There she wrote the "About New York" column and then two syndicated columns: "Life in the 30s," which drew on her experiences with her family and neighborhood, and until 1994, when she left the* Times, *"Public and Private," which explored more political issues. She is currently a contributing editor and columnist for* Newsweek. *Quindlen won the Pulitzer Prize for commentary in 1992. In addition to her two collections of columns,* Living Out Loud *(1986) and* Thinking Out Loud *(1993), Quindlen has also written four novels—* Object Lessons *(1991),* One True Thing *(1994),* Black and Blue *(1998), and* Blessings *(2002)—as well as the advice book* A Short Guide to a Happy Life *(2000). In "Evan's Two Moms," written in 1992, Quindlen emphatically argues that gay marriage should be legalized.*

AS YOU READ: *Identify the main points Quindlen uses to support her position.*

Evan has two moms. This is no big thing. Evan has always had two moms—in his school file, on his emergency forms, with his friends. "Ooooh, Evan, you're lucky," they sometimes say. "You have two moms." It sounds like a sitcom, but until last week it was emotional truth without legal bulwark.° That was when a judge in New York approved the adoption

bulwark: Strong support.

of a six-year-old boy by his biological mother's lesbian partner. Evan. Evan's mom. Evan's other mom. A kid, a psychologist, a pediatrician. A family.

The matter of Evan's two moms is one in a series of events over the last 2 year that lead to certain conclusions. A Minnesota appeals court granted guardianship of a woman left a quadriplegic in a car accident to her lesbian lover, the culmination of a seven-year battle in which the injured woman's parents did everything possible to negate the partnership between the two. A lawyer in Georgia had her job offer withdrawn after the state attorney general found out that she and her lesbian lover were planning a marriage ceremony; she's brought suit. The computer company Lotus announced that the gay partners of employees would be eligible for the same benefits as spouses.

Add to these public events the private struggles, the couples who go 3 from lawyer to lawyer to approximate legal protections their straight counterparts take for granted, the AIDS survivors who find themselves shut out of their partners' dying days by biological family members and shut out of their apartments by leases with a single name on the dotted line, and one solution is obvious.

Gay marriage is a radical notion for straight people and a conservative 4 notion for gay ones. After years of being sledgehammered by society, some gay men and lesbian women are deeply suspicious of participating in an institution that seems to have "straight world" written all over it.

But the rads of twenty years ago, straight and gay alike, have other 5 things on their minds today. Family is one, and the linchpin of family has commonly been a loving commitment between two adults. When same-sex couples set out to make that commitment, they discover that they are at a disadvantage: No joint tax returns. No health insurance coverage for an uninsured partner. No survivor's benefits from Social Security. None of the automatic rights, privileges, and responsibilities society attaches to a marriage contract. In Madison, Wisconsin, a couple who applied at the Y with their kids for a family membership were turned down because both were women. It's one of those small things that can make you feel small.

Some took marriage statutes that refer to "two persons" at their word 6 and applied for a license. The results were court decisions that quoted the Bible and embraced circular argument: marriage is by definition the union of a man and a woman because that is how we've defined it.

No religion should be forced to marry anyone in violation of its tenets,° 7 although ironically it is now only in religious ceremonies that gay people can marry, performed by clergy who find the blessing of two who love each other no sin. But there is no secular° reason that we should take a patchwork approach of corporate, governmental, and legal steps to guarantee what can be done simply, economically, conclusively, and inclusively with the words "I do."

---

tenets: Principles.   **secular:** Relating to nonreligious matters.

"Fran and I chose to get married for the same reasons that any two   8
people do," said the lawyer who was fired in Georgia. "We fell in love; we
wanted to spend our lives together." Pretty simple.

Consider the case of *Loving v. Virginia*, aptly named. At the time, sixteen   9
states had laws that barred interracial marriage, relying on natural law, that
amorphous° grab bag for justifying prejudice. Sounding a little like God
throwing Adam and Eve out of paradise, the trial judge suspended the one-
year sentence of Richard Loving, who was white, and his wife, Mildred, who
was black, provided they got out of the State of Virginia.

In 1967 the Supreme Court found such laws to be unconstitutional.   10
Only twenty-five years ago and it was a crime for a black woman to marry a
white man. Perhaps twenty-five years from now we will find it just as incredible that two people of the same sex were not entitled to legally commit
themselves to each other. Love and commitment are rare enough; it seems
absurd to thwart them in any guise.

Questions to Start You Thinking

1. CONSIDERING MEANING: According to Quindlen, what is unjust about not
   allowing gay men and lesbians to marry *legally*?

2. IDENTIFYING WRITING STRATEGIES: Quindlen ends her essay with a comparison of gay marriage and interracial marriage (paragraphs 9 and 10). How
   does she use this comparison to support her argument? Do you think it is a
   valid comparison? Why, or why not?

3. READING CRITICALLY: What kinds of appeals does Quindlen use in her essay?
   How are they appropriate or inappropriate for addressing her opponents'
   arguments? (See pp. 39–40 for an explanation of kinds of appeals.)

4. EXPANDING VOCABULARY: Define *marriage* as Quindlen would define it. How
   does her definition of the term differ from the one in the dictionary?

5. MAKING CONNECTIONS: What privileges of the majority culture are gay families and immigrant families (Tan, "Mother Tongue," pp. 397–402) sometimes denied?

Journal Prompts

1. In your opinion, is the dictionary definition of *marriage* adequate? If so,
   how do you think it should be revised? If you think the dictionary definition is fine, defend it against attack.

2. Imagine that you have the power to design and create the perfect parents.
   What would they be like? What criteria would they have to meet to live up
   to your vision of ideal parents?

---

amorphous: Having no specific shape.

Suggestions for Writing

1. Describe the most unconventional family you know. How is this family different from other families? How is it the same?

2. In your opinion, would two parents of the same gender help or hurt a child's development? Write an essay comparing and contrasting the possible benefits and disadvantages of this type of family. Use specific examples — hypothetical or gathered from your own observation or reading — to illustrate your argument.

Anjula Razdan
What's Love Got to Do with It?

Anjula Razdan *is an associate editor of* Utne *magazine, where she writes on topics ranging from international politics to pop culture. The daughter of Indian immigrants whose marriage was arranged, Razdan grew up in Illinois and currently lives in Minneapolis, Minnesota. In this selection, which appeared in* Utne *in 2003, Razdan asks her readers to consider whether arranging marriages might more effectively create lasting relationships than choosing mates based on romantic attraction. To explore this question, she draws on her own experiences and observations as well as the testimony of experts.*

AS YOU READ: *Look for Razdan's account of both the benefits and the drawbacks of arranged marriages.*

One of the greatest pleasures of my teen years was sitting down with a   1
bag of cinnamon Red Hots and a new LaVyrle Spencer romance, immersing myself in another tale of star-crossed lovers drawn together by the heart's mysterious alchemy.° My mother didn't get it. "Why are you reading that?" she would ask, her voice tinged with both amusement and horror. Everything in her background told her that romance was a waste of time.

Born and raised in Illinois by parents who emigrated from India thirty-   2
five years ago, I am the product of an arranged marriage, and yet I grew up under the spell of Western romantic love — first comes love, *then* comes marriage — which both puzzled and dismayed my parents. Their relationship was set up over tea and samosas° by their grandfathers, and they were already engaged when they went on their first date, a chaperoned trip to the movies. My mom and dad still barely knew each other on their wedding day — and they certainly hadn't fallen in love. Yet both were confident that their shared values, beliefs, and family background would form a strong bond that, over time, would develop into love.

alchemy: A medieval predecessor of chemistry that aimed to turn base metals into gold.
samosas: Small, fried Indian pastries filled with seasoned vegetables or meat.

"But, what could they possibly know of *real love?*" I would ask myself 3
petulantly° after each standoff with my parents over whether or not I could
date in high school (I couldn't) and whether I would allow them to arrange
my marriage (I wouldn't). The very idea of an arranged marriage offended
my ideas of both love and liberty — to me, the act of choosing whom to love
represented the very essence of freedom. To take away that choice seemed
like an attack not just on my autonomy as a person, but on democracy itself.

And, yet, even in the supposedly liberated West, the notion of choosing 4
your mate is a relatively recent one. Until the nineteenth century, writes historian E. J. Graff in *What Is Marriage For? The Strange Social History of Our
Most Intimate Institution* (Boston: Beacon Press, 1999), arranged marriages
were quite common in Europe as a way of forging alliances, ensuring inheri-
tances, and stitching together the social, political, and religious needs of a
community. Love had nothing to do with it.

Fast forward a couple hundred years to twenty-first-century America, 5
and you see a modern, progressive society where people are free to choose
their mates, for the most part, based on love instead of social or economic
gain. But for many people, a quiet voice from within wonders: Are we really
better off? Who hasn't at some point in their life — at the end of an ill-fated
relationship or midway through dinner with the third "date-from-hell" this
month — longed for a matchmaker to find the right partner? No hassles. No
effort. No personal ads or blind dates.

The point of the Western romantic ideal is to live "happily ever after," 6
yet nearly half of all marriages in this country end in divorce, and the number of never-married adults grows each year. Boundless choice notwith-
standing, what does it mean when the marital success rate is the statistical
equivalent of a coin toss?

"People don't really know how to choose a long-term partner," offers 7
Dr. Alvin Cooper, the director of the San Jose Marital Services and Sexuality
Centre and a staff psychologist at Stanford University. "The major reasons
that people find and get involved with somebody else are proximity and
physical attraction. And both of these factors are terrible predictors of long-
term happiness in a relationship."

At the moment we pick a mate, Cooper says, we are often blinded by 8
passion and therefore virtually incapable of making a sound decision.

Psychology Today editor Robert Epstein agrees. "[It's] like getting drunk 9
and marrying someone in Las Vegas," he quips. A former director of the
Cambridge Center for Behavioral Studies, Epstein holds a decidedly unro-
mantic view of courtship and love. Indeed, he argues it is our myths of "love
at first sight" and "a knight in a shining Porsche" that get so many of us into
trouble. When the heat of passion wears off — and it always does, he says —
you can be left with virtually nothing "except lawyer's bills."

petulantly: Irritably.

Epstein points out that many arranged marriages result in an enduring 10 love because they promote compatibility and rational deliberation ahead of passionate impulse. Epstein himself is undertaking a bold step to prove his theory that love can be learned. He wrote an editorial in *Psychology Today* last year seeking women to participate in the experiment with him. He proposed to choose one of the "applicants," and together they would attempt to fall in love — consciously and deliberately. After receiving more than 1,000 responses, none of which seemed right, Epstein yielded just a little to impulse, asking Gabriela, an intriguing Venezuelan woman he met on a plane, to join him in the project. After an understandable bout of cold feet, she eventually agreed.

In a "love contract" the two signed on Valentine's Day this year to seal 11 the deal, Epstein stipulates that he and Gabriela must undergo intensive counseling to learn how to communicate effectively and participate in a variety of exercises designed to foster mutual love. To help oversee and guide the project, Epstein has even formed an advisory board made up of high-profile relationship experts, most notably Dr. John Gray, who wrote the best-selling *Men Are from Mars, Women Are from Venus*. If the experiment pans out, the two will have learned to love each other within a year's time.

It may strike some as anathema° to be so premeditated about the 12 process of falling in love, but to hear Epstein tell it, most unions fail exactly because they aren't intentional enough; they're based on a roll of the dice and a determination to stake everything on love. What this means, Epstein says, is that most people lack basic relationship skills, and, as a result, most relationships lack emotional and psychological intimacy.

A divorced father of four, Epstein himself married for passion — "just 13 like I was told to do by the fairy tales and by the movies" — but eventually came to regret it. "I had the experience that so many people have now," he says, "which is basically looking at your partner and going, 'Who are you?'" Although Epstein acknowledges the non-Western tradition of arranged marriage is a complex, somewhat flawed institution, he thinks we can "distill key elements of [it] to help us learn how to create a new, more stable institution in the West."

Judging from the phenomenon of reality-TV shows like *Married by* 14 *America* and *Meet My Folks* and the recent increase in the number of professional matchmakers, the idea of arranging marriages (even if in nontraditional ways) seems to be taking hold in this country — perhaps nowhere more powerfully than in cyberspace. Online dating services attracted some twenty million people last year (roughly one-fifth of all singles — and growing), who used sites like Match.com and Yahoo Personals to hook up with potentially compatible partners. Web sites' search engines play the role of patriarchal grandfathers, searching for good matches based on any number of criteria that you select.

anathema: An abomination; blasphemy.

Cooper, the Stanford psychologist and author of *Sex and the Internet: A* 15
Guidebook for Clinicians (Brunner-Routledge, 2002) — and an expert in the
field of online sexuality — says that because online interaction tends to
downplay proximity, physical attraction, and face-to-face interaction, people
are more likely to take risks and disclose significant things about themselves. The result is that they attain a higher level of psychological and emotional intimacy than if they dated right away or hopped in the sack. Indeed,
online dating represents a return to what University of Chicago Humanities
Professor Amy Kass calls the "distanced nearness" of old-style courtship, an
intimate and protected (cyber)space that encourages self-revelation while
maintaining personal boundaries.

And whether looking for a fellow scientist, someone else who's HIV- 16
positive, or a B-movie film buff, an online dater has a much higher likelihood of finding "the one" due to the computer's capacity to sort through
thousands of potential mates. "That's what computers are all about — efficiency and sorting," says Cooper, who believes that online dating has the
potential to lower the nation's 50 percent divorce rate. There is no magic or
"chemistry" involved in love, Cooper insists. "It's specific, operationalizable
factors."

Love's mystery solved by "operationalizable factors"! Why does that 17
sound a little less than inspiring? Sure, for many people the Internet can efficiently facilitate love and help to nudge fate along. But, for the diehard
romantic who trusts in surprise, coincidence, and fate, the cyber-solution to
love lacks heart. "To the romantic," observes English writer Blake Morrison
in *The Guardian*, "every marriage is an arranged marriage — arranged by fate,
that is, which gives us no choice."

More than a century ago, Emily Dickinson mocked those who would 18
dissect birds to find the mechanics of song:

> *Split the Lark — and you'll find the Music*
> *Bulb after Bulb, in Silver rolled —*
> *Scantily dealt to the Summer Morning*
> *Saved for your Ear when Lutes be old.*
>
> *Loose the Flood — you shall find it patent —*
> *Gush after Gush, reserved for you —*
> *Scarlet Experiment! Skeptic Thomas!*
> *Now, do you doubt that your Bird was true?*

In other words, writes Deborah Blum in her book, *Sex on the Brain* (Pen- 19
guin, 1997), "kill the bird and [you] silence the melody." For some, nurturing the ideal of romantic love may be more important than the goal of love
itself. Making a more conscious choice in mating may help partners handle
the complex personal ties and obligations of marriage; but romantic love,
infused as it is with myth and projection and doomed passion, is a way to
live *outside* of life's obligations, outside of time itself — if only for a brief,
bright moment. Choosing love by rational means might not be worth it for

those souls who'd rather roll the dice and risk the possibility of ending up with nothing but tragic nobility and the bittersweet tang of regret.

In the end, who really wants to examine love too closely? I'd rather curl 20 up with a LaVyrle Spencer novel or dream up the French movie version of my life than live in a world where the mechanics of love — and its giddy, mysterious buzz — are laid bare. After all, to actually unravel love's mystery is, perhaps, to miss the point of it all.

Questions to Start You Thinking

1. CONSIDERING MEANING: According to the experts whom Razdan quotes, why is cyberspace an ideal venue for facilitating relationships?

2. IDENTIFYING WRITING STRATEGIES: How does Razdan use cause and effect to explain the high divorce rate in the United States?

3. READING CRITICALLY: What type of evidence does Razdan use to explore whether arranged marriages are more successful than relationships based on romantic attraction? Do you think the evidence is relevant, credible, and sufficient? Why, or why not? What other type of evidence might she have used?

4. EXPANDING VOCABULARY: In commenting on her parents' arranged marriage, Razdan asks in paragraph 3, "But what could they possibly know of *real love*?" How do you define *real love*? Do you think that Razdan would agree with your definition?

5. MAKING CONNECTIONS: The statement that "nearly half of all marriages in this country end in divorce" (paragraph 6) applies to Noel Perrin's marriage ("A Part-Time Marriage," pp. 416–18). Given his experiences, how do you think he would respond to Razdan's essay? Would he be in favor of arranged marriages?

Journal Prompts

1. Write a brief personal ad for a mate, using the writing style associated with personals. Keep in mind that the words you choose and the way you organize your ad reveal something about your personality.

2. One of the experts whom Razdan quotes mentions the myth of "love at first sight" (paragraph 9). Write about a time when you fell in love at first sight or present your opinion on whether such a thing exists.

Suggestions for Writing

1. Write an essay that uses your personal experiences and observations to develop a specific idea presented in Razdan's essay. For example, you might recall your own "date from hell" (paragraph 5), a friend's experience with an online dating service, or a matchmaker friend's success rate. Based on your experiences and observations, you might write about current dating practices or about "relationship skills" needed for a successful marriage.

2. Drawing examples from this reading and your own observations, write an essay arguing for or against arranged marriages. You might also do some research to find additional support for your argument.

Danzy Senna
The Color of Love

Danzy Senna, *born in 1970 in Boston, earned her B.A. at Stanford University and her M.F.A. from the University of California, Irvine. She teaches at the College of the Holy Cross, where she holds the William H. P. Jenks Chair in Contemporary Letters. Senna's essays and short stories have been widely anthologized, and her journalistic writing has appeared in such publications as* The Nation, Utne *magazine, and* Newsweek. *Her best-selling novel* Caucasia *(1988) won several awards, and in 2002 she received a prestigious Whiting Award, given each year to ten writers of exceptional ability and promise. In "The Color of Love," Senna, the daughter of a white mother and a black father, explores the complexities — racial and otherwise — of her relationship with her grandmother. The essay originally appeared in* O: The Oprah Magazine *in 2000.*

AS YOU READ: *Consider how her grandmother displays both love for Senna and prejudice toward her. How does Senna respond?*

We had this much in common: We were both women, and we were 1
both writers. But we were as different as two people can be and still exist in the same family. She was ancient — as white and dusty as chalk — and spent her days seated in a velvet armchair, passing judgments on the world below. She still believed in noble bloodlines; my blood had been mixed at conception. I believed there was no such thing as nobility or class or lineage, only systems designed to keep some people up in the big house and others outside, in the cold.

She was my grandmother. She was Irish but from that country's Protes- 2
tant elite, which meant she seemed more British than anything. She was an actress, a writer of plays and novels, and still unmarried in her thirties when she came to America to visit. One night while in Boston, she went to a dinner party, where she was seated next to a young lawyer with blood as blue as the ocean. Her pearl earring fell in his oyster soup — or so the story goes — and they fell in love. My grandmother married that lawyer and left her native Ireland for New England.

How she came to have black grandchildren is a story of opposites. It 3
was 1968 in Boston when her daughter — my mother — a small, blonde Wasp° poet, married my father, a tall and handsome black intellectual, in

---

Wasp: An acronym (for White Anglo-Saxon Protestant) referring to a member of the prevailing American social class.

an act that was as rebellious as it was hopeful. The products of that unlikely union — my older sister, my younger brother, and I — grew up in urban chaos, in a home filled with artists and political activists. The old lady across the river in Cambridge seemed to me an endangered species. Her walls were covered with portraits of my ancestors, the pale and dead men who had conquered Africa and built Boston long before my time. When I visited, their eyes followed me from room to room with what I imagined to be an expression of scorn. Among the portraits sat my grandmother, a bird who had flown in to remind us all that there had indeed been a time when lineage and caste° meant something. To me, young and dark and full of energy, she was the missing link between the living and the dead.

But her blood flowed through me, whether I liked it or not. I grew up to 4
be a writer, just like her. And as I struggled to tell my own stories — about race and class and post–civil rights America — I wondered who my grandmother had been before, in Dublin, when she was friend and confidante to literary giants such as William Butler Yeats and Samuel Beckett. Once, while snooping in her bedroom, I discovered her novels, the ones that had been published in Ireland when she was my age. I stared at her photograph on the jacket and wondered about the young woman who wore a mischievous smile. Had she ever worried about becoming so powerful that no man would want her? Did she now feel that she had sacrificed her career and wild Irish-woman dreams to become a wife and mother and proper Bostonian?

I longed to know her — to love her. But the differences between us were 5
real and alive, and they threatened to squelch our fragile connection. She was an alcoholic. In the evening, after a few glasses of gin, she could turn vicious. Though she held antiquated racist views, my grandmother would still have preferred to see my mother married and was saddened when my parents split in the seventies. She believed that a woman without a man was pitiable. The first question she always asked me when she saw me: "Do you have a man?" The second question: "What is he?" That was her way of finding out his race and background. She looked visibly pleased if he was a Wasp, neutral if he was Jewish, and disappointed if he was black.

My mother ignored her hurtful comments but felt them just the same. 6
She spent her visits to my grandmother's house slamming dishes in the kitchen, hissing her anger just out of hearing range, then raving, on the drive home, about what awful thing her mother had said this time. Like my mother, I knew the rule: I was not to disrespect elders. She was old and gray and would soon be gone. But I had inherited my grandmother's short temper. When I got angry, even as a child, I felt as if blood were rushing around in my head, red waves battering the shore. Words spilled from my mouth — cutting, vicious words that I regretted.

One autumn day in Cambridge, at my grandmother's place, I lost my 7
temper. I was home from college for the holidays, staying in her guest room. I woke from a nap to the sound of her enraged voice shouting at what I could only imagine was the television.

caste: Class or social group.

"Idiot! You damn fool!" she bellowed. "You stupid, stupid woman!" It 8
has to be *Jeopardy!*, I thought. She must be yelling at those tiny contestants
on the screen. She knows the answers to those questions better than they
do. But when the shouting went on for a beat too long, I went to the top of
the stairs and looked down into the living room. She was speaking to a real
person: her cleaning lady, a Greek woman named Mary, who was on her
hands and knees, nervously gathering the shards of a broken vase. My
grandmother stood over her, hands on hips, cursing.

"You fool," my grandmother repeated. "How in bloody hell could you 9
have done something so stupid?"

"Grandma." I didn't shout her name but said it loudly enough that she, 10
though hard of hearing, glanced up.

"Oh, darling!" she piped, suddenly cheerful. "Would you like a cup of 11
tea? You must be dreadfully tired."

Mary was on her feet again. She smiled nervously at me, then rushed 12
into the kitchen with the pieces of the broken vase.

I told myself to be a good girl, to be polite. But something snapped. I 13
marched down the stairs, and even she noticed something on my face that
made her sit in her velvet chair.

"Don't you ever talk to her that way," I shouted. "Where do you think 14
you are? Slavery was abolished long ago."

I stood over her, tall and long-limbed, daring her to speak. My grand- 15
mother shook her head. "It's about race, isn't it?"

"Race?" I said, baffled. "Mary's white. This is about respect — treating 16
other human beings with respect."

She wasn't hearing me. All she saw was color. "The tragedy about you," 17
she said soberly, "is that you are mixed." I felt those waves in my head:
"Your tragedy is that you're old and ignorant," I spat. "You don't know the
first thing about me."

She cried into her hands. She seemed diminished, a little old woman. 18
She looked up only to say, "You are a cruel girl."

I left her apartment trembling yet feeling exhilarated by what I had 19
done. But my elation soon turned to shame. I had taken on an old lady. And
for what? Her intolerance was, at her age, deeply entrenched. My rebuttals
couldn't change her.

Yet that fight marked the beginning of our relationship. I've since de- 20
cided that when you cease to express anger toward those who have hurt you,
you are essentially giving up on them. They are dead to you. But when you
express anger, it is a sign that they still matter, that they are worth the fight.

After that argument, my grandmother and I began a conversation. She 21
seemed to see me clearly for the first time, or perhaps she, a "cruel girl" herself, had simply met her match. And I no longer felt she was a relic. She was
a living, breathing human being who deserved to be spoken to as an equal.

I began visiting her more. I would drive to Cambridge and sit with 22
her, eating mixed nuts and sipping ginger ale, regaling° her with tales of my

---

regaling: Entertaining.

latest love drama or writing project. In her presence, I was proudly black and young and political, and she was who she was: subtly racist, terribly elitist and awfully funny. She still said things that angered me: She bemoaned my mother's marriage to my father, she said that I should marry not for love but for money, and she told me that I needn't identify as black, since I didn't look it. I snapped back at her. But she, with senility creeping in, didn't seem to hear me; each time I came, she said the same things.

Last summer I went into hiding to work on my second novel at a writ- 23 ers' retreat in New Hampshire. The place was a kind of paradise for creative souls, a hideaway where every writer had his or her own cabin in the woods with no phone or television—no distractions to speak of. But I was miserable. I could not write. Even the flies outside my window seemed to whisper, "Go out and play. Forget the novel. Leave it till tomorrow."

I woke one morning at four, the light outside my window still blue. I 24 felt panic and sadness, though I didn't know why. I got up, dressed, and went outside for a walk through the forest. But the panic persisted, and I began to cry. I assumed that my writer's block had seized me suddenly.

That night I ate dinner in the main house and received a call on the pay 25 phone from my mother. She told me my grandmother had fallen and broken her leg. But that wasn't all; she had subsequently suffered a heart attack. Her other organs were failing. I had to hurry if I wanted to say good-bye.

I drove to Boston that night, not believing that we could be losing her. 26 She would make it. I was certain. Sure, she was ninety-two, frail, unable to walk steadily. But she was lucid,° and her tongue was as sharp as ever. Somehow I had imagined her as indestructible, made immortal by power and cruelty and wit.

The woman I found in the hospital bed was barely recognizable. My 27 grandmother had always been fussy about her appearance. She never showed her face without makeup. Even in the day, when it was just she and the cleaning lady, she dressed as if she were ready for a cocktail party. At night she usually had cocktail parties; doddering° old men hovered around her, sipping Scotch and bantering about theater and politics.

My grandmother's face had swollen to twice its normal size, and tubes 28 came out of her nose. She had struggled so hard to pull them out that the nurses had tied her wrists to the bed rails. Her hair was gray and thin. Her body was withered and bruised, barely covered by the green hospital gown.

Her hazel eyes were all that was still recognizable, but the expression in 29 them was different from any I had ever seen on her—terror. She was terrified to die. She tried to rise when she saw me, and her eyes pleaded with me to help her, to save her, to get her out of this mess. I stood over her, and I felt only one thing: overwhelming love. Not a trace of anger. That dark gray rage I'd felt toward her was gone as I stroked her forehead and told her she would be okay, even knowing she would not.

---

lucid: Mentally sound.   **doddering:** Feeble.

For two days, my mother, her sisters, and I stood beside my grand- 30
mother, singing Irish ballads and reading passages to her from the works of
her favorite novelist, James Joyce. For the first time, she could not talk. At
one point, she gestured wildly for pen and paper. I brought her the pen and
the paper and held them up for her, but she was too weak for even that.
What came out was only a faint, incomprehensible line.

In death we are each reduced to our essence: the spirit we are when we 31
are born. The trappings we hold on to our whole lives — our race, our
money, our sex, our age, our politics — become irrelevant. My grandmother
became a child in that hospital bed, a spirit about to embark on an unknown journey, terrified and alone, no matter how many of us were
crowded around her. In the final hours, even her skin seemed to lose its
wrinkles and take on a waxy glow. Then, finally, the machines around us
went silent as she left us behind to squabble in the purgatory of the flesh.

Questions to Start You Thinking

1. CONSIDERING MEANING: What are the similarities and differences between
   Senna and her grandmother? How do the differences result in conflict?

2. IDENTIFYING WRITING STRATEGIES: Identify some ways Senna makes her grandmother come alive for readers. Where is her description vivid enough for
   you to see her as Senna does? Which details are particularly effective? Why?

3. READING CRITICALLY: How would you describe the tone of the essay? Support your opinion with specific passages.

4. EXPANDING VOCABULARY: In describing her grandmother, Senna explains, "I
   had imagined her as indestructible, made immortal by power and cruelty
   and wit" (paragraph 26). In your own words, define *immortal*. How can
   "power and cruelty and wit" make someone immortal?

5. MAKING CONNECTIONS: At one point in the essay, Senna suspects that her
   talented grandmother might have "worried about becoming so powerful
   that no man would want her" (paragraph 4). How does this possibility relate to the main idea in Ann Marlowe's "Pros and Amateurs" (pp. 495–99)?

Journal Prompts

1. Recall a time when you or someone you know was verbally abused. How
   did you respond?

2. At the end of her life, Senna's grandmother "gestured wildly for pen and
   paper" (paragraph 30), but she is unable to write. If she had been able to
   write a sentence or two, what do you think she might have written to
   Senna?

Suggestions for Writing

1. Senna notes that "when you cease to express anger toward those who have
   hurt you, you are essentially giving up on them" (paragraph 20). Write an

essay about a time when expressing anger had a positive effect on a relationship. Be sure to recall the events leading up to the confrontation as well as the resolution to the problem.

2. Senna suggests that her grandmother's prejudice is a result of age and ignorance. What other factors might contribute to an individual's prejudices? Write an essay presenting your views about how prejudice develops and what can be done to prevent it.

Noel Perrin
A Part-Time Marriage

*Noel Perrin (1927–2004) was born in New York City. He earned degrees at Williams College, Duke University, and Cambridge University and for over forty years taught English and environmental studies at Dartmouth College. For all his academic credentials, much of his fame as a writer comes from three volumes of essays on part-time farming—*Second Person Rural *(1980),* Third Person Rural *(1983), and* Last Person Rural *(1991). Perrin's* A Child's Delight *(1997) is a collection of essays celebrating some of his favorite but underappreciated children's books. In the following essay, first published in the* New York Times Magazine *on September 9, 1984, Perrin satirizes the postdivorce behavior of many middle-class couples and proposes a somewhat unusual remedy for the problems that plague modern marriages. In the paired selection that follows, Stephanie Coontz examines the difficulties of forming new stepfamilies and offers her own solutions.*

AS YOU READ: *Identify the problems with marriage that Perrin addresses.*

When my wife told me she wanted a divorce, I responded like any normal college professor. I hurried to the college library. I wanted to get hold of some books on divorce and find out what was happening to me.   1

Over the next week (my wife meanwhile having left), I read or skimmed   2
about twenty. Nineteen of them were no help at all. They offered advice on financial settlements. They told me my wife and I should have been in counseling. A bit late for *that* advice.

What I sought was insight. I especially wanted to understand what was   3
wrong with me that my wife had left, and not even for someone else, but just to be rid of *me*. College professors think they can learn that sort of thing from books.

As it turned out, I could. Or at least I got a start. The twentieth book was   4
a collection of essays by various sociologists, and one of the pieces took my breath away. It was like reading my own horoscope.

The two authors had studied a large group of divorced people much like   5
my wife and me. That is, they focused on middle-class Americans of the straight-arrow persuasion. Serious types, believers in marriage for life. Likely to be parents—and, on the whole, good parents. Likely to have pillar-of-the-community potential. But, nevertheless, all divorced.

Naturally there were many different reasons why all these people had   6
divorced, and many different ways they behaved after the divorce. But there
was a dominant pattern, and I instantly recognized myself in it. Recognized
my wife, too. Reading the essay told me not only what was wrong with me,
but also with her. It was the same flaw in both of us. It even gave me a hint
as to what my postdivorce behavior was likely to be, and how I might find
happiness in the future.

This is the story the essay told me. Or, rather, this is the story the essay   7
hinted at, and that I have since pieced together with much observation, a
number of embarrassingly personal questions put to divorced friends, and
to some extent from my own life.

Somewhere in some suburb or small city, a middle-class couple separate.   8
They are probably between thirty and forty years old. They own a house and
have children. The conscious or official reason for their separation is quite
different from what it would have been in their parents' generation. Then, it
would have been a man leaving his wife for another, and usually younger,
woman. Now it's a woman leaving her husband in order to find herself.

When they separate, the wife normally stays in the house they occupied   9
as a married couple. Neither wants to uproot the children. The husband
moves to an apartment, which is nearly always going to be closer to his
place of employment than his house was. The ex-wife will almost certainly
never see that apartment. The husband, however, sees his former house all
the time. Not only is he coming by to pick up the children for visits; if he
and his ex-wife are on reasonably good terms, he is apt to visit them right
there, while she makes use of the time to do errands or to see a friend.

Back when these two were married, they had an informal labor division.   10
She did inside work, he did outside. Naturally there were exceptions: she
gardened, and he did his share of the dishes, maybe even baked bread. But
mostly he mowed the lawn and fixed the lawn mower; she put up any new
curtains, often enough ones she had made herself.

One Saturday, six months or a year after they separated, he comes to see   11
the kids. He plans also to mow the lawn. Before she leaves, she says, "That
damn overhead garage door you got is off the track again. Do you think
you'd have time to fix it?" Apartment life makes him restless. He jumps at
the chance.

She, just as honorable and straight-arrow as he, has no idea of asking   12
for this as a favor. She invites him to stay for an early dinner. She may put
it indirectly — "Michael and Sally want their daddy to have supper with
them" — but he is clear that the invitation also proceeds from her.

Provided neither of them has met a really attractive other person yet,   13
they now move into a routine. He comes regularly to do the outside chores,
and always stays for dinner. If the children are young enough, he may read
to them before bedtime. She may wash his shirts.

One such evening, they both happen to be stirred not only by physical   14
desire but by loneliness. "Oh, you might as well come upstairs," she says
with a certain self-contempt. He needs no second invitation; they are up-
stairs in a flash. It is a delightful end to the evening. More delightful than

anything they remember from their marriage, or at least from the later part of it.

That, too, now becomes part of the pattern. He never stays the full night, because, good parents that they are, they don't want the children to get any false hopes up — as they would, seeing their father at breakfast.

Such a relationship may go on for several years, may even be interrupted by a romance on one side or the other and then resume. It may even grow to the point where she's mending as well as washing his shirts, and he is advising her on her tax returns and fixing her car.

What they have achieved postdivorce is what their marriage should have been like in the first place. Part-time. Seven days a week of marriage was too much. One afternoon and two evenings is just right.

Although our society is even now witnessing de facto part-time arrangements, such as the couple who work in different cities and meet only on weekends, we have no theory of part-time marriage, at least no theory that has reached the general public. The romantic notion still dominates that if you love someone, you obviously want to be with them all the time.

To me it's clear we need such a theory. There are certainly people who thrive on seven-day-a-week marriages. They have a high level of intimacy and they may be better, warmer people than the rest of us. But there are millions and millions of us with medium or low levels of intimacy. We find full-time family memberships a strain. If we could enter marriage with more realistic expectations of what closeness means for us, I suspect the divorce rate might permanently turn downward. It's too bad there isn't a sort of glucose tolerance test for intimacy.

As for me personally, I still do want to get married again. About four days a week.

Questions to Start You Thinking

1. CONSIDERING MEANING: How did Perrin's divorce affect him?

2. IDENTIFYING WRITING STRATEGIES: How does Perrin use cause and effect to support the solution he proposes?

3. READING CRITICALLY: What is Perrin's purpose in writing this essay? Do you think he is serious about his proposal for a part-time marriage? What evidence in his essay leads you to your conclusion?

4. EXPANDING VOCABULARY: Notice Perrin's use of the words *straight-arrow*, *pillar-of-the-community* (paragraph 5), *dominant* (paragraph 6), *self-contempt* (paragraph 14), *de facto* (paragraph 18), and *glucose tolerance test* (paragraph 19). How does Perrin's vocabulary fit or challenge your expectations of how a college professor writes? Find other examples to support your answer.

5. MAKING CONNECTIONS: How might Perrin react to Judy Brady's point of view in "I Want a Wife" (pp. 427–29)? By reading Brady's essay, would Perrin have a better understanding of why his wife left him to "find herself"? Would he appreciate Brady's satire?

Link to the Paired Essay

While Perrin and Stephanie Coontz ("Remarriage and Stepfamilies," pp. 419–24) both discuss a reality of many American families — divorce and re-marriage — their essays have very different purposes. Compare and contrast the tones of the two essays. For what purposes might each tone be appropriate? If you as a reader were facing the same problems these writers discuss, how would you respond to the two different tones?

■ For useful links to Web sources on topics including *families*, visit <bedfordstmartins.com/toplinks>.

Journal Prompts

1. Would you prefer a full- or part-time marriage? Why?
2. Sketch out a theory or a plan for part-time marriage. What elements or rules would be needed to make it successful?

Suggestions for Writing

1. Write an essay explaining how divorce has affected you or those around you.
2. Take a stand on the solution Perrin proposes. In a short essay, agree or disagree with the idea of part-time marriage. Is it a constructive response to problems of marital incompatibility? Why, or why not?

Stephanie Coontz
Remarriage and Stepfamilies

Stephanie Coontz *was born in 1944 in Seattle. She attended the University of California at Berkeley and the University of Washington at Seattle and has taught history and family studies at Evergreen State College in Olympia, Washington, since 1975. Coontz has explored gender roles and the American family in several books, including* Women's Work, Men's Property *(with Peta Henderson, 1986),* The Social Origins of Private Life: A History of American Families 1600–1900 *(1988), and* The Way We Never Were: American Families and the Nostalgia Trap *(1992). In this meticulously researched and documented excerpt from* The Way We Really Are: Coming to Terms with America's Changing Families *(1997), Coontz analyzes sociological, psychological, and historical data to urge a reevaluation of traditional assumptions about how "healthy" families are defined and formed. While Noel Perrin ("A Part-Time Marriage," pp. 416–18) uses personal experience with divorce to call for an expanded definition of marriage as an institution, Coontz uses analysis of statistical studies to recommend ways of handling parent-child relationships after a parent has remarried.*

AS YOU READ: *According to Coontz, what are the reasons for the difficulties stepfamilies may encounter, and what are the rewards of forming a healthy stepfamily?*

The contradictory data on stepfamilies also illustrate the problem with sweeping generalizations about family structure. While remarriage tends to reduce stresses associated with economic insecurity, some studies suggest that children in stepfamilies, taken as a whole, have the same added risks for emotional problems as do children in one-parent families; they are actually *more* likely to repeat a grade than children whose mothers have never married. Yet most stepfamilies work quite well. In a recent long-term, ongoing government study, 80 percent of children in stepfamilies were judged to be doing well psychologically — not a whole lot worse than the 90 percent in intact biological families. The large majority of stepparents and children in one national survey rated their households as "relaxed" and "close," while less than one-third described their households as "tense" or "disorganized." Sibling conflict, found in all types of families, was only slightly more frequent in families with stepfathers.[1]

The trouble with generalizing about stepfamilies is that they are even more complicated and varied than other family types because there are so many possible routes to forming them. Kay Pasley and Marilyn Ihinger-Tallman have identified nine "structurally distinct" types of remarried families, depending on the custody and visitation arrangements of each partner, the presence of children from the new marriage, and whether there are children from one or both of the remarried parents' former families. The challenges of blending a new family mount with the complexity of the combinations that are being put together.[2]

There seem to be two pieces of advice we can confidently give to parents considering remarriage. The first is *not* to marry just to find a mother or father for your child. While remarriage may be helpful for single-parent families experiencing economic distress, those with adequate financial resources may find that their children's adjustment and academic performance are initially set back. Many children take longer to adjust to remarriage than to divorce, especially when they are teens.[3]

But the second piece of advice is not to be scared off. Most stepfamilies do well, and a good relationship with a stepparent does appear to strengthen a child's emotional life and academic achievement.[4]

Although stepfamilies create new stresses and adaptive challenges, write researchers Mavis Hetherington and James Bray, they "also offer opportunities for personal growth and more harmonious, fulfilling family and personal relationships." Children gain access to several different role models, get the chance to see their parents in a happier personal situation than in the past, and can benefit from the flexibility they learn in coping with new roles and relations.[5]

The most important thing to grasp about stepfamilies is that they require people to put aside traditional assumptions about how a family evolves and functions. Since the parent-child relationships predate the marriage, each parent and child brings a history of already formed family values, rules, rituals, and habits to the new household. This situation can lead to conflict and misunderstanding. Research does not support the stereotype that children in stepfamilies normally suffer from conflicting loyalties, but there is often considerable ambiguity° about parenting roles and boundaries. For adolescents, the situation can be particularly tense. Their understandable resentment of the newcomer may cause their age-appropriate distancing from the biological parent to proceed too rapidly.[6]

Another major challenge to stepfamilies lies in the fact that traditional gender roles often conflict with the new family structure. As therapists Monica McGoldrick and Betty Carter put it, "if the old rules that called for women to rear children and men to earn and manage the financing are not working well in first-marriage families, which they are not, they have absolutely no chance at all in a system where some of the children are strangers to the wife, and where some of the finances include sources of income and expenditure that are not in the husband's power to control"—for example, alimony or child support.[7]

For stepfamilies to meet the needs of both adults and children, they have to create a new family "culture" that reworks older patterns into some kind of coherent whole, allowing members to mourn losses from the previous families without cutting off those relationships. The main barriers to doing this include leftover conflict from previous marriages, unrealistic expectations about instant bonding within the new family, and attempts to reproduce traditional nuclear family norms.[8]

As Lawrence Ganong and Marilyn Coleman point out, stepfamilies that try to function like a first-marriage nuclear family "must engage in massive denial and distortion of reality," pretending that former spouses, with their separate family histories, do not exist and cutting members off from important people or traditions in their life. This is not healthy. Nor is it realistic for the biological parent in the household to expect to have sole control over childrearing decisions. Thus stepfamilies need to have "more permeable° boundaries" than nuclear families usually maintain. And a stepparent-stepchild relationship probably *should* be less emotionally close than a parent-child relationship.[9]

Old-fashioned gender roles pose another problem for stepfamilies. *Stepmother* families have more conflicts, many specialists believe, because both women and men often expect the wife to shoulder responsibility for child care and for the general emotional well-being of the family. A stepmother may therefore try to solve problems between her husband and his children or the children and their biological mother, which sets the stepmother up to be the villain for both the children and the ex-wife. In stepfather families, a woman having trouble with her children may push her new husband to assume a disciplinary role far too early in the marriage, which tends to set back or even derail his developing relationship with the children.[10]

7

8

9

10

---

ambiguity: Something that is unclear or unspecified.   **permeable:** Able to be passed through; here it means flexible.

Therapists recommend that stepfamilies be encouraged to see the prob- 11
lems they face as a consequence of their structural complexities, not of ill
will or personal inadequacy. Indeed, many of the difficulties may actually be
a result of previous strengths in earlier family arrangements — the woman's
desire to make relationships work, for example, or the children's strong
commitments to older ties and habits. Hetherington found that sons "who
were high in self-esteem, assertiveness, and social competence before the remarriage" were most likely to start out being "acrimonious° and negative
toward stepfathers." In the long run, though, these boys were especially
likely to accept and benefit from a stepfather's addition to the household.
Boys who were close to their mothers in the single-parent family tend to re-
sent the establishment of a strong marital alliance in the new stepfamily.
Girls are more likely to welcome a close marital relationship, possibly
because it serves as a buffer "against the threat of inappropriate intimacy between stepfathers and stepdaughters."[11]

Experts agree that stepfamilies need to develop new norms permitting 12
parental collaboration across household boundaries. They need to facili-
tate° interactions between children and extended kin on the noncustodial
parent's° side of the family. They must let go of romantic fantasies about
being able to start over. They also have to become much more flexible about
gender roles. The biological parent, whether male or female, should be the
primary parent, which means that women must control their tendency to fix
everybody's emotional problems and men must control theirs to leave emotional intimacy to women. A new stepfather should resist his wife's desire to
have him relieve her of disciplinary duties; similarly, a new wife should resist a husband's pressure to take on maternal roles such as managing schedules, supervising housework, or even making sure the kids remember their
lunches on the way to school.[12]

What seems to work best is for a stepparent to initially play the role of 13
camp counselor, uncle, aunt, or even sitter — someone who exercises more
adult authority than a friend but is less responsible for direction and discipline than a parent. Behaving supportively toward stepchildren is more effective than trying to exercise control, although stepparents should back up
their partners' disciplinary decisions in a matter-of-fact manner and help to
keep track of children's whereabouts. Stepparents of adolescents have to recognize that even under the best circumstances, resistance to them is likely to
continue for some time. If stepparents understand this reaction as normal,
they can control their own natural impulse to feel rejected and to back
away.[13]

Parenting in stepfamilies requires a thick skin, a sensitive ear, and a 14
highly developed sense of balance. A successful stepfamily has to tolerate
ambiguous, flexible, and often somewhat distant relationships, without allowing any member to disengage entirely. It has to accept a closer relation-

---

acrimonious: Bitter.   **facilitate:** Help to happen.   **noncustodial parent:** The parent
who does not have primary custody of a child.

ship between biological parent and child than between stepparent and child without letting that closeness evolve into a parent-child coalition that undermines the united front of the marriage partners. And effective communication skills are even more important in stepfamilies than they are in other kinds of families.[14]

These tasks are challenging, which may be why stepfamilies take longer   15 to come together as a unified team, are more vulnerable to disruption, and often experience renewed turmoil during adolescence. But Jan Lawton, director of the Stepfamily Project in Queensland, Australia, points out that while the divorce rate among remarried families is high in the first two years, it then slows down. After five years, second marriages are more stable than first ones. And researchers have found that even modest, short-term training in communication and problem solving can dramatically increase the stability of stepfamilies.[15]

Notes

1. Barbara Dafoe Whitehead, "Dan Quayle Was Right," *Atlantic Monthly* (April 1993): 71; "School Dropout Rates for Families," *USA Today*, March 15, 1993; "Stepfamilies Aren't Bad for Most Kids," *USA Today*, August 17, 1992: 10; Frank Mott, "The Impact of Father Absence from the Home on Subsequent Cognitive Development of Younger Children," paper delivered at the American Sociological Association, August 1992; Frank F. Furstenberg Jr. and Andrew J. Cherlin, *Divided Families: What Happens to Children When Parents Part* (Cambridge, Mass.: Harvard University Press, 1991), 89; Andrew J. Cherlin and Frank F. Furstenberg Jr., "Stepfamilies in the United States: A Reconsideration," *Annual Reviews in Sociology* 20 (1994): 372.
2. Kay Pasley and Marilyn Ihinger-Tallman, "Stress and the Remarried Family," *Family Perspectives* 12 (1982): 187.
3. James Bray and Sandra Berger, "Developmental Issues in Stepfamilies Research Project: Family Relationships and Parent-Child Interactions," *Journal of Family Psychology* 7, no. 1 (1993): 86; E. Mavis Hetherington and W. Glenn Clingempeel, *Coping with Marital Transitions: A Family Systems Perspective* (Chicago: Monographs of the Society for Research in Child Development, Serial No. 227, vol. 57, 1992), 205–6; William S. Aquilino, "The Life Course of Children Born to Unmarried Mothers: Childhood Living Arrangements and Young Adult Outcomes," *Journal of Marriage and the Family* 58 (May 1996): 307.
4. E. Mavis Hetherington, "An Overview of the Virginia Longitudinal Study of Divorce and Remarriage with a Focus on Early Adolescence," *Journal of Family Psychology* 7 (1993); Kay Pasley and Marilyn Ihinger-Tallman, *Remarriage and Stepparenting: Current Research and Theory* (New York: Guilford, 1987), 105–9; Bray and Berger, "Developmental Issues in Stepfamilies Research Project," 89.
5. Alan Booth and Judy Dunn, eds., *Stepfamilies: Who Benefits? Who Does Not?* (Hillsdale, N.J.: Lawrence Erlbaum, 1994); Virginia Rutter, "Lessons from Stepfamilies," *Psychology Today* (May–June 1994): 32.
6. Lawrence H. Ganong and Marilyn Coleman, *Remarried Family Relationships* (Thousand Oaks, Calif.: Sage, 1994), 122; Pasley and Ihinger-Tallman, *Remarriage and Stepparenting*, 108; Hetherington and Clingempeel, *Coping with Marital Transitions*, 200–5.
7. Monica McGoldrick and Betty Carter, "Forming a Remarried Family," in McGoldrick and Carter, eds., *The Changing Family Life Cycle: A Framework for Family Therapy*, 3rd ed. (Boston: Allyn and Bacon, 1989).
8. John Visher and Emily Visher, *Therapy with Stepfamilies* (New York: Brunner/Mazel, 1996); McGoldrick and Carter, "Forming a Remarried Family."

9. David Demo and Alan Acock, "The Impact of Divorce on Children," in Alan Booth, ed., 201–2, *Contemporary Families: Looking Forward, Looking Back* (Minneapolis: National Council on Family Relations, 1991); Ganong and Coleman, *Remarried Family Relationships*, 123–37; James Bray and David Harvey, "Adolescents in Stepfamilies: Developmental Family Interventions," *Psychotherapy* 32 (1995): 125; Visher and Visher, *Therapy with Stepfamilies*; McGoldrick and Carter, "Forming a Remarried Family."

10. Lynn White, "Growing Up with Single Parents and Stepparents: Long-Term Effects on Family Solidarity," *Journal of Marriage and the Family* 56, no. 4 (November 1994); Rutter, "Lessons from Stepfamilies," 66; Furstenberg and Cherlin, *Divided Families*, 78; McGoldrick and Carter, "Forming a Remarried Family"; John Visher and Emily Visher, *Old Loyalties, New Ties: Therapeutic Strategies with Stepfamilies* (New York: Brunner/Mazel, 1988).

11. E. Mavis Hetherington, "Presidential Address: Families, Lies, and Videotapes," *Journal of Research on Adolescence* 1, no. 4 (1991): 341, 344.

12. Ganong and Coleman, *Remarried Family Relationships*; James Bray and Sandra Berger, "Noncustodial Father and Paternal Grandparent Relationships in Stepfamilies," *Family Relations* 39 (1990).

13. Mark Fine and Lawrence Kurdek, "The Adjustment of Adolescents in Stepfather and Stepmother Families," *Journal of Marriage and the Family* 54 (1992); Bray and Harvey, "Adolescents in Stepfamilies"; Margaret Crosbie-Burnett and Jean Giles-Sims, "Adolescent Adjustment and Stepparenting Styles," *Family Relations* 43 (October 1994); Hetherington and Clingempeel, *Coping with Marital Transitions*, 10, 200–5; Visher and Visher, *Old Loyalties, New Ties*.

14. McGoldrick and Carter, "Forming a Remarried Family"; Visher and Visher, *Therapy with Stepfamilies*; Nancy Burrell, "Community Patterns in Stepfamilies: Redefining Family Roles, Themes, and Conflict Styles," in Mary Anne Fitzpatrick and Anita Vangelisti, eds., *Explaining Family Interactions* (Thousand Oaks, Calif.: Sage, 1995); Carolyn Henry and Sandra Lovelace, "Family Resources and Adolescent Family Life Satisfaction in Remarried Family Households," *Journal of Family Issues* 16 (1995); Marilyn Coleman and Lawrence H. Ganong, "Family Reconfiguring Following Divorce," in Steve Duck and Julia Wood, eds., *Confronting Relationship Challenges*, vol. 5 (Thousand Oaks, Calif.: Sage, 1995).

15. Rutter, "Lessons from Stepfamilies," 60–62; Phyllis Bronstein, Miriam Frankel Stoll, JoAnn Clauson, Craig L. Abrams, and Maria Briones, "Fathering after Separation or Divorce: Factors Predicting Children's Adjustment," *Family Relations* 43 (October 1994): 478.

Questions to Start You Thinking

1. **CONSIDERING MEANING:** According to Coontz, what traditional expectations about how a family should work make adjusting to a stepfamily especially difficult? What solutions to these difficulties does she propose?

2. **IDENTIFYING WRITING STRATEGIES:** Coontz uses cause and effect to explain a stepfamily's problems. Trace the potential causes that she identifies. How effective is the use of cause and effect in Coontz's essay, and why?

3. **READING CRITICALLY:** Coontz begins her essay by pointing out the logical fallacies of generalizing about stepfamilies. How well does she avoid making generalizations in her own writing?

4. **EXPANDING VOCABULARY:** In paragraph 8, what does Coontz mean by "family 'culture'"? What does the word *culture* convey that a word like *atmosphere* would not?

5. **MAKING CONNECTIONS:** Could the solutions that Coontz proposes for step-families' problems be useful for the families in Anna Quindlen's essay ("Evan's Two Moms," pp. 403-05)? Why, or why not?

Link to the Paired Essay

Although Coontz and Noel Perrin ("A Part-Time Marriage," pp. 416–18) ex-plore a similar issue, they use different strategies to develop their points of view. While Perrin writes about the impact of divorce on a family that is break-ing up, Coontz analyzes the new families that form when second marriages follow divorce. How are the problems of these two family groups similar? How are they different?

■ For useful links to Web sources on topics including *families*, visit <bedfordstmartins.com/ toplinks>.

Journal Prompts

1. Think of a complicated situation or difficult problem in your family or the family of a friend. How was the situation handled?

2. Does Coontz's description of what it takes to have a successful stepfamily seem feasible to you? Why, or why not?

Suggestions for Writing

1. Coontz writes that "parenting in stepfamilies requires a thick skin, a sensi-tive ear, and a highly developed sense of balance" (paragraph 14). What do you think are the primary requirements of good parenting, whether in step-families or first-marriage families? Drawing from your own experience, write an essay explaining your idea of good parenting.

2. Do you think the family as an institution is deteriorating? Write an essay in which you take a stand — that the family is deteriorating or that the family is not deteriorating — and present evidence to support your position.

Chapter 23
Men and Women

Responding to an Image

Examine the composition of this photograph, including the overall setting and the positions of the man and woman. What are the physical characteristics of these two people? What similarities and differences do you note? What does their body language suggest? If you were to add dialogue to this picture, what might the man and woman be saying or thinking? Based on your analysis, what general point does the photograph make about gender?

Web Search

Use a search engine such as Yahoo! or InfoSeek that locates Web sites rather than specific pages to find one Web source or publication marketed for women and one marketed for men. Read a few pages of each, and compare and contrast the content. How are they similar? How are they different? Do you think they stereotype women and men? How, and for what reasons?

■ For reading activities linked to this chapter, visit <bedfordstmartins.com/bedguide> and do a key-word search:

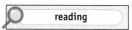

reading

Judy Brady
I Want a Wife

Judy Brady was born in 1937 in San Francisco, where she now makes her home. A graduate of the University of Iowa, Brady has contributed to various publications and has traveled to Cuba to study class relationships and education. More recently, she has edited the book 1 in 3: Women with Cancer Confront an Epidemic *(1991), drawing on her own struggle with the disease. In the following piece, which has been reprinted frequently since its appearance in* Ms. *magazine in December 1971, Brady considers the role of the American housewife. While she has said that she is "not a 'writer,'" this essay shows Brady to be a satirist adept at taking a stand and provoking attention.*

AS YOU READ: *Ask yourself why Brady says she wants a wife rather than a husband.*

I belong to that classification of people known as wives. I am A Wife. And, not altogether incidentally, I am a mother. 1

Not too long ago a male friend of mine appeared on the scene fresh 2 from a recent divorce. He had one child, who is, of course, with his ex-wife. He is looking for another wife. As I thought about him while I was ironing one evening, it suddenly occurred to me that I, too, would like to have a wife. Why do I want a wife?

I would like to go back to school so that I can become economically in- 3 dependent, support myself, and, if need be, support those dependent upon me. I want a wife who will work and send me to school. And while I am going to school I want a wife to take care of my children. I want a wife to keep track of the children's doctor and dentist appointments. And to keep track of mine, too. I want a wife to make sure my children eat properly and are kept clean. I want a wife who will wash the children's clothes and keep them mended. I want a wife who is a good nurturant° attendant to my children, who arranges for their schooling, makes sure that they have an adequate social life with their peers, takes them to the park, the zoo, etc. I want a wife who takes care of the children when they are sick, a wife who arranges to be around when the children need special care, because, of

nurturant: Kind, loving, nourishing.

course, I cannot miss classes at school. My wife must arrange to lose time at work and not lose the job. It may mean a small cut in my wife's income from time to time, but I guess I can tolerate that. Needless to say, my wife will arrange and pay for the care of the children while my wife is working.

I want a wife who will take care of *my* physical needs. I want a wife who   4 will keep my house clean. A wife who will pick up after my children, a wife who will pick up after me. I want a wife who will keep my clothes clean, ironed, mended, replaced when need be, and who will see to it that my personal things are kept in their proper place so that I can find what I need the minute I need it. I want a wife who cooks the meals, a wife who is a *good* cook. I want a wife who will plan the menus, do the necessary grocery shopping, prepare the meals, serve them pleasantly, and then do the cleaning up while I do my studying. I want a wife who will care for me when I am sick and sympathize with my pain and loss of time from school. I want a wife to go along when our family takes a vacation so that someone can continue to care for me and my children when I need a rest and change of scene.

I want a wife who will not bother me with rambling complaints about   5 a wife's duties. But I want a wife who will listen to me when I feel the need to explain a rather difficult point I have come across in my course of studies.

I want a wife who will take care of the details of my social life. When   6 my wife and I are invited out by my friends, I want a wife who will take care of the babysitting arrangements. When I meet people at school that I like and want to entertain, I want a wife who will have the house clean, will prepare a special meal, serve it to me and my friends, and not interrupt when I talk about things that interest me and my friends. I want a wife who will have arranged that the children are fed and ready for bed before my guests arrive so that the children do not bother us. I want a wife who takes care of the needs of my guests so that they feel comfortable, who makes sure that they have an ashtray, that they are passed the hors d'oeuvres, that they are offered a second helping of the food, that their wine glasses are replenished when necessary, that their coffee is served to them as they like it. And I want a wife who knows that sometimes I need a night out by myself.

I want a wife who is sensitive to my sexual needs, a wife who makes   7 love passionately and eagerly when I feel like it, a wife who makes sure that I am satisfied. And, of course, I want a wife who will not demand sexual attention when I am not in the mood for it. I want a wife who assumes the complete responsibility for birth control, because I do not want more children. I want a wife who will remain sexually faithful to me so that I do not have to clutter up my intellectual life with jealousies. And I want a wife who understands that *my* sexual needs may entail more than strict adherence to monogamy. I must, after all, be able to relate to people as fully as possible.

If, by chance, I find another person more suitable as a wife than the wife   8
I already have, I want the liberty to replace my present wife with another
one. Naturally, I will expect a fresh, new life; my wife will take the children
and be solely responsible for them so that I am left free.

When I am through with school and have a job, I want my wife to quit   9
working and remain at home so that my wife can more fully and completely
take care of a wife's duties.

My God, who *wouldn't* want a wife?   10

Questions to Start You Thinking

1. CONSIDERING MEANING: How does Brady define the traditional role of the
   wife? Does she think that a wife should perform all of the duties she outlines? How can you tell?

2. IDENTIFYING WRITING STRATEGIES: How does Brady use observation to support her stand? What other approaches does she use?

3. READING CRITICALLY: What is the tone of this essay? How does Brady establish
   it? Considering that she was writing for a predominantly female — and feminist — audience, do you think Brady's tone is appropriate?

4. EXPANDING VOCABULARY: Why does Brady use such simple language in this
   essay? What is the effect of her use of such phrases as *of course* (paragraph
   2), *Needless to say* (paragraph 3), and *Naturally* (paragraph 8)?

5. MAKING CONNECTIONS: Compare Brady's portrayal of the role of wife
   with Scott Russell Sanders's discussion of the women he observed while
   growing up ("The Men We Carry in Our Minds," pp. 430–34). What
   would the women Sanders met at college think of the kind of wife Brady
   discusses?

Journal Prompts

1. Exert your wishful thinking — describe your ideal mate.
2. Begin with a stereotype of a husband, wife, boyfriend, girlfriend, father, or
   mother, and write a satirical description of that stereotype.

Suggestions for Writing

1. In a short personal essay, explain what you want or expect in a wife, husband, or life partner. Do your hopes and expectations differ from social and
   cultural norms? If so, in what way(s)? How has your parents' relationship
   shaped your attitudes and ideals?

2. How has the role of a wife changed since this essay was written? Write an
   essay comparing and contrasting the post-2000 wife with the kind of wife
   Judy Brady claims she wants.

Scott Russell Sanders
The Men We Carry in Our Minds

Scott Russell Sanders was born in 1945 in Memphis, Tennessee. A graduate of Brown University and Cambridge University, Sanders has taught English at Indiana University since 1971. Although he is the author of novels, short story collections, and more than five children's books, Sanders is best known for his essay collections, including Paradise of Bombs *(1987),* Staying Put: Making a Home in a Restless World *(1993), and* The Force of Spirit *(2000), for which he won the Lannan Literary Award and the Great Lakes Book Award for personal nonfiction. Sanders has described his writing as "driven by a deep regard for particular places and voices . . . a regard compounded of grief, curiosity, and love." In the following essay, which first appeared in* Milkweed Chronicle *in 1984, Sanders explains how the experience of growing up in a working-class community made it difficult for him to understand the grievances of women from more privileged backgrounds.*

AS YOU READ: *Identify the privileges Sanders associated with being male when he entered college. How did his perception change?*

T his must be a hard time for women," I say to my friend Anneke. "They 1 have so many paths to choose from, and so many voices calling them."

"I think it's a lot harder for men," she replies.   2

"How do you figure that?"   3

"The women I know feel excited, innocent, like crusaders in a just cause. 4 The men I know are eaten up with guilt."

We are sitting at the kitchen table drinking sassafras tea, our hands 5 wrapped around the mugs because this April morning is cool and drizzly. "Like a Dutch morning," Anneke told me earlier. She is Dutch herself, a writer and midwife° and peacemaker, with the round face and sad eyes of a woman in a Vermeer° painting who might be waiting for the rain to stop, for a door to open. She leans over to sniff a sprig of lilac, pale lavender, that rises from a vase of cobalt blue.

"Women feel such pressure to be everything, do everything," I say. "Ca- 6 reer, kids, art, politics. Have their babies and get back to the office a week later. It's as if they're trying to overcome a million years' worth of evolution in one lifetime."

"But we help one another. We don't try to lumber° on alone, like so 7 many wounded grizzly bears, the way men do." Anneke sips her tea. I gave her the mug with owls on it, for wisdom. "And we have this deep-down sense that we're in the *right*—we've been held back, passed over, used—

---

midwife: Someone, usually a woman, who assists in childbirth.   **Vermeer:** Jan Vermeer (1632–1675), Dutch painter known for interior scenes that masterfully portray light and color.   **lumber:** Walk or move with heavy clumsiness.

while men feel they're in the wrong. Men are the ones who've been discredited, who have to search their souls."

I search my soul. I discover guilty feelings aplenty—toward the poor, 8 the Vietnamese, Native Americans, the whales, an endless list of debts—a guilt in each case that is as bright and unambiguous as a neon sign. But toward women I feel something more confused, a snarl of shame, envy, wary tenderness, and amazement. This muddle troubles me. To hide my unease I say, "You're right, it's tough being a man these days."

"Don't laugh." Anneke frowns at me, mournful-eyed, through the sassafras 9 steam. "I wouldn't be a man for anything. It's much easier being the victim. All the victim has to do is break free. The persecutor has to live with his past."

How deep is this past? I find myself wondering after Anneke has left. 10 How much of an inheritance do I have to throw off? Is it just the beliefs I breathed in as a child? Do I have to scour memory back through father and grandfather? Through St. Paul? Beyond Stonehenge° and into the twilit caves? I'm convinced the past we must contend with is deeper even than speech. When I think back on my childhood, on how I learned to see men and women, I have a sense of ancient, dizzying depths. The back roads of Tennessee and Ohio where I grew up were probably closer, in their sexual patterns, to the campsites of Stone Age hunters than to the genderless cities of the future into which we are rushing.

The first men, besides my father, I remember seeing were black convicts 11 and white guards, in the cottonfield across the road from our farm on the outskirts of Memphis. I must have been three or four. The prisoners wore dingy gray-and-black zebra suits, heavy as canvas, sodden with sweat. Hatless, stooped, they chopped weeds in the fierce heat, row after row, breathing the acrid dust of boll-weevil° poison. The overseers wore dazzling white shirts and broad shadowy hats. The oiled barrels of their shotguns flashed in the sunlight. Their faces in memory are utterly blank. Of course those men, white and black, have become for me an emblem of racial hatred. But they have also come to stand for the twin poles of my early vision of manhood— the brute toiling animal and the boss.

When I was a boy, the men I knew labored with their bodies. They were 12 marginal farmers, just scraping by, or welders, steelworkers, carpenters; they swept floors, dug ditches, mined coal, or drove trucks, their forearms ropy with muscle; they trained horses, stoked furnaces, built tires, stood on assembly lines wrestling parts onto cars and refrigerators. They got up before light, worked all day long whatever the weather, and when they came home at night they looked as though somebody had been whipping them. In the evenings and on weekends they worked on their own places, tilling gardens that were lumpy with clay, fixing broken-down cars, hammering on houses that were always too drafty, too leaky, too small.

Stonehenge: Four-thousand-year-old arrangement of enormous stones in southern England, thought to have been used for religious ceremonies and astronomical observations. **boll weevil:** A parasitic insect that bores into cotton bolls and ruins crops.

The bodies of the men I knew were twisted and maimed in ways visible 13
and invisible. The nails of their hands were black and split, the hands tattooed with scars. Some had lost fingers. Heavy lifting had given many of
them finicky backs and guts weak from hernias. Racing against conveyor
belts had given them ulcers. Their ankles and knees ached from years of
standing on concrete. Anyone who had worked for long around machines
was hard of hearing. They squinted, and the skin of their faces was creased
like the leather of old work gloves. There were times, studying them, when I
dreaded growing up. Most of them coughed, from dust or cigarettes, and
most of them drank cheap wine or whiskey, so their eyes looked bloodshot
and bruised. The fathers of my friends always seemed older than the mothers. Men wore out sooner. Only women lived into old age.

As a boy I also knew another sort of men, who did not sweat and break 14
down like mules. They were soldiers, and so far as I could tell they scarcely
worked at all. During my early school years we lived on a military base, an arsenal in Ohio, and every day I saw GIs in the guardshacks, on the stoops of
barracks, at the wheels of olive drab Chevrolets. The chief fact of their lives
was boredom. Long after I left the arsenal I came to recognize the sour smell
the soldiers gave off as that of souls in limbo. They were all waiting — for
wars, for transfers, for leaves, for promotions, for the end of their hitch — like
so many braves waiting for the hunt to begin. Unlike the warriors of older
tribes, however, they would have no say about when the battle would start or
how it would be waged. Their waiting was broken only when they practiced
for war. They fired guns at targets, drove tanks across the churned-up fields of
the military reservation, set off bombs in the wrecks of old fighter planes. I
knew this was all play. But I also felt certain that when the hour for killing arrived, they would kill. When the real shooting started, many of them would
die. This was what soldiers were *for*, just as a hammer was for driving nails.

Warriors and toilers: those seemed, in my boyhood vision, to be the 15
chief destinies for men. They weren't the only destinies, as I learned from
having a few male teachers, from reading books, and from watching television. But the men on television — the politicians, the astronauts, the gener-
als, the savvy lawyers, the philosophical doctors, the bosses who gave orders
to both soldiers and laborers — seemed as remote and unreal to me as the
figures in tapestries. I could no more imagine growing up to become one of
these cool, potent creatures than I could imagine becoming a prince.

A nearer and more hopeful example was that of my father, who had es- 16
caped from a red-dirt farm to a tire factory, and from the assembly line to
the front office. Eventually he dressed in a white shirt and tie. He carried
himself as if he had been born to work with his mind. But his body, remembering the early years of slogging work, began to give out on him in his
fifties, and it quit on him entirely before he turned sixty-five. Even such a
partial escape from man's fate as he had accomplished did not seem possible for most of the boys I knew. They joined the army, stood in line for jobs
in the smoky plants, helped build highways. They were bound to work as
their fathers had worked, killing themselves or preparing to kill others.

A scholarship enabled me not only to attend college, a rare enough feat 17
in my circle, but even to study in a university meant for children of the rich.
Here I met for the first time young men who had assumed from birth that
they would lead lives of comfort and power. And for the first time I met
women who told me that men were guilty of having kept all the joys and
privileges of the earth for themselves. I was baffled. What privileges? What
joys? I thought about the maimed dismal lives of most of the men back
home. What had they stolen from their wives and daughters? The right to go
five days a week, twelve months a year, for thirty or forty years to a steel mill
or a coal mine? The right to drop bombs and die in war? The right to feel
every leak in the roof, every gap in the fence, every cough in the engine, as a
wound they must mend? The right to feel, when the lay-off comes or the
plant shuts down, not only afraid but ashamed?

I was slow to understand the deep grievances of women. This was be- 18
cause, as a boy, I had envied them. Before college, the only people I had ever
known who were interested in art or music or literature, the only ones who
read books, the only ones who ever seemed to enjoy a sense of ease and
grace were the mothers and daughters. Like the menfolk, they fretted about
money, they scrimped and made-do. But, when the pay stopped coming in,
they were not the ones who had failed. Nor did they have to go to war, and
that seemed to me a blessed fact. By comparison with the narrow, ironclad
days of fathers, there was an expansiveness,° I thought, in the days of mothers. They went to see neighbors, to shop in town, to run errands at school, at
the library, at church. No doubt, had I looked harder at their lives, I would
have envied them less. It was not my fate to become a woman, so it was easier for me to see the graces. Few of them held jobs outside the home, and
those who did filled thankless roles as clerks and waitresses. I didn't see,
then, what a prison a house could be, since houses seemed to me brighter,
handsomer places than any factory. I did not realize — because such things
were never spoken of — how often women suffered from men's bullying. I
did learn about the wretchedness of abandoned wives, single mothers, widows; but I also learned about the wretchedness of lone men. Even then I
could see how exhausting it was for a mother to cater all day to the needs of
young children. But if I had been asked, as a boy, to choose between tending
a baby and tending a machine, I think I would have chosen the baby. (Having now tended both, I know I would choose the baby.)

So I was baffled when the women at college accused me and my sex of 19
having cornered the world's pleasure. I think something like my bafflement
has been felt by other boys (and by girls as well) who grew up in dirt-poor
farm country, in mining country, in black ghettos, in Hispanic barrios,° in
the shadows of factories, in third world nations — any place where the fate
of men is as grim and bleak as the fate of women. Toilers and warriors. I realize now how ancient these identities are, how deep the tug they exert on

expansiveness: Flexibility, openness; also connotes grandness.   **barrios:** Spanish-
speaking neighborhoods.

men, the undertow of a thousand generations. The miseries I saw, as a boy, in the lives of nearly all men I continue to see in the lives of many — the body-breaking toil, the tedium, the call to be tough, the humiliating power-lessness, the battle for a living and for territory.

When the women I met at college thought about the joys and privileges 20 of men, they did not carry in their minds the sort of men I had known in my childhood. They thought of their fathers, who were bankers, physicians, architects, stockbrokers, the big wheels of the big cities. These fathers rode the train to work or drove cars that cost more than any of my childhood houses. They were attended from morning to night by female helpers, wives and nurses and secretaries. They were never laid off, never short of cash at month's end, never lined up for welfare. These fathers made decisions that mattered. They ran the world.

The daughters of such men wanted to share in this power, this glory. So 21 did I. They yearned for a say over their future, for jobs worthy of their abilities, for the right to live at peace, unmolested, whole. Yes, I thought, yes yes. The difference between me and these daughters was that they saw me, because of my sex, as destined from birth to become like their fathers, and therefore an enemy to their desires. But I knew better. I wasn't an enemy, in fact or in feeling. I was an ally. If I had known, then, how to tell them so, would they have believed me? Would they now?

Questions to Start You Thinking

1. CONSIDERING MEANING: Why does Sanders call himself an "ally" (paragraph 21) of the women he met in college? Do you agree that he was their ally? Explain.

2. IDENTIFYING WRITING STRATEGIES: How does Sanders use the experiences he recalls to support the stand he takes?

3. READING CRITICALLY: What kinds of appeals — emotional, logical, ethical — does Sanders use in his essay? Are the appeals effective? Why, or why not? (For an explanation of kinds of appeal, see pp. 39–40.)

4. EXPANDING VOCABULARY: What qualities do you associate with "warriors" and "toilers" (paragraph 15)? Are the connotations of these terms generally positive or negative? How does Sanders use these connotations to fit the purpose of his essay?

5. MAKING CONNECTIONS: In paragraph 21, Sanders observes that the women at college "saw me, because of my sex, as destined from birth to become like their fathers, and therefore an enemy to their desires." How does Sanders's description of how these women think relate to Nicholas Wade's position on gender differences ("How Men and Women Think," pp. 447–50)?

Journal Prompts

1. Reflect on some of the men and women you knew as a child. How do they compare to the men and women Sanders remembers from his youth?

2. Do you agree that "it's tough being a man these days" (paragraph 8)? Why, or why not? Role-play: if you are female, take a man's point of view; if you are male, take a woman's point of view.

Suggestions for Writing

1. Recalling your own experience, explain the qualities of an important man you "carry in your mind." Who is this man? How did he help shape your views of what masculinity is?

2. Write an essay explaining whether men's or women's roles are more difficult in today's society. Use examples from your own experience as well as from your knowledge of current events.

Dave Barry

From Now On, Let Women Kill Their Own Spiders

Dave Barry *was born in 1947 in Armonk, New York. According to his own biographical statement, he has been "steadily growing older ever since without ever actually reaching maturity." He attended Haverford College and started his career in journalism at the* Daily Local News *in West Chester, Pennsylvania. He has been with the* Miami Herald *since 1983 and won the Pulitzer Prize for commentary in 1988. Barry is the author of numerous books, which include* Babies and Other Hazards of Sex *(1984),* Dave Barry's Complete Guide to Guys *(1995),* Dave Barry Is from Mars and Venus *(1997), and his recent* Boogers Are My Beat *(2003). The article "From Now On, Let Women Kill Their Own Spiders" first appeared in the* Miami Herald. *In this piece, Barry pokes fun at miscommunication between men and women. Identifying with both, he laughs at how the sexes inevitably bewilder and infuriate each other.*

AS YOU READ: *Try to discover what Barry is really criticizing.*

From time to time I receive letters from a certain group of individuals 1
that I will describe, for want of a better term, as "women." I have such a letter here, from a Susie Walker of North Augusta, S.C., who asks the following question: "Why do men open a drawer and say, 'Where is the spatula?' instead of, you know, looking for it?"

This question expresses a commonly held (by women) negative stereo- 2
type about guys of the male gender, which is that they cannot find things around the house, especially things in the kitchen. Many women believe that if you want to hide something from a man, all you have to do is put it in plain sight in the refrigerator, and he will never, ever find it, as evidenced by the fact that a man can open a refrigerator containing 463 pounds of assorted meats, poultry, cold cuts, condiments, vegetables, frozen dinners,

snack foods, desserts, etc., and ask, with no irony whatsoever, "Do we have anything to eat?"

Now I could respond to this stereotype in a snide° manner by making 3 generalizations about women. I could ask, for example, how come your average woman prepares for virtually every upcoming event in her life, including dental appointments, by buying new shoes, even if she already owns as many pairs as the entire Riverdance troupe. I could point out that, if there were no women, there would be no such thing as Leonardo DiCaprio. I could ask why a woman would walk up to a perfectly innocent man who is minding his own business watching basketball and demand to know if a certain pair of pants makes her butt look too big, and then, no matter what he answers, get mad at him. I could ask why, according to the best scientific estimates, 93 percent of the nation's severely limited bathroom-storage space is taken up by decades-old, mostly empty tubes labeled "moisturizer." I could point out that, to judge from the covers of countless women's magazines, the two topics most interesting to women are (1) Why men are all disgusting pigs, and (2) How to attract men.

Yes, I could raise these issues in response to the question asked by Susie 4 Walker of North Augusta, S.C., regarding the man who was asking where the spatula was. I could even ask WHY this particular man might be looking for the spatula. Could it be that he needs a spatula to kill a spider, because, while he was innocently watching basketball and minding his own business, a member of another major gender — a gender that refuses to personally kill spiders but wants them all dead — DEMANDED that he kill the spider, which nine times out of ten turns out to be a male spider that was minding its own business? Do you realize how many men arrive in hospital emergency rooms every year, sometimes still gripping their spatulas, suffering from painful spider-inflicted injuries? I don't have the exact statistics right here, but I bet they are chilling.

As I say, I could raise these issues and resort to the kind of negativity in- 5 dulged in by Susie Walker of North Augusta, S.C. But I choose not to. I choose, instead, to address her question seriously, in hopes that, by improving the communication between the genders, all human beings — both men and women, together — will come to a better understanding of how dense° women can be sometimes.

I say this because there is an excellent reason why a man would open the 6 spatula drawer and, without looking for the spatula, ask where the spatula is: The man does not have TIME to look for the spatula. Why? Because he is busy thinking. Men are almost always thinking. When you look at a man who appears to be merely scratching himself, rest assured that inside his head, his brain is humming like a high-powered computer, processing millions of pieces of information and producing important insights such as, "This feels good!"

We should be grateful that men think so much, because over the years 7 they have thought up countless inventions that have made life better for all

---

snide: Sarcastic, especially in a nasty manner.   **dense:** Slow-witted.

people, everywhere. The shot clock in basketball is one example. Another one is underwear-eating bacteria. I found out about this thanks to the many alert readers who sent me an article from *New Scientist* magazine stating that Russian scientists — and you KNOW these are guy scientists — are trying to solve the problem of waste disposal aboard spacecraft, by "designing a cocktail of bacteria to digest astronauts' cotton and paper underpants." Is that great, or what? I am picturing a utopian future wherein, when a man's briefs get dirty, they will simply dissolve from his body, thereby freeing him from the chore of dealing with his soiled underwear via the labor-intensive, time-consuming method he now uses, namely, dropping them on the floor.

I'm not saying that guys have solved all the world's problems. I'm just 8 saying that there ARE solutions out there, and if, instead of harping endlessly about spatulas, we allow guys to use their mental talents to look for these solutions, in time, they will find them. Unless they are in the refrigerator.

Questions to Start You Thinking

1. CONSIDERING MEANING: What is Barry satirizing in his essay?

2. IDENTIFYING WRITING STRATEGIES: Barry's essay is filled with rhetorical questions. Locate some of these, and consider how he answers them. What evidence does he provide to support his answers? How does this evidence affect his tone? How does it affect meaning?

3. READING CRITICALLY: What generalizations about women does Barry make in paragraph 3? How do these serve to support his main point?

4. EXPANDING VOCABULARY: Define *utopian* (paragraph 7). According to Barry, how would underwear-eating bacteria contribute to a utopian future?

5. MAKING CONNECTIONS: Both Barry and Judy Brady ("I Want a Wife," pp. 427–29) use satire, humorously attacking human mistakes and shortcomings in their essays. Compare and contrast their use of satire.

Journal Prompts

1. Put your imagination to work to suggest other inventions — besides underwear-eating bacteria — that would benefit man- (or woman-) kind. Follow Barry's model and have fun.

2. Discuss a conversation you've heard that involved man- or woman-bashing. What was the tone of the conversation? How serious were the participants? What are the effects of such remarks?

Suggestions for Writing

1. Stereotypes can be useful in literature and film, but in real life they may be damaging. Write an essay in which you examine real-life stereotypes, recalling behavior you have observed and experienced.

2. Using Barry's essay as a model, write an essay satirizing an issue you find unfair, irritating, or just amusing.

Judith Ortiz Cofer
Don't Misread My Signals

Judith Ortiz Cofer, *born in Puerto Rico in 1952, is the Franklin Professor of English and Creative Writing at the University of Georgia. A writer of diverse talents, she is acclaimed for her fiction, nonfiction, and poetry, all of which explore the intersections between her identities as a woman, an American, and a Puerto Rican. Cofer's books include the novel* The Line of the Sun *(1991), the essay collection* Woman in Front of the Sun: On Becoming a Writer *(2000), and the award-winning collections of prose and poetry* Silent Dancing *(1990) and* The Latin Deli *(1993). Her work has been featured in* The Best American Essays, The Norton Book of Women's Lives, *and the* O. Henry Prize Stories, *and she has received fellowships from the National Endowment for the Arts and the Witter Bynner Foundation. In "Don't Misread My Signals," which first appeared in* Glamour *magazine, she writes about the stereotypes she faced as a Puerto Rican girl growing up in New Jersey.*

AS YOU READ: *Identify the stereotypes that Cofer encounters due to her ethnicity and style of dress. Why do people misread her "signals"?*

On a bus to London from Oxford University, where I was earning some 1 graduate credits one summer, a young man, obviously fresh from a pub, approached my seat. With both hands over his heart, he went down on his knees in the aisle and broke into an Irish tenor's rendition of "Maria"° from *West Side Story.*° I was not amused. "Maria" had followed me to London, reminding me of a prime fact of my life: you can leave the island of Puerto Rico, master the English language, and travel as far as you can, but if you're a Latina, especially one who so clearly belongs to Rita Moreno's° gene pool, the island travels with you.

Growing up in New Jersey and wanting most of all to belong, I lived in 2 two completely different worlds. My parents designed our life as a microcosm of their *casa*° on the island—we spoke Spanish, ate Puerto Rican food bought at the *bodega,*° and practiced strict Catholicism complete with Sunday mass in Spanish.

I was kept under tight surveillance by my parents, since my virtue and 3 modesty were, by their cultural equation, the same as their honor. As teenagers, my friends and I were lectured constantly on how to behave as proper *señoritas.* But it was a conflicting message we received, since our Puerto Rican mothers also encouraged us to look and act like women by dressing us in clothes our Anglo schoolmates and their mothers found too

"**Maria**": A song from *West Side Story* about one of the main Puerto Rican characters. *West Side Story:* A 1957 Broadway musical (adapted to film in 1961) that retells Shakespeare's *Romeo and Juliet* as a clash between white and Puerto Rican street gangs.   **Rita Moreno:** Puerto Rican actress who played Anita, Maria's friend in *West Side Story.*   **casa:** Spanish for "house."   **bodega:** Spanish for "small grocery store."

"mature" and flashy. I often felt humiliated when I appeared at an American friend's birthday party wearing a dress more suitable for a semiformal. At Puerto Rican festivities, neither the music nor the colors we wore could be too loud.

I remember Career Day in high school, when our teachers told us 4 to come dressed as if for a job interview. That morning I agonized in front of my closet, trying to figure out what a "career girl" would wear, because the only model I had was Marlo Thomas° on TV. To me and my Puerto Rican girlfriends, dressing up meant wearing our mother's ornate jewelry and clothing.

At school that day, the teachers assailed us for wearing "everything at 5 once"—meaning too much jewelry and too many accessories. And it was painfully obvious that the other students in their tailored skirts and silk blouses thought we were hopeless and vulgar. The way they looked at us was a taste of the cultural clash that awaited us in the real world, where prospective employers and men on the street would often misinterpret our tight skirts and bright colors as a come-on.

It is custom, not chromosomes, that leads us to choose scarlet over pale 6 pink. Our mothers had grown up on a tropical island where the natural environment was a riot of primary colors, where showing your skin was one way to keep cool as well as look sexy. On the island, women felt free to dress and move provocatively since they were protected by the traditions and laws of a Spanish Catholic system of morality and machismo, the main rule of which was: *You may look at my sister, but if you touch her I will kill you.* The extended family and church structure provided them with a circle of safety on the island; if a man "wronged" a girl, everyone would close in to save her family honor.

Off-island, signals often get mixed. When a Puerto Rican girl who is 7 dressed in her idea of what is attractive meets a man from the mainstream culture who has been trained to react to certain types of clothing as a sexual signal, a clash is likely to take place. She is seen as a Hot Tamale, a sexual firebrand. I learned this lesson at my first formal dance when my date leaned over and painfully planted a sloppy, overeager kiss on my mouth. When I didn't respond with sufficient passion, he said in a resentful tone: "I thought you Latin girls were supposed to mature early." It was the first time I would feel like a fruit or vegetable—I was supposed to *ripen*, not just grow into womanhood like other girls.

These stereotypes, though rarer, still surface in my life. I recently stayed 8 at a classy metropolitan hotel. After having dinner with a friend, I was returning to my room when a middle-aged man in a tuxedo stepped directly into my path. With his champagne glass extended toward me, he exclaimed, "Evita!"°

Marlo Thomas: American actress who played a modern single woman on the television comedy *That Girl*, which ran from 1966 to 1971.   **Evita:** A musical and film about Eva Peron, Argentina's first lady from 1946 to 1952.

Blocking my way, he bellowed the song "Don't Cry for Me, Argentina." 9
Playing to the gathering crowd, he began to sing loudly a ditty to the tune of
"La Bamba"—except the lyrics were about a girl named Maria whose ex-
ploits all rhymed with her name and gonorrhea.

I knew that this same man—probably a corporate executive, even 10
worldly by most standards—would never have regaled° a white woman
with a dirty song in public. But to him, I was just a character in his universe
of "others," all cartoons.

Still, I am one of the lucky ones. There are thousands of Latinas without 11
the privilege of the education that my parents gave me. For them every day
is a struggle against the misconceptions perpetuated by the myth of the
Latina as a whore, domestic worker or criminal.

Rather than fight these pervasive stereotypes, I try to replace them with a 12
more interesting set of realities. I travel around the United States reading
from my books of poetry and my novel. With the stories I tell, the dreams
and fears I examine in my work, I try to get my audience past the particulars
of my skin color, my accent or my clothes.

I once wrote a poem in which I called Latinas "God's brown daughters." 13
It is really a prayer, of sorts, for communication and respect. In it,
Latin women pray "in Spanish to an Anglo God / with a Jewish heritage,"
and they are "fervently° hoping / that if not omnipotent,° / at least He be
bilingual."

Questions to Start You Thinking

1. CONSIDERING MEANING: How do people from outside of Cofer's culture
   react to her style of dress? Why do they view her clothing differently than
   Puerto Ricans do?

2. IDENTIFYING WRITING STRATEGIES: Trace the causes and effects that Cofer
   identifies. How does this strategy help her to achieve her purpose? Does she
   make it easy for you to follow the pattern of causes and effects? Why, or
   why not?

3. READING CRITICALLY: How effectively do Cofer's personal anecdotes illustrate ethnic and gender stereotyping? Which anecdotes are most powerful?
   How do they contribute to the essay's tone?

4. EXPANDING VOCABULARY: Define *microcosm* (paragraph 2). How did being
   part of a microcosm while growing up cause Cofer to clash with the larger
   American society?

5. MAKING CONNECTIONS: Both Cofer and Michael Abernethy ("Male Bashing
   on TV," pp. 463–67) explore stereotyping related to gender. (Of course,
   the stereotyping that Cofer describes also relates to ethnicity.) How
   are the tones and purposes of the two essays different? How are they
   similar?

regaled: Entertained.   **fervently:** Passionately.   **omnipotent:** All-powerful.

Journal Prompts

1. Analyze your own style of dress or another external characteristic that might cause you to be judged as a certain "type" of male or female.

2. In paragraph 5, Cofer uses the term *cultural clash*. Share a story from your own experience to exemplify this term.

Suggestions for Writing

1. In paragraph 11, Cofer criticizes "the misconceptions perpetuated by the myth of the Latina." Do you think this myth is reinforced in music, movies, and television shows? Based on your own observations, analyze the media's role in contributing to or debunking a myth about a specific cultural, ethnic, religious, or gender-related group.

2. "Rather than fight these pervasive stereotypes," Cofer writes, "I try to replace them with a more interesting set of realities" (paragraph 12). In an essay, examine Cofer's solution, providing additional solutions for eradicating a specific stereotype or stereotyping in general.

Deborah Tannen
Women and Men Talking on the Job

Deborah Tannen, *born in 1945 in Brooklyn, New York, received her Ph.D. from the University of California at Berkeley in 1979 and is now a University Professor of linguistics at Georgetown University. Tannen believes that it is her "mission" to make academic linguistic research accessible and interesting, as she has done in her many books for the general public about the way people talk to each other. Her books include* That's Not What I Meant! How Conversational Style Makes or Breaks Your Relations with Others *(1986),* You Just Don't Understand: Women and Men in Conversation *(1990), and* I Only Say This Because I Love You: How the Way We Talk Can Make or Break Family Relationships throughout Our Lives *(2001). In* The Argument Culture: Moving from Debate to Dialogue *(1998), Tannen takes a penetrating look at the way Americans argue and the sometimes disastrous consequences that follow. This excerpt is from a longer chapter in* Talking from 9 to 5: How Women's and Men's Conversational Styles Affect Who Gets Heard, Who Gets Credit, and What Gets Done at Work *(1994). Here Tannen focuses on both the causes and effects of some key differences in the way men and women negotiate, present their ideas, and express leadership on the job. In the paired selection that follows (p. 447), Nicholas Wade addresses broad differences in the ways men and women think.*

AS YOU READ: *Notice what Tannen says accounts for the differences in the ways men and women communicate.*

Negotiating Styles

The managers of a medium-size company got the go-ahead to hire a   1
human-resources coordinator, and two managers who worked well together were assigned to make the choice. As it turned out Maureen and
Harold favored different applicants, and both felt strongly about their preferences. Maureen argued with assurance and vigor that the person she
wanted to hire was the most creative and innovative, and that he had the
most appropriate experience. Harold argued with equal conviction that the
applicant he favored had a vision of management that fit with the company's, whereas her candidate might be a thorn in their side. They traded arguments for some time, neither convincing the other. Then Harold said that
hiring the applicant Maureen wanted would make him so uncomfortable
that he would have to consider resigning. Maureen respected Harold. What's
more, she liked and considered him a friend. So she felt that his admission
of such strong feelings had to be taken into account. She said what seemed
to her the only thing she could say under the circumstances: "Well, I certainly don't want you to feel uncomfortable here; you're one of the pillars of
the place. If you feel that strongly about it, I can't argue with that." Harold's
choice was hired.

   In this case, the decision-making power went not to the manager who   2
had the highest rank in the firm (their positions were parallel) and not necessarily to the one whose judgment was best, but to the one whose arguing
strategies were most effective in the negotiation. Maureen was an ardent and
persuasive advocate for her view, but she assumed that she and Harold
would have to come to an agreement in order to make a decision, and that
she had to take his feelings into account. Since Harold would not back
down, she did. Most important, when he argued that he would have to quit
if she got her way, she felt she had no option but to yield.

   What was crucial was not Maureen's and Harold's individual styles in   3
isolation but how their styles interacted — how they played in concert with
the other's style. Harold's threat to quit ensures his triumph — when used
with someone who would not call his bluff. If he had been arguing with
someone who regarded this threat as simply another move in the negotiation rather than as a nonnegotiable expression of deep feelings that had to
be respected, the result might have been different. For example, had she
said, "That's ridiculous; of course you're not going to quit!" or "If that's how
shallow your commitment to this firm is, then we'd be better off without
you," the decision might well have gone the other way.

   When you talk to someone whose style is similar to yours, you can fairly   4
well predict the response you are going to get. But when you talk to someone whose style is different, you can't predict, and often can't make sense of,
the response. Hearing the reaction you get, if it's not the one you expected,
often makes you regret what you said. Harold later told Maureen that he
was sorry he had used the argument he did. In retrospect he was embarrassed, even a bit ashamed of himself. His retrospective chagrin was like

what you feel if you slam down something in anger and are surprised and regretful to see that it breaks. You wanted to make a gesture, but you didn't expect it to come out with such force. Harold regretted what he said precisely because it caused Maureen to back down so completely. He'd known he was upping the ante° — he felt he had to do something to get them out of the loop of recycling arguments they were in — but he had not expected it to end the negotiation summarily; he expected Maureen to meet his move with a balancing move of her own. He did not predict the impact that personalizing his argument would have on her. For her part, Maureen did not think of Harold's threat as just another move in a negotiable argument; she heard it as a personal plea that she could not reject. Their different approaches to negotiation put her at a disadvantage in negotiating with him.

"How Certain Are You of That?"

Negotiating is only one kind of activity that is accomplished through talk at 5 work. Other kinds of decision making are also based as much on ways of talking as on the content of the arguments. The CEO of a corporation explained to me that he regularly has to make decisions based on insufficient information — and making decisions is a large part of his work life. Much of his day is spent hearing brief presentations following which he must either approve or reject a course of action. He has to make a judgment in five minutes about issues the presenters have worked on for months. "I decide," he explained, "based on how confident they seem. If they seem very confident, I call it a go. If they seem unsure, I figure it's too risky and nix it."

Here is where the rule of competence and the role of communication go 6 hand in hand. Confidence, after all, is an internal feeling. How can you judge others' confidence? The only evidence you have to go on is circumstantial — how they talk about what they know. You judge by a range of signs, including facial expression and body posture, but most of all, speech. Do they hesitate? Do they speak or swallow half their words? Is their tone of voice declamatory or halting? Do they make bald statements ("This is a winner! We've got to go for it!") or hedge ("Um . . . from what I can tell, I think it'll work, but we'll never know for sure until we try")? This seems simple enough. Surely, you can tell how confident people are by paying attention to how they speak, just as you can tell when someone is lying.

Well, maybe not. Psychologist Paul Ekman has spent years studying 7 lying, and he has found that most people are very sure they can tell when others are lying. The only trouble is, most can't. With a few thus-far inexplicable exceptions, people who tell him they are absolutely sure they can tell if someone is lying are as likely to be wrong as to be right — and he has found this to be as true for judges as for the rest of us.

In the same way, our ability to determine how confident others are 8 is probably quite limited. The CEO who does not take into account the individual styles of the people who make presentations to him will find it

ante: Cost or stakes.

difficult, if not impossible, to make the best judgment. Different people will talk very differently, not because of the absolute level of their confidence or lack of it, but because of their habitual ways of speaking. There are those who sound sure of themselves even when inside they're not sure at all, and others who sound tentative even when they're very sure indeed. So being aware of differences in ways of speaking is a prerequisite for making good decisions as well as good presentations.

Feasting on Humble Pie°

Although these factors affecting decision making are the same for men and   9
women, and every individual has his or her own style, it seems that women are more likely to downplay their certainty, men more likely to downplay their doubts. From childhood, girls learn to temper° what they say so as not to sound too aggressive — which means too certain. From the time they are little, most girls learn that sounding too sure of themselves will make them unpopular with their peers. Groups of girls, as researchers who have studied girls at play have found, will penalize and even ostracize a girl who seems too sure she's right. Anthropologist Marjorie Harness Goodwin found that girls criticize other girls who stand out by saying, "She thinks she's cute," or "She thinks she's something." Talking in ways that display self-confidence are not approved for girls. . . .

The expectation that women should not display their own accomplish-   10
ments brings us back to the matter of negotiating that is so important in the workplace. A man who owned a medium-sized company remarked that women who came to ask him for raises often supported their requests by pointing to a fellow worker on the same level who earned more. He consid-ered this a weak bargaining strategy because he could always identify a dif-ferent co-worker at that level who earned less. They would do better, he felt, to argue for a raise on the basis of how valuable their own work is to the company. Yet it is likely that many women would be less comfortable "blowing their own horn" than making a claim based on fairness.

Follow the Leader

Similar expectations constrain how girls express leadership. Being a leader   11
often involves giving directions to others, but girls who tell other girls what to do are called "bossy." It is not that girls do not exert influence on their group — of course they do — but, as anthropologists like Marjorie Harness Goodwin have found, many girls discover they get better results if they phrase their ideas as suggestions rather than orders, and if they give reasons for their suggestions in terms of the good of the group. But while these ways of talking make girls — and, later, women — more likable, they make women seem less competent and self-assured in the world of work. And women who do seem competent and self-assured are as much in danger of

humble pie: A colloquial expression for having to admit one is wrong.   temper: Here used as a verb meaning to moderate.

being negatively labeled as are girls. After her retirement, Margaret Thatcher was described in the press as "bossy." Whereas girls are ready to stick this label on each other because they don't think any girls should boss the others around, it seems odd to apply it to Thatcher, who, after all, was the boss. And this is the rub: standards of behavior applied to women are based on roles that do not include being boss.

Boys are expected to play by different rules, since the social organization 12 of boys is different. Boys' groups tend to be more obviously hierarchical: someone is one-up, and someone is one-down. Boys don't typically accuse each other of being "bossy" because the high-status boys are expected to give orders and push the low-status boys around. Daniel Maltz and Ruth Borker summarize research by many scholars showing that boys tend to jockey for center stage, challenge those who get it, and deflect challenges. Giving orders and telling the others what to do are ways of getting and keeping the high-status role. Another way of getting high status is taking center stage by telling stories, jokes, and information. Along with this, many boys learn to state their opinions in the strongest possible terms and find out if they're wrong by seeing if others challenge them. These ways of talking translate into an impression of confidence.

The styles typical of women and men both make sense given the context 13 in which they were learned, but they have very different consequences in the workplace. In order to avoid being put in the one-down position, many men have developed strategies for making sure they get the one-up position instead, and this results in ways of talking that serve them well when it comes to hiring and promotion. In relation to the examples I have given, women are more likely to speak in the styles that are less effective in getting recognized and promoted. But if they speak in the styles that are effective when used by men — being assertive, sounding sure of themselves, talking up what they have done to make sure they get credit for it — they run the risk that everyone runs if they do not fit their culture's expectations for appropriate behavior: they will not be liked and may even be seen as having psychological problems.

Both women and men pay a price if they do not behave in ways ex- 14 pected of their gender: men who are not very aggressive are called "wimps," whereas women who are not very aggressive are called "feminine." Men who are aggressive are called "go-getters," though if they go too far, from the point of view of the viewer, they may be called "arrogant." This can hurt them, but not nearly as much as the innumerable labels for women who are thought to be too aggressive — starting with the most hurtful one: bitch.

Even the compliments that we receive are revealing. One woman who 15 had designed and implemented a number of innovative programs was praised by someone who said, "You have such a gentle way of bringing about radical change that people don't realize what's happening — or don't get threatened by it." This was a compliment, but it also hinted at the downside of the woman's gentle touch: although it made it possible for her to be effective in instituting the changes she envisioned, her unobtrusive style ensured a lack of recognition. If people don't realize what's happening, they won't give her credit for what she has accomplished.

Not only advancement and recognition, but hiring is affected by ways of speaking. A woman who supervised three computer programmers mentioned that her best employee was another woman who she had hired over the objections of her own boss. Her boss had preferred a male candidate, because he felt the man would be better able to step into her supervisory role if needed. But she had taken a dislike to the male candidate. For one thing, she had felt he was inappropriately flirtatious with her. But most important, she had found him arrogant, because he spoke as if he already had the job, using the pronoun "we" to refer to the group that had not yet hired him. 16

I have no way of knowing whether the woman hired was indeed the better of these two candidates, or whether either she or the man was well suited to assume the supervisory role, but I am intrigued that the male boss was impressed with the male candidate's take-charge self-presentation, while the woman supervisor was put off by it. And it seems quite likely that whatever it was about his way of talking that struck her as arrogant was exactly what led her boss to conclude that this man would be better able to take over her job if needed. 17

Questions to Start You Thinking

1. CONSIDERING MEANING: According to Tannen, what are the key differences in the way men and women communicate at work? What are the major consequences of these differences?

2. IDENTIFYING WRITING STRATEGIES: Where does Tannen identify the causes and the effects of each gender's style of speech in the workplace? How does she use this cause-and-effect strategy to make her argument that women are at a cultural disadvantage in the workplace?

3. READING CRITICALLY: Tannen supports her argument with evidence apparently gained from personal interviews as well as studies by a psychologist, an anthropologist, and other scholars. Why does she draw on this wide variety of sources? Is her evidence sufficient to convince you? Why, or why not?

4. EXPANDING VOCABULARY: Define *declamatory, halting,* and *circumstantial* (paragraph 6). Why does a *declamatory* or *halting* tone provide *circumstantial* evidence about a person's level of confidence (paragraph 6)?

5. MAKING CONNECTIONS: Based on Tannen's observations about the differences between the ways men and women talk, how might she respond to Dave Barry's presentation of interactions between the sexes ("From Now On, Let Women Kill Their Own Spiders," pp. 435–37)? How might she explain the male and female communication styles evident in Barry's examples, such as a woman asking how her pants look or a man asking whether there's anything to eat in the refrigerator?

Link to the Paired Essay

Tannen explains that many of the differences between the way men and women talk are learned as children from their peers, while Nicholas Wade ("How Men and Women Think," pp. 447–50) argues that these differences may actually be the result of differences between male and female brains. Compare and contrast Tannen's and Wade's views.

■ For useful links to Web sources on topics including *men and women*, visit <bedfordstmartins.com/ toplinks>.

Journal Prompts

1. Analyze your own talking or presentation style at work or in the classroom. Does it conform to Tannen's analysis of how men and women talk?

2. What style of verbal presentation is expected at a job interview? If this expectation did not exist, how would you choose to present yourself? Explain.

Suggestions for Writing

1. Analyze the way your boss, co-workers, teachers, or classmates talk to you at work or school. How does their way of talking compare with how Tannen suggests they talk?

2. Are gender differences determined by social forces or biological factors? Write an essay in which you take a stand on this issue, drawing on Tannen's and Wade's arguments as well as other evidence to support your position. Be sure to consider and refute the arguments on the other side of the debate.

Nicholas Wade

How Men and Women Think

Nicholas Wade *was born in 1942 in England. Educated at Cambridge, Wade wrote for* Nature *magazine in London before coming to the United States in 1971. He began his U.S. career writing for* Science *magazine before joining the* New York Times *as an editorial writer. Wade is currently a reporter for the* New York Times *Science section. His several books include* The Ultimate Experiment *(1977),* The Nobel Duel *(1981), and* A World beyond Healing *(1987). He also coedited* The Environment from Your Backyard to the Ocean Floor *(vol. 2 of* The New York Times Book of Science Literacy, 1994) *and* The New York Times Book of Health: How to Feel Fitter, Eat Better, and Live Longer *(1998). His most recent book is* Life Script: How the Human Genome Discoveries Will Transform Memory and Enhance Your Health *(2001). "How Men and Women Think" was first published in the* New York Times Magazine *on June 12, 1994. While Deborah Tannen ("Women and Men Talking on the Job," pp. 441–46) believes that behavioral differences between men and women are the result of socialization, Wade suggests that they behave differently because of biology.*

AS YOU READ: *Identify the evidence that Wade uses to support his claim that gender differences might have a biological basis.*

The human brain, according to an emerging new body of scientific research, comes in two different varieties, maybe as different as the accompanying physique. Men, when they are lost, instinctually fall back on their inbuilt navigational skills, honed from far-off days of tracking large prey miles from home. Women, by contrast, tend to find their way by the simpler methods of remembering local landmarks or even asking help from strangers.

Men excel on psychological tests that require the imaginary twisting in space of a three-dimensional object. The skill seems to help with higher math, where the topmost ranks are thronged with male minds like Andrew Wiles of Princeton, who proclaimed almost a year ago that he had proved Fermat's Last Theorem° and will surely get around to publishing the proof almost any day now.

Some feminist ideologues° assert that all minds are created equal and women would be just as good at math if they weren't discouraged in school. But Camilla Benbow, a psychologist at Iowa State University, has spent years assessing biases like male math teachers or parents who favor boys. She concludes that boys' superiority at math is mostly innate.°

But women, the new studies assert, have the edge in most other ways, like perceptual speed, verbal fluency, and communications skills. They also have sharper hearing than men, and excel in taste, smell, and touch, and in fine co-ordination of hand and eye. If Martians arrived and gave job interviews, it seems likely they would direct men to competitive sports and manual labor and staff most professions, diplomacy, and government with women.

The measurement of intellectual differences is a field with a long and mostly disgraceful past. IQ tests have been regularly misused, sometimes even concocted, in support of prevailing prejudices. Distinguished male anatomists used to argue that women were less intelligent because their brains weighed less, neglecting to correct for the strong influence of body weight on brain weight.

The present studies of sex differences are venturing on ground where self-deception and prejudice are constant dangers. The science is difficult and the results prone to misinterpretation. Still, the budding science seems free so far of obvious error. For one thing, many of the field's leading practitioners happen to be women, perhaps because male academics in this controversial field have had their lives made miserable by militant feminists.

For another, the study of brain sex differences does not depend on just one kind of subvertible measure but draws on several different disciplines, in-

---

Fermat's Last Theorem: A problem that has been puzzling mathematicians for 350 years. Since this essay first came out, Wiles *has* published the proof.   **ideologues:** People who believe strongly in a certain theory.   **innate:** Present at birth.

cluding biology and anatomy. As is described in a new book, *Eve's Rib*, by
Robert Pool, and the earlier *Brain Sex* by Anne Moir and David Jessel, the foundations of the field have been carefully laid in animal research. Experiments
with rats show that exposure in the womb to testosterone indelibly imprints a
male pattern of behavior; without testosterone, the rat's brain is female.

In human fetuses, too, the sex hormones seem to mold a male and fe-   8
male version of the brain, each subtly different in organization and behavior. The best evidence comes from girls with a rare genetic anomaly° who
are exposed in the womb to more testosterone than normal; they grow up
doing better than their unaffected sisters on the tests that boys are typically
good at. There's also some evidence, not yet confirmed, that male and female brains may be somewhat differently structured, with the two cerebral
hemispheres being more specialized and less well interconnected in men
than in women.

If the human brain exists in male and female versions, as modulated in   9
the womb, that would explain what every parent knows, that boys and girls
prefer different patterns of play regardless of well-meaning efforts to impose
unisex toys on both.

The human mind being very versatile, however, any genetic propensities   10
are far from decisive. In math, for example, the average girl is pretty much as
good as the average boy. Only among the few students at the peak of math
ability do boys predominate.° Within the loose framework set by the genes,
education makes an enormous difference. In Japan, boys exceed girls on the
mental rotation tests, just as in America. But the Japanese girls outscore
American boys. Maybe Japanese kids are just smarter or, more likely, just
better taught, Japan being a country where education is taken seriously and
parents and teachers consistently push children to excel.

There are some obvious cautions to draw about the social and political   11
implications that might one day flow from brain sex research. One is that
differences between individuals of the same sex often far exceed the slight
differences between the sexes as two population groups: "If I were going
into combat, I would prefer to have Martina Navratilova° at my side than
Robert Reich,"° says Patricia Ireland, president of the National Organization
for Women. Even if men in general excel in math, an individual woman
could still be better than most men.

On the other hand, if the brains of men and women really are orga-   12
nized differently, it's possible the sexes both prefer and excel at different
occupations, perhaps those with more or less competition or social interaction. "In a world of scrupulous° gender equality, equal numbers of girls and
boys would be educated and trained for . . . all the professions. . . . [Hiring
would proceed] until half of every workplace was made up of men and half,
women," says Judith Lorber in *Paradoxes of Gender*, a new work of feminist

anomaly: Something that is unlike the general rule.   **predominate:** Be present in
greater numbers.   **Martina Navratilova:** World-renowned tennis player, retired as all-
time leader among men and women in singles titles.   **Robert Reich:** Former secretary
of labor.   **scrupulous:** Extremely careful.

theory. That premise does not hold if there are real intellectual differences between the sexes; the test of equal opportunity, when all unfair barriers to women have fallen, will not necessarily be equal outcomes.

Greek mythology tells that Tiresias, having lived both as a man and a woman for some complicated reason, was asked to settle a dispute between Zeus and Hera as to which sex enjoyed sex more. He replied that there was no contest—it was ten times better for women. Whereupon Hera struck him blind for his insolence and Zeus in compensation gave him the gift of foresight. Like Tiresias, the brain sex researchers are uncovering some impolitic truths, potent enough to shake Mount Olympus some day.

Questions to Start You Thinking

1. CONSIDERING MEANING: According to Wade, why is it difficult to do valid, reliable studies of sex differences?

2. IDENTIFYING WRITING STRATEGIES: Wade devotes much of the article to summarizing studies on sex differences. Identify the passages where he summarizes others' research as evidence to support his position.

3. READING CRITICALLY: Although Wade cites many different expert sources as evidence to support his argument, he makes a number of claims that he does not back up. Reread Wade's essay, noting when he makes a claim without referring to a source. How convincing do you find these claims? Does his lack of evidence damage his argument in any way? Why, or why not?

4. EXPANDING VOCABULARY: Define *impolitic* and *potent* (paragraph 13). Why do both describe the truths uncovered by brain sex researchers?

5. MAKING CONNECTIONS: Wade notes that "brain sex researchers are uncovering some impolitic truths" about gender differences but that these findings are "potent enough to shake Mount Olympus some day" (paragraph 13). In what ways might some people use these statements to describe Shelby Steele's position on affirmative action ("Affirmative Action: The Price of Preference," pp. 530–34)?

Link to the Paired Essay

For useful links to Web sources on topics including *men and women*, visit <bedfordstmartins.com/toplinks>.

Both Wade and Deborah Tannen ("Women and Men Talking on the Job," pp. 441–46) suggest that no matter what science is able to prove about the cause, everyday experience shows us that men and women are different. Why do both authors use common sense and everyday examples to help support the scientific research they cite? Do you find examples from everyday life to be convincing as evidence? Why, or why not?

Journal Prompts

1. Are any of your personality traits or intellectual qualities typically associated with the opposite sex? How do you feel about these traits?

2. Drawing on your own experience and observations, do you believe there are significant differences in the way men and women think? If so, do you think these differences are innate or the result of socialization? Explain.

Suggestions for Writing

1. Recall your own experience taking aptitude tests. In your opinion, did these tests accurately measure your abilities — or were they unfair because of gender bias? Write an essay explaining your responses to these tests, offering evidence to support your assessment of their fairness and accuracy.

2. Investigate some of the new findings about brain differences between the sexes reported since Wade's essay was first published in 1994. For example, what are new PET scans revealing about differences between male and female brains? Present the results of your research in an essay, pointing out where they elaborate, support, or contradict any of Wade's points.

Chapter 24
Popular Culture

Responding to an Image

Read this comic strip frame by frame, and summarize its basic story. What is the significance of its title? Overall, what is the comic strip's purpose? How does it combine text and visual images to comment on our ability to counter the effects of advertising? Why do you think the writer/artist chose to convey her message through a comic strip?

Web Search

Visit *adflip* <www.adflip.com/>, a site that archives both classic and modern print advertisements. Click on "Current Ads," and choose one that interests you. Then search one of the site's classic ad collections, looking for a similar product from a different decade. Compare and contrast the two ads. How do their visual and written components differ? What techniques or appeals do the advertisers use to sell the products? What does each ad reveal about the culture of its decade or about its intended audience? Write an essay using specific details from the ads to support your thesis or main idea about the pair.

■ For reading activities linked to this chapter, visit <bedfordstmartins.com/bedguide> and do a keyword search:

reading

Stephen King
Why We Crave Horror Movies

Stephen King *was born in 1947 in Portland, Maine, and attended the University of Maine at Orono. He now lives in Bangor, Maine, where he writes his best-selling horror novels, many of which have been made into popular movies. The prolific King is also the author of screenplays, teleplays, short fiction, essays, e-books, and (under the pseudonym Richard Bachman) novels. His well-known horror novels include* Carrie *(1974),* Firestarter *(1980),* Pet Sematary *(1983),* Misery *(1987),* The Green Mile *(1996),* Wizard and Glass *(1997), and* Hearts in Atlantis *(1999). In 2000 he published* On Writing: A Memoir of the Craft. *In the following essay, first published in* Playboy *in December 1981, King draws on his extensive experience with horror to explain the human craving to be frightened.*

AS YOU READ: *Identify the needs that King says horror movies fulfill for viewers.*

I think that we're all mentally ill; those of us outside the asylums only hide it a little better—and maybe not all that much better, after all. We've all known people who talk to themselves, people who sometimes squinch their faces into horrible grimaces when they believe no one is watching, people who have some hysterical fear—of snakes, the dark, the tight place, the long drop . . . and, of course, those final worms and grubs that are waiting so patiently underground.

When we pay our four or five bucks and seat ourselves at tenth-row center in a theater showing a horror movie, we are daring the nightmare.

Why? Some of the reasons are simple and obvious. To show that we can, that we are not afraid, that we can ride this roller coaster. Which is not to say that a really good horror movie may not surprise a scream out of us at some point, the way we may scream when the roller coaster twists through a complete 360 or plows through a lake at the bottom of the drop. And horror movies, like roller coasters, have always been the special province° of the

province: Area.

young; by the time one turns forty or fifty, one's appetite for double twists or 360-degree loops may be considerably depleted.

We also go to reestablish our feelings of essential normality; the horror   4
movie is innately conservative, even reactionary. Freda Jackson as the horrible melting woman in *Die, Monster, Die!* confirms for us that no matter how far we may be removed from the beauty of a Robert Redford or a Diana Ross, we are still light-years from true ugliness.

And we go to have fun.   5

Ah, but this is where the ground starts to slope away, isn't it? Because   6
this is a very peculiar sort of fun indeed. The fun comes from seeing others menaced—sometimes killed. One critic suggested that if pro football has become the voyeur's° version of combat, then the horror film has become the modern version of the public lynching.

It is true that the mythic, "fairy-tale" horror film intends to take away   7
the shades of gray. . . . It urges us to put away our more civilized and adult penchant° for analysis and to become children again, seeing things in pure blacks and whites. It may be that horror movies provide psychic relief on this level because this invitation to lapse into simplicity, irrationality, and even outright madness is extended so rarely. We are told we may allow our emotions a free rein . . . or no rein at all.

If we are all insane, then sanity becomes a matter of degree. If your in-   8
sanity leads you to carve up women like Jack the Ripper or the Cleveland Torso Murderer, we clap you away in the funny farm (but neither of those two amateur-night surgeons was ever caught, heh-heh-heh); if, on the other hand, your insanity leads you only to talk to yourself when you're under stress or to pick your nose on your morning bus, then you are left alone to go about your business . . . though it is doubtful that you will ever be invited to the best parties.

The potential lyncher is in almost all of us (excluding saints, past and   9
present; but then, most saints have been crazy in their own ways), and every now and then, he has to be let loose to scream and roll around in the grass. Our emotions and our fears form their own body, and we recognize that it demands its own exercise to maintain proper muscle tone. Certain of these emotional muscles are accepted—even exalted—in civilized society; they are, of course, the emotions that tend to maintain the status quo° of civilization itself. Love, friendship, loyalty, kindness—these are all the emotions that we applaud, emotions that have been immortalized in the couplets of Hallmark cards and in the verses (I don't dare call it poetry) of Leonard Nimoy.

When we exhibit these emotions, society showers us with positive rein-   10
forcement; we learn this even before we get out of diapers. When, as children, we hug our rotten little puke of a sister and give her a kiss, all the aunts and uncles smile and twit and cry, "Isn't he the sweetest little thing?"

voyeur: One who takes inordinate pleasure in the act of watching.   **penchant:** Strong inclination.   **status quo:** Existing state of affairs.

Such coveted treats as chocolate-covered graham crackers often follow. But if we deliberately slam the rotten little puke of a sister's fingers in the door, sanctions follow — angry remonstrance° from parents, aunts, and uncles; instead of a chocolate-covered graham cracker, a spanking.

But anticivilization emotions don't go away, and they demand periodic 11 exercise. We have such "sick" jokes as "What's the difference between a truckload of bowling balls and a truckload of dead babies?" (You can't unload the truckload of bowling balls with a pitchfork . . . a joke, by the way, that I heard originally from a ten-year-old.) Such a joke may surprise a laugh or a grin out of us even as we recoil, a possibility that confirms the thesis: if we share a brotherhood of man, then we also share an insanity of man. None of which is intended as a defense of either the sick joke or insanity but merely as an explanation of [how] the best horror films, like the best fairy tales, manage to be reactionary, anarchistic, and revolutionary all at the same time.

The mythic horror movie, like the sick joke, has a dirty job to do. It delib- 12 erately appeals to all that is worst in us. It is morbidity unchained, our most base instincts let free, our nastiest fantasies realized . . . and it all happens, fittingly enough, in the dark. For those reasons, good liberals often shy away from horror films. For myself, I like to see the most aggressive of them — *Dawn of the Dead*, for instance — as lifting a trapdoor in the civilized forebrain and throwing a basket of raw meat to the hungry alligators swimming around in that subterranean river beneath.

Why bother? Because it keeps them from getting out, man, it keeps 13 them down there and me up here. It was Lennon and McCartney who said that all you need is love, and I would agree with that.

As long as you keep the gators fed.   14

Questions to Start You Thinking

1. CONSIDERING MEANING: What does King mean when he says that "we're all mentally ill" (paragraph 1)? Is this a serious statement? Why, or why not?

2. IDENTIFYING WRITING STRATEGIES: How does King use analysis, breaking a complex topic into parts, to support his argument?

3. READING CRITICALLY: Why do you think King uses the inclusive pronoun *we* so frequently throughout his essay? What effect does the use of this pronoun have on your response to his argument?

4. EXPANDING VOCABULARY: Define *innately* (paragraph 4). What does King mean when he says horror movies are "innately conservative"? Does he contradict himself when he says they are also "reactionary, anarchistic, and revolutionary" (paragraph 11)? Why, or why not?

5. MAKING CONNECTIONS: How do King's reasons for our craving for horror movies relate to James Poniewozik's reasons for the popularity of reality television ("Why Reality TV Is Good for Us," pp. 468–72)? In what ways do the two writers agree or disagree about viewers' needs and about the capacity of movies or television to address those needs?

remonstrance: Objection.

Journal Prompts

1. What is your response to "sick" jokes? Why?

2. Recall a movie that exercised your "anticivilization emotions" (paragraph 11). Describe your state of mind before, during, and after the movie.

Suggestions for Writing

1. What genre of movie do you prefer to watch, and why? What cravings does this type of movie satisfy?

2. Do you agree that "the horror film has become the modern version of the public lynching" (paragraph 6)? Write an argument in which you defend or refute this suggestion, citing examples from King's essay and from your own moviegoing experience to support your position.

Veronica Chambers
The Myth of Cinderella

Veronica Chambers, *born in 1970 in the Canal Zone, Panama, was graduated summa cum laude with a B.A. in literary studies from Simon's Rock College in Great Barrington, Massachusetts. She has held several editorial posts with major magazines, and from 1996 to 1999, as an associate editor at* Newsweek *magazine, she critiqued the social significance of music and electronic media for the Arts and Lifestyle section. She is coauthor of* Poetic Justice: Filmmaking South Central Style *(1993) and a contributor to the* Young Feminist Anthology. *Her freelance writing has appeared in publications such as* Essence, *the* New York Times Book Review, *and* Vogue, *and she was awarded a prestigious research fellowship by the Freedom Forum, which she used to analyze news coverage of Asian and African Americans. Her book* Mama's Girl *is a memoir about Chambers's troubled family life and complex relationship with her mother, and* Having It All? *(2003) is a collection of essays that chronicle the lives of middle-class African American women. She has also published several children's books. In this selection, published in* Newsweek *in November 1997, Chambers explores the social and historical significance of a Disney television production of* Cinderella, *in which the fairy-tale heroine is played by an actress of African American descent.*

AS YOU READ: *Identify what Chambers claims attracts young girls to the Cinderella story. What criticism of the story does Chambers have?*

For generations, black women have been the societal embodiment of   1
Cinderella. Like Cinderella, black women (and poor white women, too) have often been relegated to the cooking and the cleaning, watching enviously as the women they worked for lived a more privileged life. Think about *Gone with the Wind.* Wouldn't Scarlett O'Hara have laughed, as the

evil stepsisters laughed at Cinderella, if Butterfly McQueen had said that *she* wanted to go to the ball, that *she* wanted to dance with Rhett Butler? For years, the idea of a black girl playing the classic Cinderella was unthinkable. But this Sunday, when Brandy, the eighteen-year-old pop singer, stars in the Disney/ABC presentation of Rodgers and Hammerstein's *Cinderella*, reparations will be made. Finally, a sister is getting to go to the ball.

The casting of Brandy as Disney's latest Cinderella is especially signifi- 2 cant because for many black women, the 1950 animated Disney Cinderella with her blond hair and blue eyes sent a painful message that only white women could be princesses. "It's hard when you don't fit the traditional view of beauty," says Whoopi Goldberg (who plays the prince's mother in the new version). "I've gotten letters from people that say if I'd just get my nose done or if I wasn't so dark, I'd be OK-looking. That's why I love this Cinderella, because Brandy is a beautiful, everyday-looking black girl."

The Disney/ABC twist on *Cinderella* is to take multiracial casting to the 3 never-never-land extreme: while Whoopi is the queen, the king (Victor Garber) is white; Bernadette Peters is the stepmother with one white daughter and one black. Whitney Houston plays the fairy godmother, in a soulful performance reminiscent of Lena Horne's° in *The Wiz*. Jason Alexander is hilarious as the prince's much maligned valet. And who plays the prince? A Filipino actor, Paolo Montalban.

Even in this postfeminist° era, where a Cinderella waiting to be rescued 4 by a prince can be seen as a wimp, the myth still appeals. There are at least a half dozen other movies in the works, including one starring Drew Barrymore, with Anjelica Huston as the wicked stepmother, for Twentieth Century Fox; Tribeca Productions' *Sisterella*; *Cinderella's Revenge* at Sony, and a Whoopi Goldberg project at Trimark.

Disney's politically correct version is sure to spark controversy in the 5 black community. "I'm genuinely bothered by the subliminal message that's sent when you don't have a black Prince Charming," says Denene Millner, author of *The Sistahs' Rules*. "When my stepson who's five looks at that production, I want him to know he can be somebody's Prince Charming." But this *Cinderella* does mirror, unwittingly, a growing loss of faith in black men by many black women. Just as Brandy's Cinderella falls in love with a prince of another color, so have black women begun to date and marry interracially in record numbers. In 1980 there were 27,000 new marriages between black women and white men. By 1990 that number had doubled, to 54,000. While black men still marry outside the race in greater numbers, interracial marriages involving black women are growing at a faster rate. "Some of it is a backlash because there are a lot of women who feel that black men have done them wrong," says Pulitzer Prize–winning poet Rita Dove. "It's also a way of taking charge and saying, 'I'm waiting for Prince

Lena Horne: Blues singer.   **postfeminist:** Relating to the assumption that the goals of the feminist movement have been achieved and that it is no longer necessary to fight actively for them.

Charming, but the important thing is that he's charming, not that he's black.'" There's an irony here: for white women the Cinderella myth is about passivity, but for black women it's about actively seeking a partner who's their equal.

With many black women heading households, the issue isn't necessarily 6 about becoming independent. Estelle Farley is a clinical research scientist in Raleigh, North Carolina. In her thirties, Farley says, "[The man I'm looking for] has to have a salary close to what I make or more. I've gone down the road with someone who didn't, and it's not a good road." bell hooks, author of the new book *Wounds of Passion*, is much more blunt. "Keep this in mind, girlfriend," says hooks. "This generation of black women is growing up in a truly integrated pop culture. Most black women under the age of thirty would rather have a rich white man than a poor black man."

Whoopi Goldberg, whose companion is the white actor Frank Langella, 7 has often been under fire for dating white men. "First off, I have dated black men," explains Goldberg. "But a woman with power is a problem for any man, but particularly a black man because it's hard for them to get power. I understand that, but I have to have a life, and that means dating the men that want to date me."

Historically, the struggle for racial equality left little room for black 8 women to indulge in Cinderella fantasies. From Reconstruction° through Jim Crow° and through the civil-rights movement, black women devoted their energies to these struggles while secretly hoping that one day their prince would indeed come. Harvard psychiatrist Dr. Alvin Poussaint remembers that during the 1960s, "many of the black women in the movement used to joke — but it was partly serious — that part of why they were fighting was so black men would be able to get good jobs and they would be able to stay at home like white women and have their men take care of them." Furthermore, in the 1970s, many black women were reluctant to embrace feminism because it seemed that just when it was about to be their turn to be Cinderella, white women were telling them that the fantasy was all wrong. "I think there was always more ambivalence about the women's movement on the part of some black women," says Poussaint. "It meant that they were losing out on their chance to be in this dependent role."

Today Cinderella, for better or worse, is much more accessible to young 9 black women. Disney vice president Anna Perez recalls, "Growing up, I loved fairy tales. But I never thought someone was going to come along and take care of me. It sure didn't happen for my mother, who raised six kids by herself." But Brandy says, "I grew up listening to the Cinderella stories; just because she was white didn't mean that I couldn't live the same dream."

What gives Cinderella such staying power is the myth's malleability, the 10 many ways in which it continues to be transformed. Author Virginia Hamil-

---

Reconstruction: The period after the Civil War when the South was rebuilding.   **Jim Crow:** Laws that legalized segregation by sanctioning "separate but equal" facilities for whites and blacks.

ton, a MacArthur "genius" award winner, is partial to a plantation myth called "Catskinella," which appears in her book, *Her Stories*. In this version Cinderella is strong and wily. The prince wants to marry her, but she makes him wait until she is good and ready. Hamilton says she loves the story because it is evidence that "when black women were at their most oppressed, they had the extraordinary imagination to create stories for themselves, about themselves."

For bell hooks, Zora Neale Hurston's classic novel *Their Eyes Were* 11 *Watching God* is the best Cinderella story going. "Janie rejects her rich husband for Tea Cake, the laborer," hooks says of the book, which Oprah Winfrey is developing into a movie. "Janie talks about how there is a jewel inside of her. Tea Cake sees that jewel, and he brings it out. Which is very different from the traditional Cinderella myth of the prince holding the jewel and you trying to get it from him."

In this latest version of Cinderella, Disney makes a subtle — some might 12 say feeble — attempt to give the myth a slightly more feminist slant. When they first meet, Cinderella tells the prince that she's not sure she wants to get to know him. She says, "I doubt if this stranger has any idea how a girl should be treated." He gives her a knowing look and says, "Like a princess, I suppose." And she looks at him, with her big brown eyes, and says, "No, like a *person*. With kindness and respect."

Questions to Start You Thinking

1. CONSIDERING MEANING: What does Chambers say is the difference between how black and white women interpret the Cinderella myth?

2. IDENTIFYING WRITING STRATEGIES: How does Chambers use cause and effect to explain the relationship between America's history of racism and the appeal of the Cinderella myth to African American women?

3. READING CRITICALLY: Chambers quotes many different women's views of the Cinderella myth. How do their credentials and opinions help shape the essay? Is this strategy effective for the point Chambers is trying to make? Why, or why not?

4. EXPANDING VOCABULARY: Define *malleability*. What does Chambers mean when she credits the endurance of the Cinderella myth to its *malleability* (paragraph 10)? What makes the story malleable?

5. MAKING CONNECTIONS: What do you think that Danzy Senna's grandmother would have thought about the Cinderella myth ("The Color of Love," pp. 411–15)? How might she have reacted to Disney's revised story with multiracial casting? What might she have learned from watching the broadcast?

Journal Prompts

1. What fairy-tale or mythical figure especially appealed to you as a child? Why? In what way — if any — did it shape your expectations of life as an adult?

2. What change in the Cinderella myth does the end of Chambers's essay suggest? Do you see it as a positive change? Why, or why not?

Suggestions for Writing

1. Does the Cinderella myth represent an ideal for you? Why, or why not?
2. Write an essay in which you analyze the influence of a character from popular culture. Is the character a positive or a negative role model? Why?

Jay Chiat
Illusions Are Forever

Jay Chiat *(1931–2002), born in New York City, was chairman of ScreamingMedia, an Internet company that built software for distributing information to corporate intranets and Web sites. He also founded TBWA/Chiat/Day, one of the ten largest advertising agencies in the world. The agency's clients have included Apple, Eveready, Nissan, Kmart, and about a hundred other companies. In "Illusions Are Forever," first published in* Forbes, *Chiat explains how advertisers greatly influence the way viewers think and feel about human experience. When a consumer imagines what a romantic moment should be like, is that idea formed by the De Beers diamond advertising campaign (or by other media images)?*

AS YOU READ: *Look for the ways in which Chiat says media can affect our perception of truth.*

I know what you're thinking: That's rich, asking an adman to define truth. 1
Advertising people aren't known either for their wisdom or their morals, so it's hard to see why an adman is the right person for this assignment. Well, it's just common sense — like asking an alcoholic about sobriety, or a sinner about piety.° Who is likely to be more obsessively attentive to a subject than the transgressor?°

Everyone thinks that advertising is full of lies, but it's not what you 2
think. The facts presented in advertising are almost always accurate, not because advertising people are sticklers but because their ads are very closely regulated. If you make a false claim in a commercial on network television, the FTC° will catch it. Someone always blows the whistle.

The real lie in advertising — some would call it the "art" of advertising 3
— is harder to detect. What's false in advertising lies in the presentation of situations, values, beliefs, and cultural norms that form a backdrop for the selling message.

piety: Religious devoutness.   **transgressor:** One who violates a law, command, or moral code.   **FTC:** Federal Trade Commission, which regulates trade and protects consumers.

Advertising — including movies, TV, and music videos — presents to us a 4
world that is not our world but rather a collection of images and ideas created for the purpose of selling. These images paint a picture of the ideal
family life, the perfect home. What a beautiful woman is, and is not. A pre-
scription for being a good parent and a good citizen.

The power of these messages lies in their unrelenting pervasiveness, the 5
twenty-four-hour-a-day drumbeat that leaves no room for an alternative
view. We've become acculturated to the way advertisers and other media-
makers look at things, so much so that we have trouble seeing things in our
own natural way. Advertising robs us of the most intimate moments in our
lives because it substitutes an advertiser's idea of what ought to be — What
should a romantic moment be like?

You know the De Beers diamond advertising campaign? A clever strat- 6
egy, persuading insecure young men that two months' salary is the appropriate sum to pay for an engagement ring. The arbitrary° algorithm is prepos-
terous, of course, but imagine the fiancée who receives a ring costing only
half a month's salary? The advertising-induced insult is grounds for calling
off the engagement, I imagine. That's marketing telling the fiancée what to
feel and what's real.

Unmediated is a great word: It means "without media," without the in- 7
between layer that makes direct experience almost impossible. Media inter-
feres with our capacity to experience naturally, spontaneously, and genuinely, and thereby spoils our capacity for some important kinds of
personal "truth." Although media opens our horizons infinitely, it costs us.
We have very little direct personal knowledge of anything in the world that
is not filtered by media.

Truth seems to be in a particular state of crisis now. When what we 8
watch is patently fictional, like most movies and commercials, it's worri-
some enough. But it's absolutely pernicious when it's packaged as reality.
Nothing represents a bigger threat to truth than reality-based television, in
both its lowbrow and highbrow versions — from *Survivor* to A&E's *Biography*.
The lies are sometimes intentional, sometimes errors, often innocent, but in
all cases they are the "truth" of a media-maker who claims to be representing reality.

The Internet is also a culprit, obscuring the author, the figure behind the 9
curtain, even more completely. Chat rooms, which sponsor intimate conversation, also allow the participants to misrepresent themselves in every way
possible. The creation of authoritative-looking Web sites is within the grasp
of any reasonably talented twelve-year-old, creating the appearance of pro-
fessionalism and expertise where no expert is present. And any mischief
maker can write a totally plausible-looking,° totally fake stock analyst's report and post it on the Internet. When the traditional signals of authority
are so misleading, how can we know what's for real?

---

arbitrary: Based on preference, not specific criteria or reason.   **plausible:** Credible,
believable.

But I believe technology, for all its weaknesses, will be our savior. The   10
Internet is our only hope for true democratization, a truly populist publishing form, a mass communication tool completely accessible to individuals.
The Internet puts CNN on the same plane with the freelance journalist and
the lady down the street with a conspiracy theory, allowing cultural and ide-
ological pluralism° that never previously existed.

This is good for the cause of truth, because it underscores what is other-   11
wise often forgotten — truth's instability. Truth is not absolute: It is presented, represented, and re-presented by the individuals who have the floor,
whether they're powerful or powerless. The more we hear from powerless
ones, the less we are in the grasp of powerful ones — and the less we believe
that "truth" is inviolable,° given, and closed to interpretation. We also come
closer to seeking our own truth.

That's the choice we're given every day. We can accept the very com-   12
pelling, very seductive version of "truth" offered to us daily by media-makers,
or we can tune out its influence for a shot at finding our own individual, confusing, messy version of it. After all, isn't personal truth the ultimate truth?

Questions to Start You Thinking

1. CONSIDERING MEANING: According to Chiat, what is truth? How does
   media affect our perception of truth?

2. IDENTIFYING WRITING STRATEGIES: Reread Chiat's opening paragraph.
   What kinds of appeals do you find? How does their use in the opening
   affect the rest of the essay? (See pp. 39–40 for an explanation of appeals.)

3. READING CRITICALLY: Chiat says, "I believe technology, for all its weaknesses, will be our savior" (paragraph 10). On what criteria does Chiat
   base this evaluation? Explain the effects of the Internet on media that
   Chiat judges valuable.

4. EXPANDING VOCABULARY: Define *pernicious* (paragraph 8). How are reality-
   based television programs pernicious? In what ways might other kinds
   of programs be pernicious?

5. MAKING CONNECTIONS: Chiat maintains that truth is threatened most
   forcefully by "reality-based television, in both its lowbrow and highbrow version — from *Survivor* to A&E's *Biography*" (paragraph 8). How
   might James Poniewozik ("Why Reality TV Is Good for Us," pp.
   468–72) or Elaine Showalter ("Window on Reality," pp. 473–76)
   counter Chiat's assertion?

Journal Prompts

1. Recall a time when someone else's version of the truth differed from
   yours. What caused the differences?

---

pluralism: A state in which minority groups have equal status within society.   **inviolable:** Incapable of being violated or destroyed.

2. Recall a case when you or someone you know has based expectations of life on media images. To what extent do these images shape our sense of reality?

Suggestions for Writing

1. Watch an episode of A&E's *Biography* or another reality-based television show. In what places might the media-maker's perception of truth have slanted the presentation? Write an essay in which you analyze the ways the program may have selected or interpreted the "truth."

2. Do some research on the media in nineteenth-century America. Then write an essay to compare and contrast the democratizing effects of nineteenth-century newspapers with those of twenty-first-century media. You may want to consider the Internet in your discussion.

Michael Abernethy
Male Bashing on TV

Michael Abernethy *was born in Bristol, Tennessee, in 1960. He holds a B.A. from Baylor University and an M.A. from the University of North Texas. He currently teaches communication studies and writing at Indiana State University, and he is also a film and television critic for* PopMatters.com. *Before becoming a full-time writer and educator, Abernethy worked in hotel and restaurant management. "Male Bashing on TV," first published on* PopMatters.com *in 2003, takes on an issue that some may find trivial. To Abernethy, however, the increasingly negative portrayal of men on sitcoms and commercials is no laughing matter.*

AS YOU READ: *Why, according to Abernethy, is male bashing on television a serious problem?*

Warning for our male readers: The following article contains big words   1
and complex sentences. It might be a good idea to have a woman nearby to explain it to you.

It's been a hard day. Your assistant at work is out with the flu and there   2
is another deadline fast approaching. Your wife is at a business conference, so you have to pick up your son at daycare, make dinner, clean the kitchen, do a load of laundry, and get Junior to bed before you can settle down on the sofa with those reports you still need to go over.

Perhaps a little comedy will make the work more bearable, you think,   3
so you turn on CBS's Monday night comedies: *King of Queens, Yes, Dear, Everybody Loves Raymond,* and *Still Standing.* Over the next two hours, you see four male lead characters who are nothing like you. These men are selfish and lazy, inconsiderate husbands and poor parents.

And the commercials in between aren't any better. Among them: A feminine hygiene ad: Two women are traveling down a lovely country road, laughing and having a great time. But wait. One of them needs to check the freshness of her mini-pad, and, apparently, the next rest area is six states away. A woman's voice-over interjects, "It's obvious that the interstate system was designed by men." 4

A digital camera ad: A young husband walks through a grocery store, trying to match photos in his hand with items on the shelves. Cut to his wife in the kitchen, snapping digital pictures of all the items in the pantry so that hubby won't screw up the shopping. 5

A family game ad: A dorky guy and beautiful woman are playing Trivial Pursuit. He asks her, "How much does the average man's brain weigh?" Her answer: "Not much." 6

A wine ad: A group of women are sitting around the patio of a beach house, drinking a blush wine. Their boyfriends approach, but are denied refreshment until they have "earned" it by building a sand statue of David. 7

Welcome to the new comic image of men on TV: incompetence at its worst. Where television used to feature wise and wonderful fathers and husbands, today's comedies and ads often feature bumbling husbands and inept, uninvolved fathers. On *Still Standing*, Bill (Mark Addy) embarrasses his wife Judy (Jamie Gertz) so badly in front of her reading group that she is dropped from the group. On *Everybody Loves Raymond*, Raymond (Ray Romano) must choose between bathing the twin boys or helping his daughter with her homework. He begrudgingly agrees to assist his daughter, for whom he is no help whatsoever. 8

CBS is not the only guilty party. ABC's *My Wife and Kids* and *According to Jim*, Fox's *The Bernie Mac Show, The Simpsons, Malcolm in the Middle*, and (the recently cancelled) *Titus* and the WB's *Reba* also feature women who are better organized and possess better relational skills than their male counterparts. While most television dramas tend to avoid gender stereotypes, as these undermine "realism," comic portrayals of men have become increasingly negative. The trend is so noticeable that it has been criticized by men's rights groups and some television critics. 9

It has also been studied by academicians Dr. Katherine Young and Paul Nathanson in their book, *Spreading Misandry°: The Teaching of Contempt for Men in Popular Culture.* Young and Nathanson argue that in addition to being portrayed as generally unintelligent, men are ridiculed, rejected, and physically abused in the media. Such behavior, they suggest, "would never be acceptable if directed at women." Evidence of this pattern is found in a 2001 survey of one thousand adults conducted by the Advertising Standards Association in Great Britain, which found two-thirds of respondents thought that women featured in advertisements were "intelligent, assertive, and caring," while the men were "pathetic and silly." The number of respondents who thought men were depicted as "intelligent" was a paltry° 14 percent. 10

misandry: Hatred of men.   **paltry:** Trivial; small.

(While these figures apply to the United Kingdom, comparable advertisements air in the U.S.)

Some feminists might argue that, for decades, women on TV looked 11 mindless, and that turnabout is fair play. True, many women characters through the years have had little more to do than look after their families. From the prim housewife whose only means of control over her children was, "Wait till your father gets home!" to the dutiful housewife whose husband declares "My wife: I think I'll keep her," women in the '50s and '60s were often subservient. (This generalization leaves out the unusual someone like Donna Reed, who produced her own show, on which she was not subservient.)

Then, during the "sexual revolution," TV began to feature independent 12 women who could take care of themselves (Mary and Rhoda on *The Mary Tyler Moore Show*, *Julia*, Alice and Flo on *Alice*, Louise and Florence on *The Jeffersons*). So now, thirty years later, you'd think that maybe we'd have come to some parity.° Not even.

Granted, men still dominate television, from the newsroom to prime- 13 time. And men do plenty on their own to perpetuate the image of the immature male, from Comedy Central's *The Man Show* to the hordes of drunken college boys who show up every year on MTV's Spring Break. What's the problem with a few jokes about how dumb men can be? C'mon, can't we take a few jokes?

If only it was just a few. The jokes have become standard fare. Looking 14 at a handful of sitcoms makes the situation seem relatively insignificant, but when those sitcoms are combined with dozens of negative ads which repeat frequently, then a poor image of men is created in the minds of viewers.

According to *Gender Issues in Advertising Language*, television portrayals 15 that help create or reinforce negative stereotypes can lead to problems with self-image, self-concept, and personal aspirations. Young men learn that they are expected to screw up, that women will have the brains to their brawn, and that childcare is over their heads. And it isn't just men who suffer from this constant parade of dumb men on TV. Children Now reports a new study that found that two-thirds of children they surveyed describe men on TV as angry and only one-third report ever seeing a man on television performing domestic chores, such as cooking or cleaning. There are far too few positive role models for young boys on television.

Moreover, stereotypical male-bashing portrayals undermine the core 16 belief of the feminist movement: equality. Just think. What if the butt of all the jokes took on another identity? Consider the following fictional exchanges:

"It is so hard to get decent employees."
"That's because you keep hiring blacks."

---

parity: Equality.

"I just don't understand this project at all."
"Well, a woman explained it to you, so what did you expect?"

"I can't believe he is going out again tonight."
"Oh please, all Hispanics care about is sex."

All of these statements are offensive, and would rightfully be objected to by advocates of fair representation in the media. However, put the word "man" or "men" in place of "blacks," "woman," and "Hispanics" in the above sentences and they're deemed humorous. Are men who ask to be treated civilly overly sensitive or are we as justified in our objections as members of NOW,° the NAACP,° GLAAD,° and other groups which protest demeaning television portrayals, whether those portrayals are on sitcoms, dramas, advertisements, or moronic TV like *The Man Show*?

Most of the shows I'm talking about are popular. Maybe that means that 17 I am being too sensitive. Yet, many U.S. viewers didn't have a problem with *Amos and Andy* or *I Dream of Jeannie*, both famous for their offensive stereotypes. These shows enjoyed good ratings, but neither concept is likely to be revived anytime soon, as "society" has realized their inappropriateness.

All this is not to say buffoonery — male or female — isn't a comic staple. 18 Barney on *The Andy Griffith Show*, Ted on *The Mary Tyler Moore Show*, and Kramer on *Seinfeld* were all vital characters, but the shows also featured intelligent males. And these clowns were amusing because they were eccentric personalities, not because they were men. The same could be said of many female characters on TV, like *Alice's* Flo, *Friends'* Phoebe, or Karen on *Will & Grace*. Good comedy stems from creative writing and imaginative characterizations, not from degrading stereotypes.

Fortunately, some people are working to change the way television por- 19 trays men. J. C. Penney recently ran an ad for a One Day sale, with a father at the breakfast table, with his infant crying and throwing things. The father asks the child when his mother will be home. Lana Whited of *The Roanoke Times*, syndicated columnist Dirk Lammers, and the National Men's Resource Center were just a few who objected to this image of an apparently incompetent and uncaring father, one who would let his child cry without making any attempt to calm him. Penney's got the message; their recent holiday ad featured a father, mother, and son all happily shopping together.

Few men I know want a return to the "good ole days." Those generaliza- 20 tions were as unrealistic as the idea that all men are big slobbering goofballs. Hope lies beyond such simplistic oppositions, in shows like *The Cosby Show* or *Mad About You*, which placed their protagonists on level playing fields. Paul Reiser and Cosby did, on occasion, do moronic things, but so did Helen Hunt and Phylicia Rashad. People — because they are people, not just gendered people — are prone to fall on their faces occasionally.

NOW: National Organization for Women.   **NAACP:** National Association for the Advancement of Colored People.   **GLAAD:** Gay and Lesbian Alliance Against Defamation.

Undoubtedly, there are men out there who are clones of Ward Cleaver, 21 just as there are men who resemble Al Bundy. But the majority is somewhere in between. We're trying to deal the best we can with the kids, the spouse, the job, the bills, the household chores, and the countless crises that pop up unexpectedly. After all that, when we do get the chance to sit down and relax, it would be nice to turn on the TV and not see ourselves reflected as idiots.

Questions to Start You Thinking

1. CONSIDERING MEANING: In Abernethy's opinion, what generates the best kind of comedy?

2. IDENTIFYING WRITING STRATEGIES: What strategies does Abernethy use to help readers understand the complexity and extent of male bashing on television?

3. READING CRITICALLY: Abernethy states that jokes about men's incompetence have become "standard fare" on television (paragraph 14). Does he provide sufficient relevant evidence to support this statement? Which of his examples are particularly striking?

4. EXPANDING VOCABULARY: In paragraph 10, Abernethy cites a study in which only 14 percent of respondents thought that men on television were depicted as "intelligent." How do you define "intelligent"? What kind of intelligence do you think Abernethy would like to see male sitcom characters display?

5. MAKING CONNECTIONS: In paragraph 18, Abernethy declares, "Good comedy stems from creative writing and imaginative characterizations, not from degrading stereotypes." How might Dave Barry ("From Now On, Let Women Kill Their Own Spiders," pp. 435–37) respond to this statement?

Journal Prompts

1. As Abernethy points out in paragraph 11, "Some feminists might argue that, for decades, women on TV looked mindless, and that turnabout is fair play." Do you agree or disagree with this attitude? Why?

2. How do you define "good comedy"? In your opinion, does stereotyping add to or detract from humor?

Suggestions for Writing

1. Is Abernethy overreacting? Using additional examples from television shows or commercials that you have seen, write an essay responding to his point of view.

2. Select a magazine geared to women and one geared to men, and then thumb through the advertisements. How are males portrayed in each magazine's ads? Does the treatment differ between the two magazines? In what ways does it support or refute Abernethy's point? Present your analysis in a comparison-and-contrast essay.

*James Poniewozik**
Why Reality TV Is Good for Us

James Poniewozik, *a native of Monroe, Michigan, is a graduate of the University of Michigan and New York University. Since 1999 he has been the media and television critic for* Time *magazine, writing on subjects ranging from the television series* The Sopranos *to the effects of September 11 on popular culture. Before joining the staff of* Time, *Poniewozik served as the media critic and media section editor for* Salon.com. *He also has written for such publications as* Fortune, Rolling Stone, New York, *the* New York Times Book Review, *and* Talk *and regularly contributes to NPR's "On the Media" and "All Things Considered." Although his reasons differ from those of Elaine Showalter ("Window on Reality," pp. 473–76), Poniewozik extols the virtues of the often criticized but hugely popular genre of reality television in the following selection from a 2003 issue of* Time.

AS YOU READ: *Determine why Poniewozik suggests that reality television characters set a good example for viewers.*

For eight single professional women gathered in Dallas, it is holy 1 Wednesday—the night each week that they gather in one of their homes for the Traveling *Bachelorette* Party. Munching snacks and passing a bottle of wine, they cheer, cry, and cackle as their spiritual leader, Trista Rehn, braves heartache, indecision, and the occasional recitation of bad poetry to choose from among her twenty-five swains.° Yet something is unsettling Leah Hudson's stomach, and it's not just the wine. "I hate that we've been sucked into the Hoover vac of reality TV," says Hudson, thirty. "Do we not have anything better to do than to live vicariously through a bunch of fifteen-minute-fame seekers?"

There you have the essence of reality TV's success: it is the one mass- 2 entertainment category that thrives because of its audience's contempt for it. It makes us feel tawdry, dirty, cheap—if it didn't, we probably wouldn't bother tuning in. And in this, for once, the audience and critics agree. Just listen to the raves for America's hottest TV genre.

"The country is gripped by misanthropy!"° — New York *Observer*   3

"Ridiculous and pernicious!° *Many kinds of cruelty are passed off as enter-* 4 *tainment!"*—Washington *Post*

"So-called reality television just may be killing the medium!"—San Fran- 5 cisco *Chronicle*

O.K., we added the exclamation points, but you get the idea. Yes, view- 6 ers are tuning in to *Joe Millionaire, The Bachelorette,* and *American Idol* by the tens of millions. Yet, to paraphrase Winston Churchill,° never have so many watched so much TV with so little good to say about it.

---

* Reported by *Time's* Amy Lennard Goehner, Jeanne McDowell, and Adam Pitluk.

swains: Admirers.   **misanthropy:** Hatred of humanity.   **pernicious:** Cruel.   **Winston Churchill:** British prime minister during World War II.

Well, that ends here. It may ruin reality producers' marketing plans for a   7
TV critic to say it, but reality TV is, in fact, the best thing to happen to television in several years. It has given the networks water-cooler buzz again; it
has reminded viewers jaded by sitcoms and dramas why TV can be exciting;
and at its best, it is teaching TV a new way to tell involving human stories.

A few concessions up front. First, yes, we all know that there's little real-   8
ity in reality TV: those "intimate" dates, for instance, are staged in front of
banks of cameras and sweltering floodlights. But it's the only phrase we've
got, and I'm sticking with it. Second, I don't pretend to defend the indefen-
sible: *Are You Hot? The Search for America's Sexiest People* isn't getting any
help from me. And finally, I realize that comparing even a well-made reality
show with, say, *The Simpsons* is not merely comparing apples with oranges;
it's comparing onions with washing machines — no reality show can match
the intelligence and layers of well-constructed fiction.

On a sheer ratings level, the latest wave of reality hits has worked a sea   9
change for the networks. And it has put them back on the pop-cultural map,
after losing the buzz war to cable for years. Reality shows don't just reach
tens of millions of viewers but leave them feeling part of a communal experience — what network TV does best, but sitcoms and dramas haven't done
since *Seinfeld* and *Twin Peaks*. (When was the last time *CSI* made you call
your best friend or holler back at your TV?) "Reality has proven that network
television is still relevant," says Mike Fleiss, creator of the *Bachelor* franchise.

This has sitcom and drama writers praying for the reality bust. "The   10
networks only have so much time and resources," says Amy Sherman-
Palladino, creator of *Gilmore Girls*. "Rather than solely focusing on convincing the Olsen twins to allow themselves to be eaten by bears in prime time,
I wish they would focus on coming up with something that would really
last." TV does seem to be in overkill mode, as the networks have signed up
dozens of dating shows, talent searches, and other voyeurfests. And like an
overheated NASDAQ, the reality market is bound to correct. But unlike earlier TV reality booms, this one is supported by a large, young audience that
grew up on MTV's *The Real World* and considers reality as legitimate as dramas and sitcoms — and that, for now, prefers it.

And why not? It would be easier to bemoan reality shows' crowding out   11
sitcoms and dramas if the latter weren't in such a rut. But the new network
shows of fall 2002 were a creatively timid mass of remakes, bland family
comedies, and derivative° cop dramas. Network executives dubbed them
"comfort" — i.e., familiar and boring — TV. Whereas reality TV — call it "discomfort TV" — lives to rattle viewers' cages. It provokes. It offends. But at
least it's trying to do something besides help you get to sleep. Some upcoming reality concepts are idealistic, like FX's *American Candidate*, which aims
to field a "people's candidate" for president in 2004. Others are lowbrow,
like ABC's *The Will* (relatives battle for an inheritance), Fox's *Married by
America* (viewers vote to help pair up a bride and groom), and NBC's *Around
the World in 80 Dates* (American bachelor seeks mates around the world;

derivative: Unoriginal.

after all, how better to improve America's image then to send a stud to other countries to defile their women?). But all of them make you sit up and pay attention. "I like to make a show where people say, 'You can't put that on TV,'" says Fleiss. "Then I put it on TV."

By and large, reality shows aren't supplanting° creative successes like *24* 12 or *Scrubs;* they're filling in for duds like *Presidio Med* and *MDs.* As NBC reality chief Jeff Gaspin says, "There is a little survival-of-the-fittest thing this ends up creating." When sitcoms started cloning goofy suburban dads and quirky, pretty yuppies, we got *The Osbournes.* And now reality TV is becoming our source for involved stories about personal relationships. This used to be the stuff of dramas like the canceled *Once and Again,* until programmers began concentrating on series like *CSI* and *Law & Order,* which have characters as detailed and individuated as checkers pieces. By the time *Survivor* ends, you know its players better than you know *Law & Order*'s Detective Briscoe after eleven years. Likewise, the WB's *High School Reunion,* which brings together classmates after ten years, is really asking whether you're doomed to live out your high school role — "the jock," "the nerd," or whatnot — for life. Last fall two scripted shows, *That Was Then* and *Do Over,* asked the same questions but with cardboard characters and silly premises involving time travel. They got canceled. *High School Reunion* got a second season.

In Britain, where reality has ruled Britannia's (air)waves for years, TV 13 writers are starting to learn from reality's success. The sitcom *The Office* uses reality-TV techniques (jerky, handheld camera work, "confessional" interviews) to explore the petty politics of white-collar workers. Now airing on BBC America, it's the best comedy to debut here this season, because its characters are the kind of hard-to-pigeonhole folks you find in life — or on reality TV. On *Survivor* and *The Amazing Race,* the gay men don't drop Judy Garland references in every scene. MTV's *Making the Band 2* — a kind of hip-hop *American Idol* — gave center stage to inner-city kids who would be portrayed as perps or victims on a cop drama.

But aesthetics° aside, the case against reality TV is mainly moral — and 14 there's a point to it. It's hard to defend the deception of *Joe Millionaire* — which set up twenty women to court construction worker Evan Marriott by telling them he was a multimillionaire — as hilarious as its fool's-gold chase can be. Even the show's Potemkin° Croesus° contends that producers hid the show's premise from him until the last minute. "The day before I left for France, I signed confidentiality papers which said what the show was about," Marriott tells *Time.* "At that point, could I really back out?" Others are concerned about the message of meanness. "There's a premium on the lowest common denominator of human relationships," James Steyer, author

---

supplanting: Replacing.   **aesthetics:** Artistic beauty and taste.   **Potemkin:** Something that appears impressive on the surface but is shabby underneath, referring to Grigori Aleksandrovich Potemkin's construction of fake villages for Catherine the Great's tours of the Ukraine and the Crimea.   **Croesus:** A very wealthy man, referring to a king of Lydia who was renowned for his riches.

of *The Other Parent: The Inside Story of the Media's Effect on Our Children.* "It's often women degrading themselves. I don't want my nine-year-old thinking that's the way girls should behave."

So *The Bachelorette* is not morally instructive for grade-schoolers. But 15 wallowing in the weaknesses and failings of humanity is a trademark of satire—people accused Jonathan Swift and Mark Twain of being misanthropes too—and much reality TV is really satire boiled down to one extreme gesture. A great reality-TV concept takes some commonplace piety of polite society and gives it a wedgie. Companies value team spirit; *Survivor* says the team will screw you in the end. The cult of self-esteem says everybody is talented; *American Idol's* Simon Cowell says to sit down and shut your pie hole. Romance and feminism says a man's money shouldn't matter; *Joe Millionaire* wagers $50 million that they're wrong.

The social criticisms of reality TV rest on two assumptions: that millions 16 of other people are being taken in by reality TV's deceptions (which the critic himself—or herself—is able to see through) or are being led astray by its unsavory messages (to which the critic is immune). When a reality show depicts bad behavior, it's immoral, misanthropic, sexist, or sick. When *The Sopranos* does the same thing, it's nuanced storytelling. We assume that viewers can empathize with Tony Soprano without wanting to be him; we assume they can maintain critical distance and perceive ironies between his words and the truth. Why? Because we assume that people who like *The Sopranos* are smarter, more mature—better—than people who like *The Bachelorette.*

And aren't they? Isn't there something simply wrong with people who 17 enjoy entertainment that depends on ordinary people getting their heart broken, being told they can't sing, or getting played for fools? That's the question behind the protests of CBS's plans to make a real-life version of *The Beverly Hillbillies* with a poor rural family. Says Dee Davis, president of the Center for Rural Strategies, "If somebody had proposed, 'Let's go into the barrio° in L.A. and find a family of immigrants and put them in a mansion, and won't it be funny when they interview maids?' then people could see that's a step too far." It's hard to either defend or attack a show that doesn't exist yet, but it's also true that the original sitcom was far harder on Mr. Drysdale than the Clampetts. And on *The Osbournes,* Ozzy—another Beverly Hills fish out of water—was "humiliated" into becoming the most beloved dad in America.

Indeed, for all the talk about "humiliation TV," what's striking about 18 most reality shows is how good humored and resilient most of the participants are: the *American Idol* rejectees stubbornly convinced of their own talent, the *Fear Factor* players walking away from vats of insects like Olympic champions. What finally bothers their detractors is, perhaps, not that these people are humiliated but that they are not. Embarrassment, these shows demonstrate, is survivable, even ignorable, and ignoring embarrassment is a skill we all could use. It is what you risk—like injury in a sport—in order

barrio: Spanish-speaking neighborhood in the United States.

to triumph. "What people are really responding to on these shows is people pursuing their dreams," says *American Candidate* producer R. J. Cutler. A reality show with all humiliation and no triumph would be boring.

And at their best, the shows offer something else entirely. One of the 19 most arresting moments this TV season came on *American Idol*, when a single mom and professional boxer from Detroit flunked her audition. The show went with her backstage, with her adorable young son, as she told her life story. Her husband, a corrections officer, was murdered a few years before. She had taken up boxing—her ring name is "Lady Tiger"—because you can't raise a kid on waitress money. Her monologue went from defiance ("You'll see my album. Lady Tiger don't stop") to despair ("You ain't going nowhere in Detroit. Nowhere") to dignified resolve for her son's sake ("We're never going to quit, are we, angel?"). It was a haunting slice of life, more authentic than any *ER* subplot.

Was Lady Tiger setting a bad example for her son on national TV? 20 Or setting a good example by dreaming, persevering and being proud? *American Idol* didn't say. It didn't nudge us to laugh at her or prod us to cry for her. In about two minutes, it just told a quintessentially° American story of ambition and desperation and shrinking options, and it left the judgment to us. That's unsettling. That's heartbreaking. And the reality is, that's great TV.

Questions to Start You Thinking

1. CONSIDERING MEANING: According to Poniewozik, what are the main reasons that "reality TV is the best thing to happen to television in several years" (paragraph 7)?

2. IDENTIFYING WRITING STRATEGIES: What criteria does Poniewozik use to evaluate reality television? In his opinion, how do traditional sitcoms and dramas fare when judged according to the same criteria?

3. READING CRITICALLY: Where does Poniewozik address arguments against reality television? Does he present sufficient evidence to support his evaluation in the face of these opposing viewpoints?

4. EXPANDING VOCABULARY: Define *individuated* (paragraph 12). What does Poniewozik mean when he finds today's fictional television characters "as detailed and individuated as checkers pieces"? Does the comparison work?

5. MAKING CONNECTIONS: How do reality shows like *Joe Millionaire* and *The Bachelorette* relate to or differ from the institution of arranged marriage that Anjula Razdan analyzes ("What's Love Got to Do with It?" pp. 406–10) or the economic trade-offs that Ann Marlowe describes ("Pros and Amateurs," pp. 495–99)?

---

quintessentially: Most representative; classic.

Journal Prompts

1. Are you offended by reality television or entertained? Explain why.

2. Would you like to participate in a reality television show? Why, or why not? Which program would you like to be on, if any?

Link to the Paired Essay

Elaine Showalter ("Window on Reality," below) contends that *American Idol* is "real" in the sense that it reflects society. Poniewozik, on the other hand, admits, "We all know that there's little reality in reality TV" (paragraph 8). Yet they both defend the genre. How do you account for this difference in point of view? In what ways is reality television "real" and "not real"?

■ For useful links to Web sources on topics including *popular culture*, visit <bedfordstmartins.com/toplinks>.

Suggestions for Writing

1. Imagine that you have the opportunity to create a reality television show. Write an essay in which you pitch the show to a television producer. Describe your show's premise, purpose, intended audience, and participants' characteristics. Include a paragraph that convinces the producer that your show, sure to be a blockbuster, is a must-have for the next television season.

2. Do additional research on the factors that have led to the success or failure of a specific reality television show. Based on what you learn from your research and from this reading, develop criteria for evaluating reality television programs. Using your criteria, write an essay that reviews, either negatively or positively, a reality television show.

Elaine Showalter
Window on Reality

Elaine Showalter *was born in Cambridge, Massachusetts, in 1941. She earned a B.A. in English from Bryn Mawr College, an M.A. from Brandeis University, and a Ph.D. from the University of California at Davis. One of the founders of feminist criticism in the United States, Showalter has written several classics in the field, including* A Literature of Their Own: British Women Novelists from Brontë to Lessing *(1977) and* The Female Malady: Women, Madness, and English Culture *(1986). She has also published numerous articles and essays and been granted Guggenheim and Rockefeller Humanities fellowships. Showalter taught in the English department at Princeton University until her recent retirement. In "Window on Reality," from a 2003 issue of* The American Prospect, *she examines the reality television show* American Idol *from a sociological perspective.*

AS YOU READ: *Consider why Showalter finds* American Idol *more than just a hokey talent contest.*

"Reality" television is generally scorned as mindless, vulgar, exploita-   1
tive, and contrived. So is it ever sociology, is it ever real? Yes, if it's
American Idol, the Fox show that recently wrapped up its blockbuster second
season. The program, for the uninitiated, pitted twelve young performers
against one another for a chance at a $1 million recording contract. True,
American Idol was adapted from a British series, *Pop Idol*, which had attracted
a record fourteen million voters and made an instant celebrity of a colorless
boy singer. True, the program's producers were motivated by only the slick-
est of intentions: to manufacture a lucrative audience for a recording star before even one CD had been released. True, the twice-weekly programs, with
their drawn-out commercial breaks and clumsily staged group numbers,
were not the material of art.

And yet, in its shape and timing, *American Idol* has provided a fascinat-   2
ing snapshot of American youth culture in the twenty-first century. At once
a competition, a talent show, a soap opera, a makeover fest, a patriotic celebration, and an election, *American Idol* showed how the postmillennial
United States is changing with regard to race, class, national identity, and
politics. As its affiliate Fox News was cheering on the Iraq War, the Fox network's *American Idol* — one of the top-rated TV shows of the period leading
up to, during, and after the Iraq invasion — offered both a mirror image and
a contradictory view of the nation's mind-set. Appealing simultaneously to
Marines, Mormons, gays, blacks, and Latinos, and to every region of the
country, *American Idol* has a legitimate claim to its label of reality TV.

Playing the Race Chord

American Idol promoted multiculturalism with an ease missing from most   3
network television, and quite distinct from its precursor.° Although the
British show began with a wide range of candidates, black and Indian aspi-
rants were quickly eliminated; despite the influence of Asian styles from
Bollywood° and Bhangra° and black styles from the Caribbean, Africa, and
American hip-hop, the British pop scene is still white. In contrast, *American
Idol* showed a youth culture and a young generation past the tipping point
of racial harmony. Sociologically the program has been what one critic
called "the Ellis Island of talent shows." In order to achieve this particular
American dream of fame, 70,000 aspirants dressed in everything from yel-
low pimp suits to preppy khakis, then flew, drove, and hitchhiked to gruel-
ing auditions in seven iconic American cities — New York, Detroit, Miami,
Atlanta, Nashville, Austin, and Los Angeles — for the second season.

Vying for only a dozen finalists' slots, an astonishing mix of blond   4
Asians, yodeling twins, inner-city rappers, hopeful ex-convicts, and desperate single mothers slept on the sidewalks and endured the blunt dismissals
of multicultural judges Randy Jackson (a black music-company executive),

---

precursor: Forerunner.   **Bollywood:** The Indian film and music industry.   **Bhangra:**
Traditional Indian dance music which has now been incorporated into modern Indian
pop music.

Paula Abdul (a Brazilian/French-Canadian recording star and choreographer), and Simon Cowell (a white British music producer whose merciless insults and fearless observations as a *Pop Idol* judge had delighted U.K. audiences). The *American Idol* finalists included several black candidates plus two from biracial families. Despite the fears of some critics that no black candidate could win, Ruben Studdard, the soulful "velvet teddy bear" from Birmingham, Alabama, who proudly displayed his 205 area code on his size XXXL T-shirt, took home the prize. Imagine a black singer as a Birmingham booster in the '60s! Ruben's distance from the racist history of the city where Martin Luther King Jr. began the civil-rights movement is a statement of how far this country has come.

In a vote so close that it recalled the 2000 presidential election, Clay 5 Aiken, a white college student from North Carolina who worked with autistic teens and had become Ruben's best friend, came in second. At his audition, one reviewer recalled, Clay looked "like Alfred E. Neuman and Howdy Doody crashed head-on." Twenty weeks later, tanned, ironed, and styled to rock-star perfection, Clay still retained his down-home charm and modesty. Guest judges alternated between Motown gods (Lamont Dozier, Gladys Knight) and white songwriters (Diane Warren, Billy Joel). Jackson's slang epithets ("dawg," as a term of affectionate greeting, was a favorite) domesticated the outlaw rapper idiom of hip-hop culture and repackaged it for middle America.

But there was a subtext to this surface of racial harmony and equality. 6 Three black or biracial finalists and semifinalists were disqualified for concealing criminal records or for behavior unfitting to *American Idols*, suggesting disparities of opportunity and continuing cultural differences. One ex-finalist, Corey Clark, accused the producers of exploiting him for ratings when a Web site revealed that he was facing trial on assault charges, and he had to tape an on-air defense interview for *American Idol* that he claimed was misleadingly edited.

U.K. and U.S.A.: The Pop Coalition

The change of venue from England to the United States not only shifted 7 racial meanings but highlighted national differences. To the British, *Pop Idol* means something specific: a mainstream, TV-packaged, youth-oriented, music-biz phenomenon. There was no conscious sense of national identity in the choice of *Pop Idol* winners Will Young and Gareth Gates. But *American Idol* had a different agenda, especially the second series, which coincided with the buildup to and climax of the Iraq War. For their charity single benefiting the American Red Cross, ten of the finalists recorded a hokey Reaganesque anthem, "God Bless the USA," which zoomed to the top of the charts. Part of the patriotic message was the presence among the finalists of husky Marine Josh Gracin, whose commanding officers hinted that he could be sent to Iraq at any moment. (He wasn't.)

Yet in the midst of all this flag waving, the edgy presence of Cowell 8 shocked the American judges into taking a tougher line, just as the critical, even whining, war coverage of the BBC balanced and challenged the excessive optimism of American news correspondents. Cowell's refusal to be kind, tactful, warm and fuzzy, or euphemistically° upbeat, made him a bracing presence on the show. Unintimidated by the politically correct, he told biracial Kimberley Locke that her performance improved as soon as she had her bushy curls straightened and highlighted. "Now," he said approvingly, "you look cute." Unmoved by the tears of losers, he was also the only judge unsoftened by the shrill audition of a five-year-old black child. "I didn't think it was any good," he said forthrightly. The studio audience regularly booed Cowell, but his candor and insistence on high standards made the pop coalition of *American Idol* work.

The Democratic Process: Elections and Parodies

In the show's finale on May 21, more than twenty-four million votes came   9
in to *American Idol*. We can't compare the percentage of response to a real election because *Idol* participants were allowed to vote more than once. But the electoral structure of the program reflected American attitudes about the political process, and perhaps even served as a mass-culture referendum on the mood of the nation. Both professional reviewers and fans chatting on the Web speculated on voting blocs, on campaigns, and on whether the voting was rigged; Cowell told *People* magazine that some of the finalists "play the role like presidential candidates. If there was a baby in the audience, they'd be running over to kiss it." Local newspapers ran opinion polls on behalf of hometown candidates. In the end, some reviewers even wondered about having the votes audited, bringing back memories of counting chads.°

With *American Idol* providing its own parody of elections, it's no wonder   10
that satirists were also attracted to the format. *The Onion* proposed a new Fox reality show called *Appointed by America*, in which contestants would vie in "a democracy quiz, a talent competition, and nation-building activities" to lead postwar Iraq. Who would it be: Ahmed Chalabi, leader of the exiled Iraqi National Congress? A *peshmurga* fighter from Kurdistan? Or Kymbyrley Lake, a cashier from Garland, Texas, who has always dreamed of "doing something to help bring about a more peaceful world"?

A third series of *American Idol* is promised for next year, with Paul Mc-   11
Cartney rumored to be a guest judge. I'd bet the Bush twins and some Democratic candidates will be in the audience, too. This reality show could be a better political photo-op than the USS *Abraham Lincoln*.

Questions to Start You Thinking

1. CONSIDERING MEANING: How does *American Idol* reflect changes in American society, specifically those within the youth culture?

---

euphemistically: Substituting vague or mild words for something harsh.   **chads:** Bits of paper punched out of data cards, used in some voting machines.

2. IDENTIFYING WRITING STRATEGIES: Showalter partly develops her point by comparing and contrasting *Pop Idol* with its *American Idol* spinoff. What details does she provide to show that Americans have made *American Idol* their own distinct hit?

3. READING CRITICALLY: How and where does Showalter address criticism of reality television? Is the placement of this information effective? Is it sufficient?

4. EXPANDING VOCABULARY: In describing *American Idol*, one critic calls it the "Ellis Island of talent shows" (paragraph 3). How do you interpret this phrase? Does it have positive or negative connotations?

5. MAKING CONNECTIONS: If Danzy Senna ("The Color of Love," pp. 411–15) and Judith Ortiz Cofer ("Don't Misread My Signals" pp. 438–40) watched *American Idol*, do you think that they would see it as an effective promotion of multiculturalism? Why, or why not?

Journal Prompts

1. What characteristics would you assign to an *American Idol* winner?

2. Showalter states that "reality" television is "generally scorned as mindless, vulgar, exploitative, and contrived" (paragraph 1). She then shows how *American Idol* rises above these criticisms. After reading Showalter's defense of the program, what adjectives would you use to describe *American Idol*? Why?

Link to the Paired Essay

Both Showalter and James Poniewozik ("Why Reality TV Is Good for Us," pp. 468–72) explore positive aspects of reality television. However, they take different approaches to their topic. Compare and contrast the two writers' purposes and writing strategies. Is one piece more convincing than the other? Why, or why not?

■ For useful links to Web sources on topics including *popular culture*, visit <bedfordstmartins.com/toplinks>.

Suggestions for Writing

1. The title of Showalter's essay, "Window on Reality," reflects her point that *American Idol* is a way to view the reality of our changing society. What other reality television shows provide a glimpse into our society, mirroring our values, desires, way of life, and so on? Write an essay in which you analyze one or more of these shows, explaining what you think that they reveal about American society.

2. Reality shows like *American Idol* are considered to be the staple of the younger generation. Write an essay for the older generation, convincing those viewers that they should also tune in. Consider your audience's assumptions, values, and potential objections as you plan your argument and present your supporting evidence.

Chapter 25
The Workplace

Fredrik Brodén

Responding to an Image

At first glance, how would you describe the overall feeling or mood conveyed by this image? Examine its composition, determining the focal point. How is the focal point related to the surrounding elements of the visual? What does this relationship tell you as a viewer? What is significant about the direction the man is facing? What symbols can you identify in the image, and what point do they make about today's workplace? Translate that point into a caption for the illustration or into a thesis for an essay.

Use a search engine such as Yahoo! or Google to find Web sites for organiza-tions that offer information on workplace rights, such as the American Civil Liberties Union (<http://archive.aclu.org/issues/worker/hmwr.html>), the Pri-vacy Rights Clearinghouse (<www.privacyrights.org/workplace.htm>), the Families and Work Institute (<www.familiesandwork.org/>), or the AFL-CIO (<www.aflcio.org/issuespolitics/>). Choose one issue that is covered by at least two sites, and analyze the stand each organization takes on that issue. How well does each site support its stand with evidence, either at the site itself or through links? If you were to add a posting to a discussion board about that issue, how would you summarize what you learned or state your own position on the issue? If you were to create a visual to accompany your posting, what would it look like?

Joe Robinson
Four Weeks Vacation

Joe Robinson *grew up in California's San Fernando Valley. After receiving a degree in journalism from California State University, Northridge, he moved to London, then returned to Los Angeles and started up a music magazine followed by* Escape *magazine, an adventure-travel publication. Robinson is also the author of* Work to Live *(2003) and the founder of the Work to Live Vacation Campaign. The campaign, which recently presented 50,000 petition signatures to the U.S. Congress, aims to change national labor laws in order to give all American workers a minimum of three weeks paid vacation after a year on the job. In "Four Weeks Vacation," first published in the* Utne Reader, *Robinson scrutinizes the American work ethic and examines how the United States and other countries view vacation time. He asks what is happening to American ideas of self and culture when so many people have so little respite from work.*

AS YOU READ: *Find out why Robinson thinks Americans need more time off and how he thinks they can get it.*

The economy may have boomed in recent years, but most Americans are ready to bust. You don't hear much about that, with the national PR machine breathlessly trumpeting the longest peacetime expansion in U.S. history. But behind the doors of the apartments, ranch houses, and brown-stones of the real folks who fuel this economy, there is a different story, one of contraction — lives and family and free time swallowed whole by work without end. Ask most working Americans how things are *really* going and you'll hear stories of burnout and quiet desperation, of fifty- and sixty-hour weeks with no letup in sight. The United States has now passed Japan as

479

the industrialized world's most overworked land. In total hours, Americans work two weeks longer than the Japanese each year, two whole *months* longer than the Germans. On top of that, while Europeans and Australians are able to relieve the grind with four to six weeks of paid vacation each year guaranteed by law, Americans average a paltry nine days off after the first year on the job (and that's totally dependent on the whims of employers). If you need some time to tend to an illness in the family or paint the house, your vacation time is pretty much shot. Forget about Tuscany, Yosemite, or even a few days at a nearby state park.

As a longtime traveler, I first became aware that the United States wasn't 2 number one in everything after encountering far too many Germans, Brits, and Danes gallivanting the globe for five and six weeks a year. (In Denmark two years ago, unions staged a nationwide general strike for a sixth week of vacation and settled for two extra days a year, plus three additional personal days for workers with young children.) We eke out 9.6 days at large U.S. companies after one year, 16 after ten years; at small business operations (where the vast majority of us work these days) it's 8 days after a year, 16 after twenty-five years! But that's only part of the story. There's the drowning number of hours — according to the Families and Work Institute, forty-nine hours is the weekly average for men (and forty-two for women), which adds up to an extra three months on the job each year beyond the alleged forty-hour week.

"The gap between Europe and America seems to be growing," says a baf- 3 fled Orvar Löfgren, a professor at Lund University in Sweden and author of an excellent history of vacations, *On Holiday* (University of California, 1999). "I'm a bit amazed at this, because Americans love having fun."

Americans started out on a level playing field with Europeans, with a 4 week to two weeks in the '30s, when paid vacations were first introduced, says Löfgren. But "there was a decision made at some stage: Do you want more pay or longer vacations? The unions in Europe went for longer vacations. The state in many European countries was very much concerned that vacations were good for you, that everyone should have holidays, that there should be legislation about vacation time. I don't think the state played the same role in the United States."

After that the Europeans shot ahead of us, adding a week more vacation in 5 the '50s, '60s, and '70s. As a result, Swedes get five weeks off by law, plus another two weeks during the Christmas holidays. And don't forget the paid public holidays, he reminds me, which are far more frequent around the world.

Meanwhile, we are spending more time on the job than in past decades. 6 The husband and wife in a typical U.S. household are now working five hundred more hours a year than they did in 1980, according to Eileen Appelbaum, research director at the Economic Policy Institute. Absenteeism due to job stress has tripled in the past five years. So has the number of people calling in sick who aren't, a phenomenon called "entitlement mentality": Workers are using sick time to take the days off they feel they deserve.

Clearly, we have hit the wall. If we have no time for family and friends,   7
no time to enjoy, explore, refresh, and recreate, no time to think that there
could be, should be something more, what exactly do we have?

One tired nation. Estimates are that about half of all U.S. workers suffer   8
from symptoms of burnout. Pam Ammondson, author of *Clarity Quest* (Fire-
side, 1999), sees the wreckage in her Santa Rosa, California–based Clarity
Quest workshops, designed to help people suffering from burnout reclaim
their lives: "I see a lot of people who work twelve to fourteen hours a day
routinely," she says. "They want to make a change, but they're too tired to
know how to do it. *Overwhelmed* is a word they use a lot.... We allow
downtime for machinery for maintenance and repair, but we don't allow it
for the employees."

The health implications of sleep-deprived motorists weaving their way   9
to the office or operating machinery on the job are self-evident. One study
conducted by the American Psychosomatic Society found that men age
thirty-five to fifty-seven who took annual vacations were 21 percent less
likely to die young than nonvacationers and 32 percent less likely to die of
coronary heart disease.

We all play our part in this marathon of overwork, seduced by the cul-   10
ture into believing that who we are is what we do. It's this lack of a nonwork
identity that allows so many of us to be consumed by the workaholic frenzy.
"Americans compared to almost any other society are encouraged to achieve
and display identity through labor," explains Mark Liechty, professor of anthropology at the University of Illinois at Chicago. "Most Americans labor
to consume and construct the self." In Europe, he points out, there's more
of a separation between identity and work; work life is "subordinate° to
other kinds of social spheres."

The leading casualty of all this is our time, that commodity° we seemed   11
to have so much of back in sixth grade, when the clock on the wall never
seemed to move. Time is the fastener of friendship and family; it gives us the
space to explore more than a button on the snooze alarm. Without it, we're
a nation of strangers, even to those closest to us — and to ourselves. Families
are taking a beating. "People are spending less time with their family," observes Barry Miller, a career counselor at Pace University in New York.
"They're not taking the time to rejuvenate and connect with their family
members. Intimate relationships are falling apart, their relationships with
their children are falling apart."

I used to think that the issue of vacation time was complicated. There's   12
the almost religious stigma° in America against government regulating the
private sector, the pressure on runaway consumers to support their shopping
habits, and the paranoia that global competitors would outpace our economy if we took half the time off that they do. But they're all just excuses and

subordinate: Less important.   **commodity:** Something of value or advantage.
stigma: A mark of shame or disgrace.

pretexts that crumble with a hard look at the facts. Business, for instance, can be regulated for the good of the citizenry without jeopardizing profits. Some of the most basic tenets of the working world come out of federal legislation, from Social Security to the minimum wage to the forty-hour week — passed by Congress in 1938 as the Fair Labor Standards Act. Business was dragged kicking and screaming every time, but today these laws enjoy universal support.

Some on the left hold that we don't really want the extra time, because   13
we're too busy consuming goods and running up our credit cards. Yet a survey by the Families and Work Institute found that 64 percent of Americans *want* to work less, up from 47 percent in 1992. As for the threat of instant economic demise once Americans get real vacations, it doesn't appear that the Swiss or Swedish economies are in danger of immediate collapse. In fact, Löfgren points out that 25 percent of Swedes are able to afford second homes in the countryside.

When I raised the vacation issue in an article six years ago, some irate   14
letter writers predicted that the Asian Tigers — Korea, Thailand, Taiwan — would eat us up if we "gave" any more vacation time. A few economic meltdowns later, we're not too worried about those Tigers anymore. We're blowing away the world's economies and have the lowest unemployment in thirty years. Why are we so insecure? What's the point of being an economic superpower if we don't have time for anything but more work?

Another impediment° to rational discussion in this debate is the idea   15
that employers are giving something away with vacation leave. But it's just the opposite. "In essence, companies get more for their money," says employment counselor Barry Miller. "Not only are they going to get more productive employees, but they're also going to get retention and loyalty. My stepson got a week off for paternity leave from his company. He is so loyal to them, he'll never leave. He has more of a commitment to them because they have an interest in him."

And besides, it's not a giveback so much as a rightful return of a fraction   16
of the hours already burned up by routine fifty-hour weeks. "Within most large companies, the long-hours culture permeates° the way things are done, and the level of stress is high," says Mindy Fried of the Center for Work and Family at Boston College. "People are incredibly burned out." Fried has just released a study showing that flexible hours can help take some of "the steam out of the kettle."

Providing a decent amount of time off also makes good business sense.   17
Employees who are burned out make costly errors, they rack up sick days, they quit or get fired, and companies have to spend extra money to train new employees. SAS Institute, a North Carolina–based software company, has reportedly saved "tens of millions" of dollars in turnover costs with an employee-friendly policy of no overtime and a thirty-five-hour week, according to a study reported in the *New York Times*.

---

impediment: Obstacle.   **permeates:** Spreads through every part of.

Opponents of a mandated vacation law always trot out the myth that it 18
would hurt productivity. While the United States does rule in productivity,
it's not by much compared to Germany, for instance. The difference in output per hour is almost negligible, and Germans manage to do it in two
months less work. Think about that one. According to the Bureau of Labor
Statistics, from 1992 to 1998, France and Sweden, both five-week-vacation
lands, matched or surpassed the annual U.S. increase in output per hour
while working vastly fewer hours.

Another common misperception is that American business would never 19
accept Euro-style multiweek vacations. Well, it already is. Four-week vacation packages for upper management are routine at major U.S. companies.
And workers with special and highly coveted skills, like high-tech experts,
negotiate lengthy vacation into their contracts. We just need to spread the
wealth.

It's important to note that with national legislation, no company will 20
find itself at a disadvantage by establishing humane vacation policies. In
Sweden, for instance, there's no possibility of Volvo gaining a competitive
advantage over Saab by offering less vacation. All employers must follow the
same law. A standardized national system also eliminates the current penalties against people who change jobs, who can't bring the vacation benefits
accrued at their last company to the new one, where they usually have to
start at ground zero again: one or two weeks. In an era when people are
changing jobs as often as cars, this may be one of the best arguments of all
for a national vacation policy.

I'd like to leave it to the free market to work all this out. But the market 21
does what's best for itself — as reflected on the next quarterly report — not
what's best, or even logical, for the long-term health of the human capital
that is its foundation. If six-day weeks and no time off was considered abu-
sive in the nineteenth century and laws were required to make things better,
the situation is equally exploitive today and also requires legislative redress.
Just as we need traffic signs at intersections, we also need them in the workplace, or we'll keep getting run over.

Which brings us to what we must do: amend the Fair Labor Standards 22
Act so that every American who has worked at a job for at least a year gets
three weeks off, increasing to four weeks after three years. That's our policy
at *Escape*, and that's what Work to Live° is pressing for. We're in the middle
of a campaign to gather as many signatures as possible to present to Congress, proving there is an enthusiastic constituency for working to *live*, not
just living to *work*. We want to create a national Internet meeting hall for
supporters of the cause. We're looking for progressive companies to join
with us, as well as activists who can lend their talents to turning this tide of
citizen support into public policy. [. . .]

Work to Live: An e-mail campaign started by *Escape* magazine to petition the U.S. Congress to change the labor laws and increase the length of paid leave.

Courage among politicians is a little like El Niño: It only shows up 23
when heat is applied. That's where we come in. Let's turn up the temperature on candidates, Congress members, and local officials. Send e-mail and
faxes, make phone calls, hit their Web sites, write letters to the editor.

While there's no doubt that we're the home of the brave—a nation 24
ready to work till it drops—can we really be the land of the free when we're
on the chain gang fifty weeks a year? I asked Orvar Löfgren to imagine what
it would be like for him in the American vacation system, no five to seven
weeks off, just that long tunnel of eleven and a half months of work every
year stretching to the grave. He considered the possibility: "I would think,
how could I survive? I would feel claustrophobic. It's a question of priorities. In Europe, vacations have become a basic facet° of the quality of life."

Why not here? We've lost sight in the overwork hysteria of what makes 25
it all worthwhile—the time to enjoy the fruits of our labor. What's the point
of it all if there's no time to live but only to exist? Having time for family,
friends, exploring, reflecting, hiking—these are the things that give meaning
to life. I don't think at the end of our days we're going to be looking back on
that great eighty-hour week we pulled back in '99. It's going to be the time
playing ball with a kid, snorkeling off Maui, lingering over coffee in a sidewalk café—the time when we had time, the most precious natural resource
of all.

A wise man once told me that the fear of dying is really just the fear of 26
never having lived.

Let's leave no doubt about it. Viva vacations!   27

Questions to Start You Thinking

1. **CONSIDERING MEANING:** According to Robinson, why do Americans
   need more vacation time?

2. **IDENTIFYING WRITING STRATEGIES:** Robinson asserts that the government
   should legislate more vacation time for American workers (paragraph
   22). Where does he deal with objections to his proposal? Is this the
   most effective placement? Why, or why not?

3. **READING CRITICALLY:** Robinson says America is "one tired nation" (paragraph 8). Trace the causal chain that accounts for this fatigue. What effects does Robinson attribute to overwork?

4. **EXPANDING VOCABULARY:** Define *gallivanting* (paragraph 2). To what
   problem did "Germans, Brits, and Danes gallivanting the globe" alert
   Robinson? What does this word suggest about the author's tone?

5. **MAKING CONNECTIONS:** What would Judy Brady ("I Want a Wife," pp.
   427–29) make of Robinson's claim that four weeks of vacation would
   make American workers more productive? How might Brady incorporate this information into her essay?

---

facet: A phase or aspect of something.

Journal Prompts

1. Would you rather have longer vacations or more money? Why?

2. What was the most expensive item you ever bought? How did you get the money to pay for it? Did you regret buying it, or was it worth the sacrifices you made?

Suggestions for Writing

1. America is perceived as a materialistic nation. Is this stereotype accurate? Write an essay in which you use your own observations to define America's national character as materialistic or nonmaterialistic.

2. Robinson asserts that it is a "lack of a nonwork identity that allows so many [Americans] to be consumed by the workaholic frenzy" (paragraph 10). Write an essay in which you consider this question: To what degree do Americans identify themselves with their work?

Steve Olson

Year of the Blue-Collar Guy

Steve Olson *was born in 1946 in Rice Lake, Wisconsin. When asked for biographical information, Olson identified himself simply as "a construction worker." Claiming that he writes "mostly for [him]self," he seems to be speaking for the average American. In the following piece, which appeared as a "My Turn" essay in* Newsweek *on November 6, 1989, Olson strives to honor the dialect and ethic of a group of Americans who are often stereotyped but rarely heard from.*

AS YOU READ: *Identify the stereotypes about blue-collar workers that Olson addresses in his essay.*

While the learned are attaching appropriate labels to the 1980s and speculating on what the 1990s will bring, I would like to steal 1989 for my own much maligned° group and declare it "the year of the blue-collar guy (BCG)." BCGs have been portrayed as beer-drinking, big-bellied, bigoted rednecks who dress badly. Wearing a suit to a cement-finishing job wouldn't be too bright. Watching my tie go around a motor shaft followed by my neck is not the last thing I want to see in this world. But, more to the point, our necks are too big and our arms and shoulders are too awesome to fit suits well without expensive tailoring. Suits are made for white-collar guys.

But we need big bellies as ballast to stay on the bar stool while we're drinking beer. And our necks are red from the sun and we are somewhat bigoted. But aren't we all? At least our bigotry is open and honest and worn

maligned: Talked badly about.

out front like a tattoo. White-collar people are bigoted, too. But it's dis-guised as the pat on the back that holds you back: "You're not good enough so you need affirmative action." BCGs aren't smart enough to be that cynical. I never met a BCG who didn't respect an honest day's work and a job well done—no matter who did it.

True enough, BCGs aren't perfect. But, I believe this: we are America's 3 last true romantic heroes. When some twenty-first-century Louis L'Amour° writes about this era he won't eulogize the greedy Wall Street insider. He won't commend the narrow-shouldered, wide-hipped lawyers with six-digit unearned incomes doing the same work women can do. His wide-shouldered heroes will be plucked from the ranks of the blue-collar guy. They are the last vestige° of the manly world where strength, skill, and hard work are still valued.

To some extent our negative ratings are our own fault. While we were 4 building the world we live in, white-collar types were sitting on their ever-widening butts redefining the values we live by. One symbol of America's opulent wealth is the number of people who can sit and ponder and com-ment and write without producing a usable product or skill. Hey, get a real job—make something—then talk. These talkers are the guys we drove from the playgrounds into the libraries when we were young and now for twenty years or more we have endured the revenge of the nerds.

BCGs fidgeted our way out of the classroom and into jobs where, it 5 seemed, the only limit to our income was the limit of our physical strength and energy. A co-worker described a BCG as "a guy who is always doing things that end in the letter 'n'—you know huntin', fishin', workin' . . ." My wise friend is talking energy! I have seen men on the job hand-nail 20 square of shingles (that's 6,480 nails) or more a day, day after day, for weeks. At the same time, they were remodeling their houses, raising chil-dren, and coaching Little League. I've seen crews frame entire houses in a day—day after day. I've seen guys finish concrete until 11 P.M., go out on a date, then get up at 6 A.M. and do it all over again the next day.

These are amazing feats of strength. There should be stadiums full of 6 screaming fans for these guys. I saw a forty-year-old man neatly fold a 350-pound piece of rubber roofing, put it on his shoulder and, alone, carry it up a ladder and deposit it on a roof. Nobody acknowledged it because the event was too common. One day at noon this same fellow wrestled a twenty-two-year-old college summer worker. In the prime of his life, the col-lege kid was a 6-foot-3, 190-pound body-builder and he was out of his league. He was on his back to stay in ninety seconds flat.

Great Skilled Workforce

Mondays are tough on any job. But in our world this pain is eased by stories 7 of weekend adventure. While white-collar types are debating the value of

Louis L'Amour (1908–1988): Best-selling author of Westerns.   **vestige:** A visible sign left by something vanished or lost.

reading over watching TV, BCGs are doing stuff. I have honest to God heard these things on Monday mornings about BCG weekends: "I tore out a wall and added a room," "I built a garage," "I went walleye fishing Saturday and pheasant hunting Sunday," "I played touch football both days" (in January), "I went skydiving," "I went to the sports show and wrestled the bear." Pack a good novel into these weekends.

My purpose is not so much to put down white-collar people as to stress 8
the importance of blue-collar people to this country. Lawyers, politicians, and bureaucrats are necessary parts of the process, but this great skilled workforce is so taken for granted it is rarely seen as the luxury it truly is. Our plumbing works, our phones work, and repairs are made as quickly as humanly possible. I don't think this is true in all parts of the world. But this blue-collar resource is becoming endangered. Being a tradesman is viewed with such disdain these days that most young people I know treat the trades like a temporary summer job. I've seen young guys take minimum-wage jobs just so they can wear suits. It is as if any job without a dress code is a dead-end job. This is partly our own fault. We even tell our own sons, "Don't be like me, get a job people respect." Blue-collar guys ought to brag more, even swagger a little. We should drive our families past the latest job site and say, "That house was a piece of junk, and now it's the best one on the block. I did that." Nobody will respect us if we don't respect ourselves.

Our work is hard, hot, wet, cold, and always dirty. It is also often very 9
satisfying. Entailing the use of both brain and body there is a product — a physical result of which to be proud. We have fallen from your roofs, died under heavy equipment, and been entombed in your dams. We have done honest, dangerous work. Our skills and energy and strength have transformed lines on paper into physical reality. We are this century's Renaissance men. America could do worse than to honor us. We still do things the old-fashioned way, and we have earned the honor.

Questions to Start You Thinking

1. CONSIDERING MEANING: Why does Olson feel there should be a "Year of the Blue-Collar Guy"? What would be the purpose of such a year?

2. IDENTIFYING WRITING STRATEGIES: How does Olson support his stand by comparing and contrasting the "blue-collar guy" with "white-collar types"?

3. READING CRITICALLY: What kind of appeal — emotional, logical, or ethical — does Olson use when he suggests that blue-collar workers need to do more bragging to their families about the work they do? Is the appeal an effective one? Why, or why not? (For an explanation of appeals, see pp. 39–40.)

4. EXPANDING VOCABULARY: Define *ballast* (paragraph 2), *eulogize* (paragraph 3), *opulent* (paragraph 4), *disdain* (paragraph 8), and *Renaissance men* (paragraph 9). How does Olson's vocabulary compare to one you might expect from a self-professed "blue-collar guy" (paragraph 1)?

5. MAKING CONNECTIONS: Would Olson consider Scott Russell Sanders ("The Men We Carry in Our Minds," pp. 430–34) an ally or a threat to his cause? Why?

Journal Prompts

1. Has a job ever influenced your self-image? When, and how?

2. Does "blue-collar" describe only men? Based on observation or imagination, describe the appearance and leisure activities of a "blue-collar woman."

Suggestions for Writing

1. Identify a group you belong to that you think should have a year of its own (for example, college students, part-time workers, parents), and write an essay taking a stand on why your group deserves such an honor.

2. Have attitudes toward blue-collar workers changed since this essay was published in 1989? Why, or why not? Write an essay responding to this question using evidence you gather from media sources and current research.

Jane Smiley
The Case against Chores

Jane Smiley *was born in 1949 in Los Angeles, California, and received her B.A. from Vassar College. She earned her M.A., M.F.A., and Ph.D. from the University of Iowa. A contributor to many leading American magazines, Smiley's work has been selected for* Best American Short Stories, The Pushcart Anthology, *and* Best of the Eighties. *The author of many books, her most recent is* Good Faith *(2003). Her earlier novel* A Thousand Acres *(1991) retells Shakespeare's* King Lear *in the contemporary Midwest. Besides winning the Pulitzer Prize, National Book Critics Circle Award, and Heartland Award, this novel has been made into a popular film. Here, Smiley uses a light autobiographical touch to discuss the serious matter of how children should be encouraged to understand work.*

AS YOU READ: *Find Smiley's reasons for opposing chores for children.*

I've lived in the upper Midwest for twenty-one years now, and I'm here to   1
tell you that the pressure to put your children to work is unrelenting. So far I've squirmed out from under it, and my daughters have led a life of almost tropical idleness, much to their benefit. My son, however, may not be so lucky. His father was himself raised in Iowa and put to work at an early age, and you never know when, in spite of all my husband's best intentions, that early training might kick in.

Although "chores" are so sacred in my neck of the woods that almost no   2
one ever discusses their purpose, I have over the years gleaned some of the reasons parents give for assigning them. I'm not impressed. Mostly the rea-

sons have to do with developing good work habits or, in the absence of good work habits, at least habits of working. No such thing as a free lunch, any job worth doing is worth doing right, work before play, all of that. According to this reasoning, the world is full of jobs that no one wants to do. If we divide them up and get them over with, then we can go on to pastimes we like. If we do them "right," then we won't have to do them again. Lots of times, though, in a family, that *we* doesn't operate. The operative word is *you*. The practical result of almost every child-labor scheme that I've witnessed is the child doing the dirty work and the parent getting the fun: Mom cooks and Sis does the dishes; the parents plan and plant the garden, the kids weed it. To me, what this teaches the child is the lesson of alienated° labor: not to love the work but to get it over with; not to feel pride in one's contribution but to feel resentment at the waste of one's time.

Another goal of chores: the child contributes to the work of maintaining 3 the family. According to this rationale, the child comes to understand what it takes to have a family, and to feel that he or she is an important, even indispensable member of it. But come on. Would you really want to feel loved primarily because you're the one who gets the floors mopped? Wouldn't you rather feel that your family's love simply exists all around you, no matter what your contribution? And don't the parents love their children anyway, whether the children vacuum or not? Why lie about it just to get the housework done? Let's be frank about the other half of the equation too. In this day and age, it doesn't take much work at all to manage a household, at least in the middle class — maybe four hours a week to clean the house and another four to throw the laundry into the washing machine, move it to the dryer, and fold it. Is it really a good idea to set the sort of example my former neighbors used to set, of mopping the floor every two days, cleaning the toilets every week, vacuuming every day, dusting, dusting, dusting? Didn't they have anything better to do than serve their house?

Let me confess that I wasn't expected to lift a finger when I was growing 4 up. Even when my mother had a full-time job, she cleaned up after me, as did my grandmother. Later there was a housekeeper. I would leave my room in a mess when I headed off for school and find it miraculously neat when I returned. Once in a while I vacuumed, just because I liked the pattern the Hoover made on the carpet. I did learn to run water in my cereal bowl before setting it in the sink.

Where I discovered work was at the stable, and, in fact, there is no 5 housework like horsework. You've got to clean the horses' stalls, feed them, groom them, tack them up, wrap their legs, exercise them, turn them out, and catch them. You've got to clip them and shave them. You have to sweep the aisle, clean your tack and your boots, carry bales of hay and buckets of water. Minimal horsekeeping, rising just to the level of humaneness, requires many more hours than making a few beds, and horsework turned

alienated: Isolated; distant or unfriendly.

out to be a good preparation for the real work of adulthood, which is rearing children. It was a good preparation not only because it was similar in many ways but also because my desire to do it, and to do a good job of it, grew out of my love of and interest in my horse. I can't say that cleaning out her bucket when she manured in it was an actual joy, but I knew she wasn't going to do it herself. I saw the purpose of my labor, and I wasn't alienated from it.

Probably to the surprise of some of those who knew me as a child, I have 6 turned out to be gainfully employed. I remember when I was in seventh grade, one of my teachers said to me, strongly disapproving, "The trouble with you is you only do what you want to do!" That continues to be the trouble with me, except that over the years I have wanted to do more and more.

My husband worked hard as a child, out-Iowa-ing the Iowans, if such a 7 thing is possible. His dad had him mixing cement with a stick when he was five, pushing wheelbarrows not long after. It's a long sad tale on the order of two miles to school and both ways uphill. The result is, he's a great worker, much better than I am, but all the while he's doing it he wishes he weren't. He thinks of it as work; he's torn between doing a good job and longing not to be doing it at all. Later, when he's out on the golf course, where he really wants to be, he feels a little guilty, knowing there's work that should have been done before he gave in and took advantage of the beautiful day.

Good work is not the work we assign children but the work they want 8 to do, whether it's reading in bed (where would I be today if my parents had rousted me out and put me to scrubbing floors?) or cleaning their rooms or practicing the flute or making roasted potatoes with rosemary and Parmesan for the family dinner. It's good for a teenager to suddenly decide that the bathtub is so disgusting she'd better clean it herself. I admit that for the parent, this can involve years of waiting. But if she doesn't want to wait, she can always spend her time dusting.

Questions to Start You Thinking

1. CONSIDERING MEANING: According to Smiley, why shouldn't children be required to do chores?

2. IDENTIFYING WRITING STRATEGIES: Where does Smiley use recall to support her argument? Is her own experience effective as support? Why, or why not?

3. READING CRITICALLY: Locate the claims Smiley attributes to those who believe chores are "sacred." How does she refute each of these claims? Do you find her argument convincing?

4. EXPANDING VOCABULARY: Define *humaneness* (paragraph 5). What does Smiley mean by "the level of humaneness"? How is "horsekeeping" better preparation for childrearing than doing household chores (paragraph 5)?

5. MAKING CONNECTIONS: What would Olson ("Year of the Blue-Collar Guy," pp. 485–87) make of Smiley's argument against chores? Does his idea of meaningful work agree with Smiley's? Do you think he would require his children to do chores? Why, or why not?

Journal Prompts

1. Describe your work ethic. What childhood influences helped shape it?

2. How should chores be divided in a household? How are they divided in yours?

Suggestions for Writing

1. What purpose should work serve in our lives? Is one kind of work more valuable than another? Does work have intrinsic value of its own? Write an essay in which you explore the value and meaning of work.

2. Smiley takes exception with parents who believe they must teach their children good work habits. Choose a commonly accepted practice in childrearing, and defend it or argue against it. Use your personal observations, experience, or expert opinions to support the stand you take in your essay.

Barbara Ehrenreich
Warning: This Is a Rights-Free Workplace

Barbara Ehrenreich, *born in 1941, holds a B.A. from Reed College and a Ph.D. from Rockefeller University. A writer and social activist, her critiques of such issues as health care policy and workplace rights have appeared in publications including* Ms., Mother Jones, The Nation, The New Republic, *and* Time, *to name a few. She is also the author of several books, including* Fear of Falling: The Inner Life of the Middle Class *(1988)*, Snarling Citizen: Essays *(1995), and* Blood Rites: Origins and History of the Passions of War *(1997). To write* Nickel and Dimed: On (Not) Getting by in America *(2001), in which she explores the harsh realities of surviving on a wage of six to seven dollars an hour, Ehrenreich spent two years waiting tables, cleaning houses, and performing other low-wage jobs. In "Warning: This Is a Rights-Free Workplace," from the* New York Times Magazine *in 2000, Ehrenreich argues that the rights of American workers have been eroded to such a degree that "what we need is nothing less than a new civil rights movement."*

AS YOU READ: *Determine what rights Ehrenreich finds to be commonly violated in the workplace.*

I f the laws of economics were enforced as strictly as the laws of physics, America would be a workers' paradise. The supply of most kinds of labor is low, relative to the demand, so each worker should be treated as a cherished asset, right? But there have been only grudging gains in wages over the last few years, and in the realm of dignity and autonomy, a palpable° decline.

palpable: Substantial; obvious.

In the latest phase of America's one-sided class war, employers have ₂ taken to monitoring employee's workplace behavior right down to a single computer keystroke or bathroom break, even probing into their personal concerns and leisure activities. Sure, there's a job out there for anyone who can get to an interview sober and standing upright. The price, though, may be one's basic civil rights and — what boils down to the same thing — self-respect.

Not that the Bill of Rights ever extended to the American workplace. In ₃ 1996, I was surprised to read about a grocery store worker in Dallas who was fired for wearing a Green Bay Packers T-shirt to work on the day before a Cowboys-Packers game. All right, this was insensitive of him, but it certainly couldn't have influenced his ability to keep shelves stocked with Doritos. A few phone calls, though, revealed that his firing was entirely legal. Employees have the right to express their religious preferences at work, by wearing a cross or a Star of David, for example. But most other forms of "self-expression" are not protected, and strangely enough, Green Bay Packer fandom has not yet been recognized as a legitimate religion.

Freedom of assembly is another right that never found its way into the ₄ workplace. On a recent journalistic foray° into a series of low-wage jobs, I was surprised to discover that management often regarded the most innocent conversation between employees as potentially seditious.° A poster in the break room at one restaurant where I worked as a waitress prohibited "gossip," and a manager would hastily disperse any gathering of two or more employees. At the same time, management everywhere enjoys the right to assemble employees for lengthy anti-union harangues.°

Then there is the more elemental and biological right — and surely it ₅ should be one — to respond to nature's calls. Federal regulations forbid employers to "impose unreasonable restrictions on employee use of the facilities." But according to Marc Linder and Ingrid Nygaard, coauthors of "Void Where Prohibited: Rest Breaks and the Right to Urinate on Company Time," this regulation is only halfheartedly enforced. Professionals and, of course, waitresses can usually dart away and relieve themselves as they please. Not so for many cashiers and assembly-line workers, some of whom, Linder says, have taken to wearing adult diapers to work.

In the area of privacy rights, workers have actually lost ground in recent ₆ years. Here, too, the base line is not impressive — no comprehensive right to personal privacy has ever been established. I learned this on my first day as a waitress, when my fellow workers warned me that my purse could be searched by management at any time. I wasn't carrying any stolen salt shakers or anything else of a compromising nature, but there's something about the prospect of a purse search that makes a woman feel a few buttons short of fully dressed. After work, I called around and found that this, too, is generally legal, at least if the boss has reasonable cause and has given prior notification of the company's search policies.

foray: Venture.   **seditious:** Rebellious.   **harangues:** Lectures.

Purse searches, though, are relatively innocuous° compared with the so- 7
phisticated chemical and electronic forms of snooping adopted by many
companies in the '90s. The American Management Association reports that
in 1999 a record two-thirds of major American companies monitored their
employees electronically: videotaping them; reviewing their e-mail and
voice-mail messages; and, most recently, according to Lewis Maltby, president of the Princeton-based National Workrights Institute, monitoring any
Web sites they may visit on their lunch breaks. Nor can you count on keeping anything hidden in your genes; a growing number of employers now use
genetic testing to screen out job applicants who carry genes for expensive
ailments like Huntington's disease.

But the most ubiquitous° invasion of privacy is drug testing, usually of 8
urine, more rarely of hair or blood. With 81 percent of large companies now
requiring some form of drug testing—up from 21 percent in 1987—job
applicants take it for granted that they'll have to provide a urine sample as
well as a résumé. This is not restricted to "for cause" testing—of people
who, say, nod or space out on the job. Nor is it restricted to employees in
"safety-sensitive occupations," like airline pilots and school-bus drivers.
Workers who stack boxes of Cheerios in my local supermarkets get tested, as
do the editorial employees of this magazine, although there is no evidence
that a weekend joint has any more effect on Monday-morning performance
than a Saturday-night beer.

Civil libertarians see drug testing as a violation of our Fourth Amend- 9
ment protection from "unreasonable search," while most jobholders and
applicants find it simply embarrassing. In some testing protocols, the employee has to strip to her underwear and urinate into a cup in the presence
of an aide or technician, who will also want to know what prescription
drugs she takes, since these can influence the test results.

According to a recent report from the American Civil Liberties Union, 10
drug testing has not been proven to achieve its advertised effects, like reducing absenteeism and improving productivity. But it does reveal who's on anti-
depressants or suffering with an ailment that's expensive to treat, and it is un-
deniably effective at weeding out those potential "troublemakers" who are
too independent-minded to strip and empty their bladders on command.

Maybe the prevailing trade-off between jobs and freedom would make 11
sense, in the narrowest cost-benefit terms, if it contributed to a more vibrant economy. But this is hardly the case. In fact, a 1998 study of sixty-
three computer-equipment and data-processing firms found that companies that performed both pre-employment and random drug testing
actually "reduced rather than enhanced productivity"—by an eye-popping
29 percent, presumably because of its dampening effect on morale.

Why, then, do so many employers insist on treating their workers as a 12
kind of fifth column within the firm? Certainly the government has played
a role with its misguided antidrug crusade, as has the sheer availability of

innocuous: Harmless.   **ubiquitous:** Everywhere; pervasive.

new technologies of snooping. But workplace repression signals a deeper shift away from the postwar social contract in which a job meant a straightforward exchange of work for wages.

Economists trace the change to the 1970s, when, faced with falling prof- 13 its and rising foreign competition, America's capitalists launched an offensive to squeeze more out of their workers. Supervision tightened, management expanded, and union-busting became a growth industry. And once in motion, the dynamic of distrust is hard to stop. Workers who are routinely treated like criminals and slackers may well bear close watching.

The mystery is why American workers, the political descendants of 14 proud revolutionaries, have so meekly surrendered their rights. Sure, individual workers find ways to cheat on their drug tests, outwit the electronic surveillance and sneak in a bit of "gossip" here and there. But these petty acts of defiance seldom add up to concerted resistance, in part because of the weakness of American unions. The A.F.L.-C.I.O. is currently conducting a nationwide drive to ensure the right to organize, and the downtrodden workers of the world can only wish the union well. But what about all the other rights missing in so many American workplaces? It's not easy to organize your fellow workers if you can't communicate freely with them on the job and don't dare carry union literature in your pocketbook.

In a tight labor market, workers have another option, of course. They 15 can walk. The alarming levels of turnover in low-wage jobs attest to the popularity of this tactic, and if unemployment remains low, employers may eventually decide to cut their workers some slack. Already, companies in particularly labor-starved industries like ski resorts and software are dropping drug testing rather than lose or repel employees. But in the short run, the mobility of workers, combined with the weakness of unions, means that there is little or no sustained on-site challenge to overbearing authority.

What we need is nothing less than a new civil rights movement — this 16 time, for American workers. Who will provide the leadership remains to be seen, but clearly the stakes go way beyond "labor issues," as these are conventionally defined. We can hardly call ourselves the world's pre-eminent democracy if large numbers of citizens spend half their waking hours in what amounts, in plain terms, to a dictatorship.

Questions to Start You Thinking

1. CONSIDERING MEANING: What arguments does Ehrenreich present against drug testing in the workplace? Why do civil libertarians oppose drug testing? Why do employees and job applicants object to the procedure?

2. IDENTIFYING WRITING STRATEGIES: How does Ehrenreich use cause and effect to develop her case against the erosion of workplace privacy? Where does she propose a solution to the problem? How does she help readers follow her line of thought?

3. READING CRITICALLY: How effectively does Ehrenreich support her assertion that workplace rights are being violated? What kind of appeals — emotional, logical, or ethical — does she use to support her claims? How effec-

tively do these appeals help Ehrenreich achieve her purpose? (For an explanation of appeals, see pp. 39–40.)

4. EXPANDING VOCABULARY: In paragraph 10, Ehrenreich says that drug tests
   discover "those potential 'troublemakers' who are too independent-minded
   to strip and empty their bladders on command." Why does Ehrenreich
   place quotation marks around "troublemakers"? How does Ehrenreich
   think these employers define a workplace troublemaker? How do you define the term?

5. MAKING CONNECTIONS: Ehrenreich writes about exploitative working conditions. Would Jane Smiley ("The Case against Chores," pp. 488–90) go as far
   as calling mandatory chores "exploitative"? Why, or why not?

Journal Prompts

1. How are workers generally treated at a place where you currently work or
   have worked in the past?

2. If you have ever had to take an employment-related drug test, how did it
   make you feel? At the time, did you consider it a violation of your privacy?
   Why, or why not? If you haven't had to take a drug test, how do you think
   you would respond?

Suggestions for Writing

1. Recall a time in the workplace or the classroom when you felt that
   your rights were violated. The situation might be something as simple
   as having to wear a uniform or as invasive as drug testing. Write an essay
   explaining what happened, how you reacted, and what consequences
   followed.

2. Select one of the workplace practices that Ehrenreich discusses. Write an
   essay arguing for or against that practice. Support your thesis with pertinent,
   reliable evidence, and consider opposing viewpoints as well. Include a variety of appeals — emotional, logical, and ethical — to make your case as convincing as possible.

Ann Marlowe

Pros and Amateurs

Ann Marlowe, *who currently lives in New York, earned her B.A. at Harvard University and her M.B.A. at Columbia Business School. As a writer and critic, she
has covered music, books, and culture for* The Village Voice, LA Weekly, The
New York Observer, The National Review, *and* Salon.com. *She has also
worked as a financial analyst, a consultant, and a magazine editor. Her first book,*
How to Stop Time: Heroin from A to Z *(1999), is a memoir describing her
experiences as a heroin addict. In "Pros and Amateurs," first published on*
Salon.com *in 2000, Marlowe makes some bold claims about the underlying reasons for the earnings gap between men and women.*

AS YOU READ: *Look for the ways that, according to Marlowe, men "pay" for sex and women "sell" themselves.*

When I first heard about *Who Wants to Marry a Multi-Millionaire?* I remembered an incident from my childhood. It might have been the first time I became aware that sex was something exchanged for money. My parents were gossiping, mainly over my head, and a scrap drifted down in my father's voice: "Why buy a cow, when milk is so cheap?" I asked what that meant, and my parents laughed. "Your father is talking about what happens when men and women live together without being married," my mom explained, in a lower voice. I didn't quite understand, but I felt the offense to my gender and seethed with anger at my father for a few minutes.

After *Who Wants to Marry a Multi-Millionaire?* I was also offended for my gender. But after years of life experience, I was equally offended by its members. I knew the evil patriarchy hadn't forced the female contestants to enter this humiliating contest, or forced millions of women to watch. (The show actually got higher ratings among women than men.) If women were willing to sell themselves on national television, and other women were entertained by it, we hadn't come very far from the gender primitivism° of my childhood, when both my parents took it for granted that sex was a good that men would, or should, pay for, and one that women could either "give away" or, well, not exactly sell, but obtain full value for bestowing.

After forty years of feminism, many women still expect men to show their intentions, and devotion, by paying for dates and presents, and still evaluate them as future providers for a family. Men still complain of "wasting money" taking women out to dinner who don't want to have sex with them. They still mutter, "When push comes to shove, we pay all the time, whether it's prostitution or dating." Girls still grow up thinking of work as an option, while boys know it as a necessity.

Conventional wisdom would have it that women have to think hard about their future spouses' earnings because of the earnings gap. In 1998 the median income for all females in the labor force was 73 percent of male income ($25,862 to $35,345). For college graduates twenty-five and older, the gap is wider, with women earning only 71 percent of what men make ($35,408 to $49,982).

But what if, rather than being hapless victims of the earnings gap, women allow it to continue, in part in order to choose their bed partners based on their incomes? What if (most) women enjoy earning less than men, because we have eroticized being on the short end of the stick? What if women, like men, effectively pay for sex—with lower earnings?

My theory is that men have by and large eroticized freedom, while women have eroticized its absence. It's not that lower female earnings lead women to evaluate men based on their earning power—it's that women want to maintain male financial dominance, so they make sure they earn

primitivism: Primitive ways.

less than men. And it's not that men are willing to support women (and their children) because they are committed to them — it's because men believe they are buying the freedom to leave that they will (for a while at least) foot the bills. This applies to prostitution, where men pay for the freedom of closing the door on the selves they show, and to family life, where all too many men are able to walk away from supporting their children.

We rarely examine the values implied by the kinds of remarks we let slip constantly — "She married badly." "He's a meal ticket," "She's too high-maintenance." Very few women would react well if a man asked their price, but many will casually boast of their boyfriend's expensive presents or recent promotion, or imply that a lover's income offsets other less stellar qualities. Not many men are proud of going to prostitutes, but even those who have never bought sex are apt to mutter that one way or another, men still pay for it.   7

Some people will howl in outrage at these ideas. Some will say it's harmful to the feminist cause to air these issues. I raise them here with the hope that discussion leads to more open lives, and better ones, with choices being made with open eyes. Some women may consciously choose a less responsible, less stressful or less remunerative° job — and that's fine, as long as it is a choice, not the result of sexism or its internalized equivalents. But just as we have learned to look at cultural factors when equal opportunity doesn't result in equal results racially, so we should inquire why so few women opt for the top of their professions, and why so many of the best and brightest women sideline themselves in their twenties, long before the tradeoff between childbearing and work becomes acute.   8

Instead of endlessly rehashing the staple women's-magazine issues, we should be exploring why women set their work and money goals relatively low, why women still represent only 13 percent of corporate officers of *Fortune* 500 companies, why so few of the dot-coms are founded by women, why of a recent list of 167 newly minted Goldman Sachs partners not even 15 percent are female. I do not think institutionalized sexism is a major part of the answer.   9

The tricky part of the sex-for-money trade is that there's a slippery slope. On one end is a man sending flowers to a woman after a first date, and on the other is the prostitute and her client. In a typical dating scenario, it isn't sex for money, exactly, but it may be sex because of money — sex because a man's behavior gives signals that he has money and is willing to spend it. It's sexy, we women often think, when a man insists on taking us out to dinner or sends flowers, when he gives jewelry, when he promises a big diamond if things work out. But we also feel it's sexy when he earns more, when he has more heft and impact in the world. "More" is always relative, and since we can't be sure of having a relationship with a tycoon — indeed, most women can be sure they won't — women increase their chances of having a relationship with a man who is more successful by being fairly unsuccessful themselves.   10

remunerative: Profitable.

You choose one of those fields that are respectable and interesting and 11 offer an absurdly low ratio of income to effort, like public-school teaching or social work; or you have a series of dead-end and nonlucrative jobs rather than a career; or you do embark on a career, say in law or banking or advertising, but you take it less seriously, and ensure that you will never make partner or the equivalent. You make it clear that your career will not come first in your life. You can even make it clear that you are going to need to be taken care of. And surprisingly enough, men respond protectively.

I say "surprisingly" because hardly any woman wants to marry a man 12 who says he will have to be supported. And in our cash-conscious society, we have few qualms° about lacking a safety net for poor children, the ill, or the disabled. Yet many a man who is not rich and doesn't expect to be rich will take on the financial responsibility for a young, able-bodied, well-educated woman who is not yet, and may not ever be, the mother of his children. Of course, there are limits. Men say, "She's too high-maintenance" about a woman they feel will bankrupt them. Women who overtly demand financial tribute are a turnoff to most men. But men almost never say (as women do), "What a great person — but we can't get married because she's a nursery school teacher and hasn't got a dime." Women who need to be supported, with humble expectations for themselves, are a turn-on.

In middle- to upper-class life, it's almost a rule: The lower paid the occu- 13 pation, the more obvious it is that the woman in it expects to attract a man to support her. Publishing? Auction houses? Private-school teaching? Classic post-deb,° waiting-to-be-wed jobs. (Office receptionist, restaurant host, public-school teaching used to be the lower- to middle-class equivalents, except that now almost all married women in these economic groups have to work.) It's not that women need to get married because they hold these jobs — in many cases, they hold these jobs because they want to get married. They're signals: "Rescue me" is the message.

Look at the equally controversial black-white earnings gap. While sub- 14 stantial numbers of blacks have moved into the middle class, the statistics also reflect the "underclass" who have not. In many inner-city neighborhoods, children emulate gangster culture and profess scorn for those who succeed in school. They're behaving in a self-defeating manner, dooming themselves to poverty, but it's understandable. They not only have few role models of conventional success, but they have little chance of achieving it. So a new culture of low expectations grows, with its own aesthetic, set up in opposition to the mainstream or elite.

Aren't there analogies to the case of women? We fail to see them be- 15 cause our eyes have not been nearly as opened to the effects of patriarchy as they have been to the effects of racism. When adult women spend substantial amounts of leisure time shopping for clothes they neither need nor can afford, or undergoing time-consuming "beauty" treatments, both men and women tend to read that as appropriate behavior. In both cases, women and African American inner-city dwellers, there are what biologists call "feed-

qualms: Doubts.   **post-deb:** After having "debuted" into high society.

back effects": The defeatist attitude leads to certain perceptions by the power structure of the group in question, and these perceptions are internalized, increasing the defeatist attitude. Multiply that by 5,000 years of patriarchal society, and you have some deeply ingrained behaviors. So deep, they tend to be called natural, by both sexes.

Nietzsche° called this process of scorning what you can't have ressenti- 16 ment. It's a status order internalized in the form of rules, like "Don't do your homework — that's not cool," or "Majoring in computer engineering will scare attractive men away," or the perennial° "If you work out too much, you'll bulk up." Women's eroticization of traditional power relationships makes evaluating a boyfriend for his earning power seem acceptable, rather than mercenary,° to most men and women. And it's one small step from assessing a man's spending power to assessing your own salability.° How far is that from selling yourself on national television?

Questions to Start You Thinking

1. CONSIDERING MEANING: According to Marlowe, why do women set low work and earnings goals?

2. IDENTIFYING WRITING STRATEGIES: How does Marlowe use comparison and contrast to make her point about attitudes toward sex and earnings? Does this strategy effectively advance her claim? Who are her intended readers, and how do you think they would react to the comparisons and contrasts?

3. READING CRITICALLY: Marlowe makes some bold generalizations that are sure to offend some readers. Does she effectively support her claims and counter possible objections? Do you find Marlowe's argument convincing? Why, or why not?

4. EXPANDING VOCABULARY: Define *high maintenance* (paragraph 12). Supply an example that Marlowe might use as support in her essay.

5. MAKING CONNECTIONS: Nicholas Wade ("How Men and Women Think," pp. 447–50) states that "if the brains of men and women really are organized differently, it's possible the sexes both prefer and excel at different occupations" (paragraph 12). How does this statement either support or refute Marlowe's claims? Whose argument about why people choose certain occupations do you side with more — Wade's or Marlowe's?

Journal Prompts

1. In general, do you think that men should pay for everything on a date? How does Marlowe's essay try to make readers think twice about this traditional arrangement?

Nietzsche: Friedrich Wilhelm Nietzsche (1844–1900), a German philosopher.   **perennial:** Persistent, perpetual.   **mercenary:** Motivated by a desire for money.   **salability:** Marketability.

2. What type of occupation do you envision for yourself? Would Marlowe say it screams "Rescue me" (paragraph 13) or "I'll take care of you"?

Suggestions for Writing

1. Based on your experience and observation, write an essay that makes a specific point about how sex is used as a means to an end in today's society. For example, you might consider how advertisers use sex to sell a product or promote an event.

2. Do you agree with Marlowe's position? If so, support her argument in an essay geared toward students just beginning high school. Your purpose should be to help your readers make informed choices about their marriage and career paths. If you disagree with Marlowe, write an essay in which you argue against one of her specific claims.

Anne Finnigan
Nice Perks — If You Can Get 'Em

Anne Finnigan *covers business and consumer issues for* Working Mother *and other magazines. Her article, which accompanied* Working Mother's *survey of the 100 Best Companies for Working Mothers, focuses on the loopholes employees encounter when they try to use the benefits their employers offer. Finnigan identifies three main difficulties faced by workers who want to obtain family-friendly benefits.*

AS YOU READ: *Identify the family-friendly benefits available to employees of the "100 Best" companies and the reasons some employees don't get them.*

You read about them here every year: Companies where you can struc-   1
ture your workday around your child's oboe recital without raising a single managerial eyebrow. Companies that let you work from home — no questions asked. Companies that pick up your dry cleaning, change your oil, even send you home at five o'clock with a hot dinner. You may work for one of those companies, a member of the *Working Mother* 100 Best list. Problem is, even though your company may offer such benefits, they don't seem to be available to you. This year's 100 Best list shows — again — that companies are doing more to accommodate their employees' work/life needs than ever before. They're pushing the envelope with innovative policies and spending hundreds of millions of dollars to make these programs work.

But there's still a long way to go, as the editors of this magazine are re-   2
minded each year after publishing the 100 Best list. We get hundreds of letters charging that for every 100 Best working mom who enjoys family-friendly benefits, dozens of others — often in the same company — are still scrambling to meet even the most basic "life" needs. There's the single mom on the swing shift whose company offers child care, but not for anyone

working off-peak hours. There are the women working at far-flung satellite offices who don't have access to the company gym or concierge services at headquarters; those niceties might as well exist in another galaxy for all the good they do them. And there's the mom who tries to take advantage of a company's advertised flextime policies, only to be told by her manager that he's not approving any such thing.

Why do work/life policies fall short for some employees? There are three 3 reasons. One: No matter what the company says on paper, the corporate culture demands a work-is-your-life commitment. Two: Managers aren't trained to turn policy into real practice, nor are they rewarded for doing so. And three: Work/life benefits are distributed inequitably, so that many workers are left out of the loop—those earning less, those laboring far from headquarters, or those whose jobs, simply by their nature, preclude some benefits.

"Many companies haven't implemented work/life options throughout 4 the entire organization," says Jennifer Chatman, a professor at the University of California at Berkeley's Haas School of Business. "The policies provide a good image and attract employees, but they're not practiced because people get informally penalized for doing anything that takes away from a less-than-one-hundred-percent effort."

Here, a look at these three problem areas, the key complaints we've seen 5 in the last year, and information on what some companies are doing to improve the situation.

1. They say it but they don't mean it. Remaking corporate culture can 6 be tougher than turning the *Titanic*. In a big company, it means changing the minds—and behavior—of tens of thousands of people. That can be especially difficult in a work-is-your-life organization, or one with a rigidly structured hierarchy° —and the requirements of certain kinds of jobs in such organizations make it even harder. A Merck employee writes:

> Did you ever interview one field sales rep to see what the stress level is like for those of us who don't have a child-care facility on site, or get reimbursed for extra hours of child care when our meetings take us away from home for a week at a time? Or that when training for field sales, a mother is away from home for nearly three months? Management turns a blind eye to these issues and replies, "You hired on to this job." Most of us were unaware of the seventy- to eighty-hour weeks we were signing on for.

"We're definitely not there yet," Merck spokesperson Maggie Beute re- 7 sponds frankly. "With 36,000 employees in the United States, it's hard to make sure all managers have great communications skills. As in any large corporation, not every manager is as excited about these policies as our CEO is. And individual managers let some people use them but don't let others, and employees feel they're being treated unfairly." One of the elements at work: a major culture shift. "Before Raymond Gilmartin joined as CEO, the organization was very top-down," says Beute. "Now we're supposed to work face to face, manager to employee."

hierarchy: A system in which persons are ranked above one another.

To address this challenge, Merck devised a team brainstorming process   8
in which employees and managers in each unit take up problems like workweeks that have stretched too long or the unavailability of flex. Beute's
group, corporate communications, did this last year. Everyone filled out a
detailed survey on how they worked, and an outside analyst pinpointed
what the unit's problems were and where time could be saved. "A few directors took some of it personally, but it got all of us around a table," says
Beute.

In Beute's case, the process paid off: Her seventy-hour weeks have been   9
cut to fifty, and she works one day a week from home. As important, "when
things get crazy now, I ask for help."

To help workers far from headquarters, Merck is putting computer kiosks   10
at all manufacturing sites, so employees have access to the latest benefits information. Workers with a hard-to-resolve problem can also call a hot line,
staffed by a chief ombudsman and four others. The ombudsmen then call
the manager's manager to see about resolving the problem, Beute says.

The hardest company cultures to change are those that value "face time"   11
above all else. "In these businesses, the attitude is 'your personal life is personal, and you need to be here when I say you need to be here,'" says Re-
becca Blank, dean of the University of Michigan's Gerald R. Ford School of
Public Policy. Also challenging: corporate cultures that are designed, 1950s
style, around the idea of a stay-at-home spouse who takes care of all the life
stuff—a pleasant fiction, since more than two-thirds of all U.S. moms are
out in the workplace. Then there's the you-married-the-company kind of
culture, where "once you're hired, you give up any life you used to have outside," as one reader wrote us.

Some kinds of businesses also find it difficult to incorporate work/life   12
practices because of the nature of the work that they do. Enterprises that require employees on site twenty-four hours a day—any kind of manufacturing, for instance—aren't the optimal candidates for work/life benefits like
telecommuting. And those companies that hire large numbers of lower-
income workers have a real challenge helping them meet their child-care
needs affordably.

In other cases, the demands of the job are so intense that they virtually   13
preclude° balance. Take the case of management consultants who can be
away from home four nights out of seven, serving clients in other states. They
may work for a company that has an on-site child-care center and flex—but
to a parent away most of the week, the company isn't likely to feel particularly family-friendly. Certain professions—including law, academia, and finance—also continue to require a fast-track work pace for those who want
to rise to the top. If employees take time off beyond a minimum maternity
leave, "they are labeled 'off-track' very quickly," says Chatman.

2. My manager won't get with the program. An employee's work/life   14
balance stands or falls on her manager's ability to turn policies into work-

---

preclude: Prevent the possibility of.

able practice. And that ability rests on how well work/life policies are supported from up top. A DuPont employee writes:

> Some of the great things mentioned in your article are just not applicable
> to most of the workers at DuPont. They are policies that are there in writing,
> but if I were to need part-time or flextime work, I would be told it wasn't
> possible. What looks good on paper isn't necessarily true in real life.

"That's one of the hardest issues facing us," admits Claudette Whiting, 15
director of work/life and diversity at DuPont, which has more than eighty
sites. "You can have the best programs in place, but you have to educate
managers to get them to use them. And you have to know what your employees need." DuPont will spend $200,000 this year to help managers at
satellite sites determine how to improve their work/life policies. Another
program trains managers in how to put such benefits into practice.

Those sorts of specific steps are virtually mandatory for firms who want 16
to make sure managers understand and use work/life programs. "Probably
three quarters of the complaints we hear begin with 'My manager won't let
me,'" says Anne Ruddy. "Many of these supervisors are under pressures of
their own. It can be tough to persuade them that employees can and should
be able to design their own schedule or be trusted to work at home. You've
got to teach them."

That's why the best of the 100 Best train their managers extensively and 17
reward them for how much programs like telecommuting and job-sharing
get used. Managers are encouraged to be innovative and to focus on what
gets done rather than where or how it's done. "Our approach to work/life is
common sense," says J. T. (Ted) Childs Jr., vice president of global workforce
diversity at IBM, which has been on the 100 Best list for fifteen years. "We
want managers to focus on results, not on face time. We don't care how,
where, or when the work gets done, but that the results are achieved." These
companies also conduct regular employee work/life surveys and make
changes based on the feedback they get.

Finally, one of the most effective ways companies can send the message 18
that they mean business about work/life is by having top-level executives
practice what they preach. When executives take a paternity or maternity
leave or cut out in midafternoon for their kid's softball game, everyone else
knows that it's really okay for them to do it too.

3. Workers like me can't get that. Aside from changing the corporate 19
culture and getting managers on board, a company's biggest work/life challenge is to make sure all policies are truly available to all employees, no
matter what their level is on the corporate ladder. For a variety of reasons,
that rarely happens. One large category of worker who frequently misses out
is the blue-collar employee, who is paid by the hour (about two-thirds of all
working mothers). "They are compelled to put in overtime under penalty of
losing their job if they refuse— and the law is on the company's side," explains Robert Reich, former U.S. Secretary of Labor and professor of social
and economic policy at Brandeis University.

The landmark Fair Labor Standards Act of 1938 requires only that a   20
company pay its workers time and a half for each hour of work beyond forty
hours in a single week, Reich says. That leaves these workers with only one
option — trying to convince their company to agree not to order them to
work overtime when spouses, kids, or elderly parents need them at home.
"Some employers do this already, as a means of attracting and keeping good
workers," Reich says. "But other companies have to be prodded." Increasingly, unionized workers are seeking such agreements within formal labor
contracts. "But it's an uphill fight," Reich says. "Less than 8 percent of working women belong to a union."

An employee of Bell Atlantic (called Verizon after its merger with GTE)   21
writes: "Members [of the union group Communications Workers of Amer-
ica] have consistently been assigned mandatory overtime to meet customer
needs. Other items such as flextime, compressed workweeks, and job-
sharing are for management employees only."

Bell Atlantic, on the 100 Best list for its third year, has made the grade by   22
investing in a wide range of family options, from on-site and community-
based child care to flex arrangements like job-sharing. But like many other
companies on the list, Bell Atlantic hasn't been able to make such benefits
available across the board, particularly at sites with unionized hourly employees. Depending on seniority, union workers can receive up to five weeks
of vacation and four excused workdays with pay, and the company's Kids in
the Workplace program provides on-site child care when employees have to
work on holidays. Winning other benefits has proven elusive,° in part because the tight labor market has made it increasingly difficult for Bell Atlantic to find enough workers to fill all the slots they have open.

"We need to have people work overtime," says Sharon Beadle, senior   23
specialist of media relations for Bell Atlantic. "Managers do make an effort
to assign it on a voluntary basis."

"What do you do if you're assigned overtime, but you have to pick up   24
your kid from day care?" responds Linda Kramer, president of the Communications Workers of America Local 1023. "These are stressful jobs, especially for young parents." When one dad had to leave on a few occasions
and was eventually fired, the union took the case to arbitration. The ruling:
The company has the right to schedule mandatory overtime, but also has
the responsibility to accommodate its workers' family issues. The union is
trying to formalize that responsibility in its new contract. But negotiating
work/life balance across the bargaining table is complicated. The adversarial
nature of labor-management relations often results in agreements that are
set in stone, while it can be more desirable to deal with work/life practices
on a case-by-case basis.

Bell Atlantic is currently working to boost the number of supervisors, in   25
the hope that improving the supervisor/worker ratio will help develop more
personal connections. "When I started at Bell thirty years ago, you could go

elusive: Remaining out of reach.

talk to your manager if you had a problem and they'd try to help you work it out—because they knew you," says Kramer. Today, because of corporate cutbacks in the early 1990s, supervisors might have thirty or more employees under them, and their managers might oversee more than 100—located in different states.

Finding the Solutions

Despite such shortcomings, it's important to note that the 100 Best compa- 26 nies are doing much more for employees than the vast majority of employers. Only 10 percent of U.S. companies offer on-site or near-site child care, according to a survey by Hewitt Associates, a benefits consulting firm; 68 percent of 100 Best companies offer such programs. Flextime, which is an option at 99 percent of the 100 Best companies, is available at only 57 percent of companies in the Hewitt survey.

And some of the 100 Best are ahead of the pack in delivering work/life 27 benefits to lower-income employees, who need them the most—and are least likely to get them. Broadening work/life's base is critical: Recent research by the Families and Work Institute shows that while lower-level workers now have access to some essentials such as job-guaranteed time off for childbirth, other options—like telecommuting, regular flex scheduling, and paid time off to care for a sick child—are still out of reach.

So what will it take to change the workplace for *all* of us? The law of 28 supply and demand may do it. The current worker shortage is giving working mothers increasing clout. And we have a new ally in our quest for balance: Younger workers, who are demanding—and getting—control over their time. The good news is that the adoption of strong work/life practices is fast becoming a bottom-line business necessity.

"It's a golden opportunity," says sociologist Arlie Hochschild, author of 29 *The Time Bind* and *The Second Shift*, "to get careers designed around family commitments." And in the best of the 100 Best, it's already a reality.

Questions to Start You Thinking

1. CONSIDERING MEANING: According to Finnigan, how successful are the "100 Best" companies in implementing family-friendly policies? What does their success suggest about the availability of such benefits at other companies or other types of jobs?

2. IDENTIFYING WRITING STRATEGIES: How does Finnigan use quotations to support her analysis of family-oriented practices? How does identification of the people she quotes lend credibility to her evidence?

3. READING CRITICALLY: How are the "100 Best" companies trying to resolve the problems with family-friendly policies? What causes their solutions to succeed or fail?

4. EXPANDING VOCABULARY: What are *flextime* (paragraph 2), *face time* (paragraph 11), *telecommuting* (paragraph 12), and *job-sharing* (paragraph 17)? Does Finnigan provide enough context for you to figure out the meaning of these terms? How has her audience influenced her word choice?

5. MAKING CONNECTIONS: How might Stephanie Coontz ("Remarriage and Stepfamilies," pp. 419–24) view the family-friendly benefits Finnigan describes? Would they relieve any of the stresses Coontz identifies? Would they increase any other stresses?

Link to the Paired Essay

Both Finnigan and Elinor Burkett ("Unequal Work for Unequal Pay," below) address the shift to family-oriented workplace policies. How do their concerns differ? How might Finnigan respond to Burkett?

Journal Prompts

1. How important will a prospective employer's family policies be when you seek a job? In what ways would you expect the importance to vary during different stages of your life?
2. Write about frustrations you've experienced in the workplace.

Suggestions for Writing

1. Finnigan points out that "more than two-thirds of all U.S. moms are out in the workplace" (paragraph 11). Write an essay exploring the effects on the workplace of the shift away from the 1950s-style family. Use your own experience and observations as resources.
2. Taking the point of view of company management, write an essay in which you explore the value of family-friendly policies. Look at both long-range and short-range effects.

■ For useful links to Web sources on topics including *the workplace*, visit <bedfordstmartins.com/toplinks>.

Elinor Burkett
Unequal Work for Unequal Pay

Elinor Burkett *taught history before becoming a reporter. She has written for the* New York Times Magazine, The Atlantic Monthly, Rolling Stone, *and* Mirabella. *Her work with the* Miami Herald *has earned her many national and state awards, and she was nominated for a 1991 Pulitzer Prize for journalism. Burkett, who lives in New York, has written several books, including* The Gravest Show on Earth *(1995),* The Right Women *(1998), and* Another Planet *(2002).* The Baby Boon: How Family-Friendly America Cheats the Children *(2000), from which this selection was taken, was inspired by Burkett's article* "Pushing Mommy Off the Track," *which appeared in* Mirabella *and won the Front Page Award from the Newswomen's Club of New York. In* The Baby Boon, *Burkett questions the fairness of corporations that cater to employees with children.*

AS YOU READ: *Look for ways Burkett feels family-friendly policies affect workers who are not parents.*

Few of the new "family-friendly benefits" have much to do with the lives   1
of most American workers. In fact, most of the highly touted innova-
tions are entirely irrelevant to them since most workers aren't the kind of
middle-class working mothers who dream up these benefits in the first
place. Look at what the "best" companies—the companies honored by
Working Mother magazine, by *Business Week,* or the Women's Bureau of the
Department of Labor, which actually printed an Honor Roll of well-behaved
corporations—are offering their employees.

Fel-Pro Incorporated is precisely the type of company Americans expect   2
not to have superb "family" benefits. This is no white-collar corporation
heavy with kid-gloves executives nor a high-tech business packed with professionals and technicians who could move to, say, North Carolina, Boston,
or Silicon Valley with a single phone call. Fel-Pro's twenty-one hundred
employees—40 percent of them female—manufacture engine gaskets,
sealants, and lubricants in the industrial section of Skokie, Illinois.

But it is a parental heaven, with on-site daycare, a summer camp for   3
kids at the company's two-hundred-acre park, subsidized in-home childcare
for those days when the baby-sitter doesn't show up or a child is ill. New
parents receive a one-thousand-dollar check as a gift for their baby and two
months of unpaid leave. Adoptive parents receive fifteen hundred dollars to
help out with the legal bills. Parents of older children can take advantage of
a special program that helps them explore college options. And if their children are outstanding students, they even receive corporate scholarships.

IBM boasts the nation's most generous family-leave policy, granting par-   4
ents three years with full benefits. It has spent millions of dollars to help its
employees with childcare, spending five hundred thousand dollars on one
North Carolina daycare center in conjunction with Duke Power, Allstate,
and American Express. Parents can carve out their work schedules any time
from 6:30 A.M. to 10:30 P.M., or opt for a "midday flex."

The largesse of major companies is dramatic. Eli Lilly provides up to ten   5
thousand dollars in financial aid for adoption. BE&K, one of the nation's
largest building contractors, owns a modular daycare center that it moves
from site to site to provide for the children of construction workers. Stride-
Rite, the shoe manufacturer, allows new parents eight weeks of paid leave
and eighteen weeks more unpaid but with full benefits and job protection.
And Hallmark lends tuition money, interest-free, to parents with five or
more years of service.

When *Working Mother* began its best companies list in 1985, editors say   6
they could find only thirty companies marginally qualified for the title of
mother-friendly. Now hundreds vie for those slots. According to Hewitt Associates' annual survey of the benefits packages of America's employers, 72
percent allow parents some sort of flexible schedules, 86 percent sponsor a
childcare benefit program, 31 percent provide family-leave benefits that are
more generous than the federal government requires, 25 percent subsidize
adoptions, and a wide array of programs, everything from after-school hot-
lines to family care days, vacation camps, and tuition reimbursement, for
the children of their workers, are spreading like wildfire.

Survey after survey confirms that same picture of a family-friendly work-   7
place movement reshaping the nature of work for American parents. A 1998
survey of more than one thousand companies conducted by the Families
and Work Institute found that 88 percent of all companies with more than
one hundred employees allow parents time off for school functions; 15 percent offer more than twelve weeks of maternity leave, and more than half
with some pay; 24 percent award scholarships or other educational assistance to the children of their employees; and 87 percent paid for at least
part of the health insurance of their employees' families.

The magazine editors, human resources officers, consultants, and politi-   8
cians who promote these programs, and themselves in the process, argue
their value not just on humanistic or moral grounds, but as wise bottom-
line decisions. Family-friendliness, they say, pays by promoting loyalty and
productivity, reducing absenteeism, tardiness, and turnover, and polishing a
company's public image. Such testimonials are legion. The Families and
Work Institute presents flow charts and graphs proving that businesses with
more "supportive workplaces" have more satisfied employees who are more
committed to the success of their employers and more likely to remain on
the job. They cite the case of the pharmaceutical giant Johnson & Johnson,
where absenteeism plummeted after the introduction of a raft of family programs. Officials at Fel-Pro claim that their turnover rate dropped from between 30 and 40 percent to 10 percent after they opened a company summer camp. Merck reports that it saves three dollars for each dollar it spends
on family programs because workers wind up less stressed, less likely to arrive at work late or leave before the end of the workday, to miss work to take
care of sick children, or to quit to stay home with the kids. John Fernandez,
a Philadelphia management consultant, posits that family-friendly programs can reduce absenteeism by as much as 19 percent and the rate of employee turnover from 8 to 3 percent.

By the time *Business Week* published the results of its first survey of   9
family-friendly corporate America in 1996, Corporate America was in full
swoon. "Disbelievers, skeptics, working stiffs, take note," proclaimed the
magazine. "Work-family strategies haven't just hit the corporate mainstream — they've become a competitive advantage. . . . It is a phenomenon,
in other words, that executives deny at their own risk."

The numbers, however, don't add up, given the demographics of the   10
American workforce. How can turnover and absenteeism drop so precipi-
tously° in response to childcare assistance, family leaves, and scholarships
for employees' kids when, according to the Bureau of Labor Statistics, only
one-third of the workforce has children at home under the age of eighteen?
How can daycare centers account for 50 percent reductions in turnover
when only 8 percent of women workers have kids under the age of six? How
can a company like Chase Manhattan Bank spend seven hundred thousand
dollars a year to run a daycare center in Brooklyn for 110 children and justify

precipitously: Steeply.

the expenditures by citing "return-on-investment" analyses showing savings of $1.5 million in avoided absenteeism alone? Were the parents of those 110 children missing that much work?

Since there are 13 million more working women without kids at home 11 than with kids — 38 million to 25 million — how can corporate America's obsession with family-friendliness possibly be improving morale? Adoption allowances, maternity and paternity leave, childcare, sick kid care, after-school care, and summer camps are entirely irrelevant to them. Those benefits don't do all that much for workers who do have kids, since the vast majority don't adopt, don't seem not to want institutional daycare, and can't take long parental leaves because they can't afford six months without income.

Rather than boosting morale, in fact, the programs are having an oppo- 12 site effect — and for logical reasons. How would you feel if you had no children and worked at Fel-Pro, where employees have access to childcentric benefits worth thousands of dollars more than the benefits you can use? Imagine what it is like to work at the *New York Times*, where parents can claim long unpaid leaves to bond with their children as a right while those without children who ask for unpaid leave to pursue *their* interests, which usually involve writing books, are subject to management whimsy, which often means that their requests are denied.

Consider what state your morale would be in if you, as a nonparent, 13 heard endlessly about your company's concern for employee morale and the balance in their lives, then discovered that the office charged with both was called Work/Family and spent most of its resources referring parents to daycare centers and planning luncheon workshops on parenting. Would you not ask how the morale of the other two-thirds of the workforce was being tended? And think what it would feel like to be on the staff at NationsBank and hear the chief executive officer call the bank a "meritocracy"° when you know that the flexible schedule of the man sitting next to you, or the five thousand dollars in extra benefits of the woman behind you, aren't rewards for meritorious work, but for reproduction.

In today's workplace, childless employees are well-versed in the Ten Com- 14 mandments of workplace etiquette in family-friendly America. They're not yet included in employee handbooks, or posted prominently on bulletin boards alongside flyers about safety or workers' compensation. But they are etched into the experience of virtually every nonparent who works alongside parents.

1. Thou shalt volunteer to work late so that mothers can leave at 2:00 P.M. to watch their sons play soccer, for a mother's time is more valuable than thine.

---

meritocracy: A system that bases rewards on ability and performance.

2. Thou shalt never complain when important meetings are broken up at 2:30 by phone calls from children reporting in after school lest thou be considered indifferent to the importance of parental bonding.

3. Thou shalt take thy vacations when no one else wants time off so parents can take theirs during the summer, over Christmas, or on any other school or "family" holiday.

4. Thou shalt not apply the phrase "equal pay for equal work" to thy company's benefits plan, although it offers mothers and fathers thousands of dollars in perks thou can't use.

5. Thou shalt willingly do two jobs for the price of one while mothers are on six-month maternity and parental leaves.

6. Thou shalt never ask for a long leave to write a book, travel, or fulfill thy heart's desire because no desire other than children could possibly be worth thy company's inconvenience.

7. Thou shalt volunteer to take frequent business trips to places like Abilene, Kansas, or Cleveland, Ohio, so that parents can spend their evenings watching *ER* after they put the kids to bed.

8. Thou shalt promote thy "family-friendly" company as a firm that cherishes women because everyone knows that women equals mothers.

9. Thou shalt never utter the words "but that's not my problem" when a parent rushes out the door during the final negotiations of a corporate merger, explaining that he has promised to take the children to the movies.

10. Thou shalt smile graciously when thy co-worker brings her three-year-old to the office and allows him to turn the papers on thy desk into airplanes.

Questions to Start You Thinking

1. CONSIDERING MEANING: What are Burkett's objections to the "family-friendly benefits" increasingly offered by American companies?

2. IDENTIFYING WRITING STRATEGIES: Where does Burkett begin to question the advantages claimed by "family-friendly" advocates? What do her preceding paragraphs describing family benefits contribute to her argument? How successful is this organizational structure?

3. READING CRITICALLY: In paragraph 8, Burkett names people who "promote these [family] programs, and themselves in the process." How do advocates of family-friendly programs promote themselves? What evidence does Burkett use to refute the claims of these advocates?

4. EXPANDING VOCABULARY: Define *demographics* (paragraph 10). What demographics does Burkett cite that conflict with successes claimed for family-friendly programs?

5. MAKING CONNECTIONS: Burkett uses demographics to support her claim that nonparent workers are treated unequally by policies that grant costly benefits to employees with children. Compare her use of such evidence with

Liu's in "The Causation Fallacy: *Bakke* and the Basic Arithmetic of Selective Admissions" (pp. 535–43). How do both writers use numbers to counter perceptions?

Link to the Paired Essay

Elinor Burkett and Anne Finnigan ("Nice Perks — If You Can Get 'Em," pp. 500–05) agree that workplace benefits for employees with children are on the rise, but they disagree on the desirability of this trend. Which writer do you find more convincing? Why?

■ For useful links to Web sources on topics including *the workplace*, visit <bedfordstmartins.com/ toplinks>.

Journal Prompts

1. Describe a practice that you find unfair in your workplace or at school.
2. When you were a child, did you have working or stay-at-home parents? What were some of the advantages or disadvantages?

Suggestions for Writing

1. Is reproduction rewarded in our society? Should it be? Write an essay that uses your own observations to support your opinion.
2. Do the advantages of family-oriented programs go beyond increased productivity in the workplace? Write an essay in which you explore the long-term effects of such programs and take a stand on whether they should be expanded or discontinued.

Education

Responding to an Image

At first glance, this cartoon may appear to be about nothing more than a school basketball game. However, a closer look reveals a deeper message. Why does the scene include two scoreboards? How does the composition of the image guide a viewer's eye to them? What does the cartoon suggest about the role of sports in today's schools, the relationship between sports and academics, or the standards for evaluating athletes and other students? Could the cartoon also be making a comment about standardized testing? Write a brief editorial that might accompany this cartoon.

The educational system is facing many challenges, two of which are highlighted in this cartoon — the role of sports in education and standardized testing. Conduct your own investigation into these and other challenges by visiting Education Week on the Web (<www.edweek.org/context/topics/>) or the National Education Association home page (<www.nea.org/>). Which of the issues highlighted on these Web sites do you consider the most important and deserving of immediate attention? Why? Use the Internet to find at least one other reliable source of information on this topic. Be able to explain how you found your source and which criteria you used to evaluate its reliability and usefulness.

■ For Web reading activities linked to this chapter, visit <bedfordstmartins.com/bedguide> and do a keyword search:

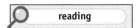
reading

William Zinsser
The Right to Fail

William Zinsser *was born in New York City in 1922. After receiving his B.A. from Princeton University in 1944, he worked as a feature writer for the* New York Herald Tribune *and later became the newspaper's drama and film critic. Zinsser has written numerous books and contributed articles to magazines including* Life, The New Yorker, *and* The Atlantic. *Although he has covered subjects ranging from American landmarks to jazz, he is probably best known for his classic guides to writing:* Writing with a Word Processor *(1983),* On Writing Well *(1976),* Inventing the Truth *(1987), and* Writing to Learn *(1988). Zinsser has taught humor and nonfiction writing at Yale University, and he currently teaches at the New School University in New York City. In "The Right to Fail," an excerpt from* The Lunacy Boom *(1970), Zinsser makes the case that failure is an important aspect of human experience.*

AS YOU READ: *Identify the benefits of failure that Zinsser presents.*

I like "dropout" as an addition to the American language because it's brief and it's clear. What I don't like is that we use it almost entirely as a dirty word.

We only apply it to people under twenty-one. Yet an adult who spends his days and nights watching mindless TV programs is more of a dropout than an eighteen-year-old who quits college, with its frequently mindless courses, to become, say, a VISTA volunteer. For the young, dropping out is often a way of dropping in.

To hold this opinion, however, is little short of treason in America. A boy or girl who leaves college is branded a failure — and the right to fail is one of the few freedoms that this country does not grant its citizens. The American dream is a dream of "getting ahead," painted in strokes of gold wherever we look. Our advertisements and TV commercials are a hymn to material success, our magazine articles a toast to people who made it to the top. Smoke the right cigarette or drive the right car — so the ads imply — and girls will be swooning into your deodorized arms or caressing your expensive lapels. Happiness goes to the man who has the sweet smell of achievement. He is our national idol, and everybody else is our national fink.°

I want to put in a word for the fink, especially the teen-age fink, because 4 if we give him time to get through his finkdom — if we release him from the pressure of attaining certain goals by a certain age — he has a good chance of becoming our national idol, a Jefferson or a Thoreau, a Buckminster Fuller° or an Adlai Stevenson,° a man with a mind of his own. We need mavericks° and dissenters and dreamers far more than we need junior vice-presidents, but we paralyze them by insisting that every step be a step up to the next rung of the ladder. Yet in the fluid years of youth, the only way for boys and girls to find their proper road is often to take a hundred side trips, poking out in different directions, faltering, drawing back, and starting again.

"But what if we fail?" they ask, whispering the dreadful word across the 5 Generation Gap to their parents, who are back home at the Establishment, nursing their "middle-class values" and cultivating their "goal-oriented society." The parents whisper back: "Don't!"

What they should say is "Don't be afraid to fail!" Failure isn't fatal. 6 Countless people have had a bout with it and come out stronger as a result. Many have even come out famous. History is strewn with eminent dropouts, "loners" who followed their own trail, not worrying about its odd twists and turns because they had faith in their own sense of direction. To read their biographies is always exhilarating, not only because they beat the system, but because their system was better than the one that they beat.

Luckily, such rebels still turn up often enough to prove that individual- 7 ism, though badly threatened, is not extinct. Much has been written, for instance, about the fitful scholastic career of Thomas P. F. Hoving, New York's former Parks Commissioner and now director of the Metropolitan Museum of Art. Hoving was a dropout's dropout, entering and leaving schools as if they were motels, often at the request of the management. Still, he must have learned something during those unorthodox years, for he dropped in again at the top of his profession.

His case reminds me of another boyhood — that of Holden Caulfield in 8 J. D. Salinger's *The Catcher in the Rye*, the most popular literary hero of the postwar period. There is nothing accidental about the grip that this dropout continues to hold on the affections of an entire American generation. Nobody else, real or invented, has made such an engaging shambles of our

---

fink: Tattletale or other contemptible person.   **Buckminster Fuller:** American inventor, architect, and engineer (1895–1983) who dropped out of Harvard to work on solving global resource and environmental problems.   **Adlai Stevenson:** American politician (1900–1965) who was greatly admired for championing liberal causes but badly lost two presidential elections.   **mavericks:** Nonconformists.

"goal-oriented society," so gratified our secret belief that the "phonies" are in power and the good guys up the creek. Whether Holden has also reached the top of his chosen field today is one of those speculations that delight fanciers of good fiction. I speculate that he has. Holden Caulfield, incidentally, is now thirty-six.

I'm not urging everyone to go out and fail just for the sheer therapy 9 of it, or to quit college just to coddle° some vague discontent. Obviously it's better to succeed than to flop, and in general a long education is more helpful than a short one. (Thanks to my own education, for example, I can tell George Eliot from T. S. Eliot. I can handle the pluperfect tense in French, and I know that Caesar beat the Helvetii because he had enough frumentum.°) I only mean that failure isn't bad in itself, or success automatically good.

Fred Zinnemann, who has directed some of Hollywood's most honored 10 movies, was asked by a reporter, when *A Man for All Seasons* won every prize, about his previous film *Behold a Pale Horse*, which was a box-office disaster. "I don't feel any obligation to be successful," Zinnemann replied. "Success can be dangerous — you feel you know it all. I've learned a great deal from my failures." A similar point was made by Richard Brooks about his ambitious money loser, *Lord Jim*. Recalling the three years of his life that went into it, talking almost with elation about the troubles that befell his unit in Cambodia, Brooks told me that he learned more about his craft from this considerable failure than from his many earlier hits.

It's a point, of course, that applies throughout the arts. Writers, play- 11 wrights, painters and composers work in the expectation of periodic defeat, but they wouldn't keep going back into the arena if they thought it was the end of the world. It isn't the end of the world. For an artist — and perhaps for anybody — it is the only way to grow.

Today's younger generation seems to know that this is true, seems will- 12 ing to take the risks in life that artists take in art. "Society," needless to say, still has the upper hand — it sets the goals and condemns as a failure everybody who won't play. But the dropouts and the hippies are not as afraid of failure as their parents and grandparents. This could mean, as their elders might say, that they are just plumb lazy, secure in the comforts of an affluent state. It could also mean, however, that they just don't buy the old standards of success and are rapidly writing new ones.

Recently it was announced, for instance, that more than two hundred 13 thousand Americans have inquired about service in VISTA (the domestic Peace Corps) and that, according to a Gallup survey, "more than three million American college students would serve VISTA in some capacity if given the opportunity." This is hardly the road to riches or to an executive suite. Yet I have met many of these young volunteers, and they are not pining for traditional success. On the contrary, they appear more fulfilled than the average vice-president with a swimming pool.

---

coddle: Indulge; satisfy.   **frumentum:** Latin word for corn or grain.

Who is to say, then, if there is any right path to the top, or even to say   14
what the top consists of? Obviously the colleges don't have more than a partial answer — otherwise the young would not be so disaffected with an education that they consider vapid.° Obviously business does not have the
answer — otherwise the young would not be so scornful of its call to be an
organization man.

The fact is, nobody has the answer, and the dawning awareness of this   15
fact seems to me one of the best things happening in America today. Success
and failure are again becoming individual visions, as they were when the
country was younger, not rigid categories. Maybe we are learning again to
cherish this right of every person to succeed on his own terms and to fail as
often as necessary along the way.

Questions to Start You Thinking

1. CONSIDERING MEANING: What does Zinsser mean when he says that "dropping out is often a way of dropping in" (paragraph 2)? Why is this especially true for young adults?

2. IDENTIFYING WRITING STRATEGIES: Identify some of the concrete examples
   that Zinsser uses to illustrate his points. Are his examples extensive and varied enough to be convincing? Why, or why not?

3 READING CRITICALLY: Zinsser is savvy enough to admit that his position is
   "little short of treason in America" (paragraph 3). Where else does he acknowledge that his advice might seem outlandish? How does he counter
   the opposition?

4. EXPANDING VOCABULARY: In paragraph 3, Zinsser writes, "Our advertisements and TV commercials are a hymn to material success." Define hymn.
   What does the word suggest about the American attitude toward material
   success? How does Zinsser feel about the American dream?

5. MAKING CONNECTIONS: If Malcolm X ("Learning to Read," pp. 517–20) were
   to write a journal response to Zinsser's essay, what do you think he would
   write? Could Zinsser have used Malcolm X as an additional example in his
   essay?

Journal Prompts

1. What is your definition of the "American Dream" (paragraph 3)?

2. Who would you like to share Zinsser's essay with in order to open up that
   person's mind about failure? Why?

Suggestions for Writing

1. In paragraph 10, Zinsser offers the following quote from a movie director:
   "Success can be dangerous — you feel you know it all. I've learned a great
   deal from my failures." Write an essay in which you recall a personal experience that illustrates this statement.

vapid: Dull.

2. Originally written in 1970, Zinsser's essay includes some examples that may not be familiar to you. Write an essay that supports and updates Zinsser's position by drawing on more current examples from history, literature, sports, current events, or popular culture. Imagine a specific audience for your essay (perhaps a sibling, a friend, or a high school class), and be sure that your examples will have an impact on those readers.

Malcolm X
Learning to Read

Malcolm X *was born Malcolm Little in Omaha, Nebraska, in 1925. After dropping out of school in the eighth grade, Malcolm X soon fell into the life of a street hustler and was convicted of robbery in 1946. He spent seven years in prison, where he used the time to further his education and study the teachings of Elijah Muhammad, founder of the Nation of Islam. During the civil rights movement of the 1960s, Malcolm X emerged as a powerful leader, drawing many followers to the black separatist movement. A pilgrimage to Mecca in 1964, however, convinced him that harmony between African Americans and the white community was possible. Adopting the orthodox Muslim name El Hajj Malik El-Shabazz, he left the Nation of Islam to found his own less radical religious and civil rights group. In 1965, he was assassinated while giving a speech. In the following excerpt from* The Autobiography of Malcolm X *(1965), which he coauthored with Alex Haley, Malcolm X describes his "homemade education."*

AS YOU READ: *Note how Malcolm X's prison studies affected his life.*

It was because of my letters that I happened to stumble upon starting to 1
acquire some kind of a homemade education.

I became increasingly frustrated at not being able to express what I 2
wanted to convey in letters that I wrote, especially those to Mr. Elijah Muhammad. In the street, I had been the most articulate hustler out there — I had commanded attention when I said something. But now, trying to write simple English, I not only wasn't articulate, I wasn't even functional. How would I sound writing in slang, the way I would *say* it, something such as, "Look, daddy, let me pull your coat about a cat, Elijah Muhammad —"

Many who today hear me somewhere in person, or on television, or 3
those who read something I've said, will think I went to school far beyond the eighth grade. This impression is due entirely to my prison studies.

It had really begun back in the Charlestown Prison, when Bimbi° first 4
made me feel envy of his stock of knowledge. Bimbi had always taken charge of any conversations he was in, and I had tried to emulate him. But every book I picked up had few sentences which didn't contain anywhere

---

Bimbi: A fellow inmate with impressive speaking skills.

from one to nearly all of the words that might as well have been in Chinese. When I just skipped those words, of course, I really ended up with little idea of what the book said. So I had come to the Norfolk Prison Colony still going through only book-reading motions. Pretty soon, I would have quit even these motions, unless I had received the motivation that I did.

I saw that the best thing I could do was get hold of a dictionary — to study, to learn some words. I was lucky enough to reason also that I should try to improve my penmanship. It was sad. I couldn't even write in a straight line. It was both ideas together that moved me to request a dictionary along with some tablets and pencils from the Norfolk Prison Colony school.   5

I spent two days just riffling uncertainly through the dictionary's pages. I'd never realized so many words existed! I didn't know *which* words I needed to learn. Finally, just to start some kind of action, I began copying.   6

In my slow, painstaking, ragged handwriting, I copied into my tablet everything printed on that first page, down to the punctuation marks.   7

I believe it took me a day. Then, aloud, I read back, to myself, everything I'd written on the tablet. Over and over, aloud, to myself, I read my own handwriting.   8

I woke up the next morning, thinking about those words — immensely proud to realize that not only had I written so much at one time, but I'd written words that I never knew were in the world. Moreover, with a little effort, I also could remember what many of these words meant. I reviewed the words whose meanings I didn't remember. Funny thing, from the dictionary first page right now, that "aardvark" springs to my mind. The dictionary had a picture of it, a long-tailed, long-eared, burrowing African mammal, which lives off termites caught by sticking out its tongue as an anteater does for ants.   9

I was so fascinated that I went on — I copied the dictionary's next page. And the same experience came when I studied that. With every succeeding page, I also learned of people and places and events from history. Actually the dictionary is like a miniature encyclopedia. Finally the dictionary's A section had filled a whole tablet — and I went on into the B's. That was the way I started copying what eventually became the entire dictionary. It went a lot faster after so much practice helped me to pick up handwriting speed. Between what I wrote in my tablet, and writing letters, during the rest of my time in prison I would guess I wrote a million words.   10

I suppose it was inevitable that as my word-base broadened, I could for the first time pick up a book and read and now begin to understand what the book was saying. Anyone who has read a great deal can imagine the new world that opened. Let me tell you something: from then until I left that prison, in every free moment I had, if I was not reading in the library, I was reading on my bunk. You couldn't have gotten me out of books with a wedge. Between Mr. Muhammad's teachings, my correspondence, my visitors, . . . and my reading of books, months passed without my even thinking about being imprisoned. In fact, up to then, I never had been so truly free in my life.   11

The Norfolk Prison Colony's library was in the school building. A vari- 12
ety of classes was taught there by instructors who came from such places as
Harvard and Boston universities. The weekly debates between inmate teams
were also held in the school building. You would be astonished to know
how worked up convict debaters and audiences would get over subjects like
"Should Babies Be Fed Milk?"

Available on the prison library's shelves were books on just about every 13
general subject. Much of the big private collection that Parkhurst° had
willed to the prison was still in crates and boxes in the back of the library —
thousands of old books. Some of them looked ancient: covers faded, old-
time parchment-looking binding. Parkhurst . . . seemed to have been princi-
pally interested in history and religion. He had the money and the special
interest to have a lot of books that you wouldn't have in a general circulation. Any college library would have been lucky to get that collection.

As you can imagine, especially in a prison where there was heavy em- 14
phasis on rehabilitation, an inmate was smiled upon if he demonstrated an
unusually intense interest in books. There was a sizable number of well-read
inmates, especially the popular debaters. Some were said by many to be
practically walking encyclopedias. They were almost celebrities. No university would ask any student to devour literature as I did when this new world
opened to me, of being able to read and *understand*.

I read more in my room than in the library itself. An inmate who was 15
known to read a lot could check out more than the permitted maximum
number of books. I preferred reading in the total isolation of my own room.

When I had progressed to really serious reading, every night at about 16
ten P.M. I would be outraged with the "lights out." It always seemed to catch
me right in the middle of something engrossing.

Fortunately, right outside my door was a corridor light that cast a glow 17
into my room. The glow was enough to read by, once my eyes adjusted to it.
So when "lights out" came, I would sit on the floor where I could continue
reading in that glow.

At one-hour intervals at night guards paced past every room. Each time I 18
heard the approaching footsteps, I jumped into bed and feigned° sleep. And
as soon as the guard passed, I got back out of bed onto the floor area of that
light-glow, where I would read for another fifty-eight minutes until the
guard approached again. That went on until three or four every morning.
Three or four hours of sleep a night was enough for me. Often in the years
in the streets I had slept less than that.

Questions to Start You Thinking

1. CONSIDERING MEANING: What prompted Malcolm X to begin studying the
   dictionary? What motivated him to continue?

Parkhurst: Charles Henry Parkhurst (1842–1933), an American clergyman and president
of the Society for the Prevention of Crime.   **feigned:** Faked.

2. IDENTIFYING WRITING STRATEGIES: How does Malcolm X use both recall and cause and effect to illustrate the power of his self-education? Which of his details seem especially focused and engaging? How does he organize them in a logical sequence?

3. READING CRITICALLY: What is Malcolm X's purpose in this essay? How do his voice and selection of details work toward achieving this purpose?

4. EXPANDING VOCABULARY: Define *rehabilitation*. What might Malcolm X consider vital to the successful rehabilitation of prisoners?

5. MAKING CONNECTIONS: Johanna Wald ("Extracurricular Drug Testing," below) suggests that academically at-risk students require "connections, attachments, and engagement" (paragraph 5) in order to succeed. While Malcolm X does not write about a traditional educational environment, he plays the role of student as he learns to read and write. In what ways did his prison studies fulfill some or all of these needs? How do "connections, attachments, and engagement" contribute to academic and social success?

Journal Prompts

1. Write about an accomplishment that you are proud of.

2. Malcolm X mentions that he sacrificed sleep to have more time to read. Write about a sacrifice that you have made for some goal or interest.

Suggestions for Writing

1. Write about a time when you taught yourself how to do something. Recall why you decided to teach yourself, the process you used, and the obstacles you had to overcome.

2. It is ironic that, as a prisoner, Malcolm X had never felt "so truly free" (paragraph 11) in his life. Write an essay in which you argue that education or knowledge is the key to freedom. Use the readings in this text and your own experiences and observations to support your point.

Johanna Wald
Extracurricular Drug Testing

Johanna Wald *holds a B.A. from Wesleyan University and an M.Ed. from Harvard University. She is the Senior Development/Policy Analyst for Harvard University's Civil Rights Project (CRP), an organization that conducts research and policy studies with the goal of renewing the civil rights movement. Wald is currently developing CRP's "school to prison" pipeline project, researching the connections between poor educational performance and juvenile crime. She has covered educational issues including zero tolerance policies and high stakes testing for* The Nation, Salon.com, *and the* Boston Globe. *In "Extracurricular Drug Testing,"* *which originally appeared in* Education Week *in 2002, Wald argues that drug testing in schools could have negative consequences for the students who would most benefit from extracurricular activities.*

AS YOU READ: *Determine the factors that, according to Wald, contribute to the success of at-risk students.*

The line of questioning pursued by justices of the U.S. Supreme Court in   1
March, as they heard oral arguments in a case involving student drug tests, suggests that the court may be poised to sanction broader use of drug testing in schools. If that happens, one almost certain consequence will be that students who want to participate in an expanded range of extracurricular activities will be required to submit to these tests. The head of the Oklahoma school board whose policy is being reviewed by the court indicated as much when she said, "We'd love to test all students, if they'd let us." And the deputy solicitor general of the United States, Paul D. Clement, said that in his opinion, schoolwide drug-testing programs would be constitutional. ("Supreme Court Hears Case on Expanded Drug Testing," March 27, 2002.)

A majority of Supreme Court justices appeared to be persuaded by the   2
argument that drug-testing policies represent, as Julie Underwood, the general counsel for the National School Boards Association, phrased it, part of a school's "arsenal to prevent drug use." To Justice Antonin Scalia, the Tecumseh, Oklahoma, district's tests represented an attempt to "train and raise these young people to be responsible adults." Justice Stephen G. Breyer seemed to agree, suggesting that the testing is "an effort to deal with the demand side of drugs."

While the logic may be persuasive in this context, might there not be   3
another, darker side to the argument? Ambitious high school students who recognize that participation in extracurricular activities gives them the leg up they need to gain admission to the college of their choice will not be deterred by required drug testing, for example. It might even be for them, as one adult suggested, the "hammer" they need to "say no to temptation." But what about marginal and disaffected° students, those who may not see college in their future? Missing in most accounts of this debate has been any consideration for what the impact of extending drug-testing programs might be on them.

These are kids for whom participation in an extracurricular activity may   4
represent more than just an add-on that pulls them into the "accept" column of an elite college. It could be the lifeboat they need to sail safely into the "survive" column in life. Yet, these are also the students most likely to opt out of extracurricular activities if participation requires an intrusive, potentially humiliating drug test.

Research is fairly clear about what academically at-risk and marginal   5
students need: connections, attachments, and engagement. The Harvard

disaffected: Alienated; resentful toward authority.

University educator Gil G. Noam has written extensively of the critical role that mentoring, the development of trusting relationships with a wide array of adults, and involvement with the community can play in such students' lives. More than anything else, he maintains, a vulnerable student needs at least one adult who believes in him and in his future. Extracurricular activities at school often are the source of such adult bonding and guidance, as well as of small measures of success for these students. Finding such "islands of competence" that can enable them to experience success may spell the difference between continued vulnerability and emotional resilience,° write Robert Brooks and Sam Goldstein in *Raising Resilient Children.*

Consider this account from a student, posted on the Web site of What 6 Kids Can Do:

> I was in a pattern of academic failure, and so they barred me from my musical theater class. Discouraged and unmotivated, I dropped out of school. . . . A year later, I found myself with a second chance, enrolled at a small alternative public high school. . . . My adviser, Carlos, who was also our softball coach, cared about what we did and where our lives were headed, and his genuine concern and advice really made a difference. . . . Like the chorus in my junior high school, that softball team mattered more than almost anything else I ever did in school. Our coach believed in us and he was there for us when we needed an adult. And that kept us motivated to work hard and come to school.

The question is, do public schools have a responsibility to try to pull in — instead of pushing out — such students?

Sadly, it feels increasingly as if they can't afford to. An overemphasis on 7 test-score-based accountability has created a perverse° incentive for administrators to try to get rid of low-performing students, rather than work with them. An assistant principal in one Midwestern city said: "We want quality more than quantity. If that means removing dead weight, we will remove dead weight."

Harsh disciplinary codes, typified by the proliferation and expansion of 8 rigid, nonnegotiable "zero tolerance" policies, have dramatically increased the number of students routinely barred from attending school, often for relatively minor misbehaviors that bear no relation to general safety. Despite studies showing how devastating these exclusions can be to children and their families, a spokesperson for Massachusetts' state department of education justified the state's swelling expulsion figures this way: "From our perspective, what these numbers show is that districts are becoming more vigilant about getting disruptive students out of the classroom in order to ensure that the rest of the students are able to learn." Even two of the U.S. Supreme Court justices spoke disparagingly of "druggies" who pollute the educational environment.

Is it any wonder that students labeled "dead weight" and "druggies" by 9 adults in positions of authority may feel alienated and disengaged from

resilience: Ability to recover quickly.   **perverse:** Faulty; wrongheaded.

school? Or that they would consider themselves of no particular value when their expulsion is seen as a bonus point for their district? When viewed alongside other school policies — high-stakes testing, zero tolerance, tracking, and restrictive special education placements, to name a few — drug testing must seem to these students less a part of their school's arsenal to prevent drug use than part of its arsenal to categorize, isolate, and exclude them.

Yet, the counselors, youth workers, and alternative education providers 10 who interact with these students after they have left the public schools routinely testify to the fact that most of these youths are neither incorrigibly° "disruptive" nor hopeless "druggies" who deserve to be discarded with such callous° disregard. Rather, they say, these students often come from damaged or dysfunctional family backgrounds, have experienced profound loss and trauma, and, like the young woman quoted above, have hit a rough spot in their lives.

In his recent book *"Being Down": Challenging Violence in Urban Schools,* 11 Ronnie Casella, an educational researcher at Central Connecticut State University, observes that, for the most part, these are students who, though capable of acting in self-destructive ways, could well "pull it together" with a little help from adults who take an interest in their lives. Unfortunately, school officials' overreliance on punitive° and heavy-handed disciplinary practices continues, he says, to "create a school system that lacks caring and students who in the end give up on themselves and simply take what is coming to them."

Studies show that participation in extracurricular activities reduces drug 12 use. It increases the chances that struggling students will find mentors who recognize and nurture their talents and abilities, and will discover "islands of competence" that boost their self-image and build their confidence. Such activities represent for these students much more than a ticket to a good college. They represent a lifeline to a hopeful future.

Why, then, would schools choose to develop an "arsenal" that is very 13 likely to further isolate those students most in need of engagement? By erecting barriers to students' participation in extracurricular activities, drug-testing programs will only exacerbate° for some students the problem that proponents claim it was meant to deter.

Questions to Start You Thinking

1. CONSIDERING MEANING: Why are at-risk students more likely than others to be negatively affected by drug testing?
2. IDENTIFYING WRITING STRATEGIES: How does Wald use cause and effect to establish her case against school drug testing?

---

incorrigibly: Hopelessly.   **callous:** Heartless.   **punitive:** Punishing.   **exacerbate:** Make worse.

3. READING CRITICALLY: Identify the logical, ethical, and emotional appeals that Wald uses to present her claim persuasively. Which appeal does she use most frequently? Explain why she may have relied on this type of appeal more heavily than on others. (For an explanation of these appeals, see pp. 39–40.)

4. EXPANDING VOCABULARY: Define *at-risk* and *marginal.* How does Wald use these terms in her essay? What are some of the characteristics of at-risk or marginal students?

5. MAKING CONNECTIONS: Compare and contrast drug testing in school and drug testing in the workplace, discussed by Barbara Ehrenreich in "Warning: This Is a Rights-Free Workplace" (pp. 491–94). Are both acceptable or unacceptable? Or is one more reasonable than the other?

Journal Prompts

1. Have you ever been asked to take a drug test for school? What was your response? If not, how would you react if you were told that you must take one to participate in an extracurricular activity?

2. Wald feels that drug testing can push students away from positive extracurricular activities. Do schools do anything else that discourages students from taking an active interest in their education?

Suggestions for Writing

1. Drawing on your own experiences or observations, write an essay explaining how mentoring or involvement in extracurricular activities can lead to a student's success.

2. Do some research on the current state of drug testing in schools, and write an essay in which you argue for or against it. Direct your essay to Supreme Court Justice Stephen Breyer, whom Wald quotes in paragraph 2.

Richard Rodriguez
Public and Private Language

Richard Rodriguez, *the son of Spanish-speaking Mexican American parents, was born in 1944 and grew up in San Francisco, where he currently lives. He earned a B.A. at Stanford University and received graduate degrees in English from Columbia University and the University of California at Berkeley. A full-time writer and lecturer, Rodriguez is an editor at Pacific News Service and a contributing editor for* Harper's Magazine, U.S. News & World Report, *and the Sunday "Opinion" section of the* Los Angeles Times. *His work has appeared in numerous publications including the* New York Times, *the* Wall Street Journal, The American Scholar, Time, Mother Jones, *and* The New Republic. *His books, which often draw on autobiography to explore race and ethnicity in American society, include*

Hunger of Memory *(1982), from which the following selection is drawn,* Days of Obligation: An Argument with My Mexican Father *(1992), and* Brown: The Last Discovery of America *(2002). In "Public and Private Language," he recounts the origin of his complex views of bilingual education.*

AS YOU READ: *Discover the ways in which learning English changed Rodriguez's life and his relationship with his family.*

Supporters of bilingual education today imply that students like me miss   1
a great deal by not being taught in their family's language. What they seem not to recognize is that, as a socially disadvantaged child, I considered Spanish to be a private language. What I needed to learn in school was that I had the right—and the obligation—to speak the public language of *los gringos.*° The odd truth is that my first-grade classmates could have become bilingual, in the conventional sense of that word, more easily than I. Had they been taught (as upper-middle-class children are often taught early) a second language like Spanish or French, they could have regarded it simply as that: another public language. In my case such bilingualism could not have been so quickly achieved. What I did not believe was that I could speak a single public language.

Without question, it would have pleased me to hear my teachers ad-   2
dress me in Spanish when I entered the classroom. I would have felt much less afraid. I would have trusted them and responded with ease. But I would have delayed—for how long postponed?—having to learn the language of public society. I would have evaded—and for how long could I have afforded to delay?—learning the great lesson of school, that I had a public identity.

Fortunately, my teachers were unsentimental about their responsibility.   3
What they understood was that I needed to speak a public language. So their voices would search me out, asking me questions. Each time I'd hear them, I'd look up in surprise to see a nun's face frowning at me. I'd mumble, not really meaning to answer. The nun would persist, "Richard, stand up. Don't look at the floor. Speak up. Speak to the entire class, not just to me!" but I couldn't believe that the English language was mine to use. (In part, I did not want to believe it.) I continued to mumble. I resisted the teacher's demands. (Did I somehow suspect that once I learned public language my pleasing family life would be changed?) Silent, waiting for the bell to sound, I remained dazed, diffident,° afraid.

Because I wrongly imagined that English was intrinsically° a public lan-   4
guage and Spanish an intrinsically private one, I easily noticed the difference between classroom language and the language of home. At school, words were directed to a general audience of listeners ("Boys and girls.") Words were meaningfully ordered. And the point was not self-expression alone but

los gringos: Spanish for "foreigner," often used as a derogatory term for English-speaking Americans.   **diffident:** Shy.   **intrinsically:** Essentially; inherently.

to make oneself understood by many others. The teacher quizzed: "Boys and girls, why do we use that word in this sentence? Could we think of a better word to use there? Would the sentence change its meaning if the words were differently arranged? And wasn't there a better way of saying much the same thing?" (I couldn't say. I wouldn't try to say.)

Three months. Five. Half a year passed. Unsmiling, ever watchful, my   5
teachers noted my silence. They began to connect my behavior with the difficult progress my older sister and brother were making. Until one Saturday morning three nuns arrived at the house to talk to our parents. Stiffly, they sat on the blue living room sofa. From the doorway of another room, spying the visitors, I noted the incongruity° — the clash of two worlds, the faces and voices of school intruding upon the familiar setting of home. I overheard one voice gently wondering, "Do your children speak only Spanish at home, Mrs. Rodriguez?" While another voice added, "That Richard especially seems so timid and shy."

That Rich-heard!   6

With great tact the visitors continued, "Is it possible for you and your   7
husband to encourage your children to practice their English when they are home?" Of course, my parents complied. What would they not do for their children's well-being? And how could they have questioned the Church's authority which those women represented? In an instant, they agreed to give up the language (the sounds) that had revealed and accentuated our family's closeness. The moment after the visitors left, the change was observed. "*Ahora,*° speak to us *en inglés,*"° my father and mother united to tell us.

At first, it seemed a kind of game. After dinner each night, the family   8
gathered to practice "our" English. (It was still then *inglés,* a language foreign to us, so we felt drawn as strangers to it.) Laughing, we would try to define words we could not pronounce. We played with strange English sounds, often overanglicizing our pronunciations. And we filled the smiling gaps of our sentences with familiar Spanish sounds. But that was cheating, somebody shouted. Everyone laughed. In school, meanwhile, like my brother and sister, I was required to attend a daily tutoring session. I needed a full year of special attention. I also needed my teachers to keep my attention from straying in class by calling out, *Rich-heard* — their English voices slowly prying loose my ties to my other name, its three notes, *Ri-car-do.* Most of all I needed to hear my mother and father speak to me in a moment of seriousness in broken — suddenly heartbreaking — English. The scene was inevitable: One Saturday morning I entered the kitchen where my parents were talking in Spanish. I did not realize that they were talking in Spanish however until, at the moment they saw me, I heard their voices change to speak English. Those *gringo* sounds they uttered startled me. Pushed me away. In that moment of trivial misunderstanding and profound insight, I felt my throat twisted by unsounded grief. I turned quickly and left the

---

incongruity: Lack of harmony or appropriateness.   ***Ahora:*** Spanish for "now."
en inglés: Spanish for "in English."

room. But I had no place to escape to with Spanish. (The spell was broken.) My brother and sisters were speaking English in another part of the house.

Again and again in the days following, increasingly angry, I was obliged 9 to hear my mother and father: "Speak to us *en inglés.*" (*Speak.*) Only then did I determine to learn classroom English. Weeks after, it happened: One day in school I had my hand raised to volunteer an answer. I spoke out in a loud voice. And I did not think it remarkable when the entire class understood. That day, I moved very far from the disadvantaged child I had been only days earlier. The belief, that calming assurance that I belonged in public, had at last taken hold.

Shortly after, I stopped hearing the high and loud sounds of *los gringos.* 10 A more and more confident speaker of English, I didn't trouble to listen to *how* strangers sounded, speaking to me. And there simply were too many English-speaking people in my day for me to hear American accents anymore. Conversations quickened. Listening to persons whose voices sounded eccentrically pitched, I usually noted their sounds for an initial few seconds before I concentrated on *what* they were saying. Conversations became content-full. Transparent. Hearing someone's *tone* of voice — angry or questioning or sarcastic or happy or sad — I didn't distinguish it from the words it expressed. Sound and word were thus tightly wedded. At the end of a day, I was often bemused, always relieved, to realize how "silent," though crowded with words, my day in public had been. (This public silence measured and quickened the change in my life.)

At last, seven years old, I came to believe what had been technically true 11 since my birth: I was an American citizen.

But the special feeling of closeness at home was diminished by then. 12 Gone was the desperate, urgent, intense feeling of being a home; rare was the experience of feeling myself individualized by family intimates. We remained a loving family, but one greatly changed. No longer so close; no longer bound tight by the pleasing and troubling knowledge of our public separateness. Neither my older brother nor sister rushed home after school anymore. Nor did I. When I arrived home there would often be neighborhood kids in the house. Or the house would be empty of sounds.

Following the dramatic Americanization of their children, even my par- 13 ents grew more publicly confident. Especially my mother. She learned the names of all the people on our block. And she decided we needed to have a telephone installed in the house. My father continued to use the word *gringo.* But it was no longer charged with the old bitterness or distrust. (Stripped of any emotional content, the word simply became a name for those Americans not of Hispanic descent.) Hearing him, sometimes, I wasn't sure if he was pronouncing the Spanish word *gringo* or saying gringo in English.

Matching the silence I started hearing in public was a new quiet at 14 home. The family's quiet was partly due to the fact that, as we children learned more and more English, we shared fewer and fewer words with our parents. Sentences needed to be spoken slowly when a child addressed his mother or father. (Often the parent wouldn't understand.) The child would need to repeat himself. (Still the parent misunderstood.) The young voice, frustrated, would end up saying, "Never mind" — the subject was closed. Dinners would be noisy with the clinking of knives and forks against dishes. My mother would smile softly between her remarks; my father at the other end of the table would chew and chew at his food, while he stared over the heads of his children.

My *mother!* My *father!* After English became my primary language, I no 15 longer knew what words to use in addressing my parents. The old Spanish words (those tender accents of sound) I had used earlier — *mamá* and *papá* — I couldn't use anymore. They would have been too painful reminders of how much had changed in my life. On the other hand, the words I heard neighborhood kids call *their* parents seemed equally unsatisfactory. *Mother* and *Father; Ma, Papa, Pa, Dad, Pop* (how I hated the all-American sound of that last word especially) — all these terms I felt were unsuitable, not really terms of address for *my* parents. As a result, I never used them at home. Whenever I'd speak to my parents, I would try to get their attention with eye contact alone. In public conversations, I'd refer to "my parents" or "my mother and father."

My mother and father, for their part, responded differently, as their chil- 16 dren spoke to them less and less. She grew restless, seemed troubled and anxious at the scarcity of words exchanged in the house. It was she who would question me about my day when I came home from school. She smiled at the small talk. She pried at the edges of my sentences to get me to say something more. (What?) She'd join conversations she overheard, but her intrusions often stopped her children's talking. By contrast, my father seemed reconciled to the new quiet. Though his English improved some-what, he retired into silence. At dinner he spoke very little. One night his children and even his wife helplessly giggled at his garbled English pronun-ciation of the Catholic Grace before Meals. Thereafter he made his wife recite the prayer at the start of each meal, even on formal occasions, when there were guests in the house. Hers became the public voice of the family. On official business, it was she, not my father, one would usually hear on the phone or in stores, talking to strangers. His children grew so accustomed to his silence that, years later, they would speak routinely of his shyness. (My mother would often try to explain: Both his parents died when he was eight. He was raised by an uncle who treated him like little more than a menial servant. He was never encouraged to speak. He grew up alone. A man of few words.) But my father was not shy, I realized, when I'd watch him speaking Spanish with relatives. Using Spanish, he was quickly effusive.° Es-pecially when talking with other men, his voice would spark, flicker, flare alive with sounds. In Spanish, he expressed ideas and feelings he rarely re-vealed in English. With firm Spanish sounds, he conveyed confidence and authority English would never allow him.

effusive: Talkative; unreserved.

The silence at home, however, was finally more than a literal silence. 17
Fewer words passed between parent and child, but more profound was the
silence that resulted from my inattention to sounds. At about the time I no
longer bothered to listen with care to the sounds of English in public, I grew
careless about listening to the sounds family members made when they
spoke. Most of the time I heard someone speaking at home and didn't distinguish his sounds from the words people uttered in public. I didn't even
pay much attention to my parents' accented and ungrammatical speech. At
least not at home. Only when I was with them in public would I grow alert
to their accents. Though, even then, their sounds caused me less and less
concern. For I was increasingly confident of my own public identity.

Today I hear bilingual educators say that children lose a degree of "indi- 18
viduality" by becoming assimilated into public society. (Bilingual schooling
was popularized in the seventies, that decade when middle-class ethnics
began to resist the process of assimilation — the American melting pot.) But
the bilingualists simplistically scorn the value and necessity of assimilation.
They do not seem to realize that there are *two* ways a person is individualized. So they do not realize that while one suffers a diminished sense of *private* individuality by becoming assimilated into public society, such assimilation makes possible the achievement of *public* individuality.

Questions to Start You Thinking

1. CONSIDERING MEANING What created the new "silence" in the Rodriguez
   household? Explain why.
2. IDENTIFYING WRITING STRATEGIES: How does Rodriguez use comparison and
   contrast to convey his experience learning English?
3. READING CRITICALLY: How does Rodriguez use dialogue to make the experience he recalls more vivid for his readers? Is this strategy effective in helping
   him achieve his purpose? Why, or why not?
4. EXPANDING VOCABULARY: Rodriguez uses the terms *private* and *public*. What
   do these words mean when used as adjectives to describe "language" and
   "identity"?
5. MAKING CONNECTIONS: Both Rodriguez and Amy Tan ("Mother Tongue,"
   pp. 397–402) are from homes in which English was spoken as a second
   language. Compare and contrast how each writer's mastery of English affected his or her mother.

Journal Prompts

1. Recall a time when your public identity was at odds with your private self.
2. Has an accomplishment that you are proud of ever had a negative effect on
   another aspect of your life or on other people around you?

Suggestions for Writing

1. If you speak a second language, write an essay recalling your experience learning it. What were some of your struggles? Can you relate to Rodriguez's experience? How do you use that language today? If you do not know a second language, write an essay in which you analyze the possible benefits of learning one. What language would you like to learn? Why?

2. According to Rodriguez, "Supporters of bilingual education today imply that students like me miss a great deal by not being taught in their family's language" (paragraph 1). Rodriguez counters this assumption by showing how his immersion in English allowed him to develop a public identity that ultimately led to his success. At the same time, however, his English-only immersion hurt his family life. Write an essay in which you take a stand on the complex topic of bilingual education, using further reading and research to support your position about how it does or does not benefit students.

Shelby Steele

Affirmative Action: The Price of Preference

Shelby Steele *was born in Chicago in 1946. His parents, an African American truck driver and a white social worker, were both civil rights activists, and Steele himself participated in the movement in the late 1960s. He attended Coe College in Iowa and later earned an M.A. in sociology from Southern Illinois University and a Ph.D. in English from the University of Utah. He has taught at San Jose State University and is currently a senior research fellow at Stanford University's Hoover Institution, where he specializes in race relations. Steele's publications include* The Content of Our Character: A New Vision of Race in America *(1990) and* A Dream Deferred: The Second Betrayal of Black Freedom in America *(1998). His work has appeared in the* New York Times, *the* Wall Street Journal, *and* Harper's, *and he received an Emmy for his PBS documentary* Seven Days in Bensonhurst *(1991). In "Affirmative Action: The Price of Preference," originally published in the* New York Times Magazine, *Steele outlines his opposition to affirmative action.*

AS YOU READ: *Identify the reasons Steele opposes college affirmative action admissions policies.*

In a few short years, when my two children will be applying to college, the affirmative-action policies by which most universities offer black students some form of preferential treatment will present me with a dilemma. I am a middle-class black, a college professor, far from wealthy, but also well removed from the kind of deprivation that would qualify my children for the label "disadvantaged." Both of them have endured racial insensitivity from whites. They have been called names, have suffered slights and have experienced first hand the peculiar malevolence that racism brings out of people.

Yet they have never experienced racial discrimination, have never been stopped by their race on any path they have chosen to follow. Still, their society now tells them that if they will only designate themselves as black on their college applications, they will probably do better in the college lottery than if they conceal this fact. I think there is something of a Faustian bargain in this.

Of course many blacks and a considerable number of whites would say 2 that I was sanctimoniously° making affirmative action into a test of character. They would say that this small preference is the meagerest recompense° for centuries of unrelieved oppression. And to these arguments other very obvious facts must be added. In America, many marginally competent or flatly incompetent whites are hired every day — some because their white skin suits the conscious or unconscious racial preference of their employers. The white children of alumni are often grandfathered° into elite universities in what can only be seen as a residual benefit of historic white privilege. Worse, white incompetence is always an individual matter, but for blacks it is often confirmation of ugly stereotypes. Given that unfairness cuts both ways, doesn't it only balance the scales of history, doesn't this repay, in a small way, the systematic denial under which my children's grandfather lived out his days?

In theory, affirmative action certainly has all the moral symmetry that 3 fairness requires. It is reformist and corrective, even repentant and redemptive. And I would never sneer at these good intentions. Born in the late 1940s in Chicago, I started my education (a charitable term, in this case) in a segregated school, and suffered all the indignities that come to blacks in a segregated society. My father, born in the south, made it only to the third grade before the white man's fields took permanent priority over his formal education. And though he educated himself into an advanced reader with an almost professorial authority, he could only drive a truck for a living, and never earned more than $90 a week in his entire life. So yes, it is crucial to my sense of citizenship, to my ability to identify with the spirit and the interests of America, to know that this country, however imperfectly, recognizes its past sins and wishes to correct them.

Yet good intentions can blind us to the effects they generate when im- 4 plemented. In our society affirmative action is, among other things, a testament to white good will and to black power, and in the midst of these heavy investments its effects can be hard to see. But after twenty years of implementation I think that affirmative action has shown itself to be more bad than good and that blacks — whom I will focus on in this essay — now stand to lose more from it than they gain.

In talking with affirmative-action administrators and with blacks and 5 whites in general, I found that supporters of affirmative action focus on its

---

sanctimoniously: Self-righteously.   **recompense:** Compensation for a loss.   **grandfathered:** Here, admitted on the basis of family ties to a school without having to meet admission standards; generally, exempted from requirements on the basis of prior circumstances.

good intentions and detractors emphasize its negative effects. It was virtually impossible to find people outside either camp. The closest I came was a white male manager at a large computer company who said, "I think it amounts to reverse discrimination, but I'll put up with a little of that for a little more diversity." But this only makes him a half-hearted supporter of affirmative action. I think many people who don't really like affirmative action support it to one degree or another anyway.

I believe they do this because of what happened to white and black 6 Americans in the crucible of the 1960s, when whites were confronted with their racial guilt and blacks tasted their first real power. In that stormy time white absolution° and black power coalesced into virtual mandates for society. Affirmative action became a meeting ground for those mandates in the law. At first, this meant insuring equal opportunity. The 1964 civil-rights bill was passed on the understanding that equal opportunity would not mean racial preference. But in the late '60s and early '70s, affirmative action underwent a remarkable escalation of its mission from simple antidiscrimination enforcement to social engineering by means of quotas, goals, timetables, set-asides and other forms of preferential treatment.

Legally, this was achieved through a series of executive orders and Equal 7 Employment Opportunity Commission guidelines that allowed racial imbalances in the workplace to stand as proof of racial discrimination. Once it could be assumed that discrimination explained racial imbalances, it became easy to justify group remedies to presumed discrimination rather than the normal case-by-case redress.°

Even though blacks had made great advances during the '60s without 8 quotas, the white mandate to achieve a new racial innocence and the black mandate to gain power, which came to a head in the very late '60s, could no longer be satisfied by anything less than racial preferences. I don't think these mandates, in themselves, were wrong, because whites clearly needed to do better by blacks and blacks needed more real power in society. But as they came together in affirmative action, their effect was to distort our understanding of racial discrimination. By making black the color of preference, these mandates have reburdened society with the very marriage of color and preference (in reverse) that we set out to eradicate. . . .

I think one of the most troubling effects of racial preferences for blacks 9 is a kind of demoralization. Under affirmative action, the quality that earns us preferential treatment is an implied inferiority. However this inferiority is explained — and it is easily enough explained by the myriad° deprivations that grew out of our oppression — it is still inferiority. There are explanations and then there is the fact. And the fact must be borne by the individual as a condition apart from the explanation, apart even from the fact that others like himself also bear this condition. In integrated situations in which blacks must compete with whites who may be better prepared, these

---

absolution: A formal setting free from guilt.   **redress:** Compensation.   **myriad:** Numerous.

explanations may quickly wear thin and expose the individual to racial as well as personal self-doubt. (Of course whites also feel doubt, but only personally, not racially.)

What this means in practical terms is that when blacks deliver them-   10
selves into integrated situations they encounter a nasty little reflex in whites, a mindless, atavistic° reflex that responds to the color black with negative stereotypes, such as intellectual ineptness. I think this reflex embarrasses most whites today and thus it is usually quickly repressed. On an equally atavistic level, the black will be aware of the reflex his color triggers and will feel a stab of horror at seeing himself reflected in this way. He, too, will do a quick repression, but a lifetime of such stabbings is what constitutes his inner realm of racial doubt. Even when the black sees no implication of inferiority in racial preferences, he knows that whites do, so that — consciously or unconsciously — the result is virtually the same. The effect of preferential treatment — the lowering of normal standards to increase black representation — puts blacks at war with an expanded realm of debilitating doubt, so that the doubt itself becomes an unrecognized preoccupation that undermines their ability to perform, especially in integrated situations.

I believe another liability of affirmative action comes from the fact that it   11
indirectly encourages blacks to exploit their own past victimization. Like implied inferiority, victimization is what justifies preference, so that to receive the benefits of preferential treatment one must, to some extent, become invested in the view of one's self as a victim. In this way, affirmative action nurtures a victim-focused identity in blacks and sends us the message that there is more power in our past suffering than in our present achievements.

When power itself grows out of suffering, blacks are encouraged to ex-   12
pand the boundaries of what qualifies as racial oppression, a situation that can lead us to paint our victimization in vivid colors even as we receive the benefits of preference. The same corporations and institutions that give us preference are also seen as our oppressors. At Stanford University, minority-group students — who receive at least the same financial aid as whites with the same need — recently took over the president's office demanding, among other things, more financial aid.

But I think one of the worst prices that blacks pay for preference has to   13
do with an illusion. I saw this illusion at work recently in the mother of a middle-class black student who was going off to his first semester of college: "They owe us this, so don't think for a minute that you don't belong there." This is the logic by which many blacks, and some whites, justify affirmative action — it is something "owed," a form of reparation. But this logic overlooks a much harder and less digestible reality, that it is impossible to repay blacks living today for the historic suffering of the race. If all blacks were given a million dollars tomorrow it would not amount to a dime on the dollar for three centuries of oppression, nor would it dissolve the residues of that oppression that we still carry today. The concept of historic reparation

atavistic: Primitive.

grows out of man's need to impose on the world a degree of justice that simply does not exist. Suffering can be endured and overcome, it cannot be repaid. To think otherwise is to prolong the suffering. . . .

But if not preferences, what? The impulse to discriminate is subtle and 14 cannot be ferreted° out unless its many guises are made clear to people. I think we need social policies that are committed to two goals: the educational and economic development of disadvantaged people regardless of race and the eradication from our society — through close monitoring and severe sanctions — of racial, ethnic or gender discrimination. Preferences will not get us to either of these goals, because they tend to benefit those who are not disadvantaged — middle-class white women and middle-class blacks — and attack one form of discrimination with another. Preferences are inexpensive and carry the glamour of good intentions — change the numbers and the good deed is done. To be against them is to be unkind. But I think the unkindest cut is to bestow on children like my own an undeserved advantage while neglecting the development of those disadvantaged children in the poorer sections of my city who will most likely never be in a position to benefit from a preference. Give my children fairness; give disadvantaged children a better shot at development — better elementary and secondary schools, job training, safer neighborhoods, better financial assistance for college and so on. A smaller percentage of black high school graduates go to college today than fifteen years ago; more black males are in prison, jail or in some other way under the control of the criminal-justice system than in college. This despite racial preferences.

The mandates of black power and white absolution out of which prefer- 15 ences emerged were not wrong in themselves. What was wrong was that both races focused more on the goals of those mandates than on the means to the goals. Blacks can have no real power without taking responsibility for their own educational and economic development. Whites can have no racial innocence without earning it by eradicating discrimination and helping the disadvantaged to develop. Because we ignored the means, the goals have not been reached and the real work remains to be done.

Questions to Start You Thinking

1. CONSIDERING MEANING: What is the general purpose of affirmative action programs? According to Steele, why don't these programs accomplish that purpose?

2. IDENTIFYING WRITING STRATEGIES: Identify the problem that Steele is writing about. How does he develop his point? Where does he present his solution? Does the solution seem plausible? Why, or why not?

3. READING CRITICALLY: How does Steele establish his credibility to write about this topic? How does he highlight the flaws of affirmative action programs and counter opposing arguments?

ferreted: Searched.

4. **EXPANDING VOCABULARY:** Define *Faustian bargain*. Why does Steele use the phrase when describing those who designate themselves as black on college applications?

5. **MAKING CONNECTIONS:** How does Judith Ortiz Cofer's solution to stereotyping ("Don't Misread My Signals," pp. 438–40) relate to Steele's proposed solution to discrimination? Are they both advancing the same solution?

Journal Prompts

1. Write about a time you or someone you know was a victim of discrimination.

2. Have you ever felt that you were owed repayment (not necessarily monetary) for a wrong that someone inflicted on you? What made you feel this way?

Link to the Paired Essay

Although Steele focuses on how affirmative action policies affect African Americans, he does mention "reverse discrimination," the focus of Goodwin Liu's essay ("The Causation Fallacy: *Bakke* and the Basic Arithmetic of Selective Admissions," below). For example, Steele quotes a business manager who said, "I think [affirmative action] amounts to reverse discrimination, but I'll put up with a little of that for a little more diversity" (paragraph 5). How would Liu respond to this comment?

■ For useful links to Web sources on topics including *education*, visit <bedfordstmartins.com/toplinks>.

Suggestions for Writing

1. Recall a time when you feel that you either received preferential treatment or suffered unjust discrimination. How did you react to the situation? How did it make you feel?

2. Do some research into recent developments in the affirmative action debate. Write an essay taking a stand on affirmative action programs. Should they be abolished, as Steele claims, or are they necessary? Is there a better solution to the problem of racial discrimination?

*Goodwin Liu**

The Causation Fallacy: *Bakke* and the Basic Arithmetic of Selective Admissions

Goodwin Liu, who holds degrees from Stanford University, Oxford University, and Yale Law School, is acting professor of law at the University of California,

* O'Melveny & Myers, LLP, Washington, D.C. B.S. 1991, Stanford; B.A. 1993, Oxford; J.D. 1998, Yale.— Ed. I am grateful to Brianne Ford for research assistance and to Robert Gordon, Linda Lye, Nathaniel Persily, David Tatel, and Ann O'Leary for thoughtful comments on earlier drafts and for encouragement and support during my writing process.

Berkeley. He has also worked as a lawyer in Washington, D.C., and as a clerk for U.S. Supreme Court Justice Ruth Bader Ginsburg. During the Clinton Administration, he served as program officer for AmeriCorps, then as special assistant to the deputy secretary of the U.S. Department of Education. His writing, which focuses on education and social-welfare policy, has appeared in the New York Times, *the* Washington Post, *and numerous legal journals. In the following excerpt from an article Liu published in 2002 in the* Michigan Law Review, *he takes a close look at affirmative action policies, arguing that their impact on white applicants is less significant than many might believe.*

AS YOU READ: *Consider how Liu defends affirmative action programs against claims of reverse discrimination.*

Although the most recent legal challenges to racial preferences in univer-   1
sity admissions vary in their details, they are unified by a common narrative — the same narrative that animated Allan Bakke's lawsuit against the Davis Medical School over twenty years ago.[1] Bakke won admission to the medical school after convincing the Supreme Court that the school's practice of setting aside sixteen out of one hundred seats in each incoming class for minority students was an unconstitutional racial quota. The record shows that Bakke was, in fact, a highly qualified applicant. His undergraduate grades and standardized test scores were excellent, far better than the averages for minority students admitted through the set-aside. Yet the medical school rejected Bakke's application, even as it admitted minority applicants in numbers large enough to fill the sixteen-seat quota. This prompted Bakke to complain that affirmative action cost him a letter of admission, and the success of his lawsuit confirms what so many people find unfair about affirmative action: By according substantial preferences to minority applicants, affirmative action causes the displacement of deserving white applicants like Allan Bakke and the plaintiffs° now following in his footsteps.[2]

This article argues that the perceived unfairness is more exaggerated   2
than real. The perception is a distortion of statistical truth, premised° on an error in logic. There is strong evidence, as Bakke's story suggests, that minority applicants stand a much better chance of gaining admission to selective institutions with the existence of affirmative action. But that fact provides no logical basis to infer° that white applicants would stand a much better chance of admission in the absence of affirmative action. To draw such an inference, as opponents of affirmative action routinely do, is to indulge what I call "the causation fallacy" — the common yet mistaken notion that when white applicants like Allan Bakke fail to gain admission ahead of minority applicants with equal or lesser qualifications, the likely cause is affirmative action.

plaintiffs: Those who bring a suit (against *defendants*).   **premised:** Based.   **infer:** Conclude.

The causation fallacy reflects white anxiety over the intensely competi- 3
tive nature of selective admissions,[3] and it undoubtedly accounts for much
of the moral outrage that affirmative action inspires among unsuccessful
white applicants. It was widely reported, for example, that what prompted
Jennifer Gratz to become the lead plaintiff in a major test case challenging
the University of Michigan's use of racial preferences in undergraduate admissions was her overriding sense that she had been displaced by less qualified minority applicants.[4] Observers of politics will recall a 1990 television
commercial that depicted the plight of applicants like Bakke and Gratz by
showing a pair of white hands crumpling a letter informing the recipient he
had lost a job to a minority applicant. "You needed that job," the voice-over
said. "And you were the best qualified. But they had to give it to a minority
because of a racial quota. Is that really fair?"[5] Michael Lind, an otherwise
thoughtful commentator on the subject, has said that "[i]n order to accommodate a few less-qualified black students, the University of Texas Law
School, like other leading law schools, must turn down hundreds or thousands of academically superior white students every year.[6] And a recent national survey confirms that affirmative action remains highly unpopular
among whites in part because of perceptions of increased competition with
minorities for employment and educational opportunities.[7]

Yet the powerful appeal of the causation fallacy is all the more reason 4
for courts and commentators to purge it from moral and legal discourse on
affirmative action, especially as the current spate of anti-affirmative action
lawsuits percolates° up to the Supreme Court. At its core, the fallacy erro-
neously conflates° the magnitude of affirmative action's instrumental benefit to minority applicants, which is large, with the magnitude of its instrumental cost to white applicants, which is small. While not the first to
observe the arithmetic error at the root of the fallacy,[8] this article is the first
to give the error a name, to expose the genesis of this error in *Bakke,* and to
examine its implications for the standing of white plaintiffs and the merits
of their claims. What this article demonstrates is that the causation fallacy,
by unduly magnifying the practical harm suffered by white applicants,
stands in the way of any rational effort to evaluate the fairness of affirmative
action. . . .

Bakke *Revisited*

Let us begin with a familiar story. In 1973, a white student named Allan 5
Bakke applied unsuccessfully for admission to the Davis Medical School at
the University of California. Bakke reapplied in 1974 and was again turned
down. At the time, the medical school enrolled one hundred new students
each year and operated a two-track admissions process consisting of a general admissions program, under which Bakke's application was reviewed,
and a special admissions program, under which various minority applicants
could seek review.[9] The special program screened minority applicants to fill

percolates: Bubbles up.   **conflates:** Combines.

a quota; it continually recommended applicants to the general admissions committee until sixteen were admitted.[10] Before the Supreme Court, Bakke argued that the "racial quota . . . prevented [him] from competing for 16 of the 100 places at the Davis Medical School and, as a result, barred him — by reason of race alone — from attending the school."[11]

Justice Powell agreed. As a preface to Bakke's legal claims, Justice Powell   6 observed that "[i]n both years, applicants were admitted under the special program with grade point averages, [Medical College Admission Test] scores, and bench mark scores significantly lower than Bakke's."[12] To make this clear, he dropped a footnote showing the following table:[13]

CLASS ENTERING IN 1974

	Science GPA	Overall GPA	Verbal MCAT (%ile)	Quant. MCAT (%ile)	Science MCAT (%ile)
Bakke	3.44	3.46	96	94	97
Regular admittees	3.36	3.29	69	67	82
Special admittees	2.42	2.62	34	30	37

After finding the quota unconstitutional, Justice Powell affirmed the   7 California Supreme Court's judgment ordering Bakke's admission.[14] The medical school had chosen not to contest Bakke's admissibility absent the quota,[15] and Justice Powell noted that "[h]ere . . . there is no question as to the sole reason for respondent's rejection — purposeful racial discrimination in the form of the special admissions program."[16] In other words, affirmative action cost Bakke his seat at the Davis Medical School.

What, if anything, is wrong with this story?   8

An Introduction to the Causation Fallacy

However neat and intelligible, the conventional rendition of *Bakke* defies   9 common sense. The reason is clear upon a closer look at the table in Justice Powell's footnote. That table unambiguously shows that Bakke's academic qualifications were far better than those of the average special admittee. His MCAT scores placed him roughly in the top 5 percent of test-takers, whereas the average scores of the special admittees placed them in the bottom third.[17] Likewise, his science grade point average was more than one full point (one letter grade) higher than the average of the special admittees.[18] These large gaps strongly suggest that the special program afforded minority applicants a substantial preference in admissions.[19]

However, although Justice Powell notes these "significant[ ]" dis-   10 parities,[20] he fails to point out what I find to be the most striking information in the table: Bakke's grade point averages and MCAT scores in 1974 were not only far better than those of the special admittees, but also significantly better than those of the *regular* admittees. Indeed, Bakke's academic indicators were high by any measure and, importantly, higher than those of the *majority* of applicants who gained admission under the regular program.[21]

How did these applicants get in ahead of Bakke? Clearly, the medical 11
school admitted students not only on the basis of grades and test scores, but also on the basis of other factors relevant to the study and practice of medicine — effective communication skills, demonstrated compassion, commitment to a particular field of research, and perhaps others. From Justice Powell's opinion, we do not learn exactly what qualities the regular admittees had that Bakke lacked, although Justice Powell noted that the chairman of the admissions committee, who interviewed Bakke in 1974, "found Bakke 'rather limited in his approach' to the problems of the medical profession and found disturbing Bakke's 'very definite opinions which were based more on his personal viewpoints than upon a study of the total problem.'"[22] The point is that many reasons, apart from racial preferences, might explain Bakke's failure to achieve a more competitive position relative to the fifty or more *regular* admittees with grades and test scores lower than his.[23]

To be sure, the sixteen-seat set-aside lowered Bakke's chance of admis- 12
sion. But by how much? One rudimentary° way to think about this question is to compare (a) Bakke's likelihood of admission as an applicant for only the eighty-four seats available through the regular admissions program with (b) his likelihood of admission had he been able to compete for all one hundred seats in the entering class. To simplify the comparison, let us assume that none of the special applicants would have been admitted ahead of any of the regular applicants.[24] In 1974, Bakke was one of 3,109 regular applicants to the Davis Medical School.[25] With the racial quota, the average likelihood of admission among regular applicants was 2.7 percent (eighty-four seats divided by 3,109 applicants). With no racial quota, the average likelihood of admission would have been 3.2 percent (one hundred seats divided by 3,109 applicants).[26] In other words, the quota increased the average likelihood of rejection among regular applicants from 96.8 percent to 97.3 percent.

Admittedly, this comparison is somewhat artificial because Bakke was 13
clearly not an average applicant. However weak his interview may have been, his test scores and grade point averages gave him a substantial edge over the majority of regular applicants. We do not know exactly how much the admissions committee had narrowed the regular applicant pool before rejecting Bakke, but we do know that Bakke received an interview and that, under the regular admissions program, "[a]bout one out of six applicants was invited for a personal interview."[27] Thus, Bakke was one of roughly 520 regular applicants interviewed (3,109 divided by six). Among these highly qualified applicants, the average rate of admission with the racial quota in place was 16.2 percent (eighty-four seats divided by 520 applicants). Without the quota, the average rate of admission would have been 19.2 percent (100 seats divided by 520 applicants).

rudimentary: Basic, elementary.

Of course, with additional criteria, it may be possible to narrow down   14
Bakke's competition to a small enough number that the effect of the quota
turns out to be substantial. The point, however, is that without precise information about how Bakke's application fared in the overall pool — and Justice Powell's opinion provides none — no reasonable basis exists to infer
that the racial quota, and not some other selection criterion, caused his application to be rejected. In a selection process where there are far more applicants than available opportunities, the likelihood of success for *any* candidate is low, even under race-neutral criteria. Reserving a small number of
seats for minority applicants, relative to the total number of seats, will not
decrease that low likelihood very much. Based on the data in Justice Powell's opinion, the most reasonable inference is that affirmative action did
not appreciably affect Bakke's chance of admission. . . .°

Conclusion

The basic arithmetic of selective admissions is an essential component of   15
any conceptual framework for judging the fairness of affirmative action. Although *Bakke* paints a compelling portrait of unfairness, it is but one part of
a more complicated picture. As it turns out, it is one small part that does not
faithfully capture Bakke's own circumstances or the circumstances of the
vast majority of unsuccessful white applicants. Stripped of the causation fallacy, the conventional affirmative action narrative unravels into several nar-
ratives, each shaped by the application of a particular admissions policy to
the attributes and qualifications of a particular applicant. Without careful
attention to the mechanics of affirmative action, it is easy to lapse into the
polarizing° terms of common discourse — minorities versus whites, qualified versus unqualified — even as those terms exaggerate the degree of racial
conflict in selective admissions and ignore the utter irrelevance of race in the
evauation of large numbers of white applicants.

Justice Powell is no doubt correct that "there are serious problems of   16
justice connected with the idea of preference itself."[28] Eventually, when the
Supreme Court revisits *Bakke*, it may well determine that the problems of
justice are so serious that racial preferences must end. On the other hand, it
may endorse Justice Powell's compromise, or it may even develop an alternative. Whatever the Court decides, it will face the task of characterizing and
explaining precisely what the problems of justice are. That explanation
might begin with an acknowledgment that *Bakke*, as a story about what happens to white applicants in race-conscious admissions, is more fiction than
fact. For it is only by purging the causation fallacy from our legal and moral
discourse on racial preferences that we may reach a principled conclusion
about the ultimate fairness of affirmative action.

. . . In the sections deleted here from the article, the author continues to present evidence
for his argument that affirmative action significantly benefits minority applicants
while not significantly burdening white applicants. He considers SAT scores and other
factors. — ED.   **polarizing:** Breaking something into two contrasting sides.

Notes

1. See *Regents of Univ. of Cal. v. Bakke*, 438 U.S. 265 (1978).

2. Although I use the term *minority* to label applicants who benefit from affirmative action and the term *white* to label those who do not, I recognize that some minority applicants do not benefit from affirmative action and that some affirmative action programs may benefit disadvantaged whites. Given this reality, it is probably more precise to use the generic terms *preferred* and *nonpreferred* applicants. But I stick to the term *minority* and *white* in order to track the usage in common discourse on affirmative action. As Bakke's claim demonstrates, that discourse typically characterizes affirmative action as pitting minority applicants against white applicants in a deep racial conflict. This article is an attempt to explain and dispel that characterization.

3. The intense competition among selective institutions for academically talented students is a relatively recent phenomenon in American higher education, largely driven by economic, social, legal, and demographic forces that have conspired over the last century to make educational opportunity more desirable and more attainable for an expanding majority of the citizenry.

4. Ethan Bronner, *Group Suing U. of Michigan Over Diversity*, New York Times, Oct. 14, 1997, at A24 ("I knew of people accepted to Ann Arbor who were less qualified, and my first reaction when I was rejected was, 'Let's sue, ... ") (quoting Jennifer Gratz); Jodi S. Cohen, *Affirmative Action on Trial; Denial Shatters Dream; Southgate Woman Key Figure in University Bias Suit*, Detroit News, Nov. 12, 2000, at A1 (profile of Jennifer Gratz); see also Kenneth J. Cooper, *Deciding Who Gets In and Who Doesn't; Schools Consider Many Factors, From Grade Average to 'Get Up and Go'*, Washington Post, Apr. 2, 2000, at A5.

5. Peter Applebome, *Subtly and Not, Race Bubbles Up as Issue in North Carolina Contest*, New York Times, Nov. 2, 1990, at A1 (quoting television commercial).

6. Michael Lind, *The Next American Nation* 166 (1995) (citing Lino Graglia, *Racial Preferences in Admission to Institutions of Higher Education*, in *The Imperiled Academy* 134 [Howard Dickman, ed., 1993]). The careful reader will note that Lind's assertion flatly defies basic arithmetic.

7. *See* Richard Morin, *Misperceptions Cloud Whites' View of Blacks*, Washington Post, July 11, 2001, at A1. This article does not address affirmative action in the employment context. Instead, it focuses exclusively on the use of racial preferences in the admissions processes of selective colleges and universities. Although the article's main statistical argument is applicable to most educational contexts where race is a factor in selective admissions, its applicability is more variable in the context of employment. The reason is that the relative magnitudes of the pertinent statistical parameters (e.g., spaces available, number of minority applicants, number of total applicants) are not as consistent across employment opportunities as they are across educational opportunities where race is a factor in selection.

8. See, e.g., Thomas J. Kane, *Racial and Ethnic Preferences in College Admissions*, in *The Black-White Test Score Gap* 453–54 (Christopher Jencks & Meredith Phillips eds., 1998); Goodwin Liu, *Affirmative Action in Higher Education: The Diversity Rationale and the Compelling Interest Test*, 33 Harv. C.R.-C.L. L. Rev. 381, 422–23 n.192 (1998); Andrew Hacker, *The Myths of Racial Division*, Guardian, May 1, 1992, at 19 (analyzing Andrew Hacker, *Two Nations: Black and White, Separate, Hostile, Unequal* [1992]) ("[I]n the end black Americans remain a relatively small minority, so there are limits to how many whites they can displace even with aggressive affirmative action recruiting"); John Iwasaki, *Affirmative Action Aids White Students Too; Stereotype False, State Study Says*, Seattle Post-Intelligencer, Nov. 19, 1995, at A9 ("[M]any white students who were denied admission did not lose out because of minority students, but because of tight limits on enrollment. In other words, many qualified white applicants probably would have been turned down even if no minority students had applied"); Gary Orfield, *Boston Needs to Strengthen Its Case for Diversity at Latin School*, Boston

Globe, Jan. 11, 1999, at A15 ("[W]hites tend to overestimate what they actually 'lose' through affirmative action....").

9. *Regents of Univ. of Cal. v. Bakke,* 438 U.S. 265, 274–76 (1978) (opinion of Powell, J.). The medical school's formal policy indicated that any applicant who identified herself or himself as "economically and/or educationally disadvantaged" could seek review under the special admissions program. Id. at 272 n.1. In fact, large numbers of disadvantaged whites applied to the special program. Id. at 275 n.5. No whites, however, were ever admitted through the special program. Id. at 276 & n.6.

10. Competition within the special program was substantial. Even discounting the disadvantaged white applicants in the pool, the special program admitted only 7.1 percent of minority applicants (sixteen out of 224) in 1973 and only 3.5 percent of minority applicants (sixteen out of 456) in 1974. Id. at 275 n.5.

11. Brief for Respondent at 63, *Regents of Univ. of Cal. v. Bakke,* 438 U.S. 265 (1978) (No. 76-811).

12. *Bakke,* 438 U.S. at 277.

13. See id. at 277 n.7. Allan Bakke also applied unsuccessfully in 1973, and the footnote includes a second table showing similar data for the class entering in 1973. The two tables in footnote 7 include a sixth column titled "Gen. Infor." I have omitted it because Justice Powell nowhere explains or relies on the data in this column.

14. Id. at 320.

15. Id.

16. Id. at 321 n.54.

17. See id. at 277 n.7.

18. Id.

19. A section not included in this excerpt discusses "why the use of averages to infer the magnitude of preference accorded to minority applicants is not entirely valid." — Ed.

20. *Bakke,* 438 U.S. at 277.

21. Id. at 277 n.7. Although the grade point averages and test scores of regular admittees in footnote 7 are means, not medians, I think it is reasonable to assume that the admittees are normally distributed around each mean.

22. Id. at 277 (quoting the record).

23. Neither Justice Powell's opinion nor the litigation record indicates exactly how many regular admittees had grades and test scores lower than Bakke's. Using the number of regular admittees who matriculated (eighty-four) as a lower bound for the number of regular applicants who were admitted, and assuming that the grade point averages and test scores of regular admittees are normally distributed around the mean, I estimate that fifty or sixty regular admittees, at a minimum, had grades and test scores lower than Bakke's. The true number is certainly much higher, because not all admittees choose to matriculate. But I am unable to estimate the true number reliably without knowing either the total number of applicants admitted under the regular program or the percentage of admittees who decided to matriculate.

24. This assumption is improbable despite the large gaps in average GPAs and MCAT scores between special and regular admittees. Special applicants at the high end of their distribution likely had GPAs and test scores at least as high as, if not higher than, those of regular applicants at the low end of their distribution. Indeed, the record shows that, whereas Bakke had an overall GPA of 3.46 and a science GPA of 3.44, *Bakke,* 438 U.S. at 277 n.7, the overall GPA of special admittees ranged up to 3.76 in 1973 and up to 3.45 in 1974, and the science GPA of special admittees ranged up to 3.89 in 1974, see Brief of Amici Curiae National Urban League et al. at 12 n.6. *Regents of Univ. of Cal. v. Bakke,* No. 76-811 (U.S. filed Jan. 14, 1977) (on petition for writ of certiorari) [hereinafter Amici National Urban League]. The assumption that none of the special applicants would have been admitted under the regular program thus establishes an upper bound for the cost of affirmative action to regular applicants like Bakke.

25. See *Bakke*, 438 U.S. at 273 n.2 (noting that 3,737 applications were submitted for the 1974 entering class); id. at 275 n.5 (noting that 628 persons applied to the special committee in 1974). 3,737 – 628 = 3,109.
26. I describe this comparison as rudimentary because it does not account for the fact that the medical school had to admit more than eighty-four or one hundred applicants in order to obtain a "yield" of eighty-four or one hundred matriculants. In other words, the average admission rates for white applicants — i.e., the likelihood of receiving a letter of admission — were higher than my rough calculations show, both with and without the quota. But without knowing the total number of admittees or the yield rates for the medical school, see supra note [23], I am unable to offer a more precise calculation.
27. Id. at 273–74.
28. *Bakke*, 438 U.S. at 298 (opinion of Powell, J.).

Questions to Start You Thinking

1. CONSIDERING MEANING: In paragraph 2, Liu refers to the "perceived unfairness" of affirmative action policies. What injustices are perceived in such policies? How does Liu support his position that attacks against affirmative action are misguided?

2. IDENTIFYING WRITING STRATEGIES: In paragraph 3, Liu quotes some opposing views, including lines from a 1990 television commercial. What do you think is his rationale for using such examples? Are they effective?

3. READING CRITICALLY: How does Liu use the *Bakke* case to make his point that reserving seats for black applicants does not place the general population of white applicants at a significant disadvantage in college admissions?

4. EXPANDING VOCABULARY: Define *causation fallacy* in your own words. How does Liu use this term to show that affirmative action does not unduly disadvantage white applicants?

5. MAKING CONNECTIONS: Liu wrote a version of this piece for the *Washington Post* titled "The Myth and Math of Affirmative Action." Veronica Chambers ("The Myth of Cinderella," pp. 456–59) also uses the word *myth* in the title of her essay. Do you think Liu and Chambers tackle the same kind of myth? Do they share the same goal of dispelling a myth? The same strategy? Are they successful in their attempts?

Journal Prompts

1. If you were a Supreme Court Justice, how might you rule in the *Bakke* case or in more recent cases arguing that affirmative action is an unfair policy?

2. How does diversity enhance the educational experience?

Link to the Paired Essay

Liu and Shelby Steele ("Affirmative Action: The Price of Preference," pp. 530–34) not only have different opinions about affirmative action but also develop their positions in different ways. Compare the types of evidence that

■ For useful links to Web sources on topics including *education*, visit <bedfordstmartins.com/ toplinks>.

each writer presents to argue his position. Which type of evidence is predominant in each essay? Do you consider one type more persuasive than another? Is one type of evidence easier to disprove or counter than another?

Suggestions for Writing

1. Write an essay detailing an experience when you were rejected, perhaps from a team, a college, or a job. How did you interpret that rejection? Did someone explain the reason for your rejection? What was your reaction?

2. Write an essay in which you propose and defend a set of college admission criteria that is fair to all applicants.

A
Writer's
Research
Manual

A Writer's Research Manual Contents

Introduction:
The Nature of Research

Does cell phone use cause brain tumors?

What steps can law enforcement take to help prevent domestic violence?

How do strict death penalty laws affect crime rates?

Is it true that about a million children in the U.S. are homeless?

Why is baseball exempt from antitrust laws?

You may have asked yourself questions like these. Perhaps you discussed them with friends, asked a teacher about the subject, or read an article about the issue. In doing so, you were conducting informal research to satisfy your curiosity.

In your day-to-day life, you also conduct practical research to help you make decisions. You may want to buy a cell phone, consider an innovative medical procedure, or plan a vacation. To become better informed, you may talk with friends, search the Internet, request product information from sales personnel, compare prices, read articles in magazines and newspapers, and listen to commercials. You pull together and weigh as much information as you can, preparing yourself to make a well-informed decision.

When one of your college professors assigns a research paper due in a month or two, you won't be expected to discover the secrets of the spiral nebula. On the other hand, you will find that research isn't merely pasting together information and opinions from other people. Instead, the excitement lies in using research to draw conclusions and arrive at your own fresh view. The key is to start your investigation as professional researchers do — with a research question that you truly want to learn more about. Like a detective, you will need to plan your work but remain flexible, backtracking or jumping ahead if it makes sense to do so. If you meet an insurmountable obstacle, you must turn around, go sideways, or set out in another direction altogether.

Whenever you use research to come to a conclusion based on facts and expert opinions — whether in your personal life, for a college class, or on the job — this research manual will provide you with effective, efficient strategies and procedures.

Chapter 27, "Planning and Managing Your Research Project."   This chapter introduces the basics for completing a research assignment, from generating ideas and developing your research question through managing your project with a realistic schedule, a working bibliography, a research archive, and a system for taking notes.

Chapter 28, "Finding Sources in the Library, on the Internet, and in the Field."   What resources are available to answer your research question? The useful tips in this chapter suggest the best ways to locate promising sources.

Chapter 29, "Evaluating Sources."   This chapter discusses the critical process of evaluating, or judging, the information you gather in order to select the best evidence for your paper. It provides questions you can use to evaluate library, Internet, and field resources as you conduct your research.

Chapter 30, "Integrating Sources."   This chapter shows how to take accurate and useful notes — quoting, summarizing, and paraphrasing. It also illustrates how to incorporate source material while avoiding plagiarism.

Chapter 31, "Writing Your Research Paper."   Here you will learn how to pull together, or synthesize, the information from your sources so that you answer your research question in a readable, trustworthy paper. At the end of the chapter you will find a sample student research paper that integrates library, Internet, and field sources.

Chapter 32, "Documenting Sources."   This chapter explains when and how to cite your sources, illustrating MLA and APA documentation styles.

Chapter 27

Planning and Managing Your Research Project

Writing a research paper is a useful skill, essential not only in an academic community but also in the workplace. Engineers rely on research studies when they write feasibility reports. Health-care workers synthesize research findings to help them decide how to treat patients. Businesses depend on market research to sell their products.

Although research writing is a practical skill — and one you'll draw on for the rest of your life — learning to conduct research efficiently and effectively can be daunting. The Internet, television, books, newspapers, and magazines shower us with facts and figures, statements and reports, views and opinions — some of them half-baked, some revealing and trustworthy. College research requires you to sort through this massive burst of words, distinguishing fact from opinion, off-the-wall claims from expert interpretations.

As you investigate a topic and write a paper based on your findings, you will build valuable skills such as these:

- You'll learn how to find a topic and develop it into a focused and answerable research question.
- You'll draw from a wide range of sources — in the library, on the Internet, and in the field.
- You'll use library, Internet, and field research techniques to complement one another.
- You'll use your sources as evidence to support your own ideas, rather than simply repeating what they say.
- You'll do critical thinking — evaluating, analyzing, and synthesizing.
- You'll learn to cite and list your sources in a form that scholars and professionals follow in writing research reports and articles.

This chapter will help you manage your research project by creating a research schedule, maintaining a working bibliography, and building a research archive. Armed with these skills and tools, you will find yourself prepared to accomplish even the most formidable research task.

Planning Your Project

A research paper is often the most engaging and complex assignment in a course. You may already have learned how to take research notes or how to make a working bibliography, but as we guide you through the research process, we'll pause to explain these special skills. Mastering them, if you haven't done so already, will speed you on your way to completing your assignment and becoming an accomplished research writer.

THE ASSIGNMENT: WRITING FROM SOURCES

Find a topic that intrigues you, and develop a focused research question about it. Answering the question will probably require you to return to writing situations you addressed in Part Two of this book, such as comparing and contrasting, explaining causes and effects, taking a stand, proposing a solution, or evaluating. After conducting whatever research is necessary, synthesize the information you assemble to develop your own reasonable answer to the research question. Then write a paper, persuasively using a variety of source material to convey your conclusions.

Having a real audience can help you select what to include or exclude as you write your report. If possible, try to use your paper to benefit your campus administration, your employer, or a particular cause or nonprofit group on campus or in your local community. Because your final paper answers your research question, it will be more than a stack of facts. Reading and digesting the ideas of other writers is just the first step. During the process of writing, you'll also bring your own intelligence to bear on what you have read.

For advice on scheduling your research project, see pp. 559–60.

You can anticipate these major stages during your research process:

The Research Process

Choose a general subject that interests you (see p. 552), following your assignment.

↓

Take an overview (see pp. 552–53), and select the specific aspect of the subject that interests you.

↓

State your research question ⟶ Manage your project
(see pp. 553–55).   (see pp. 559–65).

- Create a schedule.
- Start a working bibliography.
- Organize a research archive.
- Plan a method of recording notes.

Search for sources that might help to answer your question (see pp. 555–58 and Ch. 28), and revise your question if necessary. Then investigate in depth to discover relevant ideas, facts, statistics, expert testimony, and first-hand observation.

- Use the library catalog, databases, and reference materials.
- Search carefully on the Web.
- Interview, observe, or conduct other field research.

Evaluate the sources you find (see Ch. 29). Integrate reliable information and evidence from them to support your answer to your research question.

- Quote, paraphrase, and summarize from your sources to avoid plagiarism.
- Clarify the thesis that answers your question, and write your paper (see Ch. 31).
- Document your sources (see Ch. 32).

Generating Ideas and Forming a Research Question

> What most effectively helps long-term prisoners return to society after they have served their sentences?
>
> How accurately do standardized tests measure intelligence?
>
> What can be done to assist homeless families in Miami, Florida?

To define a narrow research question like the examples above, start with your broad interests.

CHOOSING YOUR TERRITORY

To explore, you need a territory — a subject that interests you. Perhaps your work in this very course or another one intrigues you. A psychology course might encourage you to investigate mental disorders; a sociology course, urban renewal; a geography course, tropical forests.

You'll have an easier time from the start if you can make your territory smaller than "mental disorders" or "urban renewal." "Schizophrenia" and "downtown housing renovation" are smaller territories, easier to explore and to manage as your research leads you to a more focused topic. But if you don't feel you can narrow and define your topic at this point, go ahead and start with a broad subject.

Here are a few questions to help you find a general subject:

DISCOVERY CHECKLIST

____ Can you recall an experience that raises interesting questions or creates unusual associations in your mind?

____ What have you observed recently — perhaps on your way to school or work today — that you could more thoroughly investigate?

____ In a recent conversation with friends or in class, have you encountered any new perspectives you'd like to explore?

____ What problem would you like to solve?

____ What have you read about lately that you'd like to pursue further?

TAKING AN OVERVIEW

Before launching an expedition into a little-known territory, a smart explorer first makes a reconnaissance flight to take an overview. Having seen the terrain, the explorer then chooses the very spot to set up camp — the point on the map that looks most promising. Research writers do something like that, too. Before committing themselves to a topic, they first get a broad overview to see what parts of the territory look promising and then zero in on one small area that seems most interesting.

■ For charts detailing the information you can get from print and electronic sources, see pp. 556–57.

Begin in the Library.   How do you take an overview? Say you are looking for preliminary information on schizophrenia or mental illness or (still more general) psychiatry. A good place to start is your college or local library. Most libraries subscribe to many specialized databases (like *Medline, PsycLIT, ERIC,* and the *MLA Bibliography*). You will often be able to familiarize yourself with your topic and get a good feel for the broad range of sources available by beginning your overview here.

■ For more on electronic searches, see pp. 557–58 and Ch. 28.

Go Online.   You can also browse on the Internet, visiting Web sites and reading messages posted to newsgroups or Web discussion forums. Web search engines — such as Google, and Yahoo! — can lead you to a wide range of Web pages (see p. 583 for URLs). Google (http://groups.google.com) also can help you locate newsgroups and mailing lists related to your topic. The number of sources you can locate on the Internet is vast — and growing daily — so you'll need to exercise discipline when you're online, especially in this early stage.

Talk with Experts.   Consider discussing your topic with an expert in the field. If you're curious about America's fascination with the automobile, consider meeting with a professor, such as a sociologist or a journalist, who specializes in the area. Or talk with friends or acquaintances who are particularly passionate about their cars. Or spend time at an auto show, carefully observing and talking with the people who attend.

■ For more on interviewing, see pp. 585–86 and Ch. 6.

Revisit Your Purpose and Audience.   If necessary, refine the purpose of your research and your analysis of your audience in light of what you have discovered thus far. For example, perhaps your overview of campus programs has led you to a proposal by the International Students Office for matching first-year students with host families during holidays. You'd like to find out more about such programs — what they cost, how they work, what they offer foreign students, how they contribute to their college success, and how they benefit host families as well. At first, you thought that your purpose would be to persuade community members to participate. As you learned more, however, you decided that the real challenge was to persuade the Director of Student Activities to support the project.

■ For more on purpose and audience, see pp. 13–15 and 269–70.

STATING YOUR QUESTION

Once you have staked out part of a territory to explore, you can move from the broad to the specific by asking more precise questions. Ask exactly what you want to find out, and your task will leap into focus.

BROAD OVERVIEW	Social problems in large cities
SPECIFIC QUESTION	What happens to teenage runaways on the streets of San Diego?
BROAD OVERVIEW	Contemporary architecture
SPECIFIC QUESTION	Who in America today excels at designing sports arenas?

Generate Ideas.   You might start by freewriting, mapping, or brainstorming, jotting down whatever questions come to mind. Then, select one that appears promising. Your instructor also may have some suggestions, but you will probably be more motivated investigating a question you select.

■ For more on generating ideas, see Ch. 15.

Size Up Your Question.   Ask these questions as you test for a workable research question:

- Is your question debatable? Does it allow for a range of opinions so that you can support your own view rather than explain something that's generally known and accepted?

- Is it interesting to you? Will your discoveries interest your readers?
- Is it narrow enough to allow for a productive investigation in the few weeks you have?

BROAD QUESTION	How is the climate of the earth changing?
NARROWER QUESTION	How will El Niño affect global climate changes in the next decade?
BROAD QUESTION	Who are the world's best living storytellers?
NARROWER QUESTION	How is Irish step dancing a form of storytelling?
BROAD QUESTION	Why is there poverty?
NARROWER QUESTION	What notable welfare-to-work programs exist in the southeastern United States?

Although you should restrict your topic, a question can be too narrow or too insignificant. If so, it may be impossible to find relevant sources.

TOO NARROW	How did John F. Kennedy's maternal grandfather influence the decisions he made during his first month as president?

A question may also be so narrow that it's uninteresting. Avoid questions that can be answered with a simple yes or no or with a few statistics.

TOO NARROW	Are there more black students or white students in the entering class this year?
BETTER	How does the ratio of black students to white students affect campus relations at our school?

Instead, ask a question that will lead you into the heart of a lively controversy. The best research questions ask about issues that others take seriously and debate, issues likely to be of real interest to you and your readers.

Hone Your Question.   Make the wording of your question specific and simple: identify one thing to find out, not several. A well-crafted question can lead you into your research. Its very phrasing can suggest keywords that may be useful as you search databases, the library catalog, or the Web.

QUESTION	What has caused a shortage of affordable housing in northeastern cities?
POSSIBLE SEARCH TERMS	Housing, housing shortage, affordable housing, urban housing

If your question doesn't suggest such leads, try more concrete wording.

Refine Your Question.   Until you start your research, of course, you can't know for certain how fruitful your research question will be. If it doesn't lead you to any definite facts or reliable opinions, if it doesn't start you thinking critically, you'll need to reword it or throw it out and ask a new question. But at the very least, your first question can establish a definite direction in which to start looking.

After tentatively stating a question, use these questions to refine it:

RESEARCH CHECKLIST

Questioning Your Question

___ Is the scope of your question appropriate — not too immense and not too narrow? Is your question answerable given the time you have and the length limits for your paper?

___ Can you find enough current information about your question?

___ Have you worded your question simply, so that you are seeking just one answer, not several? Have you worded your question concretely and specifically, so that it states exactly what you are looking for?

___ Does your question concern an issue that engages you personally?

Predict an Answer in a Working Thesis. Some writers find a research project easier to tackle if they have not only a question but also an answer in mind. At this stage, however, you need to be flexible enough to change your answer or even your question if your research turns up something unexpected.

■ For more on stating and using a thesis, see pp. 271–77.

You can state a proposed answer as a working thesis.

RESEARCH QUESTION   How does a school dress code benefit students?

WORKING THESIS   Instituting a school dress code decreases the incidence of school violence.

Remember that a working thesis is meant to guide your research, not hinder it. If you're not learning anything new, just finding support for what you already thought was the case, then your working thesis may be too dominant, and you may no longer be conducting true research. Because of this possibility, some writers delay formulating a working thesis until they've already done substantial research or even begun drafting. Your approach will probably depend on your research assignment, your instructor's expectations, and your own work style.

MAKING A PRELIMINARY SEARCH

You can quickly test whether your question is likely to lead to an ample research paper by spending an hour or so conducting a fast search at the library. In some ways, this search will be similar to the initial overview you conducted at the beginning of your research process. Your goal then was to discover an interesting aspect of your topic. Your goal now is to determine whether you'll find enough ideas, opinions, facts, statistics, and expert testimony to address your question and to identify the most fruitful avenues for research.

If your preliminary search turns up a skimpy list of sources or, more likely, hundreds of sources, consider asking another question. Try to pick a question that is the focus of a dozen or twenty available sources. If you need help conducting a reliable search, ask a librarian for help.

In addition, decide which types of sources to concentrate on. Some research questions require a wide range of sources. Others are better suited to a narrower range, perhaps restricted by date or discipline. Target those most likely to yield the best information to answer your question. Understanding the types of information available in various print and electronic sources can help you plan your research. See the charts on pp. 600–05.

▨ For more characteristics of the sources described in the chart below, see pp. 602–06.

▨ To review the types of evidence, see pp. 35–40.

Finding Evidence and Opinions in Print Sources	Source for Facts and Statistics	Source for Expert Testimony	Source for Opinions
Scholarly Book	Extensive facts and data on book's topic reported from reliable sources or original study	Written by expert scholars, researchers, or professionals	Book presents author's point of view supported by own and other scholarly research
Popular Nonfiction Book	Facts and data may or may not be included	Written by experts, professionals, practitioners, journalists, or informed writers	Book presents author's point of view or experience with or without support from research
Scholarly Journal	Facts and data on article's topic reported from reliable sources or original study	Written by expert scholars, researchers, or professionals	Article presents author's point of view supported by own and other scholarly research; letters or responses to articles express views of readers
News Magazine	Facts, data, and quotations in text, graphics, or sidebars may be attributed to persons interviewed, published reports, or unidentified sources	Written by freelance and staff journalists who may quote experts, participants, or observers	Articles may reflect magazine's focus or point of view; opinion features—columns, pro-con articles, and letters from readers—may represent varied views
Popular Magazine	Facts and data included in popular or catchy form may not be attributed to original source	Written by staff and freelance writers who may quote others, including popular experts	Articles may reflect magazine's focus or area of interest; columns and letters from readers may present varied views
Newspaper	Facts, data, and quotations in text, graphics, or sidebars may be attributed to persons interviewed, published reports, or unidentified sources	Written by local and wire-service journalists, columnists, and others who may quote participants, observers, or experts	Extensive opinion features include editorials (views of paper's editors), letters to the editor (views of writers), and regular or featured columns (views of columnists)
Pamphlet or Booklet	Facts and data may or may not be included	Written by experts, professionals, researchers, or interested individuals	Contents may reflect opinions and point of view of writer or sponsor
Reference Work	Extensive facts and explanations cited from reliable sources or supplied by expert authors of entries	Written by scholars, specialists, and staff experts in subject	Articles may review several or present one of the alternative approaches or views of a topic

Finding Evidence and Opinions in Electronic Sources	Source for Facts and Statistics	Source for Expert Testimony	Source for Opinions
Online Reference Site	List of topics or links may lead to specialized facts or statistics	Expert academic sources available	Academic topic links to a variety of approaches and views on research topics
Gateway Site for a Topic or Field	Site pages with facts or links, such as *Polling Report* at <www.pollingreport.com>	Expert academic and field sources available	Topic links; opinion sites, such as *Opinion-Pages* at <www.opinion-pages.org> or *Public Agenda* at <www.publicagenda.com>
Online Document Collection	Documents posted on site with facts or statistics	Expert and well-regarded authors and documents available	Documents that present arguments or essays that express opinions
Professional Web Site	Reports, newsletters, and surveys, such as MetLife Foundation's "Survey of the American Teacher" at <www.metlife.com> or *InfoNation* at <www.un.org/Pubs/CyberSchoolBus/infonation/e_i_map.htm>	Expert and professional views available, promoting sponsor or sponsor's interests	Materials, advice, and sponsored reports that support interests or views of organization
Academic Web Site	Library links to sets of facts or statistics, such as "Community Information by Zip Code" at <http://library.csun.edu/mfinley/zipstats.html>	Department or library links and lists of campus experts to interview or e-mail may be available	Possible links to campus or local newspaper with editorials and letters on current issues
Government Web Site	Agency studies and reports with extensive statistics and other facts, such as *The World Factbook* at <www.cia.gov/cia/publications/factbook>	Expert analysis of research studies, policy options, and consumer topics available	Reports or pages that reflect specific mission or objectives of agency
Online Newspaper or News Service	Reports and boxes with facts or statistics to develop news coverage or provide background	Quotations and background from participants, observers, and analysts may be available	Editorials, letters to editor, regular or featured columnists, polls of site visitors
Interest-Group or Personal Web Site	Facts and statistics that support or promote group interests	Range available from expert to partisan to oddball views	Opinions, advocacy, and personal views that shape site content

USING KEYWORDS AND LINKS

Keywords are terms or phrases that identify the topics discussed in a research source. As you look for information on the Internet or in databases, you will most likely perform keyword searches. When you enter the keywords into an electronic search engine (whether in a library catalog or on the Web), the engine will return to you a list of all the sources it can find with that keyword. Knowing how to use keywords to search is a skill useful not only in your research project but also throughout your college career and beyond.

■ To practice using keywords, visit *The Bedford Researcher* Web site at <bedfordresearcher.com>.

For a list of search engines, see p. 583.

For advanced search strategies, see p. 584.

Finding the best keywords for a particular topic and a particular search engine is essential. Start by using the main terms in your research question. As you conduct your preliminary search, jot down or print out the keywords you use, noting whether they produce too few or too many results. You are likely to find that some keywords work better than others and that certain combinations of keywords produce the best results.

As your keywords lead you to Web sites compiled by specialists or people interested in a particular area, you can browse through the information and resources gathered there. These sites often contain *links* — lists of related sites — also relevant to your research project. These links, in turn, often contain their own lists of related Web pages. By following these connections systematically, you can benefit from the work of others and rapidly expand your own knowledge. Be careful, however, not to look only for information that supports a preconceived notion. Research should be an opportunity to learn more about a topic, to answer an authentic question, not simply to collect evidence that supports what you already think.

FOR GROUP LEARNING

Collaborative Research

Conducting research as a group is a complex yet exciting job, one especially common in the workplace. It requires responsible teamwork, clear communication, and full accountability. You might work with a research team in several ways, pooling your research but writing individual papers or collaborating on the entire project. After getting a go-ahead from your instructor, fix a series of deadlines, parcel out the work, and meet faithfully according to a schedule. Everyone must do his or her share of the work. Here is a schedule for full collaboration on an eight-week research project:

• Week One: Each member of the group seeks a topic for the project.

• Week Two: The group meets and agrees on a topic and a research question that they clear with the instructor. Members choose a coordinator to call or e-mail group members in order to keep the project moving.

For details on research archives, see pp. 562–63.

• Weeks Three and Four: Each member makes a preliminary search and contributes to the group's working bibliography. The group meets to determine responsibilities — who will collect what material for the group's research archive — and all begin work.

• Week Five: Everyone continues to collect sources, read, and take notes.

• Week Six: The group meets to evaluate the material collected and to see what else is needed. Members collaborate on a rough plan or outline.

• Week Seven: The group divides up the outline, and each member writes part of the draft. Members swap drafts, read them over, and respond.

• Week Eight: The group meets to review the combined draft. All write comments and corrections on it. Then one member prepares a polished copy, and the coordinator gives the whole paper one last proofreading.

Managing Your Project

No matter what your question or where you plan to look for material, you will want to manage your project wisely. You will need a schedule to use your time efficiently, a working bibliography to keep track of where you've been and where you need to go, and a research archive to organize information from all your sources — whether photocopies, printouts, or notes.

CREATING A SCHEDULE

If your instructor doesn't give you a series of deadlines as part of your assignment, set some for yourself. You can be sure that a research paper will take longer than you expect. If you procrastinate and try to toss everything together in a desperate all-night siege, you will not be satisfied with the result. Instead, start with a clear-cut schedule that breaks your project into a series of small tasks.

SAMPLE SCHEDULE

- *Week One:* If you are not assigned a topic, start thinking about an interesting general subject. Take an overview of your topic by searching your library database and the Internet.

- *Week Two:* Begin narrowing your topic to a workable research question. Conduct a preliminary search on your research question. Start your working bibliography and your research archive.

- *Week Three:* Begin your research in earnest. Locate and evaluate your most promising sources. Take notes.

- *Week Four:* Continue narrowing your research, identifying promising sources, evaluating them as you go along, and taking efficient notes.

- *Week Five:* Begin your preliminary outline, and state your thesis. Continue to update your bibliography and research archive, putting your sources in the order in which you think you might use them.

- *Week Six:* Refine your thesis statement. Start your first draft.

- *Week Seven:* Complete your first draft. Begin thinking about ways to revise and improve it. Seek feedback from a peer editor.

- *Week Eight:* Revise and edit your draft. Check that you have presented quotations properly. Carefully go over your documentation. Finally, proofread the entire paper, checking for any errors.

■ For downloadable sample schedules (and research checklists), visit <bedfordstmartins.com/ bedguide> and do a keyword search:

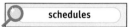 schedules

Each week you can make up a more detailed schedule, identifying tasks by the day or by the type to increase your efficiency while varying your activities.

DAILY SCHEDULE
Monday — finish library catalog
   search
Tuesday — start article indexes

ACTIVITY SCHEDULE
library search — EBSCOhost and
   InfoTrac
Web search — government sites

DAILY SCHEDULE	ACTIVITY SCHEDULE
Thursday — read printouts and add notes	reading — new printouts
Sunday night — organize files	writing — revised research question — thesis?

STARTING A WORKING BIBLIOGRAPHY

A working bibliography is a detailed list of the books, articles, and Web sites that you either plan to consult or have consulted. It has two purposes:

It guides your research by recording which sources you've examined and which you intend to examine.

It helps you document or identify the sources you have used by recording detailed information about each source.

Choose a Method for Compiling Your Working Bibliography.   Pick the method that suits you best, the one that you can use most easily and efficiently during the course of your research. Here are some options:

- Note cards, recording one source per card
- Small notebook
- Word-processing program
- Computer database
- Hand-held electronic storage tool

Keep Careful Records.   Whatever your method, the more carefully you record your tentative sources, the more time you'll save later when you compile a list of the works you actually used and cited. At that point, you'll be grateful to find all the necessary titles, authors, dates, page numbers, and URLs (Internet addresses) at your fingertips — and you'll avoid a frantic, time-consuming trip back to the library.

Start a bibliographic entry for each source you intend to consult. At this point, your information about the source may be incomplete: "Dr. Edward Denu — cardiologist — interview about drug treatments." Later, once you locate a print or Internet source or conduct field research, you'll be able to fill in the complete bibliographical information.

■ For examples of correct documentation form, see Ch. 32.

Record What You Will Need.   What should each source note in your working bibliography contain? Eventually it should include everything necessary to find the source as well as to write the final list of sources to be placed at the end of your paper.

BOOKS
1. The library call number
2. The author's full name, last name first

3. The book's title, including its subtitle if it has one, underlined or in italics
4. The publication information: place, publisher, year of publication (See Figure 27.1.)

PERIODICALS

1. The author's full name, last name first
2. The title of the article, in quotation marks, followed by the name of the publication, underlined or in italics
3. The volume number for a scholarly journal; add the issue number if each issue during the year begins with page 1
4. The date of the issue
5. The page numbers of the article (See Figure 27.2.)

ELECTRONIC SOURCES

1. The author's (or editor's) full name, if identified
2. The title of the page or document and site

Figure 27.1   *A bibliography card for a book with one author, in MLA style*

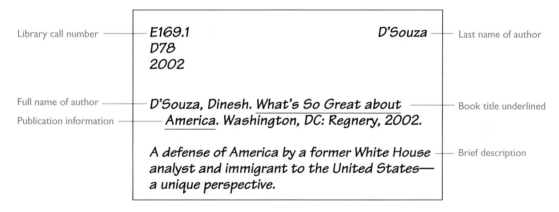

Figure 27.2   *A bibliography source note recorded on a computer for an article in a monthly magazine, in MLA style*

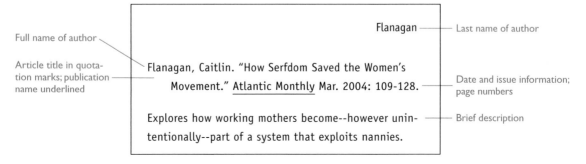

3. Information about alternate or original print publication, if any and if available
4. The date the source was created or last updated
5. The name of the sponsoring organization, if any
6. The date you accessed the source
7. The Internet address or URL (Uniform Resource Locator) (See Figure 27.3.)

FIELD SOURCES
1. The name of the person you interviewed or the setting you observed
2. Descriptive label, such as "Personal interview" or "Telephone interview"
3. The date you conducted the interview or observation (See Figure 27.4.)

You may list each item of information separately in your notes, but it is wise at this point to put the information in the correct form for a final bibliography entry in your works cited list. Keeping accurate records now will save future trips to the library.

Figure 27.3
A bibliography source note recorded on a computer for an Internet site, in MLA style

MacLeod

MacLeod, David. "Problems Affecting City Economies." 14 Nov. 2000.
    28 Feb. 2004 <http://www3.sympatico.ca/david.macleod/URBECO.htm>.

Addresses current problems in urban planning.

Figure 27.4
A bibliography source note recorded on a computer for a personal interview, in MLA style

Cardone

Cardone, Amy. Personal interview. 28 Feb. 2004.

Anecdotal evidence. Describes sports injuries in children that she's treated.

STARTING A RESEARCH ARCHIVE

You can organize information from library, Internet, and field sources by creating a research archive. An *archive* is a place where information is systematically stored. As you locate and evaluate sources, you will accumulate information for later use. If you have ever found yourself staring at a pile of books, photocopies, and printouts, wondering which one contained the fact or quotation that you wanted to use, you know the importance of organizing. You can use several techniques to create a research archive.

File Paper Copies.   To use this method, try to get all important sources in a paper format: photocopy book passages and periodical articles, print out electronic sources, and keep questionnaires and other field material. Then put these pages in a separate file folder for each source, labeled with title or subject and author. If you highlight key passages, you'll be able to locate that information even more quickly. Make sure the source and page number are identified on your copy so that you can connect them to the corresponding note in your working bibliography. If necessary, write that information on the photocopy.

Save Computer Files.   You can save Web pages, e-mail messages, posts to newsgroups and mailing lists, transcripts of chat sessions, and records from databases to a disk, a hard drive, or a network drive. Give each file a descriptive name so that you'll be able to locate the information quickly later on. You can also organize the files in different electronic folders or directories, also named so you can easily tell what each contains.

Save Favorites and Bookmarks.   You can save the locations of sites on the Web within your browser so that you can easily locate them again. Microsoft Internet Explorer calls these saved locations *favorites*, while Netscape Navigator calls them *bookmarks*. You can also annotate favorites and bookmarks with your browser and organize them into folders, much as you organize files on a computer.

Save Search Results.   If a database or Internet search was very productive but you don't have time to locate each relevant source at that moment, note the keywords you used to search. Then repeat the search at a later date. You can also print out the search results or save them to a computer file so you don't need to rerun the search.

RECORDING INFORMATION

Regardless of the techniques you use to create your archive, remember two things: copy judiciously and take notes. Some researchers say that copying (either photocopying or saving to a computer file) has done away with the need to take notes. Indeed, judicious copying can save you time as you gather materials. But simply copying everything you read is likely to waste money and time. Much of the material won't be worth saving. Further, you won't have digested and evaluated what was on the page; you will merely have copied it. Instead, make the material yours by selecting what is essential, highlighting or transcribing it by hand, perhaps summarizing or paraphrasing it.

■ For advice on quoting, paraphrasing, and summarizing in your paper, see pp. 607–14 and D3–D5 in the Quick Research Guide (the dark-red-edged pages). See also pp. 614–17 on avoiding plagiarism.

Capture the Essentials.   Record every fact, idea, quotation, and memorable phrase that you might eventually want to use. Make sure your notes are complete and accurate, ready to transfer information efficiently from your source to your draft. If you want your paper to be a sound analysis or argument based on a variety of reliable sources, you'll need to separate the useful nuggets in each source from all the rest. Your research notes are the best place to do that. A good research note includes three elements:

1. An *identifier*, usually the last name of the author whose work you're citing, followed by the location of the information — the page number or numbers, an Internet address, or a field source. (You should already have a note in your working bibliography for this source with complete publication information. If not, make one now.)
2. A *subject heading*, some key word or phrase you make up yourself to help you decide where in your paper the information might best fit.
3. The *fact, idea, opinion,* or *quotation* you plan to use in your paper.

■ For more on integrating sources, see Ch. 30.

Record all three elements so that later, when you integrate your notes into your paper or develop your ideas from multiple sources, you'll have an accurate record of what you found in each source and where you found it.

Use a Sensible Format.   Many writers find that using note cards or a word-processing program works better than taking notes on sheets of notebook paper. When the time comes to organize the material, they can reshuffle cards or computerized notes to arrive at a logical order.

Don't Crowd Your Notes.   Before you begin taking notes, skim through your source to decide what — and how much — you need to record. If you use note cards, aim to record only one note on each card. Grouping two or more ideas will complicate your task when you organize and draft your paper. If you use a computer to take notes, separate your entries clearly so that you can move them around easily later.

■ For more on critical reading, see Ch. 2.

Take Accurate and Thorough Notes.   Read the entire article or section of a book before beginning to take notes to help you avoid distorting the meaning. Put exact quotations in quotation marks, and take care not to quote something out of context or change the meaning. Double-check all statistics and lists. Make your notes and citations full enough that, once they're written, you are totally independent of the source from which they came.

Bristle while You Work.   While reading the material you are collecting, view it a little suspiciously to help you remain critical.

Keep Evaluating.   As you take notes, continue to evaluate what you read, considering what will be extremely valuable, fairly valuable, or only a bit valuable. Some researchers code the top of a note with a star (for great value) or a question mark (for questionable usefulness). Later, when they're organizing, they can see what stands out and needs emphasis. Others write notes to themselves at the bottom of a card or within the computer file.

Know When to Stop.   How many notes are enough? When you find that your sources are mostly repeating what you've learned from previous sources — and aren't any more authoritative or credible — you have probably done enough reading and note taking.

Working with Your Research Archive

As you build your research archive, you may want to create electronic "note cards." For example, you might keep a list of Web sites and the relevant information from them in a computer file that allows you to return to your sources with the click of a mouse. Or you may record information from each source in a file stored separately or within a folder. Then when you are composing a draft, you can easily keep several files open to copy and paste the source information (with citations and quotation marks around any quoted material) as you weave it into the draft. Use the File menu to create files and folders, labeled by subject, for grouping related files.

WRITING WITH A COMPUTER

For more on research archives, see pp. 562–63.

Chapter 28

Finding Sources in the Library, on the Internet, and in the Field

For more on managing your research project, see Ch. 27.

By now you have narrowed your research question, started your working bibliography, and begun your research archive. Consult your schedule so that you stay on track, and revise it if necessary. This chapter will help you continue your research by using efficient strategies for searching the library, the Web, and the field for relevant sources.

Searching the Library

Your college library is usually the best place to begin your search. From its computer terminals, your home, or your dorm room, you can access many of its resources — catalogs, indexes, and databases, for example. Although much of the library's information is stored on printed pages, the way it has been for centuries, the tools for locating these pages and, increasingly, the information itself are taking electronic form. Today's researcher needs to navigate both the print and electronic worlds.

From your library's home page, you will find access to a wide variety of resources — the online catalog, periodical databases, online reference material, guides to the Internet. Your library may also offer tours, online tutorials, or brochures explaining the library's organization and services. (See Figure 28.1 for a sample library home page.) Reference librarians are available to help you answer questions, from specifics such as "What is the GNP of Brazil?" to general queries such as "Where can I find out about the Brazilian economy?" Before you look for sources for your paper, it pays to do a little research on the library itself, starting with the following basic questions:

Figure 28.1
Sample home page from the
Tuskegee University Libraries

A. Overview of libraries and their purpose

B. Access to library holdings and resources

C. Information on specific campus libraries

Investigating Your Library

___ Where can you find a Web site or pamphlet mapping locations of library holdings, describing library resources, and explaining services?

___ Where is the reference desk, and what hours is it open?

___ How do you access the library's catalog? Can you search it or other library databases from your home computer or the campus network?

___ Where are periodicals kept, and how are they arranged?

___ What kinds of indexes or computerized databases are available, and how can you access them?

___ Can you use interlibrary loan to order material the library doesn't have?

___ How long is the check-out period for books? How do you request items, renew them, or use other circulation services?

USING THE ONLINE CATALOG

A library catalog provides information about the books, periodicals, videos, databases, and other materials available through the library. Typically, catalogs do not provide information about individual articles in periodicals. They do, however, provide you with the periodical's publication information (title, date, publisher, and so on), call number, location, and in some cases availability.

■ For more about using your research question to identify keywords, see p. 556.

Become a Flexible Searcher.   When library catalogs were limited to printed file cards, they allowed searches only by author, title, or subject. Now, electronic catalogs may greatly expand these search options, as the following chart illustrates. Consult a librarian or follow the catalog prompts to

TYPE OF SEARCH	EXPLANATION	EXAMPLES	SEARCH TIPS
Keyword	Terms that identify topics discussed in the source, including works by or about an author, and may generate long lists of relevant and irrelevant sources	• workplace mental health • geriatric home health care • Creole cookbook • Jane Austen novels	Use a cluster of keywords to avoid broad terms (whale, nursing) or to reduce irrelevant topics using same terms (people of color, color graphics)
Subject	Terms assigned by library catalogers, often following the *Library of Congress Subject Headings* (LCSH)	• motion pictures (not films) • developing countries (not third world) • cookery (not cookbooks)	Consult the *LCSH,* a set of large red books often shelved near the catalog terminals, to find the exact phrasing used
Author	Name of individual, organization, or group, leading to list of library (and possibly online) works by author	• Hawthorne, Nathaniel • Colorado School of Mines • North Atlantic Treaty Organization	Begin with an individual's last name or first, as directions indicate; for a group, first use a keyword search to identify its exact name
Title	Name of book, pamphlet, journal, magazine, newspaper, video, CD, or other material	• *Peace and Conflict Studies* • *Los Angeles Times* • *Nursing Outlook*	Look for a separate search option for titles of periodicals (journals, newspapers, magazines)
Identification Numbers	Library or consortium call numbers, publisher or government publication numbers	• MJ BASI, local call number for recordings by Count Basie	Use the call number of a useful source to find related items shelved nearby
Dates	Publication or other dates used to search (or limit searches) for current or historical materials	• Elizabeth 1558 (when she became queen of England) • science teaching 2000	Add dates to keyword or other searches to limit the topics or time of publication

find out which searches your library catalog allows. Try options that restrict a search by date, location, type of material, or other characteristics. Once you locate a relevant item, check its detailed record for alternative search terms that may help focus your search more productively. If your catalog adds online resources such as e-books or recommended Web sites to the items available at the library, use these selectively so that you are not distracted from your own research question.

■ To practice using keywords, visit *The Bedford Researcher* Web site at <bedfordresearcher.com>.

Sort Your Search Results. When your search produces a list of possible sources, click on the most promising individual items to learn more about them. See Figure 28.2 for a sample keyword search and Figure 28.3 for the sample online record for one source. In addition to the call number or shelf

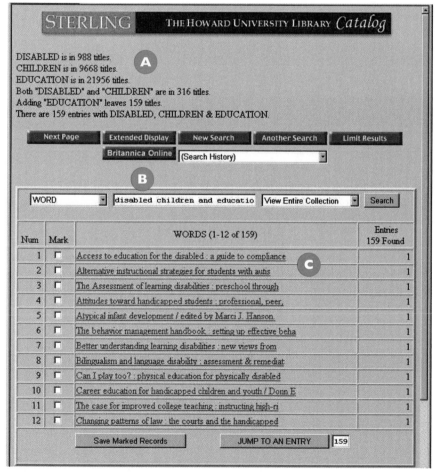

A. Number of results for individual and combined search terms
B. Keyword search window
C. Results screen (linked to full entries)

Figure 28.2
General results of a keyword search on "disabled children and education" using an online library catalog

Figure 28.3
Specific record selected
from keyword search
results

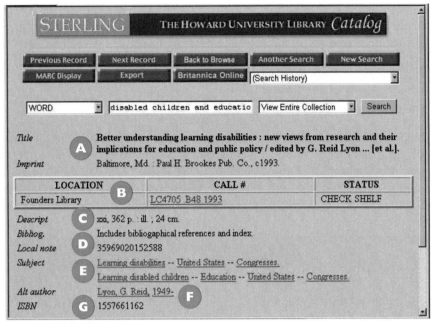

A. Book title, author, and publication information
B. Location and library call number
C. Number of pages, illustrations, height of book
D. Description of bibliography
E. Alternate subject headings (often hyperlinked)
F. Other works by the same author (often hyperlinked)
G. International Standard Book Number (ISBN)

■ For more on evaluating sources, see Ch. 29.

location, the record will identify the author, title, place of publication, and date. Often it will describe what the book contains, how long it is, and which subject headings define its scope. Though each library presents information slightly differently, the elements generally are the same. Use these clues to help you select and evaluate your options wisely.

Find Items on the Shelves.   A book's call number, like a building's address, tells where the book "resides." This number is carefully chosen so that books on the same subject end up as neighbors on the shelves. College libraries generally use the classification system devised by the Library of Congress. Its call letters and numbers direct you to items grouped in subject areas. (See Figure 28.4.) Other libraries use the older and more familiar Dewey decimal system, which files items into large categories by number. In either case, reserve some of your research time for browsing because you will almost certainly find interesting materials on the shelf next to the ones you found through the catalog. The two common classification systems are outlined here. Both have added newer fields, such as computer science, mass communications, and environmental studies, to related areas.

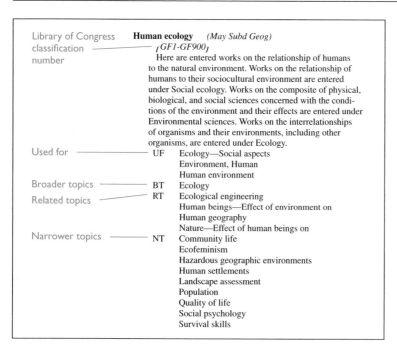

Figure 28.4
Entries from the Library of Congress Subject Headings

Library of Congress classification number — **Human ecology**   *(May Subd Geog)*
    ₍GF1-GF900₎
        Here are entered works on the relationship of humans to the natural environment. Works on the relationship of humans to their sociocultural environment are entered under Social ecology. Works on the composite of physical, biological, and social sciences concerned with the conditions of the environment and their effects are entered under Environmental sciences. Works on the interrelationships of organisms and their environments, including other organisms, are entered under Ecology.
Used for — UF   Ecology—Social aspects
                Environment, Human
                Human environment
Broader topics — BT   Ecology
Related topics — RT   Ecological engineering
                Human beings—Effect of environment on
                Human geography
                Nature—Effect of human beings on
Narrower topics — NT   Community life
                Ecofeminism
                Hazardous geographic environments
                Human settlements
                Landscape assessment
                Population
                Quality of life
                Social psychology
                Survival skills

LIBRARY OF CONGRESS CLASSIFICATION SYSTEM

A General Works
B Philosophy, Psychology, Religion
C Auxiliary Sciences of History
D History: General and Old World
E History: America
F History: America
G Geography, Anthropology, Recreation
H Social Sciences
J Political Science
K Law
L Education
M Music and Books on Music
N Fine Arts
P Language and Literature
Q Science
R Medicine
S Agriculture
T Technology
U Military Science
V Naval Science
Z Library Science

DEWEY DECIMAL CLASSIFICATION SYSTEM

000–009 General Works
100–199 Philosophy
200–299 Religion
300–399 Social Sciences, Government, Customs
400–499 Language
500–599 Natural Sciences
600–699 Applied Sciences
700–799 Fine and Decorative Arts
800–899 Literature
900–999 History, Travel, Biography

Consult Catalogs at Other Libraries.   Most college and university library catalogs are available over the Internet or through regional, state, or other consolidated catalogs. Use these catalogs to find books or other materials that you can borrow through interlibrary loan or by visiting a nearby library. If you're not sure how to access such catalogs ask a librarian. You may be able to connect directly to them via the Internet or through your own library's catalog.

For more on timeliness and other characteristics of periodicals and other sources, see the charts on pp. 600–05 and in B2 in the Quick Research Guide (the dark-red-edged pages).

To practice using databases, visit *The Bedford Researcher* Web site at <bedfordresearcher.com>.

CONSULTING DATABASES: PERIODICAL INDEXES AND BIBLIOGRAPHIES

Information on current topics often appears first in periodicals rather than books. Periodicals are journals, magazines, newspapers, and other publications issued at regular intervals. Many indexes — guides to material published within other works — exist to help you locate articles in periodicals. Bibliographies — lists of sources on a particular topic — also can lead you to relevant materials, often those you would never think to trace in a catalog.

If you have questions about which database to use or how to access it, ask a reference or subject-area librarian. Many library indexes and databases are not available free to the general public; your library selects these resources and subscribes to them so that you — and other campus researchers — can find the most current and reliable sources as quickly and easily as possible. Academic librarians, often expert research advisors, are specially trained to help you search efficiently in the most appropriate databases. They are available in person, generally at the reference desk, and often by e-mail, telephone, appointment, or live chat online.

Periodical Indexes.   In a periodical index, you'll find every article — listed by author, title, and subject — for the periodicals and time period covered by the index. The index also includes the source information you'll need to find each article in the library, usually the periodical title, date, volume or issue number, and page numbers.

Electronic indexes — often called periodical databases — are organized as a series of records or entries on a particular item, such as a newspaper or journal article. You can easily search for these records using author, title, subject, or keyword. Electronic indexes may include more information on each article than traditional print indexes do, such as a short summary or abstract or even the full text of the article, which you can print or download for later use. Electronic indexes may complement, replace, or duplicate print indexes; for instance, *MLA Online, ERIC,* and *PsychLIT* are available in both forms.

Each periodical index includes entries only for its specific collection of periodicals, so finding the right article is largely a matter of finding the right index. Before you use a periodical index, ask these questions:

RESEARCH CHECKLIST

Finding the Right Index

___ Is your subject covered in this index? Does the index cover a broad field or a very specific subject in depth?

___ Does the index cover the period you're interested in? If the index is electronic, how far back does it go? How often is it updated?

___ Does the index cover scholarly journals written for an expert audience, or popular magazines for a more general audience?

___ Does the index simply identify an article, add a summary or abstract, or supply a link to its full text?

___ Is the index an online subscription service available to students on a library terminal, campus network, or home computer? Is it a public index available on the Web and conveniently linked from the library's Web site?

___ Are older print or CD-ROM indexes, sometimes needed for historical research, available in the reference area or elsewhere in the library?

General Indexes.   Several indexes can help you if you're looking for magazine or newspaper articles addressed to the general population.

> The *Readers' Guide to Periodical Literature* started publication in 1900, so you can use the current or retrospective indexes to locate popular press coverage of events at any time in the twentieth century—for example, articles published days after the bombing of Pearl Harbor in December 1941. (See Figure 28.5 for sample entries.)
>
> The *New York Times Index*, dating back to 1851, can help you track down that newspaper's current or historical coverage of events.
>
> *EBSCOhost* and *InfoTrac* include the full text of many articles written for a fairly general audience. (See Figure 28.6 for a sample entry.)
>
> *NewsBank*, with daily updates, indexes nearly five hundred local U.S. papers.
>
> *Lexis-Nexis* carries mainly full-text articles from newspapers, wire services, and other general-interest publications.

Specialized Indexes.   Discipline-specific indexes are more likely to analyze scholarly journals with peer-reviewed articles that have been critiqued

> For more on types and characteristics of periodicals, see the charts on pp. 600–01 and B2 in the Quick Research Guide (the dark-red-edged pages).

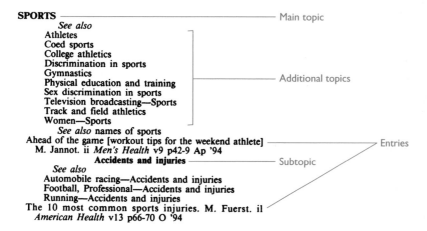

Figure 28.5
Entries from the Readers' Guide to Periodical Literature

Figure 28.6
Search result from
InfoTrac index

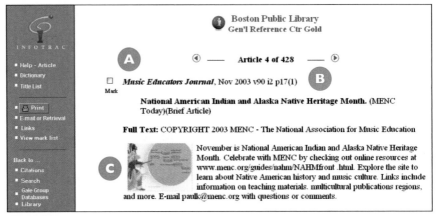

A. Publication name, date, volume number, illustrations, page number,
   total pages in article
B. Article title and author
C. Text of short article

by other experts before being accepted for publication. Such articles are aimed at a more specialized audience and provide more analysis than articles in popular magazines. If you are looking for literary criticism, research on social issues, or scientific or medical research only summarized or reported in the popular press, turn to indexes such as these:

> *Humanities Index* or *Humanities Abstracts*
>
> *Social Sciences Index* or *Social Sciences Abstracts*
>
> *Business Periodicals Index*
>
> *PAIS International* (an index focusing on public affairs)

Bibliographies.   When you use a bibliography — a list of sources on a specific subject — you take advantage of the research others have already done. Every time you find a good book or article, look at the sources the author draws on; some of these may be useful to you, too. Look for a section at the back of a book labeled "Bibliography" or perhaps "For Further Reading." If the author has quoted or referred to other works, look for a list called "References" or "Works Cited" at the end of the work. If the book or article uses footnotes or endnotes, check those, too, for possible leads.

Sometimes you may locate a book-length bibliography on your subject, compiled by a researcher and published so that other researchers (including you) won't have to duplicate the work. Bibliographies cite a wide variety of materials — including not only books and articles but also films, manuscripts, letters, government documents, and pamphlets — and they will probably lead you to sources that you wouldn't otherwise find.

For example, *Essential Shakespeare* lists the best books and articles published on each of Shakespeare's works, a wonderful shortcut when you're looking for worthwhile criticism. If you're lucky, adding the word *bibliography* to a subject or keyword search will turn up a list of sources with annotations that describe and evaluate each one.

For more on keyword searches, see pp. 580–84.

Before turning to the wealth of other library and Web resources available, take a moment to assess where you are in your research project. If you have a clear idea of what's left to accomplish, you will find it easier to stick to your research schedule and, in the final stage, to write your paper.

RESEARCH CHECKLIST

Managing Your Project

___ Are you on schedule? Do you need to adjust your timetable to give yourself more or less time for any of the stages?

___ Are you using your research question to stay on track and avoid digressions?

___ Are you keeping your materials up-to-date — listing new sources in your working bibliography and labeling and storing new material in your archives?

___ Do you have a clear idea of where you are in the research process?

For downloadable sample schedules (and research checklists), visit <bedfordstmartins.com/ bedguide> and do a keyword search:

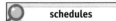

schedules

Using Other Library Resources

Many other library resources are available to you beyond what you can access from your library's home page. One of the most overlooked resources in the library is its staff. Besides knowing the library better than anyone else, librarians are constantly working with its catalog, reference books, databases, and new additions to the collections. If you need help locating or using materials, consult a librarian.

CONSULTING REFERENCE MATERIALS

The library also contains an amazing array of useful reference material, including encyclopedias, handbooks, and atlases — listed in the online catalog and sometimes available online through your library's home page. Spending some of your research time in the library, however, can still save you a lot of time and effort in the long run. Remember, the library and all of its resources — whether electronic or print — are specifically designed to help researchers like you to find information quickly and efficiently. Here you can familiarize yourself with a topic or fine-tune your research by filling in detailed definitions, dates, statistics, or facts. You can look for reference sources related to your topic in the *Guide to Reference Books,* a directory of sources arranged by discipline.

General Encyclopedias.   General encyclopedias, such as the *New Encyclopaedia Britannica* and *Encyclopedia Americana*, are written for readers who are not specialists. These references, in print or online, may be especially valuable when you first take an overview of a topic. They also can supply a missing fact here or there, and their index volumes and cross-references will help you find what you need. But when you start investigating more deeply, you will need to go to other sources as well.

Specialized Encyclopedias.   These references cover a field in much greater depth than general encyclopedias do. The following sampling of titles suggests their variety:

> *Dictionary of American History*
>
> *Encyclopedia of the American Constitution*
>
> *Encyclopedia of Human Biology*
>
> *Encyclopedia of Psychology*
>
> *Encyclopedia of Sociology*
>
> *Encyclopedia of World Cultures*
>
> *The Gale Encyclopedia of Science*
>
> *New Grove Dictionary of Music and Musicians*

Dictionaries.   In your library, you'll find large and specialized dictionaries covering foreign languages, abbreviations, and slang as well as the specialized terminology in a particular field, such as *Black's Law Dictionary*, *Stedman's Medical Dictionary*, or the *Oxford Dictionary of Natural History*. Unabridged dictionaries are often available on dictionary stands. Here you can find the most obscure words and learn what they mean as well as how to pronounce them.

Handbooks and Companions.   Between encyclopedias and dictionaries are these reference books with concise surveys of terms and topics relating to a specific subject. The articles are generally longer than dictionary entries but more concise than those in encyclopedias. Check with a reference librarian to see if specialized handbooks, such as the following, are available for your topic.

> *Blackwell Encyclopaedia of Political Thought*
>
> *Bloomsbury Guide to Women's Literature*
>
> *Dictionary of the Vietnam War*
>
> *Oxford Companion to English Literature*

Statistical Sources.   If numbers are a key type of evidence for your research, you can find sources for statistics in the library and on the Web.

- The *Statistical Abstract of the United States.* Perhaps the most useful single compilation of statistics, this resource contains hundreds of tables relating to population, social issues, economics, and so on.

- *Gallup Poll.* Good resources for public-opinion statistics, the surveys conducted by the Gallup organization are published in annual volumes, in a monthly magazine, and on the Web.

- *<www.census.gov>.* The federal government collects an extraordinary amount of statistical data and releases much of it on the Web. Check also <www.fedworld.gov> and <www.fedstats.gov> for lists of other government statistics available on the Web.

Atlases.   If your research has a geographical angle, maps and atlases may be useful. Besides atlases of countries, regions, and the world, others cover history, natural resources, ethnic groups, and many other special topics.

Biographical Sources.   Useful directories list basic information — degrees, work history, honors, addresses — for prominent people. To locate biographical sources, you can use tools such as *Biography Index* and the *Biography and Genealogy Master Index.* Biographical resources include the following:

> *American Men and Women of Science*
>
> *The Dictionary of American Biography*
>
> *The Dictionary of National Biography*
>
> *The Dictionary of Scientific Biography*
>
> *Who's Who in Politics*
>
> *Who's Who in the United States*

LOCATING SPECIAL MATERIALS

Your library is likely to have other collections of materials, especially on regional or specialized topics, but you may need to ask what's available.

Periodicals on Microform.   Most libraries have some of their resources available in microform, especially periodicals. This technology puts a large amount of printed material — for example, two weeks' worth of the *New York Times* — on a durable roll of film (microfilm) that fits into a small box or on a set of plastic sheets the size of index cards (microfiche). The machines used to read microforms often print out full-sized copies of pages.

Primary Materials on Microform.   Many libraries also have primary, or firsthand, material in microform. For example, the *American Culture Series* reproduces books and pamphlets (1493 to 1875) along with a good subject index, making it possible to view colonial religious tracts or nineteenth-century abolitionist pamphlets without traveling to a museum or rare books collection. The *American Women's Diaries* collection provides firsthand glimpses of the past through the words of women living in New England and the South and traveling west as pioneers.

Primary Materials in Digitized Format.   Firsthand materials such as diaries, letters, speeches, and interviews are increasingly available to libraries in digitized databases that can be searched using keywords, authors, titles, or other means. Examples include *Black Thought and Culture*, *Oral History Online*, and *North American Immigrant Letters, Diaries, and Oral Histories* (1840 on).

Resources from Organizations.   Many groups maintain informative Web sites. Your library may also collect pamphlets and reports distributed by companies, trade groups, or professional organizations. The *Encyclopedia of Associations*, organized by subject or group name, or the *United States Government Manual*, listing government agencies, can lead you to useful materials and contacts, especially for field research.

Government Documents.   The federal government of the United States is the most prolific publisher in the world and, in an effort to make information accessible to citizens all over the country, makes an increasing number of documents available on the Web along with indexes like these:

- *Monthly Catalog of United States Government Publications*, which is the most complete index to federal documents available
- *CIS Index*, which specializes in congressional documents and includes a handy legislative history index
- *Congressional Record Index*, which indexes reports on what happens in Congress each day

When most people think of government documents, they may think of congressional hearings, presidential papers, and reports from federal agencies — but the government has published something on practically any topic you can think of as the following sampling suggests:

Ozone Depletion, the Greenhouse Effect, and Climate Change

Placement of School Children with Acquired Immune Deficiency

Small Business and the International Economy

Strengthening Support and Recruitment of Women and Minorities to Positions in Education Administration

Violence on Television

If you plan to use government documents, reports, or statistics in your research, don't be shy about asking a librarian for help. The documents can be difficult to locate both on the shelves and on the Web.

Using the Web for Research

The Internet contains an enormous and ever-growing amount of information. For example, a quick search for information about Yellowstone National Park turns up nearly anything you might want to find: contacts for making cabin reservations, photographs of family trips to Yellowstone, the Greater Yellowstone Coalition's spirited defense of the park's ecosystem, scientific studies of regrowth following the 1988 fire, teaching modules on fire management, the Old Faithful Webcam, and technical reports such as the official Yellowstone Wildland Fire Management Plan. Unfortunately, because of the sheer bulk of this information, searching for relevant materials can be both too easy and too difficult. Finding information that is actually useful can be time consuming, but understanding a few basic principles can help a great deal.

SELECTING SEARCH ENGINES

Search engines bring the vast resources of the Internet to your computer screen, but they are not unbiased, objective searchers. Each has its own system of locating material, categorizing it, and establishing the sequence for reporting results. One search site, patterned on a library catalog or index, might be selective, designed to advance the investigations of students, faculty, and professionals. Another might carry extensive advertising but separate it from search results, while a third organizes search results so that the sites that pay advertising fees ("sponsors") pop up first in the list, even though sites listed on later pages might better match the searcher's needs. Take a close look at the practices of your favorite search engine (which may be described on an "About" page), and consider trying some others to find those that most efficiently supply the reliable sources you need.

For a list of leading search sites, see p. 583.

FINDING RECOMMENDED INTERNET RESOURCES

Instead of beginning your Web research with a few keywords and your favorite search engine, go first to online resources recommended by your instructor, department, campus library, or other reliable source. What are the advantages of well-chosen site recommendations? They save the time required to search and screen randomly chosen sites. More important, they can take you directly to respected resources that have been prepared by experts (scholars or librarians), directed to academic researchers (like you), and used successfully by others on campus. Of course, no recommendation can replace your careful consideration of the appropriateness of a resource for your research question.

For a checklist for finding recommended sources, see B1 in the Quick Research Guide (the dark-red-edged pages).

For more on evaluating sources, see Ch. 29.

How can you locate recommended sources? Browse to find collections of links to resources such as these on your library or other campus Web site:

■ See the list of search sites on p. 583. See also the Online Reference Sites and other examples in the charts on pp. 602–04 and in B2 in the Quick Research Guide (the dark-red-edged pages).

- Self-help guides or Internet databases organized by area (social sciences or business), topic (literary analysis), or type of information, such as the *Auraria Library Statistics Guide* at <http://library.auraria.edu/findit/subj_guides/statistics/statistics.html>.

- Research Web sites sponsored by another library, academic institution, or consortium such as the Internet Public Library at <www.ipl.org> or the Librarians' Index to the Internet at <www.lii.org>.

- Other research centers or major libraries with their own collections of links, such as the Library of Congress page "Newspaper & Current Periodical Reading Room" at <www.loc.gov/rr/news/othint.html>.

- Specialty search engines for government materials — <www.fedworld.gov>, <www.firstgov.gov>, or <www.google.com/unclesam> — along with advice about using them such as that on the California State University Northridge Web site at <http://library.csun.edu/subgov.html/>.

- Specialty search engines for specific materials such as images at <www.ditto.com>.

- Collections of e-books, including reference books and literary texts now out of copyright, such as *Bartleby.com* at <www.bartleby.com/> and *Project Gutenberg* at <www.gutenberg.net/index.shtml>.

- Web databases with "unrestricted access" (not online subscription services restricted to campus users) as varied as the country-by-country data of *InfoNation* at <www.un.org/Pubs/CyberSchoolBus/infonation/e_infonation.htm> and the health resources of *MedlinePlus (Pub Med)* at <www.nlm.nih.gov/medlineplus/healthtopics.html>.

- Community resources or organizations, often useful for local research and service learning reports, such as the information on Austin, Texas, at <www.lib.utexas.edu/refsites/austin.html>.

CONDUCTING ADVANCED ELECTRONIC SEARCHES

Searching the Web is similar to searching library catalogs and databases. Search engines contain millions of records on Web sites, much as a database or library catalog contains records on books, periodicals, or other materials found in a library. Generally, search engines can be searched by broad categories such as *education* or *health* or by more specific keywords.

■ For more on keywords see pp. 557–58. When you limit your search simply to keywords and broad categories, however, you may be overwhelmed with information not directly related to your research question. For example, Figure 28.7 illustrates a keyword search for sources on *foster care* on Google that produced more than 4 million entries. A keyword search may be ideal if you search for a highly specialized term or topic, such as training for distance runners. For a more general topic — such as *foster care* — you may turn up seemingly endless lists of results.

Several techniques are available for more sophisticated searches of the Web, databases, and library catalogs. Some of these techniques can expand

Figure 28.7
Results of a keyword
search for foster care
using Google, reporting
more than 4 million
entries

A. Search terms

B. Total number of entries located

C. Highlighted search terms found in entries

your search, but most researchers want to limit the scope of their searches in order to find more results relevant to their research interests. As Figure 28.8 shows, an advanced search produced fewer sources on one aspect of foster care — placing older children in foster care.

Use Wildcards.   Wildcards are symbols that tell the search engine to look for all possible endings to a word. For instance, if you search for the keyword *runner,* you'll get every entry containing that word but not entries containing only *run, runs,* or *running.* Using a wildcard symbol such as run*, you can search for all words that begin with *run,* thus increasing the range of your results. The most common wildcard symbols are an asterisk (*) for multiple letters, numbers, or symbols and a question mark (?) for single characters. Check your search engine's symbols by clicking on search tips.

Figure 28.8
Advanced search results on foster care + placing older children *using Google, reporting 52 entries*

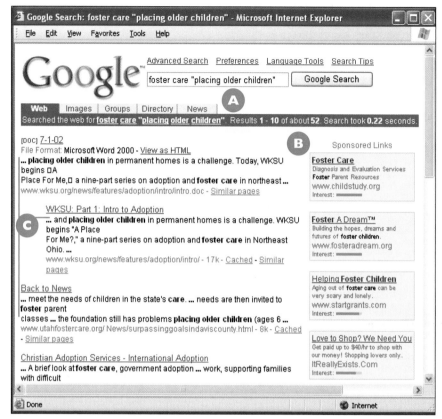

A. Search terms
B. Total number of entries located
C. Highlighted search terms found in entries

Combine Terms in Boolean Searches.   A Boolean search, named after the nineteenth-century mathematician George Boole, lets you specify the relationships between your keywords and phrases. Common Boolean search terms include *AND* (all terms must appear in a result), *OR* (one or more of the terms must appear), and *NOT* (one or more terms can appear, but another must not).

Search for: history AND California
Result: all entries containing both *history* and *California*

Search for: history OR California
Result: all entries containing *history* or *California* or both

Search for: history NOT California
Result: all entries containing *history* but not containing *California*

Search for: history AND California NOT Los Angeles
Result: all entries containing *history* and *California* but not those containing *Los Angeles*

Leading Internet Search Sites

The best search site is the one you learn to use well. Each of the search tools below uses its own particular phrasing and search designs. In addition to following general search strategies, you should note each site's "search tips" and "help" instructions.

WRITING WITH A COMPUTER

If you are uncertain about your topic, use a directory site like Yahoo!, Magellan, or WebCrawler that begins searches with categories. Next, think of searching like a zoom lens. If you zoom into "no results" or "no pages found," then you can step back and add more information until you start to focus on sites you want to explore. By tinkering with your words, you can improve your searches and locate Web pages with titles and ideas closer to your research goals. This process is much easier than starting with a general prompt and finding thousands of potential sites.

SUBJECT CATALOGS, DIRECTORIES, AND GUIDES
Ask Jeeves <www.ask.com>
Digital Librarian (Margaret Vail Anderson)
Encyclopaedia Britannica's Internet Guide
Google Directory (Open Directory Project)
     <http://directory.google.com/>
Infomine: Scholarly Internet Resource Collections
     <http://infomine.ucr.edu>
Librarians' Index to the Internet <http://lii.org/>
Michigan Electronic Library <http://mel.org/>
UC Berkeley Electronic Resources Database
     <www.lib.berkeley.edu/find/types/electronic_resources.html>
Yahoo!

■ For links to other online resources, visit <bedfordstmartins.com/bedguide>.

INDEXES WITH CONTENT GATHERED BY COMPUTER "SPIDERS" OR "ROBOTS"
AlltheWeb <www.alltheweb.com>
Alta Vista
Excite <www.excite.com/search/>
Go Network <http://search.go.com/>
Google

SITES THAT SEARCH MULTIPLE INDEXES AT ONE TIME
Dogpile
Ixquick
Metacrawler
MetaEureka
MetaFind
Search.com
SurfWax
Webcrawler

Select Limitations for Advanced Searches.   Many search engines will automatically combine terms for Boolean searches when you select the advanced search option. Google and Metacrawler, for example, allow you to limit searches to all, exactly, any, or none of the words you enter. Look for directions for limitations such as these:

- A phrase such as *elementary school safety*, requested as a unit (exactly these words) or enclosed in quotation marks to mark it as a unit
- A specific language (human or computer) such as English or Spanish
- A specific format or type of software such as a .pdf file
- A date range (before, after, or between dates for creation, revision, or indexing)
- A domain such as .edu (educational institution), .gov (government), .org (organization), or .com (commercial site or company), which indicates the type of group sponsoring the site
- A part of the world, such as North America or Africa
- The location (such as the title, the URL, or the text) of the search term
- The audio or visual media enhancements
- The file size

FINDING ONLINE DISCUSSIONS

You will find that you can locate a variety of material online, ranging from e-zines (electronic magazines) to conversations among people interested in your topic.

Searching for Electronic Publications.   Wide public access to the Internet has given individuals and small interest groups an economical publication option. Although such texts must be used cautiously, you can locate a wide range through the Etext Archives at <www.etext.org/index.shtml>. Globe of Blogs at <www.globeofblogs.com> indexes many blogs (short for Web logs), providing access to the personal, political, and topical observations and commentaries of individuals around the globe.

Searching Newsgroups and Mailing Lists.   Newsgroups and mailing lists, among the oldest forms of Internet communication, generate an enormous amount of text each day. Both types of exchange support the discussion of topics such as adult education or immigration among people with a shared interest. If you're working on a current issue, consider consulting the archives of such groups. You will need to read cautiously but may find detailed analyses by interested members of the public or acknowledged experts. Google (at <groups.google.com>) allows you to search for mailing lists and newsgroups.

Using Chat.   Major news organizations, such as ABC News, use chat to interview public figures or industry leaders in advertised sessions attended by hundreds or even thousands of participants. You can view transcripts of these sessions by visiting <http://abc.news.com> and searching under "chat." Similarly, major search sites, such as Yahoo!, host regular chat sessions on topics including entertainment and finance. Yahoo! also provides transcripts of past sessions.

Finding Sources in the Field

The goal of field research is the same as that of library and Internet research — to gather the information you need to answer your research question and then to marshal persuasive evidence to support your conclusions in your research paper. The only difference is where you conduct the research. Many rich, unprinted sources lie beyond the library and the Internet, providing opportunities to explore matters that few researchers have investigated.

If you enjoy talking with people and don't mind what news reporters call legwork, you may relish obtaining firsthand information. Almost any paper will be enriched by authentic and persuasive field sources. And you'll almost certainly learn more about your topic by going into the field and developing firsthand knowledge of it. In this section, we focus on field research techniques that have proven most useful for college students. Before you begin, however, be sure to find out from your instructor whether you need institutional approval for research involving other people ("human subjects approval").

INTERVIEWING

Interviews — conversations with a purpose — may prove to be your main source of field material. Choose your interview subjects carefully, whenever possible interviewing an expert in the field or, if you are researching a group of people, someone representative or typical. Regardless of your interview subject, preparation is central to a good interview.

■ For more on preparing for an interview, see pp. 86–89.

TIPS FOR INTERVIEWING
- Be sure your prospect is willing to be quoted in writing.
- Make an appointment for a day when the person will have enough time — an hour if possible — to have a thorough talk with you.
- Arrive promptly, with carefully thought-out questions to ask.
- Come ready to take notes. If you also want to tape-record the interview, ask permission of the interviewee.
- Really listen. Let the person open up.
- Be flexible, and allow the interview to move in unanticipated directions.

- If a question draws no response, don't persist; go on to the next one.

- At the end of the interview, be sure to confirm all direct quotations.

- Make additional notes right after the interview to preserve anything you didn't have time to record during the interview.

■ For more on recording an interview, see pp. 88–89.

Take notes even if you use a tape recorder so that you can remember the interview accurately, distill its most important points, and reconstruct it in your paper. Besides recording key points and quotations, you should note any telling details that might prove useful later — the interviewee's appearance, the setting, the mood, any notable gestures.

If you can't talk to an expert in person, your next best resource may be a telephone interview. Make a phone appointment for a time convenient for both you and your interviewee. A busy person may not be able to give you a half hour of conversation on the spur of a moment, and it is polite to ask for a time when you may call again. Have written questions in hand before you dial so you don't waste the person's time (and yours). Take notes.

Federal regulations, by the way, forbid recording a phone interview without notifying the person talking that you are recording his or her remarks.

OBSERVING

■ For more on observing, see Ch. 5.

An observation may provide essential information about a setting such as a business or a school. If so, you will need to make an appointment and, as soon as you arrive, identify yourself and your purpose. Some receptionists will insist on identification. You might ask your instructor for a statement on college letterhead declaring that you are a bona fide student doing field research. Follow-up field trips may be necessary if you find gaps in your research or if you need to test new ideas by further observation.

TIPS FOR OBSERVING

- Establish a clear purpose — exactly what you want to observe and why.

- Take notes so that you don't forget important details when you review your findings and incorporate them into your paper.

- Record facts, telling details, and sensory impressions. Notice the features of the place, the actions or relationships of the people who are there, or whatever relates to the purpose of your observation.

- Consider using a still or video camera if you have equipment available and can operate it without being distracted from the scene you are observing. Photographs can illustrate your paper and help you interpret your observations or remember details while you write. If you are filming or taking photographs in a private place, be sure to get written permission from the owner (or other authority) and from any people you film or photograph.

USING QUESTIONNAIRES

Questionnaires, as you know, are part of contemporary life. You probably filled one out the last time you applied for a job or for college. You may have responded to one in *People* or *Glamour* magazine. As a rule, when researching a particular question, professional pollsters, opinion testers, and survey takers contact thousands of individuals chosen to represent a segment of society or perhaps a broad range of the populace (diversified in geography, income, ethnic background, and education).

Because your surveys will not be this extensive, you should avoid generalizing about your findings as if they were unimpeachable facts. It's one thing to say that "many of the students" who filled out a questionnaire on reading habits hadn't read a newspaper in the past month; it's another to claim that this is true of 72 percent of the students at your school — especially when you gave questionnaires only to those who ate in the dining hall the day you were there and half of those students just threw their forms into the trash.

A far more reliable way for you to use questionnaires is to treat them as group interviews: assume that the information you collect is representative, use it to build your overall knowledge of the subject, and cull the responses for interesting or persuasive details or quotations. Use a questionnaire when you want to collect the same type of information from a large number of people, concentrate on what a group thinks as a whole rather than on what a particular individual has to say, or find an interview that would cover all your questions impractical. (See Figure 28.9 for an example of a student questionnaire.)

TIPS FOR USING A QUESTIONNAIRE

- Ask yourself what you want to discover with your questionnaire. Then thoughtfully invent questions to fulfill that purpose.

- Keep your questionnaire simple. Make it easy and inviting to fill out. Test it on classmates or friends before you distribute it to the group you want to study.

- Ask questions that call for checking alternative answers, marking yes or no, or writing a few words so that responses are easy to tally. Try to ask for just one piece of information per question.

- When appropriate, ask open-ended questions that call for short written responses. Although these will be difficult to tally and fewer people are likely to respond, the answers may supply worthwhile quotations or suggest important issues or factors when you mull over the findings.

- Write unbiased questions that will solicit factual responses. Do not ask, "How religious are you?" Instead ask, "What is your religious affiliation?" and "How often do you attend religious services?" Based on responses to the last two questions, you could report actual numbers and draw logical inferences about the respondents.

Figure 28.9   *A questionnaire asking college students about Internet use*

QUESTIONNAIRE

Thank you for completing this questionnaire. All information you supply will be kept strictly confidential.

1. What is your age? ____

2. What is your class?

    ____ First year   ____ Junior

    ____ Sophomore   ____ Senior

3. How old were you when you first began using the Internet? ____

4. How do you currently access the Internet? Indicate which of the following statements is true for you.

    ____ With my own computer   ____ Someone I live with has a computer
    with Internet access

    ____ I never use a computer   ____ With computers at the library or university lab

    ____ Other (please specify): _____

5. Approximately how many hours a week do you use the Internet? ____

6. What is your primary reason for using the Internet?

    ____ Personal   ____ School-related   ____ Work-related

7. Indicate all of the ways in which you use the Internet.

    ____ E-mailing

    ____ Recreational Web surfing

    ____ Conducting optional research for a class

    ____ Conducting mandatory research for a class

    ____ Conducting personal research (such as planning travel, evaluating
    products, or searching for a job)

    ____ Managing your financial accounts

    ____ Visiting chat rooms

    ____ Shopping online

    ____ Posting résumés or job applications

    ____ Designing or posting Web sites

    Other: _____

8. For which of the activities above do you use the Internet most? _____

    _____

9. On a scale of 1 to 5, rate how comfortable you are using the Internet.

    (not very comfortable)   1   2   3   4   5   (very comfortable)

10. Do you feel that you could benefit from further instruction in using the Internet?

    ____ Yes   ____ No   ____ Maybe

- When you get back completed questionnaires, tally the results. You can simply count short answers ("Republican," "Democrat"), but you will need to classify longer answers into groups or categories. For example, if you asked "What is your goal in life?" you might find that the responses fell into these groups: (1) to make money, (2) to serve humanity, (3) to travel, (4) to save my soul, (5) other. By classifying, you can group and count similar replies and look for patterns in the responses.

CORRESPONDING

Is there a person whose knowledge or opinions you need but who lives too far away to interview? Do you need information or resources that you might request from large corporations, organizations such as the American Red Cross or the National Wildlife Federation, branches of the military, or offices of the state or federal government? Could an elected official provide what you need? Many organizations and officials are accustomed to getting requests by mail and may employ public relations officers to answer inquiries like yours. Sometimes they will unexpectedly supply you with a bonus — free brochures, press releases, or other materials that might interest you. To tap such resources, write a letter, or send an e-mail message.

For advice on writing business letters and e-mail messages, see pp. 221–25 and 226–28.

TIPS FOR CORRESPONDING

- Plan ahead, and allow plenty of time for responses to your requests.
- Make your letter or e-mail message short and polite. Identify yourself, explain what you want to find out, and request what you need. Thank your correspondent for helping you.
- If you want specific information from an individual, send your questionnaire or a short list of pointed questions. If you e-mail your message, insert the questions from your questionnaire into the message.
- Enclose a stamped, self-addressed envelope for a reply by mail. If you are sending an e-mail message, include your e-mail address in the message.

ATTENDING PUBLIC AND ONLINE EVENTS

College organizations frequently bring interesting speakers to campus. Check the schedules of events on bulletin boards and in your campus newspaper. In addition, professionals and special-interest groups sometimes convene for a regional or national conference. These meetings can be fertile sources of fresh ideas for a student researcher. Attending a lecture or conference can be an excellent way to begin to learn the language of a discipline.

TIPS FOR ATTENDING EVENTS

- Take notes on the lectures, which are usually given by experts in the field and supply firsthand opinions.

- Ask questions from the audience or corner a speaker or two later for an informal talk.

- Record who attended the event, how the audience reacted, or other background details that could prove useful in writing your paper.

- Depending on the nature of the gathering, a speaker might distribute copies of the paper presented or be willing to send a copy to you. Conferences often publish their proceedings — usually a set of all the lectures delivered — but publication generally takes months or even years after the conference. Try the library for proceedings of past conferences.

For more on using online discussions, see pp. 584–85.

Be on the lookout, as well, for blog (Web logs) or online discussions — such as the chat sessions sponsored by Web search engines like Yahoo! or Web sites like CNN Online — that are relevant to your research topic. You can participate as an observer or perhaps even ask a question. Remember to use your chat program to record the discussion for later review. You can learn how to record a transcript by consulting the program's online help.

Chapter 29
Evaluating Sources

Locating and collecting information are only two of the many activities involved in writing a research paper. You also have to think critically about what you find. You need to evaluate — in other words, judge — your sources, exploring the ideas, opinions, facts, and beliefs they express.

■ For more on critical reading, see Ch. 2.

- Which of your sources are reliable?
- Which of these sources are relevant to your topic?
- What evidence from these sources is most useful for your paper?

As you identify, select, and read sources, you'll use evaluation from start to finish. This extremely useful skill is one that you can apply both in college and beyond.

Evaluating Library and Internet Sources

Not every source you locate will be equally reliable or equally useful to you. You will need to examine sources from the Web with special care. Like other firsthand materials, individual postings, Web logs ("blogs"), and Web sites will reflect the biases, interests, or information gaps of their writers or sponsors. Commercial and organizational sites may supply very useful material, but they'll provide only what supports their objectives — selling their products, serving their clients, enlisting new members, or persuading others to support their activities or views. Sites recommended by your library will have been screened by professionals, but each will have its own point of view or approach, often a necessary bias to restrict its focus.

Even so, your selection of sources can itself simplify evaluation. For example, when you draw information from an article in a print or online peer-reviewed journal, the process of evaluation for that article actually began

■ For exercises on evaluating Web sources, visit <bedfordstmartins.com/bedguide> and do a keyword search:

evaluate

■ For more about the characteristics of various types of sources, see the charts on pp. 600–05 and B2 in the Quick Research Guide (the dark-red-edged pages).

when the editors of the journal first read the article and then asked expert reviewers to evaluate whether it merited publication. Similarly, a serious book from a major publishing company or university press probably has been submitted to knowledgeable reviewers. Such reviewers may be asked to assess whether the article or book is well reasoned, logically presented, and competently researched. However, such reviewers can't decide if the work is pertinent to your research question or if it contains evidence useful for your paper. For this reason, a key part of the job of conducting research is thinking critically about sources so that you can select the best evidence for your purposes.

How do you know what evidence is best? Do what experienced researchers do — ask a series of key questions in order to evaluate your sources. The basic questions remain the same whether your source is print or electronic. See Figure 29.1 for a sample evaluation of a Web site that provides both informative and persuasive materials about its topic.

■ For advice on evaluating field sources, see pp. 597–98.

RESEARCH CHECKLIST

Evaluating Sources — Print and Electronic

____ What is the purpose of the publication or Web site? Is it to sell a product or service? To inform? To shape opinion about an issue or cause?

____ Who is the intended audience? Experts in the field or novices? The general public or people with a particular bias? How does this audience affect the tone and evidence in the source?

____ Who is the author of the source? Does the source provide information about the author's credentials and profession? Can you detect the author's bias or point of view?

____ Is your material a primary source (a firsthand account) or a secondary source (an analysis of primary material)? If it is a secondary source, does it use sound evidence from primary sources? Would you learn more if you looked at the primary source yourself? Is it available?

____ What can you tell about the publisher? Is it a corporation, an organization, or a government agency? Have you heard of this publisher before? Does the publication seem reputable and responsible? If the source is a Web site, what can you find out about its sponsor?

____ What kind of evidence does the source present? Is it reliable, sufficient, and relevant? Does the argument or analysis seem complete, or does it leave many questions unanswered? Is the source well constructed and logically organized? Does it supply a bibliography or a list of recommended sources? If it is electronic, does it supply appropriate, active links?

____ When was the source published? If it is a Web site, when was it created or last updated? Is the information up-to-date or out of date?

____ Is the information in the source directly relevant to your research question? Why should you use this source rather than others?

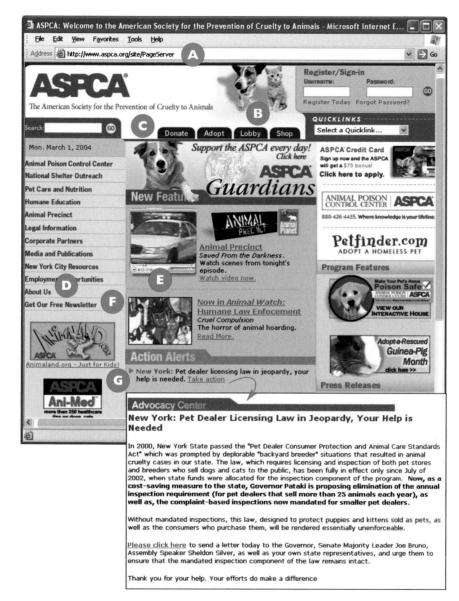

Figure 29.1
Evaluating the purpose,
audience, and bias of a
Web site offering informa-
tive and persuasive
materials

A. Identifies group as organization (.org), not school (.edu) or company (.com)

B. Uses engaging animal graphics

C. Appeals for support

D. Explains purpose of group and provides link to contact information

E. Provides special features slanted toward animal-lovers and ASPCA activities

F. Offers free newsletter to involve readers

G. Links to information about controversies and recommends action

WHAT IS THE PURPOSE?

Understanding the purpose or intention of a source will help you decide whether it might supply solid evidence for your research project. A reference book in a library serves a different purpose than a newspaper editorial, a magazine advertisement, or a Web site that promotes a product or service. Asking critical questions is crucial: Is the purpose of this source to explain or inform? To report new research? To persuade? To offer an alternative viewpoint? To sell a product? Does the source acknowledge its purpose in its preface, introduction, mission statement, or "About Us" or FAQ (Frequently Asked Questions) page?

WHO IS THE INTENDED AUDIENCE?

A source written for an audience of experts in a field is likely to assume that readers already have plenty of background knowledge. For this reason, such sources typically skip general treatments in favor of detailed discussions tailored to experts. In contrast, sources written for general audiences usually define terms and include the background explanations. For example, for your paper on current treatments for HIV, you locate an article from a well-known medical journal that discusses the most favorable chemical composition for an effective protease inhibitor drug. Instead of beginning with this article, written by a physician for other physicians, you might turn first to a source that defines *protease inhibitor* and discusses how it helps HIV patients. Considering the intended audience can help you identify sources appropriate for your project.

WHO IS THE AUTHOR?

Make every effort to learn about each author's credentials, affiliations with institutions or organizations, and reputation among peers. Try to make sure that any author who shapes or supports your ideas is reliable and trustworthy.

Bias.   A *bias* is a preference for a particular side of an issue. Because most authors have opinions on their topics, there's little point in asking whether an author is biased. Instead, ask how the author's viewpoint affects the presentation of information and opinion. What are the author's allegiances? Does the author treat one side of an issue more favorably than another? Is the author's bias hidden or stated? Having a strong bias does not invalidate what an author has written. However, if you recognize such biases early on, you may want to look for other viewpoints or approaches that will help you avoid lopsided analyses or arguments.

Print Credentials.   Check for a brief biographical note at the beginning or end of a book or article, especially in any preface or introduction. However, the best measure of someone's authority is whether his or her work meets the critical standards of other authorities. Do others cite the work of your source's author? If your instructor or someone else on campus knows the field, does he or she recognize the author? Is the author listed in a biographical database?

Web Credentials.   Learning the credentials of authors whose work is posted on the Web, on a newsgroup site, or on certain databases can be difficult. If your source is a Web site, look for a link on its home page to information about the author. If no credentials are provided, check for an e-mail address that you could use to ask the author about his or her credentials. If your source is a posting to a newsgroup or a mailing list, see what you can deduce from the writer's e-mail address and any signature file. Try a Web search for the person's name, looking for associated sites or links to or from the author's site. If you can't find out anything about the author of a posting, it is best not to use the information in your paper, although it might provide useful background.

Publication.   If your source is a weekly newsmagazine like *Time, Newsweek,* or *U.S. News & World Report,* an article is likely to have been written by a reporter who may not have a famous name and probably is not a world-renowned authority. When such magazines feature articles by experts, their credentials will usually be described alongside the article. All such magazines have good reputations for checking facts carefully and presenting a range of opinions. Be aware, however, that some magazines select facts that mirror the opinions of their editors.

Materials with No Author Identified.   If no author is given, try to identify the sponsoring organization or publisher. On a Web site, check the home page or search for a disclaimer, contact information, or an "About This Site" page. If a print source doesn't list an author, consider the nature of the publication: Is the article published in a nationally respected newspaper like the *Wall Street Journal* or in a supermarket tabloid? Is the brochure published by a leading organization in its field?

Field Research.   If you are conducting field research, you may be able to select the sources of your information. If you are investigating safety standards for infant car seats, for example, a personal interview with a local pediatrician will probably produce different information than an interview with the manufacturer's sales representative. You can also affect the results of your research by distributing a questionnaire to a certain group of people or by observing a particular setting.

IS THIS A PRIMARY OR A SECONDARY SOURCE?

A *primary source* is a firsthand account written by an eyewitness or a participant. It contains raw data and immediate impressions. A *secondary source* is an analysis of the information contained in one or more primary sources. For example, primary sources for investigating a large fire would include the statements of victims and witnesses, the article written by a journalist who was at the scene, and the report of the fire chief in charge of putting out the blaze. If another reporter used those accounts as background for a story on industrial accidents or if a historian used them in a book on urban life, these resulting works would be secondary sources.

For most research papers, you need to use both primary and secondary sources. If you find yourself repeatedly citing a fact or authority as it is quoted in someone else's analysis, go to the primary source of the information itself. For example, statistics can be used by those arguing both sides of an issue; often only the interpretation differs. Going back to the original research or statistics (published as a primary source) will help you to learn where the facts end and the interpretation begins.

WHO IS THE PUBLISHER?

Experienced researchers know that the publisher of a source — the person, organization, government agency, or corporation that prints or electronically distributes a source — plays an important role in shaping its content. Like authors, publishers often have a bias about a particular topic or issue and are likely to present their own products and services more favorably than those of competitors. Similarly, political groups, such as the Democratic Party or the National Rifle Association, are likely to publish materials that support policies favored by the organization.

For an example showing how a URL identifies a publisher, see A on p. 593.

As you evaluate a source, ask critical questions about what might motivate its publisher. Is a Web site created for commercial purposes, such as selling a product or service? Is it devoted to a specific cause? Is it sponsored by a particular organization or government agency? Is it the work of an individual who has strong opinions but little expertise? Is a newsgroup or mailing list a general-interest group or one limited to a particular topic or issue? Is a publisher noted for its works in a specific field or with a specific political agenda? Does a periodical have a predictable point of view? For example, commentary in *The Nation*, a politically liberal magazine, is likely to give you a different picture of the world than that in the conservative *National Review*.

Because these questions can be difficult, even for experienced researchers, consult with a librarian if you need help finding answers. To learn about the publisher of a Web site, try to locate a disclaimer or information about the site. If the site is sponsored by an organization or agency, look for a mission statement or "About" description (as illustrated in Figure 29.1).

HOW SOUND IS THE EVIDENCE?

The evidence in a source — its ideas, information, facts, expert or other opinions — can tell you a great deal about its reliability and usefulness for your research project. Is the evidence complete, up-to-date, and carefully assembled? Is any thesis supported by credible evidence? Is the argument or analysis convincing? Is there enough evidence to support the claims being made?

Does visual material enhance the source rather than distract from its argument or information? Does the source formally identify its own sources in citations and a bibliography? If the source leaves important questions unanswered, you might want to look elsewhere for your own evidence.

For more on evidence, see pp. 35–40.

For more about the characteristics and timeliness of various sources, see the charts on pp. 600–05 and in B2 in the Quick Research Guide (the dark-red-edged pages).

IS THE SOURCE UP-TO-DATE?

In general, you should strive to select current sources. In most fields, new information and discoveries appear every year, so the evidence in a source needs to be up-to-date or at least still timely. New information may appear first in Web postings, media broadcasts, and periodicals such as newspapers and eventually magazines, though such sources may not allow the time needed to consider information thoughtfully. Later, as material is more fully developed or examined, it may be treated in scholarly journal articles and books. In contrast, older materials can supply a historical, theoretical, or analytical focus.

IS THE SOURCE RELEVANT TO YOUR RESEARCH?

Finally, continue to question whether each of your sources is relevant to your topic, your research question, your thesis, and your ideas. An interesting fact or opinion could be just that — interesting. Instead, you need facts, expert opinions, information, and quotations that relate directly to the purpose and audience of your research paper. It's surprisingly easy to waste your time being sidetracked by a persuasive book, article, or Web site on a topic only slightly connected to your research.

For more on testing evidence, see pp. 38–39.

Why use one source rather than another? Is the information it contains useful for your purposes? Does it provide strong quotations or hard facts that would be effective in your paper? Does it tackle the topic in a relevant way? For one paper, you might appropriately rely on an article from a popular magazine; for another, you might need the findings published in a scholarly journal — the article on which the magazine article was based. As you look for the best possible sources for your purpose, always ask yourself not only "Will this do?" but also "Would something else be better?"

For more on selecting sources, see section B in the Quick Research Guide (the dark-red-edged pages).

Evaluating Field Sources

Although the general criteria for evaluating print and electronic sources may also apply to field resources, you might want to ask these questions as well:

RESEARCH CHECKLIST

Evaluating Field Sources

___ Does your source seem biased or prejudiced? If so, is this bias or prejudice so strong that you have to discount some of the source's information?

___ Does your source provide evidence to support or corroborate claims? Have you compared different people's opinions, accounts, or evidence?

___ Is any of your evidence hearsay — one person telling you the thoughts of another or recounting actions that he or she hasn't witnessed? If so, can you support your source's view by comparing it with other evidence?

___ Does your source seem to respond consistently, seriously, and honestly? If a respondent has told you about past events, has time possibly distorted his or her memory?

Each type of field research can also raise particular questions. For example, if you are observing a particular event or setting, are people aware that they are being observed? Often, knowing that they are being observed can change people's behavior. If you have tried to question a random sampling of people, do you feel that they are truly representative? Or, if you have tried to question everyone in a group, have you been thorough enough? It is important for you to think critically about field sources as well as those from the library and the Web.

Reconsidering Your Purpose and Your Thesis

As you evaluate your sources, you will critically examine each individual source, assessing its specific strengths, shortcomings, and possible contributions to your paper. Once you have gathered and evaluated a reasonable collection of sources, it's time to step back and consider them as a group — lifting your eyes from the maples, red oaks, and elms to the forest as a whole.

- Have you found enough relevant and credible sources to satisfy the requirements of your assignment? Have you found enough to suggest sound answers to your research question?

- Are your sources thought-provoking? Can you tell which information is generally accepted, which is controversial, and which may be unreliable? Have your sources engaged and enlightened you while substantiating, refining, or changing your original ideas?

- Are your sources varied? Have they helped you achieve a reasonably complete view of your topic? Have they suggested other perspectives, approaches, alternatives, or interpretations that you will want to acknowledge? Have they deepened your understanding and helped you reach well-reasoned, balanced conclusions?

- Are your sources appropriate? Do they answer your question with the kind of evidence that your readers will find persuasive? Do they have the range and depth necessary to achieve your purpose and satisfy your readers?

Use these questions to check in with yourself. Make sure that you have a clear direction for your research — whether it's the same direction you started with or a completely new one. Perhaps you are ready to answer your research question, refine your thesis, and begin to draft a paper that pulls together your own ideas and those of your sources. On the other hand, you may want to find additional sources that support or challenge your assumptions about the topic. Maybe you need to hunt for specific counterevidence that responds to strong evidence against your position — or change your working thesis to account for that evidence. On the other hand, you might want to pursue a new direction that seems more tantalizing than your original one.

The following charts, mentioned earlier in this chapter, will help you make solid source choices regardless of where you are in your research process.

Typical Features of Print Sources	Location Information	Typical Audience	Authors and Contributors	Quality Controls
Scholarly Book	Library online catalog or database	Specialists, researchers, students, professionals	Scholars, researchers, specialists, professionals	Peer reviews, editorial standards
Popular Nonfiction Book	Library online catalog, public library, or bookstore	General readers interested in book's topic	Informed writers, journalists, specialists, professionals	Reviews for publisher, editorial standards
Scholarly Journal	Library periodical index (print or online)	Specialists, researchers, students, professionals	Scholars, researchers, specialists, professionals	Peer reviews, editorial standards
News Magazine	Library periodical index (print or online) or newsstand	General readers interested in current events	Freelance and staff journalists, editorial staff	Editorial and journalistic standards
Popular Magazine	Library periodical index (print or online) or newsstand	General readers interested in magazine's focus	Freelance and staff writers, editorial staff, guest contributors	Editorial standards
Newspaper	Library periodical index (print or online) or newsstand	General or local readers	Freelance and staff journalists, editorial staff, columnists	Editorial and journalistic standards
Pamphlet or Booklet	Library collection (such as government, business, historical, or civic material)	Specialists, professionals, students, general or local readers	Range from specialists and researchers to sponsoring groups or individuals	Editorial standards of sponsor
Reference Work	Library online catalog or database	Specialists, researchers, students, professionals	Scholars, specialists, and staff experts	Selection of contributors, editorial standards

Typical Publication Time Frame	Sponsor or Publisher	Possible Purposes of Publication	Content for Researchers	Use of Source Citations
Months or years of preparation for publication probably following years of research and writing	Major or specialty publisher, or university press such as University of Chicago Press	Explore issues or topics in the field, advance knowledge, sell books	In-depth library or field research that meets academic standards	Yes—supplies in-text citations, notes, or bibliography
Months or years of preparation for publication possibly following months or years of writing	Major or specialty publisher such as Simon & Schuster	Present popular issues, explore trends, provide advice, sell books	Substantial research, investigative journalism, or opinion based on experience	Maybe—possibly identifies sources in chapters, notes, or bibliography
Months (or longer) for acceptance and publication probably following months or years of research and writing	Scholarly or professional organization or publisher such as Modern Language Association	Explore topics of concern to journal readers and specialists in the field	In-depth library or field research or professional critique that meets field's standards	Yes—supplies in-text citations, notes, and references following format used in the field
Days or weeks for publication following current or long-term investigation	Commercial or specialty publisher such as Time Warner	Cover news, promote magazine's viewpoint, sell advertising and magazines	News reports supported by facts, observation, and interviews; investigative journalism	Maybe—might name popular or expert sources mentioned or quoted but does not list sources
Days, weeks, or months for publication following long-term or immediate topic development	Commercial or specialty publisher such as National Geographic or Rodale	Cover popular topics and readers' interests, sell advertising and magazines	Current advice, expert views reduced to popular applications	Maybe—might name sources mentioned or quoted in article but does not list sources
Days or weeks for publication following current or long-term topic development or investigation	Newspaper publisher or media group	Cover news, current events, and timely issues; sell advertising and newspapers	News reports supported by facts, observation, and interviews; investigative journalism	Maybe—might name popular or expert sources mentioned or quoted but does not list sources
Days or months of preparation for publication following development of material	Government, civic, business, health, or other professional group	Supply timely and useful information in short form, promote sponsor or writer's specialty	Concise presentation of advice, information, opinion, or research findings	Maybe—might supply full, some, or no source citations, depending on purpose and sponsor
Months or years of preparation for publication probably following months or years of research and writing	Major or specialty publisher	Present accurate information on topic, sell books	Concise and accurate presentation of facts, terms, and background for topic	Maybe—may or may not list standard sources or recommend other sources

Typical Features of Electronic Sources	Location Information and Examples	Typical Audience	Authors or Expert Contributors	Quality Controls
Online Reference Site	Recommended sites such as *Michigan Electronic Library* at <http://mel.org/index.jsp>, *UC Berkeley and Internet Sources by Academic Discipline* at <http://lib.berkeley.edu/Collections/acadtarg.html>, and *Pinakes: A Subject Launchpad* at <http://hw.ac.uk/libWWW/irn/pinakes/pinakes.html>	Researchers, scholars, professionals, students	Librarians, information specialists	Site selection criteria and standards
Gateway Site for a Topic or Field	Recommended sites such as *Voice of the Shuttle* for the humanities at <www.vos.ucsb.edu> or *Social Science Information Gateway* at <www.sosig.ac.uk>	Researchers, scholars, professionals, students	Librarians, information specialists in field	Site selection criteria and standards
Online Document Collection	Research collections such as the *Electronic Text Center* at <http://etext.lib.virginia.edu> or specialized collections such as the Thomas historial documents at <http://thomas.loc.gov>	Researchers, scholars, professionals, students, general readers	Librarians, information specialists, topic specialists	Site selection criteria
Professional Web Site	Links to corporations, non-profits, and foundations on sites such as *Fortune* at <www.fortune.com> or the Foundation Center at <http://lnp.fdncenter.org/finder>	Professionals, business people, consumers, students, interested readers	Professionals, scholars, business people, organization staff	Site objectives; public or customer service standards
Academic Web Site	Lists of college or university Web pages such as those of the University of Texas at <www.utexas.edu/world/univ/state> or at <www.utexas.edu/world/comcol/state>	Students, graduates, faculty, staff, parents, visitors	Campus units, groups, and Web staff	Campus criteria for inclusion
Government Web Site	Index to federal Web sites at <www.firstgov.gov> or Google's Uncle Sam search engine at <www.google.com/unclesam>	Public visitors, other agencies, researchers, specialists	Agency information specialists, staff, and consultants	Agency mission, research and editorial standards

Typical Publication Time Frame	Sponsor or Publisher	Possible Purposes of Publication	Content for Researchers	Use of Source Citations
Immediate, daily, or regular updates	Library or information organization	Assist scholars, researchers, and students	In-depth academic, professional, or personal research	Yes (Web links) — lists sites and provides links, often grouped and annotated
Regular or irregular updates, depending on sponsor or Webmaster	Library or professional organization	Assist scholars, researchers, and students; encourage interest in specialty	In-depth academic and professional research in discipline	Yes (Web links) — lists sites and provides links, often grouped and annotated
Regular or irregular updates, depending on materials or Webmaster	Library or special-interest sponsor	Assist scholars, researchers, and students to access documents	Easy access to selected texts for researchers or readers	Yes (Web links) — identifies documents and may supply background for texts
Regular or irregular updates, depending on sponsor	Professional group, nonprofit agency, corporation, or corporate foundation	Promote interests of organization; attract and assist members, clients, professionals, or site visitors	Promotion of organization and its research, civic, economic, or other interests	Maybe — may present information, with or without sources, or may supply links
Regular or irregular updates, depending on academic unit maintaining page	College or university	Assist campus community, attract future students, promote family and public support	Promotion of campus programs and activities, including academic research	Maybe — may supply campus information without sources as well as academic texts and resource lists or links
Regular or irregular updates, depending on government agency	Federal, state, local, or foreign government division or agency	Fulfill agency objectives by providing public information and assistance	Authoritative information for citizens, policy makers, and agencies based on reliable research	Maybe — may present reports or texts with source citations as well as popular information without sources

Table continues on pages 604–605.

Typical Features of Electronic Sources	Location Information and Examples	Typical Audience	Authors or Expert Contributors	Quality Controls
Online Newspaper or News Service	Collections of links such as *NewsBank* at <www.newsbank.com/features/nptitles/nbnpmast.html>, *News & Periodical Resources on the Web* at <http://lcweb.loc.gov/rr./news/lists.html>, *Arts & Letters Daily* at <www.aldaily.com>, and *Global Spin* at <http://globalspin.org/world_news_sources.html>	General or local readers, researchers, professionals, students	Journalists, editorial staff, columnists	Journalistic and editorial standards
Interest Group or Personal Web Site	Collections of links such as those of the American Academy of Pediatrics at <www.aap.org/advocacy/washing/resources/irgd2-nlink.htm>, Global Advocacy Sites at <http://danenet.wicip.org/bcp/global_advocacy.html>, or Salon Blogs at <www.salon.com/blogs>	Issue-oriented visitors, students, researchers	Activists, concerned citizens, individuals	Individual or group objectives

Typical Publication Time Frame	Sponsor or Publisher	Possible Purposes of Publication	Content for Researchers	Use of Source Citations
Immediate updates as events occur along with archives of past coverage	Newspaper or media group	Cover news, current events, and timely issues; sell advertising	Accurate news reports supported by facts, observation, interviews, and visuals; investigative journalism	Maybe—might identify popular or expert sources mentioned or quoted but not other sources
Regular or irregular updates, depending on individual or group	Partisan group, special-interest group, or individual	Promote special interests of group or individual	Range from academic interests to partisan activism to individual interests	Maybe—may or may not identify sources of information or use reliable sources

Chapter 30

Integrating Sources

For more on using
sources in your writing,
see D1–D6 in the Quick
Research Guide (the
dark-red-edged pages).

Once you have evaluated sources that respond to your research question, you will want to record all the valuable information and persuasive evidence from the sources you choose to use so that you can easily work that material into your paper. Your paper will present and support your own ideas — your thesis about your research topic and question — with the ideas, information, and evidence from these sources. Quotation, paraphrase, and summary — all explained in this chapter — are useful techniques for capturing such information for any research paper. In addition, you will need to add this information responsibly, identifying both the ideas and the exact words from your sources in order to avoid plagiarizing.

Combining Your Sources with Your Own Ideas

Sources alone do not make for an effective research paper. Instead, the ideas, explanations, and details from your sources need to be integrated — combined and mixed — with your own thoughts and conclusions about the question you have investigated. Together they eventually form a unified whole that conveys your perspective, along with the evidence that logically supports it, to your audience. To make sure that your voice isn't drowned out by your sources, keep your research question and your working thesis — maybe still evolving — in front of you as you record information. On the other hand, to make sure that you identify and credit your sources appropriately, work carefully, treating your sources with the respect they deserve.

For more on stating a
thesis, see pp. 271–77.

You have an obligation to the researchers, scholars, and writers who came before you. You repay this obligation by citing your source materials carefully, identifying all the other writers you get information from. You do so not only for the quotations you use but also for the ideas, even those conveyed in your own words. If a writer fails to acknowledge all sources or uses another writer's words without quotation marks, he or she has *plagiarized*, a very serious offense in academic and business communities. Such a writer is suspected of a theft when he or she may merely have failed to honor a debt by citing and listing sources, as a good scholar should.

For more on citing sources, see Ch. 32.

For more on plagiarism, see pp. 614–17 and D1 in the Quick Research Guide (the dark-red-edged pages).

Quoting, Paraphrasing, and Summarizing in Your Notes

When it comes time to draft your paper, you will incorporate your source material in a variety of ways:

- Quoting: transcribing the author's exact words directly from the source
- Paraphrasing: restating the author's ideas fully but in your own words
- Summarizing: reducing the author's main point to essentials

To practice quoting, paraphrasing, and summarizing, visit <bedfordstmartins.com/bedguide> and do a keyword search:

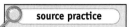

source practice

Your notes, too, should be in these three forms — and the form you pick for each bit of information should represent your best guess as to the form you will use in the final paper.

Deciding whether to quote, paraphrase, or summarize at the note-taking stage will save you time. A faithful transcription of a long quotation takes much longer than a quick summary. If you know in advance that you intend to use only the essentials, you might as well save those extra minutes. In addition, weighing each source carefully and deciding how to use it — even as you are reading — is part of the dynamic process of research. This process requires thinking critically about sources and their usefulness, not just taking a source at face value and copying it word for word into your paper. You should always be thinking about how you will use your sources — otherwise, they'll end up using you.

For more on recording notes, see pp. 560–62.

QUOTING

If you intend to use a direct quotation, copy the quotation carefully, reproducing the words, spelling, order, and punctuation exactly, even if they're unusual. Put quotation marks around the material so that when you add it to your paper, you'll remember that it's a direct quotation. (See Figure 30.1 for an example of a note card quoting a source.)

For more about quoting from sources, see D3 and D6 in the Quick Research Guide (the dark-red-edged pages).

Figure 30.1   *A sample note card giving a direct quotation from a source*

> Children and sports   Leonard 140
>   "... [in organized sports] children may be subject to intense emotional stress caused by fear and anxiety, concern about physical safety, and doubts about performances and outcomes. This anxiety may emerge if children are ignored, chastised, or made to feel that they are no good. Scanlan and Passer's study of preadolescent male soccer players showed that losing players evidenced more postgame anxiety than winning players. Children who experience anxiety in sport competition may try to avoid failure by shying away from active participation, by developing excuses, or by refusing to try new things." [Good quote!]

RECORDING A GOOD QUOTATION

1. Quote sparingly, selecting only notable passages that might add support and authority to your assertions.
2. Mark the beginning and the ending with quotation marks.
3. Carefully record each quotation. Check your copy—word by word—for accuracy.
4. Record the exact number of the page where the quotation appears in the source. If it falls on two pages, note both, marking where the page turns.

▨ For more on quotations and ellipsis marks, see C3 in the Quick Editing Guide (the dark-blue-edged pages).

Sometimes it doesn't pay to transcribe a long quotation word for word. Parts may fail to serve your purpose, such as transitions, parenthetical remarks, and irrelevant information. If you take out one or more words, indicate the omission in your note by using an ellipsis mark (. . .).

PARAPHRASING

▨ For more about paraphrasing sources, see D4 and D6 in the Quick Research Guide (the dark-red-edged pages).

When paraphrasing, you restate an author's ideas in your own words. Simply try to express them fairly and accurately. Avoid judging, interpreting, or hovering so close to them that your paraphrase is merely an echo of the original. A good paraphrase retains the organization, emphasis, and often many of the details of the original, so it may not be much shorter. Even so, paraphrasing is useful when the language of another writer is not particularly memorable, but you want to walk your readers through the points made in the original source. (See Figure 30.2 for an example of a note card paraphrasing a source.)

ORIGINAL	"In staging an ancient Greek tragedy today, most directors do not mask the actors."
TOO CLOSE TO THE ORIGINAL	Most directors, in staging an ancient Greek play today, do not mask the actors.
A GOOD PARAPHRASE	Few contemporary directors of Greek tragedy insist that their actors wear masks.

Children and sports   Leonard 140

Stress and anxiety on the playing field can result in
children backing away from participating in sports
because they fear rejection if they perform poorly.
This anxiety and stress is a result of the child's
fears of being hurt or not being good enough. A
study by Scanlan and Passer confirms these findings, showing that boys who lose in soccer have
more anxiety after losing a game than boys who
win.

Figure 30.2   *A sample note card paraphrasing the*
quotation from Leonard's book (Figure 30.1)

Paraphrase about half
the length of original
passage

Emphasis of original
maintained with word
choice and order re-
worked to avoid
plagiarism

No interpretation or
evaluation of original
passage included

WRITING A GOOD PARAPHRASE

1. Read the entire passage through several times.
2. Divide the passage into its most important ideas or points, either in your mind or by highlighting or annotating the page. Noting three or four points for each paragraph will make the task manageable.
3. Look away from the original, and restate the first idea in your own words. Sum up the support for this idea. Review the section if necessary.
4. Go on to the next idea, and follow the same procedure. Continue in this way until you reach the last point.
5. Go back and reread the entire original passage one more time, making sure you've conveyed its ideas faithfully but without repeating its words or sentence structure. Revise your paraphrase if necessary.

SUMMARIZING

Sometimes a paraphrase will unneccessarily use up space or disrupt the flow of your own ideas. Often all you need is a summary that conveys the main point of a source "in a nutshell." Summarizing alerts your readers to the most important ideas of a passage by restating them in your own words. This strategy can save a lot of space, distilling a page or more of detailed text into one or two succinct sentences. Be careful, though, that in reducing a long passage you do not distort the original meaning or emphasis. (See Figure 30.3 for an example of a note card summarizing a source.)

WRITING A GOOD SUMMARY

1. Read the original passage several times.
2. Without looking back at the passage, state the gist of it, its central point or the main sense as you remember it.
3. Reread the original passage one more time, making sure you've conveyed its ideas faithfully. Revise your summary if necessary.

■ For more about sum-
marizing, see D5 and D6
in the Quick Research
Guide (the dark-red-
edged pages). For an
extended summary of a
literary work, see pp.
211–12.

Figure 30.3   A sample note card summarizing a source

Subject heading

Identifier: person interviewed and date

Main points clearly broken out

Terse, even fragmentary, notes convey gist of key point in the interview

Reasons for moving to Las Animas	Aaron Sanchez Interview, 3-11-04

In 1964, my father Octavio and his family (father, mother, four brothers, three sisters) moved to Las Animas because they couldn't make enough money where they were living in New Mexico. The inheritance from his mother's father went to her brothers, and she got nothing. They moved to the Las Animas region, settling in a <u>colonia</u> (labor camp).

Learning to select appropriate quotations and to write useful paraphrases and summaries takes time and practice. Use the following questions to help you improve these research skills:

RESEARCH CHECKLIST

Taking Notes with Quotations, Paraphrases, and Summaries

___ For each research note, have you identified the source (by the author's last name or a key word from the title) and the exact page? Have you added a subject heading to each note?

___ Have you made a companion bibliography card or note for each new source you discovered during your reading?

___ Have you remained true to the meaning of the original source?

___ Have you quoted sparingly — selecting striking, short passages?

___ Have you quoted sources exactly? Do you use quotation marks around significant words, phrases, and passages from the original sources? Do you use ellipsis marks as needed to show where any words are omitted?

___ Are most notes in your own words — paraphrasing or summarizing?

___ Have you avoided paraphrasing too close to the source?

■ To practice quoting, paraphrasing, and summarizing, visit <bedfordstmartins.com/bedguide> and do a keyword search:

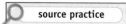
source practice

Capturing Source Material in Your Paper

Once you have written out a note, it's a great temptation to include it in your paper at all costs. Resist. Include only material that answers your research question and supports your thesis. A note dragged in by force always sticks out like a pig in the belly of a boa constrictor.

Use Sources (and Don't Let Them Use You).   When material fits, consider how to incorporate it. As we've just discussed, quoting reproduces an author's exact words. Paraphrasing restates an author's ideas in your own words. Summarizing extracts the essence of an author's meaning and states it "in a nutshell." Besides using these methods as you record your notes, you face the challenge of using them to capture and incorporate source materials into your paper.

■ For more on quoting, paraphrasing, and summarizing, see pp. 607–10 and section D in the Quick Research Guide (the dark-red-edged pages).

SUMMARIZE IN A NUTSHELL

To illustrate how summarizing can serve you, let's first look at a passage from historian Barbara W. Tuchman. In *The Distant Mirror: The Calamitous Fourteenth Century* (New York: Knopf, 1978), Tuchman sets forth the effects of the famous plague known as the Black Death. In her foreword, she admits that any historian dealing with the Middle Ages faces difficulties. For one, large gaps exist in the recorded information. Here is Tuchman's original wording:

ORIGINAL

A greater hazard, built into the very nature of recorded history, is overload of the negative: the disproportionate survival of the bad side — of evil, misery, contention, and harm. In history this is exactly the same as in the daily newspaper. The normal does not make news. History is made by the documents that survive, and these lean heavily on crisis and calamity, crime and misbehavior, because such things are the subject matter of the documentary process — of lawsuits, treaties, moralists' denunciations, literary satire, papal Bulls. No Pope ever issued a Bull to approve of something. Negative overload can be seen at work in the religious reformer Nicolas de Clamanges, who, in denouncing unfit and worldly prelates in 1401, said that in his anxiety for reform he would not discuss the good clerics because "they do not count beside the perverse men."

Disaster is rarely as pervasive as it seems from recorded accounts. The fact of being on the record makes it appear continuous and ubiquitous whereas it is more likely to have been sporadic both in time and place. Besides, persistence of the normal is usually greater than the effect of disturbance, as we know from our own times. After absorbing the news of today, one expects to face a world consisting entirely of strikes, crimes, power failures, broken water mains, stalled trains, school shutdowns, muggers, drug addicts, neo-Nazis, and rapists. The fact is that one can come home in the evening — on a lucky day — without having encountered more than one or two of these phenomena.

This passage might be summarized as follows:

SUMMARY

Tuchman reminds us that history lays stress on misery and misdeeds because these negative events attracted notice in their time and so were reported in writing; just as in a newspaper today, bad news predominates. But we should remember that suffering and social upheaval didn't prevail everywhere all the time (xviii).

As you can see, this summary merely abstracts from the original. Not everything has been preserved—not Tuchman's thought about papal bulls, not examples such as Nicolas de Clamanges or the modern neo-Nazis. But the gist—the summary of the main idea—echoes Tuchman faithfully.

Before you write a summary, an effective way to sense the gist of a passage is to pare away examples, details, modifiers, offhand remarks, and nonessential points. Following is the original quotation from Tuchman as one student marked it up on a photocopy, crossing out elements she decided to omit from her summary.

A greater hazard, built into the very nature of recorded history, is overload of the negative: the disproportionate survival of the bad side—of evil, misery, contention, and harm. In history this is exactly the same as in the daily newspaper. The normal does not make news. History is made by the documents that survive, and these lean heavily on crisis and calamity, crime and misbehavior, because such things are the subject matter of the documentary process—of lawsuits, treaties, moralists' denunciations, literary satire, papal Bulls. No Pope ever issued a Bull to approve of something. Negative overload can be seen at work in the religious reformer Nicolas de Clamanges, who, in denouncing unfit and worldly prelates in 1401, said that in his anxiety for reform he would not discuss the good clerics because "they do not count beside the perverse men."

Disaster is rarely as pervasive as it seems from recorded accounts. The fact of being on the record makes it appear continuous and ubiquitous whereas it is more likely to have been sporadic both in time and place. Besides, persistence of the normal is usually greater than the effect of disturbance, as we know from our own times. After absorbing the news of today, one expects to face a world consisting entirely of strikes, crimes, power failures, broken water mains, stalled trains, school shutdowns, muggers, drug addicts, neo Nazis, and rapists. The fact is that one can come home in the evening—on a lucky day—without having encountered more than one or two of these phenomena.

Rewording what was left, she wrote the following condensed version:

SUMMARY

History, like a daily newspaper, reports more bad than good. Why? Because the documents that have come down to us tend to deal with upheavals and disturbances, which are seldom as extensive and long-lasting as history books might lead us to believe (Tuchman xviii).

In writing her summary, the student couldn't simply omit the words she had deleted. The result would have been less readable and still long. She knew she couldn't use Tuchman's very words: that would be plagiarism. To make a compact, honest summary that would fit smoothly into her paper, she had to condense the passage into her own words.

PARAPHRASE IN YOUR OWN WORDS

Sometimes you want to include more than the essence of a source in your paper, restating the details of an author's ideas in your own words. In the following paraphrase of Tuchman's passage, notice how the writer has put Tuchman's ideas into other words but retained her major points and given her credit for the ideas.

PARAPHRASE

Tuchman points out that historians find some distortion of the truth hard to avoid, for more documentation exists for crimes, suffering, and calamities than for the events of ordinary life. As a result, history may overemphasize the negative. The author reminds us that we are familiar with this process from our contemporary newspapers, in which bad news is played up as being of greater interest than good news. If we believed that newspapers told all the truth, we would think ourselves threatened at all times by technical failures, strikes, crime, and violence--but we are threatened only some of the time, and normal life goes on. The good, dull, ordinary parts of our lives do not make the front page, and praiseworthy things tend to be ignored. "No Pope," says Tuchman, "ever issued a Bull to approve of something." But in truth, social upheaval did not prevail as widely as we might think from the surviving documents of medieval life. Nor, the author observes, can we agree with a critic of the church, Nicolas de Clamanges, in whose view evildoers in the clergy mattered more than men of goodwill (xviii).

In this reasonably complete and accurate paraphrase, about three-quarters the length of the original, most of Tuchman's points have been preserved and spelled out fully. The writer doesn't interpret or evaluate Tuchman's ideas — she only passes them on. Paraphrasing enables her to emphasize ideas important to her research. It also makes readers more aware of them as support for her thesis than if the whole passage had been quoted directly. But notice that the writer has kept Tuchman's remark about papal bulls as a direct quotation because that statement is short and memorable, and it would be hard to improve on her words.

Often you paraphrase to emphasize one essential point. Here is an original passage from Evelyn Underhill's classic study *Mysticism* (New York: Doubleday, 1990):

ORIGINAL

In the evidence given during the process for St. Teresa's beatification, Maria de San Francisco of Medina, one of her early nuns, stated that on entering the saint's cell whilst she was writing this same "Interior Castle" she found her [St. Teresa] so absorbed in contemplation as to be unaware of the external world. "If we made a noise close to her," said another, Maria del Nacimiento, "she neither ceased to write nor complained of being disturbed." Both these nuns, and also Ana de la Encarnacion, prioress of Granada, affirmed that she wrote with immense speed, never stopping to erase or to correct, being anxious, as she said, to write what the Lord had given her before she forgot it.

Suppose that the names of the witnesses do not matter but that the researcher wishes to emphasize, in fewer words, the celebrated mystic's writing habits. To bring out that point, the writer might paraphrase the passage (and quote it in part) like this:

PARAPHRASE WITH QUOTATION

Evelyn Underhill has recalled the testimony of those who saw St. Teresa at work on The Interior Castle. Oblivious to noise, the celebrated mystic appeared to write in a state of complete absorption, driving her pen "with immense speed, never stopping to erase or to correct, being anxious, as she said, to write what the Lord had given her before she forgot it" (242).

Avoiding Plagiarism

■ For more on avoiding plagiarism and using accepted methods of adding source material, see D1 in the Quick Research Guide (the dark-red-edged pages).

Here is a point we can't stress too strongly: when you write, never lift another writer's words or ideas without giving that writer due credit and transforming them into words of your own. If you do use words or ideas without giving credit, you are plagiarizing. You have seen in this chapter examples of honest summarizing and paraphrasing. Introducing them into a paper, a writer would clearly indicate that their ideas belong to the originator, Barbara Tuchman or Evelyn Underhill. Now here are a few horrible examples — paraphrases of Tuchman's passage that lift, without thanks, her ideas and even her very words. Finding such gross borrowings in a paper, an instructor might hear the ringing of a burglar alarm. The first example lifts both thoughts and words.

PLAGIARIZED THOUGHTS AND WORDS

■ For Tuchman's original passage, see p. 611.

Sometimes it's difficult for historians to learn the truth about the everyday lives of people from past societies because of the disproportionate survival of the bad side of things. Historical documents, like today's newspapers, tend to lean rather heavily on crisis, crime, and misbehavior. Reading the newspaper could lead one to expect a world consisting entirely of strikes, crimes, power failures, muggers, drug addicts, and rapists. In fact, though, disaster is rarely so pervasive as recorded accounts can make it seem.

What are the problems here? The phrase "the disproportionate survival of the bad side" is quoted directly from Tuchman's passage (line 2). The series "crisis, crime, and misbehavior" is too close to Tuchman's series "crisis and calamity, crime and misbehavior" (lines 5–6); only the words "and calamity" have been omitted. The words "lead one to expect a world consisting entirely" is almost the same as the original "one expects to face a world consisting entirely" (line 18). The phrase "strikes, crimes, power failures, muggers, drug addicts, and rapists" simply records — and in the same order — six of Tuchman's ten examples (lines 18–20). The last sentence in the plagiarized passage ("In fact, though, disaster is rarely so pervasive as recorded accounts can make it seem") is almost the same as the first sentence of Tuchman's second paragraph ("Disaster is rarely as pervasive as it seems from recorded accounts").

The student who attempted this paraphrase failed to comprehend the passage well enough to put Tuchman's ideas in his or her own words. Remember that taking useful notes from a source is a process of both understanding what you read and writing thoughtful notes that accurately convey the ideas of the source. In addition, successful research papers often require realistic scheduling and consistent maintenance of a research archive. Students who allow enough time to read, to think, and to write are likely to handle sources more effectively than those who procrastinate or rush through the research process.

For more on managing a research project, see Ch. 27.

This next example is a more subtle theft, lifting thoughts but not words.

PLAGIARIZED THOUGHTS

It's not always easy to determine the truth about the everyday lives of people from past societies because bad news gets recorded a lot more frequently than good news does. Historical documents, like today's newspapers, tend to pick up on malice and disaster and ignore flat normality. If I were to base my opinion of the world on what I see on the seven o'clock news, I would expect to see death and destruction around me all the time. Actually, though, I rarely come up against true disaster.

By using the first-person pronoun *I*, this student suggests that Tuchman's ideas are his own. That is just as dishonest as quoting without using quotation marks, as reprehensible as not citing the source of ideas.

The next example fails to make clear which ideas belong to the writer and which belong to Tuchman.

PLAGIARIZED WITH FAULTY CREDIT

Barbara Tuchman explains that it can be difficult for historians to learn about the everyday lives of people who lived a long time ago because historical documents tend to record only the bad news. Today's newspapers are like that, too: disaster, malice, and confusion take up a lot more room on the front page than happiness and serenity. Just as the ins and outs of our everyday lives go unreported, we can suspect that upheavals do not really play so important a part in the making of history as they seem to do.

■ For more on launching, capturing, and citing source material, see D6 in the Quick Research Guide (the dark-red-edged pages). For more on quotation marks, ellipses, and brackets, see C3 in the Quick Editing Guide (the dark-blue-edged pages).

After rightfully attributing the ideas in the first sentence to Tuchman, the student researcher makes a comparison to today's world in sentence 2. Then in sentence 3, she returns to Tuchman's ideas without giving Tuchman credit. The placement of the final sentence suggests that this last idea is the student's whereas it is really Tuchman's.

As you write your paper, use ideas and words from your sources carefully, and credit those sources. Supply introductory and transitional comments to launch and attribute quotations, paraphrases, and summaries to the original source ("As Tuchman observes . . ."). Whenever possible, help readers understand why you have selected your particular sources, why you find their evidence pertinent, or how they support your conclusions:

- Mention the author's name in the text to alert readers to the source of a quotation or paraphrase that follows: "According to Paula Dwight, . . ."

- Follow a quotation or paraphrase with your attribution to the author, perhaps using it as a transition to your own interpretation: ". . . or so Chen affirms. In my own view . . .".

- Add an author's background or credentials when pertinent: "As Randi Salten, president of the local teachers' organization, mentioned during the school board meeting, . . ."

- Note an author's professional expertise: "In his recent article on high-stakes testing, Raul Martinez, professor of education at Dunlap State College, observes . . ."

- Identify information from your own field research: "When interviewed about the campus disaster plan, Natalie Chan, Director of Campus Services, confirmed . . ."

- Relate one source to another: "Although Campbell identifies the challenges facing nonprofit agencies in an uncertain economy, Norton reports the steps taken by successful organizations, based on her extensive regional survey."

Rely on quotation marks and other punctuation to show exactly which words come from your sources. Use the questions in the following checklist to help you avoid plagiarizing:

RESEARCH CHECKLIST

Avoiding Plagiarism

___ Have you identified the author of material you quote, paraphrase, or summarize? Have you credited the originator of facts and ideas you use?

—— Have you clearly indicated where another writer's ideas stop and yours begin?

—— Have you checked each paraphrase or summary against the original for accuracy? Do you use your own words? Do you avoid wording and sentence structure close to that in the original? Do you avoid misinterpreting or distorting the meaning of the original?

—— Have you checked each quotation against the original for accuracy? Have you used quotation marks for both passages and significant words taken directly from your source?

—— Have you used an ellipsis mark (. . .) to show where you have omitted something from the original? Have you used brackets ([ ]) to indicate your changes or additions in a quotation? Have you avoided distorting the meaning of the original?

■ Exercise

Paraphrasing

Study one of the following passages until you understand it thoroughly. Then, using your own words, write a paraphrase of the passage. Compare and contrast your version with those of your classmates. With their help, evaluate your own version: What are its strengths and weaknesses? Where should it be revised?

■ For more exercises on incorporating sources, visit <bedfordstmartins.com/ bedguide> and do a keyword search:

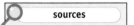
sources

PASSAGE 1

Within the next decades education will change more than it has changed since the modern school was created by the printed book over three hundred years ago. An economy in which knowledge is becoming the true capital and the premier wealth-producing resource makes new and stringent demands on the schools for educational performance and educational responsibility. A society dominated by knowledge workers makes even newer — and even more stringent — demands for social performance and social responsibility. Once again we will have to think through what an educated person is. At the same time, how we learn and how we teach are changing drastically and fast — the result, in part, of new theoretical understanding of the learning process, in part of new technology. Finally, many of the traditional disciplines of the schools are becoming sterile, if not obsolescent. We thus also face changes in what we learn and teach and, indeed, in what we mean by knowledge.

—— Peter F. Drucker, *The New Realities*

PASSAGE 2

When I look to the future of humanity beyond the twenty-first century, I see on my list of things to come the extension of our inquisitiveness from the objective domain of science to the subjective domain of feeling and memory. Homo sapiens, the exploring animal, will not be content with merely physical exploration. Our curiosity will drive us to explore the dimensions of the mind as vigorously as we explore the dimensions of space and time. For every pioneer who explores a new asteroid or a new planet, there will be another pioneer who explores from the inside the minds of our fellow passengers on planet Earth. It is our nature to strive to explore everything, alive and dead, present and past and future. When once the technology exists to read and write memories from one mind into another, the age of mental exploration will begin in earnest. Instead of admiring the beauties of nature from the outside, we will look at nature directly through the eyes of the elephant, the eagle, and the whale. We will be able, through the magic of science, to feel in our own minds the pride of the peacock and the wrath of the lion. That magic is no greater than the magic that enables me to see the rocking horse through the eyes of the child who rode it sixty years ago.

— Freeman Dyson, *Infinite in All Directions*

Chapter 31
Writing Your Research Paper

Planning and Drafting

You began gathering material from library, Internet, and field sources with a question in mind. By now, if your research has been thorough and fruitful, you know your answer. The moment has come to weave together the material you have gathered. We can vouch for two time-proven methods.

The Thesis Method.   Decide what your research has led you to believe. What does it all mean? Sum up that view in a sentence. That sentence is your thesis, the one main idea your paper will demonstrate. You can then start planning and drafting, including only material that supports your thesis, concentrating from beginning to end on making that thesis clear.

For advice on stating and using a thesis, see pp. 271–77.

The Answer Method.   Some writers have an easier time if they plunge in and start writing without first stating any thesis at all. If you try this method, recall your original research question. Start writing with the purpose of answering it, lining up evidence as you go and discovering what you want to say as you write. (Note that this method usually requires more revising than the thesis method.)

For revision strategies, see Ch. 19.

MOVING FROM NOTES TO OUTLINE TO DRAFT

Your source notes are only the raw material for your research paper. If these nuggets are to end up in a readable, unified whole, you need to put them into the proper setting, shaping and finely polishing them. Sometimes you can copy your notes verbatim into your first draft. But usually you need to rewrite, fitting them in so they don't stand out like boulders in the stream of your prose. Moving from the nuggets of information in your notes to a

619

smooth, persuasive analysis or argument is the most challenging part of the research process — and, ironically, the part on which we can give the least concrete advice. Every writer's habits of mind are different. Even so, you'll probably cycle again and again through four basic activities:

- Interpreting your sources
- Refining your thesis
- Organizing your ideas
- Putting your thoughts into the form of a draft

For more on evidence, see pp. 35–40 and section A in the Quick Research Guide (the dark-red-edged pages).

Interpreting Your Sources.   On their own, your source notes are only pieces of information. They need your interpretation to transform them into effective evidence. As a researcher and writer, you have to think critically about each fact. What does it mean in the context of your paper? Is it strong enough to bear the weight of the claim you're going to base on it? Do you need supplemental evidence to shore up an interesting but possibly ambiguous fact?

You'll also need to synthesize your sources and evidence, to weave them into a unified whole. If you've been guided by a research question or a working thesis, you may find this synthesis fairly easy. You know what the question is; you know what the general answer is; you just need to let the pieces fall into place. If your question or thesis has changed, perhaps because you have unearthed persuasive information at odds with your original direction, consider these questions:

- Taken as a whole, what does all this information mean?
- What does it actually tell you about your topic?
- What's the most important thing you've learned?
- What's the most important thing you can tell your readers?

For more on stating and using a thesis, see pp. 271–77.

Refining Your Thesis.   A thesis is a clear, precise statement of the point you want to make in your paper. It will help you decide what to say and how to say it. If your thesis is clear to your readers, it will help them interpret what you present by letting them know in advance the scope of your paper and your general message.

Explicitly stating your thesis as the first or last sentence in your opening paragraph is only one option. Sometimes you can craft your opening so that your readers know exactly what your thesis is even though you only imply it. (Check with your instructor if you're unsure whether an implicit thesis statement will be acceptable.)

If you haven't developed a thesis yet, now is the time to write one. If you've used a working thesis to guide your research, sharpen and refine it before you start drafting. Later you may need to change it even further, but a clear thesis will guide you in organizing and expressing your ideas.

Outlining and Organizing Your Draft

Word processors often offer an outline tool in the View menu. As you think critically about your organization, you can assign outline levels to your headings or to individual paragraphs, letting the word processor automatically fashion your sequence in outline form. After you have outlined your text, you can display headings by hiding text or manipulate text while you reorganize your thinking.

WRITING WITH A COMPUTER

You can also use the computer to develop a personalized system of coding using bold, italics, underlining, color, or other highlighting. Some writers like to organize their ideas around italicized questions, while others prefer bold headings. Some use a color scheme to show pro and con thinking; others highlight their main pro and con points. Think about the features on a computer that can make your ideas more visual and easier to organize.

In your thesis, try to be precise and concrete, and don't claim more than you can demonstrate in your paper. If your paper is argumentative—that is, if you take a stand, propose a solution, or evaluate something—then you should make your stand, solution, or appraisal clear.

TOPIC	Americans' attitudes toward sports
RESEARCH QUESTION	Is America obsessed with sports?
THESIS	The national obsession with sports must end.

Organizing Your Ideas. In writing your paper, it isn't enough to describe the steps you took in answering your research question or to string data together in chronological order. You aren't writing a memoir; you're reporting the significance of what you found out. Put your material together in various combinations until you arrive at an organization that fulfills your purpose.

For more on organizing and developing ideas, see Chs. 16 and 18.

If you began with a clear research question, you will not have much difficulty selecting and organizing your evidence to answer it. But research questions often change. Don't be afraid to ditch an original question that no longer works and to reorganize around a newly formed question.

For more on research questions, see pp. 553–55.

If your material seems to resist taking shape, you might arrange your notes, whether cards or computer file entries, in an order that makes sense. Then the sequence of these notes becomes a plan you can follow as you write. Or you can write out an informal or formal outline on paper or on the computer.

For more on outlining, see pp. 280–87.

Beginning to Draft. An outline is only a skeleton until you flesh it out with details. Use your outline as a working plan, but change the subdivisions or the order of the parts if you discover a better way as you draft. Compare each section of your outline with the notes you have on hand for it. If for a certain section you lack notes, reconsider your plan or return to the library, the Internet, or the field to fill the gap in your research. Even if everything hasn't fallen into perfect order, start writing anyway. Get something down on paper so that you will have something to revise. And remember that you don't have to start at the beginning; start wherever you feel most comfortable.

As you write, cultivate a certain detachment rather than swaggering in triumph over what you have discovered. Make no exorbitant claims for what you have discovered ("Thus I have shown that day-care centers deserve the trust of parents in the state of Washington"). You have probably not answered your research question for all time; you need not claim to be irrefutable.

■ For more strategies for drafting, see Ch. 17.

Try to make the connections between parts of your paper clear. For example, summarizing the previous section of your paper will remind your reader of what you have already said. This strategy is especially handy in a long paper when, after a few pages, readers' memories may need refreshing.

DOCUMENTING YOUR SOURCES AS YOU DRAFT

Right after every idea, fact, summary, and paraphrase you've drawn from your reading or field research, you need to refer your readers to the exact source of your material. Citing your sources as you draft saves fuss when you're putting your paper into final form. And it prevents unintentional plagiarism.

■ For more on documenting sources, see Ch. 32. For advice on integrating sources and avoiding plagiarism, see Ch. 3.

If you are following MLA style, note in your draft, right after each borrowed item, the name of the author and the page of the book or article you took it from. If you are quoting a field source, include the name of the person speaking, if any. If you're using two or more works by the same author, you need to add one more detail to tell them apart: the first word or words from the title will do.

An assassin outrages us not only by his deed but also by his unacceptable reason for violence. Nearly as offensive as his act of wounding President Reagan was Hinckley's explanation that he fired in order to impress screen star Jodie Foster (Szasz, "Intentionality," 5).

The title in parentheses is short for "Intentionality and Insanity," distinguishing that article by Thomas Szasz from another work by Szasz that the writer also cites — *The Myth of Mental Illness.*

When you include a direct quotation in your draft, you might as well save copying time. If your note is in a computer file, you can just copy the passage from the file and paste it right where you want it in your draft file. If it is on a note card, you can just tape the whole card into a handwritten or printed draft. If your draft looks sloppy, who cares?

As you lay the quotation into place, add a few words to introduce it. A brief transition might go something like this: *A more negative view of standardized intelligence tests is that of Harry S. Baum, director of the Sooner Research*

Center. Then comes Baum's opinion that IQ tests aren't very reliable. The transition announces why Baum will be quoted — to refute a previous quotation in favor of IQ tests. The transition, brief as it is, also tells readers a little about Baum by including his professional title. Knowing that he is a recognized authority would probably make readers willing to accept his expert view.

If no transition occurs to you as you are placing a quotation or borrowed idea into your draft, don't sit around waiting for one. A series of slapped-in summaries and quotations makes rough reading, but you can write a note to yourself in the margin or in brackets that you'll need to add a transition. Keep writing while the spirit moves you along; later, when you rewrite, you can add connective tissue.

For more on transitions, see pp. 300–03.

BEGINNING AND ENDING

Perhaps you will think of a good beginning and conclusion only after you have written the body of your paper. The head and tail of your paper might simply make clear your conclusion about whatever you have found out. But that is not the only way to begin and end a research paper.

For exercises on opening and concluding writing, visit <bedfordstmartins.com/bedguide> and do a keyword search:

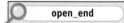
open_end

Build to Your Finish.   Depending on the kind of paper you are writing, you might prefer to start out slowly by opening with a clear account of an event to draw your readers into the paper. You could then build up to a strong finish, saving your strongest argument until the end — after you have had the chance to present all the evidence to support your thesis. For example, if your paper argues that American children are being harmed by the national obsession with sports, you might organize your paper something like this:

- Begin with a factual account of a real event, putting you and your reader on the same footing.
- Explore that event's implications to prepare your reader for your view.
- State your thesis (main idea): for example, "The national obsession with sports must end."
- Support your thesis with evidence and well-chosen sources, moving to your strongest argument.
- Then end with a rousing call to action:

    For the sake of our children and the future of our country, isn't it time that we put the brakes on America's sports mania? The youth of America have been sold a false and harmful bill of goods. Let's stop such madness and step off the carousel now. We owe that to the children of America and to ourselves.

Sum Up the Findings of Others.   Still another way to begin a research paper is to summarize the work of other scholars. One research biologist, Edgar F. Warner, has reduced this time-tested opening to a formula.

First, in one or two paragraphs, you review everything that has been said about your topic, naming the most prominent earlier commentators. Next you declare why all of them are wrong. Then you set forth your own claim, and you spend the rest of your paper supporting it.

That pattern may seem cut and dried, but it is clear and useful because it places your research and ideas into a historical and conceptual framework. If you browse in specialized journals in many fields — literary criticism, social studies, sciences — you may be surprised to see how many articles begin this very way. Of course, one or two other writers may be enough to argue with. For example, a student writing on the American poet Charles Olson starts her research paper by disputing two views of him.

To Cid Corman, Charles Olson of Gloucester, Massachusetts, is "the one dynamic and original epic poet twentieth-century America has produced" (116). To Allen Tate, Olson is "a loquacious charlatan" (McFinnery 92). The truth lies between these two extremes, nearer to Corman's view.

For more strategies for opening and concluding, see pp. 294–98.

Whether or not you fully stated your view at the beginning, you will certainly need to make it clear in your closing paragraph. A suggestion: before writing the last lines of your paper, read over what you have written. Then, without referring to your paper, try to put your view into writing.

Revising and Editing

For more revising and editing strategies, see Ch. 19.

Looking over your draft, you may find your essay changing. Don't be afraid to develop a whole new interpretation, shift the organization, strengthen your evidence, drop a section, or add a new one. Answering these questions may help you see how to improve your draft:

REVISION CHECKLIST

___ Have you honestly said something, not just heaped facts and statements by other writers that don't add up to anything?

___ Is your thesis (main idea) clear?

___ Have you included only evidence that makes a point? Do all your points support your main idea?

___ Does each new idea or piece of information follow from the one before it? Can you see any stronger order in which to arrange things? Have you provided transitions to connect the parts?

___ Do you need more — or better — evidence to back up any point? If so, where might you find it?

___ Are the words that you quote truly memorable? Are your paraphrases and summaries accurate and clear?

—— Is the source of every quotation, every fact, every idea you have borrowed made unmistakably clear?

After you have revised your research paper, edit and proofread it. Carefully check the grammar, word choice, punctuation, and mechanics — and then correct any problems you may find. Be sure you check your documentation, too — how you identify the sources of quotations and how you list the works you have cited in your paper. Here are some questions to get you started editing and proofreading your paper:

EDITING CHECKLIST

—— Have you used commas correctly, especially in complicated sentences that quote or refer to sources?	C1
—— Have you punctuated quotations correctly?	C3
—— Have you used capital letters correctly, especially in titles of sources?	D1
—— Have you used correct manuscript form?	E1
—— Have you used correct documentation style?	

▓ For more help, turn to the dark-blue-edged pages, and find the Quick Editing Guide sections noted here.

▓ For more on documentation, see Ch. 32.

FOR PEER RESPONSE

Have a classmate or friend read your draft and suggest how you might make your paper more informative, tightly reasoned, and interesting. Ask your peer editor to answer questions such as these about writing from sources:

- What is your overall reaction to this paper?

- What do you see as the research question? Does the writer answer that question?

- How effective is the opening? Does it draw you into the paper?

- How effective is the conclusion? Does it merely restate the introduction? Is it too abrupt or too hurried?

- Is the organization logical and easy to follow? Are there any places where the essay is hard to follow?

- Do you know which information is from the writer and which is from the research sources?

- Does the writer need all the quotations he or she has used?

- Do you have any questions about the writer's evidence or the conclusions drawn from the evidence? Point out any areas where the writer has not fully backed up his or her conclusions.

- If this were your paper, what is the one thing you would be sure to work on before handing it in?

For general questions for a peer editor, see pp. 328–29.

WRITING WITH A COMPUTER

Revising a Research Paper

To help you step back from a draft, begin by duplicating your file. (Use a command such as Save As or Versions from the File menu.) This step is important because it will enable you to experiment without losing your existing draft. Your software may also have a useful resource such as Track Changes in the Tools menu. By using colors and cross-outs to highlight text and record comments, this resource allows you to see the changes you make in a text. It can even automatically compare documents so that you can see how much your revision has changed from the previous draft.

Documenting Sources

For more on documenting sources, see Ch. 32.

A research paper calls on you to follow special rules in documenting your sources — in citing them as you write and in listing them at the end of your paper. At first, these rules may seem fiendishly fussy, but research papers that follow the rules are easy to read and easy to set into type. The rules also ensure that any interested reader can use complete and accurate source information to look up the original materials.

For more on using these styles, see pp. 641–55 (MLA) or pp. 655–63 (APA).

In humanities courses and the social sciences, most writers of research papers follow the style of the Modern Language Association (MLA) or the American Psychological Association (APA). Your instructor will probably suggest which style to follow; if you are not told, use MLA. The first time you prepare a research paper according to MLA or APA rules, you'll need extra time to look up exactly what to do in each situation.

CITING SOURCES IN YOUR TEXT

For more on punctuation in quotations, see C3 in the Quick Editing Guide (the dark-blue-edged pages).

For exercises on citing and listing sources, visit <bedfordstmartins.com/bedguide> and do a keyword search:

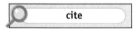
cite

When you use a short direct quotation, four lines or fewer, you must put quotation marks around the words you're using from your source and cite the author and page number. For a quotation longer than four lines, indent the entire quotation in your text, without quotation marks, and also note its source. In both cases, you may include the author's name either in the text of the essay — as in the following example of a short quotation — or in parentheses with the page number at the end of the quotation.

Johnson heavily emphasizes the importance of "giving the child what she needs at the precise moment in her life when it will do the most good" (23).

You also can indicate your source in a terse phrase — "Barbara W. Tuchman believes that ..." or "According to Tuchman ..." — and then give the page number in parentheses after your quotation, paraphrase, or summary.

LISTING SOURCES AT THE END

At the very end of a research paper, you list all the sources you have cited —
books, articles, Web sites, interviews, and other materials. This list is usually the last thing you write. If your working bibliography includes for each
source all the information needed, your list will be easy to construct.
Simply arrange the works you used in alphabetical order and type the
information about each, following the MLA or APA guidelines. The MLA
specifies that you call your list "Works Cited"; the APA, "References." Include only the works actually mentioned in your paper. Simply file away
any leftovers — notes for sources you haven't used after all — for any future
writing about the subject. Resist the temptation to use them to lengthen
your list.

■ For the source infor-
mation you need to
record, see pp. 560–62.

■ For specific MLA and
APA guidelines, see
Ch. 32.

OTHER ASSIGNMENTS

Using library, Internet, and field sources, write a research paper on one of
the following topics or another that your instructor approves. Proceed as if
you had chosen to work on the main assignment described on page 550.

1. Investigate the career opportunities in a line of work that interests you.
   Include data from interviews conducted with people in the field.
2. Write a paper discussing the progress being made in the prevention and
   cure of a disease or syndrome, including current data.
3. Discuss recent political or economic changes in another country.
4. Compare student achievement in schools with different characteristics —
   for example, those with limited or extensive computer access or those
   with low and high numbers of students who move.
5. Study the growth of telecommuting — people working in their homes
   and keeping in touch with the main office by phone, fax, and e-mail.
6. Write a portrait of life in your town or neighborhood as it was in the
   past, using sources such as local library archives, photographs or other
   visual evidence, articles in the local newspaper, and interviews with
   long-time residents or a local historian.
7. Write a short history of your immediate family, drawing on interviews,
   photographs, scrapbooks, old letters, unpublished records, and any
   other available sources.
8. Study the reasons students today give for going to college. Gather your
   information from interviews with a variety of students at your college
   and possibly from questionnaires.
9. Investigate a current trend you have noticed on television, collecting evidence by observing news shows, other programs, or commercials.
10. Write a survey of recent films of a certain kind (such as horror movies,
    comedies, or love stories), supporting your generalizations with evi-
    dence from your film watching.

WRITING WITH A COMPUTER

Using Software to Document Sources

Programs such as *Citation, EndNote, Reference Manager,* and *Pro Cite* can help you to build a database of bibliographic information and generate citations in the style required by your instructor. You can also go to <www.mla.org> or <www.apa.org/journals> to get advice and style updates for the MLA and APA documentation styles.

Applying What You Learn: Some Uses of Research

In College Courses.   In many courses beyond your English course, you will be asked to write papers incorporating library, Internet, and field research.

- Some courses require short papers using a few sources rather than a full research project, but instructors still expect you to use all your research skills — finding, evaluating, and documenting relevant sources or conducting your own field research.

- The more deeply you move into specialized courses for your major, the more independent research and thinking you will do. Some colleges require a long research paper of all seniors.

- In some courses, you may be asked to prepare a review of the literature or an annotated bibliography on a topic or research question. To do so, you will need to locate, evaluate, and summarize major sources in the field.

In the Workplace.   Many workplaces demand — and value — writing based on research that supports their products and services.

- Large companies often maintain their own specialized libraries because information and opinions are worth money and are necessary for decision-making. If you should take an entry-level job at corporate headquarters, don't be surprised to be told, "We're opening a branch office in Sri Lanka, and the V.P. doesn't know a thing about the place. Can you write a report on it — customs, geography, climate, government, state of the economy, political stability, religion, lifestyle, and all that?"

- If you start your own business, plan to spend time investigating print, electronic, and human resources to determine market segment, growth trends, budgeting, strategic planning, and product development.

- At a large city newspaper, reporters and feature writers continually conduct library and Internet research as well as field interviews and surveys. The newspaper's library of clippings on subjects covered in the past (the "morgue") is in constant use.

In the Community.   Research often benefits you or your community by answering questions, solving problems, or satisfying your curiosity.

- If you oppose plans for a nearby factory that you think might be environmentally unsound, your research on zoning laws and environmental issues will strengthen your appeal to the local planning board.

- As a volunteer at the local women's shelter, you may want to persuade board members to open a second facility by researching other community shelters, citing authoritative sources, and reporting your findings.

- Research can be a great help when you or an organization intends to purchase something — be it a new kitchen for the community center or a new car for yourself.

A Sample Research Paper

In her paper "Is Inclusion the Answer?" Sarah E. Goers grapples with the complex topic of equal access to education for disabled students. By drawing from varied sources, Goers is able to show both sides of the issue while forming her own conclusions. As a result, her paper is more than just a compilation of facts or a string of quotations. Goers sets forth a problem that troubles her, she provides evidence to support her concern, and she adds her own thoughts to the facts and ideas she has gleaned from her research.

Writer's last name, followed by page number in small roman numerals, on upper right corner of all pages of outline

"Outline" centered, one inch from top

Main idea stated in thesis

Double-spacing throughout

Sentence outline providing a skeleton of the research paper

 For more sample student research papers, visit <bedfordstmartins.com/bedguide> and do a keyword search:

🔍 **sample papers**

 ½"

Goers i

Outline

Is Inclusion the Answer?

Thesis: The full inclusion of disabled children into mainstream classrooms may not truly be in the best interest of every student.

I. The practice and degree of inclusion is debated among many groups.

    A. Teacher organizations oppose full inclusion.

        1. The American Federation of Teachers believes that special needs students learn best in separate programs.

        2. The National Education Association favors a combination of general and specialized education.

    B. Some opponents argue that inclusion will negatively affect other groups.

        1. Parents of non-learning disabled students fear that inclusion will result in less academic attention for their children.

        2. Taxpayers argue that inclusion will be too expensive to implement.

    C. Despite the debate, disabled children do have equal rights to free public education.

II. The actual implementation of inclusive practices may have negative consequences.

    A. Without promised federal funding, schools may have to spend general funds on special education, possibly at the expense of other scholastic areas.

    B. General education teachers are often not adequately prepared to accommodate special needs students.

        1. Without proper training, teachers become frustrated, and special education students do not receive the instruction that they need.

        2. General education teachers often do not receive enough assistance from special education teachers.

    C. Resources needed for specialized instruction are often inadequate in public schools.

        1. Public schools often do not employ enough teachers to provide the personalized attention that disabled students need.

        2. Supplemental learning tools are not available in many public schools.

III. Some parents of disabled students and students themselves oppose inclusion.

    A. Children are happy with special education schools, and parents don't want their learning disrupted.

    B. Parents fear that separate schools will close before solid programs are established in general schools.

IV. Pull-out programs have been proposed.

    A. Students experience the general classroom and also receive specialized instruction.

    B. Pull-out programs are subject to the same concerns raised by full inclusion.

        1. Teacher training is still needed.

        2. Adequate resources must be available in general classrooms.

    C. Disabled students deserve respect for their individualized needs.

Writer's last name and page number ¹/₂" from top of page

Writer's name

Instructor's name

Course

Date

Title, centered

▨ For more on beginning a research paper, see pp. 623–24.

Opening definition of "inclusion," citing sources in parentheses

Thesis established

▨ For more on a thesis for a research paper, see p. 619 and pp. 620–21.

Brief overview of paper's development following thesis

Double-spacing throughout

Lecturer's name identifies public address

---

¹/₂"
Goers 1

1"

Sarah E. Goers

Professor Day

English 101

28 January 2004

¹/₂" indent (or 5 spaces)   Is Inclusion the Answer?

    Inclusion is one of the most passionately debated issues in public education today. Full inclusion, defined as placing all students with disabilities in general education classes, has three main components: the integration of special education students into the mainstream classroom, educational planning and programming, and the clarification of responsibility for appropriate instruction (Heinich 292). Although the intent of inclusion is to provide the best care for all children by treating both special and general education students equally, some people in the field believe that the full inclusion of disabled children in mainstream classrooms may not be in the best interest of either type of student. Disabled children will not benefit from a general education program unless the school is prepared to accommodate their needs; if placed in a school where their needs are not met due to low funding, unprepared teachers, or a lack of necessary resources, they most likely will suffer. For these reasons, the merits of full inclusion over partial inclusion or separate programs are questionable.

    Although individual children learn differently, students classified as "special needs" require significantly different types of instruction because of their physical, mental, or emotional state. The degree of differentiated instruction that they require, and how best to provide it, is the basis of the ongoing debate about inclusion. Initially, full inclusion sounds like a wonderful step toward implementing the democratic belief that all people in all environments are to be treated as equals. In her lecture at William Rainey Harper College, however, Barbara Radebaugh explained the positions of the two major national teacher organizations on this issue.

1"

Goers 2

The American Federation of Teachers (AFT) disagrees with full inclusion, believing that special needs students learn best in separate programs where they can receive the specialized instruction their disabilities require. On the other hand, the National Education Association (NEA) favors "appropriate inclusion," a less extreme approach, in which each special needs student would receive a combination of general and special education throughout the school day (Radebaugh). In this way, students would experience the general classroom while still receiving some degree of specialized instruction.

While the teacher organizations debate the benefits of inclusion in terms of how disabled students learn best, other groups oppose inclusion because of how the changes might affect them. At a typical school, if a disabled student were to be placed in general education classrooms, the school would have to undergo changes including teacher training and a larger staff, both to assist the special needs child and to aid other students' adjustment to an inclusive environment (Block 6-7). Some opponents of inclusion include the parents of non-learning disabled students who fear that these changes will result in less attention for their own children and thus slow their academic progress. Other opponents, such as local taxpayers, cite the cost of these changes as reasons against inclusion (Rios).

In response to such arguments, protective laws have been enacted to ensure disabled persons equal access to appropriate public education, regardless of extra cost or others' fears. The Education for All Handicapped Children Act of 1975 mandates that schools must provide free public education to all students with disabilities. The main tenets of the 1975 legislation declare that all learners with handicaps between the ages of three and twenty-one have the right to a free public education and an individualized education program involving both the school and the parents. Also protecting the disabled is the Individuals with Disabilities Education Act (IDEA), which calls for serving children

No page number needed for one-page article

Point from last paragraph used for transition to new topic

Source establishes historical background

Goers 3

with disabilities in the least restrictive environment possible, and Section 504 of the Rehabilitation Act, which guarantees disabled people access to services provided by any institution that receives federal funding (Heinich 293).

Society has made great strides in protecting the rights of disabled students, and inclusion theoretically upholds their right to free and equal education. There is still concern about the actual implementation of inclusive practices, however. In California, for example, journalist Denise Rios explains a situation whereby, as more parents opt to place children with special needs in regular classrooms, "state and education officials are grappling with several issues that could affect the future of special education. At the top of their list is funding." According to Rios, financially strapped school districts use as much as 25% of their general funds to pay for federally mandated special education programs. Officials explain that this high percentage is a result of the federal government's not fulfilling its monetary promises, costing local districts in California about $600 million a year (Rios). Money must be taken from other scholastic areas to supplement the lack of funding designated for special education.

To help offset the expensive cost of integrating disabled students into the regular classroom, California officials contend that the federal government promised to fund 40% of program costs when federal mandates guaranteeing access for special education students were passed in 1975. However, government contribution has actually averaged only 7% or 8% of program costs (Rios). While money ideally should not be an issue when it comes to the well-being of students, the figures in a situation such as this are troubling. Since special education may demand a large amount of the already tight funds that most districts are working with, schools may be forced to use a high percentage of these limited resources on a minority of students, rather than the entire school. Without proper financial support from the government, money unfortunately does become an issue

For more on integrating sources, see Ch. 30.

Credentials of source author noted

Brief quotation specifies critical issue, followed by paraphrase of source

Facts and data support main point

Goers 4

when it threatens to undermine the well-being of the majority of students.

When inclusive practices are implemented, teachers as well as students are forced to undergo dramatic classroom changes. Teachers feel a great deal of pressure in this debate in that many believe that they are not adequately trained to teach students with disabilities effectively. They are concerned that special needs students will therefore not receive the instruction that they need to succeed, and these teachers may be frustrated by their inability to provide appropriate instruction (Block 7). Without significant help from special education teachers in the regular classroom, teachers fear that inclusion could result in disaster due to their frustrations, lack of appropriate training, and students' distraction levels. Linda Jacobson describes the dilemma of general education instruction: "Because special education teachers often float among classes, regular classroom teachers sometimes are left on their own." She also notes the AFT's criticism of inclusive practices when "teachers are promised resources and training to make inclusion work, but school systems often don't deliver."

Community College of Baltimore County professor Beth Hewett finds that while teachers receive information about a specific student's disability and how to offer fair classroom treatment, this information is usually only cursory. She eloquently echoes Jacobson's concerns through firsthand experience:

> Our experiences with these students often are frustrating and unsatisfying because we do not know enough about how to help them. Recognizing our limited knowledge and skills in helping students with disabilities to read and write well, we often flounder and leave teaching situations feeling that we have missed a key opportunity to help a student address a particular challenge. Many of us would welcome rescue through more practical knowledge of the problems, better training to recognize

I" indent (or 10 spaces)

Paraphrase of original source, followed by source in parentheses

Only one citation needed for quotations from the same source that appear in sequence in a paragraph

Credentials of source author noted

Direct quotation longer than four lines set off from text without quotation marks, followed by page numbers in parentheses

Goers 5

and deal with them, and access to technological tools that address special needs. We sense that our students would be equally grateful if we were better prepared. (1-2)

After observing the methods of teachers at the Landmark Institute, a private postsecondary institution renowned for its work with learning disabled students, Jacob Gaskins notes the importance of putting students through a battery of diagnostic testing and then teaching specifically to these diagnoses in a variety of modalities. In an institution like Landmark, with a student/faculty ratio of approximately 3 to 1, teachers are able to tailor their instruction to give students personal attention. The sheer number of teachers, all of whom have training specific to all types of learning disabilities, along with access to, and training in how to use, supplemental learning tools, enables them to meet the wide range of needs and disabilities they encounter (73). Because these resources are not often adequately provided in public schools, however, many teachers wonder if inclusion is truly beneficial for students who have disabilities that require specialized instruction.

Some parents of disabled students and some disabled students themselves also do not agree with full inclusion. Mary Maushard explains in her article "Special Schools Fall Victim to 'Inclusion'" that many disabled students prefer to learn in a special education school because they like the small class sizes, the nurturing staff specifically trained to teach special needs students, the family atmosphere, and the many available specialized services. The parents of these students do not want to disrupt a system which their children are happy with and are afraid that their children will "fall through the cracks" in the general educational system. Unfortunately, many special education schools are being closed due to low enrollment, mainly because those parents who support inclusion have taken their disabled children out of special schools and placed them in regular education classes.

Valuable information paraphrased after naming author earlier in paragraph and noting page number of original source in parentheses

Goers 6

Among parents who do favor inclusion, some nonetheless worry that the country is moving away from special education schools too fast for solid special education programs to be established in the general schools (Maushard).

As a solution, pull-out programs--in which disabled students are in the regular classroom for part of the day and special instruction classes for the remainder of the day--have been suggested. In this way, disabled students would have daily classroom instruction as well as one-on-one instruction. These programs offer a compromise to address the concerns of some educators that the individual needs of disabled students would be neglected when they are integrated into the general classroom (Block 7). However, while ensuring that at least part of the students' day will consist of instruction tailored to their needs, these programs do not ensure that the students' time in the general classroom will be productive. These programs are promising, but only to the extent that the students will also be receiving quality instruction in the general classroom; otherwise, they simply shorten the amount of unproductive classroom time. Thus, there is still a need for teacher training and adequate resources to help meet the needs of disabled students when they are not in the special education classes (Urbina).

Despite individual beliefs about which system is best, we can reasonably assume that the majority of society supports efforts to provide all children with the best possible care and education. When considering inclusion, it is necessary to look at the big picture by considering everyone involved. Unless the school is adequately prepared to provide proper services and meet students' individual needs, inclusion truly may not be the best solution for disabled students. If we want our children to be as successful as they possibly can be, each individual should be assessed and placed where he or she will learn most effectively, whether in a general classroom, a special education classroom, or a combination of both. While many people support inclusion because they

Possible solution or compromise follows various sides of argument

Writer gives credit to source after summarizing the ideas from the source

Electronic sources without page numbers cited only by author

For more on concluding a research paper, see pp. 623–24.

Conclusion summarizes main points and restates thesis

feel that it is wrong to exclude anyone, they must also look at the potential problems inclusion may cause. Disabled students should receive proper respect for their needs without the intrusion of policy, funding, and what others, particularly those who are uninformed about the issue, decide they want.

Goers 8

½"

1"

Works Cited

Block, Martin E. "Did We Jump on the Wrong Bandwagon?
Problems with Inclusion." <u>Palestra</u> 15.3 (1999): 4-10. 10
Dec. 2003 <http://www.palestra.com/Inclusion.html>.

Gaskins, Jacob. "Teaching Writing to Students with Learning
Disabilities: The Landmark Method." <u>Teaching English in the
Two-Year College</u> 22.2 (1995): 71-76.

Heinich, Robert, ed. <u>Educating All Handicapped Children</u>.
Englewood Cliffs: Educational Technology Publications,
1979.

Hewett, Beth. "Helping Students with Learning Disabilities:
Collaboration between Writing Centers and Special
Services." <u>Writing Lab</u> 25.3 (2000): 1-4.

Jacobson, Linda. "Disabled Kids Moving into Regular Classrooms."
<u>Atlanta Journal</u> 5 May 1994: C1.

Maushard, Mary. "Special Schools Fall Victim to 'Inclusion.'" <u>Sun</u>
[Baltimore] 13 June 1993: B1. NewsBank. Boston Public
Lib. 21 Dec. 2003 <http://www.newsbank.com>.

Radebaugh, Barbara. "NEA vs. AFT." Education 201-002 Lecture.
William Rainey Harper Coll., Palatine, IL. 21 Jan. 1999.

Rios, Denise A. "Special Students Joining Regular Classrooms."
<u>Orange County Register</u> 9 June 1994. A24. NewsBank.
Boston Public Lib. 11 Dec. 2003 <http://www.newsbank
.com>.

Urbina, Yolanda. "Full Inclusion of Disabled Children in a Regular
Classroom." 8 Aug. 1998. 15 Dec. 2003 <http://
www.lgc.edu/academic/educatn/yolanda/lai.htm>.

List of works cited on a separate page

List alphabetized by authors' last names

First line of entry at left margin

Subsequent lines indented ½"

For more on listing sources, see Ch. 32.

Documenting Sources

When you use information from other sources—written or spoken—you must *document* those sources.

- In the text of a paper, cite, or identify, the exact source (book or article with page number, person interviewed, television program, Web site) for every fact or idea, paraphrased or quoted, from sources.
- At the end of a paper, list the sources that were cited.

The purpose of citing and listing sources is twofold: (1) to give proper credit to the original writer or speaker and (2) to enable any interested reader to look up a source for further information. The mechanics of documentation may seem fussy, but the obligation to cite and list sources keeps research writers truthful and responsible.

Writers of college research papers most often follow the rules for citing and listing sources from either of two style manuals—one compiled by the Modern Language Association (MLA) and the other by the American Psychological Association (APA). MLA documentation style is generally observed in English composition, literature, history, foreign languages, and other humanities courses. APA documentation style usually prevails in the social sciences and business. If your research takes you into scholarly or professional journals in these areas, you will probably find that the articles follow a recognizable style. Other disciplines follow other style manuals: *Scientific Style and Format: The CBE Style Manual for Authors, Editors, and Publishers of the Council of Biology Editors* (1994), for instance, is used in the sciences and medicine.

You need not memorize any of the documentation styles. Instead, you should understand that you will use different styles in different disciplines, and you need to practice using at least one style to become accustomed to scholarly practices. For your composition course, more than likely your instructor will ask you to use the MLA style. The sample paper in Chapter 31 illustrates the use of this style.

This chapter is here for handy reference. We try to tell you no more than you will need to know to write a first-year research paper. Knowing MLA style or APA style will be useful at these moments:

Citing while you write. You'll use a documentation style any time you want to document (often on a note card or in your paper) exactly where you obtained a fact, statistic, idea, opinion, quotation, graph, or chart.

■ For advice on preparing a list of works cited, see pp. 646–55.

Listing all your sources. You'll use a documentation style when you prepare a final bibliography (a list called "Works Cited" or"References").

Citing Sources: MLA Style

The *MLA Handbook for Writers of Research Papers,* Sixth Edition (New York: MLA, 2003) supplies extensive recommendations for citing sources in your paper and then listing them at the end in a section titled "Works Cited." If you want more detailed advice than that given here, you can purchase a copy of the *MLA Handbook* or consult a copy in the reference room of your college library.

■ For a brief overview of MLA style, see E1 in the Quick Research Guide (the dark-red-edged pages).

PRINTED SOURCES: NONFICTION BOOKS

AUTHOR NOT NAMED IN SENTENCE

To cite a book in the text of your paper, you can place in parentheses the author's last name and the number of the page with the information used.

At least one critic maintains that Dean Rusk's exposure to Nazi power in Europe in the 1930s "scarred his mind, leading him to share Acheson's hostility to appeasement in any form anywhere" (Karnow 194).

AUTHOR NAMED IN SENTENCE

For the sake of readability and transition, you'll sometimes want to mention an author in your text. In this case, put only the page number in parentheses.

Morgan claims that one reason we admire Simone de Beauvoir is that "she lived the life she believed" (58).

AUTHOR UNKNOWN

For a source with an unknown author, use the complete title in your sentence or a word or two from the title in parentheses. If a source is sponsored by a corporation or other group, name the sponsor as the author.

According to a recent study, drivers are 42% more likely to get into an accident if they are using a wireless phone while driving ("Driving Dangerously" 32).

LONG QUOTATION

When a quotation is longer than four typed lines, indent the entire quotation one inch or ten spaces. Double-space it, but don't place quotation marks around it. If the quotation is one paragraph or less, begin its first line without any extra paragraph indentation.

> Cynthia Griffin Wolff comments on Emily Dickinson's incisive use of language:
>
> Language, of course, was a far subtler weapon than a hammer. Dickinson's verbal maneuvers would increasingly reveal immense skill in avoiding a frontal attack; she preferred the silent knife of irony to the strident battering of loud complaint. She had never suffered fools gladly. The little girl who had written of a dull classmate, "He is the silliest creature that ever lived I think," grew into a woman who could deliver wrath and contempt with excruciating economy and cunning. Scarcely submissive, she had acquired the cool calculation of an assassin. (170-71)

TWO OR THREE AUTHORS

Include each author's last name either in your text or in the citation.

Taylor and Wheeler present yet another view (25).

MORE THAN THREE AUTHORS

Give the names of all the authors, or use only the last name of the first author listed, followed by the abbreviation *et al.* (Latin for "and others"). Present the source the same way in your list of works cited.

In the years between 1870 and 1900, the nation's cities grew at an astonishing rate, mostly as a result of internal and international movement of people (Roark et al. 422).

MULTIPLE WORKS BY THE SAME AUTHOR

If you cite two or more works by the same author, use an abbreviated title to indicate which one you are citing in your text. In a paper that uses two books by Ann Charters, *Major Writers of Short Fiction* and *The Story and Its Writer,* you would cite them as follows:

Having done extensive studies of short fiction, Charters believes that "the range and quality of the writer's mind are the only limitations on a story's shape" (Story 3).

One observer notes the changing tide of short fiction, represented in part by the flood of magazine fiction which carries with it "stories of real distinction" (Charters, Major Writers 1408).

A MULTIVOLUME WORK

For a work with multiple volumes, provide the author's name and the volume number, followed by a colon and the page number.

In ancient times, astrological predictions were sometimes used as a kind of black magic (Sarton 2: 319).

INDIRECT SOURCE

Whenever possible, cite the original source. If that source is unavailable to you (as often happens with published accounts of spoken remarks), use the abbreviation *qtd. in* (for "quoted in") before citing the secondary source.

Zill says that, psychologically, children in stepfamilies most resemble children in single-parent families, even if they live in a two-parent household (qtd. in Derber 119).

PRINTED SOURCES: LITERATURE

NOVEL OR SHORT STORY

Give the page number from your own source first. If possible, include further identifying information, such as the section or chapter where the passage can be found in any edition.

In A Tale of Two Cities, Dickens describes the aptly named Stryver as "shouldering himself (morally and physically) into companies and conversations, that argued well for his shouldering his way up in life" (110; bk. 2, ch. 4).

PLAY

For a verse play, list the act, scene, and line numbers, separated by periods.

"Love," Iago says, "is merely a lust of the blood and a permission of the will" (Othello 1.3.326).

POETRY

When quoting poetry, add a slash mark to show where each new line begins. Use the word *line* or *lines* in the first reference but only numbers in subsequent references, as in the following examples from William Wordsworth's "The World Is Too Much with Us." The first reference:

"The world is too much with us; late and soon / Getting and spending, we lay waste our powers" (lines 1-2).

The subsequent reference:

"Or hear old Triton blow his wreathed horn" (14).

If a poem has multiple parts, cite the part and line numbers, separated by a period. Do not include the word *line*.

In "Ode: Intimations of Immortality," Wordsworth ponders the truths of human existence, "Which we are toiling all our lives to find, / In darkness lost, the darkness of the grave" (8.116-17).

A WORK IN AN ANTHOLOGY

For works in an anthology, cite the author of the selection — not the editor of the collection.

As Julio Marzán's "The Ingredient" opens, Vincent looks down on his neighborhood from a rooftop, realizing that "there was a kind of beauty to the view" (145).

PRINTED SOURCES: REFERENCE BOOKS AND PERIODICALS

ARTICLE IN A REFERENCE BOOK

In citing a one-page article from a work with entries arranged alphabetically, include the author's name and omit the page number.

One unusual definition of love calls it the force that enables individuals to "understand the separateness of other people" (Havell).

If a reference article is longer than one page, include the page number.

Gordon discusses Carver's "implosive" technique of ending stories just before epiphany (176).

If the article is unsigned, identify a brief title in your text or in parentheses.

She alienated many feminists with her portraits of women "who seemed to accept victimization" ("Didion").

JOURNAL ARTICLE

Follow the same format used for a book, citing author and page number.

Arthur seeks a goal "beyond the immediate context of the narrative" (Mueller 751).

In citing a one-page article, include the author's name in your text or in parentheses. Do not include the page number, which will be noted in the list of works cited at the end of the paper.

Vacuum-tube audio equipment is making a comeback, with aficionados praising the warmth and glow from the tubes, as well as the sound (Patton).

When citing articles longer than one page, provide the specific page number or numbers in the parenthetical reference.

Some less than perfect means have been used to measure television viewership, including a sensor that scans rooms for "hot bodies" (Larson 69).

For an anonymous magazine article, cite the first few words of its title. Begin with the word by which it is alphabetized in the list of works cited.

In a new take on "road rage," Newsweek reports that a consortium of businesses in London has called for a sidewalk speed lane to weed out "dawdlers" ("Speed Bump").

THE BIBLE

Note the version, book, and chapter and verse numbers for a quotation.

"What He has seen and heard, of that He testifies" (New American Bible, John 3.32).

ELECTRONIC AND OTHER NONPRINT SOURCES

WEB SITE

Treat a Web site as you would a print source, indicating the author (or, if no author, a brief title) in parentheses or in the text. Note any paragraph or screen numbers that replace page numbers.

The five-year survival rate for a woman with localized breast cancer is 93 percent (Bruckheim).

ONLINE ARTICLE

You may cite an online article in parentheses or weave it into your paper. No page or paragraph numbers are needed unless supplied online.

Robert S. Boynton's article in Atlantic Monthly Online explores the recent achievements and popularity of the new African American intellectuals.

INTERVIEW

In a recent interview, nutritionist Christina Diaz discussed how control issues can trigger eating disorders among teens.

RECORDING

Hearing Yeats reading "The Song of the Old Mother" on tape sheds new light on the poem.

Listing Sources: MLA Style

At the end of your paper, you need to list the sources from which you have cited material. When you follow the MLA style, title this list "Works Cited" and center the title at the top of a new page. Double-space the list, and alphabetize the entries by authors' last names or, for works with no author, by title. When an entry exceeds one line, indent the following lines one-half inch (or five spaces). Include only sources actually cited in your paper.

BOOKS

The information about each source is divided into three sections, each followed by a period—author or agency's name (if there is one), title, and publishing information. Give the author's name, last name first, and the title in full as they appear on the title page. (If a work has more than one author, all names after the first are given in normal order.) If the publisher lists more than one city, note only the first. Use just the first name of a publisher with multiple names: not "Holt, Rinehart and Winston," but simply "Holt." Omit initials: for "J. B. Lippincott Co.," write "Lippincott." Also omit terms such as *Press, Inc.,* and *Co.,* except when naming university presses. (Use *UP,* as in *Oxford UP.*) Use the most recent copyright date in your entry.

SINGLE AUTHOR

For an introduction to basic MLA entries, see E2 in the Quick Research Guide (the dark-red-edged pages).

Hazzard, Shirley. The Great Fire. New York: Farrar, 2003.

TWO OR THREE AUTHORS

Name the authors in the order in which they are listed on the title page.

Phelan, James R., and Lewis Chester. The Money: The Battle for Howard Hughes's Billions. New York: Random, 1997.

FOUR OR MORE AUTHORS

Give the names of all the authors, or give only the name of the first author listed, followed by *et al.* for "and others." Identify the source in the same way you cite it in the text.

Roark, James L., et al. The American Promise. Boston: Bedford, 1998.

MULTIPLE WORKS BY THE SAME AUTHOR

Use the author's name for the first entry only; for subsequent entries, replace the name with three hyphens and a period. List works alphabetically by title.

Gould, Stephen Jay. Full House: The Spread of Excellence from Plato to Darwin.
     New York: Harmony, 1996.

---. Triumph and Tragedy in Mudville: A Lifelong Passion for Baseball. New York:
     Norton, 2003.

CORPORATE AUTHOR

Name the organization as author, omitting any initial article (*a, an,* or *the*) (The name may reappear as the publisher.)

Student Conservation Association. The Guide to Graduate Environmental Programs.
     Washington: Island, 1997.

UNKNOWN AUTHOR

Start with the work's title.

Rand McNally 2003 Commercial Atlas & Marketing Guide. Skokie, IL: Rand, 2003.

EDITED BOOK

If your paper focuses on the work or its author, cite the author first.

Marx, Karl, and Frederick Engels. The Communist Manifesto. 1848. Ed. John E. Toews.
     Boston: Bedford, 1999.

If your paper focuses on the editor or the edition used, cite the editor first.

Toews, John E., ed. The Communist Manifesto. By Karl Marx and Frederick Engels.
     1848. Boston: Bedford, 1999.

TRANSLATED WORK

Hoeg, Peter. Tales of the Night. Trans. Barbara Haveland. New York: Farrar, 1998.

If your paper focuses on the translation, cite the translator first.

Haveland, Barbara, trans. Tales of the Night. By Peter Hoeg. New York: Farrar,
     1998.

MULTIVOLUME WORK

To cite the full work, include the number of volumes (*vols.*) after the title.

Who Built America? Working People and the Nation's Economy, Politics, Culture, and
 Society. 2 vols. New York: Worth, 2000.

To cite only one volume, give its number after the title. If you wish, you can add the total number of volumes after the date.

Who Built America? Working People and the Nation's Economy, Politics, Culture, and
 Society. Vol. 1. New York: Worth, 2000. 2 vols.

EDITION OTHER THAN THE FIRST

Volti, Rudi. Society and Technological Change. 4th ed. New York: Worth, 2001.

BOOK IN A SERIES

After the book title, add the series name as it appears on the title page, followed by any series number.

Berlin, Jeffrey B., ed. Approaches to Teaching Mann's Death in Venice and Other
 Short Fiction. Approaches to Teaching World Lit. 43. New York: MLA, 1992.

PARTS OF BOOKS

When citing part of a book, give the author of the section first; the editor of the book should follow the title. Give the page numbers of the selection after the publication information.

CHAPTER OR SECTION IN A BOOK

Burke, Kenneth. "A Grammar of Motives." The Rhetorical Tradition: Readings from
 Classical Times to the Present. Ed. Patricia Bizzell and Bruce Herzberg. Boston:
 Bedford, 2001. 1298-1324.

ESSAY, SHORT STORY, POEM, OR PLAY IN AN EDITED COLLECTION

Rothman, Rodney. "My Fake Job." The Best American Nonrequired Reading. Ed. Dave
 Eggers. Boston: Houghton, 2002. 117-132.

TWO OR MORE WORKS FROM THE SAME EDITED COLLECTION

The following examples show citations for articles in the collection *The Beacon Book of Essays by Contemporary American Women,* as well as the citation for the collection itself.

Cisneros, Sandra. "Only Daughter." Martin 10-13.

Martin, Wendy, ed. The Beacon Book of Essays by Contemporary American Women.
    Boston: Beacon, 1996.

Tan, Amy. "Mother Tongue." Martin 32-37.

INTRODUCTION, PREFACE, FOREWORD, OR AFTERWORD

Godwin, Mike. Foreword. High Noon on the Electronic Frontier. Ed. Peter Ludlow.
    Cambridge: MIT P, 1996. xiii-xvi.

REFERENCE BOOKS

It is not necessary to supply the editor, publisher, or place of publication for well-known references such as *Webster's, The Random House Dictionary, World Book Encyclopedia,* and *Encyclopaedia Britannica.* Omit volume and page numbers when citing an entry from a reference that is arranged alphabetically.

SIGNED DICTIONARY ENTRY

Turner, V. W. "Divination." A Dictionary of the Social Sciences. Ed. Julius Gould and
    William L. Kolb. New York: Free, 1964.

UNSIGNED DICTIONARY ENTRY

"Organize." Merriam-Webster's Collegiate Dictionary. 11th ed. 2003.

SIGNED ENCYCLOPEDIA ARTICLE

Binder, Raymond C., et al. "Mathematical Aspects of Physical Theories." The New
    Encyclopaedia Britannica: Macropaedia. 15th ed. 1993.

UNSIGNED ENCYCLOPEDIA ARTICLE

"Solstice." Encyclopaedia Britannica 2003. 2003.

PERIODICALS

ARTICLE FROM A JOURNAL PAGINATED BY ISSUE

For an article from a journal that starts each issue with page 1, provide the issue number as well as the volume number, separated by a period.

Ferris, Lucy. "'Never Truly Members': Andre Dubus's Patriarchal Catholicism." South
    Atlantic Review 62.2 (1997): 39-55.

ARTICLE FROM A JOURNAL PAGINATED BY VOLUME

For an article from a journal in which page numbers run continuously through all issues of a volume, give only the volume number, year, and page numbers.

Daly, Mary E. "Recent Writing on Modern Irish History: The Interaction between Past and Present." Journal of Modern History 69 (1997): 512-33.

SIGNED MAGAZINE ARTICLE

Give the month and year of the issue, or its specific date, after the title of the magazine.

Rushin, Steve. "Don't Mess with the Ballpoint Pen." Sports Illustrated 15 Mar. 2004: 15.

If the pages for the article are not consecutive, add a + after its initial page.

Hooper, Joseph. "The New Diet Danger." Self July 2003: 128+.

UNSIGNED MAGAZINE ARTICLE

"Speed Bump." Newsweek 11 Dec. 2000: 12.

SIGNED NEWSPAPER ARTICLE

If the newspaper has different editions, indicate the one where the article can be found.

Kolata, Gina. "Men and Women Use Brain Differently, Study Discovers." New York Times 16 Feb. 1995, natl. ed.: A1+.

UNSIGNED NEWSPAPER ARTICLE

"Plague Researcher Gets Two Years in Fraud Case." Boston Globe 11 Mar. 2004: A2.

SIGNED EDITORIAL

Jacoby, Jeff. "When Jerusalem Was Divided." Editorial. Boston Globe 8 Jan. 2001: A11.

UNSIGNED EDITORIAL

"Taking the Initiatives." Editorial. Nation 13 Nov. 2000: 3-4.

PUBLISHED INTERVIEW

Kerry, John. Interview. Newsweek 8 Mar. 2004: 26.

LETTER TO THE EDITOR

Cohen, Irving M. Letter. Atlantic Monthly Mar. 2004: 14.

REVIEW

Include the words *Rev. of* before the title of the work reviewed.

Passaro, Vince. "The Unsparing Vision of Don DeLillo." Rev. of Underworld, by Don
    DeLillo. Harper's Nov. 1997: 72-75.

OTHER PRINTED SOURCES

GOVERNMENT DOCUMENT

Generally, the "author" will be the name of the government and the government agency, separated by periods. If the document names an author or editor, that name may be provided either before the title or after it, if you supply the government agency as author.

United States. Bureau of the Census. Statistical Abstract of the United States. 123rd
    ed. Washington: GPO, 2003.

PAMPHLET

Follow the format for a book.

Metropolitan Life Insurance Company. Metlife Dental. New York: Metropolitan Life
    Insurance, 1996.

DOCTORAL DISSERTATION OR MASTER'S THESIS

If the work is unpublished, place the title in quotation marks; if published,
underline the title. Follow the title with *Diss.* (for a dissertation) or with an
apt master's abbreviation (e.g., *MA thesis*).

Beilke, Debra J. "Cracking Up the South: Humor and Identity in Southern
    Renaissance Fiction." Diss. U of Wisconsin, Madison, 1997.

PERSONAL LETTER

Finch, Katherine. Letter to the author. 15 Jan. 2004.

ADVERTISEMENT

A.G. Edwards. Advertisement. Scientific American Mar. 2004: 17.

INTERNET AND ELECTRONIC SOURCES

Here are the basic elements of an Internet or electronic citation:

- Name of the author (if known)
- Title of document and site
- Name of the editor (if any)
- Publication information, including the date or latest update

- Name of the sponsoring organization (if any)
- Date on which you last accessed the source and its URL (uniform resource locator)

Because most Internet sources do not have page numbers, these are not required. If the source numbers paragraphs or screens, use these instead.

The Einstein Papers Project. Ed. Robert Schulmann. 9 Nov. 1997. Boston U. 29 Jan.
    1998 <http://albert.bu.edu>.

Try to cite the exact URL for a source. However, if this address is so long that readers might make a mistake in transcribing it, provide the address for the site's search page or home page. Readers can use keywords to access the work.

Havrilesky, Heather. "Secrets, Lies and Copy Machines." Salon.com. 8 Mar. 2003.
    1 Apr. 2003 <http://search.salon.com>.

If a site does not have usable URLs for each page, list the address of the home page and the path you followed to reach the work — for example: *Path: Archives; By Author; A-C.*

PROFESSIONAL OR PERSONAL WEB SITE

If the author's name is unknown, begin with the site title.

EPA Laws and Regulations Page. 6 Mar. 1998. US Environmental Protection Agency.
    11 Mar. 1998 <http://www.epa.gov/epahome/rules.html>.

If no title is available, include a description such as *Home page*.

Watson, Chad J. Home page. 27 Jan. 1998. 10 Mar. 1998 <http://cc.usu.edu/
    ~slypx/index.html>.

HOME PAGE FOR CAMPUS DEPARTMENT

Supply the department, the description "Dept. home page," and the school. Note your access date and the URL.

Sociology. Dept. home page. U of California Los Angeles. 8 Oct. 2003
    <http://www.sscnet.ucla.edu/soc/>.

ONLINE BOOK

Include the original and online publication dates as well as your access date and the URL.

Wharton, Edith. The Age of Innocence. New York: D. Appleton, 1920. Bartleby.com:
    Great Books Online. 2000. 8 May 2004 <http://www.bartleby.com/1005/>.

ARTICLE IN AN ONLINE JOURNAL, MAGAZINE, OR NEWSPAPER

When citing articles from online periodicals, provide information as for
print articles; end with your date of access and the URL.

Loker, William M. "'Campesinos' and the Crisis of Modernization in Latin America."
    Journal of Political Ecology 3.1 (1996). 13 Mar. 1998 <http://
    www.library.arizona.edu/ej/jpe/volume_3/ascii-lokeriso.txt>.

If you are citing an abstract, give the word *Abstract* before the date of access.

AN ONLINE POSTING

For an online posting, begin with the author, the title (the subject line), the
words *Online posting*, the posting date, the access date, and the address.
Identify a newsgroup with the word *news* before the group's name.

Weiss, Phil. "News from Philadelphia Animation Society Meeting." Online posting.
    14 Apr. 2004. 16 Mar. 2004. <news:rec.arts.anime.fandom>.

If the posting is from an e-mail discussion list, add the name of the group or
forum (if known) after the posting date. Supply the URL for the group's Web
site or the moderator's e-mail address.

Cubbison, Laurie. "Metaphor and Cliché." Online posting. 13 Apr. 2004. H-Rhetor.
    3 May 2004 <http://www.h-net.msu.edu/~rhetor/>.

ONLINE GOVERNMENT DOCUMENT

Begin with the name of the government, followed by the agency and the rest
of the publication and access information.

United States. Natl. Inst. of Child Health and Human Dev. Natl. Inst. of Health.
    Milk Matters for Your Child's Health! 1999. 2 Oct. 2003 <http://
    www.nichd.nih.gov/milk/brochure0105/index.htm>.

E-MAIL

Moore, Jack. E-mail to the author. 11 Jan. 2004.

PUBLICATION ON CD-ROM

Sheehy, Donald, ed. Robert Frost: Poems, Life, Legacy. CD-ROM. New York: Holt,
    1997.

COMPUTER SOFTWARE

Electronic Supplements for Real Writing: 1. Interactive Writing Software. Diskette.
Vers. 1. Boston: Bedford, 2004.

MATERIAL ACCESSED THROUGH A LIBRARY OR SUBSCRIPTION SERVICE

Sataline, Suzanne. "Charter Schools Could Hit Ceiling." Boston Globe 31 Mar. 2004:
B1. NewsBank. Boston Public Lib. 5 May 2004 <http://infoweb.newsbank.com>.

If you find a source through a library subscription service, include the library name. If you find it through a subscription service that is searchable by keywords, cite the keyword or path that you followed.

"Echocardiography." Merriam-Webster Medical Dictionary. 13 Oct. 1995. America
Online. 8 June 2004. Keyword: Medical Dictionary.

OTHER NONPRINT SOURCES

AUDIOTAPE OR RECORDING

Begin with the name of the speaker, the writer, or the director, depending on your emphasis. If the recording is not on a CD, note the format.

Byrne, Gabriel. The James Joyce Collection. Dove Audio, 1996.

Yeats, William Butler. "The Song of the Old Mother." The Poems of William Butler
Yeats. Read by William Butler Yeats, Siobhan McKenna, and Michael
MacLiammoir. Audiotape. Spoken Arts, 1974.

TELEVISION OR RADIO PROGRAM

The Six Wives of Henry VIII. PBS. WGBH, Boston. 6 Mar. 2003.

"A Dangerous Man: Lawrence after Arabia." Great Performances. Perf. Ralph Fiennes
and Siddig el Fadil. PBS. WNET, New York. 6 May 1992.

FILM

Lord of the Rings: The Return of the King. Dir. Peter Jackson. New Line Cinema,
2003.

If you wish to emphasize the work of a person connected with the film, start with his or her name.

Jackson, Peter, dir. Lord of the Rings: The Return of the King. New Line Cinema,
2003.

PERFORMANCE

Whale Music. By Anthony Minghella. Dir. Anthony Minghella. Perf. Francie Swift.
    Theater Off Park, New York. 23 Mar. 1998.

A WORK OF ART

Botticelli, Sandro. The Birth of Venus. Uffizi Gallery, Florence.

SPEECH OR LECTURE

Hurley, James. Address. Opening Gen. Sess. Amer. Bar Assn. Convention. Chicago. 17
    Jan. 1987.

BROADCAST INTERVIEW

Bernstein, Richard. Interview. Fresh Air. Natl. Public Radio. WBUR, Boston. 3 Apr.
    2001.

PERSONAL INTERVIEW

Boyd, Dierdre. Personal interview. 5 Feb. 2004.

Ladner, John. Telephone interview. 20 Oct. 2003.

Citing Sources: APA Style

The American Psychological Association (APA) details the style most commonly used in the social sciences in its *Publication Manual,* Fifth Edition (Washington, D.C.: APA, 2001). As in MLA style, APA citations are placed in parentheses in the body of the text.

For advice on preparing an APA list of references, see pp. 658–63.

PRINTED SOURCES

To cite a work in APA style, you usually place in parentheses the author's last name, a comma, and the year the source was published. You must add a page number for a direct quotation from the source and may include one for a paraphrase.

AUTHOR NOT NAMED IN SENTENCE

Some experts feel that adolescent boys who bully are not merely aggressive but are depressed and acting out in an aggressive manner (Pollack, 2000).

If you paraphrase ideas from a long work, you can refer to a specific page so that your readers can easily find the reference. Use the abbreviation *p.* (or *pp.*).

Dean Rusk's exposure to Nazi power in Europe in the 1930s seems to have permanently influenced his attitude toward appeasement (Karnow, 1991, p. 194).

AUTHOR NAMED IN SENTENCE

If you name the author in your text, give only the date in parentheses.

Pollack (2000) contends that boys tend to contain their pain for fear of appearing vulnerable and inviting ridicule.

When the author's name appears in the text, put the page number in parentheses after quoted or paraphrased material.

Karnow (1991) maintains that Dean Rusk's exposure to Nazi power in Europe in the 1930s "scarred his mind" (p. 194).

LONG QUOTATION

If you quote forty words or more from your source, indent the whole quotation one-half inch (five spaces) and double-space it unless directed otherwise. Put the author's name, the publication year, and the page number in parentheses following the quotation with no additional period.

At least one critic maintains that Dean Rusk's exposure to Nazi power in Europe in the 1930s permanently influenced his attitude toward appeasement:

> Then came the moment that transformed his life and his thinking. He won a Rhodes scholarship to Oxford. More important, his exposure to Europe in the early 1930s, as the Nazis consolidated their power in Germany, scarred his mind, leading him to share Acheson's hostility to appeasement in any form anywhere. (Karnow, 1991, p. 194)

TWO AUTHORS

List the last names of coauthors in the order in which they appear in the book or article you cite. Join the names with *and* if you mention them in your text and with an ampersand (&) if the citation is in parentheses.

A group's cultural development enhances its chance for survival, providing both physical and psychological protection (Anderson & Ross, 1998).

Anderson and Ross (1998) contend that the development of a group's culture provides both physical and psychological protection.

THREE TO FIVE AUTHORS

Include all the last names in your first reference only. In any later references, use the first author's last name with *et al.* (for "and others"), whether in the text or in parentheses.

The discipline of conservation biology has developed in response to the accelerating rate at which species are being lost due to human activities (Purves, Orians, & Heller, 1999).

CORPORATE AUTHOR

There are three signs of oxygen deprivation (American Red Cross, 2002).

GOVERNMENT DOCUMENT

In the first citation in your text, give the full name of the originating agency. If the name is complicated or commonly shortened, you can add an abbreviation in brackets.

Stopping the spread of mosquito-borne diseases is essential. (Department of Health and Human Services [DHHS], 2003, p. 25).

In later citations, use just the abbreviation and the date: (DHHS, 2003).

UNKNOWN AUTHOR

Identify the source with a short title and a date.

There are questions people can ask themselves if they suspect their drinking has gotten out of hand (*Alcoholism,* 1986).

MULTIPLE WORKS BY THE SAME AUTHOR

One nuclear energy proponent insists on tight controls for the industry (Weinberg, 1972), even calling on utilities to insure each reactor with their own funds (Weinberg, 1977).

OTHER SOURCES

PERSONAL COMMUNICATIONS

Personal communications — such as personal interviews, letters, telephone conversations, memos, and e-mail — are not included in the reference list. But in the text of your paper, you should include the initials and last name of your source, with the date of the communication.

J. T. Moore (personal communication, February 10, 2004) has specific suggestions for stimulating the local economy.

WEB SITE OR OTHER ELECTRONIC DOCUMENT

When possible, treat a Web site or online article as you would treat a print source, indicating the author's name and the date in parentheses.

Breast cancer survival rates depend on early detection before the cancer has a chance to spread (Bruckheim, 1998).

For an electronic source with no author named, use the full title of the document in text or include the first word or two of the title in parentheses. When the date is unknown, use "n.d." to indicate "no date." For a source without page numbers, include any information that helps readers to locate quoted material, such as the paragraph number or the section heading.

"Interval training involves alternating short bursts of intense activity with what is called active recovery, which is typically a less-intense form of the original activity" (*Interval training*, n.d., para. 2).

Listing Sources: APA Style

In APA style, your list of sources, titled "References," appears at the end of your paper. The APA guidelines instruct you to format entries with a hanging indent: the first line is not indented, while subsequent lines are. Use a hanging indentation of one-half inch, or about five to seven spaces.

Double-space your list, organize it alphabetically by authors' last names, and use only initials for the authors' first and middle names. The year follows the authors' names in parentheses. In book and article titles, capitalize only the first word, proper names, and the first word after a colon. Italicize book titles (or, if your word processing program has no italics function, underline), but use no quotation marks or italics for article titles. Italicize journal names, and capitalize all important words. Use a shortened name for a publisher, but include *Press*. Omit the state name with larger cities.

BOOKS

SINGLE AUTHOR

Pollack, W. (2000). *Real boys' voices*. New York: Random House.

TWO OR MORE AUTHORS

Anderson, R., & Ross, V. (1998). *Questions of communication*. New York: St. Martin's Press.

CORPORATE AUTHOR

American Red Cross. (2004). *CPR/AED for the professional rescuer*. Washington DC: American Red Cross.

UNKNOWN AUTHOR

Rand McNally 2003 Commercial Atlas & Marketing Guide. (2003). Skokie, IL:
     Rand-McNally.

MULTIPLE WORKS BY THE SAME AUTHOR

Arrange the titles by date, the earliest first.

Gould, S. J. (1996). *Full house: The spread of excellence from Plato to Darwin*. New
     York: Harmony.

Gould, S. J. (2003). *Triumph and tragedy in Mudville: A lifelong passion for baseball*.
     New York: Norton.

CHAPTER OR SECTION OF A BOOK

Write "In" after the chapter title, followed by the editor's name, the book
title, and the chapter's page numbers.

Shofner, J. H. (1995). Florida's black codes. In L. Dinnerstein & K. T. Jackson (Eds.),
     American vistas: 1877 to the present (pp. 56-75). New York: Oxford University
     Press.

INTRODUCTION, PREFACE, FOREWORD, OR AFTERWORD

Godwin, M. (1996). Foreword. In P. Ludlow (Ed.), *High noon on the electronic frontier*
     (pp. xiii-xvi). Cambridge: MIT Press.

WORK IN AN EDITED COLLECTION

Tollifson, J. (1997). Imperfection is a beautiful thing: On disability and meditation.
     In K. Fries (Ed.), *Staring back* (pp. 105-112). New York: Plume-Random.

EDITED BOOK

Bolles, E. B. (Ed.). (1999). *Galileo's commandment: 2,500 years of great science
     writing*. New York: Freeman.

TRANSLATED WORK

Ishinomori, I. (1998). *Japan inc.: Introduction to Japanese economics*
     (B. Schneiner, Trans.). Berkeley: University of California Press. (Original work
     published 1986)

REVISED EDITION

Volti, R. (2001). *Society and technological change*. (4th ed.). New York: Worth.

PERIODICALS

ARTICLE FROM A JOURNAL PAGINATED BY ISSUE

Place the issue number in parentheses after the volume. Note that volume numbers are italicized along with the titles of the journals and magazines.

Lipkin, S. N. (1999). Real emotional logic: Persuasive strategies in docudrama. *Cinema Journal, 38*(4), 68-85.

ARTICLE FROM A JOURNAL PAGINATED BY VOLUME

Martin, J. (1997). Inventing sincerity, refashioning prudence: The discovery of the individual in Renaissance Europe. *American Historical Review, 102,* 1309-1342.

MAGAZINE ARTICLE

Lankford, K. (1998, April). The trouble with rules of thumb. *Kiplinger's Personal Finance Magazine, 52,* 102-104.

SIGNED NEWSPAPER ARTICLE

Stein, R. (2004, March 11). Breast-cancer drug changes suggested. *The Boston Globe,* p. A4.

UNSIGNED NEWSPAPER ARTICLE

The AMD unveils faster bargain microprocessor. (2001, January 8). *The Boston Globe,* p. C4.

SIGNED EDITORIAL

Kass, R. (1998, March 23). Wanted: An official state janitor. [Editorial.] *The Boston Globe,* p. A15.

UNSIGNED EDITORIAL

Taking the initiatives. (2000, November 13). [Editorial.] *The Nation, 272,* 3-4.

LETTER TO THE EDITOR

Yusuf, S. (2000, November 4). Pakistan's choice [Letter to the editor]. *Economist, 357,* 6.

REVIEW

Rose, T. (1998, February 24). Blues sisters [Review of the book *Blues legacies and black feminism: Gertrude "Ma" Rainey, Bessie Smith, and Billie Holliday*]. *Village Voice,* pp. 139-141.

OTHER PRINTED SOURCES

GOVERNMENT DOCUMENT

Start with the name of the agency and then give the date of publication, the title (and author, if any), identifying number, and publisher.

U.S. Bureau of the Census. (2003). *Statistical abstract of the United States* (123rd
ed.). Washington, DC: U.S. Government Printing Office.

ACADEMIC OR RESEARCH REPORT

Begin with the author (if any) and then give the date of publication, title, and publisher. If the report is numbered, include this information in parentheses after the title.

Whelan-Berry, K. S. (2002). *Implementing problem-based learning in business.*
Birmingham, AL: Samford University, Center for Problem-Based Learning.

UNPUBLISHED DOCTORAL DISSERTATION

Write out the words "unpublished doctoral dissertation," followed by information about the college that granted the degree.

Richter, P. (2004). *Improving nursing in the age of managed care.* Unpublished doctoral dissertation, University of Wisconsin, Madison.

INTERNET AND ELECTRONIC SOURCES

For Internet and electronic sources, provide as much of the following information as available:

- Name of the author or editor (if known)
- Date of publication or of latest update, in parentheses
- Document title, in italics
- Date of retrieval
- URL or online location

For current information on formatting online sources using APA style, visit the official Web site of the APA at <www.apastyle.org>.

NONPERIODICAL WEB DOCUMENT

Watkins, C., & Brynes, G. (2001). *Anxiety disorders in children and adults.* Retrieved
July 20, 2003, from http://www.baltimorepsych.com/anxiety.htm

Identify a chapter or section within a Web site as well as the main site.

Watkins, C. (2001). Separation anxiety in young children. In *Anxiety disorders
in children and adults* (chap. 1). Retrieved July 20, 2003, from http://
www.baltimorepsych.com/anxiety.htm

For a document that is part of a government agency Web site or other large
site, identify the sponsoring agency or organization before the URL.

United States Department of the Interior. Bureau of Indian Affairs. (2001, July).
Report on tribal priority allocations. Retrieved from the Bureau of Indian Affairs
Web site: http://www.doi.gov/bia/tpa/TPARept.pdf

ARTICLE FROM AN ONLINE PERIODICAL

Loker, W. M. (1996). "Campesinos" and the crisis of modernization in Latin America
[Electronic version]. *Journal of Political Ecology, 3,* 69-88.

Do not include a URL in the citation if the article also appears in a printed
journal. Instead, include "Electronic version" in brackets after the title. If
there is no print version of the article, include in your retrieval statement
your date of access and the URL.

Rothfleisch, J. (2001, February). Mid-dermal elastolysis. *Dermatology Online Journal, 7.*
Retrieved June 8, 2001, from http://dermatology.cdlib.org/DOJvol7num1/
NYUcases/elastolysis/rothfleisch.html

ONLINE NEWSPAPER ARTICLE

Stevenson, R. (2001, July 20). Panel argues for changing Social Security. *New York
Times.* Retrieved July 20, 2001, from http://www.nytimes.com

E-MAIL (INCLUDING MAILING LISTS)

APA does not recommend including these messages in your reference list, as
they are difficult or impossible for readers to retrieve. Cite them in your text
as personal communications. See p. 657.

COMPUTER SOFTWARE

Microsoft Office Excel 2003 [Computer software]. (2003). Redmond, WA: Microsoft.

ARTICLE FROM AN INFORMATION SERVICE OR DATABASE

Berger, S. (1995). Inclusion: A legal mandate, an educational dream. *Updating School
Board Policies, 26*(4), 1-4. Retrieved February 15, 2001, from ERIC database
(No. ED386789)

NOTE: If the source is an abstract, include "Abstract" in brackets after the title.

OTHER NONPRINT SOURCES

AUDIO RECORDING

Byrne, G. (1996). *The James Joyce collection* [Cassette]. Hollywood: Dove Audio.

TELEVISION OR RADIO PROGRAM

Clark, L., (2004). Descent into the ice. [Television series episode]. In P. Aspell
    (Executive Producer), *Nova*. Boston: WGBH.

MOTION PICTURE

Lustig, B., Molen, G., & Spielberg, S. (Producers). (1993). *Schindler's List* [Motion
    Picture]. Los Angeles: Universal.

PERSONAL INTERVIEW

APA guidelines omit personal interviews from the reference list because they
do not provide recoverable data. Mention such sources in your paper as personal communications. See p. 657.

A
Writer's
Handbook

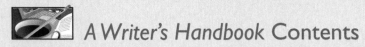

A Writer's Handbook Contents

**Introduction: Grammar, or
The Way Words Work   H-3**

Introduction:
Grammar, or The Way Words Work

Every speaker of English, even a child, commands a grammatical system of tremendous complexity. Take the sentence "A bear is occupying a telephone booth while a tourist impatiently waits in line." In theory, there are nineteen billion different ways to state the idea in that sentence.[1] (Another is "A tourist fumes while he waits for a bear to finish yakking on a pay phone.") How do we understand a unique sentence like that one? For we do understand it, even though we have never heard it before — not in those very same words, not in the very same order.

To begin with, we recognize familiar words and we know their meanings. Just as significantly, we recognize grammatical structures. As we read or hear the sentence, we know that it contains a familiar pattern of *syntax,* or word order, that helps the sentence make sense to us. Ordinarily we aren't even conscious of such an order, but to notice it, all we need do is rearrange the words of our sentence:

> Telephone a impatiently line in waits tourist bear a occupying is a booth while.

The result is nonsense: it defies English grammar. The would-be sentence doesn't follow familiar patterns or meet our expectations of order.

Hundreds of times a day, with wonderful efficiency, we perform tasks of understanding and constructing complex sentences. Why, then, think about grammar in college? Isn't it entirely possible to write well without contemplating grammar at all? Yes. If your innate sense of grammar is reliable, you can write clearly and logically and forcefully without knowing a predicate nominative from a handsaw. Most successful writers, though, have practiced for many years to gain this sense. When you doubt a word or a construction, a glance in a handbook often can clear up your confusion and restore your confidence — just as referring to a dictionary can help your spelling.

The grammatical conventions you'll find in this handbook are not mechanical specifications, but accepted ways in which skilled writers and speakers put words together to convey meaning clearly. The amateur writer can learn by following their example, just as an amateur athlete, artist, or even auto mechanic can learn by watching the professionals.

---

1 Richard Ohmann, "Grammar and Meaning," *American Heritage Dictionary* (Boston: Houghton, 1979), pp. xxxi–xxxii.

This handbook, divided into the following chapters, presents the important rules and conventions of standard written English. Exercises are provided so you can practice putting the information to use.

33. Grammatical Sentences   36. Punctuation
34. Effective Sentences   37. Mechanics
35. Word Choice

Following the handbook are convenient appendices.

QUICK RESEARCH GUIDE
Identified by the dark-red-edged pages, this concise guide introduces how to find, evaluate, and use sources in your writing. Look here also for the basics of the MLA documentation style.

QUICK EDITING GUIDE
Identified by the dark-blue-edged pages, this guide briefly discusses how to edit the common grammar, style, punctuation, mechanics, and format problems found in college writing. Check its useful tables, lists, and editing checklists as well.

A GLOSSARY OF TROUBLEMAKERS
This glossary lists words and phrases that often trouble writers. Turn here when you wonder which of two words to select (*affect* or *effect*, for example) or how to use a word correctly.

ANSWERS FOR LETTERED EXERCISES
Use these excellent tools to test yourself on a particular skill. Simply answer the lettered exercise sentences in the handbook, and then turn to the answers to see how you did.

Here are some easy ways to find information in *A Writer's Handbook*:

- Use the *table of contents* at the beginning of the handbook (p. H-2). If you needed help with quotation marks, for instance, you would first look under the chapter titled "Punctuation." By scanning the list of topics, you would quickly spot what you need: section 25, Quotation Marks, p. H-115.

- Turn to the alphabetically arranged *index* at the back of the book. Here you will find all of the key terms used in the handbook followed by the exact page that you should turn to.

- For those of you who speak English as a second language, near the back of the book is an *ESL index* listing all the ESL boxes in the handbook.

Chapter 33
Grammatical Sentences

1 *Sentence Fragments*

A *fragment* lacks a subject (naming something) or a predicate (making an assertion about the subject) or both or otherwise fails to express a complete thought. We all use fragments in everyday speech, where their context and delivery make them understandable and therefore acceptable.

> That bicycle over there.
>
> Good job.
>
> Not if I can help it.

In writing, fragments like these fail to communicate complete, coherent ideas. Notice how much more effective they are as complete sentences.

> I'd like to buy that bicycle over there.
>
> You did a good job sanding the floor.
>
> Nobody will steal my seat if I can help it.

Some writers purposefully use fragments. For example, advertisers are fond of short, emphatic fragments that command attention, like a series of quick jabs to the head.

> For seafood lovers. Every Tuesday night. All you can eat.

In college writing, though, it is good practice to express your ideas in complete sentences. Besides, complete sentences usually convey more information than fragments — a big advantage in essay writing.

sentence: A word group that includes both a subject and a predicate and can stand alone

For more on editing for fragments, see A1 in the Quick Editing Guide (the dark-blue-edged pages).

If you sometimes write fragments without recognizing them, learn to edit your work. Luckily, fragments are fairly easy to correct. Often you can attach a fragment to a neighboring sentence with a comma, a dash, or a colon. Sometimes you can combine two thoughts without adding any punctuation at all.

1a If a fragment is a phrase, link it to an adjoining sentence or make it a complete sentence.

You have two choices for revising a fragment if it is a phrase: (1) link it to an adjoining sentence using punctuation such as a comma or a colon, or (2) add a subject or a verb to the phrase to make it a complete sentence.

phrase: Two or more related words that work together but may lack a subject (*will have been*), a verb (*my uncle Zeke*), or both (*in the attic*)

FRAGMENT   Malcolm has two goals in life. *Wealth and power.* [Phrase without verb]

FRAGMENT   Schmidt ended his stories as he mixed his martinis. *With a twist.* [Prepositional phrase without subject or verb]

subject: The part of a sentence that names something—a person, an object, an idea, a situation—about which the verb in the predicate makes an assertion: The *king* lives.

FRAGMENT   *To stamp out the union.* That was the bosses' plan. [Infinitive phrase without main verb or subject]

FRAGMENT   The students taking the final exam in the auditorium. [Participial phrase without complete verb]

You can make each of these phrases express a complete thought by linking it with a neighboring sentence or by adding the missing element.

verb: A word that shows action (The cow *jumped* over the moon) or a state of being (The cow *is* brown)

REVISED   Malcolm has two goals in life: wealth and power. [A colon links *wealth and power* to *goals.*]

REVISED   Schmidt ended his stories as he mixed his martinis, with a twist. [The prepositional phrase *with a twist* is connected to the main clause with a comma.]

REVISED   To stamp out the union was the bosses' plan. [The infinitive phrase *To stamp out the union* becomes the subject of the sentence.]

REVISED   The students were taking the final exam in the auditorium. [The helping verb *were* completes the verb and thus makes a sentence.]

1b If a fragment is a subordinate clause, link it to an adjoining sentence or eliminate the subordinating conjunction.

Some fragments are missing neither subject nor verb. Instead, they are subordinate clauses, unable to express complete thoughts unless linked with main clauses. When you find a subordinating conjunction at the start or in the middle of a word group that looks like a sentence, that word group may be a subordinate clause and not a sentence at all.

subordinate clause: A group of words that contains a subject and a verb but cannot stand alone because it depends on a main clause to help it make sense: Pia, *who plays the oboe,* prefers solitude. (See 14d–14f.)

FRAGMENT   The new law will help create jobs. *If it passes.*

FRAGMENT   George loves winter in the mountains. *Because he is an avid skier.*

If you have treated a subordinate clause as a complete sentence, you can correct the problem in one of two ways: (1) you can combine the fragment with a main clause nearby, or (2) you can make the subordinate clause into a complete sentence by dropping the subordinating conjunction.

REVISED   The new law will help create jobs, if it passes.

REVISED   George loves winter in the mountains. He is an avid skier.

A sentence is not necessarily a fragment just because it opens with a subordinating conjunction. Some perfectly legitimate sentences with both main and subordinate clauses have their conjunctions up front instead of in the middle.

If you leave early, say good-bye.

Because it rained all afternoon, the game was canceled.

I c If a fragment has a participle but no other verb, change the participle to a main verb or link the fragment to an adjoining sentence.

A present participle (the *-ing* form of the verb) can serve as the main verb in a sentence only when it is accompanied by a form of *be* ("Sally *is working* harder than usual"). When a writer mistakenly uses a participle alone as a main verb, the result is a fragment.

FRAGMENT   Jon was used to the pressure of deadlines. *Having worked the night shift at the daily newspaper.*

One solution is to combine the fragment with an adjoining sentence.

REVISED   Jon was used to the pressure of deadlines, having worked the night shift at the daily newspaper.

Another solution is to turn the fragment into a complete sentence by choosing a form of the verb other than the participle.

REVISED   Jon was used to the pressure of deadlines. He *had worked* the night shift at the daily newspaper.

I d If a fragment is part of a compound predicate, link it with the complete sentence containing the subject and the rest of the predicate.

FRAGMENT   In spite of a pulled muscle, Jeremy ran the race. *And won.*

A fragment such as *And won* sounds satisfyingly punchy. Still, it cannot stand on its own as a sentence because it lacks a subject. Create a complete sentence by linking the two verbs in the compound predicate.

REVISED   In spite of a pulled muscle, Jeremy *ran* the race *and won.*

---

subordinating conjunction: A word (such as *because, although, if, when*) used to make one clause dependent on, or subordinate to, another: *Unless* you have a key, we are locked out. (See 14d–14f.)

participle: A form of a verb that cannot function alone as a main verb, including present participles ending in *-ing* (*dancing*) and past participles often ending in *-ed* or *-d* (*danced*)

compound predicate: A predicate consisting of two or more verbs linked by a conjunction: My sister *stopped and stared.*

■ For advice on punctuating linked phrases and clauses, see 14a.

If you want to emphasize the second verb, you can turn the fragment into a full clause by adding punctuation and another subject.

REVISED   In spite of a pulled muscle, Jeremy ran the race — and *he* won.

ESL GUIDELINES

verbal: A form of a verb that cannot function alone as a main verb, including infinitives (*to live*), present participles (*living*), and past participles (*lived*)

participle: A form of a verb that cannot function alone as a main verb, including present participles ending in -*ing* (*dancing*) and past participles often ending in -*ed* or -*d* (*danced*)

gerund: A form of a verb, ending in -*ing*, that functions as a noun: Lacey likes *playing* in the steel band.

infinitive: The base form of a verb preceded by *to* (*to go, to play*)

Using Participles, Gerunds, and Infinitives

A *verbal* cannot function as the main verb in a sentence but can function as an adjective, an adverb, or a noun.

Using participles
When used as an adjective, the -*ing* form expresses cause, and the -*ed* and -*d* forms express effect or result.

> The movie was *terrifying to the children*. [The movie caused terror.]

> The children were *terrified by the movie*. [The movie resulted in terrified children.]

Using verbs with gerunds and infinitives
Some verbs are followed by gerunds; others are followed by infinitives.

- Verbs that are followed by gerunds include *appreciate, avoid, consider, discuss, enjoy, finish, imagine, practice,* and *suggest,* among others.

   > My family enjoys *going* to the beach.

- Verbs that are followed by infinitives include *decide, expect, pretend, refuse,* and *want,* among others.

   > My mother decided *to eat* dinner at McDonald's.

- Some verbs, including *continue, like, love, hate, remember, forget, start,* and *stop,* can be followed by either a gerund or an infinitive.

   > I like *going* to the museum, but Nadine likes *to go* to the movies.

NOTE: Some verbs, such as *stop, remember,* and *forget,* have significantly different meanings according to whether they are followed by a gerund or an infinitive.

> I stopped *smoking.* [I don't smoke anymore.]

> I stopped *to smoke.* [I stopped so that I could smoke.]

- *Used to* (meaning "did in the past") is followed by the basic form of the verb. *Be used to* or *get used to* (meaning "be or become accustomed to") is followed by a gerund.

   > I *used to live* in Rio, but now I live in New York. [I lived in Rio in the past.]

   > I *am used to living* in New York. [I am accustomed to living in New York.]

   > I *got used to living* in New York. [I became accustomed to living in New York.]

■ Exercise 1–1

Eliminating Fragments

Find and eliminate any fragments in the following examples. Some sentences may be correct. Possible revisions for the lettered sentences appear in the back of the book. Example:

> Bryan hates parsnips. And loathes squash.
>
> Bryan hates parsnips *and* loathes squash.

■ For more practice, visit <bedfordstmartins.com/ bedguide> and do a keyword search:

fragments

a. Michael had a beautiful Southern accent. Having lived many years in Georgia.

b. Pat and Chris are determined to marry each other. Even if their families do not approve.

c. Jack seemed well qualified for a career in the Air Force. Except for his tendency to get airsick.

d. Lisa advocated sleeping no more than four hours a night. Until she started nodding through her classes.

e. They met. They talked. They fought. They reached agreement.

1. Being the first person in his family ever to attend college. Alex is determined to succeed.

2. Does our society rob children of their childhood? By making them aware too soon of adult ills?

3. Richard III supposedly had the young princes murdered. No one has ever found out what really happened to them.

4. For democracy to function, two elements are crucial. An educated populace and a collective belief in people's ability to chart their own course.

5. You must take his stories as others do. With a grain of salt.

■ Exercise 1–2

Eliminating Fragments

Rewrite the following paragraph, eliminating all fragments. Explain why you made each change. Example:

> Many people exercise to change their body image. And may become obsessed with their looks. [The second word group is a fragment because it lacks a subject.]
>
> Many people exercise to change their body image *and* may become obsessed with their looks. [This revised sentence links the fragment to the rest of the sentence.]

Some people assume that only women are overly concerned with body image. However, men often share this concern. While women tend to exercise vigorously to stay slender, men usually lift weights to "bulk up." Because of their desire to look masculine. Both are trying to achieve the "ideal" body form. The muscular male and the waifish female. Sometimes working out begins to interfere with other aspects of life. Such as sleeping, eating regularly, or going to school or work. These are warning signs. Of too much emphasis on physical appearance. Preoccupation with body image may turn a healthy lifestyle into an unhealthy obsession. Many people believe that looking attractive will bring them happiness. Unfortunately, when they become compulsive. Beautiful people are not always happy.

2 *Comma Splices and Fused Sentences*

main clause: A group of words that has both a subject and a verb and can stand alone as a complete sentence: *My sister has a friend.*

For more on editing for comma splices and fused sentences, see A2 in the Quick Editing Guide (the dark-blue-edged pages).

Splice two ropes, or two strips of movie film, and you join them into one. Splice two main clauses by putting only a comma between them, however, and you get an ungainly construction called a *comma splice.* Here, for instance, are two perfectly good main clauses, each separate, each able to stand on its own as a sentence:

> The detective wriggled on his belly toward the campfire. The drunken smugglers didn't notice him.

Now let's splice those sentences with a comma.

> COMMA SPLICE   The detective wriggled on his belly toward the campfire, the drunken smugglers didn't notice him.

The resulting comma splice makes for difficult reading.

Even more confusing than a comma splice is a *fused sentence:* two main clauses joined without any punctuation.

> FUSED SENTENCE   The detective wriggled on his belly toward the campfire the drunken smugglers didn't notice him.

Lacking clues from the writer, a reader cannot tell where to pause. To understand the sentence, he or she must halt and reread.

The next two pages show five easy ways to eliminate both comma splices and fused sentences, also called **run-ons**. Your choice depends on the length and complexity of your main clauses and the effect you desire.

Sentence Parts at a Glance

The *subject* (**S**) of a sentence identifies some person, place, thing, situation, or idea.

The *predicate* (**P**) of a sentence includes a verb (expressing action or state of being) and makes an assertion about the subject.

An *object* (**O**) is the target or recipient of the action described by the verb.

A *complement* (**C**) renames or describes a subject or object.

> S   P   C   S   P   O
> The *campus center is beautiful.* The new *sculpture draws crowds.*

2a **Write separate complete sentences to correct a comma splice or a fused sentence.**

COMMA SPLICE   Sigmund Freud has been called an enemy of sexual repression, the truth is that he is not a friend of free love.

FUSED SENTENCE   Sigmund Freud has been called an enemy of sexual repression the truth is that he is not a friend of free love.

Neither sentence yields its meaning without a struggle. To point readers in the right direction, separate the clauses.

REVISED   Sigmund Freud has been called an enemy of sexual repression. The truth is that he is not a friend of free love.

sentence: A word group that includes both a subject and a predicate and can stand alone

2b **Use a comma and a coordinating conjunction to correct a comma splice or a fused sentence.**

Is it always incorrect to join two main clauses with a comma? No. If both clauses are of roughly equal weight, you can use a comma to link them — as long as you add a coordinating conjunction after the comma.

COMMA SPLICE   Hurricane winds hit ninety miles an hour, they tore the roof from every house on Paradise Drive.

REVISED   Hurricane winds hit ninety miles an hour, *and* they tore the roof from every house on Paradise Drive.

coordinating conjunction: A one-syllable linking word (*and, but, for, or, nor, so, yet*) that joins elements with equal or near-equal importance: Jack *and* Jill, sink *or* swim

For advice on coordination, see 14a–14c.

2c **Use a semicolon or a colon to correct a comma splice or a fused sentence.**

A semicolon can keep two thoughts connected while giving full emphasis to each one.

COMMA SPLICE   Hurricane winds hit ninety miles an hour, they tore the roof from every house on Paradise Drive.

REVISED   Hurricane winds hit ninety miles an hour; they tore the roof from every house on Paradise Drive.

If the second thought clearly illustrates or explains the first, add it on with a colon.

REVISED   The hurricane caused extensive damage: it tore the roof from every house on Paradise Drive.

Remember that the only punctuation powerful enough to link two main clauses single-handedly is a semicolon, a colon, or a period. A lone comma won't do the job.

EXCEPTION: Certain very short, similar main clauses can be joined with a comma.

Jill runs by day, Tom walks by night.

I came, I saw, I conquered.

Commas are not obligatory with short, similar clauses. If you find this issue confusing, you can stick with semicolons to join all main clauses, short or long.

Jill runs by day; Tom walks by night.

I came; I saw; I conquered.

main clause: A group of words that has both a subject and a verb and can stand alone as a complete sentence: *My sister has a friend.*
subordinate clause: A group of words that contains a subject and a verb but cannot stand alone because it depends on a main clause to help it make sense: Pia, *who plays the oboe*, prefers solitude.

■ For advice on subordination, see 14d–14f.

2d Use subordination to correct a comma splice or a fused sentence.

If one main clause is more important than the other, or if you want to give it more importance, you can make the less important one a subordinate clause. When you make one clause subordinate, you throw weight on the main clause. In effect, you show your reader how one idea relates to another: you decide which matters more.

FUSED SENTENCE	Hurricane winds hit ninety miles an hour they tore the roof from every house on Paradise Drive.
REVISED	*When hurricane winds hit ninety miles an hour,* they tore the roof from every house on Paradise Drive.
REVISED	Hurricane winds, *which tore the roof from every house on Paradise Drive,* hit ninety miles an hour.

2e Use a conjunctive adverb with a semicolon and a comma to correct a comma splice or a fused sentence.

conjunctive adverb: A linking word that can connect independent clauses and show a relationship between two ideas: Armando is a serious student; *therefore*, he studies every day. (See 14.)

If you want to cram more than one clause into a sentence, you may join two clauses with a **conjunctive adverb**. Conjunctive adverbs show relationships such as addition (*also, besides*), comparison (*likewise, similarly*), contrast (*instead, however*), emphasis (*namely, certainly*), cause and effect (*thus, therefore*), or time (*finally, subsequently*). These transitional words and phrases can be a useful way of linking clauses — but only with the right punctuation.

| COMMA SPLICE | Sigmund Freud has been called an enemy of sexual repression, however the truth is that he is not a friend of free love. |

A writer might consider a comma plus the conjunctive adverb *however* enough to combine the two main clauses, but that glue won't hold. Stronger binding — the semicolon along with a comma — is required.

| REVISED | Sigmund Freud has been called an enemy of sexual repression; however, the truth is that he is not a friend of free love. |

■ Exercise 2–1

Revising Comma Splices and Fused Sentences

In the following examples, correct each comma splice or fused sentence in two ways and decide which way you believe works best. Be creative: don't correct every one in the same way. Some sentences may be correct as written. Possible revisions for the lettered sentences appear in the back of the book. Example:

> The castle looked eerie from a distance, it filled us with nameless fear as we approached.

> The castle looked eerie from a *distance;* it filled us with nameless fear as we approached.

> *Or*

> The castle, *which looked eerie from a distance,* filled us with nameless fear as we approached.

a. We followed the scientist down a flight of wet stone steps at last he stopped before a huge oak door.

b. Dr. Frankenstein selected a heavy key, he twisted it in the lock.

c. The huge door gave a groan it swung open on a dimly lighted laboratory.

d. Before us on a dissecting table lay a form with closed eyes to behold it sent a quick chill down my spine.

e. The scientist strode to the table, he lifted a white-gloved hand.

1. Dr. Frankenstein flung a power switch, blue streamers of static electricity crackled about the table, the creature gave a grunt and opened smoldering eyes.

2. "I've won!" exclaimed the scientist in triumph he circled the room doing a demented Irish reel.

3. The creature's right hand strained, the heavy steel manacle imprisoning his wrist began to creak.

4. Like a staple wrenched from a document, the manacle yielded.

5. The creature sat upright and tugged at the shackles binding his ankles, Frankenstein uttered a piercing scream.

■ Exercise 2–2

Revising Comma Splices and Fused Sentences

Revise the following passage, using subordination, a conjunctive adverb, a semicolon, or a colon to correct each comma splice or fused sentence. You may also write separate complete sentences. Some sentences may be correct. Example:

> English can be difficult to learn, it is full of expressions that don't mean what they literally say.

> English can be difficult to learn *because* it is full of expressions that don't mean what they literally say.

■ For more practice, visit <bedfordstmartins.com/bedguide> and do a keyword search:

 splice_fused

Have you ever wondered why you drive on parkways and park on driveways, that's about as logical as your nose running while your feet smell! When you stop to think about it, these phrases don't make sense yet we tend to accept them without thinking about what they literally mean we simply take their intended meanings for granted. Think, however, how confusing they are for a person who is just learning the language. If, for example, you have just learned the verb *park*, you would logically assume that a parkway is where you should park your car, of course when most people see a parkway or a driveway they realize that braking on a parkway would be hazardous, while speeding through a driveway will not take them very far. However, our language is full of many idiomatic expressions that may be difficult for a person from another language background to understand. Fortunately, there are plenty of questions to keep us *all* confused, such as why Americans commonly refer to going to work as "punching the clock."

3 *Verbs*

For help editing verbs, see A3 in the Quick Editing Guide (the dark-blue-edged pages).

Most verbs show action (*swim, eat, sleep, win*). Some verbs indicate a state of being by linking the subject of a sentence with a word that renames or describes it; they are called **linking verbs** (*is, become, seem*). A few verbs accompany a main verb to give more information about its action; they are called **helping verbs** or **auxiliary verbs** (*have, must, can*).

VERB FORMS

3a Use a linking verb to connect the subject of a sentence with a subject complement.

linking verb: A verb (*is, become, seem, feel*) that shows a state of being by linking the sentence subject with a word that renames or describes the subject: The sky *is* blue.

subject complement: A noun, an adjective, or a group of words that follows a linking verb and renames or describes the subject: This plum tastes *ripe*.

By indicating what the subject of a sentence *is* or is *like*, a linking verb (LV) creates a sort of equation, either positive or negative, between the subject and its complement. The subject complement (SC) can be a noun, a pronoun, or an adjective.

LV   SC
Julia will *make* a good *doctor*. [Noun]

LV   SC
Jorge *is* not the *one*. [Pronoun]

LV   SC
London weather *seems foggy*. [Adjective]

A verb may be a linking verb in some sentences and not in others. If you pay attention to what the verb means, you can usually tell how it is functioning.

I often *grow* sleepy after lunch. [Linking verb + subject complement *sleepy*]

I often *grow* tomatoes in my garden. [Transitive verb + direct object *tomatoes*]

> ## Common Linking Verbs at a Glance
>
> Some linking verbs tell what a noun is, was, or will be.
>
> > *be, become, remain:* I *remain* optimistic.
> >
> > *grow:* The sky is *growing* dark.
> >
> > *make:* One plus two *makes* three.
> >
> > *prove:* His warning *proved* accurate.
> >
> > *turn:* The weather *turned* cold.
>
> Some linking verbs tell what a noun might be.
>
> > *appear, seem, look:* The child *looks* cold.
>
> Most verbs of the senses can operate as linking verbs.
>
> > *feel, smell, sound, taste:* The smoothie *tastes* sweet.

3b Use helping verbs to add information about the main verb.

Adding a *helping* or *auxiliary verb* to a simple verb (*go, shoot, be*) allows you to express a wide variety of tenses and moods (*am going, did shoot, would have been*). (See 3g–3l and 3n–3p.)

The parts of this combination, called a *verb phrase,* need not appear together but may be separated by other words.

> I probably *am going* to France this summer.

> You *should* not *have shot* that pigeon.

> This change *may* well *have been* seriously *contemplated* before the election.

helping verb: A verb added to a main verb to show variations in its action (*do, can, have, will*)

main verb: The verb in a sentence that identifies the central action (*hit, stopped*)

> ## Helping Verbs at a Glance
>
> Of the twenty-three helping verbs in English, fourteen can also function as main verbs:
>
> > be, is, am, are, was, were, being, been
> >
> > do, does, did
> >
> > have, has, had
>
> The other nine can function only as helping verbs, never as main verbs:
>
> > can, could, should, would, may, might, must, shall, will

3c **Use the correct principal parts of the verb.**

The **principal parts** are the forms the verb can take — alone or with helping verbs — to indicate the full range of times when an action or state of being does, did, or will occur. Verbs have three principal parts: the infinitive, the past tense, and the past participle.

- The **infinitive** is the simple or dictionary form of the verb (*go, sing, laugh*) or the simple form preceded by *to* (*to go, to sing, to laugh*).
- The **past tense** signals that the verb's action is completed (*went, sang, laughed*).
- The **past participle** is combined with helping verbs to indicate action occurring at various times in the past or future (*have gone, had sung, will have laughed*). With forms of *be*, it makes the passive voice. (See 3m.)

In addition to the three principal parts, all verbs have a present participle, the *-ing* form of the verb (*going, singing, laughing*). This form is used to make the progressive tenses. (See 3k and 3l.) It also can modify nouns and pronouns ("the *leaking* bottle"); as a gerund, it can function as a noun ("*Sleeping all day* pleases me").

> ▓ For the principal parts of many irregular verbs, see A3 and A4 in the Quick Editing Guide (the dark-blue-edged pages).

3d **Use *-d* or *-ed* to form the past tense and past participle of regular verbs.**

Most verbs in English are **regular verbs:** they form the past tense and past participle in a standard, predictable way. Regular verbs that end in *-e* add *-d* to the infinitive; those that do not end in *-e* add *-ed*.

INFINITIVE	PAST TENSE	PAST PARTICIPLES
(to) smile	smiled	smiled
(to) act	acted	acted

3e **Use the correct forms for the past tense and past participle of irregular verbs.**

English has at least two hundred **irregular verbs,** which form the past tense and past participle in some other way than by adding *-d* or *-ed*. Most irregular verbs, familiar to native English speakers, pose no problem.

> For the forms of many irregular verbs, see A3 in the Quick Editing Guide (the dark-blue-edged pages). For the forms of *be* and *have*, see A4 in the Quick Editing Guide.

3f **Use the correct forms of *lie* and *lay* and *sit* and *set*.**

Try taking two easy steps to eliminate confusion between *lie* and *lay*.

- First, memorize the principal parts and present participles of both verbs (see the chart on p. H-17).
- Second, fix in memory that *lie*, in all its forms, is intransitive and never takes a direct object: "The island *lies* due east." *Lay*, a transitive verb, always requires an object: "*Lay* that pistol down."

> **intransitive verb:** A verb that is complete in itself and needs no object: The surgeon *paused*.
> **transitive verb:** A verb that must have an object to complete its meaning: Alan *hit* the ball.

Forms of *Lie* and *Lay*, *Sit* and *Set*

lie, lay, lain, lying: recline

PRESENT TENSE		PAST TENSE	
I lie	we lie	I lay	we lay
you lie	you lie	you lay	you lay
he/she/it lies	they lie	he/she/it lay	they lay

PAST PARTICIPLE

lain   (We have *lain* in the sun long enough.)

PRESENT PARTICIPLE

lying   (At ten o'clock he was still *lying* in bed.)

lay, laid, laid, laying: put in place, deposit

PRESENT TENSE		PAST TENSE	
I lay	we lay	I laid	we laid
you lay	you lay	you laid	you laid
he/she/it lays	they lay	he/she/it laid	they laid

PAST PARTICIPLE

laid   (Having *laid* his clothes on the bed, Mark jumped into the shower.)

PRESENT PARTICIPLE

laying   (*Laying* her cards on the table, Lola cried, "Gin!")

sit, sat, sat, sitting: be seated

PRESENT TENSE		PAST TENSE	
I sit	we sit	I sat	we sat
you sit	you sit	you sat	you sat
he/she/it sits	they sit	he/she/it sat	they sat

PAST PARTICIPLE

sat   (I have *sat* here long enough.)

PRESENT PARTICIPLE

sitting   (Why are you *sitting* on that rickety bench?)

set, set, set, setting: place

PRESENT TENSE		PAST TENSE	
I set	we set	I set	we set
you set	you set	you set	you set
he/she/it sets	they set	he/she/it set	they set

PAST PARTICIPLE

set   (Paul has *set* the table for eight.)

PRESENT PARTICIPLE

setting   (Chanh-Duy has been *setting* pins at the Bowl-a-drome.)

The same distinction exists between *sit* and *set*. Usually, *sit* is intransitive: "He *sits* on the stairs." *Set*, on the other hand, almost always takes an object: "He *sets* the bottle on the counter." There are, however, a few easily memorized exceptions. The sun *sets*. A hen *sets*. Gelatin *sets*. You *sit* on a horse. You can *sit* yourself down at a table that *sits* twelve.

■ For more practice, visit <bedfordstmartins.com/bedguide> and do a keyword search:

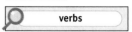
verbs

■ Exercise 3–1

Using Irregular Verb Forms

Underline each incorrectly used irregular verb in the following sentences, and substitute the verb's correct form. Some sentences may be correct. Answers for the lettered sentences appear in the back of the book. Example:

> We have already <u>drove</u> eight hundred miles, and we still have a long way to go to reach Oregon.

> We have already *driven* eight hundred miles, and we still have a long way to go to reach Oregon.

a. In those days, Benjamin wrote all the music, and his sister sung all the songs.
b. After she had eaten her bagel, she drank a cup of coffee with milk.
c. When the bell rung, darkness had already fell.
d. Voters have chose some new senators, who won't take office until January.
e. Carol threw the ball into the water, and the dog swum after it.

1. He brought along two of the fish they had caught the day before.
2. By the time the sun set, the birds had all went away.
3. Teachers had spoke to his parents long before he stole the bicycle.
4. While the cat laid on the bed, the mouse ran beneath the door.
5. For the past three days the wind has blew hard from the south, but now the clouds have began to drift in.

TENSES

tense: The time when the action of a verb did, does, or will occur

With the *simple tenses* we can indicate whether the verb's action took place in the past, takes place in the present, or will take place in the future. The *perfect tenses* enable us to narrow the timing even further, specifying that the action was or will be completed by the time of some other action. With the *progressive tenses* we can indicate that the verb's action did, does, or will continue. Using this variety of verb forms can increase the precision of your writing.

■ For advice on consistent verb tense, see 9a.

3g **Use the simple present tense for an action that takes place once, repeatedly, or continuously in the present.**

The simple present tense is the infinitive form of a regular verb plus *-s* or *-es* for the third-person singular.

Verb Tenses at a Glance

NOTE: The examples show first person only.

SIMPLE TENSES

Present	*Past*	*Future*
I cook	I cooked	I will cook
I see	I saw	I will see

PERFECT TENSES

Present perfect	*Past perfect*	*Future perfect*
I have cooked	I had cooked	I will have cooked
I have seen	I had seen	I will have seen

PROGRESSIVE TENSES

Present progressive	*Past progressive*	*Future progressive*
I am cooking	I was cooking	I will be cooking
I am seeing	I was seeing	I will be seeing

Present perfect progressive	*Past perfect progressive*	*Future perfect progressive*
I have been cooking	I had been cooking	I will have been cooking
I have been seeing	I had been seeing	I will have been seeing

I like, I go	we like, we go
you like, you go	you like, you go
he/she/it likes, he/she/it goes	they like, they go

Some irregular verbs, such as *go*, form their simple present tense following the same rules as regular verbs. Other irregular verbs, such as *be* and *have*, are special cases for which you should learn the correct forms.

I am, I have	we are, we have
you are, you have	you are, you have
he/she/it is, he/she/it has	they are, they have

You can use the simple present tense for an action happening right now ("I *welcome* this news"), happening repeatedly in the present ("Judy *goes* to church every Sunday"), or ongoing in the present ("Wesley *likes* ice cream"). In some cases, if you want to ask a question or intensify the action, use the helping verb *do* or *does* before the infinitive form of the main verb.

I *do think* you should take the job.

Does Christos *want* it?

You can use the simple present for future action: "Football season *starts* Wednesday." Use it also for a general truth, even if the rest of the sentence is in a different tense:

Columbus proved in 1492 that the world *is* round.

Mr. Hammond will argue that people *are* basically good.

ESL GUIDELINES

■ For the past forms of many irregular verbs, see A3 in the Quick Editing Guide (the dark-blue-edged pages).

The Simple Tenses

Present Tense: base form of the verb (+ *-s* or *-es* for *he, she, it*)

- Use the simple present tense to express general statements of fact or habitual activities or customs. Although it is called "present," this tense is really general or timeless.

  Zanetta *goes* to the movies every Sunday afternoon.

  You *make* wonderful coffee.

- To form negatives and questions, use *do* or *does* + base form.

  Zanetta *does not* (*doesn't*) go to the movies during the week.

  Do you still *make* wonderful coffee?

Past Tense: base form + *-d* or *-ed* for regular verbs

- Use the simple past tense to express an action that occurred at a specific time in the past. The specific time may be stated or implied.

  The package *arrived* yesterday.

  They *went* to San Juan for spring break.

- To form negatives and questions, use *did* + base form.

  They *did not* (*didn't*) go to Fort Lauderdale.

  Did the package *arrive* yesterday?

Future Tense: *will* or *be going to* + base form

- Use the simple future tense to express an action that will take place in the future. Also use *will* to imply promises and predictions.

  The students *will study* hard for their exam.

  The students *are going to study* hard for their exam.

  We *will help* you move. [Promise]

  Cell phones *will* soon *replace* most other phones. [Prediction]

- To form negatives and questions, use *will* + base form.

  José *will not* (*won't*) *graduate* this year.

  Will cell phones *replace* most other phones?

NOTE: Use the simple present, not the future, to express future meaning in clauses beginning with *before, after,* or *when*.

     INCORRECT   When my mother *will get* home, we will make dinner.

     CORRECT   When my mother *gets* home, we will make dinner.

Use the simple present to show a future action when other words in the sentence make the future meaning clear.

     The bus *departs* in five minutes.

     We *leave* for Chicago in the morning and *return* next Wednesday.

3h Use the simple past tense for actions already completed.

Regular verbs form the past tense by adding *-d* or *-ed* to the infinitive; the past tense of irregular verbs must be memorized.

> Jack *enjoyed* the party. [Regular verb]

> Akita *went* home early. [Irregular verb]

Although speakers may not always pronounce the *-d* or *-ed* ending clearly, standard written English requires that you add the *-d* or *-ed* to all regular past tense verbs.

> NONSTANDARD   I *use* to wear weird clothes when I was a child.

> STANDARD   I *used* to wear weird clothes when I was a child.

In the past tense, you can use the helping verb *did* (past tense of *do*) to ask a question or intensify the action. Use *did* with the infinitive form of the main verb for both regular and irregular verbs.

> I went.   I did go.   Why did I go?
> You saw.   You did see.   What did you see?
> She ran.   She did run.   Where did she run?

For a chart of troublesome irregular verbs, see A3 in the Quick Editing Guide (the dark-blue-edged pages).

3i Use the simple future tense for actions that are expected to happen but have not happened yet.

Although the present tense can indicate future action ("We *go* on vacation next Monday"), most actions that have not yet taken place are expressed in the simple future tense.

> George *will arrive* in time for dinner.

> *Will* you please *show* him where to park?

To form the simple future tense, add *will* to the infinitive form of the verb.

> I will go   we will go
> you will go   you will go
> he/she/it will go they will go

You can also use *shall* to inject a tone of determination ("We *shall overcome*!") or in polite questions ("*Shall* we dance?").

3j Use the perfect tenses for an action completed at the time of another action.

The present perfect, past perfect, and future perfect tenses consist of a form of the helping verb *have* plus the past participle. The tense of *have* indicates the tense of the whole verb phrase.

The action of a *present perfect* verb was completed before the sentence is uttered. Its helping verb is in the present tense: *have* or *has.*

I *have* never *been* to Spain, but I *have been* to Oklahoma.

Mr. Grimaldi *has gone* home for the day.

Have you *seen* Johnny Depp's new film?

You can use the present perfect tense either for an action completed before some other action ("I *have washed* my hands of the whole affair, but I am watching from a safe distance") or for an action begun in the past and still going on ("Max *has worked* in this office for twelve years").

ESL GUIDELINES

The Perfect Tenses

Present Perfect Tense: *has* or *have* + past participle (*-ed* or *-en* form for regular verbs)

- Use the present perfect tense when an action took place at some unspecified time in the past. The action may have occurred repeatedly.

    I *have traveled* to many countries.

    The dog *has bitten* my aunt twice.

- Use the present perfect tense with *for* and *since* to indicate that an action began in the past, is occurring now, and will probably continue.

    I *have gone* to school with Min and Paolo since fifth grade.

    Soo-Jung *has lived* next door to the Kramers for twelve years.

Past Perfect Tense: *had* + past participle

■ For the forms of many irregular verbs, see A3 in the Quick Editing Guide (the dark-blue-edged pages).

- Use the past perfect tense to indicate that an action was completed in the past before some other past action.

    Josef *had smoked* for many years before he decided to quit.

    We got rid of the dog because he *had bitten* my aunt twice.

- Particularly in speech or informal writing, the simple past may be used instead of the past perfect when the relationship between actions is made clear by a conjunction such as *when, before, after,* or *until.*

    Observers *saw* the plane catch fire before it landed.

Future Perfect Tense: *will* + *have* + past participle

- Use the future perfect tense when an action will take place before some time in the future.

    The package *will have* already *arrived* by the time we get home.

    By June, the students *will have studied* ten chapters.

The action of a *past perfect* verb was completed before some other action in the past. Its helping verb is in the past tense: *had*.

The concert *had ended* by the time we found a parking space.

Until I met her, I *had* not *pictured* Jenna as a redhead.

Had you *wanted* to clean the house before Mother arrived?

The action of a *future perfect* verb will be completed by some point (specified or implied) in the future. Its helping verb is in the future tense: *will have*.

The builders *will have finished* the house by June.

When you get the Dutch Blue, *will* you *have collected* every stamp you need?

The store *will* not *have closed* by the time we get there.

3k Use the simple progressive tenses for an action in progress.

The present progressive, past progressive, and future progressive tenses consist of a form of the helping verb *be* plus the present participle (which is formed by adding *-ing* to the infinitive). The tense of *be* determines the tense of the whole verb phrase.

The *present progressive* expresses an action that is taking place now. Its helping verb is in the present tense: *am, is,* or *are*.

I *am thinking* of a word that starts with *R*.

Is Stefan *babysitting* while Marie *is* off *visiting* her sister?

You can also express future action with the present progressive of *go* plus an infinitive phrase.

I *am going to read* Tolstoy's *War and Peace* someday.

Are you *going to sign up* for Professor Blaine's course on the sixties?

The *past progressive* expresses an action that took place continuously at some time in the past, whether or not that action is still going on. Its helping verb is in the past tense: *was* or *were*.

The old men *were sitting* on the porch when we passed.

Lucy *was planning* to take the weekend off.

The *future progressive* expresses an action that will take place continuously at some time in the future. Its helping verb is in the future tense: *will be*.

They *will be answering* the phones while she is gone.

Will we *be dining* out every night on our vacation?

ESL GUIDELINES

The Simple Progressive Tenses

Present Progressive Tense: present tense of *be* + present participle (*-ing* form)

- Use the present progressive tense when an action began in the past, is happening now, and will end at some time in the future.

    The students *are studying* for their exam.

    My sister *is living* with us until she graduates from college.

- You can also use the present progressive tense to show a future action when other words in the sentence make the future meaning clear.

    Nili *is flying* to Pittsburgh on July 8.

NOTE: Linking verbs (such as *be, seem, look*), verbs that express an emotional or mental state (such as *trust, like, guess, realize*), and verbs without action (such as *belong, have, need*) are not generally used in the present progressive tense. For these verbs, use the present tense to express a continuous state.

    INCORRECT   I think I *am liking* you very much.

    CORRECT   I think I *like* you very much.

Past Progressive Tense: *was* or *were* + present participle

- Use the past progressive tense when an action began and continued at a specific time in the past.

    Maria *was watching* the news when I arrived.

    The students *were studying* for their exam all day.

Future Progressive Tense: *will be* + present participle or present tense of *be* + *going to be* + present participle

- Use the future progressive tense when an action will begin and will continue in the future.

    Hans *will be wearing* blue jeans to the party tonight.

    The students *are going to be studying* until midnight.

---

31   **Use the perfect progressive tenses for a continuing action that began in the past.**

Use the present perfect progressive, the past perfect progressive, or the future perfect progressive tense for an action that started in the past and did, does, or will continue.

The *present perfect progressive* indicates an action that started in the past and is continuing in the present. Form it by adding the present perfect of *be* (*has been, have been*) to the present participle (*-ing* form) of the main verb.

All morning Fred *has been singing* the blues about his neighbor's wild parties.

Have you *been reading* Uma's postcards from England?

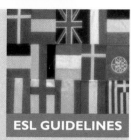

ESL GUIDELINES

The Perfect Progressive Tenses

Present Perfect Progressive Tense: *have* or *has been* + present participle (*-ing* form)

- Use the present perfect progressive tense when an action began at some time in the past and has continued to the present. The words *for* and *since* are often used in sentences with this tense.

  She *has been answering* questions all day.

  The students *have been studying* for a long time.

Past Perfect Progressive Tense: *had been* + present participle

- Use the past perfect progressive tense when an action began and continued in the past and then was completed before some other past action.

  We *had been studying* for three hours before we took a break.

  Miguel *had been ringing* the doorbell for five minutes when we got home.

Future Perfect Progressive Tense: *will have been* + present participle

- Use the future perfect progressive tense when an action will continue in the future for a specific amount of time and then will end before another future action.

  The students *will have been studying* for twenty-four hours by the time they take the exam tomorrow.

  Jenn *will have been sailing* for a week when she reaches Jamaica.

The *past perfect progressive* expresses a continuing action that was completed before another past action. Form it by adding the past perfect of *be* (*had been*) to the present participle of the main verb.

By the time Khalid finally arrived, I *had been waiting* for twenty minutes.

The *future perfect progressive* expresses an action that is expected to continue into the future beyond some other future action. Form it by adding the future perfect of *be* (*will have been*) to the present participle of the main verb.

By 2009 Joanne *will have been attending* school longer than anyone else I know.

■ Exercise 3–2

Identifying Verb Tenses

Underline each verb or verb phrase and identify its tense in the following sentences. Answers for the lettered sentences appear in the back of the book. Example:

John is living in Hinsdale, but he prefers Joliet.

■ For more practice, visit \<bedfordstmartins.com /bedguide> and do a keyword search:

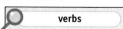

verbs

John is living [present progressive] in Hinsdale, but he prefers [simple present] Joliet.

a. He has been living like a hunted animal ever since he hacked into the university computer lab to change all of his grades.
b. I have never appeared on a reality television show, and I never will appear on one unless my family gets selected.
c. James had been at the party for only fifteen minutes when his host suddenly pitched the caterer into the swimming pool.
d. As of next month, I will have been studying karate for six years, and I will be taking the test for my orange belt in July.
e. The dachshund was running at its fastest speed, but the squirrel strolled toward the tree without fear.

1. As of May 1, Ira and Sandy will have been going together for a year.
2. She will be working in her study if you need her.
3. Have you been hoping that Carlos will come to your party?
4. I know that he will not yet have returned from Chicago.
5. His parents had been expecting him home any day until they heard that he was still waiting for the bus.

VOICE

Intelligent students read challenging books.

Challenging books are read by intelligent students.

These two statements convey similar information, but their emphasis is different. In the first sentence, the subject (*students*) performs the verb's action (*read*); in the second sentence, the subject (*books*) receives the verb's action (*are read*). One sentence states its idea directly, the other indirectly. We say that the first sentence is in the *active voice* and the second is in the *passive voice*.

3m Use the active voice rather than the passive voice.

Verbs in the *active voice* consist of principal parts and helping verbs. Verbs in the *passive voice* consist of the past participle preceded by a form of *be* ("you *are given*," "I *was given*," "she *will be given*"). Most writers prefer the active to the passive voice because it is clearer and simpler, requires fewer words, and identifies the actor and the action more explicitly.

ACTIVE VOICE   *Sergeants give* orders. *Privates obey* them.

Sometimes a verb in the passive voice would be more effective in the active voice. Normally the subject of a sentence is the focus of readers' attention. If that subject does not perform the verb's action but instead receives

The Passive Voice

Passive Voice: form of *be* + past participle (*-ed* or *-en* form for regular verbs)

- In a passive voice sentence, the subject *receives* the action of the verb instead of performing it.

  ACTIVE   The university *awarded* Hamid a scholarship. [The subject (*university*) performs the action of *awarding*.]

  PASSIVE   Hamid *was awarded* a scholarship by the university. [The subject (*Hamid*) receives the action.]

ESL GUIDELINES

- Often the identity of the action's performer is not important or is understood, and the *by* phrase is omitted.

  PASSIVE   Automobiles are built in Detroit. [It is understood that they are built *by people*.]

- When forming the passive, be careful to use the appropriate tenses of *be* to maintain the tense of the original active sentence.

  ACTIVE   Kip the clown *entertains* children. [Present tense]

  PASSIVE   Children *are entertained* by Kip the clown. [Present tense]

  ACTIVE   Kip the clown *entertained* the children. [Past tense]

  PASSIVE   The children *were entertained* by Kip the clown. [Past tense]

NOTE: Intransitive verbs are not used in the passive voice.

  INCORRECT   The plane *was arrived*.

  CORRECT   The plane *arrived*.

NOTE: The future progressive and future perfect progressive tenses are not used in the passive voice.

  INCORRECT   The novel *will be being read* by John.

  CORRECT   John *will be reading* the novel.

intransitive verb: A verb that is complete in itself and needs no object: The surgeon *paused*.

the action, readers may wonder: What did the writer mean to emphasize? Just what is the point?

  PASSIVE VOICE   *Orders are given* by sergeants. *They are obeyed* by privates.

Other writers misuse the passive voice to try to lend pomp to a humble truth (or would-be truth): for example, "Slight technical difficulties are being experienced" may replace "The airplane needs repairs." Some even use the passive voice deliberately to obscure the truth — a contradiction of the very purpose of writing.

You do not need to drop the passive voice entirely from your writing. Sometimes the performer of the verb's action in a sentence is unknown or irrelevant. With a passive voice verb, you can simply omit the performer, as in "Many fortunes were lost in the stock market crash of 1929" or "The passive voice is often misused." It's a good idea, though, to substitute the active voice for the passive unless you have a good reason for using the passive.

■ For more practice, visit <bedfordstmartins.com/ bedguide> and do a key-word search:

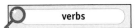

■ Exercise 3–3

Using Active and Passive Voice Verbs

Revise the following passage, changing the passive voice to the active voice in each sentence, unless you can justify keeping the passive. Example:

> The Galápagos Islands were reached by many species of animals in ancient times.

> Many species of animals *reached* the Galápagos Islands in ancient times.

The unique creatures of the Galápagos Islands have been studied by many scientists. The islands were explored by Charles Darwin in 1835. His observations led to the theory of evolution, which he explained in his book *On the Origin of Species*. Thirteen species of finches on the islands were discovered by Darwin, all descended from a common stock; even today this great variety of species can be seen by visitors to the islands. Each island species has evolved by adapting to local conditions. A twig is used by the woodpecker finch to probe trees for grubs. Algae on the ocean floor is fed on by the marine iguana. Salt water can be drunk by the Galápagos cormorant, thanks to a salt-extracting gland. Because of the tameness of these animals, they can be studied by visitors at close range.

MOOD

Still another characteristic of every verb is its **mood**: *indicative, imperative,* or *subjunctive.* The indicative mood is the most common. The imperative and subjunctive moods add valuable versatility.

3n **Use the indicative mood to state a fact, to ask a question, or to express an opinion.**

Most verbs in English are in the indicative mood.

FACT   Danika *left* home two months ago.

QUESTION *Will* she *find* happiness as a belly dancer?

OPINION   I *think* not.

3o **Use the imperative mood to make a request or to give a command or direction.**

The understood but usually unstated subject of a verb in the imperative mood is *you*. The verb's form is the infinitive.

REQUEST   Please *be* there before noon. [*You* please be there. . . .]

COMMAND   *Hurry!* [*You* hurry!]

DIRECTION   *Drive* east on State Street. [*You* drive east. . . .]

3p **Use the subjunctive mood to express a wish, a requirement, a suggestion, or a condition contrary to fact.**

The subjunctive mood is used in a subordinate clause to suggest uncertainty: the action expressed by the verb may or may not actually take place as specified. In any clause opening with *that* and expressing a requirement, the verb is in the subjunctive mood and its form is the infinitive.

Professor Vogt requires that every student *deliver* his or her work promptly.

She asked that we *be* on time for all meetings.

When you use the subjunctive mood to describe a condition that is contrary to fact, use *were* if the verb is *be*; for other verbs, use the simple past tense. Wishes, whether present or past, follow the same rules.

If I *were* rich, I would be happy.

If I *had* a million dollars, I would be happy.

Elissa wishes that Ted *were* more goal-oriented.

Elissa wished that Ted *knew* what he wanted to do.

For a condition that was contrary to fact at some point in the past, use the past perfect tense.

If I *had been* awake, I would have seen the meteor showers.

If Jessie *had known* you were coming, she would have cleaned her room.

Although use of the subjunctive mood has grown scarcer over the years, it still sounds crude to write "If I *was* you. . . ." If you ever feel that the subjunctive mood makes a sentence sound stilted, you can rewrite it, substituting an infinitive phrase.

Professor Vogt requires every student *to deliver* his or her work promptly.

ESL GUIDELINES

Conditionals

Conditional sentences usually contain an *if* clause, which states the condition, and a result clause.

- When the condition is true or possibly true in the present or future, use the present tense in the *if* clause and the present or future tense in the result clause. The future tense is not used in the *if* clause.

    If Jane *prepares* her composition early, she usually *writes* very well.

    If Maria *saves* enough money, she *will buy* some new software.

- When the condition is not true in the present, for most verbs use the past tense in the *if* clause; for the verb *be,* use *were.* Use *would, could,* or *might* + infinitive form in the result clause.

    If Carlos *had* a computer, he *would need* a monitor, too.

    If Claudia *were* here, she *could do* it herself.

- When the condition was not true in the past, use the past perfect tense in the *if* clause. If the possible result was in the past, use *would have, could have,* or *might have* + past participle (*-ed* or *-en* form) in the result clause. If the possible result is in the present, use *would, could,* or *might* + infinitive form in the result clause.

    If Claudia *had saved* enough money last month, she *could have bought* new software. [Result in the past]

    If Annie *had finished* law school, she *might* be a successful lawyer now. [Result in the present]

■ For more practice, visit <bedfordstmartins.com/ bedguide> and do a keyword search:

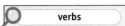

verbs

■ Exercise 3–4

Using the Correct Mood of Verbs

Find and correct any errors in mood in the following sentences. Identify the mood of the incorrect verb as well as its correct replacement. Some sentences may be correct. Answers for the lettered sentences appear in the back of the book. Example:

> The law requires that each person files a tax return by April 15.

> The law requires that each person *file* a tax return by April 15. [Incorrect: *files,* indicative; correct: *file,* subjunctive]

a. Dr. Belanger recommended that Juan flosses his teeth every day.

b. If I was you, I would have done the same thing.

c. Tradition demands that Daegun shows respect for his elders.

d. Please attends the training lesson if you plan to skydive later today.

1. If she was slightly older, she could stay home by herself.

2. If they have waited a little longer, they would have seen some amazing things.

3. Emilia's contract stipulates that she works on Saturdays.

4. If James invested in the company ten years ago, he would have made a lot of money.

4 *Subject-Verb Agreement*

What does it mean for a subject and a verb to agree? Practically speaking, it means that their forms match: plural subjects take plural verbs, third-person subjects take third-person verbs, and so forth. When your subjects and verbs agree, you prevent a mismatch that could distract readers from your message.

> For more on editing for subject-verb agreement, see A4 in the Quick Editing Guide (the dark-blue-edged pages).

4a A verb agrees with its subject in person and number.

Subject and verb agree in person (first, second, or third):

I write my research papers on my laptop. [Subject and verb in first person]

Eamon writes his papers in the lab. [Subject and verb in third person]

Subject and verb agree in number (singular or plural):

Grace has enjoyed college. [Subject and verb singular]

She and Jim have enjoyed their vacation. [Subject and verb plural]

The present tense of most verbs is the infinitive form, with no added ending except in the third-person singular. (See 3g–3l.)

I enjoy	we enjoy
you enjoy	you enjoy
he/she/it enjoys	they enjoy

Forms of the verb *be* vary from this rule.

I am	we are
you are	you are
he/she/it is	they are

> **subject:** The part of a sentence that names something—a person, an object, an idea, a situation—about which the predicate makes an assertion: The *king* lives.
>
> **verb:** A word that shows action (The cow *jumped* over the moon) or a state of being (The cow *is* brown)

4b A verb agrees with its subject, not with any words that intervene.

My *favorite* of O. Henry's short stories *is* "The Gift of the Magi."

Home sales, once driving the local economy, *have fallen* during the last year.

A singular subject linked to another noun or pronoun by a prepositional phrase beginning with wording such as *along with, as well as,* or *in addition to* remains a singular subject and takes a singular verb.

My cousin *James* as well as his wife and son *plans* to vote for Levine.

> **prepositional phrase:** The preposition and its object (a noun or pronoun), plus any modifiers: *in the bar, under a rickety table*

4c   Subjects joined by *and* usually take a plural verb.

compound subject: A subject consisting of two or more nouns or pronouns linked by *and: My mother and my sister drove home.*

In most cases, a compound subject takes a plural verb.

> *"Howl" and "Gerontion" are* Barry's favorite poems.

> *Sugar, salt, and fat* adversely *affect* people's health.

However, for phrases like *each man and woman* or *every dog and cat,* where the subjects are considered individually, use a singular verb.

> *Each man and woman* in the room *has* a different story to tell.

Use a singular verb for two singular subjects that form or are one thing.

> *Lime juice and soda quenches* your thirst.

4d   With subjects joined by *or* or *nor,* the verb agrees with the part of the subject nearest to it.

> Either they or *Max is* guilty.

> Neither Swaylhi nor *I am* willing to face the truth.

Subjects containing *not . . . but* follow this rule also.

> Not we but *George knows* the whole story.

You can remedy awkward constructions by rephrasing.

> Either they are guilty or Max is.

> Swaylhi and I are unwilling to face the truth.

> We do not know the whole story, but George does.

4e   Most collective nouns take singular verbs.

collective noun: A singular noun that represents a group of people or items, such as *committee, family, jury, trio*

When a collective noun refers to a group of people acting in unison, use a singular verb.

> The *jury finds* the defendant guilty.

When the members act individually, use a plural verb.

> The *jury do* not yet *agree* on a verdict.

If you feel that using a plural verb results in an awkward sentence, reword the subject so that it refers to members of the group individually.

> The *jurors do* not yet *agree* on a verdict.

■ For more on agreement with collective nouns, see 7e.

Count Nouns and Articles

Nouns referring to items that can be counted are called **count** (or **countable**) nouns. Count nouns can be made plural.

> *table, chair, egg*   two *tables*, several *chairs*, a dozen *eggs*

Singular count nouns must be preceded by a **determiner.** The class of words called determiners includes **articles** (*a, an, the*), **possessives** (*John's, your, his, my,* and so on), **demonstratives** (*this, that, these, those*), **numbers** (*three, the third,* and so on), and **indefinite quantity words** (*no, some, many,* and so on).

> *a* dog, *the* football, *one* reason, *the first* page, *no* chance

ESL GUIDELINES

Noncount Nouns and Articles

Nouns referring to items that cannot be counted are called **noncount** (or **uncountable**) nouns. Noncount nouns cannot be made plural.

> INCORRECT   I need to learn more *grammars*.
>
> CORRECT   I need to learn more *grammar*.

- Common categories of noncount nouns include types of **food** (*cheese, meat, bread*), **solids** (*dirt, salt, chalk*), **liquids** (*milk, juice, gasoline*), **gases** (*methane, hydrogen, air*), and **abstract ideas** including emotions (*democracy, gravity, love*).

- Another category of noncount nouns is **mass** nouns, which usually represent a large group of countable nouns (*furniture, mail, clothing*).

- The only way to count noncountable nouns is to use a countable noun with them, usually to indicate a quantity or a container.

> one *piece* of furniture
>
> two *quarts* of water
>
> an *example* of jealousy

- Noncount nouns are never preceded by an indefinite article; they are often preceded by *some*.

> INCORRECT   She gave us *a* good advice.
>
> CORRECT   She gave us good advice.
>
> CORRECT   She gave us *some* good advice.

- When noncount nouns are *general* in meaning, no article is required, but when the context makes them specific (usually in a phrase or a clause after the noun), the definite article is used.

> GENERAL   Deliver us from *evil*.
>
> SPECIFIC   The *evil* that humans do lives after them.

■ For more on using articles with count and noncount nouns, see p. H-49.

indefinite article: An article (*a* or *an*) that indicates any one of many possible items: I will make *a* cake or *a* pie.

definite article: An article (*the*) that indicates one particular item: I ordered *the* spaghetti, not *the* lasagna.

agr
4f

4f   Most indefinite pronouns take a third-person singular verb.

indefinite pronoun: A pronoun standing for an unspecified person or thing, including singular forms (*each, everyone, no one*) and plural forms (*both, few*): *Everyone* is soaking wet.

For a list of indefinite pronouns, see A6 in the Quick Editing Guide (the dark-blue-edged pages).

The indefinite pronouns *each, one, either, neither, anyone, anybody, anything, everyone, everybody, everything, no one, nobody, nothing, someone, somebody,* and *something* are considered singular and take a third-person singular verb.

> *Someone is bothering* me.

Even when one of these subjects is followed by a phrase containing a noun or pronoun of a different person or number, use a singular verb.

> *Each* of you *is* here to stay.

> *One* of the pandas *seems* dangerously ill.

4g   The indefinite pronouns *all, any,* and *some* use a singular or plural verb, depending on their meaning.

> I have no explanation. *Is any* needed?

> *Any* of the changes considered critical *have* been made already.

> *All is* lost.

> *All* of the bananas *are gone.*

> *Some* of the blame *is* mine.

> *Some* of us *are* Democrats.

For more on agreement with indefinite pronouns, see 7d.

None — like *all, any,* and *some* — takes a singular or a plural verb, depending on the sense in which the pronoun is used.

> *None* of you *is* exempt.

> *None* of his wives *were* blond.

4h   In a subordinate clause with a relative pronoun as the subject, the verb agrees with the antecedent.

subordinate clause: A group of words that contains a subject and a verb but cannot stand alone because it depends on a main clause to help it make sense: Pia, *who plays the oboe,* prefers solitude. (See 14d–14f.)

To determine the person and number of the verb in a subordinate clause whose subject is *who, which,* or *that,* look back at the word to which the pronoun refers. The antecedent is usually (but not always) the noun closest to the relative pronoun.

> I have a roommate *who studies* day and night. [The antecedent of *who* is the third-person singular noun *roommate.* Therefore, the verb in the subordinate clause is third-person singular, *studies.*]

I bought one of the two hundred new cars *that have* defective upholstery. [The antecedent of *that* is *cars,* so the verb is third-person plural, *have.*]

This is the only one of the mayor's new ideas *that has* any worth. [Here *one,* not *ideas,* is the antecedent of *that.* Thus, the verb in the subordinate clause is third-person singular, *has,* not *have.*]

4i A verb agrees with its subject even when the subject follows the verb.

In some sentences, introductory expressions such as *there* or *here* change the ordinary order so that the subject follows the verb. Remember that verbs agree with subjects and that *here* and *there* are never subjects.

Here *is* a *riddle* for you.

There *are* forty *people* in my law class.

Under the bridge *were* a broken-down *boat and* a worn *tire.*

4j A linking verb agrees with its subject, not its subject complement.

When a form of the verb *be* is used to link two or more nouns, the subject is the noun that precedes the linking verb. Nouns that follow the linking verb are subject complements. Make a linking verb agree with the subject of the sentence, not with the subject complement.

Jim is a gentleman and a scholar.

Amy's *parents are* her most enthusiastic audience.

4k When the subject is a title, use a singular verb.

When I was younger, *Harry Potter and the Sorcerer's Stone was* my favorite book.

"Memories" sung by Barbra Streisand *is* my aunt's favorite song.

4l Singular nouns that end in -s take singular verbs.

Some nouns look plural even though they refer to a singular subject: *measles, logistics, mathematics, electronics.* Such nouns take singular verbs.

The *news is* that *economics has become* one of the most popular majors.

---

relative pronoun: A pronoun (*who, which, that, what, whom, whomever, whose*) that opens a subordinate clause, modifying a noun or pronoun in another clause: The gift *that* I received is very practical.

antecedent: The word to which a pronoun refers: *Lyn* plays golf, and *she* putts well.

linking verb: A verb (*is, become, seem, feel*) that shows a state of being by linking the sentence subject with a word that renames or describes the subject: The sky *is* blue. (See 3a.)

subject complement: A noun, an adjective, or a group of words that follows a linking verb and renames or describes the subject: This plum tastes *ripe.* (See 3a.)

■ **Exercise 4–1**

Making Subjects and Verbs Agree

■ For more practice, visit
<bedfordstmartins.com/
bedguide> and do a key-
word search:

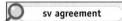
sv agreement

Find and correct any subject-verb agreement errors in the following sentences. Some sentences may be correct. Answers for the lettered sentences appear in the back of the book. Example:

> Addressing the audience tonight is the nominees for club president.
>
> Addressing the audience tonight *are* the nominees for club president.

a. For many college graduates, the process of looking for jobs are often long and stressful.

b. Not too long ago, searching the classifieds and inquiring in person was the primary methods of job hunting.

c. Today, however, everyone also seem to use the Internet to search for openings or to e-mail their résumés.

d. My classmates and my cousin sends most résumés over the Internet because it costs less than mailing them.

e. All of the résumés arrives quickly when they are sent electronically.

1. There are many people who thinks that interviewing is the most stressful part of the job search.

2. Sometimes only one person conducts an interview, while other times a whole committee conduct it.

3. Either the interviewer or the committee usually begin by asking simple questions about your background.

4. Making eye contact, dressing professionally, and appearing confident is some of the qualities an interviewer may consider important.

5. After an interview, most people sends a thank-you letter to the person who conducted it.

5 *Pronoun Case*

■ For advice on editing pronoun case, see A5 in the Quick Editing Guide (the dark-blue-edged pages).

As you know, pronouns come in distinctive forms. The first-person pronoun can be *I*, or it can be *me, my, mine, we, us, our,* or *ours.* Which form do you pick? It depends on what job you want the pronoun to do.

Depending on a pronoun's function in a sentence, we say that it is in the *subjective case,* the *objective case,* or the *possessive case.* Some pronouns change form when they change case, and some do not. The personal pronouns *I, he, she, we,* and *they* and the relative pronoun *who* have different forms in the subjective, objective, and possessive cases. Other pronouns, such as *you, it, that,* and *which,* have only two forms: the plain case (which serves as both subjective and objective) and the possessive case.

We can pin the labels *subjective, objective,* and *possessive* on nouns as well as on pronouns. Like the pronouns *you, it, that,* and *which,* nouns shift from plain form only in the possessive (*teacher's* pet, the *Joneses'* poodle).

Beware, when you are not sure which case to choose, of the temptation to fall back on a reflexive pronoun (*myself, himself*). If you catch yourself writing, "You can return the form to John or *myself*" or "John and *myself* are in charge," replace the reflexive pronoun with one that is grammatically correct: "You can return the form to John or *me*"; "John and *I* are in charge."

5a Use the subjective case for the subject of a sentence or clause.

Jed and *I* ate the granola.

Who cares?

Maya recalled that *she* played jai alai.

Election officials are the people *who* count.

A pronoun serving as the subject for a verb is subjective even when the verb isn't written but is only implied:

Jed is hungrier than *I* [am].

Don't be fooled by a pronoun that appears immediately after a verb, looking as if it were a direct object but functioning as the subject of a clause. The pronoun's case is determined by its role, not by its position.

The judge didn't believe *I* hadn't been the driver.

We were happy to interview *whoever* was running. [Subject of *was running*]

5b Use the subjective case for a subject complement.

When a pronoun functions as a subject complement, it plays essentially the same role as the subject and its case is subjective.

The phantom graffiti artist couldn't have been *he.* It was *I.*

5c Use the subjective case for an appositive to a subject or subject complement.

A pronoun placed in apposition to a subject or subject complement is like an identical twin to the noun it stands beside. It has the same meaning and the same case.

The class *officers* — Ravi and *she* — announced a senior breakfast.

---

subject: The part of a sentence that names something—a person, an object, an idea, a situation—about which the predicate makes an assertion: The *king* lives.

direct object: The target of a verb that completes the action performed by the subject or asserted about the subject: I photographed *the sheriff.*

subject complement: A noun, an adjective, or a group of words that follows a linking verb (*is, become, feel, seem,* or another verb that shows a state of being) and that renames or describes the subject: This plum tastes *ripe.* (See 3a.)

appositive: A word or group of words that adds information about a subject or object by identifying it in a different way: my dog *Rover,* Hal's brother *Fred*

direct object: The target of a verb that completes the action performed by the subject or asserted about the subject: I photographed *the sheriff.*

indirect object: A person or thing affected by the subject's action, usually the recipient of the direct object, through the action indicated by a verb such as *bring, get, offer, promise, sell, show, tell,* and *write:* Charlene asked *you* a question.

object of a preposition: The noun or pronoun that follows the preposition (such as *in, on, at, of, from*) that connects it, along with any modifiers, to the rest of the sentence: She opened the door to the *garage.*

infinitive: The base form of a verb preceded by *to: to go, to play*

For a chart of possessive personal pronouns, see C2 in the Quick Editing Guide (the dark-blue-edged pages).

5d Use the objective case for a direct object, an indirect object, the object of a preposition, or a subject of an infinitive.

The custard pies hit *him* and *me.* [Direct object]

Mona threw *us* towels. [Indirect object]

Mona threw towels to *him* and *us.* [Object of a preposition]

We always expect *him* to win. [Subject of an infinitive]

5e Use the objective case for an appositive to a direct or indirect object or the object of a preposition.

Mona helped us *all* — Mrs. Van Dumont, *him,* and *me.* [*Him* and *me* are in apposition to the direct object *us.*]

Binks gave his favorite *students,* Tom and *her,* an approving nod. [*Her* is in apposition to the indirect object *students.*]

Yelling, the pie flingers ran after *us* — Mona, *him,* and *me.* [*Him* and *me* are in apposition to *us,* the object of the preposition *after.*]

5f Use the possessive case to show ownership.

Possessive pronouns can function as adjectives or as nouns. The pronouns *my, your, his, her, its, our,* and *their* function as adjectives by modifying nouns or pronouns.

My new bike is having *its* first road test today.

The possessive pronoun *its* does not contain an apostrophe. *It's* with an apostrophe is a contraction for *it is,* as in "*It's* a beautiful day for bike riding."

The possessive pronouns *mine, yours, his, hers, ours,* and *theirs* can discharge the whole range of noun duties, serving as subjects, subject complements, direct objects, indirect objects, or objects of prepositions.

Yours is the last vote we need. [Subject]

This day is *ours.* [Subject complement]

Don't take your car; take *mine.* [Direct object]

If we're honoring requests, give *hers* top priority. [Indirect object]

Give her request priority over *theirs.* [Object of a preposition]

gerund: A form of a verb, ending in *-ing,* that functions as a noun: Lacey likes *playing* in the steel band.

5g Use the possessive case to modify a gerund.

A possessive pronoun (or a possessive noun) is the appropriate escort for a gerund. As a noun, a gerund requires an adjective, not another noun, for a modifier.

Mary is tired of *his griping*. [The possessive pronoun *his* modifies the gerund *griping*.]

I can stand *their being* late every morning but not *his drinking* on the job. [The possessive pronoun *their* modifies the gerund *being*; the possessive pronoun *his* modifies the gerund *drinking*.]

Gerunds can cause confusion when you edit because they look exactly like present participles. Whereas a gerund functions as a noun, a participle often functions as an adjective modifying a noun or pronoun.

Mary heard *him griping* about work. [The participle *griping* modifies the direct object *him*.]

If you are not sure whether to use a possessive or an objective pronoun with a word ending in *-ing*, look closely at your sentence. Which word — the pronoun or the *-ing* word — is the object of your main verb? That word functions as a noun; the other word modifies it.

Mr. Phipps remembered *them* smoking in the boys' room. [Mr. Phipps remembers *them*, those naughty students. *Them* is the object of the verb, so *smoking* is a participle modifying *them*.]

Mr. Phipps remembered *their* smoking in the boys' room. [Mr. Phipps remembers *smoking*, that nasty habit. The gerund *smoking* is the object of the verb, and the possessive pronoun *their* modifies it.]

In everyday speech, the rules about pronoun case apply less rigidly. Someone who correctly asks in conversation, "To whom are you referring?" is likely to sound pretentious. You are within your rights to reply, as did the comic-strip character Pogo Possum, "Youm, that's whom!" Say, if you like, "It's *me*," but write "It is *I*." Say, if you wish, "*Who* did he ask to the party?" but write "*Whom* did he ask?"

> *present participle:* A form of a verb ending in *-ing* that cannot function alone as a main verb but can act as an adjective: *Leading* the pack, Michael crossed the finish line.

■ Exercise 5–1

Using Pronouns Correctly

Replace any pronouns used incorrectly in the following sentences. (Consider all these examples as written — not spoken — English, so apply the rules strictly.) Explain why each pronoun was incorrect. Some sentences may be correct. Answers for the lettered sentences appear in the back of the book. Example:

That is her, the new university president, at the podium.

That is *she*, the new university president, at the podium. [*She* is a subject complement.]

a. I didn't appreciate you laughing at her and I.
b. Lee and me would be delighted to serenade whomever will listen.
c. The waiters and us busboys are highly trustworthy.
d. The neighbors were driven berserk by him singing.

> ■ For more practice, visit <bedfordstmartins.com/ bedguide> and do a keyword search:
>
>
> case

e. Jerry and myself regard you and she as the very people who we wish to meet.

1. Have you guessed the identity of the person of who I am speaking?
2. It was him asking about the clock that started me suspecting him.
3. They — Jerry and her — are the troublemakers.
4. Mrs. Van Dumont awarded the prize to Mona and I.
5. The counterattack was launched by Dusty and myself.

6   *Pronoun Reference*

Look hard at just about any piece of writing — this discussion, if you like — and you'll find that practically every pronoun in it points to some noun. This is the main use of pronouns: to refer in a brief, convenient form to some *antecedent* that has already been named. A pronoun usually has a noun or another pronoun as its antecedent. Often the antecedent is the subject or object of the same clause in which the pronoun appears.

> Josie hit the *ball* after *its* first bounce.

> Smashing into *Greg,* the ball knocked off *his* glasses.

The antecedent also can appear in a different clause or even a different sentence from the pronoun.

> Josie hit the *ball* when *it* bounced back to *her.*

> The *ball* smashed into *Greg. It* knocked off *his* glasses.

A pronoun as well as a noun can be an antecedent.

> My *dog* hid in the closet when *she* had *her* puppies. [*Dog* is the antecedent of *she; she* is the antecedent of *her.*]

6a   Name the pronoun's antecedent: don't just imply it.

antecedent: The word to which a pronoun refers: *Lyn* plays golf, and *she* putts well.

When editing, be sure you have identified clearly the antecedent of each pronoun. A writer who leaves a key idea unsaid is likely to confuse readers.

> VAGUE   Ted wanted a Norwegian canoe because he'd heard that *they* produce the lightest canoes afloat.

What noun or pronoun does *they* refer to? Not to *Norwegian,* which is an adjective. We may guess that this writer has in mind Norwegian canoe builders, but no such noun has been mentioned. To make the sentence work, the writer must supply an antecedent for *they.*

> CLEAR   Ted wanted a Norwegian canoe because he'd heard that Norway produces [*or* Norwegians produce] the lightest canoes afloat.

Watch out for possessive nouns. They won't work as antecedents.

VAGUE   On William's canoe *he* painted a skull and bones. (For all we know, he might be some joker named Gustavo.)

CLEAR   On his canoe William painted a skull and bones.

Adjective Clauses and Relative Pronouns

Be sure to use relative pronouns (*who, which, that*) correctly in sentences with adjective clauses.

- Do not omit the relative pronoun when it is the subject within the adjective clause.

    INCORRECT   The woman *gave us directions to the museum* told us not to miss the Picasso exhibit.

    CORRECT   The woman *who gave us directions to the museum* told us not to miss the Picasso exhibit. [*Who* is the subject of the adjective clause.]

- In speech and informal writing, you can imply (not state) a relative pronoun when it is the object of a verb or preposition within the adjective clause. In formal writing, you should use the relative pronoun.

    FORMAL   Jamal forgot to return the book *that I gave him.* [*That* is the object of *gave.*]

    INFORMAL   Jamal forgot to return the book *I gave him.* [The relative pronoun *that* is implied.]

    FORMAL   This is the box *in which we found the jewelry.* [*Which* is the object of the preposition *in.*]

    INFORMAL   This is the box *we found the jewelry in.* [The relative pronoun *which* is implied.]

NOTE: When the relative pronoun is omitted, the preposition moves to the end of the sentence but must not be left out.

- *Whose* is the only possessive form of a relative pronoun. It is used with persons, animals, and things.

    INCORRECT   I sat on a chair *that its* legs were wobbly.

    CORRECT   I sat on a chair *whose* legs were wobbly.

NOTE: If you are not sure how to use a relative pronoun, try rephrasing the sentence more simply.

    I sat on a chair *that had wobbly legs* [or *with wobbly legs*].

6b Give the pronoun *it*, *this*, *that*, or *which* a clear antecedent.

antecedent: The word to which a pronoun refers: *Lyn* plays golf, and *she* putts well.

Vagueness arises, thick as fog, whenever *it*, *this*, *that*, or *which* points to something a writer assumes is said but indeed isn't. Often the best way out of the fog is to substitute a specific noun or expression for the pronoun.

VAGUE   I was an only child, and *it* was hard.

CLEAR   I was an only child, and my solitary life was hard.

VAGUE   Judy could not get along with her younger brother. *This* is the reason she wanted to get her own apartment.

CLEAR   Because Judy could not get along with her younger brother, she wanted to get her own apartment.

6c Make the pronoun's antecedent clear.

Confusion strikes if a pronoun seems to point in two or more directions. In such a puzzling situation, more than one antecedent looks possible. Baffled, the reader wonders which the writer means.

CONFUSING   Hanwei shouted to Kenny to take off *his* burning sweater.

Whose sweater does *his* mean — Kenny's or Hanwei's? Simply changing a pronoun won't clear up the confusion. The writer needs to revise enough to move the two possible antecedents out of each other's way.

CLEAR   "Kenny!" shouted Hanwei. "Your sweater's on fire! Take it off!"

CLEAR   Flames were shooting from Kenny's sweater. Hanwei shouted to Kenny to take it off.

Pronouns referring to nouns of the same gender are particular offenders.

CONFUSING   Linda welcomed Lee-Ann's move into the apartment next door. Little did she dream that soon she would be secretly dating her husband.

Let meaning show you how to straighten out the grammatical tangle. If you had written these sentences, you would know which person is the sneak. One way to clarify the antecedents of *she* and *her* is to add information.

CLEAR   In welcoming Lee-Ann to the apartment next door, Linda didn't dream that soon her own husband would be secretly dating her former sorority sister.

6d Place the pronoun close to its antecedent to keep the relationship clear.

Watch out for distractions that slip in between noun and pronoun. If your sentence contains two or more nouns that look like antecedents to a pronoun, your readers may become bewildered.

antecedent: The word to which a pronoun refers: *Lyn* plays golf, and *she* putts well.

CONFUSING   Harper steered his dinghy alongside the cabin cruiser that the drug smugglers had left anchored under an overhanging willow in the tiny harbor and eased it to a stop.

What did Harper ease to a stop? By the time readers reach the end of the sentence, they are likely to have forgotten. To avoid confusion, keep the pronoun and its antecedent reasonably close together.

CLEAR   Harper steered his dinghy into the tiny harbor and eased it to a stop alongside the cabin cruiser that the drug smugglers had left anchored under an overhanging willow.

Never force your readers to stop and think, "What does that pronoun stand for?" You, the writer, have to do this thinking for them.

■ Exercise 6–1

Making Pronoun Reference Clear

Revise each sentence or group of sentences so that any pronoun needing an antecedent clearly points to one. Possible revisions for the lettered sentences appear in the back of the book. Example:

■ For more practice, visit <bedfordstmartins.com/ bedguide> and do a keyword search:

reference

> I took the money out of the wallet and threw it in the trash.
>
> I took the money out of the wallet and threw *the wallet* in the trash.

a. I could see the moon and the faint shadow of the tree as it began to rise.
b. Katrina spent the summer in Paris and traveled throughout Europe, which broadened her awareness of cultural differences.
c. Most managers want employees to work as many hours as possible. They never consider the work they need to do at home.
d. I worked twelve hours a day and never got enough sleep, but it was worth it.
e. Kevin asked Mike to meet him for lunch but forgot that he had class at that time.

1. Bill's prank frightened Josh and made him wonder why he had done it.
2. Korean students study up to twenty subjects a year, including algebra, calculus, and engineering. Because they are required, they must study them year after year.
3. Pedro Martinez signed a baseball for Chad that he had used in a game.

4. When the bottle hit the windshield, it shattered.

5. My friends believe they are more mature than many of their peers because of the discipline enforced at their school. However, it can also lead to problems.

7   *Pronoun-Antecedent Agreement*

pronoun: A word that stands in place of a noun (*he, him,* or *his* for *Nate*)
antecedent: The word to which a pronoun refers: *Lyn* plays golf, and *she* putts well.

A pronoun's job is to fill in for a noun, much as an actor's double fills in for the actor. Pronouns are a short, convenient way for writers to avoid repeating the same noun over and over.

> The sheriff drew a six-shooter; he fired twice.

In this action-packed sentence, first comes a noun (*sheriff*) and then a pronoun (*he*) that refers back to it. *Sheriff* is the antecedent of *he.*

Just as verbs need to agree with their subjects, pronouns need to agree with the nouns they stand for. A successful writer takes care not to shift number, person, or gender in midsentence ("The *sheriff* and the *outlaw* drew *their* six-shooters; *he* fired twice").

7a   Pronouns agree with their antecedents in person and number.

■ For more on editing for pronoun-antecedent agreement, see A6 in the Quick Editing Guide (the dark-blue-edged pages).

A pronoun matches its antecedent in person (first, second, or third) and in number (singular or plural), even when intervening words separate the pronoun and its antecedent.

> FAULTY   All *campers* should bring *your* knapsacks.

Here, noun and pronoun disagree in person: *campers* is third person, but *your* is second person.

> FAULTY   Every *camper* should bring *their* knapsack.

Here, noun and pronoun disagree in number: *camper* is singular, but *their* is plural.

> REVISED   All *campers* should bring *their* knapsacks.
>
> REVISED   Every *camper* should bring *his or her* knapsack. (See also 7f.)

7b   Most antecedents joined by *and* require a plural pronoun.

compound subject: A subject consisting of two or more nouns or pronouns linked by *and: My mother and my sister drove home.*

A *compound subject* is plural; use a plural pronoun to refer to it.

> *George,* who has been here before, *and Susan,* who hasn't, should bring *their* knapsacks.

If the nouns in a compound subject refer to the same person or thing, they make up a singular antecedent. Use a singular pronoun too.

> The *owner and founder* of this camp carries *his* own knapsack everywhere.

7c A pronoun agrees with the closest part of an antecedent joined by *or* or *nor*.

If your subject is two or more nouns (or a combination of nouns and pronouns) connected by *or* or *nor*, look closely at the subject's parts. Are they all singular? If so, your pronoun should be singular.

> Neither *Joy nor Jean* remembered *her* knapsack last year.

> If *Sam, Arthur, or Dieter* shows up, tell *him* I'm looking for *him*.

If the part of the subject closest to the pronoun is plural, the pronoun should be plural.

> Neither *Joy nor her sisters* remembered *their* knapsacks last year.

> If you see *Sam, Arthur, or their friends,* tell *them* I'm looking for *them.*

7d An antecedent that is an indefinite pronoun takes a singular pronoun.

Indefinite pronouns are usually singular in meaning, so a pronoun referring to one of them is also singular.

> *Either* of the boys can do it, as long as *he's* on time.

> Warn *anybody* who's still in *her* swimsuit that a uniform is required for dinner.

Sometimes the meaning of an indefinite pronoun is plural. To avoid awkwardness, avoid using such a pronoun as an antecedent.

> Tell *everyone* in Cabin B that I'm looking for *him.*

This sentence works better if it is phrased differently.

> Tell *all the campers* in Cabin B that I'm looking for *them.*

indefinite pronoun: A pronoun standing for an unspecified person or thing, including singular forms (*each, everyone, no one*) and plural forms (*both, few*): *Everyone* is soaking wet.

▪ For a list of indefinite pronouns, see A6 in the Quick Editing Guide (the dark-blue-edged pages). For more on agreement with indefinite pronouns, see 4f and 7f.

7e Most collective nouns used as antecedents require singular pronouns.

When the members of such a group act as a unit, use a singular pronoun to refer to them.

> The *cast* for the play will be posted as soon as the director chooses *it.*

When the group members act individually, use a plural pronoun.

> The *cast* will go *their* separate ways when summer ends.

collective noun: A singular noun that represents a group of people or items, such as *committee, family, jury, trio*

▪ For more on agreement with collective nouns, see 4e.

7f **A pronoun agrees with its antecedent in gender.**

If *one of your parents* brings you to camp, invite *him* to stay for lunch.

While technically correct (the singular pronoun *he* refers to the singular antecedent *one*), this sentence overlooks the fact that some parents are male, some female. To make sure the pronoun covers both, a writer has two choices.

If *one of your parents* brings you to camp, invite *him or her* to stay for lunch.

If your *parents* bring you to camp, invite *them* to stay for lunch.

For more on bias-free language, see 18.

For more practice, visit <bedfordstmartins.com/bedguide> and do a keyword search:

🔍 **pa agreement**

■ Exercise 7–1

Making Pronouns and Antecedents Agree

If any nouns and pronouns disagree in number, person, or gender in the following sentences, substitute pronouns that agree with the nouns. If you prefer, strengthen any sentence by rewriting it. Some sentences may be correct. Possible revisions for the lettered sentences appear in the back of the book. Example:

A cat expects people to feed them often.

A *cat* expects people to feed *it* often. *Or*

Cats expect people to feed *them* often.

a. Many architects find work their greatest pleasure.
b. Neither Melissa nor James has received their application form yet.
c. He is the kind of man who gets their fun out of just sipping one's beer and watching his Saturday games on TV.
d. Many a mother has mourned the loss of their child.
e. When one enjoys one's work, it's easy to spend all your spare time thinking about it.

1. All students are urged to complete your registration on time.
2. When a baby doesn't know their own mother, they may have been born with some kind of vision deficiency.
3. Each member of the sorority has to make her own bed.
4. If you don't like the songs the choir sings, don't join them.
5. Young people should know how to protect oneself against AIDS.

adjective: A word or phrase that describes, or modifies, a noun or a pronoun: The *small brown* cow leaned against the *old* fence.

8 *Adjectives and Adverbs*

An adjective's job is to provide information about the person, place, object, or idea named by the noun or pronoun. The adjective typically answers the question Which? or What kind?

Karen bought a *small red* car.

The radios *on sale* are an *excellent* value.

An adverb typically answers the question How? or When? or Where? Sometimes it answers the question Why?

Karen bought her car *quickly*.

The radios arrived *yesterday;* Denis put them *in the electronics department*.

Karen needed her new car *to commute to school*.

The common problems that writers have with adjectives and adverbs involve mixing them up: sending an adjective to do an adverb's job or vice versa.

8a Use an adverb, not an adjective, to modify a verb, adjective, or another adverb.

FAULTY   Karen bought her car *quick*.

FAULTY   It's *awful* hot today.

Though an informal speaker might get away with these sentences, a writer cannot. *Quick* and *awful* are adjectives, so they can modify only nouns or pronouns. Adverbs are needed to modify the verb *bought* and the adjective *hot*.

REVISED   Karen bought her car *quickly*.

REVISED   It's *awfully* hot today.

8b Use an adjective, not an adverb, as a subject complement or object complement.

If we write, "Her old car looked awful," the adjective *awful* is a *subject complement:* it follows a linking verb and modifies the subject, *car*. An *object complement* completes the description of a direct object and can be an adjective or a noun, but never an adverb.

Adjectives and Adverbs at a Glance

ADJECTIVES

1. Typically answer the question Which? or What kind?

2. Modify nouns or pronouns

ADVERBS

3. Answer the question How? When? Where? or sometimes Why?

4. Modify verbs, adjectives, and other adverbs

---

adverb: A word or phrase that modifies a verb, an adjective, or another adverb: The cow bawled *loudly*.

■ For more on editing adjectives and adverbs, see A7 in the Quick Editing Guide (the dark-blue-edged pages).

subject complement: A noun, an adjective, or a group of words that follows a linking verb (*is, become, feel, seem* or another verb that shows a state of being) and renames or describes the subject: This plum tastes *ripe*. (See 3a.)

object complement: A noun, an adjective, or a group of words that renames or describes a direct object: The judges rated Hugo *the best skater*.

Early to bed and early to rise makes a man *healthy, wealthy,* and *wise.* [Adjectives modifying the direct object *man*]

When you are not sure whether you're dealing with an object complement or an adverb, look closely at the word's role in the sentence. If it modifies a noun, it is an object complement and therefore should be an adjective.

The coach called the referee *stupid* and *blind.* [*Stupid* and *blind* are adjectives modifying the direct object *referee.*]

If it modifies a verb, you want an adverb instead.

In fact, the ref had called the play *correctly.* [*Correctly* is an adverb modifying the verb *called.*]

8c   Use *good* as an adjective and *well* as an adverb.

This sandwich tastes *good.* [The adjective *good* is a subject complement following the linking verb *tastes* and modifying the noun *sandwich.*]

Al's skin healed *well* after surgery. [The adverb *well* modifies the verb *healed.*]

subject complement: A noun, an adjective, or a group of words that follows a linking verb and renames or describes the subject: This plum tastes *ripe.* (See 3a.)

linking verb: A verb (*is, become, seem, feel*) that shows a state of being by linking the sentence subject with a word that renames or describes the subject: The sky *is* blue. (See 3a.)

Only if the verb is a linking verb can you safely follow it with *good.* Other kinds of verbs do not take subject complements. Instead, they need adverbs to modify them.

FAULTY   That painting came out *good.*

REVISED   That painting came out *well.*

Complications arise when we write or speak about health. It is perfectly correct to say *I feel good,* using the adjective *good* as a subject complement after the linking verb *feel.* However, generations of confusion have nudged the adverb *well* into the adjective category, too. A nurse may speak of "a well baby"; and greeting cards urge patients to "get well" — meaning, "become healthy." Just as *healthy* is an adjective here, so is *well.*

What, then, is the best answer when someone asks, "How do you feel?" If you want to duck the issue, reply, "Fine!" Otherwise, in speech either *good* or *well* is acceptable; in writing, use *good.*

8d   Form comparatives and superlatives of most adjectives with *-er* and *-est* and of most adverbs with *more* and *most.*

Comparatives and superlatives are special adjective and adverb forms that allow us to describe one thing in relation to another. Put most adjectives into comparative form by adding *-er* and into superlative form by adding *-est.*

The budget deficit is *larger* than the trade deficit.

This year's trade deficit is the *largest* ever.

The Definite Article (*the*)

- Use *the* with a specific count or noncount noun mentioned before or familiar to both the writer and the reader.

    She got a huge box in the mail. *The* box contained oranges from Florida. [*The* is used the second time the noun (*box*) is mentioned.]

    Did you feed *the* baby? [Both reader and writer know which baby.]

- Use *the* before specific count or noncount nouns when the reader is given enough information to identify what is being referred to.

    The furniture in my apartment is old and faded. [Specific furniture]

- Use *the* before a singular count noun to state a generality.

    The dog has been a companion for centuries. [*The dog* refers to all dogs.]

- Use *the* before some geographical names.

    Collectives: the United States, the United Kingdom

    Groups of Islands: the Bahamas, the Canary Islands

    Large Bodies of Water (except lakes): the Atlantic Ocean, the Dead Sea, the Monongahela River, the Gulf of Mexico

    Mountain Ranges: the Rockies, the Himalayas

- Use *the* or another determiner when plural count nouns name a definite or specific group; use no article when they name a general group.

    Hal is feeding *the horses* in the barn, and he has already fed *his cows*.

    Horses don't eat meat, and neither do *cows*.

ESL GUIDELINES

count noun: A noun with both singular and plural forms that refers to an item that can be counted: *apple, apples*

noncount noun: A noun that cannot be made plural because it refers to an item that cannot be counted: *cheese, salt, air*

The Indefinite Article (*a, an*)

- Use *a* or *an* with a nonspecific, singular count noun when it is not known to the reader or to the writer.

    Jay has *an* antique car. [The car's identity is unknown to the reader.]

    I saw *a* dog in my backyard this morning. [The dog's identity is unknown to the writer.]

- Use *a* or *an* when the noun is first used; use *the* when it is repeated.

    I saw *a* car that I would love to buy. *The* car was red with tan seats.

- Use *some* or no article with general noncount or plural nouns.

    INCORRECT   I am going to buy *a* furniture for my apartment.

    CORRECT   I am going to buy *some* furniture for my apartment.

    CORRECT   I am going to buy furniture for my apartment.

We usually form the comparative and superlative of potentially cumbersome long adjectives with *more* and *most* rather than with *-er* and *-est*.

> The lake is *more beautiful* than I'd imagined.

For short adverbs that do not end in *-ly*, usually add *-er* and *-est* in the comparative and superlative forms. With all other adverbs, use *more* and *most*. (Also see 8f.)

> The trade deficit grows *fastest* and *most uncontrollably* when exports are down and imports remain high.

For negative comparisons, use *less* and *least* for adjectives and adverbs.

> Michael's speech was *less dramatic* than Louie's.

> Paulette spoke *less dramatically* than Michael.

For a chart of comparative forms of irregular adjectives and adverbs, see A7 in the Quick Editing Guide (the dark-blue-edged pages).

Comparative and superlative forms of irregular adjectives and adverbs (such as *bad* and *badly*) are also irregular and should be used with care.

> Tom's golf is *bad*, but no *worse* than George's.

> Tom plays golf *badly*, but no *worse* than George does.

8e Omit *more* and *most* with an adjective or adverb that is already comparative or superlative.

Some words become comparative or superlative when we tack on *-er* or *-est*. Others, such as *top*, *favorite*, and *unique*, mark whatever they modify as one of a kind by definition. Neither category requires further assistance to make its point. To say "a *more worse* fate" or "my *most favorite* movie" is redundant: "a *worse* fate" or "my *favorite* movie" does the job.

> FAULTY Lisa is *more uniquely* qualified for the job than any other candidate.

> REVISED Lisa is *better* qualified for the job than any other candidate.

> REVISED Lisa is *uniquely* qualified for the job.

8f Use the comparative form of an adjective or adverb to compare two people or things, the superlative form to compare more than two.

No matter how wonderful something is, we can call it the *best* only when we compare it with more than one other thing. Any comparison between two things uses the comparative form (*better*), not the superlative (*best*).

> FAULTY Chocolate and vanilla are both good, but I like chocolate *best*.

> REVISED Chocolate and vanilla are both good, but I like chocolate *better*.

Cumulative Adjectives

Cumulative adjectives are two or more adjectives used directly before a noun and not separated by commas or the word *and*.

> She is an *attractive older French* woman.

> His *expressive large brown* eyes moved me.

Cumulative adjectives usually follow a specific order of placement before a noun. Use this list as a guide, but keep in mind that the order can vary.

ESL GUIDELINES

1. Articles or determiners

   a, an, the, some, this, these, his, my, two, several

2. Evaluative adjectives

   beautiful, wonderful, hard-working, distasteful

3. Size or dimension

   big, small, huge, obese, petite, six-foot

4. Length or shape

   long, short, round, square, oblong, oval

5. Age

   old, young, new, fresh, ancient

6. Color

   red, pink, aquamarine, orange

7. Nation or place of origin

   American, Japanese, European, Bostonian, Floridian

8. Religion

   Protestant, Muslim, Hindu, Buddhist, Catholic, Jewish

9. Matter or substance

   wood, gold, cotton, plastic, pine, metal

10. Noun used as an adjective

    telephone (as in *telephone operator*), *computer* (as in *computer software*)

■ For advice on using commas with adjectives, see 21d.

■ Exercise 8–1

Using Adjectives and Adverbs Correctly

Find and correct any improperly used adjectives and adverbs in the following sentences. Some sentences may be correct. Answers for the lettered sentences appear in the back of the book. Example:

> The deal worked out good for both of us.

> The deal worked out *well* for both of us.

a. Credit card debt is becoming increasing common among college students, who have expenses but do not work full-time.

■ For more practice, visit <bedfordstmartins.com/ bedguide> and do a keyword search:

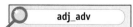

adj_adv

b. Nearly all credit card companies try to convince students to apply by offering introductory rates that are enticingly low.

c. It then is easy for students to charge many items on different cards and make only the lower minimum payments each month.

d. Unfortunately, when juggling multiple credit cards, many students lose sight of how rapid the debt is accumulating.

e. It is a well idea to charge only as much as you can pay in full each month.

1. A popular trend in television today is voyeurism, or the act of secret watching people as they go about their daily lives.

2. In the late 1990s, the popularity of MTV's *The Real World* sparked increasingly interest in this concept.

3. Music videos and commercials also began to incorporate voyeuristic elements, although, of the two, videos used the technique most frequently.

4. With the millennium came a flood of new "reality" programs all trying to capitalize more distinctively on the current trend.

5. On the program *Survivor,* contestants were filmed living on a desert island with limited supplies, while viewers at home watched breathless to see how the contestants would behave.

9   *Shifts*

Just as you can change position to view a scene from different vantage points, in your writing you can change the time or the actor to consider a subject in various ways. However, writers sometimes shift point of view unconsciously or unnecessarily within a passage, creating ambiguity and confusion for readers. Such shifts are evident in grammatical inconsistencies.

9a   Maintain consistency in verb tense.

tense: The time when the action of a verb did, does, or will occur

When you write a paragraph or an essay, keep the verbs in the same tense unless the time changes.

INCONSISTENT   The driver *yelled* at us to get off the bus, so I *ask* him why, and he *tells* me it *is* none of my business.

CONSISTENT   The driver *yells* at us to get off the bus, so I *ask* him why, and he *tells* me it *is* none of my business. [All verbs are present tense.]

CONSISTENT   The driver *yelled* at us to get off the bus, so I *asked* him why, and he *told* me it *was* none of my business. [All verbs are past tense.]

9b If the time changes, change the verb tense.

If you are writing about something that occurred in the past, use past tense verbs. If you are writing about something that occurs in the present, use present tense verbs. If the time shifts, change the verb tense.

> I *do* not *like* the new television programs this year. The situation comedies *are* too realistic to be amusing, the adventure shows *don't have* much action, and the courtroom dramas *drag* on and on. Last year the television programs *were* different. The sitcoms *were* hilarious, the adventure shows *were* action-packed, and the courtroom dramas *were* fast-paced. I *prefer* last year's reruns to this year's new choices.

The time and the verb tense change appropriately from present (*do like, are, do have, drag*) to past (*were, were, were, were*) back to present (*prefer*), contrasting this year's *present* programming with last year's *past* programming and ending with *present* opinion.

NOTE: When writing papers about literature, the accepted practice is to use present tense verbs to summarize what happens in a story, poem, or play. When discussing other aspects of a work, use present tense for present time, past tense for past, and future tense for future.

> John Steinbeck *wrote* "The Chrysanthemums" in 1937. [Past tense for past time]

> In "The Chrysanthemums," John Steinbeck *describes* the Salinas Valley as "a closed pot" cut off from the world by fog. [Present tense for story summary]

9c Maintain consistency in the voice of verbs.

In most writing, active voice is preferable to passive voice. Shifting unnecessarily from active to passive voice may confuse readers.

For more on using active and passive voice, see 3m.

| INCONSISTENT | My roommates and I *sit* up late many nights talking about our problems. Grades, teachers, jobs, money, and dates *are discussed* at length. |
| CONSISTENT | My roommates and I *sit* up late many nights talking about our problems. We *discuss* grades, teachers, jobs, money, and dates at length. |

9d Maintain consistency in person.

Person indicates your perspective as a writer. First person (*I, we*) establishes a personal, informal relationship with readers. Second person (*you*) is also informal and personal, bringing readers into the writing. Third person (*he, she, it, they*) is more formal and objective than the other two persons. In a formal scientific report, first and second person are seldom appropriate. In a

For more on pronoun forms, see 5 and also A5 in the Quick Editing Guide (the dark-blue-edged pages).

ESL GUIDELINES

Negatives

You can make a sentence negative by using **not** or another negative adverb such as *seldom, rarely, never, hardly, hardly ever,* or *almost never.*

- With **not:** subject + helping verb + **not** + main verb

  Gina did *not* go to the concert.

  They will *not* call again.

- For questions: helping verb + *n't* (contraction for *not*) + subject + main verb

  Didn't Gina go to the concert?

  Won't [for *Will not*] they call again?

- With a negative adverb: subject + negative adverb + main verb *or* subject + helping verb + negative adverb + main verb

  My son *seldom* watches TV.

  Jared may *never* see them again.

- With a negative adverb at the beginning of a clause: negative adverb + helping verb + subject + verb

  Not only does Emma play tennis well, but she also excels in golf.

  Never before have I been so happy.

---

personal essay, using *he, she,* or *one* to refer to yourself would sound stilted. Choose the person appropriate for your purpose, and stick to it.

INCONSISTENT	College *students* need transportation, but *you* need a job to pay for the insurance and the gasoline.
CONSISTENT	College *students* need transportation, but *they* need jobs to pay for the insurance and the gasoline.
INCONSISTENT	*Anyone* can go skydiving if *you* have the guts.
CONSISTENT	*Anyone* can go skydiving if *he or she* has the guts.
CONSISTENT	*You* can go skydiving if *you* have the guts.

9e Maintain consistency in the mood of verbs.

For examples of the three moods of verbs, see 3n–3p.

Closely related to shift in person is shift in the mood of the verb, usually from the indicative to the imperative.

INCONSISTENT	Counselors *advised* the students to register early. Also *pay* tuition on time to avoid being dropped from classes. [Shift from indicative to imperative]
CONSISTENT	Counselors *advised* the students to register early. They also *advised* them to pay their tuition on time to avoid being dropped from classes. [Both verbs in indicative]

9f Maintain consistency in level of language.

Attempting to impress readers, writers sometimes inflate their language or slip into slang or informal wording. The level of language should be appropriate to your purpose and your audience throughout an essay.

If you are writing a personal essay, use informal language.

INCONSISTENT   I felt like a typical tourist. I carried an expensive camera with lots of gadgets I didn't quite know how to operate. But I was in a quandary because there was such a plethora of picturesque tableaus to record for posterity.

Instead of suddenly shifting to formal language, the writer could end simply: *But with so much beautiful scenery all around, I just couldn't decide where to start.*

If you are writing an academic essay, use formal language.

INCONSISTENT   Puccini's final work *Turandot* is set in a China of legends, riddles, and fantasy. Brimming with beautiful melodies, this opera is music drama at its most spectacular. It rules!

The last sentence can be cut to avoid an unnecessary shift in formality.

■ Exercise 9–1

Maintaining Grammatical Consistency

Revise the following sentences to eliminate shifts in verb tense, voice, mood, person, and level of language. Possible revisions for the lettered sentences appear in the back of the book. Example:

> I needed the job at the restaurant, so I tried to tolerate the insults of my boss, but a person can take only so much.
>
> I needed the job at the restaurant, so I tried to tolerate the insults of my boss, but *I could* take only so much.

a. Dr. Jamison is an erudite professor who cracks jokes in class.

b. The audience listened intently to the lecture, but the message was not understood.

c. Scientists can no longer evade the social, political, and ethical consequences of what they did in the laboratory.

d. To have good government, citizens must become informed on the issues. Also, be sure to vote.

e. Good writing is essential to success in many professions, especially in business, where ideas must be communicated in down-to-earth lingo.

1. Our legal system made it extremely difficult to prove a bribe. If the charges are not proven to the satisfaction of a jury or a judge, then we jump to the conclusion that the absence of a conviction demonstrates the innocence of the subject.

■ For more practice, visit <bedfordstmartins.com/ bedguide> and do a keyword search:

shifts

2. Before Morris K. Udall, Democrat from Arizona, resigns his seat in the U.S. House of Representatives, he helped preserve hundreds of acres of wilderness.

3. Anyone can learn another language if you have the time and the patience.

4. The immigration officer asked how long we planned to stay, so I show him my letter of acceptance from Tulane.

5. Archaeologists spent many months studying the site of the African city of Zimbabwe, and many artifacts were uncovered.

Chapter 34
Effective Sentences

10 *Misplaced and Dangling Modifiers*

The purpose of a modifier is to give readers more information. To do so, the modifier must be linked clearly to whatever it is meant to modify. If you wrote, "We saw a stone wall around a house on a grassy hill, beautiful and distant," your readers would have to guess what was *beautiful* and *distant*: the wall, the house, or the hill. When you edit, double-check your modifiers—especially prepositional phrases and subordinate clauses—to make sure each one is in the right place.

For more on editing for misplaced or dangling modifiers, see B1 in the Quick Editing Guide (the dark-blue-edged pages).

10a Keep modifiers close to what they modify.

Misplaced modifiers—phrases and clauses that wander away from what they modify—produce results more likely to amuse readers than to inform them. Place your modifiers as close as possible to whatever they modify.

modifier: A word (such as an adjective or adverb), phrase, or clause that provides more information about other parts of a sentence: Plays *staged by the drama class* are *always successful.*

MISPLACED   She offered toys to all the children in colorful packages. [Does the phrase *in colorful packages* modify *toys* or *children?*]

CLEAR   She offered toys in colorful packages to all the children.

MISPLACED   We need to remove the dishes from the crates that got chipped. [Does the clause *that got chipped* modify *dishes* or *crates?*]

CLEAR   We need to remove from the crates the dishes that got chipped.

Sometimes when you move a misplaced modifier to a better place, you can make an additional change to clarify the sentence.

MISPLACED   Chuck offered cream and sugar to his guests in their coffee.

CLEAR   Chuck offered his guests cream and sugar in their coffee. [When *guests* is made an indirect object, *to* is cut.]

10b **Place each modifier so that it clearly modifies only one thing.**

A *squinting modifier* is one that looks two ways, leaving the reader uncertain whether it modifies the word before it or the word after it. A good tactic to avoid ambiguity is to place your modifier close to the word or phrase it modifies and away from any others that might cause confusion.

SQUINTING	The book that appealed to Amy *tremendously* bored Marcus.
CLEAR	The book that *tremendously* appealed to Amy bored Marcus.
CLEAR	The book that appealed to Amy bored Marcus *tremendously*.

■ Exercise 10–1

■ For more practice, visit <bedfordstmartins.com/ bedguide> and do a keyword search:

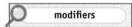
modifiers

Placing Modifiers

Revise the following sentences, which contain modifiers that are misplaced or squinting. Possible revisions for the lettered sentences appear in the back of the book. Example:

> Patti found the cat using a flashlight in the dark.
>
> *Using a flashlight in the dark,* Patti found the cat.

a. The bus got stuck in a ditch full of passengers.
b. He was daydreaming about fishing for trout in the middle of a staff meeting.
c. The boy threw the paper airplane through an open window with a smirk.
d. I reached for my sunglasses when the glare appeared from the glove compartment.
e. High above them, Sally and Glen watched the kites drift back and forth.

1. In her soup she found a fly at one of the best French restaurants in town.
2. Andy learned how to build kites from the pages of an old book.
3. Alex vowed to return to the island sometime soon on the day he left it.
4. The fish was carried in a suitcase wrapped in newspaper.
5. The reporters were informed of the crimes committed by a press release.

10c **State something in the sentence for each modifier to modify.**

main clause: A group of words that has both a subject and a verb and can stand alone as a complete sentence: *My sister has a friend.*

Generally readers assume that a modifying phrase at the start of a sentence modifies the subject of the main clause to follow. If we encounter a modifying phrase midway through a sentence, we assume that it modifies something just before or (less often) after it.

Feeling tired after the long hike, Jason went to bed.

Alicia, while sympathetic, was not inclined to help.

Sometimes a writer slips up, allowing a modifying phrase to dangle. A *dangling modifier* is one that doesn't modify anything in its sentence.

DANGLING   *Noticing a pain behind his eyes,* an aspirin seemed like a good idea. [The opening phrase doesn't modify *aspirin* or, in fact, anything.]

To correct a dangling modifier, first figure out what noun, pronoun, or noun phrase the modifier is meant to modify. Then make that word or phrase the subject of the main clause.

CLEAR   *Noticing a pain behind his eyes,* he decided to take an aspirin.

Another way to correct a dangling modifier is to turn the dangler into a clause that includes the missing noun or pronoun.

DANGLING   Her progress, *although talented,* has been slowed by poor work habits.

CLEAR   *Although she is talented,* her progress has been slowed by poor work habits.

Sometimes rewriting will clarify what the modifier modifies and improve the sentence as well.

CLEAR   *Although talented,* she has been hampered by poor work habits.

■ Exercise 10–2

Revising Dangling Modifiers

Revise any sentences that contain dangling modifiers. Some sentences may be correct. Possible revisions for the lettered sentences appear in the back of the book. Example:

> Angry at her poor showing, geology would never be Joan's favorite class.
>
> *Angry at her poor showing, Joan* knew that geology would never be her favorite class.

a. Unpacking the suitcase, a horrible idea occurred to me.

b. After preparing breakfast that morning, the oven might still be left on at home.

c. Trying to reach my neighbor, her telephone was busy.

d. Desperate to get information, my solution was to ask my mother to drive over to check the oven.

e. With enormous relief, my mother's call confirmed that everything was fine.

■ For more practice, visit <bedfordstmartins.com/ bedguide> and do a keyword search:

modifiers

1. After working six hours, the job was done.
2. Further information can be obtained by calling the specified number.
3. To compete in the Olympics, talent, training, and dedication are needed.
4. Pressing hard on the brakes, the car spun into a hedge.
5. Showing a lack of design experience, the architect advised the student to take her model back to the drawing board.

11 *Incomplete Sentences*

For advice on editing fragments, see 1 and also A1 in the Quick Editing Guide (the dark-blue-edged pages).

A fragment fails to qualify as a sentence because it lacks a subject or a predicate (or both) or it fails to express a complete thought. However, a sentence with the essentials can still miss the mark. If it lacks a crucial word or phrase, the sentence may be *incomplete*. Incomplete sentences catch writers most often in comparisons and elliptical constructions.

COMPARISONS

11a Make your comparisons clear by stating fully what you are comparing with what.

INCOMPLETE   Roscoe loves spending time online more than Diane.

What is this writer trying to tell us? Does Roscoe prefer the company of a keyboard to the company of his friend? Or, of these two people, is Roscoe (and not Diane) the online addict? We can't be sure because the writer has not completed the comparison. Adding a word would solve the problem.

REVISED   Roscoe loves spending time online more than Diane *does.*

REVISED   Roscoe loves spending time online more than *with* Diane.

11b When you start to draw a comparison, finish it.

The unfinished comparison is a favorite trick of advertisers — "Our product is better!" — because it dodges the question "Better than what?" A sharp writer (or shopper) knows that any item must be compared *with* something else.

INCOMPLETE   Scottish tweeds are warmer.

REVISED   Scottish tweeds are warmer *than any other fabric you can buy.*

11c Be sure the things you compare are of the same kind.

A sentence that compares should reassure readers on two counts: the items involved are similar enough to compare, and the terms of the comparison are clear and logical.

INCOMPLETE   The engine of a Ford truck is heavier than a Piper Cub airplane.

What is being compared? Truck engine and airplane? Or engine and engine? Because a truck engine is unlikely to outweigh an airplane, we can guess the writer meant to compare engines. Readers, however, should not have to make the effort to complete a writer's thought.

REVISED   The engine of a Ford truck is heavier than *that of* a Piper Cub airplane.

REVISED   A Ford truck's engine is heavier than a *Piper Cub's*.

In this last example, parallel structure (*Ford truck's* and *Piper Cub's*) helps to make the comparison concise as well as clear.

> For more on parallel structure, see 13.

11d   To compare an item with others of its kind, use *any other*.

A comparison using *any* shows how something relates to a group without belonging to the group.

Alaska is larger than *any* country in Central America.

Bluefish has as much protein as *any* meat.

A comparison using *any other* shows how one member of a group relates to other members of the same group.

Death Valley is drier than *any other* place in the United States.

Bluefish has as distinctive a flavor as *any other* fish.

■ Exercise 11–1

Completing Comparisons

Revise the following sentences by adding needed words to any comparisons that are incomplete. (There may be more than one way to complete some comparisons.) Some sentences may be correct. Possible revisions for the lettered sentences appear in the back of the book. Example:

I hate hot weather more than you.

I hate hot weather more than you *do. Or*

I hate hot weather more than *I hate* you.

a.   The movie version of *The Brady Bunch* was much more ironic.
b.   Taking care of a dog is often more demanding than a cat.
c.   I received more free calendars in the mail for 2004 than any year.
d.   The crime rate in the United States is higher than Canada.
e.   Liver contains more iron than any meat.

> For more practice, visit <bedfordstmartins.com/bedguide> and do a keyword search:
>
>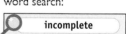
> incomplete

1. Driving a sports car means more to Jake than his professors.
2. People who go to college aren't necessarily smarter, but they will always have an advantage at job interviews.
3. I don't have as much trouble getting along with Michelle as Karen.
4. A hen lays fewer eggs than a turtle.
5. Singing is closer to prayer than a meal of Chicken McNuggets.

ELLIPTICAL CONSTRUCTIONS

Robert Frost begins his well-known poem "Fire and Ice" with these lines:

> Some say the world will end in fire, / Some say in ice.

When Frost wrote that opening, he avoided needless repetition by implying certain words rather than stating them. The result is more concise and more effective than a complete version of the same sentence would be:

> Some say the world will end in fire, some say the world will end in ice.

This common tactic produces an *elliptical construction* — one that leaves out (for conciseness) words that are unnecessary but clearly understood by readers. Elliptical constructions can be confusing, however, if a writer gives readers too little information to fill in those missing words accurately.

11e   When you eliminate repetition, keep all the words essential for clarity.

An elliptical construction avoids repeating what a reader already knows, but it should omit only words that are stated elsewhere in the sentence. Otherwise, your reader may fill the gap incorrectly.

> INCOMPLETE   How can I date her, seeing that she is a senior, I a mere freshman?

This elliptical construction won't work. A reader supplying the stated verb in the last part of the sentence would get "I *is* a mere freshman."

> REVISED   How can I date her, seeing that she is a senior and I *am* a mere freshman?

Be sure to state necessary prepositions as well.

> INCOMPLETE   The train neither goes nor returns from Middletown.

Readers are likely to fill in an extra *from* after *goes.* Write instead:

> REVISED   The train neither goes *to* nor returns from Middletown.

11f In a compound predicate, leave out only verb forms that have already been stated.

Compound predicates are prone to incomplete constructions, especially if the verbs are in different tenses. Be sure no necessary part is missing.

INCOMPLETE　　The mayor never has and never will vote to raise taxes.

REVISED　　　The mayor never has *voted* and never will vote to raise taxes.

compound predicate: A predicate consisting of two or more verbs linked by a conjunction: My sister *stopped and stared.*

11g If you mix comparisons using *as* and *than*, include both words.

To contrast two things, we normally use the comparative form of an adjective followed by *than: better than, more than, fewer than.* To show a similarity between two things, we normally sandwich the simple form of an adjective between *as* and *as: as good as, as many as, as few as.* Often we can combine two *than* or two *as* comparisons into an elliptical construction.

For more on comparative forms, see 8d–8f.

The White House is smaller [than] and newer than Buckingham Palace.

Some elegant homes are as large [as] and as grand as the White House.

However, merging a *than* comparison with an *as* comparison won't work.

INCOMPLETE　　The White House is smaller but just as beautiful as Buckingham Palace.

REVISED　　　The White House is smaller *than* but just *as* beautiful *as* Buckingham Palace.

INCOMPLETE　　Some elegant homes are as large and no less grand than the White House.

REVISED　　　Some elegant homes are *as* large *as* and no less grand *than* the White House.

■ Exercise 11–2

Completing Sentences

Revise the following sentences by adding needed words to any constructions that are incomplete. (There may be more than one way to complete some constructions.) Some sentences may be correct. Possible revisions for the lettered sentences appear in the back of the book. Example:

For more practice, visit <bedfordstmartins.com/bedguide> and do a keyword search:

🔍 **incomplete**

President Kennedy should have but didn't see the perils of invading Cuba.

President Kennedy should have *seen* but didn't see the perils of invading Cuba.

    a. Eighteenth-century China was as civilized and in many respects more so-phisticated than the Western world.

    b. Pembroke was never contacted, much less involved with, the election committee.

    c. I haven't yet but soon will finish my research paper.

    d. Ron likes his popcorn with butter, Linda with parmesan cheese.

    e. George Washington always has been and will be regarded as the father of this country.

1. You have traveled to exotic Tahiti; Maureen to Asbury Park, New Jersey.

2. The mayor refuses to negotiate or even talk to the civic association.

3. Building a new sewage treatment plant would be no more costly and just as effective as modifying the existing one.

4. You'll be able to tell Jon from the rest of the team: Jon wears white Reeboks, the others black high-tops.

5. Erosion has and always will reshape the shoreline.

12 *Mixed Constructions and Faulty Predication*

phrase: Two or more re-lated words that work together but may lack a subject (as in *will have been*), a verb (*my uncle Zeke*), or both (*in the attic*)

clause: A group of re-lated words that in-cludes both a subject and a verb: *The sailboats raced until the sun set.*

preposition: A transi-tional word (such as *in, on, at, of, from*) that leads into a phrase such as *in the bar, under a rickety table*

Sometimes a sentence contains all the necessary ingredients but still doesn't make sense. The problem may be a discord between two or more of its parts: phrases or clauses that don't fit together (a *mixed construction*) or a verb and its subject, object, or modifier (*faulty predication*) that don't match.

12a Link phrases and clauses logically.

A *mixed construction* results when a writer connects phrases or clauses (or both) that don't work together as a sentence.

> MIXED   In her efforts to solve the tax problem only caused the mayor addi-tional difficulties.

The prepositional phrase *In her efforts to solve the tax problem* is a modifier; it can't act as the subject of a sentence. The writer, however, has used this phrase as a noun—the subject of the verb *caused*. To untangle this mixed construction, the writer has two choices: (1) rewrite the phrase so that it works as a noun, or (2) use the phrase as a modifier, not a subject.

> REVISED   Her efforts to solve the tax problem only caused the mayor addi-tional difficulties. [With *in* gone, *efforts* becomes the subject.]

> REVISED   In her efforts to solve the tax problem, the mayor created addi-tional difficulties. [The phrase now modifies the verb *created*.]

To avoid mixed constructions, check the links that join your phrases and clauses — especially prepositions and conjunctions. A sentence, like a chain, is only as strong as its weakest link.

> MIXED   Jack, although he was picked up by the police, but was not charged with anything.

Using both *although* and *but* gives this sentence one link too many. The writer could unmix the construction in two ways.

> REVISED   Jack was picked up by the police but was not charged with anything.

> REVISED   Although he was picked up by the police, Jack was not charged with anything.

conjunction: A linking word that connects words or groups of words through coordination (*and, but*) or subordination (*because, although, unless*)

Mixed Constructions, Faulty Predication, and Subject Errors

Mixed constructions result when phrases or clauses are joined even though they do not logically go together. Combine clauses with either a coordinating conjunction or a subordinating conjunction, never both.

> INCORRECT   *Although* baseball is called "the national pastime" of the United States, *but* football is probably more popular.

> CORRECT   *Although* baseball is called "the national pastime" of the United States, football is probably more popular.

> CORRECT   Baseball is called "the national pastime" of the United States, *but* football is probably more popular.

Faulty predication results when a verb and its subject, object, or modifier do not match. Do not use a noun as both the subject of the sentence and the object of a preposition.

> INCORRECT   *In my neighborhood has* several good restaurants.

> CORRECT   *My neighborhood has* several good restaurants.

> CORRECT   *In my neighborhood, there are* several good restaurants.

Also avoid these common errors involving subjects of clauses.

- Do not omit *it* used as a subject. A subject is required in all English sentences except imperatives.

> INCORRECT   *Is* interesting to visit museums.

> CORRECT   *It is* interesting to visit museums.

- Do not repeat the subject of a sentence with a pronoun.

> INCORRECT   *My brother-in-law, he* is a successful investor.

> CORRECT   *My brother-in-law* is a successful investor.

ESL GUIDELINES

■ For more on conjunctions, see 14a–14c.

coordinating conjunction: A one-syllable linking word (*and, but, for, or, nor, so, yet*) that joins elements with equal or near-equal importance: Jack *and* Jill, sink *or* swim

subordinating conjunction: A word (such as *because, although, if, when*) used to make one clause dependent on, or subordinate to, another: *Unless* you have a key, we are locked out.

verb: A word that shows action (The cow *jumped* over the moon) or a state of being (The cow *is* brown)

subject: The part of a sentence that names something—a person, an object, an idea, a situation—about which the predicate makes an assertion: The *king* lives.

predicate: The part of a sentence that makes an assertion about the subject involving an action (Birds *fly*), a relationship (Birds *have feathers*), or a state of being ("Birds *are warm-blooded*)

direct object: The target of a verb that completes the action performed by or asserted about the subject: I photographed *the sheriff.*

linking verb: A verb (*is, become, seem, feel*) that shows a state of being by linking the sentence subject with a subject complement that renames or describes the subject: The sky *is* blue. (See 3a.)

For more on using active and passive voice, see 3m.

12b Relate the parts of a sentence logically.

Faulty predication refers to a skewed relationship between a verb and some other part of a sentence.

FAULTY   *The temperature of water freezes* at 32 degrees Fahrenheit.

At first glance, that sentence looks all right. It contains both subject and predicate. It expresses a complete thought. What is wrong with it? The writer has slipped into faulty predication by mismatching the subject and verb. The sentence tells us that *temperature freezes,* when science and common sense tell us it is *water* that freezes. To correct this error, the writer must select a subject and verb that fit each other.

REVISED   *Water freezes* at 32 degrees Fahrenheit.

Faulty predication also results from a mismatched verb and direct object.

FAULTY   Rising costs *diminish college* for many students.

Costs don't *diminish college.* To correct this error, the writer must change the sentence so that its direct object follows logically from its verb.

REVISED   Rising costs *diminish the number of students who can attend college.*

Subtler predication errors result when a writer uses a linking verb to forge a false connection between the subject and a subject complement.

FAULTY   *Industrial waste* has become *an important modern priority.*

Is it *waste* that has become a *priority*? Or is it *solving problems caused by careless disposal of industrial waste*? A writer who says all that, though, risks wordiness. Why not just replace *priority* with a closer match for *waste*?

REVISED   *Industrial waste* has become a *modern menace.*

Predication errors tend to plague writers who are too fond of the passive voice. Mismatches between a verb and another part of the sentence are easier to avoid when the verb is active rather than passive.

FAULTY   The idea of giving thanks for a good harvest *was not done* first by the Pilgrims.

REVISED   The idea of giving thanks for a good harvest *did not originate* with the Pilgrims.

12c Avoid starting a definition with *when* or *where.*

A definition, like any other phrase or clause, needs to fit grammatically with the rest of the sentence.

FAULTY   Dyslexia is when you have a reading disorder.

REVISED   Dyslexia is a reading disorder.

FAULTY   A lay-up is where a player dribbles close to the basket and then makes a one-handed, banked shot.

REVISED   To shoot a lay-up, a player dribbles in close to the basket and then makes a one-handed, banked shot.

12d Avoid using *the reason is because . . .*

Anytime you start an explanation with *the reason is,* what follows *is* should be a subject complement: an adjective, a noun, or a noun clause. *Because* is a conjunction; it cannot function as a noun or adjective.

FAULTY   *The reason* Gerard hesitates *is because* no one supported him two years ago.

REVISED   *The reason* Gerard hesitates *is that* no one supported him two years ago.

REVISED   Gerard hesitates *because* no one supported him two years ago.

REVISED   *The reason* Gerard hesitates *is simple*: no one supported him two years ago.

■ Exercise 12–1

Correcting Mixed Constructions and Faulty Predication

Correct any mixed constructions and faulty predication you find in the following sentences. Possible revisions for the lettered sentences appear in the back of the book. Example:

> The storm damaged the beach erosion.
>
> The storm worsened the beach erosion. *Or*
>
> The storm damaged the beach.

■ For more practice, visit <bedfordstmartins.com/bedguide> and do a keyword search:

mixed

a.   The cost of health insurance protects people from big medical bills.

b.   In his determination to prevail helped him finish the race.

c.   The AIDS epidemic destroys the body's immune system.

d.   The temperatures are too cold for the orange trees.

e.   A recession is when economic growth is small or nonexistent and unemployment increases.

1.   The opening of the new shopping mall should draw out-of-town shoppers for years to come.

2.   The reason the referendum was defeated was because voters are tired of paying so much in taxes.

3.   In the glacier's retreat created the valley.

4.   A drop in prices could put farmers out of business.

5.   The researchers' main goal is cancer.

13 *Parallel Structure*

You use *parallel structure,* or parallelism, when you create a series of words, phrases, clauses, or sentences with the same grammatical form. The pattern created by the series — its parallel structure — emphasizes the similarities or differences among the items, whether things, qualities, actions, or ideas.

> My favorite foods are roast beef, apple pie, and linguine with clam sauce.

> Louise is charming, witty, intelligent, and talented.

> Jeff likes to swim, ride, and run.

> Dave likes movies that scare him and books that make him laugh.

■ For more on editing for parallel structure, see B2 in the Quick Editing Guide (the dark-blue-edged pages).

Each series is a perfect parallel construction, composed of equivalent words: nouns in the first example, adjectives in the second, verbs in the third, and adjective clauses in the fourth.

13a In a series linked by a coordinating conjunction, keep all elements in the same grammatical form.

coordinating conjunction: A one-syllable linking word (*and, but, for, or, nor, so, yet*) that joins elements with equal or near-equal importance: Jack *and* Jill, sink *or* swim

■ For more on coordination, see 14a–14c.

A coordinating conjunction cues your readers to expect a parallel structure. Whether your series consists of single words, phrases, or clauses, its parts should balance one another.

AWKWARD The puppies are *tiny, clumsily bumping* into each other, *and cute.*

Two elements in this series are parallel one-word adjectives (*tiny, cute*), but the third, the verb phrase *clumsily bumping,* is inconsistent.

PARALLEL The puppies are *tiny, clumsy, and cute.*

Don't mix verb forms, such as gerunds and infinitives, in a series.

AWKWARD Plan a winter vacation if you like *skiing and to skate.*

PARALLEL Plan a winter vacation if you like *skiing and skating.*

PARALLEL Plan a winter vacation if you like *to ski and to skate.*

In a series of phrases or clauses, be sure that all elements in the series are similar in form, even if they are not similar in length.

AWKWARD The fight in the bar takes place *after the two lovers have their scene together* but *before the car chase.* [The clause starting with *after* is not parallel to the phrase starting with *before.*]

PARALLEL The fight in the bar takes place *after the love scene* but *before the car chase.*

AWKWARD You can take the key, or don't forget to leave it under the mat. [The declarative clause starting with *You can* is not parallel to the imperative clause starting with *don't forget.*]

PARALLEL You can *take the key,* or you can *leave it* under the mat.

13b   In a series linked by correlative conjunctions, keep all elements in the same grammatical form.

When you use a correlative conjunction, follow each part with a similarly structured word, phrase, or clause.

AWKWARD	I'm looking forward *to either attending* Saturday's wrestling match *or to seeing* it on closed-circuit TV. [*To* precedes the first part of the correlative conjunction (*to either*) but follows the second part (*or to*).]
PARALLEL	I'm looking forward *either to attending* Saturday's wrestling match *or to seeing* it on closed-circuit television.
AWKWARD	Take my advice: try *neither to be first nor last* in the lunch line. [*To be* follows the first part of the correlative conjunction but not the second part.]
PARALLEL	Take my advice: try to be *neither first nor last* in the lunch line.

> **correlative conjunction:** A pair of linking words (such as *either/or, not only/but also*) that appear separately but work together to join elements of a sentence: *Neither* his friends *nor* hers like pizza.

13c   Make the elements in a comparison parallel in form.

A comparative word such as *than* or *as* cues the reader to expect a parallel structure. This makes logical sense: to be compared, two things must resemble each other, and parallel structure emphasizes this resemblance.

> For more on comparisons, see 11a–11d and 11g.

AWKWARD	Philip likes *fishing* better than *to sail*.
PARALLEL	Philip likes *fishing* better than *sailing*.
PARALLEL	Philip likes *to fish* better than *to sail*.
AWKWARD	*Maintaining* railway lines is as important to our public transportation system as *to buy* new trains.
PARALLEL	*Maintaining* railway lines is as important to our public transportation system as *buying* new trains.

13d   Reinforce parallel structure by repeating rather than mixing lead-in words.

Parallel structures are especially useful when a sentence contains a series of clauses or phrases. For example, try to precede potentially confusing clauses with *that, who, when, where,* or some other connective, repeating the same connective every time. To do so not only helps you to keep your thoughts in order but helps readers to follow them with ease.

> No one in this country needs a government *that* aids big business at the expense of farmers and workers, *that* ravages the environment in the name of progress, or *that* slashes budgets for health and education.

Repeating an opening phrase can accomplish the same goal in a graceful series of parallel sentences.

The Russian dramatist is one who, walking through a cemetery, does not see the flowers on the graves. The American dramatist is one who, walking through a cemetery, does not see the graves under the flowers.

Sometimes the same lead-in word won't work for all elements in a series. In such cases you may be able to preserve a parallel structure by changing the order of the elements to minimize variation.

AWKWARD   The new school building is large but not very comfortable, and expensive but unattractive.

PARALLEL   The new school building is large and expensive, but uncomfortable and unattractive.

■ Exercise 13–1

Making Sentences Parallel

■ For more practice, visit <bedfordstmartins.com/bedguide> and do a keyword search:

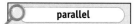
parallel

Revise the following sentences by substituting parallel structures for awkward ones. Possible revisions for the lettered sentences appear in the back of the book. Example:

In the Rio Grande Valley, the interests of conservationists, government officials, and those trying to immigrate collide.

In the Rio Grande Valley, the interests of conservationists, government officials, and immigrants collide.

a. The border separating Texas and Mexico marks not only the political boundary of two countries, but it also is the last frontier for some endangered wildlife.

b. In the Rio Grande Valley, both local residents and the people who happen to be tourists enjoy visiting the national wildlife refuges.

c. The tall grasses in this valley are the home of many insects, birds, and there are abundant small mammals.

d. Two endangered wildcats, the ocelot and another called the jaguarundi, also make the Rio Grande Valley their home.

e. Many people from Central America are desperate to immigrate to the United States by either legal or by illegal means.

1. Because the land along the Rio Grande has few human inhabitants and the fact that the river is often shallow, many illegal immigrants attempt to cross the border there.

2. To capture illegal immigrants more easily, the U.S. government has cut down tall grasses, put up fences, and the number of immigration patrols has been increased.

3. For illegal immigrants, crossing the border at night makes more sense than to enter the United States in broad daylight, so the U.S. government has recently installed bright lights along the border.

4. The ocelot and the jaguarundi need darkness, hiding places, and to have some solitude if they are to survive.

5. Neither the immigration officials nor have wildlife conservationists been able to find a solution that will protect both the U.S. border and these endangered wildcats.

14 *Coordination and Subordination*

Coordination and subordination can bring out the relationships between your ideas. Coordination connects thoughts of equal importance; subordination shows how one thought affects another. Often, conjunctions — words that link groups of words — specify these relationships. Together, coordination and subordination will help you produce sentences, paragraphs, and essays that function as a coherent whole.

conjunction: A linking word that connects words or groups of words through coordination (*and, but*) or subordination (*because, although, unless*)

14a Coordinate clauses or sentences that are related in theme and equal in importance.

The car skidded for a hundred yards. It crashed into a brick wall.

These two clauses make equally significant statements about the same subject, a car accident. Because the writer has indicated no link between the sentences, we can only guess that the crash followed from the skid; we cannot be sure. Suppose we join the two with a conjunction.

The car skidded for a hundred yards, and it crashed into a brick wall.

Now the sequence is clear: first the car skidded, then it crashed. That's coordination. To tighten the coordination, try combining the two clauses into a single sentence with a compound predicate.

The car skidded for a hundred yards and crashed into a brick wall.

Now the connection is so clear we can almost hear screeching brakes and crunching metal.

Once you decide to coordinate two clauses, there are three ways you can do it: with a conjunction, with a conjunctive adverb, or with punctuation.

clause: A group of related words that includes both a subject and a verb: *The sailboats raced until the sun set.*

compound predicate: A predicate consisting of two or more verbs linked by a conjunction: My sister *stopped and stared.*

1. Join two main clauses with a coordinating conjunction.

UNCOORDINATED Ari does not want to be placed on your mailing list. He does not want a salesperson to call him.

COORDINATED Ari does not want to be placed on your mailing list, nor does he want a salesperson to call him.

COORDINATED Ari does not want to be placed on your mailing list or called by a salesperson.

coordinating conjunction: A one-syllable linking word (*and, but, for, or, nor, so, yet*) that joins elements with equal or near-equal importance: Jack *and* Jill, sink *or* swim

conjunctive adverb: A linking word that can connect independent clauses and show a relationship between two ideas: Armando is a serious student; *therefore,* he studies every day.

■ For more on semicolons and colons, see 22 and 23.

2. Join two main clauses with a semicolon and a conjunctive adverb. Conjunctive adverbs show relationships such as addition (*also, besides*), comparison (*likewise, similarly*), contrast (*instead, however*), emphasis (*namely, certainly*), cause and effect (*thus, therefore*), or time (*finally, subsequently*).

UNCOORDINATED   The guerrillas did not observe the truce. They never intended to.

COORDINATED   The guerrillas did not observe the truce; furthermore, they never intended to.

3. Join two main clauses with a semicolon or a colon.

UNCOORDINATED   The government wants to negotiate. The guerrillas prefer to fight.

COORDINATED   The government wants to negotiate; the guerrillas prefer to fight.

UNCOORDINATED   The guerrillas have two advantages. They know the terrain, and the people support them.

COORDINATED   The guerrillas have two advantages: they know the terrain, and the people support them.

14b Coordinate clauses only if they are clearly and logically related.

Whenever you hitch together two sentences, make sure they get along. Will the relationship between them be evident to your readers?

FAULTY   The sportscasters were surprised by Easy Goer's failure to win the Kentucky Derby, but it rained on Derby day.

The writer has not included enough information for the reader to see why these two clauses are connected.

COORDINATED   The sportscasters were surprised by Easy Goer's failure to win the Kentucky Derby; *however, he runs poorly on a muddy track,* and it rained on Derby day.

Have you chosen a coordinating conjunction, conjunctive adverb, or punctuation mark that accurately reflects this relationship?

FAULTY   The sportscasters all expected Easy Goer to win the Kentucky Derby, and Sunday Silence beat him.

Because *and* implies that both clauses reflect the same assumptions, which is not the case, the writer should choose a conjunction that expresses difference.

COORDINATED   The sportscasters all expected Easy Goer to win the Kentucky Derby, *but* Sunday Silence beat him.

Coordinating and Subordinating Words at a Glance

Coordinating Conjunctions

and, but, for, nor, or, so, yet

Correlative Conjunctions

as . . . as	just as . . . so	not only . . . but also
both . . . and	neither . . . nor	whether . . . or
either . . . or	not . . . but	

Common Conjunctive Adverbs

accordingly	finally	likewise	otherwise
also	furthermore	meanwhile	similarly
anyway	hence	moreover	still
as	however	nevertheless	then
besides	incidentally	next	therefore
certainly	indeed	nonetheless	thus
consequently	instead	now	undoubtedly

Common Subordinating Conjunctions

after	even if	since	when
although	even though	so	whenever
as	how	so that	where
as if	if	than	wherever
as soon as	in order that	that	while
as though	once	though	why
because	provided that	unless	
before	rather than	until	

Relative Pronouns

that	what	who	whom
which	whatever	whoever	whomever
whose			

14c Coordinate clauses only if they work together to make a coherent point.

When a writer strings together several clauses in a row, often the result is excessive coordination. Trying to pack too much information into a single sentence can make readers dizzy, unable to pick out which points really matter.

> EXCESSIVE Easy Goer was the Kentucky Derby favorite, and all the sportscasters expected him to win, but he runs poorly on a muddy track, and it rained on Derby day, so Sunday Silence beat him.

What are the main points in this passage? Each key idea deserves its own sentence so that readers will recognize it as important.

REVISED   Easy Goer was the Kentucky Derby favorite, and all the sports-casters expected him to win. However, he runs poorly on a muddy track, and it rained on Derby day. Therefore, Sunday Silence beat him.

Excessive coordination also may result when a writer uses the same conjunction repeatedly.

EXCESSIVE Phil was out of the house all day, so he didn't know about the rain, so he went ahead and bet on Easy Goer, so he lost twenty bucks, so now he wants to borrow money from me.

REVISED   Phil was out of the house all day, so he didn't know about the rain. He went ahead and bet on Easy Goer, and he lost twenty bucks. Now he wants to borrow money from me.

■ For advice on subordination, see 14d.

One solution to excessive coordination is subordination: making one clause dependent on another instead of giving both clauses equal weight.

■ Exercise 14–1

Using Coordination

■ For more practice, visit <bedfordstmartins.com/bedguide> and do a keyword search:

coord_subord

Revise the following sentences, adding coordination where appropriate and removing faulty or excessive coordination. Possible revisions for the lettered sentences appear in the back of the book. Example:

The wind was rising, and leaves tossed on the trees, and the air seemed to crackle with electricity, and we knew that a thunderstorm was on the way.

The wind was rising, leaves tossed on the trees, and the air seemed to crackle with electricity. We knew that a thunderstorm was on the way.

a. Professional poker players try to win money and prizes in high-stakes tournaments. They may lose thousands of dollars.

b. Poker is not an easy way to make a living. Playing professional poker is not a good way to relax.

c. A good "poker face" reveals no emotions. Communicating too much information puts a player at a disadvantage.

d. Hidden feelings may come out in unconscious movements. An expert poker player watches other players carefully.

e. Poker is different from most other casino gambling games, for it requires skill and it forces players to compete against each other, and other casino gambling pits players against the house, so they may win out of sheer luck, but skill has little to do with winning those games.

1. The rebels may take the capital in a week. They may not be able to hold it.

2. If you want to take Spanish this semester, you have only one choice. You must sign up for the 8 A.M. course.

3. Peterson's Market has raised its prices. Last week tuna fish cost $.89 a can. Now it's up to $1.09.

4. Joe starts the morning with a cup of coffee, which wakes him up, and then at lunch he eats a chocolate bar, so that the sugar and caffeine will bring up his energy level.

5. The *Hindenburg* drifted peacefully over New York City. It exploded just before landing.

14d Subordinate less important ideas to more important ideas.

Subordination is one of the most useful of all writing strategies. By subordinating a less important clause to a more important one, you show your readers that one fact or idea follows from another or affects another. You stress what counts, thereby encouraging your readers to share your viewpoint.

When two sentences contain ideas that need connecting, you can subordinate one to the other in any of the following three ways.

1. Turn the less important idea into a subordinate clause by introducing it with a subordinating conjunction.

Jason has a keen sense of humor. He has an obnoxious, braying laugh.

From that pair of sentences, readers don't know what to feel about Jason. Is he likable or repellent? The writer needs to decide which trait matters more and to emphasize it.

Although Jason has a keen sense of humor, he has an obnoxious, braying laugh.

This revision makes Jason's sense of humor less important than his annoying hee-haw. The less important idea is stated as a subordinate clause opening with *Although;* the more important idea is stated as the main clause.

The writer could reverse the meaning by combining the two ideas the other way around:

Although Jason has an obnoxious, braying laugh, he has a keen sense of humor.

That version makes Jason sound fun to be with, despite his mannerism.

Which of Jason's traits to emphasize is up to the writer. What matters is that, in both combined versions, the writer takes a clear stand by making one sentence a main clause and the other a subordinate clause.

2. Turn the less important idea into a subordinate clause by introducing it with a relative pronoun such as *who, which,* or *that.*

Jason, *who has an obnoxious, braying laugh,* has a keen sense of humor.

Jason, *whose sense of humor is keen,* has an obnoxious, braying laugh.

3. Turn the less important idea into a phrase.

Jason, *a keen humorist,* has an obnoxious, braying laugh.

Despite his obnoxious, braying laugh, Jason has a keen sense of humor.

subordinating conjunction: A word (such as *because, although, if, when*) used to make one clause dependent on, or subordinate to, another: *Unless* you have a key, we are locked out.

For a list of subordinating words, see p. H-73.

main clause: A group of words that has both a subject and a verb and can stand alone as a complete sentence: *My sister has a friend.*

relative pronoun: A pronoun (*who, which, that, what, whom, whomever, whose*) that opens a subordinate clause, modifying a noun or pronoun in another clause: *The gift that I received is very practical.*

phrase: Two or more related words that work together but may lack a subject (as in *will have been*), a verb (*my uncle Zeke*), or both (*in the attic*)

14e Express the more important idea in the main clause.

Sometimes a writer accidentally subordinates a more important idea to a less important one and turns the sentence's meaning upside down.

FAULTY
SUBORDINATION

Although the heroism of the Allied troops on D-Day lives on in spirit, many of the World War II soldiers who invaded Normandy are dead now.

This sentence is factually accurate. Does the writer, however, want to stress death over life? This is the effect of putting *are dead now* in the main clause and *lives on* in the subordinate clause. Instead, the writer can reverse the two.

REVISED

Although many of the World War II soldiers who invaded Normandy are dead now, the heroism of the Allied troops on D-Day lives on in spirit.

14f Limit the number of subordinate clauses in a sentence.

subordinate clause: A group of words that contains a subject and a verb but cannot stand alone because it depends on a main clause to help it make sense: Pia, *who plays the oboe*, prefers solitude.

Often the result of cramming too much information into one sentence, excessive subordination strings so many ideas together that readers may not be able to pick out what matters.

EXCESSIVE
SUBORDINATION

Debate over the Strategic Defense Initiative (SDI), which was originally proposed as a space-based defensive shield that would protect America from enemy attack, but which critics have suggested amounts to creating a first-strike capability in space, has to some extent focused on the wrong question.

In revising this sentence, the writer needs to decide which are the main points and turn each one into a main clause. Lesser points can remain as subordinate clauses, arranged so that each gets appropriate emphasis.

REVISED

Debate over the Strategic Defense Initiative (SDI) has to some extent focused on the wrong question. The plan was originally proposed as a space-based defensive shield that would protect America from enemy attack. Critics have suggested, however, that it amounts to creating a first-strike capability in space.

■ For more practice, visit <bedfordstmartins.com/ bedguide> and do a keyword search:

coord_subord

■ Exercise 14–2

Using Subordination

Revise the following sentences, adding subordination where appropriate and removing faulty or excessive subordination. Possible revisions for the lettered sentences appear in the back of the book. Example:

Some playwrights like to work with performing theater companies. It is helpful to hear a script read aloud by actors.

Some playwrights like to work with performing theater companies *because* it is helpful to hear a script read aloud by actors.

a. Cape Cod is a peninsula in Massachusetts. It juts into the Atlantic Ocean south of Boston. The Cape marks the northern turning point of the Gulf Stream.

b. The developer had hoped the condominiums would sell quickly. Sales were sluggish.

c. Tourists love Italy. Italy has a wonderful climate, beautiful towns and cities, and a rich history.

d. At the end of Verdi's opera *La Traviata,* Alfredo has to see his beloved Violetta again. He knows she is dying and all he can say is good-bye.

e. I usually have more fun at a concert with Rico than with Morey. Rico loves music. Morey merely tolerates it.

1. Although we occasionally hear horror stories about fruits and vegetables being unsafe to eat because they were sprayed with toxic chemicals or were grown in contaminated soil, the fact remains that, given their high nutritional value, these fresh foods are generally much better for us than processed foods.

2. English has become an international language. Its grammar is filled with exceptions to the rules.

3. Some television cartoon shows have become cult classics. This has happened years after they went off the air. Examples include *Rocky and Bullwinkle* and *Speed Racer.*

4. Although investors have not fully regained confidence in the stock market, stock prices have gone up.

5. Violetta gives away her money. She bids adieu to her faithful servant. After that she dies in her lover's arms.

15 *Sentence Variety*

Most writers rely on some patterns more than others to express ideas directly and efficiently, but sometimes they combine sentence elements in unexpected ways to emphasize ideas and to surprise readers.

sentence: A word group that includes both a subject and a predicate and can stand alone

15a Normal Sentences

In a *normal sentence,* a writer puts the subject before the verb at the beginning of the main clause. This pattern is the most common in English because it expresses ideas in the most straightforward manner.

Most college *students* today *want* interesting classes.

main clause: A group of words that has both a subject and a verb and can stand alone as a complete sentence: *My sister has a friend.*

Types of Sentences at a Glance

Simple Sentences

Any sentence that contains only one main clause is a *simple sentence,* even if it includes modifiers, objects, complements, and phrases in addition to its subject and verb.

───────────────── MAIN CLAUSE ─────────────────
Even amateur stargazers can easily locate the Big Dipper in the night sky.

A simple sentence may have a compound subject (*Fred and Sandy*) or a compound verb (*laughed and cried*). Sometimes the subject of a simple sentence is not stated but is clearly understood, as is *you* in the command "Run!"

Compound Sentences

■ For lists of coordinating conjunctions, conjunctive adverbs, and subordinating words, see p. H-73.

A *compound sentence* consists of two or more main clauses joined by a coordinating conjunction such as *and, but,* or *for* or by a semicolon. Sometimes the semicolon is followed by a conjunctive adverb such as *however, nevertheless,* or *therefore.*

─────── MAIN CLAUSE ───────   MAIN CLAUSE
I would like to accompany you, but I can't.

── MAIN CLAUSE ──   ─────── MAIN CLAUSE ───────
My car broke down; therefore, I missed the first day of class.

Complex Sentences

A *complex sentence* consists of one main clause and one or more subordinate clauses.

MAIN   SUBORDINATE
── CLAUSE ──   ── CLAUSE ──
I will be at the airport when you arrive.

In some sentences, the relative pronoun linking the subordinate clause to the main clause is implied rather than stated.

MAIN   SUBORDINATE
CLAUSE   ── CLAUSE ──
I know [that] you saw us.

Compound-Complex Sentences

A *compound-complex sentence* shares the attributes of both a compound sentence (two or more main clauses) and a complex sentence (at least one subordinate clause).

MAIN   SUBORDINATE   SUBORDINATE   MAIN
── CLAUSE ──   ── CLAUSE ──   ── CLAUSE ──   ── CLAUSE ──
I'd gladly wait until you're ready; but if I do, I'll miss the boat.

15b   Inverted Sentences

In an *inverted sentence,* a writer inverts or reverses the subject-verb order to emphasize an idea in the predicate.

> NORMAL   *My peers are uninterested* in reading.
>
> INVERTED   How *uninterested* in reading *are my peers*!

15c   Cumulative Sentences

In a *cumulative sentence,* a writer piles details at the end of a sentence to help readers visualize a scene or understand an idea.

> They came walking out in heavily brocaded yellow and black costumes, the familiar "toreador" suit, heavy with gold embroidery, cape, jacket, shirt and collar, knee breeches, pink stockings, and low pumps.
> > — Ernest Hemingway, "Bull Fighting a Tragedy"

15d   Periodic Sentences

The positions of emphasis in a sentence are the beginning and the end. In a *periodic sentence,* a writer suspends the main clause for a climactic ending, emphasizing an idea by withholding it until the end.

> Leaning back in his chair, shaking his head slowly back and forth, frustrated over his inability to solve the quadratic equation, Franklin scowled.

■ Exercise 15–1

Increasing Sentence Variety

Revise the following passage, adding sentence variety to create interest, emphasize important ideas, and strengthen coherence.

■ For more practice, visit <bedfordstmartins.com/ bedguide> and do a key-word search:

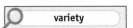
variety

> We are terrified of death. We do not think of it, and we don't speak of death. We don't mourn in public. We don't know how to console a grieving friend. In fact, we have eliminated or suppressed all the traditional rituals surrounding death.
>
> The Victorians coped with death differently. Their funerals were elaborate. The yards of black crepe around the hearse, hired professional mourners, and its solemn procession leading to an ornate tomb is now only a distant memory. They wore mourning jewelry. They had a complicated dress code for the grieving process. It governed what mourners wore, and it governed how long they wore it. Many of these Victorian rituals may seem excessive or even morbid to us today. The rituals served a psychological purpose in helping the living deal with loss.

Chapter 35
Word Choice

16 *Appropriateness*

When you talk to people face to face, you can gauge their reactions to what you say. Often their responses guide your tone and your choice of words: if your listener chuckles at your humor, you go on being humorous; if your listener frowns, you cut the comedy and speak more seriously.

When you write, you cannot gauge your readers' reactions as easily because you cannot see them. Instead, you must imagine yourself in their place, focusing especially closely on their responses when you revise.

16a Choose a tone appropriate for your topic and audience.

Like a speaker, a writer may come across as friendly or aloof, furious or merely annoyed, playful or grimly serious. This attitude is the writer's *tone* and, like a speaker's tone, it strongly influences the audience's response. A tone that seems right to a reader conveys your concern for the reader's reaction. If you ignore your reader, then your tone may be inappropriate. For instance, taking a humorous approach to a disease such as cancer or AIDS probably would create an inappropriate tone. The reader, not finding the topic funny, would likely reject what you say.

To help you convey your tone, you may use sentence length, level of language, vocabulary, and other elements of style. You may choose formal or informal language, colorful or bland words, coolly objective words, or words loaded with emotional connotations ("You pig!" "You angel!").

16b Choose a level of formality appropriate for your tone.

Considering the tone you want to convey to your audience helps you choose words that are neither too formal nor too informal. By *formal* language, we mean the impersonal language of educated persons, usually written. In general, formal language is marked by relatively long and complex sentences and by a large, often esoteric, vocabulary. It doesn't use contractions (such as *doesn't*), and the writer's attitude toward the topic is serious.

   Informal language more closely resembles ordinary conversation. Using relatively short and simple sentences, informal language is marked by common words and may include contractions, slang, and references to everyday objects and activities (cheeseburgers, T-shirts, CDs). It may address the reader as *you,* and the writer may use *I.*

   The right language for most college essays lies somewhere between formal and informal. If your topic and tone are serious (say, for a research paper on terrorism), then your language may lean toward formality. If your topic is not weighty and your tone is light (say, for a humorous essay about giving your dog a bath), then your language may be informal.

■ Exercise 16–1

Choosing an Appropriate Tone and Level of Formality

Revise the following passages to ensure that both the tone and the level of formality are appropriate for the topic and audience. Example:

> I'm sending you this letter because I want you to meet with me and give me some info about the job you do.

> I'm writing to inquire about the possibility of an informational interview about your profession.

■ For more practice, visit <bedfordstmartins.com/bedguide> and do a keyword search:

appropriate

1. Dear Senator Crowley:
      I think you've got to vote for the new environmental law, so I'm writing this letter. We're messing up forests and wetlands — maybe for good. Let's do something now for everybody who's born after us.
      Thanks,
      Glenn Turner

2. The Holocaust Museum in Washington, D.C., is a great museum dedicated to a real bad time in history. It's hard not to get bummed out by the stuff on show. Take it from me, it's an experience you won't forget.

3. Dear Elaine,
      I am so pleased that you plan on attending the homecoming dance with me on Friday. It promises to be a gala event, and I am confident that we will enjoy ourselves immensely. I understand a local recording act by the name of Electric Bunny will provide the musical entertainment. Please call me at your earliest convenience to inform me when to pick you up.
      Sincerely,
      Bill

16c Choose common words instead of jargon.

Jargon is the term for the specialized vocabulary used by people in a certain field. Nearly every academic, professional, and even recreational field—music, carpentry, law, sports—has its own jargon. In baseball, retired pitcher Dennis Eckersley once said that when he faced a dangerous batter, he would think: "If I throw him *the heater,* maybe he *juices it out* on me" (emphasis added). Translation: "If I throw him a fastball, he might hit a home run."[1]

To a specialist addressing other specialists, jargon is convenient and necessary. Without technical terms, after all, two surgeons could hardly discuss a patient's anatomy. To an outsider, though, such terms may be incomprehensible. If your writing is meant (as it should be) to communicate information to your readers and not to make them feel excluded or confused, you should avoid unnecessary jargon.

Commonly, we apply the name *jargon* to any private, pretentious, or needlessly specialized language. Jargon can include not only words but ways of using words. Some politicians and bureaucrats like to make nouns into verbs by tacking on suffixes like *-ize.*

> JARGON   The government intends to *privatize* federal land.
>
> CLEAR   The government intends to *sell* federal land to *private buyers.*

Although *privatize* implies merely "convert to private ownership," usually its real meaning is "sell off"—as might occur were a national park to be auctioned to developers. *Privatize* thus also can be called a *euphemism,* a pleasant term that masks an unpleasant meaning (see 16d).

Besides confusing readers, jargon can mislead them. Recently, technology has made verbs of the familiar nouns *access, boot,* and *format* and has popularized *interface, x amount of, database,* and *parameters.* Such terms are useful to explain technical processes; when thoughtlessly applied to nontechnical ideas, they can obscure meaning.

> JARGON   A democracy needs the electorate's *input.*
>
> CLEAR   A democracy needs the electorate *to vote and to express its views to elected officials.*

Here's how to avoid needless jargon:

1. Beware of favoring a trendy word over a perfectly good old word.
2. Before using a word ending in *-ize, -wise,* or *-ism,* count to ten. This gives you time to think of a clearer alternative or to be sure that none exists.
3. Avoid the jargon of a special discipline—say, psychology or fly-fishing—unless you are writing of such matters for readers familiar with them. If you're writing for general readers about a field—such as hang gliding—in which you are an expert, define any specialized terms. Even for fellow experts, use plain words and you'll rarely go wrong.

[1] Quoted by Mike Whiteford, *How to Talk Baseball* (New York: Dembner, 1983) 51.

■ Exercise 16–2

Avoiding Jargon

Revise the following sentences to eliminate the jargon. If necessary, revise extensively. If you can't tell what a sentence means, decide what it might mean, and rewrite it so that its meaning is clear. Possible revisions for the lettered sentences appear in the back of the book. Example:

> The proximity of Mr. Fitton's knife to Mr. Schering's arm produced a violation of the integrity of the skin.
>
> Mr. Fitton's knife cut Mr. Schering's arm.

a. Everyone at Boondoggle and Gall puts in face time at the holiday gatherings to maximize networking opportunities.

b. This year, in excess of fifty nonessential employees were negatively impacted by Boondoggle and Gall's decision to downsize effective September 1.

c. The layoffs made Jensen the sole point of responsibility for telephone interface in the customer service department.

d. The numerical quotient of Jensen's telephonic exchanges increased by a factor of three post-downsizing, yet Jensen received no additional fiscal remuneration.

e. Jensen was not on the same page with management re her compensation, so she exercised the option to terminate her relationship with Boondoggle and Gall.

1. The driver education course prepares the student for the skills of handling a vehicle on the highway transportation system.

2. We of the State Department have carefully contexted the riots in Lebanon intelligencewise and, after full and thorough database utilization, find them abnormalling rapidly.

3. In the heart area, Mr. Pitt is a prime candidate-elect for intervention of a multiple bypass nature.

4. Engaging in a conversational situation with God permits an individual to maximally interface with God.

5. The deer hunters number-balance the ecological infrastructure by quietizing x amount of the deer populace.

16d Use euphemisms sparingly.

Euphemisms are plain truths dressed attractively, sometimes hard facts stated gently. To say that someone *passed away* instead of *died* is a common euphemism — humane, perhaps, in breaking terrible news to an anxious family. In such shock-absorbing language, an army that *retreats* makes *a strategic withdrawal*, a person who is *underweight* turns *slim*, and an acne medication treats not *pimples* but *blemishes*. Even if you aren't prone to using euphemisms in your own writing, be aware of them when you read evidence from partisan sources and official spokespersons.

■ For more practice, visit <bedfordstmartins.com/bedguide> and do a keyword search:

appropriate

16e Avoid slang in formal writing.

Slang, especially when new, can be colorful ("She's not playing with a full deck"), playful ("He's wicked cute!"), and apt (*ice* for diamonds, a *stiff* for a corpse). The trouble with most slang, however, is that it quickly comes to seem as old and wrinkled as the Jazz Age's favorite exclamation of glee, *twenty-three skidoo!* To be understood in the classroom and out of it, your best bet is to stick to Standard English. Seek words that are usual but exact, not the latest thing, and your writing will stay young longer.

■ Exercise 16–3

■ For more practice, visit <bedfordstmartins.com/bedguide> and do a key-word search:

appropriate

Avoiding Euphemisms and Slang

Revise the following sentences to replace euphemisms with plainer words and slang with Standard English. Possible revisions for the lettered sentences appear in the back of the book. Example:

> Some dude ripped off my wallet, so I am currently experiencing a negative cash flow.
>
> *Someone stole* my wallet, so I am now *in debt.*

a. Our security forces have judiciously thinned an excessive number of political dissidents.

b. At three hundred bucks a month, the apartment is a steal.

c. The soldiers were victims of friendly fire during a strategic withdrawal.

d. Churchill was a wicked good politician.

e. The president's tax plan was toast; there was no way that Congress would approve it.

1. To bridge the projected shortfall between collections and expenditures in next year's budget, the governor advocates some form of revenue enhancement.

2. The course was a joke; the prof passed everyone and didn't even grade the stuff we turned in.

3. Saturday's weather forecast calls for extended periods of shower activity.

4. The caller to the talk-radio program sounded totally wigged out.

5. We anticipate a downturn in economic vitality.

17 Exact Words

What would you think if you read in a newspaper that a certain leading citizen is a *pillow of the community*? Good writing depends on knowing what words and phrases mean and using them precisely.

17a Choose words for their connotations as well as their denotations.

The *denotation* of a word is its basic meaning — its dictionary definition. *Excited, agitated,* and *exhilarated* all denote a similar state of physical and emotional arousal. When you look up a word in a dictionary or thesaurus, the synonyms you find have been selected for their shared denotation.

The *connotations* of a word are the shades of meaning that set it apart from its synonyms. You might be *agitated* by the prospect of exams next week, but *exhilarated* by your plans for a vacation afterward. When you choose one of several synonyms, you base your choice on connotation.

Paying attention to connotation helps a writer to say exactly what he or she intends, instead of almost but not quite.

> IMPRECISE   Advertisers have given light beer a macho image by showing football players *sipping* the product with *enthusiasm.*

> REVISED   Advertisers have given light beer a macho image by showing football players *guzzling* the product with *gusto.*

17b Avoid clichés.

A *cliché* is a trite expression, once vivid or figurative but now worn out from too much use. When a story begins, "It was a dark and stormy night," then its author is obviously using dull, predictable words. Many a strike is settled after a *marathon bargaining session* that *narrowly averts a walkout,* often *at the eleventh hour.* Fires customarily *race* and *gut.* And when everything is *fantastic* or *terrific,* a reader will suspect that it isn't. Clichés abound when writers and speakers try hard to sound vigorous and colorful but don't trouble themselves to invent anything vigorous, colorful, and new.

No writer can entirely avoid clichés or echoes of colorful expressions first used by someone else. You need not ban all proverbs ("It takes a thief to catch a thief"), well-worked quotations from Shakespeare ("Neither a borrower nor a lender be"), and other faintly dusty wares from the storehouse of our language. "Looking for a needle in a haystack" may be timeworn, yet who can put that idea any more memorably?

When editing your writing, you can often recognize any truly annoying cliché if you feel a sudden guilty desire to surround an expression with quotation marks, as if to apologize for it. You might also show your papers to friends, asking them to look for anything trite. As you go on in college, your awareness of clichés will grow with reading. The more you read, the easier it is to recognize a cliché, for you will have met it often before. If one turns up in your writing, replace it with something more vivid.

COMMON CLICHÉS

above and beyond the call of duty	make a long story short
add insult to injury	neat as a pin
beyond a shadow of a doubt	nutty as a fruitcake
The bottom line is . . .	old as the hills
burn one's bridges	on the brink of disaster
burn the midnight oil	pay through the nose
busy as a beaver (or a bee)	piece of cake
But that's another story.	point with pride
come hell or high water	pull the wool over someone's eyes
cool as a cucumber	sell like hotcakes
cream of the crop	a sheepish grin
dressed to kill	since the dawn of time
easy as taking candy from a baby	skating on thin ice
feeling on top of the world	a skeleton in the closet
few and far between	a sneaking suspicion
golden years	stab me in the back
greased lightning	stick out like a sore thumb
hands-on learning experience	sweet as honey
hard as a rock	That's the way the ball bounces.
In conclusion, I would like to say . . .	through thick and thin
in my wildest dreams	tip of the iceberg
last but not least	too little and too late
little did I dream	tried but true

17c   Use idioms in their correct form.

Every language contains *idioms,* or *idiomatic expressions:* phrases that, through long use, have become standard even though their construction may defy logic or grammar. Many idiomatic expressions require us to choose the right preposition. To pause *for* a minute is not the same as to pause *in* a minute. We work *up* a sweat while working *out* in the gym. We argue *with* someone but *about* something, *for* or *against* it.

For some idioms we must know which article to use before a noun — or whether to use any article at all. We can be *in motion,* but we have to be *in the swim.* We're occasionally in *a tight spot* but never in *a trouble.* Certain idioms vary from country to country: in Britain, a patient has an operation *in hospital;* in America, *in the hospital.* Idioms can involve choosing the right verb with the right noun: we *seize* an opportunity, but we *catch* a plane.

When you're at work on a paper, the dictionary can help you choose the appropriate idiom. Look up *agree* for instance, and you will probably find examples showing when to use *agree to, agree with,* or *agree that.* You can then pick the idiom that suits your sentence.

In, On, At: Prepositions of Location and Time

The prepositions *in, on,* and *at* are frequently used to express location.

> Elaine lives *in* Manhattan *at* a swanky address *on* Fifth Avenue.

- *In* means "within" or "inside of" a place, including geographical areas, such as cities, states, countries, and continents.

  > I packed my books *in* my backpack and left to visit my cousins *in* Canada.

- Where *in* emphasizes *location* only, *at* is often used to refer to a place when a specific *activity* is implied: *at the store* (to shop), *at the office* (to work), *at the theater* (to see a play), and so on.

  > Angelo left his bicycle *in* the bike rack while he was *at* school.

- *On* means "on the surface of" or "on top of" something and is used with floors of buildings and planets. It is also used to indicate a location *beside* a lake, river, ocean, or other body of water.

  > The service department is *on* the fourth floor.

  > We have a cabin *on* Lake Michigan.

- *In, on,* and *at* can all be used in addresses. *In* is used to identify a general location, such as a city or neighborhood. *On* is used to identify a specific street. *At* is used to give an exact address.

  > We live *in* Boston *on* Medway Street.

  > We live *at* 20 Medway Street.

- *In* and *at* can both be used with the verb *arrive*. *In* indicates a large place, such as a city, state, country, or continent. *At* indicates a smaller place, such as a specific building or address. (*To* is never used with *arrive*.)

  > Alanya arrived in Alaska yesterday, and Sanjei will arrive at the airport soon.

The prepositions *in, on,* and *at* are also used in many time expressions.

- *In* indicates the span of time during which something occurs or a time in the future; it is also used in the expressions *in a minute* (meaning "shortly") and *in time* (meaning "soon enough"). *In* is also used with seasons, months, and periods of the day.

  > He needs to read this book *in* the next three days. [During the next three days]

  > I'll meet you *in* the morning *in* two weeks. [Two weeks from now]

- *On* is used with the days of the week, with the word *weekend,* and in the expression *on time* (meaning "punctually").

  > Let's have lunch *on* Friday.

- *At* is used in reference to a specific time on the clock as well as a specific time of the day (*at night, at dawn, at twilight*).

  > We'll meet again next Monday *at* 2:15 P.M.

ESL GUIDELINES

preposition: A transitional word (such as *in, on, at, of, from*) that leads into a phrase such as *in the bar, under a rickety table*

ESL GUIDELINES

indirect object: A person or thing affected by the subject's action, usually the recipient of the direct object, through the action indicated by a verb such as *bring, get, offer, promise, sell, show, tell,* and *write: Charlene asked you a question.*

preposition: A transitional word (such as *in, on, at, of, from*) that leads into a phrase such as *in the bar, under a rickety table*

To, For: Indirect Objects and Prepositions

These sentences mean the same thing:

> I sent the president a letter.
>
> I sent a letter to the president.

In the first sentence, *the president* is the **indirect object:** he or she receives the direct object (*a letter*), which was acted on (*sent*) by the subject of the sentence (*I*). In the second sentence, the same idea is expressed using a **prepositional phrase** beginning with *to.*

- Some verbs can use either an indirect object or the preposition *to: give, send, lend, offer, owe, pay, sell, show, teach, tell.* Some verbs can use an indirect object or the preposition *for: bake, build, buy, cook, find, get, make.*

  > I paid *the travel agent* one hundred dollars.
  >
  > I paid one hundred dollars *to the travel agent.*
  >
  > Margarita cooked *her family* some chicken.
  >
  > Margarita cooked some chicken *for her family.*

- Some verbs cannot have an indirect object; they must use a preposition. The following verbs must use the preposition *to: describe, demonstrate, explain, introduce,* and *suggest.*

  INCORRECT   Please explain me indirect objects.

  CORRECT   Please explain indirect objects *to me.*

- The following verbs must use the preposition *for: answer* and *prepare.*

  INCORRECT   He prepared me the punch.

  CORRECT   He prepared the punch *for me.*

- Some verbs must have an indirect object; they cannot use a preposition. The following verbs must have an indirect object: *ask* and *cost.*

  INCORRECT   Sasha asked a question to her.

  CORRECT   Sasha asked her a question.

■ For more practice, visit *Exercise Central* at <bedfordstmartins.com/bedguide> and do a keyword search:

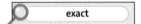

exact

■ Exercise 17–1

Selecting Words

Revise the following passage to replace inappropriate connotations, clichés, and faulty idioms. Example:

> The Mayan city of Uxmal is a common tourist attraction. The ruins have stood alone in the jungle since time immemorial.

> The Mayan city of Uxmal is a *popular* tourist attraction. The ruins have stood alone in the jungle since *ancient times.*

We spent the first day of our holiday in Mexico arguing around what we wanted to see on our second day. We finally agreed to a day trip out to some

Mayan ruins. The next day we arrived on the Mayan city of Uxmal, which is as old as the hills. It really is a sight for sore eyes, smack dab in a jungle stretching as far as the eye can see, with many buildings still covered in plants and iguanas moving quickly over the decayed buildings. The view from the top of the Soothsayer's Temple was good, although we noticed storm clouds gathering in the distance. The rain held up until we got off of the pyramid, but we drove back to the hotel in a lot of rain. After a day of sightseeing, we were so hungry that we could have eaten a horse, so we had a good meal before we turned in.

18   *Bias-Free Language*

The connotations of the words we use reveal our attitudes — our likes and dislikes, our preferences and prejudices. A *brat* is quite different from a *little angel*, a *sport utility vehicle* from a *limousine*.

Thoughtful writers try to avoid harmful bias in language. They respect their readers and don't want to insult them, anger them, or impede communication. You may not be able to eliminate discrimination from society, but you can eliminate discriminatory language in your writing. Be on the lookout for words that insult or stereotype individuals or groups by gender, age, race, ethnic origin, sexual preference, or religion.

18a   To eliminate sexist language, use alternatives that make no reference to gender.

Among the prime targets of American feminists in the 1960s and 1970s was the male bias built into the English language. Why, they asked, do we talk about *prehistoric man, manpower,* and *the brotherhood of man,* when by *man* we mean the entire human race? Why do we focus attention on the gender of an accomplished woman by calling her a *poetess* or a *lady doctor*? Why does a letter to a corporation have to begin "Gentlemen:"?

Early efforts to find alternatives often led to awkward, even ungrammatical solutions. To substitute "Everyone prefers their own customs" for "Everyone prefers *his* own customs" is to replace sexism with bad grammar. How then can we as sensitive writers minimize the sexist constraints that the English language places in our path? Although there are no perfect solutions, we can try to steer around the potholes as smoothly as possible.

18b   Avoid terms that include or imply *man*.

We all know that the obvious way to neuter *man* or a word starting with *man* is to substitute *human*. The result, however, is often clumsy.

SEXIST   Mankind remains obsessed with man's inhumanity to man.

NONSEXIST   *Humankind* remains obsessed with *humans'* inhumanity to *other humans.*

Adding *hu-* to *man* alleviates sexism but weighs down the sentence. Usually you can find a more graceful solution.

REVISED   *Human beings* remain obsessed with *people's* cruelty to one another.

Similarly, when you face a word that ends with *-man*, you need not simply replace that ending with *-person*. Take a different approach: think about what the word means and find a synonym that is truly neutral.

SEXIST   Did you leave a note for the mailman?

REVISED   Did you leave a note for the *mail carrier*?

The same tactic works for designations with a male and a female ending, such as *steward* and *stewardess*.

SEXIST   Ask your steward [or stewardess] for a pillow.

REVISED   Ask your *flight attendant* for a pillow.

18c Use plural instead of singular forms.

Another way to avoid sexist language is to use the plural rather than the singular (*they* and *their* rather than *he* and *his*). This strategy may also avoid the stereotype implied by a single individual standing for a diverse group.

SEXIST   Today's student values his education.

REVISED   Today's students value *their* education.

STEREOTYPE   The Englishman drives on the left-hand side of the road.

REVISED   *English drivers* use the left-hand side of the road.

18d Where possible, omit words that denote gender.

You can make your language more bias-free by omitting pronouns and other words that needlessly indicate gender.

SEXIST   For optimal results, there must be rapport between a stockbroker and his client, a teacher and her student, a doctor and his patient.

REVISED   For optimal results, there must be rapport between stockbroker and *client*, teacher and *student*, doctor and *patient*.

Also treat men and women equally in terms of description or title.

SEXIST   I now pronounce you man and wife.

REVISED   I now pronounce you *husband* and wife.

SEXIST   Please page Mr. Pease, Mr. Mankodi, and Susan Brillantes.

REVISED   Please page Mr. Pease, Mr. Mankodi, and *Ms.* Brillantes.

18e Avoid condescending labels.

A responsible writer does not call women *chicks, coeds, babes, woman drivers,* or any other names that imply that they are not to be taken seriously. Nor should an employee ever be called a *girl* or *boy.* Avoid terms that put down individuals or groups because of age (*old goat, the grannies*), race or ethnicity (*Indian giver, Chinaman's chance*), or disability (*amputee, handicapped*).

CONDESCENDING	The girls in the office bought Mr. Baart a birthday cake.
REVISED	The *administrative assistants* bought Mr. Baart a birthday cake.
CONDESCENDING	My neighbor is just an old fogy.
REVISED	My neighbor *has old-fashioned ideas.*

When describing any group, try to use the label or term that the members of that group prefer. While the preferred label is sometimes difficult to determine, the extra effort will be appreciated.

POSSIBLY OFFENSIVE	Alice is interested in learning about Oriental culture.
REVISED	Alice is interested in learning about *Asian* culture.

18f Avoid implied stereotypes.

Sometimes a stereotype is linked to a title or designation indirectly. Aside from a few obvious exceptions such as *mothers* and *fathers,* never assume that all the members of a group are of the same gender.

STEREOTYPE	Pilots have little time to spend with their wives and children.
REVISED	Pilots have little time to spend with their *families.*

Sometimes we debase individuals or groups by assigning stereotypical descriptors to them. Be alert for such biases, whether negative or positive.

STEREOTYPE	Roberto isn't very good at paying his rent on time, which doesn't surprise me because he is from Mexico.
REVISED	Roberto isn't very good at paying his rent on time.
STEREOTYPE	I assume Ben will do very well in medical school because his parents are Jewish.
REVISED	I assume Ben will do very well in medical school.

18g Use *Ms.* for a woman with no other known title.

Ms. is now the preferred title of polite address for women because, like *Mr.* for men, it does not indicate marital status. Use *Miss* or *Mrs.* if you know that the woman being addressed prefers this form. If the woman holds a doctorate, a professional office, or some other position with a title, use that title rather than *Ms.*

Ms. Jane Doe, Editor   Dear Ms. Doe:
Professor Jane Doe, Department of English   Dear Professor Doe:
Senator Jane Doe, Washington, D.C.   Dear Senator Doe:

For more practice, visit <bedfordstmartins.com/bedguide> and do a keyword search:

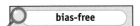

bias-free

■ Exercise 18–1

Avoiding Bias

Revise the following sentences to eliminate bias. Possible revisions for the lettered sentences appear in the back of the book. Example:

> A fireman needs to check his equipment regularly.
>
> *Firefighters* need to check *their* equipment regularly.

a. Our school's extensive athletic program will be of particular interest to Black applicants.

b. The new physicians on our staff include Dr. Scalia, Anna Baniski, and Dr. Throckmorton.

c. A Native American, Joni believes in the healing properties of herbal remedies.

d. Philosophers have long pondered whether man is innately evil or innately good.

e. The diligent researcher will always find the sources he seeks.

1. Simon drinks like an Irishman.

2. The television crew conducted a series of man-on-the-street interviews about the new tax proposal.

3. Whether the president of the United States is a Democrat or a Republican, he will always be a symbol of the nation.

4. Like most Asian Americans, Soon Li excels at music and mathematics.

5. Dick drives a Porsche because he likes the way she handles on the road. He gets pretty upset at the little old ladies who slow down traffic.

19 *Wordiness*

For strategies for cutting extra words, see Ch. 19.

Conciseness takes more effort than wordiness, but it pays off in clarity. The following list includes common words and phrases that take up more room than they deserve. Each has a shorter substitute. This checklist can be useful for self-editing, particularly if you face a strict word limit.

WINDY WORDS AND PHRASES

WORDY	CONCISE
adequate enough	adequate
a period of a week	a week

approximately	about
area of, field of	[Omit.]
arrive at an agreement, conclude an agreement	agree
as a result of	because
at an earlier point in time	before, earlier
at a later moment	after, later
join together	join
kind of, sort of, type of	[Omit.]
large in size, large-sized	large
a large number of	many
lend assistance to	assist, aid, help
merge together	merge
numerous	many
on a daily basis	daily
other alternatives	alternatives
past experience, past history	experience, history
persons of the female gender	women
persons of the Methodist faith	Methodists
pertaining to	about, on
plan ahead for the future	plan
prior to	before
put an end to, terminate	end
refer back to	refer to
repeat again	repeat
resemble in appearance	look like
subsequent to	after
sufficient amount of	enough
sufficient number (or amount) of	enough
true facts	facts, truth
until such time	until
utilize, make use of	use
very	[Omit unless you need it.]
whether or not, as to whether	whether

■ Exercise 19–1

Eliminating Wordiness

Revise the following passage to eliminate wordiness. Example:

> At this point in time, a debate pertaining to freedom of speech is raging across our campuses.

> A debate *about* freedom of speech is raging across our campuses.

■ For more practice, visit
<bedfordstmartins.com/
bedguide> and do a key-
word search:

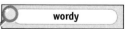

wordy

The media in recent times have become obsessed with the conflict on campuses across the nation between freedom of speech and the attempt to protect minorities from verbal abuse. Very innocent remarks or remarks of a humorous nature, sometimes taken out of context, have got a large number of students into trouble for the violation of college speech codes. Numerous students have become very vocal in attacking these "politically correct" speech codes and defending the right to free speech. But is the campaign against the politically correct really pertaining to freedom of speech, or is it itself a way in which to silence debate? Due to the fact that the phrase "politically correct" has become associated with liberal social causes and sensitivity to minority feelings, it now carries a very extraordinary stigma in the eyes of conservatives. It has become a kind of condemnation against which no defense is possible. To accuse someone of being politically correct is to refute their ideas before hearing their argument. The attempt to silence the members of the opposition is a dangerous sign of our times and suggests that we are indeed in the midst of a cultural war.

Chapter 36

Punctuation

20 *End Punctuation*

Three marks can signal the end of a sentence: the period, the exclamation point, and the question mark.

20a Use a period to end a declarative sentence, a directive, or an indirect question.

Most English sentences are *declarative,* meaning simply that they make a statement. Whatever its topic, a declarative sentence ends with a period.

> Most people on earth are malnourished.

A period also follows a *directive,* a statement telling someone to do something.

> Please send a check or money order with your application.

Some readers are surprised to find a period, not a question mark, at the end of an *indirect question.* But an indirect question is really a kind of declarative sentence: it states that a question was asked or is being asked.

> The counselor asked Marcia why she rarely gets to class on time.
> I wonder why Roland didn't show up.

Written as *direct questions,* those sentences require a question mark.

> The counselor asked, "Marcia, why do you rarely get to class on time?"
> Why, I wonder, didn't Roland show up?

20b **Use a period after some abbreviations.**

A period within a sentence shows that what precedes it has been shortened.

Dr. Robert A. Hooke's speech will be broadcast at 8:00 p.m.

▪ For more on abbreviating names, see 28e.

The names of most organizations (YMCA, PTA), countries (USA, UK), and people (JFK, FDR) are abbreviated using all capitals without periods. Other abbreviations, such as those for designations of time, use periods. When an abbreviation ends a sentence, follow it with one period, not two.

20c **Use a question mark to end a direct question.**

How many angels can dance on the head of a pin?

▪ For advice on punctuating indirect quotations and questions, see 25a. For examples of indirect questions, see 20a.

The question mark comes at the end of the question even if the question is part of a longer declarative sentence.

"What'll I do now?" Marjorie wailed.

You can also use a question mark to indicate doubt about the accuracy of a number or date.

Aristophanes, born in 450(?) BC, became the master comic playwright of Greece's Golden Age.

Often the same purpose can be accomplished more gracefully in words:

Aristophanes, born around 450 BC, became the master comic playwright of Greece's Golden Age.

In formal writing, avoid using a question mark to express irony or sarcasm: *her generous (?) gift*. If your doubts are worth including, state them directly: *her meager but highly publicized gift*.

20d **Use an exclamation point to end an interjection or an urgent command.**

An exclamation point signals strong, even violent, emotion. It can end any sentence that requires unusually strong emphasis.

We've struck an iceberg! We're sinking! I can't believe it!

interjection: A word or expression (*oh, alas*) that inserts an outburst of feeling at the beginning, middle, or end of a sentence

It may mark the short, emphatic structure known as an *interjection.*

Oh, no! Fire!

Or it may indicate an urgent directive.

Hurry up! Help me!

Because most essays appeal to readers' reason more than to their passions, you will rarely need this punctuation mark in college writing.

■ Exercise 20–1

Using End Punctuation

Where appropriate, correct the end punctuation in the following sentences. Give reasons for any changes you make. Some sentences may be correct. Answers for the lettered sentences appear in the back of the book. Example:

> Tom asked Cindy if she would be willing to edit his research paper?
>
> Tom asked Cindy if she would be willing to edit his research paper. [Not a direct question]

■ For more practice, visit
<bedfordstmartins.com/
bedguide> and do a key-
word search:

end

a. The question that still troubles the community after all these years is why federal agents did not act sooner?

b. We will ask him if he will help us build the canoe.

c. I wonder what he was thinking at the time?

d. One man, who suffered a broken leg, was rescued when he was heard screaming, "Help me. Help me."

e. If the suspect is convicted, will lawyers appeal the case?

1. What will Brad and Emilia do if they can't have their vacations at the same time.

2. When a tree falls in a forest, but no one hears it, does it make a sound.

3. If you have a chance to see the new Ang Lee film, you should do so. The acting is first-rate!

4. What will happen next is anyone's guess.

5. On what day does the fall term begin.

21   *The Comma*

Speech without pauses would be difficult to listen to. Likewise, writing without commas would make hard reading. Like a split-second pause in conversation, a well-placed comma helps your readers to catch your train of thought. It keeps them, time and again, from stumbling over a solid block of words or drawing an inaccurate conclusion.

■ For more on comma usage, see C1 in the Quick Editing Guide (the dark-blue-edged pages).

Consider the following sentence:

> Lyman paints fences and bowls.

From this statement, we can deduce that Lyman is a painter who works with both a large and a small brush. But add commas and the portrait changes:

> Lyman paints, fences, and bowls.

Now Lyman wields a paintbrush, a sword, and a bowling ball. What we learn about his activities depends on how the writer punctuates the sentence.

21a Use a comma with a coordinating conjunction to join two main clauses.

main clause: A group of words that has both a subject and a verb and can stand alone as a complete sentence: *My sister has a friend.*

coordinating conjunction: A one-syllable linking word (*and, but, for, or, nor, so, yet*) that joins elements with equal or near-equal importance: *Jack and Jill, sink or swim*

Main clauses joined by a coordinating conjunction also need a comma. The comma comes after the first clause, right before the conjunction.

> The pie whooshed through the air, and it landed in Hal's face.

> The pie whooshed with deadly aim, but the agile Hal ducked.

If your clauses are short and parallel in form, you may omit the comma.

> Spring passed and summer came.

> They urged but I refused.

Or you may keep the comma. It can lend your words a speechlike ring, throwing a bit of emphasis on your second clause.

> Spring passed, and summer came.

> They urged, but I refused.

phrase: Two or more related words that work together but may lack a subject (as in *will have been*), a verb (*my uncle Zeke*), or both (*in the attic*)

clause: A group of related words that includes both a subject and a verb: *The sailboats raced until the sun set.*

CAUTION: Don't use a comma with a coordinating conjunction that links two phrases or that links a phrase and a clause.

> FAULTY   The mustangs galloped, and cavorted across the plain.

> REVISED   The mustangs galloped and cavorted across the plain.

21b Use a comma after an introductory clause, phrase, or word.

> *Weeping,* Lydia stumbled down the stairs.

> *Before that,* Arthur saw her reading an old love letter.

> *If he knew who the writer was,* he didn't tell.

Placed after any such opening word, phrase, or subordinate clause, a comma tells your reader, "Enough preliminaries: now the main clause starts."

EXCEPTION: You need not use a comma after a single introductory word or a short phrase or clause if there is no danger of misreading.

> *Sooner or later* Lydia will tell us the whole story.

■ Exercise 21–1

Using Commas

For more practice, visit <bedfordstmartins.com/bedguide> and do a keyword search:

Add any necessary commas to the following sentences, and remove any commas that do not belong. Some sentences may be correct. Answers for the lettered sentences appear in the back of the book. Example:

> Your dog may have sharp teeth but my lawyer can bite harder.

Your dog may have sharp teeth, but my lawyer can bite harder.

a. Farmers around the world tend to rely on just a few breeds of livestock so some breeds are disappearing.

b. Older breeds of livestock are often less profitable, for they have not been genetically engineered to grow quickly.

c. For instance modern breeds of cattle usually grow larger, and produce more meat and milk than older breeds.

d. In both wild and domestic animals genetic diversity can make the animals resistant to disease, and parasites so older breeds can give scientists important information.

e. Until recently, small organic farmers were often the only ones interested in raising old-fashioned breeds but animal scientists now support this practice as well.

1. During the summer of the great soybean failure Larry took little interest in national affairs.

2. Unaware of the world he slept and grew within his mother's womb.

3. While across the nation farmers were begging for mortgages he swam without a care.

4. Neither the mounting agricultural crisis, nor any other current events, disturbed his tranquillity.

5. In fact you might have called him irresponsible.

21c Use a comma between items in a series.

When you list three or more items, whether they are nouns, verbs, adjectives, adverbs, or entire phrases or clauses, separate them with commas.

> Country ham, sweet corn, and potatoes weighted Grandma's table.

> Joel prefers music that shakes, rattles, and rolls.

> In one afternoon, we climbed the Matterhorn, voyaged beneath the sea, and flew on a rocket through space.

Notice that no comma *follows* the final item in the series.

NOTE: Some writers omit the comma *before* the final item in the series. This custom may throw off the rhythm of a sentence and, in some cases, obscure the writer's meaning. Using the comma in such a case is never wrong; omitting it can create confusion.

> I was met at the station by my cousins, brother and sister.

Are these people a brother-and-sister pair who are the writer's cousins or a group consisting of the writer's cousins, her brother, and her sister? If they are in fact more than two people, a comma would clear up the confusion.

> I was met at the station by my cousins, brother, and sister.

21d Use a comma between coordinate adjectives but not between cumulative adjectives.

Adjectives that function independently of each other, though they modify the same noun, are called *coordinate adjectives.* Set them off with commas.

Ruth was a clear, vibrant, persuasive speaker.

Life is nasty, brutish, and short.

CAUTION: Don't use a comma after the final adjective before a noun.

FAULTY   My professor was a brilliant, caring, teacher.

REVISED   My professor was a brilliant, caring teacher.

To check whether adjectives are coordinate, apply two tests. Can you rearrange the adjectives without distorting the meaning of the sentence? (*Ruth was a persuasive, vibrant, clear speaker.*) Can you insert *and* between them? (*Life is nasty and brutish and short.*)

If the answer to both questions is yes, the adjectives are coordinate. Removing any one of them would not greatly affect the others. Use commas between them to show that they are separate and equal.

conjunction: A linking word that connects words or groups of words through coordination (*and, but*) or subordination (*because, although, unless*)

NOTE: If you link coordinate adjectives with *and* or another conjunction, omit the commas except in a series (see 21c).

New York City is huge and dirty and beautiful.

Cumulative adjectives work together to create a single unified picture of the noun they modify. Remove any one of them and you change the picture. No commas separate cumulative adjectives.

Ruth has two small white poodles.

Who's afraid of the big bad wolf?

If you rearrange cumulative adjectives or insert *and* between them, the effect is distorted (*two white small poodles; the big and bad wolf*).

■ Exercise 21–2

Using Commas

Add any necessary commas to the following sentences, remove any commas that do not belong, and change any punctuation that is incorrect. Some sentences may be correct. Answers for the lettered sentences appear in the back of the book. Example:

Mel has been a faithful hard-working consistent band manager.

Mel has been a faithful, hard-working, consistent band manager.

■ For more practice, visit <bedfordstmartins.com/bedguide> and do a keyword search:

comma

a. Mrs. Carver looks like a sweet, little, old lady, but she plays a wicked electric guitar.

b. Her bass player, her drummer and her keyboard player all live in the same retirement community.

c. They practice individually in the afternoon, rehearse together at night and play at the community's Saturday night dances.

d. The Rest Home Rebels have to rehearse quietly, and cautiously, to keep from disturbing the other residents.

e. Mrs. Carver has organized the group, scheduled their rehearsals, and acquired back-up instruments.

1. When she breaks a string, she doesn't want her elderly crew to have to grab the guitar change the string and hand it back to her, before the song ends.

2. The Rest Home Rebels' favorite bands are U2, Matchbox 20 and Lester Lanin and his orchestra.

3. They watch a lot of MTV because it is fast-paced colorful exciting and informative and it has more variety than soap operas.

4. Just once, Mrs. Carver wants to play in a really, huge, sold-out, arena.

5. She hopes to borrow the community's big, white, van to take herself her band and their equipment to a major, professional, recording studio.

21e Use commas to set off a nonrestrictive phrase or clause.

A *nonrestrictive modifier* adds a fact that, while perhaps interesting and valuable, isn't essential. You could leave it out of the sentence and still make good sense. When a word in your sentence is modified by a nonrestrictive phrase or clause, set off the modifier with commas before and after it.

> Potts Alley, *which runs north from Chestnut Street,* is too narrow for cars.

> At the end of the alley, *where the fair was held last May,* a getaway car waited.

A *restrictive modifier* is essential. Omit it and you significantly change the meaning of the modified word and the sentence. Such a modifier is called *restrictive* because it limits what it modifies: it specifies this place, person, or action and no other. Because a restrictive modifier is part of the identity of whatever it modifies, no commas set it off from the rest of the sentence.

> They picked the alley *that runs north from Chestnut Street* because it is close to the highway.

> Anyone *who robs my house* will regret it.

Leave out the modifier in that last sentence — writing *Anyone will regret it* — and you change the meaning from potential robbers to all humankind.

modifier: A word (such as an adjective or adverb), phrase, or clause that provides more information about other parts of a sentence: Plays *staged by the drama class* are *always successful*.

NOTE: Use *that* to introduce (or to recognize) a restrictive phrase or clause. Use *which* to introduce (or to recognize) a nonrestrictive phrase or clause.

> The food *that I love best* is chocolate.

> Chocolate, *which I love,* is not on my diet.

21f Use commas to set off nonrestrictive appositives.

appositive: A word or group of words that adds information about a subject or object by identifying it in a different way: my dog *Rover,* Hal's brother *Fred*

Like the modifiers discussed in 21e, an **appositive** can be either restrictive or nonrestrictive. If it is nonrestrictive — if the sentence still makes sense when it is omitted or changed — then set it off with commas before and after.

> My third ex-husband, *Hugo,* will be glad to meet you.

> We are bringing dessert, *a blueberry pie,* to follow dinner.

If the appositive is restrictive — if you can't take it out or change it without changing your meaning — then include it without commas.

> Of all the men I've been married to, my ex-husband *Hugo* is the best cook.

■ Exercise 21–3

Using Commas

For more practice, visit <bedfordstmartins.com/bedguide> and do a keyword search:

Add any necessary commas to the following sentences, and remove any commas that do not belong. You may have to draw your own conclusions about what the writer meant to say. Some sentences may be correct. Possible revisions for the lettered sentences appear in the back of the book. Example:

> Jay and his wife the former Laura McCready were college sweethearts.

> Jay and his wife, the former Laura McCready, were college sweethearts.

a. We are bringing a dish vegetable lasagna, to the potluck supper.

b. I like to go to Central Bank, on this side of town, because this branch tends to have short lines.

c. The colony, that the English established at Roanoke disappeared mysteriously.

d. If the base commanders had checked their gun room where powder is stored, they would have found that several hundred pounds of gunpowder were missing.

e. Brazil's tropical rain forests which help produce the air we breathe all over the world, are being cut down at an alarming rate.

1. The aye-aye which is a member of the lemur family is threatened with extinction.

2. The party, a dismal occasion ended earlier than we had expected.

3. Secretary Stern warned that the concessions, that the West was prepared to make, would be withdrawn if not matched by the East.

4. Although both of Don's children are blond, his daughter Sharon has darker hair than his son Jake.

5. Herbal tea which has no caffeine makes a better after-dinner drink than coffee.

21g Use commas to set off conjunctive adverbs.

When you drop a conjunctive adverb into the middle of a clause, set it off with commas before and after it.

> Using lead paint in homes has been illegal, *however,* since 1973.

> Builders, *indeed,* gave it up some twenty years earlier.

21h Use commas to set off parenthetical expressions.

Use a pair of commas around any parenthetical expression or any aside from you to your readers.

> Home inspectors, *for this reason,* sometimes test for lead paint.

> Cosmic Construction never used lead paint, *or so their spokesperson says,* even when it was legal.

21i Use commas to set off a phrase or clause expressing contrast.

> It was Rudolph, *not Dasher,* who had a red nose.

EXCEPTION: Short contrasting phrases beginning with *but* need not be set off by commas.

> It was not Dasher but Rudolph who had a red nose.

21j Use commas to set off an absolute phrase.

The link between an absolute phrase and the rest of the sentence is a comma or two commas if the phrase falls in midsentence.

> *Our worst fears drawing us together,* we huddled over the letter.

> Luke, *his knife being the sharpest,* slit the envelope.

■ Exercise 21–4

Using Commas

Add any necessary commas to the following sentences, and change any punctuation that is incorrect. Answers for the lettered sentences appear in the back of the book. Example:

---

conjunctive adverb: A linking word that can connect independent clauses and show a relationship between two ideas: Armando is a serious student; *therefore,* he studies every day. (See 14.)

▨ For punctuation with a conjunctive adverb, see 22b.

parenthetical expression: An aside to readers or a transitional expression such as *for example* or *in contrast*

absolute phrase: An expression, usually a noun followed by a participle, that modifies an entire clause or sentence and can appear anywhere in the sentence: The stallion pawed the ground, *chestnut mane and tail swirling in the wind.*

■ For more practice, visit <bedfordstmartins.com/ bedguide> and do a key-word search:

 comma

The officer a radar gun in his hand gauged the speed of the passing cars.

The officer, a radar gun in his hand, gauged the speed of the passing cars.

a. The university insisted however that the students were not accepted merely because of their parents' generous contributions.

b. This dispute in any case is an old one.

c. It was the young man's striking good looks not his acting ability that first attracted the Hollywood agents.

d. Gretchen learned moreover not to always accept as true what she had read in textbooks.

e. The hikers most of them wearing ponchos or rain jackets headed out into the steady drizzle.

1. The lawsuit demanded furthermore that construction already under way be halted immediately.

2. It is the Supreme Court not Congress or the president that ultimately de-termines the legality of a law.

3. The judge complained that the case was being tried not by the court but by the media.

4. The actor kneeling recited the lines with great emotion.

5. Both sides' patience running thin workers and management carried the strike into its sixth week.

21k Use commas to set off a direct quotation from your own words.

■ For advice on using punctuation marks with quotations, see 25g–25i; for advice on using quota-tion marks, see 25a–25d and C3 in the Quick Edit-ing Guide (the dark-blue-edged pages).

When you briefly quote someone, distinguish the source's words from yours with commas (and, of course, quotation marks). When you insert an expla-nation into a quotation (such as *he said*), set that off with commas.

Shakespeare wrote, "Some are born great, some achieve greatness, and some have greatness thrust upon them."

"The best thing that can come with success," commented the actress Liv Ull-mann, "is the knowledge that it is nothing to long for."

Notice that the comma always comes *before* the quotation marks.

EXCEPTION: Do not use a comma with a very short quotation or one intro-duced by *that*.

Don't tell me "yes" if you mean "maybe."

Jules said that "Nothing ventured, nothing gained" is his motto.

linking verb: A verb (*is, become, seem, feel*) that shows a state of being by linking the sentence sub-ject with a word that re-names or describes the subject: The sky *is* blue. (See 3a.)

Don't use a comma with any quotation run into your own sentence and read as part of it. Often such quotations are introduced by linking verbs.

Her favorite statement at age three was "I can do it myself."

Shakespeare originated the expression "my salad days, when I was green in judgment."

21l Use commas around *yes* and *no*, mild interjections, tag questions, and the name or title of someone directly addressed.

YES AND NO	*Yes,* I'd like a Rolls-Royce, but, *no,* I didn't order one.
INTERJECTION	*Well,* don't blame it on me.
TAG QUESTION	It would be fun to ride in a Silver Cloud, *wouldn't it?*
DIRECT ADDRESS	Drive us home, *James.*

> *interjection:* A word or expression (*oh, alas*) that inserts an outburst of feeling at the beginning, middle, or end of a sentence.

21m Use commas to set off dates, states, countries, and addresses.

On June 6, 1979, Ned Shaw was born.

East Rutherford, New Jersey, seemed like Paris, France, to him.

His family moved to 11 Maple Street, Middletown, Ohio.

Do not add a comma between state and zip code: *Bedford, MA 01730.*

■ Exercise 21–5

Using Commas

Add any necessary commas to the following sentences, remove any commas that do not belong, and change any punctuation that is incorrect. Some sentences may be correct. Answers for the lettered sentences appear in the back of the book. Example:

> When Alexander Graham Bell said "Mr. Watson come here, I want you" the telephone entered history.

> When Alexander Graham Bell said, "Mr. Watson, come here, I want you," the telephone entered history.

a. César Chávez was born on March 31 1927, on a farm in Yuma, Arizona.

b. Chávez, who spent years as a migrant farmworker, told other farm laborers "If you're outraged at conditions, then you can't possibly be free or happy until you devote all your time to changing them."

c. Chávez founded the United Farm Workers union and did indeed, devote all his time to changing conditions for farmworkers.

d. Robert F. Kennedy called Chávez, "one of the heroic figures of our time."

■ For more practice, visit <bedfordstmartins.com/bedguide> and do a keyword search:

 comma

e. Chávez, who died on April 23, 1993, became the second Mexican American to receive the highest civilian honor in the United States, the Presidential Medal of Freedom.

1. Yes I was born on April 14 1973 in Bombay India.
2. Move downstage Gary, for Pete's sake or you'll run into Mrs. Clackett.
3. Vicki my precious, when you say, "great" or "terrific," look as though you mean it.
4. Perhaps you have forgotten darling that sometimes you make mistakes, too.
5. Well Dotty, it only makes sense that when you say, "Sardines!," you should go off to get the sardines.

21n **Do not use a comma to separate a subject from its verb or a verb from its object.**

subject: The part of a sentence that names something—a person, an object, an idea, a situation—about which the predicate makes an assertion: The *king* lives.

verb: A word that shows action (The cow *jumped* over the moon) or a state of being (The cow *is* brown)

direct object: The target of a verb that completes the action performed by the subject or asserted about the subject: I photographed *the sheriff.*

correlative conjunction: A pair of linking words (such as *either/or, not only/but also*) that appear separately but work together to join elements of a sentence: *Neither* his friends *nor* hers like pizza.

coordinating conjunction: A one-syllable linking word (*and, but, for, or, nor, so, yet*) that joins elements with equal or near-equal importance: Jack *and* Jill, sink *or* swim

FAULTY   The athlete driving the purple Jaguar, was Jim Fuld. [Subject separated from verb]

REVISED   The athlete driving the purple Jaguar was Jim Fuld.

FAULTY   The governor should not have given his campaign manager, such a prestigious appointment. [Verb separated from direct object]

REVISED   The governor should not have given his campaign manager such a prestigious appointment.

21o **Do not use a comma between words or phrases joined by correlative or coordinating conjunctions.**

Do not divide a compound subject or predicate unnecessarily with a comma.

FAULTY   Neither Peter Pan, nor the fairy Tinkerbell, saw the pirates sneaking toward their hideout. [Compound subject]

REVISED   Neither Peter Pan nor the fairy Tinkerbell saw the pirates sneaking toward their hideout.

FAULTY   The chickens clucked, and pecked, and flapped their wings. [Compound predicate]

REVISED   The chickens clucked and pecked and flapped their wings.

21p **Do not use a comma before the first or after the last item in a series.**

FAULTY   We had to see, my mother's doctor, my father's lawyer, and my dog's veterinarian, in one afternoon.

REVISED   We had to see my mother's doctor, my father's lawyer, and my dog's veterinarian in one afternoon.

21q   Do not use a comma to set off a restrictive word, phrase, or clause.

A restrictive modifier is essential to the definition or identification of what-ever it modifies; a nonrestrictive modifier is not.

FAULTY	The fireworks, that I saw on Sunday, were the best I've ever seen.
REVISED	The fireworks that I saw on Sunday were the best I've ever seen.

▨ For an explanation of restrictive modifiers, see 21e.

21r   Do not use commas to set off indirect quotations.

When *that* introduces a quotation, the quotation is indirect and requires neither a comma nor quotation marks.

FAULTY	He told us that, we shouldn't have done it.
REVISED	He told us that we shouldn't have done it.

This sentence also would be correct if it were recast as a direct quota-tion, with a comma and quotation marks.

FAULTY	He told us that, "You shouldn't have done it."
REVISED	He told us, "You shouldn't have done it."

▨ For more on quoting someone's exact words, see 25a–25c. For advice on quoting from sources, see D3 and D6 in the Quick Research Guide (the dark-red-edged pages).

22   *The Semicolon*

A semicolon is a sort of compromise between a comma and a period: it cre-ates a stop without ending a sentence.

22a   Use a semicolon to join two main clauses not joined by a coordinating conjunction.

Suppose, having written one statement, you want to add another that is closely related in sense. You decide to keep them both in a single sentence.

> Shooting clay pigeons was my mother's favorite sport; she would smash them for hours at a time.

A semicolon is a good substitute for a period when you don't want to bring your readers to a complete stop.

> By the yard life is hard; by the inch it's a cinch.

NOTE: When you join a subordinate clause to a main one or join two state-ments with a coordinating conjunction, you can generally use just a comma. Reserve the semicolon to avoid confusion when long, complex clauses in-clude internal punctuation.

coordinating conjunc-tion: A one-syllable link-ing word (*and, but, for, or, nor, so, yet*) that joins ele-ments with equal or near-equal importance: Jack *and* Jill, sink *or* swim

22b Use a semicolon to join two main clauses that are linked by a conjunctive adverb.

conjunctive adverb: A linking word that can connect independent clauses and show a relationship between two ideas: Armando is a serious student; *therefore,* he studies every day. (See 14.)

You can use a conjunctive adverb to show a relationship between clauses such as addition (*also, besides*), comparison (*likewise, similarly*), contrast (*instead, however*), emphasis (*namely, certainly*), cause and effect (*thus, therefore*), or time (*finally, subsequently*). When a second statement begins with (or includes) a conjunctive adverb, you can join it to the first with a semicolon.

> Bert is a stand-out player; *indeed,* he's the one hope of our team.

> We yearned to attend the concert; tickets, *however,* were hard to come by.

■ For punctuation with conjunctive adverbs within clauses, see 21g.

Note in the second sentence that the conjunctive adverb falls within the second main clause. No matter where the conjunctive adverb appears, the semicolon is placed between the two clauses.

22c Use a semicolon to separate items in a series that contain internal punctuation or that are long and complex.

The semicolon is especially useful for setting off one group of items from another. More powerful than a comma, it divides a series of series.

> The auctioneer sold clocks, watches, and cameras; freezers of steaks and tons of bean sprouts; motorcycles, cars, speedboats, canoes, and cabin cruisers; and rare coins, curious stamps, and precious stones.

If the writer had used commas in place of semicolons in that sentence, the divisions would have been harder to notice.

Commas are not the only internal punctuation that warrants the extra force of semicolons between items.

> The auctioneer sold clocks and watches (with or without hands); freezers of steaks and tons of bean sprouts; trucks and motorcycles (some of which had working engines); and dozens of smaller items.

■ Exercise 22–1

Using Semicolons

Add any necessary semicolons to the following sentences, and change any that are incorrectly used. Some sentences may be correct. Answers for the lettered sentences appear in the back of the book. Example:

■ For more practice, visit <bedfordstmartins.com/bedguide> and do a keyword search:

semicolon

> They had used up all their money, they barely had enough left for the train trip home.

> They had used up all their money; they barely had enough left for the train trip home.

a. By the beginning of 1993, Shirley was eager to retire, nevertheless, she agreed to stay on for two more years.

b. In 1968 Lyndon Johnson abandoned his hopes for reelection; because of fierce opposition from within his own party.

c. The committee was asked to determine the extent of violent crime among teenagers, especially those between the ages of fourteen and sixteen, to act as a liaison between the city and schools and between churches and volunteer organizations, and to draw up a plan to significantly reduce violence, both public and private, by the end of the century.

d. The leaves on the oak trees near the lake were tinged with red, swimmers no longer ventured into the water.

e. The football team has yet to win a game, however, the season is still young.

1. Although taking the subway is slow, it is still faster than driving to work.

2. When the harpist began to play; the bride and her father prepared to walk down the aisle.

3. The Mariners lost all three games to Milwaukee, worse yet, two star players were injured.

4. There was nothing the firefighters could do; the building already had been consumed by flames.

5. Chess is difficult to master; but even a child can learn the basic rules.

23 *The Colon*

A colon introduces a further thought, one added to throw light on a first. In using it, a writer declares: "What follows will clarify what I've just said."

Some writers use a capital letter to start any complete sentence that follows a colon; others prefer a lowercase letter. Both habits are acceptable. Whichever you choose, be consistent. A phrase that follows a colon always begins with a lowercase letter.

phrase: Two or more related words that work together but may lack a subject (as in *will have been*), a verb (*my uncle Zeke*), or both (*in the attic*)

23a Use a colon between two main clauses if the second exemplifies, explains, or summarizes the first.

Like a semicolon, a colon can join two sentences into one. The chief difference is this: a semicolon says merely that two main clauses are related; a colon, like an abbreviation for *that is* or *for example*, says that the second clause gives an example or explanation of the point made in the first clause.

main clause: A group of words that has both a subject and a verb and can stand alone as a complete sentence: *My sister has a friend.*

She tried everything: she scoured the library, made dozens of phone calls, wrote letters, even consulted a lawyer.

23b Use a colon to introduce a list or a series.

A colon can introduce a word, a phrase, a series, or a second main clause, sometimes strengthened by *as follows* or *the following*.

> The dance steps are as follows: forward, back, turn, and glide.

> Engrave the following truth upon your memory: a colon is always constructed of two dots.

When a colon introduces a series of words or phrases, it often means *such as* or *for instance*. A list of examples after a colon need not include *and* before the last item unless all possible examples have been stated.

> On a Saturday night many kinds of people crowd our downtown area: drifters, bored senior citizens, college students out for a good time.

23c Use a colon to introduce an appositive.

appositive: A word or group of words that adds information about a subject or object by identifying it in a different way: my dog *Rover*, Hal's brother *Fred*

A colon preceded by a main clause can introduce an appositive.

> I have discovered the key to the future: plastics.

23d Use a colon to introduce a long or comma-filled quotation.

Sometimes you can't conveniently introduce a quoted passage with a comma. Perhaps the quotation is too long or heavily punctuated; perhaps your prefatory remarks demand a longer pause. In either case, use a colon.

> God told Adam and Eve: "Be fruitful, and multiply, and replenish the earth, and subdue it."

23e Use a colon when convention calls for it.

AFTER A SALUTATION	Dear Professor James: Dear Account Representative:
BIBLICAL CITATIONS	Genesis 4:7 [The book of Genesis, chapter four, seventh verse]
BOOK TITLES AND SUBTITLES	*Convergences: Essays on Art and Literature* *In the Beginning: Creation Stories from around the World*
SOURCE REFERENCES	Welty, Eudora. *The Eye of the Story.* New York: Random, 1978.
TIME OF DAY	2:02 p.m.

23f   Use a colon only at the end of a main clause.

In a sentence, a colon always follows a clause, never a phrase. Avoid using a colon between a verb and its object, between a preposition and its object, and before a list introduced by *such as*. Any time you are in doubt about whether to use a colon, first make sure that the preceding statement is a complete sentence. Then you will not litter your writing with unnecessary colons.

> *main clause:* A group of words that has both a subject and a verb and can stand alone as a complete sentence: *My sister has a friend.*

FAULTY   My mother and father are: Bella and Benjamin.

REVISED   My mother and father are Bella and Benjamin.

FAULTY   Many great inventors have changed our lives, such as: Edison, Marconi, and Glutz.

REVISED   Many great inventors have changed our lives, such as Edison, Marconi, and Glutz.

REVISED   Many great inventors have changed our lives: Edison, Marconi, Glutz.

Use either *such as* or a colon. You don't need both.

■ Exercise 23–1

Using Colons

Add, remove, or replace colons wherever appropriate in the following sentences. Where necessary, revise the sentences further to support your changes in punctuation. Some sentences may be correct. Possible revisions for the lettered sentences appear in the back of the book. Example:

> ■ For more practice, visit <bedfordstmartins.com/bedguide> and do a keyword search:
>
>
> colon

> Yum-Yum Burger has franchises in the following cities; New York, Chicago, Miami, San Francisco, and Seattle.
>
> Yum-Yum Burger has franchises in the following cities: New York, Chicago, Miami, San Francisco, and Seattle.

a. The Continuing Education Program offers courses in: building and construction management, engineering, and design.

b. The interview ended with a test of skills, taking messages, operating the computer, typing a sample letter, and proofreading documents.

c. The sample letter began, "Dear Mr. Rasheed, Please accept our apologies for the late shipment."

d. If you go to the beach this summer, remember these three rules: wear plenty of sunscreen, drink water to replace lost fluids, and avoid exposure during the hottest hours of the day.

e. These are my dreams, to fly in a small plane, to gallop down a beach on horseback, and to cross the ocean in a sailboat.

1. In the case of *Bowers v. Hardwick,* the Supreme Court decided that: citizens had no right to sexual privacy.

2. He ended his speech with a quotation from Homer's *Iliad*, "Whoever obeys the gods, to him they particularly listen."

3. Professor Bligh's book is called *Management, A Networking Approach.*

4. George handed Cynthia a note, "Meet me after class under the big clock on Main Street."

5. Rosa expected to arrive at 4.10, but she didn't get there until 4.20.

24   *The Apostrophe*

■ For advice on editing for apostrophes, see C2 in the Quick Editing Guide (the dark-blue-edged pages).

Use apostrophes for three purposes: to show possession, to indicate an omission, and to add an ending to a number, letter, or abbreviation.

24a   To make a singular noun possessive, add -'s.

The *plumber's* wrench left grease stains on *Harry's* shirt.

Add -'s even when your singular noun ends with the sound of *s*.

Felix's roommate enjoys reading *Henry James's* novels.

Some writers find it awkward to add -'s to nouns that already end in an -s, especially those of two syllables or more. You may, if you wish, form such a possessive by adding only an apostrophe.

The Egyptian king *Cheops'* death occurred hundreds of years before *Socrates'.*

24b   To make a plural noun ending in -s possessive, add an apostrophe.

A *stockbrokers'* meeting combines *foxes'* cunning with the noisy chaos of a *boys'* locker room.

Possessive Nouns and Plural Nouns at a Glance

Both plural nouns and possessive nouns often end with -*s*.

- *Plural* means more than one (two *dogs*, six *friends*), but *possessive* means ownership (the *dogs'* biscuits, my *friends'* cars).
- If you can substitute the word *of* for the -*s'* (the biscuits *of* the dogs, the cars *of* my friends), you need the plural possessive with an apostrophe after the -*s*.
- If you cannot substitute *of*, you need the simple plural with no apostrophe (the *dogs* are well fed, my *friends* have no money for gas).

24c **To make a plural noun not ending in -s possessive, add -'s.**

Nouns such as *men, mice, geese,* and *alumni* form the possessive case the same way as singular nouns: with -'s.

> What effect has the *women's* movement had on *children's* literature?

24d **To show joint possession by two people or groups, add an apostrophe or -'s to the second noun of the pair.**

> I left my *mother and father's* home with *friends and neighbors'* good wishes.

If the two members of a noun pair possess a set of things individually, add an apostrophe or -'s to each noun.

> *Men's* and *women's* marathon records are improving steadily.

24e **To make a compound noun possessive, add an apostrophe or -'s to the last word in the compound.**

A compound noun consists of more than one word (*commander in chief, sons-in-law*); it may be either singular or plural.

> The *commander in chief's* duties will end on July 1.

> Esther does not approve of her *sons-in-law's* professions.

▦ For more on plurals of compound nouns, see p. H-142.

24f **To make an indefinite pronoun possessive, add -'s.**

Indefinite pronouns such as *anyone, nobody,* and *another* are usually singular in meaning. They form the possessive case the same way as singular nouns: with -'s. (See 24a.)

> What caused the accident is *anybody's* guess; but it appears to be *no one's* fault.

24g **To indicate the possessive of a personal pronoun, use its possessive case.**

The personal pronouns are irregular; each has its own possessive form. No possessive personal pronoun contains an apostrophe. Resist the temptation to add an apostrophe or -'s.

NOTE: *Its* (no apostrophe) is always a possessive pronoun.

> I retreated when the Murphys' German shepherd bared *its* fangs.

personal pronoun: A pronoun (*I, me, you, it, he, we, them*) that stands for a noun that names a person or thing: Mark awoke slowly, but suddenly *he* bolted from the bed.

■ For a chart of posses-
sive personal pronouns,
see C2 in the Quick Edit-
ing Guide (the dark-blue-
edged pages).

It's (with an apostrophe) is always a contraction of *it is*.

> *It's* [It is] not our fault.

24h   Use an apostrophe to indicate an omission in a contraction.

> *They're* [They are] too sophisticated for me.

> Pat *didn't* [did not] finish her assignment.

> Americans grow up admiring the Spirit of *'76* [1776].

> *It's* [It is] nearly eight *o'clock* [of the clock].

24i   Use an apostrophe to form the plural of a letter or word mentioned as a word.

■ For advice on italicizing
a letter, word, or number
named as a word, see 31e.

LETTER	How many *n*'s are there in *Cincinnati*?
WORD	Try replacing all the *should*'s in that list with *could*'s.

No apostrophes are needed for plural numbers and most abbreviations.

DECADE	The 1980s differed greatly from the 1970s.
NUMBER	Cut out two 3s to sew on Larry's shirt.
ABBREVIATION	Do we need IDs at YMCAs in other towns?

■ Exercise 24–1

Using the Apostrophe

Correct any errors in the use of the apostrophe in the following sentences. Some sentences may be correct. Answers for the lettered sentences appear in the back of the book. Example:

> Youd better put on you're new shoes.

> *You'd* better put on *your* new shoes.

■ For more practice, visit
<bedfordstmartins.com/
bedguide> and do a key-
word search:

apostrophe

a. Joe and Chucks' fathers were both in the class of 73.

b. They're going to finish their term papers as soon as the party ends.

c. It was a strange coincidence that all three womens' cars broke down after they had picked up their mothers-in-law.

d. Don't forget to dot you're *i*s and cross you're *t*s.

e. Mario and Shelley's son is marrying the editor's in chief's daughter.

1. The Hendersons' never change: their always whining about Mr. Scobee farming land thats rightfully their's.

2. Its hard to join a womens' basketball team because so few of them exist.
3. I had'nt expected to hear Janice' voice again.
4. Don't give the Murphy's dog it's biscuit until it's sitting up.
5. Isnt' it the mother and fathers' job to tell kid's to mind their *p*s and *q*s?

25   *Quotation Marks*

Quotation marks always come in pairs: one at the start and one at the finish of a quoted passage. In the United States, the double quotation mark (") is preferred over the single one (') for most uses. Use quotation marks to set off quoted or highlighted words from the rest of your text.

> "Injustice anywhere is a threat to justice everywhere," wrote Martin Luther King Jr.

◼ For more on editing quotation marks, see C3 in the Quick Editing Guide (the dark-blue-edged pages).

25a   Use quotation marks around direct quotations from another writer or speaker.

You can enrich the content, language, and authority of your writing by occasionally quoting a source whose ideas support your own. When you do this, you owe credit to the quoted person. If you use his or her exact words, enclose them in quotation marks.

> Anwar al-Sadat reflected the Arab concept of community when he said, "A man's village is his peace of mind."

In an indirect quotation, you report someone else's idea without using his or her exact words. Do not enclose an indirect quotation in quotation marks. Do name your source and accurately present what it said.

> Anwar al-Sadat asserted that a community provides a sense of well-being.

◼ For more on quoting, paraphrasing, and summarizing, see D3–D5 in the Quick Research Guide (the dark-red-edged pages).

◼ For capitalization with quotation marks, see 29j.

◼ For punctuation of direct and indirect quotations, see 21r.

25b   Use single quotation marks around a quotation inside another quotation.

Sometimes you may quote a source that quotes someone else or puts words in quotation marks. When that happens, use single quotation marks around the internal quotation (even if your source used double ones); put double quotation marks around the larger passage you are quoting.

> "My favorite advice from Socrates, 'Know thyself and fear all women,'" said Dr. Blatz, "has been getting me into trouble lately."

ESL GUIDELINES

Direct and Indirect Quotations

Avoid the problems that arise when a direct quotation (someone else's exact words) is changed into an indirect quotation (someone else's idea reported without using his or her exact words). Be sure to rephrase an indirect quotation from a source to avoid repeating its original wording.

- Be sure to change the punctuation and capitalization. You also may need to change the verb tense.

  DIRECT QUOTATION   Pascal said, "The assignment is on Chinua Achebe, the Nigerian writer."

  INDIRECT QUOTATION   Pascal said that the assignment was on Chinua Achebe, the Nigerian writer.

- If the direct quotation is a question, you must change the word order in the indirect quotation.

  DIRECT QUOTATION   Jean asked, "How far is it to Boston?"

  INDIRECT QUOTATION   Jean asked how far it was to Boston.

NOTE: Use a period, not a question mark, with questions in indirect quotations.

- Very often, you must change pronouns when using an indirect quotation.

  DIRECT QUOTATION   Antonio said, "I think you are mistaken."

  INDIRECT QUOTATION   Antonio said that he thought I was mistaken.

25c **Instead of using quotation marks, indent a quotation of more than four lines.**

■ For more on quoting and paraphrasing, see D3 and D4 in the Quick Research Guide (the dark-red-edged pages).

Suppose you are writing an essay about Soviet dissidents living in the United States. You might include a paragraph like this:

In a 1978 commencement address at Harvard University, Aleksandr Solzhenitsyn made this observation:

> I have spent all my life under a Communist regime, and I will tell you that a society without any objective legal scale is a terrible one indeed. But a society with no other scale but the legal one is not quite worthy of man either.

Merely indenting the quoted passage shows that it is a direct quotation. You need not frame it with quotation marks. Simply double-space above and below the passage, indent it ten spaces from the left margin, and double-space the quoted lines. Add source information, if needed.

Follow the same practice if you quote more than three lines of a poem.

Phillis Wheatley, the outstanding black poet of colonial America, expresses a sense
that she is condemned to write in obscurity and be forgotten:

> No costly marble shall be reared,
> > No Mausoleum's pride--
> Nor chiselled stone be raised to tell
> > That I have lived and died.

Notice that not only the source's words but her punctuation, capitalization, indentation, and line breaks are quoted exactly.

■ For advice on capitals and quotations, see 29j.

25d In dialogue, use quotation marks around a speaker's words, and mark each change of speaker with a new paragraph.

Randolph gazed at Ellen and sighed. "What extraordinary beauty."

"They are lovely," she replied, staring at the roses, "aren't they?"

25e Use quotation marks around the titles of a speech, an article in a newspaper or magazine, a short story, a poem shorter than book length, a chapter in a book, a song, and an episode of a television or radio program.

The article "An Updike Retrospective" praises "Solitaire" as the best story in John Updike's collection *Museums and Women*.

In Chapter 5, "Expatriates," Schwartz discusses Eliot's famous poem "The Love Song of J. Alfred Prufrock."

■ For advice on italicizing or underlining titles, see 31a and the chart on p. H-136.

25f Avoid using quotation marks to indicate slang or to be witty or ironic.

INADVISABLE	By the time I finished all my chores, my "day off" was over.
REVISED	By the time I finished all my chores, my day off was over.
INADVISABLE	Liza looked like a born "loser," but Jerry was "hard up" for company.
REVISED	Liza looked like a born loser, but Jerry was hard up for company.

Stick your neck out. If you really want to use those words, just go ahead. Otherwise, reword the sentence.

No quotation marks are needed after *so-called* or similar words.

FAULTY   The meet included many so-called "champions."

REVISED   The meet included many so-called champions.

25g Put commas and periods inside quotation marks.

■ For more on commas with quotations, see 21k.

A comma or a period always comes before quotation marks, even if it is not part of the quotation.

We pleaded, "Keep off the grass," in hope of preserving the lawn.

25h Put semicolons and colons outside quotation marks.

We said, "Keep off the grass"; they still tromped onward.

25i Put other punctuation inside or outside quotation marks depending on its function in the sentence.

Parentheses that are part of the quotation go inside the quotation marks. Parentheses that are your own, not part of the quotation, go outside the quotation marks.

We said, "Keep off the grass (unless it's artificial turf)."

They tromped onward (although we had said, "Keep off the grass").

If a question mark, exclamation point, or dash is part of the quotation, place it inside the quotation marks. Otherwise, place it after the closing quotation marks.

She hollered, "Fire!"

Who hollered "Fire"?

Don't close a sentence with two end punctuation marks, one inside and one outside the quotation marks. If the quoted passage ends with a dash, exclamation point, question mark, or period, you need not add any further end punctuation. If the quoted passage falls within a question asked by you, however, it should finish with a question mark, even if that means dropping other end punctuation (*Who hollered "Fire"?*).

■ For more practice, visit <bedfordstmartins.com/ bedguide> and do a key- word search:

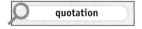

■ Exercise 25–1

Using Quotation Marks

Add quotation marks wherever they are needed in the following sentences, and correct any other errors. Answers for the lettered sentences appear in the back of the book. Example:

Annie asked him, Do you believe in free will?

Annie asked him, "Do you believe in free will?"

a. What we still need to figure out, the police chief said, is whether the victim was acquainted with his assailant.

b. A skillful orator, Patrick Henry is credited with the phrase Give me liberty or give me death.

c. I could hear the crowd chanting my name—Jones! Jones!—and that spurred me on, said Bruce Jones, the winner of the 5,000-meter race.

d. The video for the rock group Guns and Roses' epic song November Rain is based on a short story by Del James.

e. After the Gore/Bush election debacle of 2000, *Time* essayist Lance Morrow predicts, The memory of the 2000 post-election chadfest will revive an angry energy in 2004, which will produce the biggest voter turnout in history.

1. That day at school, the kids were as "high as kites."

2. Notice, the professor told the class, Cassius's choice of imagery when he asks, Upon what meat doth this our Caesar feed, / That he is grown so great?

3. "As I was rounding the bend," Peter explained, "I failed to see the sign that said Caution: Ice.

4. John Cheever's story The Swimmer begins with the line It was one of those midsummer Sundays when everyone sits around saying, I drank too much last night.

5. Who coined the saying Love is blind?

26   *The Dash*

A *dash* is a horizontal line used to separate parts of a sentence—a more dramatic substitute for a comma, semicolon, or colon. To type a dash, hit your hyphen key twice.

26a   Use a dash to indicate a sudden break in thought or shift in tone.

The dash signals that a surprise is in store: a shift in viewpoint, perhaps, or an unfinished statement.

Ivan doesn't care which team wins—he bet on both.

I didn't notice my parents' accented speech—at least not at home.

26b Use a dash to introduce an explanation, an illustration, or a series.

When you want a preparatory pause without the formality of a colon, try a dash.

> My advice to you is simple — stop complaining.

You can use a dash to introduce an appositive that needs drama or contains commas.

> Longfellow wrote about three young sisters — grave Alice, laughing Allegra, and Edith with golden hair — in "The Children's Hour."

26c Use dashes to set off an emphatic aside or parenthetical expression from the rest of a sentence.

> It was as hot — and I mean *hot* — as the Fourth of July in Death Valley.

> If I went through anguish in botany and economics — for different reasons — sociology was even worse.

26d Avoid overusing dashes.

Like a physical gesture of emphasis — a jab of a pointing finger — the dash becomes meaningless if used too often. Use it only when a comma, a colon, or parentheses don't seem strong enough.

EXCESSIVE	Algy's grandmother — a sweet old lady — asked him to pick up some things at the store — milk, eggs, and cheese.
REVISED	Algy's grandmother, a sweet old lady, asked him to pick up some things at the store: milk, eggs, and cheese.

■ Exercise 26–1

Using the Dash

Add, remove, or replace dashes wherever appropriate in the following sentences. Some sentences may be correct. Possible answers for the lettered sentences appear in the back of the book. Example:

> Stanton had all the identifying marks, boating shoes, yellow slicker, sunblock, and an anchor, of a sailor.

> Stanton had all the identifying marks — boating shoes, yellow slicker, sunblock, and an anchor — of a sailor.

a. I enjoy going hiking with my friend John — whom I've known for fifteen years.

---

appositive: A word or group of words that adds information about a subject or object by identifying it in a different way: my dog *Rover*, Hal's brother *Fred*

parenthetical expression: An aside to readers or a transitional expression such as *for example* or *in contrast*

■ For more on dashes compared with commas, see 21, and with parentheses, see 27a–27b.

■ For more practice, visit <bedfordstmartins.com/bedguide> and do a keyword search:

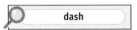
dash

   b. Pedro's new boat is spectacular: a regular seagoing Ferrari.

   c. The Thompsons devote their weekends to their favorite pastime, eating bags of potato chips and cookies beside the warm glow of the television.

   1. The sport of fishing — or at least some people call it a sport — is boring, dirty — and tiring.

   2. At that time, three states in the Sunbelt, Florida, California, and Arizona, were the fastest growing in the nation.

   3. LuLu was ecstatic when she saw her grades, all A's!

27 Parentheses, Brackets, and the Ellipsis Mark

Like quotation marks, parentheses (singular, *parenthesis*) work in pairs. So do brackets. Both sets of marks usually surround bits of information added to make a statement perfectly clear. An ellipsis mark is a trio of periods inserted to show that some information has been cut.

PARENTHESES

27a Use parentheses to set off interruptions that are useful but not essential.

> FDR (as people called Franklin D. Roosevelt) won four presidential elections.

> In fact, he occupied the White House for so many years (1933 to mid-1945) that babies became teenagers without having known any other president.

The material within the parentheses may be helpful, but it isn't essential. Without it, the sentences would still make good sense. Use parentheses when adding in midsentence a qualifying word or phrase, a helpful date, or a brief explanation — words that, in conversation, you might introduce in a changed tone of voice.

27b Use parentheses around letters or numbers indicating items in a series.

> Archimedes asserted that, given (1) a lever long enough, (2) a fulcrum, and (3) a place to stand, he could move the earth.

You need not put parentheses around numbers or letters in a list that you set off from the text by indentation.

■ For more practice, visit <bedfordstmartins.com/ bedguide> and do a key- word search:

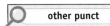
other punct

■ Exercise 27–1

Using Parentheses

Add, remove, or replace parentheses wherever appropriate in the following sentences. Some sentences may be correct. Possible answers for the lettered sentences appear in the back of the book. Example:

> The Islamic fundamentalist Ayatollah Khomeini — 1903–1989 — was de- scribed as having led Iran forward into the fifteenth century.

> The Islamic fundamentalist Ayatollah Khomeini (1903–1989) was de- scribed as having led Iran forward into the fifteenth century.

a. Our cafeteria serves the four basic food groups: white — milk, bread, and mashed potatoes — brown — mystery meat and gravy — green — over- cooked vegetables and underwashed lettuce — and orange — squash, car- rots, and tomato sauce.

b. The hijackers will release the hostages only if the government, 1, frees all political prisoners and, 2, allows the hijackers to leave the country unharmed.

c. When Phil said he works with whales (as well as other marine mammals) for the Whale Stranding Network, Lisa thought he meant that his group lures whales onto beaches.

1. The new pear-shaped bottles will hold 200 milliliters, 6.8 fluid ounces, of lotion.

2. World War I, or "The Great War," as it was once called, destroyed the old European order forever.

3. The Internet is a mine of fascinating, and sometimes useless, information.

BRACKETS

Brackets, those open-ended typographical boxes, work in pairs like pa- rentheses. They serve a special purpose: they mark changes in quoted mate- rial.

■ For advice on quoting, paraphrasing, and summa- rizing, see D3–D5 in the Quick Research Guide (the dark-red-edged pages).

27c Use brackets to add information or to make changes within a direct quotation.

A quotation must be quoted exactly. If you add or alter a word or a phrase in a quotation from another writer, place brackets around your changes. Most often the need for such changes arises when you weave into your own prose a piece of someone else's.

Suppose you are writing about James McGuire's being named chairman of the board of directors of General Motors. In your source, the actual words are these: "A radio bulletin first brought the humble professor of philosophy the astounding news." But in your paper, you want readers to know the professor's identity. So you add that information, in brackets.

> "A radio bulletin first brought the humble professor of philosophy [James McGuire] the astounding news."

Be careful never to alter a quoted statement any more than you have to. Every time you consider an alteration, ask yourself: Do I really need this word-for-word quotation, or should I paraphrase?

27d Use brackets around *sic* to indicate an error in a direct quotation.

When you faithfully quote a statement that contains an error, follow the error with a bracketed *sic* (Latin for "so" or "so the writer says").

> "President Ronald Reagan foresaw a yearly growth of 29,000,000,000 [*sic*] in the American populace."

Of course, any statement as incorrect as that one is not worth quoting. Usually you're better off paraphrasing an error-riddled passage than pointing out its weaknesses.

■ For more on brackets, see 27c.

THE ELLIPSIS MARK

27e Use the ellipsis mark to signal that you have omitted part of a quotation.

Occasionally you will want to quote just the parts of a passage that relate to your topic. It's all right to make judicious cuts in a quotation, as long as you acknowledge them. To do this, use the *ellipsis mark:* three periods with a space between each one (. . .).

Say you are writing an essay, "Today's Children: Counselors on Marital Affairs." One of your sources, Marie Winn's book *Children without Childhood* (New York: Penguin, 1984), includes this passage:

> Consider the demise of sexual innocence among children. We know that the casual integration of children into adult society in the Middle Ages included few sexual prohibitions. Today's nine- and ten-year-olds watch pornographic movies on cable TV, casually discourse about oral sex and sadomasochism, and not infrequently find themselves involved in their own parents' complicated sex lives, if not as actual observers or participants, at least as advisers, friendly commentators, and intermediaries.

You want to quote Winn's last sentence but omit some of its detail.

> "Today's nine- and ten-year-olds . . . not infrequently find themselves involved in their own parents' complicated sex lives, . . . at least as advisers, friendly commentators, and intermediaries."

If the ellipsis mark concludes your sentence, precede it with a period placed directly after the end of the sentence.

"Consider the demise of sexual innocence. . . . Today's nine- and ten-year-olds [quotation continues as in preceding example]."

27f Avoid using the ellipsis mark at the beginning or end of a quotation.

Even though the book *Children without Childhood* continues after the quoted passage, you don't need an ellipsis mark at the end of your quotation. Nor do you ever need to begin a quotation with three dots. Save the ellipsis mark for words or sentences you omit *inside* whatever you quote.

Anytime you decide to alter a quotation, with an ellipsis mark or with brackets, ask yourself whether the quoted material is still necessary and still effective. If you plan to cut more than one or two sections from a quotation, think about paraphrasing instead.

For more on quoting, paraphrasing, and summarizing, see D3–D5 in the Quick Research Guide (the dark-red-edged pages).

For more practice, visit <bedfordstmartins.com/bedguide> and do a keyword search:

other punct

■ Exercise 27–2

Using Brackets and the Ellipsis Mark

The following are two hypothetical passages from original essays. Each one is followed by a set of quotations. Paraphrase or adapt each quotation, using brackets and ellipsis marks, and splice it into the essay passage.

I. ESSAY PASSAGE

Most people are willing to work hard for a better life. Too often, however, Americans do not realize that the desire for more possessions leads them away from the happiness they hope to find. Many people work longer and longer hours to earn more money and as a result have less time to devote to family, friends, and activities that are truly important. When larger houses, sport-utility vehicles, and wide-screen TVs fail to bring them joy, they find even more things to buy and work even harder to pay for them. This cycle can grind down the most optimistic American. The only solution is to realize how few material possessions people absolutely need to have.

QUOTATIONS

a. Only when he has ceased to need things can a man truly be his own master and so really exist.
— Anwar al-Sadat

b. I like to walk amidst the beautiful things that adorn the world; but private wealth I should decline, or any sort of personal possessions, because they would take away my liberty.
— George Santayana

c. To live content with small means; to seek elegance rather than luxury, and refinement rather than fashion; to be worthy, not respectable and wealthy, not rich; to study hard, think quietly, talk gently, act frankly; to listen to stars and birds, to babes and sages, with open heart; to bear all cheerfully, do all bravely, await occasions, hurry never. In a word, to let the spiritual, unbidden and unconscious, grow up through the common. This is to be my symphony.

— William Henry Channing

2. ESSAY PASSAGE

Every human life is touched by the natural world. Before the modern industrial era, most people recognized the earth as the giver and supporter of existence. Nowadays, with the power of technology, we can (if we choose) destroy many of the complex balances of nature. With such power comes responsibility. We are no longer merely nature's children, but nature's parents as well.

QUOTATIONS

a. The overwhelming importance of the atmosphere means that there are no longer any frontiers to defend against pollution, attack, or propaganda. It means, further, that only by a deep patriotic devotion to one's country can there be a hope of the kind of protection of the whole planet, which is necessary for the survival of the people of other countries.

— Anthropologist Margaret Mead

b. The survival of our wildlife is a matter of grave concern to all of us in Africa. These wild creatures amid the wild places they inhabit are not only important as a source of wonder and inspiration but are an integral part of our natural resources and of our future livelihood and well-being.

— Former president of Tanzania Julius Nyerere

Chapter 37
Mechanics

28 *Abbreviations*

Abbreviations enable a writer to include necessary information in capsule form. Limit abbreviations to those common enough for readers to recognize, or add an explanation so that a reader does not wonder, "What does this mean?"

If ever you're unsure about whether to abbreviate a word, remember: when in doubt, spell it out.

28a Use abbreviations for some titles with proper names.

■ For advice on punctuating abbreviations, see 20b.

Abbreviate the following titles:

Mr. and Mrs. Hubert Collins   Dr. Martin Luther King Jr.
Ms. Martha Reading   St. Matthew

Write out other titles in full, including titles that are unfamiliar to readers of English, such as *M.* (for the French *Monsieur*) or *Sr.* (for the Spanish *Señor*).

General Douglas MacArthur   Senator Dianne Feinstein
President George W. Bush   Professor Shirley Fixler

Spell out most titles that appear without proper names.

FAULTY   Tomás is studying to be a dr.

REVISED   Tomás is studying to be a doctor.

When an abbreviated title (such as an academic degree) follows a proper name, set it off with commas.

Alice Martin, CPA, is the accountant for Charlotte Cordera, PhD.

Lucy Chen, MD, and James Filbert, DDS, have moved to new offices.

An academic degree that appears without a proper name can be abbreviated, but it is not set off with commas.

My brother has a BA in economics.

Avoid repeating different forms of the same title before and after a proper name. You can properly refer to a doctor of dental surgery as either *Dr. Jane Doe* or *Jane Doe, DDS*, but not as *Dr. Jane Doe, DDS*.

28b Use *a.m.*, *p.m.*, *BC*, *AD*, and *$* with numbers.

   9:05 a.m.   3:45 p.m.   2000 BC   AD 1066

The words for pinpointing years and times are so commonly abbreviated that many writers have forgotten what the letters stand for. In case you are curious: *a.m.* means *ante meridiem*, Latin for "before noon"; *p.m.* means *post meridiem*, "after noon." AD is *anno domini*, Latin for "in the year of the Lord" — that is, since the official year of Jesus' birth. BC stands for "before Christ" and BCE for "before the common era."

For exact prices that include cents and for amounts in the millions, use a dollar sign with figures (*$17.95, $10.52, $3.5 billion*).

Avoid using an abbreviation with wording that means the same thing: write *$1 million*, not *$1 million dollars*. Write *9:05 a.m.* or *9:05 in the morning*, not *9:05 a.m. in the morning*.

28c Avoid abbreviating names of months, days of the week, units of measurement, or parts of literary works.

Many references that can be abbreviated in citations should be spelled out when they appear in the body of an essay.

NAMES OF MONTHS AND DAYS OF THE WEEK

FAULTY   After their session on 9/3, they did not meet until Fri., Dec. 12.

REVISED   After their session on September 3 [*or* the third of September], they did not meet until Friday, December 12.

UNITS OF MEASUREMENT

FAULTY   It would take 10,000 lbs. of concrete to build a causeway 25 ft. $\times$ 58 in. [*or* 25' $\times$ 58"].

REVISED   It would take 10,000 pounds of concrete to build a causeway 25 feet by 58 inches.

PARTS OF LITERARY WORKS

FAULTY   Von Bargen's reply appears in vol. 2, ch. 12, p. 187.

REVISED   Von Bargen's reply appears in volume 2, chapter 12, page 187.

FAULTY   Leona first speaks in act 1, sc. 2.

REVISED   Leona first speaks in act 1, scene 2 [*or* the second scene of act 1].

28d   Use the full English version of most Latin abbreviations.

■ For the use of *sic* to identify an error, see 27d.

Unless you are writing for an audience of ancient Romans, translate Latin abbreviations into English, and spell them out whenever possible.

COMMON LATIN ABBREVIATIONS

ABBREVIATION	LATIN	ENGLISH
et al.	*et alia*	and others, and other people, and the others (people)
etc.	*et cetera*	and so forth, and others, and the rest (things)
i.e.	*id est*	that is
e.g.	*exempli gratia*	for example, such as

Latin abbreviations are acceptable, however, for source citations and for comments in parentheses and brackets.

28e   Use abbreviations for familiar organizations, corporations, and people.

Most sets of initials that are capitalized and read as letters do not require periods between the letters (CIA, JFK, UCLA). A set of initials that is pronounced as a word is called an *acronym* (NATO, AIDS, UNICEF) and never has periods between letters.

To avoid misunderstanding, write out an organization's full name the first time you mention it, followed by its initials in parentheses. Then, in later references, you can rely on initials alone. (For very familiar initials, such as FBI or CBS, you need not give the full name.)

28f   Avoid abbreviations for countries.

When you mention the United States or another country, give its full name unless the repetition would weigh down your paragraph.

The president will return to the United States [*not* US] on Tuesday from a trip to the United Kingdom [*not* UK].

EXCEPTION: Unlike *US* as a noun, the abbreviation, used consistently with traditional periods or without, is acceptable as an adjective: *US Senate, U.S. foreign policy.* For other countries, find an alternative: *British ambassador.*

■ Exercise 28–1

Using Abbreviations

Substitute abbreviations for words and vice versa wherever appropriate in the following sentences. Correct any incorrectly used abbreviations. Answers for the lettered sentences appear in the back of the book. Example:

> Please return this form to our office no later than noon on Wed., Apr. 7.

> Please return this form to our office no later than noon on *Wednesday, April 7.*

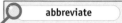

■ For more practice, visit <bedfordstmartins.com/ bedguide> and do a keyword search:

abbreviate

a. At 7:50 p.m. in the evening on election day, the media first awarded Florida to Al Gore, only to reverse that statement and declare George W. Bush the president a few hours later.

b. Biology lectures are only ninety mins. long because lab sessions immediately follow them.

c. Prof. James has office hours on Mon. and Tues., beginning at 10:00 a.m.

d. Emotional issues, e.g., abortion and capital punishment, cannot be settled easily by compromise.

e. The red peppers are selling for three dollars and twenty-five cents a lb.

1. Hamlet's famous soliloquy comes in act three, sc. one.

2. A.I.D.S. has affected people throughout U.S. society, not just gay men and IV-drug users.

3. Mister Robert Glendale, a C.P.A. accountant, is today's lucky winner of the daily double.

4. The end of the cold war between the U.S. and the Soviet Union complicated the role of the U.N. and drastically altered the purpose of N.A.T.O.

5. The salmon measured thirty-eight in. and weighed twenty-one lbs.

29 *Capital Letters*

Use capital letters only with good reason. If you think a word will work in lowercase letters, you're probably right.

■ For advice and a useful chart on capitalization, see D1 in the Quick Editing Guide (the dark-blue-edged pages).

29a Capitalize proper names and adjectives made from proper names.

Proper names designate individuals, places, organizations, institutions, brand names, and certain other distinctive things.

Miles Standish	University of Iowa
Belgium	a Volkswagen
United Nations	a Xerox copier

Any proper name can have an adjective as well as a noun form. The adjective form is also capitalized.

Australian beer   a Renaissance man   Shakespearean comedy

29b Capitalize a title or rank before a proper name.

Now in her second term, Senator Wilimczyk serves on two committees.

In his lecture, Professor Jones analyzed fossil evidence.

Titles that do not come before proper names usually are not capitalized.

Ten senators voted against the missile research appropriation.

Jones is the department's only full professor.

EXCEPTION: The abbreviation of an academic or professional degree is capitalized, whether or not it accompanies a proper name. The informal name of a degree is not capitalized.

Dora E. McLean, MD, also holds a BA in music.

Dora holds a bachelor's degree in music.

29c Capitalize a family relationship only when it is part of a proper name or when it substitutes for a proper name.

Do you know the song about Mother Machree?

I've invited Mother to visit next weekend.

I'd like you to meet my aunt, Emily Smith.

29d Capitalize the names of religions, their deities, and their followers.

Christianity   Muslims   Jehovah   Krishna
Islam   Methodists   Allah   the Holy Spirit

29e Capitalize proper names of places, regions, and geographic features.

Los Angeles   the Black Hills   the Atlantic Ocean
Death Valley   Big Sur   the Philippines

Do not capitalize *north, south, east,* or *west* unless it is part of a proper name (*West Virginia, South Orange*) or refers to formal geographic locations.

Drive south to Chicago and then east to Cleveland.

Jim, who has always lived in the South, likes to read about the Northeast.

A common noun such as *street, avenue, boulevard, park, lake,* or *hill* is capitalized when part of a proper name.

Meinecke Avenue   Hamilton Park   Lake Michigan

29f Capitalize days of the week, months, and holidays, but not seasons or academic terms.

During spring term, by the Monday after Passover, I have to choose between the January study plan and junior year abroad.

29g Capitalize historical events, periods, and documents.

Black Monday   the Roaring Twenties
the Civil War [*but* a civil war]   Magna Carta
the Holocaust [*but* a holocaust]   Declaration of Independence
the Bronze Age   Atomic Energy Act

29h Capitalize the names of schools, colleges, departments, and courses.

West End School, Central High School [*but* elementary school, high school]

Reed College, Arizona State University [*but* the college, a university]

Department of History [*but* history department, department office]

Feminist Perspectives in Nineteenth-Century Literature [*but* literature course]

29i Capitalize the first, last, and main words in titles.

When you write the title of a paper, book, article, work of art, television show, poem, or performance, capitalize the first and last words and all main words in between. Do not capitalize articles (*a, an, the*), coordinating conjunctions (*and, but, for, or, nor, so, yet*), or prepositions (such as *in, on, at, of, from*) unless they come first or last in the title or follow a colon.

◼ For advice on using quotation marks and italics for titles, see 25e and 31a.

ESSAY	"Once More to the Lake"
NOVEL	*Of Mice and Men*
VOLUME OF POETRY	*Poems after Martial*
POEM	"A Valediction: Of Weeping"
BALLET	*Swan Lake*

29j Capitalize the first letter of a quoted sentence.

Oscar Wilde wrote, "The only way to get rid of a temptation is to yield to it."

Only the first word of a quoted sentence is capitalized, even when you break the sentence with words of your own.

"The only way to get rid of a temptation," wrote Oscar Wilde, "is to yield to it."

If you quote more than one sentence, start each one with a capital letter.

"Art should never try to be popular," said Wilde. "The public should try to make itself artistic."

If the quoted passage blends in with your sentence, be sure to present every detail of your source accurately.

Oscar Wilde wrote that "The only way to get rid of a temptation is to yield to it."

■ For advice on punctuating quotations, see 25g–25i.

■ Exercise 29–1

Using Capitalization

Correct any capitalization errors you find in the following sentences. Some sentences may be correct. Answers for the lettered sentences appear in the back of the book. Example:

> "The quality of mercy," says Portia in Shakespeare's *The Merchant Of Venice,* "Is not strained."

> "The quality of mercy," says Portia in Shakespeare's *The Merchant of Venice,* "is not strained."

a. At our Family Reunion, I met my Cousin Sam for the first time, as well as my father's brother George.

b. I already knew from dad that his brother had moved to Australia years ago to explore the great barrier reef.

c. I had heard that uncle George was estranged from his Mother, a Roman catholic, after he married an Atheist.

d. She told George that God created many religions so that people would not become Atheists.

e. When my Uncle announced that he was moving to a Continent thousands of miles Southwest of the United States, his Mother gave him a bible to take along.

1. My Aunt, Linda McCallum, received her Doctorate from one of the State Universities in California.

2. After graduation she worked there as Registrar and lived in the San Bernardino valley.

■ For more practice, visit <bedfordstmartins.com/bedguide> and do a keyword search:

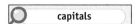

capitals

3. She has pursued her interest in Hispanic Studies by traveling to South America from her home in Northeastern Australia.

4. She uses her maiden name—Linda McCallum, PhD—for her nonprofit business, Hands across the Sea.

5. After dinner we all toasted grandmother's Ninetieth Birthday and sang "For She's A Jolly Good Fellow."

30 *Numbers*

When do you write out a number (*twenty-seven*) and when do you use figures for it (27)? Unless your essay relies on statistics, you'll generally want to use words. Figures are most appropriate in contexts where readers are used to seeing them, such as times and dates (*11:05 p.m. on March 15*).

30a In general, write out a number that consists of one or two words, and use figures for longer numbers.

Short names of numbers are easily read (*ten, six hundred*); longer ones take more thought (*two thousand four hundred eighty-seven*). For numbers of more than a word or two, use figures.

Two hundred fans paid twenty-five dollars apiece for that shirt.

A frog's tongue has 970,580 taste buds; a human's has six times as many.

EXCEPTION: For multiples of a million or more, use a figure plus a word.

The earth is 93 million miles from the sun.

30b Use figures for most addresses, dates, decimals, fractions, parts of literary works, percentages, exact prices, scores, statistics, and times.

Using figures is mainly a matter of convenience. If you think words will be easier for your readers to follow, you can always write out a number.

For examples, see Figures at a Glance on p. H-134.

30c Use words or figures consistently for numbers in the same category throughout a passage.

Switching back and forth between words and figures for numbers can be distracting to readers. Choose whichever form suits like numbers in your passage, and use that form consistently for all numbers in the same category.

For more on the plurals of figures (6's, 1960s), see 24i.

Of the 276 representatives who voted, 97 supported a 25 percent raise, while 179 supported a 30 percent raise over five years.

Figures at a Glance

ADDRESSES	4 East 74th Street; also, One Copley Place, 5 Fifth Avenue
DATES	May 20, 1992; 450 BC; also, Fourth of July
DECIMALS	98.6° Fahrenheit; .57 acre
FRACTIONS	3½ years ago; 1¾ miles; also, half a loaf, three-fourths of voters surveyed
PARTS OF LITERARY WORKS	volume 2, chapter 5, page 37 act 1, scene 2 (*or* act I, scene ii)
PERCENTAGES	25 percent; 99.9 percent; also, 25%, 99.9%
EXACT PRICES	$1.99; $200,000; also, $5 million, ten cents, a dollar
SCORES	a 114–111 victory; a final score of 5 to 3
STATISTICS	men in the 25–30 age group; odds of 5 to 1 (*or* 5–1 odds); height 5'7"; also, three out of four doctors
TIMES	2:29 p.m.; 10:15 tomorrow morning; also, half past four, three o'clock (always with a number in words)

30d Write out a number that begins a sentence.

Readers recognize a new sentence by its initial capital; however, you can't capitalize a figure. When a number starts a sentence, either write it out or move it deeper into the sentence. If a number starting a sentence is followed by other numbers in the same category, write them out, too, unless doing so makes the sentence excessively awkward.

> Five percent of the frogs in our aquarium ate sixty-two percent of the flies.

> Ten thousand people packed an arena built for 8,550.

■ Exercise 30–1

Using Numbers

Correct any inappropriate uses of numbers in the following sentences. Some sentences may be correct. Answers for the lettered sentences appear in the back of the book. Example:

> As Feinberg notes on page 197, a delay of 3 minutes cost the researchers 5 years' worth of work.

> As Feinberg notes on page 197, a delay of *three* minutes cost the researchers *five* years' worth of work.

a. If the murder took place at approximately six-twenty p.m. and the suspect was ½ a mile away at the time, he could not possibly have committed the crime.

■ For more practice, visit <bedfordstmartins.com/bedguide> and do a keyword search:

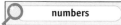
numbers

b. A program to help save the sea otter transferred more than eighty animals to a new colony over the course of 2 years; however, all but 34 otters swam back home again.

c. 1 percent or less of the estimated fifteen to twenty billion pounds of plastic discarded annually in the United States is recycled.

d. The 1983 Little League World Series saw the Roosters beat the Dusters ninety-four to four before a throng of seven thousand five hundred and fifty.

e. In act two, scene nine, of Shakespeare's *The Merchant of Venice,* Portia's 2nd suitor fails to guess which of 3 caskets contains her portrait.

1. *Fourscore* means 4 times 20; a *fortnight* means 2 weeks; and a *brace* is two of anything.

2. 50 years ago, traveling from New York City to San Francisco took approximately 15 hours by plane, 50 hours by train, and almost 100 hours by car.

3. The little cottage we bought for fifty-five thousand dollars in the nineteen-seventies may sell for $2,000,000 today.

4. At 7 o'clock this morning the temperature was already ninety-seven degrees Fahrenheit.

5. Angelica finished volume one of Proust's *Remembrance of Things Past,* but by the time she got to page forty of volume two, she had forgotten the beginning and had to start over.

31   *Italics*

Italic type — as in this line — slants to the right. In handwriting or typewriting, indicate italics by underlining. Slightly harder to read than perpendicular type, it is usually saved for emphasis or other special uses noted on page H-136.

31a   Italicize the titles of magazines, newspapers, and long literary works (books, pamphlets, plays); the titles of films; the titles of paintings and other works of art; the titles of long musical works (operas, symphonies); the titles of CDs and record albums; and the names of television and radio programs.

We read the story "Araby" in James Joyce's book *Dubliners.*

The Broadway musical *My Fair Lady* was based on Shaw's play *Pygmalion.*

The names of the Bible (King James Version, Revised Standard Version), the books of the Bible (Genesis, Matthew), and other sacred books (the Koran, the Rig-Veda) are not italicized.

For titles that need to be placed in quotation marks, see 25e.

Italics at a Glance

TITLES

MAGAZINES AND NEWSPAPERS
Ms.   the *London Times*

LONG LITERARY WORKS
The Bluest Eye (a novel)   *The Less Deceived* (a collection of poems)

FILMS
Psycho   *Crouching Tiger, Hidden Dragon*

PAINTINGS AND OTHER WORKS OF ART
Four Dancers (a painting)   *The Thinker* (a sculpture)

LONG MUSICAL WORKS
Aïda   Handel's *Messiah*

CDS AND RECORD ALBUMS
Crash   *Disciplined Breakdown*

TELEVISION AND RADIO PROGRAMS
Will and Grace   *All Things Considered*

OTHER WORDS AND PHRASES

NAMES OF AIRCRAFT, SPACECRAFT, SHIPS, AND TRAINS
the *Orient Express*   the *Challenger*

A WORD OR PHRASE FROM A FOREIGN LANGUAGE IF IT IS NOT IN EVERYDAY USE
The Finnish sauna ritual uses a *vihta,* a brush made of fresh birch branches.

A LETTER, NUMBER, WORD, OR PHRASE WHEN YOU DEFINE IT OR REFER TO IT AS A WORD
Two neon *5*'s on the door identified the club's address.

What do you think *fiery* is referring to in the second line?

When you give a synonym or translation — a definition of just a word or so — italicize the word and put its definition in quotation marks.

> The word *orthodoxy* means "conformity."
> *Trois, drei,* and *tres* are all words for "three."

31b   Italicize the names of ships, boats, trains, airplanes, and spacecraft.

The launching of the Venus probe *Magellan* was a heartening success after the *Challenger* disaster.

31c Italicize a word or phrase from a foreign language if it is not in everyday use.

Gandhi taught the principles of *satya* and *ahimsa:* truth and nonviolence.

Foreign words that are familiar to most American readers need not be italicized. (Check your dictionary to see which words are considered familiar.)

I prefer provolone to mozzarella.

31d Italicize a word when you define it.

The rhythmic motion of the walls of the alimentary canal is called *peristalsis.*

31e Italicize a letter, number, word, or phrase used as a word.

George Bernard Shaw pointed out that *fish* could be spelled *ghoti: gh* as in *tough, o* as in *women,* and *ti* as in *fiction.*

Watching the big red *8* on a basketball player's jersey, I recalled the scarlet letter *A* worn by Hester Prynne.

31f Use italics sparingly for emphasis.

When you absolutely *must* stress a point, use italics. In most cases, the structure of your sentence, not a typographical gimmick, should give emphasis where emphasis is due.

He suggested putting the package *under* the mailbox, not *into* the mailbox.

People living in affluent countries may not be aware that *forty thousand children per day* die of starvation or malnutrition.

■ **Exercise 31–1**

Using Italics

Add or remove italics as needed in the following sentences. Some sentences may be correct. Answers for the lettered sentences appear in the back of the book. Example:

Hiram could not *believe* that his parents had seen *the Beatles'* legendary performance at Shea Stadium.

Hiram could not believe that his parents had seen the Beatles' legendary performance at Shea Stadium.

a. Does "avocado" mean "lawyer" in Spanish?

■ For more practice, visit <bedfordstmartins.com/bedguide> and do a keyword search:

italics

b. During this year's *First Night* celebrations, we heard Verdi's Requiem and Monteverdi's Orfeo.

c. You can pick out some of the best basketball players in the *NBA* by the 33 on their jerseys.

d. It was fun watching the passengers on the Europa trying to dance to *Blue Moon* in the midst of a storm.

e. In one episode of the sitcom "Seinfeld," Kramer gets a job as an underwear model.

1. *Eye* in French is *oeil,* while *eyes* is *yeux.*

2. "Deux yeux bleus" means "two blue eyes" in French.

3. Jan can never remember whether Cincinnati has three n's and one t or two n's and two t's.

4. My favorite comic bit in "The Pirates of Penzance" is Major General Stanley's confusion between "orphan" and "often."

5. In Tom Stoppard's play "The Real Thing," the character Henry accuses Bach of copying a *cantata* from a popular song by *Procol Harum.*

32 *The Hyphen*

The hyphen, that Scotch-tape mark of punctuation, is used to join words and to connect parts of words.

32a Use hyphens in compound words that require them.

Compound words in the English language take three forms:

1. Two or more words combined into one (*crossroads, salesperson*)
2. Two or more words that remain separate but function as one (*gas station, high school*)
3. Two or more words linked by hyphens (*sister-in-law, window-shop*)

Compound nouns and verbs fall into these categories more by custom than by rule. When you're not sure which way to write a compound, refer to a current dictionary. If the compound is not listed in your dictionary, write it as two words.

Use a hyphen in a compound word containing one or more elements beginning with a capital letter.

Bill says that, as a *neo-Marxist* living in an *A-frame* house, it would be politically incorrect for him to wear a Mickey Mouse *T-shirt.*

There are exceptions to this rule: unchristian, for one. If you think a compound word looks odd with a hyphen, check your dictionary.

32b Use a hyphen in a compound adjective preceding a
         noun but not following a noun.

Jerome, a devotee of *twentieth-century* music, has no interest in the classic
symphonies of the *eighteenth century.*

I'd like living in an *out-of-the-way* place better if it weren't so far *out of the way.*

In a series of hyphenated adjectives with the same second word, you can
omit that word (but not the hyphen) in all but the last adjective of the series.

Julia is a lover of eighteenth-, nineteenth-, and twentieth-century music.

The adverb *well,* when coupled with an adjective, follows the same hyphenation rules as if it were an adjective.

It is *well known* that Tony has a *well-equipped* kitchen, although his is not as
well equipped as the hotel's.

Do *not* use a hyphen to link an adverb ending in *-ly* with an adjective.

FAULTY   The sun hung like a newly-minted penny in a freshly-washed sky.

REVISED   The sun hung like a newly minted penny in a freshly washed sky.

32c Use a hyphen after the prefixes *all-, ex-,* and *self-* and
         before the suffix *-elect.*

Lucille's *ex-husband* is studying *self-hypnosis.*

This *all-important* debate pits Senator Browning against the *president-elect.*

Note that these prefixes and suffixes also can function as parts of words
that are not hyphenated (*exit, selfish*). Whenever you are unsure whether to
use a hyphen, check a dictionary.

32d Use a hyphen in most cases if an added prefix or
         suffix creates a double vowel, triple consonant, or
         ambiguous pronunciation.

It is also acceptable to omit the hyphen in the case of a double *e: reeducate.*

The contractor's *pre-estimate* did not cover any *pre-existing* flaws in the house.

The recreation department favors the *re-creation* of a summer program.

32e Use a hyphen in spelled-out fractions and compound
         whole numbers from twenty-one to ninety-nine.

When her sister gave Leslie's age as six and *three-quarters,* Leslie corrected
her: "I'm six and *five-sixths!*"

The fifth graders learned that *forty-four* rounds down to forty while *forty-five* rounds up to fifty.

32f Use a hyphen to indicate inclusive numbers.

The section covering the years 1975-1980 is found on pages 20-27.

32g Use a hyphen to break a word between syllables at the end of a line.

Although many readers will prefer that you turn off your word processor's automatic hyphenation function, using it will require that you check the word divisions it generates. Words are divided as they are pronounced, by syllables. Break a hyphenated compound at its hyphen and a nonhyphenated compound between the words that make it up. If you are not sure where to break a word, check your dictionary.

FAULTY Bubba hates to be called an-
ti-American.

REVISED Bubba hates to be called anti-
American.

Don't split a one-syllable word, even if keeping it intact makes your line come out a bit too short or too long.

FAULTY I'm completely drenched.

REVISED I'm completely drenched.

■ Exercise 32–I

Using Hyphens

Add necessary hyphens and remove incorrectly used hyphens in the following sentences. Some sentences may be correct. Answers for the lettered sentences appear in the back of the book. Example:

Her exhusband works part-time as a short order cook.

Her *ex-husband* works part-time as a *short-order* cook.

a. The strong smelling smoke alerted them to a potentially life threatening danger.

b. Burt's wildly-swinging opponent had tired himself out before the climactic third round.

c. Tony soaked his son's ketchup and mustard stained T shirt in a pail of water mixed with chlorine bleach.

■ For more practice, visit <bedfordstmartins.com/bedguide> and do a key-word search:

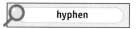

hyphen

d. The badly damaged ship was in no condition to enter the wide-open waters beyond the bay.

e. Tracy's brother in law lives with his family in a six room apartment.

1. Do you want salt-and-pepper on your roast beef sandwich?

2. Health insurance companies should not be allowed to exclude people on account of preexisting conditions.

3. Heat-seeking missiles are often employed in modern day air-to-air combat.

4. *The Piano* is a beautifully-crafted film with first-rate performances by Holly Hunter and Harvey Keitel.

5. Nearly three fourths of the money in the repair and maintenance account already has been spent.

33 *Spelling*

English spelling so often defies the rules that many writers wonder if, indeed, there *are* rules. You probably learned to spell — as most of us did — mainly by memorizing. By now you remember that there's a *b* in *doubt* but not in *spout*. You know that the same sound can have several spellings, as in *here, ear, pier, sneer,* and *weird*. You are resigned to pronouncing *ou* differently in *four, round, ought,* and *double*. Still, like most people, you may have trouble spelling certain words.

How many times have you heard someone say "ath-uh-lete" for *athlete* or "gov-er-ment" for *government?* Get the pronunciation right and you realize that the spelling has to be *arctic* (not *artic*), *perform* (not *preform*), *surprise* (not *suprise*), and *similar* (not *similiar*). The trouble is that careful pronunciation is only sometimes a reliable guide to English spelling. Knowing how to pronounce *psychology, whistle, light, gauge,* and *rhythm* doesn't help you spell them. How, then, are you to cope? You can proofread carefully and use your spell checker. You can refer to lists of commonly misspelled words and of **homonyms,** words that sound the same, or almost the same, but are spelled differently. You can also follow the spelling rules and advice about spelling skills included in this section.

> For advice on spelling and for useful spelling lists, see D2 in the Quick Editing Guide (the dark-blue-edged pages).

33a Follow spelling rules.

Fortunately, a few rules for spelling English words work most of the time. Learning them, and some of their exceptions, will give you a sturdy foundation on which to build.

EI or IE? The best way to remember which words are spelled *ei* and which ones *ie* is to recall this familiar jingle:

I before *e* except after *c*,

Or when sounded like *a*, as in *neighbor* and *weigh*.

Niece, believe, field, receive, receipt, ceiling, beige, and *freight* are just a few of the words you'll be able to spell easily once you learn that rule. Then memorize a few of the exceptions:

counterfeit	foreign	kaleidoscope	protein	seize
either	forfeit	leisure	science	weird
financier	height	neither	seismograph	

Also among the rule breakers are words in which *cien* is pronounced "shen": *ancient, efficient, conscience, prescience.*

Plurals.   Here are six useful rules:

common noun: A word that names a general class of person (*teacher*), place (*dormitory*), thing (*car*), or concept (*freedom*)

1. To form the plural of most common nouns, add *-s*. If a noun ends in *-ch, -sh, -s,* or *-x,* form its plural by adding *-es.*

attack, attacks	umbrella, umbrellas
boss, bosses	zone, zones
sandwich, sandwiches	trellis, trellises
tax, taxes	crash, crashes

2. To form the plural of a common noun ending in *-o,* add *-s* if the *-o* follows a vowel and *-es* if it follows a consonant.

radio, radios	video, videos
hero, heroes	potato, potatoes

3. To form the plural of a common noun ending in *-y,* change the *y* to *i* and add *-es* if the *y* follows a consonant. Add only *-s* if the *y* follows a vowel.

baby, babies	sissy, sissies
toy, toys	day, days

proper noun: A capitalized word that names a specific person (*Professor Graham*), place (*Milwaukee*), thing (*Cadillac*), or concept (*New Deal*)

4. To form the plural of a proper noun, add *-s* or *-es.* Proper nouns follow the same rules as common nouns, with one exception: a proper noun never changes its spelling in the plural form.

Mary Jane, Mary Janes	Dr. Maddox, the Maddoxes
Professor Jones, the Joneses	Saturday, Saturdays

5. To form the plural of a compound noun, add *-s* or *-es* to the chief word or to the last word if all the words are equal in weight.

brother-in-law, brothers-in-law	actor-manager, actor-managers
aide-de-camp, aides-de-camp	tractor-trailer, tractor-trailers

6. Memorize the plural forms of nouns that diverge from these rules. Certain nouns have special plurals. Here are a few:

alumna, alumnae	half, halves	mouse, mice
alumnus, alumni	leaf, leaves	self, selves
child, children	man, men	tooth, teeth
goose, geese	medium, media	woman, women

Suffixes.   The *-s* added to a word to make it plural is one type of *suffix,* or tail section. Suffixes allow the same root word to do a variety of jobs, giving it different forms for different functions.

1. Drop a silent *e* before a suffix that begins with a vowel.

   move, mover, moved, moving   argue, arguer, argued, arguing

   EXCEPTION: If the *e* has an essential function, keep it before adding a suffix that begins with a vowel. In *singe,* for instance, the *e* changes the word's pronunciation from "sing" to "sinj." If you dropped the *e* in *singeing,* it would become *singing.*

   singe, singed, singeing   tiptoe, tiptoed, tiptoeing

2. Keep a silent *e* before a suffix that begins with a consonant.

   move, movement   hope, hopeless

   EXCEPTION: In a word ending in a silent *e* preceded by a vowel, sometimes (but not always) drop the *e*.

   argue, argument   true, truly

3. Change a final *y* to *i* before a suffix if the *y* follows a consonant but not if the *y* follows a vowel.

   cry, crier, cried   joy, joyous, joyful
   happy, happiest, happily   pray, prayed, prayer
   hurry, hurried

   EXCEPTION: Keep the *y* whenever the suffix is *-ing.*

   hurry, hurrying   pray, praying

   Drop a final *y* before the suffix *-ize.*

   deputy, deputize   memory, memorize

4. Double the final consonant of a one-syllable word before a suffix if (1) the suffix starts with a vowel *and* (2) the final consonant follows a single vowel.

   sit, sitter, sitting   rob, robbed, robbery

   Don't double the final consonant if it follows two vowels or another consonant.

   fail, failed, failure   stack, stacking, stackable

Don't double the final consonant if the suffix starts with a consonant.

    top, topless   cap, capful

5. Double the final consonant of a word with two or more syllables if (1) the suffix starts with a vowel *and* (2) the final consonant follows a single vowel *and* (3) the last syllable of the stem is accented once the suffix is added.

    commit, committed, committing   rebut, rebuttal
    regret, regretted, regrettable

Don't double the final consonant if it follows more than one vowel —

    avail, available   repeat, repeating

— or if it follows another consonant —

    accent, accented   depend, dependence

— or the suffix starts with a consonant —

    commit, commitment   jewel, jewelry

— or, when the suffix is added, the final syllable of the stem is unaccented.

    confer, conference (*but* conferred)   travel, traveler

■ For advice on using a hyphen with a prefix, see 32c and 32d.

Prefixes.   The main point to remember when writing a word with a *prefix* (or nose section) is that the prefix usually does not alter the spelling of the root word it precedes.

    dis + appear = disappear   mis + understand = misunderstand
    dis + satisfied = dissatisfied   with + hold = withhold
    mis + step = misstep   un + necessary = unnecessary

33b Develop spelling skills.

Besides becoming familiar with the rules in this chapter, you can use several other tactics to teach yourself to be a better speller.

    1. *Use mnemonic devices.* To make unusual spellings stick in your memory, invent associations. Using such mnemonic devices (tricks to aid memory) may help you with whatever troublesome spelling you are determined to remember. *Weird* behaves *weirdly*. Rise ag*ain*, Brit*ain*! One *d* in *dish,* one in *radish.* Why isn't *mathe*matics like *athle*tics? You write a *letter* on station*ery*. Any silly phrase or sentence will do, as long as it brings tricky spellings to mind.

    2. *Keep a record of words you misspell.* Buy yourself a little notebook in which to enter words that invariably trip you up. Each time you proofread a paper you have written and each time you receive one back from your instruc-

tor, write down any words you have misspelled. Then practice pronouncing, writing, and spelling them out loud until you have mastered them.

3. *Check any questionable spelling by referring to your dictionary.* Keep a dictionary at your elbow as you write. In matters of spelling, that good-as-gold book is your best friend. Use it to check words as you come up with them and to double-check them as you proofread and edit your work.

4. *Learn commonly misspelled words.* To save you the trouble of looking up every spelling bugbear, the "Quick Editing Guide" has a list of words frequently misspelled (see D2). This list will serve to review our whole discussion of spelling, for it contains the trickiest words we've mentioned. Checkmark those that give you trouble — but don't stop there. Spend a few minutes each day going over them. Pronounce each one carefully or have a friend read the list to you. Spell every troublesome word out loud; write it ten times. Your spelling will improve rapidly.

■ Exercise 33–1

Spelling

Edit the following passage to correct misspelled words.

> The rapid growth of teknology has begun to altar traditional practice in the music bizness.
>
> The rapid growth of *technology* has begun to *alter* traditional practice in the music *business*.

Technology that inables us to download and share music via the Internet has caused considirable controversy. Napster was once a popular online tool for sharing music files free of charge. Its extrordinary popularity caught the attention not just of growing numbers of music fans but of musiciens and recording industry executives who felt they were being cheated out of sales. Others, however, including some recording artists, argued that Napster and other file-sharing services didn't hurt musicians; in fact, they offered another distribution venu, one not controled by major labels. Nonetheless, in 1999 the Recording Industry Asociation of America (RIAA) sued Napster, and in 2001 a judge told the service to block all music files that violatted copyright. Just over a year later, Napster folded. It was later revived — some say in name only. Napster customers must now pay for each song they download. Meanwhile, the RIAA is going after other file-sharing services and has even sued people who use them, a practice some beleive is counterproductive.

■ For more practice, visit <bedfordstmartins.com/bedguide> and do a keyword search:

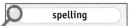
spelling

■ For helpful spelling lists, see D2 in the Quick Editing Guide (the dark-blue-edged pages).

Appendix
Quick Research Guide

When you begin college, you may feel awkward, uncertain about what to say and how to speak up. As you become a more experienced college student and writer, you will join the intellectual discussion around you by reading, thinking, and writing with sources. For many college papers, you will be expected to turn to sources such as articles, books, and Web sites for the evidence needed to support your thesis and develop your ideas about it. This expectation reflects the view that academic ideas develop through exchange: each writer reads and responds to the writing of others, building on earlier discussion while expanding the conversation.

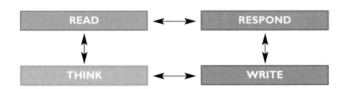

This Quick Research Guide is designed to help you succeed in several common research situations. Although conducting any research requires time to explore, to think, and to respond, efficient and purposeful research can produce greater success in less time than random searching or optimistic browsing. In addition, if you have been writing essays based on personal experience, you already are familiar with the processes involved in writing a paper that includes some research — you generate ideas, plan, draft, develop, revise, and edit.

Perhaps you are writing a paper based primarily on your own experience or observation, but you want to add a dash of supporting evidence from a source or two, using a simple research process, not a complicated one. Maybe you simply want a warm-up to build your confidence before you tackle an extensive research project. Sometimes you may need good

■ For more on writing processes, see Ch. 1, any chapter (4–11) in Part Two, or Chs. 15–19.

A-1

advice fast — perhaps because you've procrastinated, been overwhelmed by conflicting demands on your time, or feel uncertain about how to succeed as a college researcher.

To help you in all these cases, this Quick Research Guide concentrates on five key steps: defining your quest, searching for recommended sources, evaluating those you find, smoothly and gracefully adding evidence from them, and citing them correctly.

TURNING TO SOURCES FOR SUPPORTING EVIDENCE

| DEFINE YOUR QUEST | → | SEARCH | → | EVALUATE | → | ADD | → | CITE |

A *Defining Your Quest*

When your research goals are limited to finding only a few sources and using limited evidence from them, you're more likely to be successful if you try to define the hunt in advance considering questions such as these.

PURPOSE CHECKLIST

For more about stating and using a thesis, see pp. 271–77.

___ What is the thesis that you want to support or the point that you want to demonstrate?

___ Does the assignment require or suggest any specific research focus — certain kinds of supporting evidence, certain types of sources, or certain ways of presenting your material?

___ Which of your own ideas or opinions do you want to support with good evidence?

___ Which of your ideas might you want to check, clarify, or change based on your research?

___ Which ideas or opinions of others do you want to verify or counter?

___ Do you want to analyze material yourself (for example, comparing articles or Web sites taking different approaches), or do you want to find someone else's analysis?

For more about types of evidence, see pp. 35–37 and 145.

___ What kinds of evidence do you want to use — facts, statistics, or expert testimony? Do you also want to add your own first-hand observation of the situation or scene?

A1 Consider the criteria of writers and readers.

Although supporting evidence can come from many sources — your experience, observation, imagination, or interaction with others — college instructors often expect you to turn to the writings of others. In those books, articles, and reports, you can find pertinent examples, illustrations, details, and expert testimony — in short, reliable information that will show that your claims and statements are sound. That evidence should satisfy you as a writer and also meet the criteria of your college readers — your instructors and possibly your classmates.

For more about types of evidence, see pp. 36–38.

TWO VIEWS OF SUPPORTING EVIDENCE

COLLEGE WRITER	COLLEGE READER
• Does it support my thesis?	• Is it relevant to the purpose and assignment?
• Does it all seem accurate?	• Is it reliable, given academic standards?
• Is it from an up-to-date source?	• Is it current, given the standards of the field?
• Have I added enough?	• Is it of sufficient quantity, variety, and strength?
• Is it balanced and deep enough?	• Is it typical, fair, and complex?
• Will it persuade my audience?	• Does the writer make a credible case?

For evidence check-lists, see pp. 38–39 and pp. A-6–A-7.

A2 Decide what supporting evidence you need.

When you need to add muscle to your college papers, the right articles, reports, books, Web sites, and other resources can supply the facts, statistics, and expert testimony to back up your point. Sometimes you won't need comprehensive information about the topic, but you will want to hunt — quickly and efficiently — for exactly what you do need. Suppose, for example, that you are proposing solutions to your community's employment problem. Because you already have several ideas based on your first-hand observations and the experiences of people you know, your research goals are limited. First, you want to add accurate facts and figures that will show why you believe a compelling problem exists. Next, you want to visit the Web sites of local educational institutions and possibly locate someone to interview about existing career development programs.

WORKING THESIS

For the city of Aurora to achieve its full standing as one of Colorado's largest communities, many residents need more educational opportunities to improve their job skills and career alternatives.

Types of Evidence	Definition	Example	Source
Facts	Statements that can be verified objectively	When employment opportunities drop, college enrollments tend to go up because people are motivated to increase their skills.	Colorado Commission on Higher Education, "Governor's Task Force to Strengthen and Improve the Community College System: Final Report, April 5, 2004," page 16, at <www.state.co.us/cche>
Statistics	Facts stated in numbers	According to the U.S. Census Bureau, 85 percent of Aurora residents over age 25 have graduated from high school, 4.6% more than the national average. However, only 24.6% of this group have graduated from college, only 0.2% better than the 24.4% national average.	"Profile of Selected Social Characteristics: 2000" for Aurora, Colorado, and for United States, *U.S. Census Bureau Fact* at <http://factfinder.census.gov/home/saff/main.html?_lang=en>
Expert Testimony	Information from a knowledgeable person who has studied or gained experience about the topic	According to Daniela Higgins, director of the Center for Workforce Development, the Career Enrichment Program at Community College of Aurora wants to attract people looking for career advancement to improve their family resources.	"Program Provides Free College Education to People Who Need Improved Job Skills and Career Advancement," press release from Community College of Aurora at <www.ccaurora.edu/news/education.html>
Firsthand Observation	Your own unbiased, accurate eyewitness account	During my visit to Community College of Aurora to interview a workforce specialist, I observed campus publicity for programs in computer skills, paramedic and firefighter training, criminal justice, law enforcement, and early childhood education.	Your notes or your collection of campus materials

For more about these types of evidence, see pp. 35–37.

A3 **Decide where you need supporting evidence.**

Sometimes you will know exactly what your paper needs. In fact, as you plan or write a draft, you may tuck in notes to yourself—find this, look that up, add some numbers here. Other times, you may sense that your paper isn't as strong as you want it to be, but you may not know exactly what to add or where to add it. One way to determine where you need supporting evidence is to examine your draft, sentence by sentence.

- What does each sentence claim or promise to a reader?
- Where do you provide supporting evidence to demonstrate the claim or fulfill the promise?

The answers to these questions — your statements and your supporting evidence — often fall into a common alternating pattern:

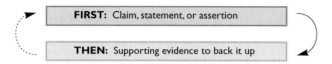

FIRST: Claim, statement, or assertion

THEN: Supporting evidence to back it up

When you spot a string of assertions in a passage without much support, you have found a place where you might need more evidence. Select your evidence carefully so that it substantiates the exact claim, statement, or assertion that precedes it.

When Carrie Williamson introduced the topic of her cause-and-effect paper, "Rainforest Destruction," she made a general statement and then supported it by quoting facts from a source. Then she repeated this statement-support pattern, backing up her next statement in turn. Using this pattern from the very beginning did more than support her opening statements; it also reassured her readers that she was a trustworthy writer who would try to supply convincing evidence throughout the rest of her paper.

■ For more about arguments based on claims of substantiation, evaluation, or policy, see pp. 141–42.

■ For the source entries from Carrie Williamson's list of works cited, see p. A-25.

The tropical rainforests are among the most biologically diverse communities in —⟍ Statement
the world. According to the Web site World Rainforest Information Portal, "more than
50 percent of all species live in tropical rainforests," and "a typical four-square-mile   ⟍ Evidence:
patch of rainforest contains up to 1,500 species of flowering plants, as many as   Statistics about species
750 tree species, 125 mammal species, 400 bird species, 100 reptile species, 60
amphibian species, and 150 butterfly species." These amazing communities that —⟍ Statement
depend on each part being intact in order to function properly and successfully are
being destroyed at an alarming rate. Each year "an area larger than Italy" (Soltani) ⟍ Evidence:
is destroyed. Many rainforest conservationists debate what the leading cause of   Facts about destruction
deforestation is. Regardless of which one is the major cause, the fact remains that ⟍ Statement identifying
both logging and slash-and-burn farming are destroying more and more acres of rain-   cause-and-effect debate
forests each year. ⟍ Statement previewing
                                                                      points to come

Besides checking for the statement-support pattern, consider your paper's overall purpose, organization, and line of reasoning. For example, evidence from sources may help you to define key terms, justify the significance of a problem or controversy, analyze causes or effects, compare similar problems or situations, back up your stand on an issue, support your solution to a problem, or interpret a literary work effectively.

The table on page A-6 shows some of the many ways this common statement-support pattern can be used.

■ For more about definition, see pp. 310–11. For more about comparing, explaining causes and effects, taking a stand, or proposing solutions, see Chs. 7–10. For more about literary analysis, see Ch. 12.

FIRST: CLAIM, STATEMENT, OR ASSERTION	THEN: POSSIBLE SUPPORTING EVIDENCE
Introduces a topic	Facts or statistics to justify the importance or significance of the topic
Describes a situation	Factual examples or illustrations to convey the reality or urgency of the situation
Introduces an event	Accurate firsthand observations to describe an event that you have witnessed
Presents a problem	Expert testimony or firsthand observation to establish the necessity or urgency of a solution
Explains an issue	Facts and details to clarify the significance of the issue
States your point	Facts, statistics, or examples to support your viewpoint or position
Interprets and prepares readers for evidence that follows	Facts, examples, observations, or research findings to define and develop your case
Concludes with your recommendation or evaluation	Facts, examples, or expert testimony to persuade readers to accept your conclusion

Use the following checklist to help you decide whether — and where — you might need supporting evidence from sources.

EVIDENCE CHECKLIST

___ What does your thesis statement promise that you'll deliver? What additional evidence would ensure that you effectively demonstrate your thesis?

___ Are your claims, statements, and assertions backed up with supporting evidence? If not, what evidence might you add?

___ What evidence would most effectively persuade your readers?

___ What criteria for useful evidence are most important to your readers? What evidence would best meet these criteria?

___ When you read through your paper, which parts sound weak or incomplete to you?

___ What facts or statistics would clarify your topic?

___ What examples or illustrations would make the background or the current circumstances clearer and more compelling for readers?

___ What does a reliable expert say about your topic or the situation that it involves?

___ What firsthand observation would add authenticity?

___ Where have peer editors suggested adding more evidence or stronger evidence?

B *Searching for Recommended Sources*

Even researchers who need specific evidence from only a source or two may turn first to the nearly limitless resources of the Internet. In this vast, disorganized arena, many resources are very reliable, but many are not because they reflect the quirks of an individual, the collective intuition of a group of like-minded people, the marketing savvy of a profit-driven business, or the beliefs of an advocate who acknowledges only part of a story. Although such sites may supply useful information, they require you to do extra work — checking all the information presented as fact, looking for biases or financial motives, and searching for what's not stated rather than simply accepting what is. When you need to conduct an efficient search, quick and focused, try to begin instead with reliable sources, already screened and recommended by professionals.

B1 Seek advice about reliable sources.

Although popular search engines can turn up sources on nearly any topic, you always need to ask whether those sources meet your criteria and your readers'. After all, your challenge is not simply to find any sources but to find solid sources with the reliable evidence you need for a college paper. Very often your instructors will help to guide your search by specifying their requirements or general expectations. In addition, the following short-cuts can help you find solid sources fast — ideally already screened, selected, and organized for you.

RESOURCE CHECKLIST

___ Has your instructor suggested to the class where you might begin? Have you talked with your instructor after class or during office hours or e-mailed to ask for specific advice about resources for your topic? Have you checked the assignment sheet, syllabus, handouts, or class Web site?

___ Have your classmates recommended useful academic databases, disciplinary Web sites, or similar resources to the class as a whole or to your writing group?

___ Does the department offering the course have a Web site with lists of resources available at the library or links to sites well regarded in that field?

___ Does your textbook Web site provide links to additional resources or information?

___ Which library databases does the librarian at the reference desk recommend for your course level and your topic?

___ Which databases or links on your campus library's Web site lead to government (federal, state, or local) resources or to articles in journals and newspapers?

___ Which resources are available on library terminals, in the new periodicals room, or in the reference area of your college library?

B2 Select reliable sources that meet your readers' criteria.

If you planned to survey common Internet hoaxes for a paper about online practices, you might deliberately turn to sources that are, by definition, unreliable. However, investigating such sources is very different from accepting and repeating their phony claims as if they were accurate supporting evidence. Generally you want to turn right away to sources that are reliable. The charts on pages A-10–A-11 explain how to recognize different types of sources, gauge their currency, and select those appropriate for a given topic or assignment.

Each type of source analyzed in these charts might be credible and useful for a paper. For certain assignments, you might be expected to use sources as varied as reports from journalists, advice from practitioners in the field, accounts of historical eyewitnesses, or opinions on civic policy. However, college instructors often expect you to turn not to popular sources but to scholarly ones — also identified as peer-reviewed or refereed sources — with characteristics such as these:

- in-depth investigation or interpretation of an academic topic or research problem
- discussion of previous studies, which are cited in the text and listed at the end for easy reference by readers
- use of research methods accepted across several fields or within a discipline
- publication by a reputable company or sponsoring organization
- acceptance for publication based on reviews by experts (peer reviewers) who assess the quality of the study
- preparation for publication supervised by academic or expert editors or by authors and professional staff

Your instructors may be more confident of the standards and quality controls of established publications, appearing in print or in simultaneous print and online versions, than of the procedures of newer or unfamiliar electronic sources. Your campus librarian can help you limit your searches to peer-reviewed journals or to check the scholarly reputation of sources that you find.

C *Evaluating Possible Sources*

You may dream that your research will instantly turn up the perfect source. Like the perfect wave, the perfect snowy slope, or the perfect day, such a source is likely to be hard to come by. After all, by what standards will you judge perfection? And what are the odds that you will find such perfection ever, much less during your limited research schedule? Instead of looking for perfect sources, most college researchers evaluate sources on the basis of their own practical needs, the standards of their readers, and the shared concern of writers and readers for reliable, appropriate evidence.

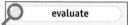 For exercises on evaluating Web sources in particular, visit <bedfordstmartins.com/bedguide> and do a keyword search:

> evaluate

C1 Evaluate sources in terms of your practical needs as a researcher.

Your situation as a writer may determine how long or how widely you can search for what you need or how deeply you can delve into the sources you find. For example, if you are worried about finishing your paper on time or about juggling several assignments at once, you will need to search efficiently, evaluating sources first in terms of your own practical criteria.

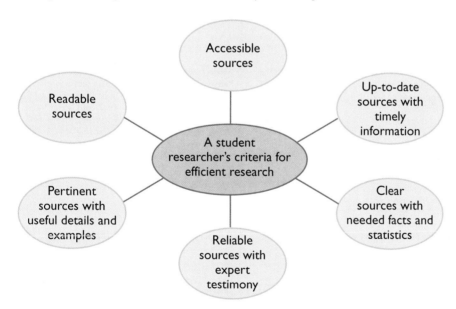

C2 Evaluate sources in terms of the expectations of your readers.

You will want to consider what your readers expect of the sources you select and the way that you use them. If you are uncertain about college requirements, you will want to find reliable sources that are easily accessible, readable,

Understanding Print Sources and Their Applications	Likely Appearance	Typical Publication Time Frame	Examples	Best For
Scholarly Book	In-depth discussion, often hardbound with a plain cover, that presents research findings, references, and few, if any, illustrations to an academic audience	Months or years, probably following months or years for research and writing	*Improving Classroom Testing, The Information Society: A Skeptical View, The Psychology of Aggression, Theodore Roosevelt and His Times*	In-depth analysis and research into established academic topics
Popular Nonfiction Book	Trendy or topical hardbound or paperback publication, often with an eye-catching cover, that conveys information, advice, or instructions to general readers	Months or years, possibly following months or years for writing	*Dude, Where's My Country?, Ten Minutes from Normal, General Ike, A Short History of Nearly Everything*	Overview of current trends or issues, informative advice, personal experience, or life story
Scholarly Journal	Quarterly or monthly text-heavy publication, often sponsored by a scholarly group, with prominent table of contents listing long articles directed to specialists	Months (or longer), probably following months or years of research and writing	*American Economic Review, Journal of the American Medical Association (JAMA), PMLA (Publications of the Modern Language Association), Science and Technology Review*	In-depth, up-to-date research on discipline-specific topics
News Magazine	Weekly or monthly publication with color cover, photographs, and short articles (sometimes collaborative) on news stories, current events, and societal trends	Days or weeks, following current or long-term investigation	*Time, Newsweek, U.S. News & World Report*	The latest news on topics of regional, national, or international significance
Popular Magazine	Colorful weekly, biweekly, or monthly publication with attention-grabbing cover, sidebars, photographs, and articles on its special interest	Days, weeks, or months, following immediate or long-term development	Range from *Atlantic Monthly, National Geographic, Psychology Today,* and *Smithsonian* to *People, Redbook,* and *US* (serious topics and in-depth stories to hobbies or celebrities)	Current information on popular issues or trends and subjects that interest readers
Newspaper	Daily, weekly, or monthly publication with oversized pages, headlines, columns, photographs, graphics, and stories on current news and timely issues	Days or weeks, following current or long-term investigation	*New York Times, Washington Post, Wall Street Journal, Chronicle of Higher Education,* your local or regional newspaper	The latest news and opinions on topics of local, regional, state, national, or international significance
Pamphlet or Booklet	Brief paperbound publications, appearing irregularly, individually, or in a series, often sponsored by a scholarly, civic, business, government, or other group or agency	Days or months, following development of material	*GE Annual Report, The Unicorn Tapestries, Children of John and Sophia Walz, Medical History of Washington County with Some Personal Recollections*	In-depth coverage of specific topics, viewpoints, advice, or recollections of groups or individuals
Reference Work	Book or multivolume encyclopedia, handbook, dictionary, directory, almanac, atlas, fact book, or other informative guide, usually in library's reference area	Months or years, probably following months or years for research and writing	*Encyclopedia of the Harlem Renaissance, Biographical Dictionary of Hispanic Americans, Oxford Dictionary of Literary Quotations, Facts on File, Atlas of World Cultures*	Concise background explanations, definitions, facts, statistics, biographies, and other specifics

Understanding Electronic Sources and Their Applications	Likely Appearance	Typical Publication Time Frame	Examples	Best For
Online Reference Site	Prominent search box, search options for fields or topics, links to specialized gateways or resources	Immediate, daily, or regular updates	*Infomine* at <http://infomine.ucr.edu>, *Internet Public Library* at <www.ipl.org>, *Librarians' Index to the Internet* at <www.ipl.org>, *WWW Virtual Library* at <http://lii.org>, *Teoma* at <www.teoma.com>	Quick access to prescreened resources and links for researchers
Gateway Site for a Topic or Field	Prominent focus on discipline or topic with search or category options	Regular or irregular updates, depending on sponsor or Webmaster	*The American Civil War Homepage* at <http://sunsite.utk.edu/civilwar>, *William Faulkner on the Web* at <www.mcsr.ole-miss.edu/~egjbp/faulkner/faulkner.html>	Quick access to prescreened resources and links on specific subjects
Online Document Collection	List of available documents, groups of documents, or search options such as author or title	Regular or irregular updates, depending on materials or Webmaster	*Bartleby* at <http://bartleby.com>, *Project Gutenberg* at <http://gutenberg.org>, *American Memory* at <http://memory.loc.gov>	Easy access to large collections of texts
Professional Web Site	Conspicuous promotion of sponsor such as scholarly or field group, nonprofit agency, corporation, or foundation (.org, .net, or .com)	Regular or irregular updates, depending on sponsor	American Educational Research Association at <www.aera.net>, Better Business Bureau at <http://bbb.org>, MetLife Foundation, search at <www.metlife.com>	Resources or specialized materials related to sponsor's interests
Academic Web Site	Attractive presentation of institution (.edu) and its academic and other units	Regular or irregular updates, depending on academic or other unit maintaining page	College Web sites such as your campus site, library home page, or department or course page	Disciplinary and cross-disciplinary resources from campus units
Government Web Site	Prominent focus on federal, state, local, or other agencies (.gov), often with links and a search box	Regular or irregular updates, depending on government agency	Government gateways at <www.first.gov>, agencies such as the Census Bureau at <http://factfinder.census.gov> or Environmental Protection Agency at <www.epa.gov>	Topic-specific statistics, reports, information about legislation and policies, consumer publications
Online Newspaper or News Service	Banner headline of news organization with breaking news, section options, and archives	Immediate updates as events occur along with archives of past coverage	Online *New York Times, Washington Post, Wall Street Journal,* or local newspapers	The latest national or international news and views
Interest-Group or Personal Web Site	Logo or banner for partisan or special-interest group, discussion group, or individual pages or blogs (Web logs)	Regular or irregular updates, depending on individual or group	Democracy for America at <www.blogforamerica.com>, Texas Young Republican Federation at <www.tyrf.org>, ArtsJournal Blog Central at <www.artsjournal.com>	Wide range of views, resources, opinions, and counterarguments which require evaluation of bias

and up-to-date — and chock full of the reliable facts, statistics, research findings, case studies, observations, examples, illustrations, and expert testimony that will persuade your readers.

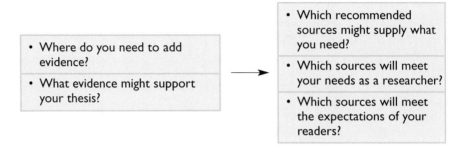

- Where do you need to add evidence?
- What evidence might support your thesis?

- Which recommended sources might supply what you need?
- Which sources will meet your needs as a researcher?
- Which sources will meet the expectations of your readers?

C3   Evaluate sources for reliable and appropriate evidence.

When you use evidence from sources to support the points that you make in college papers, both you and your readers are likely to hold two simple expectations:

- that your sources are reliable so that you can trust their information
- that the information you select from them is appropriate for your paper

After all, how could an unreliable source successfully support your ideas? And what could unsuitable or mismatched information contribute to your paper? The difficult task, of course, is learning how to judge what is reliable and appropriate. The following checklist suggests how you can use the time-tested journalist's questions — who, what, when, where, why, and how — to evaluate each print or electronic source that you consider using.

EVALUATION CHECKLIST

Who?

___ Who is the publisher of the source or the sponsor of the site? Is it a corporation, a scholarly organization, a professional association, a government agency, or an issue-oriented group? Have you heard of this publisher or sponsor before? Is it well regarded? Does it seem reputable and responsible? Is it considered academic or popular?

___ Who is the author of the source? What are the author's credentials and profession?

___ Who is the intended audience of the source? Experts in the field? Professionals? General readers? People with a special interest?

___ Who has reviewed the source prior to publication? Only the author? Peer reviewers who are experts in the area? An editorial staff?

What?

—— What is the purpose of the publication or Web site? Is it to sell a product or service? To entertain? To supply information? To publish new research? To shape opinion about an issue or cause?

—— What bias or point of view might affect the reliability of the source?

—— What kind of information does the source supply? Is it a primary source (a firsthand account) or a secondary source (an analysis of primary material)?

—— What evidence does the source present? Does it seem trustworthy, sufficient, and relevant given what you know about the subject? Does its argument or analysis seem logical and complete, or does it leave many questions unanswered? Does it identify its sources? If it is electronic, does it supply appropriate, active links?

When?

—— When was the source published or created?

—— When was it last revised or updated? Is its information up-to-date?

Where?

—— Where have you found the source? Is it a pre-screened source available through your campus library? Is it a Web site that popped up during a general search?

—— Where has the source been recommended? On an instructor's syllabus or Web page? On a library list? In another reliable source? During a conference with an instructor or librarian?

Why?

—— Why should you use this source rather than others?

—— Why is its information directly relevant to your research question?

How?

—— How does the selection of evidence in the source reflect the interests and expertise of its author, publisher or sponsor, and intended audience? How might you need to qualify its use in your paper?

—— How would its information add to your paper? How would it support your thesis and provide compelling evidence to persuade your readers?

D   *Adding Supporting Evidence to Your Writing*

■ For exercises on supporting a thesis statement, visit <bedfordstmartins.com/bedguide> and do a keyword search:

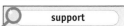

support

Sometimes researchers concentrate so hard on hunting for reliable sources that they forget what comes next. The value of every source remains potential until you successfully capture its facts, statistics, expert testimony, examples, or other information in a form that you can incorporate into your paper. In addition, you must accurately credit, both in the text of your paper and in a final list of sources, each source whose words or ideas you use. (Follow the advice of the Modern Language Association, supplied here, or whatever other system your instructor requires.) When you add source information skillfully and credit each source conscientiously, your research will probably accomplish its purpose: supporting your thesis so that your paper satisfies you and meets your readers' standards.

D1 Avoid plagiarism.

■ For exercises on incorporating source material and avoiding plagiarism, visit <bedfordstmartins.com/ bedguide> and do a keyword search:

 sources

Be sure to allow enough time to add information from sources skillfully and correctly. Find out exactly how your instructor expects you to credit sources. Even if you do not intend to plagiarize—to use another writer's words or ideas without appropriately crediting them—a paper full of sloppy or careless short-cuts can look just like a paper deliberately copied from unacknowledged sources. Instead, borrow carefully and honestly, fully acknowledging your debt to writers from whom you borrow anything.

Identify the source of information, an idea, a summary, a paraphrase, or a quotation right away, as soon as you write it in your notes. Carry that acknowledgment into your first draft and all that follow. You generally do not need to identify a source if you use what is called "common knowledge"—quotations, expressions, or information widely known and widely accepted. If you are uncertain about whether you need to cite a source, ask your instructor, or simply provide the citation.

The following chart reviews accepted methods of adding source material and identifies good research practices. These practices will help prevent common errors that may call into question your integrity or your attentiveness as a research writer.

ACCEPTED METHODS OF ADDING AND CREDITING SOURCE MATERIAL	OBJECTIVES OF METHOD	GOOD PRACTICES TO AVOID ERRORS
Quotation	Select and identify the exact words of a source in order to add its memorable, authoritative, or incisive wording to your paper.	• Supply complete identification of the source. • Provide page number locating the quotation in the source. • Use both opening and closing quotation marks. • Repeat the exact words of the source or properly indicate changes.
Paraphrase	Restate the detailed ideas of a source in your own words, with credit to the original source, in order to present and explain fully the content of a passage.	• Read carefully so that you can paraphrase accurately without distorting the source. • Supply complete identification of the source. • Provide page number locating the original passage in the source.

ACCEPTED METHODS OF ADDING AND CREDITING SOURCE MATERIAL	OBJECTIVES OF METHOD	GOOD PRACTICES TO AVOID ERRORS
Paraphrase (continued)		• Rephrase or add quotation marks to identify words from the source that slip into your paraphrase. • Apart from brief quotations, use your own words and sentences to avoid following the pattern, sequence, or wording of the original. • Clearly distinguish between the paraphrase and your own ideas to avoid confusing switches.
Summary	Very briefly express the main point of a source or passage in your own words, with credit to the original source, in order to convey its general ideas or conclusion in your paper.	• Read carefully so that you can summarize accurately without distorting the source. • Supply complete identification of the source. • Rephrase or add quotation marks to words from the source that slip into your summary. • Give specific credit to the source for ideas that you include in your discussion. • Clearly distinguish between the summary and your own ideas to avoid confusing switches.
In-Text Citation	Credit each quotation, paraphrase, summary, or other reference to a source in short form by giving the author's last name right in the paper or with the page number in parentheses (MLA style).	• Supply consistent citations without forgetting or carelessly omitting sources. • Spell names of authors and titles correctly. • Provide accurate page references.
Concluding List of Works Cited	Credit each source cited in the text with a corresponding full entry in an alphabetical list at the end of the paper.	• Provide consistent entries without forgetting or carelessly omitting sources. • Match each source citation in the text with an entry in the final list. • Supply every detail expected in an entry, even if you must return to the library to complete your source notes. • Follow the exact sequence, capitalization, punctuation, indentation pattern, and other details required by MLA or another style. • Check that each entry in your final list appears in alphabetical order.

D2   Read your source critically.

For more on critical reading, see pp. 19–22. For more on evaluating evidence, see pp. 38–39. For more on logical fallacies, see pp. 149–50.

Before you pop any outside material into your paper, read critically to evaluate the reliability and suitability of the source. If you cannot understand a complicated source that requires specialized background, don't use it in your paper. If its ideas, facts, claims, or viewpoint seem unusual, incorporate only what you can substantiate in other unrelated sources. On the other hand, if its evidence seems accurate, logical, and relevant, consider exactly how you might want to add it to your paper — by quoting, paraphrasing, or summarizing.

D3   Quote accurately.

For sample quotations, paraphrases, and summaries, see p. A-19.

For more on punctuating quotations and using ellipsis marks, see C3 in the Quick Editing Guide (the dark-blue-edged pages).

When an author expresses an idea so memorably that you want to reproduce those words exactly, quote them word for word. Direct quotations can add life, color, and authority. Be sure to quote exactly, including punctuation and capitalization. Use an ellipsis mark — three dots (. . .) mid-sentence or four dots (. . . .) counting the period concluding a sentence — to show where you leave out any original wording.

Select what you quote carefully; leave out wording that doesn't relate to your point, but don't distort the original meaning. For example, if a reviewer calls a movie "a perfect example of poor directing and inept acting," you can't quote this comment as "perfect . . . directing and . . . acting." Limit your direct quotations to compelling selections; after all, a quotation in itself is not necessarily effective evidence, and too many quotations will suggest that your writing is padded or lacks original thought.

QUOTATION CHECKLIST

___ Have you quoted only a notable passage that adds support and authority to your discussion?

___ Have you checked your quotation to be sure that it repeats your source word for word?

___ Have you marked the beginning and the ending of the quotation with quotation marks?

___ Have you used ellipses (. . .) to mark any spot where you have left out words in the original?

___ Have you identified the source of the quotation in a launch statement (see p. A-18) or in parentheses?

___ Have you specified in parentheses the page number where the quotation appears in the source?

D4   Paraphrase carefully.

For sample quotations, paraphrases, and summaries, see p. A-19.

Paraphrasing involves restating an author's ideas in your own language. A paraphrase is generally about the same length as the original; it expresses the ideas and emphasis of the original using your words and sentences. Besides avoiding plagiarism, a fresh and creative paraphrase expresses your own style without awkwardly jumping between it and your source's style.

Be careful to avoid slipping in the author's words or shadowing the original sentence structures too closely. If a source says, "President Wilson called an emergency meeting of his cabinet to discuss the new crisis," and you say, "The president called his cabinet to hold an emergency meeting to discuss the new crisis," your words are too close to those of the source. One option is to quote the original, though it doesn't seem worth quoting word for word in this case. Or, better, you could write: "Summoning his cabinet to an emergency session, Wilson laid out the challenge before them."

PARAPHRASE CHECKLIST

— Have you read the passage critically to be sure that you fully understand it?

— Have you paraphrased accurately, reflecting both the main points and the supporting details in the original?

— Does your paraphrase use your own words without repeating or echoing the words or the sentence structure of the original?

— Does your paraphrase stick to the ideas of the original without tucking in your own thoughts?

— Have you reread and revised your paraphrase so that it reads smoothly and clearly?

— Have you identified the source of the paraphrase in a launch statement (see p. A-18) or in parentheses?

— Have you specified in parentheses the page number where the passage appears in the source?

D5   Summarize fairly.

Summarizing is a useful way of incorporating the general point of a whole paragraph or section of a work. You briefly state the main sense of the original in your own words and tell where you got the idea. A summary is generally much shorter than the original; it expresses only the most important ideas — the essence — of the original.

For sample quotations, paraphrases, and summaries, see p. A-19.

SUMMARY CHECKLIST

— Have you fairly stated the author's thesis, or main point, in your own words in a sentence or two?

— Have you briefly stated any supporting ideas that you wish to summarize?

— Have you stuck to the overall point without getting bogged down in details or examples?

— Has your summary remained respectful of the ideas and opinions of others, even if you disagree with them?

— Have you reread and revised your summary so that it reads smoothly and clearly?

___ Have you identified the source of the summary in a launch statement (see D6) or in parentheses?

___ Have you specified in parentheses the page number where any specific passage appears in the source?

D6   Launch, capture, and cite each quotation, paraphrase, and summary.

Instead of dropping ideas from sources into your paper as if they had just arrived by flying saucer, weave them in so that they effectively support the point you want to make. As you integrate each idea from a source, take three steps.

1. **Launch** each quotation, paraphrase, summary, or other reference to a source with an introduction that tells readers who wrote it or why it's in your paper. College instructors are likely to favor launch statements that comment on the source, connect it to the paper's thesis, or relate it to other sources. Use strategies such as these:

- Identify the name of the author in the sentence that introduces the source:

  As Wood explains, the goal of American education continues to fluctuate between gaining knowledge and applying it (58).

- Add the author's name in the middle of the source material:

  In *Romeo and Juliet,* "That which we call a rose," Shakespeare claims, "By any other word would smell as sweet" (2.2.43–44).

- Name the author only in the parenthetical source citation if you want to keep your focus on the topic:

  A second march on Washington followed the first (Whitlock 83).

- Explain for the reader why you have selected and included the material.

- Interpret what you see as the point or relevance of the material.

- Relate the source clearly to the paper's thesis or to the specific point it supports.

- Compare or contrast the point of view or evidence of one source with that of another source.

- Supply transitions to connect several sources mentioned in a sentence or paragraph.

- Vary your introductory language (*says, claims, observes, emphasizes, studies, analyzes, interprets*) to portray accurately the contribution of the source.

For more on punctuating quotations and using ellipsis marks, see C3 in the Quick Editing Guide (the dark-blue-edged pages).

- Lead smoothly from your launch statement into the source material instead of tossing a stand-alone quotation into your paragraph without any introduction.

Sample Paraphrase, Quotations, and Summary

PASSAGE FROM ORIGINAL SOURCE

Obesity is a major issue because (1) vast numbers of people are affected; (2) the prevalence is growing; (3) rates are increasing in children; (4) the medical, psychological, and social effects are severe; (5) the behaviors that cause it (poor diet and inactivity) are themselves major contributors to ill health; and (6) treatment is expensive, rarely effective, and impractical to use on a large scale.

SAMPLE PARAPHRASE

The current concern with increasing American weight has developed for half a dozen reasons, according to Brownell and Horgen. They attribute the shift in awareness to the number of obese people and the increase in this number, especially among youngsters. In addition, excess weight carries harsh consequences for individual physical and mental health and for society's welfare. Lack of exercise and unhealthy food choices increase the health consequences, especially because there's no cheap and easy cure for the consequences of eating too much and exercising too little (51).

PASSAGE FROM ORIGINAL SOURCE

Biology and environment conspire to promote obesity. Biology is an enabling factor, but the obesity epidemic, and the consequent human tragedy, is a function of the worsening food and physical activity environment. Governments and societies have come to this conclusion very late. There is much catching up to do.

SAMPLE QUOTATIONS

Although human biology has contributed to the pudgy American society, everyone now faces the powerful challenge of a "worsening food and physical activity environment" (Brownell and Horgen 51).

As Brownell and Horgen conclude, "There is much catching up to do" (51).

SAMPLE SUMMARY

After outlining six reasons why obesity is a critical issue, Brownell and Horgen urge Americans to eat less and become more active (51).

WORKS CITED ENTRY

Brownell, Kelly D., and Katherine Battle Horgen. Food Fight: The Inside Story of the Food Industry, America's Obesity Crisis, and What We Can Do about It. Chicago: Contemporary-McGraw, 2004.

■ For more examples showing how to cite and list sources in your paper, see Section E.

2. **Capture** the source material itself.

- Quote compelling words, phrases, or sentences exactly.
- Paraphrase the connections and details by explaining them in your own words.
- Summarize to convey the gist, essence, or main sense.
- Relate sources by identifying their similarities, differences, and other relationships.

3. **Cite** each source accurately.

For sample citations, see E1.

- Name the author in parentheses (unless already named in your launch statement).
- Add the page number to locate the original passage.
- If a source has no author, begin the citation with the first words of the title.

E   *Citing and Listing Sources in MLA Style*

For exercises on citing and listing sources in MLA style, visit <bedfordstmartins.com/bedguide> and do a keyword search:

In MLA style (the format recommended by the Modern Language Association and often required in English classes), your sources need to be identified twice in your paper: first, briefly, at the very moment you draw upon the source material and later, in full, at the end of your paper. The short reference includes the name of the author of the source (or a short form of the title if the source does not name an author), so it's easy for a reader to connect that short entry in your text with the related full entry in the final alphabetical list. Because instructors expect source references to be formatted carefully, follow any directions supplied, or refer to the style manual assigned in the field.

E1   Cite sources in your text.

Right in the text, at the moment you add a quotation, a paraphrase, or a summary, you need to identify the source. Your citation generally follows a simple pattern: name the author, and note the page in the original where the material is located.

(Last Name of Author ##)   (Talia 35)   (Smitt and Gilbert 152–53)

Place this citation immediately after a direct quotation or paraphrase.

> When "The Lottery" begins, the reader thinks of the "great pile of stones" (Jackson 191) as children's entertainment.

When the author is named in your launch statement, the citation can be even simpler.

> According to Hunt, the city faced "deficits and drought" (54) for ten more years.

For quotations from poems, plays, or novels, supply line, act and scene, or chapter numbers rather than page numbers.

> The speaker in Robinson's poem describes Richard Cory as "richer than a king" (line 9), an attractive man who "fluttered pulses when he said,/ 'Good-morning'" (7–8).

If you use only one source in your paper, identify it at the beginning of your essay. Then just give page or line numbers in parentheses after each quotation or paraphrase.

Use the following checklist to improve your source citations.

CITATION CHECKLIST

___ Have you placed your citation right after your quotation, paraphrase, or summary?

___ Have you enclosed your citation with a pair of parenthesis marks?

___ Have you provided the last name of the author either in your launch statement or in your citation?

___ Have you used the title for a work without an identified author?

___ Have you added the exact page, as numbered in the source, or another location number (such as a Web paragraph, poetry line, novel chapter, or play act and scene) to identify where the source material appears?

E2 List sources at the end.

At the end of your paper, add a list of your sources called "Works Cited." For each source mentioned in the text, supply a corresponding full entry. Use this checklist to improve the accuracy of your entries.

WORKS CITED CHECKLIST

___ Have you figured out what type of source you have used? Have you followed the sample pattern for that type as exactly as possible?

___ Have you used quotation marks and underlining correctly for titles?

___ Have you used correct punctuation — periods, commas, colons, parentheses — in your entry?

___ Have you checked the accuracy of the numbers in your entry—pages, volume, and dates?

___ Have you accurately recorded the name of the author, title, publisher, and so on?

— Have you correctly typed the address of an electronic source (or supplied a simpler address for the source's search page)?

— Have you correctly arranged your entries in alphabetical order?

— Have you checked your final list against your text citations so that every source appears in both places?

The secret to figuring out what to include in a Works Cited entry generally comes down to this question about your source: What is it? Once you identify the type of source you have used, you can find a general pattern for it in this book or in your style guide. Then, using this pattern, you can examine the title page or other parts of your source to find the details needed to complete the pattern, as the following examples illustrate.

Title of book

WIN-WIN ECOLOGY

How the Earth's Species Can Survive in the Midst of Human Enterprise

MICHAEL L. ROSENZWEIG

Name of author

Name of publisher

OXFORD
UNIVERSITY PRESS

2003 ——— Year of publication

OXFORD
UNIVERSITY PRESS

Oxford   New York
Athens   Auckland   Bangkok   Buenos Aires   Cape Town   Chennai
Dar es Salaam   Delhi   Hong Kong   Istanbul   Karachi   Kolkata
Kuala Lumpur   Madrid   Melbourne   Mexico City   Mumbai   Nairobi
São Paulo   Shanghai   Taipei   Tokyo   Toronto

Year of publication ——— Copyright © 2003 by Michael Rosenzweig

Published by Oxford University Press, Inc.
198 Madison Avenue, New York, New York 10016   Place of publication

www.oup.com

Oxford is a registered trademark of Oxford University Press

All rights reserved. No part of this publication
may be reproduced, stored in a retrieval system, or transmitted,
in any form or by any means, electronic, mechanical,
photocopying, recording, or otherwise, without the prior
permission of Oxford University Press.

Library of Congress Cataloging-in-Publication Data
Rosenzweig, Michael L.
Win-win ecology : how the earth's species can survive in
the midst of human enterprise / Michael L. Rosenzweig
p. cm.
Includes bibliographical references (p.).
ISBN 0-19-515604-8
1. Nature conservation—Economic aspects.
2. Biological diversity conservation—Economic aspects.
3. Human ecology.
I. Title.
QH75 .R69 2003
333.95'16—dc 21   2002029281

1 3 5 7 9 8 6 4 2
Printed in the United States of America
on recycled, acid-free paper.

BOOK

TEXT CITATION

(Rosenzweig 7)

WORKS CITED ENTRY

Author's name   Period   Title of book, underlined

Rosenzweig, Michael L. Win-Win Ecology: How the Earth's Species Can Survive in the

Midst of Human Enterprise. New York: Oxford UP, 2003.

Period   City of   Publisher Year of Period
publication (shortened publication
name)

> ■ If you need to find formats for other types of sources, consult the current *MLA Handbook for Writers of Research Papers*, often available in the library, or check your research manual or research guide for more information.

ESSAY, STORY, OR POEM FROM A BOOK

Turn to the title page of this book and the reading selection on page 427 to find the details needed for this entry.

TEXT CITATION

(Brady 428)

WORKS CITED ENTRY

Author of   Title of selection,   Title of book or   Authors or editors
selection   in quotation marks   anthology, underlined   of book

Brady, Judy. "I Want a Wife." The Bedford Guide for College Writers. 7th ed.

    Ed. X. J. Kennedy, Dorothy M. Kennedy, Marcia F. Muth, and Sylvia A. Holladay.

    Boston: Bedford/St. Martin's, 2005. 427-29.

   City of   Publisher of book   Year of   Page numbers
publication   publication of the selection

POPULAR MAGAZINE ARTICLE

The author's name and the title generally appear at the beginning of an article. Typically, the magazine name, the date, and page numbers appear at the bottom of pages (see the *Forbes* and *Parenting* samples on p. 346).

TEXT CITATION

(Kluger 56)

WORKS CITED ENTRY

Author's name   Title of article,   Title of magazine,
           in quotation marks   underlined

Kluger, Jeffrey. "Just Too Loud." Time 5 Apr. 2004: 54-56.

                    Date of publication   Page numbers of the article

Title of journal

Volume number

Title of journal article

Number of first page of article

Year of publication

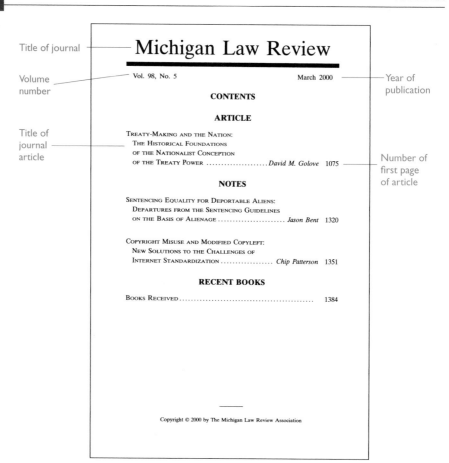

Michigan Law Review

Vol. 98, No. 5   March 2000

CONTENTS

ARTICLE

TREATY-MAKING AND THE NATION:
THE HISTORICAL FOUNDATIONS
OF THE NATIONALIST CONCEPTION
OF THE TREATY POWER .... *David M. Golove* 1075

NOTES

SENTENCING EQUALITY FOR DEPORTABLE ALIENS:
DEPARTURES FROM THE SENTENCING GUIDELINES
ON THE BASIS OF ALIENAGE .... *Jason Bent* 1320

COPYRIGHT MISUSE AND MODIFIED COPYLEFT:
NEW SOLUTIONS TO THE CHALLENGES OF
INTERNET STANDARDIZATION .... *Chip Patterson* 1351

RECENT BOOKS

BOOKS RECEIVED 1384

Copyright © 2000 by The Michigan Law Review Association

SCHOLARLY JOURNAL ARTICLE

If each issue of a journal begins with page 1, add the issue number after the volume: 98.5.

TEXT CITATION

(Golove 1077)

WORKS CITED ENTRY

Author's name

Title of journal article in quotation marks

Golove, David M. "Treaty-Making and the Nation: The Historical Foundations of the
Nationalist Conception of the Treaty Power." <u>Michigan Law Review</u> 98 (2000):
1075-1319.

Page numbers of the article

Title of journal, underlined

Volume number

Year

Colon

ARTICLE FROM A LIBRARY DATABASE

For databases like InfoTrac, the full publication information for the print source often appears at the top of the online entry. A printout of the article usually will record this information as well as your date of access and any URL provided. Note that the first page number of the print source can be followed by a hyphen if the full page range is not known.

TEXT CITATION

The page number is not included because it is not available in the online version.

See p. A-5 for the text reference from Carrie Williamson's paper.

(Soltani)

WORKS CITED ENTRY

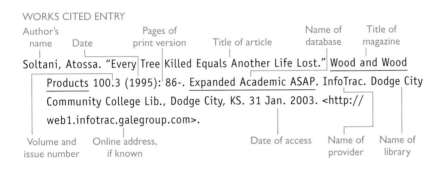

PAGE FROM A WEB SITE

The page title and site title often appear at the top of a given page. The date when a site was posted or last updated often appears at the bottom, as does the name of the sponsor. (However, sponsor information may appear as a link.) A print-out of the page will record this information as well as the date of access and URL. Note that the URL appears in the address bar of the Internet browser, as the Web pages on pp. 359 and 363 illustrate.

TEXT CITATION

The site is identified by title because it does not name an author. The page number is not included because it is not available for the Web page.

See p. A-5 for the text reference from Carrie Williamson's paper.

According to the Web site World Rainforest Information Portal, . . .

WORKS CITED ENTRY

Appendix
Quick Editing Guide

Editing and proofreading are needed at the end of the writing process because writers — *all* writers — find it difficult to write error-free sentences the very first time they try. Sometimes as a writer you pay more attention to

WRITING WITH A COMPUTER

Computers can help you edit in several ways. Grammar checkers will catch some errors, but not others. For this reason, you always need to consider the grammar checker's suggestions carefully before accepting them.

- A grammar checker cannot always correctly identify the subject or verb in a sentence; it may question whether a sentence is complete or whether its subject and verb agree, even when the sentence is correct.

- Grammar checkers are likely to miss certain problems such as misplaced modifiers, faulty parallelism, possessives without apostrophes, or incorrectly positioned commas.

- Most grammar checkers do a good job of spotting problems with adjectives and adverbs, such as confusing *good* and *well*.

You can also use your word processor to search for your own typical editing problems. Begin by keeping track of your mistakes so that you can develop an "error hit list." You then may be able to figure out how to use your software's Find and Replace capacity (probably in the Edit menu) to check quickly for some of these problems. For instance, you might search for all instances of *each* (always singular) or *few* (always plural) to see if all the verbs agree.

The computer can also help you read your draft more closely. For example, you can automatically isolate each sentence so that you are less likely to skip over sentence errors. Make a copy of your draft and select the Replace function in your software's Edit menu. Ask the software to find every period in the file and replace it with a period and two returns. This change will create a version with each sentence separated by several spaces so that you can easily check every one for fragments, comma splices, or other problems.

what you want to say than to how you say it. Sometimes you inaccurately remember spelling or grammar or punctuation. At other times you are distracted by events around you, or you simply make keyboarding errors. Once you are satisfied that you have expressed your ideas, you should make sure that each sentence and word is concise, clear, and correct.

For editing and proof-reading strategies, see pp. 336–39.

This Quick Editing Guide provides an overview of grammar, style, punctuation, and mechanics problems typical of college writing. Certain common errors in Standard Written English are like red flags to careful readers: they signal that the writer is either ignorant or careless. Use the editing checklist below to check your paper for these problems; then use the editing checklists in each section to help you focus on and correct specific errors.

EDITING CHECKLIST

Common and Serious Problems in College Writing

For advice on writing more concisely, see pp. 331–36.

Grammar Problems

—— Have you avoided writing sentence fragments?	**A1**
—— Have you avoided writing comma splices or fused sentences?	**A2**
—— Have you used the correct form for all verbs in the past tense?	**A3**
—— Do all verbs agree with their subjects?	**A4**
—— Have you used the correct case for all pronouns?	**A5**
—— Do all pronouns agree with their antecedents?	**A6**
—— Have you used adjectives and adverbs correctly?	**A7**

Sentence Problems

—— Does each modifier clearly modify the appropriate sentence element?	**B1**
—— Have you used parallel structure where necessary?	**B2**

Punctuation Problems

—— Have you used commas correctly?	**C1**
—— Have you used apostrophes correctly?	**C2**
—— Have you punctuated quotations correctly?	**C3**

Mechanics and Format Problems

—— Have you used capital letters correctly?	**D1**
—— Have you spelled all words correctly?	**D2**
—— Have you used correct manuscript form?	**D3**

A *Editing for Common Grammar Problems*

A1   Check for any sentence fragments.

A complete sentence is one that has a subject, has a predicate, and can stand on its own. A *sentence fragment* lacks a subject, a predicate, or both, or for some other reason fails to convey a complete thought. It cannot stand on its own as a sentence.

Although they are common in advertising and fiction, fragments are usually ineffective in college writing because they do not communicate coherent thoughts. To edit for fragments, examine each sentence carefully to make sure that it has a subject and a verb and that it expresses a complete thought. To correct a fragment, you can make it into a complete sentence by adding a missing part, dropping an unnecessary subordinating conjunction, or joining it to a complete sentence nearby, if that would make more sense.

FAULTY	Roberto has two sisters. Maya and Leeza.
CORRECT	Roberto has two sisters, Maya and Leeza.
FAULTY	The children going to the zoo.
CORRECT	The children were going to the zoo.
CORRECT	The children going to the zoo were caught in a traffic jam.
FAULTY	Last night when we saw Cameron Diaz's most recent movie.
CORRECT	Last night we saw Cameron Diaz's most recent movie.

subject: The part of a sentence that names something—a person, an object, an idea, a situation—about which the predicate makes an assertion: The *king* lives.

predicate: The part of a sentence that makes an assertion about the subject involving an action (Birds *fly*), a relationship (Birds *have feathers*), or a state of being (Birds *are warm-blooded*)

subordinating conjunction: A word (such as *because, although, if, when*) used to make one clause dependent on, or subordinate to, another: *Unless* you have a key, we are locked out.

EDITING CHECKLIST

Fragments

___ Does the sentence have a subject?

___ Does the sentence have a complete verb?

___ If the sentence contains a subordinate clause, does it contain a clause that is a complete sentence too?

___ If you find a fragment, can you link it to an adjoining sentence, eliminate its subordinating conjunction, or add any missing element?

▪ For exercises on fragments, visit <bedfordstmartins.com/bedguide> and do a keyword search:

fragments

A2   Check for any comma splices or fused sentences.

A complete sentence has a subject and a predicate and can stand on its own. When two sentences are joined together to form one sentence, each sentence within the larger one is called a *main clause*. However, there are rules for joining main clauses, and when writers fail to follow these rules, they create

main clause: A group of words that has both a subject and a verb and can stand alone as a complete sentence: *My sister has a friend.*

coordinating conjunction: A one-syllable linking word (*and, but, for, or, nor, so, yet*) that joins elements with equal or near-equal importance: *Jack and Jill, sink or swim*

subordinating conjunction: A word (such as *because, although, if, when*) used to make one clause dependent on, or subordinate to, another: *Unless you have a key, we are locked out.*

serious sentence errors — comma splices or fused sentences, also called run-on sentences. A *comma splice* is two main clauses joined with only a comma. A *fused sentence* is two main clauses joined with no punctuation at all.

| COMMA SPLICE | I went to the mall, I bought a CD by a new group. |
| FUSED SENTENCE | I went to the mall I bought a CD by a new group. |

To find comma splices and fused sentences, examine each sentence to be sure it is complete. If it has two main clauses, make sure they are joined correctly. If you find a comma splice or fused sentence, correct it in one of these four ways, depending on which makes the best sense:

ADD A PERIOD	I went to the mall. I bought a CD by a new group.
ADD A SEMICOLON	I went to the mall; I bought a CD by a new group.
ADD A COMMA AND A COORDINATING CONJUNCTION	I went to the mall, and I bought a CD by a new group.
ADD A SUBORDINATING CONJUNCTION	I went to the mall where I bought a CD by a new group.

EDITING CHECKLIST

Comma Splices and Fused Sentences

____ Can you make each main clause a separate sentence?

____ Can you link the two main clauses with a comma and a coordinating conjunction?

____ Can you link the two main clauses with a semicolon or, if appropriate, a colon?

____ Can you subordinate one clause to the other?

 For exercises on comma splices and fused sentences, visit <bedfordstmartins.com/bedguide> and do a keyword search:

🔍 splice_fused

verb: A word that shows action (The cow *jumped* over the moon) or a state of being (The cow *is* brown)

A3 **Check for correct past tense verb forms.**

The *form* of a verb, the way it is spelled and pronounced, can change to show its *tense* — the time when its action did, does, or will occur (in the past, present, or future). A verb about something in the present will often be spelled and pronounced differently than a verb about something in the past.

| PRESENT | Right now, I *watch* only a few minutes of television each day. |
| PAST | Last month, I *watched* television shows every evening. |

Many writers fail to use the correct form for past tense verbs for two different reasons, depending on whether the verb is regular or irregular.

Regular verbs are verbs whose forms follow standard rules; they form the past tense by adding *-ed* or *-d* to the end of the present tense form: *watch/watched, look/looked, hope/hoped*. Check all regular verbs in the past tense to be sure you have used one of these endings.

FAULTY	I *ask* my brother for a loan yesterday.
CORRECT	I *asked* my brother for a loan yesterday.
FAULTY	Nicole *finish* her English essay.
CORRECT	Nicole *finished* her English essay.

TIP: If you say the final *-d* sound when you talk, you may find it easier to add the final *-d* or *-ed* when you write past tense regular verbs.

Irregular verbs do not follow standard rules to make their forms. Their unpredictable past tense forms have to be memorized: *eat/ate, see/saw, get/got*. In addition, the past tense form may differ from the past participle: "She *ate* the whole pie; she *has eaten* two pies this week." The most troublesome irregular verbs are actually very common, so if you make the effort to learn the correct forms, you will quickly improve your writing.

> ◻ For a chart showing the forms of many irregular verbs, see pp. A-32–A-33.
>
> *participle:* A form of a verb that cannot function alone as a main verb, including present participles ending in *-ing* (*dancing*) and past participles often ending in *-ed* or *-d* (*danced*)

FAULTY	My cat *laid* on the tile floor to take her nap.
CORRECT	My cat *lay* on the tile floor to take her nap.
FAULTY	I *have swam* twenty laps every day this month.
CORRECT	I *have swum* twenty laps every day this month.

TIP: In your college papers, follow convention by using the present tense, not the past, to describe the work of an author or the events in a literary work.

FAULTY	In "The Lottery," Shirley Jackson *revealed* the power of tradition. As the story *opened,* the villagers *gathered* in the square.
CORRECT	In "The Lottery," Shirley Jackson *reveals* the power of tradition. As the story *opens,* the villagers *gather* in the square.

EDITING CHECKLIST

Past Tense Verb Forms

____ Have you identified the main verb in the sentence?

____ Is the sentence about the past, the present, or the future? Does the verb reflect this sense of time?

____ Is the verb regular or irregular?

____ Have you used the correct form to express your meaning?

> ◼ For exercises on verbs, visit <bedfordstmartins.com/bedguide> and do a keyword search:
>
>  verbs

Principal Parts of Common Irregular Verbs

INFINITIVE	PAST TENSE	PAST PARTICIPLE
be	was	been
become	became	become
begin	began	begun
blow	blew	blown
break	broke	broken
bring	brought	brought
burst	burst	burst
catch	caught	caught
choose	chose	chosen
come	came	come
do	did	done
draw	drew	drawn
drink	drank	drunk
drive	drove	driven
eat	ate	eaten
fall	fell	fallen
fight	fought	fought
freeze	froze	frozen
get	got	got, gotten
give	gave	given
go	went	gone
grow	grew	grown
have	had	had
hear	heard	heard
hide	hid	hidden
know	knew	known
lay	laid	laid
lead	led	led
let	let	let
lie	lay	lain
make	made	made
raise	raised	raised
ride	rode	ridden
ring	rang	rung
rise	rose	risen
run	ran	run
say	said	said
see	saw	seen
set	set	set
sing	sang	sung
sit	sat	sat
slay	slew	slain
slide	slid	slid
speak	spoke	spoken

INFINITIVE	PAST TENSE	PAST PARTICIPLE
spin	spun	spun
stand	stood	stood
steal	stole	stolen
swim	swam	swum
swing	swung	swung
teach	taught	taught
tear	tore	torn
think	thought	thought
throw	threw	thrown
wake	woke, waked	woken, waked
write	wrote	written

For the forms of irregular verbs not on this list, consult your dictionary. (Some dictionaries list principal parts for all verbs, some just for irregular verbs.)

A4   Check for correct subject-verb agreement.

The *form* of a verb, the way it is spelled and pronounced, can change to show *number* — whether the subject is singular (one) or plural (more than one). It can also show *person* — whether the subject is *you* or *she,* for example.

SINGULAR	Our instructor *grades* every paper carefully.
PLURAL	Most instructors *grade* tests using a standard scale.
SECOND PERSON	You *write* well-documented research papers.
THIRD PERSON	She *writes* good research papers, too.

A verb must match (or *agree with*) its subject in terms of number and person. Regular verbs (those that follow a standard rule to make the different forms) are problems only in the present tense, where they have two forms: one that ends in *-s* or *-es* and one that does not. Only the subjects *he, she, it,* and singular nouns use the verb form that ends in *-s* or *-es.*

I like	we like	Dan likes
you like	you like	the child likes
he/she/it likes	they like	the children like

The verbs *be* and *have* do not follow the *-s/no -s* pattern to form the present tense; they are irregular verbs, so their forms must be memorized. The verb *be* is also irregular in the past tense.

Problems in agreement often occur when the subject is difficult to find, is an indefinite pronoun, or is confusing for some other reason. In particular, make sure that you have not left off any *-s* or *-es* endings and that you have used the correct form for irregular verbs.

verb: A word that shows action (The cow *jumped* over the moon) or a state of being (The cow *is* brown)

subject: The part of a sentence that names something — a person, an object, an idea, a situation — about which the predicate makes an assertion: The *king* lives.

indefinite pronoun: A pronoun standing for an unspecified person or thing, including singular forms (*each, everyone, no one*) and plural forms (*both, few*): *Everyone* is soaking wet.

For a chart showing the forms of many irregular verbs, see pp. A-32–A-33.

Forms of *Be* and *Have*

THE PRESENT TENSE OF *BE*

I am	we are
you are	you are
he/she/it is	they are

THE PAST TENSE OF *BE*

I was	we were
you were	you were
he/she/it was	they were

THE PRESENT TENSE OF *HAVE*

I have	we have
you have	you have
he/she/it has	they have

THE PAST TENSE OF *HAVE*

I had	we had
you had	you had
he/she/it had	they had

For exercises on subject-verb agreement, visit <bedfordstmartins.com/bedguide> and do a keyword search:

🔍 **sv agreement**

FAULTY   Jim *write* his research papers on a computer.

CORRECT   Jim *writes* his research papers on a computer.

FAULTY   The students *has* difficulty understanding the assignment.

CORRECT   The students *have* difficulty understanding the assignment.

FAULTY   Every one of the cakes *were* sold at the church bazaar.

CORRECT   Every one of the cakes *was* sold at the church bazaar.

EDITING CHECKLIST

Subject-Verb Agreement

— Have you correctly identified the subject and the verb in the sentence?
— Is the subject singular or plural? Does the verb match?
— Have you used the correct form of the verb?

---

pronoun: A word that stands in place of a noun (*he, him,* or *his* for *Nate*)

subject: The part of a sentence that names something—a person, an object, an idea, a situation—about which the predicate makes an assertion: The *king* lives.

subject complement: A noun, an adjective, or a group of words that follows a linking verb (*is, become, feel, seem,* or another verb that shows a state of being) and that renames or describes the subject: This plum tastes *ripe*.

object: The target or recipient of the action of a verb: Some geese bite *people*.

A5   Check for correct pronoun case.

Depending on the role a pronoun plays in a sentence, it is said to be in the *subjective case, objective case,* or *possessive case.* Use the subjective case if the pronoun is the subject of a sentence, the subject of a subordinate clause, or a subject complement (after a linking verb). Use the objective case if the pronoun is a direct or indirect object of a verb or the object of a preposition. Use the possessive case to show possession.

SUBJECTIVE   *I* will argue that our campus needs more parking.

OBJECTIVE   This issue is important to *me*.

POSSESSIVE   *My* argument will be quite persuasive.

There are many types of pronouns, but only some change form to show case. The personal pronouns *I, you, he, she, it, we,* and *they* and the relative pronoun *who* each have at least two forms.

Pronoun Cases at a Glance

SUBJECTIVE	OBJECTIVE	POSSESSIVE
I	me	my, mine
you	you	your, yours
he	him	his
she	her	hers
it	it	its
we	us	our, ours
they	them	their, theirs
who	whom	whose

There are two frequent errors in pronoun case. First, writers often use the subjective case when they should use the objective case — sometimes because they are trying to sound formal and correct. Instead, choose the correct form for a personal pronoun based on its function in the sentence.

FAULTY   My company gave my husband and *I* a trip to Hawaii.

CORRECT   My company gave my husband and *me* a trip to Hawaii.

FAULTY   The argument occurred because my uncle and *me* had different expectations.

CORRECT   The argument occurred because my uncle and *I* had different expectations.

FAULTY   Jack is taller than *me*.

CORRECT   Jack is taller than *I*.

A second common error with pronoun case involves gerunds. Whenever you need a pronoun to modify a gerund, use the possessive case.

gerund: A form of a verb, ending in *-ing*, that functions as a noun: Lacey likes *playing* in the steel band.

FAULTY   Our supervisor disapproves of *us* talking in the hallway.

CORRECT   Our supervisor disapproves of *our* talking in the hallway.

EDITING CHECKLIST

Pronoun Case

___ Have you identified all the pronouns in the sentence?

___ Does each one function as a subject, an object, or a possessive?

___ Given the function of each, have you used the correct form?

■ For exercises on pronoun case, visit <bedfordstmartins.com/bedguide> and do a key-word search:

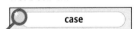

case

A6 Check for correct pronoun-antecedent agreement.

The *form* of a pronoun, the way it is spelled and pronounced, changes depending on its use in a particular sentence. The form can change to show *number* — whether the subject is singular (one) or plural (more than one). It

pronoun: A word that stands in place of a noun (*he, him,* or *his* for *Nate*) can change to show *gender* — masculine or feminine, for example. It can also change to show *person* — first (*I, we*), second (*you*), or third (*he, she, it, they*).

SINGULAR   My brother took *his* coat and left.

PLURAL   My brothers took *their* coats and left.

MASCULINE   I talked to Steven before *he* had a chance to leave.

FEMININE   I talked to Stephanie before *she* had a chance to leave.

In most cases, a pronoun refers to a specific noun or pronoun mentioned nearby; that word is called the pronoun's *antecedent.* The connection between the pronoun and the antecedent must be clear so that readers know what the pronoun means in the sentence. One way to make this connection clear is to ensure that the pronoun and the antecedent match (or *agree*) in number and gender.

A common error in pronoun agreement is using a plural pronoun to refer to a singular antecedent. This error often crops up when the antecedent is difficult to find, when the antecedent is an indefinite pronoun, or when the antecedent is confusing for some other reason. When editing for pronoun-antecedent agreement, look carefully to find the correct antecedent, and then make sure you know whether it is singular or plural. Make the pronoun match its antecedent.

FAULTY   Each of the boys in the Classic Club has *their* own rebuilt car.

CORRECT   Each of the boys in the Classic Club has *his* own rebuilt car.

            [The word *each,* not *boys,* is the antecedent. *Each* is an indefinite pronoun and is always singular, so any pronoun referring to it must be singular as well.]

FAULTY   Everyone in the meeting had *their* own cell phone.

CORRECT   Everyone in the meeting had *his or her* own cell phone.

            [*Everyone* is an indefinite pronoun that is always singular, so any pronoun referring to it must be singular as well.]

Indefinite Pronouns at a Glance

ALWAYS SINGULAR			ALWAYS PLURAL
anybody	everyone	no one	both
anyone	everything	nothing	few
anything	much	one (of)	many
each (of)	neither (of)	somebody	several
either (of)	nobody	someone	
everybody	none	something	

FAULTY   Neither Juanita nor Paula has received approval of *their* financial aid yet.

CORRECT   Neither Juanita nor Paula has received approval of *her* financial aid yet.

[*Neither Juanita nor Paula* is a compound subject joined by *nor*. Any pronoun referring to it must agree with only the nearer part of the compound. In other words, *her* needs to agree with *Paula*, which is singular.]

Indefinite pronouns as antecedents are troublesome when they are grammatically singular but create a plural image in the writer's mind. Fortunately, most indefinite pronouns are either always singular or always plural.

EDITING CHECKLIST

Pronoun-Antecedent Agreement

___ Have you identified the antecedent for each pronoun?
___ Is the antecedent singular or plural? Does the pronoun match?
___ Is the antecedent masculine, feminine, or neuter? Does the pronoun match?
___ Is the antecedent in the first, second, or third person? Does the pronoun match?

■ For exercises on pronoun-antecedent agreement, visit <bedfordstmartins.com/bedguide> and do a key-word search:

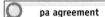   pa agreement

A7   **Check for correct adjectives and adverbs.**

Adjectives and *adverbs* describe or give more information about (*modify*) other words in a sentence. Many adverbs are formed by adding *-ly* to adjectives: *simple, simply; quiet, quietly*. Because adjectives and adverbs resemble one another, writers sometimes mistakenly use one instead of the other. To edit, find the word that the adjective or adverb modifies. If that word is a noun or pronoun, use an adjective. (An adjective typically describes which

Comparison of Irregular Adjectives and Adverbs

	POSITIVE	COMPARATIVE	SUPERLATIVE
ADJECTIVES	good	better	best
	bad	worse	worst
	little	less, littler	least, littlest
	many, some, much	more	most
ADVERBS	well	better	best
	badly	worse	worst
	little	less	least

or what kind.) If that word is a verb, adjective, or another adverb, use an adverb. (An adverb typically describes how, when, where, or why.)

FAULTY   Kelly ran into the house *quick*.

CORRECT   Kelly ran into the house *quickly*.

FAULTY   Gabriela looked *terribly* after her bout with the flu.

CORRECT   Gabriela looked *terrible* after her bout with the flu.

Adjectives and adverbs that have similar comparative and superlative forms can also cause trouble. Always ask whether you need an adjective or an adverb in the sentence, and then use the correct word.

FAULTY   His scar healed so *good* that it was barely visible.

CORRECT   His scar healed so *well* that it was barely visible.

EDITING CHECKLIST

Adjectives and Adverbs

—— Have you identified which word the adjective or adverb modifies?

—— If the word modified is a noun or pronoun, have you used an adjective?

—— If the word modified is a verb, adjective, or adverb, have you used an adverb?

—— Have you used the correct comparative or superlative form?

■ For exercises on adjectives and adverbs, visit <bedfordstmartins.com/bedguide> and do a keyword search:

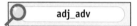
adj_adv

B *Editing to Ensure Effective Sentences*

B1 Check for any misplaced or dangling modifiers.

modifier: A word (such as an adjective or adverb), phrase, or clause that provides more information about other parts of a sentence: Plays *staged by the drama class* are *always successful*.

For a sentence to be clear, the connection between a modifier and the thing it modifies must be obvious. Usually, a modifier should be placed right before or right after the sentence element it modifies. If the modifier is placed too close to some other sentence element, it is a *misplaced modifier*. If there is nothing in the sentence that the modifier can logically modify, it is a *dangling modifier*. Both of these errors cause confusion for readers — and they sometimes create unintentionally humorous images. As you edit, be sure that a modifier is placed directly before or after the word modified and that the connection between the two is clear.

MISPLACED   George found the leftovers when he visited in the refrigerator.

CORRECT   George found the leftovers in the refrigerator when he visited.

[In the faulty sentence, *in the refrigerator* seems to modify George's visit. Obviously the leftovers are in the refrigerator, not George.]

DANGLING   Looking out the window, the clouds were beautiful.

CORRECT   Looking out the window, I saw that the clouds were beautiful.

CORRECT   When I looked out the window, the clouds were beautiful.
           [In the faulty sentence, *looking out the window* should modify *I*,
           but *I* is not in the sentence. The modifier is left without any-
           thing logical to modify—a dangling modifier. To correct this,
           the writer has to edit so that *I* is in the sentence.]

EDITING CHECKLIST

Misplaced and Dangling Modifiers

___ What is each modifier meant to modify? Is the modifier as close as possible
to that sentence element? Is any misreading possible?

___ If a modifier is misplaced, can you move it to clarify the meaning?

___ What noun or pronoun is a dangling modifier meant to modify? Can you
make that word or phrase the subject of the main clause? Or can you turn the
dangling modifier into a clause that includes the missing noun or pronoun?

■ For exercises on
misplaced and dangling
modifiers, visit
<bedfordstmartins.com/
bedguide> and do a key-
word search:

 modifiers

B2 Check for parallel structure.

A series of words, phrases, clauses, or sentences with the same grammatical
form is said to be *parallel.* Using parallel form for elements that are parallel
in meaning or function helps readers grasp the meaning of a sentence more
easily. A lack of parallelism can distract, annoy, or even confuse readers.

To use parallelism, put nouns with nouns, verbs with verbs, and phrases
with phrases. Parallelism is particularly important in a series, with correlative conjunctions, and in comparisons using *than* or *as.*

FAULTY   I like to go to Estes Park for skiing, ice skating, and to meet inter-
           esting people.

CORRECT   I like to go to Estes Park to ski, to ice skate, and to meet interest-
           ing people.

FAULTY   The proposal is neither practical, nor is it innovative.

CORRECT   The proposal is neither practical nor innovative.

FAULTY   A parent should have a few firm rules rather than having many
           flimsy ones.

CORRECT   A parent should have a few firm rules rather than many flimsy
           ones.

correlative conjunction:
A pair of linking words
(such as *either/or, not
only/but also*) that appear
separately but work to-
gether to join elements
of a sentence: *Neither* his
friends *nor* hers like pizza.

Take special care to reinforce parallel structures by repeating articles, conjunctions, prepositions, or lead-in words as needed.

AWKWARD   His dream was that he would never have to give up his routine
           but he would still find time to explore new frontiers.

> PARALLEL   His dream was that he would never have to give up his routine but *that* he would still find time to explore new frontiers.

EDITING CHECKLIST

Parallel Structure

■ For exercises on parallel structure, visit <bedfordstmartins.com/bedguide> and do a keyword search:

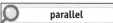

— Are all the elements in a series in the same grammatical form?
— Are the elements in a comparison parallel in form?
— Are the articles, conjunctions, or prepositions between elements repeated rather than mixed or omitted?
— Are lead-in words repeated as needed?

C   *Editing for Common Punctuation Problems*

CI   Check for correct use of commas.

The *comma* is a punctuation mark indicating a pause. By setting some words apart from others, commas help clarify relationships; they prevent the words on a page and the ideas they represent from becoming a jumble. Here are some of the most important conventional uses of commas.

1. Use a comma before a coordinating conjunction (*and, but, for, or, so, yet, nor*) joining two main clauses in a compound sentence.

   The discussion was brief, *so* the meeting was adjourned early.

2. Use a comma after an introductory word or word group unless it is short and cannot be misread.

   After the war, the North's economy developed rapidly.

3. Use commas to separate the items in a series of three or more items.

   The chief advantages will be *speed, durability,* and *longevity.*

4. Use commas to set off a modifying clause or phrase if it is nonrestrictive — that is, if it can be taken out of the sentence without significantly changing the meaning of the sentence.

   Good childcare, *which is difficult to find,* should be provided by the employer.

   Good childcare *that is reliable and inexpensive* is the right of every employee.

appositive: A word or group of words that adds information about a subject or object by identifying it in a different way: my dog *Rover*, Hal's brother *Fred*

5. Use commas to set off an appositive, an expression that comes directly after a noun or pronoun and renames it.

   Sheri, *my sister,* has a new job as an events coordinator.

6. Use commas to set off parenthetical expressions, conjunctive adverbs, and other interrupters.

The proposal from the mayor's commission, however, is not feasible.

EDITING CHECKLIST

Commas

____ Have you added a comma between two main clauses joined by a coordinating conjunction?

____ Have you added commas needed after introductory words or word groups?

____ Have you separated items in a series with commas?

____ Have you avoided putting commas before the first item in a series or after the last?

____ Have you used commas before and after each nonrestrictive phrase or clause?

____ Have you avoided using commas around a restrictive word, phrase, or clause?

____ Have you used commas to set off appositives, parenthetical expressions, conjunctive adverbs, and other interrupters?

parenthetical expression: An aside to readers or a transitional expression such as *for example* or *in contrast*

conjunctive adverb: A linking word that can connect independent clauses and show a relationship between two ideas: Armando is a serious student; *therefore*, he studies every day.

■ For exercises on commas, visit <bedfordstmartins.com/bedguide> and do a keyword search:

comma

C2   Check for correct use of apostrophes.

An *apostrophe* is a punctuation mark that either shows possession (*Sylvia's*) or indicates that one or more letters have intentionally been left out to form a contraction (*didn't*). Because apostrophes are easy to overlook, writers often omit a necessary apostrophe, use one where it is not needed, or put one in the wrong place. An apostrophe is never used to create the possessive form of a pronoun; use the possessive pronoun form instead.

FAULTY   *Mikes* car was totaled in the accident.

CORRECT   *Mike's* car was totaled in the accident.

FAULTY   The principles of the *womens'* movement are still controversial to some people.

CORRECT   The principles of the *women's* movement are still controversial to some people.

FAULTY   Che *did'nt* want to stay at home and study.

CORRECT   Che *didn't* want to stay at home and study.

FAULTY   The dog wagged *it's* tail happily.

CORRECT   The dog wagged *its* tail happily.

FAULTY   *Its* raining.

CORRECT   *It's* raining. [it's = it is]

> ### Possessive Personal Pronouns at a Glance
>
> | PERSONAL PRONOUN | POSSESSIVE CASE |
> |---|---|
> | I | my, mine |
> | you | your, yours (*not* your's) |
> | he | his |
> | she | her, hers (*not* her's) |
> | it | its (*not* it's) |
> | we | our, ours (*not* our's) |
> | they | their, theirs (*not* their's) |
> | who | whose (*not* who's) |

■ For exercises on apostrophes, visit <bedfordstmartins.com/bedguide> and do a keyword search:

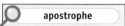

apostrophe

EDITING CHECKLIST

Apostrophes

—— Have you used an apostrophe to show that letters have been left out in a contraction?

—— Have you used an apostrophe to create the possessive form of a noun?

—— Have you used the possessive case — rather than an apostrophe — to show that a pronoun is possessive?

—— Have you used *it's* correctly (to mean *it is*)?

C3 Check for correct punctuation of quotations.

When you quote the exact words of a person you have interviewed or a source you have read, be sure to enclose those words in quotation marks.

> Derek is straightforward when asked about how his work is received in the local community: "My work is outside the mainstream. Because it's controversial, it's not easy for me to get exposure."

If your source is quoting someone else (a quotation within a quotation), put your subject's words in quotation marks and the words he or she is quoting in single quotation marks. Always put commas and periods inside the quotation marks; put semicolons and colons outside.

Substitute an ellipsis mark (. . .) — three spaced dots — for any words you have omitted from the middle of a direct quotation. If you are following MLA style, you may place the ellipsis mark inside brackets ([. . .]) when necessary to avoid confusing your ellipsis marks with those of the original writer. If the ellipsis mark comes at the end of a sentence, add another period to conclude the sentence. You don't need an ellipsis mark to show the beginning or ending of a quotation that is clearly incomplete.

"The importance of what women athletes wear can't be underestimated," Rounds claims. "Beach volleyball, which is played . . . by bikini-clad women, rates network coverage" (44).

Common errors in punctuating quotations include leaving out necessary punctuation marks or putting them in the incorrect place or sequence.

FAULTY   In the comic book *The Uncanny X-Men,* Magneto championed his fellow mutants, "people slaughtered wholesale for no more reason than" . . . "the presence in their DNA of an extra special gene".

CORRECT   In the comic book *The Uncanny X-Men,* Magneto championed his fellow mutants, "people slaughtered wholesale for no more reason than . . . the presence in their DNA of an extra special gene."

For more about quotations from sources, see D3 in the Quick Research Guide (the dark-red-edged pages).

EDITING CHECKLIST

Punctuation with Quotations

___ Are the exact words quoted from your source enclosed in quotation marks?
___ Are commas and periods placed inside closing quotation marks?
___ Are colons and semicolons placed outside closing quotation marks?
___ Have you used an ellipsis mark to show where any words are omitted from the middle of a quotation?

For exercises on using and punctuating quotation marks, visit <bedfordstmartins.com/bedguide> and do a keyword search:

quotation

D Editing for Common Mechanics and Format Problems

D1 Check for correct use of capital letters.

Capital letters are used in three general situations: to begin a new sentence; to begin names of specific peoples, places, dates, and things (proper nouns); and to begin main words in titles. Writers sometimes use capital letters where they are not needed, such as for emphasis, or fail to use them where they are needed.

FAULTY   During my Sophomore year in College, I took World Literature, Biology, History, Psychology, and French — courses required for a Humanities Major.

CORRECT   During my sophomore year in college, I took world literature, biology, history, psychology, and French — courses required for a humanities major.

■ For exercises on using capital letters, visit <bedfordstmartins.com/bedguide> and do a keyword search:

capitals

EDITING CHECKLIST

Capitalization

—— Have you used a capital letter at the beginning of each complete sentence, including sentences that are quoted?

—— Have you used capital letters for proper nouns and pronouns?

—— Have you avoided using capital letters for emphasis?

—— Have you used a capital letter for each main word in a title, including the first word and the last word?

Capitalization at a Glance

Capitalize the following:

THE FIRST LETTER OF A SENTENCE, INCLUDING A QUOTED SENTENCE
She called out, "Come in! The water's not cold."

PROPER NAMES AND ADJECTIVES MADE FROM THEM
Marie Curie   Cranberry Island
Smithsonian Institution   a Freudian reading

RANK OR TITLE BEFORE A PROPER NAME
Ms. Olson   Professor Santocolon

FAMILY RELATIONSHIP ONLY WHEN IT SUBSTITUTES FOR OR IS PART OF A PROPER NAME
Grandma Jones   Father Time

RELIGIONS, THEIR FOLLOWERS, AND DEITIES
Islam   Orthodox Jew   Buddha

PLACES, REGIONS, AND GEOGRAPHIC FEATURES
Palo Alto   the Berkshire Mountains

DAYS OF THE WEEK, MONTHS, AND HOLIDAYS
Wednesday   July   Labor Day

HISTORICAL EVENTS, PERIODS, AND DOCUMENTS
the Boston Tea Party   the Middle Ages   the Constitution

SCHOOLS, COLLEGES, UNIVERSITIES, AND SPECIFIC COURSES
Temple University   Introduction to Clinical Psychology

FIRST, LAST, AND MAIN WORDS IN TITLES OF PAPERS, BOOKS, ARTICLES, WORKS OF ART, TELEVISION SHOWS, POEMS, AND PERFORMANCES
The Decline and Fall of the Roman Empire

D2 Check spelling.

Misspelled words are difficult to spot in your own writing. You usually see what you think you wrote, and often pronunciation or faulty memory may interfere with correct spelling. When you proofread for spelling, check especially for words that sound alike but are spelled differently (*accept* and *except*, for example), words that are spelled differently than they are pronounced, words that do not follow the basic rules for spelling English words (*judgment*, for example), and words that you habitually confuse and misspell.

For a list of commonly confused words, see p. A-46. For a list of commonly misspelled words, see pp. A-47–A-49.

EDITING CHECKLIST

Spelling

___ Have you checked for the words you habitually misspell?

___ Have you checked for commonly confused or misspelled words?

___ Are you familiar with standard spelling rules, including their exceptions?

___ Have you checked a dictionary for any words you are unsure about?

___ Have you run your spell checker? Have you read your paper carefully for errors that it would miss?

For spelling exercises, visit <bedfordstmartins.com/bedguide> and do a keyword search:

spelling

If you know the words you habitually misspell, you can use your software's Search or Find functions to locate all instances and check the spelling. Consider keeping track of misspelled words in your papers for a few weeks so you can take advantage of this feature to simplify your editing.

Spell checkers offer a handy alternative to the dictionary, but you need to be aware of their limitations. A spell checker compares the words in your text with the words listed in its dictionary, and it highlights words that do not appear there. (The size of computer spelling dictionaries varies greatly, but most contain fewer entries than a typical college-level dictionary in book form.) A spell checker cannot help you spell words that its dictionary does not contain, including most proper nouns. Spell checkers ignore one-letter words; for example, they will not flag a typographical error such as *s truck* for *a truck*. Nor will they highlight words that are misspelled as different words, such as *except* for *accept*, *to* for *too*, or *own* for *won*. Always check the spelling in your text by eye *after* you've used your spell checker.

Grammar checkers may note some commonly confused words, but they often do this even when you have used the correct form. Use a dictionary to decide whether to accept the grammar checker's suggestion.

WRITING WITH A COMPUTER

COMMONLY CONFUSED HOMONYMS

accept (v., receive willingly); **except** (prep., other than)

Mimi could *accept* all of Lefty's gifts *except* his ring.

affect (v., influence); **effect** (n., result)

If the new rules *affect* us, what will be their *effect?*

allusion (n., reference); **illusion** (n., fantasy)

Any *allusion* to Norman's mother may revive his *illusion* that she is up-stairs, alive, in her rocking chair.

capital (adj., uppercase; n., seat of government); **capitol** (n., government building)

The *Capitol* building in our nation's *capital* is spelled with a *capital C.*

cite (v., refer to); **sight** (n., vision or tourist attraction); **site** (n., place)

Did you *cite* Mother as your authority on which *sites* feature the most interesting *sights?*

complement (v., complete; n., counterpart); **compliment** (v. or n., praise)

For Lee to say that Sheila's beauty *complements* her intelligence may or may not be a *compliment.*

desert (v., abandon); **dessert** (n., end-of-meal sweet)

Don't *desert* us by leaving before *dessert.*

elicit (v., bring out); **illicit** (adj., illegal)

By going undercover, Sonny should *elicit* some offers of *illicit* drugs.

formally (adv., officially); **formerly** (adv., in the past)

Jane and John Doe-Smith, *formerly* Jane Doe and John Smith, sent cards *formally* announcing their marriage.

led (v., past tense of *lead*); **lead** (n., a metal)

Gil's heart was heavy as *lead* when he *led* the mourners to the grave.

principal (n. or adj., chief); **principle** (n., rule or standard)

The *principal* problem is convincing the media that our school *principal* is a person of high *principles.*

stationary (adj., motionless); **stationery** (n., writing paper)

Hubert's *stationery* shop stood *stationary* until a flood swept it away.

their (pron., belonging to them); **there** (adv., in that place); **they're** (contraction of *they are*)

Sue said *they're* going over *there* to visit *their* aunt.

to (prep., toward); **too** (adv., also or excessively); **two** (n. or adj., numeral: one more than one)

Let's not take *two* cars to town — that's *too* many unless Lucille and Harry are coming *too.*

who's (contraction of *who is*); **whose** (pron., belonging to whom)

Who's going to tell me *whose* dog this is?

your (pron., belonging to you); **you're** (contraction of *you are*)

You're not getting *your* own way this time!

COMMONLY MISSPELLED WORDS

absence	believe	despair
academic	beneficial	desperate
acceptable	benefited	develop
accessible	breath (noun)	development
accidentally	breathe (verb)	device (noun)
accommodate	bureaucracy	devise (verb)
achievement	business	diary
acknowledgment	calendar	difference
acquaintance	careful	dilemma
acquire	casualties	dining
address	category	disappear
advertisement	cemetery	disappoint
advice	certain	disastrous
advise	changeable	discipline
aggravate	changing	discussion
aggressive	characteristic	disease
aging	chief	dissatisfied
allege	choose (present tense)	divide
all right	chose (past tense)	doesn't
all together (all in	climbed	dominant
one group)	column	don't
a lot	coming	drunkenness
already	commitment	efficiency
although	committed	eighth
altogether (entirely)	comparative	either
amateur	competition	embarrass
analysis	conceive	entirety
analyze	condemn	environment
answer	congratulate	equipped
anxiety	conscience	especially
appearance	conscientious	exaggerate
appetite	conscious	exceed
appreciate	consistent	excel
appropriate	controlled	excellence
arctic	criticism	exercise
argument	criticize	exhaust
ascent	curiosity	existence
assassinate	curious	experience
assistance	deceive	explanation
association	decision	extremely
athlete	defendant	familiar
athletics	deficient	fascinate
attendance	definite	February
audience	dependent	fiery
average	descendant	financial
awkward	describe	foreign
basically	description	foresee
beginning	desirable	forth

(continued)

COMMONLY MISSPELLED WORDS *(continued)*

forty	license	persistence
forward	lightning	personnel
fourth (number four)	literature	persuade
frantically	loneliness	physical
fraternities	loose (adjective)	playwright
friend	lose (verb)	possession
fulfill	lying	possibly
gaiety	magazine	practically
genealogy	maintenance	precede
generally	marriage	predominant
genuine	mathematics	preferred
government	medicine	prejudice
grammar	miniature	prevalent
grief	mischievous	privilege
guarantee	misspell	probably
guard	muscle	procedure
guidance	mysterious	proceed
harass	necessary	professor
height	neither	prominent
heroes	niece	pronounce
herring	ninety	pronunciation
humorous	ninth	pursue
illiterate	noticeable	quantity
illogical	notorious	quiet
imitation	nuclear	quite
immediately	nucleus	quizzes
incredible	numerous	realize
indefinite	obstacle	rebelled
independence	occasionally	recede
indispensable	occur	receipt
infinite	occurrence	receive
influential	official	recipe
intelligence	omission	recommend
intentionally	omitted	reference
interest	opinion	referring
interpret	opportunity	regrettable
interrupt	originally	relevance
irrelevant	outrageous	relief
irresistible	paid	relieve
irritable	pamphlet	religious
island	panicky	remembrance
its (possessive)	parallel	reminisce
it's (it is, it has)	particularly	reminiscence
jealousy	pastime	repetition
judgment	peaceable	representative
knowledge	perceive	resistance
laboratory	performance	restaurant
led (past tense of *lead*)	permanent	review
library	permissible	rhythm

ridiculous	supersede	unnoticed
roommate	suppress	until
sacrifice	surprise	useful
safety	suspicious	usually
scarcely	technical	valuable
schedule	technique	vengeance
secretary	temperature	vicious
seize	tendency	view
separate	therefore	villain
siege	thorough	warrant
similar	thoroughbred	weather
sincerely	though	Wednesday
sophomore	thought	weird
source	throughout	whether
specifically	tragedy	who's (who is)
sponsor	transferred	whose (possessive
strategy	traveling	of *who*)
strength	truly	withhold
stretch	twelfth	woman
succeed	tyranny	women
successful	unanimous	
suddenness	unnecessary	

D3 Check for correct manuscript form.

In case you have received no particular instructions for the form of your paper, here are some general, all-purpose specifications.

▥ For more on document design, see Ch. 20. For an example of MLA-style paper format, see p. 343.

GENERAL MANUSCRIPT STYLE FOR COLLEGE ESSAYS, ARTICLES, AND REPORTS

1. Pick a conventional, easy-to-read typeface such as Courier, Times New Roman, Helvetica, or Palatino. Make sure you have a fresh cartridge in your printer. If you handwrite your paper, make sure your handwriting is legible.

2. Print in black ink. Use dark blue or black ink if you write by hand.

3. Write or print on just one side of standard letter-size bond paper (8½ inches by 11 inches). If you handwrite your paper, use 8½-by-11-inch paper with smooth edges (not torn from a spiral-bound notebook).

4. For a paper without a separate title page, place your name, your instructor's name, the number and section of the course, and the date in the upper left or right corner of the first page, each item on a new line. (Ask whether your instructor has a preference for which side.) Double-space and center your title. Don't underline the title, don't put it in quotation marks or use all capital letters, and don't put a period after it. Capitalize the first and last words, the first word after a colon or semicolon, and all other words except prepositions, coordinating conjunctions, and articles. Double-space between the title and the first line of your text. (Most instructors do not

preposition: A transitional word (such as *in, on, at, of, from*) that leads into a phrase
coordinating conjunction: A one-syllable linking word (*and, but, for, or, nor, so, yet*) that joins elements with equal or near-equal importance
article: The word *a, an,* or *the*

require a title page for short college papers. If your instructor requests one but doesn't give you any guidelines, see number 1 under Additional Suggestions for Research Papers, below.)

5. Number your pages consecutively, including the first page. For a paper of two or more pages, use a running header to put your last name in the upper right corner of each sheet along with the page number. (Use the heading option under View or Edit.) Do not type the word *page* or the letter *p* before the number, and do not follow the number with a period or parenthesis.

6. Leave ample margins — at least an inch — left, right, top, and bottom.

7. If you use a word processor, double-space your manuscript; if you handwrite, use wide-ruled paper or skip every other line.

8. Indent each new paragraph five spaces or one-half inch.

For more about citing sources, see D6 and E1 in the Quick Research Guide (the dark-red-edged pages).

9. Long quotations should be double-spaced like the rest of your paper but indented from the left margin — ten spaces (one inch) if you're following MLA (Modern Language Association) guidelines, five spaces (one-half inch) if you're using APA (American Psychological Association) guidelines. Put the source citation in parentheses immediately after the final punctuation mark of the block quotation.

10. Label all illustrations. Make sure any insertions are bound securely to the paper.

11. Staple the paper in the top left corner, or use a paper clip as MLA advises. Don't use any other method to secure the pages unless one is recommended by your instructor.

12. For safety's sake and peace of mind, make a copy of your paper, and back up your file.

ADDITIONAL SUGGESTIONS FOR RESEARCH PAPERS

For research papers, the format is the same as recommended in the previous section, with the following additional specifications.

1. The MLA guidelines do not recommend a title page. If your instructor wants one, type the title of your paper, centered and double-spaced, about a third of the way down the page. Go down two to four more lines and type your name, the instructor's name, the number and section of the course, and the date, each on a separate line and double-spaced.

2. Do not number your title page; number your outline, if you submit one with your paper, with small roman numerals (i, ii, iii, and so on). Number consecutively all subsequent pages in the essay, including your "Works Cited" or "References" pages, using arabic numerals (1, 2, 3, and so on) in the upper right corner of the page.

For examples of MLA documentation style, see E1 and E2 in the Quick Research Guide (the dark-red-edged pages).

3. Double-space your works cited or references list, if you have one.

HOW TO MAKE A CORRECTION

Before you produce your final copy, make any large changes in your draft, edit and proofread carefully, and run your spell checker. When you give your paper a last once-over, however, don't be afraid to make small corrections in pen. In making such corrections, you may find it handy to use certain symbols used by printers and proofreaders.

A transposition mark (⌒) reverses the positions of two words or two letters:

> The nearby star Tau Ceti closely resmebles our sun.

Close-up marks (⌒) bring together the parts of a word accidentally split. A separation mark (|) inserts a space where one is needed:

> The nearby star Tau Ceti closely re sembles our|sun.

To delete a letter or punctuation mark, draw a line with a curlicue through it:

> The nearby star Tau Ceti closely ressembles our sun.

Use a caret (∧) to indicate where to insert a word or letter:

> The nearby star Tau Ceti closely reembles our sun.

The symbol ¶ before a word or a line means "start a new paragraph":

See the back inside pages of this book for a list of correction symbols.

> Recently, astronomers have reduced their efforts to study dark nebulae. ¶ That other solar systems may also support life makes for another fascinating speculation.

To make a letter lowercase, draw a slanted line through it. To make a letter uppercase, put three short lines under it:

> i read it for my History class.

You can always cross out a word neatly, with a single horizontal line, and write a better one over it.

> *closely*
> The nearby star Tau Ceti somewhat resembles our sun.

Finally, if a page has many handwritten corrections on it, print or write it over again.

Appendix
A Glossary of Troublemakers

■ For advice on spelling, see 33. For advice on conciseness, see Ch. 19.

Usage refers to the way in which writers customarily use certain words and phrases, including matters of accepted practice or convention. This glossary lists words and phrases whose usage may trouble writers. Not every possible problem is listed — only some that frequently puzzle students. Look over this brief list; refer to it when you don't remember the preferred usage.

a, an   Use *an* only before a word beginning with a vowel sound. "*An* asp can eat *an* egg *an* hour." (Some words, such as *hour* and *honest*, open with a vowel sound even though spelled with an *h*.)

above   Using *above* or *below* to refer back or forward in an essay is awkward and may not be accurate. Less awkward alternatives: "the *preceding* argument," "in the *following* discussion," "on the *next* page."

accept, except   *Accept* is a verb meaning "to receive willingly"; *except* is usually a preposition meaning "not including." "This childcare center *accepts* all children *except* those under two." Sometimes *except* is a verb, meaning "to exempt." "The entry fee *excepts* children under twelve."

advice, advise   *Advice* is a noun, *advise* a verb. When someone *advises* you, you receive *advice*.

affect, effect   Most of the time, the verb *affect* means "to act on" or "to influence." "Too much beer can *affect* your speech." *Affect* can also mean "to put on airs." "He *affected* an Oxford accent." *Effect*, a noun, means "a result": "Too much beer has a numbing *effect*." But *effect* is also a verb, meaning "to bring about." "Pride *effected* his downfall."

agree to, agree with, agree on   *Agree to* means "to consent to"; *agree with*, "to be in accord." "I *agreed to* attend the New Age lecture, but I didn't *agree with* the speaker's views." *Agree on* means "to come to or have an understanding about." "Chuck and I finally *agreed on* a compromise: the children would go to camp but not overnight."

ain't   Don't use *ain't* in writing; it is nonstandard English for *am not, is not* (*isn't*), and *are not* (*aren't*).

a lot   Many people mistakenly write the colloquial expression *a lot* as one word: *alot*. Use *a lot* if you must, but in writing *much* or *a large amount* is preferable. See also *lots, lots of, a lot of*.

already, all ready   *Already* means "by now"; *all ready* means "set to go." "At last our picnic was *all ready*, but *already* it was night."

altogether, all together   *Altogether* means "entirely." "He is *altogether* mistaken." *All together* means "in unison" or "assembled." "Now *all together* — heave!" "Inspector Trent gathered the suspects *all together* in the drawing room."

among, between   *Between* refers to two persons or things; *among*, to more than two. "Some disagreement *between* the two countries was inevitable. Still, there was general harmony *among* the five nations represented at the conference."

amount, number   Use *amount* to refer to quantities that cannot be counted or to bulk; use *number* to refer to countable, separate items. "The *number* of people you want to serve determines the *amount* of ice cream you'll need."

an, a   See *a, an.*

and/or   Usually use either *and* or *or* alone. "Tim *and* Elaine will come to the party." "Tim *or* Elaine will come to the party." If you mean three distinct options, write, "Tim *or* Elaine, *or both*, will come to the party, depending on whether they can find a babysitter."

ante-, anti-   The prefix *ante-* means "preceding." *Antebellum* means "before the Civil War." *Anti-* most often means "opposing": *antidepressant*. It needs a hyphen in front of *i* (*anti-inflationary*) or in front of a capital letter (*anti-Marxist*).

anybody, any body   When *anybody* is used as an indefinite pronoun, write it as one word: "*Anybody* in his or her right mind abhors murder." Because *anybody* is singular, do not write "Anybody in *their* right mind." (See 7d.) *Any body,* written as two words, is the adjective *any* modifying the noun *body.* "Name *any body* of water in Australia."

anyone, any one   *Anyone* is an indefinite pronoun written as one word. "Does *anyone* want dessert?" The phrase *any one* consists of the pronoun *one* modified by the adjective *any* and is used to single out something in a group: "Pick *any one* of the pies — they're all good."

anyplace   *Anyplace* is colloquial for *anywhere* and should not be used in formal writing.

anyways, anywheres   These nonstandard forms of *anyway* and *anywhere* should not be used in writing.

as   Sometimes using the subordinating conjunction *as* can make a sentence ambiguous. "*As* we were climbing the mountain, we put on heavy sweaters." Does *as* here mean "because" or "while"? Whenever using *as* would be confusing, use a more specific term instead, such as *because* or *while.*

as, like   Use *as, as if,* or *as though* rather than *like* to introduce clauses of comparison. "Dan's compositions are tuneful, *as* [not *like*] music ought to be." "Jeffrey behaves *as if* [not *like*] he were ill." *Like,* because it is a preposition, can introduce a phrase but not a clause. "My brother looks *like* me." "Henrietta runs *like* a duck."

as to   Usually this expression sounds stilted. Use *about* instead. "He complained *about* [not *as to*] the cockroaches."

at   See *where at, where to.*

bad, badly   *Bad* is an adjective; *badly* is an adverb. Following linking verbs (*be, appear, become, grow, seem, prove*) and verbs of the senses (*feel, look, smell, sound, taste*), use the adjective form. "I feel *bad* that we missed the plane." "The egg smells *bad.*" (See 8a, 8b.) The adverb form is used to modify a verb or an adjective. "The Tartans played so *badly* they lost to the last-place team whose *badly* needed victory saved them from elimination."

being as, being that   Instead of "*being as* I was ignorant of the facts, I kept still," write "*Because* I was ignorant" or "*Not knowing* the facts."

beside, besides   *Beside* is a preposition meaning "next to." "Sheldon enjoyed sitting *beside* the guest of honor." *Besides* is an adverb meaning "in addition." "*Besides,* he has a sense of humor." *Besides* is also a preposition meaning "other than." "Something *besides* shyness caused his embarrassment."

between, among   See *among, between.*

between you and I   The preposition *between* always takes the objective case. "Between *you* and *me* [not *I*], Joe's story sounds suspicious." "Between *us* [not *we*], what's going on between Chris and her [not *she*] is unfathomable."

but that, but what   "I don't know *but what* [or *but that*] you're right" is a wordy, imprecise way of saying "Maybe you're right" or "I believe you're right."

can, may   Use *can* to show ability. "Jake *can* bench-press 650 pounds." *May* involves permission. "*May* I bench-press today?" "You *may,* if you *can.*"

capital, capitol   A *capital* is a city that is the center of government for a state or country. *Capital* can also mean "wealth." A *capitol* is a building in which legislators meet. "Who knows what the *capital* of Finland is?" "The renovated *capitol* is a popular attraction."

center around   Say "Class discussion *centered on* [or *revolved around*] her paper." In this sense, the verb *center* means "to have one main concern" — the way a circle has a central point. (To say a discussion centers *around* anything is a murky metaphor.)

cite, sight, site   *Cite,* a verb, means "to quote from or refer to." *Sight* as a verb means "to see or glimpse"; as a noun it means "a view, a spectacle." "When the police officer *sighted* my terrier running across the playground, she *cited* the leash laws." *Site,* a noun, means "location." "Standing and weeping at the *site* of his childhood home, he was a pitiful *sight.*"

climatic, climactic   *Climatic,* from *climate,* refers to meteorological conditions. Saying "climatic conditions," however, is wordy — you can usually substitute "the climate": "*Climatic* conditions are [or "The *climate* is"] changing because of the hole in the ozone layer." *Climactic,* from *climax,* refers to the culmination of a progression of events. "In the *climactic* scene the hero drives his car off the pier."

compare, contrast *Compare* has two main meanings. The first, "to liken or represent as similar," is followed by *to*. "She *compared* her room *to* a jail cell." The second, "to analyze for similarities and differences," is generally followed by *with*. "The speaker *compared* the American educational system *with* the Japanese system."

Contrast also has two main meanings. As a transitive verb, taking an object, it means "to analyze to emphasize differences" and is generally followed by *with*. "The speaker *contrasted* the social emphasis of the Japanese primary grades *with* the academic emphasis of ours." As an intransitive verb, *contrast* means "to exhibit differences when compared." "The sour taste of the milk *contrasted* sharply *with* its usual fresh flavor."

complement, compliment *Compliment* is a verb meaning "to praise" or a noun meaning "praise." "The professor *complimented* Sarah on her perceptiveness." *Complement* is a verb meaning "to complete or reinforce." "Jenn's experiences as an intern *complemented* what she learned in class."

could care less This is nonstandard English for *couldn't care less* and should not be used in writing. "The cat *couldn't* [not *could*] care less about which brand of cat food you buy."

could of *Could of* is colloquial for *could have* and should not be used in writing.

couple of Write "a *couple of* drinks" when you mean two. For more than two, say "a *few* [or *several*] drinks."

criteria, criterion *Criteria* is the plural of *criterion*, which means "a standard or requirement on which a judgment or decision is based." "The main *criteria* for this job are attention to detail and good computer skills."

data *Data* is a plural noun. Write "The data *are*" and "*these* data." The singular form of *data* is *datum*—rarely used because it sounds musty. Instead, use *fact*, *figure*, or *statistic*.

different from, different than *Different from* is usually the correct form to use. "How is good poetry *different from* prose?" Use *different than* when a whole clause follows. "Violin lessons with Mr. James were *different than* I had imagined."

don't, doesn't *Don't* is the contraction for *do not*, and *doesn't* is the contraction for *does not*. "They *don't* want to get dressed up for the ceremony." "The cat *doesn't* [not *don't*] like to be combed."

due to *Due* is an adjective and must modify a noun or pronoun; it can't modify a verb or an adjective. Begin a sentence with *due to* and you invite trouble: "*Due to* rain, the game was postponed." Write instead, "*Because of* rain." *Due to* works after the verb *be*. "His fall was *due to* a banana peel." There, *due* modifies the noun *fall*.

due to the fact that A windy expression for *because*.

effect, affect See *affect, effect*.

either Use *either* when referring to one of two things. "Both internships sound great; I'd be happy with *either*." When referring to one of three or more things, use *any one* or *any*. "*Any one* of our four counselors will be able to help you."

et cetera, etc. Sharpen your writing by replacing *et cetera* (or its abbreviation, *etc.*) with exact words. Even translating the Latin expression into English ("and other things") is an improvement, as in "high-jumping, shot-putting, and other field events."

everybody, every body When used as an indefinite pronoun, *everybody* is one word. "Why is *everybody* on the boys' team waving his arms?" Because *everybody* is singular, it is a mistake to write, "Why is *everybody* waving *their* arms?" (See 7d.) *Every body* written as two words refers to separate, individual bodies. "After the massacre, they buried *every body* in *its* [not *their*] own grave."

everyone, every one Used as an indefinite pronoun, *everyone* is one word. "*Everyone* has *his or her* own ideas." Because *everyone* is singular, it is incorrect to write, "*Everyone* has *their* own ideas." (See 7d.) *Every one* written as two words refers to individual, distinct items. "I studied *every one* of the chapters."

except, accept See *accept, except*.

expect In writing, avoid the informal use of *expect* to mean "suppose, assume, or think." "I *suppose* [not *expect*] you're going on the geology field trip."

fact that This is a wordy expression that, nearly always, you can do without. Instead of "*The fact that* he was puny went unnoticed," write, "That he was puny went unnoticed." "Because [not *Because of the fact that*] it snowed, the game was canceled."

farther, further In your writing, use *farther* to refer to literal distance. "Chicago is *farther* from Nome than from New York." When you mean additional degree, time, or quantity, use *further*: "Sally's idea requires *further* discussion."

fewer, less *Less* refers to general quantity or bulk; *fewer* refers to separate, countable items. "Eat *less* pizza." "Salad has *fewer* calories."

field of In a statement such as "He took courses in *the field of* economics," omit *the field of* to save words.

firstly The recommended usage is *first* (and *second*, not *secondly*; *third*, not *thirdly*; and so on).

former, latter *Former* means "first of two"; *latter*, "second of two." They are an acceptable but heavy-handed pair, often obliging your reader to back-track. Your writing generally will be clearer if you simply name again the persons or things you mean. Instead of "The *former* great artist is the master of the flowing line, while the *latter* is the master of color," write, "Picasso is the master of the flowing line, while Matisse is the master of color."

further, farther See *farther, further*.

get, got *Get* has many meanings, especially in slang and colloquial use. Some, such as the following, are not appropriate in formal writing:

To start, begin: "Let's start [not *get*] painting."

To stir the emotions: "His frequent interruptions finally started annoying [not *getting to*] me."

To harm, punish, or take revenge on: "She's going to take revenge on [not *get*] him." Or better, be even more specific: "She's going to spread rumors about him to ruin his reputation."

good, well To modify a verb, use the adverb *well*, not the adjective *good*. "Jan dives *well* [not *good*]." Linking verbs (*be, appear, become, grow, seem, prove*) and verbs of the senses (such as *feel, look, smell, sound, taste*) call for the adjective *good*. "The paint job looks *good*." *Well* is an adjective used only to refer to health. "She looks *well*" means that she seems to be in good health. "She looks *good*" means her appearance is attractive. (See 8b, 8c.)

hanged, hung Both words are the past tense of the verb *hang*. *Hanged* refers to an execution. "The murderer was *hanged* at dawn." For all other situations, use *hung*. "Jim *hung* his wash on the line to dry."

have got to In formal writing, avoid using the phrase *have got to* to mean "have to" or "must." "I *must* [not *have got to*] phone them right away."

he, she, he or she Using *he* to refer to an indefinite person is considered sexist; so is using *she* with traditionally female occupations or pastimes.

However, the phrase *he or she* can seem wordy and awkward. For alternatives, see 18.

herself See *-self, -selves*.

himself See *-self, -selves*.

hopefully *Hopefully* means "with hope." "The children turned *hopefully* toward the door, expecting Santa Claus." In writing, avoid *hopefully* when you mean "it is to be hoped" or "let us hope." "*I hope* [not *Hopefully*] the posse will arrive soon."

if, whether Use *whether*, not *if*, in indirect questions and to introduce alternatives. "Father asked me *whether* [not *if*] I was planning to sleep all morning." "I'm so confused I don't know *whether* [not *if*] it's day or night."

imply, infer *Imply* means "to suggest"; *infer* means "to draw a conclusion." "Maria *implied* that she was too busy to see Tom, but Tom *inferred* that Maria had lost interest in him."

in, into *In* refers to a location or condition; *into* refers to the direction of movement or change. "The hero burst *into* the room and found the heroine *in* another man's arms."

infer, imply See *imply, infer*.

in regards to Write *in regard to*, *regarding*, or *about*.

inside of, outside of As prepositions, *inside* and *outside* do not require *of*. "The students were more interested in events *outside* [not *outside of*] the building than those *inside* [not *inside of*] the classroom." In formal writing, do not use *inside of* to refer to time or *outside of* to mean "except." "I'll finish the assignment *within* [not *inside of*] two hours." "He told no one *except* [not *outside of*] a few friends."

irregardless *Irregardless* is a double negative. Use *regardless*.

is because See *reason is because*, reason . . . is.

is when, is where Using these expressions results in errors in predication. "Obesity *is when* a person is greatly overweight." "Biology *is where* students dissect frogs." *When* refers to a point in time, but *obesity* is not a point in time; *where* refers to a place, but *biology* is not a place. Write instead, "Obesity is the condition of extreme overweight." "Biology is a laboratory course in which students dissect frogs." (See 12c.)

its, it's *Its* is a possessive pronoun, never in need of an apostrophe. *It's* is a contraction for *it is*. "Every new experience has *its* bad moments. Still, *it's* exciting to explore the unknown." (See 24g.)

it's me, it is I   Although *it's me* is widely used in speech, don't use it in formal writing. Write "It is I," which is grammatically correct. The same applies to other personal pronouns. "It was *he* [not *him*] who started the mutiny." (See 5.)

kind of, sort of, type of   When you use *kind, sort,* or *type* — singular words — make sure that the sentence construction is singular. "That *type* of show *offends* me." "Those *types* of shows *offend* me." In speech, *kind of* and *sort of* are used as qualifiers. "He is *sort of* fat." Avoid them in writing. "He is *rather* [or *somewhat* or *slightly*] fat."

latter, former   See *former, latter.*

lay, lie   The verb *lay,* meaning "to put or place," takes an object. "*Lay* that pistol down." *Lie,* meaning "to rest or recline," does not. "*Lie* on the bed until your headache goes away." Their principal parts are *lay, laid, laid* and *lie, lay, lain.* (See 3f.)

less, fewer   See *fewer, less.*

liable, likely   Use *likely* to mean "plausible" or "having the potential." "Jake is *likely* [not *liable*] to win." Save *liable* for "legally obligated" or "susceptible." "A stunt man is *liable* to injury."

lie, lay   See *lay, lie.*

like, as   See *as, like.*

likely, liable   See *liable, likely.*

literally   Don't sling *literally* around for emphasis. Because it means "strictly according to the meaning of a word (or words)," it will wreck your credibility if you are speaking figuratively. "Professor Gray *literally* flew down the hall" means that Gray traveled on wings. Save *literally* to mean that you're reporting a fact. "Chemical wastes travel on the winds, and the skies *literally* rain poison."

loose, lose   *Loose,* an adjective, most commonly means "not fastened" or "poorly fastened." *Lose,* a verb, means "to misplace" or "to not win." "I have to be careful not to *lose* this button — it's so *loose.*"

lots, lots of, a lot of   Use these expressions only in informal speech. In formal writing, use *many* or *much.* See also *a lot.*

mankind   This term is considered sexist by many people. Use *humanity, humankind, the human race,* or *people* instead.

may, can   See *can, may.*

media, medium   *Media* is the plural of *medium* and most commonly refers to the various forms of public communication. "Some argue that, of all the *media,* television is the worst for children."

might of   *Might of* is colloquial for *might have* and should not be used in writing.

most   Do not use *most* when you mean "almost" or "nearly." "*Almost* [not *Most*] all of the students felt that Professor Crey should receive tenure."

must of   *Must of* is colloquial for *must have* and should not be used in writing.

myself   See *-self, -selves.*

not all that   *Not all that* is colloquial for *not very;* do not use it in formal writing. "The movie was *not very* [not *not all that*] exciting."

number, amount   See *amount, number.*

of   See *could of, might of, must of, should of.*

O.K., o.k., okay   In formal writing, do not use any of these expressions. *All right* and *I agree* are possible substitutes.

one   Like a balloon, *one,* meaning "a person," tends to inflate. One *one* can lead to another. "When *one* is in college, *one* learns to make up *one's* mind for *oneself.*" Avoid this pompous usage. Whenever possible, substitute *people* or a more specific plural noun. "When *students* are in college, *they* learn to make up their minds for *themselves.*"

ourselves   See *-self, -selves.*

outside of, inside of   See *inside of, outside of.*

percent, per cent, percentage   When you specify a number, write *percent* (also written *per cent*). "Nearly 40 *percent* of the listeners responded to the offer." The only time to use *percentage,* meaning "part," is with an adjective, when you mention no number. "A high *percentage* [or *a large percentage*] of listeners responded." *A large number* or *a large proportion* sounds better yet.

phenomenon, phenomena   *Phenomena* is the plural of *phenomenon,* which means "an observable fact or occurrence." "Of the many mysterious supernatural *phenomena,* clairvoyance is the strangest *phenomenon* of all."

precede, proceed   *Precede* means "to go before or ahead of"; *proceed* means "to go forward." "The fire drill *proceeded* smoothly; the children *preceded* the teachers onto the playground."

principal, principle   *Principal* means "chief," whether used as an adjective or as a noun. "According to the *principal*, the school's *principal* goal will be teaching reading." Referring to money, *principal* means "capital." "Investors in high-risk companies may lose their *principal*." *Principle*, a noun, means *rule* or *standard*. "Let's apply the *principle* of equality in hiring."

proved, proven   Although both forms can be used as past participles, *proved* is recommended. Use *proven* as an adjective. "They had *proved* their skill in match after match." "Try this *proven* cough remedy."

quote, quotation   *Quote* is a verb meaning "to cite, to use the words of." *Quotation* is a noun meaning "something that is quoted." "The *quotation* [not *quote*] next to her yearbook picture fits her perfectly."

raise, rise   *Raise*, meaning "to cause to move upward," is a transitive verb and takes an object. *Rise*, meaning "to move up (on its own)" is intransitive and does not take an object: "I *rose* from my seat and *raised* my arm."

rarely ever   *Rarely* by itself is strong enough. "George *rarely* [not *rarely ever*] eats dinner with his family."

real, really   *Real* is an adjective, *really* an adverb. Do not use *real* to modify a verb or another adjective, and avoid overusing either word. "*The Ambassadors* is a *really* [not *real*] fine novel." Even better: "*The Ambassadors* is a fine novel."

reason is because, reason . . . is   *Reason . . . is* requires a clause beginning with *that*. Using *because* is nonstandard. "The *reason* I can't come *is that* [not *is because*] I have the flu." It is simpler and more direct to write, "I can't come because I have the flu." (See 12d.)

rise   See *raise, rise.*

-self, -selves   Don't use a pronoun ending in *-self* or *-selves* in place of *her, him, me, them, us,* or *you.* "Nobody volunteered but Jim and *me* [not *myself*]." Use the *-self* pronouns to refer back to a noun or another pronoun and to lend emphasis. "*We* did it *ourselves.*" "Sarah *herself* is a noted musician."

set, sit   *Set*, meaning "to put or place," is a transitive verb and takes an object. *Sit*, meaning "to be seated," is intransitive and does not take an

object. "We were asked to *set* our jewelry and metal objects on the counter and *sit* down." (See 3f.)

shall, will; should, would   The helping verb *shall* formerly was used with first-person pronouns. It is still used to express determination ("We *shall* overcome") or to ask consent ("*Shall* we march?"). Otherwise, *will* is commonly used with all three persons. "I *will* enter medical school in the fall." *Should* is a helping verb that expresses obligation; *would*, a helping verb that expresses a hypothetical condition. "I *should* wash the dishes before I watch TV." "He *would* learn to speak English if you *would* give him a chance."

she, he or she   See *he, she, he or she.*

should of   *Should of* is colloquial for *should have* and should not be used in writing.

sight   See *cite, sight, site.*

since   Sometimes using *since* can make a sentence ambiguous. "*Since* the babysitter left, the children have been watching television." Does *since* here mean "because" or "from the time that"? If using *since* might be confusing, use an unambiguous term (*because, ever since*).

sit   See *set, sit.*

site   See *cite, sight, site.*

sort of   See *kind of, sort of, type of.*

stationary, stationery   *Stationary*, an adjective, means "fixed, unmoving." "The fireplace remained *stationary* though the wind blew down the house." *Stationery* is paper for letter writing. To spell it right, remember that *letter* also contains *-er.*

suppose to   Write *supposed to.* "He was *supposed to* read a novel."

sure   *Sure* is an adjective, *surely* an adverb. Do not use *sure* to modify a verb or another adjective. If you mean "certainly," write *certainly* or *surely* instead. "He *surely* [not *sure*] makes the Civil War come alive."

than, then   *Than* is a conjunction used in comparisons; *then* is an adverb indicating time. "Marlene is brainier *than* her sister." "First crack six eggs; *then* beat them."

that, where   See *where, that.*

that, which   Which pronoun should open a clause —*that* or *which*? If the clause adds to its sentence an idea that, however interesting, could be left out, then the clause is nonrestrictive. It should begin with *which* and be separated from the rest of the sentence with commas. "The vampire, *which* hovered nearby, leaped for Sarah's throat."

If the clause is essential to your meaning, it is restrictive. It should begin with *that* and should not have commas around it. "The vampire *that* Mel brought from Transylvania leaped for Sarah's throat." The clause indicates not just any old vampire but one in particular. (See 21e.)

Don't use *which* to refer vaguely to an entire clause. Instead of "Jack was an expert drummer in high school, *which* won him a scholarship," write "Jack's skill as a drummer won him . . ." (See 6b.)

that, who, which, whose   See *who, which, that, whose.*

themselves   See *-self, -selves.*

then, than   See *than, then.*

there, their, they're   *There* is an adverb indicating place. *Their* is a possessive pronoun. *They're* is a contraction of *they are.* "After playing tennis *there* for three hours, Lamont and Laura went to change *their* clothes because *they're* going out to dinner."

to, too, two   *To* is a preposition. *Too* is an adverb meaning "also" or "in excess." *Two* is a number. "Janet wanted to go *too*, but she was *too* sick to travel for *two* days. Instead, she went *to* bed."

toward, towards   *Toward* is preferred in the United States, *towards* in Britain.

try and   Use *try to.* "I'll *try to* [not *try and*] attend the opening performance of your play."

type of   See *kind of, sort of, type of.*

unique   Nothing can be *more, less,* or *very unique. Unique* means "one of a kind." (See 8e.)

use to   Write *used to.* "Jeffrey *used to* have a beard, but now he is clean-shaven."

wait for, wait on   *Wait for* means "await"; *wait on* means "to serve." "While *waiting for* his friends, George decided to *wait on* one more customer."

well, good   See *good, well.*

where, that   Although speakers sometimes use *where* instead of *that*, you should not do so in writing. "I heard on the news *that* [not *where*] it got hot enough to fry eggs on car hoods."

where . . . at, where . . . to   The colloquial use of *at* or *to* after *where* is redundant. Write "*Where* were you?" not "Where were you *at*?" "I know *where* she was rushing [not *rushing to*]."

whether   See *if, whether.*

which, that   See *that, which.*

who, which, that, whose   *Who* refers to people, *which* to things and ideas. "Was it Pogo *who* said, 'We have met the enemy and he is us'?" "The blouse, *which* was green, accented her dark skin." *That* refers to things but can also be used for a class of people. "The team *that* increases sales the most will get a bonus." Because *of which* can be cumbersome, use *whose* even with things. "The mountain, *whose* snowy peaks were famous world over, was covered by fog." See also *that, which.*

who, whom   *Who* is used as a subject, *whom* as an object. In "*Whom* do I see?" *Whom* is the object of *see*. In "*Who* goes there?" *Who* is the subject of "goes." (See also 5a.)

who's, whose   *Who's* is a contraction for *who is* or *who has.* "*Who's* going with Phil?" *Whose* is a possessive pronoun. "Bill is a conservative politician *whose* ideas are unlikely to change."

whose, who, which, that   See *who, which, that, whose.*

will, shall   See *shall, will; should, would.*

would, should   See *shall, will; should, would.*

would of   *Would of* is colloquial for *would have* and should not be used in writing.

you   *You*, meaning "a person," occurs often in conversation. "When *you* go to college, *you* have to work hard." In writing, use *one* or a specific, preferably plural noun. "When *students* go to college, *they* have to work hard." See *one* and 18c.

your, you're   *Your* is a possessive pronoun; *you're* is the contraction for *you are.* "*You're* lying! It was *your* handwriting on the envelope."

yourself, yourselves   See *-self, -selves.*

Appendix
Answers for Lettered Exercises

EXERCISE 1–1   ELIMINATING FRAGMENTS, p. H-9

Suggested revisions:

a. Michael had a beautiful Southern accent, having lived many years in Georgia.

b. Pat and Chris are determined to marry each other, even if their families do not approve.

c. Jack seemed well qualified for a career in the Air Force, except for his tendency to get airsick.

d. Lisa advocated sleeping no more than four hours a night until she started nodding through her classes.

e. Complete Sentences

EXERCISE 2–1   REVISING COMMA SPLICES AND FUSED SENTENCES, p. H-13

Suggested revisions:

a. We followed the scientist down a flight of wet stone steps. At last he stopped before a huge oak door.
We followed the scientist down a flight of wet stone steps, until at last he stopped before a huge oak door.

b. Dr. Frankenstein selected a heavy key; he twisted it in the lock.
Dr. Frankenstein selected a heavy key, which he twisted in the lock.

c. The huge door gave a groan; it swung open on a dimly lighted laboratory.
The huge door gave a groan and swung open on a dimly lighted laboratory.

d. Before us on a dissecting table lay a form with closed eyes. To behold it sent a quick chill down my spine.
Before us on a dissecting table lay a form with closed eyes; beholding it sent a quick chill down my spine.

e. The scientist strode to the table and lifted a white-gloved hand.
The scientist strode to the table; he lifted a white-gloved hand.

EXERCISE 3–1   USING IRREGULAR VERB FORMS, p. H-18

a. In those days, Benjamin wrote all the music, and his sister *sang* all the songs.

b. Correct

c. When the bell *rang,* darkness had already *fallen.*

d. Voters have *chosen* some new senators, who won't take office until January.

e. Carol threw the ball into the water, and the dog *swam* after it.

EXERCISE 3–2   IDENTIFYING VERB TENSES, p. H-25

a. has been living: present perfect progressive; hacked: simple past; change: simple present   **b.** have never appeared: present perfect; never will appear: simple future; gets selected: simple present   **c.** had been: past perfect; pitched: simple past   **d.** will have been studying: future perfect progressive; will be taking: future progressive   **e.** was running: past progressive; strolled: simple past

EXERCISE 3–4   USING THE CORRECT MOOD OF VERBS, p. H-30

a. Dr. Belanger recommended that Juan *floss* his teeth every day. (Incorrect *flosses,* indicative; correct *floss,* subjunctive)

b. If I *were* you, I would have done the same thing. (Incorrect *was,* indicative; correct *were,* subjunctive)

c. Tradition demands that Daegun *show* respect for his elders. (Incorrect *shows,* indicative; correct *show,* subjunctive)

d. Please *attend* the training lesson if you plan to skydive later today. (Incorrect *attends,* indicative; correct *attend,* imperative)

EXERCISE 4–1   MAKING SUBJECTS AND VERBS AGREE, p. H-36

a. For many college graduates, the process of looking for jobs *is* often long and stressful.

A-59

b. Not too long ago, searching the classifieds and inquiring in person *were* the primary methods of job hunting.

c. Today, however, everyone also *seems* to use the Internet to search for openings or to e-mail *his or her* résumés.

d. My classmates and my cousin *send* most résumés over the Internet because it costs less than mailing them.

e. All of the résumés *arrive* quickly when they are sent electronically.

EXERCISE 5–1   USING PRONOUNS CORRECTLY, p. H-39

a. I didn't appreciate *your* laughing at her and *me*. (*Your* modifies the gerund *laughing; me* is an object of the preposition *at.*)

b. Lee and *I* would be delighted to serenade *whoever* will listen. (*I* is a subject of the verb phrase *would be delighted; whoever* is the subject of the clause *whoever will listen.*)

c. The waiters and *we* busboys are highly trustworthy. (*We* is a subject complement.)

d. The neighbors were driven berserk by *his* singing. (The gerund *singing* is the object of the verb *driven;* the possessive pronoun *his* modifies *singing.*)   *Or*
Correct as is. (*Him* is the object of the verb *driven; singing* is a participle modifying *him.*)

e. Jerry and *I* regard you and *her* as the very people *whom* we wish to meet. (*I* is a subject of the verb *regard; her* is a direct object of the verb *regard; whom* is the object of the infinitive *to meet.*)

EXERCISE 6–1   MAKING PRONOUN REFERENCE CLEAR, p. H-43

Suggested revisions:

a. As the moon began to rise, I could see the faint shadow of the tree.

b. While she spent the summer in Paris, Katrina broadened her awareness of cultural differences by traveling throughout Europe.

c. Most managers want employees to work as many hours as possible. They never consider the work their employees need to do at home.

d. Working twelve hours a day and never getting enough sleep was worth it.

e. Kevin asked Mike to meet him for lunch but forgot that Mike had class at that time.   *Or*
Kevin forgot that he had class at the time he asked Mike to meet him for lunch.

EXERCISE 7–1   MAKING PRONOUNS AND ANTECEDENTS AGREE, p. H-46

Suggested revisions:

a. Correct

b. Neither Melissa nor James has received an application form yet.   *Or*

Melissa and James have not received their application forms yet.

c. He is the kind of man who gets his fun out of just sipping his beer and watching his Saturday games on TV.

d. Many a mother has mourned the loss of her child.   *Or*
Many mothers have mourned the loss of their children.

e. When you enjoy your work, it's easy to spend all your spare time thinking about it.   *Or*
When one enjoys one's work, it's easy to spend all one's spare time thinking about it.

EXERCISE 8–1   USING ADJECTIVES AND ADVERBS CORRECTLY, p. H-51

a. Change *increasing* to *increasingly.*   **b.** Correct.   **c.** Change *lower* to *lowest.*   **d.** Change *rapid* to *rapidly.*   **e.** Change *well* to *good.*

EXERCISE 9–1   MAINTAINING GRAMMATICAL CONSISTENCY, p. H-55

Suggested revisions:

a. Dr. Jamison is an erudite professor who tells amusing anecdotes in class. (Formal) *Or* Dr. Jamison is a funny teacher who cracks jokes in class. (Informal)

b. The audience listened intently to the lecture but did not understand the message.

c. Scientists can no longer evade the social, political, and ethical consequences of what they do in the laboratory.

d. To have good government, citizens must become informed on the issues. Also, they must vote.

e. Good writing is essential to success in many professions, especially in business, where ideas must be communicated clearly.

EXERCISE 10–1   PLACING MODIFIERS, p. H-58

Suggested revisions:

a. The bus full of passengers got stuck in a ditch.

b. In the middle of a staff meeting, he was daydreaming about fishing for trout.

c. With a smirk, the boy threw the paper airplane through an open window.

d. When the glare appeared, I reached for my sunglasses from the glove compartment.

e. Sally and Glen watched the kites high above them drift back and forth.

EXERCISE 10–2   REVISING DANGLING MODIFIERS, p. H-59

Suggested revisions:

a. As I was unpacking the suitcase, a horrible idea occurred to me.

b. After preparing breakfast that morning, I might have left the oven on at home.

c. Although I tried to reach my neighbor, her telephone was busy.

d. Desperate to get information, I asked my mother to drive over to check the oven.

e. I felt enormous relief when my mother's call confirmed that everything was fine.

EXERCISE 11–1   COMPLETING COMPARISONS, p. H-61

Suggested revisions:

a. The movie version of *The Brady Bunch* was much more ironic *than the television show*.

b. Taking care of a dog is often more demanding than *taking care of* a cat.

c. I received more free calendars in the mail for the year 2004 than *I have for* any other year.

d. The crime rate in the United States is higher than *it is in* Canada.

e. Liver contains more iron than any *other* meat.

EXERCISE 11–2   COMPLETING SENTENCES, p. H-63

Suggested revisions:

a. Eighteenth-century China was as civilized *as* and in many respects more sophisticated than the Western world.

b. Pembroke was never contacted *by*, much less involved with, the election committee.

c. I haven't yet *finished* but soon will finish my research paper.

d. Ron likes his popcorn with butter; Linda *likes hers* with parmesan cheese.

e. Correct

EXERCISE 12–1   CORRECTING MIXED CONSTRUCTIONS AND FAULTY PREDICATION, p. H-67

Suggested revisions:

a. Health insurance protects people from big medical bills.

b. His determination to prevail helped him finish the race.

c. AIDS destroys the body's immune system.

d. The temperatures are too low for the orange trees.

e. In a recession, economic growth is small or nonexistent, and unemployment increases.

EXERCISE 13–1   MAKING SENTENCES PARALLEL, p. H-70

Suggested revisions:

a. The border separating Texas and Mexico marks not only the political boundary of two countries but also the last frontier for some endangered wildlife.

b. In the Rio Grande Valley, both local residents and tourists enjoy visiting the national wildlife refuges.

c. The tall grasses in this valley are the home of many insects, birds, and small mammals.

d. Two endangered wildcats, the ocelot and the jaguarundi, also make the Rio Grande Valley their home.

e. Many people from Central America are desperate to immigrate to the United States by either legal or illegal means.

EXERCISE 14–1   USING COORDINATION, p. H-74

Suggested revisions:

a. Professional poker players try to win money and prizes in high-stakes tournaments; however, they may lose thousands of dollars.

b. Poker is not an easy way to make a living, and playing professional poker is not a good way to relax.

c. A good "poker face" reveals no emotions, for communicating too much information puts a player at a disadvantage.

d. Hidden feelings may come out in unconscious movements, so an expert poker player watches other players carefully.

e. Poker is different from most other casino gambling games, for it requires skill and it forces players to compete against each other. Other casino gambling pits players against the house, so they may win out of sheer luck, but skill has little to do with winning those games.

EXERCISE 14–2   USING SUBORDINATION, p. H-76

Suggested revisions:

a. Cape Cod is a peninsula in Massachusetts that juts into the Atlantic Ocean south of Boston, marking the northern turning point of the Gulf Stream.

b. Although the developer had hoped the condominiums would sell quickly, sales were sluggish.

c. Tourists love Italy because it has a wonderful climate, beautiful towns and cities, and a rich history.

d. At the end of Verdi's opera *La Traviata*, Alfredo has to see his beloved Violetta again, even though he knows she is dying and all he can say is good-bye.

e. I usually have more fun at a concert with Rico than with Morey because Rico loves music while Morey merely tolerates it.

EXERCISE 16–2   AVOIDING JARGON, p. H-83

Suggested revisions:

a. Everyone at Boondoggle and Gall attends holiday gatherings in order to meet and socialize with potential business partners.

b. This year, more than fifty employees lost their jobs after Boondoggle and Gall's decision to reduce their number of employees by September 1.

c. The layoffs left Jensen in charge of all telephone calls in the customer service department.

d. Jensen was responsible for handling three times as many telephone calls after the layoffs, yet she did not receive any extra pay.

e. Jensen and her managers could not agree on a fair compensation, so she decided to quit her job at Boondoggle and Gall.

EXERCISE 16–3   AVOIDING EUPHEMISMS AND SLANG, p. H-84

Suggested revisions:

a. Our security forces have arrested many political dissidents.
b. At three hundred dollars a month, the apartment is a bargain.
c. The soldiers were accidentally shot by members of their own troops while they were retreating.
d. Churchill was an excellent politician.
e. The president's tax plan was doomed; Congress would not approve it.

EXERCISE 18–1   AVOIDING BIAS, p. H-92

Suggested revisions:

a. Our school's extensive athletic program will be of interest to *many* applicants.
b. The new physicians on our staff include Dr. Scalia, *Dr.* Baniski, and Dr. Throckmorton.
c. Joni believes in the healing properties of herbal remedies.
d. Philosophers have long pondered whether *humans are* innately evil or innately good.
e. *Diligent researchers* will always find the sources *they* seek.

EXERCISE 20–1   USING END PUNCTUATION, p. H-97

a. The question that still troubles the community after all these years is why federal agents did not act sooner. [Not a direct question]
b. Correct
c. I wonder what he was thinking at the time. [Not a direct question]
d. One man, who suffered a broken leg, was rescued when he was heard screaming, "Help me! Help me!" [Urgent directive]
e. Correct

EXERCISE 21–1   USING COMMAS, p. H-98

a. Farmers around the world tend to rely on just a few breeds of livestock, so some breeds are disappearing.
b. Correct
c. For instance, modern breeds of cattle usually grow larger and produce more meat and milk than older breeds.
d. In both wild and domestic animals, genetic diversity can make the animals resistant to disease and parasites, so older breeds can give scientists important information.
e. Until recently, small organic farmers were often the only ones interested in raising old-fashioned breeds, but animal scientists now support this practice as well.

EXERCISE 21–2   USING COMMAS, p. H-100

a. Mrs. Carver looks like a sweet little old lady, but she plays a wicked electric guitar.
b. Her bass player, her drummer, and her keyboard player all live in the same retirement community.

c. They practice individually in the afternoon, rehearse together at night, and play at the community's Saturday night dances.
d. The Rest Home Rebels have to rehearse quietly and cautiously to keep from disturbing the other residents.
e. Correct

EXERCISE 21–3   USING COMMAS, p. H-102

Suggested revisions:

a. We are bringing a dish, vegetable lasagna, to the potluck supper.
b. I like to go to Central Bank on this side of town because this branch tends to have short lines.
c. The colony that the English established at Roanoke disappeared mysteriously.
d. If the base commanders had checked their gun room, where powder is stored, they would have found that several hundred pounds of gunpowder were missing.
e. Brazil's tropical rain forests, which help produce the air we breathe all over the world, are being cut down at an alarming rate.

EXERCISE 21–4   USING COMMAS, p. H-103

a. The university insisted, however, that the students were not accepted merely because of their parents' generous contributions.
b. This dispute, in any case, is an old one.
c. It was the young man's striking good looks, not his acting ability, that first attracted the Hollywood agents.
d. Gretchen learned, moreover, not to always accept as true what she had read in textbooks.
e. The hikers, most of them wearing ponchos or rain jackets, headed out into the steady drizzle.

EXERCISE 21–5   USING COMMAS, p. H-105

a. César Chávez was born on March 31, 1927, on a farm in Yuma, Arizona.
b. Chávez, who spent years as a migrant farmworker, told other farm laborers, "If you're outraged at conditions, then you can't possibly be free or happy until you devote all your time to changing them."
c. Chávez founded the United Farm Workers union and did, indeed, devote all his time to changing conditions for farmworkers.
d. Robert F. Kennedy called Chávez "one of the heroic figures of our time."
e. Correct

EXERCISE 22–1   USING SEMICOLONS, p. H-108

a. By the beginning of 1993, Shirley was eager to retire; nevertheless, she agreed to stay on for two more years.
b. In 1968 Lyndon Johnson abandoned his hopes for reelection because of fierce opposition from within his own party.

c. The committee was asked to determine the extent of violent crime among teenagers, especially those between the ages of fourteen and sixteen; to act as a liaison between the city and schools and between churches and volunteer organizations; and to draw up a plan to significantly reduce violence, both public and private, by the end of the century.

d. The leaves on the oak trees near the lake were tinged with red; swimmers no longer ventured into the water.

e. The football team has yet to win a game; however, the season is still young.

EXERCISE 23–1   USING COLONS, p. H-111

Suggested revisions:

a. The Continuing Education Program offers courses in building and construction management, engineering, and design.

b. The interview ended with a test of skills: taking messages, operating the computer, typing a sample letter, and proofreading documents.

c. The sample letter began, "Dear Mr. Rasheed: Please accept our apologies for the late shipment."

d. Correct

e. These are my dreams: to fly in a small plane, to gallop down a beach on horseback, and to cross the ocean in a sailboat.

EXERCISE 24–1   USING THE APOSTROPHE, p. H-114

a. Joe's and Chuck's fathers were both in the class of '73.

b. Correct

c. It was a strange coincidence that all three women's cars broke down after they had picked up their mothers-in-law.

d. Don't forget to dot your *i*'s and cross your *t*'s.

e. Mario and Shelley's son is marrying the editor in chief's daughter.

EXERCISE 25–1   USING QUOTATION MARKS, p. H-118

a. "What we still need to figure out," the police chief said, "is whether the victim was acquainted with his assailant."

b. A skillful orator, Patrick Henry is credited with the phrase "Give me liberty or give me death."

c. "I could hear the crowd chanting my name — 'Jones! Jones!' — and that spurred me on," said Bruce Jones, the winner of the 5,000-meter race.

d. The video for the rock group Guns and Roses' epic song "November Rain" is based on a short story by Del James.

e. After the Gore/Bush election debacle of 2000, *Time* essayist Lance Morrow predicts, "The memory of the 2000 post-election chadfest will revive an angry energy in 2004, which will produce the biggest voter turnout in history."

EXERCISE 26–1   USING THE DASH, p. H-120

Suggested revisions:

a. I enjoy going hiking with my friend John, whom I've known for fifteen years.

b. Pedro's new boat is spectacular — a regular seagoing Ferrari.

c. The Thompsons devote their weekends to their favorite pastime — eating bags of potato chips and cookies beside the warm glow of the television.

EXERCISE 27–1   USING PARENTHESES, p. H-122

Suggested revisions:

a. Our cafeteria serves the four basic food groups: white (milk, bread, and mashed potatoes), brown (mystery meat and gravy), green (overcooked vegetables and underwashed lettuce), and orange (squash, carrots, and tomato sauce).

b. The hijackers will release the hostages only if the government (1) frees all political prisoners and (2) allows the hijackers to leave the country unharmed.

c. Correct

EXERCISE 28–1   USING ABBREVIATIONS, p. H-129

a. At 7:50 p.m. [*or* 7:50 in the evening] on election day, the media first awarded Florida to Al Gore, only to reverse that statement and declare George W. Bush the president a few hours later.

b. Biology lectures are only ninety *minutes* long because lab sessions immediately follow them.

c. *Professor* James has office hours on Monday and Tuesday, beginning at 10:00 a.m.

d. Emotional issues, *for example*, abortion and capital punishment, cannot be settled easily by compromise.

e. The red peppers are selling for $3.25 a pound.

EXERCISE 29–1   USING CAPITALIZATION, p. H-132

a. At our family reunion, I met my cousin Sam for the first time, as well as my father's brother George.

b. I already knew from Dad that his brother had moved to Australia years ago to explore the Great Barrier Reef.

c. I had heard that Uncle George was estranged from his mother, a Roman Catholic, after he married an atheist.

d. She told George that God created many religions so that people would not become atheists.

e. When my uncle announced that he was moving to a continent thousands of miles southwest of the United States, his mother gave him a Bible to take along.

EXERCISE 30–1   USING NUMBERS, p. H-134

a. If the murder took place at approximately 6:20 p.m. and the suspect was *half* a mile away at the time, he could not possibly have committed the crime.

b. A program to help save the sea otter transferred more than eighty animals to a new colony over the course of *two* years; however, all but *thirty-four* otters swam back home again.

c. *One percent* or less of the estimated *15* to *20* billion pounds of plastic discarded annually in the United States is recycled.

d. The 1983 Little League World Series saw the Roosters beat the Dusters *94–4* before a throng of *7,550*.

e. In act II, scene ix, of Shakespeare's *The Merchant of Venice*, Portia's *second* suitor fails to guess which of *three* caskets contains her portrait.

EXERCISE 31–1   USING ITALICS, p. H-137

a. Does *avocado* mean "lawyer" in Spanish?

b. During this year's First Night celebrations, we heard Verdi's *Requiem* and Monteverdi's *Orfeo*.

c. You can pick out some of the best basketball players in the NBA by the *33* on their jerseys.

d. It was fun watching the passengers on the *Europa* trying to dance to "Blue Moon" in the midst of a storm.

e. In one episode of the sitcom *Seinfeld,* Kramer gets a job as an underwear model.

EXERCISE 32–1   USING HYPHENS, p. H-140

a. The strong-smelling smoke alerted them to a potentially life-threatening danger.

b. Burt's wildly swinging opponent had tired himself out before the climactic third round.

c. Tony soaked his son's ketchup- and mustard-stained T-shirt in a pail of water mixed with chlorine bleach.

d. Correct

e. Tracy's brother-in-law lives with his family in a six-room apartment.

ACKNOWLEDGMENTS (continued from p. iv)

Jonathan Burns, "The Hidden Truth: An Analysis of Shirley Jackson's 'The Lottery'" and "A Synopsis of 'The Lottery.'" Reprinted with the permission of the author.

Tim Chabot, "Take Me Out to the Ballgame, but Which One?" Reprinted with the permission of the author.

Veronica Chambers, "The Myth of Cinderella" from *Newsweek* (November 3, 1997). Copyright © 1997 by Newsweek, Inc. Reprinted by permission. All rights reserved.

Jay Chiat, "Illusions Are Forever" from *Forbes* (October 2, 2000). Copyright © 2000 by Forbes, Inc. Reprinted by permission of Forbes ASAP Magazine.

Yun Yung Choi, "Invisible Women." Reprinted with the permission of the author.

Judith Ortiz Cofer, "Don't Misread My Signals" from "The Myth of the Latin Woman: I Just Met a Girl Named Maria" from *The Latin Deli: Prose and Poetry.* Copyright © 1995 by Judith Ortiz Cofer. Reprinted with the permission of the University of Georgia Press.

Michael Coil, "Communications." Reprinted with the permission of the author.

Heather Colbenson, "Missed Opportunities." Reprinted with the permission of the author.

Stephanie Coontz, "Remarriage and Stepfamilies" from *The Way We Really Are.* Copyright © 1997 by Stephanie Coontz. Reprinted with the permission of Basic Books, a member of Perseus Books Group, LLC.

Harry Crews, excerpt from "The Car" from *Classic Crews: A Harry Crews Reader* (New York: Touchstone, 1993). Copyright © 1993 by Harry Crews. Reprinted with the permission of John Hawkins & Associates, Inc.

Freeman Dyson, excerpt from *Infinite in All Directions.* Copyright © 1988 by Freeman Dyson. Reprinted with the permission of HarperCollins Publishers, Inc.

Barbara Ehrenreich, "Warning: This Is a Rights-Free Workplace," *The New York Times Magazine* (2000). Copyright © 2000 by Barbara Ehrenreich. Reprinted with the permission of International Creative Management, Inc.

Anne Finnigan, "Nice Perks If You Can Get 'Em" from *Working Mother* (October 2000). Copyright © 2000 by Working Woman Network, Inc. Reprinted with permission.

Kurt M. Fischer and Arlyne Lazerson, excerpt from *Human Development.* Copyright © 1984 by W. H. Freeman and Company. Reprinted with permission.

Robert Hartwell Fiske, "Don't Look It Up! The Decline of the Dictionary" from *The Weekly Standard* (August 18, 2003). Copyright © 2003 New Corporation, Weekly Standard. Reprinted by permission.

Robert Frost, "Putting in the Seed" and "The Road Not Taken" from *The Poetry of Robert Frost,* edited by Edward Connery Lathem. Copyright 1916, 1969 by Henry Holt and Company. Reprinted with the permission of Henry Holt and Company, LLC.

Sara E. Goers, "Is Inclusion the Answer?" Reprinted with the permission of the author. This selection includes an excerpt from Beth Hewett, "Helping Students with Learning Disabilities: Collaboration between Writing Centers and Special Services," from *The Writing Lab* 25.3 (2000).

Ellen Goodman, "Kids, Divorce, and the Myth" from *The Boston Globe Online* (September 28, 2000). Copyright © 2000 by the Boston Globe Newspaper Co./Washington Post Writers Group. Reprinted with permission.

Suzan Shown Harjo, "Last Rites for Indian Dead" from the *Los Angeles Times* (September 16, 1989). Copyright © 1989 by Suzan Shown Harjo. Reprinted with permission.

Shirley Jackson, "The Lottery" from *The Lottery and Other Stories.* Copyright © 1948, 1949 by Shirley Jackson. Copyright renewed © 1976, 1977 by Laurence Hyman, Barry Hyman, Mrs. Sarah Webster, and Mrs. Joanne Schnurer. Reprinted with the permission of Farrar, Straus & Giroux, LLC.

Stephen King, "Why We Crave Horror Movies" from *Playboy* (1982). Copyright © by Stephen King. Reprinted with permission. All rights reserved.

Dawn Kortz, "Listen." Reprinted with the permission of the author.

William Severini Kowinski, "Kids in the Mall: Growing Up Controlled" from *The Malling of America: An Inside Look at the Great Consumer Paradise* (New York: William Morrow, 1985). Copyright © 1985 by William Severini Kowinski. Reprinted with the permission of the author.

Eric Liu, "The Chinatown Idea" from *The Accidental Asian: Notes of a Native Speaker.* Copyright © 1998 by Eric Liu. Reprinted with the permission of Random House, Inc.

Goodwin Liu, excerpt from "The Causation Fallacy: *Bakke* and the Basic Arithmetic of Selective Admissions" from the *Michigan Law Review* 100, no. 5 (April 2002). Copyright © 2002 by The Michigan Law Review Association. Reprinted with the permission of the author and the *Michigan Law Review.*

Charles C. Mann and Mark L. Plummer, "The Butterfly Problem" from *The Atlantic Monthly* (January 1992). Copyright © 1992 by Charles C. Mann. Reprinted with permission.

Ann Marlowe, "Pros and Amateurs" from <salon.com/books/feature/2000/02/24/pros> (February 24, 2000). Copyright © 2000 by Salon.com. Reprinted with permission.

Jay Mathews, "Class Struggle: Is Homework Really So Terrible?" from *The Washington Post* (February 18, 2003). Copyright © 2003 by the Washington Post Writers Group. Reprinted with permission.

N. Scott Momaday, "To the Singing, To the Drums" (excerpt) from *Natural History* (February 1975). Copyright © 1975 by the American Museum of Natural History. Reprinted with permission.

Madeleine Nash, excerpt from "The Case for Cloning" from *Time* (February 9, 1998). Copyright © 1998 by Time, Inc. Reprinted by permission.

Theresa H. Nguyen, "Antiterrorist Law Violates Civil Rights." Reprinted with the permission of the author.

Steve Olson, "Year of the Blue-Collar Guy" from *Newsweek* (November 6, 1989). Copyright © 1989 by Steve Olson. Reprinted with the permission of the author.

Noel Perrin, "A Part-Time Marriage" from *The New York Times Magazine* (September 9, 1984). Copyright © 1984 by the New York Times Company. Reprinted with permission.

James Poniewozik, "Why Reality TV Is Good for Us" from *Time* (February 17, 2003). Copyright © 2003 by Time, Inc. Reprinted with permission.

Anna Quindlen, "Evan's Two Moms" from *The New York Times* (February 5, 1992). Copyright © 1992 by the New York Times Company. Reprinted with permission.

Anjula Razdan, "What's Love Got to Do with It?" from *Utne* (June 2003). Copyright © 2003 Anjula Razdan. Reprinted with the permission of the author. This essay includes Emily Dickinson, "Split the Lark—and you'll find the Music—" from *The Poems of Emily Dickinson,* edited by Thomas H. Johnson. Copyright 1951, © 1955, 1979 by the President and Fellows of Harvard College.

Reprinted with the permission of the Belknap Press of Harvard University Press.

Wilbert Rideau, "Why Prisons Don't Work" from *Time* (March 21, 1994). Copyright © 1994 by Time, Inc. Reprinted with permission.

Joe Robinson, "Four Weeks Vacation" from *Utne* (September/ October 2000). Reprinted with the permission of the author.

Richard Rodriguez, "Public and Private Language" from "Aria: Memory of a Bilingual Childhood" from *Hunger of Memory: The Education of Richard Rodriguez: An Autobiography.* Copyright © 1980, 1982 by Richard Rodriguez. Reprinted with the permission of Georges Borchardt, Inc. for the author.

Scott Russell Sanders, "The Men We Carry in Our Minds" from *Milkweed Chronicle* (1984). Copyright © 1984 by Scott Russell Sanders. Reprinted with the permission of the Virginia Kidd Agency, Inc.

Lindsey Schendel, excerpt from "How to Heal a Broken Heart (in One Day)." Reprinted with the permission of the author.

Robert G. Schreiner, "What Is a Hunter?" Reprinted with the permission of the author.

Danzy Senna, "The Color of Love" from *O, The Oprah Magazine* (2000). Copyright © 2000 by Danzy Senna. Reprinted with the permission of International Creative Management, Inc.

LaBree Shide, "ANWR: Not a Place for Profit." Reprinted with the permission of the author.

Elaine Showalter, "Window on Reality" from *The American Prospect* 14 (July 3, 2003). Reprinted with the permission of *The American Prospect*, 5 Broad Street, Boston, MA 02109. All rights reserved.

Jane Smiley, "The Case against Chores" from *Harper's* (June 1995). Copyright © 1995 by *Harper's* magazine. Reprinted with the permission of *Harper's*.

Shelby Steele, "Affirmative Action: The Price of Preference" from *The Content of Our Character.* Copyright © 1990 by Shelby Steele. Reprinted with the permission of St. Martin's Press, LLC.

Amy Tan, "The Mother Tongue" from *Threepenny Review* (1990). Copyright © 1990 by Amy Tan. Reprinted by permission of the author and the Sandra Dijkstra Literary Agency.

Deborah Tannen, "Women and Men Talking on the Job" from *Talking from 9 to 5.* Copyright © 1994 by Deborah Tannen. Reprinted with the permission of HarperCollins Publishers, Inc.

Lillian Tsu, excerpt from "A Woman in the White House" from *Cornell Political Forum* (1997). Copyright © 1997 by Lillian Tsu. Reprinted with the permission of the author.

John Updike, excerpt from "Venezuela for Visitors" from *Hugging the Shore.* Originally published in *The New Yorker.* Copyright © 1983 by John Updike. Reprinted with the permission of Alfred A. Knopf, a division of Random House, Inc.

Nicholas Wade, "How Men and Women Think" from *The New York Times Magazine* (June 12, 1994). Copyright © 1994 by the New York Times Company. Reprinted with permission.

Johanna Wald, "Extracurricular Drug Testing" from *Education Week* (May 1, 2002). Copyright © 2002 by Editorial Projects in Education. Reprinted with the permission of Editorial Projects in Education c/o Copyright Clearance Center.

E. B. White, "Once More to the Lake" from *Essays of E. B. White.* Copyright 1944 by E. B. White. Reprinted with the permission of Mr. Joel White.

Carrie Williamson, excerpt from "Rainforest Destruction." Reprinted with the permission of the author.

Malcolm X, "Learning to Read" from *The Autobiography of Malcolm X.* Copyright © 1964 by Alex Haley and Malcolm X. Copyright © 1965 by Alex Haley and Betty Shabazz. Reprinted with the permission of Random House, Inc.

William Zinsser, "The Right to Fail" from *The Lunacy Boom* (New York: Harper & Row, 1970). Copyright © 1969, 1970 by William Zinsser. Reprinted with the permission of the author.

Art and Photograph Credits (in order of appearance)

Page 23: Figure adapted from *Taxonomy of Educational Objectives, Handbook I: Cognitive Domain* by Benjamin S. Bloom et al. © 1956 McKay.

Page 45: © Larry Williams/CORBIS.

Page 57: Courtesy of Dan Jahn for Photofiler.com.

Page 62: Courtesy of Sarah Gilbert/*Iowa State Daily.*

Page 63: John Storey/Getty Images.

Page 71: Courtesy of Ben Ailes Photography.

Page 78: Beaver selection chart courtesy of LabWrite, © 2000 Miriam Ferzli, Ph.D., North Carolina State University. Used with permission. Photo of destroyed fraternity house courtesy of the *Cumberland Times-News.*

Page 79: Scott Olson/Getty Images.

Page 86: Courtesy of Northwestern University.

Page 94: Courtesy of the Boston *Metro*/Metro Publishing.

Page 95: © Jason Reblando.

Page 105: Table based on data from the U.S. Bureau of Economic Analysis and the U.S. Census Bureau.

Page 112: Chart on employment by class of worker courtesy of *Occupational Outlook Quarterly.* Chart on backup aid cameras © 2003 by Consumers Union of U.S., Inc. Yonkers, NY 10703-1057, a non-profit organization. Reprinted with permission from the October 2003 issue of *Consumer Reports®* for educational purposes only. No commercial use or reproduction permitted. To subscribe, call 1-800-234-1645, or visit us at <www.ConsumerReports.org>.

Page 113: © Fred Voetsch.

Page 124: Chart projecting global temperature courtesy of Intergovernmental Panel on Climate Change.

Page 130: Graphic on workforce changes as seen in *Business 2.0,* © 2003 XPLANATIONS by Xplane.com®.

Page 131: This advertisement has been created for the Play Fair at the Olympics campaign, Clean Clothes Campaign, Oxfam, and Global Unions; see <www.fairolympics.org>.

Page 140: © Andrew Scott/*The Chronicle.*

Page 151: Tuition-increase map reprinted by permission of the National Center for Public Policy and Higher Education. "Consume" poster © Jaivin Anzalota.

Page 152: Image courtesy of <www.adbusters.org>.

Page 160: Reprinted with permission of the Ford Foundation.

Page 168: Photo © Steve Rubin.

Page 169: © Christina Beck.

Page 170: Courtesy of Lou Beach.

Page 178: Photo by Dr. Lou Campbell, Belhaven College Theatre Department.

Page 186: Web page created by University Career Services staff at George Mason University. "Flicks in a Flash" chart © *The Boston Phoenix.*

Figure 20.1: USA Today front page courtesy of USA Today, copyright May 16, 2001. Reprinted with permission. *Wall Street Journal* front page reprinted by permission of the Wall Street Journal, copyright © 2003 Dow Jones & Company, Inc. All rights reserved worldwide.

Figure 20.3: Forbes spread reprinted by permission of *Forbes* magazine © Forbes, Inc.; Photos in spread by Jonathan Olley/Network Photographers and Mark Jenkinson, © Mark Jenkinson/CORBIS OUTLINE. *Parenting* spread from *Parenting* magazine, June/July 2003. Photograph courtesy of CORBIS.

Figure 20.4: Design by Studio InFlux/The Art Institute of Boston at Lesley University: Jenny Barrett, ManChing Cheng, Lisa Goode, Yehudit Massouda.

Figure 20.12: © 2003 Office of Community Service Learning. All rights reserved.

Figure 20.17: © 2003 Smithsonian Institution.

Figure 20.18: Courtesy of King County, Washington, Wastewater Treatment Division.

Figure 20.19: Copyright © Dorling Kindersley Ltd.

Figure 20.20: Courtesy of the Energy Information Administration.

Figure 20.21: Graphic by Matt Zang.

Figure 20.22: Copyright © 2002 *U.S. News & World Report*, L.P. Reprinted with permission.

Figure 20.23: Sara Weeks, copyright © 2002 *Health*® magazine. For subscriptions please call 1-800-274-2522.

Figures 21.2–21.5: Courtesy of Merrilee Giegerich.

Figure 21.6: Courtesy of Volkswagen of America, Inc.

Figure 21.7: Courtesy of Leo Burnett.

Figure 21.8: Courtesy of Eunjin Kim, Samsung Art and Design Institute.

Figure 21.9: Roy Paul Nelson, *Publication Design* (© 1991, the McGraw-Hill Companies). Reproduced with permission from McGraw-Hill.

Figure 21.10: Copyright © D. Reed Monroe.

Page 390: From *A True Likeness* (Columbia, S.C.: Bruccoli Clark Layman, 1986) by permission of the Estate of Richard Samuel Roberts.

Page 426: © Paul Ickovic, courtesy of Robert Klein Gallery.

Page 452: © Carol Lay, 2002.

Page 478: Fredrik Brodén Photography.

Page 512: © The New Yorker Collection 2002 Edward Koren from cartoonbank.com. All rights reserved.

Figure 28.1: Courtesy of Tuskegee University/Ford Motor Company Library.

Figures 28.2 and 28.3: Courtesy of Howard University.

Figure 28.4: Courtesy of the Library of Congress.

Figure 28.5: Readers' Guide to Periodical Literature © 2001 The H. W. Wilson Company. Material reproduced with permission of the H. W. Wilson Company.

Figure 28.6: Screen image from Gale's InfoTrac Web site, The Gale Group. Reprinted by permission of The Gale Group. Text from "MENC TODAY" news, *Music Educators Journal*, November 2003. Copyright © 2003 by MENC: The National Association for Music Education. Reprinted with permission.

Figures 28.7 and 28.8: © Google, Inc.

Figure 29.1: Copyright © 2004 The American Society for the Prevention of Cruelty to Animals (ASPCA). Reprinted with the permission of the ASPCA. All rights reserved.

Page A-22: Title page and copyright page from *Win-Win Ecology: How Earth's Species Can Survive in the Midst of Human Enterprise* by Michael L. Rosenzweig. Copyright 2003 by Michael L. Rosenzweig. Reprinted with permission of Oxford University Press, Inc.

Page A-24: Contents page from the *Michigan Law Review* 98, no. 5 (March 2000), Copyright © 2000 by The Michigan Law Review Association.

Index

I-1

Proofreading Symbols

Use these standard proofreading marks when making minor corrections in your final draft. If extensive revision is necessary, type or print out a clean copy.

∽	Transpose
≡	Capitalize
/	Lowercase
#	Add space
⌒	Close up space
℘	Delete
⸛‥‥‥℘	Stet (undo deletion)
∧	Insert
⊙	Insert period
⌃	Insert comma
;/	Insert semicolon
:/	Insert colon
⌄	Insert apostrophe
⌄ ⌄	Insert quotation marks
|=|	Insert hyphen
¶	New paragraph
no ¶	No new paragraph

Correction Symbols

Many instructors use these abbreviations and symbols to mark errors in student papers. Refer to this chart to find out what they mean.

Boldface numbers refer to sections of the handbook and the Quick Editing Guide.

abbr	faulty abbreviation **28**		⌄	comma **21, C1**
ad	misuse of adverb or adjective **8, A7**		no ,	no comma **21n–r, C1**
agr	faulty agreement **4, 7, A4, A6**		;	semicolon **22**
appr	inappropriate language **9f, 16, 18**		:	colon **23**
awk	awkward		⌄	apostrophe **24, C2**
cap	capital letter **29, D1**		" "	quotation marks **25, C3**
case	error in case **5, A5**		. ? !	period, question mark, exclamation point **20**
coord	faulty coordination **14a–c**		– ( ) [ ] . . .	dash, parentheses, brackets, ellipsis **26–27**
cs	comma splice **2, A2**		par, ¶	new paragraph **D3**
dm	dangling modifier **10c, B1**		pass	ineffective passive **3m**
exact	inexact language **17**		ref	error in pronoun reference **6, A6**
frag	sentence fragment **1, A1**		rep	careless repetition **19**
fs	fused sentence **2, A2**		rev	revise
gl	see Glossary of Troublemakers		run-on	comma splice or fused sentence **2, A2**
gr	grammar **1–9, all of A**		sp	misspelled word **33, D2**
hyph	error in use of hyphen **32**		sub	faulty subordination **14d–f**
inc	incomplete construction **11**		t	error in verb tense **3g–l, 9a–b, A3**
irreg	error in irregular verb **3e–f, A3**		tense	error in verb tense **3g–l, 9a–b, A3**
ital	italics (underlining) **31**		v	voice **3m, 9c**
lc	use lowercase letter **29, D1**		vb	error in verb form **3a–f, A3, A3**
mixed	mixed construction **12**		w	wordy **19**
mm	misplaced modifier **10a–b, B1**		//	faulty parallelism **13, B2**
mood	error in mood **3n–p, 9e**		∧	insert **D3**
ms	manuscript form **D3**		x	obvious error
nonst	nonstandard usage **16, 17**		#	insert space
num	error in use of numbers **30**		⌣	close up space **D3**
om	omitted word **11**			
p	error in punctuation **20–27, C**			

Selected Visuals for Analysis—By Topic/Genre

Directory to MLA Documentation Models

Directory to APA Documentation Models

Index to ESL Guidelines

A Guide to the Handbook

A College Writer's Activities

Write

- Generate ideas about a topic.
- Plan a thesis and organization for your purpose and audience.
- Draft coherent paragraphs.
- Develop ideas, examples, details, and evidence.
- Revise your thesis, structure, support, and connections.
- Edit and proofread sentences, words, punctuation, and mechanics.

Read

- Respond to reading by annotating or keeping a journal.
- Read text literally and analytically.
- Observe and interpret images.
- Generate ideas from reading.

Think

- Think critically as a reader and writer.
- Supply reliable facts, statistics, expert testimony, and firsthand observations.
- Test your supporting evidence.

Research

- Identify your research question and plan your project.
- Find library, Internet, and field sources.
- Evaluate your sources.
- Integrate your sources by quoting, paraphrasing, summarizing, and citing.
- Write your research paper.
- Document your sources.